Poverty in the United Kingdom

A Survey of Household Resources and Standards of Living

Poverty in the United Kingdom

A Survey of Household Resources and Standards of Living

Peter Townsend

University of California Press
Berkeley and Los Angeles

University of California Press
Berkeley and Los Angeles

Copyright © Peter Townsend, 1979

I S B N: 0-520-03871-1 (cloth)
I S B N: 0-520-03976-9 (paper)
Library of Congress Catalog Card Number 78-66023

Set in Monotype Times
Printed in Great Britain by
Hazell Watson & Viney Ltd, Aylesbury, Bucks

Contents

Preface   17
Acknowledgements   25

1   Introduction: Concepts of Poverty and Deprivation   31

Previous Definitions of Poverty   32
The Limitations of the Evidence of Poverty   39
Poverty and Inequality   43
Three Forms of Deprivation   46
Conceptions of Relativity   50
Style of Living   54
Stratification and Resources   54
Conclusion   59

2   Theories of Poverty   61

Theoretical Principles Underlying Alternative Policies   62
Minority Group Theory   64
The Sub-culture of Poverty   65
The Related Concept of a Cycle of Deprivation   70
Orthodox Economic Theory   71
Dual Labour Market and Radical Theories   77
Sociological Approaches to Inequality   80
Functionalist Explanations of Inequality and Poverty   83
The Functions of Poverty   85
Conclusion   87

3   Methods of Research   93

The Questionnaire   94
Sampling   98
Interviewing   101
Response   104
Representativeness   109
Limitations of Research   111
The Survey Method   113

4 Inequality and Poverty, 1938–68   116

Personal Incomes: Before and After Tax   117
Survey Data on Personal Income   126
Incomes Policy   128
Earnings   133
Social Stratification and Occupations   142
Assets   144
Taxation   147
Fiscal Welfare   150
Employer Welfare   152
Public Social Services   154
Poverty   160
Nutrition   167
Health   170
Conclusion   174

5 The Concept and Distribution of Resources   177

The Problem of the Recipient Unit   178
Cash Income   180
Imputed Rent   180
Distribution of Gross Income   182
The Make-up of Household Income   186
Cash Incomes of Different Types of Household   193
The Distribution of Assets   199
Assets of Different Types of Household   205
The Relationship between Assets and Income   210
The Value of Employer Welfare Benefits   215
The Value of Public Social Services   218
Private Income in Kind   223
The Interrelationship of Resources   225
Conceptual Problems of Income and Wealth   230
Summary   232

6 Three Measures of Poverty   237

Subjective and Social Definitions of Poverty   237
The State's Standard of Poverty   241
The Relative Income Standard of Poverty   247
The Deprivation Standard of Poverty   248
The Problem of Equivalence   262
Cash Income and a Poverty Line   267
Summary and Conclusion   270

7 The Incidence of Poverty   272

Short-term and Long-term Poverty   275
Size of Household   276

The State's Standard 278
The Relative Income Standard 280
The Relative Deprivation Standard 281
Definitions of the Domestic Unit and of Resources 282
Regional Poverty 284
Population and Poverty 285
Families with Children 288
Type of Household 290
Birthplace and Colour 291
Employment Status and Occupational Class 291
Assets 295
Housing Cost and Poverty 298
Summary 301

8 The Impact of Poverty 304

1. In poverty: Young family, with disabled man and woman and handicapped child 305
2. In poverty: Retirement pensioner living alone 310
3. In poverty: Chronically sick and disabled man living with elderly mother 311
4. In poverty: Young fatherless family 313
5. In poverty: Long-term unemployed man with wife and six children (two low-paid) 313
6. In poverty: Single woman supporting severely incapacitated mother 315
7. On the margins of poverty: Low-paid man with young family 316
8. In poverty: Complex household including three disabled adults, a handicapped child, fatherless family, low-paid and long-term unemployed 317
9. In poverty: Single woman supporting elderly father (immigrants) 321
10. On the margins of poverty: Motherless family (disabled adult) 322
11. On the margins of poverty: Disabled retirement pensioner, living alone 323
12. In poverty: Long-term unemployed man and wife and four children (gipsy family) 324
13. In poverty: Low-paid man and wife and three children (also long-term unemployed) 326
14. In poverty: Large fatherless family, including handicapped child 327
15. In poverty: Elderly disabled couple 328
16. In poverty: Low-paid man and wife and five children (formerly long-term unemployed) 329
17. In poverty: Chronically sick and disabled man living with elderly mother 331
18. In poverty: Chronically sick man and wife and three children 332
19. On the margins of poverty: Elderly retirement pensioners 333
20. In poverty: Three disabled adults 334
21. On the margins of poverty: Fatherless family (also immigrant) 335

9 The Rich 337

Concepts and Definitions of Riches 338
Top Incomes and Top Wealth Holdings 341
Combining Income and Wealth 345
A Definition of the Rich 347
The Rich and the Poor 357
The Configuration of Wealth and Class 359
Separate Elites or Ruling Class? 363
The Sources of Wealth 364
The Institutional Structure of Wealth 365
The Proselytization of Life-styles 366
Summary 367

10 Social Class and Styles of Living 369

The Problem of Measurement 369
Images of Class 371
Self-rated Class and Economic Circumstances 377
'Objective' Occupational Class 381
Self-rated Class and Occupational Class 382
Occupational Class and Economic Circumstances 385
The Cumulative Command over Resources 389
Occupational Class and Poverty 394
Occupational Class and Style of Living 395
Social Mobility 400
The Relationship between Social Class and Poverty 409
Summary and Conclusion 411

11 Objective and Subjective Deprivation 413

Forms of Objective Deprivation 413
Subjective Deprivation 418
The Interrelationship between Objective and Subjective Deprivation 422
Subjective Deprivation and Income 423
Personal Denials of Poverty 425
Subjective Perceptions of Poverty in Society 427
Objective Deprivation and Lack of Income 430
Summary 431

12 Deprivation at Work 432

The Concept of Deprivation 437
Deprivation and Occupational Class 443
The Character of the Job 444
Security of Work 452
Conditions of Work 453
Welfare and Fringe Benefits 455

An Index of Work Deprivation 461
Deprivation and Earnings 463
The Self-Employed 465
Work Deprivation and Poverty 466
Changes in Work Deprivation 468
Satisfaction with Work 470
Summary and Conclusion 474

13 **Deprivation in Housing** 476

The Problem of Obtaining Objective Measures of Poor Housing 476
Different Indices of Poor Housing 479
Characteristics of the Poorly Housed 486
The Housing Market 490
Poor Housing and Low Income 498
Housing Costs, Poor Housing and Poverty 503
The Ill-balanced Structure of Housing Costs 505
Access to the Housing Market: Owner-occupation 514
Access to Council Housing 519
Access to the Housing Market: Private Tenancies 522
Explanations of Poor Housing 524
Summary 526

14 **Deprivation of Environment** 529

Three Measures of Environmental Deprivation 531
Multiple Deprivation 532
Social Characteristics of the Environmentally Deprived 535
Poverty, Class and Tenure 538
Summary 541

15 **The Problems of Poor Areas** 543

The Incidence of Poverty 545
Rural and Urban Differences 549
Differences between Regions 550
Areas of High Deprivation 553
The Persistence of Deprivation 558
Towards a Theory of Area Poverty 559
Summary and Conclusion 563

16 **Social Minorities** 565

Definitions of Social Minorities 566
Thirteen Selected Minorities 568
The Incomes of Minorities 572
The Characteristics of the Poor 576
Households with Woman and Adult Dependants 578
Two Groups of Immigrant Households 579

Households with One or More Persons Born in Eire   580
Households with One or More Non-white Members   582
Large Families   584
Summary   586

17   **The Unemployed and the Sub-employed**   588

Discontinuous Employment and Poverty   590
The Levels of Unemployment and Sub-employment   595
Occupational Class and Unemployment   601
The Institutional and Personal Characteristics of the Unemployed   603
Income Support During Unemployment   607
Employment Policy   610
Summary   614

18   **The Low Paid**   618

The Concept of Low Pay   618
Low Pay and the Lowest Decile   621
Low Pay as a Percentage of the Mean   625
Low Pay and Poverty   629
The Failure of Family Income Supplements   633
Wages Councils   634
Correlates of Low Pay   635
Fluctuations in Manual Pay   639
The Instability of the Pay and Conditions of Manual Work   642
A Case-history of Low Pay, Unemployment and Poverty   643
The Dual Labour Market Theory   645
Approaches to Policy   648
Summary   649

19   **The Older Worker**   652

The Increasing Trend towards Retirement   655
Possible Explanations of Earlier Retirement   656
Changes in Activity Rates   658
The Employment Record of the Older Worker   661
Incapacity and Age   663
Skill, Training and Education   665
Trends in Social Class by Age   667
Changes in the Type of Industry and Employment   671
Earnings and Age   675
Fringe Benefits and Work Conditions   678
The Woman Worker   680
Conclusion and Summary   682

20 Disabled People and the Long-term Sick 685

The Concept of Disability 686
Two Operational Definitions 688
The Need for a New Approach to Assessment 693
The Disabled Population 695
Why Official Estimates of Handicapped are Low 699
Disability Increases with Age 705
Low Social Status of Disabled 709
Poverty 711
Deprivation 714
Subjective Deprivation 716
Some of the Problems of Disability in the Home 717
Chronic Illness or Invalidity 722
Mental Illness 725
The Disadvantages of Employment 727
Disabled Housewives 733
Explanations of Poverty among the Disabled 734
Summary 738

21 Handicapped Children 740

Different forms of Handicap 742
Poverty among Handicapped Children 745
Illustrations of Families with a Handicapped Child 746
Summary and Conclusion 750

22 One-Parent Families 753

The Total Numbers of One-Parent Families 754
Trends in Numbers of One-Parent Families 758
The Chances of Being in Poverty 759
Changes in Numbers in Poverty: the Introduction of Family Income Supplement 763
One-Parent Families Who Are Not Poor 764
Variation of Living Standards between Different Types of One-Parent Families 764
An Illustration of the Contrasts in Living Standards 767
The Consequences of Poverty 768
Explaining the Disadvantages Suffered by One-Parent Families 771
Income Rights of Different Types of One-Parent Family 773
Variations in Living Standards during the Life of the Family 775
Other One-Parent Families 776
Alternative Policies 778
Summary and Conclusion 781

23 Old People 784

Inequality between Elderly and Young 786
Inequality among the Elderly: Single and Married 795

Inequality among the Elderly: the Concept of the Fourth Generation   797
Social Class and Access to Resources   800
Low Lifelong Social Status and Poverty   801
Retirement and the Diminished Social Status of the Employed   804
Occupational Pensions and the Middle Class   807
Social Isolation and Access to Family Resources   811
Increasing Disability and Access to Resources   815
Conclusion   819

24   Eligibility for Supplementary Benefit   823

The History of Research on 'Take-Up'   824
Social Security   826
Eligibility for Supplementary Benefits   827
Implications of Estimated Numbers Eligible for Benefits   832
Characteristics of the Legally Entitled   833
Temporary and Long-term Poverty   835
Levels of Living of Recipients   836
Eligibility in Four Areas   837
Attitudes and Circumstances of those Eligible for Benefit   842
Attitudes of Recipients   845
Inadequate Payments   847
The Conflicting Functions of the Supplementary Benefits Scheme   847
Summary   848
Annex to Chapter 24   850

25   The Failure of Means-tested Benefits   860

Free School Meals   860
Free Welfare Milk   868
Educational Maintenance Allowances   869
School-uniform Grants   871
Rate Rebates   873
Rent Rebates   875
Option Mortgage Scheme   877
Explanations of Under-use   879
Summary   891

26   Conclusion I: The Social Distribution of Poverty and Trends in the 1970s   893

Measurement of Poverty   894
Changes since 1968–9   902

27   Conclusion II: The Explanation and Elimination of Poverty   913

Definitions of Poverty   913
Explanations of Poverty   916
The Principles of Policy   922

Appendix One: Methods of Sampling   927
Appendix Two: Representativeness of the Sample   955
Appendix Three: Eligibility for Supplementary Benefit   959
Appendix Four: The Value to Families of the Social Services   964
Appendix Five: Some Definitions   980
Appendix Six: The Social Grading of Occupations   986
Appendix Seven: Note on the Adjustment of Sample Findings   989
Appendix Eight: Additional Tables   991
Appendix Nine: Comments on Survey and Questionnaire   1076
Appendix Ten: Questionnaire   1084
Appendix Eleven: Statistical Tests   1168
Appendix Twelve: Method of Adjusting Distribution of Assets   1170
Appendix Thirteen: Multiple Deprivation on the Threshold of Income   1173
List of References   1177
Index   1201

List of Text Figures

1.1   Illustration of the distribution of incomes in two countries   44

2.1   The Paretian conception of income distribution   72

6.1   Deprivation index score at different levels of income   253

6.2   The relationship between income and deprivation for certain types of households   257

6.3   The percentages at three levels of income, with different deprivation scores   259

6.4   Modal deprivation by logarithm of income as a percentage of supplementary benefit scale rates   261

6.5   The establishment of equivalent income   265

7.1   The life-cycle of poverty: people of different age in income units, with income in previous year above and below the state standard   286

7.2   Mean net disposable income plus the income equivalent of wealth as a percentage of the state's poverty standard   288

7.3   Percentages in income units with net disposable income in previous year below or just above the state's poverty standard   294

7.4   Percentage in income units who are below or just above the state's poverty standard after the income equivalent of their wealth is added to non-asset income in previous year   296

10.1   The effect of adding other resources to the net disposable income of units of which people of different ages were members   392

18.1   Average percentage changes in earnings against level of earnings   642

19.1   Percentages of men aged 65 and over who are economically active   654

20.1   Two measures of limiting disablement   704

20.2   Percentages of males and females of different ages with any incapacity and with appreciable or severe incapacity   706

20.3   Percentages of males and females of different ages who have trouble with a disablement condition and have a marked or specific restriction of activity   707

A.1   Modal deprivation by logarithm of income as a percentage of mean for household type   1004

Preface

In this book I have sought to show the extent of poverty in the United Kingdom and give some explanation for its existence. Although I have drawn on a number of studies carried out in the 1970s, and on the reports in 1975, 1976 and 1977 of the Royal Commission on the Distribution of Income and Wealth, the principal source of information is the national survey carried out for the specific purpose of writing this book in 1968–9. Are the findings from that year out of date in the late 1970s? Very properly this question will be raised. The answer can take many different forms, some theoretical, some technical and some personal.

One answer is that the structure of society does not change significantly in a short span of years, except sometimes in revolutionary conditions or war, and that the research team was inevitably seeking to describe and analyse the social structure of the United Kingdom in attempting to describe and explain poverty. There are major conceptual and technical problems in doing so – in trying to revise familiar but inadequate methods of describing society and adopting *relative* measures of inequality and deprivation instead. I believe this lays the basis for cross-national and scientific work.[1] The team discussing and planning the project grappled with the problem of devising alternative measures when completing the pilot studies[2] and preparing the questionnaire. In the questionnaire we tried to develop a *comprehensive* conception of resources; measure some of them, like fringe benefits and the ownership of wealth, more reliably than in other studies; and at the same time develop operational standards, and not only indicators, of deprivation. Yet at the stage of provisionally analysing the information collected in interviews, and at the final stage of checking and integrating that analysis, there were unanticipated problems of generating as well as of digesting new conceptions, and therefore new measures of inequality and deprivation (and putting them into operational form as indicators and combined indices), so that a closer representation of that elusive structure of inequality might finally be given. We

1. As discussed in different papers in a preparatory conference before the survey. See Townsend, P. (ed.), *The Concept of Poverty*, Heinemann Educational Books, London, 1970.

2. See, for example, Marsden, D., *Mothers Alone*, Allen Lane, London, 1969; and Land, H., *Large Families in London*, Bell, London, 1970.

were trying to sustain both an account of the total social structure (as well as of the relationship between some of its component parts) and an account of poor minorities within that structure.

There are a number of different senses in which the underlying social structure can be said to have remained much the same during a period of a little under ten years. Upon analysis, social changes turn out to be technical or cultural rather than structural. People are conscious of the rapid spread of car ownership, colour television, telephones, central heating, hi-fi equipment and air travel; the introduction of new methods of production in industry and new drugs and surgical techniques in medicine; new fashions as well as materials and processes in the clothes that are worn and the goods and furnishings that are bought for the home; new types of musical and theatrical entertainment; and an array of new bodies, controls and procedures brought into existence by legislation. But while styles of living and prevalence of types of social interaction are indeed affected, the division of society into social classes, social minorities, regional and local communities, family, neighbourhood and friendship groups and networks, and administrative, professional, political and religious groups, and therefore the distribution of resources commanded by such groups, may remain largely unaltered. This is the paradox which the social scientist is bound to call attention to and explore. One of the problems is that individuals often ascribe changes occurring to them in their lifetime as changes occurring to society. Another is that the extent of social change is exaggerated by many bodies because it suits them consciously or unconsciously to do so. And a third is that even when structural changes occur, they may be of a very short-term nature only. Change may be cyclical rather than long term, and there may be periodic reversions to long-term structural dispositions. The state of conflict between major contending classes and groups in society may mean that one class or group secures an advantage at a particular point in time which is later lost or redressed by another class or group.

What has to be accepted therefore is that some 'changes', in the popular sense of the term, have little or no impact on the basic divisions or conflicts in society and do not affect its structure. Many contemporary 'changes' – in fashion, technology, legislation and, during inflation, in the interaction of earnings, taxes and prices – belie the reality of our stable structure of inequality. This reality is not easy to demonstrate. There are organizations and interests which exist, both knowingly and unknowingly, to conceal or deny it. One of the characteristics of inequality is that many of the people who have most to gain from it are not conscious of it or do not want to be reminded of it. If they happen to be conscious of it, they want and tend to believe that their privilege is ordained or natural, or meritorious, or diminishing – and extremely modest; alternatively, that others' disprivilege is inevitable or deserved – and rather modest. These beliefs are reproduced in government and administration and are reflected in decisions about the collection and presentation of knowledge about our society by social scientists.

The key question is whether, in trying to escape conventional perceptions, or, more correctly, showing that we are not entirely ruled by them, the relativity of that structure can be described independently of belief. Repeatedly in the book I have tried to show how the survey findings tie in with other, more recent, data, and how the distribution of earnings, and of net disposable incomes, happens to have remained much the same in the early 1970s as in the late 1960s. By 1976 there was, for men, a slight narrowing of differentials among both manual and non-manual workers, compared with 1968, and the earnings at the lowest decile, relative to the median, approached the level reached in the early 1960s. For women, the picture was more complicated, with some widening of differentials for both lower-paid manual workers and higher-paid non-manual workers. The over-all distribution of earnings, as shown by the New Earnings Survey of the Department of Employment, like that demonstrated from 1906 to 1960 by G. Routh[1] and by A. R. Thatcher,[2] has remained remarkably constant during the last two decades. Similarly, such *relative* figures as can be gleaned from the reports of the Family Expenditure Survey for 1957–76, especially the quantile data published in *Economic Trends*, covering the years since the poverty survey was carried out, suggest a stable structure, with no marked changes taking place in the distribution of resources between different household types or in the distribution around the mean or the median *within* any of the types or groups, especially since 1969. In the words of one statistician in the Central Statistical Office, who analysed the distribution of original, net disposable and final incomes during the period 1961–75, 'although there are variations over the years, particularly for the upper ranges of income, there is no significant trend either towards or away from more equality, the net effect being a distribution very similar in 1975 to that in 1961'.[3] All this is discussed in various sections of the book, particularly the conclusion.

Perhaps the one trend to which I call special attention, though its short-run impact is small, is the proportionate growth of the professional, managerial and executive classes, without there being much evidence of a corresponding long-term relative fall in their levels of remuneration and living standards. It is this trend, accompanied by, or perhaps even indirectly determining, the growth in the 'dependent' population of retired, unemployed and disabled people, and of

1. Routh, G., *Occupation and Pay in Great Britain, 1906–60*, Cambridge University Press, 1965.
2. Thatcher, A. R., 'The Distribution of Earnings of Employees in Great Britain', *Journal of the Royal Statistical Society*, A, 131, Part 2, 1968.
3. Harris, R., 'A Review of the Effects of Taxes and Benefits on Household Incomes 1961–1975', *Economic Trends*, January 1977, p. 105. A special review of the published data from the FES for 1953–73 concluded 'the extent of *relative* poverty has probably changed little over the past twenty years'. Fiegehen, G. C., Lansley, P. S., and Smith, A. D., *Poverty and Progress in Britain 1953–73*, Cambridge University Press, 1977, p. 31. However, as argued later in this book, there is reason from the same source to conclude there has been some *increase* in relative poverty between 1953 and 1960 and between 1960 and 1975.

school or college trainees, which our institutions and culture are having difficulty in absorbing. Whatever the inequality between top and bottom in the dispersion of resources, the proportionate accumulation of population in the upper-middle reaches of the dispersion is being accommodated only at the price of more people being pushed to the bottom. It is not simply that there are more old people, but proportionately more *retired* old people, proportionately more people near the state's pensionable ages who are being retired or made redundant, and more people being pushed into unemployment or sub-employment, all of them having very low incomes. In some respects, of course, as with the big increase in the official unemployment rate, or even the increase in the numbers retired, the proportion with low incomes has definitely grown since 1969. However, new social security and tax measures may have cushioned the fall of some members of the population, or have helped members of other groups to clamber a step or two higher in the long ladder of income distribution, and while that possibility exists, the evidence cannot be regarded as conclusive.

I regard this structural change – that is, of a simultaneous increase towards the top of the distribution of income in number and proportion of professional, managerial and executive workers, and at the foot of that distribution of economically inactive or dependent persons – as being the most important taking place in our society. It represents an advanced stage in the history of conflict between classes. Later in this book the distribution of different types of resources will be shown to be related not just to the occupational class of individuals but to that of their parents as well. The most striking example of this will be found in the case of old people (in Chapter 23). But access to, and command over, resources is not only determined by class of origin and past as well as current occupational class mediated directly therefore by family, laws of inheritance and labour market. It is also determined increasingly through the infrastructure of social policy, mainly the state's social policy. Through social policy, the upper non-manual groups exercise enormous influence. Sometimes that influence is exercised positively on their own behalf – in the comparatively low taxes raised from capital gains; the special tax reliefs and indirect as well as direct subsidies like improvement grants available to home owners; the additions to personal standards of living represented by employers' welfare benefits, especially occupational pension rights, the subsidies and tax relief available for private education and the grants and subsidies available for higher education. The economic position of such groups is positively enhanced. Sometimes that influence is exercised negatively – by creating hostility towards increases in public expenditure and hence taxation, or insisting on tighter controls of those seeking supplementary benefit; influencing the adoption and perpetuation of national minimum or subsistence-level benefits only for people with reasonably good employment records; and laying the basis for public acceptance of early retirement. In part, attitudes are directed at the working class; 'feather-bedding' is derided and 'standing on one's own feet' is extolled. In part, attitudes are directed towards the perpetuation and extension of an underclass.

If the indicative evidence since 1969 about resources is correct, and if the underlying trend towards greater inequality is continually threatening to make itself evident, then the findings have not lost any of their force or relevance.

The findings can also be considered in relation to method. The need for better measures of inequality in the distribution of incomes and wealth is as acute as it was in the late 1960s, and the book may make some contribution to those measures. Examples might be given from government sources which show what little progress has been made in documenting inequality in the distribution of resources. Richard Titmuss long ago listed the limitations of Inland Revenue data,[1] and more recently Tony Atkinson has reviewed at length the defects of official estimates which purport to show trends in the distribution of incomes and wealth.[2] The Royal Commission on Income and Wealth has tried to run in both directions at once, criticizing the official statistics but also reproducing them without amendment. The commission admitted that the official statistics were 'deficient in many respects', largely because these were 'by-products of the administrative processes of Government Departments, particularly the Inland Revenue'.[3] They had been urged to adopt alternative approaches to the definition of both income and wealth,[4] and the commission agreed that 'no single definition could be adequate for all purposes'.[5] Yet, despite going on to claim that they had followed a policy offering alternative approaches and definitions 'so that readers may make their own choice of the most appropriate statistics for the problems they wish to study',[6] in practice they made little or no use of secondary analysis or estimation to produce alternative data. Admittedly it would be difficult, though not impossible, to do so. Instead the commission provided the same official diet as before, concluding that there had been significant trends towards greater equality of distribution of both wealth and income, even in recent years.[7] Re-

1. Titmuss, R. M., *Income Distribution and Social Change*, Allen & Unwin, London, 1962.
2. Atkinson, A. B., *The Economics of Inequality*, Clarendon Press, Oxford, 1975, Chapter 4. See also Atkinson, A. B., and Harrison, A. J., *Distribution of Personal Wealth in Britain*, Cambridge University Press, 1978.
3. Royal Commission on the Distribution of Income and Wealth, Report No. 1, *Initial Report on the Standing Reference*, Cmnd 6171, H M S O, London, July 1975, p. 9.
4. By, for example, A. B. Atkinson, A. J. Harrison and C. Trinder, C. D. Harbury, the National Institute of Economic and Social Research and the Office of Manpower Statistics in their evidence reproduced in the Royal Commission on the Distribution of Income and Wealth, *Selected Evidence Submitted to the Royal Commission for Report No. 1: Initial Report on the Standing Reference*, H M S O, London, 1976.
5. Report No. 1, *Initial Report on the Standing Reference*, p. 13.
6. ibid, p. 132.
7. Compare the unqualified summary paragraph 16(a) in the first report, for example

grettably, the press seized on the broad summaries of the fall in share of the top 1 per cent and 5 per cent without much reference to the commission's qualifications, and thereby helped to maintain the unsubstantiated belief that the rich have become relatively poorer, not just in post-war compared with pre-war years, but in the 1970s compared with 1960.[1] The appointment of the Royal Commission greatly raised expectations. A complex range of official statistics were rapidly assembled in the first six of their Reports, but a breakthrough in the measurement of either resources commanded by individuals, income units, households and families, or of changes that have taken place over a period of years in the distribution of those resources, has still to be achieved.

The data collected in the annual Family Expenditure Survey, carried out regularly since 1957, are potentially more valuable than either the Inland Revenue data or the Central Statistical Office's adaptations of those data. However, as its name implies, the survey is designed to obtain more comprehensive and reliable information about expenditure than about income;[2] and the findings on income distribution are rarely presented in a form which allows a span of years or different types of household to be compared.

Despite considerable public discussion and pressure, the Board of Inland Revenue's practices have not been thoroughly overhauled. And, with the exception of certain data about different quantiles, both in the survey reports and in the

---

(which suggests a decline in the income share of the top 5 per cent), with the strong reservations about household composition, imputed rent of owner-occupiers, investment income, income in kind, fringe benefits, tax evasion and interconnections between income and wealth in Chapter 3, esp. pp. 34–54. Compare, again, the inconsistency of summary paragraph 16(b) (which suggests an increase in the income share of the bottom 20 per cent) with paragraph 346 (which stated that there was little change in their share of income and, anyway, that further study was required of the incomes of this section).

1. There are problems other than appearing to write for two audiences, moreover. The commission did not attempt to resolve certain apparent conflicts of evidence. Thus in the summary chapter of the fourth report attention was called to 'a net overall reduction in inequality' between 1972–3 and 1973–4 before and after tax, and specific reference was made to the respective shares of the top 20 per cent and bottom 20 per cent. No mention was made of the evidence reproduced earlier in the text from the FES showing what the commission admit was 'an increase in the share [of final income] of the top decile group' as well as a change in original income 'indicating a tendency towards greater inequality overall'. Tables 11 and C12–C17, which appear to tell a rather different story from the Blue Book distribution of personal incomes, are strangely not referred to in the summary chapter. Royal Commission on the Distribution of Income and Wealth, Report No. 4, *Second Report on the Standing Reference*, Cmnd 6626, HMSO, London, 1976, pp. 24–5, 73–4 and 109–14.

2. Thus, the report of the 1973 survey, published in 1974, stated, 'It must be emphasized that the survey is primarily a survey of expenditure on goods and services by households . . . Information which is obtained about income is primarily to enable households to be classified into income groups, in order that separate analyses of expenditure can be made for these groups of households' – Department of Employment, *Family Expenditure Survey, 1973*, HMSO, London, 1974, p. 3.

special analyses of the Central Statistical Office, published since November 1962 in *Economic Trends*, and a few forays into the survey data by the Department of Health and Social Security,[1] the annual Family Expenditure Survey has not been extensively developed or more imaginatively analysed and presented.

These criticisms make the decision not to collect reliable information about net disposable income in the General Household Survey all the more regrettable. Through the Social Survey Division of its Office of Population Censuses and Surveys, the government launched the General Household Survey in 1971. The purpose of the survey is to 'provide a kind of co-operative research service meeting the needs of many departments within one survey framework'.[2] In the notes prepared for interviews is the statement: 'Income is probably one of the most powerful factors influencing the way people live, their housing, employment, size of family and so on.' Yet the questions on income were reduced to a minimum and cover 'gross' income only. Both the first report, published in 1973, and the second report, published in 1975, contained few tables based on this variable, and the second is apologetic to the point of embarrassment about the shortcomings of the attempts in it to move towards a measure of any value comparatively. The long-established deficiencies of government statistics of the distribution of income remain.

In terms, then, of the continuing need to measure more exactly and more comprehensively the distribution of resources, as well as the relatively unchanging structure of inequality, I hope the findings described in *Poverty in the United Kingdom* will be felt to be relevant and not outdated.

In a report of considerable length, it may be helpful to provide as many signposts as possible for readers wishing to track down subjects of special interest to them. The table of contents on pages 5–13 gives headings of subsections as well as titles of chapters, and chapters normally have a short summary at the end. Sometimes I have chosen to include a theoretical discussion or a discussion of the implications for policy of the findings in the latter pages of chapters rather than in the concluding chapters. Illustrations of the experiences of individuals and families will be found in most chapters, and especially in Chapter 8. However, names used are not the real names and sometimes one or two other details have been changed to protect the identities of people providing information in confidence.

---

1. For example, Department of Health and Social Security, *Two-Parent Families: A Study of their Resources and Needs in 1968, 1969 and 1970*, Statistical Report Series No. 14, HMSO, London, 1971.
2. Office of Population Censuses and Surveys, Social Survey Division, *The General Household Survey*, Introductory Report, HMSO, London, 1973, p. v.

Acknowledgements

This book has been a long time in the making and I owe both a special debt to a few close friends and colleagues who at considerable cost to themselves made it possible and a general debt to many families whom we interviewed, fieldworkers, coders, assistants and statisticians who took a generous interest in the project and collaborated to bring it to fruition. It represents some fulfilment of a lifetime's ambition. In my early twenties I wrote a draft paper for Political and Economic Planning, subsequently published in 1952 under the title *Poverty: Ten Years After Beveridge*, and realized that in the years following the Second World War there was nothing that matched the accounts provided by Charles Booth and Seebohm Rowntree of social conditions in Britain at the turn of the century, although there had been a few imitative studies in the inter-war years.

My friend and colleague Brian Abel-Smith had been writing quite independently on the subject of poverty at that time, and we began working together on a pamphlet on pensions. Later we wrote together as well as separately on social security, and especially pensions, health and welfare services and the history of institutional care. In 1960–62 I had been undertaking secondary analysis of Family Expenditure Survey data, comparing the distribution of incomes with national assistance scales. Around that time we developed the idea of carrying out a national survey of poverty. After I had written a paper for the *British Journal of Sociology* in 1962, based partly on these FES data, we wrote a more extensive account of the surveys in *The Poor and the Poorest* (1965). In early 1964, shortly after I had been appointed to a Chair in Sociology at the newly founded University of Essex, we drafted what we believed to be a provisional application to the Joseph Rowntree Memorial Trust in three pages for £32,000 to undertake both a number of pilot studies and a national survey of poverty. This was approved with an alacrity which, in view of the rough-and-ready estimates of both time and cost of undertaking an unprecedently ambitious survey, was subsequently embarrassing and frankly painful – for the protracted final stages of analysis and writing had to be conducted on a shoestring. The trustees' prompt decision was a measure of their warmth and confidence. The research would not have been possible without this generous grant (and subsequent supplementary support) from the Rowntree Trust. Perhaps I should add, for the benefit of those who are prone to criticize the costs of social science research, that the eventual cost of £58,762 included about £20,000 for the pilot studies and altogether resulted in substantial books on fatherless families, large families and methods of defining and measuring poverty, as well as this report on the national survey (some further material is also being prepared).

With the help of an advisory group consisting of Sir Donald Sargent (Ministry of Social Security), Leonard Nicholson (Central Statistical Office), Miss Jean Rowntree and Ford Longman (both of the Joseph Rowntree Memorial Trust), Professor John Yudkin (Queen Elizabeth College) and Professor David Marsh (University of Nottingham), under the chairmanship of the late Professor Richard Titmuss (London School of Economics), we completed *The Poor and the Poorest*, embarked on the pilot studies of large families, fatherless families, the chronically sick and the unemployed (already described in the Preface), and later drew up drafts of the questionnaire to be used in the main study. I must also thank Professor Alan Stuart and Professor Durbin for advice and encouragement when we came to devise methods of drawing a stratified sample.

Because computing and other facilities would not in the early days have been readily available at the new University of Essex, the pilot work and the analysis of the main survey were located at both the two university institutions, though the fieldwork for the main survey and the follow-up surveys were administered from London. The Research Officers appointed to carry out the pilot studies were Hilary Land (LSE), and Dennis Marsden and John Veit-Wilson (both at the University of Essex). Adrian Sinfield had already embarked on a pilot study of unemployed men in North Shields, and after he moved to the University of Essex in 1965 he continued studying the unemployed and, with the other three, joined the planning of the main survey under the joint direction of Brian Abel-Smith and myself. For a short period Christopher Bagley also worked on the project as a research officer. Sheila Benson was appointed administrative research secretary to mobilize and direct the field and coding staff, and at a later stage Marie Brown joined the team to supervise and accompany interviewers who were to approach households throughout the United Kingdom.

The completion of the fieldwork was touch and go. We had hopes of employing a research agency to do the interviewing, but there were no precedents for the range of income, wealth, fringe benefit and social service data which we wanted to collect. At that stage only one organization, the Government Social Survey, seemed sufficiently equipped to do such a job. Dorothy Wedderburn and myself had worked with them on a national survey of the elderly in 1962. However, the Government Social Survey (now a division of the Office of Population Censuses and Surveys) was overloaded with research commissioned by the government and we therefore decided to recruit and train our own team of interviewers. We recruited a number of very experienced interviewers, not all of whom took kindly to the length of the questionnaire and its preoccupation with income. Some withdrew in the early stages.

There were twenty-five interviewers who completed more than four fifths of the interviews, including many of the follow-up interviews in four special areas (Belfast, Glasgow, Neath and Salford). They were Angela Avens, Grace Benton, Mollie Carney, Sheila Chapple, Mrs E. M. Cluley, Michael Faherty, Zara Faherty, Marion Ford, Rhoda Fraser, Jim Gatt, Mrs E. Y. Golden, Doreen Groom, Doreen Hersee, Inez Jones, Mrs B. Knight, Betty Prince, Pam Rattee, Brenda Rawlings, Mrs Sorbie, Mrs E. Taylor, Keith Travis, Susan Vinen, Janet Williams, Mrs H. Worgan and Joan Worthington. Nearly all of them were interviewers with long experience and I am grateful for their support and help. Among them I must pick out Janet Williams, who travelled throughout the United Kingdom, supervising, briefing, converting refusals and checking questionnaires in the office; the late Rhoda Fraser, who was dedicated to the project and quite exceptionally to the welfare of the families whom she interviewed; Mrs H. Worgan, who supervised the work in Scotland, and Mrs Cluley, Michael Faherty, Zara Faherty, Keith Travis and Joan Worthington, who travelled extensively and, like Janet Williams and Marie Brown, showed that people initially refusing an interview could often be persuaded to change their minds. It was the faith and persistence of these people which, in the end, brought a most hazardous task to a successful culmination.

Interviewers helping with difficult areas or for some interviews in the final stages were Faith Adams, Mrs K. Almes, Mrs Baguley, Mrs J. Bunning, Mrs Burnett, Paul Chapman, Peter Collier, Andrea Cordani, Mrs P. Coulson, J. Cullen, Mrs M. L. Doughty, Mrs Feltell, Roger Giles, Ron Halpern, Mrs Hosier, Hugh Kerr, Stasia Laudanska, Mrs J. Martin, Ian McCannagh, F. G. Moore, Mrs H. T. Parker, Mrs M. B. Pattison, Chris Pye and Mrs V. Widdett.

In the special areas, Spencer Marketing Services helped us with the screening interviews and, following special briefing and pilot sessions, later undertook in conjunction with our team many of the follow-up interviews. I am particularly indebted to Joy Marcuse, who directed the operations of this research agency. I would also like to thank Joy Restron, of Public Attitudes Surveys, for her assistance in the Newcastle region.

Andrew Hinchliffe carried out and supervised much of the coding, and Colin Jacobsen not only supervised some difficult stages of the coding but also edited and checked the questionnaires as they came in. Both kept the rest of us at full stretch in disentangling the interviews, sometimes resulting in return visits to certain households. Both showed that they were not prepared to settle for a quiet life and insisted on meaningful, as well as high professional, standards (which are not always the same thing).

In mid 1968, Brian Abel-Smith was invited by R. H. S. Crossman, newly appointed as Secretary of State for Social Services, to become his Senior Adviser at the Department of Health and Social Security. Soon after he accepted this appointment he withdrew from the project. None of us appreciated quickly enough the significance for the survey of his acceptance of this new assignment. We failed to take a decision which in retrospect might have saved one or two years, to transfer the data analysis immediately to Essex. While the LSE computer manager was extremely indulgent in permitting protracted analysis of the survey data, it was inevitable that as time went on it became difficult to administer data analysis in a separate institution. Moreover, problems of integrating the analysis at LSE with that at Essex meant, in the end, that most of the work originally conducted at LSE had to be repeated at Essex. This was a big reason for delay, for which I must accept entire responsibility. Another was, of course, that in supervising the analysis and writing a report two directors acting jointly in their vacations and during terms of sabbatical leave would have completed the report a lot more quickly than one director alone. And as I have already indicated, too few funds were available during the analysis stages to allow the report to be prepared more quickly by financing a division of labour in the writing up.

In the subsequent analysis of the data I depended heavily first on Hazel O'Hare, of the London School of Economics, and then Phil Holden, of the Department of Sociology in the University of Essex. Each of them constructed tapes, overcame the difficulties of rewriting programmes for different computers and showed immense patience with insistent requests for tabulations. To both of them and to the Essex University Computing Service I owe a major debt. John Bond, David Hughes, Tim Mason, Jennifer Nyman and Alan Walker acted as my research assistants for different periods of the analysis, and prepared material for particular chapters. I am grateful for their help and especially their sense of commitment. John Bond wrote the first draft of Appendix Four on the costing of social services and contributed substantially to Chapter 19. Dennis Marsden has written Chapter 22 (on one-parent families) jointly with me. Alan Walker wrote the first draft of Chapter 25 (on means-tested benefits) and also worked on material on children and the elderly, David Hughes prepared a substantial amount of material on housing costs for Chapter 13 and helped to elaborate Chapter 16, and Hilary Land was responsible for writing the first draft of Appendix One on methodology. Tim Mason and Jennifer Nyman worked on housing, low pay, the rich and the special areas.

Among those who have helped in the preparation of the project, answered particular questions, commented on particular chapters, or otherwise contributed to the report, and to whom I am indebted are Tony Atkinson, Richard Barron, Colin Bell, Marjorie Cowell, Susan Ferge, Amelia Harris, Alan Harrison, Colin Harbury, Geoffrey Hawthorn, Mrs Jackson, David Lockwood, Tony Lynes, John Macarthy, Della Nevitt, Geoff Norris, Frank Parkin, Nicholas Ragg, Jack Revell, Sally Sainsbury, Gurmukh Singh, Jim Spencer, Roy Wallis, Dorothy

Wedderburn, Steve Winyard and Michael Wolfson. Barbara Wootton was also a key adviser at a critical stage of the work.

A version of the introduction was published by the Cambridge University Press in *Poverty, Inequality and Class Structure*, edited by Dorothy Wedderburn. I should also like to acknowledge the help given in the course of preparation and publication of this report by Jill Norman of Penguin Books and Peter Ford. During the fieldwork and subsequent analysis I depended heavily on the secretarial services first of Wendy Morgan and then of Sue Best, Marion Haberhauer, Linda Peachey and Sandra Rowell. The University of Essex made my participation in the preparatory fieldwork and much of the writing up possible through its generous provision of sabbatical leave for its academic staff. It would be invidious also not to mention the long-standing debt I owe to staff, members of the Executive Committee and individual members of the local branches of the Child Poverty Action Group, and especially its director, since 1969, Frank Field, who have helped me better to comprehend, and appreciate the practical importance of many of the issues raised in this book.

Finally I owe certain debts of an incalculable kind to Brian Abel-Smith, who shared with me all the early planning, the organization of the questionnaire and the fieldwork, maintaining a clear-headed appreciation of what was really worthwhile in research and, after having to withdraw from the project, showing dignity when the project came under fire from certain established, including political, interests. To Sheila Benson and Marie Brown, who held the project together during its most critical stages. Marie's infectious enthusiasm communicated itself to the most hesitant interviewer and her qualities as an interviewer are, in my experience, quite unique. To Dennis Marsden, Adrian Sinfield, Alan Walker and Joy Townsend, who have given continuing help and personal encouragement during the research. And to Ruth Townsend, who helped me through so many vicissitudes during the early years of the project and never lost her sense of priorities, even when family life was put at strain by my obsession with the project. I wish this report were a more adequate return for their support.

1
Introduction: Concepts of Poverty and Deprivation

Poverty can be defined objectively and applied consistently only in terms of the concept of relative deprivation. That is the theme of this book. The term is understood objectively rather than subjectively. Individuals, families and groups in the population can be said to be in poverty when they lack the resources to obtain the types of diet, participate in the activities and have the living conditions and amenities which are customary, or are at least widely encouraged or approved, in the societies to which they belong. Their resources are so seriously below those commanded by the average individual or family that they are, in effect, excluded from ordinary living patterns, customs and activities.

The consequences of adopting this definition will be illustrated to bring out its meaning. For example, research studies might find more poverty, according to this definition, in certain wealthy than in certain less wealthy societies, although the poor in the former might be better off, according to some criteria, than the poor in the latter. Again, despite continued economic growth over a period of years, the proportion of the population of an advanced industrial society which is found to be in poverty might rise. Certainly some of the assumptions that are currently made in comparing and contrasting the more developed with the less developed societies, and in judging progress in overcoming poverty in affluent societies, would have to be revised. In the United States, for example, the assumption that the prevalence of poverty has been steadily reduced since 1959 may have to be abandoned, principally because the definition upon which prevalence is measured is rooted in the conceptions of a particular moment of history and not sufficiently related to the needs and demands of a changing society. The US government adopted a standard which was misconceived, but showed, for example, that the number of people in poverty declined from 22·4 per cent (or 39·5 million) in 1959 to 12·5 per cent (or 25·6 million) in 1971,[1] and 11·6 per cent (or

1. *Social Indicators, 1973*, the 1970 Manpower Report of the President, Social and Economic Statistics Administration, US Department of Commerce, Government Printing Office, Washington DC, 1974. See Table 5.17 in particular. The 1970 Manpower Report of the President by the US Department of Labor solemnly traces, like many other reports emanating from the US government, and also papers and books by social scientists, the fall in poverty during the

24·3 million) in 1974.[1] Students of income distribution in the United States were coming to appreciate by the late 1970s that the standard was seriously misleading.[2]

The definition also has implications for policy which should be recognized at the outset. Although all societies have ways of identifying and trying to deal with their problems, the social sciences are having an increasing influence upon decision-makers, both in providing information and implicitly or explicitly legitimating action. An important example in the history of the formulation of social policies to deal with poverty is the definition of the subsistence standard in the Beveridge Report of 1942. Beveridge adapted the definition used in measuring poverty by Seebohm Rowntree, A. L. Bowley and others in their studies of different communities in Britain, and he argued that this was the right basis for paying benefits in a social security scheme designed to abolish want.[3] For thirty years the rationale for the level of benefits paid in the British schemes of national insurance and supplementary benefit (formerly National Assistance) has rested upon the arguments put forward in the early years of the Second World War. No attempt has yet been made to present an alternative rationale, although benefits have been increased from time to time in response to rises in prices and wages. A clear definition allows the scale and degree as well as the nature of the problem of poverty to be identified, and therefore points to the scale as well as the kind of remedial action that might be taken. Such action may involve not just the general level of benefits, for example, but revision of relativities between benefits received by different types of family.

Previous Definitions of Poverty

Any attempt to justify a new approach[4] towards the definition and measurement of poverty, so that its causes and means of alleviation may be identified, must begin with previous definitions and evidence. The literature about both poverty

---

1960s and early 1970s. But since a fixed and not an up-dated poverty line has been applied at regular intervals, this fall is scarcely surprising. The same trend could have been demonstrated for every industrial society in the years since the war and, indeed for nearly all periods of history since the Industrial Revolution.

1. *The Measure of Poverty*, A Report to Congress as Mandated by the Education Amendments of 1974, US Department of Health, Education and Welfare, Washington DC, April 1976, p. 13.

2. Schorr, A. L. (ed.), *Jubilee for our Times: A Practical Program for Income Equality*, Columbia University Press, 1977, pp. 15–16.

3. *Social Insurance and Allied Services* (The Beveridge Report), Cmd 6404, HMSO, London, 1942.

4. It is new only in the sense that the implications and applications do not appear to have been spelled out systematically and in detail. The line of thought has been put forward by many social scientists in the past. For example, Adam Smith wrote, 'By necessaries I under-

and inequality are closely related and need to be considered in turn. Any explanation of the fact that the poor receive an unequal share of resources must be related to the larger explanation of social inequality. We will consider definitions, evidence about poverty and related evidence about inequality.

Previous operational definitions of poverty have not been expressed in thoroughgoing relativist terms, nor founded comprehensively on the key concepts of resources and style of living. The concern has been with narrower concepts of income and the maintenance of physical efficiency. Among the early studies of poverty, the work of Seebohm Rowntree is most important. In 1899 he collected detailed information about families in York. He defined families whose 'total earnings are insufficient to obtain the minimum necessaries for the maintenance of merely physical efficiency as being in primary poverty'.[1] Making shrewd use of the work of W. O. Atwater, an American nutritionist, reinforced by the findings of Dr Dunlop, who had experimented with the diets of prisoners in Scotland to find how nutritional intakes were related to the maintenance of body weight, he estimated the average nutritional needs of adults and children, translated these needs into quantities of different foods and hence into the cash equivalent of these foods. To these costs for food he added minimum sums for clothing, fuel and household sundries according to size of family. The poverty line for a family of man and wife and three children was 17s. 8d. per week, made up of 12s. 9d. for food, 2s. 3d. for clothing, 1s. 10d. for fuel and 10d. for household sundries. Rent was treated as an unavoidable addition to this sum, and was counted in full. A family was therefore regarded as being in poverty if its income minus rent fell short of the poverty line.

Nearly all subsequent studies were influenced deeply by this application of the concept of subsistence. With minor adaptations, a stream of area surveys of poverty based on Rowntree's methods was carried out in Britain, especially between the wars.[2] Rowntree himself carried out further studies in York in 1936 and

stand, not only the commodities which are indispensably necessary for the support of life, but whatever the custom of the country renders it indecent for creditable people, even of the lowest order, to be without.' He gave as examples linen shirts and leather shoes which 'the established rules of decency have rendered necessary to the lowest rank of people'. However, beer and ale, in Great Britain, and wine, even in the wine countries, were not necessaries because 'custom nowhere renders it indecent for people to live without them.' See *The Wealth of Nations*, Ward, Lock, London, 1812, p. 693 (first published 1776).

1. Rowntree, B. Seebohm, *Poverty: A Study of Town Life*, Macmillan, London, 1901. Charles Booth's major work in London between 1887 and 1892 was on a larger scale but employed a cruder measure of poverty. See his *Life and Labour of the People in London*, Macmillan, London (17 volumes published in 1903; first volume on East London originally published 1889).

2. See, for example, Bell, Lady F., *At the Works*, Nelson, London, 1912; Davies, M., *Life in an English Village*, London, 1909; Reeves, P., *Round About a Pound a Week*, London, 1914; Bowley, A. L., and Burnett-Hurst, A. R., *Livelihood and Poverty, A Study in the Economic and Social Conditions of Working Class Households in Northampton, Warrington, Stanley, Reading*

1950.[1] The subsistence standard was used as a measuring rod, or as a basis for recommending minimum social security rates and minimum earnings in many countries, including South Africa, Canada and Tanganyika (before the emergence of Tanzania).[2]

But the standards which were adopted proved difficult to defend. Rowntree's estimates of the costs of necessities other than food were based either on his own and others' opinions or, as in the case of clothing, on the actual expenditure of those among a small selection of poor families who spent the least. Does the actual expenditure of the poorest families represent what they *need* to spend on certain items? Neither in his studies nor in similar studies were criteria of need, independent of personal judgement or of the minimum amounts actually spent on certain goods, put forward.

In the case of food it seemed, at first sight, that independent criteria of need had been produced. But there were three major faults in procedure. Estimates of the nutrients required were very broad averages and were not varied by age and family composition, still less by occupation and activity outside work. The foods that were selected to meet these estimates were selected arbitrarily, with a view to securing minimally adequate nutrition at lowest cost, rather than in correspondence with diets that are conventional among the poorer working classes. And finally, the cost of food in the total cost of subsistence formed a much higher percentage than in ordinary experience. In relation to the budgets and customs of life of ordinary people, the make-up of the subsistence budget was unbalanced. For example, when Lord Beveridge argued in the war for a subsistence standard similar to the poverty standards of Rowntree and others, he recommended an allowance of 53s. 3d. a week at 1938 prices for a man, wife and three small children, including 31s. for food (58 per cent of the total). But in 1938 families of the same size with roughly the same total income were spending less than 22s. on food (41 per cent of the total).[3]

An adaptation of the Rowntree method is in use by the US government. The

(*and Bolton*), King, London, 1915; Bowley, A. L., and Hogg, M. H., *Has Poverty Diminished?*, London, 1925; *New Survey of London Life and Labour*, London, 1930–35; Soutar, M. S., Wilkins, E. H., and Florence, P., *Nutrition and Size of Family*, London, 1942.

1. Rowntree, B. S., *Poverty and Progress*, Longmans, Green, London, 1941; Rowntree, B. S. (with Lavers, G. R.), *Poverty and the Welfare State*, Longmans, Green, London, 1951.

2. For example, Batson, E., *Social Survey of Cape Town*, Reports of the School of Social Science and Social Administration, University of Cape Town, 1941–4; Batson, E., *The Poverty Line in Salisbury*, University of Cape Town, 1945; Pillay, P. N., *A Poverty Datum Line Study Among Africans in Durban*, Occasional Paper No. 3, Department of Economics, University of Natal, 1973; Poduluk, J. R., *Income Distribution and Poverty in Canada, 1967*, Dominion Bureau of Statistics, 1968; Bettison, D. S., 'The Poverty Datum Line in Central Africa', *Rhodes Livingstone Journal*, No. 27, 1960.

3. Based on data in Henderson, A. M., 'The Cost of a Family', *Review of Economic Studies*, 1949–50, vol. XVII (2).

Social Security Administration Poverty Index is based on estimates prepared by the Department of Agriculture of the costs of food needed by families of different composition. A basic standard of nutritional adequacy has been put forward by the National Research Council, and this standard has been translated into quantities of types of food 'compatible with the preference of United States families, as revealed in food consumption studies'.[1] This, in turn, is then translated into the minimum costs of purchases on the market. Finally, by reference to the average sums spent per capita on food as a proportion of all income (derived from consumer expenditure surveys), it is assumed that food costs represent 33 per cent of the total income needed by families of three or more persons and 27 per cent of the total income needed by households consisting of two persons.

A number of points in the argument can be examined critically. First, and most important, the index is not redefined periodically to take account of changing customs and needs. In one of her influential articles Mollie Orshansky writes, 'Except to allow for rising prices, the poverty index has not been adjusted since 1959.' Between 1959 and 1966, 'the average income of 4-person families had increased by 37 per cent but the poverty line by only 9 per cent'.[2] Yet the same writer had pointed out earlier that 'social conscience and custom dictate that there be not only sufficient quantity of food but sufficient variety to meet recommended nutritional goals and conform to customary eating patterns'.[3] In a rapidly developing society like the United States, dietary customs and needs are liable to change equally rapidly and estimates of need must be reviewed frequently. Otherwise the risk is run of reading the needs of the present generation as if they were those of the past. Foods are processed differently, and presented from time to time in new forms, whether in recipe or packaging. Real prices may rise without any corresponding improvement in nutritional content. In the United States as well as Britain household expenditure on food has increased faster than prices in the last ten or twenty years, but regular studies of nutrition have shown little change in nutritional intakes. This evidence provides the minimum case for raising the poverty line between two points in time by more than the rise in prices.[4]

1. Orshansky, M., 'Counting the Poor: Another Look at the Poverty Profile', Social Security Bulletin, vol. 28, January 1965, p. 5.
2. Orshansky, M., 'Who Was Poor in 1966?', Research and Statistics Note, US Department of Health and Education and Welfare, 6 December 1967, p. 3. The 1970 Manpower Report of the President puts the same point in a rather different way: 'Whereas in 1959 the poverty threshold represented about 48 per cent of the average income of all four-person families, in 1968 it represented only 36 per cent.'
3. Orshansky, 'Counting the Poor', p. 5.
4. Between 1960 and 1968, average expenditure per head in Britain on food increased by about 6 per cent more than prices, but the energy value of nutritional intakes by only about 1 per cent and calcium by less than 3 per cent. However, there is no satisfactory comprehensive index for nutritional intakes. See Ministry of Agriculture, Household Food Consumption and Expenditure: 1968, HMSO, London, 1970, pp. 8, 57 and 64; Household Food Consumption and Expenditure: 1966, HMSO, London, 1968, pp. 9 and 84.

No price index can cope properly with changes in ingredients, quality and availability of and 'need for' goods and services.[1] The standard that Miss Orshansky helped to work out for 1959 could only be justified in the stream of American domestic history in terms far more dynamic than the grudging movements in the price index. That the United States definition is static and historically barren is revealed in her honest admission that one of the things the Social Security Administration did not know was 'how to adjust a poverty line to conform to changes in productivity'.[2]

Secondly, nutritional needs are narrowly defined. The cost of buying a minimally adequate diet, providing families restrict the kind and quality of their purchases and exercise skill in preparing as well as in buying food, is worked out.[3] Nothing extra is allowed for eating meals out, and the amounts are enough only for 'temporary or emergency use when funds are low'.[4] There are grounds for supposing that the standards pay insufficient heed to ordinary food customs and are inappropriate for more than a temporary period. The underlying definitions of dietary adequacy are insufficiently related to actual performance of occupational and social roles. Estimates of nutritional needs in fact include a larger element for activities which are socially and occupationally determined than for activities which are biologically and physiologically determined. Moreover, the former obviously vary widely among individuals and communities. While it may seem to be

1. This applies to most goods and services and not just foodstuffs. One instance might be given from US experience. Between 1958 and 1964, the minimum price of refrigerators increased from $217 to $261. At the same time they became self-defrosting and incorporated more frozen-food storage space. But during the same period, 1958–64, partly in conformity with these changes, the Consumer Price Index showed a *decline* of 11 per cent on the price per unit. Nevertheless 'a person with $217 could buy [a refrigerator] in 1958 but not in 1964'. See Department of Economic and Social Affairs, United Nations, *Social Policy and the Distribution of Income in the Nation*, New York, 1969, p. 53.

2. Orshansky, M., 'How Poverty is Measured', *Monthly Labor Review*, February 1969, p. 41. There are few references to this conceptual problem in the American literature. Ornati does call attention to the problem, but does not suggest how a fresh 'contemporary' standard for each period of time, which he recommends, can be worked out consistently. See Ornati, O., *Poverty Amid Affluence*, The Twentieth Century Fund, New York, 1966, pp. 28–31. By the mid 1970s, government officials were aware of some criticisms of absolute definitions of poverty, but believed that the only alternative was a 'purely relative definition' of a 'fixed per cent' or a 'quasi-relative definition' of a 'fixed per cent of the median'. See *The Measure of Poverty*, p. 21.

3. 'All the plans, if strictly followed, can provide an acceptable and adequate diet but – generally speaking – the lower the level of cost, the more restricted the kinds and qualities of food must be and the more the skill in marketing and food preparation that is required' – Orshansky, 'Counting the Poor', p. 5.

4. This is a phrase used by the US Department of Agriculture in describing an 'economy food plan' costing only 75 to 80 per cent as much as the basic low-cost plan, quoted in ibid., p. 6. Later Miss Orshansky made the remarkable admission that, 'The Agriculture Department estimates that only about 10 per cent of persons spending (up to the level in the economy food plan) were able to get a nutritionally adequate diet.' See 'How Poverty is Measured', p. 38.

reasonable to average nutritional requirements, empirical studies of diets in relationship to incomes and activities have to be undertaken to demonstrate whether that procedure is in fact as reasonable as it purports to be.

Finally, the question of finding criteria for needs other than food is dodged by estimating food costs and then taking these as a fixed percentage of the total budget stated to be necessary. The percentage varies for households of different size and is lower for farm families than for other families. How, therefore, are the percentages chosen? Essentially they are a reflection of actual consumption, or, more strictly, consumption in the mid 1950s.[1] But, again, although actual behaviour is more relevant than an arbitrarily defined category of 'poor', it cannot be regarded as a criterion of need. This remains the nagging problem about the entire procedure. All that can be conceded is that at least the United States method makes more allowance (although out of date) for conventional distribution of a poverty budget between food, fuel and clothing and other items, than the Rowntree method, which expected poor families to adopt a distributional pattern of spending quite unlike other families.

The circularity in the definition of poverty by the US Social Security Administration is its weakest feature. In some respects, budgetary practice is redefined as budgetary need. But arbitrary elements are also built into the definition from the start. Miss Orshansky is refreshingly candid about this. Beginning an expository article, she writes:

Poverty, like beauty, lies in the eye of the beholder. Poverty is a value judgement; it is not something one can verify or demonstrate, except by inference and suggestion, even with a measure of error. To say who is poor is to use all sorts of value judgements. The concept has to be limited by the purpose which is to be served by the definition . . . In the Social Security Administration, poverty was first defined in terms of the public or policy issue; to how many people, and to which ones, did we wish to direct policy concern.

[Later she adds] A concept which can help influence public thinking must be socially and politically credible.[2]

1. Orshansky herself quotes a Bureau of Labor Statistics Survey for 1960–61, showing that food represented only 22 per cent of the expenditure of a household of three people, for example, compared with 31 per cent in the 1955 survey. Acknowledging that the percentage had decreased, she stated that this 'undoubtedly reflect[ed] in part the general improvement in real income achieved by the Nation as a whole in the 6 years which elapsed between the two studies'. Had the later percentages been adopted, the poverty line would have been $1400 to $1500 higher for a family of three persons, for example, and the total number of families in poverty would have been at least half as many again. See Orshansky, 'How Poverty is Measured', p. 9. The percentage chosen is a further instance of the rigidity of poverty measurement. In the last hundred years the proportion of the family budget spent on food has fallen steadily in the United States, Britain, Japan and other rich countries, and tends to be higher in countries which have a lower income per capita than the USA. See, for example, *Social Policy and the Distribution of Income*, pp. 53–6.
2. Orshansky, 'How Poverty is Measured', p. 37.

This may be shrewd but is scarcely reassuring. Socio-economic measures cannot rest only on imaginable or even politically acceptable, but must also rest on demonstrable, definitions of social conditions. These may be difficult to apply consistently. There are bound to be difficulties and disadvantages in any approach that is developed. In the final analysis, a definition of poverty may have to rest on value judgements. But this does not mean that a definition cannot be objective and that it cannot be distinguished from social or individual opinion.

In these passages Miss Orshansky confuses different purposes. The point about a good definition is that it should be comprehensive, should depend as much as possible on independent or external criteria of evaluation, should involve the ordering of a mass of factual data in a rational, orderly and informative fashion, and should limit, though not conceal, the part played by the value judgement.

Two conclusions might be drawn from this brief historical review of attempts, especially in Britain and the United States, to define poverty. The first is that definitions which are based on some conception of 'absolute' deprivation disintegrate upon close and sustained examination and deserve to be abandoned. Poverty has often been defined, in the words of an OECD review, 'in terms of some absolute level of minimum needs, below which people are regarded as being poor, for purpose of social and government concern, and which does not change through time'.[1] In fact, people's needs, even for food, are conditioned by the society in which they live and to which they belong, and just as needs differ in different societies so they differ in different periods of the evolution of single societies. Any conception of poverty as 'absolute' is therefore inappropriate and misleading.

The second conclusion which might be drawn is that, though the principal definitions put forward historically have invoked some 'absolute' level of minimum needs, they have in practice represented rather narrow conceptions of relative deprivation and deserve to be clarified as such.[2] Thus Seebohm Rowntree's

1. The review tacitly acknowledges the intellectual weakness of this approach. See Organization for Economic Cooperation and Development, *Public Expenditure on Income Maintenance Programmes*, Studies in Resource Allocation No. 3, Paris, July 1976, pp. 62–4.
2. A good example of continuing ambivalence about 'absolute' and 'relative' standards is a review in the mid 1970s of trends in poverty in relation to evidence from the Family Expenditure Survey for the years 1953 to 1973. The fact that Rowntree and others did not in practice apply the same 'absolute' standard at different dates is documented, but the authors never quite come to terms with that fact, either theoretically or operationally, and find why an 'absolute' definition cannot be sustained. While appearing to wish to keep both options open, they seem to come down in favour of an 'absolute' approach. Thus, under a subheading entitled, 'The Decline of Poverty', in the Conclusions, A. D. Smith writes, 'Our principal finding on the extent of poverty is that, on the basis of a constant 1971 absolute living standard, numbers in poverty declined from about a fifth of the population in 1953/4 to about a fortieth in 1973. A fall by a factor of eight in only twenty years is a notable improvement. But in relative terms we found little change: the net income of the poorest fifth percentile was about the same proportion of the median income in both years, so that the decline in numbers in poverty so

definition amounted in effect to a conception of nutritional deprivation relative to the level believed to be required for members of the manual working class at the turn of the century to function efficiently. That definition corresponded with contemporary Liberal interpretations of the rights and needs of labour in industrial society and was a class standard. The US Social Security Administration Poverty Index is similar in basic respects. It is a stringent view of nutritional deprivation relative to the minimally adequate diets achieved by low-income. families in 1959 who were managing their budgets economically.

The Limitations of the Evidence of Poverty

I shall now briefly review available evidence about poverty. It is certainly voluminous, but also incomplete and inconsistent. Most of it is indirect, in the sense that particular aspects of poverty, such as bad-quality housing, homelessness, overcrowding and malnourishment, the hardship of the unemployed, aged, sick and disabled and the severity of some working conditions rather than actual income in relation to community living standards have been described and discussed. One tradition is the polemical, comprehensive account of working and living conditions, as, for example, in some of the writing of Engels, Masterman and Orwell.[1] Another is the painstaking official commission of inquiry, ranging, for example, from the 1844 Report of the Commission of Inquiry into the State of Large Towns to the 1965 Report of the Milner Holland Committee on Housing in Greater London.[2] A third is the punctiliously specific research study.

For example, there have been studies of the relationship between prenatal nutritional deficiencies in mothers and organic and mental defects in their children;[3] more general studies of depression, apathy and lethargy resulting from inadequate diets and nutritional deficiency; books and papers containing evidence of the correlation between bad social conditions and restricted physical growth of children both in height and weight;[4] evidence too of the association between over-

---

measured reflects essentially the growth of the economy rather than a redistribution of income.' See Smith, A. D., 'Conclusions', in Fiegehen, G. C., Lansley, P. S., and Smith, A. D., *Poverty and Progress in Britain 1953–73*, Cambridge University Press, 1977, p. 111.

1. Compare, for example, Engels, F., *The Condition of the Working Class in England*, Panther Books, London, 1969 (first published 1845); Masterman, C., *The Condition of England*, Methuen, London, 1960 (first published 1909); and Orwell, G., *The Road to Wigan Pier*, Penguin Books, Harmondsworth, 1962 (first published 1937).

2. Report of the Committee on Housing in Greater London (The Sir Milner Holland Committee), Cmnd 2605, HMSO, London, 1965.

3. Pasamanick, B., Lilienfeld, A., and Rogers, M. E., *Prenatal and Perinatal Factors in the Development of Childhood Behavior Disorders*, Johns Hopkins University School of Hygiene, 1957.

4. See, for example, Benjamin, B., 'Tuberculosis and Social Conditions in the Metropolitan

crowding and a number of different infectious diseases;[1] and evidence of the downward drift of income and occupational status in relation to schizophrenia.[2] This kind of evidence can certainly be used by the social scientist to build up a picture of the interrelationship of different problems and very rough estimates of the amount of, as well as the relative variations in, poverty. Different indicators can be used for this purpose, such as morbidity and mortality rates, percentage of households lacking certain amenities, unemployment rates, measures of the average height and weight of schoolchildren and the percentage of families obtaining means-tested welfare benefits.[3] Perhaps insufficient work has yet been done on the correlations between indicators like these and variables such as population structure, employment structure and rateable value. Certainly elaborate work of this kind would be required to buttress any development of more general theories of poverty.

But the underlying task of developing a definition of poverty in operational terms which can be applied in different countries and regions, and which can permit measurement of a kind sensitive enough to show the short-term effect on the numbers in poverty of, say, an increase in unemployment, an unusually large increase in prices, or the stepping-up in value of social security benefits, is still in an early stage. This remains true despite a longish history of empirical work in some countries.[4] Even recent work reflects continuing reliance on the subsistence ap-

Boroughs of London', *British Journal of Tuberculosis*, 47, 1953; Miller, F. J. W., *et al.*, *Growing up in Newcastle upon Tyne*, Oxford University Press, 1960.

1. For example, Stein, L., 'Tuberculosis and the "Social Complex" in Glasgow', *British Journal of Social Medicine*, January 1952; Scott, J. A., 'Gastro-enteritism in Infancy', *British Journal of Preventive and Social Medicine*, October 1953.

2. Brown, G. W., *et al.*, *Schizophrenia and Social Care*, Oxford University Press, 1966; Goldberg, E. M., and Morrison, S. L., 'Schizophrenia and Social Class', *British Journal of Psychiatry*, 1963.

3. Methods of relating different indicators are discussed in Moser, C. A., and Scott, W., *British Towns: A Statistical Study of their Social and Economic Differences*, Oliver & Boyd, London, 1961. See also Davies, B., *Social Needs and Resources in Local Services*, Michael Joseph, London, 1968; and for an illustration of the political uses of indicators of area deprivation, the Labour Party, *Labour's Social Strategy*, August 1969.

4. American work of a systematic kind could be said to date from Dubois, W. E. B., *The Philadelphia Negro*, first published in 1899 (reissued by Schocken, New York, 1967). The early work in England of Booth and Rowntree in the 1880s and 1890s prompted a succession of studies in towns and cities. See, for example, Bowley and Burnett-Hurst, *Livelihood and Poverty*; Caradog Jones, D., *Social Survey of Merseyside*, Liverpool, 1934; Tout, H., *The Standard of Living in Bristol*, Bristol, 1938, as well as Rowntree's own subsequent work. Much the same approach was followed by Professor Geoffrey Batson in South Africa, 1941–4 and 1945. For a review of English studies, see Political and Economic Planning, *Poverty: Ten Years after Beveridge*, Planning No. 344, 1952. For a general review of surveys using the subsistence standard of measurement, see Pagani, A., *La Linea Della Poverta*, Collana di Scienze Sociali, Edizioni ANEA, Milan, 1960.

proach, despite appreciation of its inadequacy.[1] Recent quantitative analyses in different countries of the extent of poverty can be compared. In 1966 the British Ministry of Social Security found that 160,000 families with two or more children, or 4·1 per cent of such families, were living on incomes lower than the prevailing basic rates of national assistance.[2] In the same year, the US Social Security Administration, using a more generous definition of adequacy, found that 13·6 per cent of all households with children (15·6 per cent with two or more children) and 17·7 per cent of all households were poor.[3] In 1966 in Melbourne, 4·8 per cent of families with children (6·1 per cent of families with two or more children) and just over 7 per cent of all households were found to be in poverty.[4] But although the last of these three 1966 surveys copied methods used in the United States to estimate what incomes for families of different size were equivalent, they each adopted a national or conventional and not independent standard. In Britain, the Ministry of Social Security simply adopted the basic scale rates paid by the National Assistance Board, plus rent, as the poverty line, and sought to find how many families had an income of less than the levels implied by those rates. (In the 1970s, estimates derived from the Family Expenditure Survey and published in *Social Trends*[5] and elsewhere[6] have followed the same procedure.) In Australia, the legal minimum wage plus child endowment payments was treated as equivalent to the poverty line for a man and wife and two children, and adjustments were made for families of different size. In each case, standards which had al-

1. For example, a long series of studies in South Africa and Central Africa have adopted the Poverty Datum Line, developed by Batson on the basis of Rowntree's and Bowley's work. Modern research workers have a wry appreciation of its shortcomings. See Maasdorp, G., and Humphreys, A. S. B. (eds.), *From Shanty Town to Township: An Economic Study of African Poverty and Rehousing in a South African City*, Juta, Capetown, 1975.

2. Ministry of Social Security, *Circumstances of Families*, HMSO, London, 1967, p. 8.

3. Orshansky, 'Who Was Poor in 1966', Table 4. In Canada, a similar kind of approach to that used in the United States produced an official estimate of 3·85 million people in poverty in 1967, or about a quarter of the population. The proportion was highest in the Atlantic Provinces. See a brief prepared by the Department of National Health and Welfare for presentation to the Special Committee of the Senate on Poverty, The Senate of Canada, *Proceedings of the Special Senate Committee on Poverty*, 24 and 26 February 1970, pp. 18–19 and 62.

4. Estimated from Table 7.5 in Henderson, R. F., Harcourt, A., and Harper, R. J. A., *People in Poverty: A Melbourne Survey*, Cheshire, Melbourne, 1970, p. 117. Also see Henderson, R. F., Harcourt, A., Harper, R. J. A., and Shaver, S., *The Melbourne Poverty Survey: Further Notes on Methods and Results*, Technical Paper No. 3, Institute of Applied Economic and Social Research, University of Melbourne, May 1972. A further, national, survey of incomes on the basis of this work was carried out in August 1973 by the Australian Bureau of Statistics. This found a rather higher percentage in poverty (10·2) than just in the city of Melbourne (7·3), which was broadly similar to the study of 1966. See *Poverty in Australia*, Interim Report of the Australian Government's Commission of Inquiry into Poverty, March 1974, Canberra.

5. *Social Trends*, No. 7, HMSO, London, 1976, p. 123.

6. See Fiegehen, Lansley, and Smith, *Poverty and Progress in Britain*.

ready proved to be politically acceptable rather than other standards were invoked. The United States method has been described above, and though it is more complicated in that it consists of certain attempts to develop detached criteria and build rational procedures, rough and arbitrary judgements are made at the really critical stages of fixing the level of the poverty line.

In calling attention to the fact that much of the evidence about poverty depends on measures which are built, in the final analysis, on conventional judgement or experience rather than on independent criteria, such evidence must not be discounted. If there are national standards of need, expressed through public assistance scales, a minimum wage or child endowment, knowing the number of people having incomes of less than these standards none the less represents valuable information. Such information can also be collected for different countries. The moral is, however, to endeavour to distinguish between definitions of poverty which are in practice made by a society or by different groups within a society and those which depend on alternative and more scientific criteria.

A Working Party of the Organization for Economic Cooperation and Development did, in fact, attempt to assemble and compare the results obtained in five countries – Australia, Canada, France, the United Kingdom and the United States – of applying official national poverty lines.[1] This was not very satisfactory, because of differences of definition, and the working party went on to develop a 'standardized' relative poverty line which could also be applied to national data on income distribution. However, their standardization amounted only to a crude form of averaging. The income said to be required by a single non-retired person in each country was expressed as a percentage of the average per capita disposable income, and the resulting percentages were averaged. Arbitrary increments were added for larger households. A one-person household was counted as poor if income fell below 66⅔ per cent of average per capita income, a two-person household 100 per cent, a three-person household 125 per cent, a four-person household 145 per cent and so on. This method has the advantage of showing which countries have the largest, and which the smallest, number of people living below the chosen relative income standard.[2] Thus in the early 1970s there were 3 per cent in Germany, 3·5 per cent (or, if certain necessary adjustments are made for purposes of comparison, 2·5 per cent) in Sweden, 7·5 per cent in the United Kingdom and 13 per cent in the United States.[3] But no independent check or justification was offered for choosing the cut-off points.

1. *Public Expenditure on Income Maintenance Programmes*, Chapter 5.
2. This type of standard is further discussed in Chapter 6.
3. *Public Expenditure on Income Maintenance Programmes*, p. 67.

Poverty and Inequality

Any preliminary outline of available evidence about poverty must include evidence about inequality. For many countries there is a considerable amount of evidence about unequal distribution of incomes, for example, the proportion of aggregate incomes taken by the poorest 10 per cent or 20 per cent of income recipients. In one wide-ranging review, Harold Lydall found that the countries distributing employment income most equally were Czechoslovakia, Hungary, New Zealand and Australia. Those distributing them most unequally were Brazil, Chile, India, Ceylon and Mexico. Lydall attempted also to document trends in the distribution for different countries. He showed that in ten of the eleven countries for which information was available, inequality in the distribution of pre-tax incomes had not just remained stationary during the 1950s but had actually widened.[1] Most other attempts to compare distributions have been less carefully documented and have been reduced to rankings according to a single coefficient or the percentage of aggregate income taken by the upper 10 per cent of income units and by the lowest 50 per cent of income units.[2]

The methods that have been used to compare the distribution of income in different countries can be criticized on grounds that they are so crude as to be misleading. For example, the ranking of so-called developed and developing countries according to a measure of inequality, such as the Gini coefficient, can change remarkably if alternative measures, such as the standard deviation of logarithms or coefficient of variation, are used.[3] The rankings are sufficiently diverse to throw profound doubt on the accepted conclusion that inequality is greater in the developing countries. As Atkinson points out, nearly all the conventional measures are insensitive to whether or not inequality is more pronounced near the top rather than near the bottom of the distribution.[4] What is at stake is the concept of equality. An attempt is made in Figure 1.1 to bring out the ambiguities in present conceptions. In Country A, the total range of the distribution of income is not as wide as in Country B, but 97 per cent of the population of B are concentrated over a narrower range of income. In which country is income distribution more unequal? Equality might be taken to mean the range of the

1. Lydall, H., *The Structure of Earnings*, Oxford University Press, 1968, pp. 152–62 and 249–51.

2. See Ranadive, K. R., 'The Equality of Incomes in India', *Bulletin of the Oxford Institute of Statistics*, May 1965, in her critical review of data used by Kuznets, S., 'Quantitative Aspects of Economic Growth of Nations: VIII Distribution of Income by Size', *Economic Development and Cultural Change*, 11 January 1963.

3. For example, see Russett, B. M., *et al.*, *World Handbook of Political and Social Indicators*, Yale University Press, 1964; Kuznets, 'Quantitative Aspects of Economic Growth of Nations'.

4. Atkinson, A. B., 'On the Measurement of Inequality', *Journal of Economic Theory*, September 1970, pp. 258–62.

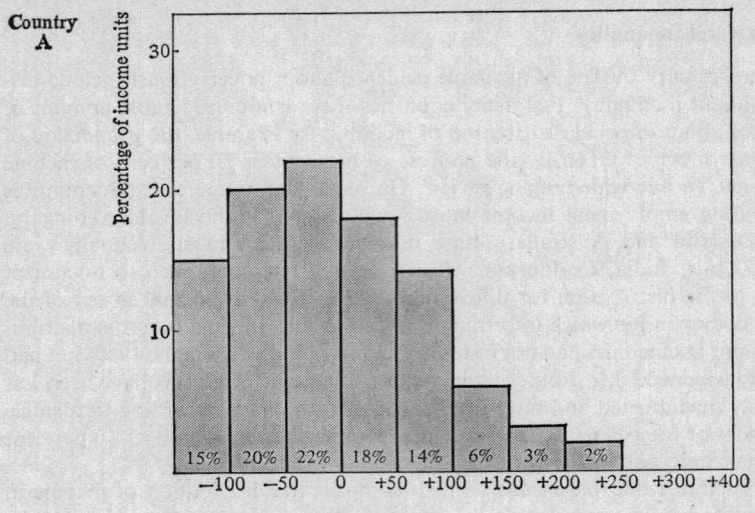

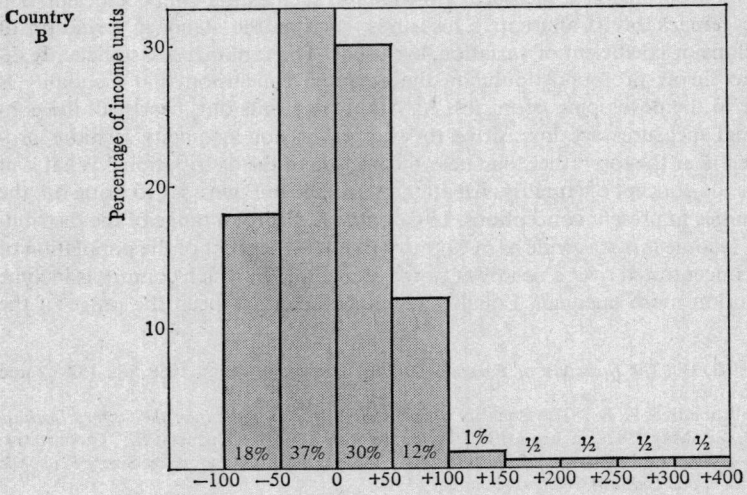

Figure 1.1. *Illustration of the distribution of incomes in two countries.*

distribution being narrow, or a high proportion of population being concentrated around the mean, or a very small proportion of population being found much below the mean. As Professor Atkinson points out, 'The degree of inequality cannot, in general, be measured without introducing social judgements.'[1]

The statistics themselves are suspect. For many countries the information for income units below taxable levels is either very sketchy or ignored. This is likely to have a big effect on conclusions drawn from comparisons made between some poor countries. Moreover, income in kind is extremely important in those countries with large agricultural populations, and yet the monetary equivalent is extremely difficult to estimate and take into account in relation to the distribution of cash incomes.

The problem is not much easier in the rich countries. Though methods of measuring income distribution have improved, estimates still have to be made for many income recipients with low incomes. In recent years information has been increasingly distorted because people manipulate income to avoid tax, for example, by converting income into assets, channelling income through children and postponing its receipt. Industrial fringe benefits, such as superannuation payments, sick pay, housing and educational subsidies, and travelling expenses in the form of subsidized transport, have become vastly more important. Like income in kind, these are not ordinarily counted in estimates of the distribution of personal incomes.[2] Apparent differences between countries in inequalities of income distribution might be wholly explained by the differential use by sections of the population of such resources. Inevitably we are driven to develop a more comprehensive definition of income and collect more comprehensive data on which to build theory. Better information about accepted styles of living in different countries is also required. The same relative level of command over resources in each of two countries might permit minimal participation in such styles in one but not in the other.

Theories and data are, of course, interdependent. Bad theories may not just be the consequence of bad data, but also give rise to the collection of bad data, or at least the failure to collect good data. Economic theories of inequality tend to misrepresent the shape of the wood, and in endeavouring to account for it, fail to account for the trees. Sociological theories of inequality tend to avoid any specific examination of the correlation between economic resources and occupational status or styles of life, and are, as a consequence, unnecessarily diffuse.

Information about poverty and inequality tends to be shaped and permeated by conventional opinion, and certainly decisions about what is or is not collected

---

1. Atkinson, A. B., *The Economics of Inequality*, Clarendon Press, Oxford, 1975, p. 47.

2. '. . . We have, at present, no means of estimating the effects of private fringe benefits on the degree of inequality of effective employment income . . . Private fringe benefits may offset a large part of the equalizing effects of progressive income taxes' – Lydall, *The Structure of Earnings*, pp. 157–8.

and how it is analysed and reported rest ultimately with governments rather than with independent social scientists in most countries. The information about incomes which is collected by tax departments or census bureaux, and about both incomes and expenditure in national surveys carried out by government statistical and labour offices, is neither under external control nor readily available for external analysis. Even when comparable information could be produced independently in a country substantial resources would be required, and these are rarely committed for such purposes either by the governments in question or by charitable foundations. When they are committed they are usually committed to people who are sympathetic to the government or to its methods of data collection and presentation.

Three Forms of Deprivation

Present national or social conceptions of poverty tend therefore to be inadequate and idiosyncratic or inconsistent, and the evidence which is collected about the phenomenon seriously incomplete. A new approach to both the definition and measurement of poverty is called for. This depends in part on adopting some such concept as 'relative deprivation'. As already argued, a fundamental distinction has to be made between actual and socially perceived need, and therefore between actual and socially perceived poverty – or more strictly, between *objective* and *conventionally acknowledged* poverty. All too easily the social scientist can be the unwitting servant of contemporary social values, and in the study of poverty this can have disastrous practical consequences. He may side with the dominant or majority view of the poor. If, by contrast, he feels obliged or is encouraged from the start to make a formal distinction between scientific and conventional perspectives, he is more likely to enlarge knowledge by bringing to light information which has been neglected and create more elbow-room for alternative forms of action, even if, in the end, some colouring of scientific procedure by social attitudes and opinion or individual valuation is inescapable.[1] At least he is

1. Gunnar Myrdal is well aware of this problem and describes it in broad terms. 'The scientists in any particular institutional and political setting move as a flock, reserving their controversies and particular originalities for matters that do not call into question the fundamental system of biases they share . . . The common need for rationalization will tend . . . to influence the concepts, models and theories applied; hence it will also affect the selection of relevant data, the recording of observations, the theoretical and practical inferences drawn explicitly or implicitly, and the manner of presentation of the results of research.' He argues that 'objectivity' can be understood only in the sense that however elaborately a framework of fact is developed the underlying set of value premises must also be made explicit. 'This represents an advance towards the goals of honesty, clarity and effectiveness in research . . . It should overcome the inhibitions against drawing practical and political conclusions openly, systematically and logically. This method would consequently render social research a much more powerful instrument for guiding rational policy formation.' See Myrdal, G., *Objectivity in Social Research*, Duckworth, London, 1970, pp. 53 and 72. Of course, this does not absolve the social

struggling to free himself from control and manipulation by the values which prevail within the constrictions of his own small society, social class or occupational group. Without pretending that the approach offered in these pages, or any alternative approach, can escape the exercise of judgement at key stages, it may open the way to cross-national usage and limit the element of arbitrariness.

On the one hand we have to examine the different elements which go to make up living standards at a point of time and how they vary over time, and on the other the sectional and collective interpretations of, or feelings about, such living standards. Throughout a given period of history there may be no change whatever in the actual inequalities of wealth and of income, and yet social perceptions of those inequalities and of any change in them may become keener. Alternatively, substantial changes in the structure of incomes in society may occur without the corresponding perception that such changes are taking place.

Examples can be uncomfortable. After the Second World War, there was for over a decade very little critical discussion of social policy in either Britain or the United States, and few studies by social scientists of the problems of minorities. Until the mid 1950s in Britain, and until the late 1950s in the United States, even the term 'poverty' had not been disinterred for the purposes of either popular or scientific discussion of contemporary society. But by the mid 1970s there had been over a decade of continuous debate, study and even action taking heed of the problem. No one can suppose that there was virtually no problem in the United States and Britain between the mid 1940s and the mid 1950s. Indeed, if the conclusions of the research undertaken by the US Social Security Administration are to be believed – that 20 per cent of the population of the United States was in poverty in 1962, 18 per cent in 1964, and only 11·6 per cent in 1974 – then the proportion must have been very substantially larger than 20 per cent around 1950. If this evidence makes any kind of sense, it only dramatizes the distinction between actuality and perception.

The distinction may also encourage sociologists to pay more attention to actuality than many have paid hitherto. The term 'relative deprivation' was coined originally by Stouffer and his colleagues,[1] and elaborated valuably first by Merton and then by Runciman,[2] to denote *feelings* of deprivation relative to others

---

scientist from giving grounds for the values he adopts for, as Alvin Gouldner has aptly argued, it 'betrays smugness and naïveté. It is smug because it assumes that the values that we have are good enough; it is naïve because it assumes that we know the values we have.' See Gouldner, A., 'The Sociologist as Partisan: Sociology and the Welfare State', in Douglas, J. D. (ed.), *The Relevance of Sociology*, Appleton-Century-Crofts, New York, 1970, p. 136.

1. Stouffer, S. A., *et al.*, *The American Soldier*, Princeton, 1949.
2. Merton, R. K., *Social Theory and Social Structure* (revised edn), Glencoe, Illinois, 1957; Runciman, W. G., *Relative Deprivation and Social Justice*, Routledge & Kegan Paul, London, 1966. Runciman's work is particularly valuable, not just because he expounds the practical relevance of the concept to contemporary problems, such as wage bargaining, but because he

and not *conditions* of deprivation relative to others. Yet the latter would be a preferable usage since differences in conditions between men underlie social structure and values, are not at all easy to define and measure, and may in fact be obscured by social belief. Little or no attempt has been made to specify and measure conditions of deprivation which some people experience relative to others in recent work, perhaps because such conditions are recognized to be complex phenomena requiring elaborate and patient fieldwork to identify precisely. The description and analysis of these conditions is important in many different ways. For example, a group of skilled manual workers may feel deprived in relation to a group of office staff, and it may be observed that their take-home earnings may be as high, or higher, than the salaries of the office staff. Before jumping too readily to an assumption that subjective and objective states are out of line, more information has to be given about pay and conditions. We have to establish what are the inequalities in actual working conditions, security of employment, promotion prospects and fringe benefits and, in addition, the extent to which some workers may be excluded from sharing in the conditions available either to other groups of workers in the same industry, or workers comparable to themselves in other industries. It is surely impossible to assess the importance of subjective deprivation as an explanatory variable independent of assessing actual deprivation.

A different example might be a group who are conscious of only small deprivation, but who are, in fact, like some sections of the retired, substantially deprived by any objective criteria. By comparison with the earnings of older people who are still at work, or with the incomes of younger people without dependants, the incomes of retired persons in different countries are very low. The great majority have few assets.[1] Moreover, their deprivation is quite widely acknowledged by the rest of society (if not by governments), and public support is readily found for proposed increases in pensions. But although some pensioners' organizations campaign for large increases in pension rates, most of the elderly themselves say they would be content with relatively small increases. Their expectations are modest.[2]

This example brings out very clearly how a distinction must be drawn not just between the actuality and perception of poverty, but also between normative and individual subjective or group perceptions. So the social scientist has to collect

---

shows its relevance to the analysis of political behaviour generally. A new edition of his book, with the addition of a postscript, was published by Penguin Books in 1972.

1. Wedderburn, D., 'The Financial Resources of Older People: A General Review', and 'The Characteristics of Low Income Receivers and the Role of Government', in Shanas, E., *et al., Old People in Three Industrial Societies*, Routledge & Kegan Paul, London, 1968.

2. See, for example, Wedderburn, D., 'A Cross-National Study of Standards of Living of the Aged in Three Countries', in Townsend, P. (ed.), *The Concept of Poverty*, Heinemann, London, 1970, p. 204.

evidence about (a) objective deprivation, (b) conventionally acknowledged or normative deprivation, and (c) individual subjective or group deprivation. The distinction between the second and third is in some ways a matter of degree. The former represents a dominant or majority valuation in society. The latter may reflect the views held by different kinds of minority group. There are various possibilities. Some individuals may feel poor, especially by reference to their previous situations in life, even when they are neither demonstrably poor nor acknowledged to be poor by society. Some retired middle-class persons, for example, have an income which is more than adequate according to either objective or conventional standards, but which is inadequate according to their own customary or expected standards. A group of manual or professional workers who have earnings considerably higher than the mean may feel poor by reference to other groups.

There are alternative ways which are open to the social scientist of defining and measuring conventionally acknowledged or normative deprivation. In the course of history, societies develop rules about the award of welfare payments and services to poor families. These rules can be said to reflect the standard of poverty conventionally acknowledged by these societies. The rates of payment under public assistance laws, for example, represent a contemporary social standard. The extent to which people in different societies in fact fall below national standards can be investigated, as in one study in Britain.[1] Similarly, societies use minimum housing standards, whether of overcrowding or amenities. These standards tend to be changed from time to time in response to political pressures. They represent conventional or elitist values rather than standards the non-fulfilment of which represents objective deprivation.[2]

Each of the three types of deprivation deserves thorough documentation and measurement, as a basis for explaining social conditions, attitudes and behaviour. But by trying to separate subjective and collective views about poverty from the actual conditions which constitute the problem, we are led to define both subjective and objective states and their relationships rather more carefully.

1. This was a secondary analysis of income and expenditure data. The social or normative standard of poverty was discussed and applied and the number and characteristics of people living below that standard identified. The authors did not claim that this was an objective or an ideal definition of poverty – though their work was sometimes subsequently misinterpreted as such. See Abel-Smith, B., and Townsend, P., *The Poor and the Poorest*, Bell, London, 1965. For a similar approach, see Ministry of Social Security, *Circumstances of Families*, HMSO, London, 1967.

2. The present definition of overcrowding adopted by the Registrar General is 1½ persons per room. A 'bedroom standard' of overcrowding has been devised which makes greater provision for family norms about the age and sex of children who share rooms. A 'minimum fitness' standard for housing was also worked out by the Denington Committee. See Ministry of Housing, Central Housing Advisory Committee, *Our Older Homes: A Call for Action*, HMSO, London, 1966.

Conceptions of Relativity

The idea of 'the relativity' of poverty requires some explanation. The frame of reference in adopting this approach can be regional, national or international, although until formal ties between nation states are stronger, or global corporations even more strongly entrenched, the international perspective is unlikely to be given enough emphasis. The question is how far peoples are bound by the same economic, trading, institutional and cultural systems, how far they have similar activities and customs and therefore have similar needs. Needs arise by virtue of the kind of society to which individuals belong. Society imposes expectations, through its occupational, educational, economic and other systems, and it also creates wants, through its organization and customs.

This is easy enough to demonstrate for certain commodities. Tea is nutritionally worthless, but in some countries is generally accepted as a 'necessity of life'. For many people in these countries drinking tea has been a life-long custom and is psychologically essential. And the fact that friends and neighbours expect to be offered a cup of tea (or the equivalent) when they visit helps to make it socially necessary as well: a small contribution is made towards maintaining the threads of social relationships. Other goods that are consumed are also psychologically and socially 'necessary' in the same sense, though to varying degrees. The degree of necessity is not uniform for all members of society, because certain goods and services are necessary for some communities or families and other goods and services for others. Repeated advertising and imitation by friends and neighbours can gradually establish a new product or a new version of an old product as essential in a community. Minority wants are converted into majority needs. People may buy first of all out of curiosity or a sense of display, but later make purchases in a routine way. The customs which these purchases and their consumption develop become socially and psychologically ingrained.

Clothing is another good example. Climate may determine whether or not any soft forms of protection are placed over the body, and how thick they are, but social convention, itself partly dependent on resources available, determines the type and style. Who would lay down a scale of necessities for the 1970s for young women in Britain consisting of one pair of boots, two aprons, one second-hand dress, one skirt made from an old dress, a third of the cost of a new hat, a third of the cost of a shawl and a jacket, two pairs of stockings, a few unspecified underclothes, one pair of stays and one pair of old boots worn as slippers, as Rowntree did in 1899?[1]

But convention is much more than ephemeral fashion. It is a style of living also governed by state laws and regulations. Industry conditions the population not only to want certain products and services, but to put up with certain disservices.

1. Rowntree, *Poverty: A Study of Town Life*, pp. 108–9 and 382–4.

The Public Health and Housing Acts and regulations control sanitation, the structure, size and layout of housing, streets and shops. A population becomes conditioned to expect to live in certain broad types of homes, and to heat and furnish them accordingly. Their environment, and the expectations of society around them, create their needs in an objective as well as a subjective sense. Similarly, society expects parents to provide certain things for their children, thereby creating needs. The goods and services provided for infants and at all stages of childhood are, through law, the school system, the mass media and so on, socially controlled. The needs which parents feel obliged to meet out of their incomes will depend, among other things, on formal rules about compulsory schooling, free schooling, free school meals and milk and free health services, as well as social norms about the wearing of shoes and school uniforms. Laws and norms are in delicate interdependence with need.

Those who question the relativity of poverty are often prepared to concede this part of the argument, but not that part dealing with food and drink. Estimates of minimum nutritional intakes required by man are believed to represent absolute requirements in every country, which have to be adjusted only marginally because of climate or geographical elevation. The cost of meeting these nutritional requirements is also believed to cover the bulk of the cost of meeting all human necessities, and therefore any difficulties produced by the relativity of the needs for accommodation, fuel, light, clothing, household sundries, furniture, play and leisure are unimportant and can be ignored.

This belief depends on a failure to perceive the relationship between nutritional intakes and social activities, and a failure to consider the resources (and not only cash incomes) used in meeting human needs other than for an adequate diet. It is certainly true that in favourable climates a man requires at least 1,000 calories a day to survive, providing he remains inert. But estimates of normal daily requirements in Western industrial societies average around 3,000 calories. Most of the difference between the estimates of the 'absolute' requirement of 1,000 calories and the 'absolute' requirement of 3,000 calories is socially determined. A man's dietary needs are determined to a predominant extent by the work expected of him and by the activities enjoined by the culture.[1] Society determines what foods he should look for, produce, or buy and eat. This fact is all too frequently forgotten in studies of 'necessary' intakes. Society also conditions the amount of energy that different sections of the population habitually expend not only at work but in community and family pursuits. The estimates of nutrients said by the Department of Health and Social Security to be necessary for an adequate diet represent crude averages which take little heed of the real activities of

---

1. Large variations in energy consumption among individuals engaged in different occupations are documented in Durwin, J. V. G. A., and Passmore, R., *Energy, Work and Leisure*, Heinemann, London, 1967.

different sections of the population.[1] The problem is not simply one of making allowances for variations in estimates of nutritional requirements for heaviness of occupation, but also for other activities – whether sporting, social or sexual – outside employment. Even the latest World Health Organization Handbook displays no sensitivity to the sociology of nutrition.[2] What is indisputable is that in Britain, despite increases in real incomes among all sections of the population throughout the 1950s and 1960s, the evidence of nutritional gains on the part of different income strata within each type of household is surprisingly small. Indeed, data from the National Food Survey demonstrate that inequalities in nutrient intakes are almost as wide as of household income and have remained remarkably constant – at least since 1945.

If poverty is relative cross-nationally or cross-culturally, then it is also relative historically. It is relative to time as well as place. Needs which are a product of laws and social norms must change as new legislation is passed, social organizations grow and coalesce, automation develops and expectations change. Within a generation the possession of a television set in Britain has changed from being a doubtful privilege of a tiny minority to being an expected right of 95 per cent of the population. But this is only one example. The Parker Morris standards for housing, like earlier housing standards, have been accepted by the government; new homes built to these standards will add items that each family will be expected to afford. In the 1880s and 1890s one room was the most that many working-class families could afford – or expect. Today, a two- or three-bedroomed house exacts larger real financial obligations. The attenuation of public transport services is brought about in some areas by the development of private transport and, if private transport becomes the norm, that can only be at greater real cost per family. Two or three weeks' summer holiday away from home is another social revolution of the mid twentieth century which, now that it has become a majority convention, adds to the needs which the average family is expected to meet.

Laws and not only conventions and structures also change the character of family needs. For example, by raising the school leaving age Parliament has imposed new obligations on families to support children for one year longer. With economic growth, though not necessarily in direct proportion to such growth, the needs which a family is expected to meet also increase. Standards rise subtly, sometimes imperceptibly, as society itself adapts to greater prosperity and responds to the changes demanded by industry, consumers, educationists and the professions. Certainly no standard of sufficiency could be revised only to take account of changes in prices, for that would be to ignore changes in the goods and

1. *Recommended Intakes of Nutrients for the United Kingdom*, Reports on Public Health and Medical Subjects No. 120, H M S O, London, 1969.
2. Passmore, R., Nicol, B. M., and Narayana, Rao M., with Beaton, G. H., and Demayer, E. M., *Handbook on Human Nutritional Requirements*, W H O, Geneva, 1974.

services consumed as well as new obligations and expectations placed on members of the community. Lacking an alternative criterion, the best assumption would be to relate sufficiency to the average rise in real incomes.

There is one further important elaboration. If needs are relative to society, then they are also relative to the set of social sub-systems to which the individual belongs. This seems to suggest that a different definition of poverty is required for every society, or indeed every relatively autonomous community. But this tends to ignore the marked interrelationship of many communities within regional and national economic, political, communication, welfare and other systems. Members of ethnic minorities can often be said to participate in commonly shared rather than exclusive activities. They use the common system of transport, work in multiracial occupations, go to multiracial schools which broadly subscribe to national cultural values, and generally adapt in many ways to the conventions and styles of life of the national society. Many of their needs will therefore be the same as of persons who are not members of such minorities and the same as of persons who are members of other minorities. But to some extent their resources will be different and their activities and beliefs relatively autonomous. A national definition of need, and more particularly of poverty, will to that extent not apply to them. Little is yet known in any quantitative sense about the degrees of cultural self-containment of different ethnic minorities. Certainly in Britain it can be said that West Indian immigrant communities are far less self-contained than Pakistani communities. Again, while both Jews and Irish preserve a corporate identity and tend to play special, though different, functions in industrial cultural life, it would be difficult to claim they live so differently and have needs which are so radically different from those of society at large that only an entirely different conception of poverty can meaningfully be applied to them. Still, in the absence of empirical evidence demonstrating degrees of integration of ethnic minorities in the wider society, this difficulty about any 'relative' conception of poverty must remain.

It would be wrong, however, to call attention only to the possible divergence of racial or ethnic sub-systems from the social system as a whole. There are differences between rural and urban communities and even between different urban communities which would compel different overall definitions of their needs. The difficulty of allowing properly for the income in kind of the country dweller (such as home-grown vegetables, free or cheap fuel, and tied accommodation), but also the lack of facilities available to the town or city dweller, especially if he is young (for example, entertainment, choice of shops and choice of indoor as compared with outdoor work) are reasonably well recognized. Inevitably both would have to be taken into account in any sophisticated investigation of poverty, not just in qualifying the results of any measure but also in applying that measure.

Style of Living

A distinction must therefore be made between the resources which are made available by society to individuals and families and the style of life with which they are expected, or to which they feel prompted, to conform. This is the set of customs and activities which they are expected to share or in which they are expected to join. However, conformity is not rigidly prescribed. People engage in the same kind of activities rather than the same specific activities, just as they select from a fairly limited and familiar range of foodstuffs or other commodities. Different but overlapping sets of activities are expected of people of different age and sex and family membership. Communities differ according to geographical situation, composition and the kind of resources that are readily available to them. The style of living of a society consists more of elements which are heterogeneous, but ordered and interrelated rather than rigidly homogeneous. Any attempt to define this style and represent it in some form of operational index, so that the conformity of a population can be measured statistically, is bound to be rough and ready. One kind of analogy could be drawn with the Retail Price Index. The price index does not show how much the cost of living may have changed between two dates for any particular family or section of the population, but only in broad terms for society as a whole. There are difficulties in applying it to retirement pensioners or to the poor generally and to different regions. Techniques have to be developed so that applications to certain groups can be qualified; or a modified index, such as the index for retirement pensioners, is developed. But nonetheless it represents a useful point of departure and a means of accumulating, and generalizing, knowledge.

Stratification and Resources

What principles must therefore govern the attempt to obtain better information? The conditions and numbers of the poor relative to others in society are to be identified. The population must be ranked in strata according to a criterion of inequality. But the criterion of cash income is inadequate. There are groups in the population with considerable income in kind, such as farmers and smallholders. There are people with small cash incomes but considerable assets, which elevate their standards of living. There are people with identical wages or salaries who differ greatly in the extent to which fringe benefits from employers add substantially to their living standards. There are people with identical cash incomes who differ greatly in the support they may obtain from free public social services, because, for example, they live in different areas.

Living standards depend on the total contribution of not one but several systems distributing resources to individuals, families, work-groups and communities. To concentrate on cash incomes is to ignore the subtle ways developed in both modern and traditional societies for conferring and redistributing benefits. Moreover, to concentrate on income as the sole criterion of poverty also implies that relatively simple adjustments, as might be made in a single scheme for negative income tax, will relieve it.

A plural approach is unavoidable. Thus, the list given below shows the types of resource arising from the principal systems of resource distribution. Even a fleeting reference to the different systems in society which distribute and redistribute resources, such as the wage system, insurance and banking, social security and services like the National Health Service, may suggest that poverty is the creation of their complex interrelationship, or perhaps, more fundamentally, of the values and norms upon which they rest or which they continuously reinforce. The practical implication is that the abolition of poverty may require comprehensive structural change in not one but several institutional systems. The problem is to establish, first, the part that the different types of resource play in determining the overall standards of living of different strata in the population, and secondly, which of the systems underlying the distribution of that resource can be manipulated most efficiently to reduce poverty. The list is as follows:

1. *Cash income:*
   (a) Earned.
   (b) Unearned.
   (c) Social security.

2. *Capital assets:*
   (a) House/flat occupied by family, and living facilities.
   (b) Assets (other than occupied house) and savings.

3. *Value of employment benefits in kind:*
   (a) Employers' fringe benefits; subsidies and value of occupational insurance.
   (b) Occupational facilities.

4. *Value of public social services in kind:*
   Including government subsidies and services, e.g. health, education and housing but excluding social security.

5. *Private income in kind:*
   (a) Home production (e.g. of smallholding or garden).
   (b) Gifts.
   (c) Value of personal supporting services.

To obtain full information about all these types of resource for a representative cross-section of households is an ambitious but necessary task. Each of the types of resource can be defined in detail and converted (sometimes though arbitrarily and with difficulty) into equivalent cash-income values. The distribution of each in the population can be examined. Individual income units and households can be ranked according to each dimension and a measure of total rank achieved.

The way can be opened for the measurement of the contribution made by different resource systems to both inequality and poverty.

The extent of rank agreement in society – that is, the proportion of units which are ranked the same on all dimensions – might be investigated. The use in stratification theory by Landecker, Lenski and Galtung and others of ideas about class and status crystallization, rank disequilibrium, congruence and so on, can, of course, be adapted for poverty research.[1]

One of the purposes of combining the ranking of resources in different dimensions would be to allow *total* and *partial* poverty to be distinguished. If resources are distributed by different institutional systems, then it follows that while some people may lack a minimal share of any of these resources, there will be others who lack a minimal share of one or two of these types of resource but have a substantial share of others. Alternatively, the level of total resources may be sufficient to avoid deprivation in one or more but not all major spheres of life. Thus in Britain there are, for example, fatherless families with identically low cash incomes, but whose other resources differ sharply. There are those who live in the slum areas of cities in very bad, overcrowded housing, with schools and hospitals of poor quality near by. And there are those who live in new council housing estates on the fringe of cities or in new towns, in good housing with spacious, modern schools and hospitals near by with modern facilities and equipment. The standards of living of these two sets of families are not at all equivalent.[2] Whether instances such as these are common is unknown.

Another advantage is to trace more clearly the differences between *temporary* and *long-term* poverty. The distribution of resources changes over time. People are promoted within the wage system; they change jobs, and become unemployed or sick; they obtain new dependants. Clearly there may be major changes in the possession of resources both in the long term, over the entire life-cycle, but also in the short term, from month to month and even week to week. The life-cycle of poverty, first described by Seebohm Rowntree, requires contemporary documentation. A proportion of the population may always have been poor, but a much larger proportion have had occasional or periodic but not continuous experience

1. The possibilities are discussed in Townsend, P. (ed.), *The Concept of Poverty*, Heinemann, London, 1970. There are two special difficulties in deriving total rank in stratification theory from individual rank dimensions. Total rank is very difficult to express if the form of distribution varies in each individual dimension. It is also difficult to express if there is no criterion according to which the different dimensions can be weighted. The conversion of values in the different dimensions into equivalent cash incomes offers a means of overcoming the second problem. However, such a conversion may overlook subtleties in the different meanings placed on the value of assets, goods and services in everyday social life, as we shall see.
2. The tendency for families of widows and children to have higher living standards than other fatherless families is traced in Marsden, D., *Mothers Alone*, Allen Lane, London, 1969. There appear to be inequalities in the ownership of assets, particularly housing and household durables, as well as in treatment under social security.

of poverty. A larger proportion still have lived or are living under the constant threat of poverty and regard some of the resources flowing to them, or available to them, as undependable. For the purposes of understanding the experience of poverty and the development of good policy, it is most important to find whether the over-confident division of the population into 'we the people' and 'they the poor' has to be modified.

Inequality, however, is not poverty. Even if inequalities in the distribution of resources are successfully identified and measured, those in the lowest 20 per cent or 10 per cent, say, are not necessarily poor. For example, the 20 per cent with the lowest incomes in Sweden are not so badly placed as the corresponding 20 per cent in the United States.[1] Some criterion of deprivation is required by which a poverty line may be drawn and the numbers and characteristics of persons and families in the population who fall below the line estimated. It may be hypothesized that, as resources for any individual or family are diminished, there is a point at which there occurs a sudden withdrawal from participation in the customs and activities sanctioned by the culture. The point at which withdrawal 'escalates' disproportionately to falling resources could be defined as the poverty line. It would be difficult to gain information about all customs and activities which make up the style of living which predominates in society, or which can be distilled, as a kind of common denominator, from the overlapping styles of different groups and classes. Instead information could be obtained for a random selection of common activities (common in the sense either that they are followed by over half the population, or at least are approved and are widespread). These would comprise an index. It should be stressed that no one indicator alone could be sufficient. Sometimes particular social customs are observed or not observed for reasons which are locked, for example, in special factors of personality or group religion. All that can be claimed is that a *pattern* of non-observance may be conditioned by severe lack of resources.

Let me set out in a little more detail the reasoning behind these statements. Just as I have argued that a wider concept of 'resources' should replace 'income' in the study of inequality and poverty, so I would argue that 'style of living' should replace 'consumption' (or more narrowly still, 'nutritional intakes') in determining what levels in the ranking of resources should be regarded as constituting deprivation. Some care is required in establishing the meaning of the concept of style of living, for it has been used in sociology in many different senses. For Weber, stratification by economic class and status could both be represented by style of living. 'Status honour is normally expressed by the fact that a special

---

1. They have about 6 per cent of pre-tax income, compared with about 4 per cent in the United States. The top quintile have about 43 per cent compared with 46 per cent. See Lydall, H., and Lansing, J. B., 'A Comparison of the Distribution of Personal Income and Wealth in the United States and Great Britain', *American Economic Review*, March 1959; United Nations, *Economic Survey of Europe in 1956*, Geneva, 1957, Chapter IX, p. 6.

style of life can be expected from all who wish to belong to the circle.'[1] But Veblen and more recently sociologists such as Warner developed the concept into a system of what amounts to supercilious and derogatory distinctions in society. Everyone, or nearly everyone, was supposed to hold similar views about what was good and desirable. Modern studies have begun to break down this unrelieved picture of a uniformly acquisitive, materialistic, consumer society, and a number of community studies in particular have shown that there are not just enclaves of traditional working-class culture but highly developed and pervasive styles of community living.[2] Tom Burns suggests that, in contemporary urban society, the principle of segregation is more and more strictly followed. In any large town or city there are social areas 'representing important expressive aspects not only of the income but of the occupations, social proclivities, educational background, and social pretensions of the people who live in them – or rather of the kind of people who are supposed to live in them'. In suburbs, neighbourhoods and even blocks of flats there were, he continued, groupings of young married couples, middle-aged people, the retired or bachelor girls and men. Consumption was the expressive aspect of style of life, and 'style of life has developed a much greater significance as a mode of organizing individual behaviour and leisure, careers and, therefore, as a form of social structure . . . Individuals do organize their lives in terms of a preferred style of life which is expressed concretely in terms of a pattern of consumption ranging from houses, and other consumer durables, to clothing, holidays, entertainment, food and drink.'[3]

Style of life is made up of very widely and very restrictedly shared elements. This must always have been so for reasons of cultural self-confidence and social control as well as individual and local community self-respect. But the mix for any particular section or group in society may be different and may change over time. There are types of behaviour which are nationally sanctioned, and even upheld in law, affecting working hours and conditions, child care, marital relations, spending and so on. There are public corporations and departments which endeavour to provide recognizably uniform services throughout the country. There are trade unions, which encourage their membership to adopt a nationally cohesive outlook and not diverse and perhaps contradictory branch opinions and activities. There are symbols of nationhood, like the Royal Family, the British policeman, a village green, a love of animals or of cricket, which are repeatedly invoked in family or local rituals. And through the mass-communication industries – television, newspapers, popular magazines, the cinema and advertising –

1. Gerth, H., and Mills, C. W., *From Max Weber: Essays in Sociology*, Oxford University Press, 1946, p. 187.

2. See, for example, Willmott, P., and Young, M., *Family and Class in a London Suburb*, Routledge & Kegan Paul, London, 1960; Stacey, M., *Tradition and Change: A Study of Banbury*, Oxford University Press, 1960.

3. Burns, T., 'The Study of Consumer Behaviour: A Sociological View', *Archives of European Sociology*, VII, 1966, pp. 321–2.

the cultural norms of society are both reflected and modified. The mass media help to standardize the kinds of leisure-time pursuits, child-rearing practices, manners and language which certain wide sections of the population will feel it is appropriate for them to adopt.

There are subtle gradations of styles of living ramifying through society as well as different mixes of national and local styles for different communities and ethnic groups. Different classes may engage in similar types of activity, such as going on a holiday or holding a birthday party for children, but do them differently. In developing an operational definition of style of living it is therefore necessary to distinguish (a) types of custom and social activity practised or approved, and home, environmental and work conditions enjoyed or expected by a majority of the national population; (b) the types of custom and social activity practised or approved by a majority of people in a locality, community, class, racial group, religious sect or work group; and (c) the specific content and manner of individual and group expression of both national and local customs or practices. It is hypothesized that, with a diminishing level of resources, people will engage less fully in the national 'style of living'. At relatively low levels of resources people find they are unable to enjoy a wide representation of consumer goods, customs and activities and are able to enjoy only cheaper versions of some goods, customs and activities. The range is reduced proportionately to falling levels of resources. The reduction is more gradual than the diminishing resources would suggest, because of the need to maintain social cohesion or integration. Through state, industry, community, church and family, means are found, for example, through mass production and the mass media, to satisfy and integrate the relatively hard up. But at still lower levels of individual and family resources, economical forms of social participation become impossible to provide. People's participation in the national style of living diminishes disproportionately. An attempt to define this operationally is outlined below (Chapter 6), and the results of applying it in the survey are presented in Chapter 7 and elsewhere in this book.

Conclusion

In this introduction previous definitions of poverty, and selected evidence about poverty and inequality, have been discussed. Historically, the most influential definitions have been those which have been expressed in terms of some absolute level of minimum needs, below which people are regarded as being poor, and which does not change through time. However, conceptions of poverty as 'absolute' were found to be inappropriate and misleading. People's needs, even for food, are conditioned by the society in which they live and to which they belong, and just as needs differ in different societies, so they differ in different periods of the evolution of single societies. In practice, previous definitions have represented narrow conceptions of relative deprivation – sometimes associated only with what is necessary for the physical efficiency of the working classes. A fuller conception of relative deprivation needs to be adopted and spelt out.

The social scientist is very frequently the victim of normative values, and his perceptions and measures tend to be permeated by them. But if he feels obliged to make a distinction, as I have suggested, between subjective, collective and objective assessments of need, then first he becomes much more aware of the forces which are controlling his own perceptions, and secondly he becomes that much more prepared to break with the conventions which restrict and trivialize his theoretical work. I have suggested two steps that might be taken towards the objectification of the measurement of poverty. One is to endeavour to measure all types of resources, public and private, which are distributed unequally in society and which contribute towards actual standards of living. This will tend to uncover sources of inequality which tend to be proscribed from public and even academic discourse. It will also lay the basis for comparisons between conditions in different societies. The other is to endeavour to define the style of living which is generally shared or approved in each society, and find whether there is, as I have hypothesized, a point in the scale of the distribution of resources below which, as resources diminish, families find it particularly difficult to share in the customs, activities and diets comprising their society's style of living.

But this does not leave measurement value-free. In the last resort the decisions which are taken to define the exact boundaries of the concept of resources and weigh the value of different types of resource have to be based on judgement, even if such judgement incorporates certain criteria of number and logical consistency. And decisions have to be taken about all the different ingredients of 'style of living', their relative importance and the extent to which they can be reliably represented by indicators used as criteria of deprivation by social scientists. Values will not have been eliminated from social research. But at least they will have been pushed one or two stages further back and an attempt made to make measurement both reproducible and more dependent on externally instead of subjectively assessed criteria.

It will be some time before theory and methodology can be put on to a respectable scientific footing. The problem of poverty has attracted a lot of concern, and also justifiable anger. Many of the attempts to document and explain it have been grounded in limited national and even parochial, not to say individualistic, conceptions. Until social scientists can provide the rigorous conception within which the poverty of industrial societies and the Third World can both be examined, and the relationship between inequality and poverty perceived, the accumulation of data and the debates about the scale and causal antecedents of the problem will in large measure be fruitless.

2
Theories of Poverty

In the social sciences it is usual to start with conceptions or definitions of a social problem or phenomenon and proceed first to its measurement and then its explanation before considering, or leaving others to consider, alternative remedies. The operation of value assumptions at each stage tends to be overlooked and the possibility that there might be interaction between, or a conjunction of, these stages tends to be neglected. What has to be remembered is that policy prescriptions permeate conceptualization, measurement and the formulation of theory; alternatively, that the formulation of theory inheres within the conceptualization and measurement of a problem and the application of policy.

While implying a particular approach to theory, Chapter 1 was primarily concerned with the conceptualization and measurement of poverty in previous studies. This chapter attempts to provide a corresponding account of previous theories of poverty. It will discuss minority group theory, the sub-culture of poverty and the cycle of deprivation, orthodox economic theory, dual labour market and radical theories, and sociological, including functionalist, explanations of poverty and inequality.

Until recently, little attempt was made to extend theory to the forms, extent of and changes in poverty as such. Social scientists, including Marx, had been primarily concerned with the evolution of economic, political and social inequality. Economists had devoted most interest to the factor shares of production and distribution rather than to the unequal distribution of resources, and where they had studied the latter, they confined themselves to studies of wages. Sociologists had kept the discussion of the origins of, or need for, equality at a very general level, or had confined their work to topics which were only indirectly or partly related, like occupational status and mobility, and the structure and persistence of local community. The social definition of deprivation, the denial by major non-governmental as well as government institutions of access of certain kinds of people to earnings or earnings substitutes, the structuring of the resource systems in relation to social stratification and even the evolution and structure of the wage system attracted little attention.

Theoretical Principles Underlying Alternative Policies

Yet this did not mean that theories were not promulgated. In public policy and in the public expression of political beliefs, if not in full-length academic studies, strongly held theories had been advanced for generations. This can be illustrated best in relation to broad policies applied historically or contemporaneously. Thus, I suggest that alternative policies for dealing with large-scale deprivation or poverty might be identified according to the following three distinct general principles: (a) *conditional welfare for the few*; (b) *minimum rights for the many*; and (c) *distributional justice for all*. Each of these, of course, carries implications for the structure of society, including the organization of industry, and occupational status and reward.

In Britain, conditional welfare for the few was represented by the development of the Poor Laws, as reflected in the Report of the Poor Law Commission of 1832–4. In the early nineteenth century, leading elites believed that poverty was necessary, for otherwise the labouring poor would not be motivated to work. But they also believed that it was pauperism, a condition of moral defect, rather than poverty, a lack of material resources, which was the problem.[1] They therefore combined fatalism, believing that 'the poor ye have always with you', and moralism, believing that it was individual weakness of character – drunkenness, improvidence, fecklessness – which brought people into poverty.[2] There were evil social influences which could corrupt the young and which could be rooted out only by stern patriarchal values. Leaders of the new settlement houses and voluntary organizations like the Charity Organization Society called attention severely to individual fault and individual misfortune.[3] There were undeserving and not only deserving poor. Early forms of case-work concentrated on the individual and advised independence and self-help. The problem was also believed to be of relatively small dimensions. Thus, before Booth and Rowntree published the reports of their surveys at the turn of the century, improved poor law administration was believed to have reduced poverty to insignificant proportions.[4] Policy was therefore intended to be one based on conditional welfare for the few. It was linked with *laissez faire* economics and the virtues of a hierarchical, market society. Far from threatening the conventional economic and social order, the

1. For example, Colquhoun, P., *On Destitution*, 1806, pp. 7–9.
2. See the clear summary in Rose, M. E., *The Relief of Poverty: 1834–1914*, Macmillan, London, 1972, esp. pp. 6–20.
3. Beatrice Webb referred scathingly to the society in her autobiography. They 'had not got the faintest glimmer of what I have called "the consciousness of collective sin"' – Webb, B., *My Apprenticeship* (2nd edn), Longmans, Green, London, 1926, p. 177.
4. For an example of this view, see Giffen, R., 'The Progress of the Working Classes in the Last Half Century', in *Essays in Finance* (2nd edn), 1887. Cited in Rose, *The Relief of Poverty*, p. 15.

policy upheld and reflected it – and therefore helped to create it. Virtue was carefully linked with work. Since level of income was also tied to amount and importance of work done, those who were not at work not only had less income but had to show eagerness to work even to secure those minimum rights. Some major features of such social policy have persisted to the present day, have been given greater emphasis by some factions than by others, and by some governments than by others, and have, of course, played a large part in many other countries besides Britain. Characteristic of such policy is the maximization of relief through charity and voluntary effort, and public expenditure kept low by the barrier of means tests.

The second principle, minimum rights for the many, began to be treated seriously as a basis for social policy in Britain at the turn of the century. It was spelt out in the Reports on the Poor Law of 1909, particularly through the example of the Webbs' notion of the national minimum, was regarded as lying behind much of the legislation of the period 1902–11, and was taken up with renewed vigour in the Beveridge Report of 1942, with its stress on insurance to provide a minimum subsistence as the basis of benefits, and by both the Coalition and Labour governments during the period 1944–8. Poverty was assumed to be a significant but not an unmanageable problem, explained predominantly by the misfortune of certain minorities who fell out of work, could not work or were not expected to work, and did not have or could not afford certain 'basic' necessities of life. The state had to intervene in the private sector to regulate, supplement and exhort, but not impose. The economic and social order needed to be properly and decently underpinned rather than radically recast. The growth of support for the principle was associated with the rise of trade unions and the Labour party and the extension of the franchise. Characteristic of such policy are redistributive taxation and universal benefits in cash and in kind which are usually limited in range and modest in value. The policy represented more a change in public attitudes towards those who were not dependent on their labour power than a transformation of the scale of productive and non-productive values.

The third principle, distributional justice for all, has not yet been clearly articulated or tried in Britain, though it might be said to have been invoked in certain areas of policy, such as medicine and public health, and some aspects of the law, and is beginning to play a considerable part in discussions about, for example, the educational system, as in the case of community schools, and services and centres for the mentally ill. Support for the principle also arises from some grass-roots activities, such as the movement for workers' control, and certain pressure groups and consumer associations. The poor are believed to be those denied the potential *per capita* share of the resources of the nation, or access to the customs, activities and pleasures generally available within society. The principle is more an aim to be striven towards, and its applications spelt out after further public discussion, than embodied concretely in historical events. Characteristic of a policy worked out according to such a principle would be the de-stratification of society through economic, political and social reorganization and the equal distribution and wider diffusion of all kinds of power and material resources.

Theories of poverty need to be related to such different policies so that they can be better comprehended. At the very least we can appreciate that there are disagreements not merely about remedies or even explanations but also conceptions and measurement (or scale) of the problem. Each of the policies presupposes a different conception of the problem, different operationalization and measurement, and different explanation. Any statement of policy to reduce poverty contains an implicit if not explicit explanation of its cause. Any explanation of poverty contains an implicit prescription for policy. Any conceptualization of poverty contains an implicit explanation of the phenomenon.

Minority Group Theory

'Minority group theory' originated in the earliest empirical studies of poverty. It is a term which can be coined to represent attempts in those studies to identify the characteristics of certain groups of poor people. For example, in his early work Rowntree said he was not aiming 'to discuss the ultimate causes of poverty. To attempt this would be to raise the whole social question.' Instead, he listed the immediate causes of primary poverty (or earnings 'insufficient to obtain the minimum necessaries for the maintenance of merely physical efficiency') as:

1. Death of chief wage-earner.
2. Incapacity of chief wage-earner through accident, illness or old age.
3. Chief wage-earner out of work.
4. Chronic irregularity of work.
5. Largeness of family.
6. Lowness of wage.[1]

Rowntree usefully identified a cycle of poverty – children, young married couples with children and old people running the highest risk of descending into poverty. But otherwise no attempt was made to relate these groups to the range and qualifying conditions for membership of the employment system; the differential wage-system and the sources of support for it in institutions and values; and the systems compensating people unable to work or excluded from earning a living.

None the less, the classification represented a significant advance, and influenced political thought away from conditional welfare for the few and towards a mini-

1. Rowntree, B. S., *Poverty: A Study of Town Life*, Macmillan, London, 1901, pp. 119–20. Rowntree also listed the immediate causes of secondary poverty as 'drink, betting and gambling. Ignorant or careless housekeeping, and other improvident expenditure, the latter often induced by irregularity of income' – ibid., pp. 141–2.

mum income for certain identifiable minorities, such as the old, the unemployed and the sick. There were advantages to be derived from indicating the processes by which families became or remained poor and the categories into which they might be divided. Later it is argued that the concept of the minority group has an important place in the evolution of theory, and, indeed, the delineation of minority groups is a major objective of the research described in this book.

As we shall see, the division of the population into different social categories and the allocation to some of relatively low resources and status demands exposition and explanation. The process by which some groups are assigned low resources or status can, of course, be negative, as the outcome of action on behalf of other groups, and not only positive. If they are disqualified from receiving new services established by the state, or new kinds or amounts of resources made possible by a growing economy, they can experience a gradual fall into deprivation without there being any explicit discrimination against them.

The Sub-culture of Poverty

The 'sub-culture of poverty' is a concept which is derived from a variety of anthropological, sociological and eugenic studies, and was expressed in its modern form by Oscar Lewis.[1] He suggested that the poorest section of society forms a sub-society or a sub-culture which is distinctive and largely self-perpetuating.

In anthropological usage the term culture implies, essentially, a design for living which is passed down from generation to generation. In applying this concept of culture to the understanding of poverty, I want to draw attention to the fact that poverty in modern nations is not only a state of economic deprivation, of disorganization, or of the absence of something. It is also something positive in the sense that it has a structure, a rationale, and defence mechanisms without which the poor could hardly carry on. In short, it is a way of life, remarkably stable and persistent, passed down from generation to generation along family lines.[2]

There were 'remarkable similarities in family structure, interpersonal relations, time orientations, value systems, spending patterns, and the sense of community in lower-class settlements in London, Glasgow, Paris, Harlem and Mexico City'.

1. Henry Mayhew came very close to the idea in his suggestion that costermongers were a residue in society from ancient wandering tribes. See Thompson, E., and Yeo, E., *The Unknown Mayhew*, Penguin Books, Harmondsworth, 1972.
2. Lewis, O., *The Children of Sánchez*, Penguin Books, Harmondsworth, 1965, p. xxiv. The key statement about the generations is repeated elsewhere, for example, in *La Vida*. 'Once it comes into existence it tends to perpetuate itself from generation to generation because of its effect on the children. By the time slum children are aged six or seven they have usually absorbed the basic values and attitudes of their sub-culture and are not psychologically geared to take full advantage of changing conditions or increased opportunities which may occur in their lifetime' – Lewis, O., *La Vida*, Panther Books, London, 1968, p. 50.

Among the economic traits were unemployment and under-employment, low wages, 'a miscellany of unskilled occupations, child labour, the absence of savings, a chronic shortage of cash, the absence of food reserves in the home, the pattern of frequent buying of small quantities of food many times a day as the need arises, the pawning of personal goods, borrowing from local money lenders at usurious rates of interest, spontaneous informal credit devices organized by neighbours, and the use of second-hand clothing and furniture'.[1]

The social and psychological characteristics included 'crowded quarters, a lack of privacy, gregariousness, a high incidence of alcoholism, frequent resort to violence in the settlement of quarrels, frequent use of physical violence in the training of children, wife beating, early initiation into sex, free unions or consensual marriages, a relatively high incidence of the abandonment of mothers and children, . . . little ability to defer gratification and plan for the future', resignation, a belief in male superiority and 'a corresponding martyr complex among women'.[2] The sub-culture of poverty was both an adaptation and a reaction of the poor to their marginal position in a class-stratified, highly individuated, capitalistic society. It would result from colonial conquest or detribalization. The sub-culture of poverty was not the same as poverty. Many preliterate peoples, many of the lower castes in India and many in a socialist country like Cuba, may live in poverty, but 'they do not have a way of life that I would describe as a sub-culture of poverty'.[3] Again, 'my rough guess would be that only about 20 per cent of the population below the poverty line . . . in the United States have characteristics which would justify classifying their way of life as that of a culture of poverty'.[4]

Much of the thesis had been expressed earlier. But the elaborate work of Oscar Lewis gave authority to statements made by governments[5] and generalizations put forward in popular reviews.[6]

The thesis has come under close examination, however. There are criticisms of method, value-loading of assumptions, ambiguity or imprecision, lack of evidence and logical inconsistency. First, his method of research was extraordinarily interesting but individual-orientated and uncontrolled. With the exception of his

1. Lewis, *The Children of Sánchez*, p. xxvi.
2. ibid., pp. xxvi–xxvii.
3. Lewis, *La Vida*, p. 54.
4. ibid., p. 57.
5. 'Poverty breeds poverty . . . The cruel legacy of poverty is passed from parents to children' – *The 1964 Economic Report of the President*, Government Printing Office, Washington DC, 1964, pp. 69–70. The 1966 and 1967 Economic Reports of the US President made strong references to the 'cycle of poverty'.
6. For example, ' . . . the real explanation of why the poor are where they are is that they made the mistake of being born to the wrong parents, in the wrong section of the country, in the wrong industry, or in the wrong racial or ethnic group . . . There are two important ways of saying this: the poor are caught in a vicious circle; or the poor live in a culture of poverty' – Harrington, M., *The Other America*, Penguin Books, Harmondsworth, 1962, pp. 21–2.

first book, *Life in a Mexican Village*,[1] his books consisted of hundreds of pages (in the case of *La Vida* of 800 pages) of vivid reportage about the lives of individuals belonging to a single extended family, preceded by short introductory sections about country, setting, family, method and the concept of the culture of poverty. His reasons for choosing the families and for investigating particular aspects of their lives were not strictly controlled and explained. Because behaviour was described almost wholly through unstructured individual self-histories, it was inevitable that the patterns of elaborate social organization, and in particular the influence upon individuals and communities of values, beliefs and institutions which are nationally or regionally controlled, should have gone largely unexamined and even unremarked. He concentrated on the family and not the sub-systems and forces of the wider society as the principal unit of analysis. For example, he wrote several books on the poor and yet nowhere discussed, so far as I am aware, the network of agencies providing jobs, training, social security and medical care and the relationships that his informants had with them.[2] Because Lewis made little use of either the survey method or census data to disentangle the different kinds of community and styles of living even within the areas in which his families lived,[3] it was difficult for him to claim that they were representative. For example, prostitution was important in the lives of all the women in the Rios family described in *La Vida*, but Lewis himself states that only 'about a third of the households [in the slum area of San Juan] had a history of prostitution'.[4]

Secondly, there is unconscious if not conscious bias. Many of the criteria used to distinguish the culture of poverty were formulated in terms of middle-class values. Otherwise Lewis would have felt obliged to demonstrate that the poor prized apathy, fatalism, inferiority, submissiveness, hopelessness and despair. He might have asked whether 'a minimum of organization' or 'family instability'

1. Lewis, O., *Life in a Mexican Village: Tepoztlán Restudied*, University of Illinois, 1951. This owed a great deal to Lewis's teacher, Redfield.
2. In replying to critics like C. A. Valentine, Lewis protested that he laid great store by the economic institutions of society and that these were more important than sub-cultural factors in explaining poverty, but his work does not reflect this retrospective view. See Lewis, O., *Cultural Anthropology*, April–June 1969, pp. 189 and 191.
3. In *La Vida*, Lewis explains that a hundred families in San Juan were selected 'with the help of social workers' and had to have low income and relatives in New York. In New York, fifty families were selected. *La Vida* itself deals with one extended family and contains only about ten pages in the introduction about all the families.
4. Valentine charges Lewis with inconsistency: 'Thus in the space of four or five pages we have the characters of *La Vida* presented, in turn, as (i) typical of the culture of the poor, (ii) following a life-style of unknown frequency and distribution, (iii) deeply affected by a specialized occupational pattern confined to one-third of their community, (iv) characterized by an extreme deviance unique in their chronicler's experience, and (v) spanning the gap between the upper and lower classes both in wealth and family patterns' – Valentine, C. A., *Culture and Poverty*, University of Chicago Press, 1968, p. 54.

were being defined independently of middle-class evaluations of organization and family stability. One might even ask why material calculated to shock middle-class sensibilities and confirm comfortable middle-class prejudices, for example on sexuality, appears to have been given greater prominence than lengthy, but duller, disquisitions by his informants on politics or sport.

A third problem was ambiguity. All the criteria used to distinguish the sub-culture of poverty were inexact. The boundaries of the sub-culture were not specified, still less quantified. Because Lewis also distinguished in *La Vida* between those who belonged to the sub-culture of poverty and the much larger class of those who lived in poverty, he disarmed the critic in advance. Evidence produced against his thesis could be said to apply to those in poverty, not those living in a culture of poverty.

Fourthly, in so far as the thesis could be regarded as testable it was difficult to confirm. After a careful study, Rossi and Blum concluded, 'All told, the empirical evidence from our review of the literature does not support the idea of a culture of poverty in which the poor are distinctively different from other layers of society.'[1] A large number of sources might be cited to demonstrate that shanty-town inhabitants and other poor individuals in different societies are part of complex forms of social organization, are generally in regular employment,[2] uphold conventional values[3] and develop cohesive family relationships. In so far as some groups of the poor do not participate much in extra-familial associations, their opportunities to do so, because of inaccessibility and prohibitions on membership (trade unions exclude shanty-town dwellers from membership in some countries, for example), may be greatly restricted. In so far as some of the poor may give the impression of defeatism, listlessness or irritability, the effects of malnutrition and of overcrowding must first be examined.[4] There is little comparative evidence for different generations. The authors of one important survey in the United States, while admitting that their data were cursory, concluded, 'Though no sweeping generalizations can be made on the basis of these few tables,

1. Rossi, P. H., and Blum, Z. D., in Moynihan, D. P. (ed.), *On Understanding Poverty*, Basic Books, New York, 1968, p. 43.
2. See, for example, the papers by Germani, G., Mar, J. M., Pearse, A., in Hauser, P. (ed.) *Urbanization in Latin America*, Unesco, Paris, 1961; or MacEwen, A., 'Stability and Change in a Shanty Town,' *Sociology*, January 1972. Unemployment tends to be highest in the poorest parts of cities, but is clearly related to general economic conditions and not just individual, family or community characteristics.
3. 'In short, distinctive, original values characteristic of a culture of poverty remain to be found. On the contrary, what has struck us particularly has been conformism of the poor and their respect for the values of society as a whole.' Labbens, J., *Reflections on the Concept of a Culture of Poverty*, International Committee on Poverty Research, Bureau de Recherches Sociales, Paris, 1966, p. 4. See also Labbens, J., *La Condition sous-prolétarienne*, Bureau de Recherches Sociales, Paris, 1965, pp. 151–71.
4. Schorr, A. L., 'The Non-Culture of Poverty', *American Journal of Orthopsychiatry*, vol. 34, No. 5, 1964.

they offer little support for a theory of poverty that rests entirely on inter-generational transmission.'[1] And an analysis of 1962 data on occupational mobility led one economist to conclude that they only lent weak support to the argument for there being a 'vicious cycle of poverty'.[2] Much of the evidence presented by Lewis was inconclusive. He emphasized the limited, parochial interests and the lack of class-consciousness of people with a culture of poverty, and yet large parts of the testimony in his books suggest the contrary.[3] Again, despite the disorganization said to be characteristic of the sub-culture of poverty, parts of his work testified to the strength and cohesiveness of social relationships in slum areas.[4]

Finally, there is the question of consistency. By definition, a sub-culture consists of a distinctive system of values, beliefs and institutions, positively established and upheld, which is at variance with the culture of the majority in a given society.[5] The case for the existence of a separate sub-culture has to be demonstrated in order further to claim transmission of that sub-culture, through methods of socialization and social control, from generation to generation. But what Lewis described was largely reaction against the dominant classes or an accommodation with them. Disorganization, instability, inferiority and fatalism are neither approved nor self-perpetuated. The concept of a sub-culture of poverty cannot be applied consistently when its supposed values are not accepted by its members. The statistical *prevalence* of certain conditions or attitudes is a very different matter, for this can have, indeed usually has, external causes. As Lewis described it, the culture of poverty is a contradiction in terms.[6]

This kind of theory tends to have an influential effect on policy and might even be interpreted as arising from the subconscious of a society which feels guilty about its inequalities but does not quite want to forsake them. It might be said to reappear in different and usually more sophisticated forms in successive generations. In the introductions to his books Lewis seems to be resurrecting the Victorian notion of the 'undeserving poor'.[7] After every allowance is made for re-

1. Morgan, J. N., *et al.*, *Income and Welfare in the United States*, McGraw-Hill, New York, 1962, p. 210.

2. Gallaway, L. E., 'On the Importance of "Picking One's Parents"', *Quarterly Review of Economics and Business*, VI, No. 2 (Summer, 1966).

3. See, for example, Valentine's discussion of these points, *Culture and Poverty*, pp. 59–63.

4. Lewis, O., 'Urbanization without Breakdown: A Case Study', in Heath, D. B., and Adams, R. N. (eds.), *Contemporary Cultures and Societies of Latin America*, Random House, New York, 1965.

5. Elizabeth Herzog made, but did not pursue, this point in 1963 in a review of the evidence for Lewis's thesis. See Herzog, E., 'Some Assumptions about the Poor', *Social Service Review*, December 1963, p. 394.

6. I am grateful to Roy Wallis for helping me to see the force of this point.

7. See Nathan Glazer's disparaging, and undocumented, account of 'the unworthy poor' and Moynihan's account of the weakness of Negro family structure as the 'principal source of most of the aberrant, inadequate or anti-social behaviour that did not establish but now serves to perpetuate the cycle of poverty'. Glazer, N., and Moynihan, D. P., *Beyond the Melting Pot*,

sourceful inquiry and talented literary reportage, it must be said that he did not discourage the recurrent prejudice that poverty is the fault of individuals and family or community groups rather than of society itself. He may have helped, even if unwittingly, to divert interest in the United States in solutions to poverty away from economic and social reconstruction to individual training and character reform, from costly redistributive policies to low-cost social work and community psychiatry.

Lewis correctly reported many of the stresses and penalties of life for the poor which affect styles of living. But what he did not do was to distinguish clearly between working-class culture and a sub-culture of poverty and relate these to the 'structure' of deviance in society.[1] Neither did he begin to disentangle the effects upon behaviour of a simple lack of resources from other cultural influences.

The Related Concept of a Cycle of Deprivation

The 'sub-culture of poverty' thesis has been reinvoked in Britain as a 'cycle of deprivation'. When Secretary of State for Social Services, Sir Keith Joseph drew attention in 1972 to the persistence of deprivation and problems of maladjustment despite improvements in living standards.

Perhaps there is at work here a process, apparent in many situations but imperfectly understood, by which problems reproduce themselves from generation to generation ... The problems of one generation appear to reproduce themselves in the next ... Do we not know only too certainly that among the children of this generation there are some doomed to an uphill struggle against the disadvantages of a deprived family background? Do we not know that many of them will not be able to overcome the disadvantages and will become in their turn the parents of deprived families?[2]

A new programme of research was to be sponsored by the Department of Health and Social Security, and a discussion paper prepared by a joint working party of the SSRC and the department was circulated.[3] The concept attracted critical attention.[4] On the one hand, its historical antecedents and the profession-

---

MIT Press and Harvard University Press, 1963, p. 64; and Moynihan, D. P., *The Negro Family: The Case for National Action*, US Department of Labor, Washington DC, 1965, p. 30.

1. Lewis seemed to have been unaware of the literature on the concentration of social pathology at the foot of the socio-economic scale, and criticisms of the belief that problem families reproduce their way of life, generation after generation, either by biological or cultural transmission. See, in particular, Wootton, B., *Social Science and Social Pathology*, Allen & Unwin, London, 1959, pp. 51–80.

2. Joseph, Sir K., in the text of a speech given to a conference called by the Pre-School Playgroups Association, 29 June 1972.

3. *Approaches to Research on Transmitted Deprivation*, a discussion paper provided by a Working Party set up by the SSRC and the DHSS for a conference at the London School of Economics on 16 April 1973.

4. The concept is reviewed comprehensively by Hawthorn, G., and Carter, H., 'The Con-

al and political controversies which they had provoked had not been listed.[1] On the other, the definition of the concept could be shown to presuppose more sharply than some other concepts in the social sciences a traditional (and controversial) political ideology.[2] Certainly the presentation of the concept reflected the government's intense interest in area deprivation policies (educational priority area, community development and urban aid programmes started in the late 1960s).

The concept of area deprivation (which is discussed more fully in Chapter 15) has a close affiliation to a 'sub-culture of poverty'. The discussion in Britain has tended to echo much of the corresponding discussion in the United States. But the assignation of responsibility for deprivation to the individual and family also has a close affiliation to the sub-culture thesis. And Sir Keith Joseph appeared to place greatest weight here, and hence to return, though in modern form, to a mixture of traditional social control and case-work policies. Theoretically, deprivation is treated as being a residual personal or family phenomenon rather than a large-scale structural phenomenon. It is difficult, as the critics have pointed out, to reconcile this treatment with the allocative outcomes of a market economy as well as its inputs, whether production processes or determination of consumer preferences and life-styles.

Orthodox Economic Theory

Only in recent years has economic theory begun to be applied to the phenomenon of poverty. In classical theory, attention was concentrated on the *aggregate* distribution of profits, rent and wages. Ricardo, for example, described the principal problem of political economy as the division of the earth's produce 'among three classes of the community, namely, the proprietor of the land, the owner of the stock or capital necessary for its cultivation, and the labourers by whose industry it is cultivated'.[3] Comparatively little attention was devoted to the explanation of the distribution of *personal incomes* and the relationship between personal incomes and aggregate shares of profits, rents and wages. Lately, increasing attention has been paid to inequality in the distribution of *earnings before tax*. So the first matter of importance for us to note is that economists have chosen to give

---

cept of Deprivation', a paper commissioned by the joint working party (forthcoming). See also Townsend, P., 'The Cycle of Deprivation – the History of a Confused Thesis', proceedings of the Annual Meeting of the British Association of Social Workers, 30 March 1974.

1. Discussed notably in Wootton, *Social Science and Social Pathology*. Sources of particular significance are the Report of the Committee on Mental Deficiency (The Wood Committee), Board of Education and Board of Control, HMSO, London, 1929; Lidbetter, E. J., *Heredity and the Social Problem Group*, Arnold, London, 1933.

2. Hawthorn and Carter, 'The Concept of Deprivation', esp. pp. 13–18.

3. Ricardo, D., *The Principles of Taxation and Political Economy*, Dent. London, 1821.

preference to factors affecting individual earnings rather than family incomes in explaining inequality.[1] A lot of early work concentrated on whether or not the distribution takes a generalizable form and whether this form is normal or skew. Three main conceptions of the form were developed – the Pareto, the normal and the lognormal. Pareto believed that the inequality in distribution of incomes for different countries and historical periods was remarkably similar. Thus he observed a correspondence in the patterns of income distribution for different

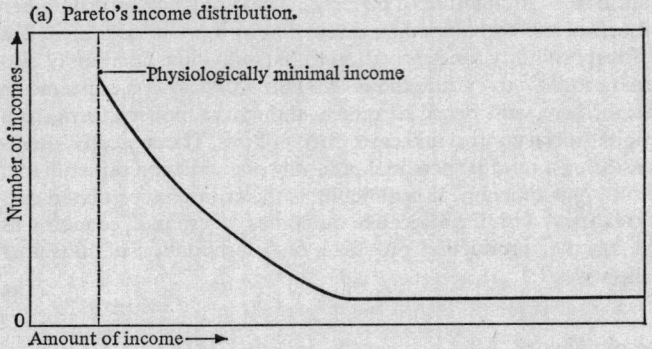

(a) Pareto's income distribution.

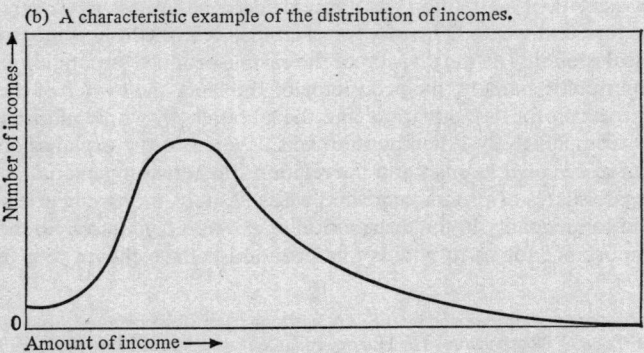

(b) A characteristic example of the distribution of incomes.

Figure 2.1. The Paretian conception of income distribution.

1. Though some have gone on to show that distributions of family incomes are also affected substantially by extra earners, less than a full year's work, and other factors. For example, Morgan, J. N., 'The Anatomy of Income Distribution', *Review of Economics and Statistics*, XLIV, August 1962.

countries which seemed to approximate to a particular law, providing it was assumed that income could not fall below a particular level represented by a physiological minimum. Pareto's Law is illustrated in Figure 2.1.[1]

The second conception of a 'normal' distribution of income is based on conceptions of the 'normal' distribution of ability, such as intelligence. Some economists have sought to reconcile the conflict between this conception and the evidence about the distribution of incomes by arguing that it none the less applies to certain occupational groups, particularly when adjustments are made to exclude part-time and seasonal employees and allow for overtime payments,[2] or that its application is modified by the distribution of inherited wealth, which would tend to confer advantages in education and career.[3]

When neither the Pareto nor the normal distribution corresponded well with the evidence, economists turned to the lognormal distribution. This produces a better fit, except at the top and the bottom of the distribution, and has led to a number of theories based on the idea that income is the product of a large number of independent random variables.[4] These are stochastic process and simultaneous multiplicative theories. Stochastic process theories account for the distribution in terms of the systematic operation under certain conditions of the laws of chance, as, for example, following a Markov chain process. They can, of course, be put forward to explain any distribution, such as a Pareto-type distribution and not just the lognormal distribution. Thus Champernowne succeeded in explaining the Pareto Law in terms of the effects over a long period of time of certain rules operating at different income ranges. He assumed that incomes were 'eternal' in the sense that new cohorts take them over as old ones die. He sought to show that the indefinite repetition of a particular matrix of transition probabilities could generate something approximating to the Pareto distribution.[5] Others have endeavoured to substitute more realistic models, taking account both of the widening variance of income in successive cohorts and of the constancy of

1. Pareto's Law has been found to apply reasonably successfully only to the upper tail of the distribution, or usually the upper 20 per cent of incomes. It also applies better to total income of households or income units than to individual components of income.
2. See, for example, Staehle, H., 'Ability, Wages and Income', *Review of Economic Statistics*, 1943; Lebergott, S., 'The Shape of the Income Distribution', *American Economic Review*, 1959; Miller, H. P., *Income of the American People*, Wiley, New York, 1955. One of the problems is that survey data tend to underestimate skewed distributions.
3. Pigou, A. C., *The Economics of Welfare* (4th edn), Macmillan, London, 1932, pp. 650–54.
4. An early pioneer was Gibrat, R., *Les Inégalités économiques*, Librairie du Recueil Sirey, Paris, 1931. For more recent illustrations, see Aitchison, J., and Brown, J. A. C., *The Lognormal Distribution*, Cambridge University Press, 1957; Roy, A. D., 'The Distribution of Earnings and of Individual Output', and 'A Further Statistical Note on the Distribution of Individual Output', *Economic Journal*, vol. 60, 1950, and Roy, A. D., 'Some Thoughts on the Distribution of Earnings', *Oxford Economic Papers*, vol. 3, 1951.
5. Champernowne, D. G., 'A Model of Income Distribution', *Economic Journal*, vol. 63, 1953.

variance of income of the whole population.[1] But, as Professor Lydall argues, the empirical basis for stochastic process theories is inadequate and too little reliance is placed on the underlying socio-economic factors known to influence the distributions.[2]

Instead of operating multiplicatively over long periods, it is, of course, possible for a large number of different factors to apply at any single time. Theories built on this idea have been called 'simultaneous multiplicative' theories. Roy, for example, feels that it would be reasonable to start with the assumption of the normal distribution of ability, but argues that there is, in fact, no single ability but several, like speed, accuracy, health and endurance, which combine multiplicatively and not additively to determine output per hour, and hence help to explain a skewed distribution of income.[3] Such theories stress the importance of individual attributes and pay little heed to the possibility of either social allocation to roles or the social definition of roles and the conditions attached to those roles.

Although there are significant variations among theorists, the core of orthodox economic theory, as it seems to have been applied to income distribution and poverty, might be said to consist of the following ingredients. The assumptions of perfect competition and market equilibrium are believed to be sufficiently borne out by the market processes of advanced capitalist economies to demonstrate a strong relationship between wages and marginal productivity. As Thurow explained, 'If an individual's income is too low, his productivity is too low. His income can be increased only if his productivity can be raised.'[4] This approach provided the initial theoretical justification for the subsequent examination of productivity components, like education, skill or ability and experience, in explaining variations in wages. It also fitted into conventional theories of demand and supply by permitting a fairly sophisticated elaboration of the productivity characteristics of the labour that was supplied. As a result, human capital theory evolved. Gordon summed it up in this way: 'Employers demand what workers supply – stocks of "human capital" embodied in individuals.'[5] The demand side of the equation was less satisfactorily elaborated, with a tendency for the units of capacity that measure demand – whether scale of operations, sensitivity to market fluctuations or even the characteristics of jobs and industries – being defined in terms of skill mixes or as exogenous variables. The values underlying the approach, whereby explanations are sought which transcend institutional and historical variations within or among societies, and therefore favour simplicity

1. For example, Rutherford, R. S. G., 'Income Distributions: A New Model', *Econometrica*, vol. 23, 1955.
2. Lydall, H., *The Structure of Earnings*, Oxford University Press, 1968, pp. 21, 25 and 43.
3. Roy, arts. cit. (1950).
4. Thurow, L. C., *Poverty and Discrimination*, Brookings Institution, Washington DC, 1969 p. 26.
5. Gordon, D. M., *Theories of Poverty and Underemployment*, Lexington Books, Lexington, Mass., 1972, p. 31.

and the quantitative treatment of variables, take institutional structures as constants, and therefore shift attention to *individual* choices in relation to education, training and mobility.

In practice, most economists present variations of the orthodox approach. One important example will be discussed at length. Professor Lydall carefully reviews previous work in his book *The Structure of Earnings*. He makes ingenious use of available data and puts forward a theory, which he plainly regards as incorporating the best features of previous theories. In doing so he makes an important qualification. The data on income for different countries which can be processed are incomes before taxes and benefits. 'This is an unfortunate practical necessity and it is difficult to see at present any way of getting round this problem satisfactorily.'[1] But it helps to explain his and other economists' preoccupation with certain variables rather than others. Lydall suggests that there are three patterns of variation in earnings which are related to ability: (a) variation in mean earning levels of occupations; (b) variation in initial abilities of individuals within occupations; and (c) variation of individual abilities with age within occupations. The stochastic combination of these three sources of variation, he says, is sufficient to explain the distribution of earnings – except for the upper levels, which depend not so much on the supply of abilities as the requirements of organizations for men to 'take responsible managerial positions'.[2] He accepts a largely genetic basis for intelligence, but also the influence upon a 'normal' distribution of home and school in preparing young people for occupational choice.

Since school achievement is dependent both on intelligence and on home environment (not to mention the quality of school education itself), and since home environment is largely a reflection of socio-economic class, which in most countries is highly skew, we have every reason to expect that 'educated ability' at the end of elementary education will be skew. This skewness will be further accentuated if intelligence itself, as we have suggested above, is slightly skew, and also, since intelligence and environment are correlated, if – as seems quite possible – intelligence and environment interact multiplicatively.[3]

In short, Lydall argues that, with the exception of the organizational factor which controls the level of high incomes, the general abilities of men in the labour force determine the distribution of incomes. These abilities are created by genetic, environmental and educational factors.

The major problem about this theory is that different factors are invoked to explain different aspects of income distribution and a consistently interrelated set of concepts is not presented. The concepts of 'managerial responsibility' and 'hierarchic organization' are believed to explain high incomes, but it could be asked why these should apply only to high incomes, at what point they cease to apply and whether there is any evidence that they apply to lower incomes? The

1. Lydall, *The Structure of Earnings*, p. 61.   2. ibid., p. 71.   3. ibid., pp. 84–5.

implications for the theory of the differences between women's and men's earnings do not appear to be appreciated. Lydall points out that 'in the developed countries the median earnings of women seem to be mostly between a half and two-thirds of the earnings of men'. He even asks 'whether this ratio is an accurate reflection of the difference of average effective abilities of men and women, or whether it is partly institutionally or sociologically determined'.[1] Rather crucially in respect of the main theory, he admits there are little or no genetic differences between the sexes in intelligence and that in the 'richest countries the average educational attainment of women is not far short of that of men'. Differentials seem to depend, he concludes, on 'social prejudice'. But if scientific investigation is to be consistent, then factors would have to be found to explain the distribution *both* of men's *and* of women's earnings. If 'social prejudice' determines women's earnings, why should not such prejudice, and therefore not only achieved ability, be explored in relation to men's earnings? The failure to explain differences in earnings between the sexes is a major deficiency of the orthodox approach,[2] and Lydall does at least recognize the need to invoke new variables. The same criticism could be made of his treatment of differences in earnings between blacks and whites. Productivity components like education and age could only 'explain' half the differentials between blacks and whites. The presentation of ability would seem, on the face of it, to be of rather less importance than social control or the scope and types of the role system and of the rules by which resources are allocated to each role. This leads us to look to stratification and organization theories for a more comprehensive explanation of the role system.

Like other economists of the broadly orthodox school, Lydall attempts to explain the distribution of income in different countries in terms of individual characteristics, and changes in such individual characteristics, instead of putting as much emphasis, or more emphasis, on social institutions, and changes in such institutions. Sometimes he even seems to suggest that changes in the earnings structure are generated by changes in individual aspirations alone. For example, in explaining the fall in dispersion of income in the United States in the 1940s, after three decades of comparative stability, he makes much of a fall in the percentage of farm workers and foreign-born workers in the labour force, combined with a fall in inequality of years of education, though even if one accepts the statistics at their face value, they suggest a gradual change over several decades that might have been expected on Lydall's own assumptions to have been reflected much sooner in the distribution of earnings. He then describes the mobili-

1. Lydall, *The Structure of Earnings*, p. 242.

2. As argued, for example, by Gordon, *Theories of Poverty and Underemployment*, pp. 38–9. Another economist found that income differentials between men and women could not be explained by controlling for variables which economists typically relate to income and productivity. See Fuchs, V. F., 'Differentials in Hourly Wages between Men and Women', *Monthly Labor Review*, May 1971.

zation of manpower into the armed forces and war industry. But instead of seeing this as taking the form of a dramatic reorganization of manpower into new systems of industrial organization, with an expansion in the scope of employment, the incursion of Keynesian economics into economic and industrial planning, revitalization of unions and the higher expectations of the government on the part of the public, all of which might have had repercussions on earnings levels, he can write, 'In many cases it gave ill-educated workers, both from farms and urban areas, an opportunity to obtain a basic training and to overcome their earlier disabilities, so that when their time for demobilization arrived, they were ready to take better jobs than they could have hoped for before the war.' Quoting a study of Ginzberg,[1] he concluded, 'Many of the unskilled men had had opportunities of vocational training previously denied to them, as well as completely new experiences which had shaken them out of old habits. Thus, since the decade of the 1940s the United States has become a much more homogeneous society than it was at any time in the previous 150 years.'[2]

The implications which Lydall draws for policy from this type of theory reveal some of the weaknesses of this approach. He believes that although in the end incomes cannot be equal because there are genetic differences in ability nonetheless much can be done by spending more on the education of the poor to improve their achieved ability, and hence their earning power. But he also admits the need of developing countries for the special skills of people who have received a secondary education and of industrial countries for university graduates. These are policies of course which tend to cancel each other out, at least so far as the effects upon income distribution are concerned. They are extremely limited and unspecific policies and reflect a basic contradiction which seems to exist in economic theory between market and welfare assumptions.

Dual Labour Market and Radical Theories

A large number of economists have now begun to adopt approaches which depart from orthodox assumptions. Some of them direct attention to the nature of the demand for labour and to forces other than individual characteristics which determine wage levels. Others direct attention to 'aspects of the labour market such as trade unions, employers' monopoly power and government intervention,which mean that there is no longer perfect competition'.[3] Studies of local conditions have favoured adoption of a concept of a segmented labour market. Evidence had accumulated in favour of there being an internal labour market within

1. Ginzberg, E., 'The Occupational Adjustment of 1000 Selectees', *American Sociological Review*, 1943.
2. Lydall, *The Structure of Earnings*, pp. 220–25.
3. As reviewed by Atkinson, A. B., *The Economics of Inequality*, Clarendon Press, Oxford, 1975, Chapter 6.

an established firm or plant, which appeared in many respects to be insulated from the outside labour market. This observation had further led to the conception of a dual labour market. On the one hand, attention was called to a 'primary' sector in which employment was stable, where pay was good and where there were strong unions. On the other, attention was called to a 'secondary' sector in which employment was unstable, where pay tended to be low, prospects of promotion poor and unions of small importance. In explaining poverty, then, emphasis was placed as much on the disadvantageous characteristics of the secondary labour market as upon the characteristics of the individuals holding such jobs. Dual labour market theory has been strongly represented in recent years in both the United States[1] and Britain.[2] It is discussed at greater length in Chapter 18. For the purposes of this chapter, however, the connections made in the presentation of the theory between pay and both income and social structure are insufficiently examined. In particular, the concept of the dual labour market is not properly related to the history of segmentation and to the long-standing occupational class division of the labour market.

It might therefore be argued, especially since some exponents of a dual labour market seem to concede further segmentation, that this theory is only a tentative step towards what has been termed 'radical' economic theory. This draws heavily on the Marxist tradition, 'but it has moulded and recast classical Marxism in response to modern social and historical developments'.[3] According to such theory, the market price of a product affects the value of an individual's marginal product, just as it does according to orthodox theory. Supply and demand, reinforced by competition, affect an individual's productivity. But the radical theory 'also postulates that the class division in society and the relative distribution among classes will affect the distribution of individual income as well. An individual's class will, ultimately, affect *both* his productivity, through the allocation of social resources to investment in the workers of his class and through the differential access of different classes to different kinds of complementary capital, *and* his relative share of final product.'[4] Employers are believed to have found it in their interest to forge a highly stratified labour market, with a major separation of non-manual and manual strata and several objectively defined economic

---

1. A good summary of US sources will be found in Gordon, *Theories of Poverty and Under-employment*, esp. Chapter 4. See also Doeringer, P. B., and Piore, M. J., *Internal Labor Markets and Manpower Analysis*, Heath Lexington Books, Lexington, Mass., 1971; Ferman, L. A., *et al.* (eds.), *Jobs and Negroes*, University of Michigan Press, 1968; Bluestone, B., 'The Tripartite Economy: Labor Markets and the Working Poor', *Poverty and Human Resources Abstracts*, July–August 1970 (the three sectors could be collapsed into the primary and secondary sectors).

2. For example, Bosanquet, N., and Doeringer, P., 'Is there a Dual Labour Market in Britain?', *Economic Journal*, 1973.

3. Gordon, *Theories of Poverty and Underemployment*, p. 53.

4. ibid., p. 65.

classes within each stratum. The employer defines separate job clusters with their own qualifications, methods of recruitment, work conditions and remuneration. A 'common consciousness about the disadvantages of jobs' is thereby discouraged.[1] Concessions can be made to some groups of workers, not just at the expense of other groups of workers, but also without surrendering the relative advantages of ownership or management. Since this process is dynamic, in respect of industrial competitors, the formation of social classes, and regulative government, some employers adapt to, rather than create, an occupational class hierarchy. The development of monopoly capitalism[2] and of multinational giant corporations, with turnover much higher than the Gross National Product, of, say, a small European country like Belgium or Switzerland, widens as well as further institutionalizes social inequality. In this way it is argued that the phenomena of urban poverty and underemployment can be explained.

Some economists think that the radical theorists' criticisms of the orthodox approach are more effective than their expositions of alternatives. Their 'challenge . . . does not begin to offer a theory of the labour market that can replace neoclassical theory'.[3] The problem is that there is disagreement on the criteria of what makes for good theory. Those who assume a competitive and perfectly functioning labour market preclude serious discussion of such factors as trade unions, employers' monopoly power and state intervention. None the less, so-called radical theory remains to be developed. There are those who have argued that non-participants in the labour force, including old people and the handicapped, are in poverty as a result of their past labour force status.[4] But little attempt has been made to analyse the low income status of minorities not in the labour force, to widen the discussion of inequality of distribution from earnings to other resources (including social security benefits as well as assets and fringe benefits),[5] further to widen the discussion of income recipients from individuals to income units and households, and, finally, to analyse the contemporary class structure in any depth. This book attempts to make some contribution to these questions.

1. Gordon, *Theories of Poverty and Unemployment*, p. 74.

2. Baran, P., and Sweezy, P., *Monopoly Capital*, Monthly Review Press, New York, 1966.

3. Cain, G. G., 'The Challenge of Dual and Radical Theories of the Labor Market to Orthodox Theory', *Proceedings of the American Economic Association*, May 1975.

4. A good summary of the radical approach is Wachtel, H. M., 'Looking at Poverty from a Radical Perspective', *Review of Radical Political Economics*, Summer 1971 (reprinted also in Roby, P. (ed.), *The Poverty Establishment*, Prentice-Hall, Englewood Cliffs, NJ, 1974).

5. There have been some 'radical' studies, however, in both Britain and America which have called attention to social security as a major component in income distribution, and have therefore shifted discussion away in part from market determinants of earnings. See, for example, George, V., *Social Security and Society*, Routledge & Kegan Paul, London, 1973, esp. Chapter 2; Kincaid, J. C., *Poverty and Equality in Britain*, Penguin Books, Harmondsworth, 1973; Coates, K., and Silburn, R., *Poverty: the Forgotten Englishmen*, Penguin Books, Harmondsworth, 1970. For the United States, see Schorr, A. L., (ed.), *Jubilee for our Times: A Practical Program for Income Equality*, Columbia University Press, 1977.

Sociological Approaches to Inequality

Despite their emphasis upon history, the work of radical economic theorists might therefore benefit from being more broadly based. Acting presumably on the unexamined assumption that the problem of explaining inequalities in the distribution of cash incomes and assets, which have to be expressed in terms of money, is the preserve of economic theory, sociologists have tended to concentrate on inequalities in occupational status and, less emphatically, power. This is doubly unfortunate, because theoretical and empirical work has not only been diverted from filling in Marx's first rough sketches of the fundamental concept of economic class, but has remained unduly generalized and ambiguous. The literature on stratification is voluminous, but also remarkably unspecific. As 'background' theories, the theories of Marx and Weber, for example, are of continuing value, but they do not, as it were, do more than set the scene for explanations of degrees of inequality within a society or of differences *between* societies in patterns of inequality.

Marx explained the evolution of social inequality and of classes through the control and use of the means of production. Society was increasingly polarized into two contending classes, each with its supporting groups. On the one hand was the class of capitalists, consisting of industrialists, merchants and bankers, with supporting groups of shareholders, salaried, managerial, technical and supervisory staff with positions of authority in industrial enterprise, and smaller groups with associated interests, such as owners of small-scale businesses and concerns (which Marx assumed would be of diminishing importance) and the surviving elements of the older aristocratic landholders. On the other was the class of productive workers who were dependent on their wages, together with the rather different supporting groups of non-productive black-coated workers and rural wage-labourers. Between these two major classes, and tending to hang on to the coat-tails of the capitalist class, were the petty bourgeoisie, people engaged in small-scale enterprises of their own, such as traders, artisans, farmers and smallholders. Although Marx recognized the existence of boundary groups and intermediate groups, he assumed that as time went on they would disappear or diminish in size. Through a series of evolutionary stages in the relationship between the productive and distributive systems private ownership would finally be eliminated. A crucial feature of Marx's approach is that inequality is neither fixed nor necessary.

Much of the criticism of Marx has centred on his failure to predict either the proliferation of different types of intermediate groups or the diminution of the central core of the proletariat, and his emphasis on the divisive character of production rather than the more graduated character of consumption. He was not concerned to explain degrees of income differentials within or even between classes. In this he resembled the classical economists. Adam Smith, Ricardo and

Malthus discussed the problem of distribution in terms of the division of the total national product between wages, rent and profit – or the aggregate shares of the factors of production. This generalized approach to wages and incomes theory has predominated in economics up to the present day. For example, Professor Hicks developed a theory of wages which, while making passing reference to the variation in abilities of labourers, was based on the assumption that labour was a homogeneous factor with a single price.[1] Or again, a text-book collection of *Readings in the Theory of Income Distribution* could be published with only one among thirty-one papers being concerned with personal income distribution, and even this was a graphical analysis.[2] Barbara Wootton finally called attention to the gross inadequacies of the classical 'cerebral' tradition and affirmed 'the grow-ing importance in contemporary wage and salary settlements of conventional and social as contrasted with purely economic forces'. She instanced the Report of the Pilkington Commission on Doctors' and Dentists' Remuneration, which recommended big increases in pay despite lack of any evidence of the need for an increase in manpower, as 'the final death blow to old-fashioned theories of supply and demand'.[3] Her concern was with the historical development of institutional machinery for settling rates of wages and salaries, such as the machinery of col-lective bargaining, statutory regulation and quasi-judicial settlement by arbitra-tion tribunals and the more diffuse operation of pressures and prejudices through professional associations, the staff associations of public services and the wider agencies of public and political opinion. She recognized that wages represented but one, although perhaps the major, factor in distribution and noted the impor-tance of dependency, fluctuating overtime and piece-work earnings, taxation and the social services in modifying the pattern.[4] Her analysis points towards the con-struction of a theory built on a multiple concept of resources and the measurement and mode of operation of each resource-system.

In some respects the need for a development of this kind of theory could be represented as the need to adapt and elaborate Marx's approach. There is a major division between manual and non-manual categories in the population,

---

1. Hicks, J. R., *The Theory of Wages*, Macmillan, London, 1935. Professor Lydall points out that, 'Much of the discussion of the problem of distribution is still carried on in these terms, despite the fact that it is well-known that many landowners are poor, many employees earn more than some capitalists, many property-owners work and many workers own property . . . Modern "neo-classical" model-builders generally do not even bother to mention that labour is a heterogeneous factor, let alone consider the implications of this fact' – Lydall, *The Struc-ture of Earnings*, p. 2.

2. See the paper by Bowman, M. J., in Fellner, W., and Haley, B. F. (eds.), *Readings in the Theory of Income Distribution*, Allen & Unwin, London, 1950.

3. See her introduction to the second edition of *The Social Foundations of Wage Policy*, Allen & Unwin, London, 1962, pp. 3–4. A later book maintained the argument: Wootton, B., *Incomes Policy: An Inquest and a Proposal*, Davis-Poynter, London, 1974.

4. Wootton, *The Social Foundations of Wage Policy*, esp. Chapter VI.

which is clear when proper account is taken of industrial fringe welfare benefits, and of some of the consequences of the interplay between tax policies (particularly affecting capital gains and relief for mortgage interest) and asset ownership. The unequal distribution of resources confers power to control the further allocation of resources and hence is a source of tension and conflict. But its nature and extent within as well as between classes has not yet been made sufficiently apparent.

This failure to develop an 'economic class' type of analysis is due partly to the influence of Weber's ideas, but also to the influence of functionalism. Each needs to be considered briefly. The neo-Weberian analysis of inequality in terms of three rather distinct concepts of economic class, status and party,[1] and the multi-dimensional approach to stratification[2] (which suggests there are different sources of inequality in modern society such as occupation, ethnic status, education, income and religion) can be criticized as being misreadings of the essentially dominant part played by economic class, or command over resources, in the sense being developed here.[3] Thus, the dimensions of status and power are conceptually distinct from economic class or power, but diffuse. I mean that it is difficult to give them agreed meanings, or meanings that can be easily operationalized. As a consequence, knowledge is clouded because causal factors cannot be traced. Put another way, responsibility is subtly dispersed. Inequality is supposed to arise not just from the particular mechanisms and principles by which those resources have been and are being allocated and maintained, but also from the general consensus about social prestige and from the general distribution of institutionalized political power. If explanation is pushed in these directions (without Marx's insights about economic influences upon value formation), we are encouraged to conclude that such inequality is 'democratic' or generally supported. We are also encouraged to conclude that inequality is necessary, because while it is not difficult to conceive of a society in which material resources are equally distributed, it is more difficult to conceive of one where there are no differences of prestige or authority.

1. See the cogent and useful chapter on 'The Three Dimensions of Social Inequality' in Runciman, W. G., *Relative Deprivation and Social Justice*, Routledge & Kegan Paul, London, 1966. See also, Parkin, F., *Class, Inequality and Political Order*, MacGibbon & Kee, London, 1971, Chapter 1.

2. See, for example, Doreian, P., and Stockman, N., 'A Critique of the Multidimensional Approach to Stratification', *Sociological Review*, 17, 1969; Townsend, P., 'Measures and Explanations of Poverty in High Income and Low Income Countries: The Problems of Operationalizing the Concepts of Development, Class and Poverty', in *The Concept of Poverty*, Heinemann, London, 1970, pp. 20–28.

3. In an interesting discussion of the relationship between poverty and stratification, Miller and Roby call attention both to the different dimensions of inequality and to the value of conceiving of income as command of resources over time. Miller, S. M., and Roby, P., 'Poverty: Changing Social Stratification', in Townsend (ed.), *The Concept of Poverty*. See also Miller, S. M., Roby, P., *The Future of Inequality*, Basic Books, New York, 1970.

This does not mean that the concept of status is not a useful adjunct to any theory of inequality, and that 'multi-dimensional' features of stratification are not bound in some measure to play a part in theory. The distinction between class and status is of value in analysing certain social systems, particularly of traditional societies; and in tracing discrepancies even in industrial societies between class and status positions and in distinguishing objective inequalities from those supposed to exist subjectively or collectively. In particular, the low status conferred by a majority on a minority group such as a racial group, may not accord with economic class or power. But when all this is fully acknowledged, it is possible to argue that the independence of status from economic class has been exaggerated. The hierarchies of material resources and status are closely correlated, particularly when overall command over resources rather than income level alone is examined. Individuals and individual groups may, of course, vary in their rankings of the population according to prestige, but the 'collective' judgement of ranking will correspond fairly closely with relative command over resources and tends to derive from it. Indeed, inconsistencies between the two may arise from the fact that the command over resources is not always conspicuously symbolized in style of living and people's experience of those richer or poorer than themselves may be limited.

Functionalist Explanations of Inequality and Poverty

The 'functionalist' approach in sociology to the problems of inequality and poverty corresponds in ideology and in some general assumptions with the approach of 'orthodox' economic theoreticians. It also reflects the assumptions introduced into political debate by elites about worth and desert. The functionalist explanation of inequality is based on differences hypothesized in the functional importance of different occupations. This theory was developed by Talcott Parsons, Kingsley Davis and W. E. Moore between 1940 and 1945,[1] and later by other sociologists such as B. Barber and M. J. Levy. It has much in common with the attribution of inequality by economists to the distribution of individual ability. The theory starts by pointing out that in all societies there are different social positions or statuses. They vary in pleasantness and difficulty and 'functional importance' for society. In order to guarantee that all positions are filled, certain rewards have to be associated with them. Hence inequality is necessary so that the positions are filled. The central point of the theory concerns motivation.

1. The best-known paper is Davis, K., and Moore, W. E., 'Some Principles of Stratification', *American Sociological Review*, April 1945. For an exchange of views on early formulations, see also the *American Sociological Review* for 1958 (Buckley and Tumin) and 1963 (Tumin and Moore); and Wesolowski, W., 'Some Notes on the Functional Theory of Stratification', in Bendix, R., and Lipset, S. M., *Class, Status and Power* (2nd edn), Free Press, New York, 1966.

Greater material rewards and higher prestige are believed to be necessary to induce people to strive to occupy certain positions. But as Wesolowski and others have pointed out, motivation depends on the cultural environment and the desire for material rewards is not so uniform in some societies as it appears to be in contemporary middle-class American society.[1] Some writers have shown that there are communities, as in Israel, where it is possible to fill positions adequately without having unequal rewards.[2] The theory does not reach the point of offering an explanation in even generalized form of differences in systems of stratification, and certainly not of amounts of reward in relation to the numbers of people occupying certain roles. And how is functional importance to be determined independently of rewards associated with a particular position? To suggest that managers are better paid than skilled manual workers because, say, they contribute more to the productive system, is not easy to settle in argument and tends to reflect value-assumptions and not consciously chosen criteria which can be measured. Moreover, even if there are differences in functional importance, how do we account for differences in degree of reward? Managers may be paid more, in part, because they are given more power than workers to make decisions on behalf of the workforce, and it may be possible to measure some differences between good and bad management. But the fact that they *are* given more power than workers does not mean that they *have* to be given more power for production to be maximized. An alternative role system might be more efficient. Functionalist theory is difficult to put into operational terms for purposes of testing. Like its economic counterpart, collective bargaining, political action and the command over resources of interest groups and classes are neglected. Inequalities in the distribution of wealth and the effects upon the distribution of incomes of the growth of fiscal policies, industrial welfare policies and social security policies are not examined. As Cutright points out, redistribution plays no part in the Davis–Moore theory of stratification or in the counter-arguments of their critics.[3]

The appeal of the functionalist approach, but also of neo-Weberian and other approaches which set considerable store by inequalities of status, rests partly on sociological and political convenience: it closely matches meritocratic 'equality of opportunity' ideology. Whereas populations can easily be persuaded to join in the game of ranking occupations according to their prestige or status, inequalities of income and of material resources generally are difficult to document. There are some people in any population who seem to object to being asked questions about such matters. This is, of course, an important fact about culture and power. The suppression of information, or, more commonly, the unconscious dissemina-

1. Wesolowski, 'Some Notes on the Functional Theory of Stratification'.
2. For example, Schwartz, R. D., 'Functional Alternatives to Inequality', *American Sociological Review*, April 1955.
3. Cutright, P., 'Income Distribution: A Cross-National Analysis', *Social Forces*, December 1967, p. 180.

tion of over-generalized, ambiguous or highly selective information about inequalities of reward is one of the methods by which social elites control the potentially disruptive effects of inequality. For these and similar reasons, sociological studies tend to be preoccupied with occupational ranking and movement between ranks instead of the actual distribution and accumulation of resources and, indeed, the connections between the two.

The Functions of Poverty

One application of the functionalist approach to the phenomenon of poverty allows us to draw general lessons. Gans has reflected at some length on the functions of poverty, taking up Merton's point that items which are functional for some sub-groups in society may be dysfunctional for others.[1] Society, he argues, is so preoccupied outwardly with the 'costs' of poverty that it fails to identify the corresponding benefits, or rather, the groups or values who benefit. He describes fifteen sets of functions, as follows:

1. Poverty helps to ensure that dirty, dangerous, menial and undignified work gets done.
2. The poor subsidize the affluent by saving them money (for example, domestic servants, medical guinea pigs, and the poor paying regressive taxes).
3. Poverty creates jobs in a number of professions (e.g. drug pedlars, prostitutes, pawnshops, army, police).
4. The poor buy shoddy, stale and damaged goods (e.g. day-old bread, vegetables, second-hand clothes) which prolongs their economic usefulness, and similarly use poorly trained and incompetent professional people, such as doctors and teachers.
5. The poor help to uphold the legitimacy of dominant norms by providing examples of deviance (e.g. the lazy, spendthrift, dishonest, promiscuous).
6. The poor help to provide emotional satisfaction, evoking compassion, pity and charity, so that the affluent may feel righteous.
7. The poor offer affluent people vicarious participation in sexual, alcoholic and narcotic behaviour.
8. Poverty helps to guarantee the status of the non-poor.
9. The poor assist in the upward mobility of the non-poor. (By being denied educational opportunities or being stereotyped as stupid or unteachable, the poor enable others to obtain the better jobs.)
10. The poor add to the social viability of non-economic groups (e.g. fund-raising, running settlements, other philanthropic activities).
11. The poor perform cultural functions, like providing labour for Egyptian pyramids, Greek temples and medieval churches.
12. The poor provide 'low' culture which is often adopted by the more affluent (e.g. jazz, blues, spirituals, country music).
13. The poor serve as symbolic constituencies and opponents for several political groups (being seen either as the depressed or as 'welfare chiselers').

1. Gans, H., 'The Positive Functions of Poverty', *American Journal of Sociology*, 78, No. 2, 1972-3.

14. The poor can absorb economic and political costs of change and growth in American society (e.g. reconstruction of city centres, industrialization).
15. The poor play a relatively small part in the political process and indirectly allow the interests of others to become dominant and distort the system.

Gans denies that he is showing why poverty should persist, only that it 'survives in part because it is useful to a number of groups in society . . . whether the dysfunctions outweigh the functions is a question that clearly deserves study'. He points out that alternatives can be found easily enough for some functions. Thus, automation can begin to remove the need for dirty work, and professional efforts can be directed, like those of social workers, to the more affluent, and those of the police to traffic problems and organized crime. But he argues that the status, mobility and political functions are more difficult to substitute in a hierarchical society, and though inequality of status might be reduced, it could not be removed. 'A functional analysis must conclude that poverty persists not only because it satisfies a number of functions but also because many of the functional alternatives to poverty would be quite dysfunctional for the more affluent members of society.' Gans believes that, unlike the Davis and Moore analysis of inequality, his argument is not conservative. By identifying the dysfunctions of poverty and discussing functional alternatives, the argument takes on 'a liberal and reform cast, because the alternatives often provide ameliorative policies that do not require any drastic change in the existing social order'.

Gans passes in a few lines over the dysfunctions of poverty and does not suggest how the functional might be distinguished from the dysfunctional. There are items which, for any single group, might be both functional and dysfunctional, though possibly to different degrees. There are problems in measuring the scope or degree of functions and dysfunctions. It is surely important to find whether poverty is functional or dysfunctional for 500 persons or 5 million persons, and whether it is seriously or only marginally functional or dysfunctional for these numbers. What is required, too, is the kind of analysis showing whether poverty applies, say, to 20 per cent of the population in one society and to 10 per cent in another, and whether and how functional analysis can explain these differences, and, moreover, whether it can explain any differences in prevalence over time. To give a list of obstacles to the removal of poverty makes a very small contribution to our understanding of the existence and conditions for removal of the phenomenon. Again, there is the problem of distinguishing between objective and subjective aspects of the phenomenon. In everyday life, people do not discuss, and are sometimes not even aware of, certain privations, as well as certain benefits. Yet they vigorously discuss, and are acutely aware of, other privations, as well as other benefits. The sociologist's job is to find and apply criteria of discrimination to these different items.

Certainly, a shopping list of functions shows that there are groups in society with a vested interest in perpetuating poverty, but the interrelationships between groups and the sources and conditions of their power might be explored with the effect of implying constructive alternatives and hence showing how specious are the claims to inevitability on the part of apologists for the existing social system. The overall effect of the approach is to convey that poverty cannot be removed but only diminished or modified.[1] It is therefore as ideological as was the statement by Davis and Moore in 1945. It would seem that functional analysis so far offers no more than preliminary descriptive classification of different groups who may, to an undefined extent, benefit from as well as suffer from poverty in society.

Conclusion

This review of theories of poverty, and of some theories of inequality which are relevant to an explanation of poverty, has made it necessary to express criticisms which imply an alternative standpoint. This might be called a 'class structuration' theory. While agreeing with certain views expressed by 'radical' economic theorists, reflecting the nineteenth-century theories of Marx, especially in relation to income from property and the importance of social classes, these views need to be clarified and spelt out in some detail, but also modified. These theorists are right to call attention to the divisions among workers in the labour market, but seem to be giving excessive weight to past labour-force status in explaining poverty, for example, among elderly and sick or disabled people.[2] Other resource systems than the wage system, and other institutions than the labour market, including the political and welfare institutions of the state, have to be brought into a general theory – even if they prove to be of lesser importance or to be indirect appendages of the labour market.

At least five priorities in the further development of theory must be identified:

1. The division of resources and not only income in society.
2. The methods, principles and systems by which these resources are produced and distributed.
3. The styles of living with which the differential ownership in the population of these

1. In his final paragraph, Gans admits that, though his analysis is more complete than early functionalism, it needs to be made more complete by an examination of functional alternatives. A conclusion would then be reached which would not be very different from that of radical sociologists 'that phenomena like poverty can be eliminated only when they either become sufficiently dysfunctional for the affluent or when the poor can obtain enough power to change the system of social stratification'. However, functional alternatives are not examined. Gans does not analyse the system of stratification, trace its origins and means of maintenance, or specify the conditions for changing it. Nor does he say how we would recognize what could be 'sufficiently dysfunctional for the affluent'. See Gans, 'The Positive Functions of Poverty', p. 288.
2. For example, Wachtel, 'Looking at Poverty from a Radical Perspective', pp. 182–8.

resources correspond (and hence the forms of deprivation which lack or denial of such resources denote).

4. The social classes who mediate the relationships of people with systems of production and distribution, and who share relatively distinct standards and styles of living.

5. The minority groups who are liable to have an unequally small share of available national resources.

Many of the chapters of this book seek to elaborate these elements of theory. The reasons for attaching importance to the concept of style of living were discussed in Chapter 1, and the significance of 'social class' requires no further comment. It will be a major theme of the book, and is treated in Chapter 10. I shall give brief illustrations of the importance of the concepts of 'resources' and 'minority groups'.

Poverty, I will argue, is the lack of the resources necessary to permit participation in the activities, customs and diets commonly approved by society. Different kinds of resources, and not just earnings or even cash incomes, have to be examined. The scope, mechanisms and principles of distribution of each system controlling the distribution and redistribution of resources have to be studied. The list below represents in simplified form the resource systems, though clearly there is a large number of sub-systems which would have to be distinguished in any full analysis. The figure is intended to illustrate the complex sources of inequality. Poverty is in part the outcome of these systems operating upon the population. Some, such as the wage and social security systems, affect large proportions of the population and account, in aggregate, for a large share of the total resources which are distributed. Others play a relatively minor role. They have developed in conjunction with the class structure and both help to re-

Type of resource	Main systems from which derived
1. Cash income:	
(a) Earned.	Wage and salary systems of private industry and the state Self-employment income system Fiscal system
(b) Unearned.	Asset-holdings (rent, dividends and interest from deposits with banks and building societies, insurance policies, land and buildings, government and company securities) Fiscal system
(c) Social security.	Social insurance and assistance Employer sick pay and pensions Family Fiscal system Court maintenance orders

Type of resource	Main systems from which derived
2. Capital assets:	
(a) House/flat occupied by family and possessions.	Family Public authority loans system Building societies and insurance companies Employer subsidy Fiscal system
(b) Assets (other than occupied house).	Employer gift Family Earnings Fiscal system Capital issues system of companies, banks and insurance companies
3. Value of employment benefits:	
(a) Employers' fringe benefits: subsidies and value of occupational insurance.	Industrial welfare system Fiscal system
(b) Occupational facilities.	Industrial planning and management Safety inspectorate Trade union
4. Value of public social services: Chiefly other than cash, including government subsidies and services, e.g. health and education, but excluding social security.	Central and local public education system Central and local public welfare system
5. Private income in kind:	
(a) Home production.	Family Personal leisure Self-employment
(b) Gifts.	Family
(c) Value of personal supporting services.	Family Community

produce but also modify that structure. They do so in terms of their scope or coverage, the scale and growth of the resources that are to be distributed, and the amounts that are distributed to those who are eligible to receive resources.

One difference that we have noted between 'radical' and orthodox economic theory is in methodology, and particularly the quantifiability of the scale and severity of poverty. There is a tendency in so-called radical theory to describe and explain *generalized* deprivation or exploitation in capitalist societies rather than historical changes or cross-national differences in magnitude.[1] There are different

1. For example, despite its analytic strengths, there are no diagrammatic models and no

theoretical possibilities. Suppose that 10 per cent of the population in Country A but only 5 per cent in Country B had been found to be living in poverty. This might be due to resources being distributed more unequally by all or most resource systems in Country A than in Country B. However, it might be due solely to differences in the relative dominance of different resource systems with the structure of 'differentials' within each remaining the same. Thus Country A might distribute more of its aggregate resources through the wage system, and transfer less (by means of taxation) to social security, than Country B. Or it is even conceivable that Country A might have systems of industrial welfare, social security and education, health and welfare which dispose of resources more equitably than Country B, but because wages and property are distributed so unequally, still experiences more poverty.

Other theoretical possibilities arise in conditions of change. Despite substantial increases in the resources distributed via social security and the other public social services, overall inequality in the distribution of resources, and perhaps of poverty as well, might grow. This might, on the one hand, be due to the disproportionate growth to prominence of industrial fringe benefits, aided and abetted by the fiscal system (the benefits being confined to a minority of the employed population), and on the other to the disproportionate growth of the dependent sector of the population which is excluded from the labour market (chiefly elderly and disabled people). Therefore, the distribution of resources *between* resource systems might be as important as the distribution *within* any single system. This is the distinctive feature of the approach to the explanation of both inequality and poverty which is recommended in this book. Essentially an attempt is made to meet the criticism that inequality tends to be conceived of 'in a piecemeal manner, rather than as a multiform and pervasive phenomenon'.[1]

In subsequent research it will be necessary for the resource systems themselves (both centrally and locally) to be examined. In the present study, it is clearly necessary to establish for a cross-section of the population what are their types of income and of other resources and to estimate the value of each 'flow' in money terms. Some households will receive substantial resources under all five headings (cash income, capital assets, and employment benefits, public social service benefits and private income in kind). Others may receive resources under only, say, two of the five headings. This is set out for the entire sample in Chapter 5. The classification of types of resource, and their magnitude in relation both to classes and minority groups, will help to demonstrate their allocative and institutional origins. Of chief importance, as we shall see, are the allocative mechanisms and amounts of employment earnings, and inherited as well as accumulated wealth.

---

tables, and few illustrative statistics, in Gordon, *Theories of Poverty and Underemployment*.

1. Goldthorpe, J. H., 'Social Inequality and Social Integration in Modern Britain', *Advancement of Science,* December 1969, p. 191.

Finally, it is hoped to establish from the present study the extent to which there are minority groups in the population with low resources who have certain specific social characteristics which, at least to a substantial degree, make them independent of social class and yet indirectly or directly support a system of classes. For example, because of age, disability or a short period of residence, some people will not come within the scope of certain resource systems, and may only qualify for a differentially small share from other systems. Thus immigrants may not qualify for certain benefits, and employees with only a few years' service may not be eligible to receive more than small amounts of money under redundancy and occupational pension agreements. Inequality and poverty are related systematically to social structure in both the demographic as well as the institutional sense. Certain minorities may account for a disproportionately large segment of the population found to be in poverty. That is one reason why it is important to examine and understand the concept of 'minority group'. But there are further reasons. In tracking and explaining the problems of industrial societies, some social scientists are prone to give almost exclusive attention to the employed population, ignoring the substantial or increasing proportions of retired, redundant, disabled and unemployed people. In understanding changes that are taking place in the pattern of inequalities, the concept of 'minority group' therefore has a useful place.

The concept of 'minority group' is essential to the elucidation of both inequality and poverty. The maintenance of inequality, and in particular of differential access to resources, presupposes the designation not merely of individuals but social groups who are not eligible for certain benefits or are not allowed opportunities to obtain certain kinds or amounts of income or accumulate certain kinds or amounts of wealth. For example, the distinction made between 'employed' and 'non-employed' or 'economically active' and 'economically inactive' and a society's attempt to manage the numbers of people allocated to, or motivated to join, each category, implies both the creation of groups marginal to the distinction and means of arranging an orderly progression of individuals from one category to the other. Ranks are thereby created.

The groups are not just individuals permanently assigned to some level or category of resources. The groups have acquired complex functions and relationships in the life of society as a whole. The pattern of their interrelationships reflects and perpetuates the basic value system and not only the economic class structure of society. This illustrates in part why the term 'structuration' seems appropriate.[1] The existence of classes conditions decisions about the development and scope of

1. Anthony Giddens has been responsible for the popularization of this term. In calling attention to the necessity of conceptualizing the structuration of class relationships, he wanted to 'focus upon *the modes in which* "economic" relationships become translated into "non-economic" social structures' – Giddens, A., *The Class Structure of the Advanced Societies*, Hutchinson, London, 1973, p. 105.

resource systems, but these, by controlling access, can also condition the identification and development of minority groups.

Nor are minority groups static. During their lifetimes, individuals move into the groups or may move between one group and another, and attain higher or lower status, with more or fewer resources, because of advancing age, length of service, change of residence or family status. The relativities in resources and status of the groups themselves may also change as a result of political or administrative action or the slow or rapid evolution of economic organization.

The groups are not 'naturally' self-selected, it should be remembered. Society itself decides who precisely are to be 'pensioners', 'immigrants', 'sick' and 'disabled', for example, and what it means to occupy that status. Definitions of, or even labels for, population groups are not always derogatory or stigmatizing. Names may be invented or blazoned at every opportunity for political effect. The use of a collective term encourages people to identify with each other and join in a common struggle; or to support a particular cause. Whether the name or the exact grouping denoted by the name finally helps or hinders a claim to fair or equal treatment or a larger income is not easy to determine. The answer may be affirmative at one stage of history, but negative at the next stage. What must be asserted is both the fact that societies recognize and, indeed, promote minority groups and that such groups exist within and help to explain a structure of inequality.

3
Methods of Research

This chapter gives an overall descriptive account of methods of research[1] and ends with a discussion of the advantages and disadvantages of surveys.

Our first practical object was to estimate the numbers in the population at different levels of living, particularly the numbers living in poverty or on the margins of poverty. Our second was to find what are the characteristics and problems of those in poverty and thus contribute to the development of an explanation for poverty.

Four phases of work were planned: special pilot research into certain minority groups who had not been studied intensively hitherto; preparatory and pilot work on the main survey, the main survey itself and follow-up surveys in poor areas of four parliamentary constituencies: Salford, Neath, Glasgow and Belfast. The pilot research which was carried out between 1965 and 1968 helped to sharpen methods of measuring unemployment and sub-employment, disability and sickness, and styles of living, including amenities at home and in the locality.[2] An international conference was held at the University of Essex in 1967, centring on methods of poverty research.[3] During the autumn of 1967 a questionnaire running to 120 pages, which was planned for the main survey, was applied to 150 households scattered in and around London. The main survey was then launched and ran for twelve months during 1968–9 in each of fifty-one constituencies in the United Kingdom. The fieldwork was completed in the early weeks of 1969. During the same period, four local surveys of a parallel nature were carried out in Salford, Glasgow, Belfast and Neath over a much shorter span, in two waves of a few weeks each in Salford and Glasgow and one wave in Belfast and Neath. Data were successfully collected for 2,052 households and 6,098 individuals in the

1. See Appendix One for further details.
2. See Marsden, D., *Mothers Alone*, Allen Lane, London, 1969; Land, H., *Large Families in London*, Bell, London, 1969; Sinfield, R. A., 'Unemployed in Shields' (unpublished mimeographed report).
3. Several members of the team on the research project, Brian Abel-Smith, Christopher Bagley, Adrian Sinfield, Dennis Marsden and Peter Townsend, contributed papers which were later published in Townsend, P. (ed.), *The Concept of Poverty*, Heinemann, London, 1970.

United Kingdom survey, and for 1,208 households and 3,950 individuals in the four local surveys. In total, therefore, there are data, mostly of a very elaborate kind, for 3,260 households and 10,048 individuals.

The Questionnaire

The questionnaire (Appendix Ten) runs to thirty-nine pages and comprises nine sections on housing and living facilities, employment, occupational facilities and fringe benefits, cash income, assets and savings, health and disability, social services, private income in kind and style of living. The commentary (Appendix Nine) explains the relationship of its design, section by section, to the purposes of the research. This design attempts to fulfil three basic conditions: (a) that information on the resources received by all individuals in the household should be reasonably comprehensive; (b) that information on styles of living and individual and family characteristics should be detailed; and (c) that the situation and diverse living conditions of social minorities, as well as of 'ordinary' families, should be properly allowed for. Housewives cannot always give reliable information about earnings, and few of them can give reliable information about the working conditions and fringe benefits of other members of the household. We also wanted to ask questions about attitudes to employment. The questionnaire was therefore designed to allow answers from individual income recipients as well as on behalf of the household as a whole. Again, the circumstances of the poor have to be described in the context of exact knowledge about the condition and living standards of other sections of the population, but these circumstances are very diverse and sometimes exceptional. Special methods are necessary to ensure that they can be accommodated in a standard questionnaire.

There are therefore a number of features of the questionnaire which are experimental. One of these is the time-span covered by a range of questions on cash income. The concept of 'normal' income seems to us to be very unsatisfactory for measuring poverty and in some respects also for measuring income. In the Family Expenditure Survey, for example, each employee gives the figure of his most recent pay and is then asked if this is the usual amount. If he says it is not, he is then asked to give an estimate of the usual amount. It seems unlikely that proper account can be taken of earnings which, perhaps because of variations in overtime, regularly fluctuate. Moreover, a man whose earnings have fluctuated and who has just received an increase in pay may say that his latest earnings are his 'usual' earnings, more because that is what he now expects to receive than because that is what he has received in the recent past. Difficulties arise especially when employees have become self-employed or vice versa, or have changed from part-time to full-time work, and when retired or non-employed people have been at work recently. There are other problems. People who are not employed at the time of the survey, and may be temporarily sick or unemployed, are categorized in terms of the earnings last received.

As the method is applied it is also inconsistent. The difficulties of obtaining earnings for the self-employed are such that they 'relate to the most recent period of 12 months for which information is obtainable'.[1] Income from investments and property relates to the twelve months preceding the interview and, 'Information on occasional bonuses paid during the last 12 months is also obtained in order to improve the informant's personal estimate of his normal earnings.' Yet legacies, payments of life assurance, gambling winnings, sale of houses, Premium Savings Bond prizes, sale of National Savings certificates and sales of stocks and shares and other assets are 'ignored'. As W. F. F. Kemsley comments wistfully, 'Since income is a flow variable it would be convenient to collect the data on earnings and other income as relating to a specific time period, and this would take care of changes in situation.'[2]

It would be absurd to pretend that the difficulties can all be met in a revised approach. The methods adopted in the Family Expenditure Survey and elsewhere are reputable and thorough. But the attempt both to establish last week's income and last year's income, as described and discussed in detail in Chapter 5, seems to avoid the difficulties of the ambiguous compromise which 'normal' income represents. The concept of 'normal' income tends to misrepresent the actual distribution of incomes, both at any single point in time and as averaged over a lengthy time-span. Inequalities are made to seem smaller than they in fact are. This is because wage-earners are more liable to experience temporary unemployment and sickness than salaried earners, and when they do, to receive relatively smaller incomes. Moreover, it is difficult to justify the averaging of occasional bonuses in 'normal' income and not, for example, the 'profit' from purchase and sales of stocks and shares, especially over periods shorter than a year. By distinguishing between current (last week's or last month's) income and income in the last year it is easier to identify households and individuals whose living standards are unstable, some of whom experience short-term or long-term poverty. These conceptual and operational problems become even harder to resolve during periods of high rates of inflation. Many people draw much higher earnings in later months than in earlier months of the year, and none the less cannot be counted among those whose earnings vary for structural reasons. In 1968–9 we ignored inflationary trends. During the twelve months of the fieldwork, earnings increased by 7·5 per cent and retail prices by 5·4 per cent.

Our attempt to trace income over a twelve-month period meant that certain social variables had to be traced for this period too. The questionnaire incorpor-

1. Kemsley, W. F. F., *Family Expenditure Survey: Handbook on the Sample, Fieldwork and Coding Procedures*, H M S O, London, 1969, p. 48.
2. ibid., pp. 47–9.

ates an employment record for each individual – showing the hours and weeks of work and the periods off work for reasons of unemployment, sickness, holidays and other reasons for both the self-employed and employed, including casual and seasonal workers.

The section on occupational facilities and fringe benefits probes the nature and adequacy of the working environment and whether or not industrial welfare benefits are a substantial supplement to earnings for many employees. A large part of adult life is passed at places of work, and we were concerned to find to what extent people experience bad working conditions as well as poor home conditions, and to what extent both are related to low earnings and, more comprehensively, to poverty of resources. A measure of working conditions was tentatively devised. For people working wholly or mainly indoors, ten items were covered: sufficient heating to be warm at work in winter; tea or coffee (whether charged or not); indoor flush WC; facilities for washing and changing, including hot water, soap, towel and mirror; place to buy lunch or eat own sandwiches (whether used or not); place to keep coat and spare set of clothes without risk of loss; place for small personal articles which can be locked; first-aid box or facilities; possibility of making and receiving at least one personal telephone call per day; and lighting which the individual can increase or reduce when necessary (e.g. light over work). Working conditions vary, and any index like this which is used for purposes of comparison should, where possible, be supplemented with accounts of individual firms, industries and groups of industries.

There was a corresponding group of questions about facilities in the home, and also questions about the environment, such as play facilities for children. In addition to measures of overcrowding, inequality in numbers of rooms and possession of a range of basic facilities, such as bath, WC and electricity, there was a measure of household durables or facilities which covers ten items: television, record player, radio, refrigerator, washing machine, vacuum cleaner, telephone, central heating, armchairs, easy chairs or settees for every member of the family plus one visitor, and carpet covering all or nearly all the floor in the main sitting room.

Very few studies of assets have ever been carried out in the United Kingdom. When H. F. Lydall came to report his 1952 survey in 1955, he pointed out that it provided the first detailed study of the distribution of personal liquid asset holdings. 'This is a subject which has been hitherto an almost completely closed book. With the exception of an inquiry undertaken on behalf of the National Savings Committee in 1948, the results of which relate only to national savings, no attempt has been made to discover the distribution of liquid asset holdings amongst persons.'[1] The general section on assets included in our questionnaire attempts to cover the subject more comprehensively than did Lydall. Two concepts were developed of readily and non-readily realizable assets. The former include savings, stocks and shares and money owed. The latter include the value of

1. Lydall, H. F., *British Incomes and Savings*, Blackwell, Oxford, 1955, pp. 1–2.

house, car, other property, including housing, business, farm or professional practice, and personal possessions such as jewellery, silver and antiques. The purpose of distinguishing between the two is to call attention to the fact that although some assets can be cashed at short notice, and indeed are often cashed for a special purpose or as a method of raising income when families enter periods of difficulty, other assets take a long time to cash and are sometimes looked on socially and psychologically as unexpendable. The distinction is, of course, not very sharp. Some people acquire paintings and jewellery and turn them into cash without compunction. Others pawn their more precious possessions when in trouble. But without asking questions about each type of asset it would be difficult to develop a rigorous classification on empirical grounds rather than arbitrary judgement. Our division follows previous practice in the sense that readily realizable assets are those referred to as 'liquid assets' by economists. Our data can be compared with those in other studies, as for example Lydall's.[1]

Efforts to collect data on non-readily realizable assets have perhaps been inhibited in the past by the difficulty of making valuations. The current values of houses, businesses and cars are sometimes difficult to estimate, and in any survey reasonable procedures to cope with diverse types of information have to be worked out. In the case of owner-occupied housing, for example, we invited the owner to give a valuation. We also asked the interviewer to do likewise and to give any reasons if his figure differed from the owner's. As a third ingredient of information, we asked what was the insured value of the house. In editing, we adopted the informant's estimate if (as in the vast majority of cases) it differed by £500 or less from the interviewer's estimate. If the estimates differed by more, we took into account the area, age of house, facilities (as given in Section 1 of the questionnaire) and the insured value of the house, as well as any information given by the interviewer, in choosing an estimate. In the case of cars, valuation was easier. The owner was asked to estimate a value and if there was any doubt he was asked the make, type and year of manufacture. In editing we consulted standard price lists for second-hand cars.

In valuing net assets, we had to estimate debts. On the one hand, the total figure for readily realizable assets, including savings, stocks and shares and money owed to the informant, might be reduced by the figure representing overdrafts or loans, rent owed, hire-purchase debt and personal debt to arrive at a realistic figure of 'net' liquidity. Information about assets before and after deducting debts might then be given. On the other hand, the figures for non-readily realizable assets might be thought to represent useful data only if debt is subtracted. Some young married couples, for example, may have a car and a house worth £6,000 and yet, because they have only just started to repay substantial loans, their 'real' assets may be calculated as less than £500. The debt on a car, which is generally being paid off through a hire-purchase agreement, can

1. See the discussion of 'personal holdings of liquid assets' in Lydall, *British Incomes and Savings,* pp. 11–14 and 61–104.

be estimated with a high degree of accuracy. The debt on a house is more difficult to estimate. We developed rather elaborate interviewing and editing procedures in an attempt to estimate the debt, exclusive of interest, on a house and deduct the figure from the estimated value of the house. The value of mortgage outstanding had to be worked out on the basis of the term of the mortgage, the number of years still to pay and how much of each monthly payment represented interest and how much represented capital repayments.

In addition to fairly well-tested operational definitions of cash income and assets, the questionnaire incorporated more experimental definitions of private income in kind, fringe benefits and value of free and subsidized social services. Previous experience showed that income in kind is invariably underestimated. We believed that this was because questions are too general and undirected and that if social relationships and exchanges could be explored in a specific and not a general fashion fuller information would materialize. The prospect of adding even more to an already extensive questionnaire deterred us from developing this principle as far as we would have wished. But some attempt was made to obtain information about the kind of personal services, especially from relatives, upon which the household depended, and to check on gifts given as well as received in the context of what was said about the most frequent contacts with relatives.

The value of social service subsidies was explored in a series of questions about benefits received during the previous twelve months – including overnight stays in hospital, consultations with G Ps, receipt of free school meals and milk, receipt of cheap welfare milk, schools and colleges attended.

The final section of the questionnaire contains a number of indicators of style of living and explores the attitudes of housewives and chief wage-earners towards poverty and changes in living standards. The intention is to relate resource levels both to behaviour and attitudes, and to find how closely subjective deprivation corresponds with objective deprivation.

One further comment about resources needs to be made. In aiming to arrive at a comprehensive, and reasonably consistent, valuation of the resources or living standards of each household and income unit we were aware from the beginning of the problem of collecting a wide range of data on debts as well as assets and incomes. But the problem of adding up the results made us increasingly aware as time went on of the problem of the *meaning* of different types of resources to various sections of the population. The social and political significance and use of economic resources deserves to attract greater attention from social scientists than it has since 1945.

Sampling

Our desire to examine conditions in considerable detail in a few poor areas, as well as nationally, together with the fact that our resources were not unlimited, determined the size of the national survey which we could undertake. It was obviously desirable that methods should be adopted to improve the chances of the sample being representative of all income groups in the population, and therefore provide a reliable basis for measuring poverty. Acting on statistical advice[1] we decided to use a multi-stage stratified design in order to draw a random sample of addresses which was likely to yield successful interviews with about 2,000 households.[2] Every household had an equal probability of selection. The sample was drawn from the 630 parliamentary constituencies of the United Kingdom, which were divided into ten regions and grouped into three strata: high income, middle income and low income. The best criterion available for this purpose was found to be the percentage of the electorate who voted Left. For example, we found that this percentage correlated with the percentage of the population who were in industry compared with other occupations; were semi-skilled and unskilled; had left school at 15 years of age or under; lacked exclusive use of a bath in the household; were overcrowded and had relatively low retail turnover. Urban constituencies, accounting for 80 per cent of the population, were grouped into three according to this voting criterion, but rural constituencies were not grouped in this way, partly because they are diverse, include a number of urban districts, and do not display such a strong link between voting behaviour and socio-economic characteristics as urban constituencies, but also because it seemed unnecessary, in view of the fact that they represent only about 20 per cent of the population. Using this sampling frame, fifty-one constituencies were selected.

At the next stage, within these fifty-one constituencies, we adopted a further method of improving the likely representativeness of the sample. Certain wards had to be selected so that interviewing could be undertaken, and it is well known that in some constituencies some wards contain poorer people than others. How could this variation be controlled in the selection of addresses? We needed a criterion by which to divide wards into groups so that addresses could be sampled representatively within these groups. Research into census data showed that the best criterion was the proportion of the population aged 25 and over who had left school at 15 or under. Using census data, percentages were worked out for every ward and county electoral division or group of parishes. Where the percentages varied widely within constituencies, the wards were grouped into two strata and within each stratum ranked in descending order of size of popu-

1. Professor Durbin and Professor Stuart of the London School of Economics acted as consultants and were responsible in particular for the proposal to stratify areas according to voting behaviour.

2. This number is generally regarded as being about the minimum for purposes of obtaining data which can be regarded as being nationally representative. A survey covering the United States population, for example, was based on a sample of 2,504 households (although there was also a supplementary sample of 296 low income households obtained from the 1960 Survey of Consumer Finances). Morgan, J. N., Martin, D. M., Cohen, W., and Brazer, H. E., *Income and Welfare in the United States*, McGraw-Hill, New York, 1962, pp. 449–50.

lation. If the percentages varied little, the wards were treated as a single stratum. A ward or county electoral division was chosen for each stratum of each constituency with probability proportional to size.

Finally, there was the problem of obtaining a full list of addresses from which to sample. The electoral register is normally used for sampling but does not provide a perfect frame of addresses. It tends to become out of date. Even if the sample can be drawn soon after publication of the register, a few months elapse between the compilation of the list and publication. Very new dwellings, dwellings which have been newly converted into two or three parts, and some dwellings occupied by households for only part of the year, as well as some in which households may have failed to make returns of information and have also escaped the careful checks made by registration officers, will not be included in the lists. Dwellings in which people live, none of whom are eligible to vote, are also not included. Gipsies and caravan-dwellers tend to be under-represented in the registers. The total deficiency at any point of time is unknown. Since we had grounds for supposing that people with low incomes were more likely to move frequently and less likely to make returns of information than others, we took the view that if the survey of poverty was to be reliable, exceptional steps should be taken to ensure that itinerants, whether rich or poor, were included in the sampling frame. The Home Secretary gave his permission for us to approach electoral registration officers for access to their records, which usually included 'partly built' as well as 'empty' addresses. In the event, we depended mostly on these basic records, but also, in some constituencies, on rating records. Our sample of addresses was laborious to compile, but certainly more comprehensive and up to date than would otherwise have been possible.

Samples were also drawn from four poor areas. We aimed to select four compact areas which could legitimately be regarded as being among the poorest in the country. For convenience of interviewing, we started with the fifty-one constituencies already chosen for the national survey and picked four, using criteria indicating that the proportion of low-income households would be well above the national average, but also giving a 'spread' geographically and in nature of the problems of poor areas. Within these four constituencies we obtained information from the census and the local councils about wards. Using criteria such as the percentage of adults leaving school at 15 years of age or younger, the percentage of children getting free school meals and average rateable value of dwellings, we selected the poorest wards of these poor constituencies from which to draw samples of addresses.

Because novel and rather elaborate methods of sampling were adopted, a full account is given in Appendix One of the procedures followed.

Interviewing

In the year before the national survey was launched, we endeavoured to commission, or develop, a research organization capable of handling a questionnaire of the demanding and complex kind which we had adopted. Other than the Government Social Survey, no research organizations in the United Kingdom had had experience, up to that time at least, of handling such detailed inquiries about incomes. Moreover, the survey methods of research organizations had been designed for surveys of the general population rather than of minority groups, and this affected design of questionnaires and field organization, and even attitudes of interviewers. Surveys which seek to establish the behaviour and attitudes of the great majority of the population can clearly be conducted according to simpler principles than surveys which seek reliable information about a variety of different minority groups.

The Government Social Survey was at that time under considerable pressure to expand its work for government departments and could not undertake fieldwork on our behalf. Instead, we developed our own organization. In the event this proved to be a more herculean task than we had anticipated. National and regional organization of a highly developed kind is required to handle interviewing based on separately issued samples for each quarter of the year for fifty-one separate constituencies, and this is difficult, and expensive, to build up from scratch for a single survey. This lay behind the organization of a very elaborate pilot survey in the late summer and autumn of 1967, and the holding of a succession of unusually lengthy briefing conferences nationally in London and regionally in places such as Belfast, Manchester and Glasgow for the interviewers.[1]

Ideally we would have wished to employ the smallest possible number of interviewers, in order to maintain uniformly high standards of interviewing and a high response rate. In practice, over four fifths of the interviews were carried out by a group of about twenty-five interviewers, upon whom we depended throughout the twelve months. But there was considerable turnover among other interviewers, partly because, though often experienced in survey work, they found the interviewing protracted, uncongenial or difficult. There were also problems administratively of fitting occasional and part-time interviewers into our quarterly schedules, when they were employed part-time or full-time by other research agencies. Many of our difficulties arose because of a shortage of really skilled interviewers in the more remote parts of the country. The fact that interviewing was carried out in each of the constituencies in all four quarters of the year added

---

1. The pilot questionnaire covered 140 duplicated pages, and considerable study and training was involved in reaching the point at which interviewers could confidently use the final questionnaire. An interviewer was also normally expected to complete three trial interviews with the final questionnaire before he began work in the survey.

to these problems and increased costs. We came to the rueful conclusion that, while our response rate was high, it would have been significantly higher if the interviewing had been concentrated in one period of the year, or concentrated for groups of the fifty-one constituencies in different periods of the year, in a kind of 'roving' programme, utilizing a small team of interviewers, who could go from one remote area to the next, as well as local interviewers.

A chief fieldwork organizer and a deputy organizer were based on London, and regional organizers were also appointed. These included some of the most highly skilled and experienced interviewers in survey work in the country, and if they had not been so devoted in giving up their spare time to training new interviewers and trudging to remote addresses, the survey would have failed. Among their duties was that of attempting to persuade householders who had initially refused to give an interview to do so. This improved the response rate by 3 or 4 per cent, and we concluded that if our resources had been greater in certain areas we could have improved it by a lot more.

Interviewers were instructed to interview the housewife and all wage-earners (and other income recipients) in the household. An average of two people was interviewed in each household, sometimes on the same occasion (separately or together) though often on one or more subsequent occasions. This means that nearly two thirds, or just over 4,000, of the 6,098 individual members of households were interviewed, most of the remainder being children. Table 3.1 shows the number of people in households who answered at least some sections of the questionnaire, compared with the number who should, ideally, have been seen.

Table 3.1. Percentages of households, according to number of people eligible for interview and actually interviewed per household.

	National Survey	
Number of people	Eligible for interview	Interviewed
1	19	25
2	58	57
3	15	12
4	6	4
5	1	1
6 or 7	0·3	0·1
Total	100	100
Number	2,024[a]	2,024[a]

NOTE: [a]Twenty-eight unclassifiable. In subsequent tables, numbers of households or of individuals will normally be given and, except in the case of sub-groups, any difference between the number given and the sample total is due to lack of information on one or other of the variables on which the table is based.

Altogether, 93 per cent of the individuals in responding households who ought properly to have been questioned directly about their incomes or other topics were in fact so questioned. Although many interviewers adopted the practice of working in the early evenings or at weekends, so that both husband and wife, for example, could be interviewed during the same call, many return visits had to be paid to interview wage-earners about incomes and conditions of work. If a return visit was difficult to arrange, or, say, a wage-earner was unlikely to be available, a special form could be left for him to complete in confidence and return. It was possible only to complete 47 per cent of questionnaires during the first call, and a further 30 per cent during a second call. As many as 23 per cent could be completed only at a third or subsequent call.

A record was kept of the total time taken up in interviewing. Table 3.2 shows the distribution. The questionnaires were completed for only 1 per cent of the households (nearly all of them being retirement pensioners living alone) in under three quarters of an hour, and only a further 17 per cent in less than an hour and a quarter. For most households, the time required was between one and a quarter and two and three quarter hours, and the mean was just over two hours. Interviews took over three hours with 12 per cent, and over six hours with some of these. The average household comprised three people.

Table 3.2. *Percentages of households, according to time taken in interviews.*

Less than ¾ hr	1
¾–1¼ hrs	17
1¼–1¾ hrs	26
1¾–2¼ hrs	24
2¼–2¾ hrs	14
2¾–3¼ hrs	8
3¼–4¼ hrs	6
4¼–5¼ hrs	2
5¼ hrs +	1
Total	100
Number	2,052

The sample of addresses was divided into four, and each quarter was issued separately to interviewers during the year. Interviewing could not begin in some constituencies until several weeks of 1968 had elapsed. The final stages of interviewing were completed during the first quarter of 1969. There was no month of the twelve months in which fewer than about a hundred interviews were completed. The interviews were distributed as follows:

1968	first quarter	23·5 per cent
	second quarter	23·2 per cent

third quarter   22·4 per cent
fourth quarter   22·3 per cent
1969 first quarter   8·6 per cent

The interviewing in the follow-up surveys which were carried out in Belfast, Glasgow, Neath and Salford was concentrated in waves. Originally two waves of interviewing from two samples of addresses in each area were contemplated, but in practice our resources did not permit a second wave of interviewing in Belfast and Neath. In Belfast and Glasgow, we commissioned Spencer Marketing Research Services to undertake the interviewing. In Neath and Salford, we organized our own teams. A special 'screening' questionnaire was used to establish whether or not households in the follow-up surveys belonged to any of a number of minority groups. If they did belong to these minority groups (about two fifths), the first interview was terminated and permission was sought for a second, at which the main questionnaire which was being used nationally was completed. If they did not belong to any minority group, an interview lasting about half an hour and designed to obtain basic information about employment, social class, health and income was completed.

Response

By the standards of income or expenditure surveys, the overall response rate was high. Nearly 76 per cent of households gave complete information, and altogether 82 per cent cooperated completely or substantially. In 1968, households cooperating in the Family Expenditure Survey represented 69 per cent, and in 1969, 67 per cent, of the effective sample (the rate being 68 per cent in 1972 and 1973 and 71 per cent in 1974).[1] As Table 3.3 shows, the response rate was lowest in the South-East and highest in Anglia and the East Midlands, but even in the South-East and Greater London was 72 per cent or better for interviews complete in all respects.

Because non-response in surveys of income tends to be substantial and may affect the reliability of the results, we asked interviewers to do their best to complete a special form giving limited information about those who refused an interview. We could not supervise the completion of these forms as efficiently as we would have wished, and had to give priority to supervising the main interviews. None the less we reached the conclusion that this exercise would be more than justified in surveys in which claims to representativeness are particularly important. With better prior planning, interviewers *could* have obtained enough information through observation, or politely by interview, to permit all major doubts about non-response to be cleared up. As it was, we were able to obtain information about the great majority of the 388 households refusing an interview.

1. Reports of the *Family Expenditure Survey*, H M S O, London, for the years specified.

Table 3.3. *Response in the survey.*

Region	Total number of households at effective addresses	Complete interviews	Incomplete interviews[a]		Refusals	Non-contact	Lost[b]	Response (complete and incomplete interviews) (%)
			A	B				
Greater London	376	271	9	9	75	12	–	76·9
South-East	402	292	8	8	90	4	–	76·6
Anglia and East Midlands	211	162	8	19	20	2	–	89·5
North-West	290	226	8	7	42	6	1	80·9
Northern, Yorks and Humberside	298	225	6	15	45	5	2	84·8
West Midlands	298	227	7	26	32	6	–	87·2
South-West and Wales	286	214	8	14	40	9	1	82·5
Scotland	230	182	5	6	32	2	3	83·9
Northern Ireland	104	87	1	2	12	1	1	86·6
Total	2,495	1,886	60	106	388	47	8	82·3
Percentage	100	75·6	2·4	4·2	15·6	1·9	0·3	–

NOTE: [a]Column A means that information is complete for one or more but not all income units in the household. Column B means that information on income and assets is not complete for any income unit in the household, although other information has been given.
[b]Eight questionnaires were completed but could not be traced at coding stage.

For example, we were able to establish the tenure of 323 of the 388 households. Owner-occupiers accounted for 54 per cent, council tenants for 31 per cent and private tenants for 15 per cent, the first two groups being rather larger, and the third smaller than the corresponding groups among responding households. Approximately 10 per cent shared the dwelling with at least one other household (compared with 8 per cent among respondents). For 17 per cent of households, there was a flight of at least four steps to the dwelling entrance – a percentage identical with that of respondents. The household composition of respondents and those who refused, where known, is compared in Table 3.4.

Table 3.4. Household composition in relation to response.

	Refusals (%)	Respondents (%)
Single person over 60	15	12
Single person under 60	6	6
Man and woman	34	26
Man, woman and children	23	24
Others with children	7	13
Others, adults only	16	19
Total	100	100
Number	286	2,027

In a number of other respects we gained information about households who refused an interview, to compare with households granting an interview or interviews. Rather fewer moved into the dwelling recently, only 6 per cent having lived there less than a year and another 5 per cent less than two years, compared with 10 per cent and 6 per cent respectively. Thirty-six per cent (compared with 30 per cent) had lived there all their lives or for fifteen or more years. Fewer chief wage-earners and housewives among refusals than among respondents were under 50. Thus 40 per cent were under 50 (compared with 55 per cent) and 25 per cent were aged 65 and over (compared with 18 per cent). Finally, we established the social class of the head of household in about half the cases where there was a refusal. (Among the others the distribution by housing tenure corresponded with the distribution given above.) We compared the distribution of occupations with that of respondents, using the Registrar General's classification. Manual occupations accounted for 55 per cent, compared with 57 per cent. Professional occupations accounted for 6 per cent (compared with 3 per cent); managerial and higher supervisory non-manual occupations 21 per cent (15 per cent); other non-manual 18 per cent (25 per cent); skilled manual 29 per cent (23 per cent); partly skilled manual 20 per cent (25 per cent); and unskilled manual 6 per cent (9 per cent). However, these more detailed figures should be treated with caution. Queries about exact occupations could not be pursued in some cases.

All in all, our evidence suggested that proportionately *more* late middleaged and older people, and couples without children, including more in the upper non-manual classes, had refused than had granted an interview. Proportionately *fewer* young adults, including fewer with children, had refused than had granted an interview. None the less, bearing in mind the respective magnitude of the numbers of refusals and numbers of respondents, the survey findings cannot have been seriously distorted. Differences in the distributions quoted would not have necessitated other than marginal corrections.

Response in the special follow-up surveys in Belfast, Glasgow, Neath and Sal-

Table 3.5. *Response at first and second stages in surveys in four areas.*

Response	Belfast		Glasgow		Neath		Salford		All four areas	
	1st	2nd	1st	2nd	1st	2nd	1st	2nd	1st	2nd
Refusing at first stage	5·9		9·8		12·0		12·7		10·3	
Non-contacts	3·0		8·6		1·1		5·5		5·2	
Interviewed, not approached 2nd stage	47·7		47·4		53·8		43·5		47·4	
Interviewed, approached 2nd stage	43·4		34·2		33·1		38·4		37·1	
Refusal at 2nd stage		9·1		12·3		17·5		5·7		10·3
Non-contact at 2nd stage		6·1		1·2		0		2·3		2·5
Interviewed, complete information		81·8		81·0		75·9		88·6		82·8
Interviewed, incomplete information		3·0		5·6		6·6		3·4		4·4
Total	100	100	100	100	100	100	100	100	100	100
Number	304	132	477	163	275	91	458	176	1,514	562

ford was also good. As Table 3.5 shows, between 82 and 91 per cent of households approached (including those not contacted) in the four areas for a screening interview agreed. Rather less than half of them were approached at a second stage for a long interview, and between 82 per cent and 92 per cent agreed. At the second stage the questionnaire which had been used in the national survey was used in all four areas. Relatively more of the households cooperating in the second stage of the survey in the four special areas than in the national survey provided complete information on income and assets. The number of people eligible for interview in households tended to be larger than in the national survey, and the proportion interviewed corresponded closely with the results given in Table 3.1. Information took rather longer to collect from households, and the average time given up to interviewing was nearly two and a quarter hours.

Table 3.6. *Response rate by region, Poverty Survey and Family Expenditure Survey.*

	Response rate (per cent)				Percentage of cooperating households	
	Poverty survey[a]	FES (1967)	Percentage of electorate (March 1966)	Percentage of population (mid 1967)	Poverty survey[b]	FES (1968)
Greater London	72·0	61·2	15·1	14·6	14·4	13·0
South-East	72·6	73·2	16·4	16·9	15·3	16·9
Anglia and East Midlands	76·7	72·5	8·7	8·9	9·4	9·0
North-West	78·0	69·5	12·4	12·3	12·0	11·6
Northern, Yorks and Humberside	76·0	71·2	14·9	14·8 ⎫	25·1	16·1 ⎧
West Midlands	78·1	71·7	9·0	9·2 ⎭		9·2 ⎩
South-West and Wales	74·9	73·6	11·6	11·6	11·7	12·3
Scotland	79·0	73·4	9·3	9·4	9·6	9·7
Northern Ireland	83·7	—	2·5	2·7	2·5	2·2
Total	75·6	70·5	100	100	100	100
Number	1,886	7,201	35·85 m	55·00 m	2,052	7,023

NOTES: [a]For purposes of comparison with the FES, only cooperating households who provided information about both incomes and assets are counted.

[b]Households providing incomplete information are included, although the regional distribution is scarcely affected by their inclusion. For purposes of comparison the figures have been recalculated to take account of the deliberate over-sampling of households in Northern Ireland. As described in Appendix One, the rural areas of the Northern, Yorkshire, Humberside and West Midlands regions were amalgamated for purposes of sampling.

SOURCES: Kemsley, W. F. F., *Family Expenditure Survey,* HMSO, London, 1969, p. 29; Department of Employment and Productivity, Report of the Family Expenditure Survey for 1968, HMSO, London, 1969, p. 81; *Social Trends,* No. 1, 1970, p. 62.

Representativeness

The sample can be regarded as providing on the whole a reasonable representation of the population of the United Kingdom. Table 3.6 shows that the proportions of cooperating households in different regions correspond well with the proportions both of the electorate and the population as a whole. The response rate even for households in the sample providing complete information on income and assets compares favourably with the Family Expenditure Survey.

The distribution by age of the sample is compared with the estimates of the Registrar General in Table 3.7. More detail will be found in Appendix Two. There is a slight over-representation in the sample of population aged under 15

Table 3.7. Percentages of non-institutionalized population and of sample, by age.

Age	Population of the UK (1969)	Poverty survey
0–14	24.3	25·3
15–29	21·1	20·6
30–39	12·0	12·4
40–49	13·0	12·4
50–59	11·9	11·7
60–69	10·4	10·3
70+	7·4	7·3
Total	100	100
Number	54,395,000	6,045

SOURCE: See Appendix Two, Table A2.1, p. 955.

and a slight under-representation of those aged 15–29, but the distributions are on the whole very similar. Certainly the poverty survey achieved better representation by age than has the Family Expenditure Survey. In 1969, 28·4 per cent of those in households cooperating in the FES were under 16 and only 11·4 per cent 65 and over. Response in the FES appears consistently to under-represent older age groups.[1]

The distribution of households by number of persons is shown in Table 3.8. By comparison with the census of 1966, one-person households in both the poverty and Family Expenditure surveys are slightly over-represented and three-

1. A special analysis of response in 1971 concluded, 'Much the most striking result to come out of this analysis is that of variation with age. It is clear . . . that there is a fairly consistent decline of response with age' – Kemsley, W. F. F., 'Family Expenditure Survey: A Study of Differential Response Based on a Comparison of the 1971 Sample with the Census', *Statistical News*, November 1975. See also Appendix Two.

person households slightly under-represented. Households of other sizes are fairly closely represented. But there were differences between the poverty survey and the census in the definition of 'household', with a consequence that in the survey relatively more of the population were allocated to one-person households.

Table 3.8. *Percentages of households of different size (census, poverty survey and FES compared).*

Number of persons	Britain		UK poverty survey	UK FES (1969)
	(Census 1966)	(Census 1971)		
1	15·4	18·1	17·7	16·1
2	30·2	31·5	29·8	31·2
3	21·2	18·9	18·9	19·8
4	17·7	17·2	17·5	18·1
5	8·8	8·3	9·1	8·3
6	4·0	} 6·0 {	4·1	3·7
7 or more	2·6		2·9	2·8
Total	100	100	100	100
Number	17.0 mil.	18·3 mil.	2,050	7,008

A large number of comparisons with official and other statistics will be found elsewhere in this book. The representativeness of the sample is further discussed in Appendix Two. For example, the census of 1966 shows that 95 per cent of the population, compared with 94·8 per cent of the sample, were born in the UK, 1·4 per cent in the Republic of Ireland, compared with 1·4 per cent of the sample, and 1·6 per cent in the West Indies, India, Pakistan and Africa, compared with 2·1 per cent.

The average rate of unemployment during 1968 as published by the Department of Employment and Productivity was 2·4 per cent, compared with 2 per cent in the survey. Altogether official returns show that 4·9 per cent of the population was dependent in part or whole on supplementary benefits in 1969,[1] compared with 5 per cent in the survey. Households living in privately rented accommodation were (as in the Family Expenditure Survey) slightly over-represented, but the representation of other tenure-groups resembled the distribution portrayed in the census of 1966. Finally, the distribution by social class of adult males in the sample resembled the census distribution.

In many different parts of the book results are compared with data from administrative and other sources. Thus estimates of the numbers employed in the

1. *Social Trends*, No. 1, 1970, p. 100.

population are compared with estimates by the Department of Employment (p. 590); numbers unemployed with those registered as unemployed (p. 595); numbers of one-parent families with estimates by the Department of Health and Social Security (p. 754); distributions of earnings with those derived from the New Earnings Survey and Family Expenditure Survey (p. 621); and many more. We consider that all these comparisons help to demonstrate the overall representativeness of the survey data.

Limitations of Research

The limitations of the research are both technical and conceptual. In general, the efforts to ensure that the sample would include representative numbers of rich and poor seem to have been reasonably successful, though obviously reservations have to be made about non-response. The fact that 16 per cent of households refused an interview, and another 7 per cent were unable to provide complete information on incomes and assets, must introduce a margin of error, quite apart from ordinary sampling errors, into the results. This is why we have endeavoured in this book not only to produce, in this chapter and in an appendix (pages 955–8), a full discussion of the question of representativeness, but also comparable evidence whenever possible or appropriate.

The question is not just whether the sample who were successfully interviewed represent the population, but whether the information provided by them was of uniformly reliable quality. This is affected by the design of the questionnaire and the emphasis given to different subjects by the interviewers. Some general questions cannot always be divided up into appropriate sub-questions. There was a difference, for example, between our approach to cash income and our approach to fringe benefits and income in kind. In the former we asked numerous questions about earnings, social security benefits, income from investments, annuities and so on. In the latter some detailed questions were asked but the sources of fringe benefits and income in kind could not be explored so exhaustively. At various points in this book, therefore, we suggest that certain figures should be treated as slight underestimates of the true figures. Thus, although a general question was asked, with prompts, about employer benefits other than occupational pensions, sick pay and subsidized meals and travel, it is likely that this procedure did not help employees to recollect some unusual types of benefit. Moreover, many people are ignorant of some benefits like sums assured on their lives or houses, or sums expected on retirement. This is, of course, partly due to the relative secrecy in which some institutions operate – because of a fear of their competitors, fragmentation of organization and even unconscious self-deception about privilege. To take a different example, the proportion of the population saying they had frequent contacts with relatives in comparison with the proportions shown by intensive studies of the family, which have been carried out in various parts of

Britain, is almost certainly an underestimate – due partly to the impossibility in a survey as wide-ranging as this one of asking questions systematically about different kinds of relatives.

In general, the design of the questionnaire and the style adopted by the interviewer 'structures' the information that it is possible to collect in a survey. Attitudes provide another example. The questionnaire contains relatively few questions about attitudes and we have endeavoured to follow the principle that useful information about attitudes can only be collected in the context of extensive information about social conditions and behaviour. Even so, the scope of the survey made difficult the design of these questions. The attitudes of men and women of all age-groups and incomes, who live in every part of the country, are not easy to explore if standard questions have to be used. Some data on desire for work and satisfaction with work, feelings of tiredness, help from relatives, subjective definitions of class, subjective deprivation and attitudes to the poor and to poverty must therefore be examined very carefully in relation to social structure and recognized to be responsive, at least in part, to the interview situation.

Because the data actually collected from interviews are structured, both by the initial preconceptions of the research workers and the social situation of the interview itself, special care has to be taken in analysing them not to bias or restrict them further, or at least to allow them to be expressed and built up in alternative ways. Attempts to set up rigorous theoretical models are sometimes inspired by the desire to compress data into forms which lend themselves to particular types of sophisticated analysis, such as linear or multiple-regression analysis.

There are a number of problems in submitting to this. Different disciplines offer different encouragement. Econometricians, for example, are used to the problems of applying highly specific theoretical models and concentrate on the problem of estimating values of the parameters within their causal structures. Sociologists usually work with much more generalized theoretical models and tend to regard empirical research principally as a means of gaining more information about possibly relevant variables. There is the problem of deciding the variables which may be relevant to a particular social condition, such as poverty. A long list may be reached, not all of which it may be possible to investigate in any single type of research. Moreover, the possibility always has to be faced that some in the list may in fact be dependent variables of independent variables so far undetected. There is the problem of clearly distinguishing the variables and finding to what extent they are intercorrelated. There is also the problem of finding whether they can be converted to some common denominator so that they can be measured and weighed in importance. Sociologists have in recent years become acutely aware of the different restrictions imposed by different types of analysis, and there have been some instructive debates about particular inquiries. For example, in the course of defending the analysis he had followed in a report on equality of educational opportunity, James Coleman admitted, '. . . if I were doing such a study now, I would seriously consider the use of multivariate cross-tabulations, with an even more open perspective toward theoretical models, in place of much of the multiple-regression analysis we used. For in the early stages of the search for knowledge about processes in a given area, it is important to use relatively open models, in which the peculiar quirks of the data that may be highly informative are not lost.'[1] At an earlier stage there was a tendency to swamp the reader with cross-tabulations, each with its chi-squared test of significance. Most lately there has been the tendency to confuse him with unnecessarily complex path analysis.[2] Although sociologists increasingly employ formal methods of reasoning,[3] there is considerable disquiet among them about the theoretical value assumptions embedded in superficially innocuous quantitative techniques,[4] about the oversimplification and therefore distortion of reality which the adoption of those techniques implies, and about the problems of using such techniques in communicating the results of sociological work to more than an infinitesimal fraction of the population.

In setting out the results of the poverty survey in the following pages we have tried to reveal some of the quirks of the data by describing in some detail individual variables and their distribution, and by using a large number of straightforward cross-tabulations to bring out some of the basic interrelationships between variables. The rule we have tried to follow is not to run before we have learned to walk. In the context of this survey, this means that there is much worth discussing about the conceptualization, operational definition and descriptive measurement of different variables in order to show the factors that are present in certain states of poverty before relevant causal models can begin to be developed.

The Survey Method

In a study such as this it is also important to express reservations about the survey method itself. Complementary methods will have to be used in order to de-

---

1. Coleman, J. S., 'Reply to Cain and Watts', *American Sociological Review*, vol. 35, No. 2, April 1970, p. 243. See also Cain, G. G., and Watts, H. W., 'Problems in Making Policy Inferences from the Coleman Report', and Aigner, D. J., 'A Comment on Problems in Making Inferences from the Coleman Report', in ibid. The report discussed is Coleman, J. S., Campbell, E. Q., Hobson, C. F., McPartland, J., Mood, A. M., *Equality of Educational Opportunity*, US Office of Education, Washington DC, 1966.

2. Boris Allan, G. J., 'Simplicity in Path Analysis', *Sociology*, May 1974.

3. For a distinctive and coherent recent account, see Boudon, R., *The Logic of Sociological Explanation*, Penguin Books, Harmondsworth, 1974.

4. The controversies following the publication of Blau, P., and Duncan, O., *The American Occupational Structure*, John Wiley, New York, 1967, are a case in point. See Crowder, N. D., 'A Critique of Duncan's Stratification Research', *Sociology*, No. 1, January 1974.

velop knowledge about poverty and theories about its causation. Studies of the mechanisms which control the structure of differentials in the wage system and the production process from which the wage system derives, the shifts of manpower between economic dependency and economic activity, and the allocation to different sectors of public expenditure, will have to be undertaken. We need to know more about the different institutions which have powers to distribute resources and about the interrelations between them. We also need to know about the interrelations between national, community, 'ethnic' and class styles of living, and the ways in which political leadership and the mass media can foster mistrust, scorn and inequitable treatment.

The survey method has certain defects because it is highly individualistic. The network of contacts in the community and at work tends to be played down and the overlapping nature of 'group' consumption is ignored. Not only is the individual in one sense an 'island' of income and spending, even within the income unit or household, but he is also, in another sense, a member of even wider 'groups' of recipients and consumers of resources – the income unit, the household, pairs of households (e.g. telephone party-lines), streets or blocks of flats (e.g. electricity, water, caretaker services, laundry, garden and play facilities), parishes and councils (rate support grant), unions (strike pay and sick pay), industries (government loans and assistance, such as agricultural support) and regions (e.g. regional employment premiums).

The survey method is also restricted because it provides a snapshot in time rather than an account of organic change, and tends to be based on assumptions about cultural homogeneity. Survey directors assume, for example, that every section of the population will understand approximately the same questions and provide an appropriate range of answers.[1]

These limitations have to be stated clearly, if only for the purposes of getting a little nearer to scientific rigour. The defects of any research method have to be spelt out so that modifications can be introduced into research, and its results properly evaluated. The limitations of the survey are very real and could profitably be discussed in relation to any major survey that is carried out. But corresponding advantages should not be forgotten. The survey method represents an attempt to extend bases of comparison to wide sections of the population, and therefore to pose questions about variation in the human condition which requires some kind of coherent explanation. The human condition is, in a sense, given priority and, within the scope of a survey individuals are accorded approxi-

1. 'The survey method favours a society with a slow rate of change and little internal conflict, highly individualistic, inner-directed and mobile, and with a high degree of correspondence between thought, word and deed. Even within such a society, the survey method is more applicable downwards than upwards, and for that reason better as an instrument of control of underdogs than of topdogs' – Galtung, J., *Theory and Methods of Social Research*, Allen & Unwin, London, 1967.

mately equal rights to representation in the analysis and description of the results. Fundamentally, then, a value is asserted. In exploring a problem and searching for an explanation for its existence, the survey director is implicitly giving priority, even over organizations, political power and process, to the human situations and predicaments of a cross-section of the population.

4
Inequality and Poverty, 1938-68

What changes had been taking place in living standards during the years preceding the survey? The evidence suggests two general phases. While there is common agreement about the first phase, there is considerable controversy about the second. There was a levelling of standards during the war years of 1939–45, maintained by the Labour government for at least the first few years after the war. Secondly, there was some reversion to former inequalities, slow at first but probably quite fast by the middle and late 1950s. In aggregate, the country was becoming more prosperous, but certain minorities were losing ground and there was some evidence that poverty (in the relative, structural, sense of that term) was growing. It is possible to go further and suggest that by the mid 1960s a new, third, phase may have begun, but it is as yet too soon to be sure. The increased emphasis on economic growth, and therefore on rewards for certain professional, managerial and skilled manual groups, at a time when there has been a disproportionately large increase of dependants in the population, may have been strengthening the living standards of the former at the expense of the latter. Part of additional resources becoming available has been taken up by the expansion in professional and managerial numbers. However, these three phases could still be regarded as short-run fluctuations within a more stable and continuing inequality, determined by the elaborate interrelationship of social institutions and values, which forms a dense and in many respects highly rigid and impermeable network.

How far can these phases be properly defined and documented? This chapter diverges from some previous attempts to trace the trends. It builds upon analyses of trends in cash incomes, but it also uses the searching criticisms that have been made of available statistics on cash incomes to prepare the ground for a more comprehensive approach. That approach cannot be conclusive, for reasons which will become obvious. I will attempt to trace the trends over the three decades up to 1968–9 in the distribution of resources in the United Kingdom. The term 'resources' is used deliberately to incorporate items which are usually excluded from the definition of the concept of income. Five broad categories are identified: cash income; capital assets; value of employment benefits in kind; value of public social services in kind; and 'private' income in kind. Special weight has to be attached to the distribution of earnings, the occupation structure (particularly in relating the retired and the unemployed to the employed population) and the effects upon the distribution of both cash incomes and overall resources of taxation and fiscal welfare. Trends in indices of poverty, nutrition and health must also be traced to provide further confirmation of any changes that may be taking place in the structure of living standards.

Personal Incomes: Before and After Tax

In the period immediately following the Second World War, the expansion of employment of women as well as continuing high rates of employment of men, the introduction of promised social reforms, and the maintenance, despite the budget of 1946, of high levels of taxation, led to the belief that Britain had abolished poverty and created a much more equal society. The difference between rich and poor, it was widely supposed, had been sharply reduced. Moreover, some interpretations of the statistics suggested that 'levelling' was continuing into the 1950s. When the evidence came to be weighed, this interpretation was first shown to be highly questionable and then likely to be the reverse of the truth. If differences in living standards and the prevalence of poverty are ever to be properly explained, then the structure of and trends in living standards have to be carefully documented.

A lot of evidence about changes in living standards must be taken into the reckoning. However, it is important at the outset to show that the way in which the evidence can be related and combined is more a matter of judgement than an automatic process of measurement. The series of conventional statistics on personal incomes are deficient. Data about some components of income are better than others. All along there has been a failure to call sufficient attention to the changing importance of each of these components, to measure them and examine their consistency. Too much reliance has been placed on trends as shown by general income statistics. The influence of fiscal and social service policies has not been adequately analysed or understood.

We will begin with a review of the general data on personal incomes, as conventionally defined, and then try to incorporate certain missing strands of information. In 1950 the Board of Inland Revenue stated that there had been 'a very considerable redistribution in incomes since pre-war' and that this redistribution was 'most marked in the case of net incomes after tax'.[1] The distinction between pre- and post-tax incomes is, of course, most important. When inflation is allowed for, the board's Report reveals only a relatively small increase in pre-tax incomes in the middle of the distribution. Any really substantial change between 1938 and 1950 is attributable to higher taxation.

Other studies have assessed the changes in more detail and have come to the

1. Board of Inland Revenue, 92nd Annual Report, Cmd 8052, H M S O, London, 1950, p. 86.

Table 4.1. *Percentages of allocated income received before and after tax by specified inter-percentile groups (Lydall).*

Inter-percen-tile group	Before tax				After tax			
	1938	1949	1954	1957	1938	1949	1954	1957
Top 1%	16·2	11·2	9·3	8·0	11·7	6·5	5·4	4·9
					(12·7)	(8·1)	(7·1)	(6·7)
2–5%	12·8	12·3	11·2	10·2	12·4	10·8	10·0	9·1
6–10%	9·0	9·5	9·5	9·8	9·5	9·6	9·7	9·5
11–20%	12·0	14·5	16·0	13·5	12·8	12·8	16·8	14·5

SOURCE: Lydall, H. F., 'The Long-Term Trend in the Size Distribution of Income', *Journal of the Royal Statistical Society*, Series A (General), 122, Part 1, 1959, pp. 14 and 31. The figures in brackets represent Lydall's adjustments to take account of some unallocated income, such as employers' superannuation and life-assurance contributions, other fringe benefits, and income unreported to the tax authorities, but not social services and undistributed company profits. Adjustments were estimated only for the top 1 per cent. The effects of indirect taxation are not allowed for in these calculations.

same conclusion, that is, between 1938 and the 1950s there was some levelling up of pre-tax incomes accompanied by more progressive fiscal measures.[1] A general 'trend' towards greater equality was postulated on the basis of piecemeal analyses and inadequate statistics. For example, 'A study of the period 1938–57 reveals a continuous trend towards greater equality in the distribution of allocated personal income . . . For the future, unless there is a catastrophic slump, the trend towards equality is likely to continue, though probably not as fast as in the past twenty years.'[2] Tables 4.1 and 4.2 summarize the data presented by Lydall and Paish respectively.[3]

But since the hypothesis of decreasing inequality seemed in the mid 1950s to run counter to other social developments, particularly the growing problems of the dependency of the old, it invited closer inspection. Professor Richard Titmuss examined the frailty of the statistics, and of the interpretations based upon them,

1. Between 1938–9 and 1948–9, the aggregate net redistribution had increased from about 8·8 per cent of the national income to roughly 13·1 per cent – Cartter, A. M., *The Redistribution of Income in Post-War Britain*, Yale University Press, 1955, p. 117. See also Seers, D., *The Levelling of Incomes Since 1938*, Blackwell, Oxford, 1951.

2. Lydall, H. F., 'The Long-Term Trend in the Size Distribution of Income', *Journal of the Royal Statistical Society*, Series A (General), 122, Part 1, 1959, p. 34. See also Paish, F. W., 'The Real Incidence of Personal Taxation', *Lloyds Bank Review*, 43, 1957.

3. It must be noted that the numbers in the table presented by Paish remain the same in the two years, even though there were about 1½ million more tax units in 1955 than in 1938. The proportionate fall is therefore exaggerated.

Table 4.2. Percentages of total personal income received before tax by different income groups (Paish).

Group of income recipients	1938	1959
First 100,000	11·7	5·3
Second 100,000	3·6	2·4
Third 100,000	2·6	1·8
Fourth 100,000	2·0	1·5
Fifth 100,000	1·6	1·3
All first 500,000	21·5	12·3
Second 500,000	6·3	5·1
Second million	8·2	7·8
Third million	6·0	6·4
Fourth million	5·1	5·7
Fifth million	4·5	5·3
Second 5 million	16·8	22·6
Remainder	31·6	34·8
Total	100	100

SOURCE: Paish, F. W., 'The Real Incidence of Personal Taxation', *Lloyds Bank Review*, vol. 43, 1957.

in detail.[1] Recipients of income were, he pointed out, ill-defined. Individuals and income units were mixed together. The increase between 1938 and 1955 in the proportion of incomes in the middle range might be attributed to a decrease in unemployment and an increase in early marriage coupled with more employment of married women, many of whom were counted with their husbands in one tax unit. The apparent levelling of pre-tax incomes might be attributed not just to a fall in incomes from investment and rent but to the employment of tax-evasion techniques. Thus a man might give away part of his capital to his heirs or dependants and by so doing raise them up into the middle ranges of the distribution of income while lowering his own apparent income.[2]

The definition of income used by the Board of Inland Revenue was, he also pointed out, limited. For example, the definition excluded important forms of capital appreciation and benefits in kind from employers. These omissions had come to be very important in the 1950s. By 1960 the incomes described by the Board of Inland Revenue represented a smaller proportion of real personal re-

1. Titmuss, R. M., *Income Distribution and Social Change*, Allen & Unwin, London, 1962.
2. In 1961 *The Economist* concluded that this process must explain the relative fall in the investment incomes of the rich (14 January 1961, p. 112); quoted by Titmuss, *Income Distribution and Social Change*, p. 75.

sources than they had in the late 1930s. This is partly indicated by Lydall (see Table 4.1). It can be seen that unallocated income increased both proportionately and absolutely between 1938 and the 1950s (compare the figures in brackets for the top 1 per cent with the other figures for their after-tax incomes).[1]

Finally, the comparisons that were made involved certain groups in society and not all. It is possible for changes to take place in the middle rather than at the extremes of a distribution. Thus, Lydall reached his conclusions on the basis of tables which covered the first, fifth, tenth, twentieth and fiftieth percentiles. When pressed about the bottom 50 per cent, he said, 'I accept this criticism in principle and agree that much more thought is needed about this matter. But the real difficulty is the lack of data on the lower incomes, especially for pre-war . . . The true situation can only be revealed by means of sample surveys in which the lowest income groups are covered equally with others.'[2] Similarly, it might be pointed out that the 'remainder' referred to in Table 4.2 (following Paish) in fact cover the bulk of the population. There is the possibility therefore of there being a redistribution from the top to the upper-middle rather than from the top to the bottom of the distribution of incomes. In recent years, Atkinson has most clearly called attention to such differences in the conceptualization of inequality.[3]

But lack of good information about the low paid and others with low incomes accounts only in part for the tendency to misinterpret the board's incomes data. The relative increase in managerial and professional occupations and the relative decrease in semi-skilled and unskilled occupations, which has probably led to a small shift in population between strata, particularly the middle strata, may have been interpreted as a form of 'levelling'.[4] In fact there have been such striking changes in the occupational structure of the United Kingdom, particularly during the period 1938–48, that related trends in the distribution of incomes must be described with caution.

Differential trends in some of the components of total income are another

1. The Royal Commission on the Distribution of Income and Wealth failed to note and thoroughly discuss this point made earlier by Lydall. See Report No. 1, *Initial Report on the Standing Reference*, Cmnd 6171, H M S O, London, 1975.

2. Lydall, 'The Long-Term Trend in the Size Distribution of Income', loc. cit., pp. 42 and 47. Lydall was in fact aware that 'scepticism has grown up about the reliability of the official figures of allocated income as an indicator of the changes in the distribution of real income'. He therefore attempted to adjust the figures given in Table 4.1 by estimating the extent to which income recipients would have benefited from unallocated personal income, namely life assurance and superannuation contributions paid by employers, investment income from life and superannuation funds, interest on national savings, miscellaneous fringe benefits and income unreported to the tax authorities. But adjustments were made only to the figures for the top 1 per cent (shown in brackets in the table).

3. Atkinson, A. B., 'On the Measurement of Inequality', *Journal of Economic Theory*, vol. 2, 1970.

4. See also the discussion in Abel-Smith, B., and Townsend, P., *The Poor and the Poorest*, Bell, London, 1965, Chapter 1.

source of confusion. One example will be given for purposes of illustration. Personal property incomes increased in aggregate by less during the period 1938–50 than did earned incomes.[1] But in the 1950s they began to catch up, as Table 4.3 shows. Over the period 1955–65, property incomes increased disproportionately to earned incomes, and increased as a proportion of total incomes from 10·6 to 13·2 per cent. Hughes estimated that if an allowance for the long-run accrual of capital gains to property owners is added, the figures would be raised to around 20 per cent. 'This suggests that the wealthiest 1 per cent in Britain in the mid 1960s secured about 14 per cent of total personal incomes from work and property, and that the next wealthiest 4 per cent took 12–13 per cent of the total.'[2] Hughes also points out that, between 1957 and 1964, taxes on capital and on property income decreased as a percentage of Gross National Product from a total of 11·7 per cent to 7·3 per cent, while there was a net increase in regressive taxes estimated at 4 per cent of GNP.[3]

Table 4.3. *Personal property income and earned income (1955–65).*

Index/£ mil.	Year	Personal property income (rents, dividends and net interest)	Earned income
1955 = 100	1955	100	100
	1960	155	133
	1965	234	184
£ mil.	1955	1,534	12,905
	1960	2,372	17,168
	1965	3,595	23,736

SOURCE: *National Income and Expenditure in 1968*, Table II, p. 4.

We must conclude cautiously that the statistics for incomes in general for the period 1938–50 and for the 1950s are insufficiently comprehensive to justify exact specification of trends in distribution. Certainly the proportion of aggregate personal cash income *after* tax received by the top 1 per cent diminished, and the proportion received by the next 4 per cent seems also to have diminished between 1938 and 1949, but the proportion received by the next 15 per cent increased (see Table 4.1). As Lydall himself showed, the decline in the income received by the

1. See, for example, Seers, D., 'Has the Distribution of Income Become More Unequal?', *Bulletin of the Oxford University Institute of Statistics*, February 1956.
2. Hughes, J., 'The Increase in Inequality', *New Statesman*, 8 November 1968, p. 820.
3. ibid., p. 821.

top 1 per cent was in fact smaller than the decline suggested by Board of Inland Revenue data – because of the increasing importance of income, like employers' superannuation contributions and unassessed profits and investment income, which was not allocated by the board. We can only conjecture to what extent this section of the population also protected themselves from high rates of taxation during the immediate post-war years, by spreading income over life and by converting certain forms of income into assets.

Studies carried out subsequently, and which cover the 1960s, also contradict the hypothesis that the trend is set towards greater equality. Some writers have argued that the criticisms of the Board of Inland Revenue's statistics of income distribution by Titmuss and others do not totally invalidate comparisons over shorter periods from the late 1940s or early 1950s onwards. Even allowing for the criticisms, the general direction of trends as shown by the statistics over periods of, say, at least ten years are thought to be reasonably reliable.[1] R. J. Nicholson presented data for the periods 1949–57 and 1957–67. As Table 4.4 shows, the proportion of income after tax received by the top 10 per cent of income recipients appears to have decreased at some stage during the period 1949–57, but, with minor fluctuations, the proportion remained about the same in the subsequent ten years. The middle-income groups gained, although not uniformly, during the two periods. But the incomes of the bottom 30 per cent of income recipients appear to have diminished during both periods. Nicholson concluded that the reduction in inequality of personal incomes came to an end in the mid 1950s, and he accepted the possibility that if certain 'tax avoidance' incomes and other claims on wealth outside personal income had increased in the late 1950s and early 1960s, 'the distribution of incomes on some wider definition may have moved towards greater inequality'.[2] Professional incomes began to increase quickly, and rents, dividends and interest comprised the most rapidly growing sector of personal income. Nicholson did not attempt to allocate about 15 per cent of personal income represented by employers' superannuation contributions, other fringe benefits, unassessed profit and investment income, particularly of professional persons and farmers, interest on national savings certificates, post-war credits, unreported income and so on.

Lydall had already shown in his study that when allowance is made for these forms of income, the share of the top income groups increases sharply. Moreover, the share is larger still when capital gains are built into the picture. From information on asset holding, Prest and Stark estimated for 1959, 'That when capital gains are allowed for in addition to pre-tax income the share of the top 1 per cent

---

1. Nicholson, R. J., 'The Distribution of Personal Income', *Lloyds Bank Review*, January 1967, pp. 11–12. It is, of course, difficult, in the absence of information about capital gains, fringe benefits and other types of income, to accept this proposition, since we do not know whether they counterbalance any trend.
2. ibid., p. 18.

Table 4.4. *Percentages of income received after tax in 1949, 1957, 1963 and 1967 by different income groups (Nicholson).*

Group of income recipients	1949	1957	1963	1967
Top 1%	6·4	5·0	5·2	4·9
2–5%	11·3	9·9	10·5	9·9
6–10%	9·4	9·1	9·5	9·5
11–40%	37·0	38·5	39·5	39·2
41–70%	21·3	24·0	23·5	24·5
Bottom 30%	14·6	13·4	11·8	12·0
Total	100	100	100	100

SOURCE: Nicholson, R. J., 'The Distribution of Personal Income', *Lloyds Bank Review*, January 1967, p. 16. I am grateful to the author for supplying further estimates for 1967. They are based on data on personal incomes published annually in the National Income and Expenditure Blue Book, which have been converted by a method described in Nicholson, R. J., *Economic Statistics and Economic Problems*. McGraw-Hill, London, 1969, pp. 292–302. The estimates must be interpreted with care, particularly for the earlier years, for the share of the bottom 30 per cent is sensitive to the method of interpolation. Only 85 per cent of personal income can be distributed by range.

of incomes rises from 8 to 14 per cent and the share of the top 5 per cent from 20 to 27 per cent.[1]

Thus, two general conclusions can be reached. One is that even if the limited CSO data on incomes are accepted, the 'trend towards equality' applied only to the upper half of incomes for 1949–57 as well as subsequent periods. As Atkinson, and before him R. J. Nicholson, had emphasized, the poor and not only the rich lost ground.[2] The second conclusion is that if a wider definition of income is used, even the trends in the upper half of the distribution become problematic. It is not just that the data are deficient. The *weighting* of the five types of resource, some of which cannot even be comprehensively measured, has been changing over time.

The Royal Commission on the Distribution of Income and Wealth has also reviewed trends for this period. In 1975 it called attention to the decline in the share of income of the top 10 per cent between 1938 and the 1950s, and went on to say that 'in general changes in the distribution of income since 1959 have not

1. Prest, A. R., and Stark, T., 'Some Aspects of Income Distribution in the UK since World War II', *Manchester School*, vol. 35, 1967. However, it should be noted that 1959 was characterized by large gains.
2. Nicholson, 'The Distribution of Personal Income'; and Atkinson, A. B., 'Poverty and Income Inequality in Britain', in Wedderburn, D. (ed.), *Poverty, Inequality and Class Structure*, Cambridge University Press, 1974, p. 66.

been very pronounced, but there has been a continuing decline in the share of the top 5 per cent . . . accounted for largely by the drop in the share of the top 1 per cent'.[1] The figures they gave for 1938–72 showed a slight fall in the percentage share of the bottom 30 per cent both before and after tax in the 1960s, compared with both 1938 and 1949, but a recovery by 1972–3. At the beginning and end of a thirty-four year period (to 1972–3), the official figures show no change in the percentage share of the bottom 30 per cent.[2]

While the Royal Commission concluded that since the end of the 1950s there had been a 'continuing decline' in the share of the top 5 per cent (principally accounted for by the top 1 per cent), two aspects of their own analysis threw this conclusion into doubt. First of all, they conceded many of the criticisms about the deficiencies of the data[3] made by Titmuss, Atkinson and others, which are discussed elsewhere in this report.[4] These consist of deficiencies in the statistics of income distribution as such *and* lack of information on resources derived from fringe benefits, capital gains and social services in kind. 'The coverage of official information on both the value of fringe and non-monetary benefits and their distribution among individuals is less than adequate for our purposes.'[5] In a later report, when discussing top employment incomes, the commission did not discuss the possible effect on income distribution of trends in the distribution of such benefits, although they did incorporate an appendix on fringe benefits.[6]

Secondly, the Royal Commission did not comment on the fact that the series on income distribution which was an alternative to the series adapted by the Central Statistical Office from the Inland Revenue's *Survey of Personal Incomes*, namely the series derived from the annual Family Expenditure Survey, did not bear out the conclusion that there had been a continuing decline in the 1960s in the percentage share of top-ranking incomes. Thus, a table in an appendix shows that the top 10 per cent had 23·5 per cent of net income in 1961, 24·7 per cent in 1968, and 23·7 per cent in 1973. There are slight variations from year to year, as one would expect from a sample survey, but no evidence of a trend in either direction.[7] In Table 4.5, with the help of the commission's staff, I have compared the top 1 per cent, next 4 per cent and next 5 per cent on the two series. Estimates of 'final' income from the FES, which takes account of indirect as well as direct

1. Royal Commission on the Distribution of Income and Wealth, Report No. 1, *Initial Report on the Standing Reference*, Cmnd 6171, HMSO, London, 1975, p. 156.
2. ibid., p. 36.
3. ibid. See, for example, pp. 37–8, 44, 127, 132 and 159.
4. In particular, Chapters 5 (p. 184) and 26 (p. 911).
5. Royal Commission on the Distribution of Income and Wealth, Report No. 1, p. 159.
6. Royal Commission on the Distribution of Income and Wealth, Report No. 3, *Higher Incomes from Employment*, Cmnd 6383, HMSO, London, 1976, Appendix H, 'Details of Particular Fringe Benefits'.
7. Royal Commission on the Distribution of Income and Wealth, Report No. 1, p. 213.

Table 4.5. *Distribution of personal income (United Kingdom): two sources compared.*

Quantile group	A	Percentage share of income after income tax (tax units; IR Survey of Personal Incomes supplemented by other data by the Central Statistical Office)				
		1949	*1959*	*1964*	*1967*	*1972/3*
Top 1%		6·4	5·3	5·3	4·9	4·4
2–5%		11·3	10·5	10·7	9·9	9·8
6–10%		9·4	9·4	9·9	9·5	9·4
Top 10%		27·1	25·2	25·9	24·3	23·6

	B	Percentage share of net income (households; CSO, based on Family Expenditure Survey)				
		1961	*1965*	*1968*	*1971*	*1972*	*1973*
Top 1%		4·4	4·8	5·9	4·4	3·8	4·4
2–5%		9·9	9·5	9·7	9·9	9·6	10·0
6–10%		9·2	9·1	9·1	9·6	9·3	9·5
Top 10%		23·5	23·4	24·7	23·9	22·7	23·9

	C	Percentage share of final income (households; CSO, based on Family Expenditure Survey)				
		1961	*1965*	*1968*	*1971*	*1972*	*1973*
Top 1%		4·6	4·5	4·2	4·2	3·8	4·2
2–5%		9·8	9·6	9·8	9·8	9·7	9·8
6–10%		9·3	9·2	9·4	9·4	9·5	9·4
Top 10%		23·7	23·3	23·4	23·4	23·0	23·4

NOTE: The estimates shown in B and C were generously provided by the staff of the Royal Commission (in a personal communication) to supplement Tables G.13 and G.15 in the first interim Report (of the Royal Commission), which gave estimates only for the top 10 per cent, next 10 per cent and so on. The estimates depend on extrapolation using the top two ranges in the FES range tables and, since the highest earnings groups also tend to be represented erratically in the FES, have to be treated with caution. *Net income* is defined as income after direct taxes and the receipt of cash benefits, and *final income* relates to the distribution after the allocation of all taxes, both direct and indirect, and certain benefits both in cash and in kind which can be allocated to specific households.

taxes and a limited measure of fringe benefits,[1] are also given. Certain reservations must be borne in mind. The FES estimates for the top 10 per cent are more reliable than for the top 5 per cent, and the figures for the top 1 per cent are distinctly hazardous.

Survey Data on Personal Income

The annual Family Expenditure Survey represents an important alternative source of information about overall trends in income distribution. For many years, data about incomes have been collected and analysed to show the burden of taxation upon, and the money value of the social services to, different income groups and types of household.[2] When allowance is made for minor fluctuations which may be largely attributable to sampling error, the incomes structure is represented as remarkably stable. Table 4.6 brings out three conclusions which can be drawn from the data for the period 1961-9: (a) except for the lagging of households with one child and the faster growth of households with three adults and two children, the 'final' incomes of different types of family have been rising at roughly similar rates during the decade; (b) as a result, the levels of income of different types of family remain in roughly the same relationship as they were in 1961 (the family with three children, for example, having 150 per cent more income than the one-person household after paying all taxes and receiving all benefits, compared with 148 per cent eight years previously); and (c) among the families within each type, there has been no pronounced change in the dispersion of incomes, the poorest 20 per cent being in 1969 at about the same and if anything a little below the level of income reached in relation to the median income in 1961. There is no evidence of a trend towards equality at low levels of living, but if anything a faint reverse trend. Compared with a very slight improvement in the incomes of the poorest couples with two children, there has been a slight deterioration in the incomes of the poorest couples with one child and four or more children and of households comprising three adults and one child and three adults and two children. The figures dip for seven out of ten categories, and although the fluctuations due to sampling must be remembered, the trends were broadly the same in 1968. These results allow for indirect as well as direct taxes.[3]

The trends have been reviewed by Semple, who was concerned to trace the effect of changes in household composition. For the period 1961-73 he concluded

1. Covering the value of meals vouchers, meal subsidies, food and other goods in kind, like concessionary coal for miners.

2. See Nicholson, J. L., *Redistribution of Income in the United Kingdom in 1959, 1957 and 1953*, Bowes & Bowes, Cambridge, 1965; *Economic Trends*, esp. February 1970 and February 1971.

3. For further discussion, see Townsend, P., *Sociology and Social Policy*, Allen Lane, London, 1975, Chapter 24. Some commentators have taken the view that there was a shift towards greater equality during 1964-70. See Stewart, M., 'The Distribution of Income', in Becker-

Table 4.6. *Income after all taxes and benefits of different types of household 1961, 1965 and 1968 (CSO Family Expenditure Survey).*

Type of household	As % of average income in 1961 for each type			As % of income received by one adult			Lowest quintile as % of median		
	1961	1965	1969	1961	1965	1969	1961	1965	1969[b]
1 adult (excl. pensioners)	100	131	160	100	100	100	70	72	71
2 adults (excl. pensioners)	100	120	153	181	167	173	70	72	69
2 adults, 1 child	100	124	147	206	194	189	74	75	73
2 children	100	120	158	230	210	227	73	75	76
3 children	100	126	162	248	238	250	78	73	78
4 children	100	121	158	276	254	271	86	77	79
3 adults	100	121	156	255	235	249	74	75	73
3 adults, 1 child	100	118	148	291	261	270	80	76	79
2 children	100	135	170	294	303	311	80	76	77
4 adults	100	121	155	333	306	322	81	78	78
All households	100	(123)[a]	(156)[a]	208	192	196	56	55	54

NOTES: [a]Estimated to maintain 1961 distribution by size of households.
[b]The figures published in Table 4, *Economic Trends*, February 1971, have been adjusted slightly to conform with income as defined for 1961 and 1965.

SOURCE: Based on *Economic Trends*, February 1970, Tables 2 and 5, and February 1971 Tables 4 and 5. Further information provided by the Central Statistical Office.

that there was 'relative stability of the income distribution both before, and after, standardization for household composition ... The apparent slight increase in equality, more evident in the highest quintile relative to the median, is *virtually eliminated* after household composition standardization'[1] (my emphasis). I have referred to Semple's analysis in the concluding chapter (p. 910) because of its relevance to what has been happening in the mid and late 1970s. However, one graph shows that between 1961 and 1969 the relative distance from the median of the highest and lowest quintiles *increased* very slightly. While the highest quintile remained about constant, the lowest quintile diminished marginally.

The FES data are based on a definition of 'final' income which approaches a

man, W. (ed.), *The Labour Government's Economic Record 1964–70*, Duckworth, London, 1972, and a review by the author of this paper in the *Listener*, 27 April 1972, and the subsequent sharp correspondence.

1. Semple, M., 'The Effect of Changes in Household Composition on the Distribution of Income 1961–73', *Economic Trends*, December 1975, p. 102.

broad conception of resources. But there are a number of limitations in the definition which may have the effect of underestimating inequality. Although a more comprehensive concept of income has been developed, the process whereby the value of benefits is allocated is still rough and ready. For example, health service benefits are averaged very crudely. The value of some social services to middle- and upper-income groups may also be underestimated. The costs of secondary education are averaged for all families with a child attending a secondary school, although children of middle-class parents are more likely than other children to be attending the costlier grammar schools. Again, improvement grants and the full value to the owner-occupier of tax relief on payments of interest on mortgages are not allocated.

Incomes Policy

The trends which I have sought to describe have been determined by an admixture of policies. One of these policies has been incomes policy. I shall discuss this policy first because the chief component of pre-tax income is earned income and the state's and other organizations' incomes policies therefore determine a predominant part of the distribution of income. But a distinction needs to be made between the incomes policies which successive governments have widely publicized and negotiated and those which the government and non-government organizations have practised. During the period under review, incomes policy as promulgated by the government was a curiously incomplete policy and it was not expressed in the context of a comprehensive statistical picture of earnings.[1] Throughout the three decades no attempt was made to relate salaries and wages to common criteria or principles, and differences in remunerating manual and non-manual work remained very unclear. In 1948, the government said that traditional differentials might be based on outdated and undesirable criteria and that the appropriate criterion was the efficient distribution of labour. No attempt was made to develop criteria of just reward.[2] Instead, comparisons were made with neighbouring professions and occupations. The Royal Commission on the remuneration of doctors, for example, took account of the pay of accountants, lawyers and university teachers.[3] The Willink Commission compared the pay of policemen with the wages of skilled manual workers.[4]

None of this is very surprising. Wage bargaining is a social and political as well

1. As Barbara Wootton has said, during the 1960s both the Conservative and Labour governments presented 'a façade of comprehensiveness' – Wootton, B., *Incomes Policy: An Inquest and a Proposal*, Davis-Poynter, London, 1974, p. 35.

2. *Statement on Personal Incomes, Costs and Prices*, Cmnd 7321, HMSO, London, 1948.

3. Report of the Royal Commission on Doctors' and Dentists' Remuneration, 1957–1960, Cmnd 939, HMSO, London, 1960.

4. Report of the Royal Commission on the Police, Cmnd 1222, HMSO, London, 1960.

as an economic process, as Barbara Wootton has argued powerfully.[1] Wages are regarded not just as cash to be spent, but as symbolic evaluation of the social worth of a role. Any attempt to change the level of one occupation relative to others has not only to be fought with an alternative reward system in mind, but tends very quickly to be converted into a wholesale political struggle against those interests representing the entire *existing* hierarchy of rewards. The creation of a clear statistical picture of earnings is fraught with political implications and tends to have been avoided by the government, and despite the introduction in recent years of an annual earnings survey, this can still be asserted. For example, the full value of fringe benefits is not added to earnings, and earnings are not standardized to take account of unsocial hours of work and risk of redundancy or unemployment.

Thus Royal Commissions have been shy of questioning the social justice of the present distribution of income. For example, the Royal Commission on Doctors' and Dentists' Remuneration made clear at the start of their report that their task was big enough without evaluating the entire occupational reward structure.[2] They contented themselves with comparing the rewards, career patterns and special problems of a chosen group of professions, explicitly linking the public medical sector with the operations of the private market. They justified this on grounds that the public services had to compete with the private market for scarce resources of skilled manpower. Perhaps the major function of such Royal Commissions is to alleviate the strains caused by the relatively inflexible mechanisms of public-sector wages policy in face of competition from the private sector. Certainly they operate more to prepare public opinion for the awkward necessity of paying out additional sums to preserve the existing reward system, rather than to appraise that system from an olympian position of detachment.[3]

Nor was a broader incomes policy framework provided directly by the government or indirectly through the ill-fated National Board for Prices and Incomes. Although the board was concerned with the full range of incomes from work, it was empowered only to *restrict* claims for higher wages that had been referred to it. In doing so, it was able in principle to recommend preferential treatment for some employed groups. The government had made gestures in the direction of the low paid. A White Paper of 1965 had already allowed exceptional increases in pay 'where there is general recognition that existing wage and salary levels are too low to maintain a reasonable standard of living'.[4] Eighteen months later, another White Paper stated that 'Improvement of the standard of living of the

1. Wootton, B., *The Social Foundations of Wages Policy*, Allen & Unwin, London, 1955.
2. Report of the Royal Commission on Doctors' and Dentists' Remuneration, p. 1.
3. It is difficult to take any other interpretation of the Report of the Pilkington Commission and the consequent reports of the review body on remuneration (the Kindersley Committee). See also the account for example by Forsyth, G., *Doctors and State Medicine: A Study of the British Health Service*, Pitman, London, 1966, Chapter 3.
4. *Prices and Incomes Policy*, Cmnd 2639, HMSO, London, 1965.

worst off members of the community is a primary social objective . . . However, it will be necessary to ensure that any pay increases justified on this ground are genuinely confined to the lowest paid and not passed on to other workers.'[1] In 1968, when increases of pay were restricted by the government to a ceiling of 3·5 per cent, the government stated that those whose earnings were 'too low to maintain a reasonable standard of living' would be given priority over other workers in being considered for such increases. The government was also prepared to concede a larger increase for the lowest paid in exceptional cases.[2] But such statements have always been worded in the most general terms and the government did not work out any viable policy for the low paid. When it invited the National Board for Prices and Incomes to advise how the criterion of low pay would be applied in practice, the board avoided any commitment to a specific amount for fear of precipitating many embarrassing claims. Instead, the pay of certain groups was shown to be low by comparison with similar groups in the same or roughly similar industries.[3]

Admittedly the board did allow wage increases considerably in excess of the 3 to 3·5 per cent norm in 1965 for adult nurses and midwives (up to 12·5 per cent), postal workers (about 13 per cent) and gas workers, road-haulage workers, prison and tax officers. Mr George Brown, citing the Priestly principle of fair comparisons for the Civil Service, said that the increase for postal workers was a 'catching-up' exercise and that there was no solution to be found by 'returning to the policy of penalizing the lower paid and weaker group of public servants'. But the problems of the pay structure were not considered as a whole and the government made no effort to deal with claims even in the public services, unless they were politically inescapable and urgent. Thus, in 1969, about a quarter of all male manual workers earning less than £15 per week were employed by local or central government, including the health and education services.[4]

The board was hampered by lack of information about low pay and discrepancies between wage *rates* (which may be fixed by Wages Councils) and earnings. Wages Councils are empowered only to raise the minimum rates and have no control over earnings. When examining the retail drapery trade, the National Board of Prices and Incomes found that the lowest paid were on rates tied to the statutory minimum fixed by the Wages Council. The board felt that the best solution was to raise the statutory minimum, so ensuring that workers with the lowest

1. *Prices and Incomes Standstill: Period of Severe Restraint*, Cmnd 3150, HMSO, London, November 1966.
2. *Productivity, Prices and Incomes Policy in 1968 and 1969*, Cmnd 3590, HMSO, London, 1968.
3. The board made recommendations for increases for the low paid, and not always for others as well, in, for example, Reports 25, 27, 29, 40, 48, 49 and 63.
4. For example, *Employment and Productivity Gazette*, June 1969, p. 518.

earnings would receive most.[1] But action generally to raise basic rates was believed to be inflationary, and inequitable. An inter-departmental committee studying the prospects of a minimum wage argued that an earnings-based minimum was better than a wage tied to basic rates. If 'the minimum were related to the basic rate it would have a very unequal, and indeed inequitable, result. It would, in fact, benefit many workers whose basic rates are low, possibly simply for historical reasons, but whose actual remuneration is high'.[2]

By December 1969, the government was beginning to recognize that the inclusion of general expressions of good intent about the low paid in its policy statements was not having tangible results. A White Paper admitted that, 'One of the weaknesses of the system of free collective bargaining has been its inability to solve the problem of the low-paid.' Among the public, low earning was increasingly regarded as inequitable, and as contributing to the perpetuation of poverty.[3] In March 1970, the board was commissioned by the government to study three low-paid industries and comment more generally on the problems of low pay. Its work was hastened after the fall of the government in June 1970, and its reports were published just before the board was finally wound up in the spring of 1971.[4] A useful range of secondary information was assembled in the general report, the results of a social survey contributed to knowledge about the low paid, but little progress was made towards spelling out a general policy. Low pay was defined very weakly as the levels below which the earnings of a tenth of all men and all women in full-time manual work were distributed.[5] This ruled out any clarification of a national objective, progress towards which might be measured from year to year. The possibilities of strengthening Wages Councils, and gradually developing a phased programme leading to the introduction of a minimum

1. Report No. 27, *Pay of Workers in the Retail Drapery, Outfitting and Footwear Trades*, Cmnd 3224, HMSO, London, March 1967.

2. Department of Employment and Productivity, *A National Minimum Wage: An Enquiry*, HMSO, London, 1969, p. 28.

3. *Productivity, Prices and Incomes Policy After 1969*, Cmnd 4237, HMSO, London, December 1969.

4. See Report No. 166, *The Pay and Conditions of Service of Ancillary Workers in the National Health Service*, Cmnd 4644, HMSO, London, April 1971; Report No. 167, *The Pay and Conditions of Service of Workers in the Laundry and Dry Cleaning Industry*, Cmnd 4647, HMSO, London, April 1971; Report No. 168, *Pay and Conditions in the Contract Cleaning Trade*, Cmnd 4637, HMSO, London, April 1971; Report No. 169, *General Problems of Low Pay*, Cmnd 4648, HMSO, London, April 1971.

5. The possibility that low pay might be defined as earnings below a fixed percentage is mentioned in paragraph 12 of the General Report, but then discussed in relation to supplementary benefit rates for a family with two children. The possibility of taking, say, 75 per cent of median or mean earnings for men in full-time work (counting salary earners as well as wage-earners) as a definition of low pay was nowhere discussed. Yet the advantage of some such definition in providing a criterion by which to measure progress from year to year, and also allow for the change taking place in the proportion of salaries to wage-earning employees, is very clear.

earnings level, were not explored. The role of a minimum wage in countries which were stated to have a more equal wage structure was not investigated. The question of supplementing earnings by means of a graduated disability pension was not considered.

None of this would be easy to understand without appreciating that the primary aim of prices and incomes policies has been to regulate aggregate demand in order to contain inflation. Policies have been developed, often in a great hurry, simply in order to freeze wages – and more particularly wages than salaries also.[1] All along, problems of equity and low pay have been of secondary importance and tend to have been given very little prominence by the government and even, as an inevitable consequence, by the board itself. In practice, the board emphasized its economic function at the expense of any social function that might have been attributed to it.[2] The possibilities of linking wage increases to productivity have perhaps been exaggerated over the necessary task of evaluating qualitative improvements in working performance and finding social and economic criteria for existing differentials in reward. To sum up, too much was expected of the National Board for Prices and Incomes. It began to contribute to a more rational discussion of incomes differentials, but (a) it was a regulatory body only, and had no authority to initiate changes in the wage system; (b) it followed government directives by construing its task as primarily one of controlling inflation, rather than dealing effectively with low pay and inequality; and (c) it was hampered in its understanding of the problems and its capacity to provide solutions by lack of information about low pay and the complexity of the wages system. In so far as Britain can be said to have an incomes policy at all, it has to be recognized, like that embodied in the National Incomes Commission and the earlier attempts to restrain wages in 1936 and 1948, as essentially a negative policy – as an attempt to regulate market processes when these are felt to be incompatible with other national goals. It remains to be seen whether the incomes policies of the mid 1970s have had any lasting effect in improving the relative position of the low paid and reducing income inequality. But for the kind of reasons given, the policies of the 1960s did not have that result, as we shall now see.

1. The failure to develop a long-term policy, and one which pays at least some heed to social objectives, is reviewed by Balogh, T., *Labour and Inflation*, Fabian Tract No. 403, Fabian Society, London, October 1970.

2. Britain is not the only country to have limited incomes policy largely to the problems of inflation. Most countries have not attempted to question or tamper with incomes differentials, and most studies of incomes policies have shied away from problems of poverty and equity, even when recognizing that they are fundamental. 'In concentrating on possible inflationary aspects the present study covers of course but a small – and by no means the most important – area of income formation and distribution. Questions of equity, of improving economic opportunity, and of tackling extreme poverty are more basic and important . . . These questions however are not the subject of this study . . .' – Turner, H. A., and Zoeteweij, H., *Prices, Wages and Incomes Policies in Industrialized Market Economies*, International Labour Office, Geneva, 1966, p. 1.

Earnings

Part of the problem of the ineffectiveness of incomes policy was a dearth of the information which would have allowed that policy to be formulated more exactly. Apart from the Board of Inland Revenue's annual returns and the limited surveys of the Family Expenditure Survey, there was not much detailed information about the distribution of earnings of manual workers until the Ministry of Labour carried out a special survey in 1960.[1] Derek Robinson, a former statistical adviser to the National Board for Prices and Incomes, suggested how the survey could be put into a form which allowed it to be brought up to date.[2] But the survey itself did not cover some employing establishments and did not give precise enough information about occupations and all ranges of earnings. A survey carried out in 1968 at last provided a good base of information about the earnings structure,[3] and since then the New Earnings Survey has begun to provide evidence of trends.

There are various ways in which changes in the earnings structure might affect the overall distribution of real personal resources. First, it may be argued that some process internal to the labour market itself is leading to a more equal distribution of wages and salaries. Differentials can be examined in broad terms of class, categories of skill and occupation. One of the problems, however, in tracing the relative levels of wages and salaries over the three decades is that the difference between them has become less clear-cut. Until 1944, the two were treated differently for purposes of income tax and unemployment insurance, but not thereafter. Some groups of manual workers have come to be paid other than weekly. Moreover it is becoming rather difficult to distinguish 'manual' and 'non-manual' among the semi-skilled and routine occupations produced by computer technology for example. Ideally we need to trace the dispersion of earnings within the major categories of occupations and as between men and women, and then attempt to construct the changes that have been taking place over time.

Between 1938 and 1950, differentials between wage and salary earners seemed to be narrowing. Most of the improvement in the position of wage earners occurred in the war. According to Seers, average wages more than doubled but average salaries increased by only 72 per cent between 1938 and 1949.[4]

For the 1950s and 1960s, on the other hand, there is no marked change in relativity between wages and salaries. Wages rose sharply as a percentage of gross national product in 1954, but otherwise the share of wages remained fairly constant throughout this period. The index of average salary earnings maintained by

1. *Ministry of Labour Gazette*, April 1961 and June 1961.
2. Robinson, D., 'Low Paid Workers and Incomes Policy', *Bulletin of the Oxford University Institute of Economics and Statistics*, vol. 29, February 1967.
3. Department of Employment and Productivity, *New Earnings Survey, 1968*, HMSO, London, 1970.
4. Seers, D., *The Levelling of Incomes Since 1938*, Blackwell, Oxford, 1957.

the Department of Employment and Productivity had increased from 100 in 1955 to 133·4 in 1960, compared with 130·1 for average weekly earnings of manual workers. During the early and mid 1960s, salaries maintained a slight lead over wages, but by 1968 both were in about the same relationship again as in 1955. The index for salaries was then 206·9, compared with 208·1 for weekly wage earnings.[1]

When the two phases are placed in longer perspective, there is little evidence of structural change. After a detailed study of occupational and pay structure between 1906 and 1960, Guy Routh concluded that 'the most impressive finding was the rigidity of the inter-class and inter-occupational relationships . . . According to our calculations the average for semi-skilled men was 86 per cent of the all-class average in 1913 and 85 per cent in 1960.'[2] The earnings of skilled and unskilled groups had also remained relatively stable. However, professional and clerical groups had lost ground and managerial groups gained slightly.

In the 1960 survey, information was collected only about the numbers of employees with earnings in specified ranges and not about either hours or occupations. The annual Family Expenditure Survey provided general data, but was not based on a sample of a size sufficient to provide detailed analyses. Between September 1968 and March 1969, the Department of Employment and Productivity therefore conducted a survey of the earnings of employees throughout Britain. Forms were completed for about 84,000 individual employees from a sample of 92,500 selected by means of national insurance numbers. In the autumn of 1968, average weekly earnings were £23 for male manual workers aged 21 and over and were just under £30 for non-manual workers. In comparison with these figures, 9·4 per cent of the manual and 4·6 per cent of the non-manual workers in the sample were earning less than £15 per week, corresponding with roughly 0·7 million and 0·2 million men respectively in the population as a whole. Table 4.7 sets out some selected results.

The median earnings of non-manual workers were about 24 per cent higher than of manual workers in 1968, but there were wide variations in both categories in the percentage of men in different occupations earning much less than the median. For example, in the manual category, 62 per cent of farmworkers earned less than £17, although the figure for all manual workers was 18 per cent. In the non-manual category, very few general managers earned as little as this, but as many as 45 per cent of routine clerks did so compared with the figure of 10 per cent for all non-manual employees. Indeed, the disproportionate growth in the number of office clerks (with relatively low earnings) among the total of non-manual employees may, in fact, have concealed a disproportionate rise in the earnings of other non-manual employees.

1. *Employment and Productivity Gazette*, June 1969, Table 129.
2. Routh, G., *Occupation and Pay in Great Britain 1906–60*, Cambridge University Press, 1965, p. x.

Table 4.7. Percentages of men aged 21 and over with different earnings (and their median earnings).

Characteristics	Less than £15	Less than £17	More than £30	More than £40	Median earnings £
All men	8	16	25	8	23·6
Manual	9	18	17	3	22·4
Non-manual	5	10	42	19	27·8
Manual aged 21–4	12	24	10	2	20·3
30–39	5	11	23	5	24·1
60–64	18	32	8	1	19·6
65 and over	37	52	6	1	16·6
Non-manual aged 21–4	20	36	5	1	18·7
30–39	1	3	52	21	30·5
60–64	5	13	40	20	26·4
65 and over	20	31	26	15	21·2
Selected occupations					
Farmworker	39	62	1	0	15·9
Coalminer (surface)	29	46	3	0	17·5
Coalminer (underground)	8	15	15	3	24·4
Shop salesman, assistant	30	46	4	1	17·0
Painter/decorator	2	13	10	2	21·7
Electrician (maintenance)	1	5	30	7	25·5
Office clerk (considerable responsibility)	3	6	28	5	25·9
Office clerk (routine)	21	45	3	0	17·4
General manager	2	3	82	67	52·8
Earnings subject to national agreement in the public sector *Manual*					
Local authority (England and Wales)	33	54	3	0	16·6
Government industrial establishments	24	40	7	1	18·2
Health services ancillary staff	29	46	4	1	17·4
Police	0	2	27	5	25·3
Non-manual					
Civil service – clerical	13	28	3	0	20·6
Civil service – executive	0	1	60	26	32·9
Primary and secondary school teachers	0	5	60	14	32·2

SOURCE: 'Results of a New Survey of Earnings in September 1968', *Employment and Productivity Gazette*, May 1969 and June 1969.

The table shows marked variations with age. High proportions of young and of elderly employees were low paid. However, the earnings of manual employees in their early twenties were higher relative to men in their thirties, than those of employees in the non-manual category. The variations by age-group apply to the employed population at a particular time and it would be wrong to infer too much from the table about the changes in earnings that individuals experience over a working lifetime. There are skilled manual workers who may be obliged to work less overtime when they get older or to take less skilled jobs. Some may even cross the manual/non-manual boundary and enter low-paid clerical occupations. There are non-manual employees who improve their earnings steadily by promotion and through increments of salary up to the sixties, but there are others who languish in an occupational backwater or who are obliged to retire early from one job and take another which is much less well paid. Little is so far known about profiles of earning experience, and yet they are highly relevant to any understanding of the problems of poverty.

One further fact brought out by the table is the large proportions of certain types of employee in the public sector who are low paid. Nearly a quarter of all manual workers whose earnings are covered by national agreements in the public sector were earning less than £17 in 1968. Not all occupations in the public sector are low paid, as illustrated in the table by police and school teachers.

Table 4.8 provides corresponding data for women. Earnings were about half those of men and the differential between manual and non-manual workers was more marked. The median earnings of non-manual employees were 31 per cent higher than those of manual employees (and were 47 per cent higher among those aged 30–39). To a large extent, this wider differential is explained by the fact that certain non-manual occupations in the public sector, such as clerical work and teaching, attract levels of pay not far short of those of men, while this is not true of manual occupations in either the public or private sectors (compare, for example, the median earnings in Tables 4.7 and 4.8 of local-authority manual workers, National Health Service ancillary staff and shop assistants). Again, some very low-paid manual occupations, such as that of kitchen hands, tend to be filled only or predominantly by women.

Variations in earnings according to age were less marked among women than among men. The median earnings of different age-groups and the distribution of earnings within these groups do not vary much at least for the age-groups between 30 and 60.

Table 4.9 shows the distribution of earnings for men and women, and for manual and non-manual employees. The dispersion of earnings among manual workers and among non-manual workers is broadly the same for each sex, but in each case the non-manual dispersion is wider than the manual. The 10 per cent in each category who receive the highest earnings in fact earn more than twice

Table 4.8. *Percentages of women aged 18 and over with different earnings (and median earnings).*

Characteristics	Less than £8	Less than £10	More than £15	More than £20	Median earnings £
All women	7	25	32	13	12·5
Manual	12	39	14	3	10·8
Non-manual	4	15	4	19	14·1
Manual					
Aged 21–4	7	33	15	3	11·2
30–39	12	39	17	4	10·9
60–64	19	51	13	3	10·0
65 and over	16	51	11	2	9·9
Non-manual					
Aged 21–4	1	8	34	5	13·5
30–39	2	7	58	28	16·0
60–64	2	7	64	39	17·2
65 and over	9	21	48	21	14·9
Selected occupations					
Kitchen hand	40	77	2	0	8·3
Shop saleswoman, assistant	20	68	6	1	9·1
Office clerk (considerable responsibility)	1	4	63	35	16·8
Office clerk (routine)	5	25	21	1	11·8
Nurse, midwife, etc.	13	25	41	19	13·8
Earnings subject to national agreement in the public sector					
Manual					
Local authority (England and Wales)	29	66	5	1	9·0
Health Services ancillary staff	3	28	8	1	11·1
Non-manual					
Civil service clerical	0	5	59	20	15·8
Primary and secondary school teachers	1	1	96	68	25·3

SOURCE: As for Table 4.7.

Table 4.9. *Earnings of full-time adult employees at different points relative to the medians (1968)*

Full-time employees	Quantiles as a % of the median				Median earnings £
	Lowest decile	Lower quartile	Upper quartile	Highest decile	
Men					
Manual	67·3	81·0	122·3	147·8	22·4
Non-manual	61·2	75·9	131·1	178·5	27·8
All	65·7	80·0	126·7	161·4	23·6
Women					
Manual	71·1	83·4	121·1	148·4	10·8
Non-manual	65·4	78·8	129·3	175·5	14·1
All	67·0	80·0	129·7	171·2	12·5

SOURCE: 'Results of a New Survey of Earnings in September 1968', *Employment and Productivity Gazette*, May 1969, p. 413.

as much, and in the case of non-manual employees nearly three times as much, as the 10 per cent with lowest earnings.

Comparative information about the earnings structures of other countries is scarce. The chief contribution is that of Lydall. His data for both the upper deciles and lower quartiles show that among male employees the distribution of earnings is less unequal in New Zealand and Australia than in the United Kingdom. Germany has a more equal distribution among male manual employees than the United Kingdom, while Sweden is roughly similar.[1] In general, inequalities are largest in countries with high proportions of their labour forces in agriculture. In Britain, an inter-departmental working party of government officials made a study of a national minimum wage, and although a summary of the minimum-wage legislation of France, the Netherlands, Canada and the United States was included, and references were made to wage regulations and negotiations in Australia, West Germany, Italy, Denmark, Norway and Sweden, no attempt was made to establish whether the low paid in Britain were relatively worse paid than their contemporaries, or whether the higher relative earnings of the lowest decile of manual employees in countries such as Australia and New Zealand were due to minimum-wage legislation.[2] The National Board for Prices and Incomes refrained from discussing the possible link, even though it pointed out both the

1. See Lydall, H., *The Structure of Earnings*, Oxford University Press, 1968.
2. Department of Employment and Productivity, *A National Minimum Wage: An Inquiry*, HMSO, London, 1969 (see esp. pp. 55–65).

more egalitarian distribution of earnings in these two countries, and the fact that there was minimum-wage legislation.[1]

What changes have been taking place in the UK structure of earnings? For a lengthy span the only useful information that exists is for manual workers. Various writers have called attention to the similarities between the distributions found in the four Board of Trade and Ministry of Labour surveys of 1886, 1906, 1938 and 1960.[2] Table 4.10 adds data from the 1968 and 1970 surveys of the Department of Employment and Productivity. While some care has to be exercised in interpreting figures from surveys which have differed in certain respects in method and scope the chief conclusion that must be drawn from Table 4.10 is of the remarkable stability in the overall dispersion of earnings of male manual workers.[3] This stability has been maintained during a period of more than

Table 4.10. *Earnings of full-time adult male manual workers, relative to the median (1886–1970).*

Date	Median £	Quantiles as a % of the median			
		Lowest decile	Lower quartile	Upper quartile	Highest decile
1886	1·21	68·6	82·8	121·7	143·1
1906	1·47	66·5	79·5	126·7	156·8
1938	3·40	67·7	82·1	118·5	139·9
1960	14·17	70·6	82·6	121·7	145·2
1968	22·40	67·3	81·0	122·3	147·8
1970	25·60	67·3	81·1	122·3	147·2

SOURCES: Bowley, A. L., *Wages and Income in the United Kingdom Since 1860*, Cambridge University Press, 1937, p. 42; Ainsworth, R. B., 'Earnings and Working Hours of Manual Wage-Earners in the United Kingdom in October 1938', *Journal of the Royal Statistical Society*, A, 115, 1949, pp. 56 and 64; *Ministry of Labour Gazette*, June 1961, p. 247; *Employment and Productivity Gazette*, May 1969, p. 411, and November 1970, p. 974.

1. The board does not discuss the evidence, fails to see any connection between Wages Council machinery and the possible introduction of a minimum wage, and concludes that, 'No false hopes should be attached to a national minimum wage' – Report No. 169, *General Problems of Low Pay*, pp. 41–2, 169 and 193.

2. For example, Crossley, J. R., 'Prices and Wages', *London and Cambridge Economic Bulletin*, June 1961; Routh, *Occupation and Pay in Great Britain*; and Thatcher, A. R., 'The Distribution of Earnings of Employees in Great Britain', *Journal of the Royal Statistical Society*, A, 131, Part 2, 1968.

3. There is evidence from other countries of similar stability. For France, for example, there was little change in the period 1948–64, despite the introduction of minimum-wage legislation in 1950. 'In relation to the average earnings of unskilled labourers (which are influenced by the minimum wage), differentials have remained remarkably constant over the last 15 years' –

140 POVERTY IN THE UNITED KINGDOM

eighty years when the level of earnings increased by a factor of over 18. It seems to conflict with the supposition that differentials between skilled and unskilled workers have narrowed. This supposition could be based on changes of wage rates rather than of earnings, and there may indeed have been a narrowing of differentials in certain occupations as well as a relative increase in the numbers in skilled occupations. But such changes seem to have been counterbalanced by a widening of differentials elsewhere or the advent of new occupations.

A number of further qualifications have to be made. The comparative stability of overall distribution of manual earnings applies only to earnings before tax and does not take account either of supplementary earnings in second jobs or earnings of more than one person in a household. Information about non-manual earnings is harder to compile and interpret. Routh has assembled some of the evidence. He found that, overall, women's earnings remained in about the same ratio to men's earnings in 1913 and 1960 as in 1906. On the other hand, he reported certain changes. Male clerks had lost ground relative to both female clerks and to male manual workers. At least up to 1960, the earnings of unskilled manual workers had increased relative to the earnings of 'higher' professional workers, from approximately 19 per cent in 1913/14 to 26 per cent in 1960. In relation to the managerial class, on the other hand, the unskilled had lost ground marginally.[1]

Although it has to be concluded from the data we have that there has not been any profound long-term change in the distribution of earnings among manual and non-manual employees, this does not rule out the possibility of short-term changes of a cyclical kind taking place within any particular 'band' of the earnings structure, nor does it rule out the long-term rise and fall, in terms of levels of earnings, of particular occupations.[2] Two important modifications need to be

---

Mouly, J., 'Wage Determination: Institutional Aspects', *International Labour Review*, November 1967. For both France and the United States, minimum-wage legislation led initially to a narrowing of differentials between unskilled and skilled workers, but within three to five years former differentials had been restored. It is, of course, possible that the initial effects could have been sustained if minimum-wage levels had been increased more rapidly in subsequent years.

1. Estimated from Tables 30 and 47 in Routh, *Occupation and Pay in Great Britain*.
2. However, 'there has been considerable long-run stability in the UK interindustry wage-structure. For example, one study of average weekly earnings in 132 industries in October 1948 and October 1959 showed that only 11 industries changed ranking by 25 places or more – that of the 20 industries ranked lowest in 1948, 15 were still among the lowest 20 in 1959; and that 11 other industries similarly maintained a position among the top 20. The coefficient of rank correlation had a value of +0·87 ... Our own examination of movements of average weekly earnings in 128 industries for full-time adult male manual workers ... indicates that only moderate changes took place between October 1960 and October 1969 in rankings of industries on the basis of their average earnings. Only 19 industries changed rankings by 25 places or more and 12 of the lowest 20 and 13 of the top 20 in 1960 were still in the same groups in 1969' – Report No. 169, *General Problems of Low Pay*, pp. 159–61.

made to the apparent 'stability' of the structure of male manual earnings, as portrayed in Table 4.10. First, reliable information on the distribution of earnings is lacking for the late 1940s and early 1950s, and there is some reason for believing that the dispersion was narrower than, say, for 1960.

Secondly, the data from the special surveys for 1960, 1968 and 1970, and from the Family Expenditure Survey for intervening years, shows that despite continuous official and other references to the difficulties of low-paid male manual workers, there is no evidence of a relative improvement taking place in their earnings during the decade. If anything, there would appear to have been a slight deterioration in their position, as Table 4.11 suggests. The figures for women manual workers are more difficult to interpret, for there is some fluctuation in the FES data for 1963–8, but the data for 1960, 1968 and 1970 suggest little change. The FES figures for male and female non-manual workers are also rather hard to interpret and are a little erratic. They disclose no consistent trend – except that the male non-manual groups when taken together seem to follow the same trend as male manual workers. It must, of course, be remembered that the Family Expenditure Survey is subject to sampling errors, and until 1967 involved a sample of a size which included only 1,500 male and 400 female manual employees and 600 and 500 non-manual employees respectively. These numbers do not allow detailed analyses of small sub-groups to be made.

Table 4.11. Gross earnings of full-time earners at the lowest decile in different categories relative to the median (1960–1970).

	1960	1963	1964	1965	1966	1967	1968 (A)	1968 (B)	1969	1970 (A)	1970 (B)
			Lowest decile as a % of the median								
Men											
Manual	70·6	70·7	71·6	69·7	68·6	69·7	68·9	67·3	68·4	67·4	67·3
Clerical	–	73·8	70·4	72·7	67·2	70·8	69·9	61·2	67·5	67·6	61·8
Managerial	–	61·5	65·9	66·0	61·7	60·5	62·8	61·2	61·4	61·9	61·8
All	–	68·9	68·9	68·1	67·0	67·8	67·4	65·7	66·1	65·2	65·4
Women											
Manual	72·0	68·5	65·1	66·5	66·3	67·2	71·8	71·1	70·5	69·2	69·0
Clerical	–	67·8	63·5	68·4	73·3	71·6	69·9	65·4	66·1	66·0	64·2
Managerial	–	44·3	53·7	51·6	49·2	55·5	55·3	65·4	57·0	64·3	64·2
All	–	66·5	62·2	64·9	67·6	66·2	69·5	67·0	66·4	65·0	66·4

SOURCES: Reports of the Family Expenditure Survey for the appropriate years, supplemented by Thatcher, 'The Distribution of Earnings of Employees in Great Britain', Table 12, p. 161. For 1968 and 1970, (A) gives the results of the FES report and (B) of the special survey carried out by the Department of Employment and Productivity, *Employment and Productivity Gazette*, May 1969, p. 413, and November 1970, p. 974.

Some confirmation of the suggestion in the FES data of a slight relative fall during the decade in the earnings of the low paid is to be found in other reports. For 1960, the Ministry of Labour listed average earnings in 128 industries. During the next six years, the average increase was 44 per cent, but the earnings of as many as seventeen of the twenty-four lowest-paid industries increased by less than that amount.[1] The differences in wage rates between unskilled and skilled workers have widened in a number of the major industries.[2] Between 1965 and 1970 the wage rates and the average weekly earnings of low-paid industries rose by less than average – though most of the lag took place in 1969–70, as a Report of the NBPI shows. 'The statutory minima laid down by Wage Councils rose ½ per cent per annum slower than average over the five years' – again because of the short fall over the last year. Wage settlements took longer in low-paid than high-paid industries.[3] Lydall has also found a tendency for the distribution of earnings to widen during the 1950s and early 1960s in other industrial countries as well as Britain. In ten of eleven countries for which information could be assembled, the distribution of pre-tax incomes had not merely remained stationary but had actually widened. They were France, Germany, the Netherlands, Sweden, Australia, Canada, Argentina, New Zealand and the United States, as well as the United Kingdom. This tendency did not apply to the distribution of earnings of male manual workers in some countries, but was marked for non-manual and female employees in most countries.[4]

Social Stratification and Occupations

One important means of checking trends in the distribution of earnings lies in the changes taking place in the occupational and class structure. During the three decades under review, there have been at least five important trends in the distribution of the population by occupation which have implications for income distribution. The proportion of men in professional, managerial and senior administrative and intermediate occupations has grown, while the proportion in unskilled and partly skilled occupations has diminished (Table 4.12). The percentage of men who are in professional occupations nearly doubled between 1951 and

1. Ministry of Labour, *Statistics on Incomes, Prices, Employment and Production*, No. 18, September 1966, pp. 26–7.
2. Though this does not necessarily imply a widening of *earnings* differentials. 'The comparisons of the time rates of wages of unskilled workers as percentages of those of skilled workers for five different activities (building, shipbuilding, engineering, railways, police) demonstrated that there was a long run narrowing of the skill differential up to the 1950s, and that the effects of the war-time wage policies and trade union growth were to narrow markedly the differential . . . More recent evidence . . . indicates that the differential has been widening over the last 20 years' – Report No. 169, *General Problems of Low Pay*, p. 162.
3. ibid., pp. 14–16.
4. Lydall, *The Structure of Earnings*, pp. 249–53.

1971. The chief novelty of the table is in showing the effects of changes in definition. The proportion of men in unskilled manual occupations has fallen from 9·7
per cent to 8·4 per cent and in partly skilled manual occupations from 23·3 per
cent to 18·0 per cent.

Table 4.12. Percentages of economically active men in different social classes, 1931,
1951, 1961, 1966, 1971 (England and Wales).

Social class (Registrar General)	1931[a]		1951[a]		1961[b]	1966[c]	1971
I	1·8	(2·2)	2·7	(3·2)	4·0	4·5	5·0
II	12·0	(12·8)	12·8	(14·3)	14·9	15·7	18·2
III	47·8	(48·9)	51·5	(53·4)	51·6	50·3	50·5
IV	25·5	(18·2)	23·3	(16·2)	20·5	20·6	18·0
V	12·9	(17·8)	9·7	(12·9)	8·9	8·8	8·4
Total	100·0	(100·0)	100·0	(100·0)	100·0	100·0	100·0
Number (000s)	13,247		14,064		14,649	15,686	15,668

NOTES: [a]Percentages have been weighted to allow for changes in classification between the
1931 and 1951 censuses and 1951 and 1961 census: the *General Report*, 1951, and the *General
Report*, 1961, give the percentage change for each social class between the two censuses, and I
have adjusted the figures accordingly to bring both the 1931 and 1951 figures up to the 1961
classification. Figures in brackets are based on the classification at that time. The reweighting
must be regarded as approximate only, since it depends on experimental coding operations
carried out with sub-samples by GRO staff.
[b]Substantial numbers who were unclassified in 1961 (518,000) have been excluded. (Only
84,034 unclassified in 1971 have been excluded.)
[c]Percentages given are for economically active and retired males. Substantial numbers who
were unclassified in 1966 have been excluded.
SOURCES: Census 1951, *General Report*, Table 66, p. 147.
   Census 1961, *General Report*, Table 55, p. 193.
   Census 1966, *Economic Activity Tables Part III*, Table 30, p. 415.
   Census 1971, *Economic Activity Tables Part IV*, Table 29, p. 96 (10 per cent sample).

Two other important trends have been the fall and rise of unemployment and
the growth of paid employment among women. Table 4.13 shows that after
dwindling during and after the Second World War, the unemployment rate increased slightly again between 1951 and 1961, and again during the later 1960s.
The number of married women entering employment continued to rise steadily
after the war, and in the late 1960s was still rising steadily. Between 1951 and
1969, the number of married women in paid employment increased by more than
2 million. The fastest increase has been among women aged 45–59, that is,
among women whose children are no longer at school. Compared with earlier

Table 4.13. Employed and unemployed population (Britain).

Working population (000s)	1951	1961	1969
Males	15,798	16,366	16,191
Females (married)	3,194	4,448	5,371
Females (others)	4,247	3,958	3,645
Registered wholly unemployed (000s)	253	341	559
As % employees	1·2	1·5	2·4

SOURCES: *Social Trends*, No. 1, 1970, pp. 72 and 74.

generations, the proportion of the population comprising middle-aged married couples without dependent children who are both earning a wage or salary is substantial. In this section of the population living standards have increased relatively.

Finally, there are two trends at either end of life. Partly because of the raising of the school-leaving age in 1944 and 1973, but also because of the continuing increase in the numbers of young people aged under 25 who are in full-time and part-time education, the number of employed people under 25 has been declining. Between 1961 and 1969, for example, the numbers of pupils at school aged 15–19 increased from 551,000 to 942,000, and the percentage of 17-year-olds at school from 12 to 19 per cent. By 1967–8, there were 520,000 students in higher education – nearly 100,000 more than only two years earlier.[1] At the other end of working life, the proportion of men remaining at work has been falling rapidly. As late as 1959, only 47 per cent of men retired at the age of 65, but by 1969 more than 70 per cent did so.[2]

Assets

The assets held by people can make a considerable difference to the standard of living implied by their incomes. Up to the mid 1930s, Campion and others had traced a reduction in the unequal distribution of property. Campion compared the periods 1911–13, 1926–8 and 1936 and, while calling attention to the inequality that remained, waxed enthusiastic about the diffusion of wealth, saying, for example, that because one third of the adult population possessed more than £100 each 'the ownership of property . . . is widespread among different classes of

1. *Social Trends*, No. 1, 1970, pp. 121 and 132.
2. Department of Health and Social Security, Report by the Government Actuary on the Financial Provisions of the National Superannuation and Social Insurance Bill, 1969, Cmnd 4223, HMSO, London, p. 21. See also Chapter 19.

the community'.[1] However, evidence about Post Office savings, home ownership and possession of durable goods showed that few working-class families had any property.[2] In 1952, the Oxford University Institute of Statistics carried out a national survey of personal holdings of liquid assets[3] as well as of income. The most striking finding was that some 32 per cent of income units had no liquid assets at all; over half had less than £20. On the other hand, 'the top 10 per cent of liquid asset holders, who are those with more than £500 each, hold between them some three-quarters of the total'.[4] This was the first reliable survey of the distribution of assets in Britain. Later surveys confirmed the broad findings and also showed that the skilled manual worker was in a less favourable position than even the least well-paid non-manual workers.[5]

The distribution of wealth appears to be more unequal in Britain than in the United States (Table 4.14), though the distribution of incomes appears to be more equal. Nearly half the spending units had less than £50 wealth in 1954, while only a quarter of American spending units had less than $500. Among the American population, ownership of physical assets, such as homes, other real estate, farms and cars, is more widespread. A much larger proportion of middle- and low-income groups in the United States own their homes. But the difference between the two countries in the distribution of financial assets is much less marked. The percentage of the population owning some liquid assets, some corporate stock and life insurance policies, is only slightly larger in the United States than in Britain.

Can any exact account be given of changes in the distribution of personal wealth over the three decades? Unfortunately, regular surveys of the kind carried out in the early 1950s by the Oxford University Institute of Statistics have not been undertaken. In the absence of a wealth tax, the government itself has not collected information about the distribution of assets. But, traditionally, economists, statisticians and others have made aggregate estimates of the distribution. As discussed in Chapter 9, these estimates are based on a technique of inflating the statistics of estates left at death with a multiplier reflecting the mortality rates applicable to the deceased property-owners. Some post-war studies using this

1. Campion, H., *Public and Private Property in Great Britain*, Oxford University Press, 1939, p. 120.

2. Runciman, W. G., *Relative Deprivation and Social Justice*, Routledge & Kegan Paul, London, 1966, pp. 75-6.

3. These assets included deposits in the Post Office Savings Bank, Trustee and other savings banks and joint-stock banks; Savings Certificates and Defence Bonds; and shares and deposits in building societies and cooperative societies.

4. Lydall, H. F., *British Incomes and Savings*, Blackwell, Oxford, 1955, p. 12.

5. Hill, T. P., 'Incomes Savings and Net Worth – the Savings Surveys of 1952-4', *Bulletin of the Oxford University Institute of Statistics*, XVII, 1955; Hill, T. P., and Straw, K. H., 'Consumers' Net Worth: the 1953 Savings Survey', *Bulletin of the Oxford University Institute of Statistics*, XVIII, 1956.

Table 4.14. Distribution of spending units by comparable ranges of net worth, United States and Britain (percentage of spending units).

Comparable ranges of net worth		United States 1953	Great Britain 1954
Negative		11	13
Zero		4	21
Under £50	($500)	10	14
£50	($500)	6	6
£100	($1,000)	10	8
£200	($2,000)	11	8
£400	($4,000)	8	5
£600	($6,000)	11	5
£1,000	($10,000)	15	8
£2,000	($20,000)	10	7
£5,000	($50,000)	4	5
Total		100	100

SOURCE: Lydall, H. F., and Lansing, J. B., 'A Comparison of the Distribution of Personal Income and Wealth in the United States and Great Britain', *American Economic Review*, March 1959.

technique at first suggested that a reduction in inequality had taken place.[1] Estimates produced annually by the Board of Inland Revenue have also maintained this interpretation.[2]

However, there does not appear to have been a large reduction in the concentration of wealth. Figures were compiled by Revell on a broadly comparable basis for 1911–60 and have been widely quoted.[3] For the three decades of our review. The percentages of total wealth owned by the top groups are:

1936–8 Share of top 1%: 56; 5%: 79; 10%: 88
1954 Share of top 1%: 43; 5%: 71; 10%: 79
1960 Share of top 1%: 42; 5%: 75; 10%: 83

1. Langley, K. M., 'The Distribution of Private Capital 1950–51', *Bulletin of the Oxford University Institute of Statistics*, XVI, 1954; Lydall, H. F., and Tipping, D. G., 'The Distribution of Personal Wealth in Britain', *Bulletin of the Oxford University Institute of Statistics*, XXIII, 1961.
2. See, for example, the Reports of the Commissioners of HM Inland Revenue, 1960–61 to 1967–8, plus *Inland Revenue Statistics*, 1970.
3. Revell, J., 'Changes in the Social Distribution of Property in Britain during the Twentieth Century', *Proceedings of the International Economic History Conference*, vol. 1, Munich, 1965. See also Revell, J., Hockley, G., and Moyle, J., *The Wealth of the Nation*, Cambridge University Press, 1967. Revell's estimates were quoted by the Royal Commission on the Distribution of Income and Wealth in their Report No. 1, *Initial Report on the Standing Reference*, Cmnd 6171, HMSO, London, 1975, p. 97.

A measured and detailed review of trends between 1923 and 1972 by Atkinson and Harrison has led them to put forward amended estimates, which indicate 'a steady arithmetic downward trend of some 0·4 per cent per annum in the share of the top 1 per cent (with a once-for-all jump between 1959 and 1960), no apparent acceleration in the arithmetic rate of decline in the share of the top 1 per cent and no apparent downward trend in the share of the next 4 per cent (but a jump upwards between 1938 and 1950, and a jump downwards between 1959 and 1960)'.[1] However, they emphasize that attempts to produce a consistent series over a long span of years have to be treated with as much caution as estimates of the concentration of wealth in any particular year. A review of Inland Revenue estimates for the 1960s also warns against uncritical acceptance of the apparent trend.[2] The estimates made on the basis of estate duty paid in any particular year are sensitive to chance variations, so that small changes from year to year cannot be treated as very significant. The estimates are also defective in excluding small estates for which probate is not required, pension rights and annuities and property held in trust. Conclusions about trends therefore have to be strongly qualified. One of the major shortcomings of statistical series on living standards is the lack of any routine collection of data on assets.[3]

All those undertaking reviews of trends have shown the continuing high concentration of wealth in Britain compared with other countries, and this has attracted much comment.[4]

Taxation

Taxation has a major influence on the actual dispersion of incomes available for spending. During the war new taxes and higher rates of existing taxes were introduced. Taxation undoubtedly played a major part in reducing the differentials between income levels during this period. Although there is a large literature on

1. Atkinson, A. B., and Harrison, A. J., *Distribution of Personal Wealth in Britain*, Cambridge University Press, 1978, p. 170.
2. Meacher, M., 'Wealth: Labour's Achilles Heel', in Bosanquet, N., and Townsend, P., *Labour and Inequality*, Fabian Society, London, 1971.
3. The problems of estimating the distribution of wealth, and the need to distinguish between accumulated and inherited wealth, are discussed in Atkinson, A. B., *Unequal Shares – the Distribution of Wealth in Britain*, Penguin Books, Harmondsworth, 1972. The Royal Commission on the Distribution of Income and Wealth has endorsed the value of specially organized surveys – but has not, at the time of writing, put one in hand. See Royal Commission on the Distribution of Income and Wealth, Report No. 1, *Initial Report on the Standing Reference*, p. 160.
4. Estimates of the share of the top 1 per cent in the United States are only a little over half the British figures. See, for example, Lampman, R. J., 'The Share of Top Wealth-Holders in National Wealth 1922–1956', *Review of Economic Statistics*, 1959. 'It seems likely that Britain has the doubtful distinction of leading the international inequality league' – Atkinson, A. B., 'The Reform of Wealth Taxes in Britain', *Political Quarterly*, January 1971.

the relationship between taxation and changes in real *aggregate* incomes, there is not very much useful information on the precise redistributive effect of changes in taxation between 1938 and 1968. In relation to some other countries, the overall tax 'burden' cannot be regarded as excessive. Table 4.15 gives a summary of the scale and structure of taxation in five countries, including social security contributions as a 'tax'. Too much should not be read into the differences. For example, West Germany raises more money than does Britain in taxes as a percentage of GNP. One major reason is that, in financing capital expenditure, Germany uses taxes while the United Kingdom tends to borrow. Taxation needs to be considered in relation to the institutional structure as well as the financial policy of each. Britain differs primarily from several European countries in obtaining less tax through employers' social security contributions and more from direct personal taxes. An attempt to compare the overall effects of taxation in the United States, West Germany and Britain shows, first, 'the similarity in the level of tax rates for positive tax payers'; secondly, 'the tendency for taxes to be proportional to income for positive tax payers' (rather than progressive); and thirdly, that, taking both government cash transfer expenditures and taxes into account, income is redistributed via the government to a larger proportion of the population of Britain than of the other two countries.[1]

Some cautious attempts have been made by J. L. Nicholson and by the Central Statistical Office to estimate from the Family Expenditure Survey the incidence of taxes and social service benefits on households of different size and in different income ranges.[2] One conclusion that can be drawn from the published data is that, for each type of family for which there are sufficient data (with one, two, three and four children), the poorer families tend to pay as high a proportion of their original incomes in all kinds of taxes as more prosperous families. In some groups, the poorer families pay a higher proportion in taxes. There was little change in the pattern for the period 1961–8.[3] During the 1960s, real incomes increased and the proportion of incomes taken in tax also increased. But the poorest among families with one child, two children and three children retained proportionately less of their original incomes in 1968 than they did in 1961. The poorest households with three adults and two children also lost ground. Those with three adults and one child and two adults and four children just about held their 1961 relativities to original income. In 1968 there was even little difference in the proportion of original income paid in tax by families of different size, being 34 per cent on average for one-child families and 33 per cent, 32 per cent and 33

1. Brown, C. V., and Dawson, D. A., *Personal Taxation, Incentives and Tax Reform*, Political and Economic Planning, London, January 1969, pp. 16–33.

2. Nicholson, J. L., *Redistribution of Income in the United Kingdom in 1959, 1957 and 1953*, Bowes & Bowes, London, 1965; *Economic Trends*, November 1962, February 1964, August 1966, February 1968, 1969, 1970, 1971, 1972, November 1972 and 1973, December 1974 and January 1976.

3. *Economic Trends*, July 1968, p. xxviii, and February 1970, p. xix.

Table 4.15. *The level and structure of taxation in five countries.*

Country	Years	Tax receipts as % GNP	Selected taxes as % personal primary income	
			Personal income tax	Social security contributions
United Kingdom	1959–61	28·1	10·6	5·0
	1962–4	29·1	11·3	5·7
	1965–6	30·6	12·8	6·4
West Germany	1959–61	34·0	9·5	13·6
	1962–4	35·2	11·4	13·8
	1965–6	34·6	10·5	13·1
United States	1959–61	27·0	12·4	5·1
	1962–4	27·6	12·6	5·7
	1965–6	27·7	12·3	6·1
France	1959–61	34·5	5·4	16·3
	1962–4	36·5	5·5	18·3
	1965–6	38·4	6·3	19·7
Sweden	1959–61	31·6	18·6	4·7
	1962–4	35·9	19·6	6·9
	1965–6	40·0	24·4	8·6

SOURCE: UN and OECD sources cited in Tables 4 and 6 in Brown, C. V., and Dawson, D. A., *Personal Taxation, Incentives and Tax Reform*, Political and Economic Planning, London, January 1969.

per cent respectively for two-, three- and four-child families.[1] Certainly on the available evidence Britain does not have a system of taxation which can be said to be 'progressive'.[2] The progressive element in direct taxation might be said to have been counter-balanced by regressive elements – such as national insurance contributions, domestic rates and tobacco taxes; and the 'progressivity' of direct taxes has diminished with the fall in the tax threshold and the abolition of the reduced rates of tax.

Secondly, the proportion of original income paid in taxes does not decrease substantially within particular income ranges with each additional dependant. For example, among households with an income of £817 to £987 per annum,

1. *Economic Trends*, February 1970, p. xix.
2. Even the official conclusion that 'all taxes combined are only mildly progressive' plainly is not true for some types of household and is not consistent for all others. See *Economic Trends*, February 1970, pp. xxvii and xix.

single-person households (not pensioner households) paid 37 per cent in taxes in 1966. Yet households consisting of two adults and of two adults and one child paid about the same proportion as this (in fact 36 per cent and 38 per cent respectively), and households with two adults and either two or three children paid 32 per cent and 31 per cent respectively. To put the same statistic into alternative form, a man and wife with three children whose income was around £19 a week in 1966 were paying only £1 less a week in total taxes than a single person or two adults of under pensionable age without dependants who were in the same income range (paying £6 per week, compared with £7).[1] Although family allowances were raised in 1968, the data for that year show much the same thing. Families with four children, for example, paid £7 per week compared with £8·50 by single adults from the same income or around £22 (original income plus cash benefits).[2]

In the early 1970s the government substituted earnings-related for flat-rate social security contributions. This suggested that the total system of taxation might become a little more progressive, but the evidence for the early 1970s from the FES does not confirm this possibility.[3] The low level of earnings on which contributions have to be paid and the ceiling on graduated contributions have limited the potentially egalitarian effect of the change. Although it would be wrong to come to a hard-and-fast conclusion without further evidence from a special survey (especially one where incomes could be checked with Inland Revenue data and information obtained about resources other than income), it seems that the tax system is barely, if at all, redistributive. The system contributes hardly at all to a more egalitarian structure of incomes, if taxes of all kinds are compared with original incomes plus cash benefits.[4] Other analysts have gone even further and have denied that taxes redistribute income from the rich to the poor.[5]

Fiscal Welfare

Just as the amounts of taxes actually paid by different income groups and families provide one test of the functions of the tax system, so the differential allocation of tax allowances provides another. Tax allowances for dependants were first intro-

1. *Economic Trends*, July 1968, pp. xxviii, xxxii–xxxvi.
2. The subsequent report of February 1970 which describes the 1968 survey does not contain data comparable with that of July 1968. See *Economic Trends*, February 1970, pp. xxviii–xxix.
3. For households with children, those with the smallest incomes pay about the same percentage of original income and in some cases a higher percentage of original income than those with higher incomes. See *Economic Trends*, December 1974, p. xxv.
4. Nicholson, J. L., 'The Distribution and Redistribution of Income in the United Kingdom', in Wedderburn, D. (ed.), *Poverty, Inequality and Class Structure*, Cambridge University Press, 1974, p. 80.
5. Field, F., Meacher, M., and Pond, C., *To Him Who Hath*, Penguin Books, Harmondsworth, 1977, pp. 238–40, but also see pp. 172–9.

duced by Lloyd George early in this century. During the past sixty years there
have been gradual extensions of the scope and amounts of these allowances. Today fiscal welfare is a major means of effecting a redistribution of resources. Two
matters need to be established. The first is that tax allowances benefit high- rather
than low-income recipients. In a memorandum to the prime minister at the end
of 1965, the Child Poverty Action Group gave examples of the combined value of
family allowances and tax allowances for children to families with different incomes and numbers of children. Family allowances were being paid at a flat rate
to the second and subsequent children in families. Table 4.16 shows that the
combined value was then three times as large for a family of three with £30 per
week as it was for a similar family with £10 per week.

Table 4.16. *Combined value of family allowances and tax allowance for children,
according to earned income and number of children (1965).*

Number of children	Annual value of combined allowances with earned weekly income of			Family allowances
	£10 £ p	£18 £ p	£30 £ p	£ p
1	12 40	44 17½	47 44	–
2	33 20	94 97½	109 49	20 80
3	59 20	147 05	174 26	46 80
4	85 20	188 27½	239 45	72 80
5	111 20	214 27½	304 64	98 80
6	137 20	240 27½	367 24	124 80

SOURCE: Child Poverty Action Group, *Memorandum to the Prime Minister*, 1965 (reprinted in
Poverty, No. 2, 1966).

Secondly, the relationship between direct payments and tax allowances has
changed. For Britain the rates for tax allowances and family allowances are given
in the table. After being introduced in 1946 and raised slightly in 1952 and then in
1956, family allowances were not raised again until 1968. Between 1957–8 and
1967–8, the cost of family allowances increased from £128 million to £160 million, but the value to families of tax allowances rose from £230 million to £630
million. In 1968, tax allowances were reduced to pay in part for increased family
allowances, and, despite inflation, were not again raised until 1971.[1]

Among other tax allowances which were of substantial value to some families
were allowances on mortgage interest paid by owner-occupiers. Between 1964–5
and 1969–70, the total value to owner-occupiers of such allowances increased

1. For a detailed account of the government's policy, see Lynes, T., 'Clawback', in Bull, D.
(ed.), *Family Poverty*, Duckworth, London, 1971.

from £90 million to £215 million.[1] These allowances are now officially recognized to be a form of housing subsidy.[2]

Finally, exemption of many forms of income from tax represents a kind of 'allowance', and changes in both the amounts and kind of income that are exempt, such as imputed rent on owner-occupied houses, capital gains and contributions to pension funds, can seriously influence the final 'dispersion' of living standards.

Employer Welfare

One marked change since 1938 has been the rapid development of employer welfare. Of course, people in certain occupations had received fringe benefits for many years. Some were manual workers. Miners received free coal, railwaymen free travel and domestic servants board and lodgings. But non-manual workers were the principal beneficiaries. In the 1950s, Richard Titmuss called attention to the rapid expansion of employer schemes for lunch expenses, subsidized housing, education, free travel and entertainment.[3] In 1952, Lydall found that 27 per cent of employees were contributing to occupational pension schemes, but while this figure covered 21 per cent of manual employees, it covered 40 per cent of non-manual employees, including well over half of professional and administrative staff.[4] To these totals should be added members of non-contributory schemes. For 1956-7, Titmuss reported that about 86 per cent of salaried staffs in the private sector belonged to some kind of occupational pension scheme compared with 20 per cent of wage-earners.[5] Some industries have continued to provide few benefits for manual workers. Even by 1970, fewer than a third of the men employed full time in the laundry and dry-cleaning industry, for example, were entitled to any form of pension.[6]

The proportion of old people actually receiving occupational pensions is fairly low. A government survey found that, in 1965, there were 48 per cent of men, 24 per cent of women on their own insurance, and only 11 per cent of widows. Even among people aged 65-9, the figures were only 58, 24 and 17 per cent respectively. Many of the amounts of pension were also very small. Forty-five per cent of men, 32 per cent of women on their own insurance and 61 per cent of the widows actually getting pensions were receiving under £2 per week, many of them under £1. More disturbing still, the average pension for former manual workers was only

1. *Hansard*, 2 March 1970.
2. See, for example, the inclusion of both housing subsidies and the value of tax relief on mortgages in *Social Trends*, No. 1, 1970, Table 100.
3. Titmuss, R. M., *Essays on the Welfare State*, Allen & Unwin, London, 1958, Chapter 3.
4. Lydall, H. F., *British Incomes and Savings*, Blackwell, Oxford, 1955, p. 117.
5. Titmuss, R. M., *Income Distribution and Social Change*, Allen & Unwin, London, 1962, p. 155.
6. Report No. 169, *General Problems of Low Pay*, p. 76.

one third of the average for former non-manual workers, being £2·25 for men and £1·75 for women.[1]

Schemes covering pay during sickness multiplied after the end of the Second World War. One for local-authority administrative, professional and technical workers was introduced in 1946, and for manual employees two years later. A number of schemes for the white-collar staff of the nationalized industries were started in this period, and between 1956 and 1958 modest schemes were started for railway and other transport workers and for mineworkers. By 1961, nearly all of the manual workers in the public sector (2½ million) but only about a third in the private sector (4½ million among 13½ million) were estimated to be covered by sick-pay schemes. Altogether 90 per cent of men in white-collar occupations but only about two fifths of manual workers were covered.[2]

However, the cover varied. First, nearly 40 per cent of men in unskilled and semi-skilled occupations who were covered by sick-pay schemes had to wait before payment could begin (usually three to six days), whereas only 4 per cent of professional and managerial staff had to wait. Secondly, 72 per cent of the unskilled could receive sick pay for only a limited number of weeks, some up to four weeks, but others up to thirteen weeks, compared with only 12 per cent of professional and managerial staff being paid for that period. Finally, although 69 per cent of men covered by schemes received full pay, or full pay less national insurance benefit, during the appropriate period, the figure varied from over 90 per cent for professional workers, administrators and managers to below 20 per cent for some groups of manual workers, for example, mineworkers who received flat-rate amounts of between £1 and £2 only.[3]

The evidence published up to the end of the 1960s suggested that, on the whole, fringe benefits reinforced rather than compensated for existing inequalities. They reflected the distribution of earnings, even within manual grades.[4] The study of three low-paid industries by the National Board for Prices and Incomes found 'no evidence from our survey to contradict this view'.[5]

1. 'Occupational Pensions – Memorandum by the Government Actuary's Department in Ministry of Pensions and National Insurance', *Financial Circumstances of Retirement Pensioners*, HMSO, London, 1966, pp. 153–63.

2. Ministry of Labour, *Sick Pay Schemes*, Report of a Committee of the National Joint Advisory Council on Occupational Sick Pay Schemes, HMSO, London, 1964, pp. 5, 10 and 51. Also see Ministry of Pensions and National Insurance, Report on an Enquiry into the Incidence of Incapacity for Work, HMSO, London, 1964.

3. ibid., pp. xxv–xxvii and pp. 44–51.

4. Reid, G. L., and Robertson, D. J., *Fringe Benefits, Labour Costs and Social Security*, Allen & Unwin, London, 1965.

5. Among full-time and part-time male employees and full-time female employees, sick-pay and pension schemes were positively related to the size of gross weekly earnings within each industry. See Report No. 169, *General Problems of Low Pay*, p. 50.

Public Social Services

The public social services have been regarded traditionally as modifying the inequalities of the private market. Certainly there is a widespread assumption that there is through them a substantial transfer of income vertically from rich to poor. However, a number of studies called attention first to the fact that much of the redistribution was 'horizontal' in different senses – from young to elderly working class, from employed to unemployed or to sick working class and even (in the case of residential care) from the married to the single. Secondly, some scholars have increasingly called attention to the need to look more broadly at the policies of the state, at the ways in which publicly subsidized and managed transport services 'support' the operation of private industry, for example, and not only at fiscal and employer welfare policies, in order to comprehend 'social' redistribution in the fullest sense. Here, attention will be confined to the 'public' social services, namely those which are conventionally defined or treated[1] by the government as social services – health, education, social security, welfare and housing. During recent years certain studies have begun to question whether some parts of these services are even mildly redistributive.[2] One of the paradoxical facts about their growth is that they have fostered a form of inequality, in that well-paid professional posts have been created on a large scale.

The public social services grew substantially between 1938 and 1968. In 1938 their cost was a little under 11 per cent of the Gross National Product of the United Kingdom (Table 4.17). By 1947, the figure had increased to nearly 13 per cent. Because of the big fall in unemployment, the total sums paid to the unemployed and their families had been reduced but the number of young children and old people had increased disproportionately. Family allowances and bigger pensions had been introduced. The war-time subsidies for school meals, welfare milk and foods were being maintained and a major housing programme had been launched to make good the destruction and lack of building in the war. By 1951, the cost of the social services reached 16 per cent of GNP, mainly because of the transfer in 1948 of health expenditure from the private to the public sector and

1. Strictly, housing is not included in the definition of social services as published in the May issue of the *Monthly Digest of Statistics* and incorporated in the annual *National Income and Expenditure* Blue Book and the Annual Abstract of Statistics. It seems often to be treated as a 'borderline' category, e.g. *Social Trends*, No. 1, 1970, Table 2; and local authority housing subsidies are counted as 'indirect' social service benefits in *Economic Trends*. Social scientists are, however, increasingly treating the social services as also including voluntary and private or occupational education, health, insurance and other services, including purchases of services from the public sector by way of charges and services subsidized directly (e.g. payments to voluntary organizations) or indirectly (employer fringe benefits allowed against tax) by the state. There are also fringe benefits for public service employees.
2. See Webb, A. L., and Sieve, J. E. B., *Income Distribution and the Welfare State*, Bell, London, 1971, esp. Chapter 7.

Table 4.17. *Expenditure of social services as percentage of Gross National Product (UK 1938–69).*

Social service	1938	1951	1959	1969	1969 (£ mil.)
Education	2·4	3·1	4·0	6·0	2,328
National Health Service	1·4	3·8	3·7	4·7	1,813
Housing	1·4	3·1	2·0	2·9	1,118
Social security	5·4	6·0	7·1	9·6	3,723
Welfare and child care	0·1	0·24	0·25	0·42	163
All social services	10·7	16·2	17·1	23·7	9,145
Current expenditure on goods and services	3·9	6·6	7·2	9·7	3,754
Capital expenditure	1·4	3·3	2·3	3·6	1,388
Transfer income	5·3	6·3	7·5	10·4	4,003

SOURCES: Estimates based on *National Income and Expenditure*, HMSO, London, 1970; *Social Trends*, No. 1, 1970; PEP, *The Cost of the Social Services, 1938–1952*, Planning No. 354, June 1953, and information supplied additionally by the Treasury and the Central Statistical Office.

the start of the National Health Service.[1] The nature and scale of this transfer had not been fully understood and there was considerable, though unnecessary, public alarm over the cost of the National Health Service which led to restrictions on expenditure during the mid 1950s. Neither the Report of the Guillebaud Committee on the costs of the service nor the news of bigger proportionate spending on health services by other countries lifted these restraints. By 1959, expenditure on the social services grew to only 17 per cent, but in the next ten years increased to a total of nearly 24 per cent. A large part of the total does not, of course, represent a direct use of resources, and the total is reduced to about 13 per cent if transfer incomes are excluded.[2]

The rise from 17 per cent to 24 per cent of GNP during the period 1959–69 in fact represents only a small improvement for the lowest income groups. Of the extra 7 per cent of GNP, nearly 1 per cent is attributable to more pupils of 15 years of age and over staying on at school and more students entering further and higher education. The main beneficiaries of this increase are middle-income families. Perhaps as much as 3·5 per cent of the increase is attributable to demo-

1. Estimates of costs before and after the war are made in Political and Economic Planning, *The Cost of the Social Services, 1938–1952*, Planning No. 354, June 1953.
2. For the purposes of examining trends historically and cross-nationally, there are advantages in comparing all forms of public expenditure on the social services with GNP. Several UN agencies, including the International Labour Office, follow this convention.

graphic change, including about 2 per cent for the rise in number of social security allowances (mainly retirement pensions and family allowances) in payment, but also more housing, home help and welfare services for the larger numbers of children and old people. The residue represents a number of improvements – an increase in hospital and school staffing ratios, the modernization of parts of the capital stock of health, education and welfare services, and a slight relative increase in the rates of benefit paid to some groups living on social security. However, the same period saw the emergence of new problems and the growth of old ones – such as racial disturbances, environmental planning, the social problems of motorway planning and high flats and new forms of homelessness and isolation.

The rate of growth of expenditure on the social services is faster than that of the economy as a whole, but this is a common phenomenon in industrial societies. In the United Kingdom the rate seems to be lower than some other countries. In the early and mid 1960s, expenditure, excluding education and housing, grew faster in Austria, Belgium, Czechoslovakia, France, Italy, Japan, the Netherlands, Sweden and New Zealand than in the United Kingdom.[1] Expenditure on education was higher, as a percentage of GNP, in eleven countries in 1955 and higher in thirteen countries in 1965, than in the United Kingdom.[2] During the 1950s, the rate of growth in the United Kingdom was a little over 3 per cent, but in the 1960s fluctuated around 5 per cent (Table 4.18). However, much of the increase was attributable to sporadic increases in expenditure on housing, particularly in the mid 1960s.[3] The rates for different services partly reflect economic vicissitudes, especially when capital expenditure represents a large proportion of the total. But current expenditure can also be affected. Part of the increase in national spending in the late 1960s is attributable to the marked rise in expenditure on unemployment benefit.

Increased expenditure on public social services may arise because of an increase in the numbers in the population who are made redundant, or retired though still physically active and willing to work; higher unit costs in surgery and acute medicine, at the expense of the care of the chronic sick; and an increase in the proportion of young people, particularly of those from middle-income fam-

1. International Labour Office, *The Cost of Social Security, 1964–1966*, Geneva, 1971; Wedel, J., 'Social Security and Economic Integration – II', *International Labour Review*, December 1970.

2. Debeauvais, M., *et al.*, *Comparative Study of Education Expenditure and its Trends in OECD Countries since 1950*, Background Study No. 2, Conference on Policies for Educational Growth, OECD, 1970. See also Edding, F., 'Expenditure on Education: Statistics and Comments', in Robinson, E. A. G., and Vaizey, J. E. (eds.), *The Economics of Education*, Macmillan, London, 1966.

3. For a discussion of the rate of growth of public expenditure, see Holmans, A. E., 'The Growth of Public Expenditure in the United Kingdom since 1950', *Manchester School of Economic and Social Studies*, December 1968.

Table 4.18. Annual percentage rate of increase in public expenditure (current and capital) at constant prices.[a]

Social service	1951–9	1959–64	1964–9
Education	4·9	5·9	4·7
National Health Service	1·9	3·2	3·3
Housing	−2·3	10·3	2·9
Social security	5·4	4·9	6·5
Welfare and child care	2·7	7·4	5·6
All social services	3·3	5·5	4·9
Social services less housing	4·3	4·8	5·3

NOTE: [a]Including subsidies for school meals, milk and welfare foods.

SOURCES: Estimates based on *National Income and Expenditure*, HMSO, London, 1970; *Social Trends*, No. 1, 1970; PEP, *The Cost of the Social Services, 1938–1952*, Planning No. 354, June 1953; and information supplied additionally by the Treasury and the Central Statistical Office. Method of revaluation based on official indices.

ilies, who enter the sixth forms of schools and colleges and universities. Certainly, compared with 1938, the functions of the public social services can be said to have diversified and become more complex. They involve very much more than the protection and subsidy of the lower income groups.

Some, but only limited information, is available about the distribution by value of the social services. The Central Statistical Office periodically reviews the relationship between incomes, taxes and social services, using the data from the Family Expenditure Survey. Table 4.19 summarizes the data for the period 1961–8. These show first that, as a proportion of original income plus cash benefits, total benefits gradually increased during the seven years; and second that total benefits form a much smaller proportion of the incomes of the high-income than of the low-income groups. On these data, the social services make a big contribution to the equalization of standards of living. The use of fixed-income groups by the CSO, however, makes comparison over the years difficult.

There are two major reservations to the figures in Table 4.19. First, a few high-income groups benefit more in *absolute* money value from the public social services than do low-income groups, and all of them benefit more from certain services. Thus, allowing for fluctuations because of sample numbers, Table 4.20 shows that, for several types of family, the middle- and high-income groups receive broadly as much in total benefits as low-income groups, sometimes more. An exception is the one-child family. While cash benefits tend to decline with income, direct benefits (which include the value of secondary and university education) tend to increase. It should also be recognized that the estimates of the benefits received by different families are, for education and health, for example,

Table 4.19. *Total social service benefits as a percentage of original incomes plus cash benefits (1961–8).*

Range of original income £ per year	Two adults and two children			All households		
	1961	1965	1968	1961	1965	1968
260—				52	55	72
315—				40	49	67
382—				36	51	59
460—	31			29	39	48
559—	28	41		23	38	44
676—	23	34	42	21	27	34
816—	19	24	32	17	24	29
988—	17	18	25	14	18	23
1,196	16	18	20	12	15	20
1,448	12	15	17	10	13	16
1,752	9	15	15	8	11	13
2,122		10	12	6	10	12
2,566			12	5	8	10
3,104			8	3	6	8
Average all ranges	18	19	18	17	19	20

SOURCE: *Economic Trends*, February 1970, p. xxxix.

based on crude averages rather than upon services actually used. Although low-income groups tend to need more medical consultations than high-income groups, the latter may use the more expensive sectors of both the health and education services relatively more heavily than the former.

Secondly, certain kinds of benefit which are of proportionately greater value to high-income than to low-income groups are not included in the Central Statistical Office's definition of social service benefits. Thus, subsidies to council housing are counted as indirect benefits in Table 4.20 (defined for each local-authority dwelling as the excess of the estimated economic rent over the actual rent paid by the tenant). But subsidies to owner-occupiers, in the form of tax reliefs on mortgage interest, averaging about £42 per annum in 1968, are not counted.[1] Similarly, the value to families of tax allowances for children is not counted, although the statistical departments of some other countries now treat this as part of social security

1. The benefit is, of course, included in total income, after all taxes and benefits, and unlike council-housing subsidies, is not counted in the value of the social services.

Table 4.20. *Average value in pounds per annum of social services to different types of household in selected income groups (1968).*

Type of family		Range of original incomes (£ per year)		
	Benefits	816–987	1,448–1,751	3,104 and above
2 adults, 1 child	Direct: cash	80	19	11
	Direct: in kind	155	140	157
	Indirect (council housing)	15	5	—2
	All	250	164	166
2 adults, 2 children	Direct: cash	116	50	48
	Direct: in kind	207	229	288
	Indirect	7	7	–
	All	330	286	336
2 adults, 3 children	Direct: cash	107	85	80
	Direct: in kind	318	335	377
	Indirect	15	5	–
	All	440	425	457
2 adults, 4 children	Direct: cash	211	136	
	Direct: in kind	455	469	
	Indirect	—1	20	
	All	665	625	
3 adults, 1 child	Direct: cash		116	39
	Direct: in kind		240	468
	Indirect		24	10
	All		380	517
3 adults, 2 children	Direct: cash		86	189
	Direct: in kind		350	430
	Indirect		8	5
	All		444	624

SOURCE: *Economic Trends*, February 1970, pp. xxix and xxx.

expenditure.[1] If the value of fiscal welfare were to be included in the total estimated benefits of the social services, the absolute and relative figures in Tables 4.19 and 4.20 for the middle- and high-income groups would be much larger.[2]

Poverty

Throughout this chapter the true living standards of the poorest sections of the population have remained shadowy. What can in fact be said about trends in the distribution of incomes at the lowest ranges? Before the Second World War there were a number of surveys of poverty in particular areas, based on the costs, for families of different composition, of attaining a defined level of subsistence. Table 4.21 shows the percentage of working-class households found to be in poverty. It should be noted that, although the operational definition of the 'poverty line' which was applied to household incomes was similar in broad principle in each of the studies, it differed in detail. The poverty line was fixed at a slightly more generous level in Seebohm Rowntree's survey of York in 1936 than in other surveys carried out in the late 1930s.

Only one survey of a similar kind was carried out after 1945, that by Rowntree and Lavers in York in 1950.[3] This survey was limited in conception and the report left many questions unanswered.[4] The number of people in poverty in York was found to be 1·7 per cent (or 2·8 per cent of working class) compared with 18 per cent in 1936.[5] A secondary analysis of the Family Expenditure Survey data for 1953–4 produced an estimate of 5·4 per cent of all households in the United Kingdom and 4·1 per cent of people living in poverty in that year, according to the Rowntree–Lavers standard. Another 4·5 per cent of households (4 per cent of people) had incomes of less than 20 per cent above this standard.[6]

By this standard, poverty seemed to have been reduced between the 1930s and the early 1950s. But although Rowntree had redefined his poverty line at a higher real level, in purchasing terms, than in 1936, he had not raised it by as much as increases in earnings.[7] It was inevitable that he should have found a much smaller proportion of the population in poverty. Moreover, it could be argued in detail that the standard reflected an out-dated conception of needs in modern society.

1. *Social Security in the Nordic Countries*, Statistical Reports on the Nordic Countries, 16, Copenhagen, 1970, e.g. pp. 16–17 and 46–7.
2. Some other benefits, such as improvement grants, are also not allocated.
3. Rowntree, B. S., and Lavers, G. R., *Poverty and the Welfare State: A Third Social Survey of York Dealing Only with Economic Questions*, Longmans, Green, London, 1951.
4. See PEP, *Poverty: Ten Years After Beveridge*, Planning, XIX, No. 344, 1952.
5. Rowntree, and Lavers, *Poverty and the Welfare State*, p. 30.
6. Abel-Smith, B., and Townsend, P., *The Poor and the Poorest*, Bell, London, 1965, p. 36.
7. For a family of five, the poverty standard was in 1936 about 69 per cent and in 1950 60 per cent of average industrial earnings. See ibid., p. 16.

It tended, in practice, to be a fixed historical standard which was ludicrously generous from the viewpoint of, say, Britain in the nineteenth century[1] or India in the twentieth century. Or it could be near destitution from the viewpoint of Britain in the 1970s or of the United States in the 1950s. The same point has been made at length about the Social Security Administration measures of poverty in the United States.[2]

None the less it can be estimated that, even if Rowntree's 1950 definition had fully reflected increases in earnings between 1936 and 1950, he would have found a diminution of poverty – from 18 per cent to probably between 6 per cent and 10 per cent. Unemployment had fallen drastically, family allowances and a more comprehensive social insurance scheme, especially for retirement pensioners, had been introduced; and welfare foods and subsidies played a much more important part in buttressing the living standards of the poor, especially families with children.

Society itself had, in practice, adopted a standard of poverty for its social security schemes. Ironically enough, this had been based on the principles of inquiry used formerly by Rowntree himself. Beveridge had defined a subsistence standard which was subsequently used in deciding social insurance benefits (though at a lower level) and national assistance benefits.[3] The basic scales, which were raised from time to time with movements in prices and earnings, offered a means of tracing changes in the prevalence of poverty. If the scales were regularly applied in field surveys of household income, the numbers and types of families in poverty according to conventional standards could be established. In fact, the data from the Family Expenditure Survey of 1953–4 and 1960 were adapted for this purpose, and the results are shown in Table 4.21. A standard of about 40 per cent higher than the basic scale rates of national assistance (allowing for income which is disregarded as well as discretionary additions to basic rates) was found broadly to represent the actual living standards experienced by recipients of national assistance. As can be seen from the tables, the proportion of the population living below this standard increased from 7·8 per cent in 1953–4 to 14·2 per cent in 1960. However, these findings are not directly comparable because one is on an expenditure basis and the other on an income basis. Allowing for this, the authors conclude cautiously that about a third of the difference between the two figures may not be real, and therefore that, to be comparable with the figure for

1. Rowntree himself showed that if he had used the standard adopted in his first study in York in 1899, he would have found only 4 per cent, and not 18 per cent, in poverty in 1936. See Rowntree, *Poverty and Progress*.
2. Ornati, O., *Poverty and Affluence*, The Twentieth Century Fund, New York, 1966, pp. 27–33.
3. *Social Insurance and Allied Services* (The Beveridge Report), Cmd 6404, HMSO, London, 1942, pp. 76–90.

Table 4.21. Percentages of households and people, and estimated total population with low levels of living (1953–4 and 1960).

Total expenditure (1953–4) or income (1960) as % of basic national assistance scale plus rent/housing costs	Percentage of households		Percentage of persons		Estimated population in United Kingdom (000s)	
	1953–4	1960	1953–4	1960	1953–4	1960
Under 80	0·5	1·3	0·3	0·9	152	471
80–99	1·6	3·4	0·9	2·9	455	1,519
100–109	1·9	4·7	1·4	2·8	709	1,467
110–19	1·7	3·1	1·4	2·4	709	1,257
120–39	4·4	5·5	3·8	5·2	1,923	2,724
140 and over	89·9	82·1	92·2	85·5	46,663	44,945
Total	100·0	100·0	100·0	100·0	50,611	52,383

SOURCE: Abel-Smith, B., and Townsend, P., *The Poor and the Poorest*, Bell, London, 1965, p. 58.

1953–4, the figure for 1960 would have to be reduced to about 12 per cent. A further difference of 2 per cent is attributable to differences in the samples surveyed.[1]

There is therefore evidence of some increase in the prevalence of poverty as conventionally defined in the 1950s. To a certain extent this is explained by demographic factors. The number of aged and of families with four or more children increased disproportionately.[2] But changes in the distribution and weight of particular forms of income are of probably greater importance. Property income and gains increased disproportionately to other forms of income, salaries moved faster than wages, and tax changes (including the extension of tax allowances) improved the net position of middle- and upper-income groups relative to lower-income groups. Most important of all, the family allowance for the second child remained at 8s. between 1953 and 1960, and the allowance for third and subsequent children increased from 8s. to only 10s., or by 25 per cent, in a period when average money

1. On an expenditure basis, the percentage in poverty increased from 8 to 12 per cent and on an income basis from 9 or 10 to 14 per cent. However, about half the increase is attributable to improvements in the representation of the aged and national assistance recipients in the sample surveyed by the government.

2. Between 1953 and 1960, the proportion of the population in the United Kingdom which was aged 65 and over increased from 11·1 to 11·7 per cent. The number of families with four dependent children increased by about 20 per cent, five children by 26 per cent and 6 or more children by 45 per cent. See Abel-Smith and Townsend, *The Poor and the Poorest*, pp. 60–61.

incomes increased by over 50 per cent. This was a crucial factor in contributing to the widening of the gap in incomes between poor families with children and others.

In 1960, 35 per cent of the people in low-income households were older people with pensions as their main source of income. Another 23 per cent depended primarily on state social-security benefits other than pensions, but 41 per cent were in households in which incomes consisted primarily of earnings. The extent of poverty varied with size of household, as Table 4.22 shows. The highest prevalence of poverty was, in fact, to be found among women pensioners living alone,

Table 4.22. *Percentages of households of different size with low levels of living (1953–4 and 1960).*

Number of persons in household	1953–4 (low expenditure)	1960 (low income)
1	38·6	52·1
2	9·6	18·2
3	4·9	7·5
4	4·6	6·4
5	5·4	10·0
6+	11·5	25·2
All sizes	10·1	17·9

SOURCE: As for Table 4.21.

fatherless families and families with four or more children. Of the $7\frac{1}{2}$ million people estimated to be living in households with low incomes in 1960, about 3 million were over the minimum pensionable ages and about $2\frac{1}{4}$ million were children. Altogether about 2 million had incomes of less than the basic national assistance scales, including about a million of pensionable age and 600,000 children. The million people of pensionable age and about half the remaining million seemed to have a *prima facie* entitlement to supplementary national assistance.[1]

During the 1950s and early 1960s, the existence of a large proportion of old people living in poverty, about one million of whom seemed to be eligible to receive supplementary national assistance, was only gradually established.[2] Well

1. Abel-Smith and Townsend, *The Poor and the Poorest,* Chapter 4 *passim,* and pp. 61–7.
2. The following three studies all estimated the numbers of the elderly eligible for, but not receiving, supplementary national assistance at between half a million and a million: Cole Wedderburn, D., with Utting, J., *The Economic Circumstances of Old People,* Codicote, Welwyn, 1962; Report of the Committee of Inquiry into the Impact of Rates on Households (The Allen Report), Cmnd 2582, H M S O, London, 1965, p. 117; Townsend, P., and Wedderburn, D., *The Aged in the Welfare State,* Bell, London, 1965, pp. 117–19 and 124–7.

over half the total of 6 million people aged 65 or more in 1962 had subsistence incomes derived wholly from the state or incomes including no more than £1 a week additional to state benefits. The median income of the retired was about half that of younger adults in the population with no dependants.[1] Some evidence was also published in the 1950s as well as the 1960s about the poverty of fatherless families, the unemployed and the sick.[2] But it was not until the mid 1960s that poverty was recognized to be a widespread problem, and one which included a large number of low-paid wage-earners and their families.[3]

The results of the empirical surveys of the old, and of the secondary analyses of budget data, were subjected to a special kind of government scrutiny – and vindicated. In 1965, a survey of retirement pensioners was carried out by the Ministry of Pensions and National Insurance. On the basis of the results, up to 750,000 old people were estimated to be living below national assistance standards. Of all widowed and unmarried female retirement pensioners, only 19 per cent had a net available income exceeding needs (as defined by the national assistance scale rates) by £1 a week or more; there were 34 per cent receiving national assistance, but another 21 per cent provisionally entitled to it. The corresponding figures for widowed and unmarried male pensioners are 33, 22 and 13 per cent; and for married pensioners 50, 18 and 11 per cent.[4]

In 1966, the ministry carried out another survey, this time of families with two or more children. There was no comprehensive register of families with one child, and they were not included in the survey,

but it is possible to make rough estimates of the number whose resources did not match their requirements, to supplement the information provided by the enquiry. In the summer of 1966 there were in all about seven million families with children. Of these – including those with one child – it seems probable that approaching half a million families, containing up to 1¼ million children, had incomes from earnings, contributory benefits, family allowances or other sources (but excluding national assistance which was paid to a substantial proportion of them) amounting to less than would now be paid to a family which qualified for supplementary benefit. About 145,000 of these families were fatherless; 160,000 were those of men who were sick or unemployed; and 140,000 of men in full-time work.[5]

1. Townsend and Wedderburn, The Aged in the Welfare State, p. 137.
2. For example, Marris, P., Widows and their Families, Routledge & Kegan Paul, London, 1958; Marsden, D., Mothers Alone: Poverty and the Fatherless Family, Allen Lane, London, 1969; Shaw, L. A., and Bowerbank, M., 'Living on a State-Maintained Income', I and II, Case Conference, March and April 1958.
3. See, for example, Land, H., Large Families in London, Bell, London, 1970, and Poverty, the journal of the Child Poverty Action Group, for 1966–70.
4. Ministry of Pensions and National Insurance, Financial and Other Circumstances of Retirement Pensioners, HMSO, London, 1966, p. 20.
5. Ministry of Social Security, Circumstances of Families, HMSO, London, 1967, p. iv.

Table 4.23 shows some of the ways in which deprivation increased according to family size in families with a father in full-time work.[1] Although the percentage of families with five, six or more children who are in poverty is much larger than that of families with two or three children, it must be remembered that there are many fewer such families in the population. They account for only 20 per cent of the families and 36 per cent of the children in poverty, compared with 64 per cent and 45 per cent respectively for families with two or three children.[2]

Table 4.23. Percentages of families in the United Kingdom (with fathers in full-time work) with certain characteristics (1966).

No. of children	In poverty (with resources less than supplementary benefit level)	Working 60 hours a week or more	With savings of £300 or more	With defective housing	Overcrowded	Wife suffers ill-health
2	3	14	22	17	5	14
3	3	19	18	19	11	16
4	7	20	16	20	19	16
5	9	24	11	19	35	23
6 or more	21	25	6	33	62	24
All sizes	4	16	19	18	11	15

SOURCE: Ministry of Social Security, *Circumstances of Families*, HMSO, London, 1967, pp. 11, 38, 40, 56, 57 and 145.

During the late 1960s, the government announced that secondary analyses of data from the Family Expenditure Survey, now based on a much larger annual sample, would be undertaken to find how many households were living below the official 'subsistence' or supplementary benefit standard. A short report on two-parent families, in which the father was in full-time work or wage-stopped, was published in July 1971.[3] This compared FES data for 1968-71 with the Circumstances of Families survey data for 1966, but not also with the Family Expendi-

1. For a detailed account of the particular difficulties of large families, see Land, *Large Families in London.*
2. One-child families are not allowed for in these figures. See *Circumstances of Families,* p. 11.
3. Howe, J. R., *Two-Parent Families: A Study of their Resources and Needs in 1968, 1969 and 1970,* Department of Health and Social Security, Statistical Report Series No. 14, HMSO, London, 1971.

Table 4.24. Number of two-parent families with incomes under the basic SBC scales plus rent, father in full-time work or wage-stopped (thousands).

	In full time work			In full-time work and wage-stopped		
Year	Families	People (children included)		Families	People (children included)	
1960[a]	85	370	(200)	–	–	–
1966[b]	95	470	(280)	110	552	(332)
1968[c]	73	334	(188)	102	500	(296)
1969[c]	96	527	(335)	122	677	(433)
1970[c]	74	336	(188)	105	505	(295)

SOURCES: [a]Abel-Smith, B., and Townsend, P., *The Poor and the Poorest*, Bell, London, 1965.
[b]*Circumstances of Families*, HMSO, London, 1967.
[c]DHSS Statistical Report Series No. 14, *Two Parent Families*, HMSO, London, 1971 (Tables 2, 10A and 10B). The self-employed below the supplementary benefit level were, in fact, excluded from the tables in the DHSS report for 1968, 1969 and 1970, and an estimate equivalent to the proportion of the employed below the level substituted. In this table an estimate for the self-employed has been restored to allow comparisons with the 1960 and 1966 figures. In the absence of actual information, this estimate for 1968, 1969 and 1970 is based on the number found in the *Circumstances of Families* survey (i.e. 11,500 additional families in each case). For later years, this figure is likely to be an underestimate since it is known that, in the late 1960s, the proportion of employed men who were self-employed increased.

ture Survey of 1966. A number of questionable adjustments were made to the survey data,[1] and Table 4.24 does not follow them. Instead it presents figures as close as possible to the original data in order to bring out the fluctuations attributable to sampling variation and other possible factors. These data do not suggest any clear rise or fall in the numbers of such families with incomes below the basic scale rates of the Supplementary Benefits Commission. In relation to known events, like the increase in family allowances towards the end of 1968, they are puzzling. However, official data for this period about the unemployed generally, the sick, disabled, elderly, fatherless families and households with men who are in paid employment but do not have dependent children, remain to be produced. Measures of poverty independent of conventional government definitions of need, as implied by SBC scales, also remain to be developed.

1. Discussed in full in Townsend, P., 'Politics and the Statistics of Poverty', *Political Quarterly*, January–March 1972.

Nutrition

One supplementary indicator of trends in poverty and inequality in living standards is that provided by nutritional data. The war certainly transformed national food habits. For example, between the mid 1930s and the end of the war the consumption per head of milk increased by a third. There were sharp increases in the consumption of milk solids, potatoes, other vegetables and wheat flour, balanced by decreases in the consumption of meat, fruit and fish.[1] Pre-war studies had called attention to widespread malnutrition. Wartime studies showed a marked improvement brought about by a national food policy of which rationing formed a significant part. 'The variation in diet between various social groups had been much reduced, and the diet of nearly all population groups was on average either very close to or above recommended nutrient requirements.'[2]

From the experience of war-time surveys, the National Food Survey was started on a national basis in 1950. Its results have shown that the narrowing of inequalities that took place in the war have been broadly maintained. But there has been surprisingly little further improvement during the 1950s and 1960s. In a careful review of the results of the food surveys between 1950 and 1960, Royston Lambert found little or no reduction in inequality. In some respects, there was cause for anxiety.

Though the intrinsic accuracy of the data may be questioned, the trends revealed by re-working the published evidence are clear enough: while the dietary levels of some groups, childless couples and Old Age Pensioners in particular, have improved since 1950, the most vulnerable groups have shown no overall improvement and in many respects are definitely worse off. In terms of an analysis by family size, there are now more segments of the population below the BMA standard and for more nutrients than in 1950. As far as numbers of the population are concerned, the indications are that at least a quarter and probably a third of the people of Britain live in households which fail to attain all the desirable levels of dietary intake. And, contrary to what is so often believed, the numbers in this situation seem to have increased since the mid fifties.[3]

A review by the Office of Health Economics registered four concerns. First, the recommended allowances for protein and calcium were not reached by sub-groups among the population, including households with a man and woman and three or more children, and households including adolescents and children. Secondly, 'the trend over time also demonstrates a slight decline in standards compared with the period of austerity in 1950'. Families with only one child had a lower nutrient intake of protein, calcium, and vitamin C than in 1950. Families with four or more children had a lower intake for protein, calcium and the vita-

1. Greaves, J. P., and Hollingsworth, D. F., in *World Review of Nutrition and Dietetics*, VI, 1966.

2. *Malnutrition in the 1960's?*, Office of Health Economics, London, 1967, p. 5.

3. Lambert, R., *Nutrition in Britain, 1950–60*, Codicote Press, Welwyn, 1964, p. 18.

mins thiamine, riboflavin and vitamin C.[1] Thirdly, results were presented in terms of the nutrients absorbed *on average* by sub-groups of the sample. Many families were bound to fall short of the average, including some in groups which *on average* minimally achieved an adequate diet. In seventeen years there had been little improvement in the National Food Survey 'in order to assess more realistically individual intake of nutrients' and collect better evidence 'on which to assess the nutritional status of the community'.[2]

Those in charge of the National Food Survey have always stressed its limitations. These arise not only in gaining good information about intakes from a sample of the population, but also in assessing adequacy. There is room for considerable disagreement about desirable intakes of nutrients, and the allowances which are recommended differ sharply in some instances from those recommended in other countries. Moreover, the National Food Survey Committee has now replaced the allowances recommended as adequate by the British Medical Association with a new set of allowances, a number of which represent a lower standard. While certain groups, such as those quoted above by the Office of Health Economics, are considered by the British Medical Association to have inadequate intakes of protein and calcium, they are now considered by the Department of Health and Social Security to have intakes which are (*on average*) perfectly adequate.[3]

While there may be disagreement over the point at which the line of nutritional adequacy may be drawn, inequalities in nutritional intakes for different groups can be shown reliably for lengthy periods. Table 4.25 compares certain low-income groups with certain high-income groups for 1956–68. Although there are some slight fluctuations from year to year, there seems to have been a very slight improvement in the intakes of the low-income families during the period, but not yet to the level recommended by the British Medical Association. But there has been very little narrowing of nutritional inequality during this period.

The possibility raised by Lambert and the Office of Health Economics that the intakes of some minority groups may have deteriorated remains unresolved. Certainly Department of Health panels have tended to produce reassuring reports about children and the elderly.[4] But the National Food Survey data have not been submitted to further analysis and presented like data on the distribution of personal incomes. One report of a survey in 1967–8 of pre-school children sug-

1. *Malnutrition in the 1960's ?*, pp. 8–11.
2. ibid., pp. 11–18 and 29.
3. Department of Health and Social Security, *Recommended Intakes of Nutrients for the United Kingdom*, Reports on Public Health and Medical Subjects, No. 120, HMSO, London, 1969; and *Household Food Consumption and Expenditure: 1967*, HMSO, London, 1969, Chapter 4.
4. For example, Department of Health and Social Security, *Interim Report on Vitamin D by the Panel on Child Nutrition*, and *First Report by the Panel on Nutrition of the Elderly*, Reports on Public Health and Medical Subjects, No. 123, HMSO, London, 1970.

Table 4.25. *Intakes of protein and calcium as a percentage of intakes recommended by the British Medical Association.*

| | High income Man and woman only | | Low income Man and woman and | | | | | |
| | | | 3 children | | 4 or more children | | children and adolescents | |
	pro-tein	cal-cium	pro-tein	cal-cium	pro-tein	cal-cium	pro-tein	cal-cium
1956	128	144	87	87	85	82	81	85
1957	127	141	87	88	80	79	79	85
1958	130	145	89	90	83	81	81	88
1959	133	151	90	93	78	77	79	86
1960	136	151	90	89	82	80	81	88
1961	138	155	90	92	87	86	83	90
1962	139	156	93	93	84	81	85	91
1963	138	153	95	94	87	83	84	87
1964	128	145	93	92	90	84	87	90
1965	136	152	95	91	86	80	82	86
1966	134	150	95	96	88	85	86	88
1967	136	147	97	97	91	89	85	89
1968[a]	(131)	(142)	(93)	(95)	(91)	(91)	(91)	(91)

NOTE: [a]A new standard of nutritional adequacy has been adopted by the DHSS and the figures given in brackets are estimates.

SOURCES: Annual Reports of the National Food Survey Committee.

gests that disturbing findings have not been fully published.[1] In a preface to the report of this survey (not published until 1975), the Chairman of the Committee on Medical Aspects of Food Policy, Sir George Godber, flatly stated, 'the results of the study produced no evidence that our pre-school children were underfed'. There were no satisfactory statistical data in the report showing variations in individual intakes according to income or occupational class. Yet a scatter diagram at the end of the report clearly showed that a very large number of children had *less than 80 per cent of the recommended daily energy intakes*.[2] The government's analyses of food survey data have remained unsatisfactory throughout the 1960s and early 1970s and could still be repeated.

1. Department of Health and Social Security, *A Nutrition Survey of Pre-School Children, 1967–68*, Report No. 10 on Health and Social Subjects, HMSO, London, 1975.
    2. ibid., p. 91.

Health

Indicators of health and disease in the population represent another important source of information about poverty and about trends in the distribution of living standards. Many different indicators might be devised. Among the most familiar are mortality rates, prevalence or incidence morbidity rates, sickness absence rates and restricted-activity rates.

One measure which has been commonly used as a guide to a nation's health is the infant mortality rate. Since the turn of the century, infant mortality has fallen from well over 150 per 1,000 live births to under 20. However, the relative disparity between the social classes did not change between 1911 and 1932,[1] and does not appear to have changed consistently between the 1930s and the 1960s. Thus, writing in 1959, Morris pointed out for England and Wales that there was 'no evidence of a narrowing of the gap between the social classes',[2] and despite the fact that the Registrar General has not published exactly comparable data for the 1960s, there are data for combinations of classes (I and II and IV and V) which do not suggest any marked change.[3] Moreover, after a narrowing of the gap between the classes in the experience of stillbirths and neo-natal deaths, compared with pre-war years, the data for Scotland suggest a reversion in the late 1960s to the same levels of inequality between social classes I and V as ruled in the late 1940s. It should be remembered that relativities in mortality rates between the classes tend to fluctuate from year to year and in the table, following conventions adopted in these matters by the Registrar General, I have given the means for periods of three years.

One other comment might be made about the trends in infant mortality over this period of three decades. Throughout, the gap between social classes I and V in their mortality experience has been wider after than during the early weeks of life.[4]

Reduction in infant mortality has been slower in Britain than in some other industrial societies. A recent review of trends between 1948 and 1968 for sixteen countries showed that England and Wales slipped from seventh to eleventh place in the ranking (Scotland fell even more sharply in ranking). Whereas the rate fell

1. Titmuss, R. M., *Birth, Poverty and Wealth: A Study of Infant Mortality*, Hamish Hamilton Medical Books, London, 1943, p. 26.
2. Morris, J. N., 'Health and Social Class', *Lancet*, 7 February 1959, p. 303.
3. Hart, J. T., 'Data on Occupational Mortality, 1959–63', *Lancet*, 22 January 1972, p. 192; Spicer, C. C., and Lipworth, L., *Regional and Social Factors in Infant Mortality*, G R O Studies on Medical and Population Subjects, No. 19, H M S O, London, 1966.
4. Titmuss noted this for the first third of the century. 'These statistics epitomize the chances of death of two infants; one born to well-to-do parents, the other to poor parents; both potential citizens of Britain. During the first few weeks of life, little separates the two children in their chances of death, but slowly at first and then with increasing effect, as week succeeds week, the gulf widens.' See Titmuss, *Birth, Poverty and Wealth*, pp. 45–6.

Table 4.26. *Number of stillbirths, neonatal and post-neonatal deaths per 1,000 live births in Scotland (1939–68).*

	Stillbirths			
	1939	1946–8	1956–8	1966–8
I	34·1	18·8	17·0	10·2
II	38·1	27·6	20·5	12·5
III	44·9	29·1	22·1	15·5
IV	38·3	32·6	26·5	15·7
V	42·7	38·5	28·8	20·0
Percentage excess of social class V over social class I	25	105	69	96
	Neonatal deaths (1st month of life)			
I	25·9	16·5	13·4	9·5
II	25·1	20·2	14·7	11·0
III	38·6	27·0	19·0	13·4
IV	34·8	29·8	20·2	15·2
V	39·9	36·5	22·8	19·5
Percentage excess of social class V over social class I	54	121	70	105
	Post neonatal deaths (2nd to 12th month of life incl.)			
I	7·6	8·1	4·0	3·1
II	14·8	12·8	5·5	3·9
III	30·2	21·4	8·2	6·7
IV	33·4	27·5	10·9	8·8
V	44·9	38·3	14·8	14·6
Percentage excess of social class V over social class I	491	373	270	371

SOURCE: Annual Reports of the Registrar General for Scotland, Part I: *Mortality Statistics.*

from 34·5 per 1,000 live births in 1948 to 18·3 in 1968, it fell from 55·9 to 17·0 in France, from 57·9 to 14·5 in Finland and from 61·7 to 15·3 in Japan. By 1968, the rate was below 14 per 1,000 in the Netherlands, Sweden and Norway.[1] In the

1. Doll, Professor Sir R., 'Monitoring the National Health Service', *Proceedings of the Royal Society of Medicine*, vol. 66, August 1973, p. 732; Scottish Home and Health Depart-

172 POVERTY IN THE UNITED KINGDOM

early 1960s, partly as a consequence of this kind of information, the Department of Health became concerned about the slow decrease in the death-rate for infants at ages between a month and a year old and undertook a study in three areas to try to identify avoidable factors contributing to death. Two paediatric assessors estimated that there were indeed avoidable factors in 28 per cent of cases – due to social, parental, general practitioner and hospital factors. The general practitioner factors included diagnostic delay or failure, slowness in reference to hospital, failure to realize severity of the situation and delay in visiting. The hospital service factors included diagnostic failures or delay, hospital-acquired infection and faulty management.[1]

There has been much less improvement in mortality rates during the course of this century at later ages. One source (the *United Nations Statistical Yearbook*) shows that while the expectation of life of males at birth in England and Wales lengthened by 2 or 3 per cent in the twenty years to 1970, it has lengthened more dramatically in other industrial nations, some of which have now surpassed, and others almost attained, the English figure. The ratio of female to male expectation of life in England and Wales has increased at all ages. The male expectation of life has increased to only a modest extent in their twenties and thirties, has barely increased at age 45, and has decreased marginally at older ages.[2]

The trends are different for people of different occupational class and need to be examined carefully. Later in this report, attention is called to the poor conditions of work in some occupations (Chapter 12). Among men aged 35–44, those in certain skilled or unskilled manual occupations have two, three or even four times as much risk of dying as men in certain non-manual occupations. But, in addition to specific occupational risks, there are general social risks which relate to occupational class and income.

Between 1949–53 and 1959–63 the risk of adult men of different social class dying appears, from data published by the Registrar General, to have become more unequal and, ten years later, there was little or no sign of any narrowing of the gap. Unfortunately the figures reproduced in Table 4.27 do not represent the real trends very accurately, because of changes introduced in 1960 in the classification of occupations, possible changes in the number and extent of discrepancies between the recording of occupations on death certificates and on census schedules, and the fact that occupations in the Census of 1961 were based on a 10

ment, Joint Working Party on the Integration of Medical Work, *Towards an Integrated Child Health Service*, H M S O, Edinburgh, 1973, p. 8.

1. D H S S, *Confidential Enquiry into Postneonatal Deaths, 1964–66*, Reports on Public Health and Medical Subjects, No. 125, London, H M S O, London, 1970, pp. 21–3.

2. D H S S, *Health and Personal Social Services Statistics for England* (with summary tables for Great Britain), H M S O, London, 1973, Table 1.6.

per cent sample. I have discussed these reservations elsewhere[1] and have argued that, because the Registrar General had already adjusted some figures to allow for changes in classification, it was possible for him to publish a revised, and more reliable, version of Table 4.27. Others had made the same plea.[2] I estimated

Table 4.27. *Standardized mortality ratios by social class: men aged 20–64 (1921–72).*

Social class	England and Wales				
	1921–3	*1930–32*	*1949–53*	*1959–63*[a]	*1970–72*[ab]
I	82	90	86	76	77
II	94	94	92	81	81
III	95	97	101	100	104
IV	101	102	104	103	113
V	125	111	118	143	137

[a]Men aged 15–64.
[b]Provisional data.

NOTES:
1. Information about occupations in the 1961 census, with which information from death certificates for 1959–63 was compared, was based on a 10 per cent sample.
2. Occupations in 1961 and 1971 were reclassified on a new basis, with the result that approximately 26 per cent would have been allocated to a different class if the 1950 basis of classification had been used. The vast majority of these were reclassified to the next ascending or descending class in rank order.
3. The standardized mortality ratios in the third column for 1949–53 have been corrected by the Registrar General and are different from the figures first published.

SOURCE: Table published in *Social Trends*, No. 6, HMSO, London, 1975, p. 26, and based on (a) 1921–30 Registrar General's Decennial Supplements, Occupational Mortality, 1951 and 1961, and (b) 1970–72 Office of Population Censuses and Surveys.

from the Registrar General's adjustments for different age-groups in social class V that, according to the 1950 classification, the figure of 143 for social class V in the fourth column of the table should read 128.[3] On both original and adjusted figures therefore there is evidence of *greater* inequality between adult men of different social class in risk of dying from 1959 onwards than earlier. Among men, inequality between social classes I and V is greater at ages 35–44 than at younger or older ages, while for married women it is greatest at ages 15–44 and for single women in the early twenties.[4]

1. Townsend, P., 'Inequality and the Health Service', *Lancet*, 15 June 1974.
2. Hart, 'Data on Occupational Mortality', p. 193.
3. Townsend, 'Inequality and the Health Service', p. 1182.
4. *Registrar General's Decennial Supplement, England and Wales 1961: Occupational Mortality Tables*, HMSO, London, 1971.

Like mortality rates, both sickness absence rates and measures of 'chronic' or 'limiting long-standing' illness show the disadvantage of the partly skilled and unskilled manual classes. Unusual care is needed in interpreting sickness absence rates. Certain studies have found high correlations between mortality and inception rates of sickness and between mortality and days of sickness.[1] Such findings are subject to reservations about particular types of diseases and causes of mortality. But although much work remains to be done to delineate the relationship between morbidity and class, different national[2] and overseas[3] studies show that the inequality between the highest and lowest classes is, in general, at least as wide according to various measures of morbidity as it is for measures of mortality. For example, in 1971 in England and Wales nearly two and a half times as many unskilled as professional men reported absence from work due to illness or injury during a two-week period, and they lost an average of four and a half times as many days from work in the year.[4]

There are other supplementary indicators of inequalities in state of health. A review of data from the National Child Development Study showed little if any change in social class differences between 1953 and the mid 1960s in the height of children. The actual figures from the two studies in fact show a slight widening of the gap, but this could be attributable to sampling variation and slight differences in method.[5]

Conclusion

Living standards depend on the total contribution of not one but several systems distributing resources directly and indirectly to individuals, families, work groups and communities. To concentrate on cash incomes is to ignore the subtle ways developed in both modern and traditional societies for conferring and redistributing benefits. Furthermore, to concentrate on income as the sole criterion of poverty carries the misleading implication that relatively simple adjustments, as, for example, through the introduction of a scheme for negative income tax, or tax credits, will relieve it.

A plural approach is unavoidable. Resources derive from a number of different

1. For example, mortality ratios are compared with inception ratios of sickness and duration ratios of sickness by Daw, R. H., *Journal of the Institute of Actuaries*, 1971.

2. See ibid., and reports of the General Household Survey, including a summary in *Social Trends*, No. 4, H M S O, London, 1973, Table 69.

3. Purola, T., Kalimo, E., Sievers, K., and Nyman, K., *The Utilization of the Medical Services and its Relationship to Morbidity, Health Resources and Social Factors*, Research Institute for Social Security, Helsinki, 1968.

4. Office of Population Censuses and Surveys, Social Survey Division, *The General Household Survey*, H M S O, London, 1973, p. 304.

5. Goldstein, H., *Human Biology*, vol. 43, 1971, p. 92; Douglas, J. W. B., and Simpson, H., *Milbank Memorial Fund Quarterly*, vol. 42, 1964, p. 20.

systems, each of which distribute and redistribute them according to a body of socially sanctioned and controlled principles. The problem is to establish the part that different types of resource play in determining the overall standards of living of different strata in the population. Five broad categories have been identified: cash income; capital assets; and the value of employment benefits, public social services and 'private' benefits in kind. The distribution of cash income was considered in relation to incomes policy and the earnings and occupational structure; and both cash income and assets in relation to taxation and fiscal welfare. Finally, supporting evidence about changes that have been taking place in the distribution of living standards – about poverty, nutrition and health – has also been included. Our means of combining quantitatively the different types of resource in order to gain some comprehension of overall inequalities in living standards is still negligible, and the combination of *some* types, as in the studies by the Central Statistical Office and the Royal Commission on the Distribution of Income and Wealth, remains primitive – as these bodies would be the first to agree.

Despite the range of statistical material which has been discussed, information on some other factors has not been included. Their importance is problematic and they cannot easily be documented. For example, the price of certain goods tends to vary for different areas and communities. The distributional structure of cash income, assets and fringe benefits could remain the same and yet inequalities in living standards could change. Whether there is any trend of a favourable or unfavourable kind among certain poor communities is unknown. However, there have been indicative studies of an illustrative kind. For an area of the United States, Caplovitz has shown the higher costs paid by the poor for some goods.[1] For Britain, Piachaud has discussed the same question.[2] Tipping has shown for the United Kingdom generally that, at the lowest levels of income, prices increased on average by 4·3 per cent more between 1955 and 1966 than they did at the highest levels of income – mainly because of a disproportionate rise in rents and fuel and light.[3] Between 1964 and 1970, Pond has estimated, the cost of living of the poorest household rose by 1·5 per cent more than that of the richest (and the differential actually grew between 1970 and 1974).[4] There may have been different effects on the cost of living in different areas of, for example, the abandonment of retail price maintenance and the development of chain stores. One fact about the differential impact of a rise in prices in the 1950s is, however, known. There were gains to low-income families from the maintenance of rationing and food subsidies for some years after the war. Food subsidies were worth

1. Caplovitz, D., *The Poor Pay More*, The Free Press, New York, 1963.
2. Piachaud, D., *Do the Poor Pay More?*, Child Poverty Action Group, London, 1974.
3. Tipping, D. G., 'Price Changes and Income Distribution', *Applied Statistics*, No. 1, 1970.
4. Pond, C., *The Low Pay Bulletin*, Nos. 1 and 5, Low Pay Unit, London, 1974 and 1976. As we have seen, there was a relative increase between the early 1950s and the early 1960s in the risk of death of adult males in social class V as compared with social class I.

more absolutely to families with children than to those without children and represented 27 per cent of the food expenditure of a family with four children, compared with 16 per cent for a married couple.[1]

Information is also needed on the changing value to different sections of the population and communities of services other than the public social services which are financed wholly or partly through taxation and local rates. This would cover public roads and transport, law and order, water, electricity and gas (such as the effects of changes from time to time in tariffs charged to different types of consumer) as well as a range of community facilities, such as libraries, playgrounds and public parks and gardens.

During the three decades under review, there was, first, a marked reduction of inequality in the distribution of resources during the war, in the sense that the proportions of the population with relatively high and relatively low resources both diminished. This structure was maintained in the years immediately following the war, but, secondly, there was a partial reversion to former inequalities in the mid and late 1950s. There was a relaxation of certain taxes for the rich, a property boom, abandonment of food subsidies and the expansion of occupational pension schemes and other fringe benefits, for example. Part of the problem of generalizing about changes in distribution over time is due to the changing structure of the population, occupationally as well as in age and family composition. Compared with the 'austerity' of the early 1950s there was some increase in poverty and a considerable growth, for example, in property incomes, by 1960. Finally, in the 1960s, there was higher unemployment, more dependency and a continuing shift of the reward system (and of the overall value of social services) to professional, managerial and higher supervisory non-manual groups, prompted not only by the unequivocal emphasis of successive governments upon economic growth, but also by professional unionization and the preoccupation of such organizations as the National Board for Prices and Incomes with productivity. The structure tended to be reinforced and there was a further slight increase in the numbers and proportion of the population in poverty or on the margins of poverty (as defined by the government), despite the introduction of new ameliorative measures by successive administrations. One indicator might, finally, be given. At 31 January 1961, for example, there were 1,844,000 recipients (not including dependants) of national assistance, or 3·6 per cent of the population, while ten years later, at the end of November 1971, there were 2,909,000 recipients, or 5·4 per cent.[2]

1. *Domestic Food Consumption, 1950*, HMSO, London, 1952, p. 73.
2. *Social Trends*, No. 5, HMSO, London, 1974, p. 121.

5
The Concept and Distribution of Resources

In measuring and explaining poverty in a society it is necessary first to describe the ownership and use made by individuals and by social groups of different types of resources which govern their standards of living. As already explained, we have identified five types: cash income; capital assets; value of employment benefits; value of public social services other than cash, and private income in kind. In this chapter these resources will be defined and their distribution described.

At the outset it should be recognized that there are risks in adopting the more elastic conception of resources preferred in this book. There are problems in measuring certain kinds of resources – particularly small amounts of income, gifts and occasional services received by only small numbers of the population. There are practical difficulties in collecting information of an exhaustive kind, and questions have to be pursued sometimes in rather general terms. We have tried to be watchful about those types of resources which might make a significant difference to the structure of inequality and the living standards of the poor in particular. We have also tried to be receptive to possible growing points and equally 'shrinking' points. The relative value of different types of resources will change over time.

The problem of relating, or weighing, the different types of resources is complicated and subtle. It seems reasonable enough to argue that an owner-occupier who has completed payments on his house has a higher standard of living than someone who is still buying his house or is paying rent, and that an imputed rental payment might be added to his income, or alternatively that housing costs should be deducted in measuring net income. But there are difficulties in deciding on what principles the weekly or monthly amount of that payment, or those costs, should be determined. There are also difficulties in treating other kinds of assets as representing income. Savings in the bank are regarded very differently by people from, say, a valuable painting of an ancestor or some engraved silverware received for a silver wedding anniversary. There are further difficulties in equating services with income, whether these are public social services paid for from taxation, or private services performed by relatives and friends. Someone

who has spent thirty expensive days and nights in a teaching hospital may have
had over £1,000 'spent' upon him, but he is not, in many senses of the term,
'better off' in the year than another man who has not had any need to enter hospital. A neighbour who helps an old woman with shopping and cleaning for an
hour each day can only with reservations be regarded as offering a service
equivalent to a paid home help or domestic servant. There is also the problem of
relating the investment value of a service to its current cash-income equivalent.
The benefits of a university education may be of some approximate current value
to a student and to his parents, but what also has to be remembered is the additional future value of such education.

These preliminary remarks indicate how hazardous is any attempt to develop a
comprehensive concept of resources. Similar difficulties have been encountered
by economists and sociologists when undertaking cost-benefit analyses and
lessons can be learned from the more absurd examples. The attempt to measure
inequality and compare material resources according to a unitary concept cannot
be carried too far. Inevitably certain limitations have to be placed on the possible
amalgamation of data. This chapter assumes that 'income' should be treated for
certain purposes as a much wider concept than it is, say, by the Board of Inland
Revenue or the Central Statistical Office, and even by critics advocating a far
more comprehensive and consistent approach, like Professor Kaldor.[1]

The Problem of the Recipient Unit

Resources are allocated to, and used by, countries, regions, communities, extended families, households, income units and individuals. It would be a mistake
to assume that all resources entering a household are pooled and used equally by
its individual members. An addition of, say, £10 per week may be made to total
household resources through the overtime earnings of the head of a household,
the part-time earnings of the housewife, or the apprenticeship earnings of an adolescent son, but these cannot be regarded as of comparable 'household' value.

1. The board's definition is criticized in a famous memorandum of dissent by a minority of
the Royal Commission on Taxation. 'In fact, no concept of income can be really equitable that
stops sh rt of the comprehensive definition which embraces all receipts which increase an individual's command over the use of society's scarce resources – in other words, his "net accre-
tion of economic power between two points in time."' See Report of the Royal Commission on
Taxation, Cmnd 9474, HMSO, London, 1955, p. 8. Kaldor has gone on to point out some of
the difficulties of widening the definition to include capital gains and other casual or non-
recurrent gains and receipts, at least in terms of measuring taxable capacity. For example, he
points out that 'it is not that capital gains *as such* provide less spending power than other forms
of profit; there are some kinds of capital gains which represent the same kind of spending
power as conventional income; other kinds which represent none at all; and yet others which
are in-between; these types moreover shade into one another gradually and imperceptibly.' See
Kaldor, N., *An Expenditure Tax*, Allen & Unwin, London, 1955, p. 45. See also his discussion
of the concept of income in economic theory in ibid., Appendix to Chapter 1.

The net increase in living standards enjoyed by each member of the household will differ, depending on who is the recipient of the additional income. Living standards vary among household members for all kinds of reasons. Historically the breadwinner was given precedence in the consumption of food, and this custom is maintained in many places. Children who have started work are often expected to get meals out, and to require relatively large sums for clothing and entertainment, including sums to meet the needs of courting before marriage. Younger dependent children have meals cheaply or freely at school and there are other public subsidies which are directed towards certain individuals rather than also to the households to which they belong. Then there are old people who sometimes comprise a semi-independent unit within the household.

To point up the implications of taking one definition of the unit which ultimately receives income rather than another, and to lay the basis for a study of the distribution and redistribution of income within the household, we have in this survey made it possible to consider resources as distributed among individuals, income units and households. The income unit is defined as any person aged 15 or over, or, if in full-time education, 19 or over, together with husband or wife and any children aged under 15 (or under 19 if in full-time education). Thus an adult living alone, a married couple, a married couple with children of school age or under, a grandparent living with married children, or a single adult living with another adult, such as a sister, will each comprise a separate income unit.

A household is defined as a single adult living alone or a group of people living together, having some or all meals together and benefiting from a common housekeeping. This is not always easy to apply, but has been found to be practicable for many purposes. Table 5.1 shows that rather less than three quarters of the households in the sample consisted of a single income unit and that only 8 per

Table 5.1. Percentages and numbers of households according to number of income units.

Number of income units	Households		Income units	
	%	No.	%	No.
1	71	1,453	51	1,453
2	20	417	29	834
3	6	132	14	397
4	2	33	5	132
5	0	9	2	45
6	0	1	0	6
Total	100	2,045	100	2,867

cent consisted of more than two income units. On the other hand, nearly half the income units in the sample shared a household with at least one other income unit.

Cash Income

Gross income is defined as all forms of current cash income, including earnings, self-employed income, casual income from work and second jobs, sick pay, holiday pay, pensions, annuities, social security payments, rent and interest from property, profit on lodgers, income from trusts, income from savings and stocks and shares, windfalls (but only that part used for living expenses), allowances from relatives, trade-union benefits, gifts of money, tax repayments, educational maintenance allowances and studentships. *Gross disposable income* is gross income less liability for income tax, surtax and national insurance contributions, and allowances elsewhere to relatives. *Net disposable income* is gross disposable income less expenses in going to work, including clothing or equipment allowed for tax purposes as well as costs of travel.

This definition is broader in certain respects than is the definition used in the Family Expenditure Survey, which excludes legacies, payments arising from insurance policies, winnings from gambling, occasional money gifts, profits from boarders and prizes from premium bonds – whether or not any of these items are used for everyday living expenses. We took the view that these items should be treated as income when it was clear that they would not be included in any current estimate of the value of assets. Information about income was obtained in depth. We endeavoured to establish income both in the previous week and the previous twelve months, and there seemed to be a distinct advantage in being able to ask income recipients systematically about the experience of the previous twelve months, beginning with employment. As will be shown later, the earnings of over two fifths of employees fluctuate, and by obtaining information about highest and lowest earnings, and then asking about 'average' earnings, it seemed that a more reliable indication of 'usual' earnings was obtained. Again, profit from lodgers or boarders was estimated less roughly than in some previous surveys.[1] Information was collected about services supplied to them, such as light, heating, laundry, cleaning and meals so that income net of expenses could be estimated.

Imputed Rent

There is one further important difference between the definition of gross income and that adopted in the analysis of the Family Expenditure Survey. In the latter

1. For example, in the survey by the Oxford University Institute of Statistics, 'People who let rooms to lodgers, without supplying food, were asked to give the total income received; and two-thirds of this was estimated to be profit'. See Lydall, H. F., *British Incomes and Savings*, Blackwell, Oxford, 1955, p. 17.

an imputed value is added to the income of heads of households living in owner-occupied dwellings. 'Although no money actually passes between the owner and the occupier of the dwelling when they are the same person, the services of the dwelling do nevertheless have value equivalent to the net income which could be obtained by letting the building commercially.'[1] But the amount used (as also for households living in rent-free accommodation) is the weekly equivalent of the rateable value, which for many of the dwellings concerned is an unrealistically low figure in relation to their potential rental value. For example, in 1970 the average weekly value was put for dwellings owned outright at £1·81, compared with average weekly outgoings of £2·66 for council tenants and £4·52 for tenants of furnished, privately owned accommodation. The weekly average even for owner-occupiers with an income of £3,000 or more was still only £3·12. The 1963 valuations of property were still being used. Total imputed rent was estimated in the Family Expenditure Survey for 1973 to be only 3 per cent of total household income from all sources, or only 6 per cent of the total income of owner-occupiers alone. In the present survey, we did not consider that rateable value reflected the real contemporary value of most owner-occupied housing and sought other means of estimating this value. The rateable or rental value of owner-occupied property, expressed as a weekly or monthly sum, and estimated either on the basis of local rateable values or local market prices, is excluded from the definition of gross income. But the value of the property is included in the valuation of assets and an equivalent 'annuity' value is included in the definition of *total* or *gross disposable resources*, which is discussed later.

One major criticism of the presentation by the Royal Commission on the Distribution of Income and Wealth of data on the distribution of incomes is that imputed rent of owner-occupation was excluded from income. Not surprisingly, the commission had received conflicting evidence about whether the benefit derived from owner-occupation should be expressed in money terms and counted with personal income. They took the view that it would be desirable in future to present alternative distributions, one including and one excluding imputed rents. They illustrated the effect of including the FES definition of imputed rent, but did not amend the artificially low estimates used in that survey or include an amended measure in the data discussed in the main body of the text. Owner-occupation is a major component of living standards, and its effect on the distribution of income is likely to have changed in recent years.[2]

1. See, for example, Department of Employment and Productivity, *Family Expenditure Survey*, Report for 1969, p. 109.
2. Royal Commission on the Distribution of Income and Wealth, Report No. 1, *Initial Report on the Standing Reference,* Cmnd 6171, H M S O, London, July 1975, pp. 7 and 40–43.

Distribution of Gross Income

Table 5.2 shows the distribution by income last week and last year of all house-holds in the sample for which information about income was complete. There are a number of factors which contribute to differences in the distribution. Earnings last week will be relatively high for some people and relatively low for others. For the employed population, earnings over the year will tend not to range so far as weekly earnings towards the extremes of the distribution, and for both the employed and non-employed the weekly average income for the previous twelve months will tend to be lower than the income for the previous week, because rates of earnings and, for example, of pensions have usually been increased during the year. Again, a fairly large proportion of people who work most weeks of the year will have been sick or unemployed or on holiday during any particular week and their incomes will be lower in that week than at other times.

Although some types of income which are paid in instalments less frequently than monthly or weekly, such as interest on savings and tax repayments, have been divided by fifty-two and added to weekly income (on grounds that they are regular additions or adjustments to income), once-and-for-all payments, like redundancy payments, grants by the Supplementary Benefits Commission of a lump sum, maternity grants and death grants have not been counted in weekly income but have been counted in annual income. Death grants are, of course, paid for persons no longer in the household. Maternity grants cover exceptional expenses which do not form part of ordinary living expenses. Lump-sum payments by the Supplementary Benefits Commission are generally made for bedding or clothing and are not often made in successive years.

However, it is important to remember that, as in all surveys of income, certain types of income could not be allocated to any specific period. This was partly because it was impractical to pursue inquiries beyond a certain point, but also because informants engaged in transactions which did not make it easy either for them or the interviewer to say exactly to what period some parts of their income applied. Thus, a high proportion of the self-employed told us that their incomes fluctuated during the year, but we could only attempt to obtain information about their annual income. To estimate their 'last week's' income, the figure for annual income was simply divided by fifty-two. Conventions such as these have tended to make the concept of last week's and last year's income less distinct than the amounts available to individuals are in reality. The extent to which income is both regular and secure is extremely important to the individual and to the household and will be discussed later.

Table 5.2 also shows the distribution according to income of the samples interviewed in the Family Expenditure Surveys of 1967 and 1968. The distributions are not exactly comparable with the poverty survey. The Family Expenditure Survey is based principally on the notion of 'usual' income which, for the sick and un-

Table 5.2. *Percentages of households with gross income per week* (*poverty survey and FES*).

Range of income	Poverty survey		FES current or usual rate p.w.	
	Last week	Average per week last year	1967	1968
Under £6	4·3	5·1	3·3	2·6
£6 but under £8	7·4	7·6	4·4	5·2
£8 but under £10	5·3	4·7	4·2	3·8
£10 but under £15	9·2	9·5	9·6	9·3
£15 but under £20	10·0	12·4	12·1	10·2
£20 but under £25	12·7	9·4	15·6	13·4
£25 but under £30	13·3	17·2	13·6	13·4
£30 but under £35	10·0	9·6	11·1	11·3
£35 but under £40	7·9	6·8	7·8	8·8
£40 but under £50	9·5	8·8	9·5	10·7
£50 or more	10·5	8·8	8·8	11·3
Total	100	100	100	100
Number	1,808	1,769	7,386	7,184

SOURCE: Department of Employment and Productivity, Family Expenditure Survey, Report for 1967, p. 86; Report for 1968, p. 82. FES figures include weekly rateable value of owner-occupied housing as an addition to income.

employed, includes latest earnings. In the poverty survey, the twelve months to which information about income refers start in early 1967 for some informants and early 1968 for others, and weekly income covers the period 1968–9. The definition of weekly income in the Family Expenditure Survey does not include certain forms of income, like windfalls, gifts of money and legacies, but does include an addition to income for imputed rent for owner-occupiers. The inclusion of the latter had the effect in 1968 of raising the income of a proportion of low-income households by an average of about £1·20 per week.[1] It will also tend to have increased the proportions in middle- and high-income groups, relative to the poverty survey. Another important point in comparing the figures is that the number of people aged 65 and over in the Family Expenditure Survey sample is about 14 per cent smaller than it should be if the sample were exactly representative of the population, while the number in the poverty survey was less than 1 per

1. In the 1968 survey, as many as 241 of the 836 households with under £10 weekly income owned their houses outright or (a tiny majority of them) were in the process of purchasing their houses. Many of these were retired people. See the Department of Employment and Productivity, Family Expenditure Survey, Report for 1968, HMSO, London, 1969, pp. 18 and 82.

cent short of the representative figure. The number of households with children in the Family Expenditure Survey sample was correspondingly 10 per cent too large. Despite the qualifications which I have expressed, the percentages of net income estimated by the Central Statistical Office (on the FES basis) to have been received in 1968 by different quantile groups of households corresponded closely with percentages produced from the poverty survey. (For detail, see Appendix Eight, Table A.1, p. 991.)

With other kinds of qualifications the data may also be compared with the Inland Revenue statistics. Table 5.3 compares the distribution by range of gross and net annual income of income units in the sample with personal incomes after tax as assessed by the Board of Inland Revenue.[1] The board counts a married couple, whether separately assessed for tax or not, as one 'person', though it admits there is a deficiency in the number of wives with earned incomes reported by their husbands' income tax districts. Corrections are made to the data to take account of this deficiency, but not for wives earning less than the deduction card limit (£5·25 in 1968–9). There are some other well-known problems about the data. For example, people who have died will have been counted for the whole year though their income was received during only part of the year; women who have married during the year will appear twice in the statistics; and children and adults with small covenants may appear as separate units. Certain kinds of income which are not taxed, such as disablement pensions, unemployment and sickness insurance benefits and some windfall income, are not included in the Inland Revenue data, but are included in the definition of income in the poverty survey. Mortgage interest and certain allowable expenses have also been deducted from the Inland Revenue figures for incomes. These differences make comparison hazardous. The Board of Inland Revenue does not provide an estimate of the number of incomes up to £275, and a figure equivalent to that found in the poverty survey has been used in order to allow other figures in the Inland Revenue distribution to be compared.[2] But the Inland Revenue totals at the next to lowest range of income are too low also because of the well-known shortfall in number of long-term sickness and unemployment beneficiaries, as well as of retirement pensioners.[3] At the highest levels of income, the fact that allowable expenses, as

1. For 1968–9, the board's income survey was based on a stratified sample of some 120,000 out of 22,130,000 incomes.

2. The estimate compares well with the estimates included in the National Income Blue Book about personal income. Thus, for 1967, the government estimates that there were 2,338,000 units with £50 income but under £250. The poverty survey suggests a figure of rather less than 3 million units with under £275 income. Estimates for the late 1960s were not included in the Blue Book. See *National Income and Expenditure 1969*, HMSO, London, 1969, Table 23.

3. The Blue Book totals for personal incomes in these ranges are substantially greater than the Inland Revenue totals. Thus, for 1967, an estimated 5,906,000 units are in the range £250–£500, compared with 3,760,000 in the range £275–£500 for 1967–8 in the corresponding Inland Revenue tables in ibid., Table 23.

well as mortgage interest, have been deducted from the Inland Revenue figures helps to explain why there were more units found in the poverty survey to have high incomes, though the tendency for different individuals in rich income units to be shown separately in the Inland Revenue tables should also be remembered.[1] Perhaps all that can safely be concluded from Table 5.3 is that the spread of incomes in the poverty survey was wide and that there was representation of the uppermost incomes.

Table 5.3. Percentages of income units with gross and net or 'after tax' income per year (poverty survey and Inland Revenue).

Range of income	Poverty survey		Inland Revenue	
	Gross	Net	1967–8 Net	1968–9 Net
Under £275	13·2	11·2	11·2[a]	11·2[a]
275—	2·0	2·4	1·3	1·2
300—	8·4	10·3	6·0	5·5
400—	7·5	8·5	8·1	7·3
500—	5·8	7·2	7·3	7·0
600—	4·4	6·8	7·8	7·2
700—	4·8	5·9	7·4	7·4
800—	5·3	6·7	7·4	6·7
900—	5·5	6·5	7·1	6·6
1,000—	12·3	12·7	15·4	15·5
1,250—	10·8	8·8	10·6	11·6
1,500—	11·7	7·7	7·1	8·9
2,000—	5·9	3·7	2·2	2·7
3,000—	1·0	1·0	0·9	1·0
5,000—	0·6	0·2		
10,000—	0·5	0·4	0·3	0·3
20,000—	0·3	0·1		
Total	100	100	100	100
Number	2,536	2,536	24,550,000	24,990,000

NOTE: [a]Numbers not known, and therefore the number equivalent in proportion to that found in the poverty survey has been estimated.

SOURCE: For Inland Revenue data: *Inland Revenue Statistics, 1971*, HMSO, London, Table 57.

1. Titmuss, R. M., *Income Distribution and Social Change*, Allen & Unwin, London, pp. 50–53.

The Make-up of Household Income

Household income is, of course, made up of the combined income of income units, if there are two or more, in the household. And the income of income units is itself made up of the combined income of individuals comprising the unit. Any

Table 5.4. Percentages of individuals, according to net disposable income for previous week of individuals, income units and households.

Net disposable income last week	Individual income			Income unit income			Household income		
	Male	Female	All	Male	Female	All	Male	Female	All
Under £5	36	65	51	3	6	5	1	1	1
£5 but under £10	11	23	17	11	18	15	5	10	8
£10 but under £12·50	8	5	7	7	8	7	4	5	4
£12·50 but under £15	10	3	6	9	7	8	5	5	5
£15 but under £17·50	10	1	5	12	10	11	9	8	8
£17·50 but under £20	8	1	4	10	9	9	8	8	8
£20 but under £22·50	5	1	3	10	9	9	9	10	9
£22·50 but under £25	4	0	2	8	8	8	9	8	8
£25 but under £27·50	2	0	1	7	7	7	8	8	8
£27·50 but under £30	2	0	1	6	5	5	8	7	7
£30 but under £35	2	0	1	6	5	6	12	10	11
£35 but under £40	1	0	0	3	3	3	6	6	6
£40 but under £50	1	0	0	3	3	3	9	8	8
£50 and over	1	0	1	4	3	3	7	5	6
Total	100	100	100	100	100	100	100	100	100
Number	2,725	2,994	5,719	2,637	2,830	5,467	2,569	2,720	5,289

theory about distribution must take account of such allocation. Many individuals, chiefly dependent children and housewives, have no income, or very little, of their own, but they live with others who do have a regular income. Table 5.4 brings out the fact that income is more dispersed for individuals than for income units, and for income units than households. The range is still enormous, even when income net of tax and work expenses is considered. The fact that fewer women than men have any individual income, and have smaller incomes even when they do have any, is also striking. As we shall see, this is true not only of those in employment and of housewives, but also of disabled and elderly women.

Table 5.5 shows the distribution of annual net disposable income for the different age-groups. Again the differences in distribution between men and women, even among the elderly, should be noted. The highest proportion of men with middle and high incomes are those in their thirties. There is a marked reduction among those in their late fifties and early sixties, and an even more marked reduction among older men. Correspondingly, the proportion with low incomes increases quite significantly among those in late middle age, and very steeply after the age of 65. Among women, more of those in their thirties than either in their twenties or forties have little or no income – explained principally by the fact that a very high proportion have two or more dependent children. In recent years, there has been a steady increase in the proportion of married women taking up employment again in their forties and fifties. The difference in income distribution between people aged 65–74 and those aged 75 and over is also fairly marked. This reflects an important difference between people of the third and fourth surviving generations.

We have seen how total household incomes come to be built up with different 'blocks' of individual incomes and those of income units. Individual incomes, and the household incomes to which they contribute, are, of course, themselves made up of different elements. The most common and substantial elements are wages and salaries, which account for 76 per cent of annual gross disposable income (less income from windfalls); but, for large numbers of households, retirement pensions and other state benefits are the major form of income. Altogether they account for a total of 10 per cent of gross disposable income and for two thirds of the income available to women aged 60 and over living alone. The differences between types of households, and the contribution of incomes from self-employment, investment, property, sub-letting and other sources is shown in Table A.2 in Appendix Eight (page 992). Despite some differences in definition and method, this table also shows that the poverty survey and the Family Expenditure Survey correspond closely in the proportions of aggregate household income drawn from different sources. The proportion for wages and salaries is slightly lower and the proportion for state benefits other than retirement and widows' pensions slightly higher in the poverty survey than in the Family Expenditure Survey. However, this is attributable at least in part to differences of

Table 5.5. Percentages of individuals of different age, according to individual net disposable income in previous year.

Individual net disposable income last year	Males aged							Females aged						
	0-19	20-29	30-39	40-54	55-64	65-74	75+	0-19	20-29	30-39	40-54	55-64	65-74	75+
Under £300	92	5	2	3	4	31	48	93	54	68	59	66	65	58
£300-	5	10	1	2	7	31	33	5	19	13	20	20	28	37
£500-	2	20	11	16	23	19	10	1	21	10	11	8	5	2
£700-	1	39	41	37	39	9	6	0	5	6	5	2	3	1
£1,000-	0	22	30	25	17	6	1	0	1	2	3	2	0	0
£1,400-	0	2	8	9	7	1	1	0	0	1	2	1	0	1
£2,000+	0	2	7	7	3	1	0	0	0	1	1	0	0	1
Total	100	100	100	100	100	100	100	100	100	100	100	100	100	100
Number	975	363	340	441	302	191	69	917	396	350	551	333	263	165

method. In the Family Expenditure Survey, 'normal' earnings are counted instead of social security benefits if the latter have been received for less than thirteen weeks. Income from other sources is also slightly higher in the poverty survey. This may be partly due to the fact that 'income from other sources' included a few additional sources of income, such as money gifts and profits from boarders.

Table 5.6 lists the different sources of income on which information was obtained for the previous twelve months, and the proportions of households and individuals receiving income from those sources. The relative aggregate importance of such income is also conveyed. One per cent of households represent about 185,000 households, and 0·1 per cent about 18,500 households. One per cent of individuals represent 554,000 persons, and 0·1 per cent represent 54,400. It was not always possible to obtain the amounts of single payments that had been made in the preceding twelve months during the interviews, particularly for households which were large and had experienced a number of changes in composition and source and rate of income.

Income from self-employment is difficult to establish in surveys. The self-employed are defined as including both persons not employed by any persons or company, and persons working in their own home for an employer (out-workers). Included are proprietors of businesses (including members of partnerships), all parochial clergy, and medical practitioners who are principals in the National Health Service and in private practice. Many of the self-employed say their income fluctuates during a year, but because business expenses and income are not recorded in terms of a weekly or monthly cycle, it is difficult to get information except for a complete financial year. Sometimes that year may have ended some considerable time before the date of a particular interview. Thus people interviewed in September 1968 may only offer information about the financial year April 1967 to April 1968. All income and expenditure surveys suffer from these limitations, and all have to adopt alternative methods of seeking the same information – that is, gross annual income for the latest available year after deducting depreciation allowances and business expenses and net annual income after deducting tax and insurance contributions.[1]

The incomes of the self-employed have not been adjusted for the time-lag, and it should be remembered that, on average, their incomes should strictly be raised by a few per cent for comparison with the incomes of the employed. Even so, Table 5.7 makes clear that their incomes are much more widely dispersed than those of the employed. There are significantly more with relatively low, and relatively high, incomes, and this fact applies to women as much as men. They range from a tinker or pedlar earning a few pounds a week to a doctor in private prac-

1. See pages 1120–21 for the alternative methods of questioning the self-employed. The methods were based on those used in the FES. See also Kemsley, W. F. F., *Family Expenditure Survey: Handbook on the Sample, Fieldwork and Coding Procedures*, HMSO, London, 1969, p. 115.

Table 5.6. *Gross disposable income for previous year, by source and amount (including windfalls).*

Types of income	Percentage of households having income	Percentage of individuals having income	Aggregate amount of such income (unadjusted) £	Aggregate amount as percentage of total income of entire sample
1. Wages (weekly paid)	61·5	34·3	1,063,692	47·2
2. Salaries (monthly paid)	22·4	9·2	429,466	19·1
3. Repayment of tax	19·4	7·6	7,048	0·3
4. Holiday pay	67·9	35·9	84,635	3·8
5. Sick pay	21·0	8·4	15,277	0·7
6. Self-employment income	7·9	3·2	155,867	6·9
7. Casual earnings and second job	6·6	2·4	17,058	0·8
8. Retirement pensions	24·4	11·9	128,116	5·7
9. Family allowances	25·6	8·8	23,811	1·1
10. Widow's pension	6·5	2·2	26,070	1·2
11. Sickness benefit	19·2	7·4	24,855	1·1
12. Unemployment benefit	5·4	2·1	9,383	0·4
13. Supplementary benefit	14·9	5·3	31,916	1·4
14. Industrial injury benefit	1·6	0·6	2,436	0·1
15. Industrial disablement pension	0·6	0·2	1,687	0·1
16. War disablement pension	1·1	0·4	3,428	0·2
17. Maternity allowance	1·5	0·5	1,534	0·1
18. Maternity grant	3·6	1·2	1,406	0·1
19. Death grant	0·8	0·3	324	0·0
20. Redundancy payment (DEP)	0·5	0·2	1,212	0·1
21. Single grant (social security)	0·8	0·3	78	0·0
22. Other (social security)	0·6	0·2	1,311	0·1
23. Pension from employer	8·8	3·1	49,104	2·2
24. Annuities	2·8	1·1	8,325	0·4
25. Gratuities	1·6	0·5	7,495	0·3
26. Trust or covenant	0·9	0·4	6,666	0·3
27. Court order	1·2	0·4	2,000	0·1
28. Allowance from relatives (armed forces)	0·8	0·2	3,304	0·1
29. Other allowances from husbands	0·3	0·1	1,041	0·0
30. Regular cash, relatives or friends	1·1	0·3	1,888	0·1
31. Money gifts	2·6	1·1	15,314	0·7
32. Trade-union benefit	2·0	0·7	2,050	0·1
33. Friendly society	0·7	0·3	326	0·0
34. Other benefits	1·7	0·7	4,957	0·2
35. Income from property	5·0	1·9	14,824	0·7
36. Profit on lodgers/boarders	0·6	0·2	583	0·0
37. Profit on letting garage	0·7	0·3	232	0·0
38. Interest received on savings	56·1	32·3	33,839	1·5
39. Interest and dividends stocks and shares	7·4	3·2	34,281	1·5
40. Awards by LEAs	1·9	0·8	9,413	0·4
41. Educational maintenance allowance	0·1	0·1	74	0·0
42. Windfalls	5·8	2·2	25,799	1·1
ALL TYPES OF INCOME	100	100	2,253,136	100

NOTE: £1,652 out of £54,374 falling under headings 26–36 inclusive could not be allocated to a specific heading and has been allocated in the same proportion as the remainder.

tice earning £15,000. It is difficult to judge the reliability of income information provided by the self-employed. We could show we were not from the tax office. On the other hand, some information on profits was as declared for tax purposes, and the reliability of that information has been questioned.[1]

Table 5.7. *Percentages of employed and self-employed, according to individual net disposable income in previous year.*

Individual net dispos-able income last year	Men		Women	
	Employed	Self-employed	Employed	Self-employed
Under £300	4	8	34	40
£300 —	8	9	34	24
£500 —	18	9	20	13
£700 —	38	24	7	9
£1,000 —	22	24	3	7
£1,400 —	6	7	1	7
£2,000 —	4	17	0	0
Total	100	100	100	100
Number	1,434	126	959	55

Can the incomes recorded in the survey be aggregated to match aggregate incomes as estimated nationally by the government? Reference has been made above in some detail to the results of the Family Expenditure Survey, and also briefly to the data reported annually by the Board of Inland Revenue. The sample data can also be grossed up and compared with aggregate figures for certain types of income published in the national income Blue Books (and also in the annual reports of the Department of Health and Social Security). With a slight adjustment for a difference in household definition, the Central Statistical Office figure of about 18½ million households in the United Kingdom has been used for purposes of estimating national totals. Table 5.8 gives some of the results. Certain reservations must be made. A number of deductions have to be made from the figures given in the Blue Books by the Central Statistical Office for the total of personal disposable income, to arrive at a figure which would be comparable with one derived from the poverty survey. Thus, the 'rent' of owner-occupied dwellings, income in kind from employers and national insurance contributions by employers can be deducted. But the resulting figure is still too high. It includes some 'in-

1. As, for example, in the evidence submitted to the Royal Commission on the Distribution of Income and Wealth by the Association of Her Majesty's Inspectors of Taxes in 1975.

Table 5.8. *Estimates of total UK personal income (poverty survey and government sources).*

Type of income	Poverty survey £m	Government estimates	
		1967 £m	1968 £m
Personal disposable income[a]	–	27,559	29,304
Personal disposable income[b]	23,880	24,265	25,766
Wages and salaries	17,363	(17,295)	(18,104)
Self-employment income	1,660	(1,724)	(1,802)
Rent, dividend interest	1,200	(1,915)	(2,003)
Employers' pensions	690	(500)	(600)
Family allowances	250	161	270
Retirement and widows' pensions	1,648	1,426	1,623
Sickness benefit	300[c]	304	348
Unemployment benefit	120[c]	127	134
War disability pensions	40	106	115
Maternity benefits	30	35	39
Industrial injury benefit	60[c]	88	96
Other national insurance benefits	16	16	19
Supplementary benefits	390[c]	385	404
Redundancy payments	13	48	61
Scholarships and maintenance allowances	100	135	148
Income tax (excluding dividends deducted at source)	4,400[d]	3,545	3,938
Employees' national insurance contributions		861	973

NOTES: The help of the Central Statistical Office was sought in compiling this table, but the CSO cannot be held responsible for the adjustments made (see also the Annex to this chapter). Personal disposable income:

[a]As defined *National Income and Expenditure 1970*, p. 24.

[b]Excluding income in kind, rent of owner-occupied dwellings, an estimate for depreciation for self-employment income, social security benefits of inmates of institutions, an estimate of pay of armed forces overseas and in non-private households, employers' contributions to occupational pensions and grants to universities and other non-profit-making bodies. The items listed comprise the total under [b], but estimates in brackets are necessarily rough and sometimes involve apportionment, e.g. taxes and contributions, between categories.

[c]Short-term benefits adjusted for information about weeks of benefit in year.

[d]Adjusted for estimate of taxes on dividends, etc., at source.

SOURCES: *National Income and Expenditure, 1970*, HMSO, London, 1970, Tables 19 and 24, Tables 37 and 40 (family allowances, supplementary benefits, war pensioners, and all national insurance benefits and other grants) and Table 47 (for breakdown of income tax and national insurance contributions).

come' represented by depreciation allowances and professional and business expenses. It includes lump-sum payments under life assurance and superannuation schemes, some of which have been, and continue to be, regarded by the recipients as 'savings', rather than as additions to income, and others of which, paid to bury the dead, are not regarded by the survivors in the household or income unit as part of their disposable income. Information on such sums is difficult to obtain in household surveys and seems not to have been obtained in full in the poverty survey (like the FES). Within the figure of income of life assurance and superannuation funds, which is counted as personal income by the Central Statistical Office, the income of private non-profit-making bodies and private trusts cannot be separated from the income of households.[1] A number of adjustments have been made to the government estimates in Table 5.8. These are explained and set out in the Annex to this chapter (pages 234–6). The aggregate figure for wages and salaries implied by the poverty survey is a little low in comparison with Blue Book estimates. The figure for self-employment income is too low, but is partly explained by the 'drift' in financial years for which information normally exists. The Blue Book estimates include an adjustment (addition to tax reserves). The figure for income from rents, dividends and interest is also low. Although it is difficult to specify the components in the national income accounts, so that precise comparisons might be drawn, the estimate in the poverty survey is probably low because, as in other such surveys, information about dividends is difficult to obtain accurately from some prosperous, particularly elderly, households. With the exception of war disablement pensions and industrial disablement benefits (which may sometimes have been incorrectly coded in interviews as retirement pensions, since the aggregate of the latter is slightly higher than expected) social security benefits of different kinds correspond with the totals expected from government data about expenditure. For example, the figures derived for family allowances, sickness benefits, unemployment benefits and supplementary benefit are close to the expected totals.

Cash Incomes of Different Types of Household

The distribution of gross income varies widely according to household composition, but also within any single type of household. Table 5.9 helps to show how the overall distribution is made up. In this table, as in other tables on household composition in this book, the numbers upon which percentages are based are unfortunately small in certain categories. We have chosen to present the full range of household types rather than a selection, partly to show the context within which certain data are set but also to indicate the kind of distribution which future surveys may set out to confirm. Percentages based on numbers under fifty

1. Maurice, R., *National Accounts Statistics: Sources and Methods,* Central Statistical Office, HMSO, London, 1968, p. 115.

Table 5.9. Percentages of households of different type with gross income for previous week.

Range of income	Man over 60	Man under 60	Woman over 60	Woman under 60	Man and woman No others	No. children 1	No. children 2	No. children 3	No. children 4+	3 adults No others	3 adults with children	4 adults	Others without children	Others with children	All	M&W FES (1968) No others	M&W FES 1 child	M&W FES 2 children	3 adults FES (1968) No others	3 adults FES Children
Under £6	(24)	3	30	5	1	0	1	0	(0)	0	0	0	1	0	4	0	0	0	0	0
£6 but under £10	(47)	3	58	28	15	1	1	0	(0)	2	0	0	6	2	13	8	0	0	1	0
£10 but under £12	(8)	0	5	9	8	0	1	1	(4)	2	0	0	3	5	4					
£12 but under £14	(3)	12	1	9	5	1	2	0	(4)	3	1	1	12	5	4					
£14 but under £16	(5)	12	2	12	4	3	6	2	(0)	2	2	0	5	6	4	31	15	11	7	2
£16 but under £18	(0)	12	1	14	3	6	5	7	(2)	2	3	0	9	0	3					
£18 but under £20	(3)	11	1	0	6	9	5	7	(2)	4	4	0	9	2	3					
£20 but under £22	(5)	11	0	3	5	9	8	11	(17)	3	2	0	3	1	5	28	43	42	21	23
£22 but under £24	(0)	13	0	2	6	9	8	9	(10)	4	7	5	3	3	5					
£24 but under £26	(0)	5	0	5	5	9	13	9	(12)	5	7	0	1	2	5					
£26 but under £28	(0)	3	0	5	4	13	6	6	(2)	5	5	5	5	1	5					
£28 but under £30	(0)	0	1	0	6	7	6	6	(6)	8	9	1	1	3	5					
£30 but under £35	(3)	3	1	3	10	14	11	16	(17)	12	15	11	8	9	10	11	17	17	13	16
£35 but under £40	(0)	5	0	0	9	5	11	5	(2)	16	11	11	3	11	8	8	10	12	16	14
£40 but under £50	(3)	2	1	2	7	7	7	15	(6)	16	22	25	5	21	9	9	8	10	21	24
£50 or more	(0)	5	0	2	5	6	7	10	(15)	17	17	41	32	28	10	6	6	8	21	21
Total	100	100	100	100	100	100	100	100	100	100	100	100	100	100	100	100	100	100	100	100
Number	38	61	190	57	483	137	174	81	48	190	130	65	66	87	1,807	1,936	741	818	674	483

NOTE: As in other tables, any percentages on a base of under 50 have been printed in brackets. The FES definition of gross income includes imputed income of owner-occupiers, and for purposes of strict comparison with the data produced by the poverty survey, the figures reproduced here will be smaller at the higher ranges of income and larger at the lower ranges.

are placed in brackets. There are a number of features of the table which should be noted. Incomes of small households do, of course, tend to bunch at the lower ranges, and of large households, particularly those with three or four adults and those generally without children, at the higher ranges. But the range is wide, especially among households consisting of a man and woman and of three adults. The most homogeneous types of household, so far as income is concerned, are households consisting of single persons or married couples of pensionable age. As the table shows, there is a big difference between the under and over 60s living alone. For selected types of households, which bulk large in the total, the data from the Family Expenditure Survey are also shown in Table 5.9. Because of differences in definition and in methods of inquiry, relatively more households in the poverty survey than in the Family Expenditure Survey, as reported above, were found to be at the lower ranges of income. The proportions of households found to be at the highest ranges of income are broadly similar, but, because the FES definition of gross income includes the imputed rental value of owner-occupied premises, the FES figures in the higher ranges would need to be reduced for purposes of strict comparison.

The mean gross disposable household income of different types of household is shown in Table 5.10, together with mean gross income. The substantial propor-

Table 5.10. *Mean gross and gross disposable household income for previous week of different types of household (£).*

Type of household	Gross income last week[a]	Gross disposable income last week[a]	Number of households
Man over 60	10·4	9·3	38
Man under 60	22·8	18·1	61
Woman over 60	8·0	7·8	190
Woman under 60	18·5	11·8	57
Man and woman	24·8	20·7	483
Man and woman, 1 child	32·3	24·6	137
2 children	30·5	25·6	174
3 children	32·7	27·6	81
4 or more children	40·5	35·8	48
3 adults	38·0	30·5	190
3 adults, plus children	39·8	33·3	130
4 adults	46·5	38·5	65
Others without children	39·6	33·7	66
Others with children	40·1	34·0	87
All	£28·9	£23·9	1,807

NOTE: [a]Adjusted for slight oversampling in Northern Ireland.

tion of income paid in tax and national insurance contributions by single person and two-person households other than the retired is evident.[1] The corresponding distribution for income last year is given in Table A.3 in Appendix Eight (page 993), together with figures drawn from the Family Expenditure Surveys for 1967–8. Despite differences in survey methodology and response, the FES mean incomes for 1968 are similar to those produced by the poverty survey. The only exception is the mean annual income of households with four or more children. In the poverty survey, the absolute number of these households was small, and by chance included three with very high incomes. In general, however, it would seem that although the poverty and family expenditure surveys produced remarkably similar *average* incomes for different households, the poverty survey seems to have included slightly more of those with relatively low and relatively high incomes.

The dispersion of income is very great for all major types of household, even after deductions for tax and work expenses. This is shown in detail in Table 5.11 in which a technique is adopted of giving the income of selected percentiles, measured from the top of the distribution.[2] Thus p 1 is the income immediately above 99 per cent of incomes found in households of each type, p 5 is the income immediately above 95 per cent of incomes, p 10 is the income immediately above 90 per cent of incomes, and so on. The median is p 50, and, as Table 5.11 shows, this is generally smaller than the mean, because of the skew distribution of incomes. If income is further expressed as a percentage of the median, then p 1, p 5, p 10 and p 20 indicate the relative dispersion of the upper tail of the distribution, and p 75, p 85 and p 95 indicate the relative dispersion of the lower tail.

The top incomes are in most instances at least twice, in some instances more than three times, as large as those of the fifth percentile. The top incomes are in most instances more than five times as large as the median incomes and more than ten times as large as the lowest incomes. Even if attention is confined to the fifth percentile, income at this level is still at least two or three times as large as the median in most instances. The table does not, of course, bring out inequalities in distribution *between* different types of household. Income for households of different size can be averaged, but this does not allow for the 'overheads' of each independent household, the 'economies' attributed to bigger households and the smaller claims upon income generally of children than of adults. The problem is discussed later in relation to measures of poverty. Here no elaborate measure is required because the existence of inequality can be demonstrated by extracting certain figures from Table 5.11 for comparison. For example, the mean income of men aged under 60 living as single householders is 32 per cent higher than that of women of the same age, and is 63 per cent of the mean income of households

1. Tax liability of income groups is shown in Table A.4, Appendix Eight, page 994.
2. This technique has been developed for employment and household incomes by Lydall, *The Structure of Earnings*, pp. 139–41 and *passim*.

Table 5.11. Net disposable income for previous year of different types of household at different percentiles of distribution.

Percentiles of net disposable household income last year	Man 60+	Man under 60	Woman 60+	Woman under 60	Man and woman	Man and woman				3 adults	3 adults and children	4 adults	Others without children	Others with children	All
						1 child	2 children	3 children	4+ children						
						£ per year									
p 1	1,374	3,917	2,775	3,510	10,300	5,186	6,151	3,479	13,537	10,436	8,641	3,010	11,314	3,895	13,537
p 5	1,208	1,642	823	1,107	1,994	2,034	2,516	2,707	9,403	2,805	3,485	2,764	3,430	3,384	2,598
p 10	1,037	1,177	542	973	1,695	1,795	2,028	2,197	2,893	2,379	2,628	2,662	2,913	3,056	2,092
p 20	642	935	443	863	1,450	1,446	1,619	1,666	1,672	1,993	2,070	2,330	2,427	2,254	1,675
p 50	399	767	338	612	963	1,135	1,128	1,225	1,042	1,450	1,564	1,951	1,142	1,674	1,076
p 75	308	603	286	416	620	944	943	971	918	1,159	1,203	1,564	784	1,190	668
p 85	286	567	259	374	505	806	846	925	770	947	1,102	1,259	644	780	459
p 95	252	351	230	271	398	730	695	808	604	666	848	1,076	448	476	308
Mean income	486	863	399	654	1,068	1,254	1,311	1,365	1,728	1,625	1,747	1,886	1,670	1,689	1,221
						Income as % of median									
p 1	344	511	821	574	1,070	457	545	284	1,299	720	552	154	990	242	1,259
p 5	303	214	243	181	207	179	223	221	903	193	223	142	300	202	242
p 10	260	153	160	159	176	158	180	179	278	164	168	136	255	183	195
p 20	161	122	131	141	151	127	143	136	160	137	132	119	213	135	156
p 50	100	100	100	100	100	100	100	100	100	100	100	100	100	100	100
p 75	77	79	85	68	64	83	84	79	80	80	77	80	69	71	62
p 85	72	74	77	61	52	71	75	76	74	65	70	65	56	47	43
p 95	63	46	68	44	41	64	62	66	58	46	54	55	39	28	29
Number	37	55	190	57	472	134	172	78	48	186	126	62	66	85	1,768

consisting of a man and woman and three children. Again, the mean income of households consisting of a man and woman and three children is smaller than of households consisting of three adults. Yet again, the incomes of half the households consisting of a man and woman are higher than a quarter of households comprising man and woman and one child, or two, three, four or more children.

An alternative method of showing inequalities in income distribution is to work out the proportion of incomes which are relatively high or relatively low. For each type of household, incomes are distributed according to whether they are high, middle or low in Table 5.12. In only one instance are there roughly as many high-income as low-income households. In general, about a fifth of house-

Table 5.12. Percentages of households of different type with relatively high, middle and low net disposable income for previous year.

Type of household	High (120% or more of mean for type)	Middle (80– 119% of mean)	Low (less than 80% of mean)	Total	Number
Man aged 60+	(19)	(19)	(62)	100	37
Man under 60	11	49	40	100	55
Woman aged 60+	13	47	40	100	190
Woman under 60	23	37	40	100	57
Man and woman	29	30	41	100	472
Man, woman, 1 child	17	51	32	100	134
2 children	20	43	37	100	171
3 children	20	42	37	100	78
4+ children	(11)	(15)	(74)	100	47
3 adults	21	42	37	100	186
3 adults, plus children	16	40	44	100	123
4 adults	25	52	23	100	61
Others without children	33	12	54	100	66
Others with children	29	37	34	100	84
All types[a]	22	38	40	100	1,761

NOTE: [a]The aggregation of incomes which are high, middle or low, according to type.

holds with high incomes are counter-balanced by about two fifths with low incomes, and, considering the smallish numbers in some sub-categories of the sample, the regularity of this phenomenon is surprising. The ratio between high and low incomes in fact indicates the length of the 'tail' of high incomes. The smaller the proportion of relatively high incomes the longer the tail.

The Distribution of Assets

More extensive information on assets was collected than in any previous survey. We agree with the recent Royal Commission that no single definition is 'ideal in all circumstances. The concept of personal wealth cannot be reduced to a single definitive statement.'[1] Our primary interest was in attempting to arrive at some measure of the effect upon living standards of the ownership of assets. There are at least four important effects. First, money assets can be realized or property sold to meet living expenses. Thus, some retired people with a low income draw savings regularly and substantially. Some men who are temporarily sick or otherwise out of work also draw upon their savings until they re-enter paid employment. Secondly, rents which are commonly paid for the use of some types of asset, such as for housing, or TV sets, or charges for the use of other assets as in fares for passenger transport, do not have to be paid because houses, TV sets and cars are owned, and the rental equivalent of these assets can be treated as an 'addition' to income. Thirdly, assets allow security to be offered to creditors and loans to be raised so that fluctuations in living standards caused by short-term changes in the flow of income can be smoothed out. Fourthly, assets allow people a wider security to take or accept risks in allocating income, to spread it over the life-cycle and to make promises to, or arouse expectations in, others so that immediate help or cooperation can be secured. Thus, a sense of obligation to an old lady because of the promise of being a beneficiary under her will may cause someone to give services far greater than may ordinarily be purchased by any income that they may be currently receiving.

An attempt has been made to produce estimates of the value of each of these. A broad distinction is drawn between 'readily' and 'less readily realizable assets'. This accords with the recently expressed view of the Royal Commission 'that different approaches to the definition of personal wealth hinge essentially on varying degrees of marketability of assets'.[2] Some assets, which are usually termed 'liquid' assets, have the common characteristic that their values are fixed in terms of money and they can be, and often are, cashed at short notice. *Readily realizable assets* are defined as deposits in savings and other banks, holdings of Savings Certificates, Defence Bonds and Premium Bonds, and shares and deposits in building societies and cooperative societies; value of stocks and shares (meaning all marketable securities whether issued by governments, municipalities, public boards or companies) and money owed (ignoring sums below £25). *Less readily realizable* assets are defined broadly to include the value of any business, farm or professional practice; owner-occupied houses and other houses, boats and caravans; cars and other saleable assets (including jewellery, silver and

1. Royal Commission on the Distribution of Income and Wealth, *Initial Report*, p. 9.
2. ibid., p. 10.

Table 5.13. Percentages of individuals, income units and households with assets.

	All assets			Amounts of assets and debts of households			
Amount	Indivi-duals	Income units	House-holds	Gross readily realiz-able assets	Money debts	Less readily realiz-able assets	Pro-perty debts
None (or in debt)	37·0	19·9	13·5	20·6	76·5	27·9	74·1
Less than £10	6·5	3·1	1·7	7·2	3·8	0·4	0·0
£10 but under £20	4·2	1·9	1·2	3·7	3·3	0·3	0·1
£20 but under £50	6·7	5·1	3·4	7·7	8·1	3·7	0·3
£50 but under £100	6·3	6·2	4·3	8·0	4·3	3·8	0·6
£100 but under £200	6·5	6·9	6·0	10·7	1·7	3·3	1·6
£200 but under £500	8·2	11·0	10·1	16·2	1·0	7·1	3·0
£500 but under £750	3·1	4·5	5·0	6·8	0·3	1·6	1·7
£750 but under £1,000	1·8	2·7	3·2	4·4	0·2	2·6	2·2
£1,000 but under £1,500	2·9	5·0	6·4	3·5	0·2	3·7	3·6
£1,500 but under £2,000	2·2	3·7	4·8	2·1	0·1	3·4	4·0
£2,000 but under £3,000	3·5	6·8	8·5	2·8	0·2	7·7	5·0
£3,000 but under £5,000	4·5	8·6	10·9	2·5	0·1	13·7	3·0
Over £5,000 but under £10,000	4·4	9·3	12·9	} 3·9	0·0	20·7	0·7
Over £10,000	2·3	5·2	8·0				
Total	100	100	100	100	100	100	100
Number	5,370	2,363	1,630	1,772	2,009	1,819	2,033

antiques, but excluding household equipment). The method of questioning individuals in the household in detail is indicated in the Questionnaire (Appendix Ten, pages 1085–1167). Money debts were deducted from money assets to obtain *net readily realizable assets*. These debts were defined as bank overdraft or loan, rent owed, hire-purchase debts (ignoring sums below £25). Similarly, outstanding 'property' debts were deducted from less readily realizable assets to obtain a net total for these assets. These debts included mortgages outstanding and money owed on cars. The total figure of assets less liabilities is termed *net assets* (and elsewhere is often referred to as *net current worth*).

Table 5.13 shows the very wide distribution of assets by value. As many as 13 per cent of households have no assets at all or are in debt. A further 11 per cent have less than £100 and another 6 per cent less than £200. Altogether nearly a third of all households in the country have no assets or under £200. These figures are higher if readily realizable assets alone are considered. Many people are owners or part-owners of the houses they occupy, but otherwise lack assets. As many as 58 per cent of all households have either no readily realizable assets or assets of under £200.

Ownership of assets varies according to type of asset. Table 5.14 shows the percentage of individuals, income units and households having different kinds of asset. The chief means by which wealth is diffused among the population is through the private ownership of dwellings, and, by means of average and aggregate value, the table shows how important this is in relation to all assets. Over three quarters of the population also live in households with money savings of some kind, the most common being in the Post Office Savings Bank and Premium Bonds. Only 4 per cent of the population, and 9 per cent of households, have stocks and shares, but the mean value of each holding is considerably in excess of the mean value of owner-occupied housing. It should also be noted that although income units or households with overdrafts is not much more than a tenth of the number with hire-purchase debts, the aggregate amount owed is nearly as large.

How do the values obtained in the survey for assets match with other estimates of national wealth? Table 5.15 compares the survey estimates with other estimates for savings, stocks and shares, business, farm or professional practices and owner-occupied housing. The two sets of estimates in the table should be regarded as indirectly rather than as strictly comparable, with the poverty survey giving better representation of wealth at the lower and middle ranges of ownership of wealth and the Board of Inland Revenue estimates giving better representation at the highest ranges. The Inland Revenue estimates are based on estates on which duty was paid in 1968. The method of estimation assumes that the estates passing on death are a representative sample both in number and value of the property of individuals. When multiplied by the reciprocals of the population's mortality rates for the various age groups, they yield an estimate of the wealth of all individuals for each age and sex group of the population. This method has

Table 5.14. Percentages of individuals, income units and households with different types of asset, and mean and aggregate amounts.

Type of assets (or debts)	Percentage with assets			Mean amount households with assets[a] £	Aggregate amount all households in sample[a] £
	Indivi- duals	Income units	House- holds		
Bank deposit account	13	20	27	424	92,432
Post Office Savings Bank	19	26	35	408	128,252
Trustee Savings Bank	10	14	18	205	36,682
Co-op savings	3	6	9	53	2,086
Any other savings bank	1	2	3	292	5,847
Shares or deposits in building society	8	11	16	610	54,264
Savings Certificates	7	10	13	111	5,660
Defence Bonds	2	3	4	173	1,900
Premium Bonds	20	26	36	46	9,251
Other savings	3	5	7	233	11,404
Having two or more of above types	21	32	39	942	603,970
All savings	54	71	78	745	954,157
Stocks and shares	4	7	9	4,746	702,378
Business, farm or professional practice	3	5	6	8,324	799,103
Owner-occupied house	16	33	45	3,267	2,424,200
Other houses, land, caravans, boats	3	5	6	3,328	342,749
Cars (vans, motor-cycles)	17	35	43	311	220,339
Personal possessions (e.g. jewellery, silver)	14	24	30	267	130,645
Other property or savings	0	1	1	669	6,020
Owed money by others	2	4	5	376	32,680
Overdraft or loan	1	2	3	564	25,377
Rent or mortgage arrears	1	1	1	12	231
Hire-purchase debts	8	17	23	81	29,709
Personal debts	1	3	4	293	16,985
Total number	4,692	2,213	1,633	—	5,539,969

NOTE: [a]For each type of saving the mean amount and the aggregate amount refer only to households with that type of savings and no other. The amount which could not be allocated is shown in the line 'having two or more of above types'.

been used by both the Inland Revenue and independent research workers for many years.[1] But the estimates 'are inevitably subject to fairly wide margins of error and are in some respects incomplete. The figures obtained from estates below the exemption limit for estate duty (£5,000 in 1968) are less reliable than those from estates paying duty because in general they do not have to be examined so thoroughly.'[2] The sampling errors for small numbers of estates among the rich and the young are considerable.

Although an attempt is made in Table 5.15 to give estimates from the two

Table 5.15. *Estimates of national value of certain types of asset.*

Type of asset	Predicted national aggregate – poverty survey		Inland Revenue estimates (1968)	Asset definition (Inland Revenue)
	£ mil.	% of Inland Revenue	£ mil.	
Bank deposit account	2,700	82	3,306	Cash at the bank on deposit
Post Office Savings Bank				Post Office and Trustee Savings Bank
Trustee Savings Bank	3,100	107	2,904	
Co-op Savings				
Any other savings bank			n.a.	
			n.a.	
Shares or deposits in Building Society	3,000	46	6,547	Shares and deposits in building societies
Savings Certificates				National Savings Certificates and Premium Bonds
Premium Bonds	1,200	50	2,404	
Defence Bonds	500	67	744	Defence, Development Bonds, Tax Reserve Certificates
Other savings	500	–	n.a.	
Sub-total	11,000[a]	69	15,905	

1. See *Inland Revenue Statistics, 1971*, HMSO, London, 1971, pp. 227–9. A comprehensive review of the deficiencies in the estimates will be found in Atkinson, A. B., *Unequal Shares: Wealth in Britain*, Allen Lane, London, 1972. See also Atkinson, A. B., and Harrison, A.J., *Distribution of Personal Wealth in Britain*, Cambridge University Press, 1978, Chapter 2.
2. *Inland Revenue Statistics, 1971*, p. 227.

Table 5.15 – contd

Type of asset	Predicted national aggregate – poverty survey		Inland Revenue estimates (1968)	Asset definition (Inland Revenue)
	£ mil.	% of Intand Revenue	£ mil.	
Stocks and shares	8,150	44	18,329	Total quoted stocks and shares including unit trusts
Business, farm or professional practice	9,265	} 167	2,636	Trade, business and professional assets
Owner-occupied house	28,050		} 22,004	Net landed property
Other houses, land, caravans, boats	3,970			
Cars (vans, motor-cycles)	2,534	–	n.a.	
Personal possessions (e.g. jewellery, silver)	1,512	} 55	} 2,896	Household goods, pictures, china, etc.
Other property or savings	76			
Owed money by others	378	–	n.a.	
Total (net of debts)	64,100	94	67,938	Adjusted net wealth less life assurance
Life assurance	10,000	76	13,008	Policies of life assurance
Grand total	74,100	91	80,946	Adjusted net wealth

NOTE: [a]All types of savings were aggregated for analysis, and the totals in this table for different types are estimated on the basis of a hand-count of a sub-sample of questionnaires.
SOURCE: Official estimates from *Inland Revenue Statistics, 1971*, Table 129, pp. 194–7.

sources which can be broadly compared, qualifications on both sides must be listed. In the poverty survey, the value of life-assurance policies, although collected, was not included in the definition of assets, for the reason that in the hands of the living they are worth only their surrender value, which is usually much less than the sum assured. Without protracted inquiry it would be difficult to reach reliable estimates of market values. Indeed, it is somewhat surprising that the full value of such policies is included in the Inland Revenue's estimates of gross and net personal wealth, especially since the board actually admits that 'an estimate based on the value of the life funds will be more realistic as the component of total personal wealth than the one given here'.[1] An estimate of the value of cars, vans and motor-cycles, net of debts outstanding, is given in the survey, but not in estate duty statistics. This was approximately £2,500 million. On the other hand, debts and income due to the deceased and 'other' assets, amounting to £6,871 million in 1968, are included in the estate-duty statistics and have not been deducted from the total given in the table. However, I have deducted the value of unquoted shares and debentures in companies, cash in the house, cash gifts and amounts standing in current bank accounts, amounting to a total of £7,022 million, from the Inland Revenue totals, either because no attempt was made to collect such information in the poverty survey, or because it is arguable whether such amounts should be treated as part of a definition of 'wealth'. There are, of course, difficulties about the components of other items.

The poverty survey's total for savings is on the low side, and not much better than such totals sought in other surveys.[2] The figure for stocks and shares is certainly low. This may be partly due to the fact that, during survey interviews, face values rather than market values are sometimes quoted by informants. Without exhaustive inquiry into the complicated portfolios of a small minority of rich people, total holdings will almost certainly be underestimated – especially of elderly men and women who leave the management of their financial affairs to a bank or solicitor. In the poverty survey, the value of household goods as such and of personal assets of under £25 in value were not sought. None the less a figure of nearly £1,600 million is reached, which suggests that the Inland Revenue total (which includes all household effects) is an underestimate. The poverty survey also produces an estimate of the value of property and land (after allowing for debts) which is considerably in excess of the Inland Revenue estimate.

Assets of Different Types of Household

Inequality of disperson of net assets is surprisingly similar between one type of household and another (Table 5.16). Slightly more households with than without children are in debt, and more single-person than other households have few assets or none, though the fractions with £200 to £1,000 fluctuate around a fifth, and with £1,000 to £5,000 between a fifth and a third for all types of households

1. *Inland Revenue Statistics, 1971*, p. 228.
2. 'The estimates of the total amount of personal capital which can be derived from this survey appear to represent only two-thirds of the true amount.' See Lydall, H. F., and Tipping, D. G., 'The Distribution of Personal Wealth in Britain', *Bulletin of the Oxford University Institute of Statistics*, xxiii, 1961, p. 85.

Table 5.16. Percentage of different types of household, according to the value of all assets.

Type of household	In debt	No assets	Under £100	£100 but under £200	£200 but under £1,000	£1,000 but under £2,000	£2,000 but under £5,000	£5,000 but under £10,000	£10,000 and over	Total	No.
Man aged 60 or over	(0)	(22)	(14)	(11)	(8)	(14)	(11)	(11)	(8)	100	36
Man under 60	3	21	16	9	19	7	12	5	7	100	57
Woman 60 or over	1	23	18	7	18	7	15	9	3	100	175
Woman under 60	4	15	9	7	22	4	22	11	6	100	54
Man and woman	3	7	9	5	19	11	25	11	9	100	456
Man, woman, 1 child	5	3	20	5	16	14	17	10	9	100	118
2 children	5	4	10	4	22	14	21	14	5	100	148
3 children	9	2	9	5	16	17	17	14	11	100	64
4+ children	(30)	(11)	(18)	(4)	(9)	(5)	(9)	(9)	(4)	100	44
3 adults	4	5	7	5	16	13	22	17	11	100	167
3 adults, plus children	9	4	10	8	19	12	15	16	7	100	116
4 adults	0	5	10	9	21	12	19	18	5	100	57
Other households without children	2	5	5	7	20	5	16	26	15	100	61
Other households with children	9	12	5	8	20	12	12	14	8	100	76
All households	5	9	11	6	18	11	19	13	8	100	1,629

(except the two with relatively low sample numbers). However, these distributions do not allow for varying sizes of households and the grouping under certain headings of combinations of persons who are dissimilar. Thus households consisting of a man and woman include young couples both in paid employment as well as elderly retired couples; and households with three adults range from married couples with an adolescent son or daughter who has left school to couples in late middle age with an aged widowed parent.

The distribution of assets is very wide for all age groups, and though more of the middle aged and elderly than of children and young adults live in households with substantial assets, the pattern varies less with age than might be expected (Table A.5, Appendix Eight, page 995). Among the oldest age groups, more men than women have substantial assets.

Table 5.17 brings out certain relationships between mean levels of assets and mean levels of income for the different types of household. It shows, first, that in relation to income the value of assets is relatively high, on average, among the smaller households, particularly those containing older people. This is particularly noticeable in the case of the three sub-types of household comprising a man and wife. But values are also relatively high in larger households peopled entirely by adults. Secondly, readily realizable assets rise and, by and large, less readily realizable assets fall, with increasing age. Among one- and two-person households, for example, the two types of assets are very broadly comparable in total value for people over 60. But for some younger households readily realizable assets shrink to only a small fraction of the value of property assets. This is explained chiefly by the fact that many young families invest first in a house and only later in life do they accumulate money savings to any considerable degree. It is also explained by the fact that older people who are owner-occupiers tend to live in property that is older and of smaller estimated value than owner-occupiers with children.

Finally, Table 5.18 shows the extreme variations in the distribution of assets within each type of household. It will be seen that there were households of two separate types within the sample which had total assets of over £200,000, and of two further types with over £100,000. At the fifth percentile, the range of assets per household lay between £10,000 and £20,000, for nearly all household types. At the tenth percentile, the range fluctuated by a few thousand pounds above and below £10,000. But when the median is reached, assets are less than, or only a little more than, £1,000 for nearly all types of household. The table shows how little wealth is owned by the poorest half of households of each type. At the ninety-fifth percentile, most types of household have no assets at all, or only negative assets.

These results can be expressed in different ways to demonstrate relativities. For each household type, Table 5.18 shows the relationship between the wealthiest and other households at different percentiles. As a proportion of the wealth of the

Table 5.17. *Mean value of all assets of different types of household.*

Type of household	Mean net disposable income last year	Gross readily realizable assets	Money debts	Less readily realizable assets	Property debts	Mean net assets	Net assets as % of net disposable income last year (mean for all households)[a]
	£	£	£	£	£	£	
Man aged 60 or over	486	1,139	0	1,445	19	2,697	831
Man under 60	863	497	5	1,503	152	1,927	203
Woman aged 60 or over	399	1,027	0	1,294	10	2,231	469
Woman under 60	654	1,095	7	1,454	120	2,449	357
Man and woman	1,068	1,374	29	3,081	359	3,980	315
Man and woman aged 60+	813	2,266	9	2,581	25	4,849	n.a.
Man and woman, one under 60	937	1,346	3	2,894	132	4,025	n.a.
Man and woman, both under 60	1,306	771	56	3,609	757	3,548	n.a.
Man, woman, 1 child	1,254	472	37	3,090	968	2,660	192
2 children	1,311	427	52	3,372	1,032	2,702	194
3 children	1,365	816	53	4,900	891	4,952	312
4+ children	1,728	3,210	98	3,080	862	4,807	112
3 adults	1,625	913	29	3,735	531	3,897	261
3 adults, plus children	1,747	767	72	5,434	528	5,828	340
4 adults	1 886	982	36	4,518	439	5,116	512
Other households without children	1,670	2,612	20	4,158	251	6,685	413
Other households with children	1,689	516	31	4,783	433	5,404	348
All households	1,221	1,062	33	3,277	483	3,823	323
Number	1,769	1,773	2,008	1,821	2,033	1,634[b]	1,537[c]

NOTES: [a]The mean of the percentage worked out within each household type for each household.
[b]The number represents only those households giving complete information on the four preceding components.
[c]The number represents households with complete information on net disposable income last year and all components of assets.

Table 5.18. Total assets in £ of different types of household at different percentiles of distribution.

Percentiles of assets	Man 60+	Man under 60	Woman 60+	Woman under 60	Man and woman	Man, woman 1 child	Man, woman 2 children	Man, woman 3 children	Man, woman 4+ children	Three adults	Three adults and children	Four adults	Others without children	Others with children	All
p1	17,151	19,393	77,819	17,960	92,200	22,070	15,665	65,887	139,121	32,740	240,920	109,269	80,106	212,514	212,514
p5	13,350	11,200	7,854	10,860	13,228	13,085	11,793	24,697	17,192	13,222	15,600	20,005	21,540	14,743	13,102
p10	7,900	7,500	5,400	9,300	9,200	8,390	7,360	13,850	8,535	10,655	8,500	9,365	14,152	7,674	8,500
p20	6,500	2,481	2,956	4,340	5,050	4,900	4,554	7,712	2,213	6,642	6,102	5,470	6,900	5,549	5,150
p50	660	245	300	550	1,500	1,041	1,360	1,299	75	2,035	1,150	1,534	4,170	966	1,065
p75	12	6	9	60	219	82	226	213	-3	432	130	250	363	75	112
p85	0	0	0	0	50	30	50	50	-21	75	25	124	175	0	8
p95	0	0	0	0	0	0	-6	-24	-63	0	-27	4	0	-20	0
Mean assets	2,697	1,927	2,231	2,449	3,980	2,660	2,702	4,952	4,807	3,897	5,828	5,116	6,685	5,404	3,823
Assets as percentage of top percentile															
p1	100	100	100	100	100	100	100	100	100	100	100	100	100	100	100
p5	78	58	10	60	14	59	75	37	12	40	8	18	27	7	6·2
p10	46	39	7	52	10	38	47	21	6	32	4	9	18	4	4·0
p20	38	13	4	24	5	22	29	12	2	20	3	5	9	3	2·4
p50	4	1	0	3	2	5	9	2	0	6	1	1	5	0	0·5
p75	0	0	0	0	0	0	1	0	0	0	0	0	0	0	0·1
p85	0	0	0	0	0	0	0	0	-1	0	0	0	0	0	0·0
p95	0	0	0	0	0	0	-1	-1	-1	0	-1	0	0	-1	0·0
Number	36	57	175	54	457	118	148	64	45	167	117	59	60	77	1,634

wealthiest, the wealth of other households falls steeply. For all types of household, even at the fifth percentile households have only 6 per cent of the assets of the wealthiest. Again, households below the median have a derisory value of assets in relation to the wealthiest households.

The Relationship between Assets and Income

The ownership of assets tends to reinforce inequalities in cash incomes. One method of examining the relationship is simply to compare the two. Table 5.19 provides a consistent correlation. For every type of household in the sample,

Table 5.19. Percentages of high-, middle- and low-income households of different types with no assets or less than £100.

Type of household	Percentage with no assets or less than £100			All levels of income	Total	No.
	High income	Middle income	Low income			
Man aged 60+	(29)	(29)	(48)	(40)	100	37
Man under 60	(0)	(30)	(59)	38	100	55
Woman aged 60+	(12)	49	38	40	100	190
Woman under 60	(15)	(24)	(48)	31	100	57
Man and woman	7	18	27	19	100	472
Man, woman,						
1 child	(9)	21	(44)	26	100	134
2 children	(3)	10	37	19	100	171
3 children	(6)	(9)	(45)	21	100	78
4+ children	(0)	(14)	(69)	(53)	100	47
3 adults	(5)	9	31	16	100	186
3 adults, plus children	(10)	14	33	22	100	123
4 adults	(7)	(25)	(21)	19	100	61
Others without children	(4)	(12)	(17)	12	100	66
Others with children	(8)	(26)	(41)	26	100	84
All types	7	21	36	25	100	1,761

NOTE: Definition of high, middle, low income as in Table 5.12.

fewer high- than low-income households lacked assets. Among all high-income households, only 7 per cent had no assets or less than £100, compared with 36 per cent of low-income households. The proportion of low-income households with children who lack assets is particularly striking. The high proportion of middle-income as well as low-income women aged 60 or over who live alone and who lack assets is also striking.

Another method is to examine dissaving and the conversion generally of assets into income to maintain or enhance living standards. After a series of questions about assets in the survey, informants were asked a general question, 'Have you in fact sold or borrowed anything worth £25 or more, or drawn out £25 or more of savings during the last 12 months to meet ordinary living expenses? I don't mean money to buy a house or other property, like a car, or to put into savings, but money for rent, housekeeping, food, clothing and leisure.' Then a series of specific items were listed: 'Sold property (including house, caravan, etc.), raised a loan on property or a life insurance policy, sold personal possessions (e.g. jewellery), sold stocks or shares, drawn savings, otherwise sold assets or borrowed money'; and amounts were entered. Altogether 14·8 per cent of households specified one or more items and as many as 13·1 per cent had drawn on savings to the extent of £25 or more. Over a third of these had drawn

Table 5.20. Percentages of households of different types dissaving in previous year.

Type of household	Amount of dissaving in year					Total	
	None or less than £25	£25–49	£50–99	£100–199	£200 or more	%	No.
Man aged 60+	(88)	(2)	(5)	(0)	(5)	100	42
Man under 60	90	5	2	3	0	100	62
Woman aged 60+	87	4	4	3	1	100	200
Woman under 60	78	10	7	2	3	100	60
Man and woman	87	3	5	2	2	100	543
Man, woman,							
1 child	91	3	2	2	3	100	152
2 children	93	3	2	2	0	100	191
3 children	88	3	4	1	3	100	90
4+ children	93	4	0	2	2	100	55
3 adults	86	3	6	2	3	100	225
3 adults, plus children	87	4	3	4	2	100	155
4 adults	86	3	6	1	3	100	87
Other households without children	76	5	10	5	5	100	82
Other households with children	85	5	8	2	1	100	105
All households	87	4	4	2	2	100	2,049

212 POVERTY IN THE UNITED KINGDOM

more than £100. The overall effect of dissaving upon the distribution of gross disposable income is small (Table A.6 in Appendix Eight, page 996) but is appreciable for some household types. Thus, more than half of the households withdrawing £100 or more were one-, two- or three-person households containing retirement pensioners. But, in relation to those having no savings of any kind upon which to draw, their numbers remain small. Table 5.20 shows that almost as many of the elderly households as of households with children do not draw on savings in the sense explored in this survey of meeting living expenses.

There are other methods of showing the relationship between the distributions of income and of assets. Current net disposable cash income and current net assets, or net worth, might be combined in a single measure of 'income net worth'. Our justification for using this method is that although traditionally the two have been treated in economic theory as distinct 'flow' and 'stock' concepts, in practice they merge. Some types of income, e.g. windfalls, bear little relationship to any on-going standard of living. They are treated as available for once-and-for-all expenditure which may or may not raise the on-going standard of living. Other types, even when received regularly, are tied specifically to an exceptional type of expenditure and not to a 'general' standard of living. Alternatively, as already pointed out, some types of assets are drawn upon regularly to support or improve living standards, or they offset living costs which are met weekly or monthly by many in the population.

They can be combined by converting net assets into an annuity value, which is then added to net disposable income. This method has been explored in previous studies.[1] The net worth of an individual or income unit could be annuitized over his, or its, lifetime so that there is nothing left at death. By calculating interest rates for assets and applying tables showing the average expectation of life for men and women of different age, an annuity value can be estimated. The method could involve a number of different types of asset,[2] and assumptions would have to be made in the case of the net worth of an income unit about the transfer of assets after death. Part of net worth could be treated as being held in trust as an estate for that purpose. In one study it was assumed that men were five years older than their wives, and that although the married couple would re-

1. Murray, J., 'Potential Income from Assets: Findings of the 1963 Survey of the Aged', *Social Security Bulletin* (US Department of Health, Education and Welfare), December 1964; Projector, D. S., and Weiss, G. S., *Survey of Financial Characteristics of Consumers*, Washington Board of Governors of the Federal Reserve System, 1966; and Weisbrod, B. A., and Hansen, W. L., 'An Income–Net Worth Approach to Measuring Economic Welfare', *American Economic Review*, vol. LVIII, No. 5, December 1968. British economists are increasingly conscious of the need to measure assets as well as income in analyses of welfare, but have not developed such analyses operationally. See, for example, Jackson, D., and Fink, A., 'Assets, Liabilities and Poverty', *Social and Economic Administration*, 1971.

2. See, for example, Projector and Weiss, *Survey of Financial Characteristics of Consumers*, pp. 38–41; and Bridges, B., 'Net Worth of the Aged', *Research and Statistics Note*, US Department of Health, Education and Welfare, September 1967.

ceive the full annuity while both were alive, the surviving widow would receive two thirds of the annuity for the remainder of her life.[1] To make such calculations meaningful in terms of on-going living standards, the annuity would have to be linked to an index of prices.

It seemed to us that, although alternative and more complex methods might be explored, there was a need to produce the simplest possible measure in order to indicate broad orders of magnitude in the distribution of 'income net worth', but also to arrive at results which would stimulate discussion. We therefore assumed that all assets produce a rate of interest of 7 per cent (slightly below the building society rate during the survey) and that the period during which an annuity is to be used is determined in the case of a single individual by the number of years he expects to live, and in the case of a married couple, by the number of years the husband expects to live, plus the years his widow expects to live (or vice versa). Income from assets is, of course, deducted from net disposable income before an addition is made for annuitized assets. For the rich, we believe this method tended to provide a very conservative estimate of the contribution made by wealth to their living standards. There are two points. One is that, unit for unit, their assets tended to be worth more than those of people with small amounts of wealth. The other is that a larger proportion of their wealth earned high rates of interest.

How important is annuitized income in relation to total income net worth? The mean net disposable income of the sample for the year previous to interview, after deducting actual income from savings, stocks and shares and other forms of assets, was £1,176. Mean income net worth, which, of course, includes the annuity equivalent figure, was £1,515. Although annuitized assets include amounts which differ in realizability, and are altogether not quite the same as cash income, they represent 29 per cent of net disposable income less property income. This proportion varies for households of different types: from about 10 per cent for households comprising man and woman and one child to about 60 per cent for women over 60 living alone. The difference between means and medians tends to widen. Thus mean disposable income per household was £1,256 (unadjusted), compared with the median of £1,076 – a difference of £180. But mean income net worth was £1,515, compared with the median of £1,260 – a difference of £255. Although proportionately this difference between these two sets of figures is small, we believe that once allowance is made for the underrepresentation of assets among the wealthiest 5 per cent, the difference becomes significantly wider.

The distributions are compared by absolute ranges in Table 5.21. The proportions of the population at the lowest relative levels are, of course, reduced by comparison with the distribution of the population according to net disposable

1. Weisbrod and Hansen, 'An Income–Net Worth Approach to Measuring Economic Welfare', p. 1319.

income last year. The proportions at the highest levels are increased. The entire distribution is shifted upwards, but in the process becomes even more unequal. For example, the proportion of households in the lowest three income groups is reduced by a third, and yet the proportion in the highest three is more than doubled. A large number of retirement pensioners with low cash incomes own their homes, but the number and the value of their property is still insufficient to have a marked effect on the distribution. When assets are converted into annuity value, the relative economic position of the elderly is improved and that of families with children diminished. This fact has implications for our understanding of poverty and inequality and will be examined later.

Table 5.21. *Percentages of income units and households according to net disposable income for previous year and 'income-net worth' for previous year.*[a]

Range of income	Net disposable income last year		Income net worth last year	
	Income units	Households	Income units	Households
Under £300	14·2	4·4	10·9	2·1
£300–	10·4	7·4	9·1	5·6
£400–	8·7	5·4	7·0	3·8
£500–	7·6	4·8	6·9	3·8
£600–	6·9	4·8	7·2	4·0
£700–	6·6	6·0	5·5	5·2
£800–	6·8	6·1	6·5	5·5
£900–	6·3	6·4	6·0	6·2
£1,000–	5·8	6·1	5·0	5·3
£1,100–	5·0	6·7	5·1	6·3
£1,200–	8·1	11·9	8·4	11·5
£1,400–	4·3	7·5	5·9	8·3
£1,600–	3·2	7·1	4·4	7·7
£1,800–	1·8	3·7	3·3	5·9
£2,000–	1·9	6·2	3·3	8·1
£2,500–	0·9	2·5	1·9	4·1
£3,000–	0·9	1·9	1·8	3·6
£4,000–	0·2	0·2	0·9	1·4
£5,000–	0·5	0·8	1·0	1·6
Total	100	100	100	100
Number	2,536	1,769	2,242	1,537

NOTE: [a]Defined as net disposable income for previous year less income from assets plus dissaving, plus annuity income from assets.

The distributions can also be compared relatively. Table 5.22 clearly shows that, when treated as a form of income, assets have the effect of increasing existing inequalities in cash incomes. The proportions of the population at the middle and upper middle ranges are reduced and the proportions at either extreme increased. Further details about those living at the lowest ranges are given in Chapter 7.

Table 5.22. Percentage of households with high, middle and low incomes, and high, middle and low income net worth.

Range	Net disposable income last year	Income net worth last year	Increase or decrease in percentage
Very high (200% or more of mean)	4·2	5·4	+1·2
High (120 to 199% of mean)	18·8	15·3	—3·5
Middle (80 to 119% of mean)	38·3	30·8	—7·5
Low (under 80% of mean)	38·8	48·5	+9·7
Total	100	100	–
Number	1,769	1,537	–

NOTE: Households are classified according to the relationship of their income (or income net worth) to the mean for their type and not the mean of the sample as a whole.

Although households containing middle-aged and elderly people depend more than other households upon assets for the maintenance of living standards, they depend on them just as unequally. For all types of household, the distribution tends to become more unequal and the proportion of households having extremely low or extremely high net income worth is usually higher than the corresponding proportion having extremely low or extremely high income (see Table A.7, Appendix Eight, page 997).

The Value of Employer Welfare Benefits

In all industrial societies benefits provided directly or indirectly by employers in kind or in the form of rights to income in sickness, retirement or termination of employment contribute substantially to the standards of living that can be commanded during life. In some countries, these benefits serve the function of tying the employee to his firm, because departure may involve their loss as well as the loss of current remuneration. In the case of pension rights, considerable sums may be involved. In some countries, the growth in importance of such benefits reflects the pressures of taxation and of unions. The employer and the employee may have a mutual interest in forms of remuneration which are not taxable. Thus, the introduction of luncheon vouchers made a larger contribution to some workers' living standards than the equivalent in wages, since they were not taxed. Again, fringe benefits which were introduced for higher-paid employees were less likely to be the subject of expressions of subjective deprivation on the part of wage-earners than corresponding increases in salary levels. They have tended to be excluded from wage negotiation. Their function in preserving and perhaps increasing inequalities in living standards remains to be properly documented.

Previous studies indicated that these benefits have become of substantial value in the United Kingdom. We therefore sought to measure them, and in the interviews asked a series of questions designed to place an exact value upon those benefits that were widely enjoyed. Questions were asked about benefits currently received, such as meals subsidies and vouchers, subsidized and free travel, the proportion of the use of a firm's car which could be said to be for personal purposes, free goods, medical expenses received or covered, shares or options to purchase shares, life insurance, educational expenses, free and subsidized accommodation. We asked about rights to sick pay in addition to any sick pay received in the previous twelve months and rights to an occupational pension. The numbers and characteristics of employees receiving or expecting such benefits will be analysed later. We appreciated that, especially for the high paid, there were benefits and amounts of benefit which could not be explored with any precision. For example, we would have liked to have discussed the personal benefit derived from business and entertainment expenses.

In estimating values difficulties were encountered, particularly with sick pay and pensions. Some employees were hazy about their expectations. Some of them, indeed, did not have any specific rights or even expectations and pointed out that they were dependent on gratuitous payments which might or might not be made. Many did not know how much of any benefit received in sickness would be paid by an employer and how much in national insurance sickness benefit. Some who could give exact amounts or proportions of usual earnings or the basic wage did not know how long payments would be made. We endeavoured to code the total amount expected, including sickness benefit, and in estimating the employer's share subsequently deducted the standard rates for flat-rate national insurance sickness benefits.

All but about 5 per cent of employees believed they knew whether or not they had entitlement to pension. Only just over a half expecting a pension could specify its size, either in cash terms or as a proportion of average or final earnings, but the proportion was much higher among middle-aged employees. In checking amounts, we made use of information about contributions from employer and employee, age at which pension was expected, and we built up a case-file about the commoner types of occupational scheme.

A mixture of 'reinforcement' questions and skilled coding in the office (with the possibility sometimes of reinterviewing) seems to be an important safeguard in obtaining information on fringe benefits from surveys. Our questions on the use of an employer's car afford an example. If an informant said he had the use sometimes of a car or van owned by his employer, we asked whether the employer paid road tax, insurance, petrol and normal repairs, what was the vehicle's current value, make and type, year and miles per gallon, and finally, how many miles the car did in a year and how many, or what proportion, were covered for personal purposes. In coding answers which were sometimes incomplete, we consulted lists of second-hand values of cars and followed rules about mileage allowances for different sizes and makes of cars, depending on what types of cost were met by the employer.

The total value of employer welfare benefits correlates highly with income. A substantial proportion of low-paid employees had no welfare benefits or benefits of very small value. Many high-paid employees had benefits of more than £200 a year, some more than £1,000. Table 5.23 shows that more men than women had

Table 5.23. *Percentages of male and female employees, with different gross earnings for previous year having different values of employer welfare benefits.*

Value of fringe benefits last year	Men with gross earnings last year						
	Under £600	£600– 799	£800– 999	£1,000– 1,199	£1,200– 1,499	£1,500+	All
£0	(66)	34	35	26	20	9	26
£1–19	(11)	17	16	17	10	6	13
£20–49	(2)	19	19	18	17	9	16
£50–99	(4)	7	16	12	20	12	14
£100–199	(6)	10	9	10	17	17	12
£200+	(11)	12	4	16	17	48	19
Total	100	100	100	100	100	100	100
Number	47	108	221	211	193	184	964

	Women with gross earnings last year					
	Under £400	£400– 599	£600– 799	£800– 999	£1,000+	All
£0	44	41	23	(14)	(3)	30
£1–19	17	32	35	(24)	(5)	26
£20–49	19	22	30	(31)	(13)	23
£50–99	6	1	5	(16)	(13)	7
£100–199	9	2	5	(6)	(30)	8
£200+	5	3	1	(8)	(30)	7
Total	100	100	100	100	100	100
Number	64	120	74	49	39	344

benefits of more than £50 value, and that for both sexes the proportion rises sharply among those with higher gross earnings. The mean value for men was £128 and for women £54. Welfare benefits are distributed more unequally than earnings.

The Value of Public Social Services

The differential use of free or subsidized public services can also substantially affect eventual living standards. Families with identical cash incomes and wealth might differ considerably in their real living standards because of different benefits derived from their use of the public services. In principle, such benefits might include passenger transport subsidies and the use of public libraries and swimming baths, but in this study the value of public goods and services received in kind by families has been restricted to those supplied by social services administered by central departments and local authorities – namely, health, education, welfare and housing services. Information was collected for each individual in the household about the use in the previous twelve months of local and central educational services (nursery schools, primary schools, different types of secondary schools and institutions of higher education), health and welfare services (period of stay in different types of hospital, general practitioner consultations at home and in the surgery, services by district nurses, home helps, health visitors and social workers, dental treatment, the receipt of hearing aids and spectacles, childbirth at home and in hospital, visits to welfare clinics, receipt of welfare milk, free school milk, free and subsidized school meals and subsidized welfare milk) and whether or not families had council or owner-occupied accommodation subsidized directly or indirectly by the government and local authorities. The questions which had to be used are listed principally in Section 7 of the questionnaire printed as Appendix Ten.

The value to families of the goods or services received during the year was then estimated, using a range of statistical information about the costs of these services published by the government. The methods of procedure are discussed in Appendix Four (page 964), and the components of total value are listed in Appendix Five: 'Some Definitions' (page 980).

There have been other attempts to measure the value to families of public social services, chiefly in order to reach conclusions about the redistributive effects of social policy. These attempts have been built on very rough assumptions, as, for example, those adopted by Barna and Cartter.[1] It may be wondered

1. Barna, T., *The Redistribution of Income through Public Finance in 1937*, Clarendon Press, Oxford, 1945; Cartter, A. M., *The Redistribution of Income in Post War Britain, A Study of the Effects of the Central Government Fiscal Programme in 1948–49*, Yale University Press, 1955, pp. 47–8 and 221–5. At a very early stage of the operation of the National Health Service, and with few empirical data available on usage, Cartter assumed, for example, that children under

whether useful conclusions can be drawn from studies which allocate social service benefits yet which are unable to depend on even approximate empirical guidance about the use of some costly social services by different income groups and types of household. Even the series of studies published by the Central Statistical Office on the basis of the Family Expenditure Survey are far from being conclusive.[1] They have failed in the last ten years to replace a number of arbitrary assumptions with assumptions which are better founded empirically. Thus, in a valuable study of the early data, J. L. Nicholson called attention to the fact that the estimates of the value of benefits which had been allocated to households 'would be improved if we had more information than we possess at present about such matters as the extent to which different households make use of the various health services [and] the benefits which individual households derive from housing subsidies'.[2] The basis of allocation, however, has not been much improved, and has been criticized powerfully by economists.[3] The Central Statistical Office's method of allocating the imputed value of social services is not sufficiently refined for services as costly as health, housing and education. Some major differences in the distribution of benefits between beneficiaries are in practice obscured. Moreover, the Central Statistical Office's definition of social services is too narrow and excludes certain major forms of tax relief which have clear welfare functions. As a result, the role of the government in redistributing resources to some in the middle and upper income groups has been minimized.[4]

The methods adopted in the present study do not overcome all the objections that might be raised against previous procedures. A number of improvements could be made. But in terms of the comments made above, two advances may be claimed. First, the value to families of social service benefits in kind is related to their actual use of social services. We were not able to estimate the cost of the specific services received by individuals, but in obtaining answers to a range of questions, were able to take account of type and frequency of service. Thus, we enumerated the number of nights spent by each individual in different types of hospital, and the number of consultations with GPs in the previous twelve months, and applied average costs to these figures. A similar method was used

15 required seven times as much medical attention as the average adult. As an introduction to overseas studies of a similar kind, see Morgan, J. N., et al., Income and Welfare in the United States, McGraw-Hill, New York, 1962, esp. pp. 300–8.

1. See Economic Trends, November 1962; February 1964; August 1966; February 1968, 1969, 1970, 1971, 1972; November 1972, 1973; December 1974; February 1976.

2. Nicholson, J. L., Redistribution of Income in the United Kingdom in 1959, 1957, and 1953, Bowes & Bowes, London, 1965, p. 2.

3. Peacock, A., and Shannon, R., 'The Welfare State and the Redistribution of Income', Westminster Bank Review, August 1968.

4. See Appendix Four for a discussion of the CSO methods. See also the elaborate account in Webb, A. L., and Sieve, J. E. B., Income Redistribution and the Welfare State, Bell, London, 1971, esp. Chapters 2 and 5.

for the value to families of children's attendance of different types of school and college. Secondly, an attempt is made to measure housing subsidies received by owner-occupiers as well as council tenants, though the estimates may err on the low side for some home-buyers by not claiming to take full account of the tax relief and housing improvement grants.

The results described below are therefore believed to be less misleading than previous estimates of the value of social service benefits in kind, but nevertheless have to be interpreted with care. Values are expressed as current public expenditure per beneficiary and not, for example, as the return during a lifetime upon an investment or as the security of non-beneficiaries.[1] Nor has more than a rough estimate been made of average current costs. Thus medical treatment may be more protracted or skilled in a particular than in a typical instance, and may be socially selective. Its value could be expressed in relation to the prolongation of working life rather than just its current cost. And someone who has never had a day's illness may enjoy security against the risk of financial catastrophe which may deserve to be expressed in the equivalent of money. Again, public legislation affords protection against certain types of financial loss, and affords indirect subsidies to private expenditure, which are not easy to document – either because such protection or subsidy is hidden or is so delicate and indirect as to be unquantifiable. For example, the benefits which independent schools obtain from their charitable status and through that proportion of grants made by various educational trusts which is attributable to tax reliefs might be allocated to parents who send their children to such schools.

A single valuation will never do entire justice to all these subtleties, and this must be recognized. All it can achieve is a greater understanding of the major methods of the allocation and reallocation of resources to different groups in the population. Even when valuations are given on alternative assumptions, it is difficult to restrict them in number or decide which is the most appropriate.

In 1969, public expenditure in the United Kingdom on the five social services: health, education, housing, welfare and social security, amounted to £9,145 million, of which £1,388 million represented capital expenditure and £4,003 million transfer incomes (mainly social security cash benefits), leaving a total of £3,754 million.[2] This is the sum which we are seeking to allocate. It represents

1. Peacock and Shannon successfully criticize the 'cost-allocation' method of the CSO without offering any satisfactory alternative. 'If we simply take, say, the cost of state education and allocate it according to some indicator of consumption by households of different composition and income group, what we are doing is measuring the benefit of education by *its cost*. What we should be attempting to do is to find some "surrogate" measure of the value of *output* rather than taking it for granted that cost of inputs is an indicator of benefit.' See Peacock and Shannon, 'The Welfare State and the Redistribution of Income', p. 40.

2. Townsend, P., 'The Problems of Social Growth', *The Times*, 10 March 1971. However, the total excludes indirect subsidies enjoyed by home owners.

Table 5.24. *Percentages of individuals living in different household income groups having different values of social services in kind.*

| | Net disposable household income last year | | | | | | | | | | | | |
Value of all social services in kind (£)	Under £400	£400–599	£600–799	£800–999	£1,000–1,099	£1,100–1,199	£1,200–1,399	£1,400–1,599	£1,600–1,799	£1,800–1,999	£2,000–2,499	£2,500+	All ranges
0	12	8	4	2	1	1	1	0	1	0	1	0	2
1–24	31	24	15	11	8	11	16	10	10	9	13	5	13
25–49	6	11	8	7	2	2	2	1	5	4	2	1	4
50–99	14	11	17	8	9	5	5	5	5	1	5	4	7
100–149	11	12	13	10	12	14	10	9	6	14	12	4	10
150–249	12	15	14	23	20	18	17	14	20	21	15	10	17
250+	14	18	27	39	48	49	49	61	52	50	52	76	46
Total	100	100	100	100	100	100	100	100	100	100	100	100	100
Number	247	305	434	649	342	367	652	456	446	226	381	367	4,872

about 10 per cent of gross disposable personal income,[1] or about 13 per cent of gross disposable personal income as defined in this survey – that is, excluding income in kind, rent of owner-occupied dwellings, pay of the armed forces and incomes of people in institutions (see note to Table 5.8, page 192). It is of approximately the same order of magnitude as total transfer incomes disbursed by the state.

The results are presented in Table 5.24. Contrary to common belief, fewer individuals in households with low than with high incomes received social services in kind of substantial value. Fifteen per cent of individuals had no benefits or benefits of less value than £25. Yet 46 per cent had benefits worth £150 per year or more. The proportion was, however, significantly larger among middle- and high-income groups than among those in households with under £1,000 a year.

Some households with relatively high absolute incomes do, of course, consist of several individuals, and some with relatively low incomes consist of single persons. The relationship between income and value of social services in kind is therefore blurred. One method of allowing for household size is to express household income as a percentage of the mean of its type. This is shown in Table 5.25. The broad conclusion was sustained. More households with relatively high than relatively low incomes received substantial value in kind through the social services.

Table 5.25. Percentages of people living in households with relatively low and high incomes who had different values of social services in kind.

| Value of all social services in kind (£) | Net disposable income as % of mean for each household type | | | | | | | | | |
	Under 50	50– 69	70– 89	90– 99	100– 109	110– 119	120– 139	140– 199	200+	All ranges
0	5	2	2	2	2	2	0	1	2	2
1–24	14	9	16	13	12	20	15	10	5	13
25–49	6	7	5	2	3	3	5	1	4	4
50–99	13	10	6	9	4	3	7	7	0	7
100–149	10	10	11	9	9	7	13	13	9	10
150–249	17	18	17	21	17	12	11	20	15	17
250+	35	44	44	43	51	53	49	47	65	46
Total	100	100	100	100	100	100	100	100	100	100
Number	453	916	1,148	511	408	342	427	478	188	4,871

The relationship between income and value of social services in kind varied with type of service. More households with low than with high incomes had no

1. *National Income and Expenditure*, H M S O, London, 1970, Table 2.

health or welfare benefits, but more also had substantial benefits. Fewer had educational benefits, and fewer who had educational benefits had benefits of substantial value. A detailed analysis showing the use made of each type of service and comparing the results of the methods adopted in the poverty survey with those adopted by the CSO in secondary analyses of FES data will be presented in a subsequent report.

Private Income in Kind

Our conception of resources included 'private' as well as employers' and 'public' income in kind. *Private income in kind* is defined as the 'profit' from home production of food, the rental value equivalent of major consumer durables, and the value of goods and services from people outside the household, including relatives and friends.[1] We decided to ignore the cash value of services carried out by members of the household for the benefit of the household itself, but not the cash value of food grown at home or obtained as a cheap or free by-product of one's own farm or business.

In many countries, produce grown on land farmed collectively by groups of people, on plots owned by a landlord or in gardens and small-holdings, is an important supplement to cash income. In assessing differences in standards of living between urban and rural areas, some estimate has to be made of its value. The proportion of the population living in rural areas in the United Kingdom is small, but a large proportion of the urban population have gardens and this can make a significant difference to some families' chances of maintaining their standard of living in adversity. We therefore felt it was important to make some estimate of the value of food grown in a garden at home or on an allotment, and we invited informants to make an estimate of the weekly average saving to them of such produce (that is, the retail value of the goods consumed less the expenses of production).

Only a tiny percentage of households estimated the net profit to them of such food at an average of more than 50p per week throughout the year (£26 in the last year). But a minority of 15 per cent said they obtained a small regular saving and, as Table 5.26 shows, relatively more of the larger than of the smaller households, and of households with children than without, drew benefit from such production. But it turns out that there is very little or no correlation with income. Although many cells in the table represent small numbers, there is no clear trend among incomes below 80 per cent of the mean for each type, compared with incomes 80 to 119 per cent of the mean, or 120 per cent and over.

1. See Appendix Five, 'Some Definitions', pages 980–85.

Table 5.26. *Percentages of different types of household, according to estimated value per week of home-grown food, and percentages of high-, middle- and low-income households with some value of home-grown food.*

Type of household	None	Up to 50p per week	Over 50p per week	Total	No.	Percentage with any value home food		
						High income	*Middle income*	*Low income*
Man aged 60+	87	13	0	100	38	(0)	(0)	(22)
Man under 60	93	7	0	100	55	(0)	(11)	(4)
Woman aged 60+	94	6	0	100	191	(4)	7	5
Woman under 60	93	7	0	100	57	(8)	(0)	(13)
Man and woman	81	18	1	100	473	15	19	23
Man, woman, 1 child	87	13	1	100	134	(9)	15	(14)
2 children	82	17	1	100	172	(14)	15	23
3 children	83	15	1	100	78	(19)	(18)	(14)
4+ children	73	23	4	100	48	(45)	(0)	(30)
3 adults	78	20	2	100	186	(20)	25	19
3 adults, plus children	82	16	2	100	125	(18)	(16)	20
4 adults	87	13	0	100	62	(13)	(6)	(28)
Others without children	88	11	1	100	66	(18)	(8)	(6)
Others with children	81	19	0	100	86	(26)	(15)	(18)
All households	84	15	1	100	1,771	15	15	18

NOTE: Definition of high, middle and low income as in Table 5.12, page 198.

The Interrelationship of Resources

We have traced the value and distribution of five types of resources: net disposable cash income, the annuity value of assets held, employer welfare benefits in kind, public social services in kind and private income in kind. We discussed earlier the interrelationship of the first two of these variables. Finally, we need to show the relative importance of each of the components of total resources, the effect that each has on the dispersion of resources and what is the distribution of resources as a whole. Certain adjustments have to be made to avoid double-counting of a few components – such as income from investments as well as their imputed annuity value, and tax reliefs on mortgage interest as well as the inclusion of that income untaxed in net disposable income.

First, their relative importance. Although net disposable income, less income from property and investments, is by far the most important component of the resources on which the population depends for its living standards, other resources are also important. Net earnings from employment and self-employment account for nearly half total resources (Table 5.27). These earnings include allowances passed on to divorced and separated wives and others. They also include holiday pay and sick pay, bonuses, commissions and repayments of tax.

The income equivalent of assets held, including the value of owner-occupied housing less any capital repayments outstanding, was more than a fifth of the total, making a substantial contribution to living standards. In the table we have attempted to adjust for incomplete data and therefore to base an estimate of annuity values on the total value of assets held, though, for reasons given earlier, our calculations of annuity values may be conservative for some types of asset. Employer welfare benefits in kind, including both current benefits and the value of sick pay and pension rights, formed about 5 per cent of the total, or 11 per cent of net earnings from employment. Employers' pensions and sick pay actually paid in cash in the last twelve months amounted to over 2 per cent of total resources, and holiday pay to 2·5 per cent. If net earnings exclusive of sick pay, holiday pay and employers' pension payments are considered, then employer cash welfare added about 10 per cent and employer welfare in kind over 11 per cent to their value. Social services in kind accounted for $11\frac{1}{2}$ per cent of total resources, and cash benefits over 7 per cent.

These results help to justify the conception upon which we embarked, for they show that resources other than cash incomes are of substantial size in the United Kingdom. In principle, the conception perhaps prepares the way for a more realistic comparison of living standards of populations in different societies. For example, there are societies where private income in kind may represent half rather than 3 per cent of living standards and where fringe benefits may be an infinitesimal addition to cash wages instead of 15 per cent. But the conception is not easy to define in practice or to measure operationally. As already indicated,

Table 5.27. Percentages and estimated value for the United Kingdom of different types of resource received in previous twelve months.

Type of resource	Percentage of gross disposable resources	Estimated UK total (£ mil.)
1. Net disposable cash income less property income		
(i) Net earnings from employment	44·5	17,400
(ii) Self-employment income	4·2	1,650
(iii) Employers pension	1·8	690
(iv) Social security cash benefits	7·3	2,850
(v) Other payments (redundancy, scholarship, and educational maintenance allowances)	0·3	120
Sub-total	58·0	22,700
2. Imputed income from assets (annuity value)[a]	22·9	8,950
3. Imputed income last year from employer welfare benefits in kind[b]	5·0	1,920
4. Imputed value last year of social services in kind	11·6	4,540
5. Imputed value last year of private income in kind	2·5	980
Total	100	39,100

NOTES: [a]With estimated addition allowing for value of life assurance (excluded from definition of assets elsewhere in this report). Slight underrepresentation in sample of wealthy, and understatement of wealth on part of those, particularly the wealthy, who responded. Readers should note that, in this table, the imputed capital value of owner-occupied housing, and not its imputed *rental* value, has been taken as the basis for calculating annuities.
[b]Adjusted for incomplete information.

there are possible extensions of the sub-items included in each type of resource. The money values of some sub-items might be defined more accurately, and more comprehensive information about some collected by methods different from, or additional to, those adopted in this survey.

Our tentative approach may encourage others to realize that the resource systems of society are more numerous than they had hitherto believed, and that if they are to be understood so that they can be controlled in the interest of serving social objectives, then special efforts have to be made by independent research workers and governments. But it is not just their relative scale in aggregate terms, but their contribution to inequality that is important. We have to ask how widely each type of resource is distributed in the population and which types of resource are distributed more unequally than others.

To take a hypothetical example: during a period of years we may be able to show that the distribution of net disposable cash incomes is less unequal, but if other resources are distributed more unequally and if their proportion of the aggregate is actually increasing, the distribution of total resources may not have changed and living standards among the population remain as unequal as they were before.

One method of presenting the distribution of different types of resource is shown in Table 5.28. In the first column net non-asset household income (that is, net disposable income less income from property and investments) is expressed as a percentage of the mean for their household type. Eight and a half per cent of households had incomes of less than half the mean and 4 per cent more than twice the mean. Subsequent columns show the effect on the relative dispersion of adding each further type of resource. The table shows that imputed income from assets and employer welfare benefits widen the dispersion, and though the addition of social service benefits and private income in kind slightly reduce the proportion of households with resources of less than half the mean, the proportion is still larger when all resources are measured than when non-asset income alone is measured. Moreover, the proportion having relatively high resources actually increases, and there is a slight shift of population away from the mean. The trend for different types of household does not always conform with this general conclusion, and the relatively small numbers of certain types within the main sample must be borne in mind. But for broad groups of households consisting of elderly single people, married couples and married couples with children, the trend is roughly the same. Table A.8 (Appendix Eight, page 998) shows the mean resources of different types of household. The various qualifications expressed in this chapter about the definition of resources should be borne in mind. The data have been set out unadjusted, and those giving information on income but not assets have been excluded from the table. The effect of this is to reduce the inequality of the dispersion, and understate the resources held by the rich. Some adjusted figures are given in Chapter 9 on the rich. One of our purposes has been to attempt a crude valuation of various kinds of resources frequently believed to be held disproportionately by the poor – private services as well as social service benefits in kind, for example – and also to measure the value of modest quantities of personal possessions, including consumer durables.

Another method of studying dispersion is to divide all households irrespective of type into five ranks according to their net disposable income, and then find how much is added to the mean income of each rank by each additional type of

Table 5.28. *The cumulative effect of different types of resource on the percentage of households having resources above and below the mean for their type (individuals in households).*

Percentage	1 Net disposable income less income from property and investments	2 Column 1 plus imputed income from assets	3 Columns 1 and 2 plus imputed income from employer welfare benefits in kind	4 Columns 1, 2 and 3 plus imputed income from social service benefits in kind	5 Columns 1, 2, 3 and 4 plus imputed income from private income in kind
Under 50	8·0	11·6	12·1	10·3	9·7
50–89	39·3	44·7	45·0	45·5	45·1
90–109	21·2	17·3	17·5	17·6	18·2
110–99	28·2	21·0	19·4	20·9	21·7
200+	3·3	5·4	6·0	5·7	5·4
Total	100	100	100	100	100
	4,391	4,391	4,391	4,391	4,391

NOTE: Those households providing information on income but not assets have been excluded from this table, since relatively more with an income of 200 per cent or more of the mean did not provide asset information.

resource. Table 5.29 gives the result, both in absolute amount of income in the previous twelve months and as a percentage of net disposable income less income from property and investment. For every type of resource the top 20 per cent received the highest absolute values (though only marginally for private income in kind). Their advantage in respect of imputed income from assets and from employer welfare benefits in kind is striking. The fact that they also received a larger amount through social service benefits in kind is more surprising. As the lower half of the table shows, the absolute values received by way of social service benefits in kind, private income in kind and even imputed income from assets did, however, form a lower percentage of net disposable income than did the values received by the two lowest ranks. Employer welfare benefits provide a striking exception.

The values in absolute amounts received by the bottom 20 per cent in employer welfare benefits, social services and private income in kind were low relative to the amounts received by other ranks, and did not add substantially to their total resources. However, though receiving the lowest absolute amounts, they derived relatively more in imputed income from assets in proportion to their net disposable incomes. This is because they included disproportionately more elderly households than other ranks. Nearly half these households had paid off mortgages on owner-occupied houses and therefore an imputed rental value on the capital value of the home (7 per cent) was applied to the full current value. Finally, the overall effect of adding four types of resource to each income rank was to add proportionately more to the incomes of the two highest and the two lowest quintiles than the middle quintile.

Table 5.29. Value for previous year in pounds of different types of resource to average household in each quintile income group.

Quintile	1 Net disposable income	2 Net disposable income less income from property and investments	3 Imputed income from assets	4 Imputed income from employer welfare benefits in kind	5 Imputed income from social service benefits in kind	6 Imputed income from private income in kind	7 Total resources
Top 20%	2,486	2,353	700	330	411	67	3,859
Second 20%	1,420	1,680	333	162	287	66	2,227
Third 20%	1,073	1,052	191	96	225	56	1,620
Fourth 20%	750	725	184	52	156	51	1,168
Bottom 20%	378	359	146	10	105	31	652

As % of net disposable income less income from property and investments							
Top 20%	106	100	30	14	17	3	164
Second 20%	103	100	24	12	21	5	161
Third 20%	102	100	18	9	21	5	154
Fourth 20%	103	100	25	7	22	7	161
Bottom 20%	105	100	41	3	29	9	181

NOTE: Column 3 gives the modified definition of imputed income, i.e. including only a low 'rental' figure for owner-occupied homes (7 per cent of current estimated capital value).

In discussions of the distribution of income and wealth, certain measures of concentration, especially the Gini coefficient, are used. Some results of applying this coefficient are given in Chapter 9 (page 344).

Conceptual Problems of Income and Wealth

The reader who has patiently followed the attempt in this chapter to set out the different resources which contribute to living standards will be keenly aware by now of the complexity of their determination. At each step difficulties in conceptualization, practical definition and measurement or estimation have been specified. What remains to be stated clearly and unmistakably is that there is no ideal or pure concept of resources, or, for that matter, income or wealth, 'out there', which if only we could measure it would settle all our disputes about inequality or about trends in inequality. What we conceptualize depends on why we want to conceptualize it, and therefore on our purposes or objectives which, in turn, reflect perceptions and values which may not be unanimously held. We have to try as best we can to make objectives clear. In the approach adopted here we have shown interest in all those resources which enable people to obtain material goods and services and styles of consumption in more or less generous measure than their fellows. We have therefore selected types of resources which some people get and others do not; we have included resources which for some are free or subsidized and for others have to be paid in full. Any attempt to move beyond conventional conceptions or definitions furnishes a kind of test of those conceptions and helps to reveal how inadequate they are. Thus the distinction so often made between 'flow' and 'stock', revenue and capital, or income and wealth, tends to lead society to underestimate the scale of inequality. The connections and cumulations are insufficiently examined and presented. While conceding lamely the artificiality of the distinction, the Royal Commission on the Distribution of Income and Wealth decided that it was impracticable to do anything very different and proceeded to develop separate analyses of the distributions of income and wealth in their first report.[1]

But the distinction made between income and wealth is not the only factor leading to the underestimation of inequality. Another is the domination of measures of value by the concept of 'marketability'. The Royal Commission on the Distribution of Income and Wealth can again be quoted. In discussing the concept of personal wealth, the commission said that it could not be reduced to a single definitive statement. The commission went on to discuss views put to them

---

1. 'We recognize that for some purposes it would be useful to include changes in capital values in the definition of income. However, we believe that for our purpose of describing, separately and at different points in time, the spread of income and the spread of wealth and the trends under both headings, it is more appropriate to define income in a way which distinguishes it clearly from wealth and, correspondingly, to deal with changes in capital value under the heading of wealth. In any case there are great practical difficulties about estimating changes in capital values' – Royal Commission on the Distribution of Income and Wealth, Initial Report, pp. 5–6. See also Report Nos. 4 and 5.

about the inclusion of certain items in the concept and they cast about for an integrating principle.

The key idea is that of marketability, and our study of this question has led us to form the view that different approaches to the definition of personal wealth hinge essentially on varying degrees of marketability of assets . . . We believe, then, that the concept of marketability lies at the heart of the debate about the scope and coverage of personal wealth.[1]

Certainly implications for our understanding of inequality can be drawn from the Royal Commission's view that it is not appropriate to include non-marketable assets (of which, as examples, they quoted communal assets, human capital and restricted assets and company assets) in the measurement of personal wealth. At least we cannot deny that the inclusion of some of the proposed items would be difficult or impracticable. But more significant is the commission's failure to note the inequality inherent in the concept of 'marketability' itself. Rich men's property is often grossly undervalued, just as large quantities of goods on the market are priced much lower than small quantities at unit cost. A glance at any estate agent's list will demonstrate the truth of this. In 1975 in south-east England, for example, a property with two small bedrooms, a small living room and a kitchen and a small garden, was commonly quoted at a price of around £10,000; yet properties with three or four times as much internal space and two or three acres of land could be found for less than £20,000. Market value is in no sense a uniformly continuous variable.

This is not the place for a definitive analysis of the conceptual and philosophical problems underlying society's use of the ideas of income and wealth. Fortunately, and partly because of the increasing influence of the work of sociologists, there is increasing acknowledgement of the limitations of official approaches to official statistics, and the categories into which they are fitted are no longer accepted as facts which are beyond question. The Royal Commission gave one example of this trend, which virtually amounted to an abdication of responsibility for the conclusions that could be drawn from their report.

We wish to make clear that what are seen as relevant facts will, in part, reflect the values of the people using them. In an area like the distribution of income and wealth there will never be one correct set of statistics. Thus we have followed a policy of offering alternative approaches and measurements based on different definitions, so that readers may make their own choice of the most appropriate statistics for the problems they wish to study.[2]

This seems to carry the principle of marketability too far. However, the commission did not put this policy into practice. Alternatives were not really worked out and presented, and the conventional measures developed over many years by

1. Royal Commission on the Distribution of Income and Wealth, Initial Report, p. 11.
2. ibid., p. 132.

the Central Statistical Office and the Board of Inland Revenue tended to prevail – in methodology and conclusions.

In the survey reported in this book, efforts have been made to develop the principles of comprehensiveness and comparability in developing measures of resources. All along we believed this would provide an alternative conception of social and economic conditions in the United Kingdom. But we have become aware that some elements in our conceptual apparatus reflect the conventional views which we have tended to question. It is very difficult to *communicate* an alternative measure of inequality without retaining some familiar categories and ingredients. And it is very difficult to *conceive* an alternative measure without drawing upon them.

Summary

This chapter shows how the concept of resources was defined in the survey and traces the five components, cash incomes, imputed as well as actual income from the ownership of wealth and three types of resources received in kind: employer welfare benefits, public social services and private income.

The spread of incomes was wide and in comparison with the government's Family Expenditure Survey and Inland Revenue data representation of high incomes was good. In comparison with census estimates of population, the representation of retirement pensioners, households with children and the long-term sick and unemployed was better than both the Family Expenditure Survey and Inland Revenue. It was a primary purpose of the survey to ensure proper representation of low-income households. When adjustments are made for differences of definition, mean incomes for different types of household correspond fairly closely with figures from the Family Expenditure Survey for 1967–8 (the period of twelve months preceding the survey).

The extent of inequality in distribution of resources is demonstrated. The top net disposable household incomes for most types of household are at least twice and, for some types, more than three times as large as those of the fifth percentile. They are, for most types of household, more than five times as large as the median and ten times as large as the lowest decile.

Assets are distributed more unequally. Among the wealthiest households were a number with more than £100,000 and a few more than £200,000. At the fifth percentile, the range lay, for nearly all types of household, between £10,000 and £20,000. At the median, the figure ranged below and above £1,000. Half the population have very little wealth. At the ninety-fifth percentile there are, for nearly all types of household, no assets at all or households are in debt.

Employer welfare benefits are also distributed extremely unequally. Some high-paid employees had benefits of more than £200 a year, some more than £1,000. More men than women had benefits of more than £50 value, and for both sexes the proportion rises sharply with increases of earnings. These benefits are distributed more unequally than either gross or net earnings, and a substantial proportion of low-paid employees had no benefits at all or benefits of very small annual value.

The value of public social services was estimated broadly by applying averages of known administrative costs to the actual use of a wide range of services, including education, health, welfare and housing, as established in the survey. Contrary to common supposition, fewer individuals living in households with low than with high incomes received social services in kind of substantial absolute value.

Private income in kind includes the net value of home-grown food. Only a small percentage of households had a value of over 50p a week and there was little or no correlation with income.

Of the five types of resource, cash incomes less income from property and investment was the largest, forming about three fifths of the grand total. Imputed income from assets comprised another fifth, and the remaining three resources the remaining fifth. But, with the exception of private income in kind, each of the other types of resource make a considerable contribution to living standards. Employer welfare benefits in kind, including both current benefits and the value of sick pay and pension rights, formed about 7 per cent of the total, or 15 per cent of net earnings from employment. Public social services in kind accounted for nearly 10 per cent of total resources, and cash benefits another 8 per cent.

Some sections of the population depended much more than others on certain types of resource. For every type of resource, the 20 per cent of households with the highest net disposable incomes received the highest money value of other types of resource. Their advantage in respect of imputed income from assets and from employer welfare benefits is striking, though not surprising, but they also had a higher value of social services in kind. Relative to income, however, the value of social services and private income in kind received by low-income households was larger.

Finally, employer welfare benefits, and imputed income from assets, tend to increase, and social services and private income in kind slightly to decrease, the dispersion of resources. But the overall effect of adding the four types of resource to net disposable incomes is slightly to increase the dispersion.

Annex to Chapter 5. Adjustment to Major Totals in Table 5.8. National Income and Expenditure.

	1967 £m	1968 £m
1. *Wages and salaries*		
Wages	12,330	13,095
Salaries	8,730	9,410
H M Forces	524	541
	21,584[a]	23,046[a]
Income tax Wages and salaries	−2,406[b]	−2,816[b]
H M Forces	−46[b]	−46[b]
Surtax Wages and salaries	−108[b]	−85[b]
	19,024	20,099
N I contributions	−861[b]	−973[b]
	18,163	19,126
Income in kind	−278[d]	−277[d]
	17,885	18,849
Adjustment for unallocated taxes, transfers	−240	−375
	17,645	18,474
Adjustment for *net* pay of servicemen overseas and institutions	−350	−370
	17,295	18,104
2. *Self-employment income*	2,812[a]	2,919[a]
Tax	−656[c]	−674[c]
	2,156	2,245
N I contributions	−82[b]	−93[b]
	2,074	2,152
Estimate for depreciation	−350	−350
	1,724	1,802

Annex to Chapter 5 – contd

	1967 £m	1968 £m
3. *Rent, dividends and interest*	3,984[a]	4,255[a]
Rent of owner-occupied dwellings	−857[c]	−933[c]
	3,127	3,322
Tax	−729	−767
Half receipts by life assurance + superannuation funds	2,398 −483	2,555 −552
	1,915	2,003
4. *Employers contributions: Other*	1,076[a]	1,189[a]
less contributions and compensation	−576	−639
leaving occupational pensions	−500	−600
5. *National insurance benefits and other grants*	3,199[a]	3,690[a]
Grants to universities	−148[e]	−165[e]
Grants to other non-profit-making bodies	−37[e]	−46[e]
Child care	−4[e]	−5[e]
Other local authority grants	−3[f]	−4[f]
Post-war credits	−17[e]	−20[e]
Other grants	−59[e]	−67[e]
	2,931	3,383
Less benefits in institutions	−100	−126
	2,831	3,257
6. *Income tax*	3,945[g]	4,388[g]
Estimate of dividends deducted at source	−400	−450
	3,545	3,938

(Items 4: −639 and −600 braced as "crude estimates")

SOURCES: As specified under Table 5.8, page 192. The help of the CSO is gratefully acknowledged in completing the estimates for this table (similar problems arise for the CSO in comparing the results of the FES with national income data). The CSO cannot, of course, be held responsible for the estimates given here.

NOTES: [a]*National Income and Expenditure, 1970*, Table 19.
[b]ibid., Table 47.
[c]Remainder of tax and surtax after allowing for items in (2), i.e.:

	1967	1968
	£3,945	£4,388
	−2,560	−2,947
	1,385	1,441

This tax is deducted proportionally from self-employment income and rent, etc.
[d]*National Income and Expenditure*, 1970, Table 24.
[e]ibid., Table 37.
[f]ibid., Table 41.
[g]ibid., Table 47; income tax and surtax on salaries, and wages, pay of HM Forces, rent of land and buildings and on dividends, interest and trading incomes.

6

Three Measures of Poverty

In Chapter 1, a distinction was made between perceived and actual poverty. This distinction will now be pursued in more detail. First, the conceptions held by families in the sample will be discussed. We will go on to consider the conception institutionalized within Britain and show how that may be used as a 'social' measure of poverty. But that is the state's definition and it may not be the right one. Therefore, we go on to consider alternative, more 'objective' measures. One is the 'relative income standard'. The other is the 'relative deprivation standard'.

Subjective and Social Definitions of Poverty

What conceptions of poverty are held by the population? In the interviews we asked the chief wage-earner or head of household: 'There's been a lot of talk about poverty. Do you think there's such a thing as *real* poverty these days?' Sixty-two per cent said there was, 3 per cent that they didn't know and 35 per cent that there was not. We went on to ask what they would describe as poverty, and we wrote down the answers. Some of these were vividly expressed and deeply felt. 'Not having any money and not being able to earn any. Hearing the babies cry because they are hungry or cold – that's poverty.' This was a 40-year-old manual worker with three children.

Such statements reflect some of the principal preoccupations of this book. In this first example might be noted the emphasis on sheer lack of resources, but also on denial of access to obtaining them. That is a seminal idea for the understanding of poverty. There is emphasis too upon the effects of lack of resources, certainly of hunger or an insufficient diet, but also of other needs. This is the corresponding idea of deprivation in relation to style of living. We did not put words into people's mouths, and inevitably the answers were haphazard. Different people took up different ideas and after an interview that was already long there was no time to explore each possible conception systematically. Neither are survey interviews the best or the only method of identifying popular conceptions and attitudes. These vary according to social situation and their expression is not felt to be relevant to some situations. We had, in any case, given priority to hard data about living conditions and behaviour.

The answers ranged widely and were not easy to categorize. Tentatively we classified the following sub-categories:

Minority group poverty

People spoke of sections or groups in the population as if that were a sufficient description or definition. They tended either to speak of *working groups*, people with low wages and/or large families and *groups who were not at work*, such as old people, the unemployed, the disabled and the sick, the unemployed and fatherless families. Thus 'the working class on low wages, the poor souls must be desperate. No wonder people go on national assistance if they are better off not working' (57-year-old labourer with wife and adolescent child). 'Old-age pensioners who are too proud to ask for anything' (retired fireman). 'Old people without any help but the pension' (40-year-old coalman with two children). Many simply listed different minorities, and some referred to gipsies and people who 'live on the streets'.

Subsistence poverty

People spoke of not having enough to feed children or go to work on; having nothing to wear or threadbare clothing; and not having the basic necessities of life. The conception of a necessary minimum income lurked in these accounts, and the emphasis was principally upon the physical necessities of food, clothing and shelter. Thus: 'Living in slum conditions; not enough money for the essentials of life' (38-year-old warehouseman with three children). 'It's not having enough food and clothes and being behind with the rent and not being able to pull up' (37-year-old railwayman with three children). 'I suppose it's simply being short of the necessaries of life – living hand to mouth and perhaps going without food and clothes' (self-employed window-cleaner of 50). 'People who have to tighten their belts because they just haven't enough to eat – or children who are very poorly clothed' (74-year-old married man). 'When you just manage to live through the day' (25-year-old student).

Starvation poverty

Some people put extreme emphasis on lack of food, malnutrition or starvation, and a number of them made specific references to overseas conditions – to Biafra, India and Morocco, for example. In calling attention to this conception, they usually denied the existence of poverty in Britain.

Relative poverty

(a) Compared with others. Some people spoke specifically with reference to conditions in the rest of society. Thus, 'Lacking the sort of things our society regards as necessities' (50-year-old hairdresser). 'Can't enjoy life like everyone else' (45-year-old carpenter with two children).

Relative poverty

(b) Historical. Some people took their standards from the past, either their own or society's past. They were drawn from all age groups, and not only the elderly. Many were people who denied there was real poverty today. Thus: 'Poverty is what we used to be like when I was a child' (23-year-old solderer in TV assembly). 'I can remember the days when I used to line up at the soup kitchen. That is why I hate having things handed down now. And there were days when I had to stop off school because it was my brother's turn for the boots' (56-year-old widow living with unmarried daughter). 'Lining up for the soup kitchen like they used to do, but there's no dire poverty now' (35-year-old widow with young daughter). 'It's on the breadline with no assistance, like before the war' (57-year-old clerk).

Poverty as mismanagement (or Rowntree's 'secondary' poverty)

Some people took the view that poverty was just a reflection of bad management, neglect or shiftlessness. Thus 'poverty arises not because of lack of money (or rather the opportunities to obtain assistance) but because of the bad management and ignorance of the working class' (40-year-old self-employed cabinet-maker with one child). 'Some people make poverty. They have adequate money if used wisely but spend it on beer and gambling and the family suffer by going short of food and clothing' (68-year-old married pensioner).

There were also a variety of answers that could not easily be categorized: 'It's not enough money'; 'It's a condition of mind'; 'It's when there are no relatives or friends to help'.

The numbers giving different descriptions are shown in Table 6.1. There were, of course, people who had multiple conceptions, and in these instances we simply took the conception which was given precedence or most emphasis. Nearly a third of heads of households, the largest fraction, saw poverty as lack of the means of subsistence. More than a quarter saw it in terms of certain minority groups, particularly retirement pensioners, but also the low paid and others. Small percentages, which none the less represented large numbers in the population, took an extreme view of poverty as starvation, and as a condition principally associated with mismanagement. A small percentage also conceived of

Table 6.1. Percentages of chief wage-earners or heads of households with low, middle and upper middle, and high incomes giving different descriptions of poverty.

| Description of poverty | Net disposable household income last year as a % of mean of household type | | | |
	Under 80	80–199	200+	All[a]
Subsistence	31	32	37	31
Minority groups (e.g. pensioners, low paid)	25	31	32	29
Mismanagement	10	7	9	8
Relative with past	7	5	0	5
Relative with others	2	3	2	2
Starvation	8	7	8	7
None to describe	9	8	5	8
Other	8	8	8	8
Total	100	100	100	100
Number	728	795	246	1,964

NOTE: [a]Including 198 unclassifiable by income.

poverty as a state of resources which were low relative to the rest of society or low relative to their own or society's past.

To what extent did these conceptions vary structurally? Certain trends are worthy of note. More heads of households with relatively high than with relatively low incomes thought of poverty in terms of a standard below subsistence. This trend was rather more marked according to class. More non-manual workers, and particularly routine non-manual workers, than manual workers regarded poverty as a standard below subsistence (Table A.9, Appendix Eight, page 999). And slightly more young and middle-aged than elderly heads of households took the same view. On the other hand, more of those with relatively low than relatively high incomes conceived of poverty as a condition belonging to the past; and slightly more of them, and of manual workers than of nonmanual workers, conceived of it as mismanagement. Finally, although roughly similar proportions of skilled manual and non-manual workers conceived of poverty as an attribute of minority groups, the proportion of partly skilled and unskilled workers saying the same was lower.

It is tempting to offer an explanation for this slightly diverse pattern. There are social pressures which dissuade large numbers of both non-manual and manual classes from seeing poverty in some ways, for example, as a condition imposed by governments or employers. After all, both classes are part of a society which explains social position predominantly in terms of individual motivation, individual qualification and individual skill. In a society which attributes high pay to individual desert and effort, some of the low paid seem likely to justify their low position, or at least reconcile themselves to it, by seeing poverty in relation to the deprivation experienced by their parents and grandparents years earlier. It is a way of maintaining self-esteem. Alternatively, self-esteem may be preserved by shifting attention from observably meagre resources to mismanagement of resources. The escape from social shame of those with little money is to plead respectable management of the little they have. By contrast, more of the high paid than low paid have experienced discontinuities in family geography, occupations and personal history. They are more likely to have status aspirations and therefore to view social problems from the perspective of finely graded living standards and thresholds of minimum accomplishment. More of them, too, are likely to have been introduced to political or institutional conceptions of poverty like that of Beveridge. More of them seem likely to identify with the state's conception of 'subsistence' and a 'national minimum'.

It is along some such lines that a theory might tentatively be developed. In this report it would be premature. The correlations found in the survey are not marked and the conceptions by no means socially distinct. More rigorous questioning might clarify the conceptions which people hold. What has to be stressed is the wide diversity among different age groups, income groups and classes.

However, a substantial percentage of the population adopts a conception of poverty as being a standard below subsistence. Another substantial percentage identifies certain minority groups which are regarded as having a very low (and broadly homogeneous) standard of living. The possibility that some individuals in these groups may be relatively prosperous is ignored. These two sections of the population reflect official conceptions of subsistence and benefit as of right as developed, for example, by the Department of Health and Social Security (in the national insurance and supplementary benefit schemes). This provides a basis for the social or state standard of poverty which has been used throughout this report and which is discussed below.

The State's Standard of Poverty

One standard of poverty which reflects the views of a large section of the population is the state's standard of poverty. All societies recognize levels of need among their populations which, through the policies of various institutions and services, they try to meet. How well the needs are, in fact, met can be a matter for empirical inquiry. But all societies also recognize other objectives which they try to pursue, such as giving adults an incentive to earn a living and be self-reliant, and sometimes these conflict with the objective of satisfying need. The extent to which different objectives are defined, pursued, reconciled and achieved can also be a matter for empirical inquiry.

At a fairly early stage in the evolution of the incomes and social security policies of most nations, cash payments are made on test of means. These are usually restricted to certain narrowly defined groups, such as the aged, or the sick and the disabled, and only later are they extended to all categories of family not containing anyone who is in paid employment and even to some categories of family in which someone *is* in paid employment. There may be different standards of cash payments within the same society. Thus, although the federal government in the United States tries to lay down certain guidelines, there is variation among individual states, not only in the amounts paid and the numbers receiving payments, but also in the standards used for payment.[1] Within many societies there are local authority schemes whereby cash payments made through national schemes may be supplemented. In Britain, local authorities vary in the standards of educational maintenance allowances, charges for home help and so on. There is therefore scope for inquiry into many complex administrative arrangements if the standard of poverty which is actually applied within any particular society is to be correctly identified.

For most practical purposes, attention can be concentrated on the ordinary scales according to which payments are made under public assistance schemes to families of different composition. By comparing the actual incomes of families with their public-assistance 'entitlement', it would be possible to show how many people were in poverty by the standard accepted by society itself. Income data have been analysed along these lines both for Britain[2] and for some other countries.[3]

In the United Kingdom, the household means test was finally abandoned in 1948. The family unit within it became eligible for assistance in 1941. The income of people in the household who are not dependants can now be ignored, except for the purpose of calculating the contribution they can afford to make towards the rent. Thus an elderly grandmother living with a young family can be considered for assistance in her own right. Allowances for rents and other housing costs are normally calculated on the assumption that each income unit in the household contributes its share.

The basic rates of payment decided for the Supplementary Benefits Commission in Britain by the government have been changed frequently because prices and wages have increased. In November 1969, they were increased for the fourteenth

1. *Monthly Cost Standards for Basic Needs Used By States for Specified Types of Old Age Assistance Cases and Families Receiving Aid to Families with Dependent Children, January 1965* Department of Health, Education and Welfare Administration, Bureau of Family Services, Division of Program Statistics and Analysis, August 1965.

2. Abel-Smith, B., and Townsend, P., *The Poor and the Poorest*, Bell, London, 1965; Atkinson, A. B., *Poverty in Britain and the Reform of Social Security*, Cambridge University Press, 1969, pp. 80–81.

3. See, for example, Taira, K., 'Consumer Preferences, Poverty Norms and Extent of Poverty', *Quarterly Review of Economics and Business*, 1969.

Table 6.2. Basic rates of national assistance/supplementary benefit in 1948, 1968 and 1978.

Type of claimant		1948 £	As % of single householder	1968 Before 7 Oct. £	From 7 Oct. £	As % of single householder	1978[a] £	As % of single householder
Single householder		1·20	100	4·30	4·55	100	15·55	100
Married couple		2·00	167	7·05	7·45	164	25·15	162
Non-householder aged	21 and over	1·00	83	3·55	3·70	81	} 12·45	80
	18–20	0·87½	73	2·90	3·05	67		
	16–17	0·75	62	2·50	2·65	58	9·55	61
Children	13–15 }	0·52½	44	{ 1·85	2·05	45	7·95	51
	11–12 }			{ 1·85	1·95	43	6·55	42
	5–10	0·45	37	1·50	1·60	35	5·30	34
Under 5		0·37½	31	1·25	1·35	30	4·40	28

NOTE: [a] Ordinary rate.

time since July 1948. After the war the rates adopted by the then National Assistance Board corresponded broadly with the subsistence standard as defined in the Beveridge Report of 1942, but they were raised fourteen times in twenty-three years, and although there have been minor changes from time to time in the relativities of certain rates,[1] no attempt has been made to redefine them. Broadly speaking, they represent the same definition of 'need' as that recommended by Beveridge. The basic rates applying in 1948, 1968 and 1978 are compared in Table 6.2. Excluding the allowance for rent, the basic rates payable to a man, wife and three children aged 12, 8 and 4 was 49 per cent of the average industrial earnings of men aged 21 and over in Ocober 1948, 52·3 per cent in April 1968 and 53·7 per cent in October 1968. During these twenty years, the 'real' value of the allowances for such a family increased by about 70 per cent – as measured by the movement in general price indices.

Some other societies recognize a very different structure of rates of benefit. For example, the rates for children are much higher in relation to adults in West Germany and some states in the United States than in Britain.[2] In these countries the

1. Bagley, C., *The Cost of a Child: Problems in the Relief and Measurement of Poverty*, Institute of Psychiatry, London, 1969, pp. 11–15.

2. ibid., pp. 16–24; Wynn, M., *Family Policy*, Michael Joseph, London, 1970, pp. 53–86.

rates for adolescent children in particular are much higher and correspond with those for adults. The social standard of poverty is relatively higher.

The basic rates cannot be used as an indication of actual family incomes without making a number of qualifications. First, higher rates are paid to the blind (and were in the past paid to some persons suffering from respiratory tuberculosis or its after-effects). Secondly, some resources are disregarded by the Supplementary Benefits Commission. For example, in 1968 up to £2 of the net weekly earnings of an adult other than a man required to register for work, up to £2 of the total of war and industrial disablement pensions, workmen's compensation and certain widows' benefits, and up to £1 of income including superannuation, sick pay, charitable payments and annuities, could be disregarded. Up to £300 of capital assets in addition to an owner-occupied house were wholly disregarded, and above this figure another £500 could be wholly and a further several hundred pounds partly disregarded. In that year, 870,000 persons drawing regular weekly payments, or 33 per cent, had income which was disregarded, averaging rather less than £1 per week. They included 355,000 with actual or assumed income from capital assets of £325 or more; 227,000 with superannuation; 69,000 with widows' pensions other than national insurance widows' pensions; 77,000 with charitable or voluntary payments; 22,000 with disability pensions; 18,000 with dependants' war pension; 164,000 with earnings; 44,000 with maintenance orders; and 34,000 others. As many as 1,178,000, or 45 per cent, had capital assets. However, some of these had only a few pounds. Altogether 55 per cent had no capital assets, but 7 per cent had £500 or more (the great majority of whom were retirement pensioners).[1] It would seem also that the commission's officers overlook modest allowances made by relatives or friends, such as 50p or £1 a week given to a pensioner by a son or daughter as itemized above under 'charitable payments'. They often ignore occasional gifts in cash or kind. A large number of persons therefore have £1 or £2 or £3 income per week in addition to the basic rates which are paid to them.

Thirdly, a large number of persons are paid more than the basic rates. Retirement pensioners other than those in hospital or local-authority residential accommodation and persons under pensionable age, other than those having to register for work, who have received supplementary allowances continuously for two years, are entitled to receive a long-term addition (now developed into the long-term rate). In 1968, this was 50p. Further additions could be made for exceptional expenses, for fuel, special diet, laundering and domestic help, for example, in excess of the fixed long-term amount. In November 1968, 527,000 persons, or 20 per cent, received an average addition of 30p. A single payment to meet some exceptional need, such as the replacement of bedding or clothing, may be made. In 1968, 470,000 such payments were made, averaging just over £5.

1. *Annual Report of the Department of Health and Social Security for the Year 1968*, Cmnd 4100, HMSO, London, 1969, pp. 328–9.

There are also exemptions from, or reimbursements of, charges for prescriptions, dentures, dental treatment and glasses supplied through the National Health Service, and supplementary benefit recipients qualify for free milk and vitamins for expectant and nursing mothers and children under school age, and free school meals for children at school.

Against these factors, which mean that families living on supplementary benefit normally have a standard of living higher than the actual basic scale rates, there are others which reduce families to a standard below the scale rates. Some persons are given allowances which provide them with an income below the basic rates. They include persons who refuse a reasonable offer of employment or who have voluntarily left their employment without just cause. In the late 1960s and early 1970s, the 'wage-stop' (since abolished) was applied to about a third of unemployed men with children. Often the allowance for a man with several children was more than £3 below, and sometimes more than £6 below, the basic rates payable by the commission.[1] The amount allowed for rent may also be reduced to a figure below the actual rent if the latter is regarded as 'unreasonable'. The number of recipients affected is not known for 1968, but in earlier years was about 1 per cent.

For all these reasons the actual cash income of persons receiving supplementary benefit can vary widely from the income defined by the basic rates. Usually it will be rather higher. A secondary analysis of FES data for 1953–4 found that single people receiving national assistance were living at a standard averaging about 26 per cent above the basic rates plus rent.[2] Evidence from the present survey, which will be discussed later, shows that the income for the preceding twelve months of those depending continuously on supplementary benefit, and the income for the preceding week of those receiving supplementary benefit in that week, was often higher than the basic rates plus housing costs. For nearly two thirds of those receiving supplementary benefit, it was, in fact, more than 10 per cent higher, and for over a quarter, more than 20 per cent higher, including a minority with an income more than 40·per cent higher. There are difficulties in drawing exact conclusions from the data, because individual circumstances may change during a short period of time, and because the contributions made to household income by different income units may be different from those assumed by the Supplementary Benefits Commission. But there is no doubt that, in practice, the incomes of the majority of households dependent on the commission fall within a range rather higher than the basic rates.

1. *Administration of the Wage Stop*, Report by the Supplementary Benefits Commission to the Minister of Social Security, H M S O, London, 1967, p. 4. During 1968, the number of unemployed persons subject to the wage-stop in Britain fluctuated between 20,500 and 32,400. However, these restricted allowances covered a total of up to 100,000 people in the families of the unemployed. See Department of Health and Social Security Annual Report for 1969, Cmnd 4462, H M S O, London, p. 336.

2. Abel-Smith and Townsend, *The Poor and the Poorest*, p. 18.

In defining the state's standard of poverty, therefore, it would be wrong to take the simple rules governing the payment of the basic rates without also paying heed to all the other rules which allow a higher standard, and sometimes a lower standard, to be applied. In practice, society approves a standard for war pensioners and the blind which is higher than (in descending rank order) widows and their families, retirement pensioners, other physically sick or disabled people, the mentally ill and handicapped, separated wives and unmarried mothers and their families and, finally, the unemployed. Any conversion of the standards into equivalent amounts of income would be arbitrary within certain limits. It would be possible, for purposes of illustration and analysis, to take, say, the income of the 20th percentile, ranked from the topmost income, in each group – on the grounds that the great majority of those in each group are 'allowed' an income up to this level. However, there are drawbacks about such a proposal, not the least of which is the lack of information about the incomes of a sufficient number representing each of these groups. In a secondary analysis of incomes data, the Department of Health and Social Security referred to these problems and made two adjustments to the basic scales in comparing family resources with their needs. First, an average addition of 5p for families with one child or two children (with 5p for each additional child) was made to cover exceptional needs grants made in the course of the year by the Supplementary Benefits Commission. Secondly, a sum of 40p per week in 1968 was added, where appropriate, for travel-to-work expenses.[1] We did not adopt these adjustments, the first because it seemed wholly arbitrary to average this type of grant and none of the other grants and allowances; the second because we were able to deduct actual expenses in travelling to work from gross disposable income.

In this study we have defined two levels of income. The first is the basic supplementary benefit rates plus housing costs for different types of household. This will usually be lower than the level allowed in practice for families by the Supplementary Benefits Commission. The second is a level 40 per cent higher. Above this level, only relatively few families in fact prove to be getting help from the commission, but the majority of families receiving help have total incomes ranging up to that level. It is also a convenient cutting-off point, since it has been used in previous research. In assessing income in relation to the basic rates, we do not disregard any form of cash income, only income in kind. Income from capital is included, but no adjustment is made for the amount of capital itself.

The cost of housing is the weekly rent, inclusive of rates. For owner-occupied housing, the weekly equivalent of mortgage interest payments and capital repayments, together with the cost of insurance (and any ground rent, if payable) but not the cost of repairs, is counted. Although the commission does not itself allow any capital repayment in calculating individual weekly allowances, such repay-

1. Howe, J. R., *Two-Parent Families: A Study of their Resources and Needs in 1968, 1969 and 1970*, HMSO, London, 1971, p. 2.

ments have been included in housing costs in three government studies comparing resources with needs.[1]

There would in practice be difficulties in excluding these amounts, whether or not there were objections in principle. 'For approximately one-third of owner-occupiers with a mortgage, information is not available to distinguish the capital and interest components of the mortgage repayment.'[2] For simplicity we have adopted previous government research practice.

With reservations, then, the supplementary benefit standard in any year can be regarded as being the state's or society's current definition of a poverty line. It is not an objectively or scientifically constructed standard, and it would be unwise to treat it as such. For example, some writers have argued that since its relationship to mean or median income varies slightly from year to year over even a short span of years, it should be standardized in relation to such income.[3] This would be to convert a social (or administrative) construct into one which is neither social nor scientific.

The Relative Income Standard of Poverty

Alternatives to the state's standard of poverty can be devised. One might be called the 'relative income standard'. Households can be placed in rank order according to their income and those with the lowest (or highest) incomes studied. The criterion of comparison is purely internal. If statements are made in terms of, say, deciles, then attention can be concentrated on the same quantitative groups in the population at different points in time or on the same quantitative groups in different populations. We may find that the poorest 10 per cent in the United Kingdom is very different in composition from the poorest 10 per cent in France, or that during a decade the poorest 10 per cent in any country changes significantly in composition. However, it would be impossible to say from time to time or country to country what changes were taking place in numbers living in poverty.

An alternative relative measure is to express income (or expenditure) as a percentage of the mean.[4] The proportion of two populations having less than 50 per cent of the mean may be significantly different, or the proportion of one population living at that level of income may change during a decade.[5]

1. Ministry of Social Security, *Circumstances of Families*, HMSO, London, 1967, p. 3. See also Ministry of Pensions and National Insurance, *Financial and Other Circumstances of Retirement Pensioners*, HMSO, London, 1966.
2. Howe, *Two-Parent Families*, p. 2.
3. ibid., p. 4.
4. Abel-Smith and Townsend, *The Poor and the Poorest*, p. 37. For an illustration of both approaches, see Miller, S. M., and Roby, P., *The Future of Inequality*, Basic Books, New York, pp. 34–7.
5. An OECD study compared the percentages of the populations of different countries

There are at least two limitations of this method. One is that income varies according to size and type of household. A distribution can be worked out for each type of household to meet this difficulty, but beyond a certain point it is difficult to allow for differentiation among households. There are numerous sub-types, and any sample of the population will include a few examples of some sub-types. The definition of 'types' is therefore governed to some extent by the number of instances of a particular kind in a sample (as well as historical knowledge about such types). And in ranking households within each type, and looking at the distribution in terms of percentage of the mean, an implicit assumption is made about the 'equivalence' of mean income for each type. Thus married couples without children and married couples with four children who each have 50 per cent of the mean for their type of family may, in fact, have a more unequal standard of living in one society than in another. In some measure the forces governing the distribution of income *within* types of household are independent of those governing the distribution *between* types of household.

The other limitation of this method is the arbitrariness of the choice of any particular percentage of the mean. Thus, on what grounds might one choose 50 per cent of mean income by which to identify relatively 'low' income rather than, say, 85 per cent? Perhaps certain criteria can be produced to justify the choice.

We decided to define the relative income standard in terms, first, of a number of types of household, and secondly, of levels of 50 per cent (very low) and 80 per cent (low) of the mean income for each type. The mean seems a more appropriate measure than the median. It is derived from the aggregate income which is distributed and therefore provides a more 'stable' reference point for measuring dispersion of incomes between countries and between two periods of time. For example, the income 'capacity' of a country might be concealed in cross-national comparisons if a tiny percentage of the population have exceptionally high incomes. Thus, the proportion of the population of this country with less income than 50 per cent of the median might be the same as of another country, and yet the proportion with less than 50 per cent of the mean might be twice as large.

The Deprivation Standard of Poverty

The third measure is that of relative deprivation. While the first measure produces an estimate of socially perceived poverty and the second a band of low incomes of

---

found to be in poverty, according to a national and a standardized definition. This standardized definition was admitted to be very arbitrary. Households were counted as poor if their incomes fell below the following percentages of mean disposable income per head: 1 person, 66·7 per cent; 2 persons, 100 per cent; 3 persons, 125 per cent; 4 persons, 145 per cent; 5 persons, 160 per cent. See OECD Studies in Resource Allocation, *Public Expenditure on Income Maintenance Programmes*, OECD, Paris, July 1976, p. 66.

somewhat arbitrary width, the third attempts to provide an estimate of objective poverty on the basis of a level of deprivation disproportionate to resources.

The measure is provisional. As explained in Chapter 1 (page 55), households are ranked according to income and a criterion of deprivation applied. In descending the income scale, it is hypothesized that, at a particular point for different types of family, a significantly large number of families reduce more than proportionately their participation in the community's style of living. They drop out or are excluded. These income points can be identified as a poverty line.

The procedure needs to be formulated. There is no unitary and clear-cut national 'style of living'. Rather, there are series of overlapping and merging community, ethnic, organizational and regional styles. By style of living I do not mean *particular* things and actions in themselves, but *types* of consumption and *customs* which are expressive of social form. Thus, the influence of national government, trading systems, education, the mass media, industry and transport systems will tend towards the establishment of diffuse cultural norms. Pakistanis in Bradford will tend or will be encouraged to adopt English habits of going away on summer holidays, patterns of child care, car-driving and travel, and patterns of consumption, even when they remain distinctive in other respects. Certain practices gradually become accepted as appropriate modes of behaviour, and even when a group performs particular rituals of religious observance or engages in particular leisure-time activity, it shares other customs with many different groups in society. What do need to be distinguished are the customs practised by a majority of the national population, and those practised by different minorities and sub-groups. Shared activities may differ in substance. Christmas may be celebrated by an exchange of gifts from Woolworth's, a few glasses of beer and a chicken from a broiler factory; or by an exchange of gifts in the best tradition of Harrods or Heal's, together with all the luxurious trappings of a country-house week-end party. The point at which a custom is no longer practised is debatable.

A national style of living has to be defined in operational terms. Many component items, including those specific to age groups, peers and generations, and to large units, such as regional communities and ethnic groups, have to be identified and examined and the elements common to, or approved by, the majority of the population distinguished. The degree of cultural integration of different groups and communities could then be tentatively assessed and perhaps measured. There are different spheres of social life – at work or school, in the home, in the immediate vicinity of the home, and elsewhere in the community, and in all of these spheres the individual's diet, health, welfare, occupation and recreation are defined. All this would represent considerable cultural inquiry.

A list of sixty indicators of the 'style of living' of the population was built up. This covered diet, clothing, fuel and light, home amenities, housing and housing facilities, the immediate environment of the home, the characteristics, security, general conditions and welfare benefits of work, family support, recreation,

Table 6.3. The deprivation index.

Characteristic	% of population	Correlation coefficient (Pearson) (net disposable household income last year)	
1. Has not had a week's holiday away from home in last 12 months	53·6	0·1892	S = 0·001
2. *Adults only.* Has not had a relative or friend to the home for a meal or snack in the last 4 weeks	33·4	0·0493	S = 0·001
3. *Adults only.* Has not been out in the last 4 weeks to a relative or friend for a meal or snack	45·1	0·0515	S = 0·001
4. *Children only* (under 15). Has not had a friend to play or to tea in the last 4 weeks	36·3	0·0643	S = 0·020
5. *Children only.* Did not have party on last birthday	56·6	0·0660	S = 0·016
6. Has not had an afternoon or evening out for entertainment in the last two weeks	47·0	0·1088	S = 0·001
7. Does not have fresh meat (including meals out) as many as four days a week	19·3	0·1821	S = 0·001
8. Has gone through one or more days in the past fortnight without a cooked meal	7·0	0·0684	S = 0·001
9. Has not had a cooked breakfast most days of the week	67·3	0·0559	S = 0·001
10. Household does not have a refrigerator	45·1	0·2419	S = 0·001
11. Household does not usually have a Sunday joint (3 in 4 times)	25·9	0·1734	S = 0·001
12. Household does not have sole use of four amenities indoors (flush W C; sink or washbasin and cold-water tap; fixed bath or shower; and gas or electric cooker)	21·4	0·1671	S = 0·001

education, health and social relations. The list is set out in Appendix Thirteen (page 1173). The corresponding parts of the questionnaire will be found in Appendix Ten (pages 1156–65). Different groups of indicators are discussed at length in Chapters 11, 12, 13, 14 and 20.

In principle, such a list might be developed, as I have suggested, from an exhaustive analysis of the amenities available to, and the customs or modes of living of, a majority of the population, in the course of which the representativeness and independence of different items and their frequency and symbolic as well as material importance would have to be discussed. In practice, we sought only to ensure that all the major areas of personal, household and social life were represented in our questionnaire. At this experimental stage, we wished to examine the relationship between participation in customary amenities and activities (as measured by indicators selected on the basis of pilot interviews and knowledge of previous studies of life-styles and amenities) and the distribution of income and other resources.

The indicators can be expressed as indicators of deprivation – for example, lacking that amenity or not participating in that activity (Appendix Thirteen, page 1173). By applying the indicators to individuals and families, a 'score' for different forms of deprivation can be added up: the higher the score the lower the participation. One would expect some indicators, like infrequent meat eating or lack of certain structural facilities in the home, to be correlated with low level of resources. But one would be less likely to expect others to be so correlated. *Prima facie*, low income might not prevent someone having an evening out once a fortnight or more, going to friends' or relatives' houses, having children's friends in to play or even having a holiday, though we would expect the occasion to be more austere. In fact, as Appendix Thirteen shows, the correlation between nearly all these indicators and different measures of resources is highly significant.

For illustrative purposes, a summary 'deprivation index' was compiled to cover major aspects of dietary, household, familial, recreational and social deprivation. This is set out in Table 6.3. The full list in Appendix Thirteen includes more items which could be applied to some sections of the population than to others. Although the scores for certain items could be reweighted to redress the balance (for example, on conditions in the home for people who were not in employment), we felt we did not have sufficient information to show how this might be done. We have therefore chosen those indicators which apply to the whole population, although with two components we considered it was appropriate to frame alternative versions for adults and children. While, in principle, we would have wished each of the indicators to apply to a minority of the population, three of the twelve in the present research in fact apply to a small majority.

The mean individual score for the entire sample was 3·5. It was 3·4 for children and 3·5 for adults; and was 3·6 for housewives. The mean score for younger adults (15–44) was however lower (3·0) than for older adults (3·5 for people aged 50–59, 4·1 for people aged 60–69 and 5·1 for people aged 70 and over).

Different items in the index reflect the fact that some customs or activities are common to the household, but others apply only to individuals within the household. No single item by itself, or pair of items by themselves, can be regarded as symptomatic of general deprivation. People are idiosyncratic and will indulge in certain luxuries and apply certain prohibitions, for religious, moral, educational and other reasons, whether they are rich or poor. Families in certain situations are not necessarily deprived if they do not have a week's holiday; or if they do not have an afternoon or evening outside the home; or if they do not have a Sunday joint, because they may have other compensating activities or customs. This is why deprivation is difficult at the margins to detect. A score of 5 or 6 or more is regarded as highly suggestive of deprivation. Twenty per cent of households scored an average of 6 or more.

Figure 6.1 shows the sharp increase in deprivation at the lower levels of net

Table 6.4. Mean scores of deprivation, according to net household income.

Range of income	Size of households					All households	
	1	2	3	4	5+	Means	No.
Under £300	5·9					5·8	69
£300–49	5·9	5·6				5·8	71
£350–99	5·4					5·4	72
£400–99	4·9	5·2				5·0	94
£500–99	4·0	5·0	4·7	(4·5)		4·7	83
£600–99	4·1	4·3				4·3	85
£700–99	4·0	4·3	4·7	(4·1)		4·4	107
£800–99		4·1	3·9	3·5	(5·2)	3·9	107
£900–99	(3·2)	3·8	3·6	(3·1)	(4·8)	3·6	115
£1,000–99		3·6	3·1	3·1	(4·1)	3·3	109
£1,100–99		3·6	2·9	3·1	(4·1)	3·4	117
£1,200–399		2·9	3·0	2·8	3·5	3·0	212
£1,400–599		2·6	2·9	3·1	3·3	3·0	130
£1,600–799	(3·4)	2·5	2·8	2·9	3·4	2·9	126
£1,800–999		(2·2)	(2·8)	(2·7)	(3·5)	2·8	66
£2,000–499		(2·7)	2·7	2·5	2·7	2·6	108
£2,500+		(1·7)	(2·2)	2·0	2·6	2·3	98
All	5·1	3·8	3·2	3·0	3·5	3·7	1,769

NOTE: In this table no means are given for groups with fewer than 10 households in each group. Means for 10–19 households are placed in brackets. It should be noted that, for households with two or more persons, scores for each person were combined and averaged.

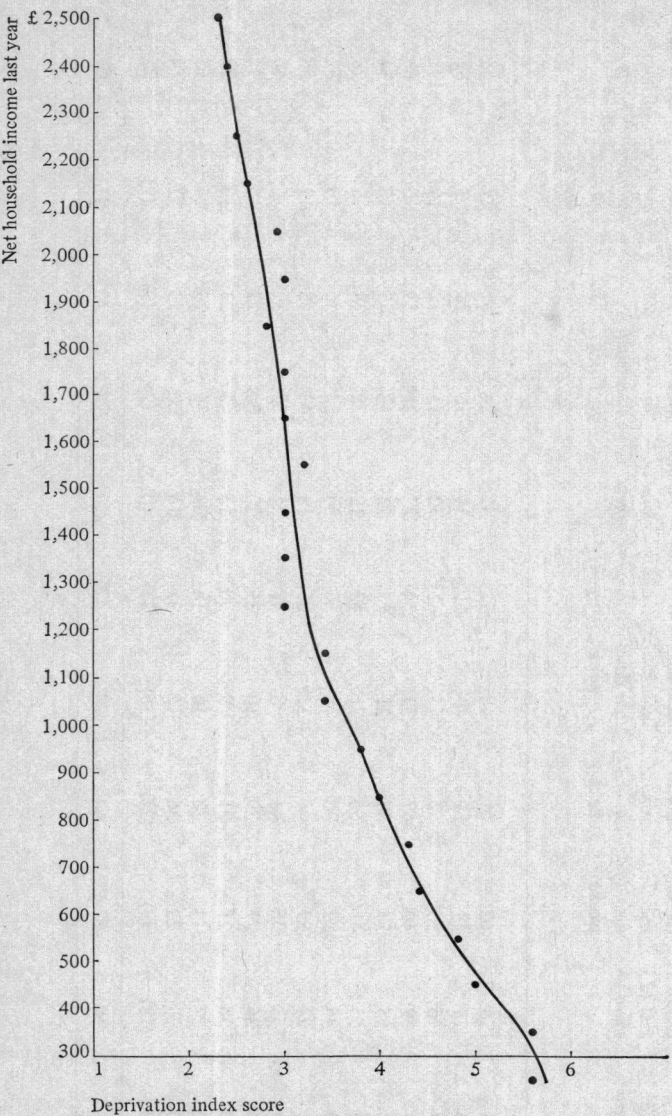

Figure 6.1. Deprivation index score for individuals in relation to household income.

Table 6.5. Percentages of people in two-person households deprived of certain activities and amenities.

Net household income last year (£)	No holiday in last 12 months	No relative or friend to meal in 4 weeks	No afternoon or evening out in 2 weeks	No fresh meat as often as four days per week	No meal with relative or friend in 4 weeks	Usually no Sunday joint of meat	Does not have sole use of 4 household facilities	No refrigerator	No cooked meal one or more days in last 2 weeks	Number of persons in households
Under 400	78	62	51	48	71	41	24	52	17	58
400–	78	48	51	49	61	34	36	78	9	88
500–	76	36	62	45	61	30	23	72	14	102
600–	59	40	57	33	54	27	21	53	6	68
700–	55	37	59	31	57	23	32	45	15	94
800–	55	41	56	21	53	18	28	38	8	78
900–	45	29	30	18	56	30	32	46	10	82
1,000–	28	29	48	12	36	18	43	46	19	58
1,100–	53	36	44	8	47	24	36	39	6	66
1,200–	36	27	29	10	35	20	20	27	6	134
1,400–	36	21	31	9	30	13	5	23	10	77
1,600–	27	14	23	16	18	23	16	19	6	62
1,800–	28	23	36	12	31	16	0	19	17	64
2,500+	(18)	(9)	(27)	(18)	(27)	(0)	(9)	(9)	(9)	22
All	50	33	44	24	47	24	24	43	11	1,053

household income. Table 6.4 further shows that the trend is similar for all sizes of household. Strictly speaking, according to our hypothesis, the deprivation 'score' would be expected to rise with household size for any level of household income (so providing a measure of what income for households of any particular size would be 'equivalent' to the income for households of a different size). Table 6.4 bears this out only in part. As pointed out above, disability tends to raise the mean score of some people, particularly single-person households, by up to one. Some income groups of similar household size include a wide variety of household types. And because the size of the sample was limited, the numbers of households in some of the cells is small. For these and other reasons, the pattern presented in the table must be treated as suggestive only.

What is the contribution made by each item in the index to the total 'score'? Table 6.5 shows the pattern for two-person households. Some customs are more strongly correlated with income than others. Thus, there is a strong correlation between income and holidays, entertainment of relatives or friends to a meal, and consumption of fresh meat most days of the week. The correlation between income and sole use of four basic household facilities is evident only at the upper ranges of income and is indeterminate at the lowest and middle ranges. As we shall see, one explanation for such fluctuations is the differential ownership of capital assets by households with the same cash income.

So far we have been able to show the relationship between diminishing income and increasing deprivation. But is there evidence of the existence of a 'threshold' of income for different types of household, below which people are disproportionately deprived? The evidence from this survey is inconclusive, but suggests that such a threshold may exist. Our evidence is strongest for one-person and two-person income units and households, and the families with one child and with four or more children. Thus Table 6.6 shows a fairly marked increase in the proportions of people who may be regarded as 'deprived' below certain levels of income, namely £400 per annum for one-person units, £600 per annum for two-person units, £800 for three-person units, £900 for four-person units, and £1,100 for five-person units. These cut-offs were checked using other indicators.

The phenomenon can be investigated more closely among particular types of household. Some results are shown in graph form in Figure 6.2. Except for men under 60 years of age, the mean score of deprivation for one-person households rises fairly sharply once income falls below £400 per annum. Among two-person households, there is a similar increase below £600 per annum. However, there is evidence of deprivation above this level of income among households consisting of two people under the age of 60. Among households consisting of a man and woman and one child, there is a sharp increase in deprivation below £800 per annum; and among households with man, woman and two children, also below £800. The trends for all types of household are shown in Table A.10 (Appendix Eight, page 1000). But it is important to remember that the underlying numbers

Table 6.6. Percentages of persons in one-person and larger income units with deprivation score of 6 or more, according to income of income unit.

Range of income	Number of persons in income unit 1	2	3	4	5+	All income units All sizes	%	No.
Under £300	36	} 50				35	14	357
£300–	37					41	10	265
£400–	19	40				25	9	219
£500–	15	43	} (29)	} 20		27	7	188
£600–	10	} 17			} (41)	15	7	177
£700–	10					15	7	168
£800–	6	} 13	} (4)			11	7	171
£900–				} 8	} (24)	12	6	161
£1,000–	} 6	} 8	} 5			10	6	147
£1,100–				} 6	} (9)	7	5	125
£1,200–		4	} 2			5	8	204
£1,400		4			} (3)	3	4	110
£1,600	} (11)	} 2				1	3	81
£1,800			} (5)	} 0		(2)	2	45
£2,000		} (6)			} (0)	(2)	2	48
£2,500+						6	3	65
Total	24	18	8	8	16	19	100	2,531

NOTE: Figures in brackets apply to fewer than 50 but more than 30 units.

are not large. Although there were 471 households in the sample consisting of a man and a woman, these should be regarded as, properly, falling into different groups according to age. There were only 213 in which both man and woman were under 60 years of age, and only 165 in which both were 60 years of age or over. Again, there were 133 households with man and woman and one child, and 171 with two children.

To pursue the investigation of the relationship between income and deprivation it is necessary to standardize for composition of household. In addition to the 'thresholds of deprivation' approach we applied two other approaches: expressing income as a percentage, first, of the mean for the appropriate household type, and secondly, of the amount the household would receive in supplementary benefit in certain contingencies. We applied the former for the following fourteen types: man over 60 years; man under 60; woman over 60; woman under 60; man and woman; man, woman and one child, two children, three children, four or more children; three adults; three adults plus children; four adults; other house-

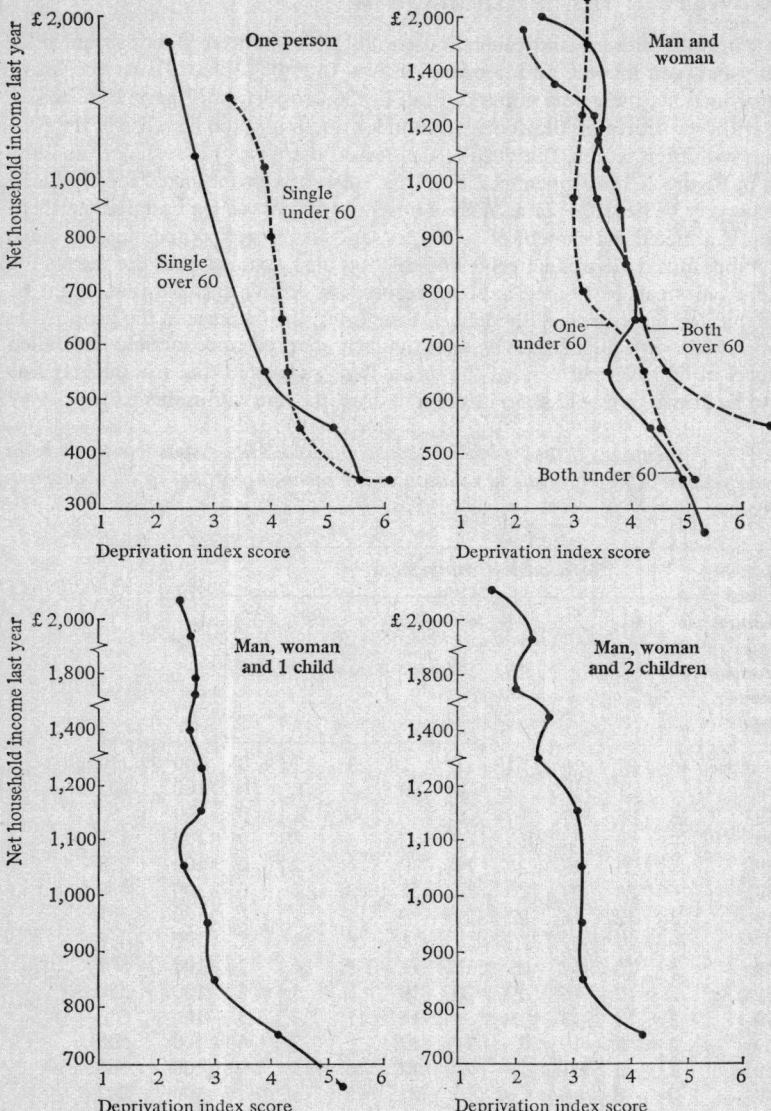

Figure 6.2. *The relationship between income and deprivation for certain types of household.*

holds without children; and other households with children. A consistent relationship between income and deprivation was found (Table 6.7). At the lower levels of income, there was a marked fall in the proportion of people in households with low scores on the deprivation index and a marked increase in the proportion with high scores. But despite this result, there was no evidence (as illustrated in Figure A.1 in Appendix Eight, page 1004) of a pronounced threshold. In part this may be because some of the household 'types' as we had defined them contained a mixed assortment of sub-types, and therefore income may not have been standardized very effectively. The method also assumes that the means for different types can be treated in some respects as equivalent. All that might be said is that for the more exactly defined categories, the increase in the proportion of households with high scores was particularly marked once income had fallen to a level of 60 to 69 per cent of the mean. This suggested that if a poverty line were to be drawn, it would seem justified to draw the line within this band.

Table 6.7. *Percentages of individuals in households with net disposable incomes in previous year at different levels in relation to the mean, according to their deprivation scores.*

Net disposable household income last year as % of mean for household type	Score on deprivation index									Total	No.
	0	1	2	3	4	5	6	7	8		
250 or more	16	27	25	12	11	3	3	3	0	100	110
200–49	6	21	34	19	6	9	3	2	0	100	105
180–99	18	35	17	16	9	3	0	1	0	100	98
160–79	7	19	34	19	13	2	3	3	0	100	134
140–59	6	23	23	21	12	9	4	2	0	100	258
120–39	6	20	24	20	14	11	3	1	0	100	433
110–19	3	12	26	22	22	9	5	1	0	100	351
100–9	3	17	19	22	17	11	6	3	1	100	418
90–99	5	15	17	22	17	13	5	4	2	100	517
80–89	2	12	16	19	20	16	8	5	2	100	580
70–79	3	11	18	19	19	13	11	4	3	100	533
60–69	2	7	19	21	17	12	9	7	6	100	508
50–59	1	3	11	13	20	12	16	15	9	100	366
40–49	0	5	8	16	15	21	15	13	7	100	242
Under 40	1	3	12	6	16	13	21	16	12	100	199
All incomes	4	13	19	17	17	12	8	5	3	100	4,852

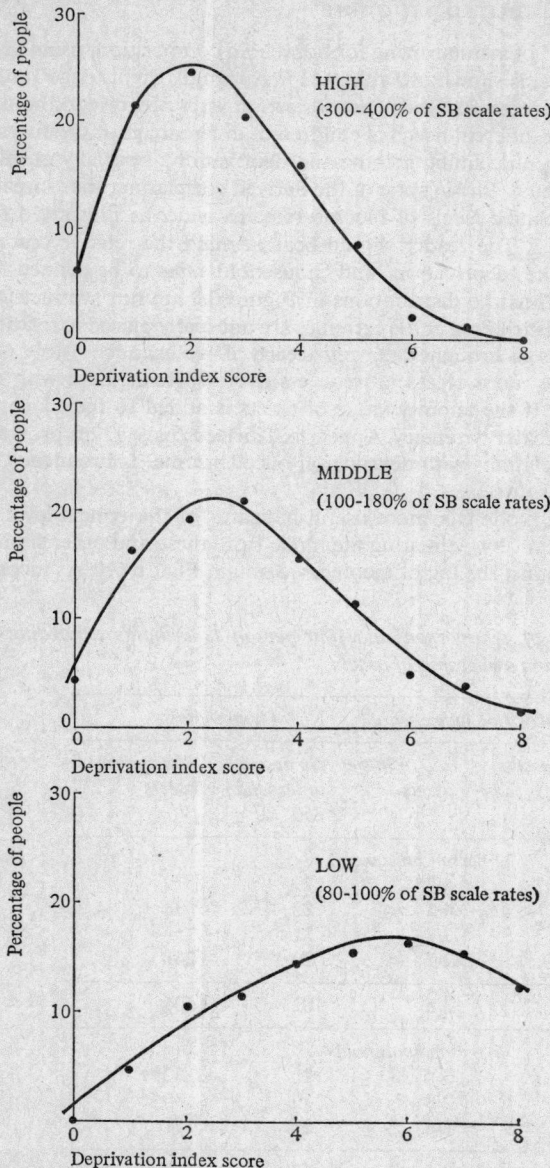

Figure 6.3. *The percentage at three levels of income with different deprivation scores.*

An alternative method of standardizing for household composition, using supplementary benefit scales, is shown in Table A.11 in Appendix Eight (page 1001). Since this method standardizes income better for certain sub-categories of household, and also allows for different needs of children of different age, it produces a better correlation between declining income and deprivation, especially at relatively low levels of income. But in spite of the derived correlation, the 'spread' of scores at different relative levels of income remains wide, as illustrated for three levels in Figure 6.3. The reader should bear in mind the relative crudity with which 'income' (like 'deprivation' and 'household') has to be defined for operational purposes. Thus the distributions in Figure 6.3 are not symmetrical and *some* of the people distributed at the extremes are unusually placed in relation to other resources. This is brought out very clearly if we examine Table 6.8. Households with £50 or more of assets were less deprived than those with no assets or less than £50. If the annuity value of assets is added to their income there is a shift towards greater symmetry. Appendix Thirteen (page 1173) provides evidence of higher correlations with deprivation once 'income' is broadened to include other types of resource.

For such reasons the mode is a more useful indicator of the typical level of deprivation than the mean. By estimating the mode from these and other similar graphs, and plotting against the log of income, we obtain Figure 6.4. As income

Table 6.8. *Deprivation of two-person and four-person households according to income in previous year and ownership of assets.*

	Deprivation index score		No. of households	
Range of income £	No assets or less than £50	£50 or more assets	No assets or less than £50	£50 or more assets
2-person households				
Under 500	5·5	4·7	29	79
500–99	5·5	4·5	22	33
600–999	5·4	3·8	31	151
1,000+	3·8	2·7	20	241
All ranges	5·1	3·5	102	504
4-person households				
Under 800	4·3	3·4	20	32
800–1,199	4·4	2·8	19	85
1,200+	4·0	2·6	21	171
All ranges	4·2	2·8	62	288

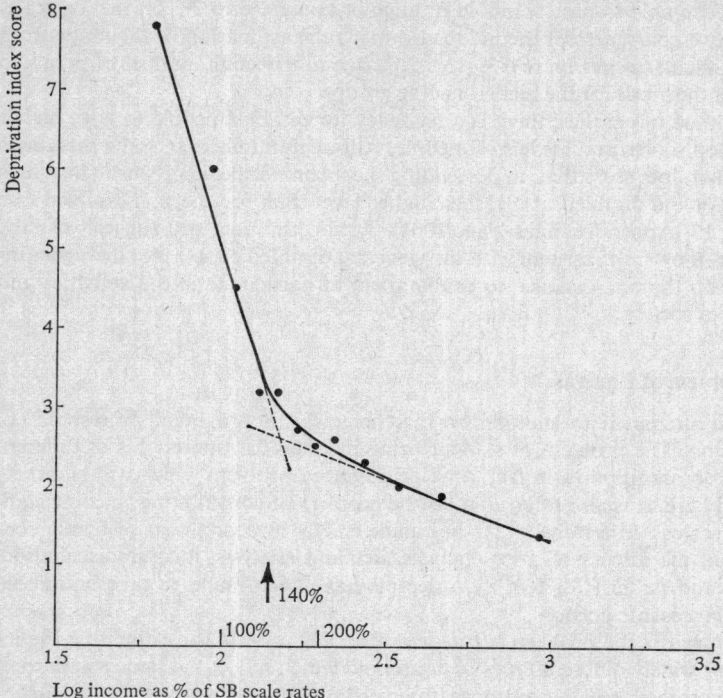

Figure 6.4. Modal deprivation by logarithm of income as a percentage of supplementary benefit scale rates.

diminishes from the highest levels, so deprivation steadily increases, but below 150 per cent of the supplementary benefit standard, deprivation begins to increase swiftly. Above and below this point the graph falls into distinct sections. Remembering that, for socio-structural or idiosyncratic, though socially permitted or encouraged reasons, some individuals do not adopt some of the values included in the index, the graph may none the less represent the expansion of social and not only material possibilities opened by increasing income. On the other hand, the swift increase in range of social activities at the higher levels of income may correspond with some diminution in the frequency or intensity of participation in different activities. The graph has been included tentatively for the following reasons. The sample size did not allow us to examine incomes more extreme than those plotted on the graph, and its shape would have been more certain if we had been able to plot points in a range of about 1·6 to 3·3 on the log scale. The relative coarseness of the index also made the estimation of the mode from graphs difficult (as in Figure 6.3, page 259) due to the small number of points to the left of the mode for the higher income groups.

As pointed out earlier, there is a tendency for disabled people to have higher deprivation scores at all levels of income. Although numbers in some categories are small, it does seem that, in descending the income scale, deprivation increases sharply for the disabled at a rather higher level than for the non-disabled (see Table A.13, Appendix Eight, page 1002). Again, the data are suggestive only. However, they are consistent with the view that disabled people require higher incomes than the non-disabled to enable them to participate in the activities and customs of society.

The Problem of Equivalence

We have attempted to standardize incomes at an approximate 'threshold' of deprivation. The problem of standardizing incomes for households of different size and composition is, in fact, a well-recognized problem which will be briefly reviewed here. It is also referred to as the problem of constructing 'income equivalence scales'. In a range of studies made chiefly by economists of family consumption, the impact of price changes, demand analysis, income distribution, poverty and patterns of fertility, attempts have been made to take household circumstances into account.[1]

First, what is the problem? It is one of finding criteria for estimating the incomes for widely different types of household which reflect the same standard of living – a rather broader purpose than estimating the equivalent 'needs' of

1. Nicholson, J. L., 'Variations in Working Class Family Expenditure', *Journal of the Royal Statistical Society* (Series A), vol. 112, 1949; Prais, S. J., 'The Estimation of Equivalent Adult Scales from Family Budgets', *Economic Journal*, 63, December 1953; Prest, A. R., and Stark, T., 'Some Aspects of Income Distribution in the U K since World War II', *Manchester School*, vol. 35, 1967; Bagley, C., *The Cost of a Child*, Institute of Psychiatry, London, 1969; Abel-Smith, B., and Bagley, C., 'The Problem of Establishing Equivalent Standards of Living for Families of Different Composition', in Townsend, P. (ed.), *The Concept of Poverty*, Heinemann, London, 1970; Wynn, M., *Family Policy*, Michael Joseph, London, 1970, esp. Chapters 2 and 3; Prais, S. J., and Houthakker, H. S., *The Analysis of Family Budgets*, Department of Applied Economics, Monograph 4, Cambridge University Press, 1955; Barten, A. P., 'Family Composition, Prices and Expenditure Patterns', in Hart, P., and Mills, G. (eds.), *Econometric Analysis for National Economic Planning*, Butterworth, London, 1964; Stark, T., *The Distribution of Personal Income in the United Kingdom 1949–1963*, Cambridge University Press, 1972; Singh, R., 'On the Determination of Economies of Scale in Household Composition', *International Economic Review*, June 1972; Seneca, J. H., and Taussig, M. K., 'Family Equivalence Scales and Personal Income Tax Exemptions for Children', *Review of Economics and Statistics*, August 1971; Blandy, R., 'The Welfare Analysis of Fertility Reduction', *Economic Journal*, March 1974; Leibenstein, H., 'An Interpretation of the Economic Theory of Fertility: Promising Path or Blind Alley?', *Journal of the Economics of Literature*, June 1974.

different types of household. Economists see one practical task in explaining and predicting shifts of demand, and another is to construct fair social security scales. The public assistance, national insurance and tax allowance rates for different dependants and types of family in different countries and at different points in the history of the United Kingdom can be compared. For example, in October 1968, the rate of benefit (including family allowances) for each dependent child of those who qualified for national insurance unemployment or sickness payments was 19·2 per cent of the rate for a married couple. But the rate for a child under 16 receiving supplementary benefit varied (according to age) from 18·1 per cent to 27·5 per cent (though, unlike national insurance, these rates do not embody an allowance for rent); and the tax allowance for a child from 33·8 per cent (for a child under 11) to 41·2 per cent (for a child aged 11–15) of the combined personal tax allowance of man and wife. Here are examples of inconsistency in treatment of families of different composition.

Without special regard to poverty or subsistence, some writers have sought to define equivalence by means of food expenditure. Engels, for example, observed in 1857 an inverse relationship between income and the percentage of total expenditure accounted for by food.[1] For Britain, Nicholson has calculated an equivalent adult scale by comparing the levels of income at which different types of family spent the same proportion of net household income on food.[2] The principle is illustrated in Figure 6.5. After plotting the expenditure on food of particular types of family with varying income on a graph, the points at which different types of family spend the same percentage can be compared. The horizontal dotted line joins two such points, and income A is treated as equivalent to income B. The lower part of the figure gives an illustration based on data drawn from the report of the Family Expenditure Survey for 1968. For every level of income, larger households committed a higher proportion of their incomes, on average, than smaller households to the purchase of food. At the lower levels of income, the percentage committed to food increased more and more sharply. If a line is drawn horizontally across the graph at the 20 per cent level, and the distance between the curves measured, then an equivalent adult scale can be represented as follows (households of man and woman being assumed to provide the standard):

1. See the account in Hobsbawm, E. J., 'Poverty', *New International Encyclopaedia of the Social Sciences*. In an 1885 paper Engels's near namesake, Engel, pioneered the development of equivalence scales. See Engel, E., 'Die Lebenskosten belgischer Arbeiter-Familien früher und jetzt', *International Statistical Bulletin*, No. 9, 1885.
2. Nicholson, J. L., *Redistribution of Income in the United Kingdom in 1959, 1957 and 1953*, Bowes & Bowes, Cambridge, 1965. For later reviews of equivalence scales, see Nicholson, J. L., 'Appraisal of Different Methods of Estimating Equivalence Scales and their Results', *Review of Income and Wealth*, 1976; and Muellbauer, J., 'Testing the Barten Model of Household Composition Effects and the Cost of Children', *Economic Journal*, September 1977.

single adult	1·13	(1·38)
man and woman	2·00	(2·00)
with 1 child	2·39	(2·37)
with 2 children	2·87	(2·72)
with 3 children	3·53	(3·08)

In brackets the approximate supplementary benefit scales (averaging for both rents and different rates for children of different age) have been given for purposes of comparison. The curves for each type of household, at least in this illustration, are remarkably equidistant. None the less it is evident that at different horizontal levels on the graph they do not maintain exactly the same proportionate relationship. And, as others have pointed out, the patterns produced by survey data are not stable from year to year.[1]

The early advocates of subsistence standards for poverty had either laid down arbitrary definitions of the needs of different types of families or had relied on crude estimates of minimum nutrition, translated into minimum market costs rather than the costs actually incurred by families.[2] A proposal that 'equivalence' could be established by finding what is the lowest household income at which a substantial minority or a majority of families actually secure minimally adequate nutrition[3] has not been put to detailed empirical test. The data collected in the national food survey are not analysed and presented in the form of distributions which would allow this approach to be scrutinized and more fully developed. Moreover, those in charge of any new empirical inquiry would have huge problems: the inquiry would have to be based on a very large sample, in order to include enough families of each type at each level of income; it would have to take account of differing, and also very broad, definitions of nutritional adequacy; and, finally, there would be the very real difficulties of measuring the actual content of people's diet partly, but not only, through their sometimes problematical accounts of food expenditure.

Neither nutritional level nor percentage of total income committed to the purchase of food can be regarded as a sufficient criterion of the satisfaction of all forms of need. One form of deprivation may often correspond with another, but we cannot take this for granted. The relationship has to be investigated and demonstrated. Without denying its importance, nutritional level has attracted disproportionate attention in the history of the study of poverty and privation throughout the world. In this study we have sought to lay stress symbolically on the *style* of consumption of food because, as a guide to deprivation, it is as im-

1. Bagley, *The Cost of a Child*, p. 10. See Table A.12, page 1001, for an example from the National Food Survey.
2. See the discussion above of the work by Rowntree and Orshansky on pages 33–9.
3. Townsend, P., 'The Meaning of Poverty', *British Journal of Sociology*, June 1954, pp. 134–5; see also Clark, R. M., 'Some Reflections on Economic Security for the Aged in Canada', in Clark, R. M., *Canadian Issues: Essays in Honour of Henry F. Angus*, University of Toronto Press, 1962, pp. 356–60.

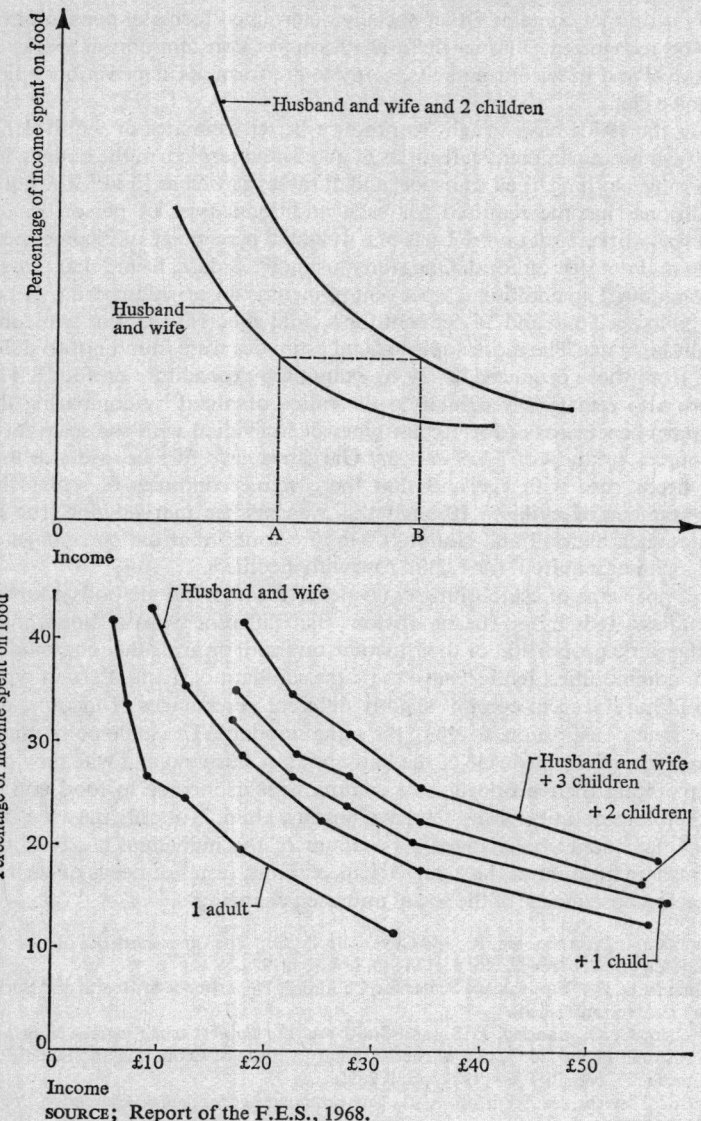

SOURCE; Report of the F.E.S., 1968.

Figure 6.5. The establishment of equivalent income.

portant as nutritional content. Other socially determined forms of consumption must also be recognized. Just as there are forms of consumption at work, at home, in travel and in leisure pursuits, so there are forms of deprivation which do not involve diet.

Studies in the 1970s have sought to produce better estimates of 'equivalent' incomes by examining different categories of goods and services in the budget, including housing, clothing, fuel, transport and durables as well as food.[1] The equivalent additional income required for each additional type of person in the household was worked out on the basis of a weighted percentage of income spent on all items and not just on food. One study, using FES data, found that a married couple required an additional 9 per cent of income for an infant child, 21 per cent for a child aged 5–7 and 36 per cent for a child aged 16–18.[2] But two comments might be made. The more sophisticated estimates were found not to differ very much from those produced solely by examining expenditure on food[1]. The results were also remarkably similar to the ratios obtained by comparing the supplementary benefit scales for certain types of individual with the scale for a married couple. A study of FES data by Garganas gave further evidence that children's needs rose with age and that there were economies of scale with increasing number of children (though this was neither marked nor true of commodities such as food and clothing). He also found that the percentage of additional income 'required' for a child rose with income.[3]

There are problems of establishing equivalence through the methods adopted in these studies.[4] It is by no means obvious that different types of households spending the same proportion of their income on food, or any other commodity or group of commodities, tend to have the same standard of living. Certain types of household may need to commit slightly different percentages of income, depending on their constitution, to share the same standard. The same point might be made in terms of the life cycle of the household. A husband and wife may not 'need' to maintain their proportionate commitment of income to food and to various other commodities once they have borne a child. Not only may the distribution of the budget be changed on account of the individual needs of the child, but also on account of the changed expectations, tastes or needs of each of the adults, as a consequence of the social unit itself changing.

1. See, for example, Van Slooten, R., and Coverdale, A. G., 'The Characteristics of Low Income Households', *Social Trends*, No. 8, HMSO, London, 1977.
2. McClements, L. D., 'Equivalence Scales for Children', Department of Health and Social Security, July 1975 (unpublished).
3. In Fiegehen, G. C., Lansley, P. S., and Smith, A. D., *Poverty and Progress in Britain 1953–73*, Occasional Paper No. XXIX of the National Institute of Economic and Social Research, Cambridge University Press, 1977, pp. 102–9.
4. For a critical review, see Atkinson, A. B., *The Economics of Inequality*, Clarendon Press, Oxford, 1975, pp. 42–5.

Again, adjustments may need to be made in deriving the scales not merely for the *number* of children, but also for the ages of both children and adults and the sex of children. For example, the distribution of the budget, and its scale, may need to be different for the retired and disabled than for non-disabled younger adults. This is already accepted conventionally through the institution of a retail price index for pensioners.

'Equivalence' seems also to vary *proportionately* at different levels of income. One study showed that 'richer' families find children relatively more costly than 'poorer' families.[1] This seems to pose a major problem. Just as the actual expenditure of poor families, for example, on clothing, cannot be averaged to derive the amount they *need* to spend (as Rowntree once did), so the actual difference in the percentage of income devoted to food (and other commodities) by poor couples with children and poor couples without children cannot be used to define what incomes are needed by couples with and without children to have the same standard of living. In the NIESR study, a child was treated as representing 21 per cent of the costs of an adult couple, but, for example, among couples with one child who had an income of over £29 per week a child's costs represented 51 per cent of the costs of an adult couple.[2] The figure of 21 per cent is a crude average reflection of *convention*[3] (derived from poor as well as rich households) and not of *need*. It reflects the distribution of income as it is rather than as it should be.

Cash Income and a Poverty Line

To find whether there is a threshold of deprivation in relation to level of income for different types of household is therefore difficult. I would wish to make two major reservations to the alternative definition of a poverty line in these pages. First, the summary deprivation index could be, as argued earlier, more 'representative' – more comprehensively and systematically built up than proved possible in the research. None the less, the range of indicators which we used was broad (see Appendix Thirteen and Chapters 11 to 14), and combinations of indicators other than those included in the summary index also produced 'thresholds' of deprivation at similar cut-offs of income. In fact we were able to demonstrate a closer correlation between different indicators of deprivation and income as converted according to our standard of relative deprivation than according to the state's supplementary benefit standard.

Secondly, deprivation has been examined in relation to incomes rather than resources. Strictly, deprivation is correlated more highly with broader concepts of resources than with income (Appendix Thirteen). But at this stage it may be premature to insist on further refinements to the alternative poverty line which the concept of relative deprivation already makes possible, when the income

1. Fiegehen, Lansley and Smith, *Poverty and Progress in Britain*, pp. 104–5.
2. ibid., pp. 105 and 142.
3. Also, 21 per cent seems low in relation to other figures quoted. See ibid., p. 103.

equivalents of assets and employer and state welfare are necessarily such rough approximations. The summary data presented in this chapter thus allow only a tentative definition of a poverty line for different types of household.

The level of income for different types of household below which deprivation increased disproportionately seemed from the evidence to be as follows:

1. For single-person households: at two thirds of that for households consisting of a man and woman, or rather higher than the proportion allowed in the UK social security system. (This conclusion is also reached by the more restricted method of deriving adult equivalence scales from the analysis of food expenditures, as discussed above, page 262.)
2. For households containing an employed adult: rather higher (10 to 20 per cent) than for households containing a retired adult.
3. For households containing a disabled person: rather higher than for households not containing such a person.
4. For households containing man, woman and child: up to about two fifths higher than the level for an elderly (non-disabled) man and woman, and about one fifth higher than for a man and woman under 60.
5. For households containing man, woman and three or more children under the age of 15: up to about double the level for an elderly (non-disabled) couple, and just under double the level for a younger couple.

Accordingly, an income standard might be constructed. The cash incomes per annum (and per week) required both to surmount the threshold of deprivation and to establish a rough equivalence between different types of households might be made up as follows (in terms of a baseline in 1968–9):

1. £156 (or £3 per week) for a household of any size.
2. £182 (or £3·50 per week) for each non-employed adult.
3. £286 (or £5·50 per week) for the chief wage-earner in the household, if any.
4. £221 (or £4·25 per week) for any supplementary earner (with employed or self-employed status of any kind).
5. £104 (or £2 per week) for a child under 10 years of age and £156 (or £3 per week) for a child under 15.
6. £104 (or £2 per week) extra for each person with appreciable, £208 (or £4 per week) with severe and £312 (or £6 per week), with very severe disablement (disablement defined as in Chapter 20).

Table 6.9 sets out the resulting scales, with the corresponding Supplementary Benefits Commission (SBC) scales. The deprivation standard is considerably below the mean gross disposable income for each type of household. It varies from about equivalent to nearly a third higher than the supplementary benefit 'standard' (and higher still for some households in which there are disabled people). However, the difference between the deprivation and SBC standards is less marked than the figures suggest. Some allowance should strictly be added to the SBC rates for the expenses of work. In fact, these expenses averaged £35 per

Table 6.9. *The relative deprivation standard of poverty in £ per annum, compared with the supplementary benefit basic scale rates, and mean household income.*

Type of household	SBC basic scale rates		Mean housing costs	SBC rates plus housing costs (cols. 1 + 3)	Deprivation standard	Mean gross disposable income last year	Col. 5 as % of col. 4
	Before 7 October 1968	After 7 October 1968					
	1	2	3	4	5	6	7
Man 60+	250[a]	263[a]	82	332	338	490	102
Man under 60	224	237	113	337	442	889	131
Woman 60+	250[a]	263[a]	77	327	338	400	103
Woman under 60	224	237	111	335	442	674	132
Man and woman, both over 60	429[a]	439[a]	72	501	520	843	104
Man and woman, one under 60	367	387	112	479	624	967	130
Man and woman, neither over 60	367	387	170	537	624	1,336	116
	'young'[b] 'older'[c]	'young'[b] 'older'[c]		'young'[b] 'older'[c]			
Man, woman, 1 child	432 463	458 494	195	627 658	728–80	1,292	116–19
2 children	510 559	540 595	191	701 750	832–936	1,358	119–25
3 children	575 655	610 697	179	754 834	936–1,092	1,404	124–31
4 children	653 751	693 804	188	841 939	1,040–248	1,769	124–33

NOTES: [a] Including the long-term additional allowance.

[b] 'Young' family: 1 child = under 5; 2 children = one under 5, one 5–10; 3 children = two under 5, one 5–10; 4 children = two under 5, two 5–10.

[c] 'Older' family: 1 child = 13–15; 2 children = one 11–12, one 13–15; 3 children = two 11–12, one 13–15; 4 children = two 11–12, two 13–15.

annum for all households in the sample, and about £50 for households with one or more persons in paid employment.[1] There is the further point that, in practice, certain types of income are disregarded by the commission's officers and certain households are awarded additional grants for exceptional needs. Later we will show that a substantial proportion of families who were currently receiving supplementary benefits had incomes higher than the deprivation standard.

Finally, attention must be called again to the fact that our measures of income unit, deprivation (through style of living) and income are all approximate. We have concentrated in this chapter upon the household, for example, rather than the income units comprising it. However, 71 per cent of households consisted of only one unit, and among households with only two income units the correspondence of deprivation, according to the index of deprivation, was fairly high. Thus at low, middle and high levels of household incomes, 86, 75 and 73 per cent respectively of the pairs of income units had the same score or a score which differed by only one. But the index itself is crude and requires further examination in relation both to multiple forms of deprivation and the combinations of individuals in households.

Summary and Conclusion

Conceptions of poverty are held by individuals and groups and institutionalized by the state. A substantial percentage of the sample saw poverty as a standard of living below a minimally defined (or subsistence) level, and so aligned themselves with the view broadly, if rather ambiguously, put into effect by the state, principally through the supplementary benefits scheme. Another substantial percentage saw poverty more as a generalized condition applying to particular social minorities, such as pensioners, the unemployed, the disabled and the low paid. In some respects, this view corresponded with the state's definition of social categories entitled under national insurance to flat-rate benefits (and the Wages Council or Trades Union Congress definitions of a minimum wage). Only a tiny percentage of the sample saw poverty as a condition relative to standards which were or were becoming widespread in contemporary society.

Three measures of poverty are outlined:

(a) The *state's* (or the social) standard (based on the rates paid by the Supplementary Benefits Commission).
(b) The *relative income* standard (a standard which allows a fixed percentage of the population with the lowest incomes to be selected, or which is at a point fixed at a low level in relation to the mean income).
(c) The *deprivation* standard (a standard of income below which people experience deprivation disproportionately to income).

1. Allowances are made for work expenses in government reports which compare incomes with supplementary benefit scales. See Howe, *Two-Parent Families*, p. 2.

Deprivation is defined relatively to the community's current style of living as established in the survey. Indicators of different forms of deprivation are listed and a summary index used in analysis.

With qualifications both about measurement and sample size, the evidence suggested that there existed a threshold of deprivation for certain types of household at low levels of income, that is, a point in descending the income scale below which deprivation increased disproportionately to the fall in income. This threshold was at levels higher than the prevailing supplementary benefit standard, especially for households with children and households with disabled people.

There are four measurement problems in undertaking further work on the relationship between income and deprivation which we have speculatively explored:

1. *The problem of defining the income unit* (*as well as the consumption unit*). Individual members of the household vary in the extent to which they pool and retain incomes for common or individual use.
2. *The problem of defining the unit of deprivation.* Correspondingly, individuals may suffer alone or together. Individual members of the household vary in the extent to which they lead separate lives and experience deprivation.
3. *The problem of measuring level* (*including type*) *of resources.* Some individuals or families live very differently from what their net disposable incomes would appear to denote – because their command over other types of resource, whether assets, or employer welfare, social service or private benefits in kind, is exceptional. For considerable sections of the population resources other than cash incomes form a significant part of living standards. The problem lies not merely in identifying such resources but in translating them into equivalent values.
4. *The problem of measuring level* (*including type*) *of deprivation.* A similar problem arises over style of living. While social surveys can help to establish what are modal activities, facilities and customs in society few individuals can be said to reflect the full list in their own lives. Their own pattern of activities may be representative only of part of the national list. Some may draw both from a national list and from a list of activities, facilities and customs which are observed or shared exclusively by some social minority. Again, styles of living divide into styles at work, at home, in travel and in leisure-time activities. Deprivation can arise in one of these spheres and not all. Deprivation can arise in income-producing and not just income-consuming situations, for example.

Theoretically, even a provisional consideration of these problems quite apart from the data adduced in this chapter, suggests how unlikely it is that we will establish any simple or consistently direct relationship between income and deprivation. The population is not divided cleanly into the deprived and non-deprived. Many people are deprived in some respects but not in others. Many are deprived for part but not all of their lives. Some also have limited access to the resources they hold, or cannot convert them into the alternative forms of resources they require to escape deprivation.

7
The Incidence of Poverty

The three measures of poverty discussed in Chapter 6 will now be applied to the data collected from the sample of households. This chapter will describe the extent of poverty among the households and population of the United Kingdom and its constituent regions in 1968-9. It will outline the relationship between short-term and long-term poverty and portray the general 'structure' of poverty among the population.

As judged by the state's or government standard, 7 per cent of the households in the sample were in poverty. By the deprivation standard, the number was 25 per cent. However, the difference between these two results is greater than it would be if the 'real' rather than the 'basic' government standard were to be used. If the government standard were to be treated not just as equivalent to the basic scale rates of supplementary benefit but were also to include the regular discretionary payments which are often added to these rates, as well as the income and assets which are ordinarily disregarded in determining eligibility, the figure of 7 per cent would be considerably higher. The 'real' standard could be applied only by making complicated adjustments for each family's circumstances. Instead, a margin of income up to 40 per cent above the 'basic' standard has been taken to show the numbers in the population who may also be in poverty or on the boundaries of poverty as defined by society.[1] Further evidence on the real levels of income of recipients of supplementary benefit and the numbers who are eligible to receive such benefit will be given later. In addition to the 7 per cent of households in poverty according to the basic government standard, there were another 24 per cent on the margins of this standard, as Table 7.1 shows. That is, these households had an annual net disposable income of only up to 40 per cent above the standard.

By the state's standard, the percentage of the people in the sample in poverty

1. The choice of 40 per cent was made for reasons given in previous research – that, in practice, the state observes a higher standard than the basic rates by disregarding (through the Supplementary Benefits Commission) certain minor amounts of income of claimants and by adding, for certain claimants, small amounts to the basic benefits. See Abel-Smith, B., and Townsend, P., *The Poor and the Poorest*, Bell, London, 1965, p. 18.

Table 7.1. *Percentages in poverty and on the margins of poverty according to three standards.*

Poverty standard	Percentage of households	Percentage of population	Estimated number (UK)	
			Households	Non-institutionalized population
State's standard (SB):*				
in poverty	7·1	6·1	1·34 mil.	3·32 mil.
on margins of poverty	23·8	21·8	4·50 mil.	11·86 mil.
Relative income standard:†				
in poverty	10·6	9·2	2·00 mil.	5·0 mil.
on margins of poverty	29·5	29·6	5·58 mil.	16·10 mil.
Deprivation standard:‡				
in poverty	25·2	22·9	4·76 mil.	12·46 mil.
Total (UK)	100	100	18·90 mil.[a]	54·4 mil.[b]

DEFINITIONS:

* Net disposable household income last year of less than 100 per cent (in poverty) or 100 to 139 per cent (on margins of poverty) of supplementary benefit scale rates plus housing costs.
† Net disposable household income last year less than 50 per cent (in poverty) or 50 to 79 per cent (on margins of poverty) of mean household income for type.
‡ Net disposable household income last year of less than a level below which deprivation tends to increase disproportionately as income diminishes.

NOTES:

[a] According to the 1971 Census, there were approximately 18,800,000 households in the United Kingdom. Our definition of 'household' (like that of the FES) was not identical with that used in the census, and we estimated that there were 18,900,000 according to that definition in 1968–9.
[b] See Appendix Two, page 955, for an explanation of estimated non-institutionalized population.

and on the margins of poverty was rather smaller than of households, being 6 per cent and nearly 22 per cent respectively. These figures represent 3·3 million and 11·9 million people, or a total of 15·2 million in nearly 6 million households in the non-institutionalized population of 54·4 million.

The relative income standard of poverty applies to those households with annual incomes below 50 per cent of the mean for their type. Over 10 per cent of households and 9 per cent of population were below this standard, representing 5 million people. Another 30 per cent had an annual income of less than 80 per cent of the mean income for their type. These two measures do not exactly overlap. About two thirds of those with incomes below the state's standard have less than 50 per cent of the mean income for their household type, but (mainly because the actual housing cost which is allowed can be relatively high) the rest are at higher levels. Altogether, about 86 per cent of those who have incomes below or less than 40 per cent above the state's standard have incomes of less than 80 per cent of the mean for their type. Again, there is substantial overlapping, but the distributions are not quite coincident.

The deprivation standard was defined on the basis of the evidence in Chapter 6 of a correlation between annual net disposable household income and deprivation, as measured by an index of deprivation. The standard was fixed at £338 for a person aged 60 and over, and £442 for a younger person living alone; £520 for a couple aged 60 and over, and £624 for a younger couple; and amounts ranging according to age of children from £728 to £780 for a man and wife and one child, £832 to £936 for a man and wife and two children, and £936 to £1,092 for a man and wife and three children. Altogether, 25 per cent of households and 23 per cent of individuals in the sample were living on incomes below the standard. They represented 4·8 million households and 12·5 million persons.

Certain adjustments should properly be made to figures for the numbers living in or on the margins of poverty, particularly to those arising from the use of the government or state standard. First, because we wanted to make general statements about the region, households were over-sampled in Northern Ireland. Since relatively more households in that region than elsewhere in the country had low incomes, a minor adjustment needed to be made to all major results concerned with levels of living. But it was hardly ever more than two or three decimal percentage points, and sometimes only one decimal point.[1] Secondly, among 2,050 households providing information in the survey, 14 per cent did not provide complete information on their cash incomes during the whole of the preceding twelve months. Since other information about them was reasonably full and some were households comprising two or more income units (where information was often complete for one unit but not the other) an adjustment could also be made to the sample findings. Thirdly, the increase of about 6 per cent in the rates of supplementary benefit during the survey made another adjustment necessary for households interviewed in late 1968 or early 1969. An account of these adjustments is set out in Appendix Seven: 'Note on the Adjustment of Sample Findings' (pages 989–90). The results (for the week preceding the interview as well as for the year as a whole) are given in Table 7.2.

The adjustments have the effect of slightly increasing the numbers found to be in poverty, but slightly reducing the numbers on its margins.[2] The final column of Table 7.2 provides revised estimates for the population as a whole. Three and a

1. See Appendix Seven, pages 989–90.
2. Unadjusted data are used elsewhere in the analysis because there is no means of distributing the adjustments for many variables.

Table 7.2. Percentages and number in poverty by the state's standard.

Period: relationship to state standard	Percentage of households		Percentage of population		Estimated population (UK)
	un-adjusted	adjusted	un-adjusted	adjusted	adjusted
Last year:					
in poverty	7·1	7·3	6·1	6·4	3·48 mil.
on margins of poverty	23·8	23·3	21·8	21·5	11·70 mil.
Last week:					
in poverty	6·7	7·1	6·0	6·3	3·43 mil.
on margins of poverty	23·7	23·1	20·8	20·6	11·21 mil.

half million people were in poverty, with another 11½ to 12 million on the margins of poverty, making over 15 million altogether, or more than a quarter of the population. The estimates vary only slightly whether we consider net household income in the week preceding the interview or in the year as a whole, though these two populations are not exactly coincident, as we shall see.

The figure of 6·4 per cent of the population below the supplementary benefit standard is higher than figures estimated from the Family Expenditure Survey for the late 1960s.[1] This is to be expected, since relatively too few households in certain minority groups with low incomes have been represented in the FES samples[2] and response is almost certainly reduced by the invitation to record expenditure for two weeks.

Short-term and Long-term Poverty

In any week of the year, some incomes will be much lower and others much larger than usual. Often this is because a wage-earner is sick or unemployed, or is

1. See, for example, an estimate of 3·4 per cent of households below the supplementary benefit standard (on certain rough assumptions) for 1969 by Atkinson, A. B., *Poverty, Inequality and Class Structure*, Cambridge University Press, 1974, p. 58; and an estimate of 5·8 per cent of households and 5·3 per cent of people for 1967 by Lansley, P. S., 'Post War Changes in the Extent of Poverty', in Fiegehen, G. C., Lansley, P. S. and Smith, A. D., *Poverty and Progress in Britain, 1953–73*, Cambridge University Press, 1977, p. 29.

2. We have already noted that the number of people aged 65 and over included in the FES for 1968 was about 14 per cent too small and the number of children about 10 per cent too large (see above, Chapter 5, page 183). This imbalance of children and old people persisted in the FES for both 1973 and 1974. Thus, in 1974, 7·7 per cent of the persons included in the FES, but 8·7 per cent in the population at large, were aged 70 and over. Twenty-eight per cent were children under the age of 16, compared with 25 per cent. And only 34 per cent aged 16 or over were economically inactive, compared with 39 per cent in the population, according to the

working varying hours of overtime. Sometimes it is due to a change of job or the loss or addition of a member of the household. Ideally we would have wished to establish income levels in relation to household membership for all periods of change during at least the previous twelve months. This was impracticable. We attempted only to find the total annual income and preceding week's income. But occasional income, like tax refunds, bonuses and windfalls, had to be assumed to be spread out over the year rather than spent in any particular period. This method of averaging income is used in all surveys and tends to smooth out the variations that exist. Our measures of the number of households and individuals who fell below the standard of income did not cover all of those who did so for certain but not all periods of the year.

Table 7.3 shows that 5 per cent of households were below the state's standard during the previous week and on average throughout the year. A further 22 per cent were on the margins of poverty or fluctuated only between poverty and the margins of poverty. Yet there was a third group experiencing poverty. Some households fell below or were on the margins of the standard during the previous week, but not on average throughout the year, and vice versa. They included families who were temporarily sick or unemployed and households in which a wage-earner was now back at work after a long spell of unemployment or sickness or had obtained an increase in pay. Either they were just emerging from poverty or just descending into it. For some, this was a once-and-for-all movement, though for others it was a recurring experience. The significance of these figures is in showing that over a third of the households and nearly a third of the population fall into one of these three groups and have recent if not present experience of poverty. Table A.14 in Appendix Eight (page 1002) gives further detail.[1]

Size of Household

Table 7.3 also shows the relationship between size of household and the state's standard of poverty. The highest incidence of poverty is found among one-person

1971 Census. The Department of Employment has not provided enough information of a social character about the sample to enable a clearer view to be taken about its representation of the poor. According to a paper prepared by the DHSS Statistics and Research Branch in October 1977 ('The Take-Up of Supplementary Benefits'), the representation of sickness and invalidity beneficiaries in 1975 was only about three quarters of the totals expected from administrative records. 'It does seem that those sick are less likely than others to cooperate in the FES.' The same paper quotes a Central Statistical Office estimate for 1964–6 which showed a tendency for those at the highest and lowest ranges of household rateable values not to cooperate in the surveys.

1. It should be noted that tables correlating data for household income last year with that for income last week are drawn from a smaller number in the sample than tables describing each of them independently. Some households giving full information, but not information com-

Table 7.3. *Percentages of households of different size in poverty and on the margins of poverty.*

Whether net disposable income below, or less than 40% above, SB scales plus housing cost, last week and last year	Size of household					
	1	2	3	4	5+	All sizes
In poverty last week and last year	10·0	5·3	2·4	2·2	4·9	5·1
In margins of poverty last week and last year	38·6	16·3	10·5	12·7	16·9	19·2
In poverty *or* on margins of poverty last week and last year	3·7	3·5	2·7	2·2	4·1	3·3
In poverty or on margins of poverty only last week	4·0	3·9	4·4	5·6	4·9	4·5
In poverty or on margins of poverty only on average last year	2·8	2·2	3·4	6·4	6·6	3·9
Not in poverty or on margins of poverty either last week or last year	40·8	68·7	76·6	70·8	62·6	64·1
Total	100	100	100	100	100	100
Number	321	508	295	267	243	1,634

households, and the lowest among three- and four-person households. The incidence rises again among households with five or more persons. Only 41 per cent of one-person households but between 63 per cent and 77 per cent of other households were not in poverty or on the margins of poverty either in the preceding week or on average during the year. Further details are given in Table A.15a in Appendix Eight (page 1003) by the separate criteria of income in the preceding week and year. The proportion in poverty and on the margins of poverty was highest for one-person households, and next for households of five or more persons. The proportion was lowest among three-person households.

The smallest households were not so liable to experience variations in living standards. More of the households with four, five or more persons than the

plete in all respects for income and assets, were included in the final sample made available for analysis. This accounts for slight discrepancies between different tables in the proportions in poverty or on the margins of poverty.

smaller households were in poverty or on the margins of poverty in the week previous to interview, but not on average during the year, and vice versa. The large households often contained two, three or more income units and their income was therefore more likely to vary. But the presence of two or more income units did not necessarily raise households out of poverty. Although more households consisting of a single income unit than of two or more units were found to be in poverty, a relatively large proportion of the latter remained in poverty or on its margins. Indeed, more households with four or more income units than with two or three units were found to be in poverty (Table A.15b, Appendix Eight, page 1003).

The State's Standard

The results of applying each of the three measures will be elaborated. Table 7.4 shows how the incomes of the sample compared with the state's standard of poverty. According to the separate criteria of last week's and last year's income, 6 to 7 per cent of households and individuals were living on incomes below the

Table 7.4. Percentages of households and persons, according to net disposable household income in preceding week and preceding year, expressed as a percentage of the supplementary benefit scales plus housing costs.

| | Net disposable household income | | | | |
| | Last week | | Last year | | |
Percentage of supplementary benefit scales plus housing cost	House-holds	Persons	House-holds	Persons	Estimated no. of persons in pop. (000s)
300+	11·0	10·1	10·8	10·4	5,658
200–99	28·6	29·5	28·8	28·4	15,450
140–99	29·9	33·6	29·5	33·3	18,115
120–39	10·8	11·4	11·8	12·9	7,018
110–19	6·8	5·1	5·9	4·5	2,448
100–9	6·1	4·3	6·1	4·4	2,394
90–99	2·9	2·7	2·9	2·2	1,197
80–89	1·4	1·1	2·3	2·2	1,197
under 80	2·4	2·2	1·9	1·7	925
Total	100	100	100	100	54,400
Number	1,803	5,271	1,764	5,146	—

standard. Most of them were under 90 per cent of the standard, some of them being under 80 per cent. The latter represented more than a million people. In addition to the estimate of three million people who were, on the basis of the sample, below the standard, another five million were up to 20 per cent and a further 7 million between 20 per cent and up to 40 per cent above the standard.

The great majority of the population were, however, far above the supplementary benefit standard, nearly two thirds being above 160 per cent and two fifths above 200 per cent of the standard. The average household commanded an income more than twice that of the supplementary benefit scale rates plus the average cost of housing in the United Kingdom.

The interviewing was organized in each area in four quarterly stages, as described in Chapter 3, and the sample was divided, in effect, into four separate random sub-samples. The results obtained for each quarter are given in Table 7.5. The *intentions* in dividing the sample into four sub-samples seem to have been broadly fulfilled. The spread of incomes was wide at all four stages and, bearing in mind variation due to sampling, broadly consistent. The percentage below the state's standard in each quarter: 5·6, 8·2, 7·5 and 5·5, and the percentage no more

Table 7.5. *Percentages of households interviewed at different periods, according to their net disposable income in preceding week, expressed as a percentage of supplementary benefit scales.*

% of supplementary benefit scales plus housing cost	First quarter 1968	Second quarter 1968	Third quarter 1968	Fourth quarter 1968 and part of first quarter 1969
300+	12·1	9·9	12·0	10·5
200–99	28·9	29·4	25·7	29·9
140–99	31·1	27·1	27·7	32·7
130–39	4·9	7·8	5·0	5·2
120–29	6·4	3·3	6·7	4·4
110–19	5·2	7·8	7·5	6·8
100–9	5·7	6·6	8·0	4·7
90–99	2·2	4·0	3·0	2·6
80–89	1·2	2·1	1·0	1·2
Under 80	2·2	2·1	3·5	1·9
Total	100	100	100	100
Number	405	425	401	572

than 40 per cent higher than that standard: 22·2, 25·5, 27·2 and 21·1, are also broadly consistent with certain historical events. For example, in October 1968 family allowances were substantially increased.

The Relative Income Standard

The incomes of the households in the sample, expressed as a percentage of the mean of each of fourteen household types to which they were allocated, is shown in Table 7.6. The dispersion is wide, with around 10 per cent having incomes below 50 per cent and 4 per cent more than 200 per cent of the mean (1·5 per cent, in fact, more than 300 per cent of the mean).

Table 7.6. Percentages of households and persons, according to net disposable household income expressed as a percentage of the mean for each household type.

Net income as % of mean	Last week		Last year		Number of persons in the population (millions)
	House- holds	Persons	House- holds	Persons	
200+	3·7	3·6	4·0	4·3	2·3
140–99	11·6	11·9	9·5	9·8	5·3
120–39	7·5	8·2	8·6	8·8	4·8
110–19	7·0	7·4	7·0	7·2	3·9
100–9	8·9	9·1	7·9	8·2	4·5
90–99	10·4	11·2	10·1	10·6	5·8
80–89	12·3	12·0	12·7	12·3	6·7
70–79	11·2	11·0	11·3	11·1	6·0
50–69	17·5	16·8	18·2	18·5	10·1
Under 50	9·9	8·7	10·6	9·2	5·0
Total	100	100	100	100	54·4
Number	1,801	5,269	1,763	5,145	–

Estimates are also given in the table, on the basis of the sample results of the numbers in the population living at different levels in relation to the mean. In addition to 5 million living in households on incomes of less than 50 per cent of the mean for their type, another 16 million were living under 80 per cent of the mean. At the other extreme, 2·3 million were living in households with incomes of more than 200 per cent of the mean, 800,000 of them more than 300 per cent.

The Relative Deprivation Standard

The proportions of households and of population surmounting and falling below the deprivation standard are shown in Table 7.7. A substantial proportion had incomes considerably below the standard, whether judged by weekly or annual in-

Table 7.7. Percentages of households and persons, according to gross disposable household income expressed as a percentage of the deprivation standard.

	Last week		Last year		
% of depriva-tion standard	House-holds	Persons	House-holds	Persons	Number of persons in the population (millions)
250+	7·9	7·6	10·0	9·8	5·3
200–49	9·2	8·5	10·5	10·1	5·5
180–99	6·4	6·7	7·3	7·5	4·1
160–79	9·8	10·3	8·9	9·1	5·0
140–59	10·8	11·4	11·8	12·6	6·9
120–39	14·5	15·7	13·9	14·9	8·1
110–19	7·2	8·2	5·8	6·1	3·3
100–9	6·7	6·7	6·6	6·9	3·8
90–99	7·1	7·9	6·4	7·0	3·8
80–89	5·4	5·0	5·9	6·0	3·3
Under 80	15·0	12·1	12·9	9·9	5·4
Total	100	100	100	100	54·4
Number	1,799	5,261	1,761	5,138	–

come.[1] As many as 10 per cent of the population were in households with gross disposable income of less than 80 per cent of the deprivation standard. A substantial section of the population were again found to have income two or three times higher than the standard.

1. Income is measured in terms of gross rather than net household disposable income, because account is already taken in the deprivation standard of the needs of work and travelling to work. This differs from the measurement of income according to the government's supplementary benefit standard, which legally applies to those not in full-time paid employment. The actual cost of working (which, according to a limited definition, averaged about £1 per week per full-time worker), have not been deducted from income instead, because this would be tantamount to treating expenditure as equivalent to needs and thereby assuming unjustifiably that the poor are not obliged to accept low-paid local work.

Definitions of the Domestic Unit and of Resources

We have shown how the proportions of the population found to be living in poverty vary, depending on whether the state's conception of poverty or an alternative, perhaps more objective, conception like that of relative deprivation described in Chapter 6 and illustrated here, is adopted as the standard. This is not the only source of variation. Much depends on whether the household or the income unit is regarded as the appropriate domestic unit receiving income and consuming goods and services, and whether resources other than cash incomes, especially assets, affect and should be regarded as affecting the results. Later chapters, on types of deprivation and different groups in the population, go into these matters in some detail. Here attention is called only to the effect of varying the definitions of both the domestic unit and resources.

Table 7.8 shows that, using the same supplementary benefit scales, more people were in units than households with incomes below those scales – 9·1 per cent compared with 6·1 per cent – and more had incomes on the margins of those scales – 23·2 per cent compared with 21·8 per cent.

According to the state's standard, the survey produces the following estimates of total population in poverty:

	Households	Income units
Number in poverty	3·3 mil.	5·0 mil.
Number on margins	11·9 mil.	12·6 mil.
	15·2 mil.	17·6 mil.

Some households in poverty had small assets which, when converted to an annuity value and added to net disposable income, lifted them above the poverty line. For example, a man of 40 with savings and possessions estimated to be worth £500 would be assumed to be receiving an annuity of about £39 per annum. A man of 65 with the same amount of savings or possessions, would be assumed to be receiving £50 per annum, or nearly £1 a week, but the table shows that even if assets were, or could be, converted into income in this way, it would still leave the majority of those in poverty or on its margins in the same position. Consider the figures in the final three columns of Table 7.8. The two percentages 9·1 and 23·2 represent 5 million and 12·6 million people respectively, or 17·6 million altogether, and the two comparable percentages of 6·8 and 16·8 represent 3·7 million and 9·1 million, or 12·8 million altogether. Thus, nearly three quarters of those in poverty or on its margins could not escape that condition even if they used, or were able to use, all their assets to buy an annuity. And, it must be added, though some of the assets included in our list – for example, most types of money savings – might be regarded as realizable in periods of hardship, others – for example, property like a car or personal jewellery – might not be so regarded.

Alternatively, it might be pointed out that owner-occupied homes and certain kinds of assets are disregarded by the Supplementary Benefits Commission, and any proposal to add a value for assets to income should be matched by the addition of the disregarded equivalent to the scales used for the purpose of measuring 'social' poverty.

Table 7.8 also shows the distribution for people in households of total resources. Again this is presented for heuristic purposes only. To non-asset income is added not only the annuity value of assets, but the value of employer welfare benefits and private services and gifts in kind, and even the value of social services in kind, including the costs of medical consultation, stays in hospital, school and college attendance, and subsidies to council housing and owner-occupied

Table 7.8. *Percentages of people in income units or households above and below the state's standard of poverty according to definition of resources.*

Percentage of supplementary benefit scales plus housing cost	Households			Income units		
	Net disposable income last year	Income net worth	Total resources	Net disposable income last year	Income net worth	Total resources
300+	10·4	21·6	34·2	12·6	22·6	37·4
200–99	28·4	30·5	34·4	26·5	29·4	33·5
140–99	33·3	28·2	22·8	28·5	24·4	19·4
100–39	21·8	15·6	7·2	23·2	16·8	6·7
Under 100	6·1	4·0	1·3	9·1	6·8	3·2
Total	100	100	100	100	100	100
Number	5,146	4,391	3,725	5,339	4,601	4,313

property. It might very reasonably be argued that it would be wrong to count the costs of many such items as a form of 'income' because they cannot be regarded as defraying living expenses even in the eyes of the Supplementary Benefits Commission. None the less, it is not without interest that, even counting all such benefits and subsidies as income, there remains 8·5 per cent of the population representing 4·6 million in poverty or on its margins.

Regional Poverty

The proportion in poverty varied among the different regions, but not so widely as sometimes supposed. By the state's standard, the poorest region was Northern Ireland, followed by the North-West of England, the South-West and Wales, and Scotland (Table 7.9). The least poor region was Greater London, which also had much the highest proportion of people living at more than twice the standard. If the alternative of the income unit and not household is used to examine poverty

Table 7.9. Percentages of population in different regions, according to net disposable household income in preceding year (in rank order of prevalence of poverty).

Region	Household income as % of supplementary benefit scales				Number of people in sample
	Under 140 (in poverty or on margins of poverty)	140–99	Over 200	All	
Northern Ireland	44·3	29·3	26·4	100	239
North-West	33·9	31·6	34·6	100	612
South-West and Wales	29·2	38·2	32·7	100	536
Scotland	29·1	31·2	39·7	100	526
Northern Yorks and Humberside	28·5	35·6	35·9	100	568
West Midlands	25·4	33·6	41·1	100	682
Anglia and East Midlands	24·9	33·6	41·5	100	497
South-East	24·2	36·8	39·1	100	797
Greater London	23·1	28·3	48·7	100	697
All regions	27·8	33·4	38·8	100	5,154

in the regions, the rank order remains virtually the same (with Scotland moving to second place and the North-West and South-West and Wales moving down a place). Poverty was widely dispersed among the nine regions. In the South-West and Wales there were estimated to be 440,000 people in income units below the state's standard, in Northern Ireland 460,000, in the South-East 490,000 and in Scotland 490,000. The remaining five regions all had more than 500,000; North-West 570,000; Greater London 570,000; Northern Yorks and Humberside 585,000; Anglia and East Midlands 585,000; and West Midlands 595,000. (Table A.16, Appendix Eight, page 1004.)

Population and Poverty

There were proportionately more elderly than young people, and more children than young and middle-aged adults who were poor. Table 7.10 shows the distribution by sex and age of those living below, and on the margins of, the state's standard, together with the proportions of each age group who were below or on the margins of the standard. More than half the poor were women and girls, and nearly two thirds of the poor were under 15 or over 65. Women were at a disadvantage at most, but not all ages. The proportion of women in poverty was higher than of men at all ages except under 15; and on the margins of poverty, higher at all ages except 30–44. The chances of living in households in poverty decreased sharply in adulthood. For both sexes, the chances did not vary much until the mid sixties, when they increased very sharply. As many as 51·6 per cent of men and 59·7 per cent of women aged 65 and over were living in households in

Table 7.10. *Percentages of people in households in poverty and on the margins of poverty according to age and sex, and percentages of males and females of different age who were in such households.*

Sex	Age	People in households with incomes according to the state's standard:		Percentage of each sex/ age-group who are:	
		in poverty	on the margins of poverty	in poverty	on the margins of poverty
Male	0–14	17·9	15·3	8·1	24·8
	15–29	3·8	5·9	2·3	12·5
	30–44	5·1	8·6	3·4	20·6
	45–64	5·1	5·6	2·8	11·0
	65+	10·9	8·1	13·8	36·8
All ages		42·8	43·5	5·4	19·5
Female	0–14	13·4	16·5	6·5	28·7
	15–29	6·7	7·7	4·0	16·2
	30–44	5·8	8·4	3·8	19·8
	45–64	10·2	9·0	5·2	16·4
	65+	21·1	15·0	16·8	42·9
All ages		57·2	56·5	6·7	23·8
Total		100	100	6·1	21·7
Number		313	1,121	313	1,121

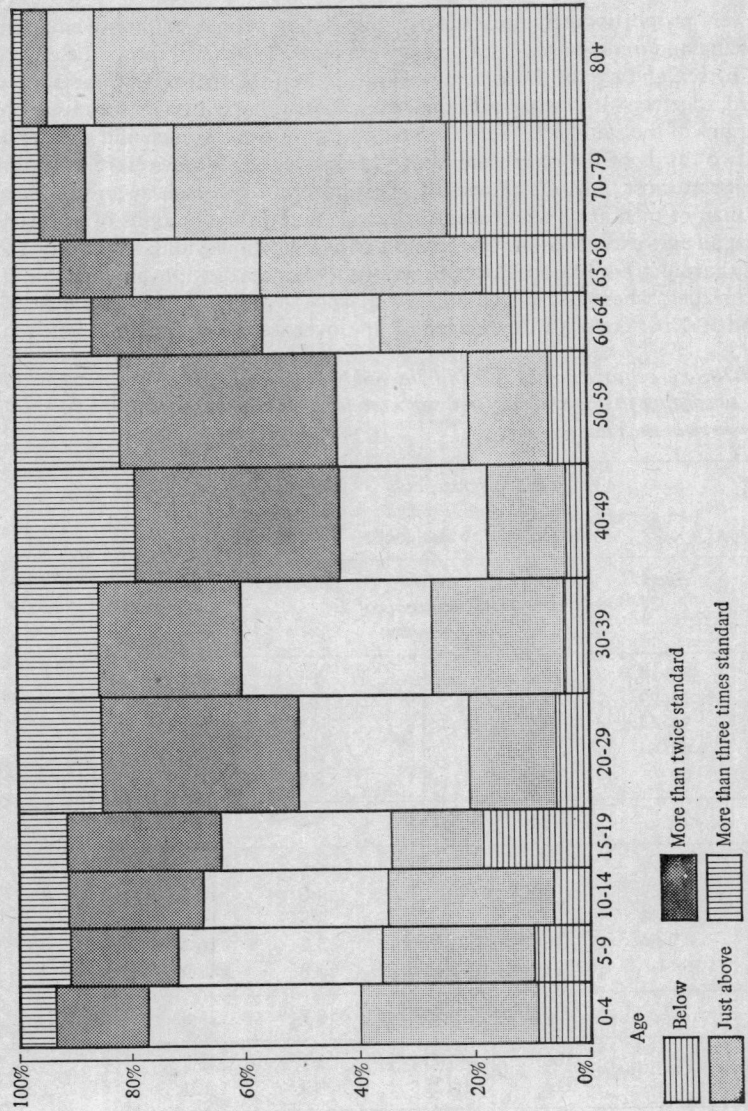

Figure 7.1. *The life-cycle of poverty: people of different age in income units with incomes in previous year above and below state standard.*

Age

Below   More than twice standard

Just above   More than three times standard

poverty or on the margins of poverty. But, in terms of popular suppositions, it should be noted that only 32 per cent of those in poverty by the standard of society itself were aged 65 and over, whereas an almost equal number, 31 per cent, were under 15. If those on the margins of poverty are added children become the largest single group.

The proportions of people of different age in income units, as distinct from households, who were in poverty or on the margins of poverty, are shown in Figure 7.1. The disadvantages of childhood and of old age are again evident, but the low incomes of (mainly manual and lower-non-manual) young people in their teens becomes an additional feature. During adult life, the proportions with incomes substantially above the state's standard reaches a peak in the forties, remaining high in the fifties and then declining sharply in the sixties. There is a sharp increase in the percentage of those with relatively low, and a decrease in the percentage with relatively high, incomes between the sixties and eighties.

By the alternative deprivation standard, more people were found to be in poverty, as already noted. This applied to each of the different age groups, but especially to children. While the supplementary benefit standard was lower than the deprivation standard for all types of household and income units, it was disproportionately low for households and units with children, especially adolescent children. By the alternative standard, more children are consequently found to be living in poverty.

Prosperity and poverty clearly change with age. This is a consequence, as we shall see, not just of the chances in middle life, for example, of earning more and having fewer dependants than in young adulthood, but also of accumulating or inheriting wealth by that stage. It is also a consequence of economic growth benefiting some age groups more than other age groups. Figure 7.2 provides in summary form a striking illustration of the fluctuating fortunes of the life-cycle. To the mean net disposable income of income units is added the annuity value of wealth. The resultant 'income' is expressed as a percentage of the supplementary benefit standard. The graph allows for direct taxes and expenses of going to work as well as dependency. By this measure, the poorest people were children under 5 and adults over 80.

The small numbers in some of the categories should be remembered. Households consisting of a man and woman have been divided into three groups according to their respective ages. The proportion of younger couples with incomes below or just above the standard was much smaller than of older couples. The two miscellaneous categories, one without and the other with children, also had fairly representative proportions with incomes below or just above the standard. The former included, for example, an elderly woman with a single adult daughter and two elderly sisters, or brother and sister. About a fifth of the latter were one-parent families; the rest included couples with two 'adult' children as well as younger children.

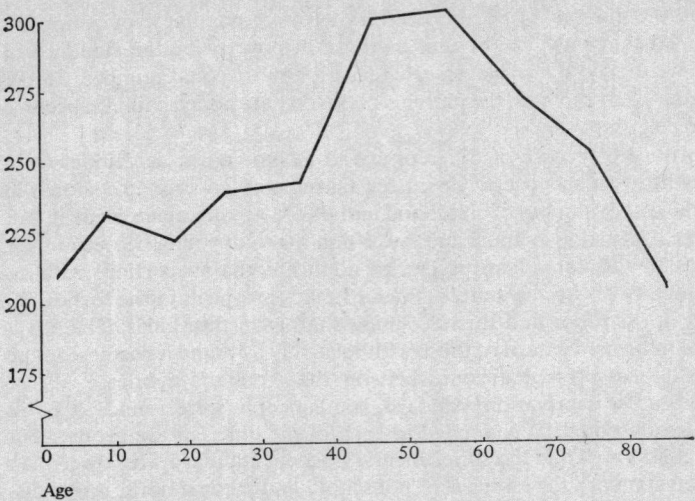

Age

Figure 7.2. Mean net disposable income plus the income equivalent of wealth as a percentage of the state's poverty standard.

Families with Children

The proportion in poverty or on the margins of poverty increases with increasing size of family. There were 21 per cent of men and women with one child, 30 per cent with two children, 31 per cent with three and 69 per cent with four or more who had a net disposable income in the previous year of less than the standard or up to 40 per cent higher. By the criterion of the preceding week's income, the figures were 20 per cent, 28 per cent, 31 per cent and 52 per cent respectively.[1] The relationship between the two criteria of last week's and last year's income is shown in Table A.17 (Appendix Eight, page 1005). This brings out the fact that elderly households tend to have stable incomes while those in which there are children are much more liable to have fluctuating incomes. Thus, 37 per cent of two-child families were in poverty, or on the margins of poverty, in the previous year as a whole, although only 28 per cent had such experience in the previous week.

1. Although the measures are not by any means identical, the roughly similar approach of the DHSS confirms this trend. As at December 1970, the number of families with less than 50 per cent more income than the 'augmented supplementary benefit level' was 10 per cent for families with one child, 14 per cent for families with two children, 22 per cent for families with three children and 35 per cent for families with four or more children. See DHSS, *Two-Parent Families: A Study of Their Resources and Needs in 1968, 1969 and 1970*, Statistical Report Series No. 14, HMSO, London, 1971, p. 8.

Marital status affected the chances of being in poverty. The poorest were those married but separated, whether legally or informally (women being poorer than men). Fourteen per cent had incomes below the state's standard, and another 22 per cent were on the margins. However, none of the small number of divorced people in the sample were in poverty and only a few were on the margins. Twelve per cent of the widowed were in poverty and another 38 per cent were on the margins. This high proportion was swelled by the number of elderly widows

Table 7.11. Percentages of households of different type with incomes in preceding week and preceding year of less than the supplementary benefit scales plus housing cost or up to 40 per cent higher.

Type of household	Last week			Last year		
	In poverty	On margins of poverty	Total no. = 100%	In poverty	On margins of poverty	Total no. = 100%
Man aged 60+	(10·5)	(50·1)	38	(8·1)	(51·3)	37
Man under 60	4·9	9·9	61	7·2	3·6	55
Woman aged 60+	16·3	60·0	190	20·0	57·9	190
Woman under 60	8·9	26·3	57	8·8	21·1	57
Man and woman	5·8	21·1	480	7·2	19·3	470
Man and woman over 60	8·4	39·3	168	9·4	33·1	166
Man and woman one over 60	3·7	31·6	54	7·6	28·9	52
Man and woman both under 60	3·3	6·4	217	1·9	7·1	213
Man, woman, 1 child	4·4	16·1	137	0·7	20·1	134
2 children	4·0	23·6	174	2·3	27·9	172
3 children	2·4	28·4	81	2·6	28·2	78
4+ children	(14·6)	(37·5)	48	(18·8)	(50·0)	48
3 adults	4·2	12·6	188	2·7	11·8	184
3 adults, plus children	2·3	15·4	130	1·6	12·8	126
4 adults	1·5	4·6	65	1·6	6·5	62
Others without children	9·0	10·6	66	7·5	15·1	66
Others with children	10·3	18·3	87	11·8	18·9	85
All types	6·7	23·7	1,803	7·1	23·8	1,764

living on very low incomes. On the other hand, the number of married and unmarried people living on incomes below the standard was slightly lower than average. Five per cent of the married were below the standard and another 19 per cent on the margins.

Type of Household

The differences between households of different type are therefore considerable. The poorest were those in which there were elderly men or women living alone and households with man, wife and four or more children. The least poor were those in which there were three or four adults and households consisting of men under 60 years of age who lived alone and married couples under the same age. The proportions having incomes in the previous week or year which were below or just above the state's standard are set out in Table 7.11. (The corresponding findings in relation to the deprivation standard are given in Table A.18, Appendix Eight, page 1006.)

The distribution is not so uneven between the different types of household according to the relative income standard. There were at least 25 per cent of

Table 7.12. *Percentages of persons in different types of households with gross disposable income below the deprivation standard.*

Type of household	Percentage of persons in each type of household in poverty	Total no. = 100%	Percentage of persons in poverty
Single person aged under 60	17·1	111	1·6
over 60	64·8	227	12·5
Man and woman both over 60	45·7	332	12·9
one over 60	23·1	104	2·0
both under 60	9·4	510	4·1
Man, woman, 1 child	5·2	402	1·8
2 children	16·3	687	9·5
3 children	25·7	389	8·5
4+ children	60·8	309	16·0
3 adults	12·5	554	5·9
3 adults plus children	19·0	603	9·8
4 adults	6·5	245	1·4
Others without children	13·9	183	2·2
Others with children	29·7	476	12·0
All types	22·9	5,137	100

households in each type who were below 80 per cent of the mean annual income for their type, but the figure is over 40 per cent for households consisting of three adults and children, man and wife and four children, older married couples and women under 60 who are living alone. (See Table A.19, Appendix Eight, page 1007.)

Because relatively higher allowances are adopted for dependent children, poverty is found to be more extensive when measured by the relative deprivation standard. Table 7.12 shows that among one-child families with two parents present there are 5 per cent in poverty, but the figure rises for families with two, three and four or more children respectively to 16 per cent, 26 per cent and 61 per cent. The percentages of elderly people living alone and in couples who are in poverty are extremely high. However, as the table shows, they account for rather less than a fifth of the people in poverty by this standard. Families with children under 15 account for well over half (that is, 58 per cent).

Birthplace and Colour

The national sample was not large enough for reliable information to be obtained about a variety of immigrant and ethnic minorities. There were 70 born in the Irish Republic, 57 in other parts of Europe, 101 in India, Pakistan, Africa and the West Indies, and 32 born elsewhere, about whom we gathered complete information on income, though, of course, there were some children of such groups born in the United Kingdom. Slightly more of those in the sample who were born in India, Pakistan, Africa and the West Indies than of those born in the United Kingdom were in poverty or on the margins of poverty, and a related analysis of people who were coloured showed the same trend. Fewer had relatively high incomes (see Table 7.13). (A fuller discussion will be found in Chapter 16.)

Employment Status and Occupational Class

There were much larger differences according to employment status. The first two columns of Table 7.13 show the household incomes as a percentage of the state's standard of all persons employed and self-employed during the year. The incomes of the self-employed are more dispersed. Not only are a larger proportion liable to have high incomes, but a much larger proportion are liable to have incomes below the state's standard. It should be remembered that the self-employed include smallholders as well as wealthy farmers, and those who keep tiny corner shops or stalls in the market as well as those who own prosperous stores. They also include general practitioners, parochial clergy and outworkers. Children and housewives are more liable than the employed to be in poverty, and the proportion of retired people both in poverty and on the margins of poverty is markedly larger than of any other major section of the population.

Table 7.13. *Percentages of people with selected characteristics living in households below and above the supplementary benefit standard.*

Characteristic	Net disposable income last year as % of supplementary benefit scales plus housing cost					Total	Number
	Under 100	100–39	140–99	200–99	300+		
Birthplace							
United Kingdom	6	22	33	29	10	100	4,895
Irish Republic	4	19	37	36	4	100	50
Elsewhere in Europe	4	18	44	16	18	100	57
India, West Indies, Africa and Pakistan	6	27	44	17	6	100	101
Colour							
White	6	22	33	29	11	100	5,020
Non-white	8	23	51	14	4	100	137
Employment status[a]							
Employed	2	12	33	40	13	100	2,242
Self-employed	10	14	23	31	22	100	148
Not employed = children	7	26	40	20	7	100	1,447
Not employed = housewives	7	25	33	26	10	100	1,027
Not employed = retired	16	42	24	14	5	100	507
Occupational status							
Professional	3	6	15	32	44	100	296
Managerial	1	9	24	43	24	100	258
Higher supervisory	4	10	33	36	16	100	508
Lower supervisory	7	18	35	31	9	100	644
Routine non-manual	1	22	35	33	9	100	388
Skilled manual	6	25	37	24	7	100	1,644
Partly skilled manual	5	29	34	28	4	100	819
Unskilled manual	15	32	32	18	2	100	503

NOTE: [a] Some people are counted twice because they changed status in the year, e.g. from employed to retired, housewife to employed, and vice versa. Students, the long-term sick and disabled and the unemployed are excluded.

Finally, as to occupational class, there is a very marked correlation between occupational class and poverty. The population was divided into eight classes, by means of a revised version of an occupational classification developed by Carr-Saunders and Caradog Jones and amended in recent years by Professor Glass and others.[1] Table 7.13 shows that nearly half of the people whose occupations or, in the case of housewives and dependent children, whose husbands' or fathers' occupations, were manual unskilled were below or on the margins of the state's standard of poverty. The figure reduces to about a third of other manual occupations, a quarter of lower-grade supervisory and routine non-manual occupations and a tenth of professional, higher administrative and managerial occupations. The corresponding increase in the proportion having incomes of more than three times the standard is also noteworthy. It should, of course, be remembered that the classification includes retired people as well as those who are the dependants of people in employment. The correlation between occupational class and poverty is more striking if the retired are excluded.

Figure 7.3 provides a summary of the differences between the non-manual and manual classes in the proportions of different age groups experiencing poverty. In the graph, the incomes of income units rather than of households have been compared with the supplementary benefit scales. The overlap of the two lines in the late teens needs to be explained. The percentage of those aged 15–19 of non-manual occupational status who are poor is almost the same as of those of manual status. Partly this is because daughters of manual workers take junior office jobs, which are classified as non-manual, and because such jobs tend to be relatively low paid. For this age group more than for most age groups the separation of the unit's (usually individual's) income from that of the household as a whole can also be misleading. But, with this qualification, and without denying the existence of serious economic disadvantage for a substantial proportion of young teenagers, the difference between people of non-manual and manual status is substantial, at all ages, and in childhood is very marked indeed. This is one of the most important findings of the entire survey and will be explored in detail in subsequent chapters. The gap is even wider when owner-occupied homes and other assets are brought into the picture, as we shall see (especially in Chapters 9 and 10).

The graph has other features. In the twenties the proportion of people of manual status who are poor is relatively low, partly because many manual workers quickly reach a peak of earnings and partly because many of their

---

1. The eight-fold classification by sociologists was developed from a seven-fold classification used by Professor Glass in Glass, D. V. (ed.), *Social Class and Mobility*, Routledge & Kegan Paul, London, 1954. This was compared with the occupational classification used by the Registrar General and with the information collected in pilot work and the first stage of the main survey. The coding of 121 occupations (slightly under a tenth of the list finally used in coding) was amended. The classification is discussed in Chapter 10 and Appendix Six.

families are not yet complete. The proportion rises in the thirties, when the number of dependants tends to be largest, and falls in the forties and fifties, when children leave school, enter paid work and leave home. Already by the early sixties, before men reach the usual pensionable age, the proportion is rising quickly. By the late sixties the number of people of manual status who are poor approaches 70 per cent, and the figure continues even to increase into extreme old age.

By contrast, relatively few young children of non-manual status are poor, nor is the same peak as for people of manual status reached in the thirties. This is

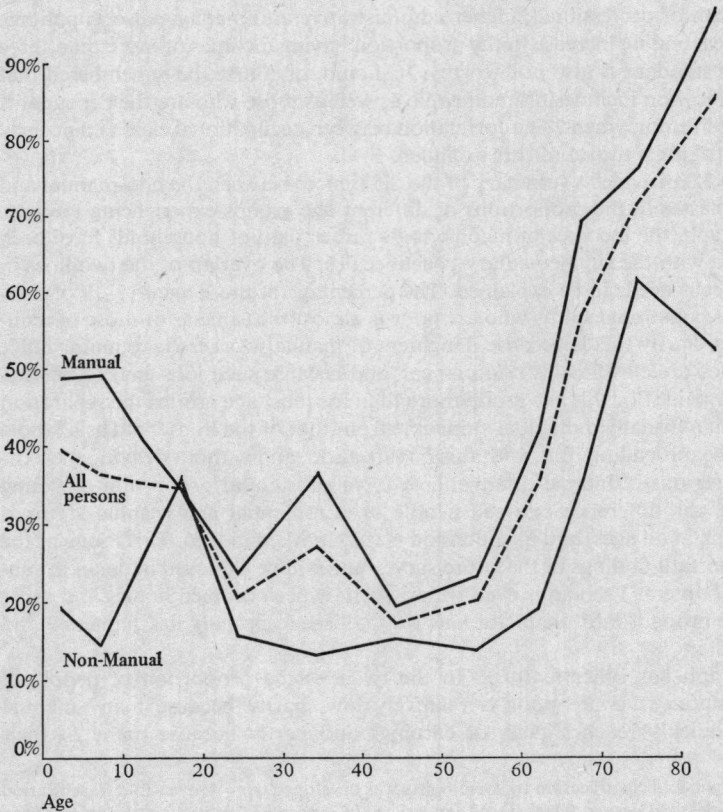

Figure 7.3. *Percentages in income units with net disposable income in previous year below or just above the state's poverty standard.*

because fewer (particularly among the non-manual workers of lower status) have large families and more are continuously employed and earn increments in middle life. Like people of manual status, the numbers who are poor rise in later life, but not sharply until the late sixties, and actually begin to diminish in the eighties.

Assets

There was a strong inverse relationship between the ownership of assets and poverty. Considerably over half those with no assets at all or negative assets were in poverty or on the margins of poverty, as Table 7.14 shows. On the other hand, nearly half those with more than £10,000 assets had an income of at least three times the social or government standard. The inclusion of owner-occupied housing in the valuation of assets accounts in large part for the fact that the proportion of people in households having more than £500 but less than £5,000 total assets who were poor or marginally poor is only a little below average. A number of these were people who were retired.

About a third of the poor and marginally poor had assets worth more than £1,000. On the other hand, about a quarter of those just beyond the margins of poverty had no assets at all, negative assets or only up to £100. Some were young people or families with above average earnings, but others included middle-aged couples living in council housing or other rented property whose children had grown up and left home and whose earnings were small. Such people had 'emerged' from poverty in the sense discussed earlier.

The relationship between other resources, especially assets or wealth, and cash incomes represents a major theme of this report. The problem of poverty might even be said to be perceptibly more pronounced when assets, for example, are brought into the picture. Earlier we showed how many were in poverty by the relative income standard – that is, had incomes of less than half the mean for their household type. Table 7.15 shows that if the annuity value of assets is added to income the dispersion of incomes becomes wider. There were 9 per cent of households having incomes, compared with 15 per cent having income net worth, of less than 50 per cent of the mean; and, at the other extreme, 4 per cent having incomes, compared with 5 per cent having income net worth, of 200 per cent or more of the mean. These tendencies apply to most types of household, as the table shows. By the criterion of having fewer than half the resources of households of the same type, then the inclusion of assets in the definition increases the proportion of the population in poverty.

Figure 7.4 takes the exercise one stage further, and can be compared with Figure 7.3. The annuity value of assets of each income unit has been added to non-asset income, and the resultant 'income' then expressed as a percentage of the supplementary benefit scales. Since more non-manual than manual families

Table 7.14. Percentages of people having different amounts of assets who were below or above the state's standard of poverty.

Net disposable house- hold income last year as % of supplementary benefit scales plus housing cost	Household assets							Zero	In debt
	More than £10,000	More than £5,000 but less than £10,000	More than £2,000 but less than £5,000	More than £1,000 but less than £2,000	More than £500 but less than £1,000	More than £200 but less than £500	More than £0 but less than £200		
300+	46	16	9	7	4	3	3	2	3
200–99	29	40	34	28	30	31	22	12	11
140–99	20	29	31	39	39	45	38	28	31
100–39	4	9	22	21	25	17	30	45	37
under 100	1	5	3	5	2	4	7	13	18
Total	100	100	100	100	100	100	100	100	100
Number	332	611	789	510	374	428	723	305	294

NOTE: The total number of people in the sample in households giving full information on assets as well as income was 4,366.

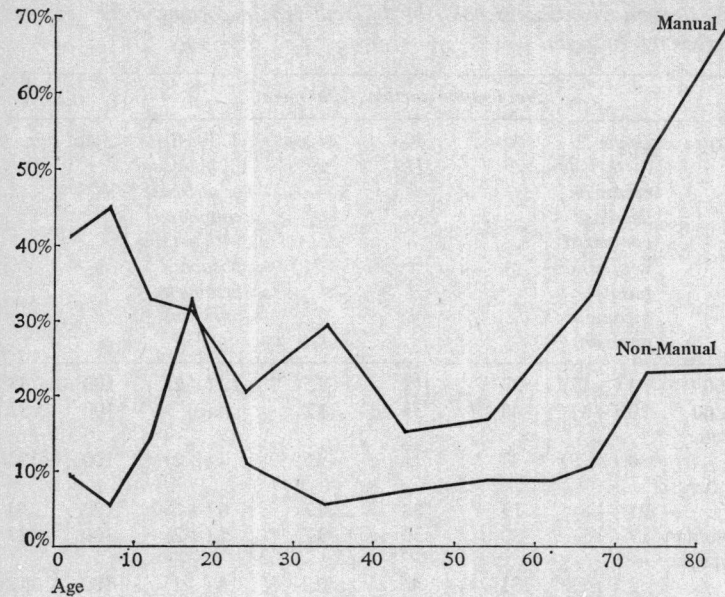

Figure 7.4. *Percentages in income units who are below or just above the state's poverty standard after the income equivalent of their wealth is added to non-asset income in previous year.*

held assets of more than negligible value, the difference between the two categories became wider for nearly all age groups, though the overlap in the late teens remained. The percentage of non-manual children remaining in poverty or on its margins was halved, whereas the percentage of manual children was only reduced by about a sixth. In old age the number of people of manual status who were poor fell more sharply, but still by less proportionately than that of people of non-manual status. This theme will be examined more fully in later chapters (especially Chapters 9, 10, 12, 17 and 18). When other types of resources as well as incomes are assessed, it becomes evident that poverty is a problem which predominantly affects the population of manual status.

Home-grown food was of only small importance to a minority of the poor. As many as 81 per cent of people with household incomes below or just above the state's standard said they had no benefit at all from home-grown food, and most of the rest put the value at less than 50p per week. Only 1 per cent of them said the value of such food was £1 or more per week.

Table 7.15. *Percentages of households of different type according to net income worth as percentage of mean.*

Household type	Net income worth as % of mean					Total	No.
	Under 50 (with % increase or decrease compared with net disposable income as % of mean)	50–79	80–119	120–99	200+ (with % increase or decrease compared with net disposable income as % of mean)		
Man aged 60+	33 (+17)	27	12	15	12 (+2)	100	33
Man under 60	10 (+1)	43	31	12	4 (0)	100	51
Woman aged 60+	30 (+29)	37	11	15	7 (+2)	100	173
Woman under 60	21 (+8)	19	38	17	6 (+2)	100	53
Man and woman	17 (−1)	30	30	17	5 (+2)	100	427
Man, woman, 1 child	2 (+1)	31	46	18	4 (+1)	100	112
2 children	7 (+3)	37	35	15	6 (+1)	100	142
3 children	3 (+1)	46	33	10	8 (+4)	100	61
4+ children	23 (+5)	54	9	9	5 (−3)	100	43
3 adults	10 (−2)	31	36	19	4 (+1)	100	157
3 adults, plus children	10 (+5)	41	35	10	4 (−1)	100	106
4 adults	4 (+2)	35	48	11	2 (+2)	100	52
Others without children	25 (+2)	29	25	14	7 (+1)	100	56
Others with children	20 (+9)	23	39	13	6 (+1)	100	71
All types	15 (+6)	33 (+3)	31 (−7)	15 (−4)	5 (+1)	100	1,537

NOTE: Selected increases or decreases in the percentages, compared with the corresponding distribution according to income, are shown in brackets.

Housing Cost and Poverty

One major weakness of the state's measure of poverty is that it includes the actual cost of housing. Three families of the same type might have identical incomes after paying rent and, if they had a net income below the supplementary benefit standard, would each be regarded as being in poverty, and yet the first might have been paying £1·50 rent a week for a rent-controlled slum flat, the second £3 for a small pre-war council flat and the third £8 a week as a mortgage repayment on a spacious owner-occupied house. The same point might be made in relation to statistical trends from year to year. If rents rise more sharply than the costs of other necessities, poverty would also tend to increase more sharply even if there were a disproportionate improvement at the same time in the quality of housing occupied by the population.

For example, we found that the income to which 81 per cent of one-person households were 'entitled' varied between £4 and £7 a week, and for most of the remaining households ranged up to £11 a week. The income to which 81 per cent of three-person households were 'entitled' varied between £10 and £16 but ranged down to £8 for some of the remaining households and up to and over £20 for others.

The fact that the Supplementary Benefits Commission generally meets rents and the interest element of mortgage repayments in full, while allowing only basic allowances for other needs, reflects the values approved by society through government. This form of expenditure is considered to be inescapable and also rather virtuous, without regard to any reduction of the general welfare which it might represent. Housing costs tend to vary more than costs such as food and, unlike some other costs, people living on supplementary benefits are not expected to be able to reduce them. By contrast, expenditure on social obligations and relationships, including entertainment of family and friends, for example, is considered as a conventional indulgence if not an extravagance. One difference between the relative deprivation and state standards of poverty is that the former does not single out housing expenditure from other forms of 'necessary' expenditure for preferment.

In fact there is wide variation in the cost of housing. In 1968–9 a fifth of all households in the sample were paying under £1 per week, but another fifth £4 or more. The dispersion was wide for all types of household (Table A.20, Appendix Eight, page 1008). Substantial minorities of households consisting of man, wife and one or more children were paying £300 a year or more. The mean housing cost was £182 in the year. This includes all payments of rent, ground rent, rates, water rates and insurance on the dwelling, and mortgage interest payments and capital repayments, less the receipt of any rent and rate rebates. The costs of repairs and decoration are also included. For purposes of comparison, the average costs of housing for each of the principal tenure groups are given in Table 7.16 both for the sample and for the corresponding samples interviewed in 1967 and 1968 in the course of the Family Expenditure Survey. Though there are slight differences in the definition of housing costs for owner-occupiers, the mean costs for each of the tenure groups are broadly similar. The proportions of households in each tenure group are also similar.

The dispersion of expenditure on housing, when expressed as a percentage of net disposable household income, was also very wide within each type of household. Although, for example, different groups of households comprising a man, wife and one child, man, wife and two children, and so on, spent on average between 14 per cent and 16 per cent on their accommodation, this figure varied from under 5 per cent (for nearly one family in every ten) to over 20 per cent (for a third of one-child families and a fifth of four child families). Nearly a half of all women in the sample who were living alone spent 20 per cent or more of their net disposable income on housing. Altogether a fifth of all households in the sample spent under 5 per cent but a quarter 20 per cent or more of their income on housing (Table A.21, Appendix Eight, page 1009).

Table 7.16. *Percentages of households according to tenure and average expenditure on housing.*

Type of tenure	Percentage of all households				Mean housing in £ p.a.		
	Poverty Survey	Family Expenditure Survey			Poverty Survey	Family Expenditure Survey	
		1967	1968	1975		1967	1968
Renting council	28	30	30	32	135	119	130
Renting, privately unfurnished	17	18	18	11	107	106	115
Renting, privately furnished	5	4	3	4	192	185	207
Living rent-free (mainly employer)	3	1	3	3	4	10	7
Owner-occupied (in purchase)	24	26	26	29	259	452[a]	305[a]
Owner-occupied (owned outright)	24	20	20	21	55	44[a]	42[a]
Total	100	100	100	100	182[b]	209[b]	180[b]
Number	2,050	7,386	7,161	7,203	–	–	–

NOTES: [a] The imputed amount of rent which had been included in the housing expenditure of owner-occupiers in the FES reports has been deducted and expenditure on 'Mortgage and other payments for purchase or alteration of dwellings' (shown in the reports under 'other payments recorded') has been included solely in the 'in purchase' category. In fact, part of this figure is attributable to other tenures, especially outright owners, but information allowing apportionment is not published. The FES figure for 1967 is out of line with that produced for subsequent as well as previous years and is probably due to a few exceptionally large payments for housing among the households sampled.
[b] This figure includes tenants' and owner-occupiers' expenditure on repairs, maintenance and decoration. These costs are not apportioned between different tenure groups in FES reports.

These big variations were not confined to the more prosperous sections of the population. Table 7.17 shows that although the housing costs of people in households living on incomes below or just above the supplementary benefit standard tended to be lower than of other groups, nearly a fifth were paying £200 or more a year. Large numbers of those with high incomes spent comparatively little on housing. Indeed, disproportionately more of them spent nothing at all on housing. These were people who, because of employer subsidies, lived free of rent, rates and the cost of repairs, or regained any costs they incurred by subletting.

Table 7.17. Percentages of people in households with a net disposable income below and above the supplementary benefit standard, according to housing cost.

| Annual housing cost (£) | Net disposable income as % of supplementary benefit scales + housing cost | | | | | |
	Under 100	100–39	140–99	200–99	300+	All
0	3	1	4	5	10	4
Under 25	7	6	4	2	3	4
26–50	17	10	6	10	11	9
51–100	30	21	16	20	30	20
101–50	25	20	22	18	18	20
151–200	7	19	20	16	10	17
201+	12	23	28	29	18	25
Total	100	100	100	100	100	100
Number	313	1,122	1,721	1,464	537	5,157

Summary

Three measures of poverty were applied to the sample. By the state's standard (the basic supplementary benefit scales plus housing costs), 7 per cent of households were found to be in poverty and 24 per cent on the margins of poverty. The corresponding proportions of people were 6 per cent and nearly 22 per cent, representing 3,320,000 and 11,860,000 people respectively.

By the relative income standard (households having an income of less than 50 per cent of the mean for their type), 10·5 per cent of the households and 9 per cent of the people, representing 5 million, were in poverty.

By the deprivation standard (households having an income of less than a level below which deprivation tends to increase disproportionately as income diminishes), 25 per cent of households and 23 per cent of people in the sample, representing 12,460,000, were in poverty.

The proportion of people in the sample with experience in the year of short-term or long-term poverty, or marginal poverty, was even higher. There were 28 per cent who were below or just above the state's standard on average during the year, but the figure increases to 36 per cent if people who dropped to these levels for at least a short period in the year are added.

The numbers found to be living in poverty depend not only on the standard of measurement but also on the definition of the domestic unit. For many purposes, an assessment of the resources of income units, rather than of households, is to be preferred. It conforms with the administrative procedures of the Supplementary Benefits Commission, for example. Seventy-one per cent of households consist of only a single income unit. The number of people found to be living in poverty (according to the state's standard) is 6·1 per cent (or 3,320,000) when the 'household' is the unit of measurement, but 9·1 per cent, (or 4,950,000), when the 'income unit' is adopted for measurement.

The numbers found to be in poverty also depend on the definition of the resources which are to be measured. For their standards of living, many people depend partly, if not wholly, on resources other than cash incomes. The possession of assets (including homes) is highly correlated with income, and even when the annuity value of assets is added to income in estimating the numbers living below the social standard of poverty, the figure quoted above, for example, of 9·1 per cent (or nearly 5 million) is reduced only to 6·8 per cent (or 3·7 million). The majority of people living in poverty or on the margins of poverty have very few other resources. Indeed, their deprivation becomes more sharply exposed once such resources are brought into the reckoning.

The incidence of poverty was highest in one-person households, then households with five or more persons, and lowest among three- and four-person households. It was highest in Northern Ireland, followed by the North-West, Wales and the South-West and Scotland, and lowest in Greater London. Children were more likely to be in poverty than adults under the pensionable ages, women more likely than men, the separated and widowed more than the married and unmarried, the self-employed than the employed, and dependants also than the employed. Poverty was also closely correlated with social class, much the highest incidence being found among unskilled manual workers and their dependants.

Poverty was more common among elderly people living alone or in couples and among families with three or more children. These are the two most serious problems revealed by this analysis. More than half the retired were in households living in poverty or on the margins of poverty by the social or government standard.

Because relatively higher allowances are adopted for dependent children, poverty is found to be more extensive among families with dependent children by the relative deprivation standard than by the supplementary benefit standard. The figure rises from 5 per cent for families with one child to 16 per cent for families with two children, 26 per cent for families with three and 61 per cent for families with four or more children. Families with children under 15 account for well over half the population in poverty, and the elderly for most of the remainder.

8

The Impact of Poverty

How does poverty affect individual families? Just as the previous chapter attempted to give a statistical summary of poverty in the United Kingdom, so this chapter will give a descriptive summary of the kind of conditions in which individual poor families lived. Such an outline is necessary because poverty is not universally recognized. People dispute its definition, and even when they agree on what it means in abstract terms, they often fail to see how that may apply to people around them. Some people who themselves live in poverty also fail to recognize or admit it.

The questionnaires used were extensive and allow a rounded, if unvarnished, account of a family's circumstances at the time of the interview and for the year preceding the interview to be written up. Interviewers were encouraged to add descriptions of informants and illustrations of what they said or did, and in nearly half the questionnaires notes and quotations were added, occasionally at length. The serial numbers of households living below or on the margins of the state poverty line were listed according to membership of 'minorities' (long-term unemployed, sick, disabled and so forth). A few of the completed questionnaires under each heading were selected at random. Summaries extracted from the questionnaires are reproduced below. Surnames and sometimes places of residence and age, but not other details, have been changed in order to protect the confidentiality in which information was offered.

I have tried to let the facts as reported by the respondents speak for themselves, rather than present them in the harshest possible light, or according to any single set of values. Of course, this does not escape subjective selection and ordering of certain material, but it does at least acknowledge the complications and inconsistencies of individual and social life. Thus some people have known poverty and emerged from it in a single year. Some manage their resources with dexterity over a limited range of social activities. Others are destitute and extravagant by turns or live and dress badly and eat well. They are moved by different social forces and constraints. The low income of some is unrelieved by any obvious compensation, while others have an owner-occupied house, a garden in which vegetables can be grown, or relatives who offer goods and money in support. All this forces the social scientist to generalize with care about the conditions in which people live and points to the broad concept of resources for which this book has argued.

What follows is not the calculated assembly of the worst instances of poverty in the entire survey. It is an account of a cross-section of the households in poverty (together with a few on the margins of poverty) according to the state's definition. The reader might like to remember that all these instances were among the 2,000 households selected entirely at random from the 17 million in the country as a whole. Because the survey was not intended to provide detailed personal histories but aimed principally at getting hard data about incomes, assets and working and other activities, the account is not comprehensive. Its purpose is just to convey the kind of people living in poverty in the United Kingdom, the problems with which they have to grapple and some of the opinions they have.

1. In poverty: Young family, with disabled man and woman and handicapped child

This is a family interviewed several times in 1968–9, and again in 1972. First, 1968.

Mr and Mrs Nelson, 35 and 32, live with their three sons of 13, 9 and 6 in a four-roomed council flat in a poor district of Oldham, overlooked by a rubber factory belching smoke all day long and near a canal. They believe the flat is a danger to their health. 'One bedroom is so damp that it stripped itself.' The living room has a fire but they can only afford a one-bar electric fire to heat the bedrooms because they are terribly damp. The fire is taken from one room to the next. At Christmas the bedroom window was smashed by a brick. Because the family cannot afford new glass, the room gets too cold and the boys sleep in one bedroom. The family had been moved out of a house which was also very damp and had been demolished in a clearance scheme two years before. They have no garden or yard, and though there is a playground attached to the flats, Mrs Nelson thinks the slides and swings are dangerous and too near to an adjoining busy main road. The flat is poorly furnished with linoleum and no carpets, no washing machine or refrigerator and just battered settees and chairs.

Mr Nelson is an epileptic. His fits began eleven years ago. He also has blood clots which keep touching the brain, and bad hearing. He can go out for a walk, but if he goes far he must have somebody with him. (Score on disability index, 11.) He tends to be in bed a week in every four, from the after-effects of fits and the blood clots on his brain. His nerves are bad, and, for example, he is afraid of holding scissors to cut his nails, in case he has a fit. His wife says that the doctor told her that not much could be done for him. He had not worked for six and a half years, when he had been a driver earning a wage well above average (then

£25–£30 p.w.), for a decorating firm. He had, in fact, served a six years apprenticeship in painting and decorating. Five years ago he had been sent to a government retraining centre, where he entered an engineering section. After three days he had an epileptic fit and the doctor said that the work, and travelling six miles each way, was too risky. Now he goes once a month to his doctor for prescriptions and a sickness certificate, and once in every four months to hospital for a check-up.

Mrs Nelson had given up her work as an office cleaner twelve months earlier to look after him. Formerly she had been a spinner in a cotton mill. She suffers badly from bronchitis and rheumatism and has pain in her chest, following a spell in hospital with fluid on the lungs two years earlier. (Score on disability index, 3.) Her health varies seasonally, and from week to week, and she feels tired all the time. She goes to the doctor three times a month for a prescription for tablets.

Their second son Jonathan, aged 9, is very thin and delicate and has intermittent deafness. He is very susceptible to colds and has had several spells in bed this year. He has been to hospital to see a specialist three times about his hearing. For much of the year he has had nasal catarrh and wakes up in the middle of the night shouting, 'I can't breathe. I can't breathe.'

The eldest son is in reasonably good health but has a so-called 'lazy eye', of which he is self-conscious. He goes to a special school. He is not mentally backward but was slow to begin to read and was considered to need such schooling. He is collected daily by school bus. The youngest child is also in fairly good health and, like the second son, goes to a neighbouring primary school. They wear plimsolls to go to school because they cannot afford shoes.

The family have little social life, partly, they say, because they moved into the district less than two years ago. Mrs Nelson sees a number of her relatives once or more a week, including a sister, her step-mother and father and her husband's mother, but there is little exchange of help. They can depend on a neighbour for emergency help, but Mrs Nelson's family seem to be keeping their distance, perhaps out of fear from the husband's epilepsy. Or perhaps the Nelsons themselves feel the need of protection from barbed gossip and want to hide in privacy. 'We keep ourselves to ourselves,' as Mr Nelson said. They have not had a summer holiday, but twice in the year Mrs Nelson has saved up and taken the children by train, just for the day, to her sister in Yorkshire. 'It gives them a good day out. Good air. It is the only holiday they are likely to get.' They have not had a meal or snack with any relative or friend in the last fortnight and have not been out any evening. Similarly they have not entertained anyone in the home. None of the children has had a birthday party and none of their friends has come in to play. They are Church of England but have not been to church in the last year.

At the time of interview (March 1968) they had £10·25 a week in sickness benefit, and £1·05 supplementary benefit, as well as 90p family allowances. Their rent of £2·60 was paid directly by the Supplementary Benefits Commission because they had got into arrears and had agreed for the council to be paid direct. Their total income appeared to be marginally below the state poverty line, and if they had been judged to be entitled (because of the poor health of three of the family) to an additional allowance, would have been more than a pound below. In the week following the interview, family allowances were to be increased by 70p, but sickness benefit and supplementary benefit reduced by the same amount. 'It is scandalous, and the government say they are trying to alleviate poverty.' They had received two single grants from the commission in the last year of £4·50 for shoes and £1·62½ for glasses. The grant for shoes was supposed to cover the cost of boys' shoes. An application for clothing was refused. Once, when Mr Nelson had recovered from a particularly bad fit and had spent a fortnight in bed, he asked for a visitor to judge an application for a grant for shoes. No visit was paid for six weeks. He said he was not embarrassed to receive supplementary benefit. 'It is a case of necessity. We cannot live without it.' They have no savings or other assets. 'There's nothing we own which would fetch a decent price.'

Wednesday is benefit day, and Mr and Mrs Nelson do not have a cooked meal on Tuesdays (and sometimes Mondays) because they have no money left. They rarely have fresh meat, but their children have free meals at school (and also free milk). The family has a pint of milk a day, which is watered down to eke it out. If Christmas so falls that the household gets two weeks' benefit, they spend it on 'giving the children a good time and starve the second week'. They have also depended a bit on a Baptist Mission which caters for the poor and needy. When Mr Nelson is well, he organizes games for poor children at the Mission on a Sunday afternoon for three hours. He is not paid for this, but at Christmas receives a big food parcel and a toy for each of the children. They cannot afford a hundredweight of coal at once and only buy it in 28-pound bags as and when they can afford them. The children receive 2½p pocket money apiece. Mr Nelson hands over his benefits to his wife, and when he is well, receives back £2, with which he buys cigarettes and has an occasional drink in the pub. They feel worse off than family or friends and feel they have never been worse off in their lives. When asked to describe poverty, Mr Nelson said, 'The circumstances we are experiencing now. Poverty is when you are living from hand to mouth and you have no security.' They had not voted at the last election and laid responsibility for poverty with the government. What could be done about it? 'Increase benefits above the subsistence level,' was Mr Nelson's reply.

*

After this interview, the family allowed the research team to take up the question of rate of benefit on their behalf. The allowance was agreed by the Supplementary Benefits Commission to be wrong and the weekly payment was increased by 35p. An exceptional needs grant of nearly £30 was also paid for clothes and bedding.

In 1972, the family was visited again. Mr Nelson is very frail. He now has sixteen or seventeen epileptic fits each day during severe episodes of epilepsy which seem to come every eight weeks or so. He was assessed for an attendance allowance but was turned down. He had been visited in the course of a disabled register survey. Mrs Nelson said, 'I asked them about a holiday for him.' As for supplementary benefit: 'After you were here last time they put everything right, but we haven't heard anything since, only when we ask them to come.' After having an exceptional needs grant in 1968, they had not received another until a grant for £12·20 was paid this year. Mrs Nelson pointed out that when her husband had fits he pulled and tore the bedding. The officer told her, 'You've had enough grants from us.' 'We need new beds. They are all falling to pieces. They were all second-hand when we got them. I've asked the WVS if they can find us any . . . The only visits we get are from the Mental Health, but the visitor has left and I don't know if we shall get another. She was nice. She tried to fix my husband up with a holiday. But it was going to cost £17 for him to go to an epileptic home for two weeks. I couldn't afford that.'

Their eldest son, Arthur, is now 17 and he took a job as a labourer with a cardboard-box firm a year ago. 'He just loves it. He's never late.' For a forty-hour week he gets a gross wage of £8·80 a week, and takes home £7·94. They were delighted because in Christmas week he got a bonus of 50p. The family's rent has increased by 45 per cent from £2·60 to £3·76. Invalidity benefit is now £15·70. To this a family allowance of 90p and supplementary benefit of £1·35 is added. Even allowing for Arthur's share of the rent, his parents' total income seems to be about 30p below the basic scales of the Supplementary Benefits Commission (including 50p long-term addition). No additional allowance is made for Mr Nelson's special needs. There has therefore been an improvement in their situation only to the extent that the eldest son now earns a small wage. About supplementary benefit and sickness benefit, Mrs Nelson commented, 'You get fed up always having to ask for everything. I hate going down. If I have to go down because the book hasn't come they say I've just got to wait until it does come.' Subsequently the income from the commission was investigated. Not only was the allowance confirmed to be an underpayment. The extra amount agreed to be necessary in 1968 for Mr Nelson's diet was no longer being paid. The underpayment was put right and the dietary allowance restored. A further exceptional needs grant was paid.

The evidence of deprivation is as strong, and in some respects stronger, than in 1968. They go to bed early to save fuel. Mrs Nelson buys second-hand clothing at jumble sales. For breakfast, she cooks porridge for the children but she and her husband have nothing. They are used to days without any cooked meal, '. . . especially Mondays and Tuesdays. We give it to the kids. We get the money on Wednesday and it doesn't last long.' They have little fresh meat. 'We have a few chops if cheap enough, perhaps once a fortnight. Arthur's that good. I like to give him a nice lamb chop as a treat sometimes.' She has no shoes for rainy weather,

'Just these boots, which are three times too big.' At Christmas, 'I got a lovely piece of lean bacon and boiled it and roasted it. It cost £1 but it was worth it. Anyway, it was a long holiday, wasn't it? My husband's sister bought a Christmas present and Arthur bought sweets for the kids and we got some second-hand toys from the welfare.' The two younger children get pocket money 'now that Arthur is working. He gives them 5p each a week.' She said that they did not go out in the evenings. 'Mr Nelson walks down to his mother's most evenings if he's feeling well enough. Sometimes she gives him money for half a pint. It does him good.' When the coal strike was on, Mrs Nelson was seriously ill at home with pneumonia. At the same time, Mr Nelson was having severe fits through the night. 'That was the worst time I have ever had.'

The problem of doing right by her children obsessed her. Her second son Jonathan is at a secondary modern school which insists on uniforms. 'The school moans at the lad because he goes in jeans, but a blue shirt alone costs £2; and the trousers are £3·15. Then there is a grey pullover and a blazer. I can't possibly afford it. There's PE equipment and swimming. I haven't any decent towels and the school complains. The headmaster keeps complaining. That's when I went to the council about a grant, and they turned me down. I bought some shoes last week for both of them, £3·25 a pair. I got the money from the TV rebate. Jonathan can't read very well and the school don't do special reading. He doesn't bother to try now and has only had one special lesson since January although the Child Guidance people said he had to have them. He still gets stomach pains. They fade and come back. The games teacher made him do games even though I sent a letter.' When asked how she described poverty, she answered, 'Not being able to buy anything for the kids . . . I'm hoping things will be better for my kiddies in time to come. I never thought life would be like this.'

There is not much change in the furnishings. One dresser which had been rather chipped and discoloured had been repainted. The living room has been papered with some wallpaper given to them by Mr Nelson's sister. A single cup and saucer stands proudly on the dresser, a memento of a relative's holiday. The interviewer was allowed to look at it, though Mrs Nelson kept a firm hold on it with one hand stretched underneath for fear it fell. 'Everything in here, except the TV, which we rent, has been given to us.' The TV is on a meter and every three months is emptied by the company. The difference between the rent and the money in the box is refunded. 'In another couple of years the TV will be mine. Then they can't take it away. I can't wait for that day.'

She has a slipped disc and has been having prolonged investigations in hospital for ulcers and gall-bladder trouble. She had just learned that very morning, however, that she is pregnant and the baby is due in eight weeks. This news had stunned her. She was bewildered by the fact that although she had had a number of X-rays as well as examinations at the hospital in the past months, no one had said anything about a baby. She had been handed a diet sheet. 'As if I can afford steak.' She had nothing for the baby and had gone that afternoon to the welfare to ask for an old pram, but was told they had none.

Mrs Nelson was as sharply critical of the government as her husband had been in 1968. The government was responsible for poverty. 'Put governments in a bag and shake them up. It doesn't matter which one you get. Each one is just as bad as the other ... They promise everything. They're going to give you this and give you that. The only thing they do give you is the transport to vote for them.'

The interviewer, a skilled and sensitive woman with long experience of field-work, herself the mother of three children, described Mrs Nelson as 'quite the bravest person I have ever met. This house is full of respect for everyone else, and affection.' Perhaps an answer to a question about holidays was most telling of all. Had the family had a summer holiday recently? 'Oh yes,' said Mrs Nelson immediately, 'we saved and saved for weeks. We put the money in that pot up there. Mind you, we had to take it out sometimes, but we managed to put it back. Then the time came, and we really did go together to see *The Sound of Music*. Oh, it was lovely – that opening scene when she was dancing on the mountains and all free. The children each had an ice-cream, and when we left we walked up the High Street and you know that wallpaper shop, well, we saw that picture, there, above our fireplace. We counted up our money. If we walked home we would just have enough for it. So next morning I walked down and bought it, and there it's been ever since. When you're fed up you can look at it and it reminds you of *The Sound of Music*.'

Mr Nelson died in 1976. He was 43.

2. In poverty: Retirement pensioner living alone

Mrs Hooton is a married woman of 65 who was separated from her husband four years ago and is living alone in a council flat in an old Victorian house in Edinburgh. She is a cheerful, plump person who was very diffident about the interview, which was twice interrupted by neighbours (both elderly) dropping in on their way home. The house is sandwiched between a car park created after the demolition of adjoining property and a busy road. She had been moved out of a private flat because of slum clearance and is now in two rooms without indoors WC or bath. There are several other elderly neighbours. There is only one electric power-point in the flat, which is sparsely furnished, with no television set but a radio. She retired from being a cloakroom attendant in a department store for nearly twenty years. Her husband had been a labourer in a paper mill.

Her pension is at a reduced rate because she elected to pay reduced contributions as a married woman. She receives only £2·80 a week, together with a payment from her husband of £1·25, making a total of £4·05. Her rent is 40p a week. She has no savings or assets of any kind. She lent a friend £7 eighteen months ago and does not expect it back. Rheumatism in her hips restricts her mobility, but she has not seen her doctor this year and is able to do most jobs in her home. (Score on the disability index, 2.)

She has one married daughter, who lives in the United States. Two married brothers are in Edinburgh. She has not seen either of them for two years. A neighbour helps her with shopping, and 'one Indian gentleman gives me curried chicken occasionally'. She feels she could count on these friends in an emergency, and sometimes gives one or other a meal. She did not have a summer holiday and seldom goes out. She has not had an evening out in the past fortnight. She has one cooked meal each day – mince or a piece of meat not more than three times a week – and she is fond of tripe. She has half a pint of milk each day. At Christmas she spent nothing on presents. 'I would have liked to, but everything was too dear.' In the winter she goes to bed at 8.30 p.m. While she thinks her situation has become worse in recent years, and is worse than it has ever been, she still considers she is as well off as others in the neighbourhood, and is 'never' poor.

She is eligible to receive supplementary benefit and the interviewer persuaded her to fill in a form and post it that day. The interviewer was subsequently able to establish that she was in fact entitled to a total allowance of £5·15 and was receiving only £4·05. On the state's definition of what was minimally adequate, her income seemed to have been more than 20 per cent deficient for four years.

3. In poverty: Chronically sick and disabled man living with elderly mother

Mrs Waterlow, a widow of 68, lives in a semi-detached council house with five rooms and a substantial garden (rent £2·65 per week) in Gloucester with her unmarried son of 49. There is no telephone or refrigerator. Mrs Waterlow lost her husband, a gardener, forty years previously, when her youngest child was five. She took in washing and cleaned and cooked 'at the big house' as a domestic help to keep them. Her son was a bricklayer, having initially served a five years' apprenticeship, but he has not been at work for fourteen months. He had a stroke, was in hospital for months, and is paralysed on one side. He goes by ambulance to an occupational-therapy centre for two hours a week, and for physiotherapy three hours a week. He is usually confined to bed or a chair and needs help to get into a chair. Normally he gets up each morning with help at 11 a.m. He cannot walk about or even use his hands and arms effectively. He can, only with difficulty, wash himself down. (Score on disability index, 17, out of a possible 18.) Astonishingly, when asked how he would describe his health, he said it was fair for his age.

His mother looks after him indefatigably, and she gets considerable support from her daughter-in-law and two married sons, who live near by and help to dress and undress her son. Her daughter-in-law comes all day on Mondays, and other days at certain hours. A married son comes in each day at weekends. She gets help with the laundry, cleaning and shopping as well. The number of working hours of support was estimated after cross-questioning at just under thirty a week. A married son gave her £25 towards an Aga cooker, and she has a steady income in kind from her family. One son gets a chicken every other week. Another brings a dozen eggs, flowers and sweets. A brother 'gives us a bottle of brandy occasionally. It lasts us six weeks.' They receive family and friends at home and do not go out. He enjoys filling in a football-pool coupon each week.

They differ in their views about living standards, she believing that her standard is about the same as ever, though she feels better off than her neighbours and about as well off as her relatives, he believing that his standard is worse than ever, and feeling much worse off than family or neighbours. She defined poverty as 'being short of food and fire and having no family to fall back on. Widows with young children are the saddest thing.' She is very conscious of the distinction between living in town and country. When asked what could be done about poverty, she said, 'It depends on the work. Then again some will work and some won't. I've never lived in a town so I don't really know. If you've a bit of land to grow food and a roof over your head you never really can say you're poor.'

After receiving earnings-related benefit of £6·50 for six months after his stroke, Mr Waterlow was reduced to flat-rate sickness benefit of £4·50, which is now his sole income. He keeps 50p (usually spent on the football-pool coupon). He said he should have received a tax rebate for the previous financial year. 'I'm still waiting for it to come through.' He accepted the interviewer's offer to write a reminder to the local Inspector of Taxes. Mrs Waterlow has a £4·50 retirement pension. Neither of them have any other form of income, except the vegetables and fruit they grow in the garden. Mrs Waterlow spent some time calculating the value of this and counted off potatoes, carrots, tomatoes, turnips, cabbage, Brussels sprouts, beans, marrow, peas, onions, radishes, lettuce, rhubarb, raspberries and strawberries. She reckoned that, on average, she would have to pay 75p a week for the vegetables and fruit they consumed in the year. She has £55 in savings and he has £12. They have no other assets. She hopes she has been left a cottage by a distant relative who died the previous week and who had promised it to her. There is a possibility it may be shared with a brother. Her share might be worth as much as £500, she believed.

The interviewer asked whether she had thought of applying for supplementary benefit, especially to cover her rent. She was appalled at the idea, and even refused to be sent some leaflets so as to think it over at her leisure. When the interviewer suggested that supplementary benefit was hers by right, she said then, if that was so, 'they would give it to me. I've always managed to keep my head above water and I always will. I don't want anything I haven't earned. Anyway, we don't need it. We manage nicely with the stuff from the garden and my married sons, and their wives couldn't be better.' By our calculations they could have qualified at that time (January 1969) for an extra allowance of at least £3·50 per week from the Supplementary Benefits Commission.

4. In poverty: Young fatherless family

Mrs Peel is 19 and lives with her boy of 18 months and her daughter of 7 months in two rooms in a smoky, industrial area of Glasgow. Her husband is serving a six-month prison sentence and will be released soon. There is no WC indoors and no bath. Both sink and kitchen have to be shared, as also the small back yard with the husband's grandfather, who rents this small house. She feels the need for at least two extra rooms. The flat is in a deplorable structural condition, with damp walls. Mrs Peel acknowledges that the place is a danger to the children's health. Her husband is a window cleaner and his wife said his earnings fluctuated a lot because of the weather. He averaged about £12 a week before going to prison. Before the birth of her children, she had been a clerical worker for a bread company. Her father had been a corporation cleaner. When her husband leaves prison in the next week they will 'have to find a new home'. She appears to be reconciled to starting afresh somewhere else. His grandfather has allowed her to stay on there only until her husband leaves prison. He does not charge her any rent.

At present she receives 6p a week (from his earnings) from her husband and she has £5·15 supplementary benefit plus 75p family allowance (June 1968). When her baby was born last year she received a £22 maternity grant, but has not received any other form of income. She has no savings or other assets and the home is very bare except for a television set. She is not embarrassed to be receiving supplementary benefits; has visited the welfare clinic and obtained welfare foods and gets welfare milk for the children at the cheap rate.

Mrs Peel sees her mother, sisters and other relatives daily, shops for them and prepares meals and in return is able to leave the children with them when necessary. She has not had a summer holiday, but has had meals with her family, has given them meals, and has been to the cinema and a pub in the last fortnight. She smokes about ten cigarettes a day, and at Christmas spent £20 extra. She is a Jehovah's Witness, but has not attended meetings lately. She feels desperately poor and says she is much worse off than her relatives and people of her age locally. In the winter she had gone to bed early because she couldn't afford a fire. The main action needed to remedy poverty, she thought, was 'more work for the people'. On our calculations, her supplementary benefit allowance was at least 75p too low.

5. In poverty: Long-term unemployed man with wife and six children (two low-paid)

Mr and Mrs Mulligan, 35 and 34, live with their six sons and daughters, 18, 15, 13, 10, 8 and 6, in a terraced house owned by the council in an industrial area of

Salford. They bought the house for £400 (£50 deposit and £1 a week for seven years) in 1955, soon after they had come from Ireland. Late in 1968, the council acquired the house under a clearance scheme and said they would give them compensation and maintain it. During the previous four months (by November 1968), the family had heard nothing. The rent is 87p per week. The house was the worst the interviewer had ever seen in his life. It consists of four small rooms and a tiny kitchen. There is a WC in the yard outside, no bath and no cooker. There is a cold tap but no washbasin or sink. It has every structural problem imaginable. Even with a coal fire in the back room, it is cold. The roof leaks, there is loose brickwork and plaster and decaying floorboards. The doors fit badly, the plaster is cracked. When the back door is closed, the vibration causes other doors to open. The larder is of rough stone, which is black and cold. There are said to be rats, mice, bugs and cockroaches. The rat catcher came a few weeks ago when, after demolition started near by, the number of vermin increased, but said he could not put poison down, because of the dangers to the children. Upstairs, both bedrooms are cold and damp. The wallpaper is peeling. The ceiling is giving way and they have stuck paper over it to delay a fall. Beds have to be covered with plastic sheets to keep the damp off them. In one bedroom, husband and wife sleep with the two youngest daughters. In the other, two sons sleep in one double bed, and two older daughters in another. The carpets downstairs have to be kept rolled up because of the damp. Mr and Mrs Mulligan are fearful of the house literally blowing down in a gale. The whole environment is dismal. The house next door is empty and in an advanced state of dilapidation. Tramps sleep there. The air in the neighbourhood is so smoky, 'it looks as if a big fire is always burning'. The children have nowhere to play indoors and nowhere safe near by.

Mr Mulligan has been unemployed for thirty-six weeks. His last job was as a building labourer. He goes round building sites repeatedly, 'but there's nothing doing'. His earnings used to vary between £9 and £24, and last earnings were £14·50. His daughter Winifred, 18, is a machinist in a clothing firm and earned £7·60 net last week. His son, Peter, 15, left school only a few months previously and is an apprentice painter. He earned only £3·20 last week. It costs him 60p per week to travel to and from work. Mr Mulligan gets £7·15 unemployment benefit. He had worked on sub-contractors' sites, 'where they don't bother much about national insurance cards, therefore I have lost benefit through not having enough stamps'. He also receives £3·20 supplementary benefit for himself, his wife and the four children not at work. He says he is not embarrassed to receive help in this way, and that the original application was his idea. His wife draws £2·90 family allowances (November 1968). His total income is over £1 below the basic supplementary benefit level – presumably because, as a labourer, he is wage-stopped. However, if household income is treated as all pooled, then for the older children at work as well as the dependent family, the standard of living is above the basic supplementary benefit rate. In fact, as in most working-class families, it is not pooled. Winifred gives £2·50 and Peter £2 to Mrs Mulligan for board (Mr Mulligan hands over £10 to his wife of the £10·35 he gets). Two weeks ago they received a 'shoe grant' of £15 from the Education Department to buy shoes for the four younger children. All four at school get free school meals. Last year they had a uniform grant for about £35 from the education committee – covering skirt and jacket, three shirts, socks, trousers, duffle coat, pullover. They were paying off a hire-purchase debt at the rate of £2 a week.

Mrs Mulligan has nervous trouble and gets very depressed. She says she is seeing her doctor for treatment. Peter has a mucous discharge from his ears and has a hacking cough. All the children had spent periods in bed recently with flu or colds, and had been seen by their doctor. They say they have no relatives living locally and neither receive nor give help, although they could count on a neighbour for emergency help if it was necessary. This may have been due to what happened in their families when they left Ireland thirteen years earlier. They had clearly lived in desperate straits in one of the worst city slum areas while they were building their family. They go regularly to church and are visited by a priest, but have no evenings out (because they cannot afford to), do not have meals out with friends or relatives, frequently go to bed early to save coal, have never given birthday parties for the children, and had no summer holiday. None of the children receive pocket money. They say they belong to the 'poor', are worse off than ever in their lives, and worse off than people living around them. They feel poor, 'all the time and everywhere'.

6. In poverty: Single woman supporting severely incapacitated mother

Miss Harris, 47, lives with her widowed mother, 87, in a two-roomed council flat with good facilities on the first floor of a block in West London. The lift is not working at present. They have radio and television, and armchairs and carpet, but no telephone, or vacuum cleaner. Miss Harris gave up her work four years earlier as a clerk in a newspaper office to stay at home to care for her mother. The mother is mentally confused, and cannot join in ordinary conversation. While she can do some personal tasks, like washing, and can climb and descend stairs, she cannot coordinate brain and fingers or hands and is unable to cook a meal, do the housework or go shopping. (Total score on disability index, 11 out of possible 18.) She is thus severely incapacitated. Her condition varies quite a lot and sometimes she becomes very agitated. She cannot be left alone in the flat. The doctor visited three times, and a social worker twice, in the previous twelve months.

Miss Harris says that relatives come every week (there are no other sons or daughters), but she does not get any help. She leads a life which is tied to the home, not having had an evening out in the last fortnight, no meals out, no summer holiday, no visit to her church and no trips to stay with relatives. She reads the newspapers and fills in football-pool coupons and watches television. She feels worse off than ever she has been in her life, and worse off than her relatives and neighbours. She described poverty thus: 'Low-paid people with lots of children are the poor people.' She thought poverty was mainly the fault of poor education. 'If people can't afford to have children, they shouldn't. Workers should look for better-paid jobs.' She has depended on supplementary benefit for the last four years (initially advised by the Employment Exchange) and now receives £4·50 (March 1968). She has an arrangement with the Supplementary Benefits Commission whereby all but 25p of her rent of £2·80 is paid direct by the commission. Her mother gets a non-contributory old-age pension and a supplementary benefit amounting to £4·50. Miss Harris said she had saved £600 up to the point when she had to stop working, and has been obliged to spend '£300 for odd bits and pieces'. (Later she said about £75 had been drawn in the previous twelve months.) She sees no way of increasing her income, although she would love to go back to work. She does not feel she can leave her mother at all, and there seems to be no one who can or does come and 'sit in', even for the occasional afternoon. The £300 left in her savings (Post Office), plus a single £1 Premium Bond, represent her and her mother's entire assets. She gave a detailed account of her weekly budget on her income of £9. She found it difficult to isolate her expenditure on the final £2 or so because it was more irregular.

Insurance stamp	65p
Papers	20p
Insurance policies	37½p
Rent	25p
Television	25p
Electricity	£1·25p
Gas	25p
Milk	60p
Hardware	50p
Food	£2·00p
Travel, clothing, washing and miscellaneous	£2·67½p
Total	£9·00

According to our calculations, her supplementary benefit allowance was too low by about 50p, even if an allowance is not added for her 'exceptional circumstances'.

7. On the margins of poverty: Low-paid man with young family

Mr and Mrs Quick, 39 and 37, live in a privately rented four-roomed terraced house in a Lincolnshire village with their two children, aged 5 and 1. His first wife had died. The W C is outdoors. The house is reasonably well furnished with carpets and armchairs, for example, but no washing machine or refrigerator. Mr Quick is a packer in a cotton mill, and worked fifty weeks last year, with two weeks' paid holiday. His normal working week is of forty-two hours. He is not entitled to sick pay or an occupational pension, and can be sacked at a week's notice. Mrs Quick gave up her work warping in the same mill just before the second child was born.

His pay varies between £12·50 and £13·50 per week, and last week his gross wage was £13·98 and take-home wage £12·90. There is a family allowance (March 1968) of 40p per week, but no other form of income, except that indirectly they appear to be subsidized by his employer, who owns the house and charges a rent of 90p per week. Mr Quick believed that the rent would normally be another £1 per week in that area. The family would have to leave the house if his job ended. They have a total of £21 in savings banks and two life-insurance policies, but otherwise no assets. This year Mr Quick had obtained a surrender value on one policy of £35. The family income is about £2 a week above the state poverty line.

They lead a very spare existence, and have not had an evening out in the last fortnight or gone on a summer holiday because they couldn't afford to. But they had given a party on the eldest child's birthday, and had paid into a Christmas club, spending about £35 extra. They are keen churchgoers, and there is a family service to which 'you can take babies'. Mrs Quick paid about 50p into a clothing club and found she missed payments occasionally. She gets three pints of milk each day. Mr Quick smokes about fifteen cigarettes a day. They believe they are worse off than the average worker and worse off than their relatives. They felt poor sometimes, 'at holiday times. We can't go away even for day trips.' Poverty was 'not having enough to eat and not enough clothes'. But if people were in poverty, it was mainly their own fault, thought Mr Quick. 'It's up to people to pull their weight', to get out of it.

8. In poverty: Complex household including three disabled adults, a handicapped child, fatherless family, low-paid and long-term unemployed

This is perhaps the most complex household in the survey. Mr and Mrs James, 54 and 52, live in a five-roomed council house in Glasgow, with one married daughter and her husband (18 and 23), three unmarried children (aged 29, 23 and 15 respectively) and five grandchildren (all the children of the unmarried daughter of 29 aged from 8 to 2). The estate is a mixture of pre-war low-standard council housing, new high flats and blocks of four or six storeys. It is a district of tallymen, overflowing dustbins, neglected gardens and an occasional broken or boarded-up window. The house is grossly overcrowded, and by contemporary standards they should have an additional four or five bedrooms. There are, in fact, four bedrooms, one living room and a tiny kitchen. The floors are of stone and walls are very damp. In the living room the wallpaper is peeling off the walls and ceiling. There are two battered rexine chairs, one small broken settee, three wooden chairs, a camp bed (on which Mrs James sleeps), a table covered by oilcloth, a television set placed on a small dresser, torn linoleum on the floor, an unkempt rug in front of the fireplace, and tattered curtains. There is a budgerigar in a colourful cage. The bedroom occupied by the married daughter Joan and her husband is 9 feet by 7 feet 6 inches and contains a three-quarter sized bed, a cot, pram and chest of drawers. The rent is £2·55 per week. They are in arrears (over £10), and have been threatened with eviction. A final warning has been served. They had been evicted previously from council property five years earlier and had moved into two rooms of a house owned by Mrs James's cousin. Mr James had to go to a model lodging house. At that time one son had to go into the army, where he has remained, and another went to a children's home until last year, when he reached the school-leaving age, and rejoined the family. Finally, they were allowed to move into this house two years earlier.

Mr James is about 5 feet 3 inches and very thin and very diffident. He is on the disablement register and cannot do heavy manual work. He lost the index finger on one hand working on the trawlers. He has anaemia, frequent migraines, severe bladder trouble, and nervous trouble. (Disability score, 6.) He admits to extreme depression and suicidal tendencies, and is being treated by his doctor, whom he has seen sixteen times in the last twelve months. He was in hospital for a week in the winter, and has also spent a fortnight in bed with flu. He is now unemployed and has had thirty-four weeks' unemployment in the last fifty-two. He worked the previous Monday, but was asked to lift heavy tyres. Because he is disabled and cannot do this, he was sacked. Before that job, he had been a floor sweeper in a government rehabilitation centre and earlier a hospital porter. His earnings varied between £8 and £9·50. Several times he had worked as a night-watchman. He had taken one such job that year with a building firm, but after one week the firm brought in 'security men with dogs' and he lost the work. He says he has no confidence in himself now, and feels everyone is against him. If he goes up for a job with three other men, he automatically shrinks back. He feels humilated by events, and does not consider that he can talk things over easily, for example, with his doctor. 'I've no courage. I should push myself forward more.'

Mrs James is a grey-faced woman and, like her daughters, bears all the marks of poverty, malnutrition and overcrowding. She weighs 6 stones 8 pounds. She had tuberculosis eight years earlier, and was in hospital. Her chest is said now to be clear, but she gets colds and flu easily and is breathless after any exertion. (Disability score 7.) In the previous twelve months she has had a total of thirty days' illness in bed. She is also hard of hearing and has suffered extremely from 'nerves' since hospitalization. She has sleeping tablets to help her sleep. Her spectacles are broken and repaired with Sellotape. Neither she nor any other member of the household has visited the optician. She finds she is desperately short of money. A fortnight earlier, the electricity meter in the coal cellar was burgled and about £30 taken. She has not yet received the electricity account for the last quarter, and says she just lives from day to day. Last week the coalman would not deliver any coal because she could not pay for it. During the winter they had commonly gone to bed early because they could not burn a fire. 'We only have one real meal a day.' The household has three pints of milk a day, including free milk. They do not have a cooked breakfast, and Mrs James says the midday meal is poorer in the week than at the weekend. On a Friday or a Saturday she will buy four pounds of stewing steak or mince for the family. She is paying off debts for linoleum, refrigerator and washing machine at the rate of £3·60 per week, and for clothing and bedding about £4 a week, spending about half this latter on a Prudential club and the rest to four separate agents or tallymen. She said she took out a 'Pru. cheque at Christmas for £15 or I would have had nothing for anyone'. Some of Mr James's clothes are in the pawnshop.

Mr Fraser, the son-in-law, is gaunt and emaciated, and has no appetite. He is also on the Disablement Register and has had a peptic ulcer for seven years. (Disability score 3.) He was sick for the first forty-four weeks of the last fifty-two and has been unemployed for the last eight weeks. He had been in hospital twice for a few days on each occasion. His last job was as a railway porter. He is seriously looking for work, and this week replied in writing to one advertisement and had been to an interview for another job. His wife Joan is about to have their first child, but is ineligible for the full maternity grant because they both have an incomplete contributions record. She has not worked in the last twelve months, and her last job was as a machinist in a clothing factory (making police uniforms).

Ann, 29, has not worked for about nine years and devotes her time to her five children. She is very passive but maternal, never goes out and gives her entire social security and family allowances to her mother. All her children have separate fathers. She wants to have nothing to do with them, receives no money from them and says it is because she wants to keep the children. Two go to a primary school a hundred yards away, and one who is aged 6 is highly strung and cries a lot. Ann feels he needs to see the doctor. Her 4-year-old is also a difficult and nervous child and sleeps badly. The health visitor has been about four times to visit the family in the last twelve months.

Mary was in the army, as a postal operator, for thirty-one weeks in the previous year, and since leaving had cared for a sick aunt in London for nineteen weeks, for which she received free board and lodging. Since returning home two weeks ago, she has been unemployed, but has been for an interview. Although pale, she is better dressed and more articulate than the other women in the house.

Richard has had four jobs since leaving school ten months ago, and has already been unemployed for twenty-four weeks. He was a slater, messenger boy, car-washer and apprentice blacksmith. Apparently he walked out of three of these jobs. His highest pay was £6·50 and lowest £3·80. He is said to have been very clever at school, has been 'in trouble' and is now supervised by a probation officer, who has been to visit him at home four times lately.

Their income is meagre, and depending on who is at home or in work, fluctuates from week to week. None of the family has any assets. Indeed, they are in debt over hire-purchase and rent arrears. Last week, Mr and Mrs James had £7·30 unemployment benefit and 25p supplementary benefit together with £2, which is an allowance paid by the son in the army. If the 15-year-old son Richard is treated as a dependant of this 'income unit', then their income (totalling £9·55) was about 10p less than a supplementary benefit entitlement (even assuming they paid no more than their 'numerical' share of the rent or had no need for an 'exceptional circumstances' addition). It is, of course, important to note that although the school-leaving age was 15 in the late 1960s, a person could not qualify for supplementary benefit in his own right until he was 16. The young married pair in the household had unemployment benefit of £7·30 last week, but were not receiving supplementary benefit (they seem to be eligible for about 30p). Ann receives £3·30 family allowances and £8 supplementary benefit, which again appears to be lower (by about 70p) than her strict entitlement. Moreover, no claim has been made at all for Mary since her return to the household a fortnight previously. Accordingly, the household is living at present at least £5 per week below the state poverty line, even assuming no extra allowances would be payable for disability and to cover part of the hire-purchase of necessary items of clothing and household equipment. They had received one exceptional-needs grant for £9 in the year.

There is a lot of family support and interchange, though little contact with neighbours. Mrs James's father visits them frequently (her mother is dead), as does Mr James's brother. Mrs James visits the cousin who gave them two rooms when they were evicted earlier. 'I live for Saturdays when I go shopping and have a pint with my cousin.' At present she sees a great deal of her daughter Mary's fiancé and his mother, who are in and out every day. Mary has meals with them on some days. She is the only one in the household who had a summer holiday (for one week). In the last fortnight, Mr James has been twice to a pub and the married couple and the 15-year-old have been to a cinema. But Mrs James and her 29-year-old daughter Ann have not been out any evening. None of the household attend church. None of them smoke, except Mrs James, who has ten cigarettes a day. Mr James occasionally has a small bet on the horses. None of the grandchildren has ever had a birthday party or had a friend in to play. The three older children (aged 4 to 8) do not get any pocket money.

They feel much worse off than ever in life and than their relatives and friends. Mr James thinks that poverty is 'when you've no money and can't afford to buy nothing. It feels rotten I can tell you. I'd like to do more for the wife. I get so fed up that, especially with this house worry, I feel like walking down to the pier and jumping off.' He hates being dependent on supplementary benefit, and when asked at a later point in the interview whether he feels poor now, said, 'All the time, especially when I have to go to Seaport House [the local Supplementary Benefits

Commission office].' He was adamant about poverty being the government's responsibility. 'I wouldn't vote for Wilson again, I'll tell you that.' He thought that the government should 'do something for the working class, more work for Scotland, for your own good'.

*

The interviewer subsequently acted with the permission of the family in contacting the local manager of the Ministry of Social Security, social workers and the manager of the Employment Exchange. She accompanied Mr James to court, and the proposed eviction was abandoned, provided arrears could be paid off at the rate of £1 a week through a social worker. Social security payments were substantially increased (by over £6) as a result of a review undertaken by the local manager of the Ministry of Social Security. In fairness, it seems that Mr James had signed a form only one week earlier to the effect that his daughters Mary and Joan were no longer living at home. But that too is understandable, since like many councils, the council does not permit overcrowding and such information could easily be regarded as undermining a tenant's security. During the following months, the interviewer kept in touch with the family and helped, by insistent pressure, to maintain the involvement of local social workers. What struck her throughout was 'the lack of real communication between this family and authority'. They seemed to be totally different in their reactions to her from the way they were in the relationships with officials and social workers.

9. In poverty: Single woman supporting elderly father (immigrants)

Miss McHale, aged 24, lives in a privately rented flat in Coventry with her father of 62, who was widowed two years previously. The flat consists of three very small rooms; there is no W C indoors and both bath and sink have to be shared. He had come from Eire only the previous year, but she had been in England for several years. She worked forty-five hours last week as a bus conductress, for a wage of £12·50 net, or £18·70 gross (income tax £5·25, national insurance contribution 78p and sick fund and club contributions 17p). Her pay fluctuates a lot, depending on the total number of hours and whether she works Sundays, for which she is paid double-time. The previous week she had worked sixty hours. Her take-home pay fluctuated during the previous twelve months between £11 and £16·50. She was sick for four weeks in the year, and then received £8·50 per week from her employers, i.e. sickness benefit deducted.

Mr McHale had scratched a living from the soil for many years as a farmer, running a 'farm' of only five acres. He had left school at the age of 12. He spoke feelingly of poverty. In his fifties, before losing his wife, he had had a job in a quarry breaking stones to line roads, and he thought it was the best job of his life. 'It was the security. It meant a wage coming in each week.' He had left the farm to his son and he had had no income whatsoever since entering the country the previous August.

Miss McHale pays a rent of £5 per week for the (partly) furnished flat. When this is deducted from her pay, they have to struggle to balance their budget. The landlord empties the meters. 'We seem to be always putting money in.' Legally, Mr McHale is still the owner of the farm cottage and five acres of land in Eire, but his son is living there and expects to inherit the property. Otherwise, neither he nor his daughter have any assets. They have no relatives living locally, but can count on help in emergencies from a neighbour. Mr McHale sometimes looks after a neighbour's children, but he does not go out in the evenings. Both attend church regularly. Miss McHale goes out fairly often with her boyfriend. They seem to manage their resources carefully, and although they do not have fresh meat frequently or eat a cooked breakfast, they seem to have sufficient food and clothing. Miss McHale said that cigarettes seemed to be all that her father needed, so far as money was concerned. He smokes twenty and she ten each day. Their income was usually below the state poverty line, and Miss McHale could claim tax allowance for her dependent father and, if the Supplementary Benefits Commission accepted that he had no income from the farm in Eire, he could qualify for a supplementary benefit allowance of at least £3·55. They were advised to take up these matters and, also because of the high rent, seek advice about an appeal against the rent or apply for council accommodation.

10. On the margins of poverty: Motherless family (disabled adult)

Mr Stewart, a man aged 52, lives with his four young children, aged 8, 6, 5, and 3, in a five-roomed council house in Nottingham. His wife died eighteen months previously and he gave up his work as a cabinet-maker two years before her death in order to care for her and the children. This meant a drop in income from around £25 to £27 (in 1966) to £11. Rather than allow them to be admitted to a children's home, he has stayed at home to look after them on his own.

He gets £11·50 from the Supplementary Benefits Commission, and £1·65 family allowances (April 1968), totalling £13·15. His rent is £2·95 a week. He is very embarrassed to receive supplementary benefit and commented on his treatment by some of the officials. Only one exceptional-needs grant had been made to the family – for £4·75 for shoes. He tries to avoid money-lenders. In a weak moment some time ago, he borrowed £20 to buy the children some clothes, and found that he had to pay £27·50 back during the next few months. He has no savings or assets.

Mr Stewart describes his health only as fair, and is having treatment from his doctor for a slipped disc and 'nerves'. (Score on the disability index, 5.) He has bad sight, sleeps badly and finds it difficult to concentrate. He is angry with his doctor, because 'she told me to remarry'. During the year he has been visited a few times by both a health visitor and a social worker. Three of his children go to a primary school, and they receive free school meals. 'A priest visited us and promised some clothes from the Catholic Needlework Guild. But nothing came.' He is spending £3 a week through a clothing club at present. But he felt that none of the children had adequate footwear for bad weather. A niece lives near by and sees the family every day. She often lends him money, but he stresses his independence and ability to stand unaided.

The family did not have a summer holiday and he could spend nothing on presents at Christmas. The family do not have a cooked breakfast and do not have fresh meat most days of the week. He gets two pints of milk a day, one of which is free. He said there were days in the last two weeks when neither he nor the children had had a cooked meal. Days, too, when they had gone to bed early through lack of coal. He gives each of the children 4p per week pocket money and cannot give up twenty cigarettes a day himself. The supplementary benefits allowance has no margin at all for any exceptional circumstances, and an allowance might have been made for his disability or need for home help.

11. On the margins of poverty: Disabled retirement pensioner, living alone

Mrs Tillson, 72, has lived in a one-roomed council flat on the ground floor of a block of flats in Leicester for the last two years. The flat does not have a yard or garden, but has good facilities (though it is not centrally heated). Until she was in her mid sixties, she worked as a cleaner in a launderette. Her husband, a lorry driver, died fourteen years ago. She is hard of hearing (but has no aid), and has severe arthritis and therefore difficulty in moving about. She can only mount stairs with great difficulty, and cannot carry a heavy shopping basket, for example. Most other personal and household tasks she can undertake only with difficulty. (Disability score 11, out of 18 – therefore 'severely' incapacitated.)

Her two daughters live near by and help her with shopping. They bring her food, which helps her budget, though she estimates the value at only about 25p a week. She has had meals with them in the past month, and has also had one or other to a meal in her flat. She has attended an old people's club and goes regularly to church (Church of England). She said she had been out four evenings in the previous two weeks. On most days of the week she affords meat, and has half a pint of milk each day. She smokes ten cigarettes a week.

Mrs Tillson finds it difficult to manage on her income and feels worse off than her relatives and worse off than previously in life. During the winter she had gone to bed early because she could not afford to burn electricity. 'I just manage to pay for the food, the TV rental and the coins for the electric fire. I've no money left for anything new for the home.' Poverty, for her, is 'having to count every penny all the time'. Action to remedy poverty 'should allow people to help themselves. I decided to move to a bed-sitter because I'd be taxed if I let two rooms.' She receives a widow's pension of £4·50 and supplementary benefit of £2·65. (She did not get the latter, which was her idea to apply for, until twelve months earlier, and still feels very embarrassed about it.) She has no savings or other assets. Her rent is £2·02½. Her supplementary allowance includes long-term addition, but no provision for an exceptional circumstances addition, for which, as a disabled pensioner living alone, she might be considered to qualify.

12. In poverty: Long-term unemployed man and wife and four children (gipsy family)

Mr and Mrs Smith, 28 and 23, are living with their four children, 6, 4, 3 and 1, in a prefabricated council bungalow of four rooms in Hampshire. They have reasonable indoor amenities and a substantial garden, but the bungalow is near a foul-smelling bog. They have a television set and arm-chairs, but no refrigerator or washing machine. He is a labourer who turns his hand to gardening, tree-felling and farm work of most kinds. He worked a short week of about thirty hours last week, but has been employed for only about twenty-six weeks in the last fifty-two. He gets different jobs in the locality, mostly piecework. The gipsy families seem to prefer working in groups of three or four. They are given a set price, say £25, for digging a field of potatoes, or clearing trees, and then divide the money between them.

Mr Smith had also worked for three weeks recently as a labourer laying cables for the Electricity Board. He said he gave it up because he didn't get paid overtime rates for working Saturdays and Sundays, and because he was only paid £12 per week for working from 7 a.m. to 5 p.m. His wife joins the working groups at certain times of the year, and sometimes the women work on their own, picking peas or potatoes. Neither he nor his wife can read or write, and they had had less than four years' schooling. They had been moving about in a van throughout the year. Mr Smith had a flexible attitude to work and to periods of hardship. 'Sometimes I get a job, sometimes I don't. If I'm hard up I borrow from one of my brothers or cousins.' The families help each other out in this way.

There is a small settlement of gipsies in a group of sixteen prefabricated bungalows – mostly large families, and most of them related. Their mother, three married sisters and many cousins live there and see them daily. They all mind each other's children at any time of day or night. Mrs Smith's sister fetches the eldest boy of six from primary school every day, for example. He also attends a Church of England Sunday school. The settlement started as a county project about four years earlier to get the gipsies off the road. There is a resident warden in one prefab whose job is to help them settle down. He sorts out legal, tax and insurance problems, and helps them read their letters. He finds employment, tries to settle disputes and collects rent. He seemed inclined to take responsibility for matters which elsewhere would be treated as interference in private life. Mr Smith said he had hated being in a house after being in the open. It was 'like wearing a hat when you are not used to it'. He believed they were never ill when they lived in the open, but since living there they were always getting colds and the two youngest children had chest trouble. Certainly this checked with information he gave about the children spending periods in bed, including fourteen days each as hospital in-patients that year. He had sinus trouble from an old 'punch-up', and his doctor had advised an operation. He also said his doctor had diagnosed stomach ulcers because he found it so difficult to swallow food, particularly in the mornings. He said that he had gone to the surgery about eight times in twelve months and the doctor had called on him five times. They had also had fairly frequent contacts with a clinic and social workers. The doctor holds a clinic in the settlement once a week. A welfare officer has visited them about five times in the last year.

The warden of the settlement happened to catch the interviewer and com-mented on the family. According to his account, the wife's sister had formerly occupied the prefab and had kept it in good condition, but this family had 'turned it into a slum. It was filthy and in a bad state of repair.' But it is difficult to determine responsibility. Three weeks earlier all their windows had been broken. The house was broken into, a family allowance book stolen and the elec-tricity meter robbed. As a result, their supplementary benefit appeared to be held, pending some attempt to establish the cause.

Up to that point they had been receiving, when Mr Smith was unemployed, £8·60 per week (£4·60 of which was in the form of food vouchers), plus £2·90 family allowance (December 1968). Their rent is £1·50 per week. They cannot grow food, although they had tried two years earlier. The ground is heathland and very stony. But by collecting wood they save a lot in fuel.

The family tend to live hand to mouth. They do not have fresh meat most days, and buy only a pint of milk a day (though they also use powdered milk). Although the social life of the settlement is fairly self-contained, they also have out-side contacts and influences. Mr and Mrs Smith have not had a summer holiday. They do not give their children a birthday party. They do not go to the cinema. But they sometimes go to bingo. They spent about £20 extra at Christmas. They pay 50p into a clothing club, and always have a Sunday joint. Interestingly, they showed absolutely no class-consciousness, and although the interviewer persisted for two or three minutes, could not understand what was meant when they were asked to say what social class they belonged to. They be-lieved their living standards were about the same as ever, and the same as their relatives and friends around them. Their income is hard to calculate. Mr Smith estimated that he earned between £10 and £12 per week when he was able to work. This seems to be an overestimate, but even if correct, means that by government standards the family live in poverty. During periods of unemployment the family appear to be wage-stopped over £3. That is, their supplementary allowance after adding family allowances is about £3 below the basic scale rates plus rent.

13. In poverty: Low-paid man and wife and three children (also long-term unemployed)

Mr and Mrs O'Reilly, 32 and 33, live in a privately rented flat of two rooms and tiny kitchen in a Fermanagh village, with a daughter of 10, a son of 7 and a daughter of 2. They are badly overcrowded and have no bath and no WC indoors. There is a tiny yard which is too small to sit outside. The house has damp walls and they have little furniture, and no washing machine or refrigerator, although there is a living-room carpet and a TV set. There is not enough space for the children to play indoors. Mr O'Reilly works a forty-four hour week on a nightshift as a labourer in a foundry. He had been unemployed for twenty-four of the last fifty-two weeks. Three years earlier, he had been a porter on a liner, and on losing that job, in which he earned £25 a week, his wage was more than halved. His wife had been a packer in a tobacco factory until three years earlier. Just when their children were growing up rapidly, and needing more food and clothes, they had experienced a serious fall in income.

Last week Mr O'Reilly earned £12·55 gross and just £10 net. It costs him about 35p to travel to and from work each week. They have family allowances (June 1968) of £1·60 in addition, but no other source of income. They pay a rent of 40p per week and have a total income about 50p below the state poverty line. During his unemployment, Mr O'Reilly had been wage-stopped. They have no savings but have a second-hand car believed to be worth £250. The two children of school age come home for dinners, because 'we can't afford school meals'. They were not aware of their eligibility for free meals.

They live near a married sister of Mrs O'Reilly and see that family every day. They can depend on each other in emergencies, but do not have meals in each other's homes. They have not had an evening out in the last fortnight, because they haven't enough money, are Nonconformists but do not attend church, do not have birthday parties for the children and have not been on a summer holiday. Mrs O'Reilly gets four pints of milk each day, and fresh meat most days of the week. She often buys second-hand clothes and also spends £1 a week on a clothing club. She admits that sometimes she misses payments. At Christmas the family spent an additional £25. She smokes about five and her husband about ten cigarettes a day.

They find it hard to manage on their income and say they are worse off than their relatives and neighbours, than the national average and than at any previous time in their lives. Mr O'Reilly gives his wife £9 of his £10 take-home pay for the housekeeping. He thinks that poverty is 'when you are so short of money you are not able to manage on your wages'. He believes that industry is responsible for not providing the right jobs, and that the way to alleviate poverty is to provide 'better jobs for the people'.

14. In poverty: Large fatherless family, including handicapped child

Mrs Merton, a divorced woman of 32, lives with her seven children, aged from 13 to 2, in a six-roomed council flat in a block in Leeds. The flat has good facilities, but the bedrooms are small and the skirtings are rising away from the floor. The underfloor heating system is believed by the council to have encouraged dry rot. The family had been moved into the flat two years earlier after being grossly over-crowded in a privately rented flat in a slum-clearance area. Mrs Merton says none of the children have a safe place to play near by, and the air in that area is always very dirty and smoky.

It is now six years since her husband, an office cleaner, left her, and after five years of proceedings she recently obtained a divorce. Her youngest child, aged 2, was conceived by another man. He has a court order to pay £2·50 per week, and this has been paid for the last three months. But during the last two weeks she re-ceived this sum from the Supplementary Benefits Commission because the father was out of work. She had to sign a form saying that if the father pays this money she will return it to the commission. Apparently the commission had prompted the application for legal aid to obtain the maintenance order.

She depends on an income of £12·75 supplementary benefit and £3·90 family allowances (April 1968). Two weeks ago, she had received one exceptional-needs grant of £9·90. She said she had been applying for a clothing grant for the last two years and had been refused on two occasions. Mrs Merton said she would prefer to go out and earn the money herself than receive it from the commission. It embarrassed her greatly to have the money. But with all her children that was impossible. Her rent is £3·40, and she spent about £20 on paint and repairs last year. She has placed sums of up to £5 in a trustee savings bank for each of the children, but apart from these sums the family has no assets whatsoever. She borrowed £58 for furniture three years previously, paid £4·50 deposit and is pay-ing 50p weekly. She has twenty weekly repayments still to make and will have re-paid £84 altogether. Her 7-year-old daughter has a bad chest complaint, which makes her breathless and prevents her playing games like other children. Her mother has to treat her as a delicate child and has to watch her constantly. Four of the children at school get free school meals, but the eldest two don't like them and come home for meals. Last year, a clothing grant from the education depart-ment allowed her to get one boy a pair of trousers and a school blazer and another boy just a pair of trousers. The school uniform was a headache, and although the blazer was quickly knocked about and outgrown, it had to last two years. She had been able to afford £1 for one boy's school outing this year. Another 'would have to wait until next year. He had his turn last year.'

She does not have any relatives living locally, but looks after, and gives meals to, a friend's children sometimes in the week. In return, her friend looks after her children when she goes to a cinema. She attends church weekly, and the children go to Sunday school (Church of England). None of the family had a summer holiday. She supplements five pints of milk a day with both tinned and powdered milk. They always have a Sunday joint of meat, and, except for herself and her eldest son of 13, all the children have a cooked breakfast. She felt that this son did not have a pair of shoes that were good enough for wet weather, but the rest did. The two eldest sons get 25p pocket money each, and younger children 5p or 7p. At Christmas, she had spent about £40 extra. But she could not afford to give any of the children a birthday party.

She felt her standard of living was about the same as ever, though she was worse off than others around her of her age. Her pride is strongly expressed. She defined poverty as 'people who won't work to help themselves. You see some people going around dirty and run down and there's no need for it.' Her flat was exceptionally clean and orderly for one which contained such a large number of children, and she gave the interviewer the impression of being extremely fond of the children and relaxed with them, and did not appear to have a 'chip on her shoulder'. As for action to relieve poverty: 'I think the prices of council houses should be lowered. And the shops shouldn't be allowed to put up their own prices on food and clothing like the little local shops around here.'

According to our calculations, her income was 30p a week below the basic scale rate that should have been allowed, or 75p if, as it seemed, she was eligible for the long-term addition. This may have been because of a failure to adjust entitlements as the children reached an age justifying a higher allowance. It would also seem that, because of the handicapped child, she might have justified an 'exceptional circumstances addition', or at least rather more generous, or frequent, exceptional-needs grants.

15. In poverty: Elderly disabled couple

Mr and Mrs Ellman, 81 and 70, have lived in a four-roomed cottage which they own in a village in Worcestershire, for forty-five years. It is very old and does not have mains sanitation. They have an outside W C with a cesspit which is emptied regularly. There is no bath, but they have regular 'wash-downs'. They have a big range in the kitchen, and because Mr Ellman gets concessionary coal, he has never sought to have an electric or gas stove. They do not have a television set, refrigerator or washing machine, but do have a radio.

Mr Ellman had been a mining power-house attendant and had retired, at the age of 64, seventeen years previously. His wife had never worked. Both consider their health good for their age. Neither was ill in bed in the last twelve months. He suffers from diabetes, pain in his back and is blind in one eye. His hearing is poor and he does not have an aid. He has difficulty in moving freely and using his hands, but can, even if with difficulty, do most activities of a light nature. (Disability score, 8.) His wife has bad rheumatism in her joints and has difficulty in doing the housework. (Disability score, 4.) She goes to the doctor's surgery regularly every month for a prescription for her husband.

She said they were 'completely independent', had no relatives to help or to see. But later it emerged that nieces and nephews came with their parents for an evening or a midday meal at least once a month. They give the children money and sweets. Moreover, they went to stay with their only married son for a fortnight in the year, and he has visited them with his wife for a period of ten days.

They have not had a summer holiday and do not go out in the evening. 'We're too old and in any case there is nowhere to go.' They are Methodists and go occasionally to church in the year, but not weekly. They have cereal and toast for breakfast and one and a half pints of milk a day. Mr Ellman smokes two ounces of tobacco a week. They find it hard to manage on their income. Their retirement pensions amount to £7·30 and a colliery pension another £1·10. This is a non-contributory pension related to length of service. The cottage is worth £1,500, according to Mr Ellman. This is the sum for which it is insured and, compared with neighbouring cottages, it is probably worth rather more. They say their housing costs last year, including rates and insurance, were only £10. This excludes a rate rebate of £1·65p. In the garden they grow fruit and vegetables and reckon they save at least 40p a week throughout the year. They depend on concessionary coal at 50p a hundredweight, and use about three hundredweight a week. Their joint savings amount to £215 (in Post Office Savings, Defence Bonds and Premium Bonds), and in answer to a range of other questions about assets, believed that two or three good pieces of furniture would be worth a total of £75. However, they feel worse off than previously in their lives, because they have been 'gradually eroding' their savings. 'Our income does not cover the cost of living and we have to delve into our savings.' Mrs Ellman thought they were worse off than the rest of her family, but not than their neighbours. She draws the pensions and pays all the bills. He receives about 50p for tobacco. She will occasionally buy him clothes, but not often. 'He is a bit old for Carnaby Street.' They do not feel poor and believe that poverty described 'the conditions that existed before the Welfare State came'. They believed that poverty was people's own fault, and that the right action to remedy it was to 'educate people so that they are aware of the allowances they are entitled to and also teach them how to manage their affairs'. None the less, they have an income below the state poverty line, and are too independent to apply for supplementary benefit.

16. In poverty: Low-paid man and wife and five children (formerly long-term unemployed)

Mr and Mrs Fisher, aged 38 and 28, live with their five children, ranging in age from 8 to 2, in two privately rented rooms in a smoky industrial area of Aberdeen. The kitchen is used as dining room and bedroom and the family is grossly overcrowded, having lived there for eight years. They have been on a council list throughout this period, and have not yet been offered a flat or house. Only one room can be heated in winter. They share the W C in the house and have no bath. The walls are very damp; the roof leaks in heavy rain and windows and doors are ill-fitting. There is no garden for the children and no safe place for the young children to play.

Mr Fisher is a bread-van salesman and longs for security of employment. He was sick for five weeks nearly twelve months earlier and was then unemployed for sixteen weeks. 'I was off sick in March and April and then my firm sent me my books.' When eventually he found his present job, it was for only £16, compared with the £25 he had earned before as a machine setter in a light engineering firm. He had in fact served a five years' apprenticeship. In the previous week he had worked sixty-eight hours. His take-home pay was £13 (deductions £2·75), but he could expect a bonus every four weeks of about £12. Family allowances amount to £3·30 (May 1968).

When unemployed, Mr Fisher had received unemployment benefit amounting to £11·55 a week, but though eligible for supplementary benefit, had not claimed any during that period. However, they got behind with the rent (90p per week) and 'were being put out', so he had obtained a single grant of £6 to tide them over. They were also paying off a big hire-purchase debt on some furniture. The two children, who go to a local primary school, have free milk there but come home for meals, 'because it is cheaper'. In fact, they qualify for free school meals, though this was not pointed out to them either during Mr Fisher's spell of unemployment or afterwards by the health visitor or social worker who has visited the home four times in the last twelve months.

The chief support for the family comes from the wife's mother, sister and brother, and the husband's brother, all of whom live locally. The mother helps look after the children when Mrs Fisher wants to go shopping. In fact, they give more help to others in the family than they receive. Mrs Fisher's sister-in-law 'is always short of money' and has borrowed money or received gifts of food worth more than £1 a week lately.

None of the family had had a summer holiday, and only the husband had had an evening out in the past fortnight (at a pub). They eat sparingly, but except for Mrs Fisher, they have a cooked breakfast and she ensures that the children have sufficient milk. She gets five pints each day. Except for the youngest, the children each get 15p pocket money. At Christmas she spent £30. For her, the husband's fall in earnings has compensations. In some ways she feels better off because 'he has less money to spend on drink and has to stay at home more'. She values the increased family allowance and uses it all for the housekeeping. They feel poor sometimes, especially in mid week, and on occasions such as Christmas. They defined poverty as 'not enough money to buy food and having no place to live and no heating'. They were clear about the chief responsibility being the government's. 'If people can't help themselves someone has to. I think there should be more help given to people in need from the government.'

17. In poverty: Chronically sick and disabled man living with elderly mother

Mrs Davis, a widow of 64, lives with a chronically sick son of 42, in an industrial area of Manchester. She suffers from bronchitis, bad nerves, poor sight and attacks of dysentery, and says she sleeps badly. Her bronchitis began twelve years previously. She had retired from domestic cleaning in a school six years previously. Her son had been a crane driver, but had been obliged to give up work nine years previously because of both a serious heart complaint and bronchitis. Now he can only walk a few yards without stopping. (His disability score on the index is 10.) He rarely goes out, though when he was seen in early April he said his condition tended to become easier in the summer. 'My doctor has told me I can never work again.'

They live in a five-roomed council maisonette on the second and third floor, into which they had been moved from a slum-clearance area a few years earlier. It had good facilities, was very clean and orderly, though simply furnished. They had fallen into poverty. She had owned a small grocery shop in the 1950s but had become bankrupt. In the late fifties, after earning very high wages, he had bronchitis and had to take a lighter, less well-paid job. He had a 50 per cent fall in earnings. Then, in 1962, he had heart trouble as well, and had to stop work entirely. Mrs Davis's husband had been disabled himself when a labourer in a local steel works and had died the previous year. About ten years ago the three of them had lived on a total income of nearly £20, which at that time was a comfortable working-class income.

She now receives a widow's pension of £4·50, and her son receives the same amount in sickness benefit. They pay a rent of £2·90 and their savings have now been reduced to under £50. 'We had less than 50p in interest last year.' He said he had withdrawn his savings gradually from a bank deposit account, and now had only £15 left. He said he had withdrawn £40 the previous year. She is paying premium for a life policy on which she expects to realize £60. She had started it upon the son's birth forty-two years ago, first at a penny a week and now at nearly 10p. She owes about £40 to a clothing club and is paying it back at the rate of 35p a week.

Her family provide some help, though she appears to be giving more in return. At present she is preparing lunch every day for a married daughter's husband and their daughter, because her daughter 'is carrying. She loses the urge to work when she is carrying.' Normally this daughter helps her mother with cleaning, one of the granddaughters helps with the shopping and a married son fetches messages and takes them out in a car to the doctor when necessary or sometimes on an afternoon's outing. Mrs Davis also gives lunch to a married son who works locally. She minds some of the grandchildren, and even has one or other of them to stay a few nights from time to time, 'to take them off their parents' hands'.

She likes going regularly to bingo and for a drink with her family to a pub, but her son at home has not been out for weeks and neither went on holiday last year. She bought a winter coat at a jumble sale last November, and both she and her son spent Christmas with her married daughter and her family. She feels they are worse off than most people around them, and are worse off than they have ever been. For example, ten years previously the household consisted not only of her son and herself, but her husband and two other working sons, and the household income was well above average, totalling £27·50 (which includes only board contributions and not total earnings of her unmarried sons). But she made a distinction between their condition and 'real' poverty, which was 'the conditions that some people used to live in during the 'thirties. Then you had no job, no proper clothing and no adequate food. There is nothing like the poverty there used to be. Nobody should be in *real* poverty if they are only prepared to use the Welfare State.' But when asked what could be done about poverty, she said, 'The government should make people more aware of the benefits that they can receive. If only they were prepared to go out and find poor people the Ministry of Social Security would be doing its job.' In fact she is eligible to receive supplementary benefit (chiefly to cover the rent), but has not applied. The interviewer tried hard to persuade her to apply, 'but she did not seem convinced. Obviously this household is living from hand to mouth but this is not reflected in the state of the home, which is neat and tidy, nor in their meals, which are nourishing and substantial.'

18. In poverty: Chronically sick man and wife and three children

Mr and Mrs Agnew are both in their forties and live with a daughter of 21, a son of 13, and a daughter of 3 in a three-roomed council house in Halifax, with WC in a small back yard, into which they had moved from a slum house three months previously. Mr Agnew was a comber in a textile mill and had been sick for nine months, suffering from bronchial asthma and severe depression. He had not been eligible for sick pay and it was no longer possible for him to return. He has repeated pain in his chest, sleeps badly and is so depressed he stays indoors most of the time and cannot face his friends. He had been a prisoner-of-war and said his condition dated from 1945 when he was released. His wife has suffered, she says, from her 'nerves' for the last ten years, and feels continuously tired, as well as getting in a rage sometimes with others. She has an NHS deaf aid. Both see their doctor regularly. Neither had been out for the evening in the previous fortnight because, they said, they had no money.

His wage had been £15 a week and their income, including sickness benefit (£7·50), family allowance (40p) and supplementary benefit (£3·05), amounts to £10·95. They have no savings or other assets of any kind. The rent is £1·50. Their

21-year-old daughter earns £12 per week gross and pays £3 a week for her board. She is saving for her marriage. He says he feels poor now – at weekends and Christmas especially, and at times 'when the children need things, like football boots, and can't have them'. Mr Agnew had asked for a supplementary grant for shoes for Mrs Agnew, and was told that the weekly allowance was supposed to cover that. 'We got a slip for £5 for a blazer and trousers for our boy at school, but that would hardly run to a shirt. And those clothes have to last nine months as well. It's a good school he goes to [a secondary modern school]. I'm not having him shabby. If the wife doesn't get some shoes soon she won't be able to go out. What will happen to the little one then? There was a lady from the NSPCC who helped us when we were in a fix. These people are lovely. They really help you. Look how we have to manage. We drew £7·50 today. There was £6·10 for food at the shop and from the rest we can get one bag of coal. We can't get two bags.' They buy all their clothing through clothing clubs, and have been missing payments lately. Mrs Agnew has not had a new winter coat in the last three years. The supplementary benefit allowance seems to be slightly below the basic entitlement, even allowing for a contribution to the rent by the daughter, and ignoring a possible additional allowance because of Mr Agnew's sickness.

19. On the margins of poverty: Elderly retirement pensioners

Mr Morgan, aged 76, lives with his wife of 60 in a six-roomed terraced house in Swansea which he owns freehold. It was bought five years previously after they had lived in it as tenants for thirty years, and is now worth about £1,500. They spent about £45 in rates and insurance last year, and about £25 on repairs. There is a tiny back yard in which it is not very pleasant to sit. Depending on the direction of the wind, there is a foul smell sometimes from a neighbouring oil works.

Mr Morgan had been a foreman in a firm building luxury coaches (earning about £15·50 in his mid sixties) and had been retired only four years. For the first twenty years of his adult life he had been a miner, but after an accident could not continue. He said bitterly that he received no compensation or pension, and not even free or cheap coal. His wife works a few hours cleaning in a local chapel, for which she receives £2·50.[1] They have a retirement pension of £8·25 per week. Since he worked until he was 72, he gets an extra 95p per week. Mrs Morgan has £50 in savings certificates, and Mr Morgan about £200 in his current bank account. Apart from the house, they have no other assets. Their debts amount to £27, the balance of repayments on a cooker and washing machine.

Mr Morgan is spry for his age, but cannot move about energetically. His wife suffers from bronchitis and rarely goes out in winter. A married son and daughter live near by and are seen daily. Often they have meals together. Neither has other-

1. The Supplementary Benefits Commission could disregard up to £2 earnings in calculating entitlement to an allowance.

wise had an evening out in the last fortnight, not because they could not afford to but because they had not wanted to. They did not have a summer holiday but went away for a long weekend to stay with a relative. Unusually, she has a cooked breakfast but he does not. Mr Morgan thinks his wife eats too much. He spends money regularly on football pools in winter but does not smoke. They spent about £10 extra at Christmas.

All their income is pooled and they do not find it difficult to manage. They consider their standard of living to be about the same as it had been before and about the same as that of their family and others around them of their age. They believe that poverty is being 'down and out', but do not believe there is any in their area. They have not applied for supplementary benefit, and though their total income seems to correspond almost exactly with their theoretical entitlement, it is possible that housing costs or extra needs might be assessed at a rate which would secure a small allowance.

20. *In poverty: Three disabled adults*

Mr Bassett, aged 65, lives with his wife, aged 52, and their son of 32 in a dilapidated terraced house in South Shields, said to be worth £1,000. There is no indoors WC or bath, and the building has numerous defects – damp walls, broken floorboards and badly fitting doors. Both mother and son are grossly overweight. She has bad legs and can scarcely walk. She can get to the bottom of the yard to go to the lavatory, but that is all. Four years previously, she had had an unsuccessful operation for a prolapse and she lives in considerable discomfort. Her son has epilepsy and has fairly frequent fits. He is physically very disabled and wears surgical boots. He had never been in employment and had not even been able to attend school regularly when young. His mother said both of them were affected by depression. He attends a training centre for the mentally handicapped and may be going on the doctor's advice to a 'holiday centre' in the summer. In early life, Mr Bassett had been a professional footballer and then a barrow salesman, selling fruit, but he had not worked for ten years. He has very bad arthritis in his legs and hips. Their doctor visits the family about once a month.

The family depend on supplementary benefit, the couple receiving £7·95 and the son £4·50, amounting altogether to £12·45. There seemed to be grounds for appealing against both assessments, for example, that the allowance of 60p per week for rates did not allow for repairs, all three seemed to be eligible for the long-term addition, and there were medical grounds for discretionary additions.

Apart from the five-roomed house which they occupy, they have no other assets whatsoever. Mrs Bassett claimed they had spent nothing at Christmas because they had nothing to spend. They have no relatives living locally and do not look to any neighbours or friends for support. Persistent questioning failed to reveal any social activities on the part of mother or son. None of the family had been on holiday for years. No friends came to the house for a snack or meal. Only the husband went out regularly. Mrs Bassett said, 'I keep £1 a week for the rates and the fuel. I give him something every day. He goes out, spends the day [i.e. 12 a.m. to 3 p.m.] in the pub and the betting shop and comes home in the afternoon with some food for the main meal. He does the cooking (and, apparently, all shopping and cleaning). I get all my son's book. He has nothing for himself. I have nothing for myself.' She said she feels poor all the time, and that poverty was 'not having enough to go round like us, trying to manage when you haven't any chance to make the money go round'.

21. On the margins of poverty: Fatherless family (also immigrant)

Mrs Mullen is a widow of 58 living with her two sons aged 16 and 15 in a privately rented flat (£2·10 per week) in Salford. Her husband died when her children were small. There are four rooms and they need another bedroom. The WC is at the end of the yard, and there is no bath. In substitution they use a zinc tub, which is placed in front of the fire. They have just installed a gas stove, found in a junk yard. Previously they had cooked on the fire. 'I had to get a stove because the food cooked on the fire upset their stomachs.' She said she could only afford to heat one room during the winter. None of the windows can be opened, and they have been painted over. The bedrooms and hallway are very damp, but 'it is paradise compared with our previous house'. The family has moved three times in the last two years, and has very little furniture – no carpets, armchairs, radio, refrigerator or washing machine, for example – and only a television set. 'It costs 55p, but I have to have it. It keeps the boys in. I can't really afford it and it may have to go back.' Mrs Mullen said she does not feel well enough to work and has anaemia. She said she had bronchitis and easily became breathless. Her hearing was also poor. She said she was also not at work because of sickness. It is now unlikely that she will either be able, or want, to go back to work. She had been a domestic cleaner until eighteen months previously. 'I have to get the boys out in the morning. Arthur [the 15-year-old who is about to leave school] comes home for dinner.' Her elder son is an apprentice with an upholstery firm and worked fifty-one weeks of the previous year. He worked forty hours the previous week for a gross wage of £5·70, or £4·90 net. It costs him about 65p to travel to and from work each week. He gives his mother £2·50 for his board.

Mrs Mullen had been widowed twice, and she said that because her second husband had worked a lot in Ireland he had not obtained enough stamps for her to qualify for a widow's pension. Instead she received a pension from the Irish Republic amounting to £3·60 a week. She also received £3·65 supplementary benefit, which she said she was a little embarrassed to receive. This seems to be a shade low (about 50p) in terms of the income for which she would be strictly eligible. Total disposable income therefore amounts to £11·50 per week. They have no savings or any other assets. 'Only my wedding ring. The boys have nothing, not even a watch.' Mrs Mullen is paying 90p per week to pay off purchases of bedding, pots and pans and a little furniture. 'I can't afford to get behind with the rent or we should soon be evicted.' Her younger son had not obtained free school meals, although eligible, and although healthy, was educationally backward and 'wild'. 'We have moved backwards and forwards between Ireland and England and his education has suffered. Last year the school inspector came to say he had had forty-two days off for playing truant. He stayed off on Fridays because he did not like the lessons that day.' Apparently a child-care officer had also called.

Mrs Mullen lives near a married son by her first marriage, and she spends a substantial part of each week minding the grandchildren, giving them meals at midday and shopping and washing. Each weekend a small grandson stays with her. 'He brings his own food.' She gets some help from her daughter-in-law in return, for example, meals. She also stayed there throughout Christmas. Mrs Mullen said she had not had a holiday since she was married forty-one years ago, and none of them had a summer holiday last year. She had not had an evening out for twelve weeks, but her sons had been out at the cinema, or a football match or a youth club, six or seven evenings in the last fortnight. She went every week to church, but the boys went less frequently.

Mrs Mullen said there were days in the last two weeks when she had no cooked meal. She had not had a new winter coat for at least three years. The house was, according to the interviewer, 'absolutely frozen' during the early evening when he was there for nearly three hours. Mrs Mullen thought her situation was worse off than ever, and that she was worse off than either her neighbours or her family. When asked how she would describe real poverty, she said, 'The state that we are living in now.'

9
The Rich

To comprehend and explain poverty is also to comprehend and explain riches. One of the major purposes of sociologists is to describe systems of stratification in different societies and explain how those systems arose, what keeps them in being and whether they are an inevitable and necessary feature of society. Through the seizure and differential inheritance or acquisition of land or wealth and political power; through the ownership, or lack of ownership, of the means of production; through the division of labour in economic and social life; and through the development of selective welfare systems as well as the restriction of the surplus benefits of production dominant groups emerge. The composition of these dominant groups varies from one society to another. In some societies, royal families rule through succession; in others, priests or military elites exercise autocratic rule, even if on behalf of an economic class; in still others, the most dominant groups are landowners, merchants or industrialists. In most instances these groups own, or control, disproportionately large, and sometimes huge, personal resources. In many societies, power may be difficult to describe with any precision, partly because it may appear to be shared between separate if related groups and partly because it may appear to depend as much upon the attitudes taken by people towards wealth or positions held in that society as upon any independently measurable characteristic of such wealth or position. None the less, power stems from wealth, and wealth usually from power and our understanding of poverty can only be deepend by any attempt to delineate wealth and its ownership.

Even to adopt the term 'the rich' as a category of social analysis is significant. It suggests that the elucidation of economic and financial factors is fundamental to the explanation of the power and position of those in the upmost stratum of society, and that access to and control over economic resources is the central theme of any account of stratification. But the term is used ambiguously, and our purpose will be to demonstrate some of the consequences of adopting alternative definitions and then to examine the sources of wealth since these will also indicate the sources of poverty.

Concepts and Definitions of Riches

Categorizing the rich depends on having regard to income or wealth or both income and wealth, composition of the household or income unit, and length of tenure of such income or wealth. The distribution of wealth is conventionally supposed to refer to the distribution of the ownership of physical and financial assets, and the distribution of income to the receipts accruing from the ownership of assets as well as earnings and social security benefits and allowances. The trouble is that assumptions are made both about the scope of income and wealth as well as the *use* to which they are put. Cash may be put under the mattress or income heavily mortgaged to pay for debts. The ownership of a house means that a substantial part of income is not paid in rent and so, if there is no mortgage, is released for other forms of consumption. Wealth and income cannot easily be distinguished and the 'confusion' sometimes attributed to classical writers like Adam Smith who tended to treat the terms synonymously may have been meritorious.

The lack of clarity can be traced first of all to poor information, not all of which is undeliberate. The information is poor because it is issued by agencies with specific and rather limited responsibilities. And such limitation is attributable to the separation of public and private sectors of economic, social and political administration; to the isolation, within each sector, of particular groups of departments, corporations and financial institutions; and, at least in part, to British values denying trespass of private property and invasion of privacy. Neither the Inland Revenue's Survey of Personal Incomes nor the Family Expenditure Survey 'is conducted specifically to collect comprehensive information on the distribution of personal income, and it is understandable therefore that they are in some respects inadequate for the purpose'.[1] The former omits incomes below the effective tax-exemption limit – the level at which a single person starts to pay tax if his income is wholly earned. It sometimes separates and sometimes combines the incomes of married couples. It excludes mortgage interest, and the imputed rental value of owner-occupied housing, thus underestimating the share of income going to the top half of the distribution. It understates investment income, fringe benefits from employers and some other forms of income. These are among the commonly agreed weaknesses.[2] The Family Expenditure Survey, on the other hand, while including low incomes, may, because of the problems of non-response, understate certain types of income, as we have found.[3] Because of the nature of the survey, it probably fails adequately to represent forms of income received once or occasionally during the year. The Department of Employment admits that self-employment and investment income are understated.

1. Royal Commission on the Distribution of Income and Wealth, Report No. 1, *Initial Report on the Standing Reference*, Cmnd 6171, HMSO, London, July 1975, p. 34.
2. ibid., p. 40.   3. See Chapter 5 above, pages 183 and 193.

The statistics on the distribution of wealth are open to greater criticisms.[1] To illustrate this, the methods on which they are based may be summarized. First is the *estate duty method* – used by the Inland Revenue for official statistics of distribution from 1960. Estimates of the wealth owned by different proportions of the population are based on information about estate duty paid to the Inland Revenue after death. The value of estates of people dying at certain ages is multiplied by the reciprocal of the mortality rates for those ages. Among the chief drawbacks to this method are (a) duty is not paid on estates of low value; (b) certain kinds of wealth, like pension rights and annuities, are excluded from wealth statistics based on estate duty; (c) valuation of estates at their *market* value understates the *real* value of, for example, company shares; and (d) because wealth can be transmitted before death, the real values held by a cross-section of the population at any particular moment of time are not adequately represented in the estimates. Some social scientists have taken great trouble to try to improve and adjust these figures.[2]

Second is the *investment income method*. This takes figures of investment income and multiplies them according to the rate of income presumed to obtain from the asset.[3] If a 10 per cent rate of income were to be assumed in a particular case, then the value of that asset would be the income multiplied ten times. The advantages of this approach are that, unlike the estate duty method, it can be applied to tax units rather than individuals and, potentially, can be linked with data about incomes. The trouble is that some forms of asset carry no income in the form of cash, others attract capital gains rather than recurrent income, and there is too little information about the 'portfolios' of people at different levels of wealth to estimate accurately what aggregate value of assets corresponds with their investment income.

Third is the *sample survey method*, as illustrated by the poverty survey and by a national sample survey of wealth carried out in 1953–4 by the Oxford Institute of Statistics,[4] through interviews with households chosen at random throughout the country. Perhaps the only other national sample survey carried out since the war was the Economists Advisory Group business research study in 1974.[5] Informa-

1. For a clear exposition, see Atkinson, A. B., *The Economics of Inequality*, Clarendon Press, Oxford, 1975, esp. Chapter 7.
2. Revell, J., 'Changes in the Social Distribution of Property in Britain During the Twentieth Century', *Actes du Troisième Congrès International d'Histoire Économique*, 1965, pp. 367–84; Meade, J. E., *Efficiency, Equality and the Ownership of Property*, Allen & Unwin, London, 1964 (also quoting figures produced by J. Revell); Atkinson, A. B., *Unequal Shares: Wealth in Britain*, Allen Lane, London, 1972; and Atkinson, A. B., and Harrison, A. J., *Distribution of Personal Wealth in Britain*, Cambridge University Press, 1978.
3. Atkinson, A. B., and Harrison, A. J., 'Wealth Distribution and Investment Income in Britain', *Review of Income and Wealth*, June 1974.
4. Lydall, H. F., *British Incomes and Savings*, Blackwell, Oxford, 1955.
5. Morgan, E. V., *Personal Savings and Wealth in Britain*, an EAG Business Research Study, Financial Times, London, 1975.

tion can be collected on individual, income unit and household or family bases, and can be linked to income. The trouble is that the distortions introduced by non-response and doubtful accuracy of information from households with complex holdings of wealth are difficult to control. A fairly elaborate questionnaire is in any event required. Because of the disadvantages of the other two methods, the Royal Commission on the Distribution of Income and Wealth did acknowledge the value of the sample survey approach at least as a supplement to them.[1] Ideally, information from rich households might be checked, providing permission is granted, with Inland Revenue data.

A brief outline of these methods shows how tricky it is to decide (a) the social unit owning, commanding or using the resources; (b) the items which are included in total resources; (c) the criteria by which different items are turned into common units of value so that they can be added together and households, families or income units ranked one above another; and (d) the length of time during which resources are received or commanded. If the resources of the rich are held disproportionately by the extended family, and can be drawn upon through trusts and settlements at later stages of life, are depersonalized in part through the company share system, are spread among a large number of resource systems, and have artificially low current market value, then the significance of restricted definitions of riches becomes clear. By restricting the size of the social unit, the range of items to be counted, the currency of convertibility and the time in which measurement is to take place, inequality is understated.

The Royal Commission upheld the principle, for example, that wealth should be defined in terms of 'marketability'. It also upheld the distinction conventionally made between income and wealth. Yet, as argued in Chapter 5 above,[2] the commission did not discuss the extent to which inequality might as a consequence be understated and society fail to keep track of changes in living standards. As Atkinson has shown, a distinction has to be made between 'realization' value of assets on the market, and 'going concern' value. Furniture, for example, could be valued according to the amount a dealer might pay for it second hand, or at its cost to replace. 'The difference between the two approaches is that the value as a going concern is likely in many cases to be higher than the realization value: for example, shares in a family business may be worth much more than the price obtainable on the market.'[3]

In this chapter, through illustrations from the poverty survey, I shall show why links between income and wealth in official statistics are desirable, and how the rich might be more clearly defined.

---

1. Royal Commission on the Distribution of Income and Wealth, *Initial Report on the Standing Reference*, pp. 74–8.
2. See pages 230–32.
3. Atkinson, *The Economics of Inequality*, p. 122.

Top Incomes and Top Wealth-holdings

An outline of the components of *net disposable income last year*, and of *assets* as defined in the survey, has been given above.[1] Despite some differences in definition and method, we found a close correspondence in income distribution with results from the government's Family Expenditure Survey. The top incomes were, for most types of household, at least twice, in some instances more than three times, as large as those of the 5th percentile. The top incomes for most types of household were more than five times as large as the median incomes, and more than ten times as large as the lowest incomes. Even if the top incomes are ignored, incomes at about the 5th percentile were still two or three times larger than the median (see Table 5.11, page 197 above). Table 9.1 shows how the distribution of net disposable income for different quantile groups compares with government estimates. Although the latter are stated to be on a tax unit basis, they are not very different from the distributions (for ten percentile groups) expressed on a household basis.[2] I have chosen to set out the government figures on a tax unit rather than a household basis only because the latter do not appear to be available for the top 1 per cent and next 4 per cent. It should be borne in mind that distributions presented on a tax unit instead of a household basis tend to be more unequal than those presented on a household basis. The top 1 per cent of households were estimated in the poverty survey to receive a rather higher proportion of aggregate income than estimated officially. The top 1 per cent received 6·2 per cent of income after tax and after allowing for work expenses and travel to work. If employer fringe benefits were to be added to income, the proportion received by the top 1 per cent would be slightly higher still. It can be seen that the next 4 per cent received nearly 10 per cent of net disposable income, and the next 5 per cent as much as 9·4 per cent. The bottom 80 per cent received 59 per cent, or a little less than estimated by the Central Statistical Office (both on a tax unit and a household basis). Finally, the bottom 5 per cent received only 1 per cent of income.

Assets were more unequally distributed than income. Two households had more than £200,000 and five others (including three giving incomplete information) more than £100,000. But the median household had only £1,065, and at the 85th percentile only £8 (Table 5.18, page 209 above). As a proportion of top wealth-holdings, the wealth of households only a little below the top was modest. Thus the households at the 5th percentile held only 6 per cent of the assets of the wealthiest household. Table 9.1 sets out the distribution in the same form as for income. The unadjusted figures are derived from those households in the sample giving full information about assets. The unadjusted information is discussed and

1. See Chapter 5, pages 180–93 and 199–205.
2. Compare Table 15 with Table G.13 in Royal Commission on the Distribution of Income and Wealth, *Initial Report on the Standing Reference*, pp. 45 and 213.

Table 9.1. Percentage shares of income and wealth received or held by quantile groups of households or tax units, comparing government estimates with the poverty survey.

	Poverty survey			Official estimates		
	Net assets of households			Net income of tax unit[b]		Personal wealth[c]
Quantile group	Net disposable income last year of households	unadjusted	adjusted[a] 1967	1967	1972–3	1972
Top 1%	6·2	24·3	(26)	4·9	4·4	28·1
2–5%	10·0	20·5	(25)	9·9	9·8	25·8
6–10%	9·4	13·9	(13)	9·5	9·4	13·4
11–20%	15·0	17·2	(15)	15·2	15·8	15·1
21–100%	59·4	24·2	(21)	60·5	60·7	17·6

NOTES: [a]Adjusting first for underrepresentation of those with high incomes also giving data on assets, and second for understatement of assets, especially stocks and shares, but also certain types of savings. (See Table 5.15, page 203 above). The value of occupational pension rights is not included here (but is included in employer welfare benefits described in Chapter 5 and later in this chapter). In adjusting Inland Revenue aggregates to balance-sheet totals, we have broadly followed the methods adopted first for the UK in 1969 by Revell, J., and Tomkins, C., *Personal Wealth and Finance in Wales*, Welsh Council, 1974, and second by the Royal Commission (Appendix K).
[b]No figures available from the Central Statistical Office for 1968–9.
[c]Estate duty figures adjusted by Royal Commission to conform with balance-sheet asset totals between included and excluded populations, assuming that 42 per cent of the increase is allocated to the population excluded from liability to estate duty.

SOURCE: Royal Commission on the Distribution of Income and Wealth, Report No. 1, *Initial Report on the Standing Reference*, Cmnd 6171, HMSO, London, July 1975, pp. 45 and 87.

analysed in various parts of this book. In the table, alternative estimates are also shown. The data have been adjusted in two respects: first, to allow for the fact that, in the responding sample, slightly more people with high than low incomes did not provide full information about assets (sometimes being one tax unit in a household with two or more units in which the other units had provided full information); and secondly, to carry out the same kind of exercise as first Professor Atkinson and then the Royal Commission on the Distribution of Income and Wealth did to allocate any difference between balance-sheet totals and totals compiled by multiplying sample survey data.

Even without any adjustment, inequality is evidently marked. The top 5 per cent owned 44·8 per cent of *net* assets, and the bottom 80 per cent only 24·2 per cent. With adjustment, the top 5 per cent owned 51 per cent or over half of net assets, and the bottom 80 per cent 21 per cent. It is hazardous to compare these distributions with government estimates. In the table I have given one illustrative set from the Royal Commission's adjusted estimates for 1972. Adjustments were not made in respect of the 1960s, and Inland Revenue data suggest that though there may have been a small decline in the holding of the top 1 per cent between 1968 and 1972, the change among other ranks was very small indeed. Moreover, the figures are stated to be for the total population aged 18 and over (though whether units are, in practice, a mixture of individuals, tax units and households remains at issue), while the poverty survey data apply to households. Again, as discussed above, valuation of the wealth holdings of the wealthiest may be under-stated by taking market values. Deduction of debts and measurement of *net* assets may also contribute to understatement of the command over resources of the rich, since substantial credit can sometimes buttress extravagant living standards for lengthy periods.

With such qualifications, the survey data can be said to furnish empirical sub-stantiation of the vast disparities in wealth-holding suggested both by official and independent estimates. Far from the wealth of the top 5 per cent being overstated because of the failure in official estimates to take account of the value of modest holdings of assets, it may have been understated in certain critical respects. Des-pite taking a deliberately broad definition of wealth, the top 5 per cent own over half of the nation's wealth – even including owner-occupied housing and personal possessions. This is a major finding. The bottom 5 per cent own little or nothing.

Table 9.2 illustrates the effect on the distribution of adding different types of resource. Each component is discussed in Chapter 5 above. Information of a de-tailed nature could not be obtained on every type of resource from all households in the sample, and the table sets out unadjusted figures only for those giving com-plete information on assets. This means that the percentages held by the top groups are slightly understated. The value of both public social services and pri-vate services in kind have been included, as has the value of standard types of consumer durables and home-grown food. These items are commonly believed to be more equally distributed than either wealth or income, and even, for example, public and private welfare services, of disproportionate value to the poor. The table shows that, despite their inclusion, they do no more than moderate to a small extent the inequality in the dispersion. In discussions of the distribution of income or wealth, it is common to use a summary measure of concentration. The most popular measure is the Gini coefficient. The results of applying it to our data are shown at the foot of Table 9.2.[1]

1. The limitations of the measure are now recognized. See, for example, Atkinson, *The Economics of Inequality*, pp. 45–9.

Table 9.2. *Absolute mean amount in pounds and percentage share of income and other resources received or held by quantile groups of households.*

Quantile	Non-asset income	and annuitized value of assets	and employer fringe benefits	and value of social services in kind	and private income in kind
Top 1%	6,053	11,246	11,517	12,062	12,331
2–5%	2,714	3,937	4,217	4,837	5,012
6–10%	2,103	2,710	2,888	3,434	3,550
11–20%	1,706	2,085	2,184	2,643	2,756
21–30%	1,421	1,683	1,752	2,137	2,233
31–40%	1,216	1,436	1,497	1,778	1,904
41–50%	1,058	1,221	1,262	1,521	1,626
51–60%	909	1,064	1,091	1,290	1,393
61–70%	760	898	925	1,071	1,180
71–80%	578	730	746	851	951
81–90%	387	511	519	611	691
91–95%	287	356	359	405	480
96–100%	184	253	254	282	323
Percentage shares					
Top 1%	5·4	8·5	8·3	7·4	6·7
2–5%	10·1	11·1	11·4	11·3	11·1
6–10%	9·4	9·7	9·8	9·9	9·7
11–20%	15·5	14·9	15·1	15·3	15·2
21–30%	12·9	12·0	12·0	12·6	12·3
31–40%	11·0	10·1	10·2	10·2	10·5
41–50%	9·6	8·8	8·6	8·8	9·0
51–60%	8·4	7·5	7·5	7·5	7·6
61–70%	6·8	6·4	6·3	6·2	6·5
71–80%	5·3	5·2	5·2	5·0	5·2
81–90%	3·5	3·7	3·6	3·6	3·8
91–95%	1·3	1·2	·1·2	1·2	1·3
96–100%	0·8	0·9	0·9	0·8	0·9
Total	100	100	100	100	100
Gini coefficient	0·34	0·37	0·37	0·37	0·36

NOTE: Households giving information on income but not assets have been excluded. An imputed rental income for owner-occupied homes has been included (see page 347).

Other components could be added to our definition of resources. For example, we included occupational pension rights but not state pension rights, on grounds that for many of those expecting substantial occupational pensions, the pension rights were treated as a form of deferred pay (often to escape tax), could sometimes be converted into a lump sum upon change of job (or during receipt of pension), frequently incorporated a lump sum upon retirement, could sometimes be used to obtain credit, and were not available to a very substantial section of the population. In these respects, they differ from state pension rights, and it is surprising that these differences attracted no commentary from the Royal Commission. The commission believed that both sets of accrued rights needed to be estimated and the effects of their inclusion in the distribution of wealth assessed, even though they 'differ in certain important respects from the more conventional forms of wealth'.[1] They took the implicit view that state pension rights should be treated in the same way as occupational pension rights. There are two objections. The Royal Commission use a 'going concern' rather than 'realization' base, and their method of valuing those rights is also not very realistic. They suggest, for example, that the total value of the accrued rights of the flat-rate retirement pension to a woman of 55–9 was £8,577 in 1975.[2] This would be news indeed to middle-aged working-class women. Unlike women with £8,577 of jewellery or savings or stocks and shares, they have no means of capitalizing on this 'asset'.

Combining Income and Wealth

Although there is an expected correlation between incomes and assets, households with the highest incomes were by no means always the households with the largest wealth. Table 9.3 shows that only just over a third of persons in households in the top 5 per cent of incomes were also in the top 5 per cent of assets; moreover, that two fifths in the top 5 per cent of assets were not even in the top 20 per cent of incomes. Nearly a quarter of persons in households in the top 5 per cent of incomes did not fall into the top 20 per cent of assets.

The households in the top 5 per cent of assets had at least £13,102, in the top 15 per cent £6,450, and in the top 25 per cent £4,200. The households in the top 5 per cent of incomes had at least £2,598 in the last year, in the top 15 per cent £1,795, and in the top 25 per cent £1,502.

When we come to consider the size and characteristics of households, we find that each of these distributions can be misleading. Thus, among top incomes there may be households containing, say, three or more persons with modest earnings who, because their net earnings are aggregated, are then categorized as rich. Among bottom incomes may be retired couples with modest state and occupational pensions who own homes of substantial size and high value of stocks and

1. Royal Commission on the Distribution of Income and Wealth, *Initial Report on the Standing Reference*, p. 88.
2. ibid., p. 92.

shares and other assets. Their low incomes would not be at all indicative of their lifetime or current standard of living (though their incomes, *together* with the income equivalent to their holdings of assets, would be so indicative). Again, among bottom assets may be young couples from rich families just setting up home who have lived their childhood in affluent households and have expectations of wealth being passed on to them as well as positions in family firms and business, or in the professions, which normally carry high expectations of wealth accumulation.

Table 9.3. Percentages of persons in households in ranked categories of net disposable income in previous year and net assets.

	Households ranked by net disposable income				
Assets	Top 5%	6–10%	11–20%	Bottom 80%	All ranks
Top 5%	2·0	0·6	0·6	1·9	5·1
6–10%	0·9	0·8	1·2	1·9	4·8
11–20%	1·2	1·6	1·4	7·0	11·2
Bottom 80%	1·4	4·0	9·2	64·3	78·9
All ranks	5·5	7·0	12·4	75·1	100·0

The survey provided illustrations of these divergencies. There were, in fact, two individuals in the lowest 5 per cent of net disposable incomes who were included in the top 5 per cent of assets. One per cent of the entire sample could be found among the bottom 5 per cent of net disposable incomes *and* among the top 60 per cent of assets. There were, however, few examples of a reverse kind. There were three, but only three, households among the top 5 per cent of net disposable incomes who were also among the bottom 40 per cent of assets. Seventy-four per cent of those among the top 5 per cent of incomes were among the top 30 per cent of assets (and 36 per cent among the top 10 per cent).

Taken separately, then, neither of the conventional measures is satisfactory for purposes of showing inequality in standards of living. At least two refinements are necessary. One is to take account of household size and composition. We contemplated a choice between two options. We had developed a measure of the different resources of the household expressed as percentages of the mean for its type. We had also developed measures expressed as a percentage of the state's poverty standard. The disadvantage of the latter was that the incomes of different types of household which were to be treated as equivalent depended on conventions established by the government, and not by independent criteria. This disadvantage also applied to the *level* of the state's poverty standard for every type of household. The disadvantage of the former was that diverse sub-types of household tended to be lumped together. This applied in part also to variations of age: for example, in the case of couples with one child the child might be an infant of a few weeks or a girl of 14. Another disadvantage was that inequalities *between* household types were ignored and the means were assumed to represent the same standard of living. Either approach would represent an improvement on conventional methods, and after experimenting with each we decided to adopt the latter.

The other necessary refinement is to combine income and wealth in one measure. The method adopted is discussed in Chapter 5 (pages 210–15). Alternatives might, of course, be proposed and developed, but it is evident that any method requires careful handling, so that the different uses made of different types of income and wealth, together with attitudes taken publicly towards these types, are called to attention when the results are described and analysed.

A Definition of the Rich

Accordingly, to non-asset income of households in the previous year was added the annuity value of their assets. Some types of asset do not augment living standards in the same way or to the same extent as others, and in choosing a rate of interest of 7 per cent and applying it to all types of asset, we were aware that we might be criticized both for underrepresenting and overrepresenting the value of assets to living standards. The rate of 7 per cent was a conservative choice. The rich tend to obtain relatively high and the poor relatively poor rates of return on their loans or investments. Some forms of capital appreciate rapidly. A complex formula would be difficult to justify, and a single rate simpler to comprehend. The rate is marginally above the rate of interest paid in 1968 by building societies, but below other rates, including returns on stocks and shares, and in relation to the capital gains element in inflation represents in practice a low rate. Thus a wholly-owned house valued at £3,000 in 1968–9 would be treated as equivalent to paying a rent of £210 a year, or £4 a week. For young or middle-aged owner-occupiers, the corresponding annuity value remained small, though for elderly people with only a short expectation of life, it could be much larger. We therefore calculated annuity values of all assets on two bases, one including the annuity value of owner-occupied housing and the other including only the imputed interest on the capital value of such housing. Except when noted, the former measure has been adopted in this book. In comparing households at different points in the dispersion of resources, however, we have preferred the latter measure. While understating the value of owner-occupied homes, some may feel it does not misplace some elderly households in the rankings.

The resulting annual 'income' was then expressed as a percentage of the state's poverty standard – the basic supplementary benefit rates plus housing cost. The percentage shares of total relative income net worth, or 'asset-linked income' as

Table 9.4. Asset-linked income (or income net worth) expressed as a percentage of the state's poverty standard, and percentage share of quantile groups of households.

Quantile group	Mean % of each group	Percentage share of the aggregate supplementary benefit equivalent of asset-linked income of all households in the sample
Top 1%	1,664	7·5 ⎫
2–5%	696	11·1 ⎬ 27.5
6–10%	440	8·9 ⎭
11–20%	334	13·4
21–30%	280	11·3
31–40%	245	9·9
41–50%	217	8·8
51–60%	191	7·6
61–70%	168	6·7
71–80%	146	5·8
81–90%	125	5·1
91–95%	109	2·2 ⎫ 3·8
96–100%	84	1·6 ⎭
Total	248	100

NOTE: The imputed interest (assumed to be a rate of 7 per cent p.a.) on the capital value of owner-occupied housing and not the annuitized value of this asset has been included.

it might be called, of different quantile groups are shown in Table 9.4.[1] All of the top 1 per cent had asset-linked income of more than 1,000 per cent of the poverty standard: their mean was 1,664 per cent. The mean of the bottom 5 per cent was 84 per cent, compared with the overall mean of 248 per cent. The income net worth of each quantile group, so standardized for household composition, can also be expressed as a percentage of the aggregate. This aggregate is the value not just in pounds of income and annuitized income combined, but that value expressed for each income unit as a percentage of the state's poverty or subsistence standard for such a unit. The top 10 per cent, in fact, had 27·5 per cent, and the bottom 10 per cent only 3·8 per cent of the aggregate. This gives a ratio of nearly seven to one. The ratio between the top 5 per cent and bottom 5 per cent was twelve to one. The ranking which we adopted had the advantage of corresponding closely with rankings according to each of net disposable household income and

1. Table A.22 in Appendix Eight, page 1010, sets out the absolute mean values of income, assets and income net worth held by different quantile groups, when the groups are ranked according to each of these criteria, but also when they are ranked according to the 'poverty criterion' of net income worth expressed as a percentage of supplementary benefit.

net assets, after allowing for household size and composition and was also reasonably all-inclusive of resources. A comparative summary will be found in Table A.22 (Appendix Eight, page 1010).

When households are more carefully ranked according to these criteria, households who are not popularly counted as 'rich' are included among the rich. The number of members of a household, and especially of dependants, can be crucial in affecting the ranking. Thus, a pensioner living alone with assets regarded by many as of only moderate dimensions might easily be found in the top 5 per cent. Again, the same might be true of a household of three people (say a couple in their early forties and an unmarried son in his early twenties) with very little wealth but each of them being in full-time employment, earning a good wage or salary. The combined income, the relatively low housing costs per person and the absence of dependants, can combine to place them in the top 5 per cent. The fact that this relative affluence may not represent previous or future years must also be remembered. The value of household assets is a more stable indicator of riches *over the life-cycle as a whole* than either current annual income or even income net worth adjusted for household composition.

Who were the richest 1 per cent? I have listed the top sixteen households. They comprised fifty-four people, fifteen being under 15, eleven being 15–39, fifteen being 40 to 59, and thirteen being 60 years of age or older. All were born in the United Kingdom. Only nine of the fifty-four had any trace of disablement. All but one of the households owned the homes in which they lived, and all had gardens, more than two thirds of them large gardens. The great majority entertained friends and/or relatives frequently in their homes, and also were guests of others. Most were living in the South-East, Midlands, Scotland and East Anglia. None lived in the North, the North-West or Northern Ireland. Nearly all adults had been educated to above the minimum school-leaving age. Most employed adults were of a professional status, and they included a bank manager, a chartered accountant, a doctor and teachers. A third of the gainfully occupied were self-employed. None of the householders was of manual status, but three young adults in the household had jobs of manual status. None counted themselves as belonging to the upper class. Ten adults said they belonged to the upper middle class, and most others said middle or lower middle class. But as many as six adults said they belonged to the upper working class and one to the working class. More than half the households owned property and businesses and nearly half had stocks and shares. A few had bank overdrafts and several were using cars owned by their firms. Inheritance seemed to have played a considerable part in explaining the assets held, and it was of some note that all except one couple saw relatives frequently and often stayed with them and vice versa.

The richest households in the sample (all except No. 12 owner-occupiers)

1. Woman of 77, retired teacher, income net worth £13,032 (assets include shares of £67,315 and twenty properties, producing a rental income of a little under £1,000 per annum).
2. Couple aged 62 and 60, professional class, retired bank manager, income net worth £18,042. Total assets of just under £100,000.
3. Couple each aged 53 with 19-year-old son and 14-year-old daughter, lower supervisory class, income net worth £20,607. (Assets £204,920.)
4. Man of 67 with wife of 36 and son and daughter aged 17 and 15, a farmer, income net worth £15,042. (Assets £109,269.)
5. Couple aged 57 and 55, professional class, income net worth £10,737 (stocks and shares of £20,000 included in assets of £70,000).
6. Elderly couple aged 83 and 66 living with resident maid. Stocks and shares amount to £60,000, and the house, other houses and savings are valued at £30,000 at least. In addition to unearned income of over £3,000, he has an army pension. (Total assets at least £90,000, but probably substantially more than £100,000.)
7. Couple in their early forties with five children ranging in age from 17 to 8. They live in a big farmhouse in 200 acres of land, and he is a company director owning a string of shops. Assets are considerably in excess of £100,000, and include valuable paintings and antiques.
8. Couple in their mid seventies with house and fourteen acres of land with an unearned income of £3,000 from ownership of butcher's business, estimated to be worth more than £20,000. Savings and other property amount to another £20,000.
9. Couple each aged 48 with six children aged from 22 to a few months, a farmer and also company director, three in family earning, income net worth £19,606. (Assets amount altogether to £212,514.)
10. Couple in early forties with child of 7, managing director of a building firm, which the husband owns and which is valued at £40,000, producing an income for him of £8,000. He also receives rents from other properties which are owned. (Total assets of at least £70,000.)
11. Woman of 77, professional class, income net worth £4,504. (Stocks and shares £4,500 in assets of £26,000.)
12. Couple aged 37 and 34, with four children aged from 7 to 2, professional class, fishing-boat owner and captain, income net worth of £10,735, privately unfurnished tenants.
13. Couple aged 80 and 68, he a former chartered accountant, owning and renting flats and houses, many valuable antiques and books, income net worth of £9,800.

14. Couple aged 53 and 51 with daughters aged 19 and 13. Managing director of clothing firm owning large house and large amount of land. (Total assets of at least £120,000.)

15. Couple aged 65 and 45 with sons of 28 and 10, dairy farmers, owning several cottages, income net worth of £11,000. (Assets at least £65,000.)

16. Couple aged 61 and 58, a farmer with a net income of £2,000 from a farm worth £26,000 which he owns (but which his son now manages). With property owned by his wife and savings, stocks and shares, their joint assets amount to at least £60,000.

The following illustrations are drawn from the wealthiest sixty households (representing rather more than the highest-ranking 3 per cent) and are arranged in order of age. At late 1970s prices, all values would be trebled.

1. After their marriage a few months previously, Mr and Mrs Pollenghast, aged 29 and 21, had moved into a five-bedroomed house in Surrey, which he estimates to be worth £13,500. He is a company director of a horticultural and agricultural machinery firm, and presently his wife is working for a private library. The firm belongs to his father and his shares are estimated to be worth £55,000. They said they had received gifts at their wedding worth over £2,000, and that in the house they had other saleable items such as guns, cutlery and jewellery worth £1,750. He has other land worth £2,500, and has £500 in a bank deposit account. He has four policies on his life, which are estimated to value £25,000. Both have cars, she a Mini and he a Ford Zephyr Estate. He draws a salary of nearly £4,000 per annum, and received £200 from a trust fund. Her salary is nearly £600. His overdraft (after the recent wedding and move into the house) is £3,000, and he also has a private debt of £500. They have daily contacts with his family and entertain and visit these and other relatives. Mr Pollenghast describes poverty as 'idleness, and also people living in bad conditions and unable to make ends meet'. He felt that poverty was due mainly to 'a lack of initiative in people', and said that the answer was to 'make people work harder, and raise the whole social level of the country in general'.
Ranked 52

2. Mr MacFraser, 32, has lived in a luxury flat in Scotland since leaving his parents' home two years previously. The flat, worth an estimated £5,500, faces south across extensive private gardens, a stone's-throw from his parents' house and a flat occupied by a brother. He is a chartered accountant, with a law degree, and has a salary of £3,500. He owns £10,000 in stocks and shares, £1,500 in savings and his life is assured for over £6,000. Recently he borrowed £710 from his bank to pay for a new car. He had an inheritance of £350 in the last year, and the possessions in his flat include antiques worth several hundred pounds. His parents paid £500 for some of his furniture and a dishwasher. He says he is upper middle class. His father is a hospital consultant. He belongs to an exclusive golf

club, which provides his chief pastime at weekends. He took a four weeks' cruise in the Mediterranean last year, and also had a holiday in Ireland. He goes to a gaming club occasionally, and has won several large sums in the previous year. Ranked 59

3. Mr and Mrs Margood, both aged 35, live with two daughters and two sons aged from 3 to 11 near a small town in Kent. The house has eight bedrooms, is in several acres of ground, and is estimated to be worth nearly £30,000. His father had been a highly skilled manual worker and he met his wife at university. Both took degrees in economics. Her father was a barrister. She taught for a time in a private school. He is now an economist in an insurance company, earning £3,500 per annum. This attracts holiday entitlement of six weeks a year in addition to bank holidays and a pension at 60 of two thirds final earnings. Through the company he pays a lower rate of interest on his house (3·5 per cent). He and his wife have £6,000 in a bank deposit account. He has shares worth £15,000, and she £100,000 in a family trust. They have an income from these sources before tax of over £10,000. Both have cars worth £2,000, and pictures and silver worth an estimated £3,000. He has overdraft facilities running to £500. He paid over £2,000 direct to the tax authorities in the previous year (showing the interviewer copies of the forms). Each of his children has £500 per annum from a family trust, and savings of over £100 in addition. Each attends a private nursery or preparatory school, two of them boarding schools; to which £1,000 in fees are paid. They are in close touch with the husband's mother and father, who live locally and are seen every day, or nearly every day. He makes his father an allowance of £350 per annum. Relatives and friends frequently stay at the house and they both entertain and visit others frequently. They recognized they were well off, and said they were better off than ever. Mr Margood gives his wife £10 a week towards her housekeeping, and she estimated she drew another £23 a week to cover food, electricity, oil and cleaning.
Ranked 58

4. Mr and Mrs Dibshoss, aged 45 and 42, live with their children aged 17, 15, 12, 10 and 8 in a big farmhouse set among 200 acres in Lincolnshire. The house has been renovated and has rooms varying from ultra-modern with abstract designs and steel sculptures to sixteenth- and seventeenth-century antiques and pictures. Mr Dibshoss is a company director. He owns a string of grocers' shops and betting shops, and though he lives on his farm and manages it, he regarded himself principally as a bookie. He admitted to clearing £10,000 net per annum (which is probably an underestimate), and said he paid £5,000 tax in addition. He estimated the farm and farmhouse as worth £50,000, and jewellery and silver at £3,000. While he refused to give individual estimates of the value of his other property (shops, savings, stocks and shares), he said they would amount to, say,

£75,000. The minimum value of assets is therefore in the region of £130,000. He owns a racehorse and four ponies, has a Land Rover and a Rover. All the children are at private schools. He said that it was 'impossible to live in poverty today. You are given enough for food and rent. What makes people poor is buying fags and booze. It's their own doing. There's no such thing as poverty.'
Ranked 7

5. A chartered surveyor and senior partner of a firm of architects aged 50 lives with his wife aged 46 and children aged 14, 12, 8, 6 and 5 in a substantial house, valued at £6,500, in two acres of land outside Birmingham. His company has a staff of sixty, and handles substantial property contracts. He has a net income of £6,000, quite apart from a stake in the firm thought to be worth at least £50,000. He and members of his family also have stocks and shares and savings worth a further £30,000, and receive rent from a number of houses he inherited from his father and which he is selling as the opportunity arises. He is a member of a top-hat pension scheme and, independent of its provisions, pays nearly £1,000 into a life assurance scheme, which assures a lump sum of £20,000 plus profits. His wife's jewellery is insured for £2,000, and in addition to a company car his wife has a small car. She is a qualified doctor, but because the children are young works just one session a week at a near-by clinic, earning about £500 a year which she keeps for clothes and other personal expenses. The eldest child is at a private boarding school (for which fees of £500 per annum are paid), and the younger children will follow in their turn. Until very recently they had had a succession of *au pair* girls, and the wife still has paid domestic help most weekdays. In the previous summer they had rented a house in France for five weeks, taking the *au pair* with the family. Both husband and wife had spent short additional holidays overseas during the year. His father had been a shopkeeper and hers a school headmaster. They regard themselves as lower middle class despite a very high standard of living. When asked, 'If there is poverty what do you think can be done about it?' the husband answered, 'If I knew that I'd try politics, but I say this sincerely, not because I pay a lot of tax myself. I don't think taxing people to the limit is any use. There must be some incentives for working hard. People basically are concerned with their own lives and families, and by improving their lot, they improve everybody's, but I know from young men who work for me that they are more and more resentful of endless fiddles by the government to get a bit more money out of all of us. The attitude now is, "I've paid for it, I'll have all I can get," and they do get all they can. No idea of doing anything for the country. The country is grabbing all it can. I don't know how it will end, but if I were younger and my business were not so involved, I'd be off to Australia or New Zealand. There is no incentive here. If you do well, make some money for your family, you are persecuted for it. It's no use thinking people are any more or any

less what they've always been. They are not a collection of saints. I know "no man is an island", but basically it's your own children you work for.'
Ranked 33

6. Mr and Mrs Chakebone are in their early fifties and have two teenage children. He is a director of a garment-manufacturing firm, said to have made a loss in the previous year, and he has a net salary of over £2,000 per annum. His share of the business is estimated to be worth £100,000, and he and his family have other assets, mainly savings and stocks and shares worth nearly another £20,000. The house is insured for £10,000, but is estimated to be worth £14,000. It is fully owned and is set in two acres of ground in Warwickshire. Mr Chakebone has been ill with a heart complaint for the last thirty weeks and has received sickness benefit through private insurance of another £48 per month in addition. He pointed out that because of his job he had access to a wide range of goods at wholesale and less than wholesale prices, and estimated that this was worth £1,000 a year to him. He and his wife regarded themselves as upper middle class. His father had been a managing director of a food firm and her father had run a drapery business. They were in daily contact with the surviving parents and a married daughter, all of whom lived near by. One child was still at private school. The other had recently left and had spent several months on holiday overseas. Mrs Chakebone described poverty as 'having no home of your own and not enough food or clothing'. She added that the poor should be educated 'to work and make the most of their ability'.
Ranked 14

7. Mr and Mrs Raynor-Blue, aged 56 and 55, live in a magnificent four-bed-roomed house in Shropshire. He is company director of a carpet manufacturing firm and draws a salary of £5,000. With a short break during the war, he had worked for the firm throughout his life and has been director for sixteen years. His father had been a master butcher. His wife had owned a profitable drapery business, which she had inherited from her father. This had been sold fifteen years earlier. They owned £20,000 in stocks and shares, £15,000 in savings in various banks, building societies and defence bonds and antiques, pictures and jewellery worth at least £15,000. The house was estimated to be worth £19,000. His life is assured for £15,000. His overdraft facility is for £1,000. He has a Rover 2000 TC paid for by the firm, and she a new Renault. The house is at the end of a long drive with huge lawns, tended by a full-time gardener. The entrance hall has a minstrel gallery and is spaciously laid out, with valuable antique furniture, paintings and silverware. They have an only son, recently married and now on his honeymoon. An elderly aunt is staying for a month and they entertain and visit relatives occasionally. Mrs Raynor-Blue is out nearly every evening and plays a big role in local voluntary agencies – the choir, the Women's Institute, Keep Fit, village suppers and church functions. Mr Raynor-Blue believed that

class was determined by one's family of birth, and both he and his wife said they were middle class. Mr Raynor-Blue does not believe in keeping money in the bank. 'The bigger the overdraft you can get, the better. It is better to play about with money today.' They believed poverty existed, but 'if they are not disabled or ill, then it is their own fault . . . There are not enough questions asked before paying out social security benefits.'
Ranked 5

8. Mr and Mrs Avis-Brown, 62 and 60, live in a detached house with a large garden in Surrey estimated to be worth £14,000, to which they moved on Mr Avis-Brown's retirement as a bank manager two years previously. His final salary was over £14,000, since he was also a director of the bank. He receives a pension of £8,000 per annum. They estimate that their stocks and shares are worth approximately £75,000. They said they had received £2,800 in dividends and interest last year. In the house they have articles such as silver, jewellery and pictures worth at least £2,000. He estimated the value of his car at £1,200. His father was a commercial traveller for a textile manufacturer, and both considered themselves to be upper middle class. They went out to dinner two or three times a week, but did not have frequent contacts with relatives, though they stayed from time to ime during the year. He pays an allowance of £500 per annum to a sister. When asked whether there was real poverty these days, he said not. 'There isn't any because there's the national assistance. It's all relative. What would be poverty to me would be a lot different to the poverty of other people. If you are really down and your living standards come from the national assistance – they give the amount necessary to live, don't they? . . . If there is any poverty, it's up to the NA – if it's genuine – to see that they get help. It's a personal matter. There's plenty of work to be got if they want it.'
Ranked 2

9. Mr Prenger, aged 67 and his wife, 36, live with their children, aged 17 and 15, in a large farmhouse with six bedrooms. The farm and farmhouse, with an acreage of several hundred acres, is estimated to be worth £220,000 (confirmed by accountant). The farm was inherited by Mrs Prenger and she felt herself to be middle class though her husband, who said *his* father was working class, said he was lower middle class. As a farmer, he claimed that the last financial year for which he could give information was a very poor year because an investment allowance was brought to an end and bad weather caused poor crops. Including an allowance for depreciation, farm expenses which were allowed amounted to over £2,750 and his net income in that year was said to be only £350. He employs one farm hand round the year. His wife keeps a kennels and divides her time between the farm and the job of boarding dogs and cats, which earns her, she estimated, an average of £250 per annum net of expenses. Mr Prenger owns two cottages worth about £6,000 on the farm land, one of which is at present empty

and the other rented for approximately £100 per annum. He has a small number of shares and about £1,000 of savings in a building society. They entertain a great deal and said their children have 'two or three friends to stay every weekend'. Both children keep horses and often go riding.
Ranked 4

10. Miss Wythenhurst, aged 77, lives in a three-bedroomed bungalow in Stirling-shire. Although others in the sample had greater wealth in absolute money value, and had larger incomes, they had dependants, whereas she had not. Her combined income and wealth was estimated to be equivalent to a figure more than forty times the supplementary benefit standard for someone living alone. She has just dispensed with the services of one housekeeper, but is about to employ another. She estimates the value of the bungalow at £6,500. Her stocks and shares of more than £65,000 yield an income of just under £3,000 per annum, and she owns about twenty houses, worth £13,650, producing a rental income after tax of £800 per annum. Other property amounts in value to £2,500, and she has jewellery and silver worth about £500. (The informant allowed the interviewer to take down extracts from her solicitor's account.) For many years she had been a teacher in a training college, having obtained an MA, but had given that up in the 1930s to nurse her mother, from whom she had inherited most of her property. Her father had owned a big store in Edinburgh. She had loaned £1,000 to a nephew to start a farm, but is paid no interest and does not give the impression of expecting to see it again. Miss Wythenhurst remains a keen churchgoer, and frequently visits the cinema and theatre. She also stays frequently with relatives and friends. She believes she is of the lower middle class. She gave an informed reply to a question about the kind of people in poverty, referring to large families, the unemployed, the families of men in prison and old people whose savings had been used up. 'I fear that the poor will always be with us, but education could still help mismanagement. Teach the young adults to look after their money and use it to the best of their abilities. That will help.'
Ranked 1

11. Colonel and Mrs Baglie are aged 83 and 66 respectively, and they live in a four-bedroomed detached house in spacious grounds near Bournemouth. His father had been the managing director of a shipping firm, and her family were 'Scottish landed gentry'. They considered they belonged to the upper middle class. They estimated that, between them, their stocks and shares were worth £60,000, and that savings (mainly invested with building societies), house and other property amounted to at least another £30,000. They still own land and houses in Scotland, from which rents are drawn. Unearned income is estimated at £3,500, in addition to the army pension. They have no children and, unusually for wealthy people, little or no contact with other relatives, seeing most of the resident maid, a non-resident gardener and a former servant, who stays with

them frequently in the year. He said that, 'No healthy person need be poor. Poverty means thinking of every penny you spend, even on food and heat . . . I think the Welfare State has done an awful lot of harm by leading the population to expect the government to do everything for them. It has undermined the feeling of responsibility that a man owes to his family. But we cannot go back to pre-Welfare State days. The country needs a good leader. [The government] should not exaggerate class consciousness.'
Ranked 6

The Rich and the Poor

One method of highlighting the characteristics of the rich is to compare them with the poor. A range of criteria were applied and are illustrated in Table 9.5. We chose to compare the top 5 per cent of households with the bottom 5 per cent. Note that our method was to rank households *after* combining non-asset income in the previous year with annuitized income, *and* after expressing the result as a percentage of the household's supplementary benefit standard. Both groups of households were smaller, on average, than other households, and each contained rather fewer than 5 per cent of the sample population. Most of the differences were of a kind that would be expected. Nearly nine tenths of the poor were of manual occupational status, and three quarters said they were working class. Nine tenths of the rich were of non-manual occupational status, and four fifths said they were middle class. Only a few of the poor owned their homes, and only a few of the rich did not. By a number of measures, far more of the poor than of the rich experienced deprivation; indeed, on the basis of selected social customs and activities, possession of household facilities and certain common consumer durables, a very high proportion, ranging from nearly half to two thirds, were deprived. Only a quarter of the poorest 5 per cent were principally dependent for an income upon earnings, compared with over two thirds. Over a third of the poor depended on supplementary benefits, and another fifth were eligible to receive supplementary benefit. A higher proportion of the poor than of the rich were aged 65 and over, and more households contained children. As the table shows, the middle-aged were disproportionately represented among the rich.[1] As would be expected among a group with a larger proportion of old people, a higher proportion also had some trace of disablement, but even when standardized for age, the proportion of disabled in poor households is still higher. The table also brings out the big difference in resources between the two. As the first three lines of the table show, if the mean assets, income and income net worth of these two groups of households are compared, the rich have 909 times, seven times and twelve times as much, respectively, as the poor.

1. The age-distribution of different groups among the richest 10 per cent is shown in Table A.23, Appendix Eight, page 1011.

Table 9.5. Richest and poorest households compared.

Characteristic	Richest 5%[a]	Poorest 5%[a]
Household resources		
1. Mean value of assets	£28,185	£31
2. Mean net disposable income	£2,934	£420
3. Mean income net worth	£4,976	£423
4. Principally dependent for income on earnings	69%	27%
5. Overdraft facilities	17%	0%

Household characteristics	Percentage of households	
6. Owner-occupiers	87	7
7. Council tenants	0	45
8. Sometimes or often short of fuel	0	22
9. No garden or too small to sit in	12	37
10. Large garden	56	5
11. Not got sole use of four household facilities	5	39
12. Fewer than 6 of 10 selected consumer durables	7	64
13. Head of manual status	12	88
14. Either chief wage-earner or housewife or both say they are working class	19	72
15. Either chief wage-earner or housewife or both say they are middle class	81	28
16. Have dependent children	20	26
17. Have one-parent families	3	14

Both groups consisted of a wide variety of types of household. Rather more of the poor than of the rich lived in single-person households, households with several children and one-parent households, and fewer lived in households consisting of three or four adults. (Table A.24, Appendix Eight, page 1011.)

The Configuration of Wealth and Class

The presentation of both distributions and case-studies show how embedded among the rich are households of professional class. Company directors and farmers are, of course, represented among those with greatest wealth (and sometimes the latter are misclassified as of lower non-manual status when they own high values of land and farm buildings and machinery). Those owning vast tracts of industry and other property are the richest people in the population, but among the top 5 per cent they are relatively few in number. The striking fact is the large representation of chartered accountants, doctors, teachers, senior ad-

Table 9.5 – contd

Individual characteristics	Percentage of individuals in such households	
18. Under 15	20	38
19. 40–59	34	10
20. 65 or more	16	25
21. Not born in United Kingdom	7	5
22. Non-white	3	6
23. Scoring 1 or more on disability index	22	37
24. Adults of 25 or over with more than 10 years education	56	5
25. Unemployed one or more weeks in year (among those available for employment)	2	16
26. Employed or self-employed	52	20
27. Receiving supplementary benefit	0	35
28. Eligible for supplementary benefit but not receiving	1[b]	22
29. Feels poor sometimes or always (among chief wage-earners and housewives only)	4	59
30. Little or no support routinely or in emergencies from family	34	24
31. Severe social deprivation (scores of 6 or more on social deprivation index)	10	58
32. Member of one or more types of social minority	39	70
33. Not had holiday away	29	79

NOTES: [a]Households ranked on criteria of non-asset income last year, plus annuitized value of assets expressed as a percentage of the government poverty standard.
[b]Two pensioners in otherwise prosperous households.

ministrative civil servants and others with professional qualifications. Some are themselves landowners or farmers, or have transferred ownership of a farm to a company in which they hold a controlling interest and from which they receive a salary. A large number who have been upwardly mobile appear to have obtained their education and their high income and status partly upon the base of parental holdings of property and middle-class living standards. Where they have manual backgrounds, there is usually a non-manual wife or other relative in the offing.

More people of non-manual than of manual status are numbered among those with top-ranking incomes, but even more among those with top-ranking assets. Non-manual groups are more distinguishable from manual groups in the wealth that they own than in the incomes they receive, and their superior living standards derive in large measure from that fact. Table 9.6 shows the higher percent-

Table 9.6. *Percentages of persons of different class in top 20 per cent of households, ranked respectively according to income, assets and income net worth as a percentage of the state's poverty standard.*

	Percentage in top 20% of households			
Class of head or chief wage-earner	(1) Net disposable household income last year	(2) Net value of household assets	(3) Income net worth as % of state's poverty standard	Number
Professional or managerial	64	67	53	410–16
Other non-manual	27	32	24	1,259–77
Manual	18	7	9	2,327–569
All classes	25	21	18	4,002–256

ages of non-manual than manual groups finding their way into the affluent ranks of society – as determined by different criteria of riches.

As indirect illustration of the close relationship between high occupational class and riches, Table 9.7 shows the striking difference in mean value of assets between income units of professional class, and other income units. Trends suggested by the presentation of means can sometimes be unrepresentative. The table therefore also shows the proportion of people in households with non-asset income last year *plus* annuitized assets of 300 per cent or more of the state poverty standard. This therefore takes account of variations in composition of households and presence of two or more income units in some households. Again, the advantages of people of professional class, and to a lesser extent of managerial class, is striking.

The advantage of professional groups over other groups was pronounced in the case of earned incomes, but was more pronounced when other resources were taken into the reckoning. Households of professional status had a mean non-asset income of 252 per cent of that of households of unskilled manual status, but the percentage rose to 369 when the annuitized value of assets was added and to 382 when the value of employer welfare benefits in kind was further added (Table 9.8). The value of private and public social services in kind reduced only slightly this differential. Readers should note that household composition is not standardized in making these comparisons. If such composition was standardized, the differential would tend to be wider. There was, as noted above, both a slight underrepresentation of high-income households among those giving further information on assets and employer fringe benefits, and some understatement of

Table 9.7. *Mean value of total net assets of income units of different occupational class.*

Occupational class of income unit	Mean assets £	People in units		Income net worth 300% or more of state's poverty standard
		No.	%	
Professional	16,516	244	5	67
Managerial	6,326	187	4	43
Higher supervisory	6,786	442	10	36
Lower supervisory	6,588	556	12	30
Routine non-manual	1,159	367	8	20
Skilled manual	1,420	1,516	33	12
Partly skilled manual	877	778	17	11
Unskilled manual	442	449	10	8

the value of assets on the part of the wealthiest households. I have therefore included 'adjusted' estimates .n the table. These are, of course, approximate only, but suggest that the ratio of advantage was really around four to one rather than around three and a half to one.

People of manual class who had reached the top ranks of income or of wealth more often came from non-manual origins than those who remained in the bottom ranks. Among heads of households or chief wage-earners of manual class who were in the top 10 per cent of households (ranked as in Table 9.5 above), nearly half had non-manual fathers; but in the bottom 10 per cent, only one in six did so. The possession of a father in a non-manual job not only gives any children chances of better schooling, a better-paid job and a home at the stage of building a family themselves in their twenties or thirties. They have chances of inheriting wealth much later in life too. This point has been made by Harbury, who has shown that inheritance, or at least the capacity of families to maintain and augment their wealth, remains of great importance, though the distinction between the accumulation and the inheritance of wealth is not easy to draw.[1]

How resources come to be related differentially to both the occupational class of the individual and the rather more complex social class of the income unit or

1. 'There was no very marked change in the creation of the personal fortunes of the top wealth-leavers of the generations of the mid-twenties and the mid-fifties of this century' – Harbury, C. D., 'Inheritance and the Distribution of Personal Wealth in Britain', *Economic Journal*, December 1962, pp. 866–7.

Table 9.8. *The cumulative effect on the mean value in the last year of the resources of households in different occupational classes.*

Social class of head of households	Non-asset income	and annuitized value of assets	and employer fringe benefits	and value social services in kind	and private income in kind	Minimum number
Professional	2,157	3,329	3,498	3,824	3,894	79
Managerial	1,585	2,072	2,197	2,483	2,544	61
Higher supervisory	1,464	2,022	2,152	2,463	2,525	145
Lower supervisory	1,133	1,607	1,702	1,933	2,016	186
Routine non-manual	1,008	1,216	1,287	1,477	1,533	103
Skilled manual	1,092	1,220	1,249	1,440	1,509	497
Partly skilled manual	1,025	1,089	1,106	1,276	1,349	244
Unskilled manual	855	903	916	1,067	1,110	154
Professional as a % of unskilled						
Professional	252	369	382	358	351	79
Professional (adjusted estimate)	[252]	[415]	[425]	[400]	[390]	79
Unskilled	100	100	100	100	100	154
Resources as a % of non-asset income						
Professional	100	154	162	177	181	79
Unskilled	100	106	107	125	130	154

NOTE: Instead of the annuitized value, a rental value of owner-occupied housing (7 per cent of the capital value) has been included in the second and subsequent columns.

the household to which the individual belongs must therefore be a major strand of the inquiry. The subject will be explored in Chapter 10 and succeeding chapters.

Separate Elites or Ruling Class?

The survey provided data, admittedly incomplete, which are relevant to the question of whether the rich consist of a power elite or a ruling class. The influential study of C. Wright Mills[1] suggested there were separate institutional areas of society, in the economy, in politics and the military, each commanded by an elite which was closely associated and integrated with the elites commanding other areas. The separateness of these elites as social entities is hard to sustain. Examination of our household questionnaires suggested less separation of areas and more homogeneously structured living patterns, social associations and attitudes than would be warranted by such a plural approach. Thus people of high occupational status but different occupations shared similar types of advantage – for example, in fringe benefits at work, or accoutrements of the home – and though there were instances of some moving into the same occupations (and businesses and farms) as their fathers, there were many more instances where they moved into different occupations, albeit of similar occupational status. Through family and local networks, and in particular through styles of living, command of, or at least high position in, some institutional spheres was converted into allegiance to a general class. It was clear that the flying start afforded by parents, and especially if reinforced by marriage to someone of similarly high status, had allowed people to maintain their position of advantage. Far more had had long years of education, and far more now owned houses and other assets of greater value than their contemporaries. Inheritance of wealth must not be interpreted just as a 'passive' factor in life chances. It provides advantage in securing admission to top private schools, supplementing education, offering the surroundings and leisure to meet well-endowed individuals of the opposite sex, secure credit and launch new businesses, offset risks and secure disproportionate representation in political bodies. But neither must inheritance of wealth be examined just as a kind of social and political springboard. There are continual threats to remove it, and the continuous actions which are taken to *defend* and *extend* it form a major part of any development of theory. Here the competitive threats of individuals or groups have to be distinguished from the threats of society. Men can become bankrupt and penniless without the system of capital or property being in any way impaired. So we have to examine both the processes of economic and social mobility *and* the processes by which the institutional infrastructure of capital or property is

1. Mills, C. W., *The Power Elite*. Oxford University Press, 1959. For a recent commentary, see Stanworth, P., and Giddens, A., *Elites and Power in British Society*, Cambridge University Press, 1974, esp. chapters by Giddens and Rex.

established and maintained – through parliamentary legislation, government regulation and administration and the formation and dissemination of cultural values.

This could, of course, take us far beyond the scope of this particular survey, but certain consequential steps may be suggested. The sociologist can examine how wealth is unequally distributed not merely by examining, as we have tried to do, the meanings of wealth and the units of ownership and the social and other characteristics of wealth-holders. He can proceed also by examining the sources of wealth, or the flows over the life-cycle; and the institutional structure of wealth.

The Sources of Wealth

Even without a specially directed series of questions, our interviews with the richest 1 per cent and 5 per cent of the sample draw attention to the considerable importance of inheritance of land and property, for example, on the death of a spouse or a parent, and also upon marriage or the establishment by a young adult of a bachelor home, in explaining substantial assets. This is in conformity with studies using other approaches,[1] and suggests that those arguing for the precedence of accumulation over inheritance, and therefore that differences in age explain a lot of inequality in the distribution of wealth, are placing the emphasis wrongly.[2] Moreover, when household assets and incomes are studied in survey conditions, the influence of family upon educational career and occupational choice and status would be hard to contravert. In various ways, people with high incomes as well as large assets have 'inherited' much from parents and family. The usual distinction between 'accumulation' and 'inheritance' is not easy to draw. It is assumed that wealth derived from invention, commerce, exploitation of land and other property, and a combination of thrift and high incomes, is attributable to individual skill, judgement and hard work. In some instances, this may be so; in most instances, skill or salary is enhanced by pledges of wealth in the first place. Our analysis shows the value of tracing riches through the life-cycle. A central question would be: from what different sources, and at what times in a man's life, did his wealth come? We would want to examine social conventions about gifts, such as upon a 21st birthday, weddings, the birth of a child; inheritance of position in a family firm; loans to start a family business or other-

---

1. Harbury, 'Inheritance and the Distribution of Personal Wealth in Britain'; Harbury, C., and McMahon, P., 'Inheritance and the Characteristics of Top Wealth Leavers in Britain', *Economic Journal*, September 1973; Todd, J. E., and Jones, L. M., *Matrimonial Property*, for the OPCS, HMSO, London, 1972. The thesis has also attracted powerful support for the United States. See, for example, Lundberg, F., *The Rich and the Super-Rich*, Nelson, 1969.

2. For example, Polanyi, G., and Wood, J. B., *How Much Inequality?*, Institute of Economic Affairs, London, 1974.

wise to assist employment; lump sums and golden handshakes after long occupational service; maintenance of interests in companies after leading roles are relinquished upon retirement; rights to property by virtue of type of employment; free or preferential issue of shares to share-holders and employees; sudden booms in the stock market or property market; and windfalls due to fluctuations in the economy or changes in the fortunes of tradition. We would expect class of origin, transmission between the generations and the accrual value of holdings obtained early in life to be major variables in the analysis of distribution -- but only by grace of the institutional structure of wealth.

The Institutional Structure of Wealth

Riches are not only inherited or made: to be riches they have to be unavailable to the vast majority of the population. A theory of riches depends not only on theories of acquisition – how much wealth is inherited, accumulated by entrepreneurial effort or earned by the exercise of scarce skills. It depends also on theories of denial of access to wealth – through selective succession, testamentary concentration, limitation of entry to the professions, monopolization of capital and property or at least severe restriction on the opportunity to acquire land and property. The law and the values and norms of society have to be examined, and also the part played by different institutions and agencies distributing wealth or controlling access to wealth. Each of them, like the building societies, the insurance companies and the banks, operate social rules by which access to the asset is controlled. If we are to understand how wealth arises and is unequally distributed, we have to explain their constitution, rules of operation and membership.[1] Over time, we can examine their relative growth and decline, and make estimates both of their share of aggregate wealth and the extent to which they contribute to the concentration of wealth among the population. The survey merely produced illustrations of their operation, and showed their combined effect on the distribution.

Some people showed us statements describing portfolios of stocks and shares and confessed how dependent they were on bank investment specialists, solicitors and brokers. Others revealed the extent of their dependence on overdraft facilities provided by a bank. Still others called our attention to different rates of interest on savings and deposits. In Chapter 13, we discuss how the most costly homes were being paid for more cheaply through endowment policies than were the least costly homes through mortgages from building societies. In investigating the institutional structure of wealth, then, we have to show not only why some people cannot become clients or customers, but why the richest customers and

1. An honourable attempt to explain the relationship of insurance companies to the structure of inequality will be found, for example, in *Your Money and Your Life: Insurance Companies and Pension Funds*, Counter Information Services, London, 1974.

clients enjoy disproportionately favourable terms. It is only by explaining both phenomena that the persistence of vast wealth can be explained. Otherwise the spread of shareholding and owner-occupation might have been expected to lead quickly to equality in the course of this century.

In practice, far from squeezing the rich, the tax system aids and abets them, in spite of concessions made to people with small amounts of savings and other forms of wealth. Until 1974, estate duty, for example, could be avoided or reduced by passing on wealth more than seven years before death, buying agricultural land, taking out insurance, or establishing trusts, and the richest people could generally employ the most astute advice. In 1974, capital transfer tax was introduced to replace estate duty.[1] Although special relief for agricultural land, business assets and woodlands has been withdrawn, and although tax is levied at progressive rates on the cumulative total of gifts made during a person's lifetime, it has so far been a mild measure and is already subject to avoidance. As with death duties, there was no tax on the first £15,000 in the mid 1970s and for higher values the rates of tax were lower than in the case of estate duty. Capital passing between husband and wife is exempt. Its longer-term effects remain to be seen, but seem unlikely to be more radical for the distribution of wealth than estate duty.[2] When first announced, the proposed wealth tax was not to be levied on amounts under £100,000.[3] In 1976, the Chancellor of the Exchequer announced deferment of the measure. There are other examples of taxes and tax allowances which are, in practice, found to be not unfavourable to the rich. Tax relief increases with the amount of interest payable on a mortgage, for example. In the case of government securities which are free of tax, the rate of interest may be low, but through such securities the tax liabilities of really wealthy people can be reduced.[4] The rich have complex types of resource which can be interchanged defensively. They have the means to employ skilled accountants and tax consultants. And, less directly, they exercise power to influence the form of the rules which are applied to them through legislation and administrative regulation.

The Proselytization of Life-styles

I have stressed the *active* defence and promotion by the rich of their resources and interests. This affords part, but only part, of the explanation of inequality and hence of poverty. It helps to show how some groups in society secure a disproportionately large share of available resources, thus diminishing the share avail-

1. *Capital Transfer Tax*, Cmnd 5705, H M S O, London, 1974. Gifts of up to £1,000 a year were exempted, and a nil rate of tax was applied to the first £15,000 of total transfers in a lifetime.
2. For a discussion of avoidance, see Field, F., Meacher, M., and Pond, C., *To Him Who Hath*, Penguin Books, Harmondsworth, 1977, pp. 157–61.
3. *Wealth Tax*, Cmnd 5704, H M S O, London, 1974.
4. See the discussion in Atkinson, *The Economics of Inequality*, Chapter 8.

able to others. Of course, this happens less from any qualities which they as individuals possess, or from any actions which they as individuals or in groups take, than from the institutionalized structure erected by society, part of which they inhabit.

There is another part of the explanation, which is the second theme of this book – the creation of a style of living. The rich are not only favoured by the system, and exploit it. They actively shape its standards or values. They set fashions which become the styles sought after by the mass of the population. Over a period of time, luxuries which they enjoy become the necessities of society (though of course they are in the interim replaced by new luxuries). They foster the values which preserve their own status and induce deference. These values are values which condone, if not positively uphold, degrees of inequality and poverty.

More precisely, the rich play a very active part (especially today through 'professional' position) in redefining standards of deprivation and poverty as the years pass. They influence public attitudes to what is accepted as 'deprivation' or 'poverty' or 'adequate living standards' or 'a civilized minimum standard'. They do so increasingly through the authority yielded to them by society by virtue of their professional qualifications and status. This is a second, distinctive, aspect of their power. In some ways they are encouraging a redefinition of poverty. They are schooling public perceptions about both the conditions which should be regarded as unacceptable and the minimum standards of life which should be conceded in deciding desert. Weber developed the idea that status groups could impose their way of life on society through domination of the educational system.[1] He did not sufficiently acknowledge the dependence of these groups on the generalized class to which they are affiliated, and perhaps the educational system must be interpreted broadly, to include certain aspects of the mass media.

Summary

The poverty survey demonstrates wide inequalities of incomes, assets and other resources. The top 1 per cent of households were found to have received 6 per cent of aggregate net disposable income in the twelve months previous to interview, with the next 4 per cent taking 10 per cent and the next 5 per cent over 9 per cent. Thus the top 10 per cent took 26 per cent of aggregate income, and the bottom 80 per cent only 59 per cent.

Assets were distributed more unequally, with the top 5 per cent owning 45 per cent of assets (i.e. *net* assets) and the bottom 80 per cent only 24 per cent, despite a wide definition of assets which included owner-occupied housing. These are unadjusted figures, and adjusted figures show that they understate the inequality in the shares of wealth which exists. We went on to demonstrate that, when multiple types of resources are examined, the unequal share of the rich remains very

1. Weber, M., *Economy and Society*, vol. 2, New York, 1968, esp. Chapter 9.

large, even when other types of resource are brought into the picture and measured – including employer welfare, social services and private services in kind.

In developing knowledge about the rich, it is clear that some method of combining the value of income and assets, reflected in living standards, and also some method of controlling statements about the rich according to the varying composition of their living units or households have to be found. Both are attempted in the chapter. The results are striking. Put most baldly, they show that the top 10 per cent have an advantage which is nearly ten times that of the poorest 10 per cent. The reader should note that the 1968-9 values quoted in this chapter more than trebled by the late 1970s.

When analysing the characteristics of the rich, the sources of wealth, the flows over the life-cycle and the institutional structure of wealth, we identified some of the connections between class and riches – through inheritance via families, denial of access to, as well as promotion of, riches via the agencies of wealth transmission, and encouragement by the wealthy of the public values underpinning the social system of rewards which has maintained, or resulted in, their own highly privileged position. Perhaps one of the surprises of the study is to reveal the considerable wealth of the professional class. Necessarily, other methods than those adopted in the survey need to be employed to develop any explanation of the structure of the riches.

There is one further concluding comment which needs to be made. This chapter has sought to demonstrate the ambiguity with which riches and the rich are commonly discussed and officially presented, and to show how these terms might be treated more consistently and clearly. This implies, of course, the formulation of theory. Broadly speaking, the rich are conventionally discussed in terms of quantiles – the top 1 or 5 per cent, for example, of either incomes or wealth, but not of both. Yet this is to conceal the manipulation and conversion from one to the other, and also depersonalizes the concept of the rich. It is almost as if wealth were being claimed to be independent of class. Some common denominator has to be found to illustrate both the flexibility of command over resources and the need for consistent measurement of scale of resources. On the basis of differences in property and market relationships, social classes come to be established and the mode of life thereby created becomes something to be defended and strengthened partly by the further exploitation of economic advantage but also through direct and indirect political action. Studies of the rich have to move beyond the processes of mobility and recruitment to the *use* of wealth and income for self-interested protection and aggrandizement. This raises not merely questions of the relationship of class to resources and to the resource allocation institutions of society – discussed in the next chapter – but questions of the relationship of classes to the formulation and administration of social policy, through law, government and local government administration and the public dissemination of views about values.

10

Social Class and Styles of Living

The concept of social class is crucial to the analysis of society and human behaviour and therefore to any explanation of the existence and scale of poverty.
Historically, the concept has played a prominent part in political and sociological
theory. In cruder senses, it also plays a prominent part in public discussion of
political and social events. It is recognized to be a more complex stratifying factor
than, say, age or sex, and emphasis is variously given in its definition and exposition to economic position, power, social status or prestige and culture. In the
survey reported in this book, we tried to obtain both objective and subjective
indicators of class membership in analysing the distribution of resources. This
chapter gives some account of these indicators and the results of using 'class' in
different senses, as an analytic variable. We developed a number of operational
classifications, which are discussed below. They are:

1. Individual unprompted self-assignation.
2. Individual prompted self-assignation.
3. The Registrar General's five-fold occupational classification.
4. A sociological eight-fold classification.
5. The combined occupational class of husband and wife.
6. The combined occupational class of husband, wife, husband's father and wife's father.

The Problem of Measurement

The state's acknowledgement of the existence of 'social class' might be said to
date from the Census of 1911, when the Registrar General sought to grade occupations according to 'social position' into eight classes. These were reduced from
1921 to five classes.[1] The criteria were arbitrary, and the classification has been
frequently criticized. In particular, manual and non-manual occupations were not
distinguished, until recently, within classes II, III and IV of the five-fold scale.
But the classification was adopted in numerous official and independent studies

1. T. H. C. Stevenson worked out the classification. His special interest was the influence of
wealth and culture on mortality and morbidity. See Stevenson, T. H. C., 'The Vital Statistics
of Wealth and Poverty', *Journal of the Royal Statistical Society*, vol. 91, 1928.

and, despite its crudity, was found to correlate significantly with many other measures of the human condition – such as housing tenure and amenities, type of education, mortality and morbidity. After the Second World War, sociologists wanted a classification more firmly based on social perceptions of occupational prestige. The Hall-Jones scale (consisting of seven ranked categories) was adopted in a pioneering study of social mobility,[1] and modified subsequently (identifying eight ranked categories). The eight-fold classification adopted in this report is essentially a further modification, as described in Appendix Six, of the scale used in these studies. Although the eight-fold classification is the one most frequently used in this book, the five-fold classification (with a division between manual and non-manual occupations within class III) has been retained to provide ready means of comparison with other work.

Strictly, both the Registrar General's and the 'sociological' scales are non-objective. They incorporate arbitrary as well as normative elements. First, occupational status is not the same as class. Social classes may be said to be segments of the population sharing broadly similar types and levels of resources, with broadly similar styles of living and some perception of their collective condition. In addition to occupation, other factors play a part in determining class – income, wealth, type of tenure of housing, education, style of consumption, mode of behaviour, social origins and family and local connections. These factors are, of course, interrelated, but none of them, taken singly, is a sufficient indicator of class. Occupation was selected historically, perhaps because it happened to be the most convenient about which to collect information. That selection has therefore exercised disproportionate influence upon both social analysis and the conditioning of social perceptions and attitudes. To put the matter baldly, by restricting investigation of the inequalities of class to the inequalities of occupational prestige (as presumed on the basis of small-scale investigations applied to the whole range of present occupations) research workers, if unconsciously, condition society to interpret, and therefore accept, inequality as one involving differences in the present distribution of occupations. As a consequence, certain differences between people which are avoidable come to be regarded as unavoidable. Similarly, aspirations for social equality are interpreted only as aspirations for upward occupational mobility. As a consequence, certain demands for structural change come to be regarded as demands only for improved opportunity and mobility.

Secondly, the ranking of occupations according to their prestige, while intended to reflect, and indeed in some measure actually reflecting, widely held perceptions, includes a number of arbitrary steps. Indeed, some critics have questioned whether 'prestige' has been treated consistently as the criterion.[2] It is im-

---

1. Glass, D. V. (ed.), *Social Mobility in Britain*, Routledge & Kegan Paul, London, 1954.
2. Goldthorpe, J. H., and Hope, K., 'Occupational Grading and Occupational Prestige', in Hope, K. (ed.), *The Analysis of Social Mobility: Methods and Approaches*, Clarendon Press, Oxford, 1972. In a later work, the authors argue at length 'against taking the results of "occu-

practical to invite samples of the population to rank the 20,000 or more occupations of the employed population; the social scientist usually confines himself to asking individuals about a small number of occupations, say thirty, which are believed to be representative, or at least common. Inferences are then made about the ranking of the remaining occupations. The identification of numbers of ranks and the criteria for differentiating between ranks are not very clear. The whole procedure is therefore a mixture of presupposition and the partial representation of social perceptions. In the Oxford studies in social mobility, Goldthorpe and Hope have now shown how the ranking of twenty occupations can be related to the ranking of 860 by asking sub-samples of informants to rank two groups of twenty occupations, one of them being the basic twenty and the other being a variable set of the same number.[1] Some social scientists in the United States have tried to avoid the hazards of a 'status' approach to the ranking of occupations by ranking them according to the combined criteria of median income and median years of schooling.[2] In Britain, Goldthorpe and Hope and their colleagues have sought to persuade pilot samples of the population to rate occupations in four separate dimensions: (a) standard of living, (b) prestige in the community, (c) power and influence over other people, and (d) value to society.[3] However, while each of these approaches achieves more consistent grading of occupations, it does so at the cost first of diverting attention from broader study of inequalities of class, and secondly of distinguishing a large, and inevitably cumbersome, number of grades.[4]

Images of Class

The conceptual and measurement problems can be illustrated by starting with the images held by individuals of social class. Towards the end of our interviews, following many questions about work, income and wealth, chief wage earners or heads of households and housewives were each asked: 'You hear of people talking about social class. If you were asked what social class you belong to what would you say?'

---

pational prestige" studies at face value – i.e. as tapping some underlying structure of social relations of deference, acceptance and derogation – and in favour of an alternative interpretation of these data in terms of the "general desirability" of occupations, understood as a synthetic, emergent judgement from a specific population' – Goldthorpe, J. H., and Hope, K., *The Social Grading of Occupations*, Clarendon Press, Oxford, 1974, p. 132.

1. ibid., pp. 48–50.

2. Occupations were assigned scores on the basis of their education and income distributions. See Blau, P. M., and Duncan, O. D., *The American Occupational Structure*, John Wiley, New York, 1967, esp. pp. 26–7 and 118–24.

3. Goldthorpe and Hope, *The Social Grading of Occupations*, pp. 27–33.

4. In the alternative grading of occupations, Goldthorpe and Hope produced a scale with 124 categories, though for some users they reduced the scale to 36 categories.

The interviewer was instructed at this stage to avoid putting names of classes into people's minds. When informants asked what the question meant, the interviewer was instructed only to repeat the question or to say, 'It's what *you* think,' or 'It's what *you* say. Everyone has their own view. What would be the name of the class you belong or are nearest to?'

This approach is not ideal. An alternative would have been to spend long periods of time with informants, noting down illustrations of their own spontaneous use of concepts of class in conversation or behaviour. But participant observation of this kind is difficult to regulate in a way which is consistent with representative measurement of a population. Some people are reticent or unobtrusive compared with others. Some who hold strong conceptions of class consciously or unconsciously avoid the use of direct terms.

The answers to the question were noted down and coded subsequently. They are set out in Table 10.1. Over four fifths of the sample assigned themselves spon-

Table 10.1. Percentages of chief wage-earners or heads of household and housewives, according to self-rating by class (unprompted).

Class	Men	Women	Men and women
Upper	0·1	0·1	0·1
Upper middle	1·6	1·4	1·5
Middle	32·3	39·4	36·1
Lower middle	5·0	3·8	4·4
Upper working	1·6	1·4	1·5
Working	50·3	42·7	46·2
Poor	1·2	1·2	1·2
Ordinary	1·1	2·3	1·8
Lower, lowest	2·0	1·8	1·9
Classless	3·5	4·2	3·9
No conception of class	1·3	1·6	1·5
Total	100	100	100
Number	1,414	1,665	3,079

taneously either to the 'middle' or 'working class', with rather fewer women than men assigning themselves to the working, and more to the middle class. Most of the replies were similarly worded and could be grouped without difficulty. Different sections of the population have different images of the class structure which are expressed in conventional terms. Strictly, we might have invited people to describe the class system before identifying their own class position. But the remarks made in the context of the interviews showed there was a difference. One section held a three-valued or multi-valued *status* model of the system, seeing the population arranged in at least three ranks of upper, middle and lower class, or a finer succession of ranks of upper, upper middle, lower middle class and so on. The other section held a two-valued *power* model of the system, of the working class and the employer class, or the rich or prosperous, or a view frequently illustrated by statements of a 'them and us' variety. 'There are only two classes,' as one builder's labourer put it to us, 'the rich and the working class.' These conceptions have been discussed elsewhere in studies of small samples of the population.[1]

Both sets of images tend to be combined crudely into a single scale in public and even scientific discussion, promoting the belief that social perceptions about class are shared more widely than they in fact are. The public conception is a clumsy amalgamation of two logically distinct perceptions – as implied by the inconsistent but accepted terms 'middle' and 'working' class. How might we begin to understand the readiness with which the mass of the population apply one of these two terms to themselves? Broadly speaking, people identifying themselves as 'middle' class imply first of all that the class system consists of at least three grades, with at least one higher and one lower class. This further implies their rejection of society dichotomously divided into rulers and ruled, rich and poor, or some similar division. The acceptance of at least three ranks also fits better with assumptions or beliefs about differences of skill and opportunities for upward mobility. And by placing *themselves* in the middle rank, they are stating, in effect, that they hold a position of superiority or advantage in society over at least one other major section; that they make no claim to the highest superiority or advantage; and that this position of modest superiority is 'central' to the membership of society – perhaps implying they are at the heart or core of society, joining the two extremes, holding an intermediate and perhaps therefore 'fair' and 'reasonable' social and political position. They are not superior and their advantages not excessive.

A similar kind of analysis is needed of the adoption of the term 'working' class. People who hold a position of disadvantage resist acknowledgement of their inferiority and refuse to designate themselves as of 'low' or 'lowest' class.[2] The

1. Most pertinently in Britain, by Bott, E., *Family Network and Social Class*, Tavistock, London, 1957, Chapter 6; Goldthorpe, J. H., Lockwood, D., Bechhofer, F., and Platt, J., *The Affluent Worker in the Class Structure*, Cambridge University Press, 1969, esp. pp. 146–56. Goldthorpe and his colleagues found among a group of Luton manual workers that a substantial number adopted a two- or three-valued 'money' model of the class structure. There were signs of this in our survey, for example, among both those identifying themselves as 'poor' and 'middle' class – and there was a substantial minority declaring that money was the most important determinant of class. This 'money' image cuts across the two principal images, and may to some extent underlie both of them. A recent pilot study in Melbourne, Australia, found income or money to be by far the most important perceived determinant of class. See Hiller, P., 'Variations in Everyday Conceptual Components of Class', *Sociology*, May 1975.

2. This has been noted in numerous studies. See, for example, Centers, R., *The Psychology of Social Classes*, Princeton University Press, 1949.

term 'working' class is in many ways a euphemism to enable them to escape acknowledgement of inferiority. It carries the imputation that other classes are non-working, and non-productive, and therefore in some deeper sense inferior classes, and also glosses over inner differences and divisions in order to represent mass solidarity and power.

No one who considers the results of this exercise can doubt the subjective distortion of reality by the illogical combination in terminology of the two typologies. On the one hand, we can note how few people unreservedly believe they belong to the 'upper' class. While the great bulk of the population adopts class imagery which assumes the existence of an upper, or a ruling class, practically no one claims to belong to such a class. In our entire sample, only four people said they were in the upper class. On the other hand, we can note how few people say they are in the 'lower' or 'lowest' class. Some of these described themselves as being 'the bottom dogs', 'the lowest dynasty' and 'the bottom end of the stick'.

There remain two minorities of great interest. Four per cent (representing, it should be remembered, well over a million adults) rejected grading. 'Snobbery, that is.' 'I don't believe in it.' 'We're all the same.' 'I'm not struck on social classes.' Some did acknowledge under further questioning that there were in practice classes in society and that they belonged to a particular class. Yet, initially in the interview, they attempted to oppose the idea, and some even in their ordinary lives to act on the presumption that society was classless.[1]

There were also those who either held a very vague idea of class, symbolized by the rating of themselves as 'ordinary', 'average', 'we pay our way', or they held no idea at all. The latter said, 'I've never thought about it,' 'That's something for other people,' or even, 'I don't belong to any clubs like that.'

We next asked people to say: 'What decides what class you're in? Is it mainly job, education, the family you're born into, your way of life, money, anything else?'

The replies are set out in Table 10.2. Interviewers were instructed to establish what individuals believed to be the most important factor determining class. Occupation did not play such a prominent part among the replies as it plays in official and scientific assessment. The most favoured factor was way of life, named by 31 per cent of respondents. Eighteen per cent thought that the family into which people were born, compared with 17 per cent specifying occupation, was the most important factor determining class. More women than men referred to way of life or family. More men than women referred to occupation. There was surprisingly small variation by age. Slightly more younger than older adults called

1. There are references to such individuals in accounts of working-class, religious and other communities, and in autobiographies. For example, Barbara Wootton wrote of her husband George that many found 'he behaved as if the classless society already existed; and what is more, he did this in a way which caused others to do likewise' – Wootton, B., *In a World I Never Made*, Allen & Unwin, London, 1967, p. 140.

attention to money as the determinant of class, and slightly fewer to style of life. Broadly similar proportions of young, middle-aged and elderly specified education, family and occupation.

Among men, more of those with relatively few years of education mentioned money and job, and fewer education and life-style, as the principal determinant of class. More women with relatively little education mentioned money and fewer job. (Table A.25, Appendix Eight, page 1012.) Overall, what seems notable is the *absence* of marked variation in the proportions of people with different amounts of education naming different determinants of class.

The pattern of answers which we secured gives, it is appreciated, only a provisional or summary representation of what people think about the determinants of class. But in view of the stress that is laid in public discussion and scientific papers on current occupation as a dominant indicator, the fact that nearly half the adults asked in the survey selected 'way of life' or 'family' as the principal factor testifies to public consciousness of what are the underlying and long-term or lifelong determinants. The difference of emphasis leads, of course, to different structures of explanation and different views about whether and how inequalities might be reduced.

Table 10.2. *Percentages of chief wage-earners or heads of household and housewives, according to principal factor believed to determine social class.*

Principal factor believed to determine class	Men	Women	Men and women
Job	22	12	17
Education	10	11	10
Family	15	21	18
Way of life	29	33	31
Money	17	16	17
Other	4	4	4
Don't know	3	2	3
Total	100	100	100
Number	1,486	1,738	3,224

Finally, we showed people a card with names or classes listed and asked them to pick out the class to which they felt they belonged. In drawing up this list, we had tacitly assumed (admittedly after extensive piloting) two of the points already demonstrated by the unprompted self-rating of class: that few people would in practice assign themselves to an 'upper' or a 'lower' class, and that in ranking themselves people were familiar with the fusion of the two perspectives of 'working' and 'non-working' class with 'upper', 'middle' and 'lower' classes. But by offering the alternative choices of 'upper middle' 'middle' and 'lower middle',

Table 10.3. *Percentages of chief wage-earners or heads of household and house-wives, according to prompted and unprompted class self-rating.*

Self-rating of class (prompted)	Self-rating of class (unprompted)				
	Upper	Upper middle	Middle	Lower middle	Upper workin
Upper middle	0·1	1·0	1·5	0·0	0·0
Middle	0·1	0·4	20·2	0·2	0·0
Lower middle	0·0	0·0	8·2	3·3	0·1
Upper working	0·0	0·0	3·1	0·6	1·4
Working	0·0	0·1	2·8	0·3	0·0
Poor	0·0	0·0	0·3	0·0	0·0
None	0·0	0·0	0·1	0·0	0·0
All	0·1	1·5	36·1	4·4	1·5

and those of 'upper working', 'working' and 'poor', we believed that more people would be prepared than by the unprompted approach to specify their own position with respect to the bulk of either the 'middle' or the 'working' class. Table 10.3 shows that there was a close correspondence between the unprompted and prompted self-assignments.

When presented with a list of the titles of social classes, nearly three fifths of the sample did not change the title of the class they had named initially. Most of the rest divided into a large and a small group. More than another fifth accepted the possibility of being more specific within the same class. Thus, some people initially saying they were middle class, now assigned themselves to the 'upper' or 'lower' middle class, and some who said they were working class now assigned themselves to the 'upper working class'. (Following other research, we had offered the term 'poor' rather than 'lower working class'.) We will examine later whether these subjective distinctions, within the two principal classes, corresponded with objective circumstances or different attitudes.

A smaller group in the sample, however, now changed their minds and assigned themselves to an entirely different class. Nearly 6 per cent of the entire sample, having first assigned themselves to the middle class, now assigned themselves to the working class (more than half of them the upper working class). A smaller number, 2 per cent, made the opposite switch from working to middle class. These figures applied equally to each sex.

Those switching from middle to working class tended to have lower incomes than the people who continued to say they were middle class, and they were distributed among broad income groups much as were those continuing to say they were working class. In other respects, they resembled those who had named them-

rating of class (unprompted) – contd

ing	Poor	Ordinary	Lower, lowest	Classless	No class	Total
	0·0	0·0	0·0	0·0	0·0	2·6
	0·0	0·3	0·0	0·7	0·5	23·3
	0·0	0·1	0·1	0·4	0·0	13·4
	0·0	0·3	0·3	0·6	0·1	18·2
	0·5	0·9	1·1	0·6	0·6	38·1
	0·6	0·0	0·3	0·1	0·2	2·5
	0·0	0·1	0·0	1·4	0·1	1·8
	1·2	1·8	1·9	3·9	1·5	100

selves all along as working class – they included a similar proportion of council tenants, nearly as many belonging to unions and nearly as few with a relatively long period of education.

Those changing from working to middle class, on the other hand, could not be said to resemble so closely other members of the class of their final choice. Fewer owned their homes; more were council tenants; fewer had substantial assets; fewer belonged to professional associations and more to unions; fewer had been educated for a relatively large number of years. They could be differentiated from the working class (to which they had originally said they were affiliated) only by the larger proportion who had experienced eleven or more years of education and who owned their homes.

Self-rated Class and Economic Circumstances

Can we give any explanation of how images of class come to be formed? The difference in the proportions of men and women assigning themselves to the middle and working classes provides a starting-point. Significantly more women than men (43 per cent compared with 35 per cent) said they were middle class, and significantly fewer (52 per cent compared with 61 per cent) said they were working class. This result is substantially, though not wholly, attributable to wives giving the title of a class different from that given by their husbands. In part this is explained by more women having, or having had, non-manual jobs (Table 10.7). But it is also a difference in the emphasis given to matters other than the job. This is suggested if we refer back to Table 10.2. More women than men said that family and way of life, and fewer occupation, determined social class. Women are therefore more likely than men to say they are middle class if they have had non-manual parents or if their style of life is 'respectable' in the sense that they own, or are paying for, their own homes, have a wide range of consumer durables, attend church locally, and live in a more desirable part of town (measured by garden space, children's play space and absence of air pollution),[1] even when their husbands, and they themselves, have manual occupations and relatively low income. Men are more likely than women to say they are working class because more take their class from the nature and amount and type of remuneration of their job, even when they have had non-manual parents. Our evidence showed all these tendencies to be significant. (Table A.26, Appendix Eight, page 1013.)

However, this might be said to be only a contributory explanation. Most husbands and wives assigned themselves to the same class, and the principal question must be the basis on which people assign themselves to the middle instead of the working class.

What differences in objective reality are there between those allocating themselves to different classes? We found a strong correlation between self-rated class and level of income and assets. Far more men and women with relatively high than relative low earnings said they were middle class (Table 10.4). In the top

Table 10.4. Percentages of chief wage-earners or employed heads of households, and wives in employment, saying they were middle or working class,[a] according to gross earnings per week.

Average gross earnings per week (last year) as % of mean	Men Middle[b]	Men Working[c]	Women Middle[b]	Women Working[c]
Under 60	6	10	10	20
60–79	17	34	15	28
80–99	24	29	19	21
100–19	18	17	15	13
120–99	26	10	28	16
200+	9	1	13	1
Total	100	100	100	100
Number	363	683	155	195

NOTES: [a]Only 5 per cent of men and 6 per cent of women in the appropriate categories gave other answers (e.g. 'poor' or 'no class').
[b]All assigning themselves to 'upper middle', 'middle' or 'lower middle' class.
[c]All those assigning themselves to the 'upper working' or 'working' class.

1. See the indices of environment in Chapter 14, pages 532–5.

band of earnings (twice or more than twice as much as the mean), only 11 per cent said they were working class. In the lowest band (under 60 per cent of the mean), 74 per cent said they were working class. Yet even these figures show there were exceptions. Some people with very high earnings said they were working class. Others with very low earnings said they were middle class.

The level of earnings does not accurately represent the standard of living. For one thing, earners have different numbers of dependants. For another, there may be supplementary sources of income and wealth, either of the earner himself or of others in his income unit or household. It is therefore pertinent to ask whether class consciousness reflects not just level (as well as type) of earnings, but of other or total material resources. Table 10.5 shows that the economic differences between those rating themselves as middle class and those rating themselves as working class become *more* pronounced when resources additional to earnings are taken into the reckoning, and when some attempt is made to weight resources according to type of household. Among those with a combined income and 'potential' income (being the annuity value of net assets) of less than 50 per cent of the mean for their type of household, only 19 per cent said they were middle class, whereas among those with twice or more than twice the mean for their type of household, 82 per cent said they were middle class. There can be no doubt that level of income and of ownership of assets are closely linked to class consciousness.

Table 10.5. Percentages of chief wage-earners or heads of households and housewives designating themselves as of middle or working class,[a] according to their net income worth as percentage of the mean for household type.

Net income worth as % of mean for household type	Middle class[b]		Working class[c]	
	Prompted	(unprompted)	Prompted	(unprompted)
0–49	6·7	(7·2)	16·0	(16·2)
50–89	30·3	(32·3)	52·6	(51·1)
90–109	18·7	(17·4)	16·0	(17·0)
110–99	33·3	(33·1)	13·8	(13·8)
200+	11·0	(10·0)	1·6	(1·9)
Total	100	100	100	100
Number	997	954	1,483	1,188

NOTES: [a]People not assigning themselves to one of these two classes comprised 15 per cent.
[b]All assigning themselves to 'upper middle', 'middle' (the vast majority) or 'lower middle' class.
[c]All those assigning themselves to the 'upper working' or 'working' class.

This is confirmed when we consider manual and non-manual groups separately. (Table A.27, Appendix Eight, page 1014.) Among both groups, the proportion identifying themselves as middle class increases when resources relative to the mean for the type of household are larger. None the less, differences in class identification between manual and non-manual groups remain. Nearly 50 per cent of the non-manual classes with *less than half* the mean income plus 'potential' income of households of their type say they are middle class. Yet only around a third of the relatively 'affluent' manual classes, with incomes and 'potential' incomes substantially above the mean, are prepared to say the same.

While size of incomes and assets, independently of occupational class, therefore *influences* self-rating by class, it is not conclusive. Why is the correlation not stronger? There are minorities in both camps. Our income data represent standards achieved during the last twelve months. For some saying they were middle class and some saying they were working class, those standards were unrepresentative of the standards experienced previously. I mean not just episodes of illness, unemployment, temporary employment or exceptional periods of overtime working, which help to place incomes in categories different from those in which they had been placed previously, but changes which may have dramatically affected living standards – such as children leaving school to take paid employment, or marrying and leaving home altogether, or persons retiring to live on much lower incomes. Our data suggest that, if resources were to be measured over, say, periods of five or ten years, rather than over one year, fewer people saying they were middle class would be found among those with relatively low resources and fewer saying they were working class would be found among those with relatively high resources. Peoples' sense of affiliation or of belonging adjusts slowly to

Table 10.6. *Percentages of people in different occupational classes, saying either that they belonged to the middle class or to the working class, who said their pay varied during the year.*

Subjective class (prompted)[a]	Percentage saying their pay varied				
	Upper non-manual	Lower non-manual	Upper manual	Lower manual	All classes
Middle	23	30	48	42	35
Working	(35)	41	58	53	52
	Total number				
Middle	120	294	157	85	656
Working	23	222	473	369	1,087

NOTE: [a]See notes to Table 10.5.

changes in economic circumstances, and does not adjust at all if those changes are temporary or cyclical (as when there are seasonal fluctuations in fortune). This argument gains support from Table 10.6, which is restricted to the employed working a full week. In each of the occupational classes, more people declaring they belonged to the working than to the middle class said their pay had varied during the previous twelve months. Expectations of a steady wage or salary, and expectations of other forms of security at work, appear to be associated with middle-class affiliation.

'Objective' Occupational Class

How far do the classes into which people put themselves correspond with the occupational classes to which they are assigned according to some social or research classification? Occupations have been classified by government departments since the early part of the twentieth century. At the time of the survey, the relevant Registrar General's classification aimed to take into account 'the standing within the community of the occupations concerned'.[1] It therefore attempts to prescribe prestige or status, and although a distinction has to be made between occupation and class, such government classifications are effectively 'some sort of amalgam of class situation and status situation'.[2] Apart from dividing occupations into status ranks, the intention was also to identify broadly homogeneous social groups.[3] Five classes were listed. To meet criticisms, and to accord with a growing practice in independent surveys, we made it possible for class III to be divided into non-manual and manual sub-classes, which was tantamount to identifying six classes altogether. Although certain individual occupations are classified differently, a comparable six-fold classification is now being used by government departments.[4]

Because the 'official' classification was not regarded as satisfactory, an alternative had been developed by sociologists.[5] We decided to adopt this alternative

1. General Register Office, *Classification of Occupations, 1960*, H M S O, London, 1960, p.v. This is now superseded by Office of Population Censuses and Surveys, *Classification of Occupations, 1970*, H M S O, London, 1970.

2. Bechhofer, F., 'Occupation', in Stacey, M. (ed.), *Comparability in Social Research*, Heinemann, London, 1969, p. 100.

3. This was made more explicit in the definition of socio-economic groups (of which there were sixteen). Ideally, 'each socio-economic group should contain people whose social, cultural and recreational standards and behaviour are similar' – *Classification of Occupations, 1960*, p. xi.

4. The first report of the General Household Survey, for example, collapsed fifteen of the socio-economic groups into six classes. O P C S, Social Survey Division, *The General Household Survey*, Introductory Report, H M S O, London, 1973, pp. 61–2. Earlier surveys had simply divided the Registrar General's class III (or both III and IV) into non-manual and manual groups. See, for example, Harris, A. I., *Labour Mobility in Great Britain, 1953–1963*, Government Social Survey, SS,333, March 1966, p. 49.

5. Hall, J., and Jones, D. Caradog, 'Social Grading of Occupations', *British Journal of*

and, after modification (as described in Appendix Six), an eight-fold classification was applied to the results of the survey. Table 10.7 compares the two scales for the employed population only. A feature of the distribution is that proportionately more employed women than men were in non-manual occupations. But among both non-manual and manual workers, more women than men are to be found in jobs of lower-ranking class. Thus 93 per cent of professional persons at the top of the non-manual classes, and 90 per cent of skilled workers at the top of the manual classes, were men.

Table 10.7. Two occupational classifications.[a]

Registrar General's classification	Men	Women	Sociological classification	Men	Women
I Professional and managerial	4·6	0·6	Professional	5·2	0·7
			Managerial	4·6	2·0
II Intermediate	15·0	17·7	Supervisory – high	9·3	8·6
			Supervisory – low	14·0	11·8
IIIa Skilled non-manual	14·7	37·1	Routine non-manual	6·2	33·9
IIIb Skilled manual	35·9	8·1	Skilled manual	34·4	5·9
IV Partly skilled	21·9	27·1	Partly skilled manual	16·4	24·5
V Unskilled	7·9	9·4	Unskilled manual	9·9	12·7
Total	100	100		100	100
Number	1,718	1,071		1,734	1,072

[a]See Appendix Six, page 986.

Self-rated Class and Occupational Class

Self-assignment to class was highly, but not uniformly, correlated with occupational class. Eighty-four per cent of professional persons, compared with only 13 per cent of unskilled manual workers, assigned themselves to the middle (or upper or lower middle) class (Table 10.8). For each occupational class of lower rank, and for both men and women, the proportion was smaller. Compared with the next highest class, the sharpest reduction was found among skilled manual workers. Within each occupational class, more women than men said they were middle class. The fact that some manual workers' wives had been, or were, in non-manual occupations may contribute to this phenomenon, but cannot account for its consistency in all classes.

Sociology, March 1950; Moser, C. A., and Hall, J. R., 'The Social Grading of Occupation', in Glass (ed.), *Social Mobility in Britain.*

Table 10.8. Percentages of men and women of different occupational class[a] who said they were middle class, or working class.

| | Self-rating (prompted) | | | |
| | Middle class[b] | | Working class[c] | |
Occupational class	Men	Women	Men	Women
Professional	81	86	15	12
Managerial	69	72	29	26
Supervisory – high	62	68	38	30
Supervisory – low	50	55	47	43
Routine non-manual	45	47	54	51
Skilled manual	22	30	76	68
Partly skilled manual	16	23	82	74
Unskilled manual	11	15	86	82

NOTES: [a]Married women classified according to husband's occupation, even when themselves employed.
[b]Including 'upper middle' and 'lower middle'.
[c]Including 'upper working class' and 'poor'.

Occupational class, like net disposable income or net income worth, only contributes, if strongly, to an explanation of class identification. Thirty-one per cent of the men, and 34 per cent of the women, assigning themselves specifically to the 'middle' class, had manual occupations. Twenty-five per cent of the men and 28 per cent of the women, assigning themselves to the working class, had non-manual occupations.

The next table shows some of the factors which play a substantial part, or some part, in shaping images of class membership (Table 10.9). Income and occupation play a substantial part, as we have seen, and are closely related. It is not just size of income or type of occupation. Expectations of a steady income, fringe benefits and security of employment are important concomitants. But self-ratings are also associated with extent of education, type of tenure, membership of organizations and occupational associations, style of life and extent of deprivation. For purposes of illustration, we have chosen groups, wherever possible, at the extremes of different continua. (Table A.26, Appendix Eight, page 1013, reproduces some of the same results, controlling for manual and non-manual occupations.) Our evidence shows quite clearly that, while peoples' sense of affiliation to a class springs from their associations, relationships and extent of education, as would be commonly conceded; it also springs from both their relative command or lack of resources and their relative enjoyment of social customs and activities.

The development and expression of class consciousness is in some ways a process by which excess or denial of resources become embedded in social structure

Table 10.9. *Percentages of men and of women*[a] *with selected characteristics who said they were middle class or working class.*

Selected characteristics	Self-rating				Total numbers	
	Men		Women			
	Middle[b]	Work-ing[c]	Middle[b]	Work-ing[c]	Men[d]	Women[d]
All	35	63	43	55	1,549	1,845
8 or fewer years education	23	75	26	74	168	196
15 or more years education	86	12	91	9	59	66
Renting council accommodation	20	78	24	72	438	514
Owner-occupier	48	50	56	42	767	895
Member of trade union	24	74	40	60	565	90
Member of profes-sional association	80	18	(77)	(22)	133	49
Not attending church in last year	30	68	35	63	796	768
Attending church in last month	40	57	51	47	392	470
Highly deprived (deprivation index = 7+)	13	84	21	77	102	170
Not deprived (deprivation index = 0)	67	29	68	29	69	62
Below 50% of mean net income worth	20	79	26	72	210	334
200% or more of mean net income worth	80	20	79	21	92	107

NOTES: [a]Chief wage-earners or heads of households and housewives only.
[b]Including 'upper middle' and 'lower middle'.
[c]Including 'upper working class' and 'poor'.
[d]Including a few individuals not assigning themselves to any class.

and behaviour, and gross inequalities more easily accepted by both rich and poor. Examples of the conceptions of rich and poor will be found in Chapters 9 and 8 respectively. We did not make it our business to explore beliefs and attitudes in any detail, and the reader needs to bear in mind the importance of public attitudes in supporting the unequal distribution of resources. The following statements could be said to illustrate the conceptions of poverty held by some rich people. Poverty is believed to be a regrettable but necessary misfortune of those who do not put aside enough savings, mismanage their incomes or are not prepared to work. However, it is also believed to be a much less harsh condition than it used to be, because of Welfare State measures, and the poor often lead a 'contented if simple life'. On the other hand, the rich see their own privileges as natural rights or the proper reward of their work. Privileges and disprivileges alike are transmuted indiscriminately by their inheritors into more tolerable artefacts.

Occupational Class and Economic Circumstances

An analogous argument can be applied to the results of assigning people to classes on the basis of their occupations. Just as there is a correlation between peoples' perceptions of class and their economic circumstances, so there is a correlation between the class into which they can be placed by virtue of their occupation and these circumstances. Whether we consider only earnings, or take a more comprehensive definition of income and consider total income flowing to the income unit, or even income including the 'potential' income denoted by wealth, whether for the individual income unit or the household as a whole, there remains a marked and, with one interesting exception, consistent, class gradient. This can be shown in terms both of distributions and averages. Thus, the vast majority of people in upper non-manual occupations received gross earnings above the average for their sex, compared with small minorities of those in manual occupations (Table 10.10). When incomes from all sources are taken into account, when the income of a spouse, if any, is added, and when the net disposable incomes of income units and even the net income worth of income units in the previous year are expressed as percentages of supplementary benefit rates, thereby standardizing for size of income unit and dependency, the picture of marked inequality remains. A single cut-off point is chosen for each type of resource in Table 10.10 but the picture faithfully represents the whole distribution.

The only inconsistency in the ranking of earnings applies to men in routine non-manual and skilled manual occupations. Numerically, the former comprise a small section – only one in eight of all non-manual workers or 5 per cent of all employed and self-employed men. In the employed population as a whole, there are seven times as many men who are skilled manual workers. The four higher grades of non-manual workers tend to have distinctly higher earnings than skilled

Table 10.10. *Percentages of people of different occupational class with earnings, incomes and net income worth, above selected levels.*

Occupational class	Gross earnings last week equal to mean or higher for each sex independently[a]		Income last year of income unit 200% or more of state's standard of poverty[b]		Net income worth last year of income unit 300% or more of state's standard of poverty[b]	
	Men	Women	Men	Women	Men	Women
Professional	90	(100)	78	75	72	70
Managerial	91		66	67	44	47
Supervisory – high	62	82	54	52	36	39
Supervisory – low	34	52	42	37	33	29
Routine non-manual	13	37	48	37	22	16
Skilled manual	29	30	38	30	17	14
Partly skilled manual	18	23	36	26	16	10
Unskilled manual	10	11	27	16	11	3

NOTES: [a]Employed and self-employed working 1,000 hours or more in year.
[b]Occupational class of chief wage-earner in income unit.

manual workers, as both Tables 10.10 and 10.11 suggest. But routine non-manual workers were found to have a lower mean, and fewer of them had relatively high earnings, than skilled manual workers. However, this is less significant than it may seem on the surface. Similar data have misled certain sociologists and many political commentators in the post-war years, and there has been a vigorous controversy, based partly on the kind of incomplete statistics illustrated in the first column of Table 10.10, about the 'embourgeoisement' of the working class.

The first points which need to be borne in mind affect *rate* and *totality* of remuneration from employment. Routine non-manual employees work many fewer hours in the course of a year than do skilled manual employees, 66 per cent, compared with 29 per cent, working fewer than 2,000 (see Table 12.4, page 451). When converted to an hourly rate, mean earnings are virtually the same. Re-weighting for arduousness, danger or discomfort and skill of work would tend to leave the balance of advantage with routine non-manual occupations. And, as Table 10.11 shows, those in the non-manual occupations derive more value (in fact from one and a half to nearly seven times as much value) from employer fringe benefits.

The advantage of people in non-manual occupations becomes more pronounced when the annuity value of their assets is added to their incomes, and their advantage remains pronounced even when the incomes of all members of the household are added together.

Table 10.11. *Mean earnings in preceding week, income and income net worth in previous year, of males of different occupational class.*[a]

	£					
	Gross earnings last week	Fringe benefits last year	Income of income unit last year	Income net worth of income unit last year	Income of household last year	Income net worth of household last year
Professional	51·05	451	2,916	3,809	3,015	3,888
Managerial	36·14	303	1,656	2,490	1,864	2,337
Higher supervisory	28·29	209	1,395	1,854	1,658	2,160
Lower supervisory	26·40	225	1,093	1,706	1,478	2,296
Routine non-manual	17·64	107	948	1,102	1,423	1,653
Skilled manual	21·44	65	1,037	1,146	1,361	1,494
Partly skilled manual	19·20	56	920	965	1,269	1,352
Unskilled manual	16·54	38	716	719	1,160	1,208
As a percentage of skilled manual						
Professional	238	694	281	332	222	260
Managerial	169	466	160	217	137	156
Higher supervisory	132	322	135	162	122	145
Lower supervisory	123	346	105	149	109	154
Routine non-manual	82	165	91	96	105	111
Skilled manual	100	100	100	100	100	100
Partly skilled manual	90	86	89	84	93	90
Unskilled manual	77	58	69	63	85	81

NOTE: [a]Working 30 hours or more in previous week.

The boundary between non-manual and manual classes is of special interest, and I have already commented above on the gross earnings and fringe benefits respectively of routine non-manual workers and skilled manual workers. Different measures of resources and of the income and spending unit to which the individual belongs are brought together in Table 10.12. By the measure of the gross earnings of mén employed full-time in the week previous to interview, skilled manual workers received 25 per cent more than routine non-manual workers. When males under 21 are excluded, the differential falls to 18 per cent. Even counting employed youths, the mean net disposable income for the previous year of all skilled manual workers was 18 per cent more than routine non-manual workers. If we refer to the non-asset income of the income unit, the figure is a

POVERTY IN THE UNITED KINGDOM

shade lower, and once we refer to different measures of the resources of the household, even including measures of the value of social services, the differential moves against the skilled manual worker and in favour of the routine non-manual worker. The middle part of the table shows that these results are partly attributable to differences in asset holdings and entitlement to employer fringe benefits.

Table 10.12. *The mean resources of male routine non-manual and skilled manual workers.*[a]

Type of resource, and period	Routine non-manual	Skilled manual	Skilled manual as % of routine non-manual
I Gross earnings last week (full-time)	£17·1[b]	£21·3[b]	125
Gross earnings last week (aged 21 and over)	£19·0	£22·4	118
Net disposable income of individual last year	£749	£883	118
Non-asset income of income unit last year	£896	£1,024	114
Non-asset income of household last year	£1,513	£1,439	95
Total resources of household last year	£2,028	£1,902	94
II Annuity value of assets of individual	£119	£98	82
Annuity value of assets of household	£246	£192	78
Value of employer's fringe benefits for the individual last year	£107	£65	61
III Net disposable income last year of household as % of supplementary benefit rate	225	214	95
Total resources of household last year as % of the mean of the household type	103	88	85
Total numbers on which means based	56–108	382–596	–

NOTES: [a]Working 30 hours or more in previous week, *and* 1,000 or more hours in previous year.
[b]Note that slight differences between Tables 10.11 and 10.12 are due to seasonal and temporary workers being included in the former.

In the bottom part of the table, I have given the results of two methods of standardizing the resources of the two classes – one in relation to the scale rates of the Supplementary Benefits Commission (which therefore standardizes between households of different size and composition), and one in relation to the mean resources of the type of household to which each worker belongs. In the former case, the skilled manual worker has slightly but significantly, and in the latter markedly, lower resources than the routine non-manual worker.

These statements about men are further complicated when we turn to consider routine non-manual workers who are women, and the economic relationship of both male and female employees to income units and households.

Among employed women, routine non-manual workers comprise 34 per cent, or relatively more than five times as many as among employed men. They were six times the numbers of female skilled manual workers and, among women working full time, more than all the female manual workers combined. Their mean earnings were higher than those of female skilled manual workers, and proportionately more had relatively high earnings. The age distribution of routine non-manual workers is distinctive in the case of both men and women. A disproportionately large number, especially of women, are in their teens or twenties. This has a number of consequences for their economic position. Fewer of them than of skilled manual workers are married or have dependent children. More tend to be in households comprising two or more income units. The final two columns of Table 10.11 illustrate the consequences: if fringe benefits at the place of work and position in income unit and household are taken into account, living standards overall tend to be higher than those of skilled manual workers. If account were also to be taken of greater security of employment, greater expectation of promotion and higher earnings through increments and (partly as a consequence) easier access to loans, the differences in living standards would be greater still.

The Cumulative Command over Resources

Membership of occupational classes therefore denotes greater significance for living standards than is implied by nominal rates of earnings. It denotes different chances of being in receipt of resources like sick pay, occupational pensions, earnings-related sickness and unemployment benefits and employer welfare benefits in kind. It also denotes different chances of being able to accumulate wealth and, indirectly through the family, different chances of passing on and inheriting wealth. Finally, it tends to denote different family building practices, risks of unemployment, sickness and disablement, and therefore different dependency obligations during life. The problem for people in manual families is not just low earnings, or unstable earnings, or lack of entitlement to fringe benefits, or even difficulty of acquiring assets. It is the disproportionately greater chance of having to support dependants – including sick and disabled as well as children. More manual than non-manual workers marry young and have children earlier. More are exposed to the risks of interruption of earnings because of unemployment or sickness; and this also means they are more likely to have a member of the household or family in that situation to whom help has to be given. More older manual than non-manual workers have had large families in the past and have therefore given up a large part of their lives, and their incomes, to the needs of dependants, and have had less opportunity to save. In descending the occupational scale, earnings are lower; other sources of income are fewer and the amounts of such income smaller; assets are fewer and less valuable; and claims tend to be made on available resources by more people.

Our data demonstrate the *cumulative* command over resources of the higher occupational classes. Although some of the details of our method of cumulation (explained in Chapter 5 and Appendix Six, and also discussed in Chapter 9) can be discussed critically and perhaps, in subsequent studies, modified, there is no doubt that the method helps both to place apparently inconsistent findings of previous studies into perspective and to bring out clearly the economic significance of social stratification.

It becomes possible even to trace the contribution towards social inequality of different types of resources. Thus Table 10.13 shows the mean non-asset income of upper non-manual, lower non-manual and manual classes, and how that mean is affected when different types of resource actually received or enjoyed by these classes are added successively. For example, assets added £892 in annuity value, employer fringe benefits £150, social services in kind £309 and private services in kind £65, to the income of the average upper non-manual household. These amounts corresponded with £98, £23, £178 and £68 respectively for the average manual household. The final figure, it should be noted, includes the estimated value of services of relatives in the home. The fact that the average upper non-manual household derived £131 more in the year than the average manual household from the social services in non-cash benefits is explained in large measure by disproportionate use of free or subsidized educational facilities, particularly after the age of 15. Assets add substantially to inequality, even adopting a relatively conservative method of estimating their value in the form of an annuity and bearing in mind our underestimation of absolute values owned by the richest households in the sample. What is perhaps surprising, as the lower half of Table 10.13 shows, is the relatively inconsequential effect of social service and private non-cash benefits upon the unequal distribution of resources. Lower non-manual households, for example, gained *proportionately* nearly as much as manual households from social service non-cash benefits. For them the value of social services received or used in the year added 14 per cent to the cumulative total of non-asset income, annuitized value of assets and employer welfare benefits, compared with 15 per cent for manual households.

Table 10.13. The cumulative effect on the mean value in the previous year of the resources of households in non-manual and manual classes.

Social class of head of household	Non-asset net disposable income	and annuitized value of assets	and employer fringe benefits	and value of social services in kind	and private income in kind	Mini-mum number
	£	£	£	£	£	
Upper non-manual	1,889	2,781	2,931	3,240	3,305	140
Lower non-manual	1,214	1,653	1,754	2,002	2,071	434
Manual	1,032	1,130	1,153	1,331	1,397	895
As a percentage of the mean manual value						
Upper non-manual	183	246	254	243	237	140
Lower non-manual	118	146	152	150	148	434
Manual	100	100	100	100	100	895
As a percentage of non-asset income						
Upper non-manual	100	147	155	172	175	140
Lower non-manual	100	136	144	165	171	434
Manual	100	109	112	129	135	895

NOTE: In this table, non-asset income is reduced by the value of tax relief on mortgage interest (which is included in the value of social services in kind), and the imputed rental income of owner-occupied housing (assumed to be 7 per cent per annum of the capital value) and not the annuitized value of such housing has been included in the second and subsequent columns.

Cumulative economic power must also be shown in relation to both age and dependency. Table 10.14 shows what were the inequalities between individuals of different age in non-manual and manual income units, and the accompanying graph (Figure 10.1) illustrates the more striking trends. The estimates refer to income units. This has the advantage that working adults other than married women are classified according to their own occupation, and not that of the head of household. It also has the advantage that the value of social service and other benefits enjoyed exclusively by one income unit in households with two or more income units are not artificially averaged out for the household as a whole. On the other hand, some costs, like rent, have been allocated arbitrarily, for want of information, to units in such households.

The advantage of non-manual over manual income units is greatest in old age and childhood, and least in the twenties. In relation to the poverty standard, the net disposable incomes of adult cohorts within the non-manual classes tend to rise with age, whereas within the manual classes they actually fall between the twenties and the thirties and do not quite recover in the forties and fifties (when children can be expected to be no longer dependent). This pattern persists when other resources are added. In the non-manual class, a relative peak of affluence is reached in the early sixties, and this becomes pronounced in relation to younger adults of that broad class once employer welfare benefits and the annuitized value of assets are counted as resources. This is true also of the manual class, though to

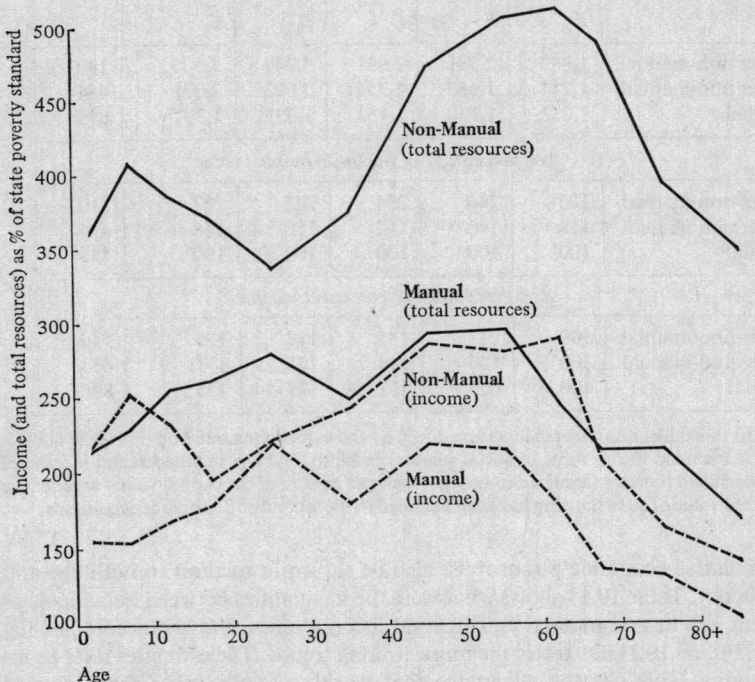

Figure 10.1. The effect of adding other resources to the net disposable incomes of units of which people of different age were members.

Table 10.14. *Mean cumulative resources of members of income units according to age, expressed as a percentage of the state's poverty standard for net disposable income.*

Cumulative resources	Age												All ages
	0-4	5-9	10-14	15-19	20-29	30-39	40-49	50-59	60-64	65-69	70-79	80+	
Non-manual													
Net disposable income last year	217	252	233	190	223	244	287	281	290	207	162	139	240
– plus employer welfare benefits	231	266	250	200	234	259	311	327	324	208	162	139	258
Income net worth plus employer welfare benefits	306	347	316	283	266	321	404	446	485	458	380	352	350
– plus private services in kind	316	357	326	293	275	330	414	458	502	471	386	343	360
– plus social services in kind	351	398	375	355	317	361	446	477	509	486	393	357	394
Manual													
Net disposable income last year	155	154	169	179	221	180	219	216	177	135	130	103	181
– plus fringe benefits	158	157	173	185	225	185	223	225	189	136	130	103	186
Income net worth plus employer welfare benefits	168	169	187	188	233	199	245	256	220	185	193	148	207
– plus private services in kind	174	175	195	193	240	206	255	268	229	197	195	150	215
– plus social services in kind	211	224	248	252	271	241	286	283	238	210	210	167	247
Non-manual lowest number	143	150	124	153	281	242	239	198	74	68	81	21	1,774
Manual lowest number	262	226	214	180	348	300	328	319	159	150	170	55	2,711

a lesser extent. For both non-manual and manual classes, the effect of including social service benefits is to reduce the age differentials among adults.

But perhaps the most striking conclusion that can be drawn from both Table 10.14 and Figure 10.1 is the marked difference between non-manual and manual groups at all ages, especially once employer welfare benefits and the annuitized value of assets are counted as resources, and even after allowing for social service benefits.

Occupational Class and Poverty

The pervasive and cumulative inequality between non-manual and manual classes is, of course, reflected in the proportions living in poverty. The proportion of people in income units with incomes below or just above the state's standard of poverty rises steadily with falling occupational class, rising from 9 per cent of those in the professional class to 59 per cent in the unskilled manual class (Table 10.15). It should be remembered that the percentages are of people of all ages, including the retired, the unemployed and the disabled. The effect of adding the 'potential' income of assets to net disposable income tends to be smaller, in reducing these proportions, for the manual than for the non-manual groups, as the summary figures in brackets suggest. For example, the proportion of the unskilled manual class in poverty or on its margins diminishes from 59 per cent only to 54 per cent. It can also be seen that the proportions of low supervisory and routine non-manual classes in poverty or on its margins diminish more sharply, and the proportions with an income of three or more times the poverty standard increase more sharply than the equivalent proportions among the manual classes. The steep increase of poverty in relation to descending occupational class is also shown if the alternative measure of the deprivation standard is adopted, as illustrated in the table.

Occupational Class and Style of Living

The differences between occupational classes extend to other structures. The inequalities in the distribution of resources produced by the system of employment may be said to be causally related to the disposition of different social institutions, and to the behaviour associated with those institutions, and with their sub-divisions. Inequalities in resources are reflected and reinforced by these institutions, though the direction of causal impulses is hard to identify. Thus the educational system tends to be graded in conformity with the occupational hierarchy, and the type and length of education as well as the qualifications obtained are related to occupational class. Table 10.16 provides an example. The educational hierarchy reinforces or legitimates the occupational hierarchy not only by providing qualifications for those entering occupations of high rank but by providing incontest-

Table 10.15. Percentages of people of different occupational class according to the net disposable income in previous year (and net income worth)[a] of their income unit, expressed as a percentage of the state's standard of poverty and of the deprivation standard.

	Professional	Managerial	Supervisory High	Supervisory Low	Routine non-manual	Skilled manual	Partly skilled manual	Unskilled manual
I Income last year (and net income worth) as % of supplementary benefit rates plus housing cost								
Below or just above standard (under 140%)	9 (7)	13 (4)	17 (9)	30 (13)	31 (19)	35 (26)	38 (31)	59 (54)
Above (140–299%)	45 (24)	62 (52)	64 (54)	58 (58)	60 (63)	56 (59)	55 (55)	36 (38)
Substantially above (300% or more)	46 (69)	25 (43)	18 (37)	12 (29)	9 (18)	9 (15)	7 (13)	4 (8)
Total	100 (100)	100 (100)	100 (100)	100 (100)	100 (100)	100 (100)	100 (100)	100 (100)
Number	299 (244)	259 (184)	518 (441)	664 (553)	414 (363)	1,686 (1,507)	858 (774)	532 (447)
II Gross disposable income as % of the deprivation standard								
Below 100	5	6	11	19	27	28	30	54
100–199	22	49	56	60	58	57	59	40
200+	73	45	34	21	14	15	10	6
Total	100	100	100	100	100	100	100	100
Number	299	259	518	664	415	1,686	858	532

NOTE: [a]The percentages in brackets are of people in income units with combined values of net disposable incomes and annuitized assets.

Table 10.16. *Percentages of employed and self-employed men and women of different occupational class with selected characteristics.*

Selected characteristics	Profes-sional	Mana-gerial	Supervisory		Routine non-manual	Skilled manual	Partly skilled manual	Un-skilled manual	All classes
			High	Low					
11 or more years of education									
men	76	58	52	41	38	15	9	8	27
women	—	—	83	44	36	17	10	7	31
Owner-occupiers									
men	81	64	77	68	45	38	35	25	48
women	—	(67)	62	61	49	46	32	31	46
Attended church in last month									
men	43	35	23	24	19	20	22	23	23
women	—	(57)	50	39	28	32	28	30	33
Membership of trade union									
men	5	17	29	31	34	60	62	40	47
women	—	—	25	6	13	29	40	(16)	21

Numbers

Education								
men	89	76	159	241	105	593	278	165	1,706
women	6	21	87	126	356	63	258	134	1,051
Tenure								
men	90	79	162	243	108	596	284	171	1,733
women	7	21	92	127	363	63	262	136	1,071
Churchgoing								
men	89	79	161	240	104	592	281	166	1,712
women	7	21	92	127	355	63	258	135	1,058
Membership of trade union[a]								
men	61	53	157	149	97	561	270	153	1,501
women	4	12	77	69	260	45	164	32	659

NOTE: [a]The self-employed and those working less than 30 hours a week are excluded.

able differentiation among those in employment by virtue of background, preparation and quality of experience. Those low in the occupational hierarchy not only lack particular qualifications but, before employment, have already been familiarized with what it means to be of low rank and have been induced to lower their career expectations. This is ironic in the case of qualifications which have no special relevance to the occupations practised.

And the more that the educational system is itself differentiated, or rather 'stratified', the more will there be a tendency for the occupational class system and other systems to be differentiated or stratified. Each system has influenced the other. Different patterns of cultural interest and even of language evolve and contribute towards social distinctiveness.

Another example is the system of tenure. The type of house in which people live and its situation in relation to others helps to confirm that distinctiveness and what expectations they have of other classes. With the rapid increase in home ownership, tenure in itself is becoming less strongly associated with class. As part of a historical process such ownership is becoming less a symbol of high non-manual class and more a system itself consisting of distinctive strata. For example, in some declining industrial areas, working-class owner-occupiers have taken over terraced homes from landlords, and a combination of inheritance of housing and downward occupational mobility is helping to disperse owner-occupation among the entire range of occupational classes. As we will see in Chapter 13, both the council and owner-occupied sectors of housing are dividing into more distinct strata. To give just one illustration, 67 per cent of the homes owned by professional and managerial persons were worth £5,000 or more in 1968–9; whereas 64 per cent of the homes owned by partly skilled and unskilled persons were worth less than £3,000, most of them less than £2,000. The difference is one of structure, amenities, size and location.

A similar process of structuration may be affecting trade unions. Trade-union membership has been a very marked characteristic of manual occupations and has been associated with distinctive sets of attitudes and behaviour. The characteristics, rewards and obligations of manual work have shaped union culture, which in turn has helped to set the manual classes apart from the non-manual classes. The growth of white-collar unions has begun to diversify the functions of the unions, however. In future, differentiation seems likely to be more internal than external. There is likely to be more of a separation of unions into distinct strata, with stronger and weaker brethren and a less homogeneous style. The growth of internal differences may therefore offset any apparent merging of manual and non-manual interests – in this case of the evolution of the unions, as much as in the cases of owner-occupation or, to take another example, comprehensive schools. The *power* of occupational differentiation, and the power of the differentiation as it has operated within families for generations and is expressed by inequalities in the distribution of resources, is likely to reproduce itself in other institutions as well as in style of living and behaviour. The hierarchy of occupational prestige cannot be treated as an independent dimension of social stratification.[1]

The prestige of people depends primarily on the material and political privileges they hold by virtue of their occupational class – though account would have to be taken of consistency of membership throughout life. Prestige or status is an important force legitimating existing social inequality.

The social estimation of honour and prestige, normally expressed by style of life, induces respect and acceptance among the poor. It also induces self-righteousness among the privileged. But symbols of prestige, flowing from the material advantages of high occupational rank and wealth, which may be enough to keep the poor at a respectful distance, may not be so convincing to those who possess them and are thoroughly familiar with them. To enjoy their privileges, the rich are induced to believe strongly in both their merits and their distinctiveness. This is a complex historical process of cultural and ideological differentiation, of which many examples might be given. Thus, in the survey, a strong relationship between occupational class and institutionalized religious practice was found, as illustrated in Table 10.16.

Just as means are generally found to justify, and therefore preserve, inequality, so means have to be found to enjoin allegiance to society as a whole. People are not only members of classes with unequal interests; they need to collaborate to defend themselves against external enemies and trade competitors and threats to social order, and to develop services required universally. The more divisive is inequality, the greater must be the bonds of nationalism, or of sanctions or rewards in favour of citizenship. Links between classes, common attitudes and even common activities have to be fostered. Through such mechanisms as occupational mobility, fostered aspirations for material goods and enforced participation in the national culture, social conformity is paradoxically superimposed upon social inequality.

There is a loosely defined set of customs, material goods and social pleasures at any point in a nation's history which can be said to represent general amenities or to which all or most people in that society are agreed to be entitled. Those who have few of these amenities can be said to be deprived. Earlier, to explore the meaning and operation of deprivation in society, we described a selected list of such amenities or customs. Table 10.17 shows that there is a systematic inverse association between occupational class and social and material deprivation.

1. The direction of this argument is to question the multi-factor theory of stratification associated with the Weberian tradition in sociology. Weber himself writes of the content of status in a way which implies it is reducible in part to class, though in part to political power. Weber, M., *The Theory of Social and Economic Organization* (edited by Talcott Parsons), Free Press, New York, 1964. This is discussed by Mann, M., 'Economic Determinism and Structural Change', University of Essex, unpublished paper, March 1974.

Table 10.17. *Percentages of males and females of different occupational class having little or no, and having severe deprivation.*

	Little or no deprivation (score 0 or 1)		Severe deprivation (score 6, 7 or 8)		Total number	
	Males	Females	Males	Females	Males	Females
Professional	42	35	1	1	167	164
Managerial	27	31	4	6	138	137
Supervisory – high	25	25	3	4	251	280
Supervisory – low	28	23	8	12	375	422
Routine non-manual	19	15	12	14	157	303
Skilled manual	15	11	12	21	878	842
Partly skilled manual	8	7	22	24	453	459
Unskilled manual	2	3	43	46	277	259

Social Mobility

In the course of working life, people may not only change jobs but take jobs of different prestige, and remuneration, in the occupational hierarchy. They may or may not hold jobs of the same prestige as those held by their fathers. And they may or may not marry someone holding a job, or whose father may be holding a job, of the same prestige as their own. Without offering more elaborate permutations, these statements suggest why at any point in time two individuals of the same occupational status may have different real prestige in the community, different sets of social relationships and different standards of living.

Such permutations not only help to explain some of the paradoxes in people's class identification, described above, but also outcomes of poverty and deprivation. Resources can be inherited, taken at the age of majority or acquired through marriage. The different amounts of earnings and other forms of income and wealth which we have shown to be associated with occupational class are associated no less with the occupational class of one's parents, spouse and spouse's parents than with the class to which, by virtue of one's own occupation, one is assigned. These structural interrelationships may have a direct association with the likelihood of being poor. For example, if one of two people with identical low earnings comes from a family of high occupational class, inherits a house and other possessions and still receives gifts in cash or kind, or can borrow, from relatives, unlike the other, he or she is that much less likely to be living in poverty than the other.

In the survey, all chief wage-earners or heads of households and housewives were invited to tell us the main occupation of their fathers. This was coded on the

eight-fold basis in exactly the same way as their own occupations, with the purpose of comparing the results. There proved to have been a considerable amount
of occupational mobility, judged by this rather crude criterion. Of course, the
larger the number of occupational categories into which the population is divided,
the higher will be any rate of mobility. For example, if we consider all eight occupational classes, then 41 per cent of men were of higher occupational class, 29 per
cent lower and 31 per cent of the same occupational class as their fathers. The
corresponding percentages of women were 42, 29 and 29 respectively. But if these
classes are collapsed into just non-manual and manual classes, then 19 per cent
of men were of higher occupational class, 14 per cent lower and 67 per cent of the

Table 10.18. Percentages of chief wage-earners or heads of households and housewives, according to their own and their fathers' occupational class.

Occupational class	Percentage		Number	
	Men	Women	Men	Women
1. Upper non-manual, father same	2·3	1·8	35	32
2. Upper non-manual, father lower non-manual	5·7	5·3	86	94
3. Upper non-manual, father manual	3·1	3·5	47	61
4. Lower non-manual, father upper non-manual	1·5	1·4	23	24
5. Lower non-manual, father same	13·1	14·1	200	250
6. Lower non-manual, father manual	15·6	16·8	236	296
7. Upper manual, father non-manual	9·0	8·0	137	142
8. Upper manual, father same	15·6	15·0	238	265
9. Upper manual, father lower manual	8·4	8·4	128	149
10. Lower manual, father non-manual	5·1	5·4	78	96
11. Lower manual, father upper manual	9·7	10·1	147	178
12. Lower manual, father same	11·0	10·2	167	180
Total	100	100	1,522	1,767

Table 10.19. *Percentages of chief wage-earners or heads of households and housewives of different combined occupational class and class of origin, with selected characteristics.*

Selected characteristics	Upper non-manual			Lower non-manual			Upper manual			Lower manual		
	Father same	Father lower non-manual	Father upper manual	Father upper non-manual	Father same	Father manual	Father non-manual	Father same	Father lower manual	Father non-manual	Father upper manual	Father same
1. With 11 or more years education	91	74	36	(77)	48	24	19	10	6	13	5	4
2. Owner-occupier	73	77	73	(64)	71	61	49	36	36	33	31	25
3. Home valued £5,000 or more[a]	(82)	71	50	(68)	39	31	22	12	13	5	8	4
4. Good environment[b]	64	68	46	(40)	44	32	27	20	16	16	14	15
5. Full or fairly full range consumer durables[c]	87	85	76	(54)	56	52	37	33	33	20	22	18
6. Little or no material and social deprivation[d]	66	60	56	(57)	45	41	32	33	27	13	18	15
7. Net disposable household income last year 300% or more of state's poverty standard	40	40	27	(8)	13	12	11	8	7	4	3	4
8. Net income worth 300% or more of state's poverty standard	(72)	61	48	(42)	40	28	23	14	11	11	13	9

Numbers on which percentages are based

1.	64	180	107	47	438	524	274	497	273	172	319	338
2.	67	181	108	47	451	532	279	503	279	173	324	346
3.	49	137	78	28	316	322	138	182	101	57	99	88
4.	58	159	93	40	376	449	227	418	229	130	273	267
5.	67	170	106	46	435	517	268	486	263	156	300	307
6.	67	181	108	47	451	532	278	501	279	174	325	347
7.	53	159	91	37	371	449	245	452	254	152	287	310
8.	46	129	67	31	316	387	219	404	227	132	261	268

NOTES: ^aOwner-occupiers only.
^bScoring 0 on the environment index (see page 535).
^cWith 8 or more of list of 10 durables.
^dScoring 0–2 on deprivation index (see page 250).

same class as their fathers (the corresponding percentages of women being 20, 13 and 66).

The categories shown in Table 10.18 have been selected partly because the numbers in the sample do not permit finer discrimination for purposes of analysis. Our hypothesis will be that within four broad occupational classes obtained by dividing each of the manual and non-manual grades into two sub-categories, resources will tend to vary according to the occupational class of the father.

The hypothesis tends to be borne out over most of the scale, though only fitfully within the lower non-manual group. A range of data have been condensed in Table 10.19. They reveal quite clearly for each of the upper non-manual, lower non-manual and upper manual groups that those whose fathers belonged to the upper non-manual class, or to the non-manual classes as a whole, were more likely to be owner-occupiers, and to have homes worth £5,000 or more if they were; and to have a combined household income and 'potential' income (from the annuity value of their assets) three or more times the state's poverty standard.

The picture is much less clear-cut for income than for wealth, as the table suggests. Not only do those whose origins were in the higher non-manual classes have a better chance of living in a home which they themselves own, but they have other forms of assets or 'wealth' which enhance living standards. Thus, for each of the upper non-manual, lower non-manual and manual classes, those whose fathers belonged to the upper non-manual group, or to the non-manual group as a whole, were more likely to live in a congenial environment (with large gardens, good play facilities for children and an absence of air pollution); to have little or no material and social deprivation, and even to have a relatively full range of consumer durables in the home. For the lower manual class as well, those with non-manual fathers were more likely to have had a lengthy education.

The measures we have presented help to show the cumulative force of occupational class, and therefore of the resources to which people have direct or indirect access by virtue of the class to which they belong, throughout life. The chances of living in a preferred type of area, living in an owner-occupied home with a garden and good play facilities, going to a school which provides high chances of educational advancement, entering a relatively high-paid and prestigious occupation, and having a large variety of possessions, seem to be due not only to one's occupational class, but *also*, whatever one's age (as we shall find in Chapter 24 on 'Old People'), to the occupational class of one's father. Occupational class controls the number of different types as well as levels of resources to which people have access, and controls, too, peoples' sense of belonging and allegiance. Otherwise it would be hard to explain the trends illustrated in Table 10.20. Non-manual workers are less likely to say they are middle class if their fathers are, or were, manual workers, and manual workers are less likely to say they are working class if their fathers are, or were, non-manual workers.

The trends illustrated in the table suggest a principle which could be pursued

Table 10.20. Percentages of chief wage-earners and heads of households or house-wives of different occupational class and class of origin, who said they were middle class, and mean individual income and annuity value of assets.

Combined class (occupational class of self and father)	Percentage saying they were middle class		Mean net disposable income last year of individual	Mean annuity value of individual assets	Number on which per-centages based	
	Men	Women	£	£	Men	Women
1. Upper non-manual, father same	(93)	(87)	1,286	1,179	30	31
2. Upper non-manual, father lower non-manual	77	87	1,113	603	80	91
3. Upper non-manual, father manual	(62)	61	841	411	45	56
4. Lower non-manual, father upper non-manual	(86)	(90)	(776)	(215)	22	21
5. Lower non-manual, father same	61	66	641	417	180	239
6. Lower non-manual, father manual	45	47	601	174	219	282
7. Upper manual, father non-manual	32	38	552	150	123	134
8. Upper manual, father same	17	30	545	85	230	248
9. Upper manual, father lower manual	21	23	526	77	121	139
10. Lower manual, father non-manual	15	25	457	61	75	88
11. Lower manual, father upper manual	19	25	450	61	139	170
12. Lower manual, father same	8	13	430	46	154	171

more deeply. There are other sources of wealth or other barriers to wealth. There is the occupational class of one's wife or husband; one's mother, and one's mother-in-law. And there is the question of career mobility: of how far the occupational class of individuals has been the same throughout their adult lives. We should expect, according to a range of criteria, that someone who achieves professional status only in his late forties is unlikely to have resources equal to those of someone who has held that status since his mid twenties. At the two extremes will be someone whose high (or low) social position is defined by virtue of the high (or low) position held throughout life by himself, his father and mother, and his wife's father and mother.

Occupational class within a household may be said to be 'reinforced' if the spouse's and both fathers' occupational classes are the same as a man's or woman's occupational class. The outcome can even be measured in the resources of the household. Two illustrations will be given. First, Table 10.21 shows the

Table 10.21. *Mean income net worth as a percentage of the state's poverty standard, according to the occupational class of both husbands and wives.*

Occupational class of husband and wife	Income net worth expressed as % of state's poverty standard	Number
Both upper non-manual	(527)	26
Husband upper non-manual, wife lower non-manual	413	266
Husband lower non-manual, wife non-manual	307	567
Husband non-manual, wife manual	311	245
Husband upper manual, wife non-manual	217	428
Husband lower manual, wife non-manual	204	186
Both upper manual	204	105
Both manual, one upper manual	199	566
Both lower manual	187	451

NOTE: Except for the topmost category, some categories have been combined because numbers in cells were small.

mean income net worth of households in which the occupational classes of husband and wife can be differently combined. As can be seen, there is a tendency for income net worth to be higher the higher the occupational class of each spouse.

Secondly, Table 10.22 shows the mean annuity value of assets for households

Table 10.22. *Mean annuity value of household assets, according to number of non-manual characteristics of chief wage-earner, head of household or housewife.*

| Number of non-manual charac-teristics[a] | Mean annuity value of household assets | | | |
	Husband in non-manual occupation	Husband in manual occupation	All house-holds	Total number of informants
	£	£	£	
Four	906	–	906	324
Three	1,091	285	988	398
Two	617	312	460	544
One	202	117	132	773
None	–	92	92	718

NOTE: [a]The four occupations were those of husband, wife, husband's father and wife's father.

in which the occupational class of husband, wife and their respective fathers could be obtained, totalling four items of information. For all households, and independently for those where the husbands had non-manual and manual occupations, the annuity value of assets tended to be higher the higher the number of non-manual occupations among the four.

Table 10.23 goes on to compare the proportions found to be in poverty according to the different indicators of social class put forward in this chapter. The material basis of the subjective and occupational classifications which have been discussed is further illustrated and the individual's command over resources may be seen to be linked not just to his or her occupational class but to that of husbands and wives and respective families of origin.

Table 10.23. *Percentages in or near poverty according to different indicators of social class (chief wage-earners or heads of households and housewives only).*

Indicator of social class	Percentage in poverty or on margins accord-ing to state's standard	Percentage in poverty accord-ing to depriva-tion standard	Number
Self-rated class (unprompted) No. = 2,864			
Upper middle	(20)	(9)	34
Middle	23	18	1,004
Lower middle	16	9	124
Working	33	26	1,375
'Poor', 'ordinary' or 'lower'	46	38	140

Table 10.23. – contd

Indicator of social class	Percentage in poverty or on margins according to state's standard	Percentage in poverty according to deprivation standard	Number
Self-rated class (prompted) No. = 3,068			
Upper middle	13	11	75
Middle	24	19	704
Lower middle	20	13	409
Upper working	22	14	548
Working	38	32	1,188
Poor	78	67	82
Registrar General's classification No. = 4,142			
I Professional and managerial	20	8	188
II Intermediate	18	14	695
III Skilled (non-manual)	17	13	547
III Skilled (manual)	30	23	1,489
IV Partly skilled	42	37	878
V Unskilled	56	49	282
Sociological (eight fold) No. = 4,095			
Professional	8	5	260
Managerial	9	5	206
Supervisory – high	13	7	416
Supervisory – low	26	17	534
Routine non-manual	31	28	234
Skilled manual	32	27	1,404
Partly skilled manual	36	27	652
Unskilled manual	59	53	389
Occupational class characteristics of family No. = 3,114			
Husband, wife, husband's father and wife's father all non-manual	11	4	400
Three of four non-manual	11	7	441
Two of four non-manual	19	15	618
One of four non-manual	34	27	843
None of four non-manual	35	31	812

NOTE: For self-rated class, husband and wife were classified separately if their answers were different. For the Registrar General's and the sociological scales, husband and wife were both classified according to the chief wage-earner's or head of household's occupation.

The Relationship between Social Class and Poverty

Finally, the implications of these findings need to be discussed. The occupational class is both a reflection of the homogeneity of rewards, privileges and dis-privileges and status conferred in the past upon the incumbents of particular occupations, and a potent influence upon developments and adjustments in the allocation of resources in changing conditions. Knowledge of a man's occupational class governs others' behaviour towards him and, most importantly, governs the behaviour of those, such as employers, personnel managers, building society officials, estate agents, bank managers, housing managers and supplementary benefit officials, who have powers to decide who is to be allowed access directly or indirectly to different types of resource. Occupational class has the function of helping to generalize particular inequalities into a structured inequality with social form and consistency. Its association with particular types and levels of reward; particular chances of having inherited, or being likely to acquire, wealth; and particular kinds and degrees of power reinforces its meaning and establishes a pattern so pervasive and compelling that it seems to carry a natural authority. It is easy, therefore, to comprehend how it acts as a kind of social seal upon, and legitimates, the many thousands of diverse acts of generosity and meanness, or privilege and disprivilege, which take place every day in society. In one fundamental sense, it can be seen as a social invention to justify or excuse greed.

But though occupational classes can be demonstrated to exist, by virtue of differences of reward, wealth and behaviour, and can be demonstrated to inter-relate, say, with the educational system, other public social services and family origins, they cannot be said to be identical with social classes. The roles of citizen, family member and community member modify occupational roles and therefore occupational class roles. And although occupational class is governed by economic class and is closely connected with other forms of stratification, it does not subsume them.

Poverty, then, is institutionalized and even legitimated by the occupational class structure. Occupational class helps to explain the low pay of the low paid, because low pay is a feature and a consequence of an elaborate hierarchical structure, the principles of which depend on the hierarchy and its acceptability to the population. The senses in which low pay is a feature of an elaborate structure will be discussed in Chapter 17. It can be explained only by reference to that structure, and remedied only by altering that structure in key respects. The poverty to which, as we have shown, half the people in the unskilled manual class are exposed is not just the combined result of low pay and an above-average share of dependants. It is the result, too, of the denial of access to other than intermittent or insecure forms of employment, with few rights or no rights to sick pay, paid holidays and other benefits, lack of assets, greater chances of becoming sick or disabled, and poorer coverage under the provisions of the national insurance and industrial injuries schemes.

The structure of inequality is not only heavily reinforced and interdependent. It is tolerated more readily by the poor and more self-righteously by the rich or prosperous than the facts would seem to warrant. Our findings begin to suggest how this arises. Those who are relatively prosperous say they belong to the middle class. They recognize superiority over a lower class and want to establish their social distance from them, but implicitly recognize that they themselves have superiors. For some of the wealthy this is convenient, because by claiming middle-class status they assume their wealth and their status to be more modest than it is. And by not setting claims to extreme social distance, they are enabled to deny that there are others in society at the extreme from them, living in conditions of deprivation. For their part, the poor distinguish their condition from that of poverty – perhaps largely because of imputations of blame. They are encouraged to espouse the status of 'the working class'. This image of their class is less revolutionary in its implications.

At the end of the eighteenth century, Sir Frederick Eden wrote *The State of the Poor, or an History of the Labouring Classes in England from the Conquest*. It was only in the course of the nineteenth century that the more euphemistic term 'the working class' gained favour. With that term securely established, the revival of the term 'poor' in the 1960s and 1970s has now come to be associated in the public mind with a largely workless (aged, sick, disabled, unsupported mothers), and supposedly small, minority. Indeed, the image of the class structure adopted by some calling themselves 'working class' presumes there is an inferior workless underclass as well as an opposed or superior employer class.[1] At a time of rapid development in many societies of a huge dependent underclass, traditional working-class consciousness can operate as a legitimating force for the deprivation of that underclass and for the relative privileges enjoyed by the working class. This can be regarded as a source of division and hence of weakness. Instead of uniting against the rich to ensure a fairer distribution of resources, the relatively poor find themselves discriminating against each other for a share of the resources which remain to them.

The larger definition of 'the poor' adopted by Sir Frederick Eden might none the less be as appropriate today as it was in the eighteenth century – even if lesser and greater poor have to be recognized, and discussed, more clearly today. For that definition would facilitate a more realistic description of the class structure and its causes. Eden, for example, could write easily of the necessary connections

1. Goldthorpe and his colleagues report that a significant minority of the manual workers they studied saw themselves as belonging to an intermediate class with a residual class below them 'made up of deprived, undeserving or disadvantaged persons'. See Goldthorpe, J. H., Lockwood, D., Bechhofer. F., and Platt, J., *The Affluent Worker in the Class Structure*, Cambridge University Press, 1969, p. 149.

between industry and poverty. 'What divides the rich from the poorer is not the ownership of land or of money, but rather the command of labour.' 'Without the most distant idea, then, of disparaging the numberless benefits derived for the country from manufactures and commerce, the result of this investigation seems to lead to this inevitable conclusion that manufactures and commerce are the true parents of our national poor.'[1]

Summary and Conclusion

Social class is strongly and uniformly correlated with poverty. We are able to show this by taking subjective as well as objective indicators of social class, and by pursuing the measurement of resources beyond the conventional limits of net disposable income.

First, subjective indicators. The 'working' and the 'middle' class tend to have different images of the class system, which are combined, uneasily and not very logically, in public usage. Members of the former often adopt a two-valued power model (such as 'the rich and the workers'), and of the latter a three-valued *status* model of three ranks of upper, middle and lower class, or a finer succession of ranks of upper, upper middle, lower middle class and so on. Very few people assign themselves to an 'upper' or even 'upper middle' class, and relatively few consider themselves to be of 'lower', 'lowest' or 'poor' class. The correlation between self-rated class and level of earnings is strong and is stronger when resources additional to earnings are taken into the reckoning. Our data suggested that the correlation would be stronger still if living standards were to be measured in relation to an extensive period of the life-cycle.

Although present occupational class is related to self-rated class, it is by no means uniformly coincident. Some people with manual jobs say they are middle class, for example, and they tend to be people with relatively high assets, above-average years of education, owner-occupiers rather than tenants and say their fathers have been or are in non-manual rather than manual occupations. We found, therefore, that class consciousness is strongly rooted in economic circumstances, as they are and have been experienced, when these are defined broadly and measured over long periods of the life-cycle.

We have also argued that the images of class which are held do play an important part in legitimating the unequal distribution of resources. Those who assign

1. I owe these quotations to Marx, who referred with respect to Eden as 'the only disciple of Adam Smith throughout the eighteenth century who produced anything of importance' and who adopted some of his themes. Marx agreed that in the sixteenth century the propertyless were more inclined to become vagabonds and robbers and beggars than workers, and that in 'the pre-history of capital, state coercion to transform the propertyless into *workers* at conditions advantageous for capital' was extreme. See Marx, K., *Grundrisse*, Penguin Books, Harmondsworth, 1973, pp. 735–7. The passages from Eden's work are from *The State of the Poor, or an History of the Labouring Classes in England from the Conquest*, vol. I, Book I, pp. 1–2 and 57–61.

themselves to the middle class accept the existence of a class of lower rank and tend to regard their own position in the world as natural or inevitable if not deserved. Some deny or underestimate their material advantage. It is particularly noteworthy that nearly all those in the topmost 5 per cent of wealth (whether defined in terms of value of assets or net disposable income per head) regard themselves as of 'middle' class.

Secondly, 'objective' indicators. Irrespective of self-rating, people can be assigned to a position on a scale on the basis of their present or last or main occupation in life. We found that according to criteria of earnings, net disposable income of income unit and imputed annual value of household resources, occupations ranked by prestige or general desirability comprise a more consistent, or regular, hierarchical system than has appeared to be the case in some other studies. We found a sharp difference in command over resources between people in non-manual and people in manual occupations, and this applied even to a small borderline group of male routine, non-manual workers, when compared with male skilled manual workers. Inequalities in earnings are widened when hours of work and weeks of work are standardized, and the value of employer welfare benefits and of home ownership and other assets are brought into the picture.

At all ages, but particularly in late middle age, there is a huge difference between non-manual and manual classes in the annual value of their total resources, when measured in relation to the state's poverty standard. Even when the value of social services in kind is added to total resources, relative inequality is only slightly moderated.

In descending the occupational class scale, there is an increase in the proportion living at a level three times or more the poverty standard. Compared with 9 per cent of those of professional class, we found 59 per cent of unskilled manual workers who were in or on the margins of poverty, according to the state's standard, and 5 per cent and 54 per cent respectively were in poverty, according to the deprivation standard. We must conclude, therefore, that the nature and degree of differentiation of occupational class is a predominant determinant of poverty – especially, as we have seen, when we take into account the class origins and occupational experience of both husband and wife.

Of perhaps most importance in the analysis has been the distinction we have been compelled to make between the occupational class of individuals and the social class of families, income units and households. The latter can be shown to depend in part on the class origins as well as the combined occupational histories of their members. Thereby structures, and hence the prevalence of poverty, can be better explained.

In the remainder of this book I will attempt to show in some detail the nature of the occupational hierarchy and how it relates to the experience of deprivation of different poor minorities.

11

Objective and Subjective Deprivation

Deprivation takes many forms in every society, and in the next four chapters some of the principal forms will be discussed. People can be said to be deprived if they lack the types of diet, clothing, housing, environmental, educational, working and social conditions, activities and facilities which are customary, or at least widely encouraged or approved, in the societies to which they belong. They fall below standards of living which either can be shown to be widespread in fact or are socially accepted or institutionalized. As we have argued, these two standards are unlikely to be one and the same thing. Perceptions of deprivation lag behind material progress or are distorted by class and other vested interests.

A third standard of deprivation can in principle be distinguished, which tends to be implicit in any attempt to define the first standard. People may not fall below a standard of living which can be shown to be widespread, but they may fall below a standard which *could be* widespread, given a reorganization of the institutions and redistribution of the means available in that society. This standard tends to be adopted more readily as an assumption in discussion about societies of the Third World than about industrial societies.

The previous chapter sketched in outline some of the components of styles of living in British society and the extent to which they are diffused, particularly among different social classes. This chapter will first demonstrate what forms of objective deprivation exist in British society and how many people experience them. Because forms of deprivation are so numerous, I will, for convenience, reserve for discussion in subsequent chapters forms of deprivation at work, in housing and environment, and concentrate attention here on material and social forms of deprivation. The chapter will go on to show whether, in what form, and how many, people *feel* deprived, and then show whether such feelings are consistent with different objective measures of deprivation, and in particular whether they are consistent with low incomes and resources.

Forms of Objective Deprivation

Different indices of deprivation were included in the survey. Those affecting work, housing and environment will be principally discussed in Chapters 12, 13

Table 11.1. Percentages of men and women, and people of different age and occupational class, who were materially and socially deprived in different senses.

Indicators of material and social deprivation	All males and females	Males	Females	Age						Occupational class (8-fold)			
				0–4	5–14	15–29	30–49	50–64	65+	Professional and managerial	Other non-manual	Skilled manual	Partly skilled and un-skilled manual
1. Short of fuel to keep warm at some or all stages during last 12 months	5·2	4	6	8	8	4	4	4	6	0	3	5	11
2. Fewer than 6 items in a selected list of 10 durables in household (incl. TV and refrigerator)	21·0	20	21	26	17	21	15	18	41	2	19	32	39
3. No television in household	8·1	8	9	7	6	8	6	6	16	6	9	11	11
4. No refrigerator	41·3	40	42	44	37	42	35	39	58	14	37	54	61
5. Does not have fresh meat most days of the week	19·2	18	21	19	18	14	15	20	36	7	15	18	30
6. At least one day without cooked meal in last fortnight	6·3	5	8	4	2	5	5	11	13	4	6	6	8

7. Less than three pints of milk per person per week	12·9	–	–	14	14	15	12	10	11	7	10	14	18
8. Household does not usually have a Sunday joint	20·1	19	21	22	18	18	17	18	33	15	16	19	26
9. Does not have cooked breakfast most days of week	66·7	62	72	73	64	67	69	68	66	59	70	72	78
10. Inadequate footwear for both wet and fine weather (excl. infants)	2·1	1	3	6	3	2	1	1	2	0	1	3	4
11. Second-hand clothing bought sometimes or often by housewife	10·4	11	10	15	16	10	10	7	6	5	8	10	17
12. *Housewife only.* No new winter coat in last 3 years	–	–	33	–	–	14	27	34	58	21	28	33	43
13. Household spent less than £10 last Christmas	11·4	10	13	8	7	8	6	12	36	3	8	11	20
14. Not had holiday away from home in last 12 months	50·0	49	50	60	45	47	45	48	68	27	42	54	65
15. *All aged 15 and over.* Not been out for meal or snack to relatives or friends in last 4 weeks	45·1	48	42	–	–	34	46	49	55	28	38	47	58

Table 11.1. – contd

Indicators of material and social deprivation	All males and females	Males	Females	Age 0–4	5–14	15–29	30–49	50–64	65+	Occupational class (8-fold) Professional and managerial	Other non-manual	Skilled manual	Partly skilled and unskilled manual
16. All aged 15 and over. Not had relative or friend for a meal or snack in last four weeks	33·4	36	31	–	–	22	34	32	37	21	28	33	45
17. Children 3–14. Not had friend to play or tea in last 4 weeks	35·9	39	33	35	36	–	–	–	–	22	34	30	53
18. Children 3–14. Not had party last birthday	56·1	60	52	51	58	–	–	–	–	44	45	60	71
19. Children 3–14. Pocket money 10p or less	43·3	44	42	68	41	–	–	–	–	47	41	41	49
20. Not had afternoon or evening out in last fortnight (e.g. pub, sports match, cinema, theatre, dancing, bingo)	40·1	35	43	36	50	21	34	47	60	37	37	40	44
21. Not enough money to have evening out in last fortnight	5·2	5	5	4	7	3	6	5	6	1	4	4	8

NOTE: Numbers on which percentages based for all males and females of all ages vary between 5,814 and 6,078; for any age group, the minimum number is 510; and for any class group the minimum number is 630 in the case of all sex and age groups, though it is 201 for housewives and 169 for children aged 3–14.

and 14, though some key items will be anticipated in the ensuing discussion. Table 11.1 sets out a long list of items which can either be shown in practice to constitute, or according to conventional opinion do constitute, deprivation. These do not, of course, provide a comprehensive list of forms of material and social deprivation, and information about them might sometimes have been collected differently, or in more detail. Each one of them really needs to be considered in relation to other items rather than singly in reaching an overall judgement of what constitutes deprivation.

Six per cent of the sample had missed at least one day with a cooked meal in the previous fortnight; 5 per cent said they had been short of fuel and 2 per cent had inadequate footwear for both fine and wet weather. As many as 40 per cent had not had an afternoon or evening out in the previous fortnight, including 5 per cent who also said this was because of lack of money. Ten per cent of housewives said that there was no one outside the household upon whom they could rely for help in an emergency, such as illness; 10 per cent that they bought second-hand clothing sometimes or often, and 33 per cent that they had not bought a new winter coat for at least three years. Thirty-six per cent of children had not had a friend to tea or to play in the previous four weeks, and 56 per cent had not had a party on their last birthday. Eight per cent of households lacked a television, and 41 per cent a refrigerator; as many as 21 per cent had fewer than six of a selected list of ten common durables or fitments in the home.

Different forms of deprivation were highly correlated, and we developed two indices, a deprivation index and a durables index, to examine those people experiencing a number of different forms. Table 11.2 shows that 28 per cent of males and 30 per cent of females had at least five of ten selected forms of deprivation, and 7 and 9 per cent respectively had seven or more. More children than young or middle-aged adults were deprived, and more old people, particularly those aged 75 and over, than young people.

Although more of the elderly than of the young, and more children than young adults, experience deprivation, the pattern varies according to type of each sub-component of deprivation. The results of applying a general index will therefore tend to vary according to the sub-components chosen. As we argued in Chapter 6, however, if efforts are made to include among the sub-components a widely representative cross-section of indicators of styles of living, the arbitrariness of the index can be minimized. A higher percentage of children than of all other age groups lived in households which were short of fuel, depended in some measure on second-hand clothing and had inadequate footwear (Table 11.1). A higher percentage of middle-aged than of young adults had not had an evening out or been to relatives or friends, or received them in their homes, than young adults, but the percentage lacking material possessions or facilities in the home was about the same as of young adults, and in some instances was lower.

For all types of deprivation, except the payment of small amounts of pocket

Table 11.2: *Percentages of males and females of different age deprived in none or one or more of ten respects.*

Deprivation index	Males aged 5-19	20-29	30-39	40-54	55-64	65-74	75+	All ages
0	3	6	5	5	4	3	1	4
1-2	34	37	37	33	32	21	12	33
3-4	25	25	25	24	22	36	15	26
3-4	33	33	34	30	30	30	32	36
5-6	20	19	19	17	23	29	31	21
7+	7	3	5	8	5	12	22	7
Total	100	100	100	100	100	100	100	100
Number	841	392	381	500	342	218	80	2,752

Deprivation index	Females aged 5-19	20-29	30-39	40-54	55-64	65-74	75+	All ages
0	4	7	4	4	2	1	0	4
1-2	34	38	34	34	28	16	11	30
3-4	24	28	34	24	28	10	12	26
3-4	38	33	40	40	44	33	22	36
5-6	18	13	18	18	20	22	23	21
7+	8	3	8	7	7	15	31	9
Total	100	100	100	100	100	100	100	100
Number	788	415	364	570	358	281	172	2,989

NOTE: Items in deprivation index comprise list as set out in Table 6.3, page 250.

money to children, there was a correlation, and usually a very marked correlation, with occupational class (Table 11.1). Compared with people of professional and managerial class, far more of those in the unskilled or partly skilled manual classes lacked durables in the household, were short of fuel, did not eat fresh meat frequently, drank very small quantities of milk and had not been on a summer holiday.

Subjective Deprivation

To what extent did people *feel* deprived? A variety of questions were asked in the survey. How well off do you feel these days on your income, compared with the rest of your family, other people round here of your age and the average in the country? On the whole, is your situation getting better or worse? Do you think you were as well off, say, ten years ago as you are now? Do you find it specially difficult to manage on your income? Do you think you could genuinely say you are poor now? The exact form of the questions will be found in the questionnaire reproduced at the end of this book. Other questions were directed at satisfaction with work and pay and are discussed in Chapter 12.

A summary of response is given in Table 11.3. In no case does the proportion of the entire sample expressing a sense of deprivation fall below about 15 per cent – representing over 8 million in the population. More chief wage-earners and housewives tended to feel worse off by comparison with other members of their families living outside the household than by comparison with the national average for people of their age or others in their immediate localities. As many as 30 per cent of chief wage-earners or heads of households said they found it specially difficult to manage on their incomes; and as many as 41 per cent over the age of 33 said they were not as well off as they were ten years previously. Eight per cent, representing 4½ million, said they felt poor all the time; and another 18 per cent sometimes. On the other hand, more people felt better off than felt worse off than ever, the numbers being 34 and 18 per cent respectively. This evidence suggests that expressions of deprivation are more widespread among individual families than is assumed collectively in discussion publicly of social problems.

The data on subjective attitudes present a rather different picture according to social structure from those on material and social conditions. Let us first consider variations according to age. Although more of the elderly than of the young felt poor or worse off than their families, their neighbours or the national average, the difference is in some instances not as marked as one might expect. The number feeling poor increased only gradually from 23 per cent of the under-thirties to 36 per cent of the over-sixty-fives. However, there was a marked increase with age in the proportion of the population saying that their own situation was worse than it had ever been; and a very marked decrease in the proportion saying that it was better than ever. Among all age groups, more people felt worse off in relation to the rest of their families than in relation to their neighbours or the national average.

Secondly, variations in attitude according to class corresponded in some but by no means all respects with the picture presented by different objective measures. The number of people in unskilled and partly skilled manual classes who said they felt poor sometimes or often was 41 per cent, compared with only 7 per cent of those in professional and managerial classes. When asked to relate their situation to that of the rest of the family, neighbours, the national average and their own previous living standards, the differences tended to be less marked. A substantial proportion of people in professional and managerial classes said they were worse off, for example, than the rest of their families. A fifth felt they were worse off than previously in their lives. Nearly a fifth found it difficult to manage on their incomes.

The correlation between different expressions of deprivation was high, but neither was it complete, nor did those expressing extreme deprivation in one respect always even admit less extreme deprivation in other respects. Thus, 39 per

Table 11.3. Percentages feeling deprived in different senses.

Types of subjective deprivation	All men and women	Men	Women	Age				Occupational class (8-fold)			
				Under 30	30–49	50–64	65+	Profes-sional and mana-gerial	Other non-manual	Skilled manual	Partly skilled and un-skilled manual
Chief wage-earners and housewives only											
Compared with rest of family feels:											
better off	22·7	26	20	32	26	20	10	38	28	20	15
about the same	46·9	47	46	42	51	46	44	39	45	51	48
worse off	27·4	24	30	25	20	31	41	19	24	27	33
No. =	3,418	1,560	1,858	525	1,355	914	607	366	1,040	1,077	858
Compared with others around locality, feels:											
better off	20·3	22	19	26	22	18	14	35	24	17	14
about the same	58·1	58	58	55	59	58	59	49	54	64	61
worse off	14·7	13	16	12	12	18	19	8	13	14	20
No. =	3,425	1,563	1,862	525	1,353	915	614	369	1,039	1,077	859
Compared with average in country, feels:											
better off	19·9	22	18	20	25	18	10	51	25	12	10
about the same	52·1	51	53	60	52	54	44	32	52	61	51
worse off	20·5	20	21	13	16	21	35	10	15	20	30
No. =	3,420	1,559	1,861	523	1,349	916	614	367	1,038	1,076	855

Own situation felt to be:											
better than ever	34·3	37	32	53	41	32	7	42	38	35	27
worse off than ever	18·5	17	19	8	14	22	32	20	16	19	20
known better and worse times	14·5	14	14	12	13	15	19	8	13	15	18
about the same as ever	31·3	30	33	25	30	31	40	28	30	30	34
No. =	3,430	1,566	1,864	525	1,355	918	614	368	1,043	1,079	860
Chief wage-earner or head of household over 35											
As well off as 10 years ago:											
No	41·1	42	38	–	46	40	36	47	42	42	36
Yes	56·8	56	59	–	51	58	62	51	57	55	60
No. =	1,564	1,145	419	–	575	535	438	155	471	475	413
Chief wage-earner or head of household of any age											
Finds it specially difficult to manage on income:											
Yes	29·8	28	36	24	27	30	38	17	25	29	41
No	69·5	72	62	76	72	69	62	82	74	70	58
No. =	2,027	1,553	474	255	761	556	370	209	616	633	515
Feels poor now:											
all the time	7·9	6	13	7	5	9	12	3	6	8	13
sometimes	17·6	17	21	16	17	15	24	4	14	19	28
never	73·4	76	63	77	77	76	62	93	80	72	58
No. =	2,006	1,547	459	252	745	556	439	205	611	631	504

NOTE: Those giving 'don't know' as answers are excluded from the table, and totals therefore of percentages do not quite add to 100.

cent of those saying they found it difficult to manage on their incomes also said they never felt poor; and although 91 per cent of those who said they felt poor all the time also said it was difficult to manage on their incomes, 9 per cent said they did not. Much of this would be explained by the different conceptions held by people about what it means 'to manage' and 'to be poor'.

We sought to examine people saying they felt deprived in several different respects. Table 11.4 shows that more women than men among chief wage-earners

Table 11.4. *Percentage of men and women feeling deprived in none or one or more of five respects.*

Number of types of subjective deprivation acknowledged	Men	Women
None	47	31
1	24	23
2	14	16
3	9	17
4	4	10
5	2	5
Total	100	100
Number	1,556	472

NOTE: The five items were feeling that income was worse compared with (a) relatives; (b) people of their age in the locality; (c) the national average and (d) previously in their lives; and (e) finding it difficult to manage on their incomes.

or heads of households felt deprived in one or more respects, feeling worse off than their families, neighbours, the national average or than previously in their lives, or finding it difficult to manage on their incomes.

The numbers of chief wage-earners or heads of households feeling deprived in one or more respects were widely distributed by type of household. More people aged 60 and over who lived alone, and more heads of households with four or more children, and fewer heads of households with two or three children, than other types of household felt deprived in at least three respects.

The Interrelationship between Objective and Subjective Deprivation

The relationship between objective and subjective deprivation was marked. This can be shown first without direct reference to income and other resources. For example, the larger the number of types of deprivation from which people suffered the more numerous were the types of subjective deprivation acknowledged (Table 11.5). The progression is marked, and consistent. Among those scoring 0 or 1 on

Table 11.5: Percentages of chief wage-earners or housewives with different degrees of objective deprivation who felt deprived in none or one or more of five respects.

How many of five types of subjective deprivation acknowledged	Deprivation index (maximum score 10)				
	0-1	2-3	4-5	6-7	8 or more
None	58	52	36	26	18
1-2	32	36	44	36	31
3-5	10	12	19	38	51
Total	100	100	100	100	100
Number	305	717	628	305	72

NOTE: For components of objective and subjective deprivation, see Tables 6.3 (page 250) and 11.4.

the deprivation index, nearly 58 per cent of chief wage-earners or heads of households replied in the negative to each of five questions about whether they were worse off than their relatives, their neighbours, the national average or their previous circumstances, and felt poor sometimes or always. Among those scoring 8 or more on the deprivation index, over half answered positively to at least three of the five questions.

The same trend applies to other grouped data about deprivation, for example, the lack of different durables or fitments in the household (Table A.28, Appendix Eight, page 1014) and to most of the individual items listed in Table 11.1.

Subjective Deprivation and Income

The broad correspondence between objective and subjective deprivation can be explained only by demonstrating the link between objective deprivation and income or other resources and going on to explore ways in which the latter help to shape attitudes. This link can be shown first in relation to individual items. Thus two thirds of chief wage-earners or heads of households who said they always felt poor, and a half of those who sometimes felt poor, compared with a fifth of those never feeling poor, had net disposable incomes which were below or on the margins of the state's standard of poverty (Table 11.6). Indeed, nearly 90 per cent of those always feeling poor and 80 per cent of those feeling poor sometimes, had household incomes below the mean of their type (Table A.29, Appendix Eight, page 1015). Again, over half those saying they had difficulty managing on their incomes, compared with a fifth of those not feeling any difficulty, lived at this same low standard (Table A.30, Appendix Eight, page 1015).

Table 11.6. *Percentages of chief wage-earners or heads of households saying they felt poor always, sometimes and never whose household incomes last year were below and above the state's standard of poverty.*

Net disposable household income as % of supplementary benefit scales plus housing cost	Always poor		Sometimes		Never	
Under 100	19	(19)	11	(9)	6	(4)
100–39	46	(40)	42	(39)	16	(15)
140+	35	(40)	46	(52)	78	(81)
Total	100	(100)	100	(100)	100	(100)
Number	153	(417)	328	(967)	1,343	(3,725)

NOTE: Percentages in brackets apply to all persons in such households.

The majority of people, then, reflected in their attitudes to their living standards the resources which they in fact had at their command. This can be illustrated in considering answers to the question how well off they felt in relation to the average in the country. Table 11.7 shows that nearly half those with less than 50 per

Table 11.7. *Percentages of chief wage-earners and housewives with low and high net income worth who said they were better off or worse off than or the same as the average in the country.*

Compared with the average in the country	Net income worth last year as % of the mean of household type					
	Under 50	50–89	90–109	110–99	200+	Total
Better off	7	11	18	40	48	20
The same	42	59	63	43	30	53
Worse off	47	23	13	11	11	21
Don't know	4	7	6	6	11	7
Total	100	100	100	100	100	100
Number	342	1,126	425	546	142	3,423

cent of the mean net income worth last year of households of their type felt worse off, and only 7 per cent better off. These figures were almost reversed among people with net income worth above the national mean.

Personal Denials of Poverty

The whole direction of our analysis so far has been to call attention to the strong relationship not just between objective deprivation and resources but with subjective deprivation as well. The myth of the contented poor is not borne out by the data. Some saying they were deprived, however, had relatively high incomes. When attention is concentrated only on a single expression of deprivation, this point can be illustrated quite dramatically. Thus, about half the chief wage-earners or heads of households with incomes below the state's poverty standard, or on the margins of that standard, said they never felt poor. Moreover, 3 per cent with incomes more than twice the standard none the less said they always felt poor, and another 9 per cent felt poor sometimes. Or again, 56 per cent of those below the standard said they did not have difficulty in managing on their incomes, and 17 per cent of those with incomes of more than twice the standard none the less said they *did* have difficulty in managing. The point can also be made in relation to Table 11.7. A small proportion of those with net income worth of less than half the mean of their household type felt worse off than, and over two fifths the same as, the national average.

These inconsistencies must not be exaggerated. In some measure they can be shown to be functions of the definition of income and of the income unit, the stability or regularity of income, and restricted study of a single question on subjective attitudes instead of a cluster of related questions, as well as the well-known problems of obtaining reliable information about on-going attitudes and income in surveys at a single point in time. This is not to deny the fact that some people feel they can manage and others feel they cannot on the same low incomes, or that some feel poor on incomes which are relatively high. But before resorting to theoretical supposition about groups in the population who seem to live at one standard and yet reflect another in their attitudes, close attention needs to be directed to the conventions and problems of measurement. And more evidence of a preliminary nature giving grounds for the existence of special social factors or pressures in such cases needs to be presented.

I pointed out above that some of the people with the lowest incomes who said they never felt poor none the less said they felt deprived in some other respect related to income. If the measure of net disposable income in the previous year is restricted to the income unit, the percentage of those with incomes below or on the margins of the state's standard who said they never felt poor was 53 per cent. If, however, four other criteria of subjective deprivation are considered in combination, the percentage falls to 35, and if six are considered, the percentage falls to 21, as in Table 11.8. Our evidence therefore illustrates the care with which subjective perceptions of financial status have to be treated. Single indicators of subjective states may be hit and miss (that is, they may not evoke reliable representations of general states); in the way they are worded, indicators may not

Table 11.8. Percentages denying any form of deprivation.

Numbers of forms of subjective deprivation	Incomes less than, or on the margins of, the state's poverty standard	Incomes of 140% or more of the state's poverty standard
One (whether feels poor)	51	84
Four[a]	35	61
Six[b]	21	51

NOTES: [a] The first four items in Table 11.3.
[b] Adding the sixth and seventh items in Table 11.3.

be interpreted uniformly throughout the population; informants may not use the same reference groups in responding to 'indicator' questions; and, finally, representations of subjective states may need to depend on *degree* as well as number of types of subjective deprivation.

Indicators or measures of resources are equally subtle. Measures adopted in this survey do not cover all the types of resource available to some families in their specific situations. Incomes fluctuate from week to week or month to month. Households lose and gain sources of income and people have different perceptions of time in relation to income.

Despite all these reservations, there remains a genuine problem = even if more limited in scope than hitherto believed by many social scientists = of people with extremely low resources who deny feelings of deprivation. How can this be explained? We will consider those below the state's standard of poverty who said they never felt poor.

We found that they had three distinguishing features:

First, *stability of personal circumstances*. By comparison with others living at the same low standard and saying they felt poor sometimes or always, they had experienced fewer personal changes. More of them had lived at the same address for fifteen years or more. More were of the same social class as their fathers. More said they were as well off as ten years earlier. To these might be added a point about stability in health. When allowing for age, fewer had any degree of incapacity.

Secondly, *frequent social contacts*. More gave hospitality to relatives and friends, went on a summer holiday and had evenings out. To a large extent, this also explains the disproportionately large number of men who were not yet retired among them. So, paradoxically, although they seem to have had more opportunity to become aware through social interaction of their own low standards of living, such interaction seemed to have dispelled some of their own sense of deprivation.

Thirdly, *other feelings of deprivation*. They were not lacking in any sense of deprivation. Over two thirds of the people with incomes below the state's poverty standard, and who denied they ever felt poor, none the less admitted that they were worse off than relatives or neighbours or worse off than they had been in the past. By comparison with people with higher incomes, more of them said it was difficult to manage on their incomes, or felt worse off by comparison with relatives or neighbours.

Subjective Perceptions of Poverty in Society

Did subjective deprivation correspond with perception of the extent and causes of poverty? One might suppose that more of those who felt poor would have recognized the existence of poverty in society, and that many more of them would have adopted sympathetic attitudes towards the problem. On the whole, our evidence contraverts such supposition. Table 11.9 shows there were similar

Table 11.9. *Percentages of chief wage-earners or heads of households feeling poor always, sometimes and never who believed there was real poverty today.*

Real poverty today	Always poor	Sometimes poor	Never poor
No	38	36	35
Yes	61	59	63
Don't know	1	4	3
Total	100	100	100
Number	157	351	1,459

proportions among those feeling and not feeling poor who failed to recognize the existence of poverty today. The specific question was: 'There's been a lot of talk about poverty. Do you think there's such a thing as real poverty these days?' When we came to examine those who were objectively poor, by the criterion of net disposable income, we found that slightly fewer recognized the existence of poverty, compared with those who were not poor.

Broadly similar findings applied to their attitudes towards the poor. We had asked chief wage-earners or heads of households to describe poverty, and we also asked what they thought could be done about the problem. We attempted to code the different answers they gave in terms of attitude. We identified the following:

1. *Punishing attitudes to poverty*, for example, blaming it on large families, irresponsible unemployed and people 'who live on the Welfare State' (30 per cent).
2. *Punishing attitudes involving immigrants only* (4 per cent).
3. *Expansive or sympathetic attitudes towards all the poor or to different sections* (31 per cent).

4. *Expansive or sympathetic attitudes towards retirement pensioners only* (23 per cent).
5. *Pessimistic or fatalistic attitudes towards eliminating poverty:* 'there will always be those who won't work', 'people who can't fend for themselves', 'the poor will always be with us', 'there are always going to be people who are hopeless at managing. Nothing can be done' (8 per cent).
6. *Optimistic attitudes:* the government was doing something about it; the problem was diminishing and prosperity becoming widespread (13 per cent).
7. *Other attitudes:* teaching people to manage their incomes better, educating people to work harder, helping poorer countries, stop helping poorer countries (1 per cent).

This must be recognized to be only a rough method of categorizing opinion. Some items in the list tend to merge conceptually with others, and there were, of course, statements betraying different kinds of attitude and sometimes inconsistent attitudes. About 11 per cent of statements contained at least two of the above list and were counted twice.

There was not much variation between these expressions of attitude towards poverty and personal admissions or denial of poverty. There was a tendency for people who considered themselves to be poor to be more expansive towards poverty and the poor in general, as well as to retirement pensioners in particular, but it was not marked. There was an equivalent tendency for people who considered themselves to be poor to be less punishing towards those in poverty, and also to be less optimistic about the possibility of eliminating the problem. When we turned to compare these attitudes with the objective criterion of net disposable incomes, there was, again, surprisingly little variation. Fewer of those with incomes below than above the state poverty line thought that poverty existed (54 per cent compared with 62 per cent), and among those who did believe that it existed, slightly more (about a third) took punishing attitudes towards the poor, and slightly less (about a quarter) took an expansive attitude towards the poor in general, though more of them continued to take an expansive attitude towards retirement pensioners. However, these figures have to be treated with caution, not only because of the difficulties of categorizing the descriptive answers that were given to the questions, but also because of the fact that a third of respondents denied there was any poverty and therefore did not express any attitudes towards the phenomenon. What has to be remembered is that many people conceived of poverty as applying to conditions experienced only in their youth or by their parents or grandparents.

A further set of data, however, is not subject to quite so many uncertainties. Chief wage-earners or heads of households were asked to say whose fault it was if there were any people in poverty: the government, education, industry in not providing the right jobs, the people themselves who were in poverty, anything else, or a combination of these. The results are given in Table 11.10. The distribution of attitudes among those who felt poor all the time was rather different from those never feeling poor, but still not markedly different. Thirty per cent,

Table 11.10. Percentages of chief wage-earners or heads of households feeling poor always, sometimes and never who blamed different factors for poverty.

Fault for poverty	Always poor	Sometimes poor	Never poor
People themselves	30	38	44
Government	22	14	9
Education	4	5	6
Industry	3	3	2
Combinations of above	33	36	32
Other	7	5	6
Nothing	1	–	1
Total	100	100	100
Number	146	340	1,412

compared with 44 per cent, blamed people who were themselves poor, and 22 per cent, compared with 9 per cent, blamed the government. Among all sections of the population there was a tendency to adopt individualistic rather than institutional explanations of poverty. Among those sections of the population who said they never felt poor, the blame for poverty was more frequently laid at the door of individuals than it was among those feeling poor sometimes or always. Conversely, there was less inclination among the former to blame the government.

These findings must be interpreted with caution. The survey method is not the best to elucidate attitudes which are subtle and which tend to vary with situational context. Indeed, at the design stage of the survey this assumption was consciously adopted, and though efforts were made to introduce meaningful attitude questions at appropriate points in the interviews, priority was given throughout to objective measures of resources and behaviour. Little previous work had been done to elucidate the problem and the data afford some basis for further work.

How might the pattern of findings which have been described be interpreted? We have found a marked objective basis, in terms of both measures of material or social deprivation and relative scale of incomes or other resources, for expressions of subjective deprivation. But these perceptions of personal circumstances appear to be largely sealed off from more general or abstract perceptions of society. Some of the poor have come to conclude that poverty does not exist. Many of those who recognize that it exists have come to conclude that it is individually caused, attributed to a mixture of ill-luck, indolence and mismanagement, and is not a collective condition determined principally by institutionalized forces, particularly government and industry. In this they share the perceptions of the better-off. Divided, they blame individual behaviour and motivation and unwittingly lend support to the existing institutional order. Perhaps the two straws of hope in our analysis are that there are significant proportions among them who are prepared to look to the government for the blame for poverty and who are prepared to adopt expansive attitudes to their fellows.

Objective Deprivation and Lack of Income

The direction of this analysis leads unavoidably back to the substantial and all-important relationship that can be established between measures of objective deprivation and low income. It can be seen for both individual and grouped items. Thus, 43 per cent of housewives who said they often bought second-hand clothing were in households with incomes below the state's standard of poverty, compared with 26 per cent of those never buying such clothing. Forty-four per cent of those not obtaining a new winter coat in the previous three years were in the same situation, compared with 21 per cent.

The relationship tends to be stronger when different items are grouped. Thus there was a high correlation between net income worth (and total resources) and the number of selected durables and fitments in the home (Table A.31, Appendix Eight, page 1016). The correlation remains marked when different social customs and activities are brought into the picture. Table 11.11 gives emphatic endorse-

Table 11.11. *Percentages of people with low and high net income worth who were deprived in none or one or more of ten respects.*

Deprivation index	Net income worth last year as % of the mean of household type				
	Under 50	50–89	100–109	110–199	200+
0	0	2	4	8	15
1–2	9	25	39	51	50
3–4	23	40	41	33	23
5–6	37	24	16	7	8
7+	31	9	1	2	4
Total	100	100	100	100	100
Number	480	1,866	706	841	225

NOTE: For list of ten items, see Table 6.3.

ment to the effects of lack of resources, not only in restricting the number of everyday possessions in the home, but on diet, hospitality in the home, summer holidays, afternoons and evenings out and other social activities. Among people whose resources were less than half the mean for their household type, 68 per cent were deprived in five or more of ten respects, compared with only 12 per cent of those with more than twice the mean. Only 9 per cent were deprived in fewer than three respects. Under personal perceptions of deprivation, therefore, rest a whole range of objective manifestations of deprivation; and under them rest sheer lack of money resources and wealth.

Summary

This chapter sets out to trace the connections between objective and subjective forms of deprivation. It starts by identifying different kinds of deprivation and shows that a substantial proportion in the population, including relatively more children and old people, especially the latter, experience several kinds.

A substantial proportion also feel poor in different senses. For example, 8 per cent of chief wage-earners and heads of households, representing 4¼ million, said they felt poor all the time, and 41 per cent of those aged 35 and over said they were not as well off as they had been ten years previously.

Objective and subjective forms of deprivation were found to be strongly correlated. The attitudes of the great majority of the sample towards their own living standards reflected the resources which they in fact had at their command. The myth of the contented poor is not borne out by the data. Although half of those living in poverty said, in answer to one question, that they never felt poor, most of them none the less recognized in other ways that they were worse off than people with high or middle incomes, or than they had been themselves in previous life. The poor who expressed least deprivation tended to be people whose personal circumstances had remained stable and who had more frequent, possibly compensatory, social contacts.

The marked tendency of the poor to admit to feelings of poverty and other forms of subjective deprivation did not, on the whole, extend to their perceptions of poverty in society at large. Compared with the rest of the population, slightly fewer believed there was any poverty. Among those who did believe in its existence, slightly more took punishing attitudes towards the poor in general, though not towards retirement pensioners. And though more of them attributed poverty to the fault of the government and fewer to the fault of people who were themselves poor, they tended to believe that it was individually caused through a mixture of ill-luck, indolence and mismanagement, rather than being a collective condition induced by institutional forces such as government and industry.

The whole direction of the analysis, however, has been to show the powerful relationship between objective manifestations of deprivation, and sheer lack of money resources and wealth, which underlies perceptions of personal deprivation.

12

Deprivation at Work

Deprivation arises in different social settings and needs to be understood and explained in relation to these settings. Much of individual life is passed at work, at home and in the immediate environment of the home. The next three chapters, including this chapter, will attempt to show in what senses and to what extent deprivation arises in each of these three.

Conceptions of deprivation at work are ill-developed. The hazards of working in certain industries have been carefully documented for many years,[1] as have hours of work and conditions in which strikes and other conflicts between management and labour have occurred. Theories of management and industrial relations have also been evolved on the basis of specific studies of organizations, such as the assembly line and work-incentive schemes.[2] But attempts to investigate how far conditions of work in one industry are characteristic of conditions in another, and to develop common standards of comparison, especially in relation to trends over time, have scarcely been made at all, or only fragmentarily.

In the literature on social conditions and in public discussion, people readily *generalize* about diets, clothing, leisure-time pursuits, housing conditions and even environmental conditions. Standards of comparison are readily adopted. For example, defined standards of overcrowding, facilities and amenities are applied nation-wide to housing of different tenure in different localities. As a

1. See, for example, *Report of the Commissioners Appointed to Inquire into the Working of the Factory and Workshop Acts*, C. 1443, HMSO, London, 1876; *Final Report of the Departmental Committee Appointed to Inquire into and Report upon Certain Miscellaneous Dangerous Trades*, C. 9509, HMSO, London, 1899; *Safety and Health at Work*, Report of the Robens Committee 1970–72, Cmnd 5034, HMSO, London, 1972; Kinnersly, P., *The Hazards of Work: How to Fight Them*, Workers' Handbook No. 1, Pluto Press, London, 1973. Violations of the Factory Acts in the early and mid nineteenth century, as reported by the inspectors, were extensively quoted by Marx in his *Capital: A Critique of Political Economy*, Lawrence & Wishart, London, 1970–72 edition (from the edition of 1887).

2. Walker, C. R., and Guest, R. H., *The Man on the Assembly Line*, Harvard University Press, 1952; Trist, E. L., Higgin, G. W., Murray, H., and Pollock, A. B., *Organizational Choice: Capabilities of Groups at the Coal Face under Changing Technologies*, Tavistock, London, 1963; Woodward, J., *Industrial Organization: Theory and Practice*, Oxford University Press, 1965.

result, measures exist of the numbers in the population who live in overcrowded or slum housing, even when those measures are subject to doubt and criticism. Such standards do not really exist for the world of work. There are no measures of the number in employment who have bad or deprived conditions of work, the industries or areas in which they are to be found, and the degree to which they also experience bad housing conditions and low incomes. As a result, we lack adequate means of understanding important changes taking place among the employed and the population generally. Improvements in pay and employer welfare benefits, and improvements in industrial relations or working conditions in particular firms or industries, may distract attention from the disservices introduced by new forms of technology and the insecurities and hazards of new or enlarged forms of marginal employment.

Concepts of deprivation at work are required partly to demonstrate and investigate inequalities among the employed, and partly to compare correspondence or disjunction between conditions at work and conditions outside work. Why have they not been adequately formulated? The reasons would have to be sought in the history of the social sciences, the trade unions, and the social policies of the state. Social scientists have given emphasis in their research, on the one hand, to the social survey based on interviews in the home, and, on the other, to specific places of employment. Comparative studies of the employed would, in any case, be difficult because of the huge range by size and composition of workforces and the sheer diversity of type of employment. The trade unions have been concerned with better pay, full employment and the protection of working practices rather than the achievement of pleasant as well as safe working conditions.[1] And, in its social policies, the state has been concerned with minimal forms of intervention to reduce accidents, malpractices and industrial diseases rather than guarantee equity and well-being generally among the employed.

The work of the Factory Inspectorates affords an important illustration. At the time of the survey, there were nine separate groups of statutes dealing with safety and health at work. They were separately administered by five central government departments with seven separate central inspectorates. The oldest and largest inspection agency is the Factory Inspectorate within the Department of Employment. Its work dates from the appointment in 1833 of the first four factory inspectors to enforce the 1833 Act to Regulate the Labour of Children and Young Persons in the Mills and Factories of the United Kingdom. In the early 1970s, there were over 700 inspectors, but they covered some 200,000 establishments under the Factory Act and, with local authority inspectors, 750,000

1. Evidence given to the Donovan Commission suggested that workers were not generally concerned with working conditions, preferring to have money in their pockets. Figures on unofficial strikes, for example, do not suggest that working conditions or arrangements are a common cause of disputes. The commission's report contains no direct reference to physical working conditions. See *Report of the Royal Commission on Trade Unions and Employers' Associations, 1965–1968*, Cmnd 3623, H M S O, London, 1968.

sets of premises under the Offices, Shops and Railway Premises Act. There are also the Mines and Quarries Inspectorate (Department of Industry), Agricultural Safety Inspectorate (Agriculture Departments), Explosives Inspectorate (Home Office), Nuclear Installations Inspectorate (Department of Industry), Radio-chemical Inspectorate (Department of Environment) and Alkali and Clean Air Inspectorate (Department of Environment).

The Robens Committee found that this 'tangle of jurisdictions' led to a variety of problems.

On the one hand the separately administered statutes, taken together, cover nothing like the whole of the working population. On the other hand, some of them overlap in ways that can create uncertainty and confusion. Worse, the fragmentation of the legislation and its administration makes the task of harmonizing, servicing and up-dating the various statutory provisions extremely difficult; and it diffuses and compartmentalizes the expertise and facilities that are available to deal with occupational hazards.[1]

The committee rejected rigorous enforcement. The criminal courts were concerned more with events in history than with curing the underlying weaknesses that had brought them about. The process of prosecution was lengthy and did not often lead to really effective remedies. The full utilization of legal sanctions was therefore inappropriate and undesirable. 'But in any case it is not feasible. There are far too many workplaces, and far too many regulations applying to them, for anyone to contemplate anything in the nature of continuous official supervision and vigorous enforcement.'[2] The committee supported the view of the Chief Inspector of Factories that persuasion was more important than a strict application of all the sanctions of the law.[3] They believed that the traditional concepts of the criminal law were not readily applicable to employers in their capacity of responsibility for working arrangements. Instead, the watchword was to be 'self-regulation'. The committee advocated the encouragement of voluntary codes of practice under unified statutory control exercised by a Health and Safety Commission and Executive. Under the Health and Safety at Work Act 1974, a Health and Safety Commission was set up in October 1974. A Health and Safety Executive, in which the various Inspectorates were merged, followed in 1975. An estimated extra 5 million people were brought within the scope of safety legislation, but there has been little increase as a consequence in the staffing of the Factory Inspectorate. To some critics, the recommendations of the Robens Committee and the response of the government seemed to be little more than an administrative streamlining of a system aimed at persuading and encouraging industry to observe standards which are both imprecisely defined as well as limited in scope. Certainly the Robens Committee had not attempted to collect evidence about safety and health in relation to general working conditions. It might also be added

1. Report of the Robens Committee, p. 9.   2. ibid., p. 64; see also Chapter 9.
3. *Annual Report of the Chief Inspector of Factories for 1969*, Cmnd 4461, HMSO, London.

that the perspectives of the Factory Inspectorate have become narrower rather than broader with the passage of time. The 1913 report, for example, discusses sanitation, washing facilities, meals facilities, lighting and temperature, and such matters attracted attention especially in the two wars. The Factory Inspectorate was made part of the Health and Safety Executive in 1975, and the wider issues of work conditions and amenities are now less likely to be regarded as priorities in its work.

However, there have been signs within government departments of the need for a broader approach to the quality of working life. For example, a report commissioned by the Department of Employment called attention to the stress created by 'some features of a variety of modern work systems' such as 'forced, uniform pacing, especially if the pace is high; repetitiveness and very short time cycles, leading to monotony, triviality and meaninglessness in work; large impersonal structures of organization, working arrangements and relations; objectives which seem distant and unreal to the worker (even if in fact vital to him)'.[1] The report also recommended a survey of workers' occupational circumstances, expectations and subjective reactions on the lines of a 1970 study by the US Department of Labor.[2]

The changing problems of statutory control of exposure to accidents and industrial disease also suggest how the problems of deprivation at work in general may be changing and have to be understood in a broader context. The Robens Committee took the view that, although there had been a fall in the annual rate of fatal accidents per 100,000 people employed in factories from 17·5 in the first decade of the century to 4·5 in the 1960s, the recent evidence was not encouraging. 'If we look at the annual figures for work fatalities over the decade 1961–1970, no unequivocally clear trend is discernible; and the number of all reported accidents rose steadily during the first half of the decade.' The committee suggested that we may have reached 'some sort of plateau in occupational safety and health performance', and that the increasing scale and complexity of modern industry may be creating new hazards. They gave, as examples, the rapid increase in the use of toxic substances, and materials with explosive or flammable properties. In 1968 alone there were 113 deaths from asbestosis.[3] But the committee were unable to compile a complete picture of work fatalities, because 5 to 6 million workpeople, or 20 per cent of the workforce, did not fall within the scope of any occupational safety and health legislation. Neither did they attempt to pursue the interrelationship between fatal accidents, non-fatal accidents, deaths and injuries arising from prescribed industrial diseases and occupational mortality and morbidity =

1. Wilson, N. A. B., On the Quality of Working Life, A Report Prepared for the Department of Employment, Manpower Papers No. 7, HMSO, London, 1973, p. 43.
2. Herrick, N. Q., and Quinn, R. P., 'The Working Conditions Survey as a Source of Social Indicators', Monthly Labor Review, April 1971.
3. Report of the Robens Committee, pp. 3–4.

for each of which independent sets of statistics exist. In evaluating developments, they neglected, above all, to take account of the changing distribution of non-manual and manual employees in the workforce, and hence failed to perceive the scale of the risks to which the *diminishing* proportion of employees with manual jobs are exposed. The importance of reports on occupational mortality to a better understanding of the work situation as well as to the circumstances outside work remains to be plumbed. Thus, in the five years 1959–63, *more* men in unskilled occupations died at every age than in the five years 1949–53, from cancer of the lung, vascular lesions of the central nervous system, arteriosclerotic and degenerative heart disease, motor-vehicle accidents and other accidents. 'The most disturbing feature of the present results when compared with earlier analyses is the apparent deterioration in social class V . . . Whilst the mortality of all men fell at all ages except 70–74, that for social class V . . . men rose at all ages except 25–34.'[1] One measure of differential exposure to death is that if men and women aged 15–64 of unskilled occupational status had experienced the same chances of death as those of professional status during the five years 1959–63, 40,000 would not have died.

From the official mortality tables sharp differences can be shown for individual occupations. Thus, for men in the prime of life (aged 35–44), the mean annual death rate per 100,000 in 1959–63 was as follows[2] for selected occupations:

High rates

Electrical engineers	828
Kitchen hands	553
Deck and engine-room ratings	544
Labourers in textiles	493
Labourers in engineering	432
Labourers in chemical trades	345
Railway porters	339
Coal miners (face workers)	332
Fishermen	327
Surface workers (quarries)	320
Crane and hoist operators	318
Labourers in foundries	318
Machine-tool operators	278
Agricultural workers	221

Low rates

Government ministers, MPs and senior government officials	169
Roundsmen (milk, bread, etc.)	168

1. The Registrar General's Decennial Supplement, England and Wales, 1961, *Occupational Mortality Tables*, HMSO, London, 1971, p. 25.
   2. ibid.

Police officers and men	152
Sales managers	146
Teachers	135
Managers in mining and production	129
Technical and related workers	113
Local authority senior officers	105
Civil service executive officers	104
Managers in building and contracting	83

It must be remembered that occupations so designated were usually the *latest* and not necessarily the *main* occupations in working life, and that factors connected with work were not the only factors explaining these rates.

The Concept of Deprivation

As a consequence of the problems briefly reviewed above, a concept of work deprivation needs to be developed. This would take account of the nature of the work itself and its security, amenities and rewards, including welfare or fringe benefits and not only earnings.

If the hazards to health at work are to be adequately understood, then the question of whether or not minimum levels of safety from exposure to the risk of accident or prescribed industrial disease are satisfied is too restricted. Broad conditions and amenities have to be described and analysed. A satisfactory work situation *prevents* risks of accident or disease. It also *promotes* health, high standards of industrial practice and relations and social integration.

Accordingly, we tried to arrange information from our informants under the following broad headings, keeping the question of pay for the moment separate:

1. The job itself, and especially its relative severity.
2. The security of the job.
3. The conditions and amenities of the work.
4. Welfare or fringe benefits.

It must be remembered that, unlike certain other concepts, like that of deprivation at home, the concept of work deprivation has not attracted sustained study and measurement and our attempts to operationalize it must be treated as preliminary.

Under the first heading, the *job itself*, the indicators adopted in the survey were: whether place of work was mainly indoors or outdoors; the proportion of working time standing or walking about; the number of hours of work; and working early or late hours of the day. These give a limited reflection of the nature and severity of the job, and it would, of course, be possible in subsequent research to attempt to measure degree of physical and mental exertion, dexterity or agility, involved; the length and variability of work shifts; the repetitiveness or variability of the working process; and pace.

Under the second heading of *job security*, the indicators were the number of weeks of unemployment or short-time employment in the previous year, and the period of entitlement to notice.

Under the third heading of *job amenities*, we developed a ten-point index for those working indoors and an eight-point index for those working outdoors. The former included the following items:

1. Sufficient heating in winter to be warm at work.
2. Tea or coffee (whether charged or not).
3. Indoor flush WC.
4. Facilities for washing and changing, including hot water, soap, towels and mirror.
5. Place to buy lunch or eat sandwiches (whether used or not).
6. Place to keep coat and spare set of clothes without risk of loss.
7. Place for personal articles which can be locked.
8. First-aid box or facilities.
9. Possibility of making at least one personal telephone call a day.
10. Lighting which the individual can increase or reduce (e.g. light over his work).

The latter included:

1. Dry and warm place to shelter in heavy rain.
2. Tea or coffee (whether charged or not).
3. Facilities for washing.
4. Indoor place to eat sandwiches or midday meal.
5. Safe and dry place for coat, spare set of clothes.
6. First-aid box or facilities.
7. Possibility of making at least one personal telephone call a day.
8. Lavatory (including earth closet or chemical closet).

Again, other indicators such as noise, air pollution, excessive heat or light, vibration, isolation from workmates, pressure, exposure to radiation, humidity, might have been added.

Under the fourth heading of *employer welfare benefits*, we obtained as much information from the employee as we could about sick pay, subsidized and free meals, occupational pensions, entitlement to paid holidays and other fringe benefits. Our coverage was more comprehensive than in the case of the character, security and conditions of the job, because we also sought to arrive at estimates of the total value of fringe benefits to relate to levels of remuneration. Our problem was that, while nearly all employees knew whether or not they were entitled to particular benefits, they were sometimes hazy about exact levels, particularly of pensions and sick pay, expected.

Table 12.1 sets out the numbers of employed men and women experiencing deprivation at work in these four senses. Fewer women than men work outdoors, work long hours or work shifts late in the evening or at night. This is largely a function of their occupations; proportionately more women than men have routine non-manual and lower supervisory occupations, and fewer have skilled and unskilled manual jobs. Large proportions of both men and women are not entitled to different employer welfare or fringe benefits, and many have only limited entitlement. The number of persons subject to only one week's notice, as testified by the employee, may be higher than they in fact are. The Contract of Employ-

Table 13.1. *Percentages of men and women experiencing different kinds of deprivation or difficulty at work.*

Type of deprivation or difficulty			Number of base	
	Men	Women	Men	Women
The character of the job				
1. Working mainly or entirely outdoors (incl. transport)	31	4	1,679	726
2. All working time standing or walking about	57	42	1,515	677
3. At work before 8 a.m. or working at night	36	15	1,558	880
4. Working 50 or more hours last week	24	4	1,559	912
Security				
5. Unemployed more than 2 weeks in last 12 months	5	4	1,720	1,048
6. Subject to 1 week's notice or less	44	51	1,395	626
Conditions and amenities				
7. Working conditions very poor or poor	23	15	1,408	665
Welfare or fringe benefits				
8. No wages or salary during sickness	37	35	1,516	679
9. Paid holidays of two weeks or less	56	61	1,706	1,044
10. No meals paid or subsidized by employer	(76)	(69)	1,510	663
11. No entitlement to occupational pension	43	61	1,423	614

NOTE: The base numbers used in calculating percentages vary for the following reasons. Items 5 and 9 cover people who were employed and self-employed for one week or more in the previous year, including people working few hours. Items 3 and 4 are restricted to people working in the previous week (including the self-employed). The remaining items apply only to the employed working at least thirty hours a week for one or more weeks in the previous twelve months.

Table 12.2. *Percentages of employed men and women of different occupational class according to various forms of work deprivation.*

A. Men

	Professional	Managerial	Supervisory – high	Supervisory – low	Routine non-manual	Skilled manual	Partly skilled manual	Unskilled manual
The character of the job								
1. Working mainly outdoors (incl. transport)	6	8	16	12	20	37	30	63
2. All working time standing or walking about	2	16	27	28	32	69	79	89
3. At work before 8 a.m. or working at night	15	19	15	20	19	46	50	55
Security								
4. Unemployed more than 2 weeks in last 12 months	0	0	2	5	5	4	6	16
5. Subject to 1 week's notice or less	5	2	12	23	33	52	56	77
6. Claimed to have experienced big fall in earnings in working life	13	11	15	14	21	17	20	18
7. Pay varies	26	35	34	36	48	62	64	60
Conditions and amenities								
8. Working conditions very poor or poor	2	12	6	10	11	29	27	40
9. % of those working indoors whose working conditions very poor or poor	2	(12)	7	6	9	27	21	27

A. Men

	Profes-sional	Mana-gerial	Super-visory – high	Super-visory – low	Routine non-manual	Skilled manual	Partly skilled manual	Unskilled manual
10. % of those working out-doors whose working conditions very poor or poor	–	–	–	–	–	34	(45)	47
Welfare or fringe benefits								
11. No wages or salary during sickness	3	6	11	14	22	47	50	63
12. % of those entitled to sick pay who receive less than usual earnings	7	8	5	8	12	44	50	41
13. Paid holidays of 2 weeks or less	34	49	28	60	50	77	74	91
14. No meals paid or subsidized by employer	47	49	73	74	84	82	77	81
15. No cover for occupational pension	10	2	18	21	36	54	49	76
16. % with right to occupational pension who cannot expect it until 65 or later	50	(56)	62	61	63	84	86	(84)
17. % with right to occupational pension who expect it to be less than 50% final earnings	36	(45)	48	39	48	67	80	(75)
Highest number on which percentages based[a]	89	78	161	242	106	589	281	171

NOTE: [a]Item 4. Numbers for items 9, 10, 12, 16 and 17 apply only to a sub-sample and are much lower. As elsewhere, a percentage based on a number between 30 and 49 is given in brackets. No percentages are given on a base below 30.

Table 12.2.—contd.

B. Women

	Supervisory— high	Supervisory— low	Routine non-manual	Skilled manual	Partly skilled manual	Unskilled manual
The character of the job						
1. Working mainly outdoors (incl. transport)	6	4	0	2	10	(0)
2. All working time standing or walking about	43	38	26	50	53	(64)
3. At work before 8 am or working at night	6	18	4	28	25	21
Security						
4. Unemployed more than 2 weeks in last 12 months	3	2	5	3	6	4
5. Subject to 1 week's notice or less	12	26	48	(62)	72	(92)
6. Experienced big fall in earnings in working life	9	12	4	7	8	1
7. Pay varies	25	22	27	42	45	24
Conditions and amenities						
8. % of those working indoors whose working conditions very poor or poor	14	10	18	(19)	20	(27)
Welfare of fringe benefits						
9. No wages or sick pay during sickness	11	19	25	56	67	(50)
10. Paid holidays of 2 weeks or less	30	59	74	84	81	90
11. No meals paid for or subsidized by employer	58	68	77	71	64	(68)
12. No cover for occupational pension	15	41	61	84	82	(93)
Highest number on which percentages based	92	127	357	662	259	1833

ment Act 1963 provides that all employees with a minimum period of service are entitled to notice of dismissal, varying from one week for up to two years' continuous service to four weeks for service of over five years.[1] Soon after this legislation was passed, there were signs of non-manual employees being granted more generous rights and of the legislation providing a floor upon which differentiation between manual and non-manual grades was reasserting itself.[2] Our data from employees on minimum entitlement to notice suggest, however, that when length of service is taken into account, some employees underestimate their entitlement. Alternatively, there may be more exceptions in practice to the legislation than has so far been publicly appreciated; or some employers may not be communicating these legal rights to their employees, or may not be observing them in their dismissal practices.

Deprivation and Occupational Class

Deprivation at work is broadly related, we found, to occupational class. A major difference in character, security, conditions and fringe benefits of work exists between manual and non-manual grades. That is perhaps the most important conclusion to be drawn from our examination of the conditions and terms of employment. But there are two supplementary conclusions. Among non-manual grades, especially among women, there are in some aspects of conditions and terms of employment, marked differences between the lower grades, especially routine non-manual grades, and professional and managerial grades. And, among manual grades, the unskilled are markedly more disadvantaged in some aspects than the skilled and partly skilled. The findings from the survey are summarized in Table 13.2. Through the eight occupational ranks there is a tendency for the incidence of deprivation to increase. But, in most instances, there is a marked difference between routine non-manual and skilled manual workers. Thus, only 33 per cent of routine non-manual male employees, compared with 70 per cent of skilled manual male employees, spent all or nearly all their working time standing or walking about; 22 per cent, compared with 46 per cent, worked early in the mornings or late in the evenings or at night; 23 per cent, compared with 47 per cent, did not expect to receive payments from the employer during sickness; and 34 per cent, compared with 54 per cent, had no cover for occupational pensions. In these respects there were similar differences between women in routine non-manual and women in skilled manual occupations.

1. The employee was entitled to one week's notice once he had been employed continuously for twenty-six weeks (later reduced to thirteen weeks by the Industrial Relations Act 1971). But employees normally expected to work less than twenty-one hours a week, and certain categories of employees working longer hours, are excepted.
2. Wedderburn, D., 'Workplace Inequality', *New Society*, 9 April 1970, and Craig, C., *Men in Manufacturing Industry*, Department of Applied Economics, Cambridge, 1969.

The significance of these findings rests not so much in their novelty as in their comprehensiveness. They cover all types of employment for a nationally representative sample of both men and women, and cover eight occupational ranks. They confirm other research on manufacturing industry,[1] and for certain aspects of employment, broad categories of manual and non-manual occupations.[2]

The Character of the Job

Manual work has distinctive features. About a third of skilled and partly skilled and nearly two thirds of unskilled male manual workers spend all or nearly all their working time outdoors. Ten per cent of skilled and partly skilled are engaged in transport – lorries, vans, buses and trains (Table A.32, Appendix Eight, page 1017). A disproportionately large number of male manual workers also spend all or nearly all their working time standing or walking about, not only because more work outdoors, but also because among those working indoors this is a characteristic of manual work. This difference between manual and non-manual grades applies to women as well as men. But while fewer working-class women than men spend all or nearly all of their working time on their feet, more women than men in the upper non-manual grades do so (Table A.33, Appendix Eight, page 1018). This is partly a function of the demands of occupations such as nursing and teaching. Among men, there are two peaks according to age. More young men aged 15–24 and more aged 60 and over than at ages 25–59 spend all or nearly all their working time on their feet. This is, to some extent, due to the disproportionate number of males of these ages engaged in manual work. Among women, the pattern is different, rising from a low proportion in the teens and twenties to a high proportion in the fifties. Over a third of employed women under 30 spend none, or very little, of their working time on their feet, compared with fewer than a fifth in their fifties (Table A.34, Appendix Eight, page 1019).

Manual workers more often work 'unusual' hours. In the survey, we asked for an account of the times in the day people had worked during the previous week. While a majority of non-manual men worked only during the period 8 a.m. to 6 p.m., the figure for skilled manual men was 40 per cent, partly skilled 33 per cent and unskilled 34 per cent. Significantly higher proportions of manual workers started work before 8 a.m., often at 7 a.m., though sometimes sooner, and significantly more of them worked at night, starting work after 6 p.m. Though more women than men worked in the 'usual' period between 8 a.m. and 6 p.m., there was a similar tendency for more manual than non-manual workers to start work

1. Craig, *Men in Manufacturing Industry*; Wedderburn, 'Workplace Inequality'; Wedderburn, D., and Craig, C., 'Relative Deprivation in Work', in Wedderburn, D. (ed.), *Poverty, Inequality and Class Structure*, Cambridge University Press, 1974.

2. For differences in working hours between manual and non-manual workers, see the reports of the Department of Employment's New Earnings Survey (as illustrated later).

before 8 a.m. or after 6 p.m. (Table A.35, Appendix Eight, page 1020). We did not inquire in addition about shift work, but the Department of Employment's New Earnings Survey shows for 1970, for example, that 22 per cent of manual, compared with 4 per cent of non-manual workers, received shift payments.[1] Some workers find social compensations in shift working, but many find they have no choice. Broadly, shift working can be said to interfere with normal family and social life.

Manual workers generally work longer hours. In the sample, 38 per cent of male non-manual employees, compared with 11 per cent of manual employees, had worked fewer than forty hours in the previous week (Table A.36, Appendix Eight, page 1021). The difference is only marginally reduced if the self-employed are included. Far more of the self-employed than of the employed are in non-manual occupations, and a large number of them work relatively long hours. (See, for example, Table A.39, Appendix Eight, page 1024.) They include shopkeepers living on the premises, however, and their conception of 'hours of work' usually incorporates, for example, time spent on call in an adjoining living room.

The difference between manual and non-manual employees in number of hours of work has been documented in successive annual surveys by the Department of Employment. For example, the report of the 1972 New Earnings Survey, covering 175,000 employees throughout Britain, showed that among men over 21 working full time, manual workers averaged 46·0 hours and non-manual workers 38·7 hours per week. Among women over 18 working full time, the respective percentages were 39·9 and 36·8.[2] The distributions are summarized in Table 12.3.

Much but not all of the difference is due to manual employees working overtime hours. In its surveys, the department has found that more manual than non-manual employees receive overtime pay (in 1972, for example, 57 per cent of male manual workers drew overtime pay for an average of over ten hours' overtime, whereas only 17 per cent of male non-manual workers drew overtime pay, for an average of under six hours' overtime). None the less, the normal basic week was two and a half hours longer for manual than for non-manual workers among both sexes.

Inequality in duration of work between manual and non-manual employees is even greater when any calculations are made of the hours worked in the year. This is because of different entitlement to paid holidays and different practices in permitting employees to take unpaid leave, to be late or take time off in the day. For example, 72 per cent of male and 53 per cent of female non-manual workers were entitled to more than two weeks' paid holiday, compared with 26 per cent and 25 per cent respectively of manual workers. Indeed, 25 per cent of both male

1. Department of Employment and Productivity, *New Earnings Survey, 1970*, HMSO, London, 1971.

2. Excluding those whose pay was affected by absence. Department of Employment, *New Earnings Survey, 1972*, HMSO, London, 1973, p. 38.

Table 12.3. Percentages of male and female employees according to number of working hours a week (Britain, 1972):

Number of hours	Men			Women		
	Full time over 21[a]		All men[b]	Full time over 18[a]		All women[c]
	Non-manual	Manual		Non-manual	Manual	
Not over 39	63·1	7·5	29·0	72·8	28·2	71·9
Over 39, not over 49	32·2	65·8	53·3	26·8	69·1	27·3
Over 49, not over 60	4·1	21·1	14·1	0·4	2·4	0·7
Over 60	0·6	5·5	3·5	0·1	0·4	0·1
Total	100	100	100	100	100	100
Number	29,644	57,330	97,901	22,318	12,283	58,180

NOTES: [a]All those working thirty hours or fewer are excluded.
[b]Includes young men under 21 employed full time and men aged 21 and over employed part-time.
[c]Includes young women under 18 employed full-time and women aged 18 and over employed part-time.

SOURCE: Table 15, Department of Employment, New Earnings Survey, 1972, HMSO, London, 1973.

and female non-manual workers were entitled to five weeks' paid holiday or more. As for unpaid holiday, we found that although only 3 per cent of men and 12 per cent of women had as much as one week's unpaid leave, the number of non-manual workers taking three or more weeks leave was 3 per cent among men and 3 per cent among women, compared with 1 per cent and 3 per cent respectively of manual workers. Other studies have shown marked differences between manual and non-manual workers in the extent to which they have to clock in to record attendance or have pay deducted for any lateness.[1]

The outcome in working hours for manual and non-manual employees in a full year is difficult to chart, for two reasons: First, the two broad occupational classes are differentially placed with respect to part-time (and seasonal) employment. More women of manual than of non-manual occupational class are working part time.[2] In the survey, while only 4 per cent of both male non-manual and

1. Wedderburn, D., and Craig, C., 'Relative Deprivation in Work', pp. 144 and 146.
2. According to the Department of Employment's Report on the New Earnings Survey for 1972, for example, 47 per cent of female manual employees aged 18 and over, compared with 23 per cent of non-manual employees, were employed part time. Moreover, 31 per cent and 23

manual workers had worked fewer than thirty hours in the previous week; the numbers of female workers were 35 per cent and 49 per cent respectively (Table A.36, Appendix Eight, page 1021). Any comprehensive analysis of the relative disadvantages of paid employment would have to include some reference to questions such as children or other dependants in the home; and to what extent women can elect to take paid work or are compelled to do so; and would prefer to take full-time rather than part-time employment if it were available. Judging by the criterion of household composition, substantially more women of non-manual than manual status lacked dependants in the home and were potentially employable. Few expressed any preference for paid employment. And few women of manual class who were working fewer than thirty hours a week said they would work longer hours if they had the opportunity.

Secondly, the two occupational classes are also differentially placed with respect to continuity of employment. More manual than non-manual workers are exposed to the risks of both prolonged unemployment and sickness. A substantial minority of the former have work records characterized by interruption (Table A.37, Appendix Eight, page 1022).

Thirteen per cent of those working in the previous year told us that in their working careers they had experienced at least one spell of eight weeks or more off work because of sickness or disability; and another 5 per cent because of unemployment. The figures were significantly higher for men than for women; and for manual than for non-manual workers. Seventeen per cent of male manual workers had experienced such a spell of sickness, compared with 12 per cent of non-manual workers. These figures are likely to be underestimates, since we were unable to probe this question fully. We also found that previous experience of at least eight weeks' sickness or unemployment was associated with low current earnings – even within broad occupational classes.

Five per cent of the employed population had been off work sick or disabled for a spell of at least eight weeks in the previous twelve months (excluding those not working a single week in the previous year). Among this group, 31 per cent declared that their work was wholly or partly responsible. They comprised forty-two individuals in the sample, all but four of whom were manual workers. The reasons given by most of them were recorded and are listed below. The reasons given by a few more people who were off work for at least six weeks have been added:

Man; 31; textile machinist	Accident while starting machine – causing broken arm.
Woman; 26; boxmaker	All-electric factory dried atmosphere, and increased catarrh.

---

per cent respectively of these part-time employees were working fewer than 17 hours a week. See *New Earnings Survey*, 1972, pp. 144 and 146.

Man; 47; miner	Because of my chest I had pleurisy and I work in the colliery underground.
Man; 65; steel erector	It was all outside work. You were continually exposed to all the elements, rain, sleet and snow.
Man; 53; builder's labourer	I had a heavy job and was doing a lot of lifting. I slipped a disc and had to have an operation. [Registered disabled]
Man; 34; GPO telephonist	My main job was a strain, and I was also doing another job in my spare time. [He had twenty-three weeks' nervous trouble]
Man; 58; labourer in metal works	I was a foundry worker. The boiler blew up and injured me. [Has since been labourer]
Man; 54; labourer in brewery	I had a bad stomach. The doctor thought the fumes at the brewery caused it.
Man; 47; labourer in biscuit factory	I slipped while working and loading and injured my back.
Man; 22; bus driver	I got ulcers or some kind of stomach trouble through irregular meals.
Man; 55; technical writer	Because of pressure of work I went back too soon after my last illness.
Man; 40; roller, aluminium works	My hand was injured at work.
Man; 45; foreman for council on building sites	My index finger was bent as a result of an accident and I had to have an operation.
Man; 55; cleaner in bakery	Moving large barrels caused a back injury (also chronic asthma and bronchitis).
Woman; 36; worker in dispatch department	I had a nervous breakdown. Maybe it was not really anything to do with the job, except the fact of trying to do a job at all was too much with four children and having to park Tony out and then rush backwards and forwards doing meals. Perhaps it triggered off the breakdown. [Had recently spent several months in a mental hospital and had had a hysterectomy. Husband a polio victim]
Man; 41; railway porter	I had heavy weights to lift. I have thrombosis and the doctor told me not to do any heavy work.
Woman; 21; tarpaulin proofer	The job was going for my nerves. My doctor advised me to leave.
Man; 51; fruit market porter	Very heavy lifting and I might have strained my heart.

Man; 59; acetylene burner in steelworks	Because of the severe heat there.
Woman; 50; school cook	There was a lot of heavy lifting. I was the school cook and worked in the kitchens.
Woman; 48; potato peeler (fish and chip shop)	I was working in water [potato peeler].
Man; 45; bricklayer in steelworks	I walked into a pipe and injured my neck causing a slipped disc.
Woman; 55; textile worker	My doctor said it was because there was poor ventilation at my place of work. I have a weak chest and it brings on a bad cough.
Man; 42; miner	I have sinus trouble and working in coal dust aggravates this.
Man; 55; scaffolder	I slipped at work and injured my back.
Man; 37; foundry engineer	I worked in a foundry. I had a bad chest for seven years previously. Then I got pneumonia and the doctor said I must leave my job.
Man; 58; postal worker	Coal fell on me years ago in the colliery causing a slipped disc. I haven't had a new accident. The old trouble keeps coming back.
Man; 36; labourer in iron foundry	There was a works accident, loose machinery. When I checked it, it fell on my hand.
Man; 59; dock labourer (ship canal)	Heavy work in the docks led to a hernia.
Woman; 53; cleaner in stores	Some water left on the stairs caused my accident.
Man; 43; cable foreman (cable manufacturers)	It was because I was working out of doors for so long in bad weather.
Man; 37; maintenance fitter	It was because I was not used to the pits. Shift work and travelling three hours every day.
Woman; 45; poultry worker	I worked in very old buildings with no heat and kept being ill with lumbago and colds.
Man; 26; labourer in tea factory	I was a paint sprayer, leaving job after recovery from disability. It gave me dermatitis on my hands and later spread to my feet.
Man; 39; docker in harbour	Stomach ulcers, not eating at proper times.
Man; 56; lorry driver	Diesel fumes and long hours affected my health.

Man; 62; assistant storekeeper	I worked all the time with dust from plastic goods which affected my lungs.
Man; 64; superintendent engineer (of corporation)	I was called out during the night to mechanical breakdowns and I got ill.
Man; 38; coach driver	I had concussion and broken arms when a crane in the docks dropped some cases on me.
Man; 61; janitor (general labouring) in a foodstuff packet manufacturing company	There were a lot of chemicals used at work and the fumes got on my chest.
Man; 58; factory odd-job man	I was a road sweeper and I got bronchitis because of the dust.
Man; 48; steel erector	I cracked a rib leaning over a high counter. We were working at high pressure.
Woman; 38; packer in cardboard factory (then factory worker 'stretching alloys')	I slipped and broke my ankle. In my other job I worked shift hours and the strain gave me nervous trouble. [Evidence of consultations with GP and ten visits to hospital out-patients]
Man; 35; electrician for general contractor	I slipped a disc while carrying a tool box.
Man; 49; steel erector	My nylon shirt was caught in some machinery – a moving drill. My chest was burnt and my neck and back muscles wrenched.
Woman; 41; greengrocer's assistant	The draught might have caused my pleurisy.
Man; 60; self-employed property repairer	I got bronchitis working outside so much.
Man; 50; self-employed private hire contractor	I had a car accident while driving my car [for private hire]. The exhaust pipe burnt a hole in my back.
Man; 53; director in family credit clothing business	I had a great deal of worry over SET and too much responsibility. [Had major intestinal operation; in hospital 30 days]
Man; 47; bricklayer	I injured my back from a fall.
Man; 37; electrical welder	A knee cartilage was damaged at work.
Woman; 19; mantle sewer for garment manufacturer	Dermatitis caused by handling chemicals and cloth.
Man; 37; electrical setter and wirer	I lost part of a finger whilst at work. It troubles me and I have to be off work periodically.

Although further information about these instances would have been valuable, they call attention both to the diverse hazards and frequent poor conditions of manual work. They also suggest uncertainty or ignorance on the part of many about the hazards involved with dust, noise and chemicals. And although working conditions may sometimes have been blamed wrongly for ill-health, the tendency to underestimate, or want to underestimate, the seriousness of some conditions is also noticeable. Sometimes from good motives, doctors as well as employers withhold information. When we came to compare two groups of people who had been off work sick for at least eight weeks – those saying the job was wholly or partly responsible and others – more of the former were found to experience work deprivation (in terms of conditions at work, and also job severity, insecurity and lack of fringe benefits). Since the great majority of both groups were manual workers, this was not explicable broadly by occupational class. The total numbers were, however, too few (135) to allow detailed examination.

Table A.38 (Appendix Eight, page 1023) shows the number of weeks worked in the previous twelve months by the employed and self-employed. Among men, more manual than non-manual workers tended to the extremes of the distribution. More had worked for at least forty-nine weeks of the year; more had worked fewer than twenty-six weeks. When the self-employed are excluded, these tend-

Table 12.4. *Percentages of employed men and women of different occupational class, according to total numbers of hours worked in the previous twelve months.*

Number of hours worked last year	Professional	Managerial	Supervisory high	Supervisory low	Routine non-manual	All non-manual	Skilled manual	Partly skilled manual	Un-skilled manual	All manual
Men										
2,400 or more	17	18	15	15	16	16	25	21	22	23
2,000–399	21	23	27	30	18	25	47	47	44	46
under 2,000	62	57	58	55	66	59	29	32	34	31
Total	100	100	100	100	100	100	100	100	100	100
Number	58	44	149	148	94	493	515	253	138	906
Women										
2,000 or more		18		16	16	16	(46)	23	10	22
1,400–999		41		57	53	51	(26)	34	15	27
under 1,400		42		27	31	32	(28)	42	74	51
Total		100		100	100	100	100	100	100	100
Number		74		79	285	438	(46)	182	106	334

encies become more marked. Among women, manual and non-manual workers worked roughly similar numbers of weeks.

Estimates of the total hours worked in the previous twelve months are set out in Table 12.4. (The employed are distinguished from the self-employed in Table A.39, Appendix Eight, page 1024.) Despite greater susceptibility to interruptions of employment because of sickness and unemployment, and, at least among women, restriction of opportunity sometimes to work a full week, more manual than non-manual employees had relatively high totals of working hours in the year. Nearly twice as many male non-manual as manual workers worked fewer than 2,000 hours. The difference between male routine non-manual and skilled manual employees is particularly sharp, bearing in mind other data in this chapter relevant to the controversy about the 'embourgeoisement' of the working class.[1]

Security of Work

Manual workers are more likely than non-manual workers to be unemployed, and to experience long spells of unemployment in the course of a year. The survey showed that more had experienced a change of job within the last five years, and that of these between twice and three times as many had been made redundant. Significantly more also changed jobs for health reasons.[2]

Substantially fewer had a right to a reasonable period of notice of dismissal. For example, whereas 75 per cent of non-manual male employees, and 55 per cent of female employees, had the right to at least one month's notice of dismissal, only 24 per cent and 11 per cent respectively of manual employees had a corresponding right. Routine non-manual workers were less likely to have that right than other non-manual workers.

To the risks of inadequate notice of dismissal, redundancy and unemployment have to be added the insecurities flowing from fluctuating hours of work. Because earnings are tied to number of hours of work, earnings will often depend on the number of overtime hours that can be worked. These cannot be predicted much in advance, and depend especially on health and family circumstances. Forty-five per cent of earners told us that their rate of pay varied, including 55 per cent of manual workers, compared with only 32 per cent of non-manual workers. We

1. See, for example, Goldthorpe, J. H., Lockwood, D., Bechhofer, F., and Platt, J., *The Affluent Worker in the Class Structure*, Cambridge University Press, 1969; Runciman, W. G., 'Embourgeoisement, Self-Rated Class and Party Preference', *Sociological Review*, vol. 12, No. 2, July 1964. See also Chapter 10 above, pages 386–8.
2. In a national survey covering a period of ten years, more manual than non-manual workers had changed jobs. Among men, the highest proportion was found among unskilled manual workers, 16 per cent of whom had had at least six jobs. Proportionally twice as many male manual as non-manual workers had been sacked or made redundant from their last job. See Harris, A. I., assisted by Clausen, R., *Labour Mobility in Great Britain 1953–1963*, Government Social Survey, SS333 March 1966, pp. 58 and 137.

Table 12.5. Percentages of employed men and women of different occupational class according to period of entitlement to notice.

Period entitled to notice	Men				Women[a]	
	Non-manual		Manual		Non-manual	Manual
	Profes-sional and managerial	Other	Skilled	Other		
1 week or less, or none	4	21	52	63	36	73
2 weeks	0	9	20	20	9	16
Month	45	59	27	15	45	11
More than a month	51	10	2	2	10	0
Total	100	100	100	100	100	100
Number	103	388	527	396	424	231

NOTE: [a]Since there were only seventeen women of professional and managerial class, and forty-two of skilled manual class, they have been combined respectively with other non-manual and manual classes.

sought details about highest and lowest pay in the preceding twelve months. Altogether 61 per cent had received pay at some point in the year of at least 20 per cent lower than at another. More manual than non-manual employees experienced substantial variation. More of them also experienced a *fall* rather than a rise in pay. (This is discussed more fully in Chapter 18.)

Conditions of Work

Altogether, 20 per cent of the employed population, representing over $4\frac{1}{2}$ million in the population, have poor conditions of work. This assessment is based on the ten indoors and eight outdoors criteria which were applied separately in the survey (page 438). The detailed breakdown, together with population estimates, is set out in Table 12.6. The criteria are provisional, and no doubt could be improved in future research. The self-employed and those employed in transport, many of whom have poor working conditions, were excluded from the assessment. Proportionately more working outdoors than indoors, and more men than women, were found to have poor conditions. Only just over half the employed population enjoyed good conditions.

Some of the items in the work conditions index were more generally available than others. For example, among people working indoors, 3 per cent did not have access to an indoors flush W C, whereas 7 per cent had no facilities for washing or changing, 11 per cent had insufficient heating in winter, 17 per cent had no place to hang a coat or keep other articles without risk of loss, 26 per cent could not make or receive a telephone call and 42 per cent were unable to control the lighting over their work (Table A.40, Appendix Eight, page 1024). In a number of directly comparable respects, more of those working outdoors than indoors lacked facilities. For example, 10 per cent worked without access to a first-aid box or facilities (compared with 4 per cent), 29 per cent had no facilities for washing

Table 12.6. *Percentages and estimated number of employed men and women working indoors or outdoors (excluding transport) according to their working conditions.*

Working conditions	Men			Women		
(Index score) Out-doors Indoors	Outdoors[a]	Indoors	Outdoors and indoors	Outdoors[a]	Indoors	Outdoors and indoors
Very poor (0–3) (0–4)	17	7	10	–	6	6
Poor (4–5) (5–6)	23	10	13	–	9	9
Adequate (6) (7–8)	14	29	26	–	33	32
Good (7–8) (9–10)	46	53	52	–	51	52
Total	100	100	100	100	100	100
Number	341	1,067	1,408	12	653	665
Estimated number in employed population (000s)						
Very poor	620	860	1,480	–	440	460
Poor	860	1,140	2,000	–	660	680
Adequate	500	3,420	3,920	–	2,350	2,350
Good	1,730	6,200	7,930	–	3,660	3,750
Total	3,710	11,620	15,330	130	7,110	7,240

NOTE: [a]It has been assumed that the conditions of those working outdoors in more than one place of employment are proportionately the same as of those in a single place of employment. Our series of questions were not applied to the former. People employed in transport are excluded from the table.

(compared with 7 per cent) and 31 per cent could not obtain tea or coffee, whether charged or not, during the day (compared with 8 per cent).

Partly, but not only, because more worked outdoors, significantly more manual than non-manual workers had poor or very poor working conditions: 31 per cent, compared with 8 per cent. Among both male and female employees, significantly fewer routine non-manual than other non-manual employees also enjoyed good conditions (Table A.41, Appendix Eight, page 1025). During individual interviews, our attention was also called to conditions which are not represented in the work conditions index. There were men and women working continuously in dusty conditions, for example, in steel works, cotton factories and brickworks. Some had to endure extremes of noise or temperature.

Welfare and Fringe Benefits

Employers have increasingly augmented earnings by providing benefits in kind at work and cash benefits in sickness or upon termination of employment.[1] Welfare is an increasingly important extension of security and an increasingly important adjunct of cash earnings. Partly this may be because of the developing formalization of collective bargaining to determine wages and conditions of employment: 'fringe benefits, as non-wage remuneration of different kinds, were thus provided within a different framework'.[2] Partly it may be because of the search for economical methods of conferring benefits upon, and securing the allegiance of, the increasing number of white-collar workers at a time when income taxes have been perceived to be high.

Two thirds of employees (63 per cent of men and 65 per cent of women) expected to be paid when sick. The fraction rises slightly (66 per cent of men and 68 per cent of women) when those working less than thirty hours are excluded. The total for men bears out the trend suggested by two other national surveys carried out at dates before and after our survey, though the total for women is a little higher than that derived from a 1971 survey.[3]

The period for which employees are entitled to sick pay varies, and we sought only to estimate level of sick pay (including sickness benefit) as a percentage of earnings during an initial period of one month's sickness. Statements made in

1. For a historical introduction, see Reid, G. L., and Robertson, D. J., *Fringe Benefits, Labour Costs and Social Security*, Allen & Unwin, London, 1965, esp. Chapter 2.
2. ibid., p. 27.
3. In a 1961–2 survey in Britain, 57 per cent of men and 59 per cent of women were found to have some cover for pay in sickness. In a 1971 survey, the percentages were 69·6 and 58·2 respectively (or 70·6 and 71·1 for full-time workers). Ministry of Pensions and National Insurance, *Report of an Enquiry into the Incidence of Incapacity for Work*, Part I: *Scope and Characteristics of Employers' Sick Pay Schemes*, HMSO, London, 1965, p. xiii; OPCS, Social Survey Division, *The General Household Survey*, Introductory Report, London, HMSO, London, 1973, p. 201.

interview were subsequently checked according to amounts normally paid under national insurance, including amounts for dependants.

Table 12.7 shows that rather fewer than half of male employees, though rather more than half of female employees, expected to have an income in the first month

Table 12.7. Percentages of employed men and women of non-manual and manual class according to entitlement to sick pay.

Entitlement to sick pay	Men			Women		
	Non-manual	Manual	All	Non-manual	Manual	All
No entitlement	12	51	37	23	50	35
Under 50% earnings[a]	0	4	2	1	2	2
50–99% earnings[a]	6	19	14	7	12	9
100% earnings[a]	81	26	46	69	35	54
Total	100	100	100	100	100	100
Number	518	934	1,481	350	280	640

NOTE: [a]National insurance sickness benefit added to sick pay and combined total expressed as percentage of gross earnings.

of sickness, including sickness benefit, equivalent to average gross earnings. The difference between non-manual and manual employees is, however, marked for both sexes. Not only are many more manual than non-manual employees ineligible for sick pay. Fewer of those eligible expect to receive the equivalent of average earnings. Manual workers more commonly have to serve a qualifying period before being entitled to sick pay; are not paid during the first days of sickness; and are ineligible to receive sick pay for longer than three months.[1]

There was no pronounced difference between those covered and those not covered by sick-pay arrangements in the numbers off work because of sickness or days illness in the year (Table A.42, Appendix Eight, page 1026). The study in 1961–2 by the Ministry of Pensions found a slightly higher inception rate among men who were not covered than who were covered by sick-pay arrangements, but the same average days of incapacity. Among women who were not covered, inception rates were lower but average number of days of incapacity greater. A 1972 survey found 'that sick pay schemes do not tend to increase the number of days lost from work in a year due to illness or injury'.[2]

1. Ministry of Pensions and National Insurance, *Report of an Enquiry in the Incidence of Incapacity for Work*, Part I, pp. xix–xxiii.
2. ibid., pp. xxxii–xxxiii; OPCS, *The General Household Survey*, Introductory Report, pp. 307–8.

Substantially more male than female employees were members of an occupational pension scheme, but again the difference in coverage of manual and non-manual workers was marked, fewer than half of male and fewer than a quarter of female manual employees being members. Fewer manual than non-manual workers who were members expected pensions of as much as 30 per cent of final earnings. Only just over a million manual workers, in a total of 13 million, expected to earn an occupational pension of 50 per cent or more of final earnings (Table 12.8). When relating pensions expected by people in the sample to their age, we found that fewer people in their forties and fifties than in their twenties and thirties expected a pension of as much as half of earnings. The present low coverage and amounts of occupational pensions received by the elderly (described in Chapter 24) are therefore unlikely to change materially for many years to come. Indeed, although coverage among the employed population grew during the 1950s and 1960s, there is evidence which suggests that in the late 1960s it

Table 12.8. Percentages of employed men and women of non-manual and manual class, according to entitlement to occupational pension.

Occupational pension as percentage of expected final salary or wage	Men			Women		
	Non-manual	Manual	All[a]	Non-manual	Manual	All[a]
No cover for pension	19	56	43	48	76	61
Under 30%	13	22	19	8	11	8
30–49%	22	9	14	25	8	18
50–59%	15	6	9	11	3	8
60%+	31	7	15	7	2	5
Total	100	100	100	100	100	100
Number	501	914	1,423	325	280	614
Estimated number in employed population (000s)						
No cover for pension	1,024	5,587	6,632	1,699	2,320	4,084
Under 30%	730	2,189	2,962	294	338	555
30–49%	1,176	926	2,124	882	240	1,186
50–59%	817	599	1,416	403	87	523
60%+	1,710	653	2,363	261	65	338
Total	5,457	9,954	15,497	3,539	3,050	6,686

NOTE: [a]Includes some not allocated by occupational class.

actually declined among manual workers of both sexes, though continuing to rise among non-manual workers.[1] And the rates of inflation experienced in the 1970s mean that, without introducing new policy measures, the real value of occupational pensions paid to existing and prospective pensioners will depreciate rapidly in relation to other forms of income. Although more people now in their forties and fifties will expect to receive an occupational pension than are receiving one today, or will receive a pension of higher initial value than those being paid to existing occupational pensioners, only part of the total value of occupational pensions will be guanteed against inflation by the contracting-out provisions of the state pension scheme which began in 1978. In payment, small additional pensions are likely to fall drastically in their real value.

A summary account of levels of pensions expected does not exhaust the inequalities which exist between manual and non-manual employees. Whereas 33 per cent of non-manual employees with entitlement to an occupational pension expected to receive a lump sum upon retirement, only 21 per cent of manual employees did so. Since fewer manual than non-manual employees expected to receive a pension in the first place, entitlement to a lump sum is in general rare among manual employees. Altogether, only 9 per cent expected to receive a lump sum upon retirement. Fewer than half of them, compared with nearly two thirds of the equivalent group of non-manual workers, expected to receive a lump sum of as much in value as the final year's earnings. Among men, 17 per cent of non-manual workers (including 27 per cent of professional and managerial workers) said they were entitled to a lump sum equivalent to at least the value of the earnings in their final year before retirement. Among women, the comparable figure was 19 per cent. These benefits are a major source of the accumulation of wealth.

The combined value of lump sum and occupational pension can be very substantial for professional workers and executives in both public services and private industry. When Sir William Armstrong, Head of the Home Civil Service and Permanent Secretary to the Civil Service Department, retired in 1974 at the age of 59, he became entitled to a tax-free lump sum of £25,000 and a pension of £8,500 (or half his final salary) which rises in line with the rise in earnings. These amounts were not affected by his appointment to the chairmanship of the Midland Bank at a salary of £35,000.[2]

Another inequality is age at which the pension starts. Of men entitled to occupational pensions, 35 per cent of non-manual workers (including 42 per cent of professional and managerial workers) were entitled to them at ages under 65, mostly 60, compared with 13 per cent of manual workers. A substantial minority, or one in six, of male non-manual workers, were expecting to draw a pension at 55. Of women entitled to occupational pensions, the great majority among both

1. *Occupational Pension Schemes, 1971*, Fourth Survey by the Government Actuary, H M S O, London, 1972.
2. *The Times*, 28 June 1974.

manual and non-manual groups expected to draw a pension at 60; however, 13 per cent of non-manual employees expected to draw pensions at 55 compared with 5 per cent of manual employees.

There are other welfare benefits which augment incomes while at work. A large proportion of employees have meals which are subsidized by the employer, 24 per cent of men and 31 per cent of women. The subsidy takes three forms: luncheon vouchers, cheap meals in canteens or restaurants and repayment or payment of some or all of the costs of meals out, usually as a charge against business expenses. In the survey, we asked about all three. Among men, more non-manual than manual workers enjoyed a subsidy, 30 per cent (including more than half professional and managerial workers) compared with 20 per cent. Among women, about the same proportions of both manual and non-manual workers (just under a third) enjoyed a subsidy (Table A.43, Appendix Eight, page 1026). The value of the subsidy was greater on average for non-manual than for manual workers. Among men, for example, 36 per cent of non-manual but only 19 per cent of manual workers estimated the value at more than £1 per week.

Five per cent of all employees, representing 1·2 million in the employed population, had the personal use sometimes or often of a car owned by the employer. Fewer than one in ten of these were women. However, the respective numbers of non-manual and manual workers was 14 per cent and 2 per cent. In nearly all cases, the employer paid road tax, insurance and repairs, and for nearly four fifths also paid petrol. We also explored what value was derived by the individual from other goods and services provided free or cheaply by the employer. Based on the numbers in the sample, we estimated that 5·2 million obtained cheap or free goods; 0·5 million cheap or free travel other than for purposes of work; 0·3 million medical expenses; 0·6 million educational expenses for themselves or their children (mostly themselves); 0·2 million shares or options to purchase shares; 0·8 million life insurance; 0·2 million loans for the purchase of a car; 0·5 million clothing, and 0·9 million other goods and services. These estimates are, of course, subject to considerable sampling errors. Altogether, 32 per cent of employees, representing 7·7 million, received goods and services other than the use of an employer's car. Again, non-manual workers were much more likely than manual employees to experience these advantages, and to receive goods or services of substantial value, though some large groups of manual workers had specific benefits. Thus, employees of British Rail could secure rail tickets at concessionary prices, and employees of the National Coal Board obtained coal free or cheaply.

Some employees have housing subsidies from their employers. These take three principal forms: loans or grants to purchase a home, subsidized rented accommodation and rent-free accommodation. A small proportion, 3 per cent, of the sample who were living in owner-occupied homes, representing ¾ million, said they had benefited from a loan or grant. More searching inquiry might have revealed that this figure was an underestimate. Loans had usually been made at lower rates of interest than those applied by building societies, and enabled employees more easily to find the deposit on a home, or make up a mortgage to a level they could afford. A substantial proportion of people renting a home, 14 per cent, representing about 1½ million, were living in accommodation owned by an employer. Over four-fifths of them said they rented their homes for less than the rent they would expect to pay elsewhere. Finally, a further small proportion of the entire sample, also representing rather less than 1½ million, were living in rent-free accommodation owned by an employer. In the entire sample, there were therefore nearly 6 per cent, representing over 3 million people, whose accommodation was in different ways subsidized by an employer.

That some manual workers, such as agricultural workers and caretakers of schools and firms, live in homes owned by an employer has been recognized in previous studies,[1] though its extent has not previously been documented. That so many non-manual workers gain help from employers with their housing has not attracted much notice or investigation. Table 12.9 sets out the differences between

Table 12.9. *Percentages of population of non-manual and manual class living in accommodation subsidized by an employer.*

Form of subsidy by employer	Percentage of population			Estimated number (000s)		
	Non-manual	Manual	All[a]	Non-manual	Manual	All[a]
Loan or grant for owner-occupation	2·2	0·6	1·3	540	190	740
Rented cheaply from employer	3·0	1·7	2·2	750	560	1,340
Rent-free, owned by employer	2·8	2·1	2·4	690	710	1,410
All forms of subsidy	7·9	4·4	5·8	1,980	1,460	3,490

NOTE: [a]Including some not allocated by occupational class.

the population of non-manual and manual class in the extent to which different forms of subsidy are enjoyed. More non-manual than manual workers are helped by employers, and they tend to receive help of greater monetary value. Altogether, about 2 million in the population are helped, compared with 1½ million people of manual class.

1. It is, of course, by no means always an advantage. The tied cottage has on the whole been a grave disadvantage to the agricultural worker, and legislation in 1976 does not suggest that his problems have been overcome. See Newby, H., 'Tied Cottage Reform', *British Journal of Law and Society*, Summer 1977.

Finally, substantially more non-manual than manual workers had holidays with pay of three weeks or more, 54 per cent of men and 47 per cent of women, compared with 21 per cent and 19 per cent respectively. (Table A.44, Appendix Eight, page 1027). During this century, the entitlement of both non-manual and manual workers has steadily increased (though sharp inequalities between the two groups remain).[1] The period of holiday actually taken in the previous year differed sometimes from actual entitlement (as indicated in Table 12.2), both because periods of entitlement for some types of worker, like schoolteachers, are hard to define and include weeks when work is carried on, and because some employees have changed jobs, and because employees do not always take the holidays to which they are entitled. Among professional and managerial employees, around a fifth had taken five or more weeks' paid holiday.

An Index of Work Deprivation

We have discussed four different forms of work deprivation. They are, of course, correlated, and some attempt must be made to show the groups in the population who are exposed to multiple forms of work deprivation. From the data collected under the four sub-headings, we constructed an index according to which each employee could be ranked. In constructing the index, we sought to be as comprehensive in coverage as possible and to reflect the four component items (severity, security, conditions and fringe benefits of job) about equally. A score was allocated as follows:

Subject to one week's notice or less	= 1
All working time standing or walking about	= 1
Poor (or very poor) working conditions[2]	= 1 (or 2)
Working before 8 a.m. or working at night	= 1
No wages or salary during sickness	= 1
No entitlement to occupational pension	= 1
No entitlement to holiday with pay, or less than 2 weeks	= 1
Possible maximum	= 8

Table 12.10 brings out more sharply than most of the individual measures the difference between non-manual and manual employees in exposure to deprivation. Not only is there a big difference between the two groups considered as a whole, but even at the margins the difference is sharp or the overlap small. Thus, 73 per cent of male routine non-manual employees scored 2 or fewer, but 67 per cent of male skilled manual workers scored 3 or more on the index. If a score of 3

1. For a historical account, see Cameron, G. C., 'The Growth of Holidays with Pay in Britain', in Reid and Robertson, *Fringe Benefits, Labour Costs and Social Security*.
2. Depending on the score on the work conditions index described earlier.

Table 12.10. Percentages of employed men and women of different occupational class according to total work deprivation.

A. Men

Total deprivation (score)		Professional	Managerial	Supervisory High	Low	Routine non-manual	All non-manual	Skilled manual	Partly skilled manual	Unskilled manual	All manual
None	(0)	74	67	40	38	27	44	6	5	6	6
Slight	(1–2)	23	28	46	44	45	41	27	33	16	26
Substantial	(3–4)	3	4	13	17	23	14	45	46	36	44
Severe	(5)	0	2	1	1	2	1	14	15	19	15
Very severe	(6+)	0	0	0	0	3	1	8	5	24	10
Total		100	100	100	100	100	100	100	100	100	100
Number		62	54	158	155	106	535	584	284	169	1,037

B. Women

Total deprivation (score)		Professional	Managerial	Supervisory High	Low	Routine non-manual	All non-manual	Skilled manual	Partly skilled manual	Unskilled manual	All manual
None	(0)	–	–	41	33	36	37	21	23	36	27
Slight	(1–2)	–	–	47	49	40	44	29	40	39	33
Substantial	(3–4)	–	–	12	17	21	18	42	35	20	31
Severe or very severe	(5+)	–	–	0	1	2	1	8	11	4	9
Total		–	–	100	100	100	100	100	100	100	100
Number		5	16	92	89	356	558	62	254	132	448

or more is taken as representing relative work deprivation, then 16 per cent of non-manual but 69 per cent of manual workers were found to experience such deprivation.

Deprivation and Earnings

The different indices of deprivation which have been described are correlated not just with occupational class but also with level of earnings. First, pay was closely associated with class. In proceeding through the ranks of each occupational class, the proportion of employees with gross earnings below the mean tended to increase. The relatively large proportion of male routine non-manual workers with pay of under 80 per cent of the mean provide a significant exception.[1] Whereas hardly any manual workers had gross earnings of more than twice the mean, 43 per cent of professional men did so (Table 12.11). Manual workers accounted for 75 per cent of those with earnings below the mean and 45 per cent above the mean.

Secondly, within each occupational class, those with lower earnings were more likely to have poor working conditions and security. On our measures of working conditions there was an association, though usually slight, for each sex, among upper and lower non-manual and skilled manual groups; but there was no association among partly skilled and unskilled groups. According to length of entitlement to notice, the association was more consistent and usually strong. Within broad occupational classes, more of those with relatively high than with relatively low earnings were entitled to relatively long notice.

Among the worst instances of deprivation in relation to earnings were those employed at home, especially those who were engaged in piecework. 'Homeworkers' are difficult to define. We estimated that, on the broadest definition, the numbers working 'at home' throughout the United Kingdom were 150,000 employed and 390,000 self-employed men, and 280,000 employed and 330,000 self-employed women – about 150,000 of the total of 1,150,000 doing so as a second job. However, many of these worked on their own account in businesses adjoining, in or over their homes – including general practitioners, shopkeepers, music teachers and publicans. If we consider the employed, they fall into two groups. First, there were those paid to provide services – numbering about 300,000. They included insurance and clothing club agents, many of whom were poorly paid on a stringent commission basis and who were often intermediaries on the one hand in life assurance and property insurance arrangements at extraordinarily high rates of payment, or on the other hand, hire-purchase arrangements at very high rates of interest. There were also housekeepers, home helps, foster-parents, child-minders, caretakers and nurses and attendants. Secondly, there were homeworkers who, in the words of the Commission on Industrial Relations, 'receive

1. See the discussion in Chapter 10, pages 386–8.

Table 12.11. Percentages of employed men and women[a] of different occupational class with gross earnings in previous year below and above the mean.

A. Men

Gross earnings last year as percentage of mean	Professional	Managerial	Supervisory High	Supervisory Low	Routine non-manual	All non-manual	Skilled	Partly skilled	Unskilled	All manual
Under 80	4	(4)	15	28	67	26	38	55	76	48
80–99	4	(4)	24	31	20	21	33	27	13	28
100–99	45	(78)	56	39	12	44	28	18	10	23
200 or more	47	(13)	5	2	1	9	1	0	0	1
Total	100	100	100	100	100	100	100	100	100	100
Number	55	45	140	139	86	465	523	254	136	913

B. Women

Gross earnings last year as percentage of mean	Professional	Managerial	Supervisory High	Supervisory Low	Routine non-manual	All non-manual	Skilled	Partly skilled	Unskilled	All manual
Under 80	–	–	(12)	18	40	31	(52)	51	(77)	56
80–99	–	–	(6)	23	23	20	(17)	26	(11)	22
100–99	–	–	(57)	57	34	42	(27)	23	(11)	22
200 or more	–	–	(24)	2	2	7	(2)	0	(0)	0
Total	100	100	100	100	100	100	100	100	100	100
Number	3	8	49	60	223	343	40	135	35	210

NOTE: [a]All 15 and over working 1,000 hours or more in year (or an average of twenty hours for fifty weeks). Note that self-employed are excluded.

work and payment directly from a manufacturing establishment and who work in their own homes', and those paid to provide services. They were estimated on the basis of the survey to number between 100,000 and 150,000, and included clothing machinists, dressmakers, lampshade and toy-makers, workers filling and addressing envelopes, or sorting and packing different manufactured articles, and those repairing machines and household gadgets. There may have been supplementary second jobs which we missed – though we did in fact ask for this information from each adult in the household. One of the worst instances was of a slightly disabled man making lampshades for about twelve hours every week for £1·50. A machinist averaged £5 a week for twenty-five hours' work. There is evidence from other sources of the miserable rates of pay of homeworkers and lack of supervision of conditions of work.[1]

The Self-Employed

The self-employed comprised 6 per cent of the 'economically active' population in 1971, or 7 per cent of those actually in employment (8 per cent of men and 4 per cent of women).[2] In the sample, the self-employed comprised 7 per cent of those working at least one week in the preceding twelve months. Thirty-six per cent worked outdoors, and as many as 70 per cent spent all or nearly all their time standing or walking about. Many men worked long hours, 56 per cent claiming to work fifty or more hours a week, including 33 per cent claiming to work sixty hours or more. By contrast, fewer than a quarter of women claimed to work fifty hours or more. (See Table A.39, Appendix Eight, page 1024, which gives data for the year.) The dispersion of earnings was much greater than in the case of the employed. As Table 12.12 shows, proportionately more earned both considerably less and considerably more than the mean. Low earnings were not uniformly correlated with relatively few working hours. A third of the men with low pay worked fifty-five hours or more a week.

There was reliable evidence that proportionately more of the self-employed than of the employed lived in poverty or on the margins (24·5 per cent compared with 14·1 per cent).[3] They included poor farmers, smallholders, stallholders, pedlars and shopkeepers, and persons engaged as 'outworkers' in their own homes. However, a substantial proportion were prosperous. Over half (56 per cent) combined home with business in the same dwellings, whether farm, shop, professional practice or other form of business. This enabled many to offset

1. See, in particular, Brown, M., *Sweated Labour: A Study of Homework*, Low Pay Unit, London, December 1974; and Field, F., '70 Years On: A New Report on Homeworking', *Low Pay Bulletin*, August–October 1976.

2. *Social Trends*, No. 4, H M S O, London, 1973, p. 85.

3. Those having an income in the previous year of less than 140 per cent of the supplementary benefit scale rates plus housing cost. Full income data for the year were obtained from 2,242 employed and 171 self-employed persons respectively.

Table 12.12. *Percentages of self-employed and employed men and women,*[a] *according to their gross earnings as percentage of the mean.*[b]

Gross earnings as % of mean	Men		Women	
	Self-employed	Employed	Self-employed	Employed
Under 50	19	4	(29)	9
50–59	7	10	(0)	8
60–79	17	29	(26)	23
80–99	12	25	(3)	21
100–19	13	15	(6)	16
120–99	18	14	(10)	18
200–99	6	2	(26)	4
300+	8	1	(0)	1
Total	100	100	100	100
Number	121	1,270	31	528

NOTES: [a]Men aged 21 and over, women aged 18 and over, working thirty or more hours a week.
[b]For employed and self-employed combined, for each sex separately.

against tax part of the family's accommodation, lighting, heating and telephone charges. The asset value of nearly half these premises was put at £5,000 or more. Over half the self-employed (61 per cent) had a car for their business, and in nearly all instances (57 per cent), the business paid for road tax, insurance, petrol and repairs. About half (48 per cent) said they saved money through getting goods cheaply through their businesses. Relatively few of the self-employed, however, had made private arrangements for welfare benefits. Only 12 per cent had taken out pension cover, and 25 per cent cover for cash benefits during sickness.

Work Deprivation and Poverty

Just as most indices of work deprivation were found to correlate with low earnings, so they correlated with poverty. Employees who were not entitled to much or any notice, or to any holiday with pay, who were working outdoors or working unusual hours, as well as employees receiving low pay, were more likely to be members of households or of income units whose income (or income plus annuity value of assets) was below, or on the margins of, the state's poverty line. For example, 61 per cent of employees living in household poverty, and 32 per cent on the margins of poverty, had not had a holiday with pay in the previous twelve months, compared with only 17 per cent of other employees (Table A.45, Appendix Eight, page 1027). The situation of those living in poverty is therefore one compounded with deprivation at work and, as we shall discuss later, with other forms of deprivation – in housing, and environmental and social conditions. None the less, poverty and deprivation are by no means mutually inclusive. Many people with high earnings, or high incomes and assets, experience deprivation in certain aspects of life. To pursue the example just quoted, while fewer of the poor than the non-poor in the sample had had holidays with pay, *most* (70 per cent) of those not having a holiday with pay were living in households with incomes markedly higher than the state's poverty line.

Table 12.13 brings together different forms of deprivation experienced at work and relates them to income of the income unit, expressed as a percentage of the

Table 12.13. Percentages of employed poor and non-poor according to index of total work deprivation.

Work deprivation (index)	Men					
	Net disposable income last year of income unit as % of the state's poverty standard					
	Under 140		140–99		200+	
	Non-manual	Manual	Non-manual	Manual	Non-manual	Manual
Little or no deprivation (0–2)	(67)	23	81	31	87	33
Substantial (3–4)	(29)	50	18	44	11	42
Severe deprivation (5 or more)	(4)	27	1	25	1	25
Total	100	100	100	100	100	100
Number	24	122	101	245	341	558
	Women					
Little or no deprivation (0–2)	71	(57)	75	62	82	59
Substantial (3–4)	26	(41)	23	26	17	31
Severe deprivation (5 or more)	3	(2)	2	12	1	10
Total	100	100	100	100	100	100
Number	58	44	101	103	341	260

supplementary benefit standard. The two are plainly connected, but by no means as strongly as many might suppose. Income units in poverty are more likely to include people experiencing insecurity, poor working conditions and lack of fringe benefits at work. On the other hand, extremes of deprivation at work are sometimes combined, as, for example, in the case of highly paid construction workers, quarrymen, miners and foundry workers, with relatively prosperous living standards. So the apparent paradox has to be understood and weighed. Many in financial poverty also experience work deprivation; but many experiencing severe work deprivation have incomes substantially in excess of poverty standards. Thus 60 per cent of the men and 62 per cent of the women with severe work deprivation belonged to units with incomes of twice or more than twice the state's poverty standard. Most were manual workers putting up with a great deal in order to make good money.

There are three significant results in comparing poverty with work deprivation. Only 5 per cent of non-manual compared with 13 per cent of manual employees were members of income units in or on the margins of poverty by the state's standards. Secondly, most in poverty were also severely deprived at work. As many as 71 per cent of male (29 per cent of non-manual compared with 79 per cent of manual) employees living in or on the margins of poverty also experienced severe work deprivation. But thirdly, the severely deprived at work included only a small minority with poverty incomes. Only 14 per cent of all men experiencing severe work deprivation were in income units in or on the margins of poverty. So although earnings low enough to make people liable to poverty generally imply that they are also severely deprived at work, the reverse does not hold. Among employees with incomes substantially in excess of poverty levels, there is none the less a high risk of severe work deprivation. This is significantly correlated with occupational class. Nineteen per cent of non-manual employees in units with incomes twice, or more than twice, the poverty standard experienced severe work deprivation, compared with a corresponding figure of 68 per cent of manual employees.

Changes in Work Deprivation

To what extent is the work situation improving for different groups? By historical standards, there have been certain changes affecting all groups. The numbers of working hours in the day, days in the week, and weeks in the year, have diminished, as has the span of working life; and rights to paid holidays, sick pay and other welfare benefits have been extended. But, even by historical standards, there are some contrary trends. Among manual groups, shift working is increasing. 'The underlying trend in the percentage of the manual labour force on shifts in manufacturing has been about 1 per cent per annum.'[1] The extension of shopping hours, the growth of restaurant and holiday facilities, and trends particularly in the construction and power industries suggest that more manual

1. National Board for Prices and Incomes, *Hours of Work, Overtime and Shift Working*, Cmnd 4554, H M S O, London, pp. 64–5.

workers may be working unsocial hours. As mentioned earlier, after recording a growth in the number and proportion of both manual and non-manual employees entitled to an occupational pension, the Government Actuary found a *decrease* in the coverage of male and female employees between 1966 and 1971, though a continuing small increase in the coverage of non-manual employees.[1] Accident rates have also remained high. During the 1960s, the number of accidents increased, though they diminished in the early 1970s.[2] The rates are not given separately for manual and non-manual workers. And although factors other than the conditions of work play a large part in explaining trends in mortality rates, the fact that more men in unskilled manual groups at all ages between 35 and 74 died in the five years 1959–63 than in the five years 1949–53 is of major significance.[3] There were striking increases, for example, in the numbers dying from arteriosclerotic and degenerative heart disease, motor-vehicle and other accidents and lung cancer. Between 1948–50 and 1968–70, the expectation of life of men aged 45 in the United Kingdom barely changed, from 27·0 years to 27·1 years.[4] During this period, that is, during the years between 1949–53 and 1959–63, the death rates per 100,000 at all ages declined to a greater proportionate extent among social classes I and II than among III and IV and, as already noted, actually *increased* among most age groups in social class V.[5]

Underlying such trends is the presumption that, although health conditions may have improved for many manual workers in recent years, either they have deteriorated for others, or more manual workers than hitherto are exposed to risks in certain types of new industry.

Other trends may be taking place of a relative kind. Thus, the Contract of Employment Act 1963 conferred certain rights to periods of notice on large numbers of employees, but the Act seems to have resulted in a parallel acceleration in the rights granted to non-manual workers. A similar acceleration in the terms of redundancy of non-manual workers seems to have occurred after the Redundancy Payments Act 1965.[6] These examples show the care with which the structure of inequality needs to be documented and traced over a span of years. Events which seem to imply a reduction of the differences in working conditions and terms of service between manual and non-manual workers may not have this outcome.

1. *Occupational Pension Schemes, 1971.*
2. Report of the Robens Committee, pp. 3 and 161–2.
3. The Registrar General's Decennial Supplement, England and Wales, 1961. *Occupational Mortality Tables*, H M S O, London, 1971, p. 25.
4. Department of Health and Social Security, *Health and Personal Social Services Statistics for England* (with summary tables for Great Britain), H M S O, London, 1973, Table 3.9.
5. I am grateful to the Chief Medical Statistician (July 1974) for data supplementing that in the Decennial Supplement published in 1971. The data provides percentage changes in death rates, on a standardized definition of occupational class, for age groups within classes.
6. Wedderburn, D., 'Inequality at Work', in Townsend, P., and Bosanquet, N., *Labour and Inequality*, Fabian Society, London, 1972, pp. 181–2.

Further privileges conferred upon, or gained by, non-manual groups may maintain their advantage over manual groups, despite general advances in the number and scale of employee rights.

Satisfaction with Work

In the survey, therefore, measures of the character of work, its security, conditions and fringe benefits, were obtained. As already discussed, some fringe benefits, like subsidized meals, are virtually extensions of pay, while others, like sick pay and occupational pensions, are extensions of security. What of employees' attitudes towards their work? An attempt was made to obtain subjective measures parallel to the objective measures of character of work, security, conditions and pay. Ideally, we would have wished to pursue attitudes to the working situation in much greater detail, as, for example, in other recent British studies.[1] For reasons of time we asked four general questions:

Are you satisfied,
Neither satisfied nor dissatisfied,
or dissatisfied,
 (i) with the pay?
 (ii) with facilities at work (like heating, canteen, etc.)?
 (iii) with the security of the job (like amount of notice and prospect of keeping the job)?
 (iv) with the job itself?

The difficulties of adopting this approach to workers' attitudes can be readily appreciated in considering the general distribution of replies, as set out in Table 12.14. As in other studies, the majority of workers tend to give favourable answers. When asked to rate levels of satisfaction, answers tend to be positive. At first sight, this suggests an inconsistency between the frequencies and degrees of objective and subjective deprivation. But, as argued in the previous chapter,[2] this can be explained partly as a function of the respective correspondence or specificity of objective and subjective measures. Objective measures which are adopted in surveys, even of the complex kind described here, do not comprehensively represent the material circumstances of any specific work situation. Nor are attitude questions built up in sufficient detail either to cover different aspects of the work situation, towards which attitudes may vary, or ensure consistency of understanding. A worker may express satisfaction with a poor job because it is better than his last job; or because, given his age or disability, he considers himself lucky to have a job at all; or because it is as good as any job someone in his position can expect. And he will tend to convey satisfaction with a job in general –

1. See, in particular, Goldthorpe, J. H., Lockwood, D., Bechhofer, F., and Platt, J., *The Affluent Worker: Industrial Attitudes and Behaviour*, Cambridge University Press, 1968.
2. See pages 425–6.

Table 12.14. *Percentages of employed men and women of non-manual and manual status according to their satisfaction with their jobs.*

Aspect of job	Men			Women		
Degree of satisfaction	Non-manual	Manual	All	Non-manual	Manual	All
Pay						
Dissatisfied	31	30	30	20	18	19
Neither dissatisfied nor satisfied	18	19	18	13	14	13
Satisfied	52	51	51	67	68	67
Total	100	100	100	100	100	100
Number	507	967	1,474	350	296	646
Facilities						
Dissatisfied	10	16	14	11	13	12
Neither dissatisfied nor satisfied	9	16	14	10	10	10
Satisfied	82	68	73	79	77	78
Total	100	100	100	100	100	100
Number	482	851	1,333	349	282	631
Security						
Dissatisfied	6	16	13	5	8	6
Neither dissatisfied nor satisfied	8	10	9	9	10	9
Satisfied	86	74	78	87	83	85
Total	100	100	100	100	100	100
Number	508	952	1,460	352	289	641
Job itself						
Dissatisfied	7	6	6	8	5	5
Neither dissatisfied nor satisfied	12	13	13	14	9	9
Satisfied	81	81	81	78	87	85
Total	100	100	100	100	100	100
Number	508	962	1,470	257	297	654

especially in answer to broad questions – but dissatisfaction with features of that job. The very fact that people operate within any particular occupational situation is likely to predispose them in general allegiance towards it. They *want* to believe that that situation is for the best and that there is no easy alternative. There are both social as well as psychological pressures in favour of them expressing general approval of what they are doing. The social pressures exist to ensure order, stability and continuity of work and other behaviour in society. In addition, 'There is considerable psychological pressure upon the individual to say that he finds his job acceptable: to say otherwise may well be tantamount to admitting that he does not find *himself* acceptable.'[1]

More manual than non-manual workers were dissatisfied with facilities and security of work, and though rates of satisfaction were greater than the objective data about deprivation seemed to warrant, this subjective difference did at least broadly correspond with objective differences. But as many non-manual as manual workers expressed dissatisfaction with their level of pay, despite their higher levels of pay. In the case of men, as many also expressed dissatisfaction with the job itself and, in the case of women, slightly more expressed dissatisfaction with the job. Among men, the highest rates of job satisfaction were found among professional workers, and the lowest among unskilled manual workers. Altogether, 38 per cent of male non-manual employees, compared with 43 per cent of manual employees, expressed dissatisfaction with at least one of the four matters relating to their jobs which were investigated. The figures for women were 28 per cent and 33 per cent respectively. In general, more women than men expressed satisfaction with their jobs.

A more direct check on the correspondence between objective and subjective deprivation is to find whether those with poor working conditions, security and levels of pay tended to express dissatisfaction. The indices selected in Table 12.15 show there was such a correlation. A tentative method of comparing indices of total work deprivation and job satisfaction is presented in Table A.46 (Appendix Eight, page 1028), which further supports this result. Therefore there exists evidence of a relationship between poor material conditions and subjective deprivation. But the correlation is by no means uniform. How far this is because our objective measures were partial and our subjective measures too generalized remains problematical. Certainly these matters deserve exploration in further research before too much effort is needlessly invested in explaining disjunction between objective status and subjective feelings which may turn out to be more apparent than real. None the less, the evidence to some extent supports those who have argued both that manual workers tend to adopt *instrumental* attitudes towards their work, in terms of the rewards they seek to enrich life outside work,

1. Goldthorpe *et al.*, *The Affluent Worker*, p. 11, citing Blauner, R., 'Work Satisfaction and Industrial Trends in Modern Society', in Galenson, W., and Lipset, S. M. (eds.), *Labor and Trade Unionism*, New York, 1960.

Table 12.15. Percentages of male and female employees of different occupational class and job characteristics who were dissatisfied with selected characteristics of their jobs.

Job charac-teristics	Percentage				Total number			
	Men		Women		Men		Women	
	Non-manual	Manual	Non-manual	Manual	Non-manual	Manual	Non-manual	Manual
Dissatisfied with facilities								
Indoor facilities good[a]	7	3	(28)	5	307	248	43	243
Indoor facilities poor or very poor[a]	(27)	36	(34)	7	26	137	44	80
Dissatisfied with pay								
Gross earnings 120% or more of mean	24	24	21	(17)	157	85	112	24
Gross earnings under 80% mean	35	32	15	22	119	426	106	106
Dissatisfied with job security								
Subject to notice of *more* than month	6	(0)	3	–	93	18	39	1
Subject to week's notice or less	11	18	9	5	83	503	146	156

NOTE: [a]As defined in work conditions index. See page 438.

rather than take intrinsic satisfaction in the job and the conditions in which it is performed; and that the attitudes brought to work are shaped substantially by such workers' experiences, and needs, in the home and the family, which for many are of greater emotional significance.[1] Many manual workers have low expectations of their work situation and feel less able to control that situation than they do their lives outside work. Not expecting much, they are less likely to demand the kind of equality of treatment they expect as members of a household or a local community, or as citizens, patients or even consumers. Despite membership of trade unions, many feel powerless (except in bargaining for pay) in *this* situation, by comparison with many other situations. With the qualifications already made about the *validity* of some favourable responses to general questions about job satisfaction, this is the best interpretation that can be offered to explain both the relatively low number of negative responses and the rather greater dissatisfaction expressed about pay than other aspects of the work situation.

Summary and Conclusion

This chapter calls attention to the importance of the concept of 'occupational hierarchy' in explaining work deprivation. Much of human life is lived at work, and deprivation can be experienced in the work situation even when it is not experienced in other social situations. This chapter argues that social conceptions of deficiencies in the work situation tend to be restricted to questions of industrial ill-health or hazards, the characteristics of particular types of industry or forms of employment, and specific rather than interconnected features of employment. As a consequence, society fails to perceive certain kinds of problem or how severe they are, and is insufficiently aware of the possibilities of systematic causation. Despite differences in the kind of products, services rendered, size, organization and locality of plant and type of technology, there are social forces which reproduce the same kinds of inequality or deprivation in the work situation in a variety of different contexts.

The chapter sought to assess the severity and nature of the job itself; its security; its conditions and amenities; and the welfare or fringe benefits often associated with it. In each instance, manual workers were found to be at a marked disadvantage compared with non-manual workers. The dichotomy between non-manual and manual work is clearly the most important fact to emerge from this analysis of the work situation of the employed population. Manual workers work longer hours and more weeks of the year, have shorter holidays, are more likely to work outdoors and to have poor amenities at work, are more likely to spend all their working time standing or walking about, are more liable to unemployment, redundancy and very short periods of notice of dismissal, and are

1. Goldthorpe *et al.*, *The Affluent Worker*, Chapter 8.

much less likely to receive sick pay, occupational pensions and other fringe benefits.

Within these two broad non-manual and manual sections of the employed population, there are other differences to which attention has been called. Among non-manual employees, especially women, considerably more professional and managerial than other workers, especially than routine non-manual workers, have certain privileges. And among manual workers, considerably more skilled and partly skilled than unskilled workers have certain privileges.

A number of indices of the work situation have been described. They include period of entitlement to notice, 'usual' hours of work, fraction of working time spent standing or walking about, entitlement to sick pay, paid holidays and occupational pensions, and poor conditions and amenities at work. When these different factors are combined, we found that 12 per cent of the employed population could be said to be very deprived, and another 30 per cent deprived, in their work situation. Deprivation was correlated with occupational class. None of those in professional and managerial groups, but 43 per cent of unskilled male manual workers, were very deprived. Within occupational classes, those with low pay tended to be more deprived.

Fewer employees expressed dissatisfaction with the security of work, its conditions and the job itself than the objective facts seemed to warrant, though this may have been partly a function of general instead of specific questioning during our interviews. Employees expressed dissatisfaction with level of pay more than they did other aspects of their work situation. There was a strong, but by no means uniform, correspondence between objective and subjective deprivation.

The quality of the work situation has to be assessed not just in relation to past but also present employment. Changes in legislation and improvements in employer provisions encourage commentators to reach complacent conclusions about progress. Analyses which depend only on comparisons with past standards fail to take account of differential advances that may have been taking place, particularly between non-manual and manual grades, within the employed population. Evidence of trends in mortality, accidents and the distribution of fringe benefits suggests that inequalities in the work situation may in recent years not have narrowed, and in some respects have widened, as between manual and non-manual groups.

13

Deprivation in Housing

Urban and rural poverty and the problems of the slums cannot be understood or explained without a knowledge of the operation of the different institutions of the housing market and the ownership of land, together with a knowledge of the social allocation, cost and use of all accommodation. This chapter aims to elucidate the latter. It will start by analysing the distribution of poor housing (identified by three separate criteria), and housing costs according to type of tenure, social class and household type, and will go on to examine the interrelationship between poor housing, housing costs and poverty. Finally, some of the reasons for the existence and scale of poor housing and the present structure of costs are discussed.

The Problem of Obtaining Objective Measures of Poor Housing

Historically, three standards or measures of poor housing have been used: of inadequate structure, amenities and space in relation to the numbers of users. As in our previous analysis of poverty and deprivation, a distinction must be made between standards as they are perceived socially and standards which in some sense of the term can be said to be objective. This is basic to any understanding of 'the housing problem', and can be illustrated historically and contemporaneously. Thus the standards which have been used historically can be shown to have changed. For example, Octavia Hill and other reformers who were concerned to improve the housing of the working classes adopted as a standard the assumptions that privies and a water tap could be shared by several households on the same landing, and that it was justifiable for a family with one or two or even several children to live in a single room.[1] During this century, successively more

1. In 1883, Octavia Hill argued that 'good-sized' single rooms should be built to meet the needs of (a) 'The small families of unskilled labourers', and (b) 'the larger families of unskilled labourers who have one or two children old enough to work, and who can afford to take a second or even a third room, but whose wages do not allow of their paying for the more elaborate appliances provided in tenements intended for artisans' – Hill, O., *Homes of the London Poor* (2nd edn), Macmillan, London, 1883, pp. 14–15.

generous standards have been adopted officially as a result of the recommendations in 1919 of the Tudor Walters Committee, in 1944 of the Dudley Committee and in 1961 of the Parker Morris Committee.[1] In the same way, the official census definition of overcrowding was changed in 1961 from two or more persons per room to over one and a half, and shows signs of being changed again in the 1970s.[2]

Social perceptions of housing standards or needs tend therefore to change with the passage of time. However, the process by which this comes about has not been carefully traced and is little understood. Evidence collected by research workers and others about deprivation and ill-health, for example, has undoubtedly had a marked effect on public opinion, and hence on social standards. The work of Chadwick and Simon on the relationship between overcrowding and infectious disease paved the way for Public Health Acts, just as work on pollution at Billingham,[3] the problems of high flats[4] and hypothermia among the elderly[5] may contribute to changes in modern standards. But such evidence has often been interpreted less seriously by housing administrators and the public than it deserves, or has even been framed in terms which compromise with conventional opinion. More depended in the past on the gradual recognition among the population and particularly among elites of changes in styles of living in the home, the spread of new kinds of equipment and facilities and the development of new attitudes about policy strategies engendered by the general system of social values. Thus the Parker Morris Committee recognized that home conditions as well as expectations had changed since the Dudley Committee reported in 1944, but made little or no attempt to examine systematically the distribution of practices, methods and expectations of a method of deriving new standards. Their report represents more the results of a kind of osmosis among the members of the committee, by which a consensus judgement about what seems practicable and attainable to reasonable men is reached. It is neither a searching and comprehensive examina-

1. Ministry of Housing and Local Government, *Homes for Today and Tomorrow*, Report of a Sub-Committee of the Central Housing Advisory Committee (The Parker Morris Report), HMSO, London, 1961.

2. 'In 1961, 2·1 per cent of households in England and Wales, and 3·8 per cent in Great Britain, were overcrowded by this measure; by 1966 the proportions had fallen to 1·2 per cent and 2·1 per cent respectively, and by 1971 (according to GHS data) to 0·6 per cent and 1·0 per cent. *Under these circumstances consideration should be given to the adequacy of such a measure.*' (my emphasis) – Office of Population Censuses and Surveys, Social Survey Division, *The General Household Survey*, Introductory Report, HMSO, London, 1973, p. 113.

3. Gregory, P., *Polluted Homes*, Bell, London, 1965.

4. Jephcott, P., *Homes in High Flats*, Oliver & Boyd, London, 1971.

5. Report of the Committee on Accidental Hypothermia, Royal College of Physicians, London, 1966. See also report of research being undertaken at the Centre for Environmental Studies (Annual Report, 1971), and Wicks, M., 'Death in a Cold Climate', *Guardian*, 18 February 1974.

tion of the housing situation, nor a full assessment of the capacities or resources available in society to meet housing needs.

Social perceptions of housing problems are very restricted. They are conditioned, and in effect distorted, by the rules and fashions accepted in Parliament, the press and elsewhere by which housing is discussed. Housing problems come to be defined in ways which are acceptable to ruling elites, particularly the government, and are measured according to procedures devised by government and local-authority services. The problems are, for example, seen as problems of attaining a minimum or threshold standard defined at some point in the past, and without regard to inequalities, or even interrelationships, within the existing system, rather than as problems of maximizing welfare and restraining privilege in housing in terms of today's resources and styles of living. The philosophy of a historic national minimum underpinning a free market pervades statements of policy, but also administration and the presentation of information, including statistical information, about the problems. There are tendencies among officials to underestimate the true scale and severity of housing problems,[1] to use outdated fixed standards of measuring them instead of relative standards,[2] and to overlook or even conceal the extent and growth of privileged housing among the wealthier sections of society, which may lead indirectly to relative impoverishment elsewhere in the system.[3] This must not be regarded so much as calculated deception as an inevitable consequence of the limited roles and functions that officials are expected to play in administering housing, their unconscious as well as conscious efforts to represent problems as within their powers to manage, and their need to represent their administrative achievements in the best possible light. This suggests how a restricted perception of a particular problem in society is arrived at, circulated and reinforced. Nevertheless, the conclusion must be faced. Emerging as well as continuing inequalities in housing are minimized.

1. The local-authority returns on the numbers of slum dwellings, both in 1954 and 1965, were subsequently shown to underestimate the scale of the problem. A Ministry of Housing survey carried out by public health inspectors found that there were 1·8 million unfit dwellings in England and Wales in the mid 1960s, and not 820,000, as counted by the local authorities. See 'House Conditions Survey, England and Wales, 1967', Economic Trends, No. 175, H M S O, London, 1968. A Scottish survey came to the conclusion that the true number of unfit dwellings was at least twice the official figure. See Scotland's Older Houses (The Cullingworth Report), H M S O, Edinburgh, 1967.

2. The best example historically is the repeated claim by Ministers of Housing that the back of the slum-clearance problem was going to be broken within the next five years or ten years, ranging, for example, from Sir Hilton Young in 1933 to Mr Harold Macmillan in 1955 and Mr Julian Amery in 1971. No account seemed to be taken of 'twilight' houses that become slums as time goes on, or of the periodic redefinition of the meaning of 'slum' as society becomes more prosperous.

3. For example, government White Papers on housing in 1971 and 1973 did not examine the effects of changes in owner-occupation on the rest of the housing market, nor the effects of the acquisition of second homes on homelessness in certain areas.

Perceptions of housing problems tend also to be biased in favour of physical rather than social manifestations. Any review of the literature on housing, particularly official surveys of conditions in the census and by central departments, will show that disproportionate attention is given to physical appearance, amenities and layout compared with social and economic allocation and use and financial cost. Again, this might be charitably explained: visual eyesores are easier than the special social and financial problems that certain kinds of family have in restrictive physical settings to communicate to councillors, officials and the public. They dominate the preoccupations, training and organization, for example, of the architectural and planning professions.

Certain lessons can be drawn from any attempt by social scientists to understand how housing problems come to be perceived and discussed in society. They can use the standards defined by society itself in its legislation and administrative regulations, or implicit in its policy decisions, to find how far these standards are actually fulfilled. They can also see that such standards are socially created and both differ from those prevailing in other societies and apply only to a particular historical period, being replaced at a subsequent stage. In principle, they must strive to adopt an alternative or objective standard which will allow them to compare the situations in different countries or in the same country at different moments of history.

In what follows, therefore, an attempt will be made to document poor housing as subjectively and socially perceived, but also to strive towards an alternative standard, principally by applying measures of housing within a distributional framework.

Different Indices of Poor Housing

Poor housing has traditionally been defined first in terms of structural defects. A series of Housing Acts has sought to define 'unfit' or slum housing, and official measures have been produced both locally and centrally. In practice, the designation is imprecise and lends itself to misapplication to suit administrative planning convenience.[1] In the poverty survey, we were not able to use an inde-

1. As the Minister of Housing states, the term 'slum' is 'variously applied to houses unfit for human habitation, unfit houses beyond repair at reasonable cost and houses in clearance areas' (parliamentary written answer, February 1971). The criteria are set out in Section 4 of the Housing Act 1957, as amended by Section 71 of the Housing Act 1969: 'In determining . . . whether a house is unfit for human habitation, regard shall be had to . . . (a) repair, (b) stability, (c) freedom from damp, (d) natural lighting, (e) ventilation, (f) water supply, (g) drainage and sanitary conveniences, (h) facilities for . . . preparation and cooking of food and for the disposal of waste water (plus internal arrangements of dwelling, added by the 1969 Act) and the house shall be deemed unfit for human habitation if and only if it is so far defective in one or more of the said matters that it is not reasonably suitable for occupation in that condition.' The phrase 'is not reasonably suitable' is, of course, open to flexible interpretation.

pendent and consistently applied measure and simply asked informants whether their housing had any structural defects, carefully prompting answers on such specific questions as rising damp, damp walls or ceilings, loose brickwork or plaster, roofs which leaked, windows and doors which fitted badly or did not open or close, and floorboards or stairs which were broken. Twenty-two per cent of households, representing about 13 million people, declared there were defects. This compares with under 12 per cent of dwellings found to be unfit, and under 35 per cent defined as fit but requiring more than £125 repairs in the official Household Conditions survey of February 1967.[1] When asked whether such defects were felt to be a danger to their health, nearly a third, representing over 7 per cent of the entire sample and 4 million in the population, said they were.

Secondly, poor housing has been defined traditionally in terms of inadequate housing facilities, such as lack of piped water, a bath and a W C. The 1969 Housing Act provided improvement grants for homes with a life of at least fifteen years that needed to be brought up to a five-point standard of having an internal W C, fixed bath or shower, wash-basin, hot and cold water at three points and a sink. In February 1967, it was estimated that 25 per cent of all dwellings in England and Wales failed to satisfy the first four of these criteria (about two fifths of these being unfit for human habitation).[2] According to the Census of 1966, about 20 per cent of households in Britain lacked sole use of a bath or shower, and by 1971 this figure was estimated in the General Household Survey to have declined to 12 per cent.[3] The comparable figure established in the poverty survey was 17 per cent (Table 13.1). In 1971 there were, according to the General Household Survey, 15 per cent lacking sole use of a W C inside the accommodation, or 17 per cent inside the building.[4] The corresponding figure in the poverty survey was 16 per cent. We sought to combine information about the 'basic' facilities of internal W C, sink or wash-basin, fixed bath or shower and gas or electric cooker which had been used in previous censuses, and evolved a 'housing facilities index'. A score of 2 was assigned to the household for each of these four facilities if it was lacking entirely, and 1 if it was shared, thus allowing us to grade the extent to which households satisfied this social standard of sole access to these basic facilities. As Table 13.1 shows, 21 per cent of households failed in one or more respects to satisfy the standard.

Again, any fixed standard becomes rapidly outdated. In the case of housing facilities, this is beginning to be recognized more readily than with some other standards, simply because of the speed with which changes have occurred. Thus data about central heating were collected in the General Household Survey, and the authors of the report point out, 'in 1960 only 8 per cent of households in Greater London, and 5 per cent in the rest of England and Wales, had any form

1. *Economic Trends*, No. 175, Table 5, p. xxxii.   2. ibid.
3. *The General Household Survey*, Introductory Report, pp. 137 and 139.
4. ibid, p. 139.

of central heating; by 1971 these figures had risen to 30 per cent and 36 per cent respectively'.[1] Ideally, a more objective standard could be produced, first, by attempting to list *all* household facilities, including any new facilities being intro-duced into homes – which in the 1970s might, for the United Kingdom, include air-conditioning and ventilation units, immersion heaters, built-in kitchen work-ing surfaces and cupboards, double-glazed windows, two or three electric points in every room, sink grinder units and calcifiers (low temperature incinerators which sterilize and dehydrate putrescible refuse and reduce its bulk). Secondly, the possession of these facilities could be shown within a distributional frame-work, in relation to the mode and the mean. This would allow relative changes as well as changes by historical standards to be better traced. Some care would of course have to be taken in redefining the respective possession of facilities, which are a kind of 'fixture' in the home and which are left when the occupant moves, and consumer durables, like refrigerators and washing-up machines.

We could not fulfil these principles in the survey, but added questions on cen-tral heating and telephones, which were at the time, and still are, rapidly being converted from the privilege of a minority to the expected possession of the majority of the population. Table 13.1 shows that, at the time, these minority facilities were far more common among the middle than the working class. A measure of the number of rooms usually heated in winter was also introduced. We asked how many of the total number of living, dining and bedrooms were usu-ally heated during the evenings in winter, whether by coal, gas or electric fire, paraffin stove or central heating. It is, of course, difficult to express the results in a form equally appropriate for different types of household living in different num-bers of rooms. We found that 44 per cent of households usually heated only one room in winter, and that another 24 per cent, having four rooms or more, heated only two. Since it might be argued that some people – for example, single people living in centrally heated bedsitters – should not be treated as 'deprived', we have also presented the results in terms of those with all or four fifths or more of their accommodation heated, those with three fifths to four fifths, those with half, or just under or just over a half, those with between a fifth and two fifths, and those with under a fifth. As Table 13.1 shows, 48 per cent had under two fifths of their accommodation heated.

A third traditional definition of poor housing is inadequate space, or high den-sity. The 1935 Housing Act, for example, gave a statutory definition of over-crowding, not permitting more than two people to occupy a single room, three for two rooms, five for three rooms, seven for four rooms, and so on. Implicitly, every room was treated as if it was available for sleeping. The standard was not one regarded as desirable but as a minimum. Although occupancy rates had con-tinued to fall, the Housing Act of 1957 reiterated this definition. By 1964, only 0·5 per cent of households in England and Wales were overcrowded in this

1. *The General Household Survey*, Introductory Report, p. 136.

Table 13.1. Percentages of households and persons in households having different characteristics who experienced or felt different kinds of housing deprivation.

	House-holds	Males and fe-males	Males	Fe-males	Age						Occupational class			
					0–4	5–14	15–29	30–49	50–64	65+	Profes-sional and mana-gerial	Other non-manual	Skilled manual	Partly skilled and un-skilled manual
With structural defects	22	24	24	24	28	27	27	22	22	19	18	17	28	31
Poor housing facilities	21	18	18	17	18	15	19	15	18	24	4	11	20	29
– no sole use internal WC	16	13	14	12	13	10	15	11	14	17	2	8	14	23
– no sole use sink or wash-basin	3	3	3	2	2	2	4	2	3	1	0	2	2	4
– no sole use fixed bath or shower	17	13	13	13	13	9	15	11	14	19	3	8	15	22
– no sole use gas or electric cooker	4	3	3	3	3	3	3	3	2	4	1	2	2	6
No electricity for both power and lights	2	2	2	2	2	2	2	2	2	3	0	2	1	4
Accommodation less than 1 room per person	3	3	4	3	8	7	4	2	1	0	0	1	3	9
Accommodation less than bedroom standard	11	18	19	17	31	28	22	17	10	4	5	13	19	29
Only 1 room (or none) heated in winter	44	40	39	40	41	34	38	34	45	51	14	30	46	54

Less than 40% of accommodation heated	48	48	47	48	46	46	45	43	53	58	31	43	51	59
No central heating	83	82	82	82	80	79	83	78	86	90	46	78	89	94
No telephone in household	69	68	67	68	74	65	71	64	65	74	16	53	81	91
No vacuum cleaner	22	19	19	20	23	17	23	14	16	29	3	13	19	35
Insufficient internal play space for children[a]	5	19[a]	20[a]	18[a]	20[a]	19[a]	–	–	–	–	1	13	24	31
Moved twice or more in the last 2 years	4	3	3	3	4	3	8	3	0	0	3	3	3	3
Need expressed for additional room(s)	25	34	35	33	53	50	38	39	14	8	31	32	38	34
Serious housing problem now	6	7	8	7	13	9	7	7	5	5	2	5	8	13
Serious housing problem since head aged 21	21	24	24	23	23	30	25	26	21	14	11	21	27	29
Structural defects felt to be danger to health	7	8	8	8	11	10	10	7	8	6	2	5	9	16

NOTE: [a]Children aged 1–10 only.

statutory sense,[1] and, as is now recognized, it has become 'irrelevant as a measure of satisfactory conditions'.[2] An alternative 'bedroom standard' was adopted by the Government Social Survey in 1960.[3] This depended on allocating bedrooms according to the composition of the household:

1. A married couple was presumed to need one room.
2. Each additional person aged 21 and over was presumed to need one room.
3. Others under 21 were presumed to share with one other, or to occupy a room alone if there was no other with whom to share, but persons aged 10–20 were not expected to share with someone under 20 if he or she was of the opposite sex.

This standard is arbitrary and is not related to family customs. It presumes, for example, that two boys of 17 and 19 can share a room and a girl of 9 with a boy of 9, but not a girl of 9 and a boy of 10; and that two rooms are needed both for a boy of 11 and a girl of 10, and for two boys and two girls all aged 15–20. No allowance is made for a bedroom for visitors. While acknowledging vaguely that future work might lead to the adoption of a 'living standard', and perhaps also take account of the purpose to which the available rooms are put, the standard has none the less been treated in the analysis of the General Household Survey as a 'convenient yardstick' that has gained acceptance by adoption in previous surveys.[4]

Official surveys showed that the number of households in England and Wales with fewer rooms than the bedroom standard declined from 11 to 6 per cent between 1960 and 1971, and in Scotland from 21 to 15 per cent between 1965 and 1971.[5] In the poverty survey, applying to the United Kingdom as a whole, there were 11 per cent. In both official and independent surveys, the percentage of population was much larger than of households. In the poverty survey, 17·7 per cent of the sample, representing nearly 10 million people, lived in accommodation with insufficient bedrooms.

The official presentation of statistics about density in terms of the bedroom standard does, in fact, go some way towards showing density in a full distributional framework, and hence paves the way for an understanding of relative deprivation. But results are still presented in terms which cut short the distribution at its extremes. Thus, 21 per cent of households in Britain were shown in 1971 to have two 'or more' bedrooms above the standard.[6] There is, of course, a substan-

1. Woolf, M., *The Housing Survey in England and Wales*, Social Survey, SS372, Ministry of Housing and Local Government, March 1967.
2. *The General Household Survey*, Introductory Report, p. 112.
3. Gray, P. G., and Russell, R., *The Housing Situation in 1960*, Social Survey, SS319, Central Office of Information, May 1962.
4. *The General Household Survey*, Introductory Report, p. 114.
5. ibid., p. 114. There was a further decline in England and Wales, from 6 to about 4 per cent (or from 990,000 to 710,000). Department of the Environment, *Housing Policy*, Technical Volume: Part I, H M S O, London, 1977, p. 67.
6. *The General Household Survey*, Introductory Report, p. 115.

tial minority with three or more rooms above the standard. The poverty survey found 1 per cent with four or more bedrooms above the standard. Similarly, the Census of 1966 found that there were 34 per cent of households in Britain with a ratio of 'under 0·5' persons a room, and by 1971 this figure was 37 per cent.[1] Again, the point might be made that the full extent of inequality is not revealed through this processing of the data. Thus, it is possible to estimate from some of the detailed tables in the census report of 1966 that there were 100,000 people in England and Wales living, at one extreme, in just over 30,000 rooms, while there were 100,000 living, at the other extreme, in 750,000 rooms.[2] According to the poverty survey, while there were 3·3 per cent living in overcrowded conditions (on the criterion of two or more persons to a room, including living rooms, dining rooms and bedrooms), there were, at the other extreme, 1·9 per cent with four or more rooms for every person.

The need for better standards of space has been recognized by committees of inquiry, such as the Parker Morris Committee, and is widely felt among the population. Altogether, as many as 25 per cent of households, representing 17 million people, felt the need for at least one additional room, more than a third of them for two or more additional rooms. Subjective deprivation in this sense was greater than according to most other indices applied in the survey, and though common among the poor and the working class, tended to be marked also among upper income groups and middle classes. The figure stands up to comparison with other data. It was highly correlated, for example, with low ratios of rooms to persons. As Table A.47 in Appendix Eight (page 1029) shows, two thirds of those judged by the bedroom standard to have too few bedrooms wanted more rooms, and almost none wanted fewer. By contrast, very few of those judged by this standard to have more than enough bedrooms in fact wanted more. The great majority thought their accommodation was adequate, and as many as a quarter wanted fewer rooms.

Another measure of subjective deprivation is how seriously housing needs are rated. We asked whether the family had a *serious* housing problem now. Six per cent of heads of households or chief wage-earners said they did, nearly a third specifying overcrowding and over a fifth damp. Others specified inadequate basic facilities and various structural defects, and some a need to move elsewhere. Interviewers were inclined to believe that people were reluctant to regard their housing problems as 'serious', and that some in accommodation with marked deficiencies in structure, or who were overcrowded, stated they did not have a serious problem.

1. *The General Household Survey*, Introductory Report, p. 127.
2. Calculated from General Register Office, *Sample Census, 1966, England and Wales, Housing Tables*, Part I, p. 9. Census data on numbers of rooms must, however, be treated with reservations. In 1966, households having only one room were underestimated by 52 per cent. see Gray, P., and Gee, F. A., *A Quality Check of the 1966 Ten Per Cent Sample Census of England and Wales*, Social Survey Division, OPCS, HMSO, London, 1972.

To these attempts to measure structural defects, inadequate housing facilities and overcrowding respectively in terms of subjective, social and more objective standards, we also added as an index of deprivation insufficient indoor play-space for children. People with children aged 1–10 were asked whether the children had enough good places to play indoors without troubling the neighbours. Seventeen per cent of such families or five per cent of households of all types, representing nearly a million families in the United Kingdom, said they had not (Table 13.1).

Finally, evidence of deprivation experienced by people in the past was also collected. After asking whether households had a serious current housing problem, we asked whether they had experienced one, and for how long, since the head of the household had reached the age of 21. Twenty-one per cent declared they had experienced such a problem, including 9 per cent specifying overcrowding, 4 per cent inadequate basic facilities, 2 per cent damp or other structural defects, 3 per cent the need to move elsewhere, and 3 per cent other types of problem. As many as 20 per cent said this had lasted for ten or more years, a further 16 per cent for five to nine years, and only 31 per cent for under two years. Housing stress is, of course, typified as much by pressure or need to move as by poor conditions in the home. Four per cent of the entire sample had moved at least twice in the previous two years, 1 per cent four or more times.

Characteristics of the Poorly Housed

The problems of housing are distributed more widely than is sometimes supposed. Table 13.2 shows that Scotland, the South-West and Wales, and Northern Ireland, in that order, had the largest proportion, between 30 per cent and 34 per cent, of households with structural defects, but the two regions with the smallest proportions, the North-West and Anglia and the East Midlands, each had 17 per cent. Households with structural defects were not concentrated in rural rather than urban areas or conurbations, and although there were more in low-income than in other areas, the differences were not very large.

By other measures of poor housing, some regions, such as Greater London and Anglia and the East Midlands, ranked higher than, or nearly as high as, Scotland and the South-West and Wales, although Northern Ireland was ranked worst by all measures. It is unlikely, then, that the explanation of poor housing is to be sought according to specifically regional or even area characteristics, at least of large areas. Two other points have to be noted in considering regional and area differences. In some instances, the proportion of households with poor housing is smaller, and in some instances higher, than the proportion of population in such households. In Northern Ireland, a strikingly higher proportion of people than of households had inadequate housing facilities and insufficient bedrooms. In some other regions, the proportion of population living in poor facilities is smaller than

Table 13.2. Percentages of households in regions and areas with poor housing (percentages of individuals in brackets).

Region	With structural defects	Inadequate housing facilities		Insufficient bedrooms	
Scotland	34	20	(15)	17	(28)
South-West and Wales	30	26	(18)	7	(14)
Northern Ireland	30	45	(53)	24	(41)
Northern Yorks and Humberside	22	25	(24)	8	(15)
Greater London	21	24	(20)	12	(19)
South-East	19	13	(9)	6	(9)
West Midlands	18	13	(11)	12	(18)
Anglia and East Midlands	17	24	(21)	10	(18)
North-West	17	16	(12)	9	(18)
Rural	24	17	(13)	8	(13)
Urban	23	22	(18)	10	(18)
Conurban	21	22	(20)	12	(20)

of households. This is explained by the tendency in most areas for more small households, including old people, to be in housing with poor facilities. In Northern Ireland, both old people and families with children are in poor housing. It should also be noted that some regions ranking low in defects had large populations. For example, although the proportions of households with structural defects was much smaller in Greater London and the South-East than in Scotland, each of these regions accounted for as many of the total households with defects, as did Scotland.

Poor housing was widely distributed by household type. By nearly all criteria, households with a man and woman and four or more children showed to great disadvantage, but in some respects they were run close or overtaken by other types of household. Some of the larger types of household, with four adults, three adults with children, and with four or more children, were more likely to be in accommodation with structural defects (Table 13.3). But even among households with a man and woman and only one or two children, the percentage with structural defects was not much lower than the average. Table 13.3 shows, however, that single-person households were much more likely than households with children to have inadequate housing facilities, though the latter, especially households with three or more children, were much more likely to have insufficient rooms, by social standards.

This difference is important for our understanding of housing problems and

Table 13.3. *Percentages of households of different type with poor housing.*

Type of household	With structural defects	Inadequate housing facilities	Insufficient bedrooms[a]	Less than two fifths of accommodation heated	Serious housing problem now
Man over 60	(20)	(37)	(0)	(65)	(3)
Man under 60	18	56	0	37	2
Woman over 60	22	32	1	54	5
Woman under 60	22	37	0	45	2
Man and woman	20	23	1	49	5
Man, woman, 1 child	20	19	12	37	7
2 children	16	13	9	42	9
3 children	25	10	20	46	9
4+ children	27	20	38	55	13
3 adults	19	14	5	56	6
3 adults + children	25	11	23	43	4
4 adults	30	13	17	44	6
Others without children	20	19	26	52	1
Others with children	33	15	50	40	11
All types	22	21	11	48	6

NOTE: [a]According to the bedroom standard.

can be highlighted by other data. Sixty-four per cent of single-person households, a high proportion of whom were elderly people, compared with 44 per cent of households consisting of a man and woman, and 36 per cent consisting of a man, woman and children, had only one room or none usually heated in winter (Table A.48, Appendix Eight, page 1029). But relatively few single-person and two-person households felt the need for an additional room, and relatively many would have liked to have had fewer rooms. Table 13.4 shows that families with children felt keenly the pressures for more space. Over half those with three or more children, and over two fifths of those with one or two children, would have liked additional rooms. Hardly any of them wanted fewer rooms.

In total, those wanting to have extra rooms represented just under 5 million households in the population, dividing approximately as follows: 1·7 million wanting two or more rooms extra, 1·8 million wanting an extra bedroom, 1·1 million wanting an extra living room and a further 100,000 wanting an extra bathroom. The number preferring to have fewer rooms is also substantial, being 1·8 million, dividing between 0·9 million preferring to have one fewer room and 0·9 million at least two fewer rooms.

Variation in experience of deprivation by household type partly explains variation by sex and age. Males and females did not differ much in experience of deprivation. Slightly more males than females were overcrowded, and fewer had poor housing facilities. This is explained by the disproportionately large number of women among the elderly population who were living alone, sometimes in several

Table 13.4. *Percentages of households of different type who would have liked additional or fewer rooms.*

Household	Would have liked				
	2 or more rooms extra	1 room extra	1 room fewer	2 or more rooms fewer	Total number
Man over 60	(0)	(2)	(15)	(17)	41
Man under 60	3	11	6	10	62
Woman over 60	1	1	8	13	197
Woman under 60	5	10	7	12	60
Man and woman	7	8	6	6	536
Man, woman, 1 child	17	24	3	2	151
2 children	16	30	1	0	189
3 children	13	43	1	0	89
4+ children	28	31	0	0	54
3 adults	3	10	6	5	221
3 adults, plus children	14	29	1	1	154
4 adults	5	20	1	2	87
Others without children	2	20	5	2	80
Others with children	24	22	4	0	106
All types	9	16	5	5	2,027

rooms, and who tended to live in housing with poor facilities. The trends in incidence of poor housing at the oldest ages are similarly explained. The most important finding with respect to age is that relatively more children and young adults than middle-aged and older people were in overcrowded households and had housing with structural defects. More also experienced serious housing problems, and structural defects felt to be a danger to health (Table 13.1). The constraints of space were felt so widely that families who included more than half the children in the country expressed a wish for additional rooms. Children were at a slight disadvantage compared with the middle aged in heating standards. According to a variety of measures, the middle aged were least deprived. Few of the elderly were overcrowded, and relatively few said there were structural defects felt to be a danger to health.

The Housing Market

Much the most important structural factor found to be associated with housing deprivation was social class. By all criteria, except for frequent moves, we found a consistently falling incidence of deprivation with higher occupational status, as Table 13.1 shows. In many instances, the differences between the professional or managerial and the partly skilled or unskilled manual classes were very marked: 5 per cent of the former had insufficient bedrooms, compared with 29 per cent of the latter; 2 per cent had structural defects felt to be a danger to health, compared with 16 per cent; and, most striking of all, 1 per cent insufficient play-space for children indoors, compared with 31 per cent. Quite how social class comes to be correlated with poor housing will be discussed later in this chapter.

Poor housing is, in substantial part, explained by the evolution of the structure of the housing market, as reflected by type of tenure or ownership. Our next step then is to spell out the relationships between poor housing and type of tenure. In the nineteenth century, the great majority of housing was owned by private landlords and rented to families. During the present century, the proportion has dwindled, and in recent years has dwindled fast. In England and Wales in 1947, for example, privately rented accommodation still accounted for 61 per cent of the total,[1] but by the time of the Census of 1961 was about 28 per cent, and in 1966 was 22 per cent. For the United Kingdom as a whole, a figure of 22 per cent was reached in the poverty survey.

This decline is broadly attributable, on the one hand, to the effect of public housing policies, which have sought to control private rents, establish public authorities to build and manage housing and, through financial and other measures, and at the behest of growing numbers of non-manual workers, encourage owner-occupation; and on the other hand, it is attributable to the adaptations of the institutions of private capital to such state and local policies in order to find alternative means for making profit. With the spread of owner-occupation, building companies and insurance companies have grown in importance and the building societies have become a powerful source of wealth.[2] Owner-occupied housing now accounts for a half, and council housing nearly a third, of the total housing stock.

Table 13.5 shows the percentages of households of different types of tenure displaying various indices of poor housing. According to a number of criteria, strikingly more households in privately rented unfurnished accommodation than in other types of tenure and fewer owner-occupiers, particularly those still paying a mortgage, had poor housing. By minimal social standards, such as the posses-

1. See *Council Housing, Purposes, Procedures and Priorities*, Ninth Report of the Housing Management Sub-Committee of the Central Housing Advisory Committee, Ministry of Housing and Local Government, London, 1969.
2. Greer, R., *Building Societies?*, Fabian Society, London, 1974.

Table 13.5. *Percentages of households of different tenure with poor housing.*

Type of poor housing	Owner-occupier		Rented			Rent free (mainly through employment)	All types
	Fully owned	Paying mortgage	Local authority	Privately (furnished)	Privately (unfurnished)		
With structural defects	12	14	27	21	41	25	22
Inadequate housing facilities	16	9	8	60	55	25	21
Insufficient bedrooms (by bedroom standard)	5	9	13	16	14	11	11
Need for additional room(s)	10	34	26	42	26	26	25
Less than two fifths of accommodation heated	52	31	50	30	57	45	48
Serious housing problem now	4	2	6	9	14	8	6
Serious housing problem since age 21	9	18	39	11	17	15	21
Insufficient play-space indoors for children aged 1–10	15	7	27	(21)	28	–	17
Number	474	477	559	109	323	68	2,020[a]

NOTE: [a]Including ten renting privately with farm or business.

sion of four traditionally approved facilities, the percentage of council tenants in poor housing was relatively small, but by some other standards was much larger than might be expected. The percentage with structural defects and insufficient internal play-space for children, for example, was substantially higher than for households as a whole.

The relative disadvantage of private tenants has attracted considerable attention in previous studies and is well established.[1] This survey adds to the data available, but also calls attention to many serious problems among council tenants. Twenty-seven per cent of households occupying council property declared that their housing had structural defects. They accounted for 33 per cent of the population in such property. These figures deserve to attract notice and concern.

A larger proportion of the total population in structurally defective housing were in council housing than in all other rented property. Thus, although 41 per cent of privately unfurnished tenures had structural defects and accounted for 43 per cent of population in such tenures, the numbers in defective housing formed only just over half the corresponding number in council tenures. Indeed, there were more people altogether in defective council housing than in all other defective rented property, whether furnished or unfurnished.

This finding must be examined closely. There are marked differences in household composition among the different tenures. There are relatively more households with children among council tenures, and fewer among private tenures, whether furnished or unfurnished, as Table A.49, Appendix Eight (page 1030), shows. Privately furnished accommodation is characterized by a strikingly large proportion of single people under 60, and privately unfurnished accommodation by strikingly large proportions of single people over 60 and of households consisting only of a man and a woman, which together comprise 54 per cent of total households in such accommodation. This helps to explain the importance of our findings relating to council accommodation. Table 13.6 shows the proportion of different types of family living in different tenures who declared they had housing defects. For all types of household, a larger proportion of privately unfurnished tenants than other householders stated there were defects, but again, more council tenants than owner-occupiers, of each type of family, stated there were defects. In the case of council tenants with children, the proportion was higher than of those without children. Their dwellings accounted for 43 per cent of all dwellings containing children which were said to have defects, compared with 24 per cent of the dwellings of tenants of privately unfurnished accommodation. One important reservation must be entered. Evidence of degree of defect was not col-

1. For example, Report of the Committee on Housing in Greater London (The Sir Milner Holland Committee), Cmnd 2605, H M S O, London, 1965; Rose, H., *The Housing Problem*, Heinemann, London, 1968; Donnison, D., *Housing Policy Since the War*, Codicote Press, Welwyn, 1962; Cullingworth, J. B., *English Housing Trends*, Bell, London, 1965.

Table 13.6. *Percentages of different types of household within types of tenure with structural defects.*

Household type	Owner-occupier		Rented		
	Fully owned	Paying mortgage	Local authority	Privately (furnished)	Privately (unfurnished)
Man or woman over 60	13	a	17	a	33
Man and woman	10	16	22	(13)	41
Man, woman and children	(4)	11	30	(17)	55
Other households without children	11	16	29	a	35
Other households with children	11	15	38	a	(58)
All types	12	14	27	21	41
Percentage of all defective housing[b] in such tenures	12	15	34	5	30

NOTES: [a]Total number under 20. Percentages in brackets have base of under 50.
[b]The percentages across the page do not add to quite 100 because a small number were in rent-free accommodation, not included in the table.

lected, and other studies have shown that private tenures are more liable than other tenures to suffer from serious defects.[1] We also found that whereas 6 per cent of council tenants said they had a serious problem now, the figures were 9 per cent and 14 per cent respectively for tenants of privately furnished and unfurnished accommodation.

The conclusion that, in absolute terms, council housing includes more people than privately rented housing with experience of deprivation, is reinforced by the data about space. More couples and couples with children who were living in privately rented than in council accommodation felt a need for extra rooms; but this tendency was not sustained for some other types of household, and overall the total percentages of council tenants and tenants of privately unfurnished accommodation expressing a need for more rooms were the same. Expressed need for more accommodation was substantial in all forms of rented accommodation. As Table 13.7 shows, among those expressing such a need, more were living in council housing than in all other types of rented accommodation.

Table 13.7 also brings out the high proportion of owner-occupiers paying mortgages, particularly those with children, who expressed a need for extra rooms. The concern among those with children was broadly the same as among council tenants. But, as we shall show, the evidence is that either by their own sub-

1. See, for example, the House Conditions Survey, *Economic Trends*, No. 175.

Table 13.7. *Percentages of different types of household within types of tenure expressing need for more accommodation, and the percentage in fact with insufficient bedrooms, according to the bedroom standard.*

Household type	Owner-occupier		Rented		
	Fully owned	Paying mortgage	Local authority	Privately (furnished)	Privately (unfurnished)
Man or woman over 60	0	a	4	a	1
Man and woman	5	16	11	(61)	21
Man, woman and children	(27)	47	45	(52)	67
Other households without children	20	23	19	a	20
Other households with children	36	40	49	a	42
All types	10	34	26	39	26
Percentage of all households expressing need in such tenures[b]	10	32	29	9	17
Percentage with insufficient bedrooms					
Man or woman over 60	0	a	1	a	0
Man and woman	1	0	0	(4)	1
Man, woman and children	8	8	16	(22)	43
Other households without children	6	11	14	a	17
Other households with children	(30)	24	40	a	(46)
All types	5	10	14	23	15
Percentage of all households with insufficient bedrooms in such tenures[b]	12	21	35	8	21

NOTES: [a]Total number under 20. Percentages in brackets have base of under 50.
[b]The percentages across the page do not add to quite 100 because a small number were in rent-free accommodation, not included in the table.

jective definition of play-space required for their children, or by social standards of need for extra space, they were much less deprived. The lower half of Table 13.7 shows that they were in fact less overcrowded, by social standards, than those living in council accommodation.

This illustrates the critical importance of housing policies. The government can restrict council building and encourage owner-occupation through its subsidy and other financial measures. But this will not deal with the problems of those in council homes and, unless it were to take measures to help owner-occupiers only with growing families (such as by raising space standards in new private building, and offering special mortgage facilities or tax reliefs), the government would do little to remedy the problems in the owner-occupied sector. At a time of rapid inflation of house prices, owner-occupiers without children, or those whose children are growing up and leaving home, are in the most commanding position to improve their housing status. Their homes have been paid for, or nearly paid for, and have appreciated rapidly in value. As our data show, a significant minority of those without children feel a need for more space. If housing policies are relatively indiscriminate, as they have been in recent years, there will be little improvement in the use of housing stock. Councils can, of course, ease some existing problems by facilitating transfers between council tenants. But the evidence collected in this survey shows that what they can do must be limited. By conventional standards, council housing is already more economically used than any other type of tenure, except the relatively small privately furnished sector. I mean that, by the bedroom standard, this type of housing has the least amount of under-occupied accommodation. This is confirmed by official surveys.[1] And however flexible the transfer policy, it is circumscribed by the reasonable right of tenants to continue living in localities which have become familiar to them even when their children have grown up. And the council stock is being overtaken rapidly by rising housing standards.

Our analysis suggests that, with the decline of privately rented housing, council housing is beginning to take its place as the sector with the largest numbers of deprived houses. This is partly due to the ageing of many estates faster than the rate of modernization. It is also due to the fact that many estates were built according to low threshold standards of previous generations, and have been built by threshold standards in recent years which have often neglected garden space for the family and play-space for the children, and have not kept pace in standards of accommodation and structure with new building in other sectors.

This can be partly substantiated with reference both to the 'stratification' by age of council housing and the poor standards of some recent homes. At the time of the survey, just over a third of council housing had been built before the Second World War, just under another third between 1946 and 1954, and the final third in 1955 or afterwards. As might be expected, more of the older housing was found

1. In 1971, 27 per cent of owner-occupied property and 20 per cent of privately unfurnished rented property, compared with only 12 per cent of council housing, had two or more rooms in excess of the bedroom standard. A higher proportion of the first two types of tenure than of the latter had one room in excess of the standard. (*The General Household Survey*, Introductory Report, p. 116.) Between 1971 and 1975, the percentage of owner-occupied accommodation with two or more rooms in excess of the bedroom standard increased and the percentage of council accommodation decreased. (*Housing Policy*, Technical Volume, Part I, p. 67.)

to have inadequate housing facilities, by conventional standards, but as many as 22 per cent of the tenants of post-1955 housing reported there were structural defects, a higher percentage than, for example, of owner-occupiers paying mortgages and about the same percentage as of tenants of housing built between 1946 and 1954. And more tenants in the newest type of council housing than in older council housing said there was insufficient indoor play-space for children, insufficient outdoor play-space, and expressed a need for extra rooms.

The explanation lies partly in the trend in recent years of building flats rather than houses. When we turn to examine *type* of housing, there are some significant differences in the proportions with poor housing. Two thirds of owner-occupiers are in detached or semi-detached houses, compared with half of council tenants and a quarter of private tenants (Table 13.8). The advantage of owner-occupation even here is concealed, because 42 per cent of owner-occupiers are, in fact, living in detached houses, compared with only 1 per cent of council tenants.[1] Between a fifth and a third of owner-occupiers, council tenants and private tenants live in terraced housing, but 27 per cent of council tenants, compared with only 18 per cent of private tenants and as few as 5 per cent of owner-occupiers, live in self-contained flats in blocks of buildings or houses. The proportion of council tenants in flats in blocks has been increasing rapidly. We found that, in council housing built before the war, between 1946 and 1954, and since 1955, the percentage living in flats was 20 per cent, 20 per cent and 42 per cent respectively. Despite the fact that more of the flats than of the houses had been built in the last thirteen or fourteen years, the proportion of tenants declaring there were structural defects was the same in the former as in the latter. More of each of the major types of council housing were said to have defects than of the corresponding owner-occupied categories, though fewer than of privately tenanted categories (with the notable exception of flats). More, too, said that they had a serious housing problem now.

In the possession of four traditional household facilities, council accommodation compares favourably with privately rented accommodation, and, for terraced houses but not semi-detached or detached housing and flats, with corresponding owner-occupied property. But, in terms of bedroom accommodation, it compares unfavourably with owner-occupied property for all three types.

Table 13.8 also breaks down the proportions of poor housing already reported for the different tenures. Thus owner-occupiers living in terraced housing (and also the small numbers living in rooms and other dwellings, such as caravans) were more likely than those living in detached or semi-detached houses to have structural defects, inadequate housing facilities and insufficient bedrooms, and their inclusion in the owner-occupier group raises the average incidence of poor housing among the group. Private tenants living in terraced houses (and also in furnished and unfurnished rooms and other kinds of accommodation) were

1. Estimated from Table 5.12, *The General Household Survey*, Introductory Report, p. 99.

Table 13.8. Percentages of owner-occupiers, council tenants and private tenants in different types of housing and percentages of households within such types with various indices of poor housing.

Type of housing	Type of tenure		
	Owner-occupiers	Council tenants	Private tenants[a]
Detached or semi-detached house	66	50	25
Terraced house	25	22	34
Self-contained flat in block	2	22	7
Self-contained flat in house	3	5	11
Self-contained with shop/business	1	0	2
Furnished or unfurnished rooms	1	0	14
Other	2	1	7
Total	100	100	100
Number	950	557	510
Percentage with structural defects			
Detached or semi-detached house	9	27	37
Terraced house	21	27	41
Self-contained flat	(19)	26	26
Percentage with inadequate household facilities			
Detached or semi-detached house	4	6	27
Terraced house	26	10	59
Self-contained flat	(8)	5	16
Percentage with insufficient bedrooms (by the bedroom standard)			
Detached or semi-detached house	3	10	11
Terraced house	9	18	17
Self-contained flat	(4)	17	6

NOTE: [a]Including small number of those living rent free. It should be noted that there were substantial minorities of private tenants in unfurnished or furnished rooms and in other kinds of dwellings who are not included in the lower half of the table. Almost all of them had inadequate housing facilities.

similarly situated. For each type of housing, they compared unfavourably with the other tenures by almost all criteria.

These figures help to show that within the owner-occupied sector as well as within the other two major types of tenure, there are big variations in amenities, size and quality of housing. Each sector has a deprived element. This is, of course, partly the outcome of the operation of different forces in the housing market historically in different areas. Thus, in Scotland, the proportion of owner-occupied and privately rented housing is relatively low and council housing relatively high. In Greater London, the proportions of council and owner-occupied housing are relatively low and privately rented housing relatively high. And in the South-West and Wales, the proportions of council housing and privately rented housing are relatively low and owner-occupied housing, particularly housing owned outright, relatively high. In Wales, a very high proportion of owner-occupied accommodation is in terraced housing, much of it of relatively poor quality and low value. Such housing assumes functions in the local economy and community structure fulfilled elsewhere by privately rented housing and serves to complicate, and perhaps partially obscure, the national picture of tenure. In an area of declining industry and outward migration, private landlords no longer found it profitable to build houses for rent and terraced housing was gradually sold at low costs, leasehold and freehold.

Poor Housing and Low Income

Poor housing is also related to low incomes and the structure of housing costs. The type and size of the housing stock is the result of the historical operation of the housing market and of public housing policies, and has, of course, been indirectly related to the rents or the mortgages people could afford, or were induced, to pay. In the short run, deficiencies of stock are difficult to remedy, and those with the lowest incomes tend to find that they can only afford the cheapest, and in certain respects worst, housing. But we should expect the association to be complicated. People moving into bad housing because their incomes are low and because they feel they have no other choice may subsequently experience an improvement in living standards which is not regarded as leading, or cannot lead, to the rapid acquisition of a home of better standard. We found in Chapter 7 how many people fall below and rise above the state's poverty line even in a single year. This is the result not just of fluctuating earnings, but of adolescent children starting work, a child being born, a member of the household marrying and moving away. Household incomes fluctuate. A contribution to that income, say by an adolescent child, may not be treated by the household head as sufficient to justify a search for a better home. People become attached to localities and have obligations to friends and relatives. There are expenses involved in moving, and vacant homes of the kind wanted are perhaps difficult to find, or difficult to find time to look for. Finally, measures of poor housing are necessarily diverse and not all can be documented in a single study or easily combined and weighted. Thus, a home close to a motorway or at a busy traffic intersection may be of good structure, spacious and have good facilities, but none the less be shunned by people with incomes high enough to command a home elsewhere. For such reasons, the association between income and bad housing may be less close than might be assumed and is likely to be demonstrated better for potential movers and those who have recently moved than the population at large.

Table 13.9 shows the association between poverty, as judged by social stan-

Table 13.9. *Percentages of poor, marginally poor and non-poor households with different types of poor housing.*

Type of poor housing	Net disposable income last year as % of supplementary benefit scales plus housing cost		
	Under 100	100–39	140+
With structural defects	19	27	20
Having only 1 room heated in winter	56	60	38
Inadequate housing facilities	31	27	18
Having no sole use indoor WC	19	18	15
Not having electric power and lighting	4	4	1
Insufficient internal play-space for children aged 1–10[a]	(26)	18	16
Moving at least twice in last 2 years	6	3	4
Insufficient bedrooms (by bedroom standard)	13	10	10
Serious housing problem now	5	8	4
Number[b]	126	416	1,214

NOTES: [a]Total numbers of households with children aged 1–10 being 31, 119 and 368 respectively.
[b]The numbers for some entries were, in fact, up to four short of these totals.

dards, and poor housing. More households in poverty for the year as a whole, or more when combined with households on the margins of poverty, than other households, tended to be in poor housing. This was true for each measure, but in several instances the association was not very marked. For households who were very poor, housing facilities, heating and internal play-space were the respects in which they fared relatively worst.

An alternative measure of income which we employed was the relative income standard, expressing net disposable household income as a percentage of the mean of its household type. For some criteria of poor housing, namely structural defects, inadequate housing facilities and insufficient internal play-space for children, the 'gradient' of deprivation was steeper according to this measure, than according to the state's standard of poverty, as Table 13.10 shows. There

Table 13.10. Percentages of low-, middle- and high-income households with poor housing.

	Percentage of households		
Type of poor housing	Net disposable household income last year as % of the mean of household type		
	Under 80	80–119	120+
With structural defects	25	23	18
Inadequate housing facilities	28	22	9
Insufficient internal play-space for children aged 1–10[a]	29	16	7
Insufficient bedrooms (by bedroom standard)	11	9	11
Only 1 room (or no rooms) heated in winter	57	43	27
Number[b]	690	692	409
	Percentage of people		
With at least 1 of above 5 deficiencies	72	61	47
Number	1,735	1,949	1,173

NOTES: [a]Numbers of children of this age, totals for columns being 398, 378 and 183 respectively.
[b]The numbers for some entries were, in fact, up to four short of these totals.

was a similar association for indices of deprivation of the immediate environment.[1]

It is difficult to decide what would be a satisfactory method of combining the different indices of poor housing to find whether multiple deprivation is experienced by a considerable section of the population and how such deprivation compares with income. Clearly people in poverty were more likely also to be in poor housing. Equally clearly, substantial numbers of households not in poverty, and indeed with relatively high incomes, were none the less experiencing different forms of housing deprivation. This is illustrated in Table 13.11, where five principal indicators are combined.

1. See Chapter 14, page 538.

Table 13.11. *Percentages of poor, marginally poor and non-poor households with multiple types of poor housing.*

Number of types of poor housing[a]	Net disposable income last year as % of supplementary benefit scales plus housing cost		
	Under 100	*100–39*	*140+*
4 or 5	7	3	2
3	26	13	6
2	17	20	14
1	36	37	34
None	14	28	44
Total	100	100	100
Number	310	1,081	3,642

NOTE: [a]The five types are listed in Table 13.10.

This measure of multiple deprivation can also be compared with income as expressed as a percentage of the supplementary benefit standard. On five criteria of poor housing, 86 per cent of those in poverty, 72 per cent on the margins of poverty and 56 per cent of those with higher incomes had inadequate housing in at least one respect (Table 13.11). Fifty per cent and 36 per cent respectively had inadequate housing in two or more respects, compared with only 22 per cent.

A further conclusion is that, independent of annual income, tenure is correlated with certain forms of poor housing. Table 13.12 underlines the critical importance of type of tenure in contributing to the likelihood of deprivation. At each range of income, relative to the mean of household type, owner-occupiers are consistently at an advantage over both council tenants and private tenants. Among 121 owner-occupiers in the sample with children aged 1–10, whose incomes were all 20 per cent or more above the mean income for their type of household, not one said there was insufficient indoor play-space. About a fifth of both private and council tenants at this level of income said such space was insufficient. At the lower levels of income, the differences are also marked. The same conclusion emerges from other data, such as data on structural defects (Table 13.12). Only 13 per cent of owner-occupiers with relatively high incomes declared that their homes had defects, the proportion being double this figure for each group of tenants. A measure of multiple deprivation, as applied to tenure and level of income, will be found in Table A.50, Appendix Eight (page 1031).

We can adopt one final method to help us understand the combined effect of income and type of tenure on housing standards. The data so far presented take no account of wealth, which may underlie the indices for income and make it possible for some people on the same incomes to command better housing stan-

Table 13.12. Percentages of children with insufficient internal play-space and percentages of households with structural defects in low-, middle- and high-income households of different tenure.

Type of poor housing/tenure	Net disposable household income last year as % of mean of household type		
	Under 80	80–119	120+
Insufficient indoor play-space for children			
Council tenants	31	33	(19)
Private tenants	39	15	(21)
Owner-occupiers	23	5	0
Total number of children			
Council tenants	202	112	26
Private tenants	67	55	29
Owner-occupiers	116	187	121
With structural defects			
Council tenants	24	30	26
Private tenants	39	37	26
Owner-occupiers	16	10	13
Total number			
Council tenants	223	209	60
Private tenants	165	154	84
Owner-occupiers	269	309	249

dards than others. The concept of income net worth includes annual income and the annuity value of assets, including savings and other investments, but also fully or partly owned housing (in the case of people paying mortgages, only that part of the value of the house so far paid off is counted). Once this concept is applied and the net income worth of each household expressed in terms of a percentage of the mean net income worth of its type, a very marked association with poor housing standards can be demonstrated (Table 13.13). Nearly half the population with net income worth of less than half the mean were found to have inadequate housing facilities, and over a third to have insufficient indoor play-space for children, compared with figures of only 3 per cent and 2 per cent respectively for people with twice or more than twice the mean. Forty per cent had housing with structural defects, compared with 9 per cent. But again, even this measure does not wholly reflect the advantage of owner-occupiers. At similar levels of net income worth, more owner-occupiers than council and private tenants possessed good facilities and amenities in their homes. (See, for example, Table A.51, Appendix Eight, page 1031.)

Table 13.13. *Percentages of people in households with low, average and high net income worth with poor housing.*

Type of housing	Net income worth as % of the mean of household type				
	Under 50	50–89	90–109	110–99	200+
With structural defects	40	27	17	15	9
Insufficient indoor play-space for children[a]	35	27	10	9	(2)
Inadequate housing facilities	46	24	9	6	3
Having only 1 room heated in winter	73	49	31	22	19
Insufficient bedrooms (by bedroom standard)	15	22	15	11	11
With at least 1 of above 5 deficiencies	90	72	51	38	35
Only 1 room per person	28	35	34	18	18
In flats or rooms, not houses[b]	24	20	16	8	10
With fewer than 8 of 10 common types of durables or fittings in the home[c]	89	70	47	28	19
Number	517	1,989	748	884	236

NOTES: [a]Only children aged 1–10. Total numbers, reading across page, being 93, 402, 127, 129 and 43 respectively.
[b]Excluding a few flats attached to shops or businesses, but including small numbers living in dwellings, e.g. caravans or huts, other than rooms or flats.
[c]Television, radio, refrigerator, washing machine, vacuum cleaner, telephone, record player, central heating, upholstered chairs for each person, carpet in living room.

Multiple housing deprivation is sharply, and systematically, related to the oc-cupational class of the household. Whereas 83 per cent of people in households of unskilled manual status lived in homes with at least one of the four (or five, in the case of people with children aged 1–10) possible defects about which we were able to collect information (25 per cent having three or more defects) only 25 per cent of people in professional households lived in homes with any defects. Most of these lived in homes with only one, and none of them in homes with as many as three defects. (See Table A.52, Appendix Eight, page 1032.)

Housing Costs, Poor Housing and Poverty

Housing costs are by no means aligned with income. First, such costs have to be defined. Included are rent and rates (deducting any rent rebate or allowance and any rate rebate), water rates, ground rent and payments for insurance of structure but not contents; receipts from sub-letting part of the dwelling or a garage, net of expenses; expenditure on repairs, maintenance and decoration; and, in the case of owner-occupiers, interest payments on loans or mortgage and repayments of loan or mortgage. This is close to the working definition employed by such bodies as the Supplementary Benefits Commission (which we have used elsewhere in this report),[1] but it poses a number of problems. Thus, owner-occupiers are incurring the costs not only of providing themselves with accommodation but of an investment which will appreciate in value or which will represent, in later life, a form of savings that will materially assist their standard of living (because they will have paid off a mortgage and will not be obliged to pay rent). In this respect as well as others, they are paying for something more than are tenants. Moreover, they are not only paying costs for greater benefits. Tenants are prevented from paying some costs even if they wanted to. Thus owner-occupiers can finance structural adaptations which tenants, in the terms of their tenancies, cannot contemplate.

It is therefore inevitable that comparisons between households of different types of tenure in their housing costs should have to be made with extreme care. Tenants and owner-occupiers are not buying like commodities. All that can be done is for the reader to be taken through a series of comparisons and methods of standardization in order to demonstrate myths about cost which are currently perpetrated. Throughout we try to confront the problem of comparing 'real' housing costs. In much conventional analysis, unreal costs are quoted. Thus, in Family Expenditure Survey reports the weekly equivalent of the rateable value is substituted for interest payments, capital repayments and payments for alterations, and the costs of repairs and maintenance.[2]

When households in the sample were ranked according to the level of their net disposable income in relation to the state's poverty standard, surprisingly little variation was found in mean absolute costs from the bottom to the top rank. The richest households, with incomes of more than three times the poverty standard, were spending only £40 more per annum, on average, than households in poverty. And, in proportion to income, the richest households spent least on housing.

1. The main difference is that tenants' expenditure on repairs, maintenance and decoration is added, and owner-occupiers' expenditure on repairs, maintenance, decoration and alterations is substituted for a standard allowance for repairs. (We discounted expenditure on alterations or improvements where this could be ascertained but sometimes made an estimate.) Elsewhere in this book, for purposes of comparing living standards with SBC scale rates, we have adopted the SBC's method of defining housing costs.

2. Average weekly housing costs, incorporating rateable value, are given for different income groups *and* tenure groups in the 1975 report, but the costs of purchase or alteration of dwellings, including mortgage payments, are not given for different tenure groups and are appended in a few tables only under 'Other payments recorded'. See Department of Employment, *Family Expenditure Survey 1975*, HMSO, London, 1976, pp. 18–19 and 24.

Only a third of these households spent more than 6 per cent of their income on housing, and the average was 6·6 per cent. The poorer the household the greater the proportion of income needed to meet housing costs. The poorest households were spending an average of 25 per cent of their incomes on housing (Table 13.14).

Table 13.14. Mean absolute and relative annual housing costs, and mean number of major housing deficiencies of households with incomes below and above the state's poverty standard.

Net disposable household income as % of supplementary benefit scale rates plus housing costs	Mean annual housing cost (£)	Housing cost as % of net disposable household income	Mean number of housing deficiencies[a]	Total number
Under 100	121	25	1·8	120
100–39	138	21	1·3	413
140–99	178	16	} 0·9 {	507
200–99	183	12		491
300+	161	7		177

NOTE: [a]Maximum 4 in the case of households without a child aged 1–10, and 5 in the case of households with such children.

No household with an income more than twice the state's poverty standard was spending as much as this percentage on housing. The types of household which were spending in excess of 30 per cent were not at all typical of those usually thought of as being in housing stress. They included widows living alone in council houses, young couples repaying a mortgage where the chief wage-earner had been made redundant, and young men and women who were in furnished rooms in London, some of whom had moved there only recently to take a job. Poor housing is common among households in poverty or on its margins, and yet housing costs are high. The structure of costs requires fuller investigation.

The Ill-balanced Structure of Housing Costs

A fuller outline will be given of housing costs. They can be looked at in absolute terms in relation to the quality of accommodation occupied and the type of tenure. They can be looked at in relation to income. And finally they can be looked at in relation to the acquisition of wealth and property rights throughout life rather than at a moment of time. The housing market must be perceived as an institution which is doing far more than mediating housing supply and demand. It reproduces, and indeed creates, inequality within society.

The absolute cost of housing varies widely according to tenure. Thus, families in process of purchasing their homes were incurring costs, on average, of just over twice those of families in council tenancies (£306 per annum, compared with £147), but those owning their homes outright were incurring costs of only three fifths of those in council tenancies (£89 compared with £147) (Table 13.15). Those

Table 13.15. *Mean annual housing costs of households in different types of tenure.*

Type of tenure	Mean annual housing cost		Total numbers	
	£	As % of net disposable income last year of household	Absolute cost	Relative cost
Renting from council	147	16·6	541	476
Renting, privately (unfurnished)	119	14·6	317	284
Renting, privately (furnished)	195	18·9	102	95
Home buyer	306 (270)[a]	21·1 (18·5)[a]	448	390
Home owner	89	10·8	448	379
All types[b]	164	15·6	1,931	1,685

NOTES: [a]Excluding tax relief on mortgage interest.
[b]Including a small number of households living rent free.

with the lowest absolute housing costs are families who own their homes outright. The definition of costs, it should be remembered, includes full account for the costs of repairs, decoration and maintenance. The differential between buyers and council tenants is reduced if tax relief on mortgage interest is deducted from buyers' housing costs. But even without any adjustment for such tax relief, there were council tenants paying far more for their housing than families buying their own homes. As Table 13.16 shows, 17 per cent of council tenants were paying more than £200 per annum in 1968–9, while 18 per cent of people buying their homes were paying less than this figure (and 6 per cent were paying less than £125). Relative costs are similarly diverse. Twenty-eight per cent of council tenants were paying more than 20 per cent of net disposable household income on housing, while 9 per cent of home buyers paid less than 10 per cent (Table 13.17).

This establishes a paradox which we can only partially resolve in the following pages. Council tenants are conventionally believed to pay low costs and owner-occupiers high costs for their housing because the former are supposed to be helped most by the community at large. Yet, on alternative reasonable definitions,

Table 13.16. *Percentages of households of different types of tenure according to annual housing costs.*

Type of tenure	Housing costs per annum (£)						Total	Number
	0–74	75–124	125–99	200–99	300–99	400+		
Rented, council	8	29	46	16	1	0	100	542
Privately rented (furnished)	11	10	36	32	9	3	100	104
Privately rented (unfurnished)	35	31	20	9	4	1	100	320
Home buyer	1	5	16	33	25	20	100	448
Home owner	49	24	23	3	0	0	100	448
Rent free, and others	83	7	9	1	0	0	100	75
All	23	21	27	16	7	5	100	1,937

this belief could be said to be unfounded and in some respects the reverse of the truth.

In the first place, absolute costs are related to the quality, spaciousness and convenience of housing. For example, although buyers in general had costs which were 108 per cent higher than council tenants (before deducting tax relief on mortgage interest), they also had more accommodation. When we standardized costs crudely by numbers of rooms, we found that buyers with four and five

Table 13.17. *Percentages of households of different type of tenure according to the relative cost of their housing.*

Type of tenure	Relative housing costs (housing cost as % of net disposable household income)					Total	No.
	Under 5	5–9	10–19	20–29	30+		
Rented, council	3	20	48	20	8	100	476
Privately rented (furnished)	4	12	41	30	12	100	97
Privately rented (unfurnished)	14	25	37	15	9	100	287
Home buyer	1	8	39	36	17	100	390
Home owner	31	31	24	7	5	100	379
Rent free, and others	80	8	11	0	0	100	61
All	14	20	37	20	10	100	1,690

rooms (the most numerous sizes for council tenants) had costs which were only 93 per cent and 67 per cent respectively higher than the tenants. Again, standardization for 'basic' amenities (of the kind discussed above) would have further reduced the differential. As we have already seen, there are other respects than numbers of rooms and amenities – according to which home buyers enjoy better accommodation and which deserve to be taken into the reckoning (difficult as that may sometimes be) in comparing their costs with those of council tenants.

Secondly, housing costs of the two groups relative to their income are, on average, very similar even before the value of certain offsetting benefits, other than tax relief on mortgage interest, are deducted from buyers' costs. The average home buyer had housing costs which represented 21·1 per cent of his net disposable income. If tax relief on mortgage interest is deducted, the figure becomes 18·5 per cent, compared with 16·6 per cent for the average council tenant. But the validity of this comparison does, of course, depend on the measure of income. Thus one convention – followed, for example, in the FES reports – is to add the imputed rental income of house ownership to net disposable household income.[1] It is not easy to justify any particular estimate of such income, but if the FES estimate for 1968[2] is added to our figure of mean disposable household income, then the percentage represented by housing costs is reduced for the home buyer from 21·1 per cent to 19·5 per cent (or if tax relief on mortgage interest is deducted, from 18·5 per cent to 16·8 per cent).[3] Another question is whether or not the net incomes of all members of the household should be added together in order to obtain a measure of the burden of housing costs. It is sometimes argued on legal as well as social grounds that the earnings of an adolescent child should not be counted as household income like the additional earnings of the head of a household in which there are no such children. This has the effect of reducing the relative housing costs of council tenants more than of home buyers. When housing costs are expressed as a percentage of the net disposable income of the head of the household's income unit, they rise from an average of 21·1 per cent to 21·6 per cent for home buyers, but from 16·6 per cent to 18·8 per cent for council tenants.

Thirdly, the difference between both the absolute and the relative housing costs of the two groups changes with length of residence. The biggest difference be-

1. The reasoning is that, though no money passes between the occupier and the owner of a dwelling when they are the same person, the services of the dwelling nevertheless have a value equivalent to the net income which would be obtained by letting the dwelling to a tenant.
2. This was only the equivalent of rateable value. See Department of Employment and Productivity, *Family Expenditure Survey Report for 1968*, HMSO, London, 1969, p. 19.
3. Strictly, it might also be argued that no tax is paid on this imputed income and that the notional tax relief should be deducted from housing costs in the same way as tax relief on mortgage interest. Until 1963, house owners paid tax on their imputed rental income from ownership (Schedule A taxation). Even then they were considerably undertaxed since the imputed rent was calculated on 1936–7 rating valuations.

Table 13.18. *Mean annual housing costs of tenants and owner-occupiers according to length of residence.*

Type of tenure	Mean annual housing cost (£)				
	Under 2 years' residence	2 years and less than 5 years	5 years and less than 15 years	15 years or more	All periods
Renting, council	143	152	148	144	147
Renting, privately (unfurnished)	181	160	107	92	119
Renting, privately (furnished)	217	198	148	76	195
Home buyer	375	334	268	215	306
Home buyer (less tax relief)	319	292	241	207	270
Home buyer (less tax relief and capital gain)	217	181	134	120	165
Home owner (owned outright)	119	98	90	84	89
Home owner (less capital gain)	23	11	9	3	7
Owner-occupied (both buying and owning outright)	324	265	188	109	198
	Mean annual housing cost as a % of net disposable household income				
Renting, council	19	17	16	15	17
Renting, privately (unfurnished)	18	18	16	15	16
Renting, privately (furnished)	22	21	15	11	20
Home buyer	24	24	18	17	21
Home buyer (less tax relief)	20	21	16	16	18
Home buyer (less tax relief and capital gain)	14	13	9	9	11
Home owner (owned outright)	10	12	9	12	11
Owner-occupied (both buying and owning outright)	22	21	14	13	16
Percentage of all owner-occupiers owning outright	20	29	44	81	50

tween buyers and tenants is found among those with less than two years' residence at their address. Even without discounting the value of tax relief on mortgage interest, it can be calculated (Table 13.18) that the housing costs of home buyers fell from a level which was 162 per cent higher on average than the costs of council tenants, for households with less than two years' residence, to only 49 per cent higher, for households with more than fifteen years' residence. It must be remembered that length of residence is not the same as period during which a mortgage has been repaid, and that some households whose residence has been short, for example, will have sold a former house and taken out a new mortgage on their present home at a smaller absolute and relative housing cost than a new buyer. This will tend to reduce the average costs of those whose residence has been short. On the other hand, some households whose residence is lengthy will have been offered the opportunity to buy their homes only in recent years, and their absolute and relative housing costs may be high. This will tend to increase the average costs of those whose residence has been lengthy.

It can be argued that this comparison between buyers and tenants according to length of residence is unfair to tenants, because their costs have been compared with home buyers and not outright owners as well as buyers. Among all owner-occupiers, only 20 per cent with less than two years' residence, but 81 per cent of those with fifteen or more years' residence, owned their homes outright (Table 13.18). A young couple buying a house on a mortgage may have higher costs than a council tenant on average during the term of their mortgage, but may live a further twenty years or more in the house. The housing costs of owner-occupiers might therefore be converted into annual lifetime costs before being compared with the on-going costs of council tenants. To obtain approximate estimates, it is justifiable to amalgamate the costs of buyers and outright owners.[1] Once the two categories of owner-occupiers are combined, the average absolute housing costs of owner-occupiers in the sample are not very much higher for those with between five and fifteen years' residence than for council tenants with the same residence, and after fifteen years' residence are only 75 per cent of the costs of council tenants. Relative housing costs are lower for owner-occupiers than for council tenants (and private tenants) after five years' residence.

Finally the home buyer acquires an asset which appreciates in real value during purchase and afterwards, and therefore represents a benefit which might be regarded as offsetting costs during the period of acquisition. Between 1968 and the first quarter of 1975, average new house prices increased by 161 per cent and the prices of existing dwellings by 158 per cent,[2] compared with an increase in the

1. This means that people who have inherited a home from parents, for example, as well as people who have repaid a mortgage, will be included. It is difficult in principle to distinguish the former from the mass of owner-occupiers. Some will be benefiting from mortgages repaid by parents who have died prematurely.
2. Building Societies Association, *Facts and Figures, Quarterly Bulletin*, July 1975, p. 11.

Retail Price Index of only 84 per cent. If the price of an existing dwelling of average value (£4,290) had increased in line with the Retail Price Index, the dwelling would have been £7,894 in 1975 instead of £11,081 (the value in fact quoted by the Building Societies Association). It might therefore be said that, in purchasing terms, the owner had benefited by £3,187 in that period of a little under six years, or by over £500 per annum at 1975 prices (or a little under £350 per annum at 1968 prices). In fact, of course, the value grew unevenly during these years.[1] According to figures issued by the Building Societies Association, the price rose on average by about £85 more between 1968 and 1969 than would have been justified by the retail price index.[2] Although the average increase in value during the 1960s and early 1970s was higher than in 1968–9, we have applied this average figure of £85 (though in proportion to estimated house values) in adjusting the housing costs of owner-occupiers before comparing them with those of council tenants.

Any reader who has followed this series of conditional statements, and who has some appreciation of the complex structure of the housing market, will understand the tentativeness of the estimates given in Table 13.19. Quite deliberately I have refrained from complicating the discussion by comparing the housing costs of private tenants with those in other tenures (partly because their numbers have been declining rapidly) and by calling attention to the variation around the mean costs of both home owners and tenants. What I have sought to show is that, when society's conventions in categorizing types of tenure and housing costs are examined, the burden assumed to be borne by the average owner-occupier becomes instead a comparative benefit. In any real meaning of 'cost' – that is, after averaging cost over the lifetime, allowing for taxation foregone, allowing for the annual appreciation in real value to the buyer (and to his children) of the asset which is being acquired, and after standardizing (in so far as this is possible) for items being purchased and rented, the average owner-occupier pays less *absolutely* as well as *relatively* for his housing than the council tenant.[3]

1. This period includes the exceptional boom in house prices between 1971 and 1973, but it should be noted that house prices increased in every year of the 1960s by more than retail prices.
2. Building Societies Association, *Facts and Figures*, edn cit., pp. 7 and 11.
3. In 1977, the Department of the Environment itself made estimates of the comparative costs of council tenants and owner-occupiers for the period 1967–76. For 1968–9, the cost borne on average by a public-authority tenant, including costs of upkeep not included in the rent, but after excluding a general exchequer subsidy of £44, was put at £104 per annum. The costs borne by the average owner-occupier were also put at £104 per annum, excluding transaction costs *and* repayments of mortgage principal, but excluding tax relief on mortgage interest estimated at £24. If repayments of mortgage principal are added to the second figure, it would become about £125 per annum, and if average payments of rates are added, the figures become, respectively, about £135 and about £170. Although the Department of the Environment's estimates were reached by different methods, they reflect the same relativity as the figures of £147 and £178 derived from the poverty survey in the last column of Table 13.19. See

Table 13.19. Mean annual housing costs of council tenants and home owners, on different assumptions of cost.

Type of tenure/ assumptions about cost	Mean annual housing cost (£)				
	Under 2 years' residence	2 years and less than 5 years	5 years and less than 15 years	15 years or more	All periods
Council tenants	143	152	148	144	147
Home buyers:					
(i) No deduction for tax relief	375	334	268	215	306
(ii) Deducting tax relief[a]	319	292	241	207	270
(iii) Further deducting capital gain in 1968–69[b]	217	181	134	120	165
(iv) Further deducting estimated cost of additional amenity[c]	(167)	(149)	(105)	(106)	(136)
All owner-occupiers:					
(i) No deduction for tax relief	324	265	188	109	198
(ii) Deducting tax relief[a]	278	234	171	106	178
(iii) Further deducting capital gain in 1968–9[b]	177	130	73	24	84
(iv) Further deducting estimated cost of additional amenity[c]	(138)	(110)	(59)	(19)	(69)

NOTES: [a] Calculated on information supplied by mortgagor about annual mortgage interest. The mean corresponds closely with government estimates.
[b] The estimated gain of £85 on the average existing dwelling at 1968 prices (£4,290) has been applied as a percentage (2 per cent) to the estimated total value of each dwelling.
[c] The mean number of rooms in council tenancies has been divided by the mean number in owner-occupied dwellings, and the resulting fraction applied to the costs of owner-occupation in order to derive a 'standardized' cost. This is an admittedly crude method of standardization (and therefore the estimates are bracketed) which can be said to understate the value of owner-occupied accommodation. (Thus no account is taken, say, of access to garden or convenience or status of siting.)

While the costs of council tenants are distributed fairly evenly, in both absolute and relative terms, over the lifetime, the costs of owner occupation are, except in the case of those inheriting their homes, concentrated in the early years of such occupation. This financial hurdle could be said to have developed so as to regulate the social allocation and the distribution by tenure of the housing stock. During the 1970s, the pattern of housing costs has become even more ill-balanced, both between owner-occupiers and tenants, and between mortgagors in the early years and mortgagors in the final years of repayment. An important paper published in 1973 showed that, partly because of the high rate of inflation in the late 1960s, the comparative costs of owning and renting in Scotland narrowed more rapidly with length of residence than in earlier years.[1] The increase in the rate of inflation, and the uneven consequent pattern of increases in interest rates in the early 1970s, and especially in 1974–6, have accelerated this trend. Just as repayments in the early years have increased relatively to income, so repayments in the later years of a mortgage term have been reduced. During the late 1960s and early 1970s, average initial mortgage repayments upon a house of average price varied between 24 and 27 per cent of average earnings. In 1973, with the rise in house prices, the figure jumped to 39 per cent, and in 1974 to 43 per cent, before falling back slightly in 1975 to the still high figure of 37 per cent.[2] For buyers of several years' standing, some benefited from delays in putting up interest rates, including those with concessionary rates on housing loans from employers, and all benefited from the fall in real value of repayments of capital. Even if inflation were to average only 5 per cent during a mortgage term of twenty years, the capital repayments would amount to only 38 per cent of what they would have been without any inflation at all.[3] And in the middle of 1974, when the rate of inflation exceeded 15 per cent, interest rates were around 11 per cent.

The pattern of housing finance has come under increasingly critical examination.[4] There is little doubt, from the evidence on absolute and relative costs, that revenue for either public subsidies or public and private investment in the housing

---

Department of the Environment, *Housing Policy*, Technical Volume, Part II, HMSO, London, 1977, pp. 19–23.

1. Hare, P. H., 'Comparing the Costs of Owning and Renting in Scotland', *Housing Review*, May–June 1973.

2. Building Societies Association, *Facts and Figures*, edn cit., p. 12.

3. Greer, *Building Societies?*, p. 7.

4. Nevitt, A. A., *Housing, Taxation and Subsidies*, London, Nelson, 1966; Nevitt, A. A., *Fair Deal for Householders*, Fabian Research Series, No. 297, Fabian Society, London, 1971; Crouch, C., and Wolf, M., 'Inequality in Housing', in Townsend, P., and Bosanquet, N., *Labour and Inequality*, Fabian Society, London, 1972; Ball, M., 'Owner-Occupation', and Boddy, M., 'Building Societies and Owner-Occupation', in Edwards, M. *et al.* (eds.), *Housing and Class in Britain*, Political Economy of Housing Workshop of the Conference of Socialist Economists, (c/o F. Gray, University of Sussex), London, 1976; Lansley, S., and Fiegehen, G., *Housing Allowances and Inequality*, Fabian Society, London, 1973.

stock could be substantially increased and made more equitable. Major structural changes in housing finance (and in categorization of tenure) would be required. Through direct and indirect subsidies, those who need help least – namely, owner-occupiers who are no longer repaying mortgages, are in the latter stages of a mortgage term, no longer have dependants, but have taken out new mortgages for more costly homes, and have high incomes but are repaying housing loans at rates heavily subsidized by their employers – are receiving help most at the present time through housing and taxation policies. Under-occupation is being subsidized. The problem of redistributing housing subsidies is therefore two-fold – from the middle-aged to the young, and from the well-endowed section of owner-occupiers to poorer occupiers in different forms of tenure.

Access to the Housing Market: Owner-occupation

We have discussed in turn the characteristics of the available housing stock and the distribution by type of tenure, the resources of the occupiers, and the costs which they have to meet. There remains one further ingredient to explain how deprivation in housing arises. This is the social system of rules by which housing is brought into use and allocated or made available. Our methods of research were limited and did not allow the provision and allocation of housing to be explored, but that process can be illustrated in certain particulars.

The production of housing of different types is very much in the hands of the government, through its control of housing finance. By various means, the Chancellor of the Exchequer can control both the total amount of accommodation built or improved and the distribution by type of tenure. The social system of allocation has two principal sub-systems: the private housing market and the subsidiary system of public housing. There are, of course, many different components of each, and some of them can be suggested here only in outline.

First and foremost, how do families acquire the privileged status of owner-occupation? Inheritance plays a substantial part. Society has been relatively lenient in shaping the rules by which gifts of property are made to relatives and passed on to heirs after death. Capital transfer taxation was introduced in 1974. Capital passing between spouses is exempt, as is the first £15,000 of capital transferred; and the rates of tax on the next slices of capital are lower than former estate duty. Estate duty could be avoided if property was passed on five or more years before death. But while inheritance has played an important part in conferring the status of owner-occupation and deserves to be thoroughly investigated, it has not yet assumed the importance it will undoubtedly have in the future. Until comparatively recent times, only a small minority of the population owned their homes. Even after the Second World War, only a quarter of homes were owner-occupied. The rapid increase in the proportion owes more to the financial power and lending rules of building societies and insurance companies than to inheritance. In 1950, the building societies had 1·5 million borrowers, and by 1973 4·2 million.[1]

A very large proportion of the population are debarred from becoming owner-occupiers, either because their parents did not own housing which could be passed on or because their incomes have been too low, the amount of capital security which they can offer too small or their age and occupational status fall outside the conditions laid down for eligibility for loans. Although building societies, insurance companies and local authorities apply a wide range of different rules of eligibility for capital loans, and the rules also vary regionally,[2] it was broadly true at the time of the survey that loans were not made to families with less than a net disposable income of about £1,200 a year (and this normally had to be the usual earned income of the head of the household rather than an income made up by overtime earnings or the income of others in the household). This effectively ruled out more than half the population who were not already in owner-occupied housing, some of whom, it must be remembered, were retired and now themselves had low incomes. Mortgages for women were also hard to come by.

In general, working-class households are not considered so good a risk as non-manual households, and households with single women are not considered so favourably as those with single men, even when they have the same basic income.[3] These groups find it difficult to raise a loan, or, if they do raise one, the ratio of the loan to annual income will tend to be lower. The decisions taken by building societies affect general housing policies. The societies help to define 'twilight areas' and hasten their decline by refusing to give loans on properties within certain areas. Their interpretation of the adequacy of *types* of income, and also of acceptability of social status and locality, have the effect of reinforcing class differences in the opportunities which exist for acquiring housing, even where class differences in cash incomes may be very small or may even overlap. This was brought out in our analysis of resources in relation to class in Chapter 10 (pages 385–94).

Table 13.20 gives a crude representation of the outcome of these lending policies in relation to occupational class. The percentage of households who are owner-occupiers falls from a peak of 88 per cent for the professional occupations to 20 per cent for the unskilled manual occupations. The percentage falls sharply between the lower supervisory and routine non-manual classes and again between the routine non-manual and skilled manual classes. The gradient provided by

1. Building Societies Association, *Facts and Figures*, edn cit., p. 3. See also Greer, *Building Societies?*, p. 7.

2. Studies of the policies of building societies and local-authority loans have been made for particular areas. See, for example, the study of Newcastle in Boddy, M. J., 'The Structure of Mortgage Finance: Building Societies and the Social Formation', *Transactions of the Institute of British Geographers*, N S I, 1975.

3. For an introduction to some of the difficulties experienced by women, see Tunnard, J., *No Father, No Home?*, Child Poverty Action Group, London, 1976.

Table 13.20. *Percentages of households of different occupational class with annual income above certain levels, and percentage who are owner-occupiers.*

Occupational class	Percentage whose net disposable household income was higher than		Percentage who are owner-occupiers
	£1,200[a]	140% of supplementary benefit scale rates plus housing cost	
Professional	92	91	88
Managerial	84	89	66
Supervisory, high	69	83	73
Supervisory, low	52	72	64
Routine non-manual	55	70	48
Skilled manual	45	66	38
Partly skilled manual	45	63	32
Unskilled manual	36	42	20

NOTE: [a] Approximately the qualifying level for a loan from a building society at the time.

particular levels of net disposable household income is, by comparison, much more gradual, as the table shows.

Within the owner-occupier sector, classes also subdivide according to the value of the dwelling. The percentage of professional and managerial households in homes valued at less than £3,000 in 1968–9 was negligible, whereas there was a

Table 13.21. *Percentages of chief wage-earners or heads of households and housewives, according to the value of owner-occupied homes.*

Value of house	Non-manual		Manual	
	Professional and managerial	Other	Skilled	Other
£5,000 or more	67	36	15	6
£4,000–999	20	21	19	11
£3,000–999	9	22	26	19
£2,000–999	1	13	18	29
Under £2,000	2	7	22	35
Total	100	100	100	100
Number	264	666	421	244

majority of manual-class households in homes of such value (Table 13.21). Manual households outnumber professional and managerial households in the ratio of five to one, but twice as many of the former as of the latter owned or were in purchase of dwellings of a value of £5,000 or more. The conflicting interests of tenure groups, for example, in relative shares of state subsidies, are hence predominantly class interests.

Owner-occupiers do not comprise a uniform class and tend to sub-divide into strata according to market value of house. Those with larger incomes and greater capital security are not only able to obtain larger loans for larger and more valuable property, but also have opportunities to reduce the proportionate amounts they pay in taxes and the total net amount of repayments over periods of years. There are many schemes which might be instanced, one of the most common of which is to take out an endowment assurance policy, with or without profits, usually through a life office, but also through certain building societies, instead of a straight mortgage from a building society. Under the normal repayment method of a building society, a borrower makes regular repayments of a loan, plus interest on the loan, for the years for which the loan is advanced. If he dies before the repayments are completed, his heirs have to meet the outstanding capital value of the loan or continue repayments.

Under the endowment method, the borrower pays a larger premium to cover the cost of meeting any sum outstanding on his death, but he has the advantage of being able to claim tax relief, not only on the interest on the loan (which he shares with the ordinary purchaser of a mortgage from a building society), but also on the regular premiums which are made towards the repayment of capital. This is because tax relief can be claimed on premiums paid for life assurance, and since he has taken out a life assurance policy with the insurance company for the amount of the loan required for his house, he can claim on these premiums. If he takes out a policy 'with profits', his premiums are larger still, but if, as in recent years, bonuses from the profits on the investment value of each of the premiums paid are substantial they offset, over time, much of the total outlay. Expectations differ for purchasers of different age, source and amount of income and different amounts already insured, but in 1967 The Times estimated that a man of 35 borrowing £5,000 with repayment over twenty-five years on the standard rate of tax would have a total outlay over the whole period of only £5,500 if he took out an endowment policy with profits, compared with around £9,000 if he used a building society mortgage on its own.[1]

Why, then, do not all intending owner-occupiers adopt this method, which, on the evidence,[2] is an astonishingly cheap method of securing a substantial loan?

1. 'House-Buying: Mortgage or Endowment', The Times, 7 January 1967.
2. See, for an example from the literature of the choices open to house purchasers in the mid 1960s, 'How Life Assurance Can Help with House Purchase', Insurance Mail, February 1964. I am grateful to Michael Malin of the Life Offices Association for introducing me to the

We can set aside the question of access to the relevant information, though, of course, this plays some part. The principal factors are that the life offices erect a higher hurdle than do the building societies for admission to straightforward mortgage schemes, in terms of checks on health, and financial status, and the initial payment of a survey fee to engage a valuer to inspect the property, and, above all, the real costs in the early years are relatively higher (though much smaller in later years). This is because the repayments made by an ordinary borrower from a building society consist predominantly of interest on the loan in the early years and predominantly of capital repayments in the later years. Because tax relief is paid only on the interest, the total net cost rises.

The finance houses are reluctant to enlarge membership of the endowment schemes too quickly for fear, among other reasons, of raising too steeply the cost to their existing members of obtaining loans and acquiring assets. Borrowers with young families and high initial housing costs also shrink from imposing upon themselves the additional costs in the early years of an endowment scheme. The result is that endowment policies tend to be restricted to people needing large loans for the purchase of their homes. In the poverty survey, most of those recently obtaining loans of £5,000 and more adopted this method. There were very few examples in the survey of people with less than these sums adopting the endowment method.

One further means of access to owner-occupation is by means of a low-interest loan arranged through an employer. Nearly fifty households in the sample, representing some 500,000 in the United Kingdom, claimed to be beneficiaries of a low rate of interest. They were principally the staff of the clearing banks, insurance companies and building societies. Even by 1976, the rates were as low as from 2·5 to 5 per cent, compared with the lending rate of 12·25 per cent recommended by the building societies.[1]

I have dwelt on one process by which families obtain their own houses, not only to show how it is that people move into the best housing available in Britain, but also to show how most people are restricted in their choice to what is left and how arbitrary are some of the rules. This is necessary in order to explain how deprivation arises. Admission is almost like admission to different socially exclusive clubs, the size and quality of which are determined indirectly by the arbitrary standards of the market and by the financial and tax policies of the government, instead of a body of fair principles discussed and formulated in public. For example, some of the rules applied by building societies and life offices are more social than strictly financial, debarring people with disabilities and working-class families with fluctuating incomes. Again, the total effect of different tax

subtleties of life-assurance schemes, although he is not, of course, responsible for the interpretation I have placed upon them.

1. Stone, M., 'Who Gets Those Cheap Mortgages?', *The Times*, 11 December 1976.

concessions for owner-occupiers is not analysed by the government or defended in relation to other types of housing subsidy. There would be nothing to prevent society from working out how owner-occupation could be quickly changed from being a privilege for around half of the population to being a universal right, or how the opportunities of owner-occupiers to advance their existing privileges could be restricted in order to release resources for the improvement of housing in the other sectors.

But the full implications of owner-occupation for standards of housing in society cannot be understood by concentrating attention only at a single moment of time on the rules and incomes governing admission to that status. As discussed above, in periods of inflation and of steadily increasing real incomes, access to that status takes on a very different light. The houses appreciate steadily in value, repayments of loans form a diminishing proportion of real incomes and are eventually paid off. This has a number of important results. It means that, in relation to people occupying other types of tenure, many of those owning their own homes have low housing costs and thereby higher living standards on the same cash incomes; more of their resources are released from direct repayments of loan and interest for expenditure on repairs and modernization, and, through the acquisition of a saleable asset, on the power to move into a more desirable home (it is one of the cheapest, if not the cheapest, form of saving) or obtain a loan for a second home. A high rate of inflation makes present policies in housing finance even less related to government intentions than they were in the late 1960s.

Access to Council Housing

Potential householders denied access to owner-occupation stay in council housing, if they inherit the parents' tenancy or can wait until they qualify for a council house or, more commonly, begin family life in a furnished or unfurnished tenancy while obtaining qualifications for admission to the council sector. Of council tenants, 31 per cent told us that they waited only a year or less than a year, or inherited a tenancy, 24 per cent waited two years, 28 per cent three or four years, and 18 per cent five or more years. Their reasons for obtaining a tenancy when they did are set out in Table 13.22. A half were in bad housing, were overcrowded or had reasons of ill-health. Over 60 per cent had been in council housing for more than ten years, including 14 per cent for more than thirty years. Substantially more council tenants had experienced a serious housing problem in adult life than either private tenants or owner-occupiers (39 per cent, compared with 15 per cent and 14 per cent respectively) (see also Table 13.5, page 491). These data afford some inkling of the direction of the flows into and between sectors. The historical expansion of council housing has drawn far more families from poor housing in the privately furnished and unfurnished sectors than has the expansion of owner-

Table 13.22. Percentages of council tenants, according to reasons for getting tenancy.

Reason	Council tenants
Inherited	5·5
Bad housing	23·5
Health of member of family	9·5
Overcrowding	18·2
Compulsory purchase	0·9
Solely reached top of list	23·9
Other	18·6
Total	100
Number	528

occupation. Other national data show that over a half of those in unfurnished and a third in furnished private accommodation who want to move have applied to the local council, compared with less than a fifth of each group who have taken steps to buy a home.[1]

The poorest families in the sample tended to be in council and private unfurnished accommodation. Contrary to impressions given in the media, families in council tenancies were found to be poorer than in any other form of tenure (Table A.53, Appendix Eight, page 1032). More were in poverty or on the margins of poverty; and fewer had incomes as much as three or more times as high as the state's poverty standard. Within the council sector there were, as well as other forms of tenure, marked differences between regions. Costs in Scotland were, on average, only a little more than half those in Greater London (Table A.54, Appendix Eight, page 1033).

Council housing tends to consist of ranks by status. Locally, this may develop partly for reasons independent of the age or construction of the property. Some estates are far from shopping facilities and work, acquire disreputable reputations for vandalism or noise, or are sited among other buildings or communities which are felt to be uncongenial. But the status of housing depends also on the age, type and desirability of the property itself. We have already shown that a higher proportion of new than of older council accommodation is in flats, and that, in some respects, the incidence of defects in this new housing was as high as or higher than in older property. But, in general, many of the facilities of new council housing have improved with rising standards and new houses as well as some types of flats are sought after. Council housing is predominantly working class. Only 19 per cent of the occupants in the sample belonged to non-manual classes, and most of these belonged to the lower-non-manual categories. There was not a

1. *The General Household Survey*, Introductory Report, p. 172.

single member of the professional class in the sample to be found living in a council flat or house, for example. We found a slight association between social class and age of housing. As Table 13.23 shows, rather more of the non-manual than manual groups were in the newest housing. But this may to some extent reflect

Table 13.23. Percentages of council tenants moving into accommodation in previous two years, and percentages of all council tenants of different occupational class who were in pre-war and post-war housing.

When accommodation built	Moving into tenancies in last two years			All council tenancies		
	Non-manual	Skilled manual	Partly skilled and unskilled manual	Non-manual	Skilled manual	Partly skilled and unskilled manual
Pre-war	(29)	39	46	37	33	36
1946–54	(21)	37	26	25	36	34
1955 or later	(50)	24	29	38	32	30
Total	100	100	100	100	100	100
Number	28	113	90	337	710	661

the national increase of the proportion of the population in non-manual classes, and may be partly obscured by changes in occupational status of the occupants rather than demonstrate deliberate allocation of tenants.

As an approximate check we therefore singled out tenants who had taken up their tenancies in the previous two years, and Table 13.23 suggests that more new tenants in non-manual than manual groups are moved, or move, into the newest housing, and more of the partly skilled and unskilled than of either the non-manual or skilled manual groups into pre-war housing. However, the numbers of such tenants in the sample were small, and include, of course, tenants exchanging homes with other council tenants, or moving from one council tenancy to another by arrangement with the housing department. These findings must therefore be treated with caution, and can only be regarded as justifying further investigation. There is the possibility that accommodation is allocated more according to social status than according to need. In most localities, council-housing departments are aware of estates which are less desirable or sought after than others, and they adopt assumptions about the kind of people who will or will not respect the amenities and rules. This is evident enough among the temporary homeless and 'problem family' categories, and has been studied at length.[1] But the financial needs of councils can also determine allocation, because subsidies for new housing can be reduced if the tenants can bear increased rents. One of the effects of the Housing Finance Act 1972 is to give councils more incentive to place better-off tenants in more expensive accommodation, reduce the total paid in rebates and hence intensify the trend towards social stratification in council housing.[2]

Access to the Housing Market: Private Tenancies

We can take up the story for tenants of private accommodation. Their housing situation is, in many respects, more deprived than that of their counterparts in other sectors. We found that of about 400 households in both unfurnished and furnished accommodation, sixty-two, or 15 per cent, said they (or part of the household) were on a council housing list. Of these, half declared the house had structural defects (and, in nearly all cases, inadequate housing facilities as well). Another third had inadequate housing facilities. They represented nearly 600,000 households in the population. Most of this minority were young couples or couples with one or two children, though a few were pensioners awaiting special accommodation. Over half were found to have been on a council list for three years or more, including a fifth for more than ten years. It should be remembered that only a quarter of privately rented accommodation (Table A.49, Appendix Eight, page 1030) is occupied by households with children. Privately rented accommodation seems to serve three functions: as temporary accommodation for young married couples starting a family who cannot afford to buy a home of their own and who cannot yet qualify for a council home; as permanent accommodation for older couples, whose children have married and left home, some of whom have been protected in the past by legislation on rent control, and who have little prospect of or desire for a house of their own or a council tenancy; and finally, as a kind of Hobson's choice of uncertain duration for single people, some of them young, some of them middle aged, and for migrants, families who have been evicted from council accommodation and others whose family status is tenuous or fluctuating. A sprinkling of all such accommodation occupied by middle-class people is to be found in the better quarters of all major cities – for example Belsize Park, Bayswater and Chelsea in London – but the bulk is in

1. Hull is the subject of Gray, F., 'Selection and Allocation in Council Housing', *Transactions of the Institute of British Geographers*, NSI, 1976. This quotes comments of housing inspectors on new tenants; for example, 'fair only – suitable for pre-war property'. See also a study of Colchester by Walker, A., *A State of Disrepair*, Colchester Poverty Action Group, 1976.

2. For a detailed analysis of the effects of the Act, see Parker, R. A., *The Housing Finance Act and Council Tenants*, Poverty Pamphlet No. 9, Child Poverty Action Group, London, 1972.

rather run-down quarters for the working class in local 'zones of transition' – for example, in Islington, Notting Hill, Brixton and Camden Town.

Part of our second category of established older couples, whose children have left home, are in accommodation owned by an employer and are scattered geographically. Eleven per cent of those renting privately were in such accommodation, the great majority of whom, four fifths, said it was rented more cheaply as a consequence. For example, more than a third estimated the accommodation would cost another £200 a year or more if they had to rent it in the normal way, and another third more than £50. Two fifths belonged to non-manual and three fifths to manual groups. In addition to these households, there is a further category living rent free in accommodation owned by an employer.

In total, we found nearly 100 households in the sample, or nearly 5 per cent, living in accommodation owned by an employer, or 20 per cent of all tenures other than ówner-occupied or council owned. They represent nearly a million households in the country.

Privately rented accommodation is very complex in quality and varies in degree of security, but, by and large, tenants are much more insecure than in the other sectors. The constraints on their ability to pay means that there is a good chance that they will find themselves in the older properties, probably built before the First World War, which are in a poor condition of repair and have a low standard of amenity. Two groups in different situations may be distinguished: the fallen or life-long poor, and the aspirant poor. Some people with low incomes have never experienced any other form of housing than privately rented homes, and in middle or old age have no prospect of moving into the other housing classes, and indeed may have difficulty in maintaining their foothold as property is sold and rent control lifted. They have been faced with rents rising relative to earnings, and of having to pay relatively higher rents even as rent allowances have been introduced in the 1970s to meet part of the so-called 'fair' rents.[1]

Other people have 'fallen' into the poorest types of privately rented housing because of a combination of low or reduced income (because of disability, retirement, unemployment, redundancy or bankruptcy) and social adversity, such as divorce or separation, bereavement and even punitive or disengaging action by the community against mental illness or handicap and deviant life-styles. Owner-occupied housing is compulsorily purchased, or mortgage repayments cannot be maintained by widows, or families are evicted from council housing because of arrears of rent. To these groups might be added those reaching retirement or becoming widowed in employer-owned property, who have to find alternative

1. For an anticipatory statement of the consequences of the Housing Finance Act 1972, see Nevitt, *Fair Deal for Householders*. In practice, the take-up of rent allowances by tenants in the private sector has been very small. In 1975, only 20 to 25 per cent of tenants in unfurnished and 10 per cent in furnished private accommodation of those believed to be eligible for rent allowances were drawing them. See *Hansard*, 17 February 1975, cols. 303–4.

accommodation. Some of the 'fallen' or downwardly mobile poor cannot compete, in the rents they can afford, with the aspirant or upwardly mobile poor, and so they resort to lodging houses or rooms which are too small for the families comprising many of the latter to want – residential accommodation owned by the local authorities or simply the streets. In the late 1960s and early 1970s, the official number of homeless families in Britain increased.[1] Official statistics continue to be criticized as being underestimates. For example, they continue to underestimate the numbers of single and married people without children, some of whom are admitted into residential homes for the elderly and disabled.[2]

The aspirant or upwardly mobile poor consist of two groups: first, new households of young married couples and couples with young children whose incomes are low and who are biding their time until they qualify for a council house or flat or save enough money to put down for a house of their own; and secondly, migrant workers, including coloured immigrants, who have nowhere else to go and whose status as potentially stable new households may yet be indeterminate. Each of these two groups may be said to be in the process of acquiring higher incomes, savings and possessions and eager to make their way as quickly as they can into housing sectors with greater security and higher status.

Explanations of Poor Housing

What also has to be faced in understanding the situation of disadvantaged groups in the privately rented sector, in some parts of the council sector (such as temporary accommodation for homeless families and low-status estates), and even in a few instances in owner-occupied property, is that they result from the maintenance of certain values of society – such as the belief in the sanctity of private property, the virtue of making reasonable profits in a market economy, the need to pay rents on time and so on. Just as the threat or fact of unemployment is widely understood to be a means of restraining wage demands, so the threat or fact of eviction and homelessness has to be understood as a means of maintaining levels of rent and respect for property. The plight of certain people in bad housing is an object-lesson in conformity for the rest of society. It is also a consequence of some of the rules of business practice. Building societies with socially respected but stringent rules about eligibility for loans, and who believe they confer moderate rates of interest upon their clients, create the conditions for the operation of

1. In England and Wales, the number of homeless persons in temporary accommodation was 13,000 in 1966, 21,000 in 1969 and 24,000 in 1970. See *Social Trends*, No. 2, 1971, p. 126. By 1973, the figure reached 30,000. In 1974, new statistical returns began to be made by local authorities in London, and this was extended to the rest of England in 1975. The early returns continued to show an increase. See *Social Trends*, No. 7, 1976, p. 159.
2. A substantial proportion of those admitted to residential homes are not 'infirm' and in need of 'care and attention', but have, in fact, for various reasons, lost houses or tenancies. See Townsend, P., *The Last Refuge*, Routledge & Kegan Paul, London, 1962, p. 326.

predators who lend money at extortionate rates of interest to people desperate for a home. The price the latter pay is both a consequence of the restrictiveness of the building societies and one factor among many which encourage borrowers to accept the terms which the societies impose upon them. Thus, one study of three areas of older terraced housing in Birmingham in 1972–4 showed that the clearing banks, fringe banks and finance companies were a more common source of loans than building societies or local authorities, and that, owing to higher interest rates, monthly repayments were often twice or more than twice as high as repayments to a building society.[1] A similar point can be made about extortionate rents and deplorable conditions in the privately rented sector. These characteristics derive directly from the interest of landlords in maintaining high rents elsewhere, of councils which have created high barriers for applicants for homes, and of the mass of owner-occupiers and other tenants eager to maintain and extend their own rights and privileges.

However, just as unemployment fluctuates in a capitalist economy, so the *amount* and *degree* of housing deprivation can also fluctuate as a result of changes in the respective powers of different interest groups and of the adoption by society as a whole, and particularly governments, of new policies and rules about housing. I am suggesting here that elementary sociological explanations of a functional kind, like that put forward in previous paragraphs, are inherently fatalistic, and while providing insights into the reasons for the existence of bad housing, offer no deeper insights into reasons for its extent or degree and therefore of the ways in which it can be reduced and eliminated. But once we grasp the point that bad housing is functional for those in privileged housing, it is possible to go on to explore how the structure of privilege can directly affect the amount and type of bad housing and, indeed, how that structure must be changed if there are to be real as opposed to supposed improvements in bad housing. For an explanation to be a good explanation, it must be presented with sufficient empirical substantiation and detail to offer lessons for policy which can be easily read.

The preceding analysis has revealed the strong association between three variables: social class, type of tenure and income (and especially of the more comprehensive concept of net income worth), and different criteria of poor housing. I have tried to explain explicitly or implicitly how this arises and how these variables are interrelated. The scale and degree of deprivation in housing in society has three principal sources:

1. The processes by which the housing stock comes to consist of different characteristics, of structure, size or space, indoor and outdoor facilities or amenities, in relation to the household membership, and is distributed unequally and augmented.
2. How resources, especially incomes and wealth of members of the household, come to be distributed, and how these resources are maintained, restricted or increased.

1. Karn, V., *Priorities for Local Authority Mortgage Lending: A Case Study of Birmingham*, Centre for Urban and Regional Studies Research Memorandum, 52, 1976.

3. How costs and systems of rules of allocation and occupancy come to be related to groups of housing.

These three are, of course, closely related and mutually reinforcing, but they also operate independently. At a single moment in time, the housing stock of most rich societies has characteristics like those described in this chapter. It is unequally distributed and the distribution is continually being influenced and reshaped. Building regulations affect the quality of structure of new buildings and modifications in the density and surroundings of existing buildings. New technical processes are developed and new materials used by building companies. Conditions for improvement grants and slum clearance and urban planning schemes change the amount and quality of the stock. Legislation and tax policies affect the ownership of stock and hence the standards by which it is managed, maintained and modernized.

The second factor has direct and indirect effects. Increase in the resources of the poorest half of the population, through higher wages, more redistribution through social security, new laws on inheritance and higher taxation on wealth, can lead to investment in repairs, decoration and modernization, as well as pressure for more desirable types of housing.

The third factor determines how many and which kind of people are to be found in different types of housing, and hence how well the available space in such housing is utilized. Thus there are, as we have shown, social and not only financial determinants of standards. If society were to adopt greater inducements for people in under-occupied property to move to smaller accommodation, and then impose controls over the allocation of, or opportunity to move into, spacious accommodation on the part of single persons and married couples without children, inequalities in density of occupation would be reduced. If tenants had more of the security and other privileges enjoyed by owner-occupiers, such as some financial return after maintaining a tenancy in good condition for many years, a say in who is to inherit the tenancy, and the power to redecorate or make minor alterations subject only to local planning regulations, many would be prepared to invest in the maintenance and improvement of their homes.

These examples are given only to suggest which institutions, agencies and bodies of rules combine to make up the three causal factors identified above. This framework of explanation would need to be filled in.

Summary

This chapter documents different types of deprivation in housing as established in the survey and in different official studies. Twenty-two per cent of households experienced structural defects, 21 per cent inadequate housing facilities, and 11 per cent insufficient bedrooms, by conventional social standards. Another 44 per cent had only one of their rooms (or none) heated in winter, and 5 per cent had insufficient internal play-space for children. According to these five measures, 13 million, 11 million, 10 million, 22 million and 4 million people respectively in the United Kingdom were deprived. Sixty-one per cent, representing 33 million, experienced at least one type of poor housing. Eleven per cent, representing 6 million, experienced three or more types of poor housing. Twenty-five per cent of households expressed a need for additional rooms, and 6 per cent declared they had a serious housing problem now.

By most criteria, households consisting of a man and woman and four or more children experienced the worst housing. Single-person households were more likely than households with all numbers of children to have inadequate facilities and only one room heated in winter, but the latter, especially with three or more children, were much more likely to have insufficient rooms. A substantial proportion of households with children had need for more space, by both social and subjective standards.

Much the most important structural factor found to be associated with housing deprivation was occupational class. By nearly all criteria, we found a consistent relationship between lower incidence of deprivation and higher class. This was in part explained by the type of tenure associated with class. Strikingly more households in privately rented unfurnished accommodation than in other types of tenure, and fewer owner-occupiers, especially fewer of those still paying a mortgage, had poor housing.

The relative disadvantage of tenants living in privately rented accommodation has been documented in other studies and is well recognized. But in the poverty survey we found that, with the decline of such accommodation, council housing is taking its place as the sector accounting for the largest numbers of deprived dwellings. There were signs of the evolution of different grades or strata of housing in the council sector, to which people may be allocated on social and not only financial grounds.

Poor housing is also explained by low incomes. More households living in poverty or on the margins of poverty also experienced poor housing than did other households. For those in poverty, housing facilities, heating and indoor play-space for children were the respects in which they fared relatively worst.

Inequality in the distribution of net income worth is even more strongly associated with deprivation in housing. Nearly half the population with net income worth of less than half the mean were found to have inadequate housing facilities, and over a third to have insufficient indoor play-space for children, compared with only 3 and 2 per cent respectively for people with twice or more than twice the mean. But, at similar relative levels of income and net income worth, more owner-occupiers than council and private tenants possessed good facilities and amenities in their homes.

Owner-occupiers who fully owned their homes had much lower absolute and relative housing costs than tenants. Most owner-occupiers paying mortgages paid more absolutely in current terms than tenants for their homes, but a substantial proportion paid less than the average tenant relative to their incomes. When account is taken of tax reliefs on mortgage interest, inflation and capital gains, owner-occupiers were paying less absolutely as well as relatively to income than council tenants on their lifetime housing costs. This is perhaps one of the most interesting outcomes of the entire survey. The homes they were paying for tended also to be of much higher housing standards – for example, detached housing, space, facilities and possession of gardens. The paradox that the poor pay most for their housing poses a major question for housing policy.

The scale and degree of deprivation in housing in society is broadly determined by three factors:

1. *The quality, amount and distribution of the housing stock:* the processes by which different characteristics of structure, size or space, indoor and outdoor facilities or amenities, in relation to household membership, come to be distributed unequally among the national housing stock and are maintained and developed.
2. *The distribution of resources:* the resources, especially the income and wealth, of members of the household, and how these resources are maintained, restricted or increased.
3. *The relationship of resources to the structure of costs of housing and access to housing:* the social system of rules by which housing comes to be allocated, the institutions and policies which are developed in relation to the finance of housing and the system of rights and obligations according to which accommodation is occupied.

The processes by which the housing stock comes to be created and augmented, access to resources controlled and modified, and the rules by which people are allocated to, or find themselves in, different standards and types of housing, are tentatively described.

14

Deprivation of Environment

Traditional measures of bad housing have not paid much heed to the defects of the immediate environment. Yet outdoor space and facilities are as important as indoor facilities to some types of families or to all families at certain stages of the year. A brand-new home may have no garden and no easy access to an outside space for leisure, or it may be sited in an area affected by pollution or a long way from shops, pubs, cafés and transport facilities. A mouldering country cottage with a small shed and cesspit outside fulfilling the function of a toilet may have a large garden and orchard, with easy access to fresh supplies of milk, vegetables, fruit and chickens from local farms.

Social awareness of the importance of environmental conditions has become more acute in recent years in Britain. A general question on whether the environment was satisfactory was added to the 1967 Housing Conditions Survey.[1] A number of studies of improvement possibilities sponsored by the Ministry of Housing and Local Government in the mid and late 1960s called attention to the environment,[2] and in 1971 central departments were reorganized and the Department of the Environment created. Departmental research groups have begun to experiment with methods of relating different measures of environmental deficiencies, but government departments have as yet been shy both of adopting comprehensive scales and of discussing them publicly. It would be difficult at present to identify a 'social' standard of environmental conditions, except implicitly.

Independent research workers have attempted, in the past, to develop integrated measures of quality of housing, and recently to work towards some operational measure of environmental deficiency. Thus, there have been attempts to devise a comprehensive housing index covering different features of structure

1. 'House Conditions Survey, England and Wales, 1967', *Economic Trends*, No. 175, HMSO, London, 1968.

2. For example, one study examined the following environmental factors: whether the home overlooked open space or whether there was open space within 440 yards, whether there was noisy or obnoxious industry adjacent or opposite, whether there was heavy traffic along the road, a railway line within 100 feet or a bus stop within 200 yards. See Ministry of Housing and Local Government, *The Deeplish Study: Improvement Possibilities in a District of Rochdale*, HMSO, London, 1966.

and amenities.[1] Efforts have also been made to add environmental deficiencies to these scales – for example, offensive smells, air pollution, noise, absence of grass and trees, presence of litter and parked vehicles.[2] But this work gives the impression of being an *ad hoc* process which does not put social perceptions strictly to the test by virtue of a comprehensive examination of dwellings and local environmental stock, facilities and services which impinge on family life and behaviour. 'Research into housing lacks sophistication . . . [It] is partial and requires to be pieced together. A conception has yet to be developed that sees man in relation to his physical environment.'[3] The value assumptions upon which experimental indices of poor environmental conditions are based are usually neither expressed explicitly nor critically discussed. As a consequence, deficiencies short of some presumed social standard are listed without any very clear attempt to specify the mean or median or to show the kind of privileges enjoyed by those living in spacious and well-appointed amenities. Standards, and therefore data about poor housing and environmental conditions, are still too detached from any moorings. They lack reference points in a period of rapidly changing conditions. What is required is a concept of 'environmental deprivation' which includes, for example, the lack of, or difficulty of access to, gardens, play-spaces, parks, water, shopping facilities, health centres and so on, and exposure to noise and dirt.

Social standards that have been implicitly applied, and objective standards, might begin to be formulated if social scientists were to examine in general terms the total effect now and in the past of loosely framed legislation, administrative control and guidance in the form of circulars, advisory pamphlets, grants and planning permission, local by-laws and regulations and local administrative practices. Control of environmental conditions has developed piecemeal. For example, different Royal Commissions and government committees have made recommendations about the heights of buildings in relation to open space, the space at the rear of the dwellings, and the powers that local authorities ought to have to control drainage and overcrowding and the replacement of dwellings.[4] Through elected

1. See, for example, Chapman, D., *The Home and Social Status*, Routledge & Kegan Paul, London, 1955; Duncan, T. L. C., *Measuring Housing Quality: A Study of Methods*, Occasional Paper No. 20, Centre for Urban and Regional Studies, University of Birmingham, 1971, esp. pp. 38–43.
2. For example, Medhurst, F., and Lewis, J. P., *Urban Decay: An Analysis and a Policy*, Macmillan, London, 1969.
3. Schorr, A. L., *Slums and Social Insecurity*, Nelson, London, 1964, p. 21.
4. For example, the 1885 Commissioners on the Housing of the Working Classes recommended: '1. That upon the lines of existing enactments in the Acts of 1862 and 1878 rules of more general application be framed to control the height of buildings in relation to the open space which should be required to be provided in front of the buildings, either in the form of land exclusively belonging to each building and kept free from erections, or in the form of an adjoining street. 2. That in the rear of every new dwelling-house or other building to be controlled by rules ordinarily applicable to dwelling-houses, and whether in old or in new streets, there be provided a proportionate extent of space exclusively belonging to the dwelling-house

councils, communities have sought to superimpose their conceptions of minimum environmental standards upon the different physical manifestations of their predecessors' policies. Control over developments has tended to remain more in local hands than has control over the development, for example, of education and health services, and has been influenced by the interests of property owners and local residents in general. By the 1950s, there was still remarkably little central definition of environmental standards and, indeed, the emphasis was upon physical and not social standards. For example, the Ministry of Housing and Local Government's guidelines issued to local authorities about the density of residential dwellings in the 1950s suggested that the principal factors affecting density of houses were type of house, garden size, space for daylight and sunlight, space for privacy, space for access and space for trees and small green spaces.[1] The social needs of different types of population, households, families and workgroups were not formulated. Some attempt is required to show, through analysis, what social standard of environmental facility is in practice being applied, and what alternative objective standard might be devised, in order to demonstrate inequalities between and within areas in the extent to which they satisfy the range of social needs of their inhabitants. In the pages which follow we can offer no more than a number of illustrations to demonstrate the value of making a thoroughgoing attempt to lay bare the privileges and disprivileges of the environment.

Three Measures of Environmental Deprivation

The first step in conceptualizing environmental needs is to consider the needs of the family or household in the immediate environment of the home. The size of gardens to which there may or may not be access is not usually documented nationally. This was our first measure of environmental deprivation. We found that 6 per cent of households had access to neither a garden nor a yard, and a further 12 per cent and 8 per cent respectively had access only to a yard and did not have sole use of a garden. Altogether 26 per cent of households, and 22 per cent of the persons in the sample, representing 12 million persons, did not have sole use of a garden. And 8 per cent of people, representing 4 million persons, had gardens which were too small for the household to sit out in the sun, or smaller than about ten feet square.

Our second measure of environmental deprivation was whether the parents of

---

or building; that this space be free from erections from the ground level upwards, that it extend laterally throughout the entire width of the dwelling-house or building; that for the distance across the space from the building to the boundary of adjoining premises a minimum be prescribed; and that this minimum increase with the height of the dwelling-house or building.' See The First Report on . . . Housing of the Working Classes, London, 1885, pp. 32–3.

1. Ministry of Housing and Local Government, *The Density of Residential Areas*, HMSO, London, 1952, p. 6.

Table 14.1. *Percentages of households and of people of different age and social class, with different forms of environmental deprivation.*

Form of environmental deprivation	Households	Males and females	Males	Females
No sole use of garden	26	22	22	22
Garden or yard too small to sit in sun (smaller than 100 sq ft)	9	8	9	8
Children aged 1–4 No safe place to play near home	34	34	36	32
Children aged 5–10 No safe place to play near home	34	34	34	33
Air always or sometimes dirty, smoky or foul-smelling	27	27	28	26

children aged 1–4 considered there was no safe place for the child to play in proximity to the home, and, for parents of children aged 5–10, whether there was no safe place near by to which the child could go unaccompanied to play. As Table 14.1 shows, a third of the children in each age group were believed to have inadequate outdoor play facilities. Parents could treat their garden as an adequate place in which to play, but we found, in fact, that a substantial proportion even of those with a garden as large as, or larger than, the size of a tennis court did not regard it as a suitable or adequate play-space.

Our third measure of environmental deprivation was air pollution. Heads of households or housewives were asked whether the air in the neighbourhood was clean or was dirty, smoky or foul-smelling. Twenty-seven per cent, representing $14\frac{1}{2}$ million, said it was sometimes or always dirty, smoky or foul-smelling. According to each one of the three indices, therefore, a substantial minority of the population experienced environmental conditions which were deficient by social standards.

Multiple Deprivation

The three selected indicators of environmental deficiency were found to be highly correlated. Young children aged 1–4 living in homes without sole use of a garden were more than twice as likely as children in households with a garden, however

Age						Occupational class			
0–4	5–14	15–29	30–49	50–64	65+	Professional and managerial	Other non-manual	Skilled manual	Partly skilled and unskilled manual
26	19	26	20	21	25	11	17	22	31
11	6	10	8	7	8	1	6	9	14
34	–	–	–	–	–	25	27	35	44
–	34	–	–	–	–	35	32	33	34
31	26	29	27	24	26	17	22	31	34

small, to lack access to a place near the home where they could play safely (58 per cent, compared with 27 per cent). They were also three times more likely to be living in polluted surroundings (63 per cent, compared with 21 per cent). All households without sole use of a garden were more than twice as likely as households with a garden to be living in polluted surroundings (47 per cent, compared with 22 per cent).

Table 14.2 shows the extent to which households with and without young children experienced multiple deprivation. Eleven per cent of children aged 1–4, and 5 per cent aged 5–10, lived in households which experienced all three deficiencies, and a further 16 per cent and 15 per cent respectively experienced two. Only two of the three indicators applied to households without children aged 1–10, and 10 per cent of these experienced both inadequate garden space and polluted air.

Young children whose families had sole use of a large garden had a marked advantage in other respects over other children. Table 14.3 shows that the size of garden was highly correlated not only, as one might expect, with there being a safe place to play, but also with unpolluted air. Seventy per cent of those whose families had sole use of a large garden, compared with only 23 per cent of those with the use of only a small garden or yard, or no garden or yard at all, had a safe place to play and unpolluted surroundings. Only 1 per cent, compared with 37 per cent, had neither a safe place to play nor unpolluted surroundings. The same

Table 14.2. *Percentages of people with none, or one, or more of three selected forms of environmental deprivation.*

Number of environmental deficiencies[a]	Percentage of persons in households		
	Children aged 1–4	Children aged 5–10	No children aged 1–10
3	11	5	–
2	16	15	10
1	30	32	29
None	44	48	61
Total	100	100	100
Number	452	617	4,514

NOTE: [a] No sole use of garden or yard; or garden/yard too small for household to sit in sun; no safe place to play near by; air polluted sometimes or always.

Table 14.3. *Percentages of children aged 1–4 living in homes with gardens of different size who did not have a safe place to play near by and with some or a lot of air pollution.*

	Size of garden or yard		
Whether safe place to play, and air sometimes or always polluted	None or small *No sole use of garden or yard, or too small for household to sit in sun (under 10 ft sq)*	Medium *Over 10 ft sq, but not as large in size as tennis court*	Large *Size equivalent to tennis court or larger*
Neither safe to play nor unpolluted	37	14	1
Not safe to play but unpolluted	17	22	15
Safe to play but polluted	22	15	14
Both safe to play and unpolluted	23	49	70
Total	100	100	100
Number	107	224	121

trends applied to children aged 5–10 (see Table A.55, Appendix Eight, page 1034).

Finally, we compiled two indices: one for households in which there were children aged 1–10 inclusive, and the other for households without children of this age. A score was compiled as follows:

Air sometimes dirty, smoky or foul-smelling	1
Air always dirty, smoky or foul-smelling	2
Garden smaller in size than tennis court but large enough to sit in	1
Garden too small to sit in	2
No garden or yard	3
No safe place near home for child to play	2
Maximum score, households with children under 11	= 7
Maximum score, other households	= 5

A high proportion of people in households with young children experienced substantial deprivation – 53 per cent having a score on the environmental deprivation index of 3 or more and 12 per cent of 5 or more.

Social Characteristics of the Environmentally Deprived

Lack of adequate garden and play-space are in large measure a function of the standards adopted historically by the housing market and in public housing policies, but air pollution is a consequence of the more general interplay historic-

Table 14.4. Percentages of people, in households with and without children under 11 years, according to their degree of environmental deprivation.

	Households	
Score on environment index	With children under 11 years of age[a]	Without children under 11 years of age[b]
0	8	25
1	15	37
2	24	21
3	31	12
4	10	4
5	9	1
6	3	–
7	0	–
Total	100	100
Number	2,630	3,154

NOTES: [a] Maximum score 7.
[b] Maximum score 5.

Table 14.5. *Percentages of people in different regions with different forms of environmental deprivation.*

Region	Air always or sometimes polluted	No garden or yard or too small[a]	No place for young children to play near by[b]	Number	
				All persons	Children 1–4
Northern, Yorks and Humberside	59	28	55	681	53
North-West	35	26	56	676	56
Greater London	28	31	29	800	55
Northern Ireland	26	31	(31)	283	26
South-East	26	7	29	888	55
Anglia and East Midlands	21	20	23	607	57
West Midlands	20	10	30	806	50
Scotland	15	26	31	609	61
South-West and Wales	12	15	20	637	54

NOTES: [a] Too small for household to sit in sun (10 feet square).
[b] Children aged 1–4 only.

ally and at the present time of land use and control. The distribution of deficiencies varied widely by region, as Table 14.5 shows. By far the largest proportion of population experiencing air pollution was to be found in the Northern, Yorkshire and Humberside region, as many as 27 per cent saying the air was always, and another 32 per cent saying it was sometimes, dirty, smoky or foul-smelling. This region was also among the five regions with the largest percentages of population lacking adequate garden space, and was one of the two regions with least adequate play-space near the home for young children. The North-West, Northern Ireland and Greater London ranked high on all three dimensions and Scotland and the South-East high on two dimensions. The South-West and Wales region as a whole produced the lowest or near to lowest percentages. All nine regions are, of course, extensive and each contains areas in which very high proportions of population experience environmental deficiencies.

Fewer old than middle-aged adults, and fewer young single than young married adults, had access to a garden, and more shared a garden or yard. Some old people who were council tenants had bed-sitting rooms on the ground floor of blocks of flats, and among owner-occupiers old people were more likely than others to be living in older types of terraced houses without gardens. A substantial proportion of single adults under 60 lived in privately rented furnished rooms or unfurnished flats and shared gardens with other tenants or had no access at all

Table 14.6. *Percentages of households of different type with or without gardens or yards and percentages of people with sole use of garden, according to its size.*

Garden/yard	Single person 60 and over	Under 60	Man and woman	Man, woman and children	Other households without children	Other households with children
Neither garden nor yard	10	15	7	6	4	2
Shared yard	5	7	4	2	3	2
Shared garden	14	32	8	5	5	3
Sole use yard	11	5	7	10	7	8
Sole use garden	59	42	74	77	81	84
Total	100	100	100	100	100	100
Number	236	122	534	480	384	261
Sole use yard or garden						
Too small to sit in sun	12	11	10	7	8	9
Medium size	64	58	60	61	57	53
Large	23	32	30	32	36	38
Total	100	100	100	100	100	100
Number	169	57	859	1,737	1,097	1,245

to a garden or yard. Although over three quarters of households with children had sole use of a garden, some of these (rather fewer than 1 in 10) had gardens which were too small to sit in the sun. Eighteen per cent of households consisting of man, woman and children had neither a garden nor a yard, or only sole or shared use of a yard (Table 14.6).

Environmental deprivation tends to vary sharply with class (Table 14.1). Seventeen per cent of persons of professional or managerial occupational class, compared with 34 per cent of persons of partly skilled and unskilled class, experienced some or a lot of air pollution. The corresponding figures, among those with sole use of a garden or yard, whose garden or yard was too small to sit out in the sun were 1 per cent and 14 per cent respectively; and children aged 1–4 with no safe place to play near the home, 25 per cent and 44 per cent respectively. There was one exception, as the table shows. There was no significant variation by class in the proportion of children aged 5–10 who had no safe place to play near the home.

Poverty, Class and Tenure

There tended to be some association between poverty, as judged by the state's standard, and different forms of environmental deprivation. Thus, 30 per cent of those with incomes of less than the supplementary benefit standard, compared

Table 14.7. Percentages of people poor, marginally poor and non-poor, by the state's standard, with different forms of environmental deprivation.

Form of environmental deprivation	Net disposable household income last year as % of supplementary benefit scales plus housing cost		
	Under 100	100–39	140+
No sole use of garden	30	26	19
Garden or yard too small for household to sit in the sun	10	11	7
No safe place for children aged 1–4 to play near by	(47)	30	35
No safe place for children aged 5–10 to play near by	(40)	20	36
Air always or sometimes polluted	35	23	28
Number of persons	312	1,121	3,713
Number of children 1–4	32	129	253
Number of children 5–10	45	138	354

with 19 per cent of those with incomes distinctly above that standard, lacked sole use of a garden. In other instances, namely no safe place to play for children and air pollution, there was little or no correlation, or it was slight. It should be remembered that the quality and costs of housing are ignored in applying the supplementary benefit standard and that a wide range of incomes are included in the final column of the table. The findings reported in Table 14.7 are less clear-cut than might be expected and invite elucidation.

We have already seen that the variation in environmental deprivation by occupational class was marked. Indeed, within each of the broad income groups defined by the supplementary benefit standard, namely, the poor, the marginally poor and the non-poor, environmental deficiencies tended to be more widespread among those of lower than higher occupational class (Table A.56, Appendix Eight, page 1035).

This is largely explained both by variation in tenure and in value of assets held.

Table 14.8. Percentages of people in different types of tenure who experienced different forms of environmental deprivation.

Form of environment deprivation	Owner-occupiers		Renting			
	Fully owning	*Paying mortgage*	*Council*	*Privately (furnished)*	*Privately (unfurnished)*	*Rent free*
No sole use of garden or yard	7	3	15	58	24	18
Garden or yard too small for household to sit in sun	8	6	5	22	21	2
No safe place for children aged 1–4 to play near by	(47)	31	27	(42)	59	–
No safe place for children aged 5–10 to play near by	22	40	26	(39)	48	(33)
Air always or sometimes polluted	23	26	26	26	44	14
Number all persons	1,202	1,694	1,819	262	802	197
Children 1–4	30	177	158	24	55	18
Children 5–10	63	232	219	23	64	21

Table 14.8 shows that more private unfurnished tenants than people in other tenures experienced polluted surroundings and lack of a safe place for young children to play, and more of them and of private furnished tenants than others lacked exclusive access to a medium-sized or large garden. Rather more council tenants than owner-occupiers lacked sole use of a garden or yard, but in other respects the proportions of people in these two types of tenure who experienced the environmental deficiencies which we had selected for study were not widely different.

Table 14.9. *Percentages of people in households with and without children under 11 years experiencing a substantial degree of environmental deprivation.*

	% scoring 3 or more on environment index[a]		Number of base	
Characteristic	With children under 11 years	Without children under 11 years	With children under 11 years	Without children under 11 years
State poverty standard				
below supplementary benefit standard	87	20	136	163
100–39% of standard	63	16	620	471
140–99% of standard	49	19	959	743
200+% of standard	42	16	592	1,376
Income net worth				
below 50% of mean income net worth of household type	75	25	180	321
50–89% of household type	62	21	996	973
90–119% of household type	53	19	352	393
120–99% of household type	30	10	308	555
200+% of household type	14	6	100	136
Occupational class				
Professional	18	8	183	154
Managerial	31	15	141	146
High supervisory	41	6	253	705
Low supervisory	47	12	388	434
Routine non-manual	41	18	149	319
Skilled manual	60	18	880	918
Partly skilled manual	69	20	416	529
Unskilled manual	77	21	220	349

NOTE: [a] As defined above, page 535. Only two items apply to households without children under 11 years of age, and the maximum score is 5 compared with 7 for households with such children.

Once the value of assets held, including the value of owner-occupied property wholly or partly paid off is taken into account, however, the relationship between environmental deficiencies and social and economic factors is easier to explain. More than half the children aged 1–4 of those with net income worth of less than half the mean for households of their type, compared with only 12 per cent of those with twice or more than twice the mean, had no safe place near by in which to play. The wealthier households were able to halve their chances of living in polluted surroundings. And among the wealthiest group with twice or more than twice the mean net income worth for their household type, the lowest incidence of environmental deprivation was to be found among owner-occupiers. (See also Table A.57, Appendix Eight, page 1036.)

Table 14.9 illustrates our discussion. The table brings out the particular disadvantages of poor families with young children. For these households, the association with environmental deprivation is more marked when we examine their income net worth than when we examine their net disposable income (both being expressed as a percentage of the state's poverty standard for ease of comparison). And because manual workers have worse access than non-manual workers to wealth in general and owner-occupation in particular, their children are much more likely to experience poor environmental amenities.

Summary

This chapter extends the analysis of deprivation from housing to the immediate environment and should be read in conjunction with chapter 13. Three measures are applied: existence and size of garden adjoining the home; frequency of air pollution; and whether or not children aged 1–4 and 5–10 have a safe place to play outside. As many as 22 per cent of the population, representing 12 million, lacked sole use of a garden, and 8 per cent, representing 4 million, had gardens which were too small for the household to sit out in the sun. Twenty-seven per cent, representing 14½ million, experienced some degree of air pollution, including 8 per cent who said the air in the neighbourhood was always dirty, smoky or foul-smelling. Over a third of children aged 1–10 were said to have no safe place in which to play in the immediate environment of the home.

The three measures were highly correlated. For example, households without sole use of a garden were more than twice as likely as households with a garden to be living in polluted surroundings. As many as 11 per cent of children aged 1–4 experienced all three forms of deprivation.

By far the largest proportion of population experiencing air pollution were to be found in the Northern, Yorkshire and Humberside region. This region was also one of the five regions with the largest percentages of population lacking adequate garden space, and was one of the two regions with least adequate play-space for young children near the home.

Environmental deprivation varies sharply by occupational class. For example, 17 per cent of persons of professional or managerial status, compared with 34 per cent of persons of partly skilled and unskilled status, experienced some or a lot of air pollution. Twenty-five per cent of children aged 1–4 of the former, compared with 44 per cent of children of the latter, had no safe place to play near the home.

There was an association between poverty, as judged by the state's standard, and certain forms of environmental deprivation. But this association was not strong and tended to be masked by variation in tenure and assets held within each of the three broad groups of poor, marginal poor and non-poor. When the value of assets held, including the value of owner-occupied property wholly or partly paid off, was taken into account with income, and the distribution among the non-poor examined, wealth and environmental deprivation could be shown to be inversely correlated to a very marked extent. Thus, the chances of living in polluted surroundings were halved for the wealthiest households. More than half the children aged 1–4 of those with net income worth of less than half the mean for households of their type, compared with only 12 per cent of those with twice or more than twice the mean, had no safe place near by to play. Our data showed that over two thirds of the families of manual workers with young children had a marked degree of environmental deprivation. This is a finding which can only in part be put right by improved industrial location policies and urban planning. Young working-class families would seem to need a better share of resources and better access to homes with gardens and other environmental amenities.

15
The Problems of Poor Areas

The idea that society's ills are concentrated in certain areas and communities has a long history. It arises from notions of association and contamination, congregation, inheritance and environmental influence. Destitute, poor or criminal people are believed to seek refuge in certain areas because there is nowhere else for them to go. Those already living there are believed to be contaminated by the anti-social values and practices of those coming into their midst, just as disease spreads in crowded conditions. Children are believed to have no chance of escaping the limitations of the families, environment and culture into which they are born and live. For such reasons, poverty, criminality and disadvantage are believed to be heavily concentrated and deeply rooted in particular communities.[1]

The idea is important historically and contemporaneously.[2] It affects government policies as much as explanations of poverty. Thus, the assumption in the United States that there were geographical 'pockets' of poverty in scattered areas in which there was both economic recession or depression and inadequate housing and welfare services led to the 'grey areas' programme of the Ford Foundation in the early 1960s and the community action programmes financed by the US government in its War on Poverty in the mid and late 1960s.[3] In the

1. 'In these horrid dens the most abandoned characters of the city are collected and from them they nightly issue to pour upon the town every species of crime and abomination' – Laing, S., *National Distress: Its Causes and Remedies*, London, 1844, p. 11; quoted in Dennis, N., *People and Planning*, Faber & Faber, London, 1970, p. 334.

2. In part, of course, the idea derives from the history of community studies. Throughout history, the expectation that geography or locality will determine the nature of social relations has been kept alive and nurtured. Communities are assumed to have more independence, and to have characteristics, sets of relations and behaviour far more idiosyncratic than they can be shown to have. In recent years there has been considerable criticism within sociology of the traditional treatment of community as a locale. See, for example, Pahl, R. E., 'The Rural Urban Continuum', *Readings in Urban Sociology*, Pergamon, Oxford, 1968; and Gans, H., *The Urban Villagers*, Free Press, New York, 1962.

3. For early accounts, see Marris, P., and Rein, M., *Dilemmas of Social Reform: Poverty and Community Action in the United States*, Routledge & Kegan Paul, London, 1967; Moynihan, D. P., *Maximum Feasible Misunderstanding: Community Action in the War on Poverty*, Arkville Press, New York, 1969.

United Kingdom, the same idea has taken root in a cluster of policies developed in the late 1960s. First, following the publication of the Plowden Report in 1967,[1] Educational Priority Areas were designated as deserving additional resources. 'Positive discrimination' became a fashionable concept. Schools in designated areas were supposed to receive larger capital sums, equipment grants and teaching staffs, and higher salaries were to be paid. Yet no basis for the measurement of deprivation either in areas or schools was laid down as the first stage in discriminating who should be helped.

Next followed the Urban Programme. In 1968, the government announced action to help 'areas of severe social deprivation in a number of our cities and towns' to 'meet their social needs and to bring their physical services to an adequate level'.[2] Urban aid projects included nursery education, day nurseries and child care, community centres, family-planning and other advice centres, play schemes, care of the aged, various miscellaneous schemes for the homeless, the mentally handicapped and alcoholics, and help for voluntary organizations such as the Salvation Army and the Samaritans.

During the late 1960s and early 1970s, local authorities with relatively large numbers of immigrants began to receive grant aid. Finally, the Community Development Project, first announced in July 1969, was 'a neighbourhood-based experiment aimed at finding new ways of meeting the needs of people living in areas of high social deprivation'. It was assumed that problems of urban deprivation had their origins in the characteristics of local populations – in individual pathologies – and that these could best be resolved by better coordination of the social services, and encouragement of citizen involvement and community self-help.[3] Twelve local project teams were set up between January 1970 and October 1972 in Coventry, Liverpool, Southwark, Glyncorrwg (Glamorgan), Canning Town (Newham), Batley (in the West Riding), Paisley, Newcastle, Cleaton Moor (Cumberland), Birmingham, Tynemouth and Oldham to identify needs, promote coordination and foster community involvement.

These schemes were either allowed to run down or were succeeded by new schemes developed in the mid 1970s. For example, two new types of special area – 'Housing Action Areas' and 'Priority Neighbourhoods', in addition to 'General Improvement Areas' – were introduced under the Housing Act 1974.[4] Housing Action Areas were intended to be areas of housing stress in which poor physical

1. Central Advisory Council for Education (England), *Children and Their Primary Schools*, HMSO, London, 1966.

2. Mr James Callaghan, *Hansard*, 22 July 1968, col. 40.

3. *The National Community Development Project*, Inter-Project Report 1973, CDP Information and Intelligence Unit, February 1974.

4. See, for example, Department of the Environment, *Housing Act 1974: Renewal Strategies*, Circular 13/75, HMSO, London, 1975; *Housing Act 1974: Parts IV, V, VI, Housing Action Areas, Priority Neighbourhoods and General Improvement Areas*, Circular 14/75, HMSO, London, 1975.

and social conditions interacted, and Priority Neighbourhoods adjacent areas where problems were likely to increase if no action were to be taken. Guidance was issued to local authorities showing what kind of indicators could be used to identify such areas.[1]

All these programmes make assumptions, however vaguely, about the spatial and social distribution of deprivation. In the following pages, the variation in the extent of poverty and certain forms of deprivation will be examined among regions, urban and rural areas and four poor districts, with the intention of mapping the range of problems experienced, contributing to the task of explaining variation in poverty and offering provisional guidelines for policy.

The Incidence of Poverty

The survey establishes beyond reasonable doubt the wide dispersion of poverty. This can be seen by comparing the findings both for regions and for selected types of area (Table 15.1). If we add together both the numbers with incomes below the state's poverty standard and those with incomes just above that standard, Northern Ireland was found by a large margin to be the poorest region, followed by Scotland, the North-West, Wales and the South-East, and the Northern, Yorks and Humberside region. Greater London and the South-East contained the smallest proportions of poor. It should be remembered, however, that the differential would not be so sharp (though it would remain) if we were to adjust incomes for their purchasing value. The relativity between regions for the populations of all ages also holds for the different age groups. (See Table A.58, Appendix Eight, page 1037). Scotland had the highest proportion of persons with high incomes as well as the second highest proportion with low incomes. Anglia and the East Midlands comprised another region with substantial proportions of the population at the extremes of poverty and wealth. None the less, as Table 15.1 shows, substantial minorities living in poverty were to be found in all regions.

We next compared the proportions of poor and marginally poor in rural and urban areas and conurbations. It will be surprising to some that the population in poverty, or on its margins, was as high or nearly as high as in urban areas. (By the alternative deprivation standard, the result was the same: 24 per cent were assessed to be in poverty, compared with 26 per cent in conurbations and 27 per cent in other urban areas.) There were proportionately more rich people in rural areas than in other types of area, but rather fewer in the next rank of prosperity. Rather fewer children but more middle aged than elsewhere, and roughly the same numbers of young adults and elderly people, were poor or marginally poor (Table A.59, Appendix Eight, page 1037). The survey also allowed a check to be made on two criteria of area poverty: the percentage of voters voting left (at the

1. Department of the Environment, Area Improvement Note 10, *The Use of Indicators for Area Action, Housing Act, 1974*, H M S O, London, 1975.

1966 General Election),[1] and the percentage leaving school early. As the table shows, there was a correlation, but by no means a marked one. Even in the large number of constituencies with a relatively low left-voting percentage, there were 9 per cent of the population living below the state's poverty standard, and another 23 per cent on the margins. And even in those areas with the fewest people who had left school early (accounting for less than a quarter of the population), there were 9 per cent below and 19 per cent on the margins of the standard.

From the viewpoint of area deprivation policies, the data for areas smaller than constituencies are perhaps the most telling. We divided the wards and districts in the fifty-one constituencies which we had visited into four groups according to the fraction of households in the sample who were living below or just above the

Table 15.1. *Variation in the incidence of poverty by region and area.*

Type of region or area	Percentage of persons in income units with net disposable income last year, as % of state standard					Total	Number
	Under 100	*100–39*	*140–99*	*200–99*	*300+*		
Degree of urbanization							
Rural	9	21	34	19	17	100	930
Urban	8	25	27	28	11	100	2,400
Conurban	10	22	28	28	12	100	1,992
Region							
Greater London	8	19	26	32	15	100	716
South-East Anglia and East	6	21	33	28	12	100	809
Midlands	11	18	32	25	14	100	526
South-West and Wales	8	26	32	21	13	100	555
West Midlands	8	22	28	29	13	100	704
North-West	9	27	27	28	10	100	621
Northern, Yorks and Humberside	10	23	32	24	12	100	586
Northern Ireland	18	31	18	28	4	100	244
Scotland	9	29	25	21	17	100	561
Left-wing vote in constituency							
80% or more	8	28	29	26	9	100	1,353
Over 65% but under 80%	9	18	29	29	15	100	1,176
Under 65%	9	23	28	26	14	100	2,793

1. The reasons for adopting this criterion are discussed in Appendix One, page 931.

Table 15.1. – contd

Type of region or area	Percentage of persons in income units with net disposable income last year, as % of state standard					Total	Number
	Under 100	100–39	140–99	200–99	300+		
Fraction of low incomes in area							
Very high (half or more)	14	36	25	18	7	100	1,275
Rather high (two fifths or more)	12	20	31	25	12	100	849
Rather low (a fifth or more)	7	20	29	31	13	100	2,629
Very low (under a fifth)	3	11	32	28	26	100	569
% leaving school early in area							
High (60% or more)	9	27	27	26	10	100	2,312
About average (50–59%)	8	22	30	26	14	100	1,804
Low (under 50%)	9	19	29	28	15	100	1,206
Selected poor areas[a]				⏜			
Belfast (2 wards)	14	36	36	14		100	750
Glasgow (polling districts in 3 wards)	13	35	36	15		100	907
Salford (4 wards)	13	25	36	26		100	905
Neath (1 urban ward and 1 rural district)	4	23	42	31		100	606

NOTE: [a]For persons in household units.

state's poverty standard (strictly, with net disposable incomes plus housing costs in the twelve months previous to interview of less than 150 per cent of the state's poverty standard). By definition, the correlation between the proportion of income units living below or close to the poverty standard and the 'poorest' areas was marked. But, even in the poorest group of areas, a quarter of the people interviewed were relatively prosperous, and in the richest group of areas 14 per cent had incomes around the poverty standard. Indeed, the reader will see from Table 15.1 that two groups of areas with 'rather low' or 'very low' fractions of low incomes accounted for 2,629 plus 569 persons respectively, making 3,198 persons altogether, or 60 per cent of the sample. None the less these areas accounted for 46 per cent, or nearly half of the poor and marginally poor in the national survey.

These data are so important for national understanding and action that they need to be presented in greater detail. In the survey, 28 per cent of the population in *households* (as distinct from *income units*) were living below or marginally above the state's standard of poverty. For the fifty-one constituencies in the entire sample, the range was (with one exception) between 12 per cent and 46 per cent, though sampling error is considerable. The ten constituencies with the largest proportions of poor accounted for 20 per cent of the population surveyed and 32 per cent of the poor. The ten constituencies with the smallest percentages of poor accounted for 19 per cent of the population surveyed and 10 per cent of the poor. For interest, the list is set out in Table A.60, Appendix Eight (page 1038). Despite the liability to extremely large sampling error, most of the constituencies which might be expected to have the largest percentages in poverty are to be found at the head of the list, and those with the smallest percentages at the foot of the list. Thus, constituencies with largest percentages of poor tended to be those with high percentages of manual workers (Table A.60, Appendix Eight, page 1038) or retirement pensioners or both. Conversely, the constituencies with the smallest percentages of poor tended to be those with more non-manual and non-elderly populations. The picture of wide dispersion of poverty, despite higher incidence in some constituencies, is not substantially altered when different criteria of deprivation are examined – such as housing facilities, number of consumer durables in the house and social customs and activities.

Four constituencies which, on different criteria, seemed at the first stage of the sampling to be the poorest among the fifty-one, had been chosen for further separate study. (For methodology, see Appendix One, pages 951–4, and Chapter 3.) These constituencies were Salford East, Belfast North, Neath and Glasgow Shettleston. The poorest districts within these constituencies (in the case of Belfast two alternative districts outside the constituency were chosen) were then selected according to the percentage of children in them receiving free school meals, and addresses sampled at random for visits and requests for interviews. For each of the four areas, data on income were successfully obtained for between 600 and 900 individuals. The percentage of poor and marginally poor was lowest in Neath, with 27 per cent, and highest in Belfast, with just under 50 per cent, the other two areas, Salford and Glasgow Shettleston, being intermediate, with 37 per cent and 48 per cent respectively. In these four poor areas (three of them highly deprived) the percentage of the population in households with incomes of more than twice the state's poverty standard varied from 16 to 31.

We can certainly conclude that there are areas with about twice as many poor and marginally poor as there are in the nation as a whole. These areas also have a disproportionately high prevalence of other types of deprivation. But there are two major reservations: (a) the majority of poor are not to be found in areas which even account for 20 per cent of the population; and (b) there are substantial minorities of relatively prosperous people even in the poorest districts of the country.

Rural and Urban Differences

The percentage of the population in rural areas who were poor or marginally poor was not markedly different from that in urban and conurban areas (Table 15.1). In other respects, there was less evidence of deprivation in rural Britain,

Table 15.2. Percentages of people in different types of area with different characteristics.

	Percentage of persons having characteristic		
Characteristic	Rural	Urban	Conurban
More than 10 years' education	29	25	24
Work indoors	56	71	76
Council tenants	21	33	32
Owner-occupiers	54	48	46
Poor household facilities	6	9	6
Socially deprived (scoring 6 or more)	15	17	16
Fewer than 6 of 10 selected consumer durables	15	24	20
Poor environmental conditions (3 or more on index)	1	9	17
Employed and self-employed with non-manual occupations	47	45	46
Persons aged 15–39 with disablement condition	5	8	6
Persons aged 40–59 with disablement condition	11	15	17
Persons aged 60 and over with disablement condition	29	33	35

taken as a whole, than in urban Britain. Thus, markedly fewer of the population lacked gardens, and almost none complained of air pollution. Slightly fewer lacked a reasonable number of consumer durables. Roughly the same proportion as in urban Britain were socially deprived and had poor housing facilities. Fewer of those who worked indoors had bad conditions of work, but more worked outdoors, and some of them had dangerous work or very poor conditions. More owned their homes and substantially fewer had council tenancies. Perhaps surprisingly, slightly more of the adults had had more than ten years' education, and about the same proportion had non-manual occupations (Table 15.2).

However, the picture derived from rural areas is by no means uniform. A larger proportion of the population than elsewhere were found to live in low-income areas, but a larger proportion also lived in high-income areas. This is because there are relatively prosperous farming areas, areas containing large numbers of upper non-manual commuters, and popular tourist holiday areas, as well as declining and poor rural areas. The relationship between different sectors of the economy and the extent of poverty in rural areas remains to be elaborated.[1] Nearly a third of the rural population, compared with a quarter elsewhere, lived in areas where over 50 per cent of the population had low incomes; and yet nearly a fifth, compared with less than a tenth, lived in areas where fewer than 20 per cent of the population had low incomes.

This means that the areas cannot be treated as autonomous or self-sufficient in terms of either economy or culture. To a large extent, their functions, and therefore their prosperity, is decided externally. The pattern of inequality can be inferred to be set nationally, and area variations in the extent of poverty arise through variation in mix of industry and use and value of land, employment level, deviation of the wage structure of the local labour market from the national labour market, the distribution of type of housing tenure and types of house location, and the deviation of the local housing market from the national housing market. These factors tend to condition distortions or unrepresentativeness of local population and hence community structure. One example is rural depopulation, leaving relatively few young people in an area. Migration from the area is a function partly of tight farming control over housing, and upper non-manual control over land-use planning. Alternatively a large number of additional elderly people may be attracted into certain rural and seaside areas. This immigration is fostered negatively by the elderly being denied employment and other functional roles in their home areas, and positively by the combined efforts of local trading interests and property speculators in the areas of settlement. When those with the largest economic interests in an area decide to go elsewhere, to concentrate their interests or to exercise them irrespective of the social consequences, there tend to be large numbers of families and individuals who, because of ties to relatives or community or housing, or simply because of cost, cannot extricate themselves to leave for a more prosperous area. The general argument briefly outlined here, therefore, is that the observed variations in poverty in rural and urban areas must be explained in terms of access to economic resources.

Differences between Regions

This geographical pattern of economic subservience and superiority results in some marked regional disparities. The regions reproduce national customs, conventions, structures and therefore inequalities. But just as country areas can serve the interests of urban areas and vice versa, and then fall into place in a larger framework of inequality, so regions do the same. Although much less independent or autonomous than nation-states, regions tend to take embryonic form as

1. A study by Howard Newby of agricultural workers in East Anglia makes evident the dependence of one large group of workers. See Newby, H., *The Deferential Worker*, Allen Lane, London, 1977.

backward and advanced sub-systems of society – in some respects like the developing and developed societies of the world – though they are rarely as unequal or as closely bound by economic, political and cultural ties. Few large countries lack regions which can be described as economically underdeveloped. Like many of the countries of the Third World, however, the relative poverty of these regions can fairly be said to be a function of the rich regions' prosperity.

In the United Kingdom, the population living in the South and South-East have distinct advantages over the population living in other regions. This is documented in various official and independent reports.[1] The poverty survey produced new types of data on deprivation. The ranking of the nine principal regions according to various criteria is summarized in Table 15.3. Three reservations must

Table 15.3. Ranking of regions according to various criteria.

Criterion of ranking (% of population in each case)	Northern Ireland	Scotland	Northern, Yorks and Humberside	Southern, West and Wales	North-East	West Midlands	Anglia and East Midlands	Greater London	South-East
Income unit in poverty or marginal poverty	1	2	3	4	5	6	7	8	9
Socially deprived (scoring 6 or more on index)	1	2	5	4	3	7	6	8	9
Fewer than 6 of 10 selected consumer durables in home	1	2	5	4	3	7	6	8	9
Poor household facilities	1	6	7	5	2	8	3	4	9
Overcrowded (according to bedroom standard)	1	2	7	8	5	4	6	3	9
Poor environmental conditions	3	9	2	8	1	6	7	5	4
Home not owner-occupied	2	1	7	5	6	4	8	3	9
Adults fewer than 11 years' education	1	2	4	7	3	5	6	8	9

1. See the annual *Regional Statistics*, produced by the Central Statistical Office, and the reports of the Family Expenditure Survey and the General Household Survey. In 1974 and 1975, average weekly household income was highest in Greater London and the South-East – the former being 35 per cent and the latter 42 per cent larger than that in Northern Ireland. See *Social Trends*, No. 7, 1976, HMSO, London, 1977, p. 128.

be entered. The number and boundaries of regions have been changed in official conventions in recent years, and some of the regions as defined in this study cover rather extensive geographical areas. Again, ranking depends in some instances on the precise 'cut-off' point of deprivation which has been chosen for purposes of comparison. And ranking sometimes conceals extremely small differences between regions. Thus a difference of three percentage points sometimes covered three or even four regions. None the less, on different criteria of deprivation, the advantage of the South and South-East, and the disadvantage of Northern Ireland, and to a lesser extent of Scotland and the North, is unmistakable. Perhaps 'environmental conditions' is the least reliable indicator since interviews were clustered in constituencies, some of which were widely subject to air pollution.

Table 15.4. *Percentages of people in different regions with different characteristics.*

Individual characteristics	Greater London	South-East	Anglia and East Midlands	South-West and Wales	West Midlands	Northern, Yorks and Humberside	North-East	Northern Ireland	Scotland
Persons aged 15–39 with more than 10 years' education	47	47	36	40	34	32	28	30	23
Persons aged 40–59 with more than 10 years' education	30	27	24	22	18	16	17	13	17
Persons aged 60+ with more than 10 years' education	15	18	20	15	9	12	6	6	11
Employed and self-employed with non-manual occupations	57	51	38	48	40	42	44	43	46
Council tenants	25	25	28	25	42	29	25	22	50
Owner-occupiers	42	60	56	48	45	52	49	35	23
Socially deprived (scoring 6 or more)	10	9	13	18	11	15	23	40	25
Fewer than 6 of 10 selected consumer durables	15	8	22	24	21	22	26	50	26
Poor environmental conditions (3 or more on index)	18	20	15	9	16	28	53	26	7
With disablement condition	11	11	8	16	13	12	11	15	14

The rankings help to sum up the regional structure of inequality, but are not very informative. Some of the most informative indicators are brought together in Table 15.4. A high proportion of the employed population in the South, South-East and Greater London were in non-manual occupations. Many women were included, the great majority of whom were in non-manual occupations. If we consider occupational status of the head of household, the high ranking of the South and South-East remains pronounced. Regional inequality is therefore closely associated with the unequal class structure. With the reservation that the findings may have been affected by migration, the inequalities in educational experience seem to have persisted for three generations. Certainly more of the elderly in the South than the North had had more than ten years' education, and though more younger people in all regions had had an education of this length, the difference between regions remains very large. There also tended to be more disablement in the North than in the South, which was not explained by differences in age structure.

Areas of High Deprivation

The themes developed above for rural and urban Britain and for the major regions can also be developed for quite small areas. The separate surveys in four areas covered groups of only from 5,000 to 8,000 households. Four wards were selected in Salford East, certain polling districts in the three wards of Glasgow Shettleston, two wards (one mainly Roman Catholic and the other mainly Protestant) in Belfast, and one urban ward and one rural district in the constituency of Neath.[1]

With the exception of Neath, the percentage found to be in poverty or on the margins of poverty by the state's standard was high, being 38 for selected areas of Salford, 48 for Glasgow Shettleston and 50 for Belfast. The figure for the United Kingdom as a whole was 28. Table A.61 in Appendix Eight (page 1039) shows that these higher percentages applied to each age group and nearly every type of household. Families with children were disproportionately at risk. Over half the children in these areas were living in or near poverty. I will review some of the factors which contribute to the excess in these poor districts and also discuss some of the correlates of that high incidence of poverty. Table 15.5 first of all shows the age distribution and household composition of the samples in each of the areas compared with the United Kingdom. The percentage of children was relatively larger, and of adults aged 25–64 relatively smaller in the three city areas. The number of elderly averaged about the same as in the United Kingdom, but was relatively larger in Belfast and Glasgow and relatively smaller in Salford. In looking at the lower half of the table, it is evident that the additional children in poverty are only in small part to be traced to there being more couples with

1. The criteria of selection are discussed in Appendix One, pages 951–4.

four or more children. The relatively exceptional category is the miscellaneous group of households with children. These were mainly one-parent families and couples with a widowed parent and children – anyone 15 or over counting as an adult. In the four areas, we found that 13 per cent of families with children were

Table 15.5. *Percentages of population of four areas and of the United Kingdom by age and household type.*

Age	Neath	Salford	Belfast	Glasgow Shettleston	All 4 areas	United Kingdom
0–14	25	31	29	31	30	25
15–24	16	15	15	14	15	14
25–54	22	23	18	24	22	25
45–64	26	22	24	18	22	23
65+	11	9	13	13	11	12
Total	100	100	100	100	100	100
Number	709	1,028	782	1,040	3,559	6,045
Household type						
Single person under 60	1	2	4	3	2	2
Single person 60 or over	3	4	5	7	5	4
Man and woman	15	15	13	17	15	18
Man, woman and 1 child	8	10	4	8	8	7
Man, woman and 2 children	12	15	6	10	11	13
Man, woman and 3 children	4	5	6	10	7	7
Man, woman and 4+ children	5	9	8	10	9	6
3 adults	14	8	8	7	9	11
3 adults and children	11	9	17	9	11	12
4 adults	5	5	7	4	5	6
Others without children	4	4	6	3	4	4
Others with children	19	15	15	13	15	10
Total	100	100	100	100	100	100
Number	671	937	736	953	3,297	6,077

NOTE: In this and other tables giving results for the four areas, adjustments have been made to allow for losses at the second stage of interviewing. This has rarely involved a change of more than one to any particular percentage figure, and only in a minority of instances even a change of one.

one-parent families, compared with 7 per cent in the United Kingdom, and 10 per cent of children, compared with 7 per cent, were in such families (see page 760).

The level of economic activity in these areas was lower. For example, as many as 19 per cent of males aged 50–64 had not worked in the previous year. Levels of unemployment and incapacity were disproportionately high for both sexes. More men and women of working age were registered unemployed, and as many as 10 per cent of households were found to include an adult who had been unemployed for eight weeks or more in the previous year, compared with 4 per cent for the United Kingdom as a whole. There were also more households with an adult under 65 who had been sick or injured for eight weeks or more in the previous year – 18 per cent, compared with 9 per cent. These are, of course, both important factors in increasing the prevalence of poverty (given the low level of alternative income support for people not in employment).

But, in addition to the high proportion of people sick or injured from work and the high proportion of people who were unemployed, both the distorted occupational structure of the population living in these districts and the high proportion of people of manual class who were low paid contributed further to the excess of poverty. Table 15.6 shows the paucity of people of non-manual occupational class living in the special areas. Only 14 per cent of their populations could be classified as non-manual, and most of these were in the routine non-manual occupations with lowest pay and status. By contrast, 86 per cent were of manual class, 24 per cent being of unskilled manual class, compared with 10 per cent who were in this class in the population of the United Kingdom as a whole.

Did the difference in distribution by occupational class in fact account for the

Table 15.6. Percentages of population of four areas and of the United Kingdom, by occupational class.

Occupational class	Neath	Salford	Belfast	Glasgow Shettle-ston	All four areas	United Kingdom
Professional	1	0	0	0	0	6
Managerial	1	0	0	0	0	5
Higher supervisory	6	2	2	1	2	10
Lower supervisory	4	4	2	2	3	14
Routine non-manual	7	7	11	9	8	8
Skilled manual	41	41	37	43	41	31
Partly skilled manual	24	24	17	20	21	16
Unskilled manual	16	23	32	24	24	10
Total	100	100	100	100	100	100
Number	695	1,016	764	1,018	3,495	5,925

excess of poverty? We estimated that if the UK population were of similar occupational structure to the populations of the four areas, the percentage in or on the margins of poverty by the state's definition would have been increased from 28 to 35 (compared with 42 per cent in the four areas). It may therefore be concluded that the difference in class structure contributed substantially – about a half – to the additional poverty experienced in the four areas.

Even allowing for the much larger proportion of the population of manual workers and their families – and especially unskilled and partly skilled manual workers – the risk of poverty was greater in the special areas. Earnings tended to be lower: for example, 8 per cent of households included men earning under £14 per week, compared with 4 per cent nationally. There were fewer, and smaller, supplementary sources of income, and fewer working-class people had assets worth £200 or more. Fewer, too, were owner-occupiers (just over a fifth, compared with two fifths who were council tenants and two fifths who were tenants of privately rented properties, nearly all unfurnished). These factors stem essentially from the form of the economy and of the housing market taken in the local area – both as it had been in the past and as it was now.

Two factors contributing to excess poverty are only indirectly related to the economy. They are the level of dependency and the low incomes of the non-working population. The *slightly* larger number of families with four or more children, and the markedly larger number of one-parent families than in the United Kingdom as a whole, were mentioned above. They suggest there was a larger problem of dependency in these areas than elsewhere. However, a comprehensive conception of dependency would need to refer, on the one hand, to the greater likelihood of loss or interruption of family support, and on the other to the greater likelihood of major dependency through illness, injury or disability. Dependent groups in the population often acquire, or are given, sets of characteristics, and are treated as social minorities. The significance of this concept to social structure and the explanation of poverty is developed in Chapter 16.

Areas such as the four selected are among the sources of migrant, especially unskilled, labour. They are declining areas industrially, and young adults tend to migrate, especially if they are earning better than average and looking for good housing. At the same time, those losing their homes in other areas because of rent arrears and loss of earnings due to illness, disability or unemployment, and wives who are separated from their husbands and have little money, are driven to look for cheap housing – which can be found there. And because the areas tend to provide for a disproportionate number of manual jobs which are heavy, dangerous or generally have poor amenities, and also have bad housing and poor environmental amenities, the incidence of illness and disability is high and the dependency ratio tends to be larger. Fewer people, with disproportionately low incomes, come to be maintaining more than their fair share of dependent people. We obtained the results in Table 15.7 from the different surveys. These data are not sur-

Table 15.7. *Percentages of households in four areas and the United Kingdom with disabled people.*

Type of dependant in household	% of all households	
	4 areas	United Kingdom
Disabled child	2·6	1·3
Disabled adult under 65	14·5	9·7
Person sick or injured for more than 8 weeks in past 52 (under 65)	18·1	8·7
	% of population	
Severely disabled 30–49	5·0	1·5
50–64	13·7	8·9
65+	30·1	28·7

prising in relation to mortality data from the selected areas. Compare, for example, mortality rates for Salford for 1959–63 with those for other towns.[1]

We also found that the incomes of the non-working population were lower in the four areas than elsewhere. Initially this seemed puzzling, because most of them were receiving social security benefits at national rates. The explanation was to be found, first, in the fact that fewer of the non-working population had sources of income supplementary to social security – occupational pensions in the case of retired people, pay during sickness, interest from savings and other unearned income, maintenance allowances from husbands, and tax rebates. Secondly, although dependent on state benefits, more were receiving relatively small amounts. Because more lacked other sources of income, more were dependent on supplementary benefit and fewer had earnings-related sickness and unemployment benefit. Some were receiving reduced rates of national insurance benefit because their contribution records had been incomplete. There were fewer retirement and widow pensioners who were entitled to supplementary benefit but not drawing it

Table 15.8. *Selected death rates in four towns.*

	Death rate per 1,000 population[a]			
	Salford	Oxford	Ipswich	Croydon
Infants under 1 year	28	17	18	18
Men aged 45–64	20	12	11	13
Women aged 45–64	10	6	7	6

NOTE: [a] Per 1,000 live births for infants under 1 year.

1. The Registrar General's Decennial Supplement, England and Wales, 1961. *Area Mortality Tables*, HMSO, London, 1967, Tables 1 and 2.

than in the United Kingdom as a whole. None the less, about a quarter of retirement pensioners who were eligible for such benefit, and about a sixth of widow pensioners, were not receiving it. The pattern for sickness and unemployment beneficiaries was less favourable. Larger proportions of both groups of beneficiaries than in the United Kingdom were entitled to supplementary benefit. Despite the fact that many received this benefit, large percentages did not, as the figures in Table 15.9 show.

Table 15.9. Percentages of certain groups in four areas and the United Kingdom who were eligible for supplementary benefit.

National insurance category	Percentage eligible to receive supplementary benefit		Percentage of those eligible who are receiving it	
	4 areas	United Kingdom	4 areas	United Kingdom
Retirement pensioners	57	46	77	57
Widow pensioners	40	43	85	65
Sickness benefit recipients	55	27	69	52
Unemployment benefit recipients	69	50	45	48

Further evidence on social-security benefits is discussed in Chapter 24. Our information on the incomes of those receiving supplementary benefits suggested that fewer than in the nation as a whole were receiving 'exceptional circumstances additions' and more of the unemployed and sick were wage-stopped. For these various reasons, more 'state beneficiaries' and their dependants than in the United Kingdom as a whole had incomes below the state's poverty standard, or very little more than that standard.

The Persistence of Deprivation

This summary of comparative statistics cannot convey the impact upon any observer of the poverty to be found in these areas. In my first visit to Belfast in 1968 (incidentally, just before the disorder and bloodshed that has persisted right through the 1970s), I was struck not only by the evident poverty in Catholic and Protestant areas alike, but by scenes which seemed to belong more to the 1930s – of red-haired boys using scales on a cart drawn by an emaciated pony to sell coal by the pound, teenage girls in a second-hand clothing shop buying underslips and skirts, and some of the smallest 'joints' of meat in butchers' windows that I had ever seen. Here, as in the other areas, working conditions, housing and the immediate environment of the home were often raw and harsh. This is not to say, of course, that there were not also some superbly laid-out and kept homes, shops and workshops. But, by various of our measures, the deprivation in these areas was undeniable. Over two thirds of families with children in the four areas had insufficient bedroom space, and over two thirds declared that there was no safe place for their young children to play in near the home. Nearly two thirds of all homes were said to suffer from structural defects, and as many as 86 per cent of the working men interviewed in the second stage of our surveys were found (on the basis of the ten criteria discussed in Chapter 12, page 438) to have poor or bad working conditions (compared with 21 per cent in the United Kingdom as a whole).

These conditions were not temporary. Others, like Robert Roberts in his compact and masterly *The Classic Slum*,[1] have traced their origins. The high incidence of poverty is not something recent, or, as the analysis earlier in this chapter makes clear, so easily explained as to be quickly remediable. Moreover, there is illustrative evidence that such conditions persisted for some years following the survey. In 1972, Marie Brown, the fieldwork supervisor for the poverty survey, decided to base a short dissertation on repeat interviews with a cross-section of twenty families originally interviewed in Salford in 1968. In the earlier year, eight of the twenty households were in poverty and nine on the margins. In the later year, the numbers were six and nine respectively. More families than at the earlier date were scored on some indicators of deprivation, and more described themselves as poor. The study was limited in size and scope, but illustrates well the effects of long periods spent at or around the poverty line. One man described such a situation as, 'It's not living. It's not even existing. It's just shuffling along somehow, from day to day.'[2]

Towards a Theory of Area Poverty

Our consideration of poverty and deprivation in rural and urban parts of the country, regions and selected small areas has shown the wide dispersion of deprivation, and yet, at the same time, both the relatively greater concentration of deprivation in certain, especially city, areas and the wide degree of inequality within any single area, however small. Other studies can be cited in support of these findings. For example, the Inner London Education Authority identified one sixth of its schools as being schools with special difficulties or educational priority schools. Twenty-five per cent of the pupils, or more than double the average, were defined to be poor readers. However, 'While the incidence of poor readers was higher than expected, three quarters of the pupils were not poor readers. In fact 5 per cent were identified as good readers.'[3] Similar points could

1. Roberts, R., *The Classic Slum: Salford Life in the First Quarter of the Century*, University of Manchester Press, 1971; reprinted by Penguin Books, Harmondsworth, 1973.

2. Brown, M., *An Intertemporal Comparison of Some Low Income Households*, Department of Social Administration, London School of Economics (unpublished thesis), p. 27.

3. Little, A., 'Schools: Targets and Methods', in Glennerster, H., and Hatch, S. (eds.), *Positive Discrimination and Inequality*, Fabian Society, London, March 1974, pp. 14–15.

be made about the distribution of free school meals and of academic performance at 11. 'Altogether, for every two disadvantaged children who are in EPA schools five are outside them. And in the EPA schools themselves, disadvantaged children are outnumbered by children who are not disadvantaged.'[1]

Another example is a study of information derived from the census about the extent and location of areas of urban deprivation in Britain. In 1971, there were 120,000 enumeration districts in Britain. In one study, eighteen indicators of housing facilities, overcrowding, employment and car-ownership were selected from census data for 88,000 of these enumeration districts, each averaging 163 households or 470 persons, though there could be as few as fifty persons. The data were weighted with respect to housing and material possessions, and for that reason might be expected to produce a high degree of concentration or overlap. Thus 1 per cent of districts had male unemployment rates of 24 per cent. On the other hand, 5 per cent of the districts (or over 4,000) accounted for only 16 per cent of the total unemployed, and 15 per cent of districts for only 36 per cent. As Sally Holtermann concludes, 'the degree of spatial concentration of individual aspects of deprivation is really quite low'.[2] She went on to ask to what extent districts with a high rate of deprivation on one indicator had a high rate on another indicator. Although there were many areas with high levels of two or three kinds of deprivation, the spatial coincidence was 'far from complete'.

Such findings confirm that an area strategy cannot be the cardinal means of dealing with poverty or 'under-privilege'. However we care to define economically or socially deprived areas, unless we include nearly half the areas in the country, there will be more poor persons or poor children living outside them than in them. There is a second conclusion. Within all or nearly all defined priority areas, there will be more persons who are not deprived than there are deprived. Therefore discrimination based on ecology will miss out more of the poor or deprived than it will include. It will also devote resources within the areas predominantly to people (or children) who are not poor or deprived. This applies even if enough areas are designated (which they have not been by existing programmes) and even if the right areas are designated (which they have not been).

An institutional theory of poverty is therefore required, drawing on labour market theory, industrial location and land-use theory, and housing market theory, as they relate to both the national and local occupational class structure, and social security theory as that relates to minority status but also class position. The theory would be expressed in terms of the process, on the one hand, whereby resources are unequally allocated or withheld; and on the other, whereby styles of living are generated, emulated and institutionalized. This process is essentially a

1. Barnes, J. H., and Lucas, H., 'Positive Discrimination in Education: Individuals, Groups and Institutions', ILEA, London, 1973, p. 37.

2. Holtermann, S., 'Areas of Urban Deprivation in Great Britain: An Analysis of 1971 Census Data', Social Trends, No. 6, HMSO, London, 1975, p. 39.

national process. To look only at minute enumeration districts is to evade the interconnections between the relatively (and not uniformly) rich in the suburbs and the relatively (and not uniformly) poor in the city areas. And whether we look at the low paid, retirement pensioners, sick and disabled persons, one-parent families and even the unemployed, they are not only dispersed geographically, but their resources, *and* their customs and style of consumption and activity, are determined in the main by *national* institutions, organizations and policies. This implies remedial action through a complex policy of structural change rather than area supplementation.

In putting such a view forward, the possibility that relatively deprived areas are functional to the operation of a market economy, and the protection of business interests, even declining business interests, must not be neglected. The area deprivation policies of recent years relate, in some respects, to policies of longer standing which, while having declared aims of *restoring* spatial equity, and perhaps in part actually *serving* such aims, in major part actually reinforce inequality and dependence. This can arise by the labelling of areas, and, through their loss of status, scare off potential development. It is a risk which we must endeavour to trace and document, knowing all the difficulties.

We can understand this by examining, for instance, central grants to local authorities. For the financial year 1976–7, the government's rate support grant to the local authorities has been estimated at about £6,000 million. More than three fifths of this sum is represented by the 'needs' element of the grant, but it would be wrong to suppose that resources are allocated substantially in accordance with any reasonable definition of needs. In practice, many of the indicators of need are very crudely defined, and they are weighted by a piece of technical wizardry which obscures the bureaucratic conservatism of the exercise.[1] Past expenditure is not only treated as an indicator of need but is the most powerful indicator in the formula. Here, then, is an example of a major instrument of social policy failing to become an instrument of radical change. The landed and market interests which have shaped and which, by their control over the rating system and the local distribution of public resources, seek to perpetuate and even accentuate inequalities between communities, are not seriously threatened.

We can also understand better the ineffectiveness of area deprivation policies by examining regional development and industrial location policies.[2] By 1970, the government was spending £314 million a year on preferential aid to industry

1. There are thirty variables used in a multiple regression calculation of 'needs', and these are set out in three pages of definitions in the *Rate Support Grant Order, 1975*, House of Commons Paper 31. The method has been criticized by Davies, B., 'Territorial Injustice', *New Society*, 13 May 1976.

2. For accounts of the development of regional policies, see McCrone, G., *Regional Policy in Britain*, Allen & Unwin, London, 1969; Richard, H. W., *Elements of Regional Economics*, Penguin Books, Harmondsworth, 1969; Fisk, T., and Jones, K., *Regional Development*, Fabian Society, London, 1972.

in the Special Development, Development and Intermediate areas. A committee under Sir Joseph Hunt on the 'intermediate areas' identified a more comprehensive set of criteria for assessing an area's needs for assistance. They included above-average rates of premature retirement, a slow growth of personal incomes, a low or declining proportion of women at work as well as a high rate of unemployment and low earnings. But the diversification of criteria leads to the dispersion instead of the concentration of resources, because a much larger number of areas become eligible for aid. Resources are spread thinly, and may make comparatively little difference to the prosperity of individual areas. Forty-four per cent of the national workforce live in the assisted areas. Some commentators have argued that policies have had a negative rather than a small positive effect because they have helped to accelerate the decline of the inner city.[1]

Declining industries become low-paying industries, and, unless new industries take their place, workers who become redundant stay unemployed or migrate, leaving disproportionate numbers of the elderly, the middle aged and the poor behind. The outflow can sometimes even lead to labour shortages – at least for the low paid. The value of houses falls, properties are not kept in repair and some houses as well as factories become derelict. A combination of low-paid work and the availability of some types of housing allows immigrant communities – including those from Eire as well as the black Commonwealth – to become established in certain areas. The depressed standard of old council estates and of so-called 'short-life' housing give further examples of local populations being stratified sharply according to status, income and amenities. The decline of an area in relation to others within a region will tend to produce some extreme effects – of overcrowding, streets taken over by squatters or sheer, unrelieved squalor – which lowers the reputation to outsiders of the area as a whole. Lacking a sufficient basis for raising rates to meet the greater needs of such communities for services and cash benefits, local authorities cannot develop policies to direct resources to the poor. Nor have sufficient powers been taken centrally to ameliorate or limit the downward spiral of poverty into which some communities are drawn.

Just as some areas are declining, others are experiencing a boom. The decline or the deprivation of some areas is not explicable except in relation to the advance or the affluence of others – whether regionally or nationally. The conditions within each type of area have to be related to some standard, or, alternatively, to other parts of the economy or the social structure as distributed spatially. Advancing prosperity is converted into new and more generous forms of consumption and display. The activities and possessions of a select few become, in time, the expected rights of the bulk of society. The attainable life-style of the majority is continually changing, and hence new obligations are imposed upon the poor and new needs are generated and acknowledged. Action to control and disperse the growing wealth of areas already wealthy is, therefore, a necessary

1. Falk, N., and Martinos, H., Inner City, Fabian Society, London, May 1975, pp. 12–13.

part of a strategy to reduce poverty, and even more necessary than action to augment the low resources of the poor. Policies have to be devised which simultaneously check the aggrandisement of the rich areas and the impoverishment of the poor areas. These are primarily industrial, employment, housing and land policies.

Summary and Conclusion

The dispersion of poverty is wide. Although the survey showed there are higher proportions of the population in poverty in some areas than in others, there are relatively prosperous people in even the poorest areas, and substantial numbers of poor people in the richest areas. The areas considered were regions, rural and urban areas, constituencies grouped according to various criteria, and four specially chosen small areas, three of them in the poorest quarters of the poorest cities in the United Kingdom.

Northern Ireland was found by a large margin to be the poorest region, followed by Scotland, the North-West, Wales and the South-West, and the Northern, Yorks and Humberside region. Greater London and the South-East contained the smallest proportions of poor. Scotland had the highest proportion of persons with high incomes as well as the second highest proportion with low incomes. Anglia and the East Midlands comprised another region with substantial proportions of the population at the extremes of poverty and wealth.

The proportion in poverty or on its margins was as high or nearly as high in rural as in different groups of urban areas, despite the higher proportion of the rich in such areas.

When constituencies were ranked according to the percentage of the adult population leaving school early, and the percentage voting left at the previous General Election, there was a correlation of the expected kind with poverty, but it was by no means marked. When we grouped the 126 wards and districts of the constituencies visited into four ranks according to the proportion of units interviewed with low incomes, the highest rank had relatively three times as many poor or marginally poor people as the lowest. But the two lowest ranks, with 60 per cent of the sample, included 46 per cent of the poor in the survey.

Four small areas were selected for separate follow-up surveys. Three were the poorest districts of three of the poorest cities of the United Kingdom. In these three, the percentage of poor and marginally poor varied from 38 to nearly 50, compared with 28 for the population in household units in the United Kingdom as a whole. On the other hand, the percentage of relatively prosperous people varied from 14 to 26, compared with 39. In studying the results of the four area surveys, we suggested that the excess proportion in poverty and on the margins of poverty was substantially the consequence of the relationship of the populations to the economy and the housing market. Substantially more were of manual than of non-manual occupational class, were unemployed, had low earnings and poor working conditions and, living in poor housing in often crowded conditions, had poor health. To this set of factors should be added high dependency ratios (loss or lack of family wage-earners and disproportionately large numbers of sick and disabled people and one-parent families) and the relatively low incomes of many in the non-working population (some of the components here being short-comings of social security schemes). The analysis calls attention to national control of the rules of access to resources.

Areas or communities cannot be treated as autonomous or self-sufficient in terms either of economy or culture. Their functions and distribution of prosperity are in the main decided externally. The pattern of inequality within them is set nationally, and area variations in the extent of poverty arise through variation in the mix of industry and use and value of land; employment level; deviation of the wage structure of the local labour market from the national labour market; the distribution of type of housing tenure and types of house location; and the deviation of the local housing market from the national housing market. It is the national structure of unequal resource allocation, especially in its outcomes for classes and social minorities on the one hand and the sponsorship of styles of living and modes of consumption by powerful market and state institutions on the other, which primarily explains area deprivation. National action to remedy poverty – through incomes policy, full employment, less specialization of work roles, higher social security benefits, new forms of allowances and rate support grants and a more redistributive tax structure – is implied.

16
Social Minorities

A recurrent theme in the literature is that poverty is due either to individual failing or to individual misfortune. At the end of the nineteenth century, society was torn by the dispute between these two and the consequent division into 'undeserving' and 'deserving' poor. Charles Booth stated at one point that he had embarked on his great survey of London life and labour with the express intention of resolving the dispute one way or the other. He produced evidence to show that, whatever they did, the great majority of the poor could not escape poverty. Through his and others' influence, attention was instead diverted to misfortune, to the problems of maintaining income in sickness, unemployment, widowhood and old age, though the 'secondary' poverty attributable to drink, improvidence and mismanagement still occupied a prominent place in the analysis.[1]

Misfortune was itself understood as something which could befall the individual and against which he should safeguard himself rather than something which was socially created. It was not determined systematically through the organization of industry and housing, the fostering of social attitudes and values and the production and distribution of resources. This aspect of poverty was conceived in terms of chance or fate. The wise individual would save in prosperity, and the wise society would create institutions to enable him to do so. Only gradually has this conception widened to include the responsibility of society to provide the institutions whereby minimum security would be available to all citizens on certain terms.

But certain individual characteristics which have long been recognized to be associated with poverty are directly or indirectly 'social'. By virtue of some characteristic which itself may be in society's power to confer, people are excluded directly or indirectly from the receipt of a full share of different types of resource.

1. See Booth, C., *Life and Labour of the People in London*, vol. 2, Macmillan, London, 1904, pp. 230–31. By 'secondary' poverty, Rowntree meant a state in which income was in theory enough to maintain physical efficiency but was misspent. The 'immediate causes' were mainly due to 'drink, betting and gambling; ignorant or careless housekeeping and other improvident expenditure, the latter often induced by irregularity of income'. See Rowntree, B. S., *Poverty: A Study of Town Life*, Macmillan, London, 1901, pp. 141–2.

Their individual situation is one which is stigmatized, that is, they are disqualified from full social acceptance.[1] They are relegated to membership of a minority which, in some specific sense, is treated as inferior by the rest of the population. I do not mean that minorities are necessarily treated with contempt. They may be patronized, like many of the disabled or elderly (as illustrated by the term 'senior citizens'), or treated with genuine sympathy but as having a right only to modest comfort rather than to equal income. As Chapter 6 showed, large numbers in the population conceived of 'poverty' primarily as the conditions experienced by particular minorities.

Definitions of Social Minorities

The term 'social minority' is needed in analysing poverty and requires discussion before the results of applying it in the survey are presented. It is used here in a different sense from that sometimes understood. Individuals or families which have some characteristic in common which marks them off, or is perceived to mark them off, from 'ordinary' people, and which prevents them from having access to, or being accorded, certain rights which are available to others, and who are therefore less likely to receive certain kinds or amounts of resources, can be defined as belonging to a social minority. This definition is broader than sometimes understood and links at least two social categories. There are distinct ethnic and racial minority groups, whose members have a common history and culture and carefully induct offspring into conformity with the beliefs and values of the group. They have close relationships among themselves, whether they are tightly or only loosely integrated with the rest of society. They can usually be shown to have been depressed into poor housing and poor jobs, and are in a relatively disadvantaged position in society and may feel it keenly. This type of social minority is well recognized and studied by social scientists.

Secondly, there are those who are assigned to a special category or status on account of their appearance, physical condition, manner or speech, their family or residential situation or their position in relation to the labour market, and who are regularly treated as second-class citizens. Their identity as members of groups is uncertain or ambiguous. Their social position is often very exposed. Some have a well-developed sense of group consciousness, and may have a network of relations with similar households or families, though this is rarely, if ever, as extensive as in an ethnic community. Others may be unaware of families or persons with identical problems and may turn in upon themselves, and lead an extraordinarily self-contained or individuated existence. Some minorities may even be regarded as an aggregation of indivuals, leading their lives mainly in isolation of each other. Their social roles are in various ways supplementary: dependent, sub-

1. In the sense defined by Goffman, See Goffman, E., *Stigma: Notes on the Management of Spoiled Identity*, Penguin Books, Harmondsworth, 1968.

servient or acquiescent. They may be objects of pity. Frequently they resist acknowledgement of membership of a minority. Rarely do they believe they are cul-
turally separate. Many develop defensive or self-protective behaviour. Some
elderly and disabled people, homeless families, social security claimants, one-
parent families and even large families, as well as people living in different types
of hospitals and other institutions, display these traits. Some at least of these
minorities, such as the elderly retired, may be regarded as coming into existence
as a result of industrial and social change.

This second category which I have described can only with reservations be
defined by sociologists as consisting of genuine social groups. For example, while
ethnic or racial status may apply equally to all members of a household and even
many residents in a single locality, other kinds of minority status, like disability
or unemployment, may apply specifically to just one member. This has many repercussions, since life-long affiliation to minority status is rarely shared with other
members of one's family or other generations within one's immediate social environment. There is the risk of friction and dissension within the household, and
though other members of the household often compensate the individual for his
stigmatized existence, they tend also to be contaminated by it. The household
as a whole acts and feels differently from other households and is also regarded
differently by the outside community. Its consciousness is dominated more by
inferiority than difference. Geographically, these minorities are distributed thinly.

Social minorities of this second type are dependent less upon the clash of cultures and self-induced characteristics of their members than upon the evaluation
of their characteristics by society. They come to embody negatively the positive
values of society. Through its legislation, bureaucratic procedures and provisions
in welfare, social security and employment, society expresses its values about
certain kinds of individuals. Willing toil, self-reliance, educational qualifications,
up-to-date occupational training and experience, skill, thrift and attachment to
home, marriage and family are among the cardinal values of British society.
People who fall out of work, become old or are turned out of positions of occupational authority; are deserted by their husbands or wives; beget a handicapped
child or a child out of marriage; are crippled after an accident at work; or fleeced
by an unscrupulous landlord or employer, are prone to be treated with condescension, suspicion about their motives and implicit criticism of their behaviour.
Many are unfairly regarded by sections of the public as work-dodgers, Welfare
State scroungers, inadequate has-beens, or unfortunates who cannot survive the
highly principled competitiveness of the market. If society prizes certain virtues,
those who patently lack them are bound to be given short shrift and often suspected of not attempting to acquire them. How otherwise could populations feel
comfortable with the unemployed, the poor and the dispossessed in their midst?

But they are not just negative examples of what society prides or values, and
therefore passive recipients of whatever treatment and resources which the major-

ity cares to mete out. In the capacity of objects of pity they are recipients of tenderness and compassion, and attract political support, often fainthearted but sometimes powerful. Their rights and their status become central questions of political dispute and of the good society. It is rather as if, having deprived them of their entitlement to full participation in community life and resources, and having established their existence crudely in the public mind, society expresses its regret and guilt for their condition through the media of pressure-groups, movements and campaigns, and restores, in part, those resources of which they have been deprived. There is a continual political struggle therefore for position and dignity – on the part of the minorities themselves, but also between contesting political factions, in fulfilling for these minorities their own images of the good society. Embryonic minorities, recognizing their deprivation, struggle to get themselves publicly identified so that they might attract political support. Ironically, such struggle, far from alleviating their conditions, may reinforce or deepen them.

Some minorities are still barely recognized. Only in the late 1960s and early 1970s did the deprivation of the one-parent family, the long-term hospitalized, the disabled and the single woman with an adult dependant, for example, come to be discussed more than cursorily. Tenants deprived of reasonable living conditions by the selective or inflexible operation of either the private housing market or council housing, and communities of consumers in poor districts who are exploited by supermarkets and tallymen alike, are embryonic minorities still requiring adequate description and analysis. What is important is the classification of groups and the definition of their relative numbers and conditions.

Thirteen Selected Minorities

Some social minorities, like the families of prisoners, are too small to be separately identified in a sample of the size described in this book. Thirteen minorities were distinguished and defined for special study in the survey. They were selected deliberately because they had been picked out previously by social scientists for study, or were the subject of popular discussion, or because we hypothesized that the incidence of poverty among them would be higher than average. Some of these minorities, such as large families, can be defined fairly easily.

Others, such as the disabled and women and their adult dependants, are difficult to define and rather complex operational specifications are required. The full list is set out below:

1. *One-parent family.* Households in which there was a child, one of whose parents was not also resident.
2. *Woman and adult dependent.* Households in which there were two or more adults, one of whom was an unmarried, separated, divorced or widowed woman who was partly or wholly supporting the other or others (usually related to her), none of whom was in

employment, by means of either income from employment or an unearned income which was larger than that of the dependant(s).

3. *Large family.* Households in which there were four or more dependent children belonging to the same family.

4. *Unemployed.* Households in which there was an adult of under 65 years of age who had been unemployed for eight weeks or more during the previous twelve months, consecutively or altogether.

5. *Households affected by the long-term sickness or injury of an adult under 65.* Households in which there was an adult under 65 who had been ill or injured for eight weeks or more, and off work, during the previous twelve months, consecutively or altogether.

6. *Households in which there was a disabled adult under 65.* Households in which there was an adult scoring 5 or more according to a special index of disability, or scoring 1 or more and having a disablement condition: epilepsy, mental handicap, breathlessness or pain in the chest; difficulty in physical movement; having a severe nervous condition (such as depression, inability to concentrate or sleep); inability to read; inability to hear or join in ordinary conversation.

7. *Households in which there was a 'borderline' disabled adult under 65.* Households in which there was an adult scoring 1 to 4 according to a special index of disability, *or* having a disablement condition (as listed above), *or* having disability only for certain times of the year.

8. *Households in which there was a disabled child.* Households containing a child of under 15 years of age who, through illness or disability, had been continuously confined to bed or to the house for at least eight weeks; those with a disablement condition (as listed above); and those attending a special school, training centre, club, day or occupation centre, out-patients' department etc., for reason of long-term illness or handicap.

9. *Households in which there was a severely handicapped adult over 65.* Households in which there was an adult of 65 years of age or over scoring 9 or more according to a special index of disability, *or* had been confined to bed or the house continuously for eight weeks or more.

10. *Households with low-paid female earners.* Households in which women aged 21–59 were earning less than £8 gross per week for at least 30 hours' work. This figure was about two thirds of the median for women.

11. *Households with low-paid male earners.* Households in which men aged 21–64 were earning less than £14 gross per week for at least 30 hours' work. This figure was a little lower than two thirds of the median for men of this age.

12. *Households in which there was a non-white person.*

13. *Households in which there was someone born in Eire.*

The largest of these minorities was found to be that comprising households with a disabled adult under 65, and the smallest comprising those with women and their adult dependants. Table 16.1 shows the percentage of households and of population living in such households in the United Kingdom as a whole and in four poor areas. There are a number of important findings. Long-term disability and sickness affects a very large proportion of the population. There are over a

Table 16.1. *Percentages and number of households in the United Kingdom, and percentages of households in four areas, with at least one member of a social minority.*

Household characteristics	Households in the UK		Households in four special areas[a]	Population in households in the UK	
	%	Estimated number (000s)	%	%	Estimated number (000s)
1-parent family	3·1	586	4·5	4·2	2,285
Women and adult dependants	0·9	170	0·3	0·8	435
Large family (4 or more children	4·4	832	6·6	10·4	5,658
Unemployed 8 weeks or more (under 65)	4·2	794	10·1	5·4	2,938
Sick or injured 8 weeks or more (under 65)	8·7	1,644	18·1	10·6	5,766
Disabled adult (under 65)	9·7	1,833	14·5	9·7	5,277
Borderline disabled (under 65)	18·7	3,534	12·7	20·2	10,989
Disabled or handicapped child	1·3	246	2·6	2·2	1,197
Elderly incapacitated (over 65)	7·1	1,342	–	5·4	2,938
Low-paid woman (under £8 per week)	3·8	718	3·1	4·6	2,502
Low-paid man (under £14 per week)	4·5	850	7·8	6·0	3,264
Non-white	2·5	472	0·4	3·3	1,795
Born in Eire	3·0	567	3·1	3·2	1,741
One or more of above characteristics	49·3	9,318	49·0[b]	53·6	29,158
None of above characteristics	50·7	9,582	51·0	46·4	25,242
Total	100	18,900	100	100	54,400
Number of households/ persons	2,047	–	1,238	6,084	–

NOTES: [a] An upwards adjustment has been made to allow for losses at the second stage of sampling. See Chapter 3, page 107.
[b] Allowing for the elderly incapacitated interviewed only at the first stage.

million people in households with a handicapped child; 3 million in households with an incapacitated elderly person; over 5 million in households with a disabled adult under 65, and 5¾ million in households with someone who has been sick or injured for at least eight weeks. The borderline disabled comprise an even larger section of the population. The implications for living standards and social needs are clearly of major significance.

Many of the minorities account for a higher proportion of population than of households. This is particularly true of large families who make up nearly 10 per cent of the population, but is also true of the low-paid, one-parent families, the unemployed, and, to a lesser extent, the sick and disabled. However, the elderly incapacitated tend to be found in smaller than average households.

The levels of pay for men and women over 21 which we chose to consider were arbitrary. The figure of £14 gross pay for men was the figure being advocated by some unions at the time as a minimum wage. In September 1968, the lowest decile earnings of male manual workers was, according to a major survey by the Department of Employment and Productivity, £15·1. The lowest decile earnings for female manual workers was £7·7, and for all full-time adult female workers £8·4.[1] We found 4 per cent of households (representing 2·5 million population) in

Table 16.2. Numbers of households belonging to different numbers of social minorities.

Household characteristic	Number of minority characteristics							
	1	2	3	4	5	6	8	All
1-parent family	23	21	14	4	–	1	1	64
Woman and adult dependants	4	12	0	2	–	–	–	18
Large family (4 or more children)	37	19	19	9	–	1	1	86
Unemployed 8 weeks or more (under 65)	35	30	16	5	2	–	1	89
Sick or injured 8 weeks or more (under 65)	40	84	34	16	2	1	1	178
Disabled adult (under 65)	77	87	24	12	2	–	1	203
Borderline disabled (under 65)	215	113	42	12	1	1	–	384
Disabled or handicapped child	9	9	6	1	–	–	1	26
Elderly incapacitated (over 65)	111	23	9	4	1	–	–	148
Low-paid woman (under £8 per week)	28	34	8	7	–	1	1	79
Low-paid man (under £14 per week)	38	37	19	10	2	1	1	108
Non-white	27	12	4	1	–	–	–	44
Born in Eire	27	11	9	1	–	–	–	48
Number of characteristics	671	492	204	84	10	6	8	1,475
Number of households	671	246	68	21	2	1	1	1,010

1. Department of Employment, *New Earnings Survey, 1968*, HMSO, London, 1970, p. 5.

which there was a female adult earner with less than £8, and 4½ per cent (representing 3·3 million) in which there was a male adult earner with less than £14 a week.

I have also shown in the table the comparable percentages obtained from the four poor areas surveyed within Belfast, Salford, Neath and Glasgow (described in the previous chapter, page 553). As might be expected, these areas contained more unemployed. They also contained more, but not markedly more, one-parent families and large families. But the most striking difference was in the proportion of sick, injured or disabled. There were more handicapped children and adults under 65 who were sick or injured or disabled to an appreciable or severe extent (for reasons of economy, the four local follow-up surveys did not include the elderly incapacitated).

About 67 per cent of the households comprising these minorities in the national sample belonged to only one, but others belonged to two, three, four or more minorities. Table 16.2 lists the numbers and shows that members of one minority, for example, the sick or injured and the low paid, were much more likely than others to fall into at least one other category. Altogether, 49 per cent of households and 54 per cent of population could be classified as belonging to at least one social minority. They represented over 29 million persons. Even if the large category of borderline disabled are excluded, the number is still over 18 million.

Nearly half the people in the sample were not in any social minority. They included relatively more of young and middle-aged adults, the employed and the self-employed, but relatively fewer children and markedly fewer adults in their fifties and early sixties. Because people with marked disability only among those aged 65 and over were assigned to minority household status, they also included more of the elderly and retired.

The Incomes of Minorities

How far were these characteristics associated with low income or poverty? The proportions within these minorities with low incomes tend to be relatively large, as Table 16.3 shows. By the test of low income, one-parent families are worst off, with the elderly incapacitated next in ranking. Bearing in mind the low absolute numbers in some minorities in the sample, the proportion with low income was higher in all instances than among households not belonging to any minority. Altogether, 50 per cent of households classified in one or more minorities had low income, compared with 31 per cent of other households in the sample.

The extent of poverty, as measured by the supplementary benefit standard, also tended to be greater. The second column in the table shows the proportion of each minority with an income in the year previous to interview which was below or up to 40 per cent above the supplementary benefit scale rates plus cost of housing, and the next column includes those who had an income which fell within these limits in the week, though not in the year, previous to interview. The minority

Table 16.3. Percentages of households belonging to certain social minorities with relatively low incomes or incomes below or just above the state's standard.

Household characteristic	% with low income[a]	% with income below (under 100%) or just above (100–39%) the state's standard		% with income last year below the deprivation standard	Total numbers[c]
		Income last year[b]	Income last year and/or last week		
1-parent family	73	44 [17]	51	32	54
Woman and adult dependants	(64)	(28) [0]	(50)	25	14
Large family (4 or more children)	53	51 [17]	60	53	69
Unemployed 8 weeks or more (under 65)	49	28 [8]	34	20	74
Sick or injured 8 weeks or more (under 65)	44	31 [6]	37	33	144
Disabled adult (under 65)	46	37 [7]	41	39	177
Borderline disabled (under 65)	45	26 [7]	31	22	328
Disabled or handicapped child	(63)	(47) [26]	(47)	(44)	19
Elderly incapacitated (over 65)	64	64 [14]	68	68	129
Low-paid women (under £8 per week)	45	30 [11]	30	29	64
Low-paid men (under £14 per week)	58	37 [12]	44	46	81
Non-white	(36)	(33) [6]	(33)	32	33
Born in Eire	(39)	(22) [5]	(32)	25	41
At least one characteristic	50	34 [9]	40	29	857
None of above characteristics	31	28 [5]	32	22	911
All	40	31 [7]	36	25	1,768

NOTES: [a] Defined as having less than 80 per cent of the mean of households of their type: man 60 or over; man under 60; woman under 60; man and woman; man, woman and 1 child; 2 children; 3 children; 4 or more children; others without and others with children. Each social minority was distributed among at least three, and sometimes all or nearly all of these household types.
[b] The figures in square brackets are those under 100 who are included.
[c] These numbers apply to the first two columns but are slightly lower (totalling 1,634) for the final column.

with the largest proportion of poor or marginally poor were the elderly disabled, followed in ranking by large families, one-parent families and low-paid men. However, poverty among some minorities, for example, households in which a member of the household had been sick or unemployed for 8 weeks or more in the year, and the coloured and Irish minorities, is not very much different from the population not falling into any of these minorities. This is discussed below. Altogether, 34 per cent of those in one or more minorities, compared with 28 per cent of those who were not in any minority, were in poverty, or on the margins of poverty, by the state's standard.

Much did, of course, depend on the extent to which households consisted of two or more income units. A large proportion of the low paid were in fact members of households in which there was at least one other earner. This helps to explain why the incidence of poverty was about average in households in which there were low-paid women and only a little over average in households which included low-paid men. The standards of living of different minorities are discussed in greater detail in subsequent chapters.

Just as membership of a social minority is correlated with low income, so membership of two or more minorities is correlated more strongly still with low income. The increase in poverty among people living in households belonging to three or more minorities is quite striking, as Table 16.4 shows. The picture provided by

Table 16.4. Percentages of people in households belonging to different numbers of social minorities who had incomes below, just above and substantially above the state's standard.

Number of social minorities to which household belongs	Net disposable income last year as % supplementary benefit scales plus housing cost			Total	Number
	Under 100	100–39	140+		
None	3·0	20·1	77·0	100	2,448
1	7·0	22·1	71·0	100	1,687
2	9·1	23·0	67·9	100	723
3 or more	17·7	30·8	51·5	100	305
All	6·0	21·7	72·3	100	5,163

the criterion of income last week rather than last year is very similar. (See Table A.62, Appendix Eight, page 1040.)

In the four poor areas there were approximately the same total proportion of households with minority characteristics. Fewer borderline disabled people were identified (and this, I should point out, *may* have been a function of using different teams of interviewers in some of the areas). There were also few non-white people in the areas visited. On the other hand, there were significantly more long-term sick and disabled and unemployed people, low-paid men and one-parent families. But more of the households belonging to different minorities (with the exception of the low paid) were living in poverty or on the margins of poverty (Table 16.5). Large families and the elderly incapacitated were especially at risk, and many more of the unemployed were in poverty.

Table 16.5. Percentages of households belonging to certain minorities who were in poverty or on the margins of poverty.

Household characteristic	Household income last year below 140% of the supplementary benefit standard			
	National sample of the UK	Four poor areas	Number	
			National sample	Four areas
1-parent family	44	(51)	54	45
Woman and adult dependants	(28)	–	14	3
Large family (4 or more children)	51	63	69	67
Unemployed 8 weeks or more (under 65)	28	58	74	100
Sick or injured 8 weeks or more (under 65)	31	43	144	182
Disabled adult (under 65)	37	48	177	147
Borderline disabled (under 65)	26	40	328	128
Disabled or handicapped child	(47)	(52)	19	27
Elderly incapacitated (over 65)	61	70[a]	129	80[a]
Low-paid women	30	(17)	64	36
Low-paid men	37	30	81	77
Non-white	(33)	–	33	4
Born in Eire	(22)	(43)	41	30
All households belonging to minorities	34	45	857	512
All households not belonging to minorities	28	41	911	548

NOTE: [a] Estimated in part.

The association between minority status and low income is also one between minority status and occupational class. Altogether, 54 per cent of the people in the sample fell into at least one minority. The figure is lower for most of the middle class, however, and higher for the partly skilled and unskilled among the working class. It ranges between 40 and 51 per cent for the professional, managerial, senior administrative and supervisory non-manual occupations, is 60 per cent for routine non-manual occupations, 53 per cent for skilled, 60 per cent for partly skilled and as high as 72 per cent for unskilled occupations. By all the tests so far provided in this book, unskilled manual workers and their families were exceptionally vulnerable to many of the conditions associated with poverty.

The Characteristics of the Poor

Some of the groups we have discussed were very small. To what extent did membership of minorities account for all those living in poverty? Much does, of course, depend on which definition we use. By the state's standard, there were 124 households in the sample with an income of less than the supplementary benefit scales plus housing cost, and another 423 with an income of less than 40 per cent above this level. The social minorities that we have considered account for less than 50 per cent of all households, but for 63 and 51 per cent respectively of these two groups, as Table 16.6 shows. Moreover, they account for 77 per cent of the population living below the standard and 56 per cent of the population living just above it.

The table also lists the proportions of poor and marginally poor households and persons belonging to each of the minorities. Large families account for the largest proportion of those living below the state's standard. Even if they were not counted as a social minority, the majority of them would be found in one or more of the other categories. Next in ranking are the borderline disabled, followed by low-paid men, the elderly incapacitated, disabled adults under 65, one-parent families and the chronic sick under 65. Each of these groups cover more than 10 per cent of those below the standard. It is also important to note that households with low-paid women, a handicapped child and someone who has been long-term unemployed each account for just a little less than 10 per cent of those below the standard. At the time of the survey, the unemployment rate was lower than it became in the mid 1970s and people with substantial recent experience of unemployment are likely to account for a very much higher proportion of people in poverty.

Who are the poor not included in any of these minorities? It should be noted that we did not count either the retired or the moderately disabled elderly as such in the minorities for special study – on grounds that some disability in old age is very common and that both society and individuals expect some adjustment to the physical limitations of ageing. In fact, all but a handful of those unaccounted for who lived below the supplementary benefit standard (fifty-nine out of seventy-three) were people in households consisting of men or women over 60 years of age living alone or in couples.

However, these groups do not explain most of the unaccounted marginally poor. Less than a third of those living on incomes which were above but not as much as 40 per cent above the supplementary benefit standard who belonged to

Table 16.6. *Percentages of households and of people living below and just above the state's standard who belong to different social minorities.*

Household characteristic	Net disposable household income last year in relation to the state's standard			
	Under 100%		100–39%	
	Households %	Population in households %	Households %	Population in households %
1-parent family	7·3	11·2	3·5	4·8
Woman and adult dependants	0·0	0·0	0·9	0·8
Large family (4 or more children)	9·7	24·9	5·4	12·6
Unemployed 8 weeks or more (under 65)	4·8	8·0	3·5	5·2
Sick 8 weeks or more (under 65)	7·3	10·5	8·3	11·0
Disabled adult (under 65)	10·5	11·5	12·5	12·5
Borderline disabled (under 65)	20·2	22·7	14·4	15·1
Disabled or handicapped child	4·0	8·9	0·9	2·0
Elderly incapacitated (over 65)	14·5	12·1	14·4	10·8
Low-paid woman (under £8 per week)	5·6	9·6	2·8	4·3
Low-paid man (under £14 per week)	8·1	16·3	4·7	8·4
Non-white	1·6	2·6	2·1	2·8
Born in Eire	1·6	2·2	1·7	1·8
One or more of above characteristics	62·9	76·7	51·3	56·3
None of above characteristics	37·1	23·3	48·7	43·7
Total	132·3	132·3	124·2	135·6
Number of characteristics	164	513	525	1,522
Number of households/people	124	313	423	1,123

no defined minority were in these households. Significantly, more than half of them (287 out of 491 in the sample) were in households consisting of man, woman and children. These were people living on low, but not the lowest, earnings, where there was no supplementary earner. Particularly when they had children in their teens, or had relatively high housing costs, they were pushed towards poverty.

The concept of the social minority therefore helps only in part in constructing an explanation of poverty. We have seen that some of the groups were relatively strong but others relatively weak predictors of poverty. No doubt additions and refinements could be made. We have identified some minorities by devising crude cut-off points, such as eight weeks' sick or unemployed (a figure chosen officially to mark 'long-term' unemployment). For some minorities, like one-parent families and the low paid, the household may not be the best unit for analysis. Thus, two or more income units in the same household may or may not pool all their income or consume jointly. Yet we are judging living standards as if all of them were. Later chapters will illustrate these points in more detail.

Four of the minorities, small numerically in the sample, will be discussed briefly in turn in this chapter. Other minorities will form the subject-matter of the next seven chapters.

Households with Women and Adult Dependants

In the national sample of 2,050 households, there were eighteen in which there were women with adult dependants, not all of whom supplied information about income and wealth. A definition has been given earlier (page 568). There are likely to be between 150,000 and 200,000 such women in the United Kingdom. With their dependants, they are likely to comprise a total of 350,000 to 400,000 people. The Society for the Single Woman and Her Dependants has done much in recent years to call attention to their problems. I will first give an illustration.

Mrs Ive is 51. She cares for her 93-year-old widowed mother who is severely disabled (incapacity score, 16), and together they live in a council house. The mother is not confined to bed, but cannot walk more than a few yards outdoors without help. The daughter had to give up work as a cashier some years ago in order to look after her parents. For several years she received no income for her services, but now the county council pays her for eighteen hours' work a week as a home-help to her mother. The job, however, is in fact a full-time one 'from 8 a.m. to 10.30 p.m.'. The cost to the council of the daughter's wage is £4·27, of which they are repaid £1·20 weekly (through the application of a local means test) by the mother. The only other significant source of income is supplementary benefit, which both individuals receive, although it took three years of persuasion to convince the mother that she should apply. Last year, to supplement their income, the mother spent £50 of her bank deposit savings. Neither of the two women had a holiday last year, nor have they had a night out for entertainment in the past two weeks. The daughter says that they can manage on their income, but are not 'living high'.

Most of the households belong to at least one other minority group – in the example given above, to the elderly incapacitated. This makes for difficulties in identifying problems specific to the group. Nevertheless, half the households in our admittedly small sub-sample conform to the general type illustrated above: namely, a middle-aged woman either single or separated who lives with her widowed mother, the latter often disabled. One may speculate, then, that the greatest hardship arises when the daughter is unable to take employment outside the home because of the constant attention or supervision needed by the parent. In this case, it is the daughter who suffers the greater disadvantage in terms of style of living relative to others of her age and sex. According to the index described earlier (page 250), a relatively high proportion of those in the sample were deprived, as Table 16.7 shows. Our data on the low income and wealth of this min-

Table 16.7. Percentages of persons in selected minorities who were deprived by the criterion of the deprivation index.

Type of minority	Percentage of people in household scoring 6 or more according to deprivation index	Total number in households
Woman and adult dependants	(33)	45
Large family	31	569
Non-white	42	180
Born in Eire	19	182
Total national sample	16	5,710

ority (Table 16.9) probably under-represent the hardship suffered, because the extra expenses of dependency, and loss of income because of dependency, are not allowed for. As discussed elsewhere about the disabled, expenses are incurred for extra expenses, and there is an implicit case for extra resources to compensate for activities and pleasures foregone. Although women and their adult dependants are deprived in terms of income, resources and style of living relative to the rest of the population, it should be borne in mind that this may reflect in some measure the high proportion of dependants who are elderly and incapacitated elderly.

Two Groups of Immigrant Households

The problems faced by any immigrant to the United Kingdom are sufficiently general to make it worthwhile to consider, at the most abstract level, all immigrant households (that is, households containing at least one immigrant) together.

Although different solutions will be dictated by different traditions, opportunities and knowledge, all newcomers have to come to terms with a common set of problems of a kind, or degree of difficulty not normally faced by the native population. The immediate and principal aims of the immigrant are to obtain adequate employment and housing, and to maintain or form a set of social relationships with persons usually described in a rather question-begging fashion in sociological literature as 'significant others'. Although information is available from the survey on each of these themes, we did not seek to ask immigrants whether they defined themselves as a group for the purposes of mutual support or local political action. One important dimension of the immigrants' position was thus left unexplored.[1]

Two minority groups will be compared with the population as a whole. In age, the minorities differ sharply from the remainder of the population (Table 16.8).

Table 16.8. *Percentages of people who live in two social minority households compared with the total population.*

Age	Characteristic of at least 1 person in household		
	Born in Eire	Non-white	Total national sample
Under 19	37	47	32
20–49	44	48	38
50 and over	19	5	29
Total	100	100	100
Number	192	196	6,039

This has repercussions on household composition – there being relatively fewer households consisting of retirement pensioners and more with single men and women below retirement age. This is the result of young immigrants arriving in large numbers in the United Kingdom in the late 1950s and 1960s.

Households with One or More Persons Born in Eire

Despite these qualifications, the hypothesis that the Irish minority is an economically disadvantaged one is not supported by the results obtained from the small sub-sample in the survey. For example, 19 per cent of the group were either below or on the margins of the state's standard of poverty (Table 16.9), compared with 32 per cent of the population as a whole. When the annuity value of assets is

1. An example of a study of immigrant groups in a particular area and their interrelations with one another and their English neighbours is Rex, J., and Moore, R., *Race, Community and Conflict*, Oxford University Press, 1967.

Table 16.9. Percentages of people in selected social minorities in or on the margins of poverty, according to two criteria.

Standard		Percentage of people in households containing:				
		Woman and adult dependant(s)	Large family	At least 1 person		All in survey
				non-white	born in Eire	
Income unit income last year as % of supplementary benefit standard plus housing cost	under 100	(32)	21	14	7	9
	100–39	(27)	41	21	12	23
	140+	(41)	38	65	80	68
Total		100	100	100	100	100
Number		37	567	159	168	5,339
Net income worth last year as % of supplementary benefit standard	under 100	(15)	18	14	4	7
	100–39	(26)	40	19	11	17
	140+	(59)	42	67	85	76
Total		100	100	100	100	100
Number		27	472	139	147	4,599

added to income, the proportion deprived by the state's standards remains smaller than among the sample as a whole. When age is allowed for, the group is broadly homogeneous in income or resources with the remainder of the population. This is, perhaps, surprising in view of the social composition of the group, 36 per cent of whom are in households with heads belonging to the partly skilled and unskilled manual classes (compared with 26 per cent in the total population), since these are particularly vulnerable to low income and resources (see Table A.63, Appendix Eight, page 1041). Over 25 per cent of employed males in the group were engaged in the building and construction industry as labourers, foremen, riggers and so on, and it may be that the relatively prosperous condition of this fluctuating industry at the time of the survey has given an unduly favourable impression of the group's position in society.

   In terms of housing tenure, the position of this minority is remarkably similar to the native population with 30 per cent of persons living in council houses and a further 46 per cent in houses either mortgaged or owned (47 per cent in the population as a whole). This supports the overall impression of a group well-integrated in an economic sense into the host society.

Households with One or More Non-white Members

The heterogeneity of households containing non-white people complicates the interpretation of the various statistics beyond the general difficulties mentioned earlier. The largest national sub-groups are the West Indians and Pakistanis, but there are also Africans, Indians and others. There were 182 persons in the sample, or 3 per cent, who were non-white, and 128, or 2·1 per cent, who were born in the West Indies, Pakistan, India or Africa, compared with a figure of 2·7 per cent of the population who, according to the 1971 Census, were of New Commonwealth ethnic origin. There was some suggestion from our limited numbers that more were in income units living in poverty, or on its margins. In relation to poverty the group has an advantageous age structure, but a disadvantageous occupational structure. Only 5 per cent of the sub-sample were aged 50 or over, compared with 29 per cent of the total sample. A relatively high proportion were in partly skilled and unskilled manual occupations, 43 per cent compared with 26 per cent in the sample as a whole. When account was taken of class of employment, there was no evidence that the hours worked by men in these households differed from the average.

Asset holdings and numbers of consumer durables were low, and households with non-white members also tended to have lower values of income in kind – whether from employers or from other sources. However, we found that when age was allowed for, the value of social services in kind per household was similar to the value in general. Table 16.9 shows that when the annuity value of assets is added to income, a lower percentage of non-white people than others had resources comfortably above the poverty standard.

There were other indicators of deprivation. A high proportion had high scores on the style of living or deprivation index (Table 16.7). The validity of the scale is, however, a matter for debate when applied to the lives of persons whose goals and order of priorities may be radically at variance with the community in which they find themselves.[1] It is probable that, by citing one particular national group or another and their customs that arguments could be made against particular items on the scale. Despite these objections, the figure of 42 per cent scoring 6 or over, which is almost three times as high as that of the total sample, is very high. One cannot assume, for instance, that if a household retreats into itself that it does so for its own reasons, since the attractiveness of alternative activities is conditioned not only by monetary resources but also by the recognition of those beyond the household.

In housing, the group are distinctive. Only 7·5 per cent lived in council housing (compared with 30 per cent of the total population).[2] This will be partly the

---

1. See Chapter 6, page 250, for a discussion of the scale, its purpose and limitations.
2. A study of 1,000 coloured people in England in 1974–5 found that there were only 8 per

result of an absence of residence qualifications for recent arrivals to a town or city but, in comparison with the numbers in Eire–Irish households who live in this type of accommodation (also 30 per cent) who must have overcome this problem, the proportion is low. Numbers are made up by private furnished lettings, where 19 per cent live, as compared with 4 per cent in the total population. A higher proportion of people living in this type of tenure than in any other type of tenure have poor amenities. The proportion in owned or mortgaged houses is, perhaps surprisingly, slightly higher than the average (42 per cent in mortgaged houses). Calculations of housing cost as a percentage of net disposable income for income units find the group scarcely distinguishable from the population in general. However, this does not take account of what they get for their money. For example, the houses are much less likely to be in an attractive environment.

An illustration may help to convey the circumstances and attitudes of many in the group. Mr and Mrs Charles, both in their late thirties, came from the West Indies eight years previously. They live in a privately rented London flat of only five rooms (for which they pay £4·50) with their seven children (four sons and three daughters), ranging in age from 16 to 2. Two of the children had been born in Britain. The house has a leaky roof and they would like to move to larger accommodation. They have been on a council list for five years. Both work full time, she in the day as a domestic worker in a hospital and he at night as a labourer. He is not eligible for either sick pay or an occupational pension. His net earnings were £21·75 and hers £14·05, both in the previous week. Both said these were on the high side. On average they brought home £17 and £13 respectively. In addition, family allowances amounted to £5·90. He had been out of work recently for eleven weeks, and she for five weeks. During that period he had drawn supplementary benefit, but said he was very embarrassed to receive it. They have placed small amounts for each of the children in the Post Office Savings Bank, but otherwise have no assets. The older children attend a local secondary modern school and the younger children a primary school. Three of the children come home for lunch, two of them because the parents had been told that the lists for school dinners were full. Strictly they would have been entitled to free school meals for much if not all of the preceding year, at least while Mr Charles or Mrs Charles were off work. Their eldest daughter helps to look after the younger children, but in the main this falls on Mr Charles's mother who lives nearby and comes in every day to prepare meals. They have other relatives, including a grandmother, who live locally and whom they see frequently. Their time is taken up with work and family. They couldn't compare their situation with that in the West Indies. They came to give their children a better chance in life. 'You can't compare. In lots of ways we are worse off than our relations at home and than we

---

were before. If it wasn't for the children we would go back.' She said she felt poor now all the time. Mr Charles is an intelligent man who is bitter about the fact that coloured people are always treated as stupid and given the worst jobs. He seemed to be a very strict disciplinarian in the home, anxious lest his eldest daughter fall into bad company, and he wanted her to stay at school as long as possible. 'When she leaves she will only get a job at the bottom, unless she nurses, which we hope for.' All the children go to Sunday school, and on the day I called all the children were well dressed. The house was well above average. Mr Charles had decorated the two downstairs rooms. I was served tea on a tray with handmade lace cloth made by Mrs Charles. She said that at the hospital she was always given the rough jobs in the canteen, everyone 'thinking you don't know anything. I would love to be able to show them that I can lay a table for a banquet. Back home in St Kitts I used to work in the best hotel and always lay up for the most important guests and do the flower arrangements.' Mr Charles regretted not being able to get back into the building trade. 'It's the unions won't recognize anything can be learned outside this country.' Although the family were all in good health and had no medical problems, his ambition was to get out into the country and bring his children up in a more healthy environment, away from the temptations and bad company of the towns.

A summary of the position of this group is difficult; the numbers in our subsample were small – though drawn from a large number of areas. In relation to age, employment, occupational class, tenure and indicators of deprivation the results do, however, reflect the findings of substantial studies carried out in the early 1970s,[1] while adding data about incomes and other resources – which tend not to be collected, at least with any degree of precision, in other studies.

Large Families

Large families have become fewer in number and are often picked out for special social comment. Table 16.9 demonstrates their poor position in respect of income and other resources. Readers will find data about them, along with a discussion of household types, throughout this book. In some ways, the comparison with the population as a whole is misleading because of the substantial number of low-income retirement pensioners in the latter. Yet comparisons standardizing for age show them to even greater disadvantage.[2]

The composition by occupational class of the group is of special interest. Table

1. For example, Smith, D., *The Facts of Racial Disadvantage*, Political and Economic Planning, London, 1976: Community Relations Commission, *Urban Deprivation, Racial Inequality and Social Policy: A Report*, H M S O, London, 1977.
2. The survey confirms in many different respects the smaller pilot study: Land, H., *Large Families in London*, Bell, London, 1969. See also Ministry of Social Security, *Circumstances of Families*, H M S O, London, 1967.

Table 16.10. Percentages of persons in each occupational class who belong to a large family.

Whether member of family	Profes-sional	Mana-gerial	Supervisory high	Supervisory low	Routine non-manual	Skilled manual	Partly skilled manual	Un-skilled manual
			Occupational class of household					
In large families	16	11	6	6	5	11	18	20
Not in large families	84	89	94	94	95	89	82	80
Total	100	100	100	100	100	100	100	100
Number	225	189	330	424	201	890	505	288

16.10 shows a kind of U-shaped distribution of large family membership by class. The families tend to divide into two groups. Altogether, 19 per cent of those in large families belong to upper non-manual classes, most of them in receipt of a higher than average income. Most of the remaining 81 per cent were in income units living below or just above the state's standard: Table 16.9 shows that as many as 62 per cent of the whole group were in poverty or on the margins of poverty. The disadvantage of the large family households can be traced to high costs rather than lack of access to resources through the employment system. It seems likely from evidence presented elsewhere that a number of the manual workers would be earning lower wages than at the time of the birth of the last child. This might be because they had passed the age of peak earnings for manual workers or because they had developed a minor disability.

Many of the children in poverty were in large families. While accounting for about a sixth of all children in the sample, the numbers in or near poverty were a little under a third (Table 16.11).

The number of children under 15 who needed to be cared for makes it unlikely that the mother will have outside employment; in those households, 14 per cent of females in the age range 15–60 worked thirty or more hours per week, whereas for the total female population the figure was 35 per cent. The effect of this is counteracted by the greater probability that the men in such households will work overtime. Thirty-six per cent of men worked fifty hours or over, as against 24 per cent in the rest of the male population going to work. This bears out the findings of a government study in the late 1960s.[1]

The striking feature of the group's housing situation is the high percentage – 46 –

1. As illustrated above, Chapter 4, p. 165.

Table 16.11. *Percentages of children aged 0–14 in income units living in poverty or on the margins of poverty.*

Household type	Children aged 0–14	
	In income units with incomes last year below or on the margins of the state's standard	*All*
With 4 or more children	29	16
Other	71	84
Total	100	100
Number	475	1,280

in council housing. The proportion living in owner-occupied homes was correspondingly lower. Partly because of this high percentage, the housing costs of these large households, expressed as a proportion of disposable income, followed the standard distribution. However, despite the higher percentage in council housing, more were in need of additional bedrooms, and fewer had good household amenities.

Working-class households with four or more dependent children suffer disadvantage in many different respects and, among families, run the highest risks, except for one-parent families, of being in poverty. The major non-means-tested benefits provided by the state, namely family allowances and income-tax allowances, had patently failed to redress the imbalance in resources and income of these families.

Summary

In this chapter we have sought to examine the relationship of different social minorities to poverty. A social minority is defined as a group of households or families which have some characteristic in common which marks them off from 'ordinary' families and prevents them from having access to, or being accorded, certain rights which are generally available. Membership of one or more of these minorities is hypothesized to increase the risk of people being in poverty. Thirteen minorities are defined in this chapter, accounting altogether for just under half the households and over half the population of the United Kingdom. A higher proportion of several of them, namely the elderly incapacitated, large families, households in which there was a handicapped child and a disabled adult under 65, one-parent families and households in which the male wage-earner was low paid, had incomes of less than, or only a little above, the state's standard of poverty. Households which belonged to two or three minorities instead of one minority were more likely to be in poverty.

In this chapter, four of the minorities, based on numerically small sub-samples, were briefly discussed. The other, larger, minorities will be discussed in the next seven chapters. Relatively more women with an adult dependant or dependants were found to be deprived. Households with one or more members who were born in Eire were found to contribute disproportionately to the partly skilled and unskilled occupational classes, but none the less to have percentages in poverty or on the margins of poverty smaller than in the population as a whole. Fewer, however, were in late middle or old age. If age were to be standardized, income and asset distribution would be approximately the same as the population as a whole.

The proportion of non-white persons living in poverty or on the margins of poverty was rather higher than the population as a whole. They are a youthful population, containing few late middle-aged and elderly people, and if this were allowed for, substantially more of them would be in poverty. Moreover, fewer than in the population as a whole had sizeable assets or other types of resource, fewer were in non-manual occupations, and larger numbers were deprived on different indicators.

We found a U-shaped distribution of membership of large families by social class, with proportionately more of professional and managerial, as well as partly skilled and unskilled manual families, than of lower non-manual families, having four or more children. Income and asset distribution also tended to be unequally distributed, but the vast majority of manual worker large families were in poverty or on its margins.

The form of analysis allowed more to be said about people living in poverty. Seventy-seven per cent belonged to at least one minority. Most of the others were elderly people living alone or in couples, who also had some, though not marked, disability. Fifty-six per cent of the people in the band of incomes just above the state's standard belonged to at least one minority, but among the rest only a third were elderly people living alone or in pairs; over half were in households consisting of children.

Poverty is not concentrated overwhelmingly among any particular minority of the population and has its roots in many parts of the social and economic structure. This is perhaps the chief finding of this chapter. However, there are two supplementary findings. Disability, among children, adults under the pensionable ages and the elderly, is a problem experienced in families by an unexpectedly large proportion of the population. The needs of dependent children are also very marked – in the families of the low-paid, whatever their size, one-parent families, the long-term unemployed and especially families with four or more children.

17
The Unemployed and the Sub-employed

The next two chapters examine the association between poverty and both the employment situation in general and low pay in particular. A majority of people living in or on the margins of poverty are dependent for their main source of income upon earnings. This is one of the most striking results of the survey. The fact that a large proportion of the poor are in work is not exactly a new phenomenon. Seebohm Rowntree found it to be true of York both in 1899 and 1936,[1] and secondary analysis of government survey data showed it to be true of the United Kingdom as a whole in 1953–4 and 1960.[2] But its scale is bound to be regarded with discomfiture in any society setting considerable store by the work ethic and self-help. If there are people in full employment who none the less cannot earn enough even to maintain themselves and their families according to society's own definition of subsistence, that would seem, on the face of it, to pose awkward questions about the 'efficiency' and acceptability of the wage system.

Our analysis must start with the fact that about 49 per cent of the resources on which the population depends for its living standards are net earnings from employment and self-employment, and another 7 per cent derives from employer pensions and fringe benefits received directly or indirectly by virtue of employment.[3] Some of the remaining 44 per cent, including, for example, flat-rate and earnings-related unemployment insurance benefits and redundancy payments, could also be argued to be indirectly dependent on the employment situation of the worker. None the less, even 56 per cent is the bulk of the total and although a society could choose to control differently the living standards of the population (for example, by separating work from income and by paying incomes or available goods and services equally to all citizens or according to criteria of need, in-

1. In 1899, about 77 per cent, and in 1936, about 43 per cent, of those in poverty were primarily dependent on wages. See Rowntree, B. S., *Poverty: A Study of Town Life*, Macmillan, London, 1901; and Rowntree, B. S., *Poverty and Progress*, Longmans, Green, London, 1941.

2. About 40 per cent in poverty in 1960 were primarily dependent on wages. See Abel-Smith, B., and Townsend, P., *The Poor and the Poorest*, Bell, London, 1965. See also *The Circumstances of Families*, H M S O, London, 1967.

3. See Chapter 5, page 226.

cluding age and dependency), the fact is that, in the United Kingdom today, the relationship between employment and income is crucial in understanding and explaining the distribution of resources and the special condition of poverty.

In this chapter and the next I shall argue that unemployment and low pay must not be treated as discrete phenomena. Neither can be understood or explained except in the context of both the occupational and wage structure as a whole. People of working age, first, are not divided sharply into the employed on the one hand and the unemployed on the other. Each are differentiated into grades according to their experience and expectations of security and continuity or regularity of employment. At one extreme are the continuously unemployed who want work. At the other are people with continuous experience of employment who have 'tenure' and little prospect of loss of employment or of loss of earnings, even in sickness, until the day of their retirement, and even then an occupational pension closely related to final earnings. In between will be the upwardly mobile, with rising expectations of work security; the downwardly mobile, with increasing exposure to the risks of unemployment and redundancy; the seasonal and the part-time workers with poor security who would like to work full-time throughout the year; people with recurrent experience of unemployment; people with experience of more than one change of job because of redundancy; and those with family dependency who have a fitful and often exploited experience of the labour market. These groups of workers have arisen historically because of the needs, constraints and fluctuations of the labour market and their numbers vary according, among other things, to the officially defined unemployment rate. Society 'regulates' their numbers, as it does the numbers of wholly unemployed. The concept of the sub-employed has been applied to include both certain groups of workers who are underemployed or vulnerable to loss of job, and those actually unemployed.[1] It is perhaps best treated as covering unemployed, discontinuously employed, temporary, seasonal and marginal (e.g. part-time or second job) workers. This has the advantage of suggesting that some of the problems of the unemployed are shared with certain groups of people who have an insecure foothold in work, and that remedies for the conditions of both may have to be found if any realistic policies are to be developed to protect the occupational and income rights of the unemployed.

Secondly, people in employment are not divided sharply into the low paid and the rest. There are fine gradations of pay within occupations, and even sometimes

1. The US Department of Labor adopted 'subemployment' and 'underemployment' to measure the extent of 'employment hardship'. The subemployed were defined to include low-wage workers, those in part-time work who expressed a desire for a full-time job, the unemployed and those who had given up looking for a job. See US Department of Labor, *Manpower Report of the President, 1968*, Government Printing Center, Washington, DC, 1969, pp. 35–6. See also Cohen, M., 'Some Alternative Measures of Sub-employment', *US Bureau of Labor Statistics*, 9 September 1968; and Stein, R., 'Subemployment Measures', *US Bureau of Labor Statistics*, 7 May 1969.

within the same occupations of particular firms, as well as within and between industries. Any line that is drawn will leave many people only a few pence better off than 'the low paid', and some among the latter substantially worse off than others. Again, pay that may be relatively low in a region or in an industry may not be low for the country as a whole. Much therefore depends on the reference group selected with which to compare level of pay. And since people move into and out of employment, change jobs and experience marked fluctuations in earnings, the population categorized as 'low paid' will change appreciably from year to year and even from week to week. Much therefore also depends on the time period over which the level of pay is to be judged. The problem of fixing on a concept of low pay which can be easily defined and agreed in practice is fundamentally the problem of separating part of an intricately interwoven structure from the whole, rather like separating tissue from a muscle in the human anatomy. My point is to suggest the difficulty of tracing defect except to the whole organism and therefore of recommending restorative treatment other than by treating the whole organism.

Discontinuous Employment and Poverty

I shall start by demonstrating that there is a systematic association between the likelihood of poverty and the greater discontinuity of employment. The estimates from the survey of the population in employment can be compared with census data about the 'economically active' and also with the 'working population' as defined by the Department of Employment. According to the Census, there were in Britain 15,994,000 males aged 15 and over in 1966, and 15,917,000 in 1971, who were economically active. This suggests a figure of about 15·95 million in 1969, or about 16·40 million for the United Kingdom as a whole, the same as the poverty survey estimate for the latter. For women, census data and the survey estimates do not correspond so closely, being 9.31 million and 10·11 million respectively. However, about 1 million included in the latter (the survey estimate) had been employed for fewer than twenty-six weeks in the year and had not been off work because of sickness or unemployment. Many of these would not have fallen within the census definition of 'economically active'.[1] Indeed the fact, that

1. The census definition of the economically active includes persons aged 15 and over who were in employment at any time during the week before the census day, together with those who were out of employment during that week but who were intending to get work. The sick would be included, but only if their jobs awaited them upon their return. There are therefore at least two points which differentiate the total from the estimates given above from the poverty survey. Those employed during the twelve months of the poverty survey would have included additionally: (a) persons who had worked during the year but no longer intended to work (e.g. retired and disabled people, and women giving up work for childbirth and other reasons); and (b) persons who were sick and no longer intended to work, or had no job to go back to, but had worked in the year.

at one time around a million women have worked at least one week in the preceding fifty-two but less than half those weeks suggests how much industry may depend on women working for relatively short spells.[1]

The Department of Employment gave estimates of the working population for the last three quarters of 1968 and the first quarter of 1969 which averaged about 16·3 million for males and 8·95 million for females, giving a total of 25·25 million for Britain. These figures would be equivalent to about 16·8, 9·2 and 26·0 million respectively for the United Kingdom as a whole. The poverty survey estimates are 16·4, 10·1 and 26·5 million respectively for the United Kingdom. Until June 1971, however, the Department of Employment gave estimates of the working population based on a count of national insurance cards. It is known that some cards were exchanged belatedly and some people may have been wrongly collated in the working population. In June 1971, when the Census of Employment was introduced, new estimates were 120,000 lower for male and 260,000 lower for female employees. The department explained that 'the old count of national insurance cards included many [though presumably not all] employees who work for part of the year only, and who would not have been in employment in the particular week in June when the census was taken ... Another difference is that a person who had two regular jobs with different employers in the week of the census was counted twice in the census but only once in the card count.'[2]

In the survey, a record for the preceding twelve months was completed for all adults who had worked for at least one week in the year. The number of weeks at work, sick, disabled, unemployed, on paid or unpaid holiday and off work for other reasons (for example, caring for someone ill or children on holiday from school, childbirth, taking up or resuming full-time study) were listed. Except for holidays, the principal interruptions of employment were for sickness and unemployment. Table 17.1 presents a summary. Eighty-two per cent of men and 45 per cent of women had been employed in the year. As many as 12 per cent of employed men, and 11 per cent of women, had lost at least five weeks during the year because of unemployment, sickness or both unemployment and sickness. Another 22 per cent of both employed men and women had lost from one to five weeks for these reasons. There were others who had worked fewer than twenty-six weeks, or who, though working most of the year, had worked short time.

The table therefore identifies some of the groups occupying points on a continuum from 'whole' year full-time employment to 'whole' year non-employment. What the table also illustrates is the relatively worsening financial situation of the

1. Some were young entrants to employment or retirees. Thus, a quarter were aged 15–19 or over 60. This still leaves substantial numbers in their twenties, thirties, forties and fifties entering or leaving paid employment. (Of the third of a million men working fewer than twenty-six weeks in the preceding year, nearly two thirds were aged 15–19 or 65 and over, and most of the others were in their twenties.)
2. *Department of Employment Gazette*, September 1974, p. 838.

groups occupying different points between the two extremes. Our data on net disposable incomes include income other than earnings, and allow for the effects of personal taxation. Differences in the composition of income units are allowed for in our measure of income as a percentage of the appropriate supplementary bene-

Table 17.1. *Percentages and estimated number of males and females aged 15 and over according to continuity of employment in the previous twelve months and risk of experiencing poverty.*

Continuity of employment in previous 12 months	Percentage		Estimated number in population (000s)[a]		Percentage of those in each category in income units in poverty or on margins of poverty[b]	
	Males	Females	Males	Females	Males	Females
Sick or disabled, 1–4 weeks (no employment)	15·3	9·4	3,070	2,120	15	9
Sick or disabled, 5–25 weeks (no employment)	5·6	3·0	1,110	670	22	26
Sick or disabled, 26 or more weeks (no unemployment)	0·4	0·3	80	60		
Unemployed, 1–4 weeks (no sickness or under 5 weeks' sickness)	2·3	0·5	460	110	(35)	–
Unemployed, 1–4 weeks (5 or more weeks' sickness)	0·3	0·0	60	0		
Unemployed, 5–25 weeks (no sickness or under 5 weeks' sickness)	2·4	1·2	470	280		
Unemployed, 5–25 weeks (5 or more weeks' sickness)	0·5	0·3	30	70	30	(32)
Unemployed, 26 weeks or more (whether or not weeks sick)	0·6	0·3	120	60		
Employed, 1–25 weeks (no sickness or unemployment)	1·8	4·8	360	1,070	(68)	42
Employed, 26 weeks or more (no sickness or unemployment)	52·6	25·2	10,550	5,670	14	13
[All employed in 12 months]	81·7	45·0	16,380	10,110	17	17

Table 17.1.—contd.

Continuity of employment in previous 12 months	Percentage		Estimated number in population (000s)[a]		Percentage of those in each category in income units in poverty or on margins of poverty[b]	
	Males	Females	Males	Females	Males	Females
Not employed in year, aged 15–19	4·5	3·7	900	840	27	34
Not employed in year, aged 20 or over but under pensionable age	3·3	28·5	660	6,420	75	36
Not employed, of pensionable age	10·5	22·8	2,100	5,120	70	71
[All not employed in 12 months]	18·3	55·0	3,660	12,380	61	51
Total	100	100	20,040	22,490	22	35
Number	1,909	2,249	–	–	–	–

NOTES: [a] Rounded to nearest 10,000. To conform with the Registrar-General's estimates of the number of males and females in the United Kingdom aged 15 and over, the numbers in the sample of this age (for whom the information in this table was available) were multiplied by 10,500 in the case of men and 10,000 in the case of women. No other adjustments have been made to sub-groups.
[b] Net disposable income of income unit in previous year of less than 140 per cent of supplementary benefit standard plus housing cost.

fit standard. Although there are substantial variations of income within most groups, especially in relation to occupational class, the general trend must be stressed. Despite sick-pay arrangements and private insurance, national insurance benefits, including retirement pensions, redundancy payments, earnings-related benefits, and the possibility of a husband or wife in the income unit going out to work in the event of absence from work, the chances of being in poverty or on the margins of poverty rise remorselessly with increasing distance from the status of someone who has worked full time (with the exception of holidays) throughout the year. Fourteen per cent of men, and 13 per cent of women, who had worked twenty-six weeks or more in the year (most of them forty-five or more weeks) were in income units in poverty or on the margins of poverty. But 70 per cent of non-employed men and 71 per cent of non-employed women of pensionable age were in a comparable situation, and as many as 75 per cent of non-employed men aged 20–64. With the exception of people employed throughout the year who had none the less experienced from one to four weeks' (mostly one or two weeks') sickness, those in intermediate groups were more likely to be poor the fewer their weeks in work. The pattern is complicated only by the question of different combinations of earnings in different married income units. Sometimes both man and wife may be earning, sometimes only one of the pair and sometimes neither. As the table shows, more non-employed women of working age than of those working most of the year are poor, but far fewer than of non-employed men. This is because more have a spouse in paid employment.

The figures in the last two columns of the table are given in relation to only one point in the dispersion of incomes, and for persons in income units, not households. The same trend, however, characterized other points in the dispersion – for example, at the basic poverty level and at a level three times or more than three times the poverty level. If the income of the household as a whole rather than of income units is taken into the reckoning, the numbers in the groups with different work records in, or on the margins of, poverty are smaller. For example, some old people live with more prosperous younger relatives and some unmarried young adults with more prosperous parents. But, partly because most households consist of only one income unit, the trend remained the same. Thus, the number of men working twenty-six weeks of the year or more who were in households below or on the margins of the poverty line was 14 per cent, compared with 22 per cent for men who had experienced five or more weeks of sickness, 20 per cent for non-employed youths aged 15 to 19, and 59 per cent for non-employed men aged 65 and over.

The picture presented in Table 17.1 depends on the number of weeks in the year unemployed, employed, sick or disabled or not employed, and not on current employment status. Table A.64 in Appendix Eight (page 1041) shows rather more clearly for both currently employed and not employed that more of those with the longest spells of unemployment in the year were living in poverty or on the margins of poverty.

In a society, therefore, in which incomes, despite their complexity, generally favour the employed, the factors which control the *size* of different groups of the employed and non-employed are as important as those which determine the *levels* of incomes which are distributed. Without any change in the relativities of different types of income, the proportion of the population in poverty can increase or decrease according to a change in the relative numbers of employed and non-employed, and therefore in access to employment. Expressed in policy terms, employers can sometimes achieve the same result by restricting or reorganizing manpower as by opposing wage increase. Historically, the access of adolescent children and older people to employment has been increasingly restricted by legal means and social convention. There seems also to have been a tendency in recent decades for the number with lengthy interruptions of employment in the year because of sickness or disability to increase. The number of wholly unemployed has fluctuated less consistently and trends in the numbers of 'marginal' workers have been more problematic.

Quite apart from changes in the size of the different components of a system – in this case, the occupational role structure of the economy – the system itself may subdivide or sub-groups may coalesce. One example is the explicit attempts of some socialist states to abolish unemployment. Another is the emergence in both market economies and socialist states of a retired category of the population. In theory, therefore, there can be a marked distinction between the employed and the non-employed, each group having relatively homogeneous conditions and living standards. Alternatively, the splitting of each group into different sub-groups might come to form a hierarchy in which the employed merge almost imperceptibly with the non-employed. The facts seem to correspond more closely with the latter model.

The Levels of Unemployment and Sub-employment

There is a close relationship, therefore, between people's employment category, defined in terms of degree of access to continuous full-time employment, and their likelihood of being in poverty. And once each category is examined, each is found to fall into sub-categories differentially placed in access to income. What are the reasons for this fine grading by income opportunity? On the one hand, in its values, society is constantly discriminating between the undeserving and deserving in each situation. Such discrimination has three principal sources: the class structure, whereby rewards and privileges are graded according to social superiority and inferiority; secondly the work ethic, whereby a need is felt to inculcate the importance of productive work, but also, thirdly, from a need which is also felt to close ranks and integrate. In each disadvantaged group, there have to be those who are potentially capable of being readmitted to positions of advantage and can be treated as potentially good citizens. Moreover, if there are, for reasons of economic and industrial necessity, large numbers of people going through the turnstiles, it is convenient to establish principles of queuing, so that rules exist to define those who are at the head of the queue and can be readmitted in an orderly fashion. For these different reasons, the population as a whole, and the labour force in particular, are rather finely stratified.

The wholly unemployed are at one extreme of the continuum. In the sample, those unemployed in the week prior to interview comprised 2·8 per cent of men and 1·1 per cent of women employed at all in the year.[1] These figures compare

1. These rates would be about $3\frac{1}{2}$ per cent and $1\frac{1}{2}$ per cent if the figures of those employed in the year were adjusted to conform with official statistics on the basis of national insurance cards. If people in the sample were not at work in the previous week they were asked, 'Why weren't you at work last week?' Our counts refer only to those who said they were unemployed.

with an average in Britain in 1968–9 of 3·2 per cent and 1·0 per cent respectively.[1]

These rates require explanation. Those published by the Department of Employment are based on the numbers registered as unemployed. When people become unemployed, they sign on at the employment exchange and call there twice a week to establish their entitlement to unemployment benefit or supplementary benefit. The statistics of unemployment are therefore a kind of by-product of the administration of unemployment benefit, and as such have been severely criticized.[2] They do not reflect unregistered unemployment and hence give a misleading picture of changes in the labour market. They are not adequately related to occupational or skill groups or to social characteristics. They therefore underestimate the extent of unemployment and afford severely limited opportunities for analysis and explanation.[3]

For April 1966 and 1971, the census found many more unemployed than were then registered with the Department of Employment. Reporting in November 1972, a government inter-departmental working party conceded that there were 'some 100,000 males and 130,000 females [who] described themselves as either seeking work or waiting to take up a job but were not registered as unemployed'.[4] For April 1971, the figures were put at 100,000 and 300,000 respectively of those who were 'neither sick nor registered as unemployed'.[5] The difference in the rates, if these estimates are added to the registered unemployed, is shown in Table 17.2. A careful estimate of the situation in 1970 suggested that a household survey would have shown an unemployment rate of half as much again among men instead of the official rate.[6] However, the General Household Survey for 1971 found

There may have been others who were registered as unemployed but giving other reasons for not working. Our denominator for both sexes is relatively larger than that used by the Department of Employment.

1. *Department of Employment Gazette*, Unemployment series.

2. US Department of Labor, Bureau of Labor Statistics, *Monthly Labor Review*, March 1965, April 1967, and September 1970; *National Institute Economic Review*, 1971. See also Bosanquet, N., and Standing, G., 'Government and Unemployment, 1966–1970: A Study of Policy and Evidence', *British Journal of Industrial Relations*, 1972.

3. 'The question at issue is whether the unemployment statistics are adequate. An examination of the record since 1966 suggests that they are not. They have not allowed a proper appreciation to be made of some important changes in the period. They have understated the general downturn of the demand for labour and they have not given an adequate picture of its incidence by industry and occupational group. In the first case this is because of the unsatisfactory quality of the data at present collected, in the second it is because we lack any relevant data. The evidence suggests two directions for change. First, unemployment data should be collected on a household survey basis. Secondly, attempts should be made to calculate rates for specific occupational groups, particularly the unskilled' – ibid., pp. 189–90.

4. *Unemployment Statistics*, Report of an Inter-Departmental Working Party, Cmnd 5157, HMSO, London, November 1972, p. 23.

5. ibid., p. 23.

6. *National Institute Economic Review*, May 1971.

Table 17.2. *Percentages of employees who were unemployed.*

Year	Britain (Department of Employment)[a]		Britain (Census)[b]	
	Men	Women	Men	Women
1966	1·7	0·8	2·4	2·1
1967	2·9	1·2	–	–
1968	3·2	1·0	–	–
1969	3·2	0·9	–	–
1970	3·5	1·0	–	–
1971	4·6	1·4	5·2	4·9
1972	5·0	1·6	–	–
1973	3·6	1·1	–	–
1974	3·7	1·2	–	–
1975	6·0	2·7	–	–
1976	7·2	4·0	–	–
1977	7·8	4·4	–	–

NOTES: [a] Not seasonally adjusted. Monthly average. The denominator used in calculating the percentage rate is the appropriate mid-year estimate of total employees (employed and unemployed).
[b] The numbers of unregistered unemployed as estimated by a government inter-departmental working party have been added to the numbers of registered unemployed.

SOURCE: Department of Employment Gazettes; *Unemployment Statistics*, Cmnd 5157, HMSO, London, 1972.

that only $7\frac{1}{2}$ per cent of the men (though as many as 54 per cent of women) *looking for work* were not registered.[1]

What might be said to be the *real* level of unemployment? In addition to the registered unemployed, there are those of working age who are looking for work but not registered at an employment exchange. The numbers in the poverty survey were small, but suggested a figure of 220,000 for the United Kingdom – a figure very close to the 1966 Census figure of 230,000 given above. Of those not working *either* in the week of the interview *or* in the previous week and saying they were looking for work, only a third were actually registered for work. The following were the reasons given for not registering with the employment exchange:

Man; 46; former painter and decorator. Had two fingers cut off in accident two years previously for which he received £1,600 compensation. He had difficulty working and attended an Industrial Rehabilitation Unit for six weeks. 'It was pathetic, no use at all. The Ministry of Labour sent me to six jobs for disabled people. I didn't get them.' He says he does not register now and is looking for a job himself because he has had no

1. Office of Population Censuses and Surveys: Social Survey Division, *The General Household Survey*, Introductory Report, HMSO, London, 1973, p. 206.

help. Maybe he is one of those on the Disabled Persons Register who are not included in the unemployment series.[1]

Man; 70; former garage odd-job man. 'I don't know. Always being at work I've had a fear of these places. It seems as if you're trying to beg for something.'

Man; 72; former builders' labourer. 'I'd lose my pension if they knew I was working.'

Man; 76; former windscreen fitter. 'I'm too proud to go there.'

Wife; 17; 4-month baby; former shop assistant. Husband earns only £7 a week as welder's apprentice. 'My husband doesn't want me to work. Anyway, I want to look for my own job. The ones they give you are no good.'

Wife; 22; child of one year; former shorthand typist. 'My husband is only a machinist. I'm looking for part-time work in the evenings.'

Wife; 27; child of four; former presser in cleaners. 'I'm only sort of half working. My husband doesn't want me to work.'

Wife; 28; three children under 10. 'I want work either in evenings or in the day if we can live in, because of the children. There's no work available. The exchange don't help people like me.'

Wife; 33; child of 3; former clothing cutter. 'I'm on a waiting list for a vacancy serving school meals. The hours will suit me. [Her child is at nursery school.] I will finish at 3 p.m.'

Wife; 39; three children aged 6–12. 'It didn't occur to me [in looking for a part-time job to go to the exchange].'

Wife; 40; three children aged 10–16; former clerk. 'I haven't bothered. I'm not that desperate. I'd take a job if a nice one cropped up locally.'

Wife; 43; 1-year-old child; former telephone wirer. 'They don't seem to have anything for you. They don't seem to bother unless you're getting unemployment money.'

Wife; 44; two children of 11 and 21; former telecommunications inspector. 'I've never been down. I want part-time work; I've never thought of going.'

Wife; 45; formerly primary-school teacher. 'I don't want a full-time job yet. I'm recovering from hepatitis.'

Wife; 47; daughter of 21 and grandchild aged 6; former egg-breaker for dried-egg factory. 'You've got to have so many stamps. I haven't got them. The employment exchange is no use. They never get you a job.'

Wife; 52; no children; former head waitress. 'Because they do not have vacancies for the position I want.'

Wife; 53; children aged 18 and 22; former paper-sorter. 'I was just looking for part-time work and I don't pay the full stamps so there's not much point in my going there.'

Wife; 54; son of 20 at work; former shop assistant. 'I'm not looking that hard and I don't think there's a very great chance of getting a job.'

Wife; 60; formerly armaments factory worker in war; husband a colliery surface worker. 'I'm too old. There's no work in this area for young women let alone old ones.'

Single woman; 62; former company secretary on estate. 'I don't think they deal with the kind of work I want.'

In addition to the unregistered unemployed who stated they were looking for work were various categories of non-employed people of socially defined working

1. *Unemployment Statistics*, p. 18.

age. They could be regarded as ranging from, at one extreme, non-incapacitated people without conventional types of obligation to dependants in the home, who were not looking for work only because there was little work to be had, or no appropriate work, in their locality, to severely incapacitated people, at the other extreme, who would have had great difficulty in following most forms of employment. Their attitudes to the question of getting work could be said to be conditioned by both conventional values about people with their characteristics and status taking paid employment, and the opportunities that were actually offered to them in their neighbourhoods. Although they could be classified elaborately, people under pension age who were not working at all in the year and whose productive energies could conceivably be tapped could be said to fall into four groups: (a) relatively non-incapacitated men, most of them being in their fifties and early sixties; (b) young, non-incapacitated women, mostly married, without dependants; (c) middle-aged and older non-incapacitated women, mostly married, without dependants; (d) relatively incapacitated men and women who could be employed productively in a limited range of occupations, or in sheltered conditions. The first, and, in part, the third group, are discussed in Chapter 19. A distinction is drawn between the second and third of these groups primarily because there are substantial numbers of middle-aged and older women who have not had much, if any, previous experience of paid employment.

The extent to which these groups are, or might be, drawn into paid forms of employment depends very much on the employment system of a society and the views that are held conventionally about the desirability of creating employment for them. And I have not added young married women with dependants, for many of whom a different case could be made. In Britain, dramatic changes in employment occurred during both world wars, and the fact that changes at other times have been more gradual should not prevent us from recognizing how society, through both its values and its institutions, directly controls the definition of both the scope of, and the terms of eligibility for, paid employment.

There are at least two other groups who might be included in any definition of 'real' unemployment, namely, the unemployed of pensionable age and the underemployed. (In principle, a group of sick who might be more quickly restored to health might also be included.) The marked reduction during this century in the proportion of men aged 65 and over who are in paid employment is discussed in Chapter 23. Here it should only be noted that the numbers of retired but still physically and mentally active men (and women) of pensionable age have been growing rapidly and are very large, and that the evolution of 'retirement' status is a social convention of recent origins.

Finally, among those employed during a year there are the under-employed. Some are under-employed in the sense they would choose to have *more* paid employment (including some who have actively sought more). They would like to work longer hours or more weeks of the year. Others work relatively few hours or relatively few weeks, and although given present assumptions they may not express a wish to work more, their family situation and health would seem to make it possible. Under-employment might be the subject of a special inquiry. We found that among those persons who had worked fewer than thirty hours in the previous week, 37 per cent of men and 17 per cent of women said they would have liked to work longer hours, some of them with reservations, but 19 per cent and 4 per cent unconditionally. Another fifth of men and women said they could not work longer, and the rest did not wish to do so.

On the basis of the survey, we estimated there were 200,000 men and 560,000 women expressing a wish to work longer hours. (These figures are subject to wide sampling errors.) About a third of the men were young, but the majority were middle aged or of pensionable age. Just over half the women were in the age groups 40–59, but nearly half were in their twenties and thirties. More than half the women had dependent children, including some who were unsupported mothers.

Estimates are given below of different categories of employment and unemployment on the basis of the survey findings (figures in 1,000s, with numbers of men in brackets):

1. Employed or self-employed during the year	26,490	(16,380)
2. At any time saying they were not at work in the previous week because of unemployment	570	(450)
(including those not registered with employment exchange)	220	(30)
3. Unemployed		
(a) Unemployed for at least one week of the year (registered and unregistered)	1,800	(1,270)
(b) As (a), including self-employed	1,900	(1,330)
(c) Unemployed for at least 10 of previous 52 weeks	700	(450)
4. Non-incapacitated people not actively seeking work (scoring less than 3 on disability index)		
(a) Men under pensionable age	168	(168)
(b) Women under 50 (without dependants in household, other than husband)	900	–
(c) Women 50–59 (without dependants in household, other than husband)	220	–
(d) Men and women of pensionable age	2,512	(1,092)
5. Relatively incapacitated men and women under pensionable age (excluding women with dependent children)	461	(241)
6. Under-employed (i.e. working less than 30 hours and expressing a wish to work longer hours)	730	(170)

Far more people than are unemployed at any single time experience unemployment in the course of twelve months. While the rates derived for each age group in the poverty survey are subject to a wide margin of error, they are consistently

Table 17.3. *Percentages of males and females employed for one or more weeks during the previous twelve months who were unemployed in the week previous to interview and at least one week during the previous twelve months.*

Age	Males		Total number	Females		Total number[a]
	Percentage unemployed			Percentage unemployed		
	week previous to interview	for one or more weeks during year		week previous to interview	for one or more weeks during year	
15–19	6·2	17·7	130	0·8	8·4	119
20–29	3·2	10·2	372	1·6	5·8	257
30–39	1·2	6·1	342	0·6	5·4	167
40–54	2·1	5·7	436	0·3	3·3	337
55–64	4·3	6·4	282	2·5	5·1	118
65+	0·0	3·3	61	3·1	(6·2)	32
All ages 15+	2·8	7·8	1,623	1·1	5·1	1,030

NOTE: [a] The self-employed are entirely excluded from the table. Twelve men and two women not employed during the year but stating they were unemployed are included.

smaller than the percentage of each age group experiencing unemployment during the year. Table 17.3 shows that more than three times as many men and five times as many women who were unemployed in the previous week had been unemployed at some stage during the year. The high rates for those in their teens and twenties are particularly striking.

Occupational Class and Unemployment

A high proportion of manual workers, and especially unskilled workers, live in the shadow of unemployment. While the unskilled accounted for only 9 per cent of the male labour force experiencing no unemployment in the previous twelve months, they were 17 per cent of those experiencing from one to nine weeks unemployment in the year, and 39 per cent of those with ten or more weeks' unemployment. By contrast, professional and managerial employees, accounting for a slightly larger proportion of the labour force (10 per cent), scarcely featured at all among the unemployed. Only one of the 155 male members of a professional association in the entire sample had experienced any unemployment in the previous year.

The risk of a man being unemployed for at least one week in the year rose from

Table 17.4. *Percentages of unemployed and employed men and women who were of different occupational class, and percentages of different classes who were unemployed.*

Occupational class	Number of weeks employed in year					Percentage of economically active who were unemployed in year		Number of economically active in sample	
	Males			Females		Males	Females	Males	Females
	over 10	1–9	none	1 week or more	none				
Professional or managerial	(0)	0	10	4	2	0	–	167	27
Other non-manual	(20)	21	30	44	55	5	4	509	576
Skilled manual	(17)	44	34	4	6	7	3	589	62
Partly skilled manual	(24)	17	17	38	24	9	8	281	259
Unskilled	(39)	17	9	11	13	18	5	171	133
Total	100	100	100	100	100	7	5	1,717	1,057
Number	49	75	1,596	55	1,002	–	–	–	–

NOTE: All those employed or self-employed one week in year are included in the economically active. Also included are twelve men and two women not employed during the previous fifty-two weeks but saying they were unemployed.

zero, among professional and managerial groups, to 2 per cent, among higher supervisory grades, 6 per cent or 7 per cent among lower supervisory grades, routine non-manual workers and skilled manual workers, 9 per cent among partly skilled, to 18 per cent among the unskilled.

The pattern is not quite the same for women. More unemployed during the year than continuously employed were manual workers (53 per cent, compared with 43 per cent), but there was no marked relationship, as there had been for men, between declining occupational status and rising risk of unemployment. However, unemployment among women is much harder than among men to define and measure, especially since a high proportion of women work only for certain weeks of the year, or fewer than thirty hours a week. Women with a cleaning job occupying twenty hours a week, for example, who also have family dependants at home, do not always categorize interruptions of paid employment as 'unemployment'. Such interruptions are due not only to the fluctuating needs and fortunes of their families, but also to the marginal and often fitful nature of their employment.

The Institutional and Personal Characteristics of the Unemployed

The unemployed have characteristics which derive from the disproportionate numbers among them who are manual workers, particularly unskilled manual workers. But it is important to recognize that their liability to unemployment derives more from the marginal or insecure character of their employment and their (consequent) lack of resources than from any characteristics which can be claimed to be exclusively personal to them. Thus, Table 17.5 shows for both men and women that more of those who were unemployed in the year than the continuously employed had experienced poor working conditions and insecurity of work. They were less likely to have had any rights to fringe benefits or to belong to a trade union. They were also much less likely to possess assets of even low value and consumer durables of different kinds. Significantly fewer owned their own homes. Fewer had incomes around or above the mean for their household type.

The differences between the sometime unemployed and the continuously employed in conditions of work, working rights and security, as well as in level of assets and annual income, were bigger the larger the number of weeks of unemployment in the year. Because of their small numbers, I have not in the table differentiated between women, as I have between men, with ten or more weeks' and from only one to nine weeks' unemployment, but similar trends were discernible. Note the evidence for men, however. If short-term unemployment were a more or less random occurrence, one would not expect to find such marked differences between those experiencing a little unemployment and those remaining continuously in employment. While the fluctuations in business fortunes and the economy may indeed lead to the laying off or redundancy of some highly paid, skilled and previously secure workers, a substantial part of unemployment, even of short duration, must be 'structurally' determined in the sense that there exist many marginal jobs with poor rates of pay, working rights and working conditions which also carry a high risk of short-term unemployment.

Some indicators of the family situation and the personal characteristics of the recently or currently unemployed are also given in the table. Rather more of the unemployed are young, have children and have not lived for as much as a year at their present address. People who migrate may be less likely to obtain secure jobs. Certainly they are less likely to be acquainted with informal as well as formal networks of information about vacancies. Without residential or local connections, they are more likely only to be given temporary or low-paid work. This applies to people who have come from other regions of the country as well as from overseas.

Table 17.5. *Percentages of unemployed and employed males and females with different characteristics.*

Characteristic	Weeks unemployed in previous 12 months[a]				
	Males			Females	
	10 or more	1–9	none	1 or more	none
Work:					
At latest (last or present) place of employment:					
1. Poor or very poor working conditions[b]	(55)	46	22	(29)	15
2. Subject to one week's notice or less	(85)	75	40	(73)	48
3. No sick-pay entitlement	(74)	66	34	(66)	33
4. No occupational pension entitlement	(78)	77	40	(82)	60
5. Not a member of a trade union	(65)	68	46	(88)	76
Household resources:					
6. Assets under £200	(70)	48	24	(43)	24
7. Income last week less than 90 per cent of mean of household type	61	50	39	44	33
8. Fewer than 6 of list of 10 consumer durables	53	29	17	18	15
9. Not owner-occupier	74	65	51	68	54
Family situation:					
10. Children in household	41	63	47	44	36
11. Less than one year at present address	20	17	12	20	11
12. Poor environmental conditions[c]	(20)	28	21	(23)	22
Personal characteristics:					
13. Under 30 years of age	36	57	27	47	33
14. With disablement condition(s)	14	13	9	21	10
15. With moderate, appreciable or severe disablement[d]	12	11	6	8	8
16. Fewer than 11 years' education	86	84	72	60	69
17. Not born in UK	9	8	8	14	6
18. Health said to be poor or only fair	(25)	17	13	17	13
Highest number on which % based	58	76	1,612	59	1,015
Lowest number on which % based	36	56	1,246	33	576

NOTES: [a] Refers to those employed and self-employed for at least one week in previous twelve months, plus twelve men and two women not employed in the year saying they had been unemployed throughout the year.
[b] According to scores on work condition index (see page 438). Estimates included for those working outdoors at more than one place of work.
[c] See index described, page 535.   [d] See pages 692 and 697.

As one might expect, the differences in ownership of assets and other house-hold resources between women continuously in employment and women with at least one week's unemployment is less pronounced in the table than it is in the case of men. It was the man's, rather than the woman's, relationship to the labour market which determined the family's comparative affluence. But the data suggest that women who were susceptible to unemployment tended to be in families which were, for other reasons, relatively poor.

In the survey, age and disablement were less potent factors than they have seemed to be in other surveys.[1] Partly this may be because we were studying those with any unemployment in the year and not only the currently unemployed; certainly more of the latter consist of older or disabled persons and certainly older or disabled persons feature prominently among the long-term unemployed. But our evidence would also suggest that rather less emphasis may need to be attached to personal factors like age and disability in analyses of unemployment and more to underlying institutional factors. So far as disablement is concerned, we say this for two reasons. Among all men aged 40–54 with some, appreciable or severe disability, for example, 77 per cent were employed throughout the year, more than two thirds of them without any spell of unemployment. Among men aged 55–64, the figure is still 68 per cent, and the non-employed in this age group include men who have retired. And, to give the second reason, only 11 per cent of men unemployed during the year had some, appreciable or severe disability (that is, scoring 3 or more on the disability index).[2] While in no way underestimating the severity of unemployment among the disabled, we must beware of building disablement (and associated ill-health) into being a dominant causal factor of unemployment. Once unemployment or sub-employed roles are defined and numbered, disablement is a supplementary allocative factor – no more.

Scrutiny of official surveys in 1961, 1964 and 1973 would seem to bear this out.[3] The categories adopted in the surveys to which the unemployed were allocated were not logically coherent, but in 1973, for example, slightly less than a third of the unemployed men who were studied were said to have poor prospects of getting work on account of their age and/or their physical or mental condition. The figures do not appear to have been checked against any more objective measure, but even at face value they represent a minority of the sample. Moreover, a

1. Hill, M. J., Harrison, R. M., Sargeant, A. V., and Talbot, V., *Men Out of Work: A Study of Unemployment in Three English Towns*, Cambridge University Press, 1973.
2. The figure would be higher, however, if sickness or susceptibility to ill-health were included. Thus, 51 per cent of men aged 45–64 who were seeking work, compared with 21 per cent working, reported 'limiting long-standing illness' in the General Household Survey of 1971. See *General Household Survey*, Introductory Report, p. 278.
3. 'Characteristics of the Unemployed, 1961', *Ministry of Labour Gazette*, April and September 1962; 'Enquiry into the Characteristics of the Unemployed, October, 1964', *Ministry of Labour Gazette*, November 1965; 'Characteristics of the Unemployed: Sample Survey, June, 1973', *Department of Employment Gazette*, March 1974.

substantial proportion of these men were found to be in work after a check some months later.

Perhaps the single best method of putting this into proportion is to compare either fluctuations historically in the unemployment rate or variations in the rate between regions or areas. In Britain there were, for example, 331,000 unemployed on the registers on average in 1966, but 521,000 in 1967. In 1955 there had been 213,000, but in 1972 844,000. It would be hard to believe that age or disability played much part in explaining these fluctuations, especially those occurring over a short time span.

Similarly, *in any year* (irrespective of the rate of unemployment) there are big differences between areas in unemployment rates. On 14 October 1974, for example, there were 0·9 per cent unemployed in High Wycombe, 1·4 per cent in Aberdeen, 1·5 per cent in Northampton, 1·6 per cent in Bury, 4·2 per cent in Hull, 6·3 per cent in Sunderland and 10·3 per cent in Londonderry.[1] Variations in the distribution of the economically active population by age or disability cannot account for more than a tiny part of such marked variations. While it may seem unnecessary to spell out these statistics. it remains true that in official and independent studies of the unemployed, disproportionately great attention is paid to the personal characteristics, including age and disability, of the unemployed.

A recent study illustrates very well the difficulties of relating any evidence that is conscientiously collected about the structure of unemployment to popular stereotypes about its causes. An attempt in three towns to examine 'voluntary unemployment' was obliged, by its methodology and terms of reference, to devote extensive attention to the characteristics and attitudes of the unemployed, but the authors were yet able to point out that in an area of low unemployment (Hammersmith) even the disadvantaged (defined according to age, skill or health) were able to get jobs again fairly quickly. The 'personal' variables were of relatively small importance, either in explaining the rate or the length of unemployment. 'Vulnerable groups in that area tended to suffer very much shorter spells of unemployment than in the other two areas (Coventry and Newcastle).'[2] In their final chapter, the authors felt obliged to return to an examination of the economic and employment institutions which had not featured in their empirical work.

The chief argument of this chapter is that it is not just men's *general* relationship to the labour market, as conditioned by the development of a market economy, which has to be analysed if we are to explain the facts of unemployment, sub-employment and associated poverty. Social and not merely industrial forces have created a more finely differentiated *hierarchy* of roles – both in employment and in unemployment – together with a set of discriminating rules by which the characteristics of those who will normally be recruited to these roles are defined.

1. *Department of Employment Gazette*, November 1974, pp. 1054–5.
2. Hill, M. J., Harrison, R. M., Sargeant, A. V., and Talbot, V., *Men Out of Work: A Study of Unemployment in Three English Towns*, Cambridge University Press, 1973.

In studying poverty, too much attention has been paid to the characteristics of the unemployed instead of to the characteristics and determinants of the job (or role) structure.

It is through case-studies that we can understand the powerlessness of the individual to change the job structure or its biases of recruitment. They can be invoked as examples in support of the general argument.

Mr Bradshaw was a bachelor of 60 who had been unemployed for thirty-four of the previous fifty-two weeks when first interviewed in May 1968. He lived in a two-roomed flat in Nottingham and was on the Disabled Persons Register. Four years earlier, as a lorry driver for British Rail, he had had a coronary and was partially paralysed on his left side. He was then forced to take a succession of light temporary jobs and had been last in a routine clerical job in the Town Hall.

In the summer of 1968, he obtained work as a weighbridge clerk with a scrap merchant, and held this job for two years, earning £16·30 gross (£13·10 after deductions) at the final stage. He then became unemployed for most of the next two years (having one clerical job at the time of the 1971 Census for ten weeks). For many months he had tried hard to get work:

'I was offered 15p an hour as a watchman from 7 p.m. to 7 a.m., seven days a week. It was like going to prison for seven nights a week. I can't use the language to you I used to them. I used to tramp all around town looking for work – writing (they never bothered to answer, never got any replies, waste of postage). It takes all the guts out of you. You're on the scrap heap now if you're over 30. They don't want to know. They make excuses about the superannuation scheme. That last job I had I saw in the news. I rang up right away. They told me my age was against me but that Saturday morning there was a knock at the door, and there was the Manager. He said, "Can you start on Monday?" What a lift that was, I can tell you. I thought, "I'm made for life now." Then came this takeover and that was that. I must have applied for over 1,000 jobs.'

He gets (1972) £8·20 supplementary benefit (which includes an allowance for a diabetes diet). He had been obliged to return his TV set to a rental firm because he could not afford the rental of 50p per week.

'I scratch along. I just make it. I can't afford cinemas or anything like that. This enforced idleness has been a bit of a let-down, I can tell you. Somehow, I've got so that I accept it, but it's not living. It's no joke to know you're no use. It doesn't seem right that all your time is spent just keeping yourself alive . . . Somebody said the poor are always with us. Was it Jesus Christ? It might have been Ted Heath. I don't know. Big money rules the world, not Christianity or charity. It always has and it always will.'

Income Support during Unemployment

Income protection during unemployment is poorer than during other types of adversity, like sickness, injury, disablement or widowhood. Nearly a third of those in the poverty sample who were unemployed at the time of interview or in the previous twelve months were in income units in poverty or on the margins of poverty (see Table 17.1 above). About a quarter of the currently unemployed were receiving supplementary benefit, but another third were not receiving such benefit and were assessed as eligible. However, some of them (about a third) were members of households consisting of two or more income units or had a spouse who was earning.

Why did over half have incomes so low that they were found to be, or would have been, entitled to supplementary benefit? First, fewer than half those unemployed on the particular day of interview were drawing unemployment insurance benefit. Official statistics in the 1970s bear this out. In November 1972, for example, 352,000 of the 790,000 persons registered as unemployed in Britain were drawing unemployment benefit (including 85,000 also drawing supplementary benefit), but another 273,000 were dependent upon supplementary allowances alone.[1] Secondly, because of the rules restricting eligibility for insurance benefit, and the rules, particularly the four-week rule,[2] restricting eligibility for supplementary allowances, some of the unemployed were entitled, at least for a time, neither to insurance benefit nor supplementary allowances. On 6 November 1972, the Department of Health and Social Security estimated that 165,000 persons, or 21 per cent (including 123,000 men), were receiving neither benefit nor supplementary allowance.[3] Finally, extra types of allowance were and are far less likely to be paid to the unemployed, even the long-term unemployed, than other types of beneficiary. Thus, after six months' sickness but not unemployment, higher rates of dependence allowance are paid under national insurance. After two years' sickness but not unemployment, an additional 'long-term' supplementary allowance is paid. Fewer of the unemployed than of other groups receiving supplementary benefit are granted exceptional circumstances additions and exceptional needs grants. For example, although in 1972 many were *already* better off by virtue of long-term additions, 19 per cent of retirement pensioners, 20 per cent of widows and 33 per cent of the sick and the disabled receiving both national insurance and supplementary benefit were also receiving exceptional circumstances additions, compared with only 6 per cent of the unemployed.[4] Some of the unemployed actually have their allowances reduced below the basic rate. Thus, in 1969, 31,000 of the 228,000 in receipt of supplementary benefit were subjected to the 'wage-stop' and their allowances were reduced.[5] Again, although in theory those with entitlement to unemployment insurance benefit can also receive earnings-

1. DHSS, *Social Security Statistics, 1972*, HMSO, London, p. 21.
2. For a reasoned and comprehensive criticism of this rule, see Meacher, M., *Scrounging on the Welfare: The Scandal of the Four Week Rule*, Arrow, London, 1974.
3. *Social Security Statistics, 1972*, p. 21.
4. ibid., p. 143.
5. See Elks, L., *The Wage Stop*, Child Poverty Action Group, London, 1974.

related supplements, only 36 per cent (or 16 per cent of all the unemployed) were receiving such supplements in November 1972. This pattern has persisted through the 1970s.

The total effect has been to build a form of discrimination into the administration of social security.[1] In 1972, the incomes, including supplementary benefit, of a range of differently constituted families of the unemployed were lower – by about 10 per cent – than those of corresponding families of the sick and disabled.[2] The incomes of those unemployed who were not receiving supplementary benefit are not included in this comparison. There were, for example, 24,000 families with two children receiving supplementary benefit who had an average total weekly income of only £17·73. This compared with an average of £48·13 for all families with two children in Britain in 1972.[3] The former was only 37 per cent of the latter. What is even more striking is that *the figure is only 65 per cent of the lowest decile.*[4] The principle of less eligibility has survived remarkably intact.

Although the estimates from the poverty survey of the numbers of unemployed eligible for supplementary benefits are subject to substantial sampling error, they suggest that at least as many again as are receiving benefits may be eligible for them.[5] This statement allows for the fact, as shown in Table 17.6, that the numbers receiving such benefits were proportionately fewer than in the general population: we have discounted this difference in making the statement. The evidence is discussed further in Chapter 24.

Existing policy is infused with relatively punitive values which the evidence shows to be inappropriate. Any analysis of trends in registered unemployment relative to the number and regional pattern of vacancies; of the avowed interest of many sections of industry in 'regulating wage demands' by creating and perpetuating a 'pool' of the unemployed; of society's implicit interest in scapegoating so as to preserve crude forms of the work ethic; of the lack of hard evidence in the available literature of any substantial degree of 'scrounging'; of the history of work deprivation and vulnerable personal characteristics of the unemployed; and, finally, of the telling evidence of the reluctance of many of the

1. Early in the 1970s measures restricting the payment of unemployment benefit had been introduced. In 1971, for example, benefit was no longer paid retrospectively for the first three days' interruption of employment. The measure passed into legislation in that year followed a period of cutting down the numbers receiving discretionary extras through the supplementary benefits system. See Townsend, P., *The Scope and Limitations of Means-Tested Social Services in Britain, Proceedings of the Manchester Statistical Society*, 29 March 1972, p. 27.
2. *Social Security Statistics, 1972*, pp. 146–7.
3. *Family Expenditure Survey*, Report for 1972, HMSO, London, 1973, p. 84.
4. ibid., p. 88.
5. A government survey in 1966 suggested that some 50,000 men with two or more children were unemployed, and that as many as 41,000 received, or were eligible for, supplementary allowances. Of these, 16,000 or 39 per cent were not receiving such allowances. About a third of them had been unemployed three months or more. See *The Circumstances of Families*, pp. 13–14.

Table 17.6. *Estimated number of unemployed receiving and eligible for supplementary benefit.*

Whether income unit receiving or eligible for supplementary benefit	DHSS, May 1969 (000s)	Poverty survey (000s)
Receiving, also with national insurance benefit	62	} 150
not with national insurance benefit	129	
Not receiving, income too high to be eligible or spouse earning	} 381	210
Not receiving, eligible		210
Total	572	570

SOURCE: DHSS, *Social Security Statistics, 1972*, HMSO, London, 1973, p. 19.

unemployed even to apply for the grudging or miserly benefits offered by the state, demonstrates the need for a much more consistent, and generous, system of income support for the unemployed. In some respects, the existing system could be said to have connived at, if not actually determined, the rise in the number of unemployed in the late 1960s.

Employment Policy

So far as the unemployed are concerned, the social security system might be said to have grown up partly to temper the hardships experienced by many people, especially among manual employees, in a fluctuating market economy, and partly to regulate and grade the queues waiting to re-enter employment. The Department of Employment does not seek to control the total number and distribution of jobs according to the edicts of a full employment policy. That would entail a wide-ranging and very ambitious strategy. Its objectives are more narrowly drawn in conformity with both economic theory about 'frictional' unemployment and social stereotypes about a core of 'hard to employ'.

The job-recovery system is even less effective for the unemployed than the system of income protection. We were struck by its haphazardness. We asked all those who were unemployed, both at the time of interview and during the previous weeks, and who were looking for work, what steps they had taken. A third were registered with the exchanges, but, as shown above, were not often enthusiastic about the help they were given. All but a handful were looking in the local papers for a job. Others told of intensive search for a job, looking regularly at advertisements in shop windows or posted outside factories and offices; writing unsolicited letters as well as replies to advertisements; calling in at likely shops or offices and leaving name and address; inquiring in person at factories and sites;

and, in particular, making and following up inquiries through relatives and friends.

There was usually a difference between the short-term and long-term unemployed, especially when this corresponded with younger and older potential workers. The former were more active, more particular about what they would accept, and more optimistic about success. In refusing initial offers of a job, a few were risking a longer spell out of work because they wanted a change rather than return to their last place of employment. Some were so determined to seek re-engagement at their last place of employment that they were, at first, unwilling to contemplate anything else. Older men were more devastated by redundancy and, especially if they had been unemployed for several weeks or months, more despairing about finding a job again. Yet, despite discouragements, some of them persisted against all the odds. 'I spent two or three hours every day going around the building sites. Today I walked all the way to X [a town five miles away] and back in answer to an advert, but they weren't starting anyone until the New Year. Yesterday I went to the Corporation. They took on two young Pakistanis, but I was turned away.'

There is evidently a remorseless adjustment with time in job-search behaviour. Men gradually become less specific about their wants, become ready to accept jobs with lower pay and status, and experience depression but also bitterness against others. 'Sometimes when they say no and turn their backs I feel like going berserk.' This adjustment corresponds with a kind of structural stratification of the unemployed, differing in characteristics, behaviour and attitudes. The strata are defined not so much in terms of the length of current unemployment as of the total recent experience, both current and recurrent, of unemployment, together with the threat of unemployment or lay-off in jobs marginal to the labour market.[1]

Bankruptcies, mergers and fluctuations in business operations primarily determine lay-offs. Selective dismissal on the basis of lack of individual skill or

1. In a detailed review of the causes of long-term unemployment, Adrian Sinfield shows that, while studies of redundancy have shown that most men laid off find alternative work quickly, this does not apply to all and is not inconsistent with greater risk of unemployment subsequently. 'A man needs luck or a period of labour shortage to establish himself else he becomes fixed on a downward spiral with less and less security in each job. The next stage may be the day or casual labour office and the stage after "skid row".' The workings of the labour market 'suggest a hypothesis of gradual downward displacement. As the number of unemployed in any given area decreases, the greater vulnerability of the disabled, the aged, the unskilled and poorly educated and the victims of discrimination becomes evident. There is talk of the residual groups that are left unemployed as those better qualified in skill, health, etc. return to jobs first . . . In this gradual process of downward displacement those least able to compete may find themselves unable to get back to jobs they previously held.' This illustrates very well the relationship between process and structure – in this case the stratification of both employed and unemployed. See Sinfield, A., The Long-Term Unemployed, Organization for Economic Cooperation and Development, Paris, 1968, pp. 41–50.

effort seem to account for a small proportion of interruptions of employment.[1] Once unemployed, a man stands more chance, on the 'last in, first out' principle, of being laid off in his next job than the average employed person. And once he has experienced at least two periods of lay-off within a short period, he may acquire the reputation of someone who cannot keep, or doesn't want, a job. He may have to swallow his pride and accept an insecure, ill-paid job even to re-establish a claim to continuous employment.

The administration of unemployment benefit on behalf of the Department of Health and Social Security seems to serve the interests of employers better than of the unemployed. The threat of withdrawal of benefit is used both implicitly and explicitly to coax, if not to force, men to apply for jobs which they may not want and whose conditions and rates of pay may be bad, on the pretext that voluntary unemployment is not insurable and this is what must be done to protect society from the workshy. At least in elaborating the functions of the Department of Employment, this possibility must not be neglected, and detailed analysis is necessary of the process of job referral.[2] This would demand close analysis of the institutional structure of local and national labour markets.

The very fact that so many employees are subject to short notice (which is highly correlated with occupational class) suggests how small is the control that individuals can exert over unemployment.

Any attempt to establish the relative importance of voluntary and involuntary unemployment bears this out. In a national survey in 1971, for example, 'Over half the men were unemployed because they had been dismissed from their previous job and, if to these are added those who left their last job because of ill-health or because the job was temporary, 88·5 per cent of the unemployed men had lost their previous job involuntarily.'[3]

The fact that a substantial proportion of real unemployment is unregistered unemployment, especially among women, suggests, too, that the receptivity of employers and the public employment exchanges to expressed public need, and demand, for work is not all that it might be. This also tilts the balance of responsibility from individual to institutions.

Finally, the scale and character of retraining programmes demonstrates so little faith in the importance of the level of individual skill that the programmes must be seen, despite avowed aims, for what they are: as half-hearted attempts to divert attention from institutional responsibility for unemployment.

1. Sinfield, *The Long-Term Unemployed*, pp. 38–42. Sinfield quotes, for example, an official US survey finding that 'three of every four of the long-term unemployed had been laid off for economic as opposed to non-economic reasons'.

2. For evidence of pressure from exchange staff, see Daniel, W. W., *A National Survey of the Unemployed*, Political and Economic Planning, Broadsheet No. 546, October 1974, pp. 94–7.

3. *The General Household Survey*, Introductory Report, p. 211. Although home and family commitments were common reasons given by women for leaving work, as many as 52 per cent also left involuntarily.

Thus, 40 per cent of those in employment during the poverty survey said they had changed jobs in the last five years, representing about 11 million employees. Of these, only 16 per cent said they had received any form of retraining, most of them in-service training. Our estimates for the population came to a total of 1,710,000, made up as follows:

In-service training	1,300,000
Industrial rehabilitation units, etc.	150,000
Other	260,000

We then checked with all men aged 30–64 whether they had 'been on a trade, industrial rehabilitation or Government training course of any kind in the last five years'. This eliminated in-service training after appointment to a job, and referred only to subsequent training in a job or training during interruption of employment. We derived the following estimates, which gave a total of 580,000:

Government training courses	150,000
Armed services training	70,000
Other employer training courses	300,000
Other courses	60,000

Only a fifth of those taking a government training course and only a quarter of those taking other training courses said that it helped them to get a better job. Only 7 per cent of all men aged 30–64 who had experienced at least one spell of eight or more weeks' unemployment said they had been on a government training course.

A more comprehensive policy of income protection would, in addition to reducing deprivation, contribute to people's prospects of re-establishing themselves in employment, and thus help to prevent long-term unemployment. Similarly, a government employment policy which abandoned half-hearted retraining and instead created and controlled jobs to which the unemployed were deliberately recruited, would also reduce long-term unemployment.

At bottom, a false economic theory of unemployment has been adopted in policy, both employment policy and social-security policy. Employment policy *accommodates* rather than reduces or prevents unemployment; correspondingly, social security policies help the short-term skilled but actually deprive and punish the long-term unskilled.

In much economic theory, unemployment in the post-war years has been characterized as of two types: 'frictional' or 'structural' unemployment, and 'residual' or 'hard-core' unemployment. This conception has the effect of underestimating the seriousness of unemployment in a market economy, by explaining away part of the phenomenon as extremely short-term and inevitable, and the other part as wholly attributable to personal shortcomings. Transitory, short-term, frictional unemployment is 'considered as relatively harmless, in the sense that it

involves no major obstacle to the speedy re-employment of the workers concerned . . . For the vast majority of workers the only risk of involuntary unemployment remaining under modern conditions is that connected with structural
adjustments in the economy.' The second category consists of people who 'seem
intrinsically difficult to employ on account of some deficiency which cannot be
readily eradicated'.[1] Another writer states, 'The post-war experience of many
nations of northwestern Europe, whose full or overfull employment prevailed in
the first half of the 1960s, suggests that there is considerable residual unemployment beyond frictional joblessness.'[2]

This conception seems to have exerted considerable influence upon the policies
of the Department of Employment, which has decided, in effect, to devote less
time proportionately to the unemployed as such and more time to men in work
wanting to move from one employer to another.[3] In recent years, the Supplementary Benefits Commission has developed its own team of Unemployment
Review Officers. Anxiety has been expressed at this shift of priorities and the
implication that the far less experienced (and lower-status) commission will
increasingly take on responsibilities for the long-term unemployed.

The Employment Exchanges were set up to assist the unemployed . . . There is a fundamental value issue at stake here, which should be widely debated . . . The British employment service developed out of a recognition that unemployment was an economic problem, a problem that could not be left to the Poor Law, with its conception of worklessness
as a consequence of idleness and sloth. But today there is a danger that a distinction will
be made between those whose unemployment is just a temporary problem of movement
from one job to another, and those whose unemployment results from a seriously disadvantaged position in the labour market, in such a way that the latter becomes the
prime concern of the organization which has taken over the legacy of the Poor Law,
while the former get the benefit of all the modern developments in methods of counsel-
ling, placing and training for employment.[4]

Summary

This chapter has shown an association between unemployment and poverty. In
itself, this is neither a new nor an unexpected finding. But we have shown that the
association exists not only for the unemployed at the time of their unemployment
but also for the much larger number of those who have experienced spells of unemployment (however short) in the recent past. Either they have failed to secure
jobs with earnings high enough to raise their families comfortably above the
poverty line, or they are victims of recurrent sickness and/or unemployment and

1. Hauser, M. M., and Burrows, P., *The Economics of Unemployment Insurance*, University
of York Studies in Economics, No. 3, Allen & Unwin, London, 1969, pp. 10 and 27.
2. Reubens, B. G., *The Hard to Employ: European Programs*, Columbia University Press,
New York and London, 1970, p. 1.
3. 'People and Jobs', *Department of Employment Gazette*, December 1971.
4. Hill *et al.*, *Men Out of Work*, pp. 147–9.

are never in work long enough to establish standards of living which are, on average, above that line.

It is with this statement that the survey can be said to contribute something fresh to the study of unemployment. There are not two broad states of employment and unemployment, but a hierarchy of states from whole-time secure employment to continuous unemployment. Corresponding especially with occupational class, there are ranks of both employed and unemployed who are differentiated, on the one hand, by security of employment and various rights to welfare, or lack of such rights, associated with the status of their employment, and on the other, by eligibility for different forms of social security as well as by length or frequency of unemployment. There are, to distinguish only five ranks: those with a high degree of secure tenure of employment, with no recent experience of unemployment; those subject to short notice but no recent experience of unemployment; the currently sub-employed and unemployed, with recent experience only of single or occasional short spells of unemployment; the sub-employed and unemployed with recurrent or recent lengthy spells of unemployment; and the long-term unemployed.

We also probed the meaning of 'unemployed', and showed that official measures underrate the real extent. Thus, the 1971 Census showed that there were 400,000 more unemployed than were at the time on the registers. The number would, of course, be much higher if the under-utilized productive capacity of non-employed women with or without dependants, the disabled, the non-incapacitated 'retired' elderly and the under-employed were to be included. The exclusion of these groups from the potential employed population is, of course, socially defined.

For men, the likelihood of unemployment rises sharply with falling occupational status. While the unskilled accounted for only 9 per cent of the male labour force experiencing no unemployment in the previous twelve months, they were 17 per cent of those experiencing one to nine weeks' unemployment in the year and 39 per cent of those with ten or more weeks' unemployment. By contrast, professional and managerial employees, accounting for a slightly larger proportion of the labour force, had experienced virtually no unemployment at all in the year.

A distinction has to be made between the institutional factors which define the roles, including 'unemployment', in the occupational hierarchy, and the socio-structural factors which define who is to occupy them. A household survey cannot contribute more than a limited understanding of the former: other methods of research, which would include, for example, a survey of firms and of their inter-relationship in the local labour market, would need to be undertaken.[1] But we

1. At the University of Essex we have sought to pursue in greater depth the limited findings about the sub-employed from the national survey. See Norris, G., 'Employment Participation and Household Incomes in Two Local Authorities in England', and 'Subemployment Amongst Men', evidence submitted to the Royal Commission on Income and Wealth, 1977.

have shown that the jobs last held by the unemployed were in very poor or poor working conditions, with much greater likelihood of being subject to only one week's notice, far smaller chance of having any rights to fringe benefits and smaller chance of being unionized. The differences between the sometime unemployed and the continuously employed in conditions of work, working rights and security, and also in annual income, level of assets and number of durables in the home, were greater the greater the number of weeks of unemployment in the year. The marginality of jobs at the lower end of the hierarchy, and the tenuousness of income protection and job recovery services during unemployment, are defined by social institutions and values. The incidence and severity of unemployment have institutional causes external to the individual.

Given a role structure with a permanent, or at least long-term, place for the unemployed, there tend to be conventions about those who are selected for unemployment. They are predominantly those from marginal employment – namely, those lacking formally defined skills and educational qualifications; among the short-term unemployed therefore proportionately more young and among the long-term unemployed proportionately more older and disabled workers; and marginally more migrants from overseas. The state's social security and employment-exchange systems act as mechanisms to grade the unemployed according to desert for jobs, retraining or income, and to adjust them to their status and to a willingness to take jobs of lower pay and status than those formerly occupied. This facilitates, among other things, the conferment of seniority rights in large sections of industry. Despite evidence of the lack of jobs and opportunities, many of the public hold relatively punitive attitudes towards the unemployed; discretionary additions to benefit are rarely awarded; there are institutional checks even on types of benefit which are ordinarily available to other groups in adversity; and a very high proportion of the unemployed either do not receive supplementary benefits to which they appear to be entitled, or they receive less than the basic rates. Certainly nothing emerges from our data to justify the view that many people remain unemployed because it is more lucrative than working.

Finally, employment and social security policies tend to reinforce the misconception of economic theory that unemployment is of two types: 'frictional' and 'residual'. There are signs that employment exchanges, which were set up in 1909 primarily to help the unemployed, are becoming more concerned with those wishing to change jobs. The Department of Employment appears to be taking a resigned attitude to longer-term unemployment, which appears to be left increasingly as an administrative problem to the legacy of the Poor Law – the Supplementary Benefits Commission.

Since our national survey was carried out, the rate of unemployment has increased markedly. Studies in the mid 1970s have called attention to its harsh consequences and the need for new measures to expand employment as well as to introduce improvements in social security benefits.[1] Our findings that there is a hierarchy of states, differentiated sharply by income, from whole-time secure employment to continuous unemployment, and a tendency substantially to understate 'real' unemployment, imply some growth of poverty and perhaps a greater 'spread' of inequality during the 1970s. This is discussed further in Chapter 26.

1. See, for example, Sinfield, A., 'The Social Costs of Unemployment', in Jones, K., and Baldwin, S., *The Yearbook of Social Policy in Britain, 1976*, Routledge & Kegan Paul, London, 1978; Field, F. (ed.), *The Conscript Army: A Study of Britain's Unemployed*, Routledge & Kegan Paul, London, 1977; and Barratt Brown, M., *et al.*, *Full Employment*, Spokesman Books, London, 1978.

18

The Low Paid

Low pay has some of the same roots as unemployment. Just as people of working age are not divided sharply into the employed on the one hand and the unemployed on the other, so they are not divided sharply into the adequately and low paid. Pay is differentiated into grades just as jobs are differentiated into strata according to their security and continuity, or indeed according to their other attributes. If we are to understand and explain low pay in itself as well as in its consequences for poverty, two things are therefore necessary: to study every level of pay in the earnings hierarchy, and to study all the occupational and social concomitants of the different levels.

The Concept of Low Pay

There have been three approaches to the definition of low pay, by estimating the income 'needs' of the individual or an average or standard family, by showing whether the pay of the occupational group or industry to which the individual belongs is low compared with other groups of industries, and by finding whether the pay of the individual is low compared with other individuals in the earning population as a whole.

The 'needs' approach is to compare income from employment with a standard of individual, family or household needs. Seebohm Rowntree was one of the first to make this approach explicit in his *The Human Needs of Labour*.[1] Low pay becomes the pay below that required to maintain the unit of comparison – individual or family – at a certain standard of living. The problem is, of course, that workers differ in the number of their dependants, and pay which is sufficient to meet the needs of one person or two persons may be wholly insufficient for five or six. The concept has persisted socially, partly because the 'needs' of an average family of man and wife and two or three children has been a convenient yardstick for trade unions wanting to raise basic wage levels. It has also reflected social values about the desirability of wives staying at home to rear the children and care

1. Rowntree, B. S., *The Human Needs of Labour*, Nelson, London, 1918; rev. edn, Longmans, Green, London, 1937.

for returning menfolk, and about the desirability of restricting family size. The idea that a wage should be enough to support a family survived the introduction of family allowances, because Sir William (later Lord) Beveridge argued that a man's wage should normally be expected to cover the man's wife and the first child in the family,[1] though he had at least argued for separate subsistence support for the second child. The introduction of Family Income Supplement in 1971 represented a further erosion of the number in the family expected socially to be supported by the wage. Society now conceded that the wage could no longer be regarded as sufficient in all instances to support even a family of three. In the course of this century, therefore, attachment to the family-needs approach to low pay has grown and later weakened.

A second approach has been to examine the pay received by members of different professions, occupations and industries, and compare their pay with other professions, occupations and industries. The emphasis here has been on elucidating the pay, conditions of work, security, expectations, qualifications, prestige and status of the *average* member, or *representative* members of the group, with average or representative members of other groups. Thus, the Royal Commission on Medical Remuneration confined themselves to looking at the pay and conditions of other professions.[2] And, in a succession of reports on manual workers, the National Board of Prices and Incomes confined themselves to looking at the pay and conditions of other manual workers in different industries.[3] The pay of non-manual groups is rarely compared with that of manual groups. Moreover, top salaries are not even compared with the middle reaches of the same professions or industries.[4] Another point about this *group* approach to low pay is that the publicity often given during a strike or during arbitration, as in the Wilberforce Committee's deliberations during the miners' strike of 1972, amounts to a test of the prestige in which the group is held socially, so that decisions can be made about pay increases.

The third approach is to compare individual pay with that of other individuals in the general hierarchy of earnings. This can be done by taking a cut-off point at some level of the total dispersion of pay, say, the lowest decile or lowest quintile,

1. *Social Insurance and Allied Services* (The Beveridge Report), Cmnd 6404, HMSO, London, 1942.
2. Report of the Commission on Doctors' and Dentists' Remuneration (The Pilkington Report), Cmnd 939, HMSO, London, 1960.
3. For example, National Board for Prices and Incomes, Report No. 25, *Pay of Workers in Agriculture in England and Wales*, Cmnd 3199, HMSO, London, 1967; Report No. 166, *Pay and Conditions of National Health Service Ancillary Staff*, Cmnd 4644, HMSO, London, 1971; Report No. 167, *Pay and Conditions of Workers Employed in the Laundry and Dry Cleaning Industry*, Cmnd 4647, HMSO, London, 1971; Report No. 168, *Pay and Conditions in the Contract Cleaning Trade*, Cmnd 4637, HMSO, London, 1971.
4. See the Reports of the Review Body on Top Salaries, Cmnd 4836, 5001, 5372, 5595 and 5846, HMSO, London, December 1971–December 1974.

or a percentage of the mean or median. Each index has advantages and disadvantages, and incorporates particular values. Thus the identification of the earnings of each decile helps to 'fix' the shape of the curve of income dispersion but discounts any further degree of dispersion among the tenth with lowest earnings. And because the distribution of earnings is heavily skewed, earnings (including deciles) which are expressed in relation to the median are 'higher' than when expressed in relation to the mean. The implicit policy 'recommendation' in taking a level of pay in relation to the median is that pay should be raised in relation to the average *worker*. The implicit policy recommendation in taking a level of pay in relation to the mean is stronger. More of the population are shown to be below the mean than the median, and the smaller percentages imply a bigger gap to be filled.

To the difficulty of deciding level of pay has to be added that of defining 'pay' and deciding whose pay is to be compared. The dispersion of earnings received for a working hour or in a week is different from that received in a year or in the course of an occupational career, and different, too, if fringe benefits are excluded from, or included in, the calculations. The exclusion of the value of fringe benefits, for example, will tend to make the dispersion of earnings much less unequal. And doubts can arise about the inclusion in the group whose earnings are being compared of young people under 21 or 18, part-time workers, women as well as men, non-manual as well as manual workers, self-employed as well as employed people, and people from Northern Ireland, Scotland or Wales as well as from different regions of England.

There is no escape from expressing values in the definition of the low paid. Two examples might be given. It is common to define 'full-time' work as work of thirty hours a week or more, and common also to compare the weekly pay of such full-time workers. But since, for example, routine non-manual workers work fewer hours than manual workers, the real difference between them in their rate of earning, which might be brought out by calculating an *hourly* rate of earnings, is obscured. And if comparisons were restricted to hourly rates of earnings, the inequality between the non-manual worker earning a particular hourly rate for thirty hours and a manual worker forced to work sixty hours, including overtime at a much higher rate, to bring his average up to the same hourly rate, would remain.

Another example is the division between male and female earnings. If male and female rates of earnings are kept distinct, similar proportions of both sexes may be found to be low-paid relative to the median or mean for their sex. But the distinction is a conventional one, even if condoned by most social scientists, and is no easier to defend in principle than, say, the production of separate pay distributions for immigrants, Jews or Roman Catholics. By including both men and women in the distribution, a majority of women and a small minority of men will be found to be low paid. This radical approach does itself have two limitations. On the one hand, it ignores what was implicit in the family-needs approach to low pay – namely, that whether we like it or not, more men than women have dependent children and adults to support from their earnings. On the other, it ignores the 'costs' of the non-employed. In the same way that more men may be 'low paid' according to criteria internal to male earners than criteria applied to both males and females, so more men and women may be 'low paid' according to criteria internal to the employed of both sexes than to those applied to the employed and non-employed as a whole. The incomes of the non-employed should be considered in any comprehensive analysis of the low paid. This argument leads back to the suggestion that, among alternative conceptions of low pay which deserve to be operationalized, one is in relation to the standard of gross disposable income per head (with possibly some adjustment for young children).

Low Pay and the Lowest Decile

When called upon in 1970 to report on the general problems of low pay, the National Board for Prices and Incomes adopted the third of the approaches listed above, with some reference both to the first and second approaches. The position of men and women were considered separately. 'Otherwise the problem of low pay would be practically synonymous with that of low pay among women, and this would ignore the social significance of the fact that men's earnings are normally the main source of family incomes.'[1] The board went on to define low pay 'where men and women in full-time jobs have average weekly earnings which are lower than the bottom decile of all men and women in full-time manual work in Great Britain. For part-time workers, the comparison is made in terms of the hourly earnings of part-time workers.'[2]

The application of this approach to earnings in 1968–9 is shown in Table 18.1, in which the results from three separate sources, the New Earnings Survey, the Family Expenditure Survey and the poverty survey, are compared. The first of these three surveys analysed earnings data for the pay week which included 25 September 1968; the second earnings distributed evenly throughout the four quarters of 1968; and the third earnings spread through most of 1968 into the early part of 1969. For this reason, one might expect the figures from the first study to be a little higher than the other two. All three surveys are subject to sampling error. The first was of a much larger sample than the other two, and the second a rather larger sample than the third. For this reason alone, one would expect a degree of variation in the results. There are a number of small differences affecting the definitions of pay, manual and non-manual employees

1. National Board for Prices and Incomes, *General Problems of Low Pay*, Cmnd 4648, Report No. 169, HMSO, London, 1971, p. 4.
2. ibid., p. 5.

Table 18.1. *Distribution of gross weekly earnings in 1968 (or 1968–9): data from three sources compared.*

Earning population	Survey	Lowest decile	Lower quartile	Median	Upper quartile	Highest decile
		£ per week				
Full-time men, manual	NES	14·6	17·8	22·0	27·2	33·6
	FES	14·1	17·3	21·2	26·0	31·6
	PS	14·4	16·9	19·9	24·6	31·0
Full-time men, all	NES	15·1	18·4	23·2	29·5	38·0
	FES	14·7	17·9	22·3	28·2	36·4
	PS	14·8	17·5	21·3	27·1	35·4
Full-time women, manual	NES	7·3	8·8	10·6	13·0	16·1
	FES	7·0	8·4	10·2	12·1	13·9
	PS	6·7	7·9	9·8	13·0	15·9
Full-time women, all	NES	8·0	9·7	12·2	15·9	21·4
	FES	7·7	9·3	11·4	14·4	19·0
	PS	7·0	8·7	11·5	15·4	20·3

SOURCE: DEP, *New Earnings Survey*, *1968*, HMSO, London, p. 187. Note that, for purposes of comparison, the Department of Employment and Productivity compared NES with FES data using Basis B (defined on p. 3).

and 'full-time' employees, which *may* also account for some of the variation.[1] Unlike the Family Expenditure Survey and the poverty survey, the New Earnings Survey does not include Northern Ireland, and this will tend to make the earnings figures for the latter relatively higher than the former.

But perhaps the most important reasons for any differences in the results may be (a) the construction of the samples, and (b), probably to a much lesser extent, the source of information on earnings. In the New Earnings Survey, a very large sample was obtained by approaching employers after identifying employees at random by using the final digits of numbers on national insurance cards. But

1. For example, 'the manual group thus includes some groups of wage-earners, such as shop assistants, policemen, and some security, institutional and catering workers, who for Census of Population and other purposes are classified as non-manual workers' – Appendix 2, Definitions, in DEP, *New Earnings Survey, 1968*. HMSO, London, 1969, p. 181. Some commissions, bonuses and advances of pay, applying to a different or longer period than the pay periods were included in the NES but excluded from figures of last week's earnings in the poverty survey (they were, however, *included* in estimates of annual earnings).

only 92,500 of an estimated total of 116,000 employees, or 79·7 per cent, were in fact pursued through employers. The explanation offered by the Department of Employment is important, and suggests why the low paid may be underrepresented in the sample of employees who were contacted.

Much of the difference was to be expected because, for various reasons, at any particular time a substantial proportion of employees in the working population are not in employment. These are not solely the registered wholly unemployed, but also those who only take employment intermittently or at particular times of the year, such as many married women and students; those temporarily incapacitated by sickness or injury and not retained on employers' payrolls; and those attending courses at government training centres and industrial rehabilitation units. All cards due for exchange are not exchanged promptly, and it was impracticable to wait for any which were not exchanged within three months. The remainder of the difference arose because some employees were inadvertently overlooked when their cards were exchanged and others were identified but their employer was not.[1]

So far as I am aware, no estimates have been made of these different categories.

This has been quoted at length because, among the population who are economically active during a year, a substantial section, up to a fifth, of people who are bound to include a disproportionate number of the lowest paid, appear not to be represented in what is intended to be a comprehensive annual review of earnings carried out by the Department of Employment. This, together with the return of information by employers rather than earners themselves, may explain the rather higher earnings figures obtained from that source than through surveys of households. More relatively low-paid employees were found in both the poverty survey and the Family Expenditure Surveys than in the New Earnings Survey, as Table 18.2 shows. In recent years, the Family Expenditure Survey has continued to differ from the New Earnings Survey in this way. Although the sample for the poverty survey was much smaller than the annual New Earnings Survey, it seems to have been more representative of the employed population.

Like other bodies,[2] the National Board of Prices and Incomes seemed to have been baffled by the problem of defining low pay and therefore of establishing clear national objectives and clear criteria for the effectiveness of policy measures. The criterion of the lowest decile, which was chosen for special studies carried out before the board was wound up, and has since featured prominently in reports of the annual surveys carried out by the Department of Employment, has a number of

1. *New Earnings Survey, 1968*, p. 185; see also p. 3.
2. An interdepartmental working party made little effort to discuss possible definitions and criteria. 'What constitutes "low income" is essentially a matter of subjective judgement and ...there is no universally accepted definition of social need in either absolute or relative terms'. And the working party went on to propose a figure of £15 per week as 'the highest level likely to be envisaged for a national minimum' – DEP, *A National Minimum Wage: An Inquiry*, HMSO, London, 1969, p. 13.

Table 18.2. *Percentages of full-time male and female employees with different amounts of gross weekly earnings: data from three sources compared.*

Gross earnings	Male employees 21 and over				Female employees 18 and over			
	NES[a]	FES		PS	NES[b]	FES		PS
	1968	1968	1969	1968–9	1968	1968	1969	1968–9
Under £10	1·5	1·0	0·9	1·1	27·9	34·7	26·4	36·3
£10 but less than £15	8·3	10·1	6·6	11·1	42·4	43·3	42·1	36·9
£15 but less than £20	23·4	24·6	21·5	29·3	17·5	13·2	19·0	17·0
£20 but less than £30	43·6	44·4	43·0	39·7	9·1	6·5	9·7	6·9
£30 but less than £35	10·2	8·5	12·1	8·4	1·6	0·8	1·2	1·2
£35 but less than £40	5·3	4·3	5·6	3·4				
£40 but less than £45	2·8	2·6	4·1	2·1				
£45 but less than £50	1·7	1·4	1·8	1·7	1·5	1·5	1·6	1·6
£50 but less than £60	1·6	1·5	1·9	1·1				
£60 or more	1·7	1·5	2·4	2·2				
	100	100	100	100	100	100	100	100
	47,460	4,598	4,289	1,260	19,186	1,702	1,607	514

NOTES: [a]Excluding an estimated 400 with no earnings.
[b]Excluding an estimated 100 with no earnings.

SOURCES: *New Earnings Survey, 1968*, H M S O, London, p. 36 (Basis A).

Family Expenditure Survey, 1969; data on 'actual' as distinct from 'normal' earnings kindly provided by the Statistics Division of the Department of Employment. The comparable series for 1968 of 'actual' earnings was not available, but 1968 'normal' earnings have been adjusted in the light of differences in the distribution of 'normal' and 'actual' earnings in both 1967 and 1969.

disadvantages. It expresses a point just above the lowest tenth in the earnings dispersion. It therefore cannot act as an indicator of any changes in the number or proportion of the low paid, except indirectly by inference from any change that is denoted in its relativity to other points in the dispersion. It tells us nothing about the dispersion of earnings *among* the lowest tenth or their mean earnings. It also represents a technical concept which seems to suggest that low pay is something whose discussion has to be restricted to technical experts.

A definition based on a percentage of average earnings is clearly preferable. It allows a target to be set – the narrowing of the spread of earnings so as to eliminate all low pay which falls below a stated percentage of the average. The only objection to this raised by the National Board for Prices and Incomes – that the choice would have to be arbitrary – applies as strongly to their choice of the lowest decile. For example, why should the lowest decile rather than vigintile or even median be chosen?

Low Pay as a Percentage of the Mean

Table 18.3 illustrates some of the different results that can be obtained by applying different definitions of low pay. In 1968–9, a figure of £15 a week had been quoted as a figure for a minimum wage by both the Trades Union Congress and a government interdepartmental working party.[1] The table shows that if this figure had been applied to the adult employed population as defined by the Department of Employment, 12 per cent of men and 73 per cent of women, or proportionately six times as many, were low paid. The corresponding figures produced from the New Earnings Survey for 1968 were 10 per cent and 70 per cent respectively (Table 18.2).[2] But we have noted the disadvantages of taking any absolute amount in pounds to define low pay. Instead, the criterion of 60 per cent of the mean was applied. The reasons for this are given below. The criterion is applied in two ways in the table. First of all, like the figure of £15, it is applied to male and female earnings jointly. The figure for mean earnings takes account of the earnings of both sexes. The result is that 4 per cent of men and 57 per cent of women are low paid by this criterion. Secondly, the figure of 60 per cent is applied separately to male and female earnings, with the result that 11 per cent and 20 per cent respectively are found to be low paid. We argue below that there is good reason to develop *both* these approaches in analyses of the pay structure. Compared with the first, the second transforms the picture of low pay. The percentage of low paid who are women slumps from 85 per cent to 43 per cent. On average, the gross weekly pay of full-time adult males was over 80 per cent higher than of females. In consequence, more men and fewer women were found to have earnings below 60 per cent of the mean when that mean applied to the earnings of each sex separately than when it applied to the earnings of both.

One other possibility is illustrated in the table. Because the distribution of earnings is skewed, the median is lower than the mean, and if we were to define low pay as 60 per cent of the median instead of 60 per cent of the mean, the proportion found to be low paid among each sex would be much smaller, as the table shows.[3] The effects for the whole earnings distribution of taking the median rather than the mean are compared in Table A.65 (Appendix Eight, page 1042).

The fact that gross pay is averaged over the year in the table also needs to be explained. *Mean* weekly earnings in the year (or total annual earnings) are less widely distributed than earnings for any particular pay period of a week or a month. This is because some workers' earnings fluctuate substantially from per-

1. DEP, *A National Minimum Wage*, p. 13.
2. By April 1972, the figure for men had fallen to 1 per cent and for women to 26 per cent. Six per cent and 58 per cent respectively had less than £20 a week. See Department of Employment, *New Earnings Survey, 1972*, HMSO, London, 1973, p. 25.
3. If the mean of gross earnings plus the value of fringe benefits is taken instead of the mean of gross earnings, then the percentage of 'low paid' is, again, larger, since fringe benefits are more unequally distributed than earnings.

Table 18.3. *Percentages of employees*[a] *who were low paid, according to different definitions.*

Definition of low pay	Percentage			Numbers in sample		
	Male employees aged 21+	Female employees aged 21+	All employees	Male employees aged 21+	Female employees aged 18+	All employees
1. *Absolute* Gross pay last week was less than £15	12·2	73·2	30·0	1,192	493	1,685
2. *Relative, sexes combined* Average gross weekly earnings last year less than 60% of mean earnings for earnings of men and women combined	4·1	57·1	19·9	1,186	502	1,688
3. *Relative, for each sex separately* Average gross weekly earnings last year less than 60% of mean for earnings of own sex	11·0	19·7	13·6	1,186	502	1,688
4. *Relative, for each sex separately* Average gross weekly earnings last year less than 60% of the median earnings of own sex	4·1	9·6	5·7	1,186	502	1,688

NOTE: [a]Self-employed and males under 21 years of age and females under 18 years of age excluded, following conventions adopted by the Department of Employment. Those working fewer than thirty hours in the previous week and fewer than 1,000 hours in the previous year have also been excluded. The fact that categories of earners are more broadly defined in some other parts of this report should be noted.

iod to period and are averaged out.[1] For employees working with the same employer throughout a year, and for those changing their jobs but remaining in the same type of occupation, there are good grounds for considering pay received during the year rather than for isolated pay periods. For the much smaller number who have had different kinds of jobs, the mean weekly pay received during the whole year is less relevant. In calculating average earnings, we have also preferred to count sick pay and holiday pay and the appropriate number of weeks for which such pay was received. That this is a relatively conservative procedure should be recognized. We considered averaging pay to cover weeks for which pay was not received as well as weeks for which it was. There is much to be said for the proposition that earnings should be expected to cover weeks of unpaid sickness or holiday for those who have no rights to pay during these periods. But the treatment of the long-term sick, housewives who take jobs only in the school terms, and those intermittently unemployed between jobs, for example, becomes problematical. National insurance and other social security benefits, or husbands' earnings, become major sources of income in periods when such people are not in work.

Below which point in the percentage distribution might low pay be said to begin? We decided there were three grounds for looking at male and female earnings together as well as separately. A large number of the jobs occupied by women are distinct in type and conditions. For example, proportionately more are non-manual, more are routine and hours are shorter. Fewer on comparable earnings experience work deprivation. Fewer also experience social deprivation outside work.

The last two of these three reasons are illustrated in Table 18.4. According to a tentative index of work deprivation (see page 461), more male than female employees were deprived. This held at different levels of pay in relation to the mean earnings of each sex (and jointly). More low-paid male than female employees were also deprived socially. Because the style of living of employed wives is much more likely than that of employed husbands to be conditioned by the earnings of the spouse and not the earnings of themselves alone, the association between earnings and social deprivation can be seen to be much less marked for female than for male employees.

The table gives two examples of the relationship between pay and deprivation. There was an inverse association between higher pay and greater likelihood of work deprivation. Two thirds of men and over half of women with weekly earnings of less than 80 per cent of the mean for their sex were substantially or severely deprived. There was little difference among men between those with earnings below 60 per cent and those with between 60 and 80 per cent of the mean in the number who were deprived. But, among women, there was a marked difference

1. This is pointed out, for example, by Lydall, H., *The Structure of Earnings*, Oxford University Press, 1968, Chapter 3.

Table 18.4. *Percentages of male and female employees with different earnings who experienced substantial or severe deprivation at work or socially.*

Form of deprivation	Gross weekly earnings of full-time employees last year as % of mean for own sex						
	Under 60	60–79	80–99	100–19	120–99	200+	Total
Substantial or severe work deprivation (scores of 3 or more on index)							
men	67	65	56	44	32	8	53
women	61	49	44	33	24	(12)	41
Severe social deprivation (scores of 5 or more on index)							
men	38	35	22	15	5	(5)	23
women	32	26	23	16	16	(12)	22
Total numbers: work deprivation:							
men	221	345	361	218	200	49	1,394
women	99	128	115	81	111	24	558
social deprivation:							
men	248	366	372	235	225	68	1,514
women	105	130	120	80	115	32	584

between these two ranges. A rather similar pattern is evident in the case of social deprivation. While further work may produce reason for choosing a higher point, such as 80 per cent, in relation to the mean, we believe that 60 per cent can be defended as a justifiable cut-off point for low pay. (The discussion in Chapter 12, pages 461–5, on the relationship between deprivation and earnings within occupational classes, is also relevant.)

Because the choice of a cut-off point is bound to be controversial, its advantages and limitations should be stated clearly. The choice depends on the following argument. Levels of pay must be studied not in absolute amounts of money nor only in relation to some limited reference group (such as a profession, industry or even wage-earners as a whole), but in relation to the sum received by the average member of the employed population, including both non-manual and manual workers. The choice of a figure substantially below the mean, such as 60 per cent, has the advantage not just of being demonstrably low but of posing implicit questions about the fairness or justice of the earnings distribution as well the practicability of redistributive measures to achieve the modest objective of bringing earnings up to at least that level. The earnings of women have to be considered along with those of men, but also separately, because the relationship between earnings and deprivation for the sexes *is* different both at work and outside work. Employees with earnings of less than 60 per cent of the mean for their sex are much more liable to be deprived than those with higher earnings both at work and outside work, according to a fairly generous spread of indicators, including conditions and facilities at work, the severity and insecurity of work, entitlement to employer welfare benefits, dietary customs, housing facilities and conditions, and experience of holidays, and afternoon or evening outings or enjoyments. Low pay is thus defined by both the relatively poor conditions and facilities of work and of social life outside work. Some of the factors may partly explain the lowness of pay – and others represent its consequences.

Other criteria could, of course, be taken into the reckoning (such as danger, noise, dusty conditions, intensity of effort, repetitiveness, stress, skill), and this must be acknowledged readily. There will always be problems of deciding the weight that should be accorded to individual criteria and how far the same criteria should be applied to different industries, regions and work situations. Essentially a distinction should be maintained between low pay as a societal condition and as a condition relative to some sub-group in society. We have sought to develop ways of defining and appraising the former.

Low Pay and Poverty

The lower individual earnings are, the more likely will income units and households be to live in poverty or on the margins of poverty. Table 18.5 shows the trends for the sample. The correlation is not, in itself, surprising. What may be surprising is that it is not more marked. Within income units, a wife's wage may lift the unit out of poverty. Within households, the wage of an adolescent child who is earning may, if income is aggregated, lift the household out of poverty. Again, the correlation during the year is obscured because of variation in the number of weeks during which people earn. Thus, an above-average earner may have been sick for a long period, and if he failed in that period to receive sick pay (and supplementary benefit), the year's income for the unit or the household might fall to a poverty level. Finally, the number of dependants varies. A man with low earnings may not be in poverty if he lives alone and has a low rent. A man with above-average earnings may be in poverty if he has a large family and a high rent.

The fact remains that, in 1968–9, as many as 14 per cent of men experiencing no interruptions of employment for sickness or unemployment were living in, or on the margins of, poverty. They represented 1,450,000 working men among a total of 10,400,000 in the entire male workforce who had experienced no interruptions of employment in the year. There were, of course, others, usually in full-time employment, who had been unemployed or off sick for at least a week during

Table 18.5. *Percentages of male and female employees aged 20 and over[a] with different levels of earnings who were in income units and households in poverty or on the margins of poverty.*

Gross earnings as % of the mean for each sex	Percentage of employees				Total numbers[c]	
	Living in households in or on margins of poverty[b]		Living in income units in or on margins of poverty[b]			
	Males	Females	Males	Females	Males	Females
Last week						
Under 50	(41)	46	(68)	60	32	59
50–59	29	(22)	57	(37)	58	27
60–79	23	16	42	34	308	94
80–99	19	8	36	40	338	106
100–19	10	9	21	32	218	75
120–99	4	6	13	27	232	124
200+	7	(3)	7	(18)	57	37
All levels	16	13	31	35	1,243	522
Last year						
Under 50	(35)	(41)	(37)	(43)	26	34
50–59	28	(17)	29	(12)	83	24
60–79	24	9	23	12	305	86
80–99	16	6	16	4	328	87
100–19	10	4	9	5	197	69
120–99	3	5	3	7	184	98
200+	(2)	(0)	(2)	(0)	42	22
All levels	16	9	16	10	1,165	420

NOTES: [a]Working thirty or more hours in previous week and at least 1,000 hours in the year.
[b]Under 140 per cent of supplementary benefit scale rates plus housing cost.
[c]For households; numbers for income units slightly larger.

the year, and who were also living in, or on the margins of, poverty. They accounted for a proportion representing another 1,310,000 working men.

Consideration of the contribution made by married women to family income reinforces these statements. But for the earnings of wives, far more men would find that their earnings did not match the subsistence requirements laid down by the government for themselves and their families. The proportion of people of different age in income units in poverty rises if the wife is in part-time rather than full-time work, and more sharply if she is not at work at all. Table 18.6 shows clearly the change in percentage in poverty according to different combinations of the employment status of husbands and wives. It also reinforces one major theme of Chapter 17 that poverty is related to *degree* of access to paid employment.

Studies of women's employment have frequently called attention not only to a smaller emotional investment on the part of women than of men in employment, but to their lesser need for the income from employment. Married women have been said to take employment for companionship, or for 'pin money', rather than to help pay for the necessities of life. Our evidence shows that their motives may often be far more serious than these studies have suggested, and that for a very substantial proportion of married women (our figures suggest about a quarter), paid employment may, in fact, raise their family incomes out of poverty or near-poverty.

Conversely, the contribution made by married women's employment to the reduction of family poverty calls attention more sharply to the inadequacies of the earnings of men with families. If married women's earnings were discounted, the proportion of families of men in full-time work who are in poverty or near-poverty would increase by over 50 per cent.

Low pay therefore has a direct, immediate effect on the numbers in or on the margins of poverty. But it also has specific indirect effects. It may influence future life chances. The figures in the tables represent the situation only at a particular moment of time. They give a snapshot of the circumstances of individuals who are at different points in their own and their families' life-cycles. Low pay in the past can cause indebtedness for years to come, prevent the accumulation of assets, reduce capacity to overcome such sudden adversity as sickness or unemployment when it arises, result in under-nutrition, restrict activities and social experience, and hence leaves permanent scars.[1] As we shall show in Chapter 23, position in the occupational hierarchy in working life affects a person's chances of surmounting the poverty line in old age.

Low pay may also have certain indirect current effects. As part of what we will demonstrate below to be a larger pattern of labour market disadvantage, it may contribute to the acceptance or even creation of various forms of deprivation in the work situation. Certainly it is correlated strongly with those forms of deprivation.

It is sometimes argued that a more equal distribution of earnings would not add much to the living standards of the mass of the population, and hence would not greatly reduce existing poverty. This argument does not hold water. As an exercise, we investigated what would be the effect of raising the earnings of men in poverty to the net weekly mean. Allowing for taxation, we estimated that the

1. See also Atkinson, A. B., 'Low Pay and the Cycle of Poverty', in Field, F., *Low Pay*, Arrow Books, London, 1973.

Table 18.6. *Percentages of individuals in income units in poverty or on the margins of poverty, according to the economic activity of married couples.*

Economic activity of married couples	Percentage with income less than 140% of the supplementary benefit standard						Number
	%						
	0–14	15–29	30–49	50–64	65+	All ages	All ages
1. Husband and wife working 1,000 or more hours last year	14	3	7	4	–	7	762
2. Husband working 1,000 or more hours, wife under 1,000	25	(16)	21	6	–	19	362
3. Husband working 1,000 or more hours, wife none	38	29	29	16	10	31	2,119
4. Husband and/or wife otherwise having some form of work	(12)	(14)	(8)	(17)	53	23	161
5. Neither husband nor wife at work	62	(63)	45	52	67	61	582
All units with married couples	35	23	22	19	60	29	3,986

NOTE: Unmarried adults and adults and children in one-parent families are not included in this table.

number of working men without experience in the previous twelve months of unemployment or sickness who were in or on the margins of poverty would be reduced from 1,450,000 to under 300,000 – most of the latter being men with three or more (usually older) children and/or relatively high housing costs.

The Failure of Family Income Supplement

Another way of illustrating the same point is to show how little the Family Income Supplement scheme affects the incomes of the low paid. The scheme was directed at families of the low paid who were in poverty and who were not eligible to receive supplementary benefit. It received Royal Assent in December 1970 and came into operation on 3 August 1971. The Conservative government introduced the scheme instead of making a general increase in family allowances which the Prime Minister had appeared to promise in the election of June 1970. It was much cheaper, costing only £10 million in 1972–3 (or 3 per cent of the cost of family allowances) and £13 million in 1973–4 (or under 4 per cent). The supplement helps low-income families with children where the breadwinner is in full-time work. Half the amount by which a family's gross income falls below a prescribed amount is paid in benefit up to a maximum weekly amount. In October 1972, average male industrial earnings were £35·92 a week, but 50,000 of the 51,000 two-parent families then claiming supplement had incomes below £28 per week (including 25,000 with three, four, five, six or more children).[1] At that time the prescribed amount for a family with two children was as low as £23·50, and even for a family with six children was £32·50, or considerably less than the mean. Despite intensive publicity, the government has admitted that only about half those qualifying for supplement have claimed it.[2]

The scheme has therefore fallen into disrepute. Our data on earnings suggest the government's estimates of families eligible for supplement have been too low, and therefore that 'take-up' has been overestimated. For example, data collected in the poverty survey suggested there might be between 250,000 and 300,000 families with incomes (including average weekly earnings in the year from full-time work) falling below the prescribed amounts for at least several weeks.[3] The failure of the scheme to reach the low paid for whom it is intended may be even greater than has been publicly admitted by government ministers.[4] There are two

1. DHSS, *Social Security Statistics, 1972*, HMSO, London, 1973, p. 134.
2. By the mid 1970s the fraction was believed to have increased to three quarters. But the estimate was found to depend upon about twenty cases of individuals found to be eligible to receive FIS (including those who were also receiving it) in the annual Family Expenditure Survey.
3. The prescribed amounts for 1972 were expressed as a proportion of average industrial earnings and then applied to the figure for October 1968.
4. For a running account of the Family Income Supplement scheme, see *Poverty*, the quarterly journal of the Child Poverty Action Group.

further arguments. The prescribed amounts are extremely low, and the help that is even in principle given to the low paid is insufficient to allow more than a minority comfortably to surmount the poverty line.[1] Moreover, the evidence we have given in this chapter of fluctuating earnings does not suggest that a scheme tied to rigid qualifying rules relating to five weeks' earnings is likely to cover needs successfully.[2]

Wages Councils

Another major policy measure to help the low paid has existed in statutory form since 1909. There were forty-six wages councils in the mid 1970s, covering retail distribution, hotels and catering, clothing, laundries, hairdressing and other trades, which set legally enforceable minimum wage rates for over 3 million workers. The trouble is that the majority of wages councils have approved very low statutory minimum rates and that the Department of Employment's Wages Inspectorate, which is responsible for enforcing the minimum rates, has not followed a strong enforcement policy. One study concluded that this is due to the inadequate size of the inspectorate, lack of knowledge of the wages council scheme among workers, the policy of persuasion and lack of adequate sanctions.[3]

For 1968, the Report of the New Earnings Survey showed that 22·6 per cent of full-time male manual workers covered by all wages board and council orders earned under £15 per week, compared with 9·4 per cent of all male manual workers. The corresponding figures for women earning under £10 per week were 54·7 per cent and 39 per cent respectively. Non-manual workers covered by wages board and councils were no better placed.[4] Later reports for the early 1970s from the earnings survey do not suggest any change in the pattern. Indeed, evidence was published for particular trades of payments below the legal minimum and of other practices requiring searching examination and regulation.[5] None the less, partly on the basis of recommendations from bodies such as the Commission for Industrial Relations, the government has abolished, instead of strengthening, certain wages councils. Statutory regulation of wage rates might have been treated

1. An official survey in 1972 showed that 29 per cent of recipients would have been below the supplementary benefit standard but for Family Income Supplement payments, but that even after these payments, 13 per cent were still below that standard. See Knight, I. B., and Nixon, J. M., *Two-Parent Families in Receipt of Family Income Supplement, 1972*, DHSS. Statistical and Research Report Series No. 9, HMSO, London, 1975, p. 13.
2. A survey of recipients showed that 'circumstances had changed for over three quarters of the total FIS sample' and that the scheme was not 'sensitive to the increased needs or reduced income of recipients over a period of time'. See ibid., p. 72.
3. Winyard, S., *Policing Low Wages*, Low Pay Unit, London, 1976, p. 28.
4. DEP, *New Earnings Survey, 1968*, HMSO, London, 1970, pp. 33 and 47–8.
5. For example, Brown, M., and Winyard, S., *Low Pay in Hotels and Catering*, Low Pay Unit, London, 1975; Brown, M., *Sweated Labour: A Study of Homework*, Low Pay Unit, London, 1974.

as a useful precedent for the development of legislation on minimum earnings. However, our brief review of direct government policies to assist the low paid – incomes policy (see also the discussion in Chapter 4), wages councils and Family Income Supplement – suggests that they have at most had marginal effect. Indirect measures of family support – through taxation, family allowances and national insurance – have had more effect.

Correlates of Low Pay

Why were certain jobs so low paid? The characteristics of jobs and not only those occupying them have to be documented. Low-paid jobs are separately associated with poor conditions, vulnerability to early notice, lack of entitlement to fringe benefits and, in the case of men, unsocial working hours (Table 18.7).

When poor working conditions, unsocial hours, insecurity, lack of entitlement to holidays with pay and to fringe benefits are taken together in the form of an index, the correlation with earnings becomes much more marked. As many as 64 per cent of the low paid, compared with only 5 per cent of the high paid, were found to be substantially or severely deprived in their work situation – that is, scoring 3 or more on the index. At higher levels of earnings, the proportion who were deprived fell sharply (see Table A.66, Appendix Eight, page 1043).

Low earnings were also found to be correlated with poor health and disability, youth and late middle age, migrants (both those born overseas and those moving house lately), and relatively small number of years of education. In these respects, the findings are orthodox.[1] Had we included persons aged under 20 and persons working for fewer than thirty hours in the series presented in the table, some of these findings (e.g. age) would have been more marked. But these characteristics may not so much determine level of pay as the people who are recruited to low-paid jobs. There may be unidentified causal factors of an institutional kind. Certainly the correlations are not marked. In the sample, there is wide variance of earnings within education groups. This corresponds with evidence from other studies.[2] It indicates that improving workers' education and training would not necessarily eliminate low earnings.

In relation to family situation, high-paid and low-paid men and women are dif-

1. For other countries and not only the UK, see, for example, Bosanquet, N. *Low Pay: An International Comparison of Patterns and Policies*, OECD, Paris, 1973; and Bluestone, B., Murphy, W., and Stevenson, M., *Low Wages and the Working Poor*, Institute of Labor and Industrial Relations, University of Michigan – Wayne State University, October 1971. For a review of both 'personal characteristics' and structural or institutional variables, see the collection of papers in Field (ed.), *Low Pay*. For a review of British materials which places stress on age (including health and physical capacity) and skill (including education and training) as factors in low pay, see Bosanquet, N., and Stephens, R. J., 'Another Look at Low Pay', *Journal of Social Policy*, July 1972.

2. See, for example, Thurow, L., *Poverty and Discrimination*, Brookings Institution, Washington, DC, 1969.

Table 18.7. *Percentages of low and high paid, and all, men and women aged 20 and over,[a] with specified job, family and personal characteristics.*

Selected characteristics	Men			Women		
	Low paid (under 60% of mean)	High paid (200% or more of mean)	All	Low paid (under 60% of mean)	High paid (200% or more of mean)	All
Job characteristics						
1. Working entirely or mainly outdoors	39	7	23	0	(3)	2
2. Working unsocial hours[b]	37	11	39	16	(18)	17
3. Poor or very poor working conditions[c]	24	7	23	27	(5)	15
4. No sick-pay entitlement	54	5	36	68	(5)	34
5. No occupational-pension entitlement	62	10	41	93	(14)	60
6. Working 30–39 hours last week	24	25	17	65	(32)	47
7. Working 50 or more hours last week	17	33	23	7	(11)	5
8. Subject to one week's notice or less	60	9	41	74	(8)	47
9. Experiencing deprivation at work[d]	64	5	52	50	(10)	40
Family situation						
10. Children in household	38	62	48	43	(20)	29
11. Less than 1 year at present address	19	13	12	11	(7)	14
Personal characteristics						
12. 20–29 years of age	42	5	26	20	12	36
13. 50 or more years of age	32	28	28	35	(35)	22
14. With disablement condition(s)	17	5	9	16	(8)	12
15. With moderate, appreciable or severe disablement[e]	10	5	6	15	(15)	8
16. Fewer than 11 years' education	71	23	73	81	(27)	64
17. Not born in UK	11	7	8	6	(7)	8
Highest number on which percentage based	102	61	1,337	102	40	581
Lowest number	80	54	1,204	57	28	435

NOTES: [a]Those working fewer than thirty hours in previous week have been excluded.
[b]Working at night; or hours regularly begin before 8 a.m.
[c]According to scores on work condition index (see page 438). Estimates included for those working outdoors at more than one place of work.
[d]Work deprivation index (scores 3 or more) (see page 461).   [e]See pages 692 and 697.

ferently placed. Fewer low- than high-paid men were in households with children, but for women this finding was reversed. As in a government survey,[1] our data showed that, with increasing numbers of dependent children, more men worked long hours, and they were predominantly in their thirties, forties and early fifties, when earning rates were highest. On the other hand, more working- than middle-class mothers with children were in paid employment, some certainly because they felt compelled by the low, irregular or fluctuating incomes of their husbands to take work, and others to augment low living standards. They worked relatively few hours (see, for example, item 6 in the table). Perhaps the need of married women with children to work near home and leave work early largely explains why disproportionate numbers among them were either in ill-paid jobs or had relatively low weekly earnings.

Slightly fewer unionized than non-unionized workers were low paid. However, this is partly a function of industry and type of occupation. Fewer in the service industries, for example, were union members. When occupational class is controlled, unionized workers of both sexes were found to have an advantage in terms of mean weekly earnings. A weighted average in the case of men gives an advantage of 12·5 per cent, and in the case of women of 34·4 per cent. These are higher estimates than those produced in national studies in the United States,[2] though it should be noted that our data are not standardized by industry. For non-manual workers, we have counted members of professional associations and of unions together, and because of small numbers in some categories, too much should not be read into the results. For professional and managerial occupations, the data are too few to draw conclusions, and men in the lower supervisory occupations represent an exception to the general pattern. Unionized men in this class had weekly earnings of only 95 per cent of non-unionized men. But, for both sexes, membership of unions gives a clear advantage in earnings on average for routine non-manual workers of more than a tenth. And for both sexes, the advantage of manual workers is marked, as Table 18.8 shows. Male union members received gross earnings 17·3 per cent higher than non-union members; female members received 32 per cent more. We found that the broad trends of these results were not materially affected when we standardized for age and years of education.

To a considerable extent, the association between low pay and poor conditions or insecurity of work is a reflection of an association between both these factors

1. The percentages of men working more than forty-five hours a week were 56, 58, 63, 62 and 68 respectively for those with two, three, four, five and six children. See Ministry of Social Security, *The Circumstances of Families*, H M S O, London, 1967, p. 40.

2. 'When personal characteristics, occupation and industry are taken into account, the estimated wage for union members is $5.20, compared to $4.84 for non-union workers – a difference of 7·4 per cent' – Duncan, G., 'Non-Pecuniary Work Rewards', in Morgan, J. N. (ed.), *Five Thousand American Families – Patterns of Economic Progress*, vol. II, Survey Research Center, Institute for Social Research, University of Michigan, 1974, p. 185.

Table 18.8. Mean gross weekly earnings in previous year of union and non-union members of each occupational class?

Occupational class	Men Union[a] (£)	Non-union (£)	Union/ non-union as %	Women Union[b] (£)	Non-union (£)	Union/ non-union as %	Number in sample Men Union	Non-union	Women Union	Non-union
Professional	54·03	53·93	100·2	–	–	–	37	16	–	–
Managerial	36·87	35·29	104·5	–	24·33	–	30	14	–	6
Supervisory high	29·36	27·59	106·4	23·71	14·71	161·2	73	65	34	14
Supervisory low	22·99	24·31	94·6	17·36	13·50	128·6	43	66	14	42
Routine non-manual	18·69	16·88	110·7	13·28	11·53	115·2	30	45	34	178
Skilled manual	23·05	19·60	117·6	13·77	8·63	159·6	308	197	13	26
Partly skilled manual	20·55	17·71	116·0	11·88	9·57	124·1	151	95	56	75
Unskilled manual	17·89	15·07	118·7	11·66	7·81	149·3	57	68	5	24

NOTES: [a]The table applies only to those working 1,000 hours or more in the previous year. Of the total of 2,060 for whom average weekly earnings were available, 185, or 9 per cent, could not be classified either on grounds of occupational class or membership of unions or professional associations.
[b]In the case of non-manual workers members of unions *and* professional associations.

and low occupational class or status. But this is by no means the whole story. At the same level of earnings we found that fewer manual than non-manual workers had good working conditions (Table A.67, Appendix Eight, page 1044), entitlement to relatively long periods of notice and rights to fringe benefits. In other words, manual workers had to endure worse working conditions, longer hours, less security and fewer fringe benefits to earn the same money as non-manual workers. Within both skilled and other manual classes, for example, we found that more high than low earners worked unsocial hours (Table A.68, Appendix Eight, page 1045).

None the less, within broad occupation classes (formed by splitting both manual and non-manual groups into two further groups), low pay tended to be associated with poor working conditions, the shortest periods of notice (Table A.69, Appendix Eight, page 1046) and lack of fringe benefits.

The implication of these findings is that the level of earnings is not only determined by the nature of the job, or its value to an employer, but by the material correlates which largely govern its status. Any variation in working conditions, entitlement to notice, range in relation to custom of working hours and conferment of fringe benefits will tend to correspond with variation of earnings. The prevalence of low pay will therefore depend on statutory and non-statutory measures to limit work deprivation.

Level of earnings is also associated with continuity of employment. Fewer of those who were continuously employed than of those who had been unemployed for short or long periods of the year, or employed only seasonally or for fewer than twenty-six weeks of the year, were low paid (Table 18.9). People experiencing short or long periods of sickness were not markedly at a disadvantage.

Table 18.9. Percentages of discontinuously and continuously employed males and females aged 15 and over who were low paid.

Continuity of employment in previous 12 months	Percentage with average gross weekly earnings of less than 60% of mean		Total number	
	Males	Females	Males	Females
Sick or disabled, 1–4 weeks (no unemployment)	10	11	272	142
Sick or disabled, 5 or more weeks (no unemployment)	19	(17)	104	46
Unemployed, 1–4 weeks (whether or not additional weeks of sickness)	(24)	–	49	7
Unemployed, 5 or more weeks (whether or not additional weeks of sickness)	26	(24)	61	25
Employed, 1–25 weeks (no sickness or unemployment)	(41)	(23)	17	31
Employed, 26 weeks or more (no sickness or unemployment)	14	18	941	327
All employed in previous 12 months	15	17	1,444	528

Fluctuations in Manual Pay

There is another good reason for shifting our attention from the characteristics of persons to the characteristics of jobs in explaining low pay. The population receiving different amounts of pay is much less stable than the structure of pay – understood in the sense of the frequency of amounts of pay relative to the mean or median. Some of the low paid remain low paid, at least for several years, but others soon experience higher levels of pay. There is a considerable movement across any boundary by which low pay is defined. In the survey, for example, 54 per cent of men and 33 per cent of women said their pay varied. For non-manual workers, the figures were 37 per cent and 27 per cent respectively, and for manual workers 63 per cent and 41 per cent. For rather more than a quarter of these men and women, the lowest pay had been less than 50 per cent of the highest pay received during the previous twelve months.

There is a great deal of movement between strata; especially during periods longer than twelve months. This is illustrated for the years 1970–72 in Table 18.10. Fewer than half of the lowest paid tenth of male manual employees in 1970 stayed

Table 18.10. *Percentages of full-time male manual employees in relation to the lowest paid tenth* (*1970–72*).

Whether above or below

£17·7 in 1970	£19·8 in 1971	£22·0 in 1972	%
above	above	above	83·2
above	above	below	2·7
above	below	above	2·4
above	below	below	1·7
below	above	above	3·1
below	above	below	1·0
below	below	above	1·3
below	below	below	4·6
Total			100
Number			27,752

SOURCE: DEP, *New Earnings Survey, 1972*, HMSO, London, 1973, p. 259.

in the lowest tenth in 1971 and 1972. Another group started in the lowest tenth, rose above that tenth, and then fell back again. Altogether, as many as 17 per cent of male manual employees were in the lowest tenth in at least one of the three years.

The fact that a substantial proportion of manual employees are liable to be low paid for at least some considerable period of a short span of years is only one (if major) consequence of the insecurity of the wage system for manual workers. Far fewer non-manual employees experience fluctuations of earnings; far fewer experience any decrease of earnings; and far fewer experience really substantial decreases of earnings. This can be illustrated from official earnings data. Between 1971 and 1972, 54 per cent of male manual employees, earning £40–45 a week, compared with only 11 per cent of non-manual employees, experienced a *decrease* of earnings. As many as 21 per cent had a cut of £10 per week or more, compared with 3 per cent. The same difference existed between female manual and non-manual employees (Table 18.11). The higher the earnings the higher the proportion of manual workers who were liable to experience drastic reductions in the

Table 18.11. *Percentages of manual and non-manual employees with selected earnings in April 1971 who experienced a change of earnings by April 1972.*

Change of earnings	Males aged 21 and over working full-time, earning £40–45 p.w.		Change of earnings	Females aged 18 and over working full-time, earning £25–30 p.w.	
	Non-manual	Manual		Non-manual	Manual
Decrease			Decrease		
over £20	1	3	over £8	2	4
£15–20	1	6	£6–8	1	3
£10–15	1	12	£4–6	1	6
£5–10	3	16	£2–4	2	10
£0–5	5	17	£0–2	4	13
No change	2	0	No change	2	2
Increase			Increase		
£0–5	32	20	£0–2	10	21
£5–10	36	13	£2–4	33	19
£10–15	13	5	£4–6	29	9
£15–20	3	3	£6–8	9	5
over £20	3	4	over £8	7	8
Total	100	100		100	100
Number in sample	1,856	1,240		1,551	203

SOURCE: DEP, *New Earnings Survey, 1972,* HMSO, London, 1973, p. 264.

following year. Thus, among the most affluent male manual employees in 1971, those earning £60 per week or more, 36 per cent experienced a fall of £20 per week or more by the following year, and 55 per cent a fall of £10 per week or more.[1]

On average, non-manual employees with the same earnings as manual employees can expect to be earning more twelve months later; and on average, male manual employees with relatively high earnings can expect to be earning less twelve months later. Both these findings are clearly illustrated in Figure 18.1.

1. *New Earnings Survey, 1972,* p. 264.

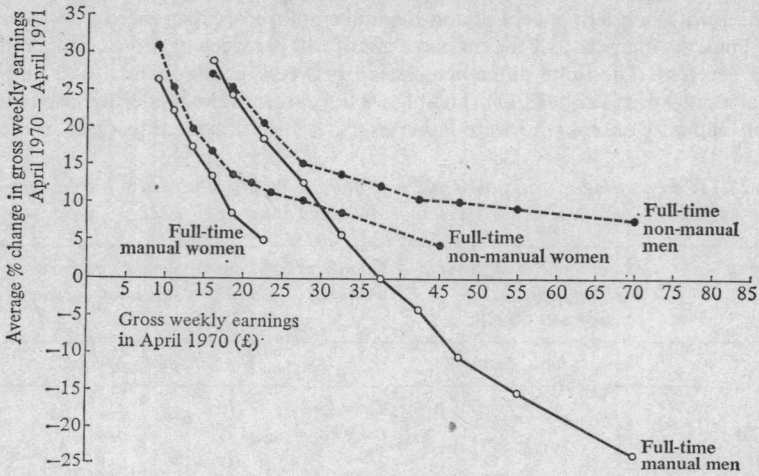

Figure 18.1 *Average percentage changes in earnings against level of earnings.*

SOURCE: Department of Employment, *New Earnings Survey, 1972,* HMSO, London, p. 262.

The Instability of the Pay and Conditions of Manual Work

The variability, indeed the instability and insecurity, of conditions and of pay during the careers of the great majority of manual workers remains to be thoroughly documented. Even those who do not change their jobs for periods of five or ten years can experience marked fluctuations of earnings, can be subject to short notice and may have poor conditions of work as well as few or no rights to fringe benefits. In Chapter 17 we found that three times as many men and five times as many women as were unemployed in the week previous to interview had been unemployed for a week or more during the previous twelve months. Among male manual workers, 9 per cent had been unemployed during the year. It may be that, during a period of three years, the number unemployed would be at least double that figure. In this chapter we have seen that during the three years 1970–72, 17 per cent of male manual workers were among the poorest tenth in at least one of the (relatively brief) survey periods in those three years. Even allowing for overlap, it is very likely that between a quarter and a third of manual workers are either unemployed or low paid according to the Department of Employment (i.e. below the lowest decile of earnings) for at least part of a period of three years. Perhaps during ten years the fraction may rise to over a half.

A Case-history of Low Pay, Unemployment and Poverty

The story of one man and his family, living in Manchester, with whom we kept in touch between 1968 and 1972, illustrates several of the points about the low paid made in this chapter and the unemployed in the last chapter.

When we first visited Mr Hanniman in 1968, he and his family would have had an income of little more than the state's poverty line but for his wife's earnings. Both he and his wife were then 34, with two children of 10 and 8, living in a ground-floor council flat with one living room and three bedrooms. His take-home pay as a builder's labourer for the previous week was £12·10, though during the year it had fluctuated between £12 and £15, averaging about £12·50. His wife was then a machinist with a clothing manufacturer. Her previous week's take-home pay had been £7, but because she was paid according to piece-work rates and demand fluctuated considerably, her earnings during the year had varied between £5 and £18 per week. One had worked for fifty-one weeks in the year and the other fifty weeks. When a third child was born at the end of that year, Mrs Hanniman gave up full-time work. She did 'outwork' and had an industrial sewing machine. But the flow of work was irregular and ill-paid – 'That stopped in 1971. They haven't even enough work for machinists in the workshop.'

Mr Hanniman worked as a labourer with several firms, and then in 1969 obtained a job as a chainmaker for coal belts. He had £25 a week take-home pay and regarded this as a very good job. 'I had one job from leaving school for ten years and then had many jobs. I never got the chance to settle. I fell to pieces. Then I got this job as a chainmaker. But after two years it folded up. I always seemed to be the first to go when there was a redundancy. When I went for jobs it was always, "We'll let you know" or "Sorry, it's taken".' After many months' unemployment, constantly looking for work, he went on a course at a government training centre. 'I know this course is my last chance. Either I get a job now or I go under.' When visited in April 1972, he had been at the training centre for six months. At that time the income for man and wife and four children was made up of £2·90 family allowance and £18·98 supplementary benefit (allowing £1·98 for bus fares and money for meals at the training centre).

Mrs Hanniman was fully aware of the effects of this work history upon her husband. 'He has no confidence and has trouble with his nerves. Everything was getting him down. He picks on everything. When I tell him, he says, "I know I do".'

Two years earlier she had lost a baby of six months through pneumonia. Whether or not this was related to their poverty is, of course, debatable, but she gave various illustrations of that poverty. 'The H P people don't want to know you if you're on t'dole. I want a washer very much, but they need a £10 deposit. I have asked them to alter my electric meter so that I get less electric and save the deposit that way, but they won't.' . . . They have not been on holiday for eight years. 'The children are going mad to go away. Oh, I would love to give them a holiday.' The family have fresh meat only at the weekends.

When Mrs Hanniman was asked whether she'd had a new winter coat in the four years since we had first met her in 1968, she said, 'No. All my clothes are what I've had given me' . . . 'I've not been able to get myself a purse. I can't afford it. But what good is a purse to me? I've nowt to put in it . . . It's the children, you see. They can't understand why they can't have things. You feel awful when they keep moithering on for things that they can't have. It's him too. He would love to give us everything. He's a good man and never kept us short when he had it to give . . . Look at my cooker. I'll have to wait until I can afford some Brillo and Ajax, we'd have to go short of food. People say being poor is no excuse for being dirty, but I say if you're poor and feeding your family properly you can't be clean. Stands to reason. If you buy those things it comes off the food.'

On the day we saw her in 1972, she was visited by two men from a local shop who came to examine a loaf in which she had found a maggot. She was told that she could visit the shop to replace the bread and choose a 'nice cake' in addition. Our interview was interjected with remarks like, 'Fancy a nice cake on Tuesday. He did say that, didn't he? You heard him, didn't you? The kids will be that excited.' Excitement at having a cake on a Tuesday could fairly be regarded as symptomatic of a state of poverty.

*

I have quoted this example at some length because it illustrates the existence of the hierarchies of employment and earnings, and the way in which employment security and level of earnings combine with the extent of family dependency to bring about prosperity or poverty. The vulnerability of a man at the foot of the occupational hierarchy in an unskilled manual job, especially when his wife is completing her family, is evident. They start with few assets (in their case £32 savings, few household durables and a second-hand car worth £40). As an unskilled manual worker in a relatively insecure industry, he is subject not only to a week's notice but a working life characterized by relatively short spells with different employers. While his wife is young and strong, the family small and she able to get work, they can keep their heads above water, but only just. Their situation is highly precarious. And so it proves. She loses her job at a time of contraction of employment and has a third baby, loses another, and then has a fourth child. He strives to better himself and manages to obtain a reasonably good job. But when business is obliged to contract a man like him in his late thirties with only two years' service and an unskilled background is almost bound to be at the head of any queue for redundancy. Once redundant, it becomes that much harder, at a time of higher or rising unemployment, to find any job, least of all a secure job. Displacement from work is a handicap not just because it can result in unemployment but because it remains a source of discrimination. Employers often assume the loss of job is the fault of the individual rather than of his former employer or the fluctuations of the economy. Therefore he may have difficulty in finding work, or in retaining it, and in obtaining promotion. He is likely to be particularly subject to the practice of 'last in, first out', and once he has lost jobs two or three times, especially if he is in his thirties or forties, he becomes the object of further discrimination. For the rest of his working life he is liable to carry scars which are supposed to have been self-inflicted, so remorselessly do we translate institutional into individual causation.

The Dual Labour Market Theory

The situation of the sub-employed and low paid is sometimes explained in terms of dual labour market theory. Classically, the labour market was assumed by economists to be a single system in equilibrium, meaning that workers with similar training and ability would receive the same earnings. If some jobs were paid more, everyone would flock into them and equality would quickly be restored by the competitive process. In this model the price of labour is determined by 'pure' market forces unencumbered by restrictions and preferences imposed by employers, groups of workers or governments. This conception of a perfectly competitive labour market has been frequently criticized, most devastatingly by Barbara Wootton in her *Social Foundations of Wage Policy*, and modern economists increasingly favour a concept of a segmented labour market.[1] Sometimes emphasis is placed on segmentation due to different degrees of control by trade unions,[2] or geographical,[3] occupational[4] and industrial[5] segmentation. Sometimes emphasis is placed on there being an internal labour market within a firm or plant which is largely insulated from the outside labour market. Jobs are arranged in a hierarchy with entry limited to certain points at the bottom of the hierarchy, and most vacancies higher up the hierarchy are filled by promotion. As a result, most jobs are protected from external competition. This model has been used to help explain large variations in pay observed within single occupations in a local labour market.[6]

Sometimes the model has been developed into the concept of the dual labour

1. For a succinct review, see Atkinson, A. B., *The Economics of Inequality*, Oxford University Press, 1975, Chapter 6.

2. Kerr, C., 'The Balkanization of Labour Markets', in Bakke, E. W. (ed.), *Labor Mobility and Economic Opportunity*, John Wiley, New York, 1954.

3. Robinson, D., *Local Labour Markets and Wage Structures*, Gower Press, London, 1970.

4. Reder, M. W., 'The Theory of Occupational Wage Differentials', in McCormick, B. J., and Owen Smith, E. (eds.), *The Labor Market*, Penguin Books, Harmondsworth, 1968.

5. Mackay, D., *et al.*, *Labour Markets under Different Employment Conditions*, Allen & Unwin, London, 1971.

6. 'Seventy-five jobs in a local labour market of forty firms were examined: the large majority showed enormous spreads of average hourly earnings for the same job' – Robinson, *Local Labour Markets and Wage Structures*, p. 20.

market, which consists of a primary sector, itself largely incorporating an internal labour market, and a secondary sector.[1] The primary sector is characterized by stability of employment, strong trade unions and high pay. The secondary sector is characterized by unstable employment, poor prospects of promotion, low pay and a low level of unionization. Little mobility between the two sectors is assumed to take place. Although the division between the two sectors leaves certain industries and firms wholly, or almost wholly, in one sector or the other, the division normally cuts across both industries and firms.[2]

The virtue of the dual labour market theory is that it restores the demand side of the labour market to an important place in theories about the determination of wage levels. Many economic explanations of low pay are heavily supply orientated: they concentrate on personal characteristics, including age, health, skill, intelligence, education and training. In the 1960s, many economists came to adopt the so-called 'human capital' approach.[3] Yet personal characteristics are clearly subsidiary in any explanation of expansions or contractions of the labour force, or of its subdivision into secure and less secure groups. Through the concept of the secondary labour market the problems, for example, of the unemployed can more easily be explained. They tend to comprise a kind of 'reserve' army for this market. And who would attribute wage or salary increases, and any change as a consequence in differentials as well as earnings levels relative to other industries, to the personal characteristics of the workforce?

The disadvantage of the theory is that it is oversimplified and insufficiently related to the occupational class structure. Some low-paid jobs are stable and have low turnover rates. This applies particularly to two groups: (a) 'family' employers with few employees; and (b) public services, including nationalized industries. Some high-paid jobs, especially in building and construction, are very unstable and have high turnover rates; these industries have a high proportion of temporary and marginal jobs. The characteristics of the two posited markets do not coalesce nearly as often as hypothesized. The variations are perhaps best understood as compensations or privations affecting pay, or security, or work conditions, but not affecting all or even most of the characteristics defining occupational class position.

1. Doeringer, P., and Piore, M. J.. *Internal Labour Markets and Manpower Analysis*, Heath Lexington Books, Lexington, Mass., 1971; Bosanquet, N., and Doeringer, P., 'Is There a Dual Labour Market in Britain?', *Economic Journal*, 1973; Bluestone, B., 'The Tripartite Economy: Labor Markets and the Working Poor', *Poverty and Human Resources Abstracts*, July-August 1970.

2. Some writers have added a third sector – the 'irregular' economy consisting of undeclared second jobs, undeclared activities within the self-employment, subcontracted activities, as well as illegal activities like gambling, peddling or prostitution. See Ferman, L. A., *The Irregular Economy*, Institute of Labor and Industrial Relations, University of Michigan – Wayne State University, mimeo, 1969; Bluestone, 'The Tripartite Economy', loc cit.

3. For example, Becker, G. S., *Human Capital*, National Bureau of Economic Research New York, 1964.

In some hands, the theory gives spurious justification to deprivation. Among other things, the secondary labour market is presumed to be a necessary creation of employers having to adjust their policies according to fluctuations in product demand. There have to be employees who can be easily dismissed, it is supposed, if the market contracts. A group of temporary jobs and employees defined in various ways as temporary workers allows that contraction to be effected with least difficulty and disruption. Therefore there has to be a pool of temporary jobs. with a pool of people willing to take them. But this applies only if the presumption already exists that there are greater and lesser jobs, and greater and lesser people filling those jobs. Otherwise contraction might take the form of a shorter week shared by everyone. It also ignores statutory regulation of the market and the existence of massive public services.

Although little attempt has yet been made to trace and explain the origins and history of the hypothesized dual labour market, some writers seem to suppose it is largely a post-war phenomenon, arising because of the need in modern economic conditions to establish a primary sector. However, there is clear evidence of segmentation at much earlier stages[1] -- which implies long-standing *occupational class* division of the labour market. It may be that knowledge of the occupational class structure of work organizations and the social class structures of local and national communities determine, to a very substantial extent, decisions on changes in work organization, work conditions and earnings, and hence perpetuate those structures.

It was not one of our objects to collect evidence of a possible segmentation of the labour market into internal and external markets, or into primary and secondary sectors, but the evidence presented in Chapters 12 and 17 and this chapter of the marked division between non-manual and manual workers, and of a more graduated segmentation into classes of each of these groups, certainly appears to reduce the possible significance of either the distinction between internal and external markets or primary and secondary sectors.

The rather amorphous structure of a dual labour market may indeed depend on the existence of occupational classes. The manifestations, for example, of an internal labour market may simply be reflections, to be found in any established firm, of the occupational class hierarchy at large. The form of the market probably draws heavily on the historical examples of the class structure of the traditional community, and the system of employer-employee relationships within the family firm, based on benevolent paternalism on the one hand and grateful compliance or acquiescence on the other. The policy responses of employers using or organizing the market to new situations are likely to be governed by their

1. As pointed out by Barron, R. D., and Norris, G. M., 'Sexual Divisions and the Dual Labour Market', in Barker, D. L., and Allen, S., *Dependence and Exploitation in Work and Marriage*, Longman, London, 1976. They cite as an example, Rowntree, B. S., and Lasker, B., *Unemployment: A Social Survey*, Macmillan, London, 1911.

knowledge of existing inequalities or differences of circumstance and values they hold about those differences. Moreover, through the home, the school and the further education system, the tentacles of occupational class reach out to affect many of the personal characteristics of those whom the different labour markets will recruit. Many of the personal characteristics which are listed to account for differences in working skills and propensities, as well as levels of pay, are themselves a product of occupational class differences. Both job-opportunity structure and many personal strengths and shortcomings thus stem from the same origins.

Approaches to Policy

In the mid 1950s, the growing importance in contemporary wage and salary settlements of conventional and social, as contrasted with purely economic forces, began to be recognized. As Barbara Wootton declared. 'The pattern of income distribution is essentially a political question.'[1] In the 1960s, successive governments attempted to develop an incomes policy without giving any evidence, as argued in Chapter 4 above (pages 128–32), that incomes other than wages were going to be controlled or that practical alternatives to collective bargaining were even being considered.

Yet if low pay in the sense defined in this chapter is to be eliminated, and poverty thereby reduced, an incomes policy which is comprehensive will have to be considered. Existing measures for the low paid include Wages Councils and Family Income Supplement. As we have seen, they have had minimum effect. In the short term, there is no doubt that some improvements could be made in Wages Council machinery,[2] and that poverty could be reduced by substantially increasing family allowances. An Incomes Gains Tax could pave the way for a fairer structure of incomes[3] and minimum earnings legislation might make a small contribution to a fairer structure. But in the absence of strenuous attempts to introduce alternative principles of distribution across the whole range of incomes, the latter may have only a marginal effect or actually have negative effects, as appears to have been the case in some countries.[4]

In the long term, low pay can be eliminated only by recognizing that it is but

1. Wootton, B., *The Social Foundations of Wages Policy*, Allen & Unwin, London, 1955, p. 166.
2. See, for example, Winyard, *Policing Low Wages*, and issues of the *Low Pay Bulletin*, 1974–6.
3. Wootton, B., *Incomes Policy: An Inquest and Proposal*, Davis-Poynter, London, 1974.
4. Bosanquet, N., *Low Pay: An International Comparison of Patterns and Policies*. For the United States, 'Minimum wage legislation has had practically no effect on raising the wage of the peripheral sector employee. Minimum wage standards have always been set so low that even where wages have been raised by legislation, the effect on a worker's total income is slight' – Bluestone, Murphy and Stevenson, *Low Wages and the Working Poor*, p. 424.

one of the institutional ramifications of class inequality, and therefore by tracing the ramifications to the institutions themselves and reconstructing them accordingly. The most critical inequality in incomes is that between incomes from employment and incomes in non-employment, and the most critical inequality in status is that between people in, and people outside, paid employment. Paradoxically, therefore, the low paid can be helped most by indirect measures designed to increase the relative income and status of those outside paid employment, including redefinition of the roles of the workforce, improvements in the work situation, and full employment (giving opportunities for occupation as of right to the non-employed, including the disabled and elderly).

In the early stages of a radical programme, new forms of taxation, like incomes gains tax, could encourage the process of social adjustment. But experience suggests that the institutions of inequality respond to such devices by offsetting their effects. Increases in the rates of tax, for example, have often been countered either by disproportionate increases in the gross salaries paid, or by a proportion of remuneration being switched to fringe benefits. In making its recommendations, the Review Body on Top Salaries has taken careful account of increases in gross salary required to produce the same *real* net salary at different dates.[1] Quite apart from actions by managements to assist the high paid in ways other than through salaries, this is a good example of the methods by which government intentions in incomes policies are subtly contraverted.

Summary

Three approaches to the definition of low pay have been tried – by comparing earnings with the 'needs' of the individual or family, with the earnings of occupational groups or industries, and with other individuals. In outlining these approaches, the view taken here is that there is no escape from expressing values in the definition of the low paid. Measures adopted in government studies are criticized and grounds are given for adopting instead a measure of 60 per cent of the mean weekly earnings during a year. That level is correlated with both deprivation at work and social deprivation.

Because of variation in income other than earnings, in the income of a spouse, in the number of dependants and in housing costs, the correlation between low pay and poverty is not found to be marked. Among the low paid, those with children (especially with three or more) are most likely to be in poverty. We found that, but for the employment of married women, far more families of men in full-time work would have been in poverty or on the margins of poverty.

Far less emphasis is placed in our analysis than is usual upon the personal

1. Review Body on Top Salaries, Report No. 6, *Report on Top Salaries*, Cmnd 5846, H M S O, London, 1974, Appendix M.

characteristics of the low paid in explaining wage differentials. There are two reasons. First, the surface correlations between level of pay and personal characteristics are quite weak. For example, we found there were considerable numbers of people with relatively few years of education, who were not born in the United Kingdom, who were older and even in poor health who were numbered among those with relatively high earnings. And even allowing for a range of 'personal' factors of these kinds, women's earnings remain much lower than men's earnings. This difference is perhaps an incontrovertible reason for abandoning any idea that the level of earnings is individually 'deserved'.

Secondly, certain kinds of evidence make necessary a distinction between the characteristics of jobs and the characteristics of the people who occupy them. While the hierarchy of pay is in many respects resistant to change, the number of people passing up and down the hierarchy is quite large – for example, we found that over half the men and a third of women experienced variations in pay, a substantial proportion among them quite marked variations, in the course of a single year. Again, this applies much more to manual than to non-manual workers. And data from an annual Department of Employment survey for periods of three years shows that those who are low paid are not a stable group, and even that male manual workers who are high paid usually experience a drastic reduction of pay during the following year.

It would be hard to believe from this evidence that personal characteristics, or even the distribution of such characteristics generally in the population, play more than a very minor part in determining pay structures. More important are the material attributes of jobs – which greatly influence the regard in which particular jobs and classes of job are held.

Low pay is associated with various forms of deprivation in the work situation – poor working conditions, small period of entitlement to notice, unsocial working hours, and lack of fringe benefits. The severity and scope of low pay must therefore depend in part on statutory and non-statutory measures to limit work deprivation. These measures could usefully be studied in future research and could be improved or augmented as a deliberate act of government policy. Conditions and terms of work are therefore important, and not just the strengthening of Wages Council legislation or the introduction of minimum-earnings legislation.

In explaining the incidence and scope of low pay, current dual labour market theory has the advantage of restoring to importance the demand side of the labour market. Classically, the labour market was assumed to be a single system in equilibrium, where personal characteristics such as age, education, skill and training were paramount. By contrast, the dual labour market is presumed to consist of a primary sector, characterized by stable employment, strong unions and high pay (itself largely incorporating an internal labour market) and a secondary sector characterized by unstable employment, poor prospects of promotion, low pay and a low level of unionization.

The theory is oversimplified and insufficiently related to the occupational class structure and the evolution of the labour market to that structure. Some low-paid jobs are stable and have high turnover rates, while some high-paid jobs have the opposite characteristics. Our analysis has called attention to the wide range of material attributes which stratify occupations, especially manual occupations, and indeed depreciate them.

19
The Older Worker

The older worker has not yet attracted much notice in the development of the sociology of work.[1] This is surprising, because of his significance for theories of change. On the one hand, seniority rights closely associated with age have been steadily established in industry, public administration and the professions, and a career 'structure' has come to characterize many types of work. On the other, a growing army of redundant and retired but active people of late middle age has been created partly by technological and scientific innovation and partly by the expanding educational opportunities for the young. These two trends are marked and might appear to be contradictory. How are they to be reconciled and explained? This chapter puts forward the hypothesis that they are causally related, and is based on a dual comparative perspective. Younger workers are compared with older workers and the structure of the workforce is compared at different points of time.

What is happening to the older worker can best be understood in terms of two possible developments in industrial society as a whole. One development might be described as follows. Society might become more of an 'unequal technocracy'. There may be highly paid elites of young wage-earners and salary-earners in various forms of skilled manual and non-manual employment. Except for a smallish sub-section of the middle aged, who fill key managerial, supervisory, professional and training posts, most of them and of the elderly will fall into a number of groups which are marginal to, or outside, the labour market. Thus there may be a large section of the middle aged, especially women, in unskilled service occupations with low pay and status; a large section of redundant and prematurely retired middle-aged people living on modest pensions (but also a small sub-section living on very high pensions and substantial capital gains); and a class of frail elderly people living on meagre pensions supplemented by public assistance or its

1. Compare, for example, Durkheim, E., *The Division of Labor*, The Free Press, Glencoe, 1964, with Caplow, T., *The Sociology of Work*, McGraw-Hill, New York, 1954. In Britain there has been some, though not a great deal of, documentary and empirical work, notably by F. Le Gros Clark. See, for example, Le Gros Clark, F., and Dunne, A. C., *Ageing in Industry*, Nuffield Foundation, London, 1955.

equivalent. This would be a society in which adults were more commonly split into the proficient and the redundant. The retired, the redundant and marginal workers would meet the costs of paying for the rewards and status of the proficient through relatively reduced living standards. At the same time, social and industrial order and the values of the class system would be maintained by the device of strengthening the seniority rights accorded to a proportion of the middle aged. In any case, seniority rights have rapidly improved as a means of restricting lateral mobility of the highly skilled and managerial elements in the workforce at a time of rapid industrial change, including in particular the growth of large firms.

A number of assumptions underlie this likely development. One is that *two* older generations are taking the place of the so-called third generation. A four-generation social structure is evolving, partly because of greater longevity but also because the children who are produced are borne by mothers earlier in the life-cycle.[1] There is a more noticeable division among the elderly between the active and the frail, or among those who may be separated in age by twenty or even thirty years.

Another assumption is that an increasing part of the third generation is retiring while still active. This will be discussed below. And yet another is that men who are made redundant are not only expected, in terms of pay and seniority rights, to start at the bottom again in any new employment, but increasingly have to compete for the kind of service occupations often filled by women. As a consequence, they are poorly rewarded. Redundant middle-aged men are having to compete with an increasing number of middle-aged women who have been released not only from child-rearing but, through relaxation of social norms, from strict allegiance to the role of housewife. Redundancy of middle-aged men and depression of their subsequent pay and status is, in some respects, a response offered by the market to the pressures for equal pay and access to employment on the part of women. Finally, in this form of society the majority of the third generation who are retired are assumed to draw, in relation to the earnings of younger employed adults who do not have dependants, very modest pensions. The fourth generation are assumed to draw even smaller pensions. By the time the third generation becomes the fourth generation, their incomes will also have declined, relatively to those of the employed population.

A second possible development would be for society to become more 'community orientated'. Far-reaching assumptions might be made about the reconstruction of the distribution of power, rewards or status in society. Thus, through greater public control of employment opportunities, more middle-aged and older

1. In 1962, 23 per cent of people over 65 with children in Britain, 23 per cent in Denmark and 40 per cent in the United States had great-grandchildren. See Shanas, E., *et al.*, *Old People in Three Industrial Societies*, Routledge & Kegan Paul, London, 1968, p. 141. There is good reason to suppose that these figures are increasing (ibid., pp. 168–74).

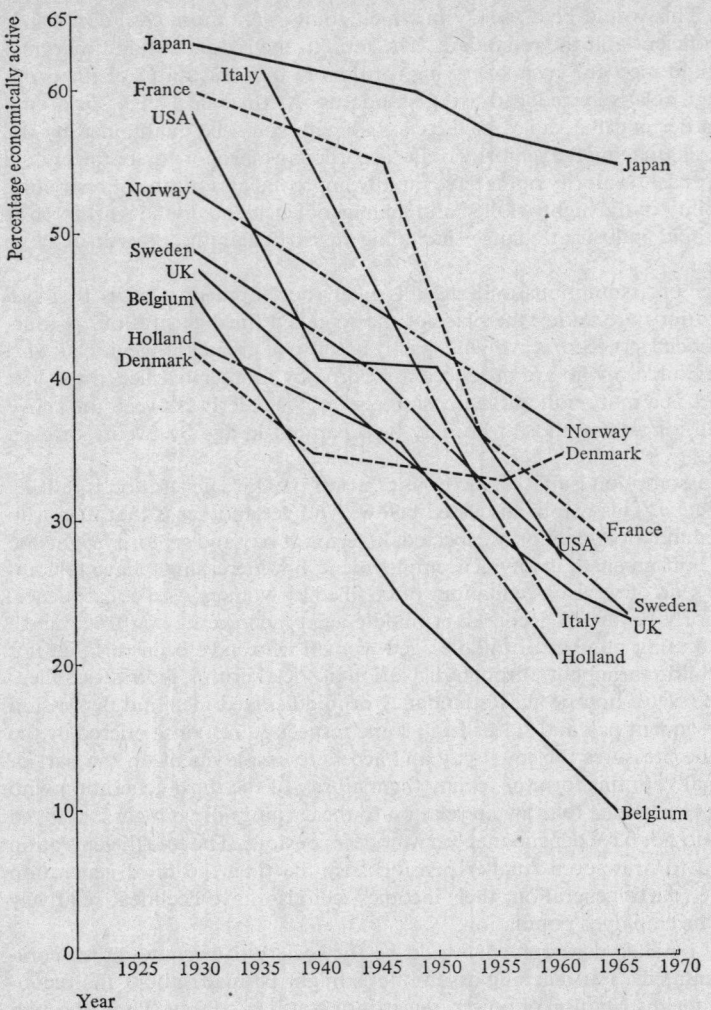

Figure 19.1. *Percentage of men aged 65 and over who are economically active.*

SOURCE: International Labour Office, *Yearbook of Labour Statistics, 1938, 1949, 1959, 1969.*

NOTE: Some of the national statistics are based on estimates made by official sources in different countries, though others are drawn from census material. Among the qualifications that need to be made about the figures on which the graph is based are the following. *Japan*: 1955,

people would be offered work and work would be organized more commonly in work teams of men and women drawn from all the adult age groups. Thus, the still active members of the third generation might increasingly move to service occupations; some of which would be of new types, which would be generated deliberately by government. These would include relatively prestigious social service occupations designed to improve the quality of community life and the environment. But a deliberate attempt would be made to 'spread' the performance of skilled and interesting work. The more disabled members of the third and fourth generations would also have opportunities of participating in an occupational programme, though this might have to be restricted in many instances to sheltered workshops, outwork, play-centres, the household and the immediate environment of the home. Finally, the resources made available to the fourth generation would be increased by special measures, such as disability supplements, rent allowances and housing maintenance services and allowances. In these ways, occupational, social and financial divisions between the young and the old could be minimized.

The extent to which reality approximates to either of these models will depend on whether or not some current trends in industry and economic and fiscal policy are checked and social as much as economic values stressed in policy.

The Increasing Trend towards Retirement

The proportion of the elderly population who are economically active has been falling rapidly, as shown in Figure 19.1. The direction of the trend is the same for all industrial societies. Although the fall has been relatively small in Japan and has ceased, temporarily at least, in Denmark, its extent has been very similar for the United States, France, Belgium, Sweden, the Netherlands, Norway, Italy and the United Kingdom.[1] From 40 to 65 per cent of men who were employed by 1930, the proportion had diminished to 10 to 38 per cent (excluding Japan) by the

---

persons only over 15 years of age; the number of economically active does not include 659,073 unemployed. *France*: 1931: estimated in part; 1954: excluding personnel stationed abroad. *United States*: 1960: based on 25 per cent sample. *Denmark*: 1955: based on 17 per cent sample of census. *Sweden*: 1965: the number of economically active excludes persons on compulsory military service, persons seeking work for the first time, and those unemployed for more than four months. *United Kingdom*: 1931: estimated in part; 1966: based on 10 per cent sample of census.

1. Part of the difference between countries is due to the adoption of different retirement or pension ages and part to the structure of the economy. The proportion of men remaining at work tends to be higher in countries with a relatively large part of the labour force engaged in agriculture. This is also related to the question of self-employment. The proportion of the self-employed who remain economically active after the age of 65 is relatively large.

1960s. During the 1960s and early 1970s, this trend continued. In the United Kingdom, for example, there was no slackening of the trend in the late 1960s. The percentage of men aged 65 to 69 last birthday who were not retired was 27 in1964 and 16 in 1971. By the late 1970s, it was officially predicted, only about 7 per cent of men in this age group would remain at work.[1]

Possible Explanations of Earlier Retirement

How is the fall in numbers remaining at work to be explained? In any comprehensive examination of this question, at least four sets of variables would have to be considered: (a) characteristics of individuals, including their age, health, education and training; (b) the different attitudes held towards work and retirement by individuals, families and other social groups; (c) internal structural factors concerned with the distribution of the workforce in relation to business enterprise and profit; and (d) external factors concerned with the social definition of the scope of paid employment, including the values held by society about work and retirement. We will illustrate these four possibilities.

The first is whether there has been any change in the characteristics of the individual elderly. Provisionally we might argue that, among the population aged 65 and over, the proportion aged 75 and over has tended to grow. This factor in itself will have contributed to the overall reduction in the percentage remaining at work. But it is only a small factor in the explanation. Thus, in the United Kingdom, those aged 75 and over formed 18 per cent of all those aged 65 and over in 1911 and 25 per cent in 1969. We might also argue that, until the introduction of pensions, men were obliged to work virtually until they dropped; now that they can retire at 65 (or some other age, such as 60 or 67), many who are no longer fully fit choose to do so. The trouble with this sort of explanation is that the fall in proportions at work is not closely correlated with the introduction of pension schemes. There are countries in which the value of the pension which is available has not changed much during a period of thirty or more years, at least in relation to earnings levels, and why the effects are taking so long to make themselves felt would have to be explained. Moreover, there is the complicating problem of disability. The time has long since passed when it was possible to argue that the introduction of pensions allowed only the disabled and those in ill-health to retire. The numbers of 'active' retired people are now quite large. This concentrates attention on whether it is structural factors within industry or the workforce,

1. DHSS, Report by the Government Actuary on the Financial Provisions of the National Superannuation and Social Insurance Bill, Cmnd 4223, HMSO, London, December 1969, p. 21. Strictly, some of those who are 'retired' are earning although receiving pensions. This explains the differences between the percentage not technically 'retired' and the percentage 'economically active' (Table 19.1) on the basis of census questions. Some are working very few hours. Between the ages of 65 and 70, a man who retires and draws a retirement pension may take paid work. Beyond certain levels of earnings, his pension has been reduced.

or social controls rather than individual characteristics or attitudes, which are shaping retirement practices. Pension ages, for example, do not appear to have been chosen on the basis of knowledge of the onset of disability. The ages chosen either by societies or the managers of occupational pension schemes do not correspond even roughly with a change in the statistical distribution of capacity or health at successive ages. But these have been treated as axiomatic in much research on retirement and the elderly and the characteristics of representative samples of the population just under the pensionable ages, for example, have attracted scant attention. For such reasons, changes in retirement practices have been 'explained' in terms of individual instead of organizational or social characteristics and values. Among samples of those of pensionable age, the non-retired have been found to include more active people than the retired and explanation has ceased. But the significant facts that some disabled people remain at work and, correspondingly, that some active people under the pensionable ages are not in the workforce, suggests that this explanation is too facile.

Much the same is true of explanations built on individuals' attitudes towards retirement. There are difficulties enough in obtaining reliable information about attitudes, but for different countries there is evidence of substantial minorities of the retired who would prefer to be at work (and sometimes vice versa).[1] The relationship between individual attitudes and retirement is complex. Attitudes change as the day of retirement approaches and recedes. Attitudes depend also on a variety of unspoken assumptions about the availability and kind of alternative employment and the social and 'occupational' as well as financial consequences of retirement, which need to be made explicit if any consistent interpretation is to be produced. And attitudes change according to the 'level' of self-revelation. People sometimes admit different things to strangers than to their intimates and to anyone else than to themselves.

Some of the structural factors internal to industry which are involved in explanations of retirement are familiar. The replacement of unskilled jobs by smaller numbers of skilled jobs, the decline and even the disappearance of certain types of industry and the reduction in the relative importance of small firms and the self-employed during the emergence of the giant corporation, have all attracted notice in accounts of unemployment and retirement. The contracting industries are those which tend to have older workforces. Research into redundancy and redeployment shows that it is the older men who are more likely to remain unemployed.[2] Periods of high unemployment would seem likely to correspond with an accelera-

1. Shanas *et al.*, *Old People in Three Industrial Societies*, pp. 320–45 and 447.

2. A study of the closing of a colliery in Durham showed that (a) the workforce contained a relatively high proportion of employees in late middle age; (b) the proportion of men still unemployed six months after closure was very high among the oldest age groups and was strikingly correlated with advancing age. See DEP, *Ryhope: A Pit Closes*, HMSO, London, 1970, pp. 11 and 67.

tion in the numbers of people of pensionable age leaving work, and correspond also with an acceleration in the numbers of people retiring earlier than the usual pensionable age. Despite the need for detailed analysis of trends, this cannot be more than a fitful part of the story, however. For example, the retirement rate increased steadily in Britain during the very low rates of unemployment in the 1950s and early 1960s. There are at least two possible effects of industrial re-organization upon the older male worker. In accordance with the decline in relative numbers of unskilled and semi-skilled in the workforce, and possibly also because of the return to the workforce of larger numbers of middle-aged women, some unskilled and semi-skilled male manual workers may find themselves forced into unemployment. Older skilled manual and non-manual workers who become redundant may be able only to obtain unskilled jobs.

This brief preliminary discussion may help to suggest lines of inquiry. Cohort analysis of the distribution by occupational status needs to be related for succes-sive points in time to the structural changes taking place in individual industries as well as the occupational system as a whole. The characteristics and attitudes of people of different age, both at work and not at work, also need to be examined and related.

Changes in Activity Rates

The trends in relation to employment below as well as above the pensionable ages will first be presented. Table 19.1 shows recent changes in the proportions of people of different age in the United Kingdom who are in paid employment. The 'economically active' are defined to include the unemployed and the short-term sick as well as those in paid employment. As already stated, the proportion of men aged 65 and over remaining at work has continued to fall steadily, but there has also been some reduction of activity rates among men in late middle age, certainly since 1961. By contrast, there was a pronounced increase in the percentages of older married and widowed women who were economically active, even of women aged 60 and over.

Since 1966, unemployment has increased and the rates in Table 19.1 conceal this change. In 1971, the monthly average was 799,000 in the United Kingdom, compared with 346,500 in 1961.[1] Proportionately more older than younger work-ers are usually unemployed for long periods. There is also evidence of a propor-tionate increase of men in late middle age who are chronic sick and who draw national insurance sickness benefit. Table 19.2 shows the change in a short span of years. To a certain extent, the classification of older men as unemployed rather than retired, or as sick rather than unemployed, is fortuitous. Government sur-veys of the unemployed have shown that a high proportion are in fact sick or

1. *Social Trends*, No. 6, HMSO, London, 1975, p. 85.

Table 19.1. *Economic activity rates, Britain, 1951–71.*

Sex	Age		Percentage of each age (or age and marital status) group economically active		
			1951	1961[a]	1971[b]
Males	20–24		94·9	93·2	90·3
	25–29		97·6	97·9	97·2
	30–34		98·3	98·7	98·2
	35–44		98·6	98·8	98·4
	45–54		97·8	98·6	97·7
	55–59		95·0	97·1	95·4
	60–64		87·7	91·0	86·6
	65–69		47·7	39·9	30·5
	70 and over		20·3	15·2	10·9
Females	20–24	single	91·1	89·5	82·1
		married	36·5	41·8	45·8
		widowed	66·8	62·7	50·5
	25–34	single	86·9	89·5	85·8
		married	24·4	29·5	38·4
		widowed	67·8	68·4	60·2
	35–44	single	81·0	85·1	85·1
		married	25·7	36·4	54·2
		widowed	63·8	71·7	70·9
	45–54	single	74·8	81·7	82·6
		married	23·7	35·3	56·8
		widowed	54·1	66·7	73·9
	55–59	single	63·9	75·1	76·4
		married	15·6	26·0	45·1
		widowed	39·1	51·8	62·2
	60–64	single	34·9	39·2	33·3
		married	7·2	12·7	24·8
		widowed	19·3	28·2	33·7
	65 and over	single	11·8	10·9	8·2
		married	2·7	3·4	6·3
		widowed	4·9	5·6	5·7

NOTES: [a]Not completely corrected for bias.
[b]Ten per cent sample.

SOURCE: *Social Trends*, No. 6, HMSO, London, 1975, p. 84.

Table 19.2. Number (thousands) of men, and percentage of each age group, drawing sickness (invalidity) benefit for more than six months.

Year	20–24	45–49	50–54	55–59	60–64	65+
Numbers						
1959	3	21	33	57	83	4
1965	2	20	34	63	115	6
1969	4	28	34	70	138	9
1973	2	26	44	65	146	15
Percentages						
1959	0·2	1·3	2·0	4·0	8·2	1·9
1965	0·1	1·4	2·1	4·0	8·6	2·7
1969	0·2	1·7	2·5	4·6	10·0	5·5
1973	0·2	1·7	2·8	4·7	10·6	5·2

SOURCES Department of Health and Social Security (private communication) and *Social Security Statistics 1974*, HMSO, London, 1975, pp. 32–3. The statistics are for dates in May or June of each year. The 1959 figures, unlike those for later years, are based on age as given six months beforehand, and are therefore slightly higher than they should be for purposes of strict comparison.

handicapped.[1] Men with chronic mental or physical handicaps sometimes refuse to acknowledge any suggestion that they are different from other men of their age and endeavour to maintain registration with the employment exchange. A large proportion of the men who draw sickness benefit for a lengthy period intend to re-enter employment. There are also disabled men who desire work and who look for work although they do not seek to be placed on the disabled persons' register at the employment exchange. Moreover, over 11,000 disabled persons classified as 'unlikely to obtain employment other than under special conditions' are excluded from the unemployment figures.[2]

The fact that the numbers drawing sickness benefit for long periods have been growing may be attributable less to a proportionate increase in the incidence of clinically verifiable chronic disease than to the classification of some redundant workers as sick instead of unemployed (or retired). To some men, the status of 'sickness' may be preferable to that of 'unemployability'. The long-term sick also have fewer difficulties than the long-term unemployed in obtaining help at all and discretionary additions from the Supplementary Benefits Commission.

The data imply that, in the United Kingdom, the proportions of men under as

1. A special survey of the unemployed by the Ministry of Labour in 1964 found that 60 per cent of the men were 'poor placing prospects on various personal grounds'. This curious terminology in fact included a large number who were disabled or had a history of ill-health. See also Sinfield, R. A., *The Long-term Unemployed*, OECD, Paris, 1968, p. 35.

2. *Employment and Productivity Gazette*, July 1971, p. 626.

well as over the pensionable ages who are economically active may continue to decrease, while the proportions of women may continue to increase. Indeed, it might be hypothesized that, because substantial reductions can no longer be made in the male labour force of pensionable age, the rate of withdrawal from the labour force of men aged 55–64 will actually rise.

What are the factors contributing to this situation? Is it that more older men are sick and disabled or that more of that proportion who have always been disabled are choosing to draw sickness benefit and avoid the stigma of unemployment? Is it that older men particularly lack the educational qualifications and occupational skills which are felt to be required in the modern labour force – in which case it would be difficult to explain the growth of women's employment, unless this is linked with the brutal fact that their labour is cheaper? Is it, more generally, that the labour force needs of the industries which are expanding can be met without recruiting older workers made redundant in the industries which are contracting? Or is it that these trends have even deeper causes, such that they make it possible, through the reduction of the relative incomes of a larger proportion of the middle aged, for class *differentials* to be preserved at a time when more young people are ascending into the upper middle class.

The Employment Record of the Older Worker

We will examine the individual characteristics of older workers and their place in the social structure, and go on to consider their industrial situation. The survey data correspond with census and Department of Employment and Productivity data, but allow the picture to be filled out in some respects. Table 19.3 shows the

Table 19.3. *Percentages of older men and women who were economically active.*

Employment status	40–54	55–64	65–74	75+
Men				
Employed	86	79	26	5
Self-employed	12	10	4	1
Not employed in year	2	11	70	94
Total	100	100	100	100
Number	506	345	217	81
Women				
Employed	58	32	11	1
Self-employed	4	4	2	–
Not employed in year	38	64	87	99
Total	100	100	100	100
Number	578	361	283	176

proportions of men and women of different ages who were employed, self-employed and not working at all during the twelve months preceding the survey. As many as 11 per cent of the men aged 55–64 did no work in the year. This includes men sick or unemployed throughout the year. The corresponding figure from the 1966 census is just under 10 per cent.

Among the economically active, fewer of the older than of the younger men experienced any unemployment in the year, for example, 6·4 per cent of men aged 55–64, compared with 10·2 per cent of employed men aged 20–29 (Table 17.3, page 601, above). The difference between older and younger men was, however, mainly in experience of very short spells of unemployment. Younger men's unemployment in the year was frequently limited to a few weeks, and similar percentages of younger and older workers had spells of more than eight weeks.

On the other hand, proportionately more of the older employed men had been off work sick, and 10 per cent had been off work sick for more than five weeks. But

Table 19.4. *Percentages of employed men of different age according to weeks of sickness in year.*

Number of weeks	20–29	30–39	40–54	55–64	65–74
None	71	70	74	67	63
1–2	19	15	12	12	14
3–5	4	8	7	12	16
6–9	3	4	4	2	4
10 or more	3	4	4	8	4
Total	100	100	100	100	100
Number	369	342	435	274	57

NOTE: Self-employed excluded.

the trends with age in absence because of sickness, as shown in Table 19.4, are less marked than might be expected. Two thirds of employed men aged 55–64, and even of men aged 65–74, had not been off work during the previous twelve months.[1]

The volume of work, as measured by the numbers of hours worked in the week is also sustained. Although fewer employed men aged 55–64 worked more than sixty hours a week, slightly fewer of them worked less than forty hours. The tendency for women of comparable age to work fewer hours and for a substantial proportion of them to work less than thirty hours a week is, however, very marked

1. Between 1954–5 and 1967–8, the average number of days of certified sickness per annum of employed men and women of different age increased, for example, of men aged 50–54 from 16·2 to 18·9 and men aged 55–59 from 25·3 to 26·9. The higher average for older than for younger employees is attributable to the more lengthy absence of a very small percentage however. See Central Statistical Office, *Social Trends*, No. 1, HMSO, London, 1970, p. 112.

Among the relatively small number of elderly people remaining at work, there is a marked increase, for both sexes, in the number working under thirty hours (Table 19.5). It also seems that, in addition to the contraction during the 1960s in numbers aged 65 and over of men remaining at work, there has also been a reduction in the proportion of them working forty or more hours a week.[1]

Table 19.5. Percentages of employed men and women in certain age groups, according to hours worked in previous weeks.

Hours	Men			Women		
	40–54	*55–64*	*65+*	*40–54*	*50–64*	*65+*
1–9	0·4	0·3	10·9	7·9	12·4	(31·2)
10–19	0·6	0·3	20·0	11·4	11·5	(15·6)
20–29	1·3	0·6	25·4	23·5	27·4	(21·8)
30–39	15·2	13·1	10·9	24·5	21·2	(15·6)
40–49	53·2	63·2	20·0	27·4	22·1	(6·2)
50–59	17·8	14·8	5·4	1·9	1·7	0
60+	11·4	6·8	7·2	3·1	3·5	(6·2)
Total	100	100	100	100	100	100
Number	455	277	55	314	113	32

Incapacity and Age

The sickness and working record of men in their fifties and early sixties seems exceptionally good in relation to the evidence we collected about physical incapacity. In the national survey, an incapacity index was developed, based on experience in a number of previous surveys.[2] This was an elaborate method devised to enable adults and children aged 10 and over to be classified carefully and as objectively as possible according to the degree to which they had difficulty in managing personal and household needs without help. Table 19.6 presents the results for the economically active and, where possible, for the economically inactive, of different age. The freedom of young men from even slight incapacity is striking. By contrast, the proportion of men with slight incapacity rises sharply with age after the age of 40. There is also a substantial minority of men in employment with some or appreciable incapacity, rising from 8 per cent (age 40–54)

1. Only about a third worked fewer than thirty hours in 1962, compared with well over half in 1968–9. Shanas *et al., Old People in Three Industrial Societies*, p. 303.

2. See Shanas *et al., Old People in Three Industrial Societies*, Chapters 2 and 3, for an account of the history and use of an index applied to the elderly. See also Sainsbury, S., *Registered as Disabled*, Bell, London, 1970. See Table 20.2, page 692 below, for the list of activities included in the index.

Table 19.6. Percentages of economically active and inactive men and women of different ages, according to degree of incapacity.

Degree of incapacity (score)		Economically active					Economically inactive					
		20–29	30–39	40–54	55–64	65–74	20–29	30–39	40–54	55–64	65–74	75+
Male												
None	0	97	94	83	65	47				(24)	24	9
Slight	1	1	3	5	14	23				(3)	21	9
	2	1	1	5	6	11				(11)	15	4
	3	1	1	2	4	7				(3)	3	11
Some	4	0	0	1	3	5				(8)	8	11
	5	0	0	1	1	2				(11)	11	7
	6	0	0	2	2	2				(3)	4	5
Appreciable	7–8	0	0	1	3	4				(8)	6	8
or severe	9+	0	0	1	3	0				(29)	8	37
Total		100	100	100	100	100				100	100	100
Number		369	342	435	274	57				37	151	76
Female												
None	0	95	89	78	57	(27)	91	91	66	42	15	5
Slight	1	2	5	9	12	(20)	3	5	8	16	17	5
	2	½	1	5	6	(20)	1	2	4	12	14	4
	3	1	1	2	2	(17)	1	0	4	4	5	8
Some	4	0	1	2	4	–	2	2	3	3	5	9
	5	1	1	2	8	(10)	1	0	4	5	7	9
	6	0	1	1	3	(3)	1	0	1	4	10	5
Appreciable	7–8	½	0	1	6	(3)	0	0	4	6	10	15
or severe	9+	0	1	0	2	(0)	0	0	4	8	17	40
Total		100	100	100	100	100	100	100	100	100	100	100
Number		257	167	336	117	30	157	154	218	231	247	174

NOTE: Self-employed not included among economically active.

to 16 per cent (age 55–64). The great majority of men aged 65–74 remaining in employment have little or no incapacity.

On the other hand, the evidence for the economically inactive is not quite as might be expected. For example, although a large proportion of the men aged 55–64 are severely incapacitated, over a third have little or no incapacity. The numbers in the sample are small, but if representative mean that nearly 15,000 men in the population with little or no incapacity are inactive. Again, proportionately more of the men aged 65–74 who are not than of those who are in the labour force are incapacitated to a marked or a severe degree; none the less 60 per cent, representing over 90,000 men in the population (with another 20,000 aged 75 and over) have little or no incapacity.

Skill, Training and Education

Incapacity is one factor which helps to explain patterns of work and retirement in late middle life and old age, but is clearly not the only one. For example, as already noted, the numbers of women aged 40–59 in employment has been rising, a considerable proportion of whom are significantly incapacitated. What part is played by other individual characteristics, such as skill, training and education?

The distribution of economically active older men and women by occupational class is shown in Table 19.7. Thirty per cent of men aged 55–64, compared with 23 per cent aged 40–54, were in occupations classified as unskilled or partly

Table 19.7. Percentages of economically active men of different age according to occupational class.

Occupational class	Men			Women	
	40–54	*55–64*	*65+*	*40–54*	*55–64*
Professional	7	5	3	3	1
Managerial	7	4	1	5	3
Supervisory – high	9	9	4	10	3
– low	16	13	10	11	13
Routine non-manual	6	7	7	11	8
Skilled manual	32	32	30	33	41
Partly skilled manual	15	18	14	18	21
Unskilled manual	8	12	30	9	9
Total	100	100	100	100	100
Number	478	305	70	336	117

skilled. Although the numbers in the survey were small, we also noted that a fifth of the unskilled among those aged 55–64 were already economically inactive and around a seventh of those in supervisory and lesser supervisory non-manual occupations. By contrast, less than a tenth of the people in skilled manual, managerial and professional occupations were economically inactive at these ages. There seems therefore to be some tendency for people in the supervisory but less well-paid non-manual jobs as well as unskilled manual jobs to retire prematurely.

The age groups differ in their educational experience. Fewer of the older than of the younger workers have had ten or more years' education. Table 19.8 shows

Table 19.8. Percentages of economically active men according to years of education.

Years of education	20–29	40–54	55–64	65+	Men of all ages
Under 5	3	4	2	3	3
6 or 7	0	1	3	4	1
8	1	4	9	31	5
9	3	54	59	46	34
10	54	15	9	11	30
11	17	10	9	1	14
12	10	4	2	1	5
13 or 14	7	4	3	0	4
15+	5	4	4	3	3
Total	100	100	100	100	100
Number	385	494	308	71	1,770

the changes in distribution for the older age groups. The table chiefly represents the changes that took place when the upper limit of compulsory schooling was raised first to 14 and then to 15.

We found that the percentage with apprenticeship training was about 10 among those still economically active over the age of 65 but varied between 15 and 20 among younger age groups. The majority of these had been apprentices for between five and seven years. Among those over 65, there was little evidence that those with longer education or any form of apprenticeship tended to remain economically active. Among people aged 55–64, those who had served apprenticeships tended not to be among the economically inactive, and this finding reflects the fact that nearly all skilled manual workers remained active at these ages, as reported above. Rather more of the economically inactive had experienced very little education, but the tendency is slight and the absolute numbers in the sample are small. In general, activity rates in late middle and old age did not offer much obvious correlation with years of education or apprenticeship training.

Among these middle-aged workers there was little evidence of retraining by employers or government. All men aged 30–64 were asked whether they had been on a trade, industrial rehabilitation or government training course of any kind in the previous five years, whether or not they had changed jobs. We found that 4·4 per cent had done so, representing rather less than 600,000 men in the country. However, over half of these had gone on a course arranged by employers, and some on courses arranged in the armed services, and by voluntary associations. Only a quarter, representing 150,000, had gone on a course arranged by the government. Most of these had gone in their thirties or early forties. The percentages by age are shown in Table 19.9. When the men who had been on

Table 19.9. *Percentages of men of different ages who had been on a training course in the previous five years.*

Training course in last 5 years	30–39	40–49	50–59	60–64
Yes	6·4	3·8	4·1	1·6
No	93·6	96·2	95·9	98·4
Total	100	100	100	100
Number	371	345	318	126

training courses were asked whether that had helped them get a better job, three quarters said it had not.

In developing a rounded picture of the relationship between general educational and specific vocational skills and the place of older men in the labour force, it will be important to investigate 'skill' in wider senses, and with specific reference to work situation. Some of the findings by Welford, for example, might be checked in relation to the allocation of roles in particular industries.[1] Reliability and steadiness of performance as well as time-keeping, and the ability to sustain heaviness of work as well as utilize experience can often afford compensation to an employer which more than off-sets diminished speed and agility with age.

Trends in Social Class by Age

Analyses of trends in social class distribution by age suggest both that each succeeding generation of young workers tend to have jobs of higher occupational status than their predecessors, but also that there is some downward mobility as well as upward mobility in later working life. It would seem that some skilled manual and non-manual workers, forced out of their present jobs, are displacing some of those who have had unskilled manual jobs, who themselves are forced into, or are accepting, premature retirement.

Table 19.10 shows the composition of the male labour force by age and social class at successive censuses between 1951 and 1971. Because there have been major changes in official classification, and our method of standardization is necessarily rough, the actual figures in the table must be treated with care. The principal trends revealed are, however, reliable enough. The proportion of partly skilled and unskilled workers declined in the 1950s and continued to decline in the 1960s, but the rate of decline was smaller. The same is broadly true for different age groups. There is a long-term trend in favour of a larger non-manual labour force, but the trend in the skilled manual labour force is more debatable. At the younger ages, there has been a remarkably swift increase in the proportion who

1. Welford, J., *Skill and Age: An Experimental Approach*, Nuffield Foundation: Oxford University Press, 1961.

Table 19.10. Percentages of men aged 25+ in five social classes in 1951, 1961 and 1971 (England/Wales), according to 1960 (and 1970) classification of occupations.

Age	Year	Professional I	Intermediate II	Skilled III	Partly skilled IV	Unskilled V
25–34	1951	2·1	7·9	54·5	26·8	8·6
	1961	5·3	12·9	55·9	18·4	7·5
	1971	7·5	18·1	53·2	15·2	6·1
35–44	1951	2·1	12·6	49·0	26·7	9·8
	1961	4·3	16·6	53·4	18·8	6·9
	1971	6·2	20·7	50·5	16·1	6·6
45–54	1951	1·9	13·1	43·5	28·5	12·9
	1961	3·3	18·8	48·5	21·1	8·2
	1971	4·8	21·3	48·8	17·9	7·3
55–59	1951	1·8	14·0	39·9	29·5	14·7
	1961	2·9	17·8	45·0	23·5	10·8
	1971	4·0	20·5	46·3	20·2	9·1
60–64	1951	1·7	13·6	38·3	30·0	16·3
	1961	2·6	17·5	42·7	24·5	12·7
	1971	3·7	18·7	45·3	21·4	10·9
65–69	1951	1·9	13·3	42·6	29·1	15·0
	1961	2·7	17·9	41·8	24·5	13·1
	1971	3·4	17·2	43·2	22·5	13·7
70+	1951	1·9	14·7	46·1	25·4	11·8
	1961	3·2	19·2	41·7	24·0	11·9
	1971	3·3	19·4	44·0	21·6	11·8
Total	1951	1·9	11·9	47·1	27·5	11·5
	1961	3·9	16·8	49·3	21·0	9·0
	1971	5·2	19·7	48·7	18·1	8·3

NOTE: An attempt has been made in this table to allow for changes of classification brought about after the introduction of the 1960 Classification of Occupations. (There were only a few further changes in the 1970 Classification and the figures from the 1961 and 1971 Censuses did not need to be adjusted before being compared.) However, for 1951 we have changed the figures for each age group by the proportion suggested for all age groups in an exercise reported in *The General Report*, General Register Office, Census 1961, Great Britain, HMSO, London, 1968, p. 193. The 1961 data were reclassified for a sample using the 1951 Classification and compared with the 1961 data classified according to the 1960 Classification of Occupations. We have worked back to the 1951 data for social classes and changed the figures for each class by the proportion suggested by the results of the exercise carried out by the GRO. The 1951 figures given above must be treated as approximate only. But they are more nearly comparable with the 1961 and 1971 Census results than the figures published in the 1951 Census reports.

SOURCES: General Register Office, Census 1951, England and Wales, *Occupation Tables*, HMSO, London, 1956; General Register Office, Census 1961, England and Wales, *Occupation Tables*, HMSO, London, 1966, Table 20; Office of Population Censuses and Surveys, Census 1971, Great Britain, *Economic Activity Tables*, Part IV, HMSO, London, 1975, Table 29.

are professional, managerial and senior administrative workers. Among older workers, the proportions in the highest two classes have also continued to rise beyond the levels reached by the corresponding cohorts ten years earlier. However, the percentage of men aged 55–64 who were unskilled manual workers in 1971 was higher than the corresponding percentage of men aged 45–54 who were such workers in 1961.

The changes among older workers are brought out in Table 19.11, which shows the increase or decrease between 1951 and 1971 in the percentage of each age

Table 19.11. *Increase or decrease in the percentage of economically active men in different social classes between 1951 and 1971 (England and Wales).*[a]

Age	I	II	III	IV	V
25–34	+5·4	+10·2	−1·3	−11·6	−2·5
35–44	+4·1	+8·1	+1·5	−10·6	−3·2
45–54	+2·9	+8·2	+5·3	−10·6	−5·6
55–59	+2·1	+6·5	+6·4	−9·3	−5·6
60–64	+2·0	+5·1	+7·0	−8·6	−5·4
65–69	+1·5	+3·9	+0·6	−4·6	−1·3
Total	+3·3	+7·8	+1·6	−9·4	−3·2

NOTE: [a]Adjustments made throughout for changes in classification, on the basis of Table 55, Census 1961, Great Britain, *General Report*, HMSO, London, 1966. The changes were assumed to apply in equal proportion to each age group.

SOURCES: General Register Office, Census 1951, England and Wales, *Occupation Tables*, HMSO, London, 1954; Census 1961, England and Wales, *Occupation Tables*, HMSO, London, 1966; Census 1961, Great Britain, *General Report*, HMSO, London, 1966; Census 1971, *Economic Activity Tables* (Ten Per Cent), Part IV, HMSO, London, 1975.

group falling into the Registrar General's five categories. As in the previous table, the data should be treated with caution, because adjustments have had to be made for changes in administrative classification between the two dates. The actual proportion of men who were in unskilled and partly skilled occupations declined – and among those in occupations in social classes I, II and III increased – for all age groups except men aged 25–34 in class III. The percentage of older workers in professional occupations increased slightly during the two decades, while the percentage of younger workers in those occupations rose strikingly.

These changes mask what has happened to different cohorts of workers as they have grown older. Table 19.12 suggests that during the 1950s there was a movement at the younger ages from manual, particularly partly skilled and unskilled, occupations into intermediate occupations, particularly certain types of senior administrative and managerial, supervisory and self-employed occupations. At older ages, the flow into administrative, supervisory and self-employed occupa-

Table 19.12. Increase or decrease in the percentage of each cohort of men of a particular age belonging to each social class (England and Wales), 1951–61 and 1961–71.

Age of cohort in 1951	1961	I	II	III	IV	V
25–34	35–44	+2·2	+8·7	−1·1	−8·0	−1·7
35–44	45–54	+1·2	+6·5	−0·5	−5·6	−1·6
45–54	55–64	+0·9	+4·5	+0·3	−4·5	−1·1
55–64	65–74	+1·1	+4·8	+2·6	−5·5	−3·0
1961	1971					
25–34	35–44	+0·9	+7·8	−5·4	−2·3	−0·9
35–44	45–54	+0·5	+4·7	−4·6	−0·9	+0·4
45–54	55–64	+0·5	+0·8	−2·7	−0·3	+1·8
55–64	65–74	+0·6	+0·6	−0·3	−1·9	+1·0

SOURCES: As for Table 19.11.

tions was smaller. During the next ten years, there continued to be upward mobility into classes I and II, though the movements at older ages was small. The class losing its percentage share now became social class III rather than IV. Older men were now also moving into social class V. There were signs of a bi-modal trend. However, these indicators of movement must be treated with reserve. There are the problems noted above of making adjustments for changes in administrative classification. And although each age group in 1951 is compared with an age group ten years older in 1961, and the same for 1961 and 1971, these are by no means exactly comparable populations. There will have been losses because of death, disability, illness, retirement, long-term unemployment and emigration, and gains because of immigration, recovery from long illness and re-entry into the workforce of some unemployed and disabled people.

In examining movements between 'skilled', 'partly skilled' and 'unskilled' occupations, it is important to keep in mind the changing realities of occupations to which these labels are attached. Some types of labourers (such as building and agricultural labourers) are today expected to display familiarity with, as well as knowledge of, a wide variety of machinery, including dumper trucks, bulldozers, cranes, combine harvesters, tractors and milking machines. It would be difficult to classify some of them as 'unskilled' according to practical criteria.

Some evidence of greater mobility in the early and the late stages than in the middle stages of working life emerged from a question we asked all those aged 30 and over: 'What was the best job you have ever had in your life?' More men aged 40–49 than either younger or older men named the same job that they currently held. Partly skilled and unskilled men in their thirties, and in their fifties and sixties, were more likely than those in their forties to name a different job of similar occupational status or a skilled manual or non-manual job. For example, 20 per cent in their thirties, and 29 per cent in their fifties and sixties, compared with 16 per cent in their forties, said the best job they had held had been a skilled manual or non-manual job. There was a similar peak in middle life for women workers, though this applied not just to the forties but throughout the fifties as well. Only about a third of both men and women in their sixties declared that their present job was their best job.

Changes in the Type of Industry and Employment

The skills that individuals can offer are not the only or even very important factors determining the employment of older workers. Industry itself has experienced profound changes in size, technology and organization, and is governed by changing values. In the ten years up to 1961, the number of women in employment rose by 12 per cent, but of men by only 4 per cent. These increases were more pronounced in many of the expanding occupations, such as the professions, technical occupations, administration and management, and clerical, typing, commercial and financial work (Table 19.13a). On the other hand, there were big decreases in the declining industries, like mining, agriculture and textiles. There

Table 19.13a. Changes in occupation, men and women, 1951–61 (England and Wales), and percentage aged 55 and over (1961).

Occupation	Numbers of men		Numbers of women		Percentage aged 55 and over (1961)	
	1961	% of 1951	1961	% of 1951	Men	Women
Total occupied population 15 and over	14,649,000	104	7,045,400	112	19·9	14·7
1. Fishermen	10,800	70	–	–	18·7	0·0
2. Agriculture, horticulture and forestry	741,400	77	70,800	73	27·3	18·7
3. Mining and quarrying	469,600	79	200	15	21·3	–
4. Workers in treatment of non-emalliferous mining products	76,600	94	40,200	87	a	a
5. Coal, gas and coke, chemical and allied trades	108,800	117	10,000	90	17·4	11·6

Table 19.13a – contd.

Occupation	Numbers of men 1961	% of 1951	Numbers of women 1961	% of 1951	Percentage aged 55 and over (1961) Men	Women
6. Engineering (manu-facturing) and allied trades	2,460,600	109	199,600	101	14·9	10·8
7. Textile workers	144,600	73	245,400	68	26·4	17·6
8. Tanners, etc.	83,600	71	65,200	100	26·4	14·7
9. Makers of textile goods	96,800	80	364,400	83	23·8	14·0
10. Food, drink and tobacco	134,800	90	65,600	78	18·8	12·5
11. Woodworkers	428,400	99	12,000	90	15·6	10·0
12. Paper-workers	200,800	124	84,400	104	15·9	10·4
13. Makers of other products	94,200	111	43,400	107	14·6	9·9
14. Building workers	838,200	100	1,000	72	18·9	36·0
15. Painters and decorators	283,000	95	9,200	88	18·6	14·3
16. Administrators and managers	525,600	129	67,600	147	22·2	23·7
17. Transport and communications	1,400,000	100	147,600	113	18·7	6·5
18. Commercial and financial	1,462,400	119	910,600	120	17·7	14·8
19. Professional and technical	1,108,000	155	674,600	129	14·0	13·3
20. Defence services	486,200	71	13,600	69	0·3	0·6
21. Entertainers and sport	77,000	94	21,800	100	a	a
22. Personal service	492,400	106	1,555,800	106	29·5	26·1
23. Clerks and typists	956,200	111	1,725,400	136	21·2	7·6
24. Warehousemen, packers, etc.	398,800	114	213,600	118	28·2	12·4
25. Crane and tractor drivers	226,000	100	1,800	91	25·0	10·8
26. Workers in unskilled occupations	1,193,600	107	437,000	115	27·4	14·8

NOTE: ªDirectly comparable figures not available. Some other percentages are not precisely comparable and are approximations.

SOURCE: General Register Office, 1961 Census, England and Wales, *General Report*, HMSO, London, 1968, Table 54; and *Occupation Tables*, HMSO, London, 1966, Table 8, p. 261.

Table 19.13b. Changes in occupation, men and women, 1966–71 (Britain), and percentage aged 55 and over.

	Number of men	1971 as % of 1966	Number of women	1971 as % of 1966	Numbers aged 55 and over		Percentage aged 55 and over	
					Men	Women	Men	Women
Total occupied population 15 and over	15,883,900	99·3	9,137,530	103·1	3,288,210	1,696,940	20·7	18·5
1. Farmers, etc.	643,040	84·7	96,770	92·2	195,320	21,530	30·4	22·2
2. Miners, etc.	256,230	68·7	520	179·3	69,460	150	27·1	28·8
3. Gas, coke workers	126,200	98·6	13,230	75·2	22,760	1,730	18·0	13·0
4. Glass, ceramics	63,810	92·3	28,860	81·8	11,950	5,160	18·7	17·9
5. Furnace, forge	159,620	80·2	8,920	73·0	32,550	1,550	20·4	17·4
6. Electrical, etc.	529,140	100·2	88,220	101·7	55,540	7,770	10·5	8·8
7. Engineering and allied	2,501,040	101·6	295,740	96·5	377,590	41,460	15·1	14·0
8. Woodworkers	415,330	91·2	12,290	95·3	77,610	1,880	18·7	15·3
9. Leatherworkers	57,190	78·7	57,160	90·0	15,430	9,940	27·0	17·4
10. Textile	143,130	88·8	166,790	68·5	30,590	43,520	21·4	26·1
11. Clothing	78,440	92·5	329,840	86·2	20,770	56,560	26·5	17·1
12. Food, drink, etc.	266,730	93·6	113,810	92·8	58,740	19,350	22·5	17·0
13. Paper and printing	219,100	98·5	95,870	84·6	39,160	13,510	17·9	14·1
14. Other products	206,090	99·5	108,700	84·4	31,470	15,630	15·2	14·4
15. Construction	551,860	93·3	1,610	83·4	121,140	380	22·0	23·6
16. Painters and decorators	279,200	89·5	8,600	80·9	62,930	1,680	22·5	19·5
17. Drivers, etc.	307,320	97·4	3,750	108·1	71,440	570	23·2	15·2
18. Labourers	1,103,630	92·3	137,180	143·9	306,540	34,240	27·8	25·0
19. Transport and communications	1,267,430	95·0	155,750	94·8	248,470	14,120	19·6	9·1
20. Warehousemen, etc.	502,900	94·2	295,410	89·9	154,650	52,280	30·8	17·7
21. Clerical	1,073,360	96·5	2,485,340	108·6	257,930	108,250	24·0	4·3
22. Sales	1,182,780	96·0	1,064,470	92·5	272,340	220,940	23·0	20·7
23. Service workers	910,770	104·9	2,037,000	95·9	281,690	594,180	31·0	29·2
24. Administrators and managers	846,310	119·4	78,110	136·6	178,240	15,000	21·0	19·2
25. Professional, technical	1,683,340	115·0	1,066,520	117·1	251,940	366,580	15·0	12·8
26. Armed forces	239,790	100·4	12,010	98·6	1,750	110	0·7	0·9

SOURCES: Census 1971, *Economic Activity Tables,* Part II; HMSO, London, 1975, Table 5; Part IV, HMSO, London, 1975, Table 35.

does, however, seem to be some evidence that in many of the declining industries the contraction of the women's labour force has been greater than of the men's labour force. Conversely, in several of the expanding industries (with the very notable exception of professional and technical occupations), the increase in the women's labour force has been greater than of the men's labour force.

Although there has been an overall decline in the number of partly skilled and unskilled workers, slowing down in the 1960s, the number has fallen dramatically in some industries, such as railways. Thus, an analysis of changes between 1961 and 1966 showed a marked reduction in numbers of porters, ticket collectors and lengthmen, for example, whereas there were during the same period increases in numbers of office cleaners, caretakers, domestic helps and ward orderlies in hospital.[1] A contraction within manufacturing industries has been accompanied by expansion in service occupations – especially within city areas.[2]

Unfortunately, because of changes in definition of occupations and the introduction of new occupations, it is difficult to trace changes continuously for all or even most occupations from 1951 to 1971, and the Registrar General has not been able to standardize and publish numerical estimates of the changes which have occurred throughout that period. Table 19.13 has therefore been divided into two parts which show trends for the first ten and last five years of the period of twenty years. Several of the totals in each part are not directly comparable with the corresponding entry in the other part. However, some trends, like the decline in textile, mining and agricultural occupations, have plainly continued throughout the 1960s. These declining occupations account for a disproportionately large number of workers, both male and female, over 55. On the other hand, some of the expanding occupations, such as services, administration and clerical work, include a substantial and fast-growing proportion of women. The proportion of female clerical workers and typists over 55 is tiny, but there are more than average proportions of women of that age in services, sales and administration (Table 19.13b). These jobs have been created with pay and conditions which have persuaded women, including older women in their fifties, to apply for them. Many, of course, are not in places where there are older men seeking work, but some are, and yet they are presented in a form which excludes such men from applying for them or where men, at least, are not expected to apply. Those who return to paid employment after many or several years' absence, nearly all of whom will be women, are unlikely to be union conscious and do not expect to receive high rates of pay. Even if indirectly more than directly, women are under-cutting

1. DEP, 'Employment Changes in Certain Less Skilled Occupations, 1961–66', *Employment and Productivity Gazette*, April 1969, pp. 308–11. See also Knight, R., 'Changes in the Occupational Structure of the Working Population', *Journal of the Royal Statistical Society*, vol. 130, Part 3, pp. 408–22.

2. Pahl, R. E., 'Poverty and the Urban System', in Chisholm, M., and Manners, G. (ed.), *Spatial Problems of the British Economy*, Cambridge University Press, 1971.

older men. There is a relationship therefore between the weakening employment position of many older male workers and both the changing occupational structure and the increasing availability of relatively cheap female labour.

During the 1970s, a much higher rate of unemployment, combined with a rate of employment of men aged 65 and over which had reached a very low level, provoked new demands for a lowering of the pensionable age. For example, backbenchers in Parliament introduced a Bill in 1976 to reduce the pensionable age of men to 60.[1] In some respects these demands can be regarded as rationalizations of what had already occurred – increasing numbers of older men had been made redundant and had found it difficult to get back into work. Earlier retirement also continued to be thought of by leading union officials and Members of Parliament as a desirable as well as an expedient objective. A lower retirement age, they believed, would reduce the numbers listed as unemployed and allow attention to be concentrated, in discussion about economic and manpower policies, on the needs of younger men. The assumptions being made by these influential figures – that the economy could not be organized with higher numbers of men and women employed; that earlier retirement is preferable to a shorter working week; that older men want to retire earlier, even when still physically active; and that it is better to dispense with older workers than, for psychological and social as well as economic reasons, to retain a balance of such workers and younger workers – could all be challenged. The problems for individuals and society of creating a considerable section of the population who are still physically active but under-employed (and perhaps under-occupied) have not been faced.

Earnings and Age

Rates of earnings help to reveal the labour market position of older workers. Median earnings tend to be highest for men in their thirties, but are almost as high for men in their forties, as Table 19.14, which is drawn from the results of three national surveys by the Department of Employment, shows. Median earnings fall for men in their fifties and fall again for men in their early and their late sixties. This applies to both manual and non-manual workers, and to skilled, partly skilled and unskilled among the manual workers.[2] But while there seems to be a marked downward drift in earnings of the majority of men at successive ages after the thirties, there is evidence of continued high earnings among the top 10

1. On 14 July 1976, Mr Gwilym Roberts, MP for Cannock, moved 'That leave be given to bring in a Bill to provide that the pensionable age of men be reduced to 60 by not later than 1 January 1985.' See Hansard, 14 July 1976, cols. 663–5.

2. In 1968 median earnings were highest for manual workers among those aged 30–39, and were £24·1 compared with £21·6 for men in their fifties and £19·6 for men in their early sixties. The peak of median earnings was reached among non-manual workers aged 40–49, and comparable weekly amounts were £31·1, £29·5 and £26·4 respectively – DEP, *New Earnings Survey*, *1968*, HMSO, London, 1970, p. 103.

Table 19.14. *Earnings (in pounds) of all men employed full time, 1968, 1970, 1975.*

Age	Lowest decile			Median			Highest decile		
	1968	1970	1975	1968	1970	1975	1968	1970	1975
15–17	5·0	6·1	16·3	7·2	8·8	23·1	10·9	13·3	34·6
18–20	9·0	10·4	23·4	13·2	15·4	35·6	21·1	24·7	54·4
21–24	13·9	16·0	33·3	19·7	22·9	47·1	28·8	33·0	67·8
25–29	16·1	18·6	38·6	23·4	27·0	55·2	34·5	29·0	79·7
30–39	17·5	19·7	40·6	25·9	29·7	60·4	40·2	45·9	91·8·
40–49	16·7	19·1	40·0	25·5	29·4	59·8	41·4	47·6	96·3
50–59	15·3	17·5	37·5	23·0	26·8	55·5	38·4	45·2	90·3
60–64	14·0	16·0	33·9	20·6	23·8	49·8	33·9	38·9	77·4
65+	10·0	12·9	26·8	17·5	20·2	44·2	30·6	34·8	73·4
All	15·5	15·8	34·1	23·6	26·3	54·3	38·1	42·8	86·5

SOURCE: Department of Employment and Productivity, *New Earnings Survey, 1968*, HMSO, London, 1970, p. 31; *Department of Employment Gazette*, January 1971, p. 48; *New Earnings Survey 1975*, HMSO, London, 1976, p. E35.

per cent or so (though some of this may be non-manual workers receiving promotion and increments and replacing high-paid manual workers, whose capacity or opportunity to get high rates of overtime pay has faded). Indeed, the earnings at the highest decile were higher in each of the three years we examine in Table 19.14 for men in their forties than in their thirties, and were only a little lower among men in their fifties. With advancing age, therefore, there is a loss of status and of earning power among a large number if not a majority of men, but a consolidation or maintenance of status and earnings among the best paid, especially non-manual workers. It is likely that, because part-time workers are excluded from these calculations, and because of the tendency of the New Earnings Survey to under-represent the low paid (see Chapter 18, pages 621–4), the disadvantages of older workers are not fully brought out here.

Our national survey allows the changes with age to be traced clearly. Among men in their forties, 42 per cent earned more than the mean, compared with 40 per cent in their thirties, 26 per cent in their twenties and only 20 per cent in their early sixties. As many as 17 per cent of men in their fifties earned less than 10 per cent of the mean, and in their early sixties 31 per cent (Table 19.15). The distribution of the actual amounts for different age groups is shown in Table A.70 (Appendix Eight, page 1047). The numbers of men in the sample aged 65 and over who were employed and for whom information about earnings was available was small, but nearly all had earnings below the mean and nearly half below 60 per cent of the mean. However, a number of these were working considerably fewer

Table 19.15. Percentages of men of different age employed full time, according to the percentage of mean earnings that their earnings represented (gross weekly earnings).

Percentage of mean gross earnings	Age					
	20–29	30–39	40–49	50–59	60–64	65+
less than 50	5	4	5	5	9	(35)
50–59	11	6	7	12	22	(10)
60–79	30	24	25	32	29	(40)
80–99	27	27	22	21	20	(5)
100–19	12	17	19	13	9	(5)
120–59	11	13	11	10	6	(5)
160–99	2	4	6	3	2	(0)
200+	1	6	6	4	3	(0)
Total	100	100	100	100	100	100
Number	319	338	322	285	107	20

than forty hours. One further exercise was to compare the mean earnings of different age groups, standardized by occupational class and number of hours employed.

In the survey we also endeavoured to find whether people who were in, or who had been in, employment, had ever experienced a big fall in earnings. The individual was left to decide what he would regard as a 'big' fall. The results are given in Table 19.16. The great majority aged 65 and over were retired. Because some of them had been retired for several years, their information may not be so reliable

Table 19.16. Percentages of men saying they had experienced a big fall in earnings.

Experience of big fall in earnings	Age				
	30–39	40–49	50–59	60–64	65–69
No	80	80	83	77	81
Yes	20	20	17	23	19
Total	100	100	100	100	100
Number	376	349	329	134	123

as that for younger workers. About a fifth of men in all age groups below the pensionable ages said they had experienced a big fall in earnings. According to this broad criterion, it does not seem that more men experienced a fall in earnings in their fifties than earlier.

Fringe Benefits and Work Conditions

The mean value of fringe benefits increases with age for both manual and non-manual employees (Table 19.17). For men in their fifties and sixties, this helps to offset the decline, relative to younger men, in their earnings. However, the fact that information was not always complete for fringe benefits, and that the value of certain benefits, such as the use of an employer's car or the provision of accommodation, were received by only a small minority of workers, should be remembered. While fringe benefits slightly redress inequalities in average earnings between younger and older workers, they reinforce the tendency among older workers for remuneration to be exceptionally unequal. Older male non-manual employees derive substantially greater benefit than do manual employees from fringe benefits, as Table 19.17 shows.

Table 19.17. Mean value of fringe benefits of non-manual and manual employees of different age, expressed as a percentage of their gross earnings.

Age	Men		Women	
	Non-manual	Manual	Non-manual	Manual
15–29	9·3	4·1	6·1	2·5
30–49	14·0	4·9	7·8	5·4
50–64	29·4	9·9	17·4	25·5
All ages	17·2	6·5	8·8	10·0
Number	355	600	197	144

NOTE: Calculations made only for employees for whom information on fringe benefits i every particular was gained.

There is little official information on cover according to age. The inquiry by the Ministry of Pensions in 1961–2 found that cover increased slightly among older male workers. Altogether 57 per cent of men were said to be covered by some kind of sick-pay arrangement. For men aged 55–63, however, the figure was 62 per cent, whereas for men aged 25–34 it was 55 per cent.[1]

Table 19.18 shows the cover for selected fringe benefits of both manual and

1. See Ministry of Pensions, Report of an Enquiry into the Incidence of Incapacity for Work, H M S O, London, 1964, p. xiii.

Table 19.18. *Percentages of non-manual and manual male employees of different age with selected fringe benefits.*

Age	Sick pay		Occupational pension		Paid holiday		Numbers[a]	
	Non-manual	Manual	Non-manual	Manual	Non-manual	Manual	Non-manual	Manual
Men								
15–29	82	41	77	34	49	14	160	337
30–39	89	49	82	41	58	23	176	200
40–49	89	46	86	49	57	25	152	192
50–59	91	62	77	61	55	30	129	173
60+	(87)	63	(79)	42	59	21	53	130
Women								
15–29	79	26	54	12	33	10	246	113
30–39	77	(38)	47	(27)	38	17	103	77
40–49	76	53	50	20	44	20	139	112
50–59	(84)	(42)	(49)	(16)	42	19	79	97
60+	(92)	(36)	(69)	(0)	(37)	12	35	51

NOTE: [a]Numbers giving information on paid holiday.

non-manual workers according to age. There is a marked difference in the proportions of manual and non-manual employees receiving sick pay and occupational pensions, and the expected growth in cover among middle-aged and older groups. The rise up to the fifties in the percentage with fringe benefits among manual workers is offset to some extent by downward occupational mobility, especially among skilled manual workers, a matter which was discussed earlier.

Conditions of work are known to vary widely, but quantifiable indices of these conditions have not been developed. In the UK survey, an experimental index of

Table 19.19. *Percentages of employed men of different age according to work conditions.*

Index of conditions at work		20–29	30–39	40–54	55–64	65–74
Very poor	0–4	4	2	3	4	(10)
Poor	5–6	10	9	10	6	(10)
Adequate	7–8	33	30	24	31	(45)
Good	9–10	53	59	63	59	(35)
Total		100	100	100	100	100
Number		227	238	280	185	20

both work conditions and work deprivation was compiled. This is discussed fully in Chapter 12 (pages 438 and 461). Table 19.19 illustrates one of these measures. There is no consistent trend with advancing age. In the context of our previous discussion, it is likely that some skilled manual workers who have high rates of pay in their thirties or forties but poor work conditions, move into partly skilled or unskilled work at lower rates of pay but more adequate work conditions in their fifties and sixties. This may offset the general tendency for lower rates of earnings to be associated with poorer conditions of work.

The Woman Worker

We have suggested that the entry or re-entry of large numbers of middle-aged women into the labour force may be making it more difficult for some men in their fifties and early sixties to retain existing status and jobs and pay, relative either to younger men or to women of comparable age with whom they are directly or indirectly competing. It is important to realize that 'competition' between the sexes is more indirect than direct. In a number of industrial contexts, there is plainly no clash of interests because of the very different nature of employment which men and women are expected to fill. But the reorganization of industry and the growth of new industries are bound to reflect the opportunities which now abound for firms to utilize relatively cheap womanpower instead of relatively expensive manpower.

The reasons for the expansion of employment of women, of course, lie in part in changing patterns of social structure, particularly earlier marriage and childbirth, smaller families, earlier completion of child-rearing and changing social norms about the roles of women. They also lie in the nature of the 'lighter' jobs made possible by scientific innovation and the service occupations increasingly made necessary by social, particularly urban, organization. Many of these jobs have long been regarded as the preserve of women, and more women are attracted into them as they expand in number.

We have seen (Table 19.1, page 659) the increase since the war in the proportions of women of different age, particularly aged 45–54, who are economically active. There have been increases among married and widowed (though not unmarried) women even at the older ages. A large proportion work part time, and few of them, unlike men, work more than fifty hours a week. A surprisingly large minority, about a fifth, of middle-aged female workers, have at least some trace of incapacity, and some of them have marked incapacity. The distribution of educational experience among the economically active is very similar to that of men. However, practically none of them (0·6 per cent among those aged 40–54, and none over this age) claimed to have had any apprenticeship training.

About the same proportions of employed women as of men, 3 per cent aged 40–

54 and 4 per cent aged 55–64, said they had been unemployed in the year, most of the latter for more than ten weeks and most of the former for under five weeks. Again, about the same proportions of women as for men, 28 per cent aged 40–54 and 29 per cent aged 55–64, had been off work sick during the year, and the spells off work were roughly comparable in duration. Fewer older than younger women had been off work sick, but they tended to be off work longer.

Married women in more than 5 million families are now in paid employment and their earnings enhance family living standards. Fewer women than men tend to be in professional, managerial and supervisory occupations in middle age, and more in skilled and partly skilled manual occupations. But even allowing for this and the smaller number of hours worked, their gross earnings are much smaller. For 1968, the Department of Employment found that the median earnings of all women working full time was £12·5, compared with £23·6 for men. In 1975, the corresponding figures were £33·4 and £54·3. In relation to the earnings of men of the same age, women's earnings among both manual and non-manual groups are higher in the twenties than they are in the thirties and forties. They begin to rise again in the fifties, and by the sixties reach, or approach (for non-manual employees) the levels reached in the early twenties (Table 19.20). In the poverty survey, the proportion of women earning more than £12 a week reached a peak in the thirties and then fell off markedly, partly because substantially more women over this age worked part-time (Table 19.5, page 663) and more of them took up, or returned to, manual employment (Table 19.7, page 665). For full-time employees, the New Earnings Survey showed relatively little variation by age among women between 20 and 64, if manual and non-manual groups are considered separately. The majority of women workers have jobs of low non-manual status or of partly skilled manual status, with few opportunities of promotion.

Even when, as in the case of many non-manual employees, they are on incremental scales, the departure of young women to raise families before they have reached the top of their wage or salary scales and the entry of middle-aged women into employment at the foot of these scales results in little observed variation by age in earnings. When more and more women have held employment for the bulk of adult life, it is likely that the lowest earners among women will be, like men, those in their fifties and sixties.

The evidence of a connection between the growth of employment for women and the pressure upon older men to retire early is at this stage tenuous. The fall in employment of older men began in the inter-war years, when the female labour force was roughly static, although, of course, there was heavy male unemployment during many of these years. But after the war, when the unemployment rate was very small, the proportion of men retiring by 65–9 increased as steadily as the proportion of women entering the labour force also increased. On the face of it, this is a paradox which requires better explanation. A much more detailed analysis of

Table 19.20. Median earnings of women of different age, expressed as a percentage of men's median earnings at that age (New Earnings Survey, 1968 and 1975).

Age	Percentage			
	Manual		Non-manual	
	1968	1975	1968	1975
21–24	55·2	64·4	72·2	78·9
25–29	51·6	59·9	62·8	69·5
30–39	45·2	56·4	52·5	57·5
40–49	46·4	57·4	52·1	53·7
50–59	49·5	59·2	58·6	59·0
60–64	51·0	63·4	65·2	68·8
65+	59·6	62·2	70·3	66·7

NOTE: Full-time employees paid for a full week.

SOURCES: Department of Employment and Productivity, *New Earnings Survey, 1968*, HMSO, London, 1970, p. 32, and *New Earnings Survey, 1975*, HMSO, London, 1976, p. E35.

trends in the labour force, industry by industry, needs to be made, particularly of patterns of employment for each sex and patterns of retirement and redundancy. All we can do is call attention to the suggestiveness of the trends and ask whether a larger number of physically active middle-aged males will be pensioned off to facilitate occupational opportunity for women?

Conclusion and Summary

This chapter has called attention to the vulnerability of the older worker, especially the man, during industrial and social change. We have traced the decline in the proportion of men over 65 remaining in paid employment and have predicted that now that the numbers have reached such low proportions, there is likely to be an acceleration in the withdrawal from the labour force of men aged 55–64. This withdrawal has so far been small, though we have brought forward data to show that it may take the form of increases in the number classified as chronic sick and unemployed as well as retired.

We have suggested that this process of withdrawal may be accelerated first by the rigidity of class and income differentials in a society in which the annual rate of recruitment to higher education and to the professional and managerial classes has increased in recent years. Thus, the national salary bill increased by 198 per cent, but the wages bill by only 106 per cent between 1955 and 1969.[1] As a per-

1. *National Income and Expenditure, 1970*, HMSO, London, 1971.

centage of all income from employment, salaries increased from 34 to 42. Yet there is no corresponding evidence in general of depreciation of salary levels relative to wages. Secondly, the withdrawal of middle-aged men from the labour force may be accelerated by the pressures from married women, particularly of middle age, to enter or re-enter employment or, rather, of employers eager to accommodate them at lower wages. We have hypothesized that the differentials in earnings between the occupational classes is being preserved by the employment of more women at rates of remuneration much below those of men, by the reduction of the proportion of men in late middle age who are employed and by the acceleration of downward mobility in middle age, through redundancies, reduction of recruitment opportunities for older men and failure to expand and create *effective* retraining facilities for men of this age.

The evidence is, however, inconclusive. Older men (i.e. aged 55–64) are vulnerable in the sense that their earnings are lower, and more of them have low earnings than men, say, in their thirties; more of them experience two or more weeks of sickness in the year, and substantially more of them have some degree of incapacity. However, despite some reduction of overtime earnings, the survey data did not show that more of them worked fewer than forty hours a week or had markedly inferior educational or apprenticeship skills. Trends in social class by age show both that each succeeding generation of younger workers tend to have jobs of higher occupational status than their predecessors, but also that there is some downward mobility as well as upward mobility in later working life. Some skilled manual and non-manual workers who are obliged to leave their jobs are displacing some unskilled workers who are forced into or are accepting premature retirement. But the proportion aged 55–64 is still small. In some of the declining industries, the contraction of the women's labour force has been greater than of the men's labour force. In several of the expanding industries, on the other hand, the increase in the female labour force has been correspondingly greater. Moreover, the increase in service occupations, particularly in city areas, has tended to expand the employment of older women with relatively low earnings, at the expense, if indirectly, of older men, who are squeezed into insecure jobs or into premature retirement. Some pensioners have been willing to accept, and employers to offer, poor rates of pay for a small number of hours, to keep within the earnings rule and not suffer any loss of benefit.

Research on a larger cross-section of the population may help to clarify the trends, for there are a number of cross-currents. On the one hand, the development of seniority rights in large organizations and the disproportionate increase of such organizations seems to be strengthening the situation and earnings of some employed men in the older age groups – even if they are becoming more dependent that previously on the firm. Thus, the mean value of fringe benefits to men in their fifties and sixties, for both manual and non-manual employees, particularly non-manual employees, is much greater than for younger men. On the other hand, redundancies from certain types of skilled job and the lagging of pay and conditions in the older industries, together with the demand for employment of women, is tending to increase the proportion of older male workers occupying low-paid and insecure jobs. These trends can amount to a major new source of inequality and of poverty in society.

20

Disabled People and the Long-term Sick

The financial and social consequences and the sheer scale of the problem of disability have been underestimated in the United Kingdom as much as in other
industrial countries. Partly this is because of the dominance of clinical and administrative criteria of disability, which have caused the disabled to be seen as a heterogeneous collection of people with different medical needs instead of a group having predominantly similar, if complex, educational, occupational, financial,
housing and social needs.[1] Partly it is because the professional organization of
welfare activities on behalf of the disabled has been ill-developed inside and outside government. This chapter will show that limited access to resources on the
part of people who are, or have become, disabled accounts for a substantial proportion of poverty. The concept of disability will be discussed and its extent measured, so that its different effects can be examined in turn.

When the survey was being planned, no comprehensive information existed and
pilot work had persuaded us that disability was closely related to poverty and that
substantial efforts had to be committed to its elucidation.[2] Fortunately that and
other work and pressures had also persuaded the government to undertake a national survey and the results of the two surveys can in some respects be compared.[3]

1. See, for example, *Handicapped Children and Their Families*, Carnegie United Kingdom
Trust, Dunfermline, 1964, esp. pp. 10–11 for the categorization of groups; or Sections VI, VII
and VIII of Farndale, J. (ed.), *Trends in Social Welfare*, Pergamon Press, Oxford, 1965.
2. At the University of Essex in the mid 1960s, two pilot studies of the disabled were undertaken by Sally Sainsbury and Michael Humphrey, and another pilot study of the mentally
handicapped by Lucianne Sawyer. A pilot study of the chronic sick by John Veit Wilson also
preceded this national survey. See Townsend, P., *The Disabled in Society*, Greater London
Association for the Disabled, London, 1967; Sainsbury, S., *Registered as Disabled*, Bell, London, 1970.
3. Harris, A. I., with Cox, E. and Smith, C. R. W., *Handicapped and Impaired in Great
Britain*, Part I, and Buckle, J. R., *Work and Housing of Impaired Persons in Great Britain*, Part
II, and Harris, A. I., Smith, C. R. W., and Head, E., *Income and Entitlement to Supplementary
Benefit of Impaired People in Great Britain*, Part III, an inquiry carried out by the social survey
division of the Office of Censuses and Surveys on behalf of the Department of Health and
Social Security and other government departments, HMSO, London, 1971, and December
1972. The inquiry was announced on 23 October 1967 by the Minister of Health and followed a

The Concept of Disability

From the start, the different meanings of disability should be recognized.[1] There are at least five concepts. First, there is anatomical, physiological or psychological abnormality or loss. In this sense, the disabled are people who have lost a limb, or part of a limb, or part of the nervous system through injury or surgery. Some are blind, or deaf or paralysed, or are physically damaged or abnormal in specific, usually observable, respects by comparison with their compatriots of like age and sex. Such loss or abnormality may have a considerable or an inconsequential effect on activity. Thus someone with discoloured skin tissue, a humped back, a phobia, or even a missing finger may perform as well as an 'ordinary' person of similar age over a vast range of activities.

Secondly, there is chronic clinical condition altering or interrupting physiological or psychological process – such as bronchitis, arthritis, tuberculosis, epilepsy, schizophrenia and manic depression. The two concepts of loss or abnormality and of chronic disease tend to merge, for just as a loss may have irreparable or unchanging effects, so long-continued disease usually has some lasting physiological or anatomical effect.[2]

Thirdly, there is functional limitation of ordinary activity, whether that activity is carried on alone or with others. It is therefore not quite coincident with a limitation of role, in the sociological sense, though, of course, it is very close to it. The simplest example is incapacity for self-care and management – such as being unable or finding it difficult to walk about, negotiate stairs and wash and dress. But by considering different reference groups, an estimate can also be made of the individual's relative incapacity for household management and performance of different general roles as husband, father or mother, neighbour or friend, as well as of any limitation of capacity to follow specific occupational roles.

A fourth meaning is pattern of behaviour which has elements of a socially deviant kind.[3] This pattern of behaviour can be determined by an impairment or pathological condition – such as a regular physical tremor or limp, or an irregularly recurring fit. Thus, activity might not necessarily be limited, or only limited, but different. But the behaviour may not be determined only or even at all by physio-

---

great deal of pressure by the Disablement Income Group and others about the desirability of a new pension scheme.

1. The following passage draws on a similar passage in the author's paper, *The Disabled in Society*, pp. 3–6.
2. See also the analysis by Nagi, S. Z., 'Some Conceptual Issues in Disability and Rehabilitation', in Sussman, M. B. (ed.), *Sociology and Rehabilitation*, American Sociological Association, Washington, D C, 1966, esp. pp. 100–3.
3. Goffman, E., *Stigma: Notes on the Management of Spoiled Identity*, Penguin Books, Harmondsworth, 1968; Freidson, E., 'Disability as Social Deviance', in Sussman (ed.), *Sociology and Rehabilitation*.

logical impairment, but by a mixture of what society expects of someone in certain situations and what the individual falls into doing. Sociologists have called attention to the concepts of the sick role and of illness behaviour.[1] Society expects the blind or the deaf or the physically handicapped to behave in certain approved or stereotyped ways. Individuals come to learn what is expected of them by nurses and doctors, and by their families and neighbours. Individuals can be motivated towards such behaviour when their physical or neurological condition does not compel it. A family or sub-culture can condition it. There are cultural differences in disability behaviour. People of different nationality or ethnic group vary in their stoicism in face of pain or impairment.[2] People may also be motivated to simulate deafness, blindness and other types of impairment. People with little or no impairment may play the disabled 'role'. Those with the same kind and even degree of impairment may see it differently. One might act up to the limit of his capacities, even at the risk of exposing his abnormality. Another might refrain from actions of which he is capable. In each case, the sociologist would explore variations in social conditions and processes for an explanation for the difference.

Finally, disability takes on the rather general meaning of a socially defined class and status. In some respects this can be 'subjective', and in others 'objective'. An individual who is 'disabled' is not just impaired, or limited, or different in his activities; he occupies a position in the social hierarchy determined by the kind of resources allowed to people like himself and a (usually) corresponding status which the disabled, when recognized as such, occupy in that particular society. By virtue of the social perception of disability, he attracts a mixture of deference, condescension, consideration and indifference. Resource or class level may not be defined very clearly or consistently, and the proportion of the population who are accorded the status of 'disabled people' may vary in different societies. There are populations which do not recognize or identify mild forms of mental handicap, schizophrenia or infirmity, for example. In working-class British society, euphemisms for certain handicaps are used. People have 'nerves' or are 'hard of hearing' or are 'a bit simple'. The technical, conclusive and often stigmatizing labels are avoided. A place is not taken in a rank of a hierarchy. This may mean that special needs may be overlooked and social resources withheld; but it may also mean that people are not set apart like lepers or treated with aloof condescension. Disability usually means inferior and not just different status.[3] Social perception is at least in part related to material conditions and opportunities. Society designs

1. See, for example, Mechanic, D., 'The Concept of Illness Behaviour', *Journal of Chronic Diseases*, vol. 15, 1962; Mechanic, D., 'Response Factors in Illness: The Study of Illness Behaviour', *Social Psychiatry*, vol. 1, August 1966.

2. See, for example, Zborowski, M., 'Cultural Components in Responses to Pain', *Journal of Social Issues*, vol. 8, 1952; Jaco, E. G. (ed.), *Patients, Physicians and Illness*, The Free Press, New York, 1958.

3. See ten Broek, J., and Matson, F. W., 'The Disabled and the Law of Welfare', *California Law Review*, vol. 54, No. 2, May 1966, p. 814.

688 POVERTY IN THE UNITED KINGDOM

buildings and methods of transport, organizes occupations and develops codes and rules which circumscribe social behaviour – and hence 'creates' disability. The status of 'disabled person' is governed loosely by general public opinion and more exactly by the rules of entitlement to social security, the definition of interest on the part of voluntary associations, employers and public services, membership of clubs and centres and the special sets of relationships with doctors, nurses and social workers.

Each of these conceptions of disability can be pursued fruitfully to achieve a fuller understanding of the phenomenon and therefore of policies of aid and service which would be effective. Each has its drawbacks. For example, the isolation and study of particular clinical conditions is necessary if advances in medical treatment and prevention are to be made, but may in the process emphasize the separateness rather than the similarity of many disabled conditions, with consequential confusion, fragmentation of effort and injustice.

Each of the conceptions can be considered subjectively as well as objectively. We might list them for convenience as conceptions of (a) 'impairment' (combining the first two, which might be regarded as merging); (b) 'functional incapacity'; (c) 'disability deviance'; and (d) 'disability status' and 'class'. The individual and the group may take a different conception, in any of these respects, from that of society as a whole, and attempts to provide independent or objective criteria may produce a different conception still. This amounts to saying that individual, collective and objective assessment of disability, or of impairment, functional incapacity, deviance and social rank may not be concordant. For example, although society may have been sufficiently influenced in the past to seek to adopt scientific measures of disability, so as to admit people to institutions, or regard them as eligible for social security or occupational and social services, these measures may now be applied in a distorted way, or may not be applied at all, or may even be replaced by more subjective criteria by hard-pressed administrators, doctors and others. At the least, there may be important variations between 'social' and objective assessments of severity of handicap.

Two Operational Definitions

Two measures which corresponded with the conceptions listed above of 'impairment' and 'functional incapacity' were developed in some detail in the survey.[1]

1. During 1966–7 there were consultations among a number of research workers engaged on studies of disability. Present at one meeting at the end of 1966, arranged by the directors of the poverty survey, were Walter Holland, who was in charge of a study of the disabled from St Thomas's Hospital, Margot Jefferys, supervising with Michael Warren a series of studies of impairment of function, particularly of the upper and lower extremities, from Bedford College, London, and Sally Sainsbury, undertaking a pilot study of the disabled in Essex, Middlesex and London. There was common agreement that the local-authority registers of the handicapped were grossly deficient and that methods had to be devised to establish the true num-

First, we asked whether each person in the household suffered from any condition which prevented him from doing things which an ordinary person of the same age might expect to do – prompting whether he or she had any trouble with chest or lungs, back or spine, joints, sight, hearing, speech, nerves, fits or blackouts, diabetes, a mental handicap or anything else, and also presenting the individual with a similar list on a card. Depending on the answer, further specific questions sought to confirm whether or not, in the informant's opinion, the condition really did have a restricting effect on activity (see page 1141). This approach allowed vague or general claims to disablement to be tested. It was comprehensive, if summary, and searching, and meant that clinical conditions were often called to our attention which might otherwise have been missed or their effects underestimated. Our objective was to find whether the individual really did claim to have one or more disabling conditions. People saying they had trouble with the chest or lungs were asked whether they became breathless or had any pain or fits of coughing when they hurried. People saying they had trouble with the back or spine or joints were asked whether they had any difficulty in moving freely and fully and using their hands. Those saying they had trouble with nerves were asked four specific questions about depression, anger, concentration and sleep. They were also asked whether they were consulting a doctor. Such supplementary questions had been found in research previously by doctors and epidemiologists to be reliable indicators of serious disabling conditions.

Table 20.1 presents the full list and shows the proportions of males and females in the sample having trouble with different bodily and mental faculties; and also, among them, those saying further that in one or more specific respects their activity was restricted. Thus 6·2 per cent said they had trouble with chest or lungs, and most of these, representing 4·7 per cent of the entire sample, also said they became breathless or had pain or fits of coughing. The incidence of trouble with chest or lungs was higher among males than females, but with back or spine, speech, fits and mental handicap was about the same among males as among females. Trouble with joints, nerves, sight, hearing and diabetes was, however, more common among females than males. The proportion of women having trouble with nerves was much higher than of men, and this applied to all age groups over the age of 20. The relative excess was maintained after supplementary questions had been put, and was also confirmed in the proportions saying they were seeing their doctors about this condition. About four fifths of the men and three quarters of the women saying they had trouble with nerves also said they were seeing a doctor about their trouble. Altogether more than a fifth of the population had trouble of one sort or another, and 12 per cent a definitely disabling condition. It

---

bers. All were experimenting with functional tests or criteria, though there was disagreement about the extent to which the same set of criteria could be applied to groups of people suffering from widely different types of disability.

should be noted that this latter figure is a slight underestimate, because people saying they had some other trouble than the items listed in Table 20.1 were not asked any specific supplementary questions and were therefore excluded from the total with a marked or specific disablement condition.

Table 20.1. Percentages of males and females with disablement condition.

Trouble with	% with condition said to give trouble			% with marked or specific restriction of activity		
	Males	Females	Males and females	Males	Females	Males and females
Chest or lungs	7·0	5·5	6·2	5·1	4·3	4·7
Back or spine	3·5	3·9	3·7	1·8	1·8	1·8
Joints	3·9	6·2	5·1	2·6[a]	3·3[a]	3·0[a]
Nerves	2·0	6·7	4·4	1·5	6·0	3·8
Sight	2·1	3·5	2·8	1·8	2·6	2·2
Hearing	2·1	3·0	2·6	1·6	2·6	2·1
Speech	0·4	0·4	0·4	0·3	0·4	0·3
Fits or blackouts	0·6	0·6	0·6	0·7	0·7	0·7
Diabetes	0·5	0·6	0·6	0·5	0·7	0·6
A mental handicap (apart from nerves)	0·5	0·4	0·5	0·5	0·4	0·5
Any other trouble	3·9	5·3	4·6	–	–	–
At least one of above	20·6	25·3	23·0	9·9	14·3	12·2
Total number	2,895	3,069	5,964	2,888	3,059	5,947

NOTE: [a]Estimated on basis of incomplete information.

Secondly, questions about a selected list of activities were designed to establish the degree to which the individual was limited in caring for himself and managing a household. This approach was based on early work with the aged,[1] and had been developed in pilot research with the disabled of all ages.[2] Irrespective of the

1. Townsend, P., *The Last Refuge*, Routledge & Kegan Paul, London, 1962, pp. 257–61 and 464–76; Shanas, E., *et al.*, *Old People in Three Industrial Societies*, Routledge & Kegan Paul, London, 1968.
2. Sainsbury, *Registered as Disabled*, pp. 26–49. This research was carried out in 1965. In 1966, a survey of disabled adults aged 16–64 was undertaken in the United States which developed both the health impairment and functional definitions of disability. Some of the results of this survey were published in 1968, but most papers on the results have been published in the period 1970–72. The two most general papers are Haber, L. D., 'Prevalence of

type of illness or disability from which people might be suffering, it was hypothesized that they could be ranked according to degree of capacity to perform ordinary activities. Thus disability itself might best be defined as inability to perform the activities, share in the relationships and play the roles which are customary for people of broadly the same age and sex in society. One problem is to distinguish what are the different activities, relationships and roles. We can group activities into those which (a) maintain personal existence, such as drinking, eating, evacuating, exercising, sleeping, hearing, washing and dressing; (b) provide the means to fulfil these personal acts, such as obtaining food, preparing meals, providing and cleaning a home; (c) are necessary to immediate family and household relationships, such as sexual, marital and parental relationships; (d) are necessary to external social relationships, at work, in the neighbourhood, travelling and as one of a crowd; and (e) are necessary to the instrumental roles performed at home and work as a member of society. Many specific activities might be listed. It is evident that some would correlate with others very closely and questions about a selected cross-section might give, for any individual, a broad approximation of his capacities as a whole. We chose to concentrate on the first two of these five groups – that is, on personal and household activities – partly because it is difficult in a national survey to provide an adequate framework of questions about relationships inside and outside the home, and also about possible as well as actual roles performed, but also because these groups of activities tend to underlie and correlate with instrumental and expressive social activities.

Table 20.2 presents the list of activities included in our index, which was produced on the basis of both previous and pilot research.[1] People were asked whether they had difficulty in carrying out any of these activities. If they had difficulty a score of 1 was registered; if they could not carry out the task at all, a score of 2 was registered. The table shows that over a quarter of the sample had difficulty with at least one item, and substantially more women than men had difficulty. In fact, the only item over which fewer women than men had difficulty was that of preparing a hot meal.

While this is not the place for a full discussion of the index adopted, its limitations, and also some of its principal advantages, should be mentioned. Only a selected cross-section of activities are included; difficulty with each activity is given

Disability among Non-Institutionalised Adults under Age 65: 1966 Survey of Disabled Adults', *Research and Statistics Notes*, US Department of Health, Education and Welfare, Social Security Administration, Office of Research and Statistics, 20 February 1968; and Allan, K. H., and Cinsky, M. E., 'General Characteristics of the Disabled Population', *Social Security Survey of the Disabled: 1966*, Report No. 19, US Department of Health, Education and Welfare, Office of Research and Statistics, July 1972.

1. The items were chosen from a list of sixty-four examined in a pilot study. Subjective reports on whether difficulty was experienced with particular activities were found to correlate significantly with the time taken by individuals in performing those activities. See Sainsbury, S., *Measuring Disability*, Bell, London, 1974.

Table 20.2. *Percentages of males and females who have difficulty with certain activities.*

Activity	Percentage who have difficulty or cannot perform activity			Total number		
	Males	Females	Males and females	Males	Females	Males and females
Washing down (whether in bath or not)[a]	3·2	5·3	4·3	2,315	2,535	4,850
Removing a jug, say, from an overhead shelf[a]	4·5	8·9	6·8	2,313	2,532	4,845
Tying a good knot in string[a]	2·4	4·3	3·4	2,311	2,532	4,843
Cutting toenails[a]	4·8	8·4	6·7	2,313	2,531	4,844
Running to catch a bus[b]	19·5	27·3	23·6	2,313	2,524	4,837
Going up and downstairs[b]	9·0	14·2	11·7	2,312	2,524	4,836
Going shopping and carrying a full basket of shopping in each hand[b]	11·3	22·4	17·1	2,304	2,521	4,825
Doing heavy housework, like washing floors and cleaning windows[c]	12·0	19·2	15·8	2,047	2,276	4,323
Preparing a hot meal[c]	4·0	3·4	3·7	2,048	2,277	4,325
At least one of above	21·6	32·1	27·1	2,264	2,485	4,749

NOTES: [a]Excludes children in sample under 10 (numbering 1,065).
[b]Excludes children under 10 and bedfast.
[c]Excludes children under 16 and bedfast.

equal weighting; and changes in individual capacity from day to day or season to to season are ignored. These are just three limitations. A more comprehensive approach would have to include a greater number of activities and weight some activities more heavily for some sections of the population than for others, not just by sex and age, but according to variations in pattern of activity among different classes, communities and ethnic groups. Although people were rated according to present abilities (in the case of the short-term sick, immediately before their sickness), we did ask about variations in disability, and these are discussed below.

The advantages also need to be recognized. The social conception and assessment of disability has had an erratic history. Some kinds of disability have been treated indifferently or stigmatized, while others, like blindness, have attracted wide public sympathy. Both medicine and social service have been susceptible to fashion and fragmentation. Just as there have been consultants for particular diseases and hospitals for particular parts of the body, so there have been a wide variety of statutory and voluntary organizations for different types of handicap, some of them far better staffed and financed than others. As a consequence, local authorities compiled registers of the handicapped which were not only incomplete but were divided quixotically into registers for the blind, deaf, and a general register for the physically handicapped. In social security those disabled in war were, and are, favoured by comparison with those disabled in industry and civil life. Yet, in recent years, society has begun to evolve a more unified conception of disability. Thus, an attendance allowance has been introduced for all severely disabled people and not just for war and industrial injury pensioners, even if it is paid at only two rates, a higher and a lower rate, compared with three rates paid under the industrial injuries disablement scheme and four rates under the war pensions scheme. The Chronically Sick and Disabled Persons Act 1970 has encouraged local authorities to adopt a more comprehensive approach to registration.[1] And the reorganization of local social services departments, following legislation also passed in 1970, together with a more general course of basic training of social workers, has helped to integrate methods of help.

The Need for a New Approach to Assessment

There is, then, an important relationship between society's conception of a problem, and the policies which are followed in relation to that problem. Yet the assessment, or operational definition, of disability is still not subjected to the critical attention is deserves. We are imprisoned within outdated conceptions, and are even unimaginative about alternative forms of assessment. Consider various methods of assessment in Britain. In the mid 1960s the McCorquodale Committee on the Assessment of Disablement reiterated the principle that assessment should be determined by 'means of a comparison between the condition of the disabled person and that of a normal healthy person of the same age', and they recognized that this involved measures of loss of faculty but made no efforts to collect information about either the disabled or 'normal healthy people'. Nor did the

1. But that legislation was, in the end, drawn up ambiguously and delayed and even softened in implementation. See Jaehnig, W., 'Seeking Out the Disabled', in Jones, K. (ed.), *The Yearbook of Social Policy in Britain, 1972*, Routledge & Kegan Paul, London, 1973.

committee review the rationale of current medical assessment. They gave attention to problems which only affected a small minority of the disabled – such as amputations and loss of limb or eye – and even for these problems did not provide any empirical or even reasoned substantiation for percentage assessments. The committee accepted, for example, the loss of both four fingers and of a leg below the knee as equivalent to 50 per cent disability. The following were each treated as equivalent of 30 per cent disability: the loss of three fingers; the amputation of 'one foot resulting in end-bearing stump'; the amputation 'through one foot proximal to the metatarso-phalangeal joint'; and the loss of vision in one eye.[1] Most informed observers agree that this approach is inappropriate for many kinds of disability and has no bearing on questions of severity of disablement or restriction of function.

A second example of administrative assessment is the Department of Employment's Register of Disabled Persons. To qualify, a person must

(i) be substantially handicapped on account of injury, disease (including a physical or mental condition arising from imperfect development of any organ), or congenital deformity, in obtaining or keeping employment or work on his own account otherwise suited to his age, qualification and experience; the disablement being likely to last for 12 months or more; (ii) desire to engage in some form of remunerative employment or work . . . and have a reasonable prospect of obtaining and keeping such employment or work.[2]

No detailed criteria for 'substantially handicapped', 'handicapped in obtaining or keeping employment', 'desire' for work, 'reasonable prospect' of obtaining work and even what is 'suited' to age, qualification and experience have been spelt out and related to empirical evidence by the Department of Employment or independent workers.[3] Society therefore has no clear idea of the numbers of people who deserve, and are getting, help.

A third example is the attendance allowance, introduced in 1971. At the higher rate, the allowance is paid to someone who

is so severely disabled physically or mentally that he requires from another person, in connection with his bodily functions, frequent attention throughout the day and prolonged or repeated attention during the night; or . . . is so severely disabled physically or mentally that he requires continual supervision from another person in order to avoid substantial danger to himself or others.[4]

1. Report of the Committee on the Assessment of Disablement (The McCorquodale Report), Cmnd 2847, H M S O, London, December 1965.
2. Disabled Persons (Employment) Act 1944.
3. The Department of Employment did not seek to fill these gaps during its 'comprehensive review' of its policies and services for helping disabled people to obtain and keep suitable employment. See The Quota Scheme for Disabled People, Consultative Document, 1973.
4. Section 4, National Insurance (Old Persons' and Widows' Pensions and Attendance Allowance) Act, 1970.

An Attendance Allowance Board was set up to advise the government on procedures and administration. A medical report has to be completed for every applicant, detailing whether he or she can without help or only with help

(i) change position whilst in bed; (ii) get out of bed; (iii) walk; (iv) use stairs; (v) dress and undress; (vi) wash; (vii) bathe; (viii) shave (men); (ix) eat; (x) drink; (xi) go to the toilet.

Other questions ask about the frequency of help at night and in the day. A modified list is applied to children. This approach represented an important innovation in that it paved the way for the identification of disability according to a set of functional criteria and allowed the classification of the disabled into groups with different degrees of incapacity.

The argument for identification according to functional criteria were also accepted in a national survey mounted in 1968–9 by the government. People were classified into eight categories of handicap in terms of their ability to undertake such activities as feed themselves, change position in bed, get to and use a W C, put on shoes and socks or stockings and do up buttons and zips.[1]

These developments have two principal advantages. Attention is called to the wide range of different effects of disability, with the possibility that social resources will be mobilized less erratically to deal with them or offset them. And although the risks of misclassification must be considerable, degrees of disability are more accurately identified, so that fairer methods of compensation are devised, and benefits and services can be allocated according to some scale of priorities.

The Disabled Population

The number of disabled in the United Kingdom is larger than believed by the government. The poverty survey produces estimates which, even allowing for differences of definition, are considerably larger than estimates for the same year accepted by the government on the basis of one of its own surveys.[2] In view of its importance, this finding must be explained in detail and with care.

First, Table 20.3 shows that 12·2 per cent of the non-institutionalized population both said they had a disablement condition and went on to specify that it prevented them doing things which were normal for someone of the same age. They represented over 6½ million in the United Kingdom, of whom nearly 1½ million had two or more disablement conditions. More women than men had such conditions. It is, of course, important to remember throughout the subsequent analysis

1. Harris *et al.*, op. cit., esp. Appendix D.
2. The estimates were made on the basis of a statement of policy in 1974. Social Security Act 1973, *Social Security Provision for Chronically Sick and Disabled People,* House of Commons Paper 276. 1974.

Table 20.3. Estimated number and percentage having disablement conditions restricting activity and specifying limiting effects on activities (United Kingdom).

Number of disablement conditions	Estimated number in non-institutionalized population (1,000s)[a]		Percentage			
	Males	Females	Males	Females	Males	Males and females
None	23,800	23,950	47,750	90·0	85·7	87·8
1 or more	(2,650)	(4,000)	(6,650)	(9·9)	(14·3)	(12·2)
1	2,080	3,100	5,180	7·8	11·1	9·5
2 or more	570	900	1,470	2·1	3·2	2·7
Total	26,450	27,950	54,400	100	100	100
Number in sample	–	–	–	2,888	3,079	5,967

NOTE: [a]Excluding persons residing in hospitals, residential hostels and homes, children's homes and prisons.

that disabled people living in most types of non-private households, especially those living in hospitals and residential homes or hostels, are not included. Many of these are elderly, and national estimates have been made of the distribution by incapacity of elderly people in institutions.[1]

Secondly, the findings from applying the incapacity index are given in Table 20.4. The estimates for each specific score on the index must, of course, be treated with caution because they are subject to considerable sampling error. But when different categories are grouped together, the estimates may be treated as reliable to a high degree of probability. There are approximately 1,100,000 persons who are severely incapacitated (with a score of 11 and over), and nearly another 2 million who are appreciably incapacitated (with a score from 7 to 10 inclusive). It will be seen that nearly 12 million in the population who are aged 10 and over call attention to some incapacity, however slight. Yet some of them did not specify any disablement condition in answering the alternative series of questions. If the numbers of these people, shown in the table, are deducted, the total who are severely incapacitated (with a score of 11 or more) and appreciably incapacitated (with a score of 7–10) is reduced from approximately 3,095,000 to 1,935,000. Even this lat-

1. For the elderly in psychiatric and non-psychiatric hospitals and residential homes, see Townsend, P., 'The Needs of the Elderly and the Planning of Hospitals', in Canvin, R. W., and Pearson, N. G. (eds.), The Needs of the Elderly for Health and Welfare Services, University of Exeter, 1973. For the elderly in residential homes, see Carstairs, V., and Morrison, M., The Elderly in Residential Care, Report of a Survey of Homes and their Residents, Scottish Health Service Studies No. 19, Scottish Home and Health Department, Edinburgh, 1972.

Table 20.4. Percentages and numbers of people (aged 10 and over) with different degrees of incapacity.

Incapacity score		Percentage			Estimated number (000s) UK			Estimated number (000s) specifying effects of disablement condition		
		Males	Females	Males and females	Males	Females	Males and females	Males	Females	Males and females
0	Slight	79·1	69·0	73·8	17,160	16,180	33,340	725	950	1,675
1		5·8	7·3	6·6	1,250	1,720	2,970	205	405	610
2		3·4	4·6	4·1	740	1,090	1,830	225	380	605
3		2·0	2·6	2·3	440	600	1,040	120	195	315
4	Some	2·0	2·4	2·2	430	560	990	250	205	455
5		1·7	3·2	2·5	375	740	1,115	240	450	690
6		1·2	2·2	1·7	265	500	770	160	205	365
7		1·2	1·9	1·5	255	440	695	165	220	385
8	Appreciable	0·5	1·4	1·0	120	335	455	105	165	270
9		0·6	1·5	1·1	135	340	475	85	205	290
10		0·6	1·0	0·8	130	235	365	105	110	215
11		0·6	0·9	0·8	135	205	340	130	150	280
12		0·1	0·7	0·4	30	160	190	30	130	160
13		0·1	0·4	0·3	30	100	130	10	55	65
14	Severe and very severe	0·3	0·2	0·3	65	55	120	20	45	65
15		0·3	0·3	0·3	55	65	120	25	65	90
16		0·1	0·3	0·2	20	65	85	10	35	45
17		0·1	0·1	0·1	30	20	50	10	20	30
18		0·2	0·2	0·2	35	35	70	30	10	40
Total		100	100	100	21,700	23,450	45,150	2,650	4,000	6,650
Number		2,373	2,603	4,976	-	-	-	-	-	-

NOTE: Estimates of population are rounded to the nearest 5,000.

Table 20.5. *Thousands in the United Kingdom who are estimated to be handicapped.*

Degree of handicap	Government survey	Degree of incapacity (and whether disablement condition(s) specified separately as limiting activities)			Poverty survey
		Score			
Very severe	161	Very severe	(15+)	(i) 1 or more disablement conditions	205
				(ii) No condition specified	120
Severe (score 12 or over)	366	Severe	(11–14)	(i) 1 or more disablement conditions	570
				(ii) No condition specified	210
Appreciable (score 6–11)	633	Appreciable	(7–10)	(i) 1 or more disablement conditions	1,160
				(ii) No condition specified	830
Minor (score 1–5)	699	Some	(3–6)	(i) 1 or more disablement conditions	1,825
				(ii) No condition specified	2,090
No handicap (score 0) non-motor disorders	757	Little or none	(0–2)	(i) 1 or more disablement conditions	2,890[a]
motor disorders	540				
Total	3,155			Total	9,900

NOTE: [a]This figure includes approximately 180,000 children aged 0–9.

ter figure is substantially in excess of the figure estimated in the government survey, which, for purposes of broad comparison, is approximately 1,160,000.[1] The discrepancy has serious implications and therefore requires discussion.

Some of the key figures derived from the two surveys are brought together in Table 20.5. Although the difference between the two is largest among the groups who are least disabled, it is still considerable among the very severely, severely and

1. Harris *et al.*, op. cit., p. 17, adding an estimate for Northern Ireland.

appreciably handicapped or incapacitated, and remains considerable even when those not in fact both specifying a disablement condition and saying it limits their activities are subtracted from the estimates derived from the poverty survey.

Why Official Estimates of Handicapped are Low

Why are the government survey estimates relatively low? First, children under 16 are not included in them. Children under 10 were not included in the attempts in the poverty survey to assess degree of incapacity and are not therefore included in the poverty survey estimates. But those with a disablement condition, estimated at approximately 180,000, are included, as has been noted. Children aged 10–15, assessed for both incapacity and disablement, are included with adults. They account for only about 100,000 of the total of 9,900,000.

Secondly, the authors admit that some people with impairment are not included.

While the total sample will reflect the incidence of locomotive impairment, whether this impairment is a handicap or not, it only covers those who are handicapped due to mental or sensory impairments. A man who is totally deaf, or blind or mentally impaired, would not be included unless he feels his impairment limits in some way his getting about, working, or taking care of himself, or he also has some physical impairment. The same conditions apply to disorders such as diabetes or epilepsy.

It is later suggested that groups including the blind 'may well be understated', either because people may not consider the impairment to be a handicap or unwilling to admit to their condition.[1] This seems *prima facie* unlikely in the case of the blind, and although the government's survey widens the category to include diseases of the eye and partial blindness, the estimates fall short even of the numbers of blind and partially sighted on the registers of local authorities at the end of 1968. In other instances, the numbers estimated in the government survey seem astonishingly small. For example, 27,000 were estimated to be mentally handicapped, yet in 1968 there were 111,000 mentally handicapped people under the care of the local authorities in Britain alone,[2] and it is known that there are many handicapped people not in contact with the local authorities. An estimate of 252,000 was derived from the poverty survey. Again, 72,000 were found to be suffering from mental illness and nervousness, and although there are no comprehensive statistics of people with mental illness in the community, there were, in 1968, 91,000 in the care of the local authorities and 247,000 *new* outpatients as well as 19,000 new day patients who attended hospital.[3] Yet again, the government survey found 30,000 with diabetes, 41,700 with epilepsy, migraine and dizziness, and 1,187,000 with diseases of the bones and organs of movement (including arthritis,

1. Harris, *et al.*, op. cit., pp. 3–4, and 9.
2. *Social Trends, 1971*, H M S O, London, p. 105.   3. ibid., p. 105.

osteoarthritis and rheumatoid arthritis), while the roughly comparable estimates in the poverty survey – all of them specifically referred to in the questionnaire as conditions affecting activity – were 315,000, 350,000 and 4,670,000 respectively. Even allowing for substantial numbers included in the latter whose degree of handicap may have been mild, the figures from the government survey seem worryingly small.

Thirdly, the definition of degrees of handicap may be a little severe in the government survey but cannot account for much of the discrepancy. The list of activities about which questions are asked is admittedly different from that used in the poverty survey. The chief difference is that the latter includes items which refer to the running of the home as well as to self-care,[1] but the approach is similar in principle and a number of the questions are the same or very similar (involving mobility, control of the body and manual dexterity). In broadly relating the two sets of estimates in Table 20.5, I have tried to allow for the heavier scoring of items in the government's survey,[2] but also for the inclusion of more 'difficult' housekeeping items in the poverty survey. Thus scores of up to 2 in the incapacity index used in the latter have been discounted. It is likely, however, that a substantial proportion of the final two categories ('some' and 'little or no' incapacity) should be discounted in roughly comparing the two sets of estimates.

Finally, and perhaps most importantly, the methods adopted in the government survey seems to have led to underestimation of the handicapped. A large sample of 100,000 households were screened by post. It is possible that a substantial proportion of the handicapped, including some who were severely handicapped, were missed in the survey. Some may have been missed through failure to respond to letters, though personally I do not believe this to be an important factor; some may have been missed because of the design of the postal questionnaire; but probably most were missed because of the lack of skilled probing that can be carried out in interviewing, particularly when two or more methods rather than a single method of approach are employed. Response to the postal questionnaire was 85·6 per cent, and although there was no reason, from a scrutiny of the types of response day by day, to believe the impaired were more likely than the non-

1. The authors of the government survey justify the restriction to self-care because, although 'there may be other ways of classifying degrees of handicap taking into account other factors such as the effect of impairment on work and housekeeping ... the only function which applies to the whole sample is self-care.' – Harris et al., op. cit., p. 257. It might be objected, however, that among the items listed shaving is certainly not undertaken by all men, and it would not usually be regarded as equivalent in difficulty to 'combing and brushing hair', which was asked of all women. Putting on shoes and stockings clearly depends also on type of shoes and stockings, and buttons and zips are not necessary, even if common, aspects of dress.

2. Difficulty in doing certain items was scored 2 and other items 4, compared with 1 in the poverty survey; and inability to undertake the activity without help was scored either 3 or 6 compared with 2. The criteria by which 'minor' activities were distinguished from 'major' activities and thus counted 3 rather than 6 were not satisfactorily defined. See Harris et al., op. cit., pp. 258–61.

impaired either to reply or not to reply, it is, of course, possible that relatively more impaired people, especially living alone, were among the non-respondents. At the subsequent interviewing stage about 89 per cent of eligible informants were seen, so the final response from the two-stage approach can be said to represent around 76 per cent of the impaired[1].

The postal questionnaire and covering letter had to be designed to maximize response, and therefore both had to be simply expressed. The opening sentence of the letter states, 'The Government Social Survey is anxious to find out whether people aged 16 or over, including the elderly, can get about and look after themselves, whether they have difficulty, but manage on their own, or whether they have or might need help.' This seems very straightforward and comprehensible, but it is arguable that a direct reference to handicap from the start might have conveyed the objects of the survey more clearly to more people; thus: 'The Government Social Survey is anxious to find out exactly how many in the population have minor, appreciable or severe handicap of any kind.' The one-page postal questionnaire is addressed to the whole household, and it might have been better if there had been a questionnaire for each person, or alternatively, a column for *each* person against the questions on that page so that the chances of omission could have been reduced.[2] The questions, moreover, are not in the form elaborated in the questionnaire at interviewing stage (there is, for example, no reference to getting to and using the WC, and the reference in the postal questionnaire to 'kneeling and bending' does not re-emerge in the interviewing). The first question in a series affecting handicap asks, 'Has anyone lost the whole or part of an arm, leg, hand or foot by having an amputation, or accident, or at birth?' This might predispose some respondents into believing that the other questions were aimed entirely or mainly at people with handicap of this observable kind. The question is, too, the only one which is not wholly related to limitation of activity. Thus, someone with an amputated finger might say he had no restriction as compared

1. Harris *et al.*, op. cit., pp. 240–42.
2. In these respects, the survey of disability carried out in 1966 in the United States was more satisfactory. The Bureau of the Census had adopted a two-stage postal and interviewing approach and the Government Social Survey followed suit (though no reference is made anywhere in the report to this corresponding work in the US). The covering letter sent out in the US was more directly addressed to both 'healthy' and 'impaired' households. Thus it began, 'The Bureau of the Census has been asked by the US Department of Health, Education and Welfare to collect information on the extent to which health problems may affect the normal, day-to-day activities of individuals. The results of this survey will be of great importance to both public and private organizations engaged in planning and research in the area of health . . .' Entries had to be made in separate columns *for every individual in the household* and simple Yes/No answers had to be ticked: 'Does your health limit the *kind* of work you can do? Does your health limit the *amount* of work you can do? Does your health keep you from working altogether? (For women) Does your health limit the amount or kind of housework you can do?' Then people were asked to describe the condition causing any limitation and a check-list of possible conditions was printed on the back of the questionnaire.

with someone else of his age. And the possibilities of turning the question into a short-list of questions of a kind like our disablement conditions index (or giving a check-list as in the US study), are not developed. Our evidence shows that some people who are in fact functionally handicapped may be missed by a selected list of questions about activities, as presented in the government's postal questionnaire. In using a more comprehensive list in the poverty survey (shown in Table 20.2), 4·2 per cent of the sample aged 10 and over, representing 1,863,000 people, said they had no difficulty with any of the ten items, but declared at another stage of the interview that they had a disablement condition which prevented them from doing all the things which it was normal for people of their age to do.

But even those who might respond positively to a list of questions about functional activities in an interview do not all do so if they are approached by post or if the postal questionnaire is not comprehensive. This seems to be the chief explanation for the government shortfall. Of the 100,000 addresses originally approached in order to assemble a sub-sample of the disabled, rather less than 98,000 proved to be eligible. Of these, 82,516 responded and a sub-sample of 13,541 (16·4 per cent) seemed to include at least one impaired person. My belief is that among the 68,975 households *not* approached for an interview, there were bound to be a substantial number of impaired persons. Indeed, even within the 16·4 per cent of households followed up for interview there were '100 persons, found at the interviewing stage, who had been permanently impaired at the time of the postal survey but who had been omitted from the postal form'.[1] Without following up a sample of the respondents who returned questionnaires saying they were not impaired, it was wrong to conclude that the postal survey had successfullly screened out nearly all the impaired.[2] During an interview, questions about impairment can be probed and check-lists can be scrutinized and explained. Interviewers can explain wording to informants. The poverty survey demonstrates both the value of the interviewing of a full random sample and a 'double-banking' method of approach to ensure that the numbers of disabled are not underestimated.

There is independent evidence supporting the conclusion that the figures from

1. Harris *et al.*, op. cit., p. 242.
2. The decision to screen postally was based partly on the pilot experience of the Bedford College research team. But that experience was extraordinarily slender as the basis for a major decision on a national survey. Thus, only 31 households among 335 responding to a postal questionnaire but saying none of their members were impaired were visited in pilot research, as a check. Three of these refused an interview. In each of the remaining 28 only one member of the household was tested, and yet three impaired people were found. Although it may seem absurd to estimate on such a slender basis, even that experience would suggest that at least 10 per cent of households completing a postal form about impairment negatively in fact include at least one impaired person. Applied to the estimates given above, about 7,000 (i.e. 10 per cent of the 68,975 saying no one was impaired) might therefore be added (or over 50 per cent) to the 13,541 impaired in the sub-sample. See Jefferys, M., Millard, J. B., Hyman, M., and Warren, M. D., 'A Set of Tests for Measuring Motor Impairment in Prevalence Studies', *Journal of Chronic Diseases*, vol. 22, 1969, pp. 303–19

the government survey are likely to be underestimates. In a national study of people aged 65 and over, the numbers found to be very severely or severely incapacitated and appreciably incapacitated were approximately 580,000 and 950,000 respectively,[1] compared with 337,000 and 378,000 respectively in the government's national survey of the handicapped. The sampling and interviewing in the study of the elderly were carried out by the Government Social Survey. Another study of the elderly in 1965–6 by the Government Social Survey produced estimates of proportions of people in different areas having difficulty with a variety of functions (getting out of doors on own, getting up or down stairs on own, getting about house on own, getting in and out of bed on own, washing, bathing and dressing) which corresponded so closely with the national figures obtained in 1962 survey that it is difficult to believe that the latter were seriously wrong.[2] These two studies correspond with the results of the poverty survey rather than those from the government's survey of handicap.

More recent national data also throw doubt on the government's estimates of the disabled population. The introductory report of the General Household Survey pointed out that 20 per cent of persons aged 15 and over had some limiting longstanding illness, compared with only 8 per cent in the 1968–9 survey of the handicapped and impaired who had any specific impairment, or had problems with specific activities, or had some other permanent disability which stopped or limited their working or getting about or taking care of themselves.[3] While different definitions were used in these two surveys, this large discrepancy could not be satisfactorily explained, For 1972, a total of 12·1 per cent of the population of all ages in households covered by the General Household Survey were said *both* (a) to suffer from a long-standing illness, disability or informity, and (b) to be limited in their activities as a consequence compared with most people of their own age.[4] This formulation is close in principle to the two-stage formulation adopted in the poverty survey described above, and the results similar. A total of 12·2 per cent in the poverty survey (Table 20.1) were found to have a disablement condition. The General Household Survey data for different age groups also correspond closely with the poverty survey, as shown in Figure 20.1.

1. Townsend, P., and Wedderburn, D., *The Aged in the Welfare State*, Bell, London, 1965, p. 25. An estimate has been added for both Northern Ireland and the increase in the population aged 65 and over between 1962 and 1968.

2. Compare, for example, Harris, A. I., assisted by Clausen, R., *Social Welfare for the Elderly: A Study of Thirteen Local Authority Areas in England, Wales and Scotland*, vol. I, H M S O, London, 1968, Table 19, p. 84, with Townsend, P., 'The Needs of the Elderly and the Planning of Hospitals', Table 3, which gives a more elaborate account of the proportions of people of different age in both stages of the 1962 survey who had difficulty in performing certain activities.

3. Office of Population Censuses and Surveys, Social Survey Division, *The General Household Survey*, Introductory Report, H M S O, London, 1973, p. 270.

4. Office of Population Censuses and Surveys, Social Survey Division, *The General Household Survey, 1972*, H M S O, London, 1975, p. 190.

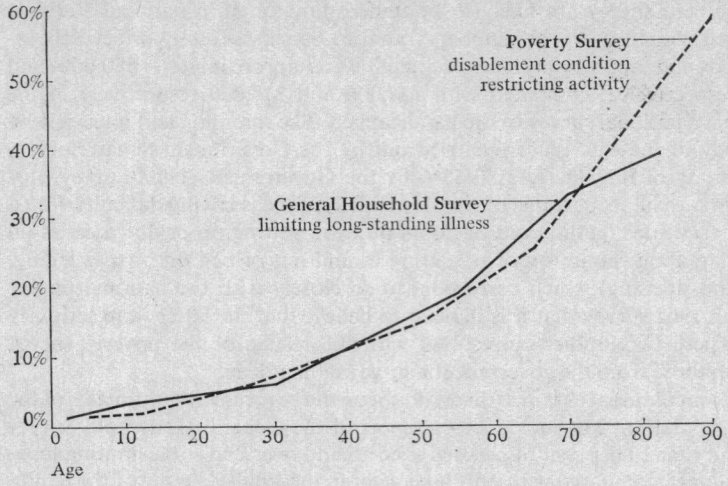

Figure 20.1. *Two measures of limiting disablement.*
SOURCE: *General Household Survey, 1972*, HMSO, London, p. 190.

Localized surveys of younger adults have also produced much higher rates of prevalence. A research team working in North Lambeth in 1966 and 1967 found that 7·2 per cent of men and 9·7 per cent of women aged 35–74 were disabled in the sense that they were unable to perform unaided defined activities essential to daily life.[1] Comparable estimates from the government's survey in 1968–9 are approximately 2·3 per cent and 3·4 per cent. Even if those with 'minor handicap' are added to the latter figures, they are still considerably below the North Lambeth rates.

Secondly, the results for the adult population under 65 are different from those obtained in other countries. The British government's survey produced estimates of 3·9 per cent of those aged 16–64 who were impaired, including only 1·2 per cent who were 'very severely, severely or appreciably handicapped'. The US survey, however, which was also based on a first-stage postal questionnaire, produced estimates of 17·2 per cent long-term disability among adults aged 18–64, including 5·9 per cent who were severely disabled.[2] Among the severely disabled there were two thirds who were unable to work at all whose functional limitations

1. Bennett, A. E., Garrad, J., Halil, T., 'Chronic Disease and Disability in the Community: A Prevalence Study', *British Medical Journal*, 26 September 1970.
2. Haber, L. D., 'Prevalence of Disability Among Non-institutionalized Adults Under Age 65: 1966 Survey of Disabled Adults', *Research and Statistics Note*, US Department of Health, Education and Welfare, 20 February 1968, p. 12.

involved 'moderate loss, severe loss', or who were 'functionally dependent'.[1] The latter represented 3·6 per cent of the entire population of this age. The discrepancies between the two countries are too great to be plausible. On the other hand, the poverty survey produces estimates which in certain respects are broadly comparable with the US estimates. There were 3·3 per cent aged 15–64 who were appreciably, severely or very severely incapacitated, according to the incapacity index. Altogether there were 12 per cent of this age with a disablement condition.[2]

A national survey carried out in Denmark in 1960–61 found that 6·5 per cent of the population aged 15–61 were *physically* handicapped.[3] Allowing for the exclusion of the mentally ill and handicapped, and of those aged 62–4, the figure is about double the corresponding figure obtained from the British government's survey. Yet certain disabling conditions, such as bronchitis, are known to be more prevalent in Britain. So while differences in the prevalence of handicap between countries should be expected, the British rate again seems suspiciously low.

Careful scrutiny of the estimates derived from the poverty survey, and also of other research in Britain, the United States and Denmark, therefore all point to the same general conclusion. Even when allowances are made for differences of definition and measurement, the government's estimate of the handicapped population of Britain, which was derived from a government survey, are, for the severely and appreciably handicapped and the moderately handicapped, only about half the real figure.

Disability Increases with Age

There is a strong correlation between incapacity and advancing age. As Figure 20.2 shows, the rate of those who are appreciably or severely incapacitated fluctuates around 1 per cent up to the forties and then rises for both sexes in the fifties and more sharply for women than men in the sixties and subsequently. By the early seventies, over a fifth of men and a quarter of women are appreciably or severely incapacitated.

While the proportion of women who are appreciably or severely incapacitated does not begin to outstrip that of men until the fifties, the proportion with minor

1. Allan, K. H., and Cinsky, M. E., 'General Characteristics of the Disabled Population', *Social Security Survey of the Disabled: 1966*, Report No. 19, US Department of Health, Education and Welfare, Social Security Administration, Office of Research and Statistics, July 1972, pp. 9 and 27.

2. After a modification in method, the General Household Survey is now producing estimates of those with limiting long-standing illness which broadly correspond to the United States data about prevalence. See, for example, *General Household Survey*, Introductory Report, pp. 270–71.

3. Andersen, B. R., *Fysisk Handicappede i Danmark* (The Physically Handicapped in Denmark), vol. 2, Report No. 16 of the Danish National Institute of Social Research, Copenhagen, 1964, p. 109.

or some incapacity outstrips that for men from the twenties onwards. The differences between the sexes are shown in Figure 20.2. (See also Table A.71, Appendix Eight, page 1048.)

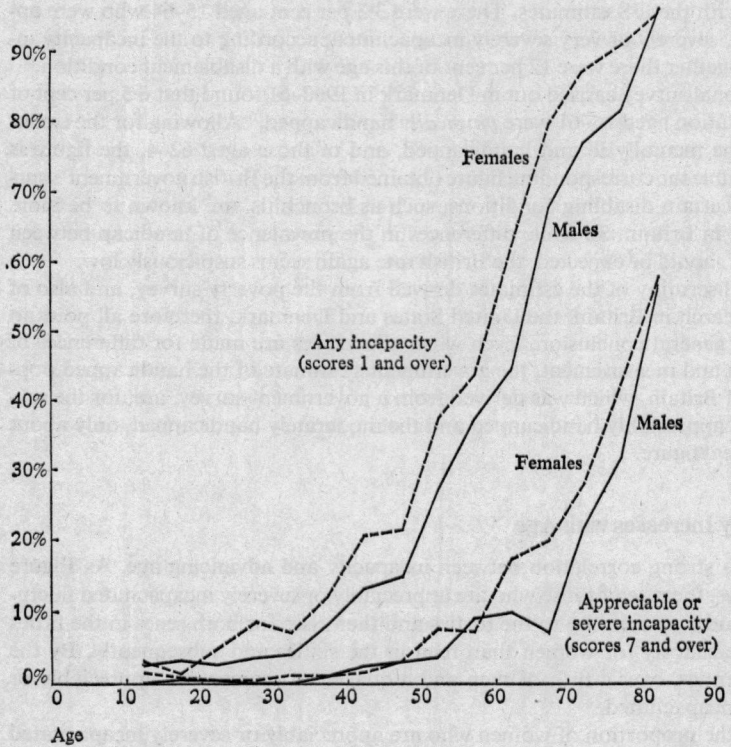

Figure 20.2. Percentages of males and females of different ages with any incapacity and with appreciable or severe incapacity.

There are approximately 325,000 people aged 10–49 who are appreciably or severely incapacitated, but they form only 10·5 per cent of all who are incapacitated to such a degree. But when those of this age with some incapacity (scores of 3–6 on the incapacity index) are added, the total is increased to 1,165,000. This is a substantial number of young people and people in early middle age. As many as 1,945,000 (or 63 per cent) of the total of 3,095,000 who are appreciably or severely incapacitated are aged 65 or over. As many as 3,835,000 (or 55 per cent) of the total with some, appreciable or severe incapacity are of this age (Table A.72, Appendix Eight, page 1049).

The alternative measure of number of disablement conditions is also strongly correlated with age. The proportion with one or more conditions rises steadily for each successive age group. But whereas among age groups over 50 the proportion of women and of men with one or two or more disablement conditions is broadly the same, substantially more women than men aged 20–29, 30–39 and 40–49 called attention to a disablement condition which restricted their activities. (See Fig. 20.3, and Table A.73 in Appendix Eight, page 1050.) We found that much

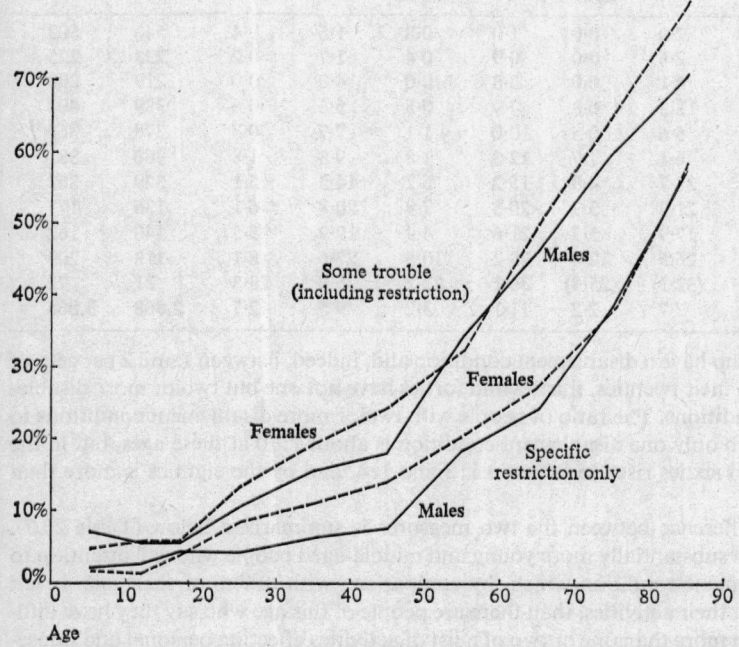

Figure 20.3. *Percentages of males and females of different ages who have trouble with a disablement condition and have a marked or specific restriction of activity.*

of this difference was due to the higher incidence of incapacitating mental anxiety among women of this age. The relatively higher incidence among women continues into older age groups, but more of the men than of the women are incapacitated by chest and lung troubles.

Table 20.6 shows that there are significant minorities of even the young age

Table 20.6. *Percentages of males and females of different ages who have one or more disablement conditions which limits their activities.*

Age	Males		Females		Males and females		Total number in sample	
	1 disablement condition	2 or more disablement conditions	1 disablement condition	2 or more disablement conditions	1 disablement condition	2 or more disablement conditions	Males	Females
0–9	2·0	0·0	1·0	0·8	1·5	0·4	540	502
10–14	2·6	0·0	0·9	0·4	1·7	0·2	233	225
15–19	4·1	0·0	3·8	0·0	4·0	0·0	219	208
20–29	3·3	0·8	7·9	0·5	5·6	0·6	389	407
30–39	5·6	0·5	10·0	1·1	7·7	0·8	378	360
40–49	6·1	1·7	12·3	1·8	9·3	1·8	360	381
50–59	13·7	4·9	15·2	5·2	14·5	5·1	329	363
60–64	21·3	3·7	20·3	7·9	20·8	6·1	136	177
65–69	17·9	5·7	21·6	4·9	19·9	5·3	140	162
70–79	26·5	12·4	28·2	10·5	27·6	8·1	113	209
80+	(32·3)	(25·8)	36·1	22·2	35·0	23·3	31	72
All ages	7·7	2·2	11·1	3·2	9·5	2·7	2,868	3,066

groups who have a disablement condition and, indeed, between 1 and 2 per cent of people in their twenties, thirties and forties have not one but two or more disablement conditions. The ratio of people with two or more disablement conditions to those with only one disablement condition is about 1:10 at these ages, but in the fifties and sixties rises to between 1:3 and 1:4, and by the eighties is more than 1:2.

The difference between the two measures is summarized below (Table 20.7). There are substantially more young and middle-aged people who call attention to a disablement condition which, by comparison with others of their age, is felt to restrict their activities, than there are people of this age who say they have difficulty with more than one or two of a list of activities affecting personal and household care and mobility. Among the elderly this situation is more or less reversed. More of them admit to difficulty in carrying out several personal and household tasks than actually specify a disablement condition.

The two measures produce roughly the same total numbers, but whereas 68 per cent of those assessed according to the first measure in Table 20.7 are aged 60 or over, the figure is only 48 per cent according to the second measure. The fall is larger for women than for men (Tables A.72 and A.74, Appendix Eight, pages 1049–50).

Table 20.7. *Estimated number of disabled people in the non-institutionalized population of the United Kingdom (thousands).*

Age	Having some, appreciable or severe incapacity (with scores of 3 or more on incapacity index)	Having disablement condition with specific or marked effect on activities
0–9	–	185
10–19	160	240
20–29	200	460
30–39	225	585
40–49	580	755
50–59	1,090	1,240
60–69	2,000	1,480
70+	2,755	1,705
All ages	7,010	6,650

NOTE: Population estimates rounded to nearest 5,000.

Low Social Status of Disabled

Is marital status related to incapacity? The distributions of incapacity scores among single and married men were not markedly different, for each of the age groups 15–29, 30–49, 50–59 and 60 and over. The same may be said of single and married women over 30. Thus, among women aged 30–49, 6 per cent of the married, compared with 5 per cent of the single, had some, appreciable or severe incapacity; among women aged 60 and over, were 49 per cent and 51 per cent respectively. But among women aged 15–29, 9 per cent of the married, compared with 2 per cent of the single, had some degree of incapacity, including minor incapacity.

Widows and widowers were worse placed than either the single or the married. Their numbers in the sample under age 50 for women, and under age 60 for men, were too few to allow generalization. Over these ages, the proportions with appreciable and severe incapacity were larger than of other men and women, even when their greater average age is allowed for.

The correlation between disability and occupational class is marked. Table 20.8 shows that a significantly higher proportion of the manual than of the non-manual classes had minor, some, appreciable or severe incapacity. The disadvantage of both men and women in the unskilled manual class is particularly striking.

The correlation between disablement conditions and class is even more marked. Among men, those belonging to the non-manual classes who had a disablement condition which limited their activities numbered 7·4 per cent, compared with 11·2 per cent of manual classes. Among women, there were 10·8 per cent and

16·2 per cent respectively. As Table 20.9 shows, there was, for males, a higher proportion of manual than non-manual people who had a disablement condition among every age group except one, and for females, among every age group except two. When specific occupational classes are examined, the disadvantage at

Table 20.8. Percentages of males and females aged 10 and over in different occupational classes, according to incapacity.

Sex incapacity (score)	Profes- sional and higher mana- gerial	Mana- gerial	Supervisory Higher	Lower	Routine non- manual	Skilled manual	Semi- skilled manual	Unskilled manual
Men								
None (0)	88	90	87	84	82	85	80	70
Minor (1–2)	8	4	6	7	7	5	10	14
Some (3–6)	3	4	3	5	5	5	7	8
Appreciable or severe (7+)	1	2	4	4	4	4	3	6
Total	100	100	100	100	100	100	100	100
Number	177	146	279	397	166	940	483	298
Women								
None (0)	85	78	83	80	76	72	72	58
Minor (1–2)	7	8	7	8	8	9	11	20
Some (3–6)	6	8	6	7	9	10	9	9
Appreciable or severe (7+)	2	5	4	5	7	9	8	13
Total	100	100	100	100	100	100	100	100
Number	175	148	297	440	317	910	485	273

different ages of the unskilled and semi-skilled is quite marked (Table A.75, Appendix Eight, page 1051), though the disadvantage of some age groups in the routine non-manual class should be noted. There is, of course, a tendency for young daughters and middle-aged wives of manual workers to take non-manual jobs, which may partly explain why some in this 'class' have a disablement condition.

Table 20.9. Percentages of non-manual and manual males and females of different age, with one or more disablement conditions.

Age	Percentage with disablement condition				Total number in sample			
	Males		Females		Males		Females	
	non-manual	manual	non-manual	manual	non-manual	manual	non-manual	manual
0–9	1·3	2·6	1·0	2·1	227	310	209	288
10–19	1·7	3·8	3·2	1·9	179	265	218	207
20–29	2·9	4·9	7·0	9·7	139	243	214	186
30–39	4·6	7·5	8·6	13·6	175	200	174	184
40–49	8·3	7·0	11·3	17·6	156	200	186	188
50–59	13·8	21·9	14·0	23·0	138	187	143	204
60–69	25·0	25·5	20·2	30·7	83	184	114	202
70+	36·4	45·6	45·3	42·0	44	92	95	162
All ages	7·4	11·2	10·8	16·2	1,141	1,681	1,353	1,621

Poverty

Not only do disabled people have lower social status. They also have lower incomes and fewer assets. Moreover, they tend to be poorer even when their social status is the same as the non-disabled. This will now be demonstrated. Table 20.10 shows the distribution of cash incomes in relation to the state's standard of poverty. With increasing incapacity, proportionately more people lived in households with incomes below, or only marginally above, that standard. Fewer lived in households with relatively high incomes. More than half those with appreciable or severe incapacity were in households in or on the margins of poverty, compared with only a fifth of those with no incapacity.

More of the incapacitated than of the non-incapacitated are aged 65 and over, and it might be supposed that the correlation shown in the table is explained more by the low incomes associated with advancing age than disability as such. But while changing age distribution underlies the correlation, poverty is still associated with increased incapacity, even when age is held constant. Indeed, when attention is paid to the income of the income unit rather than of the household as a whole, and to household stocks, and assets, the association between poverty and disability is more marked. Nearly three times as many people aged 40 and under pensionable age who were appreciably or severely incapacitated as of those who were not incapacitated were in units with incomes close to or under the poverty line. The increase in risk of poverty with increase in incapacity was marked even

712 POVERTY IN THE UNITED KINGDOM

Table 20.10. Percentages of people with different degrees of disability living below and above the state's standard of poverty.

Net disposable house-hold income last year as % of supplementary benefit scales plus housing cost	Degree of incapacity (score)					
	None (0)	Minor (1–2)	Some (3–4)	Some (5–6)	Appreciable (7–10)	Severe (11+)
Under 100	5	11	12	11	11	12
100–39	19	25	29	36	39	46
140–99	36	27	26	24	23	24
200+	41	37	33	29	27	18
Total	100	100	100	100	100	100
Number	4,026	453	189	185	197	109

among those of pensionable age (Table 20.11). Another method of examining the effects of disability is to examine income according to the level of disability of the most disabled member of the income unit (Table A.86, Appendix Eight, page 1059). There is a marked inverse relationship between increasing income and disability.

More of the incapacitated than of the non-incapacitated, for each major age group, were in debt or had no assets or had less than £100. Fewer had assets over

Table 20.11. Percentages of people of different age with different degrees of incapacity who were living in income units with incomes in previous year below or on the margins of the state's standard of poverty.

Age	Degree of incapacity (score)			
	None (0)	Minor (1–2)	Some (3–6)	Appreciable or severe (7+)
15–39	25	(30)	(64)	a
40–pensionable age	15	22	30	49
Pensionable age and over	48	62	65	73
All ages 15 and over	23	41	52	68
Number all ages	2,802	464	389	311

NOTE: [a]Equals number below 20.

£5,000. Fewer of the disabled were owner-occupiers, held a personal bank account, owned a car or had personal possessions other than furniture or clothing (such as jewellery, silver and antiques) worth £25 or more.

The next table is perhaps the most compact illustration that the survey can offer of the deleterious effects upon living standards of disability. In this the annuity values of the assets owned by the incapacitated and non-incapacitated are added to their net disposable incomes for the previous twelve months, and the resulting 'income net worth'[1] is expressed as a percentage of the state's standard of poverty, that is, the supplementary benefit rates which were in force at the time of the survey, plus housing cost (Table 20.12). A significantly higher proportion of the incapacitated than of the non-incapacitated, within each major age group, had

Table 20.12. *Percentages of people of different age and degrees of incapacity in units whose income net worth[a] was below or only marginally above the state's standard of poverty.[b]*

Age	Degree of incapacity (score)			
	None (0)	Minor (1-2)	Some (3-6)	Appreciable or severe (7+)
15-39	21	(31)	(44)	c
40-pensionable age	9	13	27	43
Pensionable age and over	28	36	35	52
All ages	17	25	33	50
Total number, all ages	2,434	416	342	266

NOTES: [a]Annuity value of assets plus net disposable income in previous year (less any income from savings and property) for income units.
[b]Supplementary benefit scales for income units of different size and composition plus actual cost of housing.
[c]Number below 20.

an income net worth of below, or only marginally above, the state's standard of poverty. The incapacitated were at a disadvantage throughout the income scale. For example, among those in their fifties, only 20 per cent of those with appreciable or severe incapacity, compared with 31 per cent of those with some incapacity and 56 per cent of those with no incapacity had an income net worth of more than 250 per cent of the supplementary benefit standard.

One result of this analysis had not been anticipated. Although the measure of incapacity that was adopted was based on previous research by the author and

1. For a discussion of the concept and measurement of 'income net worth', see Chapter 5, pages 210-15.

others, it was admittedly crude. We did not expect those with scores of 1 or 2 to be very different in various respects from those with no score at all. After all, they admitted difficulty with only one or two of nine activities listed, and it did not seem likely that significantly larger proportions of them would have had lower incomes, fewer assets and so on. But a number of tables show that even marginal incapacity, crudely measured, is associated with lower living standards and with different forms of deprivation.

Deprivation

Deprivation as a consequence of, or in conjunction with, low income and low assets takes many forms. Some indices are summarized in Table 20.13. More of the incapacitated than of the non-incapacitated had poor housing facilities. This was not just because a higher proportion of the incapacitated were older people. After all, more late middle-aged and old people become outright owner-occupiers, and some of the most infirm widowed elderly had left their homes to live with their children. We found that more of the incapacitated in each age group had poor housing[1] (Table A.76, Appendix Eight, page 1051).

According to other measures too, more of the incapacitated than the non-incapacitated lived in poor housing. Despite a tendency to be older and to live in smaller accommodation, more lacked heating in winter for at least half their accommodation. Fewer lived in structurally sound dwellings. The only measure of housing according to which the incapacitated did not show to disadvantage was overcrowding. This was because more were older, widowed or lacking dependent children. Even so, nine per cent were overcrowded, ranging from 22 per cent of those in their twenties, 19 per cent in their thirties and forties, 10 per cent in their fifties and 5 per cent of those aged 60 and over. These percentages corresponded closely with the percentages among the non-incapacitated.

The depreciation of the necessities and comforts of life because of disability is complex to trace, if pervasive. During the interviews we had asked whether or not there were any or all of a list of ten consumer durables or fitments in the home. The incapacitated had fewer than the non-incapacitated (Table 20.13). The deficiency was marked among the older age groups, but applied at all ages – although small numbers in the sample at the younger ages have to be remembered. In late middle and old age there was strong evidence of an association between increased incapacity and reduced stock and fitments in the home. Altogether, 35 per cent of those with appreciable or severe incapacity had fewer than five of ten listed items (television, record player, radio, refrigerator, washing machine, vacuum cleaner, telephone, central heating, armchairs or easy chairs for each member of the household, and living-room carpet) in the home, and only 10 per cent had nine or all

1. See also Buckle, *Work and Housing of Impaired Persons in Great Britain*, op. cit., pp. 74–81.

Table 20.13. *Percentages of non-incapacitated and incapacitated experiencing certain forms of deprivation.*

Form of deprivation	Degree of incapacity			
	None (0)	Minor (1–2)	Some (3–6)	Appreciable or severe (7+)
Does not have sole use of four basic housing facilities[a]	18	20	25	26
Not had week's holiday away from home	50	58	60	73
No sole use of garden or yard	12	13	17	19
Less than half rooms heated in winter	59	70	64	65
Deficient in household durables[b]	11	17	24	35
No electricity	2	2	2	4
Fresh meat fewer than 4 times a week	16	27	31	39
Missed cooked meal at least one day in last fortnight	5	10	11	18
Short of fuel	5	5	5	11
No relative to meal or snack during last four weeks	32	39	35	38

NOTES: [a]Indoor WC, sink with tap, bath and cooker.
[b]Having fewer than 5 of 10 listed items, as set out at the foot of page 714.

ten of the items, compared with 11 per cent and 25 per cent respectively of the non-incapacitated.

More of the incapacitated also had dietary deficiencies and experienced certain kinds of social deprivation. A few measures are given for illustration in Table 20.13. Thus, significantly more of the incapacitated than of the non-incapacitated had missed cooked meals and eaten fresh meat infrequently. Nearly three quarters of those with appreciable or severe incapacity, compared with half of the non-incapacitated, had not had as much as a week's holiday away from home in the previous twelve months.

In all these instances there is no particular reason why incapacitated people should be worse off than the non-incapacitated. In principle, they can go on holiday, visit friends or enjoy a garden like other people. What we have found, however, is not a different pattern of activity and relationships on their part but, rather, a systematic association between incapacity and deprivation. The more severe the incapacity the greater the deprivation. This can be illustrated best by our index of social deprivation. As explained earlier, an index comprising items which included not going on a summer holiday, not receiving relatives or friends for a meal or a snack in the house during the preceding fortnight, not having adequate housing facilities and not having a refrigerator, as well as not eating customary types and amounts of food, was compiled. The higher the score out of a total of 10, the greater the deprivation. As Table 20.14 shows, there was a markedly significant

Table 20.14. *Percentages of people with minor, some, appreciable, severe or no incapacity with different levels of deprivation.*

Deprivation index[a]	Degree of incapacity				
	None (0)	Minor (1–2)	Some (3–6)	Appreciable (7–10)	Severe (11+)
0–1	19	11	10	6	1
2–3	40	36	31	27	15
4–5	28	32	34	29	35
6–7	11	18	21	32	32
8 or more	2	3	5	7	17
Total	100	100	100	100	100
Number	4,279	521	419	210	117

NOTE: [a]Items as specified on page 250.

and progressive association with incapacity. Thirteen per cent of people having no incapacity, compared with nearly half those with severe incapacity, had scores on the index of 6 or more. Nearly 60 per cent of the former had scores of 3 or less, compared with 16 per cent of the latter.

Subjective Deprivation

Evidence has been offered of the lower incomes and greater objective deprivation of the disabled among all age groups. But evidence can also be offered of more of them *feeling* deprived, even at similar levels of income. This may reflect their difficulties in conforming with social norms as consumers. It may reflect greater anxiety, depression or pessimism among them as a consequence of physical and mental limitations. Or it may reflect the greater costs of disability. For any one of these contingencies it would be possible to put forward a case for additional income – whether to meet higher prices or restricted range of consumer choice, to compensate for measurable handicap or to meet the costs of meeting additional needs. Certainly a higher proportion of the incapacitated than of the non-incapacitated said they had difficulty in managing their incomes, even at levels of income above the supplementary benefit standard, as well as below that standard (Table 20.15). A higher proportion also said they felt poor (Table A.77, Appendix Eight, page 1052).

Table 20.15. Percentages of non-incapacitated and incapacitated in units with incomes above and below the state's standard of poverty who said they had difficulty in managing on their incomes.

Net disposable income last year as % of supplementary benefit scales plus housing cost	Degree of incapacity (score)			
	None (0)	Minor (1–2)	Some (3–6)	Appreciable or severe (7+)
Under 140	46	52	54	62
140–99	25	36	29	33
200+	14	22	14	30
All	24	38	39	53
Total number	1,189	247	206	164

NOTE: Heads of households or chief wage-earners only.

Some of the Problems of Disability in the Home

The problems of poverty and of objective and subjective deprivation will be illustrated with individual examples drawn from our interviews, both for those with incomes below the goverment's poverty standard and for those with higher incomes. (See also the listed illustrations between pages 305 and 335 in Chapter 8, Nos. 1, 3, 6, 8, 11, 15, 17, 18 and 20.)

1. Disability in late middle age

Mr and Mrs Donaldson are both aged 60 and live in a four-roomed council flat in South London. Although both were in paid employment, Mr Donaldson had been off work sick on two or three occasions in the year, totalling thirteen weeks, and works only with difficulty. His wife works part time. In the previous week he had worked thirty-two hours and she twenty hours. He had been a printing compositor until an illness laid him low. He says it started in the war when he experienced fits of deafness, loss of speech and giddiness when attached to a heavy anti-aircraft gun battery. Then he said he was accused of malingering and was put on guard duty, when he was court-martialled for failing to challenge an officer returning to camp. He was in hospital for two years in 1963 and was operated on for the removal of varicose veins and had five other operations. He had electro-convulsion therapy, and after leaving hospital was told he would only be fit to work part-time for the rest of his life. After leaving hospital he took a so-called rehabilitation course. 'It was no use whatsoever.' It only made it worse because he was taught such menial things and was among many handicapped people. Eventually his former employers gave him a much less well-paid job as a copyholder. He said his earnings dropped from £25 per week to about £14. He cannot stand for more than fifteen minutes without becoming giddy, and has been taken to hospital several times after having a fit or blackout. His fits are characterized by speechlessness, deafness, foaming at the mouth, or giving the appearance of being drunk, and he says that though sometimes fully conscious and aware of what is going on, he is unable to speak or hear. He had spent about fifty days in bed from illness in the last twelve months. He can only get to work by using two buses, and he and his wife have had little help from the council in finding a flat nearer his work. They had been offered three separate flats in tower blocks. His employers do not allow him sick pay for odd days off in the week, and because his job is not skilled he is dissatisfied with it. Last week his net earnings were £13·85 and those of his wife £4·80. This is about average for the weeks when he can work. When off work for an entire week at a time, he can claim £2 from the compositors' sick club. He said he had applied for a rent rebate and would normally have qualified, but because the council take account of eight weeks' earnings, and because he had had unusually little illness in this period, the rebate had not been granted. He and his wife have about £350 in a trustee savings bank. Their flat is comfortably furnished, and they said they could do with one room fewer. A son who married only last year lives near by and they see him and his wife quite frequently and help each other with shopping, occasional meals and gifts. They had not had an evening out in the last fortnight, but had had a fortnight's summer holiday. Mr Donaldson believed their situation was worse than it had ever been, but that they were about as well off as others in the neighbourhood. He did not think they could be considered as poor, and thought that 'some people are getting too much money from the government on false pretences, whilst other more deserving cases don't get anything or don't get enough'.

2. Extreme disability in middle age and old age

Mr and Mrs Millen, both 47, live with a son of 23 and Mr Millen's father, aged 80, in a semi-detached council house in a southern town. Mrs Millen was said to have acute diabetes (believed, however, by the interviewer to be leukaemia) and had been bedfast throughout the previous twelve months (incapacity score 17). The condition had begun five years earlier. The father had Parkinson's disease and was severely incapacitated, spending most of his time in bed or sitting by the bed (incapacity score 18). He had recently returned from a stay of three weeks in hospital. Mr Millen earned £12 net a week as a Gas Board meter reader, and the son

£13 as a french polisher. The father had a retirement pension and also a war disability pension amounting to £8·10, but Mrs Millen had no source of income. Housing facilities were good and the family had a small garden. Mrs Millen's mother calls every day, as does Mr Millen's sister, to prepare meals, shop and look after the invalids.

3. Chronic sickness in middle age

Mr and Mrs Newtonstone, 60 and 58, live in a semi-detached pre-war council house in a Yorkshire town. He is confined to bed much of the time and needs help to sit in a chair (incapacity score 15). He says that nine months earlier, while working as a labourer in a smelting works, an ulcer burst, and after fifteen weeks in hospital he has spent another five months at home in the present condition. During that period his GP has called about once a fortnight. Two of their daughters visit every day to help with shopping and other minor tasks, though Mrs Newtonstone bears the brunt of the work. One of the neighbours has also been very helpful. Their total income is now £9·35 sickness benefit, and the firm continues to pay £1·50, although he received full pay only for the first month of hospitalization. Rent amounts to nearly £3 a week. They had not applied for supplementary benefit, but were very bitter about people 'on the assistance' who were 'car-owners' or who were 'black prostitutes and our own people have to go short'. Until recently Mrs Newtonstone had earned a wage as a canteen worker, so in a short period they have experienced a sharp fall in income. She had not been out for an afternoon or evening for many weeks. They had not been on holiday and were aware they led a very restricted life.

4. Severe disability in middle age

Mr and Mrs Ophelia, 55 and 56, rent a council bungalow in Northern Ireland. They have lived in poverty and on the margins of poverty for years. She is stone deaf in one ear and also suffers from depression, weeping frequently. He has a serious heart condition and is also a diabetic, having been off work, confined to the house for several years (incapacity score 14). He has been ill in bed throughout the last twelve months, and is visited once a week by the GP. He had been a farm labourer. At the time of interview (January 1969) they had £7·30 sickness benefit and received in addition £2·20 supplementary benefit, including an exceptional circumstances addition for a diabetic diet. They have no money assets whatsoever, and only two of a list of ten household durables. They have several married children living locally and are visited every day, getting various kinds of help, and the wife, despite her own condition, returns some of that help. They have not had a holiday this year, and say they cannot afford any extras.

5. Severe disability in old age

Miss Hulpermatch, 89, lives alone in one room in Bristol. She is one of the most incapacitated people in the sample found to be living alone (incapacity score of 14). She gets up for one hour a day and sits in an armchair near the window. She suffers from spinal curvature, arthritis, poor hearing and sight and stomach trouble. Everything she eats makes her feel sick. A district nurse calls weekly and a home help three times a week. The doctor has been five times in the last twelve months. Two other tenants in the house give an average of three hours' help to her every day. One of these is an ex-seaman of 70 who used to store his belongings in her second room for 2s. 11d. a week. When he retired she let him move into the room, still at a sub-letting charge of 2s. 11d. – though he appears to perform many small services in exchange. She pays the other tenant to give her meals. She also has a niece next door who brings food and other gifts. She proclaimed strong opinions. 'I have never voted in my life. I did not believe in woman's suffrage when it was introduced and I have not changed my mind since.' Until she retired at the age of 60 she had sold vacuum cleaners. In 1960 a woman friend who had lived with her for fifty years died, and she had been alone ever since. She does not feel poor. 'I would be poor if I was able to eat three good meals a day because I could not afford to pay for them. But I can't eat so I'm not poor.' She lives in squalid surroundings with no electricity, no functioning bathroom, and has to share toilet facilities. She has a radio but no television and no access to a garden. Pension and supplementary benefit amount to £6·10, of which 60p is said to cover additional medical expenses.

6. Disability in young adulthood and early old age

Mr and Mrs Dobey, 66 and 63, live with a mongol son of 35 in a five-roomed council house in Lincoln. There is no W C indoors, but otherwise facilities are adequate. The house is sparsely furnished and there is no washing machine or refrigerator. They have a small garden at the back. Mr Dobey had been a labourer working with the county council and had been retired for just over a year. He had left school at 12 and held one job most of his working life. 'I had to cycle to work each day, starting at five o'clock in the morning, and I wasn't a minute late in thirty-two years. When I started at 12 I worked for 1s. 6d. per week.' He suffers from bronchitis and can only do physically demanding tasks with difficulty (incapacity score 5). He had spent three weeks in bed this year and obtained a prescription every week from his doctor (by sending a stamped addressed envelope) His son attends an adult training centre and seems very happy. The family gives the impression of being very integrated and contented. Mrs Dobey says she puts food before luxuries and warmth and makes sure they have fresh vegetables every day and salads in summer. She buys three pints of milk every day, always has a

Sunday joint, and they also have fresh meat three or four times in the week. She pays a lot of attention to diet and is anxious to keep her son's weight down. They have a beautiful garden which last year won the local prize for the best garden, and that offers plenty of occupation. They did not have a summer holiday or go away to stay with relatives during the previous twelve months, but had had relatives to stay with them for a fortnight. In the evenings they do not go out, except for Mrs Dobey's weekly trip to play bingo. They go to church (Church of England) every Sunday. A married son lives next door and they see the family every day. They took the view that poverty applied to 'old people having a job to manage' and felt that it could be reduced by 'making the devils work harder. The family allowance should be taken away and put on the pension. The young have it too easy and the old have it hard now.' Mr and Mrs Dobey have a combined retirement pension of £7·37½ a week, plus a council pension paid monthly, which is equivalent to £3·45 per week. Their rent is £1·10 a week. They have no savings and their only assets are life insurance policies amounting to a total of about £400. Their son receives supplementary benefit allowance of £4·50. Their total income is rather less than £3 above the state poverty line. They take the view that they could not manage financially without Mr Dobey's occupational pension.

7. Extreme disability in late middle age

Miss Sulman, 25, lives with her mother, 61, in a small semi-detached house owned by themselves in a country town in Suffolk. The mother suffers from chronic arthritis and is bedfast (incapacity score 18). She cannot move of her own accord, or even wash her face and hands. The doctor visits about once a fortnight and a home help five days a week. Mrs Sulman spent about ten weeks in hospital this year. She has not been away on holiday, but a friend has been to stay for a fortnight while her daughter took a holiday. Miss Sulman is a secondary modern schoolteacher with net weekly earnings of about £60 a month (gross £83) or £15 per week. Mrs Sulman has a widow's pension of £4·60 a week and supplementary benefit of another 90p. Miss Sulman sleeps in the same room and makes her mother comfortable during the night, gets breakfast and prepares an evening meal. The home help cleans and prepares a midday meal.

8. Severe disability in middle age

Mr and Mrs Fullmester, aged 56 and 55, live in a tiny terraced house owned by themselves in a rundown area of Liverpool. A lodger lives temporarily in a top room. Mrs Fullmester is usually confined to bed and can only sit in a chair by her bed. She has a heart complaint, enormously swollen legs and weighs 27 stone (incapacity score 16). During the last year she spent twelve weeks in hospital. She is visited weekly by a local-authority bath attendant, but the main task of caring for her has been assumed by her daughter, who lives locally and comes each day, shopping, preparing meals and cleaning for her. Although known to the council, she is not on the register of the handicapped. Her husband has a job as a driver's mate and his take-home pay for the previous week was £13·50.

Chronic Illness or Invalidity

We have considered four groups of disabled people: children, young adults, the middle aged and the elderly. Merging with them, although more distinct than many would suppose, as we will show, are the chronically ill. Chronic or long-term illness is difficult to define. There are the questions of the *duration* of the illness; expectation of recovery; medical or administrative classification of illness; and whether ill in the sense of being in bed or confined to house or simply having a condition which results in absence from work or school. In the survey we measured:

1. Weeks off work in previous twelve months for reasons of sickness. As a check on this question, the number of weeks making up fifty-two at work, on holiday, unemployed, etc., were listed.
2. Numbers ill on day of interview, and (for economically active people and school children):
   (a) weeks off work;
   (b) weeks off school.
   And for all those currently ill or unwell, the number confined to bed or house, and number of weeks. As a check on these questions, people were asked whether they were seeing a doctor regularly and asked to name the illness.
3. Days illness in bed in previous twelve months. As a check, people were asked about consultations with a doctor.
4. Those with long-term illness or disablement condition (adults aged 15–64 only). Years since long-term sickness or condition started. As a check for this, questions were asked about the year and job held at the time.

For the sample as a whole, Table 20.16 shows how many were chronically ill according to different criteria (see Table A.78, Appendix Eight, page 1053 for more detail). More males than females had been ill for ten weeks or more at the time of the survey, in the sense that they had been off work or school or had been confined to the house or to bed for that period because of illness. They represented three quarters of a million people, nearly half a million of whom were under pensionable age. More than half were in their thirties, forties and fifties. On the strict criterion of spending fifty or more days in bed in the previous twelve months, the numbers of males and females were proportionately about equal.

Nearly a million economically active men and women were found to have had ten weeks or more off work ill during the previous fifty-two weeks, proportionately

Table 20.16. Percentages and estimated number in population of men and women chronically ill.

Definition of chronic illness	Percentage Males	Females	Estimated total numbers in population (000s)
Currently off work or school or confined to bed or house ill for more than 10 weeks	1·6	1·2	760
Employed and self-employed off work ill for 10 weeks or more in last 52	3·9[a]	3·2[a]	945
50 or more days ill in bed in last 12 months	0·6	0·6	340
Has chronic illness or condition	13·1[b]	14·9[b]	4,860

NOTES: [a]Those not employed in course of year excluded from base.
[b]Applies only to those aged 15–64.

more of them being men. More men than women have heavy manual work and work in bad or poor conditions, and there are greater pressures upon them both to sustain paid employment and perhaps occupy the status of someone who is sick rather than someone who is unemployed when both might reasonably be applied.

Finally, people representing nearly 5 million between the ages of 15 and 64 said they had a chronic illness or condition, proportionately more of them being women than men. About half of them had been ill for ten or more years.

There was less overlap between current long-term illness and incapacity or disability than might have been expected. For both our measures of appreciable or severe incapacity (with scores of 7+) and disablement conditions, the vast majority, 81 per cent and 90 per cent respectively, were not currently ill. Only 12 per cent and 7 per cent respectively had been ill for ten weeks or more. Only 5 per cent of those with one disablement condition, and 14 per cent with two or more, had been ill off work or confined to house or bed for ten weeks or more (Table A.79, Appendix Eight, page 1054).

Many people ill for long periods did not have a disablement condition, or rather, because of its uncertain degree or outcome, not one which had yet been recognized medically or socially. Of those who had been ill for ten weeks or more, 60 per cent had a disablement condition. This was about the same percentage as were appreciably or severely incapacitated. The estimated numbers of disabled and chronically ill in the population as a whole are given in Table A.80 (Appendix Eight, page 1054). There were over 400,000 people with appreciable or severe incapacity who had been ill for over ten weeks.

Prolonged current illness is associated with low income. Nearly twice as many people who had been ill for over ten weeks as of those who had not been ill live in income units with incomes below or on the margins of the supplementary benefit standard. The majority of the former had, in fact, been ill for more than thirty weeks. Altogether more than half of those with long-term illness had incomes assessed for the previous twelve months as under or just above the poverty standard, compared with under a third of those not currently ill (Table 20.17). This pronounced association also applies to the larger category of people with

Table 20.17. Percentages of people experiencing different numbers of weeks of current illness living in units with incomes below and above the state's standard of poverty.

Net disposable income last year as % of supplementary benefit scales plus housing cost	Weeks' illness		
	None	1-9	10 or more
Under 100	9	7	15
100-39	23	16	43
140-99	29	36	14
200+	39	41	28
Total	100	100	100
Number	5,167	100	72

chronic illness or condition, of whom 64 per cent of the sample said the condition had begun five or more years earlier (24 per cent saying it had begun twenty or more years earlier). As many as 35 per cent were in or on the margins of poverty, compared with 22 per cent of the rest of the population.

There is further national evidence of the impoverishing effects of illness, and particularly of chronic illness. A survey by the Department of Health and Social Security in the early 1970s found that the percentage of those ill for six months who were below or on the margins of a notional supplementary benefit assessment was more than half as much again as the corresponding percentage of those ill for only one month (46 per cent compared with 28 per cent). This government study showed that nearly half the people who had been ill for both six months and twelve months were in or on the margins of poverty. Compared with the period immediately preceding their illness, more than half had sustained a fall in income of more than £5, most of whom of more than £10. The risk of poverty was highly correlated with lack of sick pay.[1]

1. Martin, J., and Morgan, M., *Prolonged Sickness and the Return to Work*, an inquiry carried out in 1972-3 for the Department of Health and Social Security of the circumstances of people who have received incapacity benefits for between a month and a year, and the factors affecting their return to work, HMSO, London, 1976, pp. 43, 58 and 61.

Mental Illness

Following advice about methodology from epidemiologists, people saying they suffered from mental anxieties and problems, along with those suffering from other disabling conditions, were identified in the survey. Nearly 7 per cent of women, compared with 2 per cent of men, said they had trouble with nerves. These persons (numbering 268 in the sample) were then asked whether they were affected for example,

    (i) by depression or weeping so that you can't face your work or mix with other people? [53 per cent affirmative]
    (ii) by getting in a rage with other people? [30 per cent]
    (iii) by being unable to concentrate? [37 per cent]
    (iv) by sleeping badly? [58 per cent]
or (v) by none of these? [12 per cent]

These criteria had been found to correlate very significantly in other research with those diagnosed as requiring psychiatric treatment or supervision. It can be seen that the great majority specified one or more of these criteria. Moreover, 77 per cent of the total saying they had nervous trouble said they were seeing a doctor

Table 20.18. Percentages of males and females of different age having trouble with nerves.

Nervous trouble	Age (males)						
	0–14	15–29	30–39	40–49	50–59	60+	All ages
None	99·6	99·4	97·4	97·3	95·9	95·9	98·0
Trouble	0·3	0·0	1·0	0·5	0·9	0·9	0·5
Trouble with specified effect	0·1	0·6	1·6	2·2	3·2	3·2	1·5
Total	100	100	100	100	100	100	100
Number	749	621	383	364	339	438	2,894
	(females)						
None	99·7	96·2	92·4	89·9	88·8	88·3	93·2
Trouble	0·1	0·3	0·8	1·8	0·5	1·3	0·7
Trouble with specified effect	0·1	3·5	6·8	8·3	10·7	10·4	6·0
Total	100	100	100	100	100	100	100
Number	709	624	367	387	374	634	3,095

about it or were having treatment, and one in four of the others, representing a further 6 per cent, said they *should* consult a doctor about it. These two checks therefore appeared to provide strong support for the use of this measure.

Among all age groups over 15, more women than men complained of nervous trouble, and more said they suffered as a consequence from depression, anger or lack of concentration or sleep. The percentage complaining of nervous trouble also tended to increase with age – though after the fifties there was little further change. On the basis of the findings, we estimated that approximately 2,400,000 in the non-institutionalized population were suffering from nervous trouble, 2,100,000 of whom specified one or more particular effects.

We found that significantly more of those in the sample complaining of trouble with nerves than not so doing were in or on the margins of poverty. This also applied at each age, and especially to people in late middle age (Table 20.19). Conversely, significantly fewer were in units with incomes of twice, or more than twice,

Table 20.19. *Percentages of people with and without depression or other nervous troubles, whose income was below or on the margins of the state's poverty standard.*[a]

Incapacity	Depression and other nervous troubles	No nervous trouble reported
None (0)	20·5	26·9
Minor or some (1–6)	49·5	34·4
Appreciable or severe (7+)	69·0	66·4
All	46·4	31·6
Age		
15–39	33·9	25·1
40–49	23·8	16·2
50–59	49·0	17·6
60+	62·2	57·5
All ages	46·2[b]	31·5[b]
Incapacity	Number in sample	
None (0)	95	4,057
Minor or some (1–6)	95	646
Appreciable or severe (7+)	58	256
All	248	5,079

NOTES: [a]Net disposable income last year under 140 per cent of the supplementary benefit scale rates plus housing cost.
[b]Including children under 15.

the state's poverty standard. The data also suggest that at different levels of incapacity people indicating they were suffering from a psychiatric condition were poorer than people who did not.

Hitherto, evidence of the low incomes of mentally ill people and ex-mental hospital patients has been sparse. Attention has been called to the problems of the single and homeless, particularly men, living in lodging-house areas of the major cities.[1] But psychiatric illness reduces earning power, prevents close relatives from taking paid employment, imposes additional expenses and creates the need for additional, for example, diversionary, spending.[2]

The Disadvantages of Employment

What brings about the low resources of disabled people? Major controlling factors are the economic and social expectations and obligations governing access to employment and, once in employment, access to types of jobs and levels of earnings. We will demonstrate four specific disadvantages: fewer are employed; fewer have high earnings and more have low earnings; more hours tend to be worked to secure the same earnings; and slightly fewer have good conditions of work.

Table 20.20 shows that a larger percentage of non-incapacitated than of incapacitated men and women of different ages were employed or self-employed during the twelve months preceding the survey. A work record was compiled for everyone working at least one week in the year. While there were few non-incapacitated men in their twenties, thirties, forties and fifties who were not employed, the numbers began to fall in the early sixties and fell steeply after 65. We estimated from the sample that there were, in the population, probably between 200,000 and 300,000 men under 65 (half of them over 30) not employed during the previous twelve months (including registered unemployed) who were not incapacitated, even to a minor extent. (Those at school and college are excluded.) There were also some 50,000 men under 65 with minor incapacity who were not employed, as well as 345,000 with some or with appreciable incapacity who were not employed (see Table A.81, Appendix Eight, page 1055). This gives some indication of the scope for an adequate employment policy for disabled people.

Our estimates are subject to large sampling errors but are derived from a sample of the entire population. We estimated that there were 1,220,000 men and 1,245,000 women with some, appreciable or severe incapacity who were under pensionable age. The unemployment 'rate' was, on this basis, 28 per cent for men and 56 per cent for women. The rate would, of course, be higher if disabled people of pensionable age, whether employed or not employed, were to be inclu-

1. McCowen, P., and Wilder, J., *Lifestyle of 100 Psychiatric Patients*, Psychiatric Rehabilitation Association, London, 1975.
2. See the review by Hughes, D., *How Psychiatric Patients Manage Out of Hospital*, Disability Alliance, London, 1978.

Table 20.20. *Percentages of non-incapacited and incapacitated men and women of different age employed (including self-employed) during the previous twelve months.*

| | Degree of incapacity | | | | | | | |
| | Men | | | | Women | | | |
Age	None (0)	Minor (1-2)	Some, appreciable and severe (3+)	All	None (0)	Minor (1-2)	Some, appreciable and severe (3+)	All
15-19	60 ⎫			59	56 ⎫			56
20-29	97 ⎬ 91	(94)	65	96	63 ⎬ 57	50	57	62
30-39	100 ⎭			99	49 ⎭			50
40-49	99	(100)	(81)	98	68	(64)	(54)	66
50-59	98	97	69	94	57	44	34	50
60-64	92	(89)	(69)	85	36	29	18	27
65-69	(46)	36	(27)	36	(26)	(11)	11	14
70+	(28)	(6)	6	10	(11)	(14)	2	5
All ages	90	68	42	82	57	35	17	46
Total number all ages	1,644	216	267	2,127	1,568	310	490	2,368

NOTE: Percentages not calculated on base of less than 20, and placed in brackets on base numbering 20-49.

ded in the calculation. By contrast, the Department of Employment statistics of unemployment among the disabled are based on a limited register of the disabled.[1] None the less, the unemployment rate among those registered has been higher than among the economically active as a whole in all years since the war, and increased in the late 1960s and early 1970s. Thus the rate was 8·9 per cent in 1948, reached a low point of 5 per cent in 1955 and was 7 per cent in 1958, 8 per cent in 1962, 10 per cent in 1968, 11·4 per cent in 1970 and 14·9 per cent in 1972.[2]

A surprisingly large number of men who were appreciably or severely incapacitated (with scores on the incapacity index of 7 or more) were employed. We estimated that there were 300,000. The great majority were satisfied with their jobs, and with conditions of work. While more needs to be known about their employment, the fact that they were employed gives encouragement to energetic efforts to employ others of equivalent incapacity.

In every age group, fewer women than men were at work. There was a substantial number under 60 years of age in the sample who were not incapacitated and who were neither employed nor self-employed. They represented nearly 5½ million in the population (Table A.81, Appendix Eight, page 1055). Those not at work and having minor or more severe degrees of incapacity represented a further 725,000 and 695,000 respectively. But, again, there were appreciably or severely incapacitated women aged under 60 in paid employment, representing 110,000 in the total population.

Altogether, 11 per cent of employees had one or more disablement conditions, rising from 3 per cent of those in their late teens to 16 per cent of those in their fifties and 23 per cent in their sixties (Table A.82, Appendix Eight, page 1056).

About the same numbers of self-employed as employed had a disablement condition, 12 per cent compared with 11 per cent, but not consistently for every age group. (Table A.82, Appendix Eight, page 1056.) According to the alternative measure, 19 per cent of the self-employed (19 per cent of men and 21 per cent of women), compared with 12 per cent of the employed, were incapacitated to a minor or greater degree.

Earnings of the disabled at work were significantly lower than of the non-disabled. Table 20.21 shows that, according both to the measure of incapacity and number of disablement conditions, more of those with incapacity or a disablement condition had relatively low earnings, and fewer had relatively high earnings for the year as a whole. Again, the difference between the non-incapacitated and those with only minor incapacity was significant. For example, there were 35 per cent of employed men with no incapacity, compared with 45 per cent with minor incapa-

---

1. The department has admitted that only about half of the disabled people in employment are registered, while about three quarters of unemployed disabled people are registered. Department of Employment Consultative Document, *The Quota Scheme for Disabled People*, HMSO, London, 1973, p. 10.

2. *Hansard*, 25 November 1974.

Table 20.21. Percentages of non-incapacitated and incapacitated men and women, and men and women with and without a disablement condition with gross earnings in previous year as a percentage of the mean.[a]

Gross earnings last year as % of mean	Degree of incapacity			Women
	Men			
	None (0)	Minor (1-2)	Some, appreciable or severe (3+)	None (0)
Under 60	11	11	17	14
60–79	24	34	26	18
80–99	26	26	31	21
100–39	26	22	15	29
140+	13	7	10	18
Total	100	100	100	100
Number	1,200	121	87	427

NOTE: [a]Men and women aged 20 and over and working 1,000 or more hours in the year.

city, who had earnings for the year as a whole below 80 per cent of the mean.

This finding is not much affected either by the tendency of some disabled to be off ill for more weeks of the year than the non-disabled or by the inclusion of small numbers of employees working fewer than thirty hours a week. More men with than without a disablement condition had relatively low earnings in the week preceding the survey (Table A.83, Appendix Eight, page 1056). More full-time male employees had gross earnings under £15 and full-time female employees under £10 (Table A.84, Appendix Eight, page 1057).

Up to the age of 40, the earnings of men with any incapacity score were distributed much the same as for other men, but their numbers in the sample were very small. In the forties and fifties, more had low earnings. For example, 21 per cent of men in their fifties with minor incapacity (scoring 1 or 2) and 23 per cent of those with some, appreciable or severe incapacity (scoring 3 or more) compared with 12 per cent with no incapacity, had earnings in the week previous to the survey of below 60 per cent of the mean. The corresponding percentages with earnings of more than 140 per cent of the mean were 5 per cent, 7 per cent and 12 per cent.

A higher proportion of the lowest than of the highest paid had some degree of incapacity, as Table 20.22 shows. If a comprehensive state scheme of income maintenance for the disabled were introduced, the problems of poverty and relative

Table 20.21 – contd

	Number of disablement conditions			
	Men		Women	
Minor, some, appreciable or severe (1+)	None	1 or more	None	1 or more
24	10	19	15	20
17	25	25	18	32
18	27	26	21	19
23	25	22	29	22
9	13	8	17	7
100	100	100	100	100
75	1,269	129	440	54

lack of resources among the disabled both in employment and not in employment would be reduced. But although incapacity is associated more strongly with low than with high pay, clearly it does not explain low pay.

Slightly more of the incapacitated than of the non-incapacitated worked under thirty hours in the week preceding interview. But the great majority worked as many hours, and, indeed, about a quarter of the men worked more than fifty

Table 20.22. *Percentages of low paid and high paid with some degree of incapacity.*

| | Low paid | | High paid | |
| | Earnings last week as % of mean | | Earnings last week as % of mean | |
	Under 60	60–79	140–99	200+
Men	25	17	9	(13)
Women	20	16	(5)	(6)
Total men	165	297	67	37
Total women	96	128	40	34

Table 20.23. Percentages of people with different earnings and hours of work who were incapacitated to any degree.[a]

Number of hours worked last week	Percentage with incapacity: average gross earnings last year as per cent of mean[b]				
	Under 60	60–79	80–99	100–139	140+
30–39	24	10	9	8	5
40–49	19	16	15	13	9
50+	27	17	10	15	5
All hours[c]	22	16	13	13	7
Number working all hours	310	521	437	447	233

NOTES: [a]With scores of 1 or more on incapacity index.
[b]In relation to mean for own sex.
[c]Including those working under thirty hours, whose numbers were too few to compute separately.

hours, roughly the same proportion as of the non-incapacitated (Table A.85, Appendix Eight, page 1058). Significantly more of the low than of the high paid working approximately the same number of hours had some degree of incapacity. Put another way, for the same numbers of hours' work, the incapacitated had relatively lower earnings. This is shown in Table 20.23 for people working different numbers of hours. The finding applies both to men and women. Seventy per cent of incapacitated men with gross earnings of below 60 per cent of the mean, and 81 per cent below 80 per cent, were working more than forty hours a week.

Table 20.24. Percentages of non-incapacitated and incapacitated with differing conditions of work.

Conditions of work (index)[a]	Men: degree of incapacity		Women: degree of incapacity	
	None	Minor, some or appreciable	None	Minor, some or appreciable
Very poor (0)	39	39	12	12
Poor (1–6)	8	8	10	13
Fair (7–8)	17	25	28	35
Good (9–10)	36	28	50	40
Total	100	100	100	100
Number	1,180	211	484	75

NOTE: [a]For a list of the ten items, see page 438.

Finally, slightly fewer of the incapacitated than of the non-incapacitated enjoyed good conditions of work, as measured by an admittedly crude index (Table 20.24). (The ten items are listed on page 438.) There did not appear to be much variation according to degree of incapacity.

Disabled Housewives

In the mid 1960s, public attention was called to the plight of disabled housewives in the United Kingdom. Partly because of the historical exclusion of married women from the obligation to pay national insurance contributions, even when employed, and a consequent lack of entitlement to benefits in their own right, housewives when disabled usually had no claim to benefit. Pressure groups like the Disablement Income Group quoted stark anomalies in the social security system, and the public became aware of the fact that people who were equally disabled were treated very unequally. They might be getting a relatively high weekly benefit if they were disabled in war or industry, a relatively low benefit if they were long-term sick, or nothing at all if they were the wives of men in paid employment, even if considerable sums had to be found, or were needed, for aids and services. Following the announcement of government proposals, including one for a non-contributory invalidity pension in September 1974, M Ps staged a protest at the exclusion of married women, and gained the government's agreement in principle that a small category of housewives should become entitled to a reduced rate of invalidity pension. A non-contributory invalidity pension scheme was introduced in November 1977.

The poverty survey adds to previous knowledge about housewives in at least two respects – in giving estimates of numbers, according to severity of incapacity, *and* risk of being in poverty relative to other married women. We estimated that there were approximately 2,100,000 married women with some, appreciable or severe incapacity, including 715,000 who were appreciably or severely disabled. Two thirds of the latter were aged 60 and over, but we estimated that some 195,000 were aged under 60, including approximately 65,000 under the age of 50. For the reasons discussed earlier, for the disabled population in general, these estimates are higher than those produced in the corresponding government survey.[1] The government had accepted an estimate of only 40,000 disabled housewives who would qualify for benefit.[2]

Married women who are disabled are significantly more likely to be in or close to poverty than women who are not disabled. As Table 20.25 shows, there is a systematic relationship between income and severity of disablement, despite the fact that any direct association must be blurred by the inclusion of the husband's

1. See pages 699–705 above.
2. Social Security Act 1973, *Provision for Chronically Sick and Disabled People*, op. cit., p. 14.

Table 20.25. *Estimated numbers of disabled housewives, and percentages whose incomes were above and below the state's poverty standard.*

Aged	Estimated number (000s)[a] of married women			
	No incapacity (0)	Minor incapacity (1–2)	Some incapacity (3–6)	Appreciable or severe incapacity (7 or over)
15–29	2,390	110	75	10
30–39	2,300	135	100	10
40–49	2,070	285	175	45
50–59	1,230	550	285	130
60+	485	585	570	520
All	8,480	1,670	1,200	715

%	Percentage in income units with income expressed as a % of supplementary benefit scale rates plus housing cost			
0–99	4·0	11·5	8·4	11·5
100–39	16·8	23·1	32·1	35·9
140–99	30·4	26·9	23·7	21·8
200+	48·9	38·5	35·9	30·8
Total	100	100	100	100
Number	925	182	131	78

NOTE: [a]Estimated to nearest 5,000.

earnings and other income. This relationship exists at younger and not only older ages. Thus 29 per cent of married women aged 15–59 in the survey with some, appreciable or severe incapacity were in or close to poverty, compared with 19 per cent of married women of that age with no incapacity. The corresponding figures for the over-sixties were 54 per cent and 38 per cent.

Explanations of Poverty among the Disabled

In general, the greater poverty of disabled people is explained by their uneven or limited access to the principal resource systems of society – the labour market and wage system, national insurance and its associated schemes, and the wealth-accumulating systems, particularly home ownership, life insurance and occupational pension schemes; by the indirect limitation which disability imposes upon the capacities of relatives, pooling personal resources in full or part in the household or family, to earn incomes and accumulate wealth themselves; and by the failure of

society to recognize, or to recognize only unevenly or fitfully, the additional resources that are required in disablement to obtain standards of living equivalent
to those of the non-disabled.

Part of this explanation applies to other minorities and is discussed in a number
of the chapters in the latter part of this report, and particularly the conclusion.
Here attention will be called to matters which could be demonstrated or illustrated for the disabled and long-term sick from the survey. First, we have seen how
disability restricts access to employment. It is not just that employers are less likely to employ people who are disabled or that people are less likely to apply for
jobs which they are incapable of carrying out. Disablement restricts the range of
possible choice of jobs – because journeys would take too long, and transport is
non-existent or costs too much; because redundancy or dismissal from certain
types of job makes other employers reluctant to recruit, often unjustly; and because employment is organized inflexibly so that the disabled cannot be accommodated into its operations. There are two aspects of work organization. It could
be said to have been planned 'thoughtlessly' because some types of potential employees have been excluded. Or put more strongly, by excluding part of the population potentially employable, it could be said to 'create' disablement. More of
the earnings of those disabled people who are employed are low and, indeed, they
tend to work more hours to secure the same earnings as the non-disabled. Conditions of work are sometimes bad – presumably because a number of disabled
feel that as beggars they cannot be choosers and because some employers operate
with 'marginal' workers who have poor pay and/or poor conditions of work, and
who may include other minorities as well as the disabled. After disablement, people are often re-employed at much lower rates of pay in jobs which are called,
sometimes euphemistically, 'light'; or for a time they are allowed to retain pay
and seniority rights while being deprived of responsibility, before being obliged,
or persuaded, to accept redundancy or premature retirement. A substantial sum
at 55 or 60 can have its immediate attractions, but by comparison with a non-
disabled man who serves out his full term of employment to 65, the financial
'reward' (assassed over the rest of life, including pension as well as lump sum on
retirement, and related to years of working service) may be puny. These are only
some of the ways in which remuneration, responsibility and reward from employment are reduced.

The social security system has a number of disadvantages. Except for those with
relatively large families, incomes are normally much below those of people currently in employment, even when they are of comparable age. The war pensions
and industrial injury schemes are sub-systems which are relatively more generous
than other contributory and non-contributory national insurance schemes, but
they are limited access schemes: the majority of disabled people have no entitlement. Within the sickness insurance system, contribution rules sometimes reduce
the incomes received initially by the sick or disabled. After six months, entitle-

ment to earnings-related supplement ceases. Subsequently invalidity benefits do not do much to cushion the fall in income experienced by most men who have been receiving earnings-related sickness benefits. Of course, some disabled men start off at a disadvantage, because their employment has been interrupted before its final termination, and entitlement to earnings-related benefit has been reduced, or because of disability has brought them to a level of pay which has been so low for so long that they may not be entitled to any supplement at all. Long-term receipt of sickness and invalidity benefit or supplementary benefit is also subject to a series of checks and investigations by special officers of the Department of Health and Social Security. While efforts are made to administer these in a humane way, they often reflect popular prejudices about abuse of the social security system and are not informed by professional instruction about the nature and additional needs of different forms of disablement. Additional allowances are received by a minority. Thus, in November 1974, only 27 per cent of sick and disabled people receiving supplementary benefit were also receiving an 'exceptional circumstances addition'.[1]

Other resource systems than the social security system have rules and administrative procedures which obstruct or limit access. People with a disablement condition have difficulty in obtaining life insurance, or have to pay high premiums. Building societies and banks are reluctant to make loans, or only at special rates. Motor insurance cover may be difficult to obtain. In general, credit, and therefore the means to accumulate wealth on a small as well as a large scale, is restricted.

Disability can also have the indirect effect of reducing the resources or access to resources of the immediate family. The best-documented instances are those of wives and daughters who give up work, or lose time from work or can only accept low-paid work near by, because of the disability or illness of a husband, child or parent. By introducing the invalid care allowance for those of working age who can show they have been obliged to give up paid employment, though not for wives, the government has conceded the principle.[2]

Many of the harsh and inconsistent features of the employment and wage system, the social security and other resource systems, merely reflect popular prejudices and low standards of information. Neighbours are sceptical of men who appear to have nothing wrong with them. They suppose they should be back at work and that they are living on the state. Often they do not know that the man may be epileptic, diabetic, manic depressive or have a terminal cancer, and has been medically advised not to work or cannot get work; or they may not understand what these conditions involve, psychologically and socially no less than clinically.

1. DHSS, *Social Security Statistics, 1974*, HMSO, London, 1975, p. 156.
2. Social Security Act 1973, *Social Security Provision for Chronically Sick and Disabled People*, op. cit.

It may be possible in some circumstances to change the resource systems of society without directly attacking popular prejudices and malinformation. Changing them may also have some effect on reducing those prejudices and improving that standard of information. But, in the long run, much will depend on the level of public education and on determined efforts to make employment and other occupations and pursuits more rather than less widely available to people of all ages.

Although invalidity benefit became payable from September 1971 as a replacement of sickness benefit after six months' incapacity for work, it added only small amounts to the incomes of most of the minority of disabled people who qualified for such benefit. The benefit includes an invalidity pension which was at first paid at the same rate as sickness benefit, but later at a higher rate. In late 1978, for example, the single rate was £19·50 a week, compared with £15·75 a week. The rate of £19·50 was the same as for the retirement pension. An invalidity allowance could be granted in addition to the invalidity pension – £4·15 per week if incapacity began before the age of 35, £2·60 before 45, £1.30 before 60 for men or 55 for women, and nothing if after that age. The amounts are not related to degree of disablement, and four men, all aged 61 with equally severe disablement, might be receiving different amounts and, presuming they lived into their 80s, would go on receiving these different amounts for the next twenty years irrespective of any change in the severity of their disablement.

The new benefits for disabled people introduced in the early 1970s increased certain incomes relative to the non-disabled, but did not increase them much for more than a minority. They further complicated the anomalous structure of state support. The attendance allowance, first introduced in 1971, was paid in 1976 at a higher rate to 139,000 people and at a lower rate to 121,000.[1] The non-contributory invalidity pension was expected to be paid to 150,000 (in addition to patients in psychiatric hospitals), the vast majority of whom have their supplementary benefit reduced, leaving them with the same amount of income as before. The invalid care allowance was planned for only 11,000 recipients, and the mobility allowance (paid by 1978 at a rate of £10 a week) for only 100,000.[2] Most blind, mentally ill and mentally handicapped people, as well as all those of pensionable age, do not qualify for this allowance. Organizations representing disabled people have argued in detail that government schemes of income support are uneven and inequitable, and that a comprehensive scheme of allowances graded according to severity of disablement is necessary.[3]

1. *Social Security Statistics, 1976*, HMSO, London, 1978, p. 96.
2. Social Security Act 1973, *Social Security Provision for Chronically Sick and Disabled People*.
3. Disability Alliance, *Poverty and Disability: The Case for a Comprehensive Income Scheme for Disabled People*, London, 1975; see also Disablement Income Group, *Realizing a National Disability Income*, London, 1974.

Summary

The scale of disability in the United Kingdom has so far been underestimated. The survey produces estimates which, even allowing for differences of definition, are considerably larger than government estimates for the same year. Twelve per cent, representing over 6½ million, both said they had a disablement condition and that it prevented them doing things which were normal for people their age. According to an alternative measure, 15½ per cent of people aged 10 and over, or 7 million, had some, appreciable or severe incapacity, including 1·1 million with severe incapacity. Although nearly 3 million of the 7 million were aged 70 and over, and nearly 2 million in their sixties, over 2 million were under 60 years of age.

More of the working than the middle class, particularly unskilled manual workers and their families, are disabled. Increasing incapacity is correlated with falling cash incomes and 58 per cent of those with appreciable or severe incapacity, compared with 24 per cent of the non-incapacitated, were in households with incomes below or close to the government's supplementary benefit standard. At successive ages, greater incapacity was associated with greater risk of being poor.

The incapacitated also had fewer assets and personal possessions of different kinds, and when the value of these are taken into account, the gap between the living standards of the incapacitated and non-incapacitated widens. Indeed, the difference is marked for people at every age (see in particular, Table 20.12, page 713).

These differences corresponded with differences in measures of various forms of deprivation. Compared with the non-incapacitated, more of the incapacitated lived in poor housing, had poor facilities, missed cooked meals, ate meat infrequently, were short of fuel and lacked winter heating. Fewer had been on a week's summer holiday. More confessed to difficulties in managing on their incomes.

Prolonged current illness is also associated with low income. Nearly twice as many people who had been ill for over ten weeks as of those who had not been ill lived in income units with incomes below or on the margins of the supplementary benefit standard.

The vast majority of people with a disablement condition were not currently ill, and of those who had been ill for ten weeks or more, only 60 per cent had a disablement condition. On the basis of the survey, it was estimated that there are at any one time three quarters of a million people who have been ill off work or school or ill in bed or confined to the house for ten weeks or more, including over 400,000 with appreciable or severe incapacity.

Significantly more of those in the sample complaining of trouble with nerves than not so doing were in or on the margins of poverty. This applied at each age. A disproportionately large number of them were women. There was evidence, too, of the mentally ill being poorer than other people at similar levels of incapacity.

Four specific disadvantages of the employment system are demonstrated: fewer of the incapacitated than of the non-incapacitated are employed; fewer have high earnings and more have low earnings; when they secure the same earnings, they tend to have to work longer hours; and slightly fewer have good conditions of work.

We estimated there were 2,100,000 married women with some, appreciable or severe incapacity, including 715,000 who were appreciably or severely disabled. These women were more likely than other married women to be in income units in or close to poverty.

The principal argument of the chapter is that poverty among disabled people is explained by society denying them access to different kinds of resource. This is discussed in relation to the employment and wage system, the social security system and other resource systems. There are multiplier effects of deprivation from disability which are not fully recognized. Disabled people often need a higher income than the non-disabled to secure comparable living standards. People are unable to get work and their relatives sometimes have to give up work too, or are obliged to accept low-paid jobs. They are prevented from sharing, or sharing to the same extent, the activities and pleasures of most people of their age.

21

Handicapped Children

Comparatively little systematic work has been carried out in the United Kingdom to establish the total numbers of handicapped children of different kinds, and to establish their family and social situations and needs. Although the poverty survey was insufficient in scale to discover large numbers and allow a full picture to be given, it does, in certain respects, provide a more accurate estimate of numbers and proportion in the population and a preliminary account, for different types of handicap, of standards of life and circumstances.

The government's survey of the handicapped in 1968-9 excluded children under the age of 16. There are at least three independent sources of information.[1] First, the Department of Health estimates the number cautiously at 150,000,[2] and Table 21.1 gives the numbers of handicapped on local-authority registers and receiving certain types of service. But there are a number of deficiencies in these statistics. Some children are counted twice – for example, some of those in the care of local-authority mental-health services and those awaiting admission to special schools. A few small groups of physically handicapped and chronic sick children in ordinary schools and in hospitals are not separately identified. And there are wide variations in the numbers registered in different regions and areas. These variations have been shown by research and special administrative measures to be due more to laxity of administration in registering children than to variations in prevalence. Many handicapped children are not known to any service. More strenuous efforts have been made in Scotland than in England to locate the handicapped, and though the Scottish Home and Health Department admitted in 1973 that there was still some way to go, far more physically handicapped children have been registered there than in England although the latter had nearly ten times the popula-

1. There have been a series of studies of illness and handicap among children in Britain, but these have not attempted to measure the duration and degree of handicap of different types of condition. See, for example, Spence, J., *et al.*, *A Thousand Families in Newcastle-upon-Tyne*, Oxford University Press, 1954, and Miller, F. J. W., *et al.*, *Growing Up in Newcastle-upon-Tyne*, Oxford University Press, 1960.

2. Report of the Committee on Local Authority and Allied Personal Social Services (The Seebohm Report), Cmnd 3703, HMSO, London, 1968.

tion. According to Scottish experience there should be 80,000 to 100,000 handicapped children, excluding children who are mentally handicapped, deaf, blind or partially sighted, on the English local registers. In 1971 there were fewer than 6,000.[1] Even if the Department of Health and Social Security total is revised conservatively on the basis of that experience, the numbers of handicapped children must be considerably in excess of 200,000.

Table 21.1. *Numbers of handicapped children in the United Kingdom estimated from official sources.*[a]

Number of mentally handicapped children in hospital	7,100
Registered blind	2,300
Registered partially sighted	3,300
Registered deaf and partially deaf	6,300
Handicapped (general classes) on local authority registers	15,700
Number physically handicapped and delicate children in special schools	19,500
Number of educationally subnormal children in special schools	59,000
Additional number attending special schools, formerly training centres	21,400
Number educationally subnormal children awaiting admission to special schools, and those receiving education in their own homes	10,400[b]
Numbers in care of local-authority mental-health services	31,300

NOTES: [a]Estimates have in some instances been made in proportion to the population of children, for Northern Ireland and also Wales.
[b]England and Wales only.

SOURCES: *Census of Mentally Handicapped Patients in Hospital in England and Wales at the end of 1970*, HMSO, London, 1972; *Digest of Health Statistics 1970*, HMSO, London, 1971; DHSS, Annual Report for 1971, HMSO, London, 1972; *Health of the School Child 1966–68*, HMSO, London, 1969.

Secondly, the National Children's Bureau found in a survey of 7-year-olds that 2·6 per cent were congenitally handicapped and another 1·6 per cent had been injured after accidents, had progressively disabling illnesses, were severely or partially deaf or were otherwise in need of special educational treatment.[2] If these two percentages are applied to children of all ages, a total in the United Kingdom of more than 500,000 children is reached. However, some will be only slightly handicapped, for the National Child Development Study, as the bureau's follow-up survey is called, includes medical examinations but does not establish functional effects.

Thirdly, a major survey in 1964 and 1965 of the education, health and behaviour of 9- to 12-year-old children living in the Isle of Wight, undertaken with extensive cooperation of the medical and local authorities, offers an alternative

1. DHSS, *Annual Report for 1971*, HMSO, London, 1972, p. 240.
2. Davie, R., *et al.*, *From Birth to Seven*, Longmans, Green, London, 1972.

source of estimation. Among the total population on that island of children aged 10–12, 5·7 per cent were identified as having physical disorders, including (in order of prevalence) asthma (2·3 per cent); eczema (1·0 per cent); epilepsy (0·6 per cent); cerebral palsy (0·5 per cent); other brain disorders (0·4 per cent); orthopaedic conditions (0·3 per cent); heart disease (0·2 per cent); severe deafness (0·2 per cent); diabetes (0·1 per cent); neuromuscular disorders (0·1 per cent); and miscellaneous disorders (0·4 per cent).[1] However, some of these, especially with transient asthmatic attacks, had no difficulty with everyday activities. The authors classified the children according to severity of handicap: after allowances are made for incomplete information, it seems that 1·1 per cent were moderately, severely or extremely handicapped, in the sense that they had difficulty or discomfort or restriction or inability to perform ordinary activities, or needed substantial regular help with dressing, washing, bathing or feeding, or needed help with all or nearly all ordinary activities; a further 2·2 per cent were slightly handicapped, in the sense that while they had no difficulty with everyday activities, they did have difficulty or discomfort or restriction in performing any strenuous activities, or had a limp or wore surgical shoes or other aids, or had dietary restrictions; and finally, 2·4 per cent who had a chronic condition but, except for transient episodes, no limitation of daily or even strenuous activities.[2] These proportions apply, of course, only to children aged 10–12, and children living on the Isle of Wight. If they are applied to all children aged under 16 in the United Kingdom, they would produce population totals of 157,000, 314,000 and 343,000 in the three categories respectively.

This evidence leads to the conclusion that there must be at least 400,000 children in the United Kingdom whose activities are restricted because of handicap, 150,000 of them substantially or seriously.[3] But, by the nature of the evidence, this conclusion must be imprecise, and there is an obvious need for more comprehensive work which identifies the incapacitating effect of the different types of handicap, and goes on to show what financial and social needs arise as a consequence.

Different Forms of Handicap

There were 1,543 persons, or 25 per cent, in the present sample who were aged under 15. A variety of questions sought to show how many had any trouble from

1. Rutter, M., Tizard, J., and Whitmore, K., *Education, Health and Behaviour*, Longmans, Green, London, 1970, pp. 285–96.
2. In ibid., chronic handicap is defined a little inconsistently (compare, for example, the emphasis on pp. 275–8 on conditions lasting twelve months with the emphasis on p. 288 on inability to undertake ordinary or strenuous activities). The totals allocated to degrees of handicap in Table 18.3 (p. 289) were aggregated and adjusted in terms of information on p. 286 about children with asthma and eczema. See ibid., pp. 288–91.
3. A review of previous evidence will also be found in Bradshaw, J., *The Financial Needs of Disabled Children*, Disability Alliance, London, 1975, pp. 2–5.

ill-health, injury or disablement and, in particular, how many had a marked handicap. Table 21·2 lists the percentages and estimated numbers in the population with a disablement condition who were handicapped in various other senses.

Over 5 per cent, representing 780,000 in the total population, had a disablement condition giving trouble. Over a third had trouble with chest or lungs, several of whom had asthma, and about a quarter had trouble with speech, hearing or eyesight. About a tenth were specifically said to have a mental handicap other than nerves, the equivalent rate in fact being 5 per 1,000 for all children under 15, in fact slightly higher for children under 10 and slightly lower for children aged 10–14. Others had a range of different conditions, including spinal trouble, trouble with joints, diabetes and mental illness. Three children suffered from a kidney disorder, including one with four kidneys.

The numbers in the sample with differing disabling conditions correspond closely with estimates derived from other sources. For example, the rate per 1,000 produced by children found to be having trouble with chest or lungs is 22, and the corresponding rate for children aged 5–15 with asthma, published in the Seebohm Report, was 23,[1] and for children aged 7 in the National Child Development Study was 27.[2] The rate per 1,000 for the mentally handicapped was 6, compared with rates for the 'severely subnormal' of 3·5 and 2·7 respectively.[3]

The parents of the children were also asked one or more questions to check whether the condition had a restricting effect on activity (see also pages 688–91 above). When they answered positively, this was counted as confirming the existence of a disablement condition. This procedure gives a *minimum* estimate of those in fact having a disablement condition which has a marked or specific restriction on activity. Had there been time to ask further questions, other forms of restriction on activity might have been established. Altogether, 2 per cent of children were so identified, representing 265,000 in the total population. Here, as elsewhere in this chapter, the small numbers on which our estimates are based are subject to considerable sampling errors. We have chosen to put forward the estimates, however, on two grounds: first, that the sample has been shown to correspond very closely in its structure to the structure of the population, as demonstrable from the census and other sources; and secondly, that there is a lack of reliable information about handicapped children.

Questions about incapacity were asked of children aged 10–14 but not of younger children. An entirely different set of questions would have been required for very young children, and we were aware that the questions that were used for ac-

1. Packman, J., and Power, M., 'Children in Need and the Help they Receive', Appendix Q in the Report of the Committee on Local Authorities and Allied Personal Social Services, HMSO, London, 1968.

2. Younghusband, E., *et al.* (eds.), *Living with Handicap*, National Children's Bureau, London, 1970, p. 82.

3. ibid.

Table 21.2. *Percentages and estimated number of children aged under 15 who had different forms of handicap.*

Characteristic	%	Estimated number in non-institutionalized population (000s)
1. Health said by parent to be poor for age	1·1	155
2. (a) Having trouble with a disablement condition	5·4	780
(b) Having a disablement condition with marked or specific restriction of activity	1·8	265
3. Ill off school and/or at home or in bed for 10 weeks or more	0·2	30
4. (a) Normally confined to bed	0·2	35
(b) Not confined to bed but cannot walk unaided	0·2	35
5. (a) Attending training centre	0·2	35
(b) Attending special school	0·3	65
6. (a) *Of those aged 10–14* slight incapacity	0·6	25
some incapacity	0·9	35
appreciable or severe	1·3	55

NOTE: The figures are subject to considerable sampling errors and are put forward for reasons given in the text.

tive older children and adults would have had to be modified for children aged, say, 7–9. Otherwise incapacity might merely have been equated with immaturity. But the problem is deeper even than this, because children do not all develop at the same pace in conformity with their chronological age.[1] Previous research on handicap among young children shows how difficult it is to assume that differences among children can be measured simply by varying sets of questions to children according to their chronological age. Slow development can be mistaken for incapacity and vice versa, as parents of mentally handicapped children have found.[2] In principle, measures for the very young (and perhaps very old) either have to be related to modal behaviour at that age or to standard adult activity. Agreed research procedures which apply functional criteria to young children are likely to be important explanatory tools and also devices for the allocation in policy of services and other benefits.

Among children aged 10–14, relatively few were found to have incapacity: 0·6

1. Further research between 1974 and 1976 financed by the DHSS, on functional assessment scales, including research on children, was undertaken by Alan Walker at the University of Essex.
2. Jaehnig, W., *Mentally Handicapped Children and Their Families*, unpublished Ph.D. thesis, University of Essex, 1974.

per cent slight (representing 25,000), 0·9 per cent some incapacity (35,000) and 1·3 per cent appreciable or severe incapacity (55,000).

Parents were reluctant to say that the health of their children was generally poor for their age, and only just over 1 per cent did so. These included a disproportionately high number of children with disabling conditions, but not all. Again, the combined numbers of children found to be attending special schools and training centres, of just under 100,000 compared fairly closely with annual totals produced by central and local departments.[1]

In order to examine standards of living of households in which there was a handicapped child, we employed strict criteria of handicap. We included the *immobile*, those who were normally confined to bed or to the house or off school for at least ten weeks; the long-term ill, those confined to bed or to the house or off school for at least ten weeks; those with a *marked disablement condition* (epilepsy, mental handicap, deafness, blindness, etc.); those *attending a special school, training centre, day or occupational centre, outpatients' department, etc.*, for reason of long-term illness or handicap. No child was counted as having a disablement condition without also being said to suffer some specific impairment of function (i.e. becoming breathless; having fits of coughing; or having difficulty in moving freely or in moving hands, hearing ordinary conversation; joining in ordinary conversation outside the family; reading ordinary print, even with glasses) or, in the case of a psychiatric condition, being known to be receiving treatment by a doctor or believed to require such treatment.

Poverty among Handicapped Children

Twenty-eight children were so identified, living in twenty-six households comprising a total of eighty-three people in the total sample of 6,098. The numbers are small, and for this reason any comparison between their distribution among different income groups and that of the rest of the population must be regarded as provisional only. However, if twenty-eight children found to be handicapped among 1,500 is representative, then there are 250,000 in the United Kingdom. The proportion in any particular income group is, of course, subject to substantial sampling error. But, for the reasons given above (page 743), we believe it right to put forward the figures. Table 21.3 suggests that substantially more people in such households are in poverty, and fewer have relatively high incomes. About half in the sample were in, or on the margins of, poverty by the supplementary benefit standard. Nearly a third were in poverty by the deprivation standard.

A supplementary measure was of incapacity among children aged 10–14. Nearly twice as many children living in income units in which at least one of the chil-

1. For example, 19,955 children were in junior training centres in 1968 and 57,000 day pupils in special schools, in England and Wales. Department of Education and Science, *Statistics of Education, 1968*, vol. 1, H M S O, London, 1969.

746 POVERTY IN THE UNITED KINGDOM

Table 21.3. *Percentages of people in households with a handicapped child, other people, and all children, who are in poverty.*

| | Net disposable income last year | | | | | |
| | As % of supplementary benefits scale plus housing cost | | | As % deprivation standard of poverty | | |
%	People in households with handicapped child	People in other households	All children	People in households with handicapped child	People in other households	All children
Under 100	25	6	7	55	23	29
100–39	25	22	27	} 36	57	57
140–99	25	29	40		57	57
200+	24	43	26	8	20	14
Total	100	100	100	100	100	100
Number	83	5,076	1,332	5,063	1,263	1,355

dren had a score on the incapacity index of 1 or more as other children were in or on the margins of poverty (Table A.87, Appendix Eight, page 1059). But their numbers in the sample were small.

Over three quarters of the families were working class, dividing equally between parents with skilled manual and those with partly skilled manual and unskilled manual jobs, thus suggesting the likelihood of a higher proportion in these less numerous classes. Three of the families were professional or managerial, and the remainder other non-manual classes.

The children belonged to a range of different types of families: nine in households with parents and one, two or three children, five in households with parents and four or more children, twelve in households with three adults and children, and the remainder in other types of household.

Illustrations of Families with a Handicapped Child

1. Tom

Tom, 11, lives with his mother and father, in their late thirties, and three younger brothers of 8, 2 and 1, in a four-roomed flat above an unoccupied shop in a northern city (rent £2·50). There is no garden. He has asthma and a hole in the heart and he cannot run about or climb stairs without becoming breathless. He attends a special school. Two of his brothers also have chest troubles. The family live in poverty, having an income less than 90 per cent of the supplementary benefit standard. Their income consists of £10 sickness benefit plus £2·90 family allowances. They were not receiving supplementary benefit. They had no assets, and although the home was very clean, there was little furniture. They had only one of the durables (a television set) on our list. The flat was structurally damp and they felt over-crowded. Tom's father has not worked for two years and was previously a cloth-ing cutter. He has had a series of stomach operations and had part of his stomach removed. He has spent a period of twenty-six days in hospital this year and has spasms of acute pain. He has applied to go on a government resettlement course, but will not be accepted until declared fit. His wife has anaemia and finds the de-mands of sick husband and children a strain. Until the birth of her two youngest children, she had worked as an auxiliary nurse. The family have not had a holiday and had not had an evening out lately, though the mother and two of the children go regularly to a Catholic church. Rarely do they eat fresh meat, except for the two older children who have free meals at school. At the time of interview (Jan-uary), husband and wife were going to bed early to save fuel 'for next day when the children would be up'. She said her husband gave her the entire £10. 'He scarcely spends any money on himself – five shillings a week. Newspapers, that's all.' They felt poor 'all the time. We haven't two pennies to rub together.'

2. Gillian

Gillian, aged 13, had acute rheumatic fever three years earlier and has to be watched carefully. She is delicate, had had twenty-eight days' illness in bed in the previous twelve months, and is in frequent regular contact with the GP. She has difficulty in performing everyday activities such as washing, bending down, stretching, going up and down stairs and running. Her parents are in their mid forties and also have an older son of 16, who is at a Government Training Centre, and two younger daughters. The father works for the Electricity Board as a patrol-man and earned £11·95 after deductions the previous week. The house is terraced in a village in Scotland, and has no WC indoors. Both husband and wife's par-ents live locally and see the family daily. Even allowing for the 16-year-old's low earnings (after expenses), the family's income is on the margins of the state pov-erty line.

3. Vivien

Vivien is 4, the youngest of a young family consisting of husband and wife and five children all under 10. They live on the margins of the state poverty line on a wage of £15 in a council house in Norwich. Vivien is mentally handicapped and has a speech defect. She has been given a place in an ordinary nursery class be-cause she is backward. Vivien had been to see a doctor at the hospital twelve times in the year prior to interview, and had been visited once by the children's officer in the same period. She had not been on holiday or away from home in the past twelve months, although the family does go on picnics sometimes.

4. Ann

There are two daughters aged 8 and 6, the eldest of whom, Ann, has been in bed for sixteen weeks after an operation to her back and is encased in plaster, except for her head and legs. Ann suffers from spina bifida, and her hearing and speech are impaired. She normally attends a special school. Her parents, 34 and 32, were among the most prosperous parents with a handicapped child in the survey. They own a semi-detached house worth £3,500 in Gloucestershire, with all amenities except central heating, and had spent £400 improving it in the last twelve months. The father is an electrician and his wife a nurse working two nights a week at a mental hospital. His take-home pay in the previous week was £17 (for a short week), but he normally earns about £25 a week. His wife earns about £33 a month. They have a car and are paying a substantial sum for furniture in hire purchase. Except for her night work at hospital, when her husband can, of course, look after their daughter, the wife does not go out and their social life is severely restricted.

5. Michael

Michael, 10, lives in a semi-detached council house with a small garden, in a Midlands city, with his parents in their forties and five older brothers and sisters. He has a weak heart and also a chest complaint and spent twenty-one days in hospital this year. He is taken to an out-patients' department for a check every few months, and has difficulty in joining in ordinary activities, including climbing stairs and running. He attends a special school. His father is a Post Office sorter, earning a low wage, but three of the older children are at work and contribute to household expenses. The chief problem is that the mother is frequently ill, has St Vitus's Dance, migraine, arthritis and is mentally unstable. She sleeps badly and says she weeps from depression all the time. She has been in mental hospital for a fortnight this year, has also had twenty-four days altogether ill in bed and attends an out-patients' department regularly for treatment.

6. Tony

Tony is 10. He lives with his mother and father, older sister and grandfather. His father, a maintenance worker with a water-softener firm, has take-home earnings of about £17. They had moved as owner-occupiers into a six-roomed detached house in mid Wales only six weeks previously, and extensive repairs remain to be undertaken. Tony has a spinal disablement, such that he has difficulty in moving freely and using his hands. He also has kidney trouble for which he needs to have frequent injections, and to see the doctor regularly. He experiences difficulty in, for example, reaching overhead and bending down, say, to cut his toenails. Also he finds it impossible to run anywhere and to carry a light load in each hand. He attends the local state primary school, but comes home to dinners because his mother prefers it. He had spent six nights in hospital in the year prior to the interview, visited the hospital doctor three times, and been to his own doctor's surgery seven times. Although he had not been away from home in the past twelve months, or out in the evening in the past two weeks, Tony has friends in to play and there is a garden.

7. Jenny

Jenny, 12, has a condition affecting her joints and cannot move freely. She cannot carry a shopping basket or run to catch a bus, and has difficulty climbing stairs, washing down and engaging in other activities. Her brother of 11 is mentally backward and attends a special school. Their parents are in their forties and have a third child, a daughter of 4. In addition to the two handicapped children, the mother has the care of her father, 76, who is severely incapacitated with arteriosclerosis. The family occupies a modern five-roomed council house with a substantial garden (Bristol), and the father has net earnings of about £20 a week as a sales representative.

8. Joan

Joan is 13 and has a brother of 15 and a twin sister. Her father is a shop assistant earning about £13 a week, and her mother has cleaning work in a factory for £6 a week. The family lives in a self-contained flat in London on the second floor of a large council block (there is a lift). Joan has four kidneys; consequently she is a delicate child and frequently ill. Because of her condition she must regularly attend hospital for check-ups, and had spent ten days there during the twelve months prior to interview. She had also spent a total of fifty-six days at home in bed due to illness, being visited by the doctor each day. She had been to the doctor's surgery a further twelve times. Joan had been dancing with her sister in the previous fortnight and had a friend at home to play.

9. Mary

Mary, 12, has attended a boarding school for the mentally handicapped since she was five. She sees her parents and older brother of 15 at home during school holidays. Her father is a miner, working underground for about £18·50 a week. Her mother is a canteen assistant, earning £10 a week, and her brother is a shop assistant, earning £5. According to her father, Mary has some sort of muscular disease, but he does not know what it is. Mary is severely handicapped because she is completely unable to reach overhead, tie a knot, cut her toenails or carry light loads, and finds it hard to wash herself and go up and down stairs.

*

In the four area samples surveyed in Belfast, Neath, Glasgow and Salford, there were twenty-nine households in which there was a handicapped child (following the same definition as that given above). Five of these had a net disposable income in the previous year of below the state's poverty standard, and another eleven of less than 40 per cent above that standard – amounting to more than half the families altogether. Only two of these families had an income of more than twice the poverty standard.

Summary and Conclusion

The data obtained in the poverty survey about handicapped children were limited but, first, help to confirm that the number of handicapped children is much larger than is officially estimated, and secondly, suggest that disproportionately large numbers of the families affected are in, or on the margins of, poverty – whether defined according to the deprivation standard or whether by the state.

The chapter also suggests how urgent it is to obtain *comprehensive* evidence about all children, on a national basis. It must be comprehensive in the sense that it is restricted neither to a particular cohort nor to particular types of disability, must identify *degrees* of incapacity and changes in degree over time, and must show the various family and social problems to which handicap give rise. Little is known about numbers with different degrees of handicap. Some children may be only mildly handicapped and require little more parental supervision and care than children who are not handicapped. Others place severe psychological, physical and financial demands on their parents. Some need special aids, frequent replacements of shoes and clothing, a special diet, a specially designed home environment, or regular subsidies for transport.[1]

One reason why a comprehensive approach is urgent is that the pattern of handicap is changing and therefore shaping the need for a new grouping of treatments and services in adulthood as well as childhood. During the past fifty years, cerebral palsy and spina bifida have begun to replace poliomyelitis and heart disease as principal causes of handicap. The change is, of course, based largely on the development of new drugs and methods of surgery, but also on the acceptance

1. These have been discussed more fully in Bradshaw, *Financial Needs of Disabled Children*, pp. 5–7. Also see Baldwin, S., 'The Financial Problems of Families with Handicapped Children: An Evaluation of the Attendance Allowance', Family Fund Project Paper, November 1974; and Baldwin S., *Disabled Children – Counting the Costs*, Disability Alliance, London, 1977.

by more of the medical profession and of the public of malformation, at least among children. The numbers of handicapped children who survive the critical weeks after birth is likely to increase.

A working party on children with special needs, under the chairmanship of Dame Eileen Younghusband, concluded:

Overall national planning of services and provision for handicapped children – and adults – is at the present time conspicuous by its absence ... There is an urgent need for effective machinery for co-ordinated appraisal, clarification of priorities and policy determination in relation to the total well-being of handicapped children.[1]

Another reason why a comprehensive approach is urgent is that while such an approach to a maternity service has been achieved within the National Health Service, nothing comparable has yet been devised for children. This will involve new forms of organization and training for doctors[2] and unification of educational and community services for children. There have been a number of recent studies and pressures questioning the policy of placing many handicapped children in special schools.[3] There is illustrative evidence that the educational content of that experience is sometimes neglected[4] and its emotional and social content limited.[5] The transfer of junior training centres for mentally handicapped children to education authorities makes acute the balance of choice between ordinary and special school. And the fragmented and inadequate methods of registering handicapped children implies the need for the new social service departments of local councils to replan the services they can provide for families.

Some progress has been made in outlining successive stages of child development in statistical terms, but attempts to understand handicap must be based in large measure on estimates of incapacity at successive ages. Prediction of handicap is very restricted, especially for mental handicap.[6] The most remarkable discovery from the many longitudinal studies of children now completed is the variability in the pattern of individual development. Some children develop at a steady rate, others show large fluctuations from year to year.[7] The course taken in handicap needs to be traced and can be classified as static non-adaptable, static adaptable, degenerative, regenerative or intermittent. If the relative importance of these

1. Younghusband, E., et al. (eds.), Living with Handicap, National Children's Bureau, London, 1970, p. 23.
2. Chamberlain, R. N., 'Children in the Integrated National Health Service', Lancet, 4 November 1972.
3. For example, Eckstein, H. B., and Macnab, G. H., Lancet, (i) 1966, p. 842; and 'The Handicapped Child at School', editorial note in Lancet, 11 March 1967.
4. See Rawlings, H. E., 'The Handicapped Child at School', Lancet, 15 April 1967.
5. Hunt, P. (ed.), Stigma, Chapman, London, 1966.
6. See, for example, Yarrow, L., in Glass, D. C. (ed.), Environmental Influences, New York, 1968.
7. See the review of 'Influences in Child Development', Lancet, 4 November 1972.

types of handicap are to be elucidated, base-lines have to be established from some kind of cross-sectional study at a preliminary stage of research.

Some major disabilities are not in practice identified in early infancy and only come to light, or develop, much later. Muscular dystrophy, for example, may not become apparent until a child begins to walk, and severe mental handicap may not be diagnosed among children under 5, or even under 10. The reported incidence is only 0·5 per 1,000 under 5 years of age, compared with 3·5 per 1,000 at 15–19. As the Tunbridge Committee stated in a recent report on *Rehabilitation*: 'Disability in children is rarely easy to analyse in the early years. The early identification of disability is best achieved by a periodic developmental assessment for all children.'[1]

Finally, a comprehensive approach is required if the different financial needs of families are to be properly compared and explained, and a government policy to be formulated to meet those needs and remedy the situation found in this survey. In 1972, public interest was aroused on behalf of 400 Thalidomide children and pressure put on the Distiller's Company to provide adequate compensation. The government also announced the allocation of £3 million in the first instance, to be administered by the Joseph Rowntree Memorial Trust on behalf of severely congenitally disabled children, including the Thalidomide children. But the latter comprise only about 1 in 1,000 handicapped children, and the group which the government was indirectly helping with limited grants was also only a small minority.[2] Moreover, the attendance allowance which had been introduced in 1970 had by 1973 been taken up by only 2,000 of the parents with severely handicapped children, and parents of infants under the age of 2 are not eligible. Any attempt to consider all handicapped children must imply a more rational approach to a state system of allowances, and one with a better-ordered sense of priorities. Such a system will need to include a principal system of maintenance allowances, perhaps on the model of family allowances, though related as a percentage of a maximum allowance according to degree of incapacity, supplemented by different grades of attendance allowance (there are four rates of attendance allowance in the war pension scheme), special allowances for the expenses of extra clothing, transport and services, and a more equitable system of compensation (following the report of the Pearson Commission).

1. DHSS, Central Health Services Council, *Rehabilitation*, Report of a Sub-committee of the Standing Medical Advisory Committee, HMSO, London, 1972, p. 55.
2. In October 1974, a further allocation of £3 million was made. By 1975, about £4 million had been distributed to 17,000 families as lump-sum grants for items ranging from adaptations and cars to clothing grants.

22
One-Parent Families

with Dennis Marsden

This chapter will explore the economic and social disadvantages of one-parent families. They are a minority, albeit a substantial one, in a society in which, by numerical standards, marriage has become increasingly popular,[1] and in which the two-parent family, headed traditionally by the man, has been regarded as the most appropriate group for rearing children. Previous studies have established how, in consequence of their atypical membership and their apparent transgression of traditional standards of family life, one-parent families tend to suffer severe disadvantages.[2] Those studies have also shown that some families among them suffer more than others and are by no means regarded by the public as equally deserving. By manipulation of levels of, and access to, income support, in ways which will be discussed in more detail below, attempts have been made to control what is felt to be undesirable deviation from normal standards of behaviour. As a result, income support for the families reflects differing degrees of public esteem for parents of different marital status.

The national and special area samples will be used to illustrate how the living standards of such families are affected by social disapproval of their minority status and also change during the cycle of home-building and child-rearing. The national sample produced sixty one-parent families (including motherless families), and the special area samples an additional forty-nine one-parent families. Our data therefore refer to a total of 109 families. We also obtained individual

1. The Finer Committee summed up its popularity in the following way: 'Among women born in various nineteenth century quinquennia, a steady proportion amounting to 860-880 in each 1000 had married by the ages of 50–54 years. By contrast, a more sophisticated nuptuality calculation based on the marriage registrations of 1951–1955 showed that as many as 945 women in each 1000 (that is, some 75 in each 1000 more than in the Victorian period) would be likely to marry before they were 50.' By the 1960s the figure touched 960. See Report of the Committee on One-Parent Families (The Finer Report), Cmnd 5629, HMSO, London, 1974, p. 25.

2. For example, ibid.; Hunt, A., *et al.*, *Families and Their Needs*, HMSO, London, 1973; Marshall, R., *Families Receiving Supplementary Benefit*, DHSS Statistical and Research Report Series No. 1, HMSO, London, 1972; George, V., and Wilding, P., *Motherless Families*, Routledge & Kegan Paul, London, 1972; Marsden, D., *Mothers Alone*, Allen Lane, London, 1969 (rev. edn, Penguin Books, Harmondsworth, 1973).

information for the 211 children in these families which could be compared with information about the much larger number of children in two-parent families.

The geographical dispersion and wide range of social situations among one-parent families make the collection of representative data on different types of family very difficult, and these numbers cannot be regarded as sufficient for detailed analysis. However, while small, they are drawn from a large total number of households and can be regarded as broadly representative of one-parent families throughout the United Kingdom (and the group from the area samples of some of the poorest areas of country). When the national survey was being planned, the lack of information at that time about fatherless families led us to devote one of the preliminary pilot reports to that subject.[1] That work was part of a general sustained pressure which led the government to set up a special Committee on One-Parent Families, under Mr Justice Finer, which reported in 1974.[2] Special studies were carried out for the committee, and other official and privately conducted studies now provide further information on the social and economic conditions of one-parent families.[3] These various studies comprise a valuable yardstick in interpreting the findings from our own survey and will be reviewed in conjunction with those findings in the following pages.

The Total Numbers of One-Parent Families

Until comparatively recently, there was, significantly, no collective name for, and no official estimate of the numbers of, one-parent families.[4] It now transpires that, at any one time, rather less than one in ten of all families with dependent children have only one parent by reason of death, divorce, separation or births outside marriage. The largest group are the separated, followed by the divorced and the widowed, then motherless families and finally unmarried mothers. In the United Kingdom, nearly two thirds of a million parents, at least five in every six of whom are mothers, are looking after 1 million children single-handed.

Table 22.1 compares national estimates produced from the 1971 Census and by the Department of Health and Social Security for the Finer Committee with estimates from the survey. Bearing in mind the inclusion of Northern Ireland in the survey, and the substantial sampling error to which small sub-samples in the survey are subject, the total estimates from the two sources are not very dissimilar. What needs to be remembered is that the survey estimate is based on a definition which is rather narrower than official estimates based principally on the census. Since variations of definition can lead to substantial differences in the estimated

1. Marsden, *Mothers Alone*.   2. The Finer Report.
3. Hunt, *Families and Their Needs*; Marshall, *Families Receiving Supplementary Benefit*; and George and Wilding, *Motherless Families*. See also the Finer Report, vol. 2, Appendices.
4. The book by Wynn, M., *Fatherless Families*, Michael Joseph, London, 1969, appeared in 1964, making a case for common treatment and producing the first composite estimate; but it was not until 1967 that government reports began to present statistics on fatherless families.

Table 22.1. *Estimated numbers of one-parent families with dependent children.*

Family status	Census 1971 (Britain)		DHSS estimates for Britain,[a] 1971 (000s)		Survey estimates UK,[b] 1968–9 (000s)	
	Families	Children	Families	Children	Families	Children
Female:						
Unmarried	49	77	90	120	105	160
Married but separated	187	354	190	360	170	355
Divorced	131	213	120	240	90	135
Widowed	119	235	120	200	90	180
Male:						
Unmarried, separated, divorced or widowed	116	187	100	160	80	180
All 1-parent	601	1,066	620	1,080	535	1,010

NOTES: [a]These are estimates made by the Statistics and Research Division of the DHSS for the Finer Committee, which were based on a 1 per cent sample of census forms for 1971 and adjusted in the light of information from other sources, especially the General Household Survey of 1971 and 1972. See Report of the Committee on One-Parent Families (the Finer Report), Cmnd 5629, HMSO, London, 1974, p. 22 and Appendix 4.
[b]Information collected and coded individually by interviewers and checked subsequently in the office against other information. Note that in some respects the definition of one-parent family is narrower than in the census. The total sample for which data were obtained was 6,084 and, since the total non-institutionalized population for the UK in 1968–9 was estimated to be 54,400,000, sample numbers have been multiplied by $\dfrac{54,400,000}{6,084}$ and a population estimate is given to the nearest 5,000.

numbers of one-parent families, we will briefly describe the sources of these estimates.

Special efforts were taken to ensure that one-parent families could be identified. In the survey, the interviewer established the sex, age and marital status of everyone in the household, and then asked of each person whether or not they had stayed in the home last night. This was particularly useful in correctly classifying both membership of the household and marital status. In the case of married people whose husbands or wives were away, the interviewer also asked how long it was since they had been at home or since they had been living together as man and wife. The answers usually allowed the interviewer to decide whether the separation was believed to be permanent or temporary. Married people were classified as follows:

1. Married, present, last night.
2. Married, away, last night.
3. Married, separated, no court order.
4. Married, separated, court order.

In the case of husbands or wives who had been away for thirteen weeks or more, or who were away and were not expected back within that period, they were not counted as members of the household. If their spouses had children and expected their partners home or clearly believed they were living together as man and wife, they were not counted as a one-parent family.

The interviewer also put questions for each dependent child in the household to establish whether one or both natural parents were present. This enabled us to classify separately those children who had both one natural and one legal or accepted stepfather or stepmother (there were twenty-eight in the sample representing some 250,000 children in the population) and children neither of whose natural parents were living in the household, including children with both parents dead. These children were adopted or fostered (there were fifteen in the sample, representing some 135,000 in the population). The distribution of dependent children, according to the presence or not of both parents in the household, is shown in Table A.88 (Appendix Eight, page 1060), both for the UK sample and the samples in four special areas.

Accordingly, we defined a one-parent family as an income unit in which there was only one natural or adoptive parent together with her or his dependent children at school or of pre-school age. The parent was not counted as heading a one-parent family unless no adult of the opposite sex was living there (or had lived there for at least three months) as the parent's partner (whether as common-law or legal spouse) or as father or mother of the children.

In two respects, this definition is stricter than that used by the Department of Health and Social Security, and therefore produces lower total numbers of families and children. Students, including those under 19 in receipt of a local education authority grant, are not counted as dependent children, whereas the official definition includes children 'under the age of 19 and undergoing full-time education or training'.[1] And the criteria to exclude parents temporarily separated from their husbands or wives seem to have been more specific than in the census, which excludes persons from the household who are not 'normally' resident. As the department has admitted, 'This may lead to an over-statement of the number of permanently separated parents with children, for the borderline between permanent and temporary separation is not distinct.'[2] Husbands in prison, in the armed forces or at sea are given as examples. Identification of separated status is particularly difficult since spouses themselves will, in some instances, be unable to

1. Finer Report, vol. 2, p. 78.   2. ibid.

decide or unwilling to report whether the separation is temporary or permanent.[1] We believe that our attempt to distinguish between people who are separated (i.e. no longer living as husband and wife) and people who are married and expecting a husband or wife to resume membership of the household, but not within a total period of at least thirteen weeks, and to count these categories in defining one-parent families, is socially realistic. Nearly a third of the families whose head was married but 'separated' were in this latter category – a fraction identical with that produced by the General Household Survey.[2]

On the other hand, the survey estimate of unmarried mothers is *larger* than that made by the Department of Health and Social Security, and is likely to be nearer the true figure. The department has stated baldly that both the 1966 and 1971 census analyses 'understate the probable number of unmarried mothers; the figure is clearly too low as it is exceeded in both years by the number of unmarried mothers in receipt of supplementary benefit'.[3] Consequently, the department adopted a central estimate of 90,000 (a figure higher than those produced in the General Household Survey for 1971 and 1972). Our data are, of course, based on interviews with income units and not just households, and depend on a more comprehensive set of questions, and in this respect on a fuller checking procedure, than in either the census or General Household Survey.

Widowed and divorced mothers tend to have older children than other lone mothers, and because of the exclusion of mothers with student children as well as a few in fact saying that they shared the household with an adult of the opposite sex, the survey estimates are lower than the official estimates. The estimate of lone fathers is also lower and represents rather less than one in seven of the total, compared with one in six of the official estimate. In the General Household Survey,

Table 22.2. Estimated numbers of children of different ages in one-parent families.

Age	DHSS estimates, Britain, 1971 (000s)	Survey estimates, UK, 1968–9 (000s)
0–4	260	285
5–9	370	350
10–14	330	230
15–18	120	145
Total	1,080	1,010

1. See Marsden, *Mothers Alone*, pp. 140–41 and 341–2. There are also problems with other groups who may not report their marital status correctly. As well as concealment of illegitimacy, divorced women are apt to report themselves to be widowed. See *Registrar General's Statistical Review of England and Wales*, Part III, 1963, pp. 21–7.
2. See the Finer Report, vol. 2, p. 81.   3. ibid., p. 80.

the corresponding fraction was one in six for 1971 and one in nine for 1972.[1]

The total estimated numbers of children of different age in one-parent families from the two sources are listed in Table 22.2. In the survey, 7·4 per cent of family units consisted of one-parent families. They comprised 6·8 per cent of all dependent children at school or of pre-school age.

Trends in Numbers of One-Parent Families

Strangely, while commenting at length on various demographic trends, the Finer Committee did not attempt to develop any conclusions about trends in the numbers of one-parent families.[2] The numbers of husbands dying during the period when children are dependent has fallen rapidly, not only because mortality among young and middle-aged adults has greatly declined, but because there has been a shift to families with two and three children, younger marriage and childbirth, and a compression of fertility. Three quarters of all children are now born within eight years of their mother's wedding. Early in this century, more marriages were broken by death than by divorce. With the growth of equality before the law, this position has now been reversed. There were 110,722 petitions for divorce in England and Wales in 1972, compared with 27,478 annually in 1956–60.[3] Much of this increase is attributable not so much to evidence of the breakdown of more marriages as an increase in the numbers of those separating who are not deterred from seeking a formal dissolution, including many who want to marry again.

Between the 1950s and 1970s, there has been scarcely any change in the numbers of married women in England and Wales taking matrimonial proceedings in magistrates' courts (varying only by 1,000 or 2,000 for different years above and below a figure of 26,000).

As a proportion of all live births, illegitimate births increased from around 5 per cent per annum in the 1950s to over 8 per cent in the early 1970s. A large number of such births are to married women, to women living in a stable partnership, or to women who marry soon after the birth. Nearly a fifth of such births are reregistered subsequently as legitimate and about another quarter result in adoptions. Hitherto only a minority of illegitimate children born in any year have gone on to live in fatherless families, and as a result the proportion of unmarried mothers with older children is as yet very small, possibly because of the social stigma and financial difficulties hitherto suffered by unmarried mothers;

1. *The General Household Survey*, Introductory Report, HMSO, London, 1973, p. 72; and *The General Household Survey, 1972*, HMSO, 1975, p. 23.
2. Thus in a forty-three page chapter on demographic data, there is no discussion of overall trends in numbers. There is, however, a brief reference on later pages to the effect that there has been an increase in recent years, but nothing like as large as the increase in numbers of lone parents dependent on supplementary benefit, which is mainly attributable to a switch by many mothers from relying on earnings to relying on benefit. See the Finer Report, pp. 247–9.
3. ibid., p. 41.

although it might be anticipated that any change in these respects would permit more lone mothers to keep and raise their children in a single-parent household.

Little is known about trends in the numbers of motherless families (about one in six or seven of one-parent families). The number sharing households with their relatives is high,[1] and others are heavily dependent on relatives living outside the household for domestic support. There seems to be a very slight tendency (much publicized) for more fathers to seek and be granted custody of their children and to bring them up themselves.

The influence of access to earnings and entitlement to social security benefits upon numbers of one-parent families cannot be neglected. The living standards of widowed mothers has greatly improved and enhanced their remarriage prospects, although, by the same token, they do not need to remarry to achieve a decent living standard. Apart from abolition of the earnings rule, and special tax concessions (since extended to other families), widows receive a weekly allowance for each child (including family allowance) which is much higher than other national insurance scale rates for children (in 1976 being 84 per cent higher). For other one-parent families, conditions remain difficult. Supplementary benefit payments have tended to increase relative to the women's median earnings, for although maintenance and family allowances are deducted, the value of these has declined, and supplementary benefits include an allowance for housing costs which have risen steeply, especially for one-parent families. This relative movement of supplementary-benefit rates and wage rates has meant that during the 1960s an increasing proportion of lone parents other than widows became dependent,[2] preferring to stay at home and look after their children, perhaps working part time rather than take a lower wage working full time. This trend of growing dependency among fatherless families was a major influence which led to the setting up of the Finer Committee in 1969.

The Chances of Being in Poverty

By comparison with two-parent families, more one-parent families have relatively low incomes and substantially more of them live in poverty or on its margins. This can be demonstrated from both the survey and government studies. In the survey, more of the children than of children in two-parent families were found to live in households with income smaller than the minimum scales of the Supplementary Benefits Commission (Table 22.3). Taking income of the income unit in the previous year as the criterion, nearly half the families and three fifths of the children were in poverty or on its margins. They represented 265,000 families and

1. George and Wilding, *Motherless Families*, p. 4–7.
2. See Wynn, M., 'FIS and Fatherless Families', *Poverty*, No. 16/17, Child Poverty Action Group, for a discussion of dependency among widows and other lone mothers.

Table 22.3. Percentages of one-parent and two-parent families and children in those families, according to level of income of income unit in relation to the state's poverty standard.

Net disposable income last year as % of supplementary benefit scales plus housing cost	Families		Children in families[a]	
	1 parent	2 parents (married)	1 parent	2 parents (married)
Under 100	25	4	34	7
100–39	24	22	25	27
140–99	31	41	26	37
200–99	15	24	11	20
300 or more	5	8	4	9
Total	100	100	100	100
Number	55	637	104	1,337
Four special areas				
Under 100	(33)	10	53	14
100–39	(35)	30	20	37
140–99	(24)	44	19	38
200 or more	(9)	16	6	11
Total	100	100	100	100
Number	46	363	96	842

NOTE: [a]Forty-one children in the national and twenty in the four area samples with neither parent present, or with one present, the other being a step-parent, or with both parents being unmarried, have been excluded.

nearly 600,000 children respectively in the general population. In the four special areas, there were proportionately more one-parent families than in the nation as a whole – 13 per cent[1] compared with 7·4 per cent in the national sample (and 10 per cent[1] of children in such families compared with 6·8 per cent). Over two thirds of these families, and three quarters of the children in them in the four areas, were in poverty or on the margins of poverty. Again these fractions were much higher than in the case of two-parent families (Table A.89, page 1060).

Government data confirm the disproportionately large numbers with low incomes, but do not suggest such a large number below the state's poverty line.

1. These are estimates which have been adjusted to take account of losses at the second stage of interviewing. See Chapter 3, page 107.

Thus the Finer Committee quote mean figures for the period 1969–71 of 200,000 fatherless families receiving supplementary benefit, plus 43,000 not receiving benefit who are living below the supplementary-benefit level and another 22,000 having resources of less than £2 higher than that level. Allowing for an estimated 15,000 motherless families in poverty or on its margins (including about 7,000 actually receiving supplementary benefit), the total number of one-parent families living on supplementary benefit, or below or within £2 of that standard, was 280,000 or approximately 45 per cent.[1] This official figure of 280,000 compares with the figure of 265,000 derived from the survey which is given above. The former includes all the families receiving supplementary benefit, however, and not only those whose net disposable income was less than 40 per cent higher than the basic scales.

Another measure of low income is obtained by comparing the mean income of the two groups of families. A 1970 study in five areas by the Social Survey Division of the Office of Population Censuses and Surveys found that 'in all areas (Dorset, Dundee, Glamorgan, Halifax, Haringey) the mean usual income and the mean adjusted income (allowing for size of family) of fatherless families are less than half those of two-parent families'.[2]

In the survey, 43 per cent of one-parent families lived in households consisting of two or more income units.[3] This compares with 22 per cent of two-parent families. But even if it is assumed that household incomes are pooled, the number of families in or on the margins of poverty only falls from 49 to 40 per cent (and of children in those families from 59 to 49 per cent) (Table A.89, page 1060).

Do many of the poorest families have assets which indirectly help them to raise their low living standards to tolerable levels? The short answer is no. When the potential income represented by the value of all assets, expressed as an annuity, is added to net disposable incomes, the number of children of lone parents living at a level below, or just above, the supplementary benefit basic scale rates is reduced only from 59 to 54 per cent. Indeed, one of the critical problems of many one-parent families is the total or almost total lack of assets of any kind – whether savings, houses or even consumer durables in the home. Nearly half the one-parent families, compared with only 13 per cent of two-parent families, had assets of no value at all or were actually in debt (though some lived in households with other income units having assets). Another 17 per cent had less than £100. Only 11 per cent had more than £5,000, compared with 21 per cent of two-parent families.

Many of the families living below or just above the state's poverty standard al-

1. Finer Report, p. 254; and vol. 2, Appendices 9 and 10.
2. Hunt et al., Families and Their Needs, p. 31.
3. This corresponds closely with other estimates. The government's Family Expenditure Survey produced an average figure of 46 per cent for the three years 1969 to 1971. See Finer Report, vol. 2, Appendix 10, p. 331.

Table 22.4. *Percentages of one-parent families and of dependent children in such families[a] in the United Kingdom and in four special areas, according to eligibility to receive supplementary benefits.*

Eligibility of income unit for supplementary benefit	United Kingdom				Four Areas			
	1-parent families		2-parent families		1-parent families		2-parent families[b]	
	Families	Children	Families	Children	Families	Children	Families	Children
Unclassifiable	2	4	1	2	0	1	1	1
Currently receiving benefit	28	38	1	1	49	54	7	9
Could not claim	48	39	94	92	35	26	83	78
Ineligible (income too high)	15	10	2	2	8	14	5	5
Eligible but not receiving	7	9	1	2	8	5	4	6
Total	100	100	100	100	100	100	100	100
Number	60	112	744	1,509	49	96	400	920

NOTES: [a]Including children aged 15 and over at school.
[b]Parents married.

ready receive supplementary benefit. Table 22.4 shows that 28 per cent of one-parent families in the survey, accounting for 38 per cent of dependent children in such families, were said to be receiving benefit. The figures represented 150,000 families and 385,000 children in the population. These totals correspond fairly closely with administrative totals for the same period. In 1968, for example, there were, according to official sources, approximately 360,000, and in 1970 420,000, dependent children in one-parent families receiving supplementary benefit.[1] But there were an additional 9 per cent, representing 90,000, who were in 35,000 families eligible for supplementary benefit but not receiving it.

The table also shows that a higher proportion of one-parent families in the four poor areas than in the United Kingdom as a whole were dependent on supplementary benefits. It brings out the difference between one-parent and two-parent families in income status.

1. There were 182,000 fatherless and 6,000 motherless families receiving benefit in 1968, and 212,000 and 6,000 respectively in 1970, with an average of 1·91 and 2·26 children. See Finer Report, vol. 2, Appendix 9, pp. 313 and 316.

Changes in Numbers in Poverty: the Introduction of Family Income Supplement

The Family Income Supplement scheme was introduced subsequent to the survey.[1] What effect will this have had on poverty and dependency on supplementary benefits among one-parent families? Both in proportion receiving and not receiving but eligible for benefit, children in one-parent families are at a disadvantage when compared with other children. But even those children in families unable to claim benefit are at a disadvantage. Their mothers (or fathers) are in full-time employment, but usually earning less than parents in two-parent families, and sometimes so much less that they are in poverty. In 1968–9 we estimated the numbers of such children to be 100,000. The introduction of Family Income Supplement was intended to help such groups. The incomes of one-parent and two-parent families in full-time employment with low incomes is supplemented by one half of the amount by which their gross weekly income falls below prescribed levels. Because the prescribed amounts were set a lot higher than the supplementary benefit scale rates for one-parent families, the effect was to 'raise the disposable income of one-parent families whose incomes were already higher than the supplementary benefit level – that is, the supplements increased the positive net resources of lone mothers who work rather than transferred families from negative net resources to positive net resources' (or from an income position below to an income position about the supplementary benefit level).[2]

There is little evidence that the distribution of one-parent families above and below the income represented by the supplementary benefit standard has changed since 1968–9. Only 37,000 one-parent families with about 62,000 children were receiving family income supplement at 31 December 1974. The average amount received per family was £3·41 a week.[3] As conceded by the Department of Health and Social Security, many of these would not beforehand have been in poverty or on its margins. Moreover, although the survey estimate of 580,000 dependent children and 265,000 mothers or fathers in one-parent families in poverty or on its margins would have been reduced because of the introduction of the Family Income Supplement scheme, these numbers will also have *increased*, first, because one-parent families have themselves increased (without much change in the proportions of families having incomes of different amounts relative to the supplementary benefit scales), and secondly, because many one-parent families have ceased to rely on full-time employment and have applied for supplementary benefits. The Department of Health and Social Security reported that one-parent families drawing supplementary benefit increased from 188,000 in November 1968 to 269,000 in November 1974, or by 43 per cent.[4]

1. The Family Income Supplements Act 1970 became effective from August 1971.
2. Finer Report, vol. 2, Appendix 10, p. 355.
3. DHSS, *Social Security Statistics, 1974*, HMSO, London, 1975, p. 142.
4. The 1974 figure includes 5,000 prisoners' wives. See ibid., p. 148.

One-Parent Families Who Are Not Poor

One-parent families come fairly representatively from both non-manual and manual occupational classes (defined in terms of the husband's or former husband's or, in the case of unmarried mothers and motherless families, father's occupation), the proportions among one-parent families being 46 per cent and 54 per cent respectively, compared with 45 per cent and 55 per cent of married parents. But a small proportion of predominantly non-manual lone parents had relatively high incomes and other resources.

Thus one in three non-manual lone parents had incomes in excess of 200 per cent of supplementary benefit scale rates, and one in six had an income over 300 per cent, while less than one in fifteen manual lone parents had an income over 200 per cent of the rates and none had an income as high as 300 per cent. Similarly, almost one in three of non-manual lone parents had assets of more than £5,000 (several in excess of £10,000), compared with less than one in fifteen manual lone parents.[1]

The presence of comparatively well-off one-parent families invites further elucidation. Although numbers in sub-groups are small, it is worth returning at this point to the individual interview schedules to explore in more detail which families are better and worse off. Usually we quote data from the national survey, and only quote the special areas when the data are of particular interest.

Variations of Living Standards between Different Types of One-Parent Families

Families headed by men tended to be better off. Only one man had an income below 140 per cent of supplementary benefit, and he was unemployed[2] (as, incidentally, was the only other father who had more than two children). Two of the three richest families, with incomes over 300 per cent, and in one case over 600 per cent, of supplementary benefit, were headed by men. Thus our data repeat the earlier finding that motherless families are better off because they depended principally upon a man's wage.

In fact, a high proportion of lone mothers, that is, 57 per cent, also were in paid employment, compared with only 34 per cent of other mothers (and the difference is more striking if it is remembered that the families of lone mothers contained a disproportionately large number of young children); and a higher proportion worked full-time (thirty hours or more), 40 per cent as against only 14

1. In this respect, the families from the special areas were very different: less than 10 per cent were from non-manual origins, while half were partly skilled or unskilled manual workers' families. The low socio-economic status of the families was also reflected in their lack of assets: only two families had more than £1,000; three quarters of them had nothing.
2. In the special areas samples, there was also only one man with an income below 140 per cent of the supplementary benefit standard. He, too, was unemployed.

per cent of other mothers.[1] However, with one or two notable exceptions, such as a woman GP working very long hours, these lone mothers could not make enough money from their earnings alone to take them very far above the poverty level: one mother received only £8 for thirty-seven hours work, and over one in three of mothers who worked full time still fell below 140 per cent of supplementary benefit rates, though none fell below 100 per cent. We will discuss further below how opportunities to work to supplement other small incomes were not always available and were distributed unevenly between mothers of different marital status in ways which tended to increase rather than decrease inequalities between the various types of family.

Among families headed by women, the widows were relatively better off. All the widows had full state pensions, and one third had additional income from their husbands' occupational pension schemes. One half worked full time and one third worked part time, and almost half these widows, who tended to be older, had some income from a working son or daughter who shared the household with them. As a result, none of them depended on supplementary benefit. Apart from the motherless families, the only other lone parent whose income exceeded 300 per cent of supplementary benefit was a widow. The only very poor widow was a young woman with four young children who could only work part time.

This pattern of relatively better incomes among widows was also found in the special area samples. Although more of the widows, like other types of families in these areas, had relatively low incomes, only two of thirteen widowed mothers had an income smaller than 140 per cent of the supplementary benefit standard.

Lacking pensions, none of the other groups of mothers in either the national or four area samples received very much support directly or indirectly from their children's fathers. For example, the average amount received per family was less than £2: one woman who received £5 for herself and her six children, actually returned £1·25 to her husband because he took the oldest child for a day. Plainly the collection of maintenance from fathers by legal procedures was no solution to the income problems of the divorced, the separated and the unmarried.

Included among lone mothers in the national sample were seven women not formally separated, whose husbands were away in prison or working at a distance from home. One husband had been in prison for eighteen months, another was in the navy and had not been home for thirteen months, and a third had been in a mental illness hospital for over a year, though he visited his home for occasional days and nights. Another three were in the army or merchant navy and were not expected back for periods longer than three months. The seventh was a husband who was said to live elsewhere, who visited his wife occasionally. In four of these

1. Rather fewer mothers in the special area samples (42 per cent) were in paid employment (30 per cent worked full time). This may reflect poorer employment opportunities in those areas.

families, the money remitted by the father was insufficient to raise the family above the state's poverty line, and in a fifth sufficient only to surmount that line marginally.

Lacking support from the fathers, the situation of divorced women was rather varied, with almost equal proportions of them being relatively comfortable and rather poor. The better off had fewer dependent children and were working full time. About one third had incomes from working children, though, because the children were still young, such incomes do not appear to have boosted the living standards of the whole households by very much. In the four special areas, there were proportionately fewer prosperous divorced mothers and proportionately more who had manual working origins.

Motherless families, widowed and divorced mothers were the only groups to have any substantial capital assets. Between a quarter and a third of these lone parents, compared with none of the separated and unmarried mothers, had assets in excess of £5,000, which meant that they were more likely than other groups to have adequate housing and household goods. On the other hand, it must not be forgotten that there were divorced mothers who had lost the marital home during the divorce, or who came from poorer circumstances initially, so that, as a group, divorcees are likely to show a wider range of inequality of assets than any other. In the four area samples, very few one-parent families had any assets, but those who had were widows: one had over £5,000, and another over £1,000.

The living standards of the unmarried mothers were to some extent protected (or in some instances their poverty was concealed) because all of them in the sample lived with relatives. This enabled some mothers of very young children to go out to work, which gave them an adequate income, although it postponed the expense and problems of homebuilding. On the other hand, there were two unmarried mothers who did not work but who acted as housekeepers for rather little reward: one of these was judged to live at a standard considerably below supplementary benefit rate. Another risk of continuing to live with relatives after the birth of an illegitimate child is overcrowding – well over half of these particular families were overcrowded.[1]

Of all one-parent families, the very poorest tended to be separated wives living alone on supplementary benefits supporting large families. Over a third of them, with an average of more than three children each, had incomes below the basic supplementary benefit rates. Moreover, they were usually drawing supplementary benefit allowances. (To underline these results from the national sample, we found in the four area samples that seven out of fourteen separated wives who lived with only their children had incomes below the supplementary benefit standard, and yet six of these seven were drawing supplementary benefit allowances.) From the interviews (and following similar findings from our pilot work),[2] a consider-

1. A finding echoed in the pilot report, Marsden, *Mothers Alone*, pp. 120–24.
2. ibid., pp. 263–4.

able part of the explanation appears to be that the supplementary benefit allowances of these mothers took into account maintenance allowances which their husbands were supposed to be paying them (in one instance an unpaid court order, but in the remaining instances hypothetical rates of undeclared income from the husband) – incomes which, however, there was no evidence of the women receiving. These poorer mothers almost invariably had separated from husbands who were partly skilled or unskilled manual workers. There was only one separated wife whose income exceeded 200 per cent of the supplementary benefit scale rate.

We have not been able to follow up for these sub-groups the changes in the lone parent's contacts with relatives during the home-building and child-rearing cycle. Twenty-three per cent of the lone parents said they saw relatives most days of the week, and another 44 per cent at least weekly. These proportions were similar to those of other parents. But more of the lone parents also lived with relatives, so on the whole they had more intense, though not necessarily more successful, interaction with members of their families. This applied especially to unmarried mothers. Once again, separated wives, who are in an intermediate position in the family cycle, appeared to be the least fortunate in neither living with an older relative, like a number of the unmarried mothers, nor having support from a younger adult (including an elder child), like the widows and some of the divorced mothers.

An Illustration of the Contrasts in Living Standards

It is difficult to quote families 'typical' in most of the respects described above, since, as has been pointed out, in each marital status there is a considerable range. Nevertheless, the following two contrasting examples of one-parent families drawn from the national sample are roughly representative of the extent of variation to be found in income, social security protection, wealth and possessions, and family situation – variations which are due to class situation and stage of home-building, as well as to marital status. Other illustrations will be found in Chapter 8 (pages 313–36).

1. Mrs Meare

Mrs Meare was a widow, aged 52, with a son of 16 and a daughter of 11. Her husband, a tax inspector, had been dead less than three months, so she was drawing a widowed mother's allowance for herself and her family at the higher rate of £17 a week, together with a family allowance of 90p a week (before long this income would fall to £8·15). In addition, she had a pension from her husband's occupational scheme of £51·85 a month, and she worked for twenty-five hours a week as a teacher to earn £38 a month. The family lived in a semi-detached house which she estimated to be worth over £6,000 and which cost £20 a month in mortgage and rates, and only £800 remained to be paid off. This meant that their living standard was currently almost two and a half times the basic rate of supplementary benefit for a family of her size and composition. Her son had savings of £567, her daughter had £357, and although Mrs Meare herself had only £200 at the moment, she would shortly receive £3,000 from her husband's insurance. They had no regular contacts with any kin, nor did they exchange services or gifts with others. However, they had all the consumer durables on our check-list, and in addition ran a car worth about £200. They were not deprived of any items of food, clothing, or entertainment. The son was at a direct-grant school, where the fees were £150 per year, and the daughter was at a state grammar school. Mrs Meare said she never felt poor.

2. Mrs Fitch

Mrs Fitch, aged 30, had left her husband, an electrical fitter, a year before, and had gone back to her parents' home where she lodged in one furnished room, sharing bathroom and kitchen with the rest of the family. With a son aged 2 and a daughter aged 1, she badly needed an extra bedroom. Her husband had hoped to make voluntary payments of £7 a week, but had done so for only four months of the previous year, when he had been in work. At the moment she was drawing £6·15 supplementary benefit and 40p family allowance, out of which she was supposed to pay £2·75 for her room, a sum which included coal and one meal a day for herself and the children. She had tentatively asked friends about finding work for herself, but had so far done little about work because of problems with child-minding. Without work, her standard of living remained at only four fifths of the basic rate of supplementary benefit for her family. However, she did see her parents and grandparents almost daily, and exchanged services with them like cooking, washing, sewing and ironing, and received help with the children which she estimated at fifteen hours of services a week altogether. She also received gifts for the children worth about 50p a week. She had no savings, and of the items on the list of consumer durables she possessed only three: a radio, a washing machine, and adequate carpeting. She had had no holiday, could not afford to go out in the evenings, and her diet was poorer than that of her children. She rarely ate a proper breakfast or ate meat, for example. She said she sometimes felt poor, at weekends, with some of her friends, and when holiday times came along.

The Consequences of Poverty

In examining the situation of one-parent families, then, we have to appreciate that, like the disabled or the elderly, there are striking inequalities between sub-groups among them as well as a disproportionately large number who are in, or

Table 22.5. Percentages of adults in two-parent and one-parent families experiencing certain difficulties or deprivations.

| Characteristic | 2-parent families | Type of 1-parent family | | | | All in four special areas |
		Un-married and separated mothers	Widowed and divorced mothers	All lone mothers	All lone parents	
Net income worth of household below 140% supplementary benefit level	19	(58)	(21)	(45)	(28)	–
Not owner-occupier	49	(86)	(62)	75	72	90
Structural defects	24	(45)	(21)	34	29	78
Housing facilities poor or very poor	4	(21)	(4)	13	13	29
Household with too few bedrooms	19	(55)	(33)	45	41	57
Fewer than 6 consumer durables in list of 10	15	(38)	(15)	28	27	51
No holiday away from home in last 12 months	47	(79)	(64)	73	70	80
No evening out in last fortnight	39[b]	(52)	(62)	57	56	73
Moderately or severely deprived according to 8 criteria[c]	24	(48)	(32)	41	41	89
Minimum base number[a]	1,480	29	24	53	60	49

NOTES: [a]For some items the number is slightly fewer.
[b]Mothers only.
[c]As listed on page 250.

on the margins of, poverty. The fact that the incomes of many are low, and are relatively lower than of two-parent families, has many outcomes. Table 22.5 lists a variety of characteristics in which fewer adults in one-parent than in two-parent families have customary facilities and benefits. Fewer own their own homes, fewer own a representative selection of consumer durables, fewer take a holiday during the year away from home and fewer have an afternoon or evening out in the course of a fortnight. (In the final column of the table, the even greater deprivation of one-parent families in the four poor areas is starkly illustrated.) Moreover, Table 22.5 clearly reveals the clustering of deprivation among the unmarried and the separated, and the slightly better position of families headed by widows, divorced mothers and lone fathers. The widowed and divorced are deprived relative to two-parent families on some but not all counts, whereas the unmarried and separated are substantially deprived on all counts. Only in the matter of going out in the evening do the widowed and divorced appear more disadvantaged than the unmarried and the separated. This may be partly explained, as can some other deprivations, in terms of the mother's age and stage in the family cycle, as well as in terms of lack of cash and child-care resources. In the survey, most of the widowed and divorced mothers were in their forties and early fifties, most of the married but separated mothers were in their thirties and early forties, and most of the unmarried mothers were in their twenties and thirties.

Multiple deprivation is, of course, also suffered by the children in one-parent families. Table 22.6 lists some corresponding respects in which more children in one-parent than two-parent families were deprived. There is strong evidence of the relatively deleterious effects upon children.[1]

Subjective aspects of deprivation are also important to examine. In correspondence with objective deprivation, lone parents proved to be more likely than other parents to feel deprived. Seventy-six per cent of them, compared with only 22 per cent of other parents, said they were worse off than their close relatives. Similarly, 42 per cent, compared with 12 per cent of other parents, felt they were worse off than their neighbours. And 37 per cent, compared with 18 per cent, felt they were worse off than the average in society.

Comparisons with the past to some extent mirrored the differences in living standards, not only between one-parent and two-parent families but also between lone parents of different marital status. Thus, 36 per cent of all lone parents, compared with 13 per cent of other parents, felt they were worse off than they had been in the past. However, about a third of widowed and divorced mothers, and a quarter of single mothers, compared with almost none of the separated wives, felt themselves to be better off. Indeed, three quarters of all separated wives with dependent children said they were financially worse off as an immediate consequence of the separation, though between that time and the date of the interview some of these felt their situation had improved.

Finally, an indication of the diffidence of one-parent families in asserting their rights appears in the difference between the objective and subjective indices of overcrowding (Table 22.6). Although substantially more children in one-parent families were objectively overcrowded, expressions of need for additional accommodation were about as common among two-parent as one-parent families.

1. See, in particular, parental anxiety about children's health and behaviour in Ferri, E., and Robinson, H., *Coping Alone*, National Foundation for Educational Research (for the National Children's Bureau), London, 1975.

Table 22.6. *Percentages of children in one-parent and two-parent families experiencing different forms of deprivation.*

Characteristic	Children in families			
	Percentage		Total number	
	1 parent	2 parents	1 parent	2 parents
Household with two or more bedrooms too few[a]	26	8	112	1,509
Household with one bedroom too few[a]	31	18	112	1,509
Additional accommodation wanted	50	49	112	1,491
Housing facilities poor or very poor	8	6	112	1,492
Structural defects	34	27	112	1,491
Household with fewer than 6 durables in list of 10	33	18	103	1,427
No safe place for child to play (aged 1–10)	43	34	69	974
Not had holiday away from home in last 12 months	57	49	108	1,483
Not had birthday party (aged 3–14)	75	56	71	1,182
No pocket money (aged 5–14)	17	3	42	702
Moderately or severely deprived according to 8 criteria[c]	48	25	89	1,231

NOTES: [a]According to the bedroom overcrowding index. See page 484.
[b]Head of household or housewife expressing need for additional rooms of different type.
[c]As listed on page 250.

Possibly the awareness that society is not exactly generous in acknowledging their needs disposes some one-parent families not to be as assertive about their needs or rights as two-parent families.

Explaining the Disadvantages Suffered by One-Parent Families

A comprehensive explanation of the deprivations experienced by one-parent families would entail a searching analysis of work, marriage and the family. From the studies which have been conducted, it can be established that, in general, what might be called the 'structural' economic disadvantages of the one-parent family stem from the conditions of the labour market, where the father is regarded as the family bread-winner with the mother as, at best, a subsidiary earner. Thus, the average full-time earnings of men have remained fairly constant at nearly twice those of women, a differential which expresses not only higher rates of pay for men but also men's easier access to a range of more highly paid jobs, and women's conditioned reluctance to aspire to much traditionally male work. Most two-parent families will have a man's wage, and increasingly also will benefit from a woman's wage.[1] But, by contrast, one-parent families have only one parent's, usually a woman's, earning power. Moreover, the earning power of the lone parent, whether a woman or a man, tends to be curtailed by obligations to care for the children – obligations which conventionally press more heavily on mothers (although fathers too may experience them), and which are reinforced and made more inconvenient by the continuing lack of alternative public or private child-care facilities. Even for lone fathers who manage to continue to work, their work interest and careers have been shown to be restricted by family obligations.[2]

Further economic disadvantages accrue particularly to fatherless families because the greater financial power and status of men is embodied in the structure of property and house-ownership, credit and mortgage facilities, the ability to command better housing tenancies, and so on. In fact, resources and status of all kinds tend to be channelled to families primarily through the employed male head, whom the majority of one-parent families are, of course, currently lacking.

Related to this structure of male priority, the one-parent family also suffers economically for its supposed transgressions of marital and family norms. A society which sets great store by the institution of marriage will tend to reward the married and to withhold rewards from the non-married, or even to punish the non-married, if they should seek to obtain the pleasures of the married state without incurring its formal, and social, obligations.

Examples of discrimination against the non-married in favour of the married could be documented in all sorts of institutional rules, and in less formal behavioural rules concerning hospitality and the practice of gossip about the non-married. But discrimination appears most importantly in the property, tax and social security laws.

The provision of adequate social security and even legal recognition for one-parent families has hitherto been inhibited by fears that any such support or recognition might tend to perpetuate and increase the numbers of such families and so erode the institution of marriage. For example, the law has been slow to grant married women any economic rights to their husband's income in or outside the marital home, and in particular there has been only a very tardy development of rights to matrimonial relief and financial support for the wife to live apart from her husband.[3] There has been a corresponding reluctance to provide financial support for one-parent families through social security of various types. The

1. The Finer Report discusses in detail these structural disadvantages. See Part 3, pp. 21–63.
2. George and Wilding, *Motherless Families*, Chapter 4.
3. There is a detailed discussion of the history of the obligation to maintain in the Finer Report, vol. 2, Appendix 5.

role of a parent, of either sex, caring for children at home, could have been recognized by some form of income, yet it seems that the provision of such an income would run counter to prevailing male superiority in marriage, and also against the higher standing of industrial work as compared with child-care.

A similar reluctance to recognize the right of mothers to live with their children apart from the children's fathers appears in the unwillingness of local authorities to permit fugitive wives to enter hostels for the homeless – they are frequently officially classified as not homeless.[1] And there is evidence that, in the allocation of tenancies, local authorities have failed to make special provision for one-parent families, or have even actively discriminated against them.[2]

Income Rights of Different Types of One-Parent Family

Within the overall climate of discrimination against one-parent families, there occur variations between different types of family which affect both their formal rights to income and their informal access to help of various kinds. These variations are primarily distinctions of marital status, but also they represent discrimination between families of different social class. Widows constitute no direct threat to marriage, yet they first received a pension only as recently as 1925, and it was not until the 1960s that a combination of pension increases, tax concessions and the removal of the earnings rule brought working widows with full pensions more or less up to the economic level of the average two-parent family. Even so, widows have to be aged 40 or over to qualify for a widow's pension (though widow's benefit is paid for the first twenty-six weeks and widowed mother's allowance thereafter to widows with a dependent child if a woman is widowed under the age of 40), and if the woman herself has not worked or not contributed adequately to the national insurance fund, the amount of the pension is dependent on her husband's work record, and even upon the circumstances of his death:[3] in other words, she is still not treated as an individual with needs and rights of her own.

Nevertheless, in the achievement of parity with two-parent families, widows remain far ahead of other one-parent families in attaining social security support.[4] From time to time during the present century, there has been discussion of an 'end of marriage' allowance, on the lines of a widow's pension, but the discussions have foundered on the problems, already mentioned, of how the allowance for separated spouses could be justified on criteria of need and desert which are as clear, and as acceptable to the public, as those provided by the death of the

1. For example, Greve, J., *Homelessness in London*, Scottish Academic Press, 1971, p. 140; and Glastonbury, B., *Homeless Near a Thousand Homes*, National Institute for Social Work Training Series, No. 21, Allen & Unwin, London, 1971, pp. 212–13.

2. Glastonbury, *Homeless Near a Thousand Homes*, p. 68.

3. Wynn, *Fatherless Families*, p. 28.

4. Hunt *et al.*, *Families and Their Needs*, p. 32.

husband. Failing such an allowance, some legal rights of one-parent families to income maintenance are provided by a number of overlapping jurisdictions.

There are three overlapping legal and administrative systems: divorce law, separation procedures, and supplementary benefits administration. During the last century or so, divorce law has been made more accessible to people without resources and more equally available to women as well as men. Thus, legal and financial barriers to divorced mothers and their children receiving maintenance from the father have been removed or at least lowered, with the result that the divorcing population now represents a wider cross-section of all classes of the population than it did previously. Unfortunately, the same cannot be said of separated husbands and wives. Separation procedures come under the summary jurisdiction of magistrates' courts. Originally designed as a redress against wife-beating, separations have remained linked with the administration of the criminal law, and reforms, such as changes in admissible grounds, have proceeded more slowly than in divorce law. It has only recently been established that the population using magistrates' courts in order to separate are basically people lacking a knowledge of the law and lacking income. Today the magistrates' courts have been comprehensively described as a separate, unreformed, inferior, discriminatory law for the poor.[1] A substantial proportion of partly skilled and unskilled manual workers' wives who use such courts for matrimonial relief do not go on to divorce but remain separated for long periods. And unmarried mothers, who can claim affiliation orders only for their children, have even less legal protection than separated wives.

The third administrative and legal system for some one-parent families originated in the old Poor Law and has been developed under successive systems of public assistance, national assistance and supplementary benefits. The state has gradually assumed the duty of supporting women and children whose resources fall below a given level: in principle, mothers are now allowed to stay at home and care for their children and are not formally required to register for work. However, the Supplementary Benefits Commission, which administers these provisions, has a statutory duty to attempt to reclaim any support for one spouse and children from the other spouse, if the latter is working. They have interpreted this duty by pressing mothers to apply for court orders, or by themselves suing the liable relative, through the *magistrates'* courts. Thus, for families with low incomes, the residual Poor Law administration enshrined in the practice of the Supplementary Benefits Commission tends to reinforce the unreformed matrimonial jurisdiction.[2]

1. McGregor, O. R., *et al.*, *Separated Spouses*, Duckworth, London, 1970, Chapter 5. Reforms are now being proposed by the Law Commission.
2. In some ways, Appendix 5 of the Finer Committee's Report, which describes and analyses these three jurisdictions in relation to public attitudes about marriage and the family, is the most crucial explanatory section of the entire document.

By the late 1960s, attempts by mothers to seek maintenance by direct legal action had been rendered increasingly irrelevant as a factor in the living standards of one-parent families. Maintenance awards through the courts proved inadequate because the wage-earner could not in most instances earn enough to support two households: the amounts awarded by the courts have been low and the higher awards have almost invariably fallen into arrears.[1] As a result, although separated spouses have gone to court ostensibly to get maintenance and permission to live apart, in fact their freedom to live apart has been determined by whether or not they could establish a right to support from the state through supplementary benefits, which are paid at a rate above the level of court orders. Indeed, this has become such a recognized practice that many inadequate or irregularly paid court orders are now signed over by the mothers to the Supplementary Benefits Commission for collection.

A large section of the Finer Report on one-parent families was concerned with sorting out the glaring anomalies of this continued anachronistic overlapping of jurisdictions between the two types of court and the Poor Law.

Although there are formal social security provisions for the support of all fatherless families, in practice, both formally and informally, there may be discrimination against or among one-parent families of various statuses, in the ease with which access to benefits is granted and amount of benefit determined. Thus part of the incomes of widowed mothers, such as part of the allowance for each child, can be disregarded in working out their entitlement to supplementary benefits and, as a consequence, they are more generously treated than other claimants. Again it may be assumed that maintenance payments to women from separated husbands are paid regularly when they are not. As a consequence, some women have difficulty in securing a subsistence benefit in certain weeks, or they experience delays in payment. Unmarried and separated mothers may be pressed to work. Until 1975, lone fathers who wished to stop work and stay at home because they felt this would be the best way to care for their children, had to bargain individually with officials. (And it might be suspected that, in spite of official recognition of the father's right to choose, this unofficial bargaining will continue.) In other ways, the exercise of officials' powers of discretion, or their witting or unwitting departures from discretionary rules, may work not only to hinder one-parent families' access to benefit, but also to reduce those benefits below the state subsistence level.[2]

Variations in Living Standards during the Life of the Family

There are further variations between one-parent families of different types because they tend to have reached a different stage in the cycles of home-building

1. McGregor, *Separated Spouses*, Chapters 6 and 7.
2. Marsden, *Mothers Alone*, pp. 261–5.

and child-rearing when they first lose a man's income, and because of the different positions these 'incomplete' nuclear families occupy in the wider kinship network of the extended family.[1]

Motherless families, of course, have not usually lost a man's wage, and although income prospects may be damaged, most men continue to work. Their problem is to secure care of the children and of the home, either by paying for services or by finding time from work themselves, or both. It also seems likely that motherless families which stay together will usually comprise rather older children. Some lone fathers see themselves as needing child-care and domestic help from female relatives, rather than cash, though such help is sometimes spasmodic and inadequate.[2]

As well as being more representative of a cross-section of income groups and classes of fatherless families, widows and divorcees tend to be older than other lone parents, and tend therefore to have gone further with home-buying and home-building.[3] They are also more likely to have older children so that the mothers themselves can work, and the working children can contribute to their own upkeep. However, by the same token, these older mothers may be less likely to receive support from *their* parents and may themselves be expected to give support to their adult children.

In contrast, many unmarried mothers are unlikely even to have begun homebuilding, and the start of a family brings major problems of accumulating the necessary goods for the child and the home, as well as finding reasonably secure and adequate accommodation at a low rent.

Separated wives, like the unmarried mothers, tend to be younger (though by no means all these mothers are young) and to come from poorer families which may have been starved of resources during the early stages of home-building. While some mothers are 'readopted' by their own parents,[4] and receive a great deal of help, others may find themselves cut off from their parents, yet with still a long way to go to get together a home of their own. There is also some evidence that they tend to have more, younger, dependent children, which makes it difficult for them to work.[5]

Other One-Parent Families

We have so far discussed the special problems only of families with parents who are no longer married. These problems also apply to some parents who remain

1. Marsden, *Mothers Alone*, pp. 29–30, and Chapter 7.
2. George and Wilding, *Motherless Families*, pp. 140–48.
3. Marsden, *Mothers Alone*, p. 33; Marshall, *Families Receiving Benefit*, p. 8; Hunt *et al.*, *Families and Their Needs*.
4. Marsden, *Mothers Alone*, pp. 121–4.   5. ibid., pp. 23 and 344.

married (or consider themselves to remain married). Fathers may work away from home or be sent to gaol, while both fathers and mothers sometimes enter hospital for long periods. A few examples have been listed above (page 756).[1]

Financially, these families may be in as bad a situation as the separated wives who cannot trace their husbands. Whether or not they also lack good accommodation and consumer durables will depend on the other factors discussed above. Unless a woman whose husband works away has taken out a maintenance order, she has no legal right to an adequate share of his income and is dependent on his sense of responsibility which, with the attenuation of distance and pressures of additional living costs, may be weakened.

Little is known about the social situation of women left alone with children for 'socially honourable' reasons, such as husbands working away or in hospital. Yet it seems likely that they will experience some of the inconvenience, discrimination and stigma which tends to result from the absence of a man in the home. Thus, it has been reported that the problems experienced by prisoners' wives are not a consequence of guilt or shame, since these feelings pass quickly and are subsumed in the loss of status in not having a man about the house.[2]

There is no provision under the national insurance scheme for protection of the needs of the family if the father (or mother) is sent to prison. The family can claim supplementary benefit, but usually finds more difficulty than other one-parent families in obtaining benefits under the discretionary powers of the Supplementary Benefits Commission, and certainly is greatly restricted in meeting the expenses of travelling to the prison. In the case of a parent in hospital, entitlement to national insurance benefit will depend on contribution record. Most married women will have no entitlement. The benefit of those who are entitled to national insurance is reduced after eight weeks in hospital, and reduced again to a 'pocket money' rate after one year; but for that first year, dependants' rates of benefit continue to be paid in full. However, the rates generally provide an income much lower than average family income and few employers make sickness payments for very long (see Chapter 12 above). Many families soon find themselves in poverty or on the margins of poverty, and in some ways are worse off than other one-parent families. Not only do they spend money to maintain contacts with the parent in hospital. They cannot adjust budgets, as, for example, on

1. In the national sample, there were seven fathers said to be working away, while in the special areas, two men worked away, and three were in prison. If these numbers were to be representative, there would be about 10,000 in the population for each one in the sample.

2. 'Loss of status was certainly perceived as a crisis for most wives, but again this seemed directly related to the physical absence of the husband rather than to his criminality or imprisonment. Amongst working-class and lower middle-class families it is the expected norm for women to be married, and inability to appear in public with a husband was felt to place them in an invidious position' – Morris, P., *Prisoners and Their Families*, Allen & Unwin, London, 1965, p. 210.

accommodation, to conform with their more restricted size. And the fact that many long-stay patients themselves have low standards of living and entitlement to very low earnings or amounts of 'pocket money' should not be forgotten.

Alternative Policies

The deprivation of one-parent families is therefore the result not just of irregular or inadequate payment of maintenance allowances on the part of husbands or fathers, but of disadvantages structured by society and multiplied: of inadequate support for families with dependent children; the low earning power of women; the disprivileged status of the non-married, especially with children; and the lack of income rights of women within marriage, in caring for home and children, and qualifying for benefits under national insurance. To put all these things right would cost a great deal – and incidentally transform the nature of the society in which we live. For the poverty of one-parent families is inextricably bound up with the problems generally of women in society and of young families, and, in the ultimate analysis, cannot be met independently.

In certain passages of its Report, as, for example, in an appendix when they explained why Beveridge's proposal for a separation benefit had foundered,[1] the Finer Committee seemed to accept this kind of analysis. But they shrank from drawing the far-reaching implications for policy. They put forward an income solution in only two parts. They recommended that an extra £1 a week be paid in addition to family allowances (or child benefit) for each child and, inconsistently, that adults should receive a new means-tested allowance. In accepting a universal child allowance, they had conceded that few one-parent families were well off, and that even these families were at a financial disadvantage compared with two-parent families. It is therefore puzzling, if the savings are small, that they proposed an administratively wasteful means test. It is also puzzling that they did not seriously consider applying a flat-rate benefit to every family and taxing it back from the 10 or 20 per cent who were most prosperous. Methods might have been devised along these lines, both to save administrative costs and to ensure that all rather than, say, half of those entitled to benefit were to receive such benefit. Only one unsatisfactory paragraph in the entire report of 519 pages was devoted to the possibility of 'clawback'.

The committee recognized the 'basic unsuitability' of supplementary benefits received by over a quarter of a million one-parent families, and claimed that, under their new proposals, 'over 90 per cent of all one-parent families who now draw supplementary benefit for three months or more would no longer need it'.[2] However, the value of rescuing many thousands of families from the Supplementary Benefits Commission only to assign them to an alternative means-tested scheme seems debatable, to put it mildly. The committee did not discuss take-up

1. Finer Report, vol. 2, pp. 136–49.   2. Finer Report, vol. 1, p. 288.

or show how a separate administration would appear less 'hostile or intrusive' to families or 'involve as little burden and as little embarrassment as possible for the claimant'.[1] They did not collect or present any evidence about the operation of the Family Income Supplement scheme, and yet accepted it as a sufficient model for the guaranteed maintenance allowance. In particular, they did not demonstrate how the administration of the allowance could be disentangled successfully from the Supplementary Benefits Commission.

The right strategy would seem to be (a) to separate administration of benefit from the establishment of lone-parent status and the collection of any debts from errant husbands (or wives) and fathers; (b) to steer resources as much to families in general as to one-parent families in order to limit discrepancies between them; and (c) to base both general and special support on the principle of paying benefits as of right instead of on test of means.

Lone parental status might be better and more coherently defined legally – for widowed people immediately, perhaps for some persons where 'permanent' separation can be demonstrated easily, after a period of less than two years, and for others perhaps by affidavit after two years' absence of the other parent. 'Provisional' lone parental status might be established for married parents whose husbands or wives have been absent for at least, say, thirteen weeks, where housekeeping and child-care allowances cannot be, or are not being, paid regularly. Examples would be husbands or wives who are in prison or hospital. The way would then be cleared for either the abolition or relaxation of the cohabitation rule operated by the Supplementary Benefits Commission. In principle, a lone mother (or father) should be entitled to an allowance in her (or his) own right when caring for dependent children except when receiving a regular income from another adult with whom she (or he) is sharing the household, which in practice covers, or is a substantial contribution towards, the upkeep of the family home or children. To protect the interests of the children and encourage stable cohabitation,[2] any allowance for children in a one-parent family which is *additional* to allowances for children in two-parent families might be continued for a period of at least, say, two years after the start of the cohabitation. What we have in mind is the common instance of a man with financial obligations to children of his former marriage living elsewhere who cannot easily meet the financial needs of the children of his new-found partner, even though he might reasonably be expected to contribute towards her needs.

There is a strong argument for transitional additional benefits for all one-parent families, and these could be on the lines of the existing relatively advantageous widows' benefits (with some improvements), since the analogy between

1. Finer Report, vol. 1, p. 308.
2. For a fuller discussion of problems in abolishing or modifying existing cohabitation rules, see Marsden, D., 'Cohabitation', discussion paper for seminar on Cash Allowances for One-Parent Families, *National Council for One-Parent Families*, November 1976.

the situation of widows and other one-parent families would be easier to establish in public debate. However, we believe that in the long run there should for all types of family be a policy of income support with the following three components: first, *larger maintenance allowances for all children*, whether in one-parent or two-parent families. The government's child benefit scheme must be greatly strengthened and varied according to age of child. The Child Poverty Action Group has proposed, for example, allowances ranging from 6·5 per cent to 11 per cent of average male industrial earnings per child according to age.[1]

Secondly, *allowances for the care of children*. The married man's tax allowance can be withdrawn, at a saving estimated in 1976–7 at over £1,300 million per annum, and a home responsibility cash allowance paid at two rates – a higher rate for those caring at home for young children, for a large family or for disabled dependants, and a lower rate for those caring at home only for one older child or two older children. These rates might be fixed, say, at 15 per cent and 5 per cent respectively of average male industrial earnings, and financed from an earnings-related contribution from employers and employees. The invalid care allowance scheme introduced in 1976 for a few thousand people provides a precedent.

Finally, *an allowance for the upkeep of the family home*. The services of a housewife are usually unpaid, and are assumed to be covered by the husband's wage or, more exactly, his housekeeping allowance. The definition in law of a wife's entitlement to a housekeeping alllowance, or to a specific claim on his wage would not only protect the position of some married women with children who do not receive adequate allowances from their husbands, but would make it much easier to define and justify politically the payment by the state of a similar allowance to lone parents. A lone parent not in paid employment could become eligible for a 'home upkeep' allowance, again financed by social security contributions and fixed initially at, say, 10 per cent of average male industrial earnings.[2]

It might be argued that, with the development of such major proposals to restructure rights to income, the present clumsy structure of gross wages which are allocated primarily by market processes, and clawed back by taxation so that those outside the market may obtain a fair income, could become overstrained. Already we are reaching a situation when people do not appreciate that they are not so much 'earning' their gross wages as facilitating, by the transfer of a proportion of those wages, the necessary upkeep of a large population (including 'productive' housewives) who do not have access to the market (or otherwise to paid employment). If we lived in a society in which personal taxes from wages were much smaller and aggregate taxes from employers (and from personal wealth) were much larger, there might be less resistance to the payment of adequate incomes (through tax transfers) to those unable to earn a wage. The present

1. See Lister, R., *Social Security: The Case for Reform*, CPAG, London, 1975, pp. 60–61.
2. For fuller discussion, see Townsend, P., 'Problems of Introducing a Guaranteed Maintenance Allowance for One Parent Families', *Poverty*, No. 31, Winter/Spring 1975.

wage-system may have to be replaced, either by a statutory income policy or by a mixture of such a policy and a much larger network of free services.

General measures which reduce inequalities are more likely also to reduce the poverty of social minorities, including one-parent families, than measures designed specifically for them. Policies identified too exclusively with one-parent families may end up by stigmatizing them more and reinforcing their poverty.

Summary and Conclusion

Using a slightly stricter definition of one-parent family than the Department of Health and Social Security (the latter also being adopted in 1969–74 by the Finer Committee), we estimated that there were approximately 535,000 one-parent families, with 1,010,000 dependent children, in the United Kingdom at the time of the survey. This group was found to be one of the poorest groups in the entire population, 49 per cent of the families, and 59 per cent of the children, being in or on the margins of poverty as defined by the state. These figures contrasted with 26 per cent of two-parent families (and 34 per cent of children in those families).

We have sought to show that the explanation for this contrast lies in three related matters: the manner in which relations between the sexes are institutionalized in society, particularly in marriage; the direct effects of social policies for lone parents in the past and in the present; and the selective operations of the labour market. For it is only by invoking these three that both the relative poverty of one-parent families in general and the varying circumstances of different subgroups among them, or the constituent structure of their poverty and deprivation, can be understood.

Explanation has to be pursued first, then, through the inequalities which arise and are sustained by society between the sexes. This begins in the home with the expectations in the family that girls rather than boys will be allocated domestic work and nursing responsibilities, for example, and in schools with the expectations that more boys than girls will obtain high-status education and, later, professional, academic and vocational training. The dependency of women for resources upon men within marriage and the family, and the expectation that they will normally carry the primary responsibilities for child care (and outside marriage the responsibility of caring for any child that may be conceived), consolidate that inequality and ramify through many different sets of relationships and institutions. The risks of a woman finding herself to be a lone mother in poverty begin, in other words, with the manner in which relations between the sexes are institutionalized, particularly in marriage, so that wives have restricted access to resources, except through their husbands.

Secondly, explanation has to be pursued through the history and present effect of direct social policies for lone parents, including protection by the courts and taxation laws, as well as education, welfare and housing services and social security payments, which, in Britain, are made up principally of national insurance benefits for widowed mothers and supplementary benefits. The story here, with the possible recent exception of widowed mothers, is of the tendency for a principle of 'less eligibility' to operate – of aid falling short of that required to establish parity of status and of living standards with married parents, especially when lone mothers are compared with married mothers.

Finally, explanation has to be pursued through the lesser opportunities of lone parents to secure alternative resources through the labour market. Their availability for certain forms of employment tends to be restricted; their employment tends to be interrupted more frequently for reasons of illness, and change of home; and they are less able than married persons to pursue a 'career'. Lone fathers are only a tiny fraction of the total – and their families' living standards are not always drastically reduced. The overwhelming majority are women dependent on local labour-market opportunities and vulnerable to contractions in the economy.

These disadvantages tend to have a different outcome for people of different age, who are at a different stage of the family-building cycle, and they combine to stratify the group of lone parents. In the survey, most of the widowed and divorced mothers were in their forties and early fifties, most of the married but separated mothers were in their thirties and early forties, and most of the unmarried mothers were in their twenties and thirties. More of the older women had had an opportunity to establish a home or accumulate possessions. The widowed mothers comprised a more representative cross-section of manual and non-manual classes, and were likely to include representative numbers owning their homes or substantial amounts of other assets. The divorced mothers included those whose situation was stable and, relative to the separated, more of those from non-manual classes. The separated mothers were predominantly working class, and a substantial number of them had been starved of resources before the eventual separation.

Inequalities between the sexes in marriage, social policy and the labour market reflected class inequalities. The three systems of law carefully identified and described by the Finer Committee[1] – the law of divorce, the law which the magistrates administer as between husband and wife, and mother and putative father, and the law of supplementary benefits, which is the successor of the Poor Law – not only reflect among lone parents the general inequalities between the classes, but help to account for the different status and treatment of different types of one-parent family. There was an almost exact representation of non-manual and manual occupational classes (defined in terms of the husband's or former husband's or, in the case of unmarried mothers, father's occupation) among one-parent families as a whole, being 46 and 54 per cent respectively, compared with

1. Finer Report, p. 9 and Part 4.

45 and 53 per cent of married parents. A small proportion of non-manual parents had relatively high incomes and other resources.

The existence of a relatively prosperous group of one-parent families has to be accounted for in any explanation of the generally low resources of one-parent families. This is why analysis of the relationship between class and the institutions of marriage, work and family, and also the history of social policies for one-parent families, is so important.

The lesson for policy of this analysis is that a variety of measures of income support need to be adopted to reduce the differential incomes received by one-parent and two-parent families. While not ruling out the case for transitional additional benefits for lone parents and for children in their families, we conclude that (a) higher rates of child benefit for children in all types of family should be paid and varied as a percentage of earnings according to age; (b) an allowance for the care of young children, and certain other special categories of dependants, should be introduced; and (c) an allowance should be paid, or underwritten in the legal rights of a mother with children in respect of her husband, for the upkeep of the family home.

23
Old People

This chapter aims to elaborate and in part explain our finding that a relatively high proportion of the population in the oldest age groups are living in poverty. The finding is important, because the proportion of people in these age groups is large and has been growing steadily throughout this century. In 1911, there were fewer than 3 million people of pensionable age in the United Kingdom, in 1951 fewer than 7 million, and in 1975, 9½ million; and although this last total is expected to be about the same at the end of the century, there are expected to be more persons aged 75 and over among them.[1] The finding is disturbing because the problem of poverty among the elderly has been recognized socially for at least 100 years,[2] has been emphasized in a succession of local and national studies carried out by government bodies as well as by independent research workers since the war,[3] and yet has resisted the attempts of successive governments to alleviate substantially still less eliminate it. Moreover, the problem is by no means peculiar to Britain and seems to be characteristic of market economies and state socialist societies alike.[4]

1. *Social Trends*, No. 7, HMSO, London, 1976, p. 62.
2. Charles Booth dated the early agitation for old-age pensions from the late 1870s, with the publication of a pamphlet by Hookham, entitled 'The Outline of a Scheme for dealing with Pauperism: The Question of the Day', and his own work contributed to the concern expressed about the large minority of old people who were paupers. See Booth, C., *Pauperism: A Picture; and the Endowment of Old Age: An Argument*, Macmillan, London, 1892; *The Aged Poor: Condition*, Macmillan, London, 1894; and *Old Age Pensions and the Aged Poor*, Macmillan, London, 1899. See also Collins, D., 'The Introduction of Old Age Pensions in Great Britain', *Historical Journal*, VIII, 2, 1965.
3. Townsend, P., *The Family Life of Old People*, Routledge & Kegan Paul, London, 1957, esp. Chapter 12; Cole Wedderburn, D., with Utting, J., *The Economic Circumstances of Old People*, Codicote Press, Welwyn, 1962; Townsend, P., and Wedderburn, D., *The Aged in the Welfare State*, Bell, London, 1965 (see the list of studies in Appendix 1); Ministry of Pensions and National Insurance, *Financial and Other Circumstances of Retirement Pensioners*, HMSO, London, 1966.
4. See, for example, Epstein, L. A., 'Income of the Aged in 1962: First Findings of the 1963 Survey of the Aged', *Social Security Bulletin*, XXVII, March 1964; Orshansky, M., 'Counting the Poor: Another Look at the Poverty Profile', *Social Security Bulletin*, XXVIII, January 1965; Shanas, E., *et al.*, *Old People in Three Industrial Societies*, Routledge & Kegan Paul,

Paradoxically, although public opinion often seems to favour substantial government intervention to guarantee more support for the elderly, the measures that are enacted are often delayed and do not match in generosity that opinion. The problem persists, and can even be shown in some societies to have grown. The failure may not just be a failure of governments to commit the necessary resources to alleviating or meeting the problem, but *explaining* why they have not done so or are not prepared to do so. In other words, the underlying failure may be one of analysing, explaining and therefore understanding the persistence of the problem in the first place.

This provides the theme of this chapter and conditions its organization and structure. The general hypothesis of the chapter is that the propensity to poverty in old age is a function of low levels of resources, and restricted access to resources, relative to younger people. Restriction and inadequacy of resources is determined by different causal factors. State pensions and other cash benefits comprise the most important source of income for the elderly, and the initial rate of state pensions, and the amounts of substitute or supplementary benefits which are paid, after the pensionable age or upon retirement, are low relative to the earnings of younger adults. State help is conditional upon retirement from paid employment, and this status is imposed upon elderly people at a fixed chronological age, or they are persuaded to accept it as a social norm. The choice of continuing in paid employment rather than retiring and drawing a pension is also restricted by the tendency for earnings to fall in late middle age and to be very low for people over the pensionable ages, as well as by high rates of redundancy and unemployment late in life. The initial rates of occupational and private pensions are, with some exceptions, also low relative to the earnings of young adults; some, but not all, of these pensions are conditional upon retirement; certain forms of state aid are reduced to take such income into account; and the numbers of elderly, and particularly of widows, who are entitled to these pensions, or have had opportunities to contribute to any scheme, is greatly restricted. The resources held by most of the elderly fail to keep pace in value with the resources of other groups in society: either certain forms of asset held, such as household goods and equipment and certain types of incomes from savings, and occupational pensions, depreciate in value absolutely or relatively to the rise in real living standards, with increasing length of retirement, or many do not have, and have not in the past had, an opportunity of obtaining, types of resource which are newly becoming available to younger people. Greater exposure to certain forms of social desolation and isolation, brought about by the death of a spouse, the loss of close relatives or friends, and the decay of industries or city centres, as well as by retirement, tends to deprive the elderly of access to alternative or subsidiary resources

London, 1968; Csenh-Szombathy, L., and Andorka, R., *Situation and Problems of the Pensioners of Budapest*, Central Statistical Office, Research Group for Population Studies, 1965–6.

and sometimes leads to additional costs. Liability to disablement also restricts access to resources and, in the absence of compensating cash benefits and services, leads to additional costs for many which outweigh the savings consequent upon retirement.

Such are the major factors, although there are others, which must feature in our analysis. They will be discussed below in relation both to inequalities between the elderly and the non-elderly and inequalities among the elderly. Historically, the emergence of certain types of resource for the elderly, the definition of categories eligible to receive them and the amounts that are available, respresent the outcome of the continuing struggle to preserve or enhance class interests, directly or as a by-product, through the social policies of the state and of other institutions. The historical evolution of this complex can only be touched on below.

Inequality between Elderly and Young

One tendency of research in recent years has been to limit explanation by studying the elderly as if they were independent of the economy and the polity and even of the general structure and value system of society. As a consequence, the principal causes of their problems have been attributed to individual and limited associational factors: to the special problems of individual adjustment to ageing, individual adjustment to physical decrescence, and individual adjustment to retirement. The only significant exception to the indifference in explanation shown towards the wider institutions of society is the blame that has been attributed to the family, an alleged weakening of family ties or decline in the importance of the extended family brought about by the functional necessity to industrial society of the 'structurally isolated conjugal family'.[1] This approach has stressed adjustment to, and detachment from, social roles during the later stages of life, with the basis of society, or its economic and social institutions, as largely given.[2] It does not question that basis or ask whether the fundamental problems of ageing are attributable to the unequal and barbarous effects of the operation, including the neglect, of economic and social institutions at a particular stage of the evolution of industrial societies. With some noteworthy exceptions,[3] too little attention

1. This concept was developed in particular by Talcott Parsons. Functional theories of family change and of changes in the situation of the elderly exerted a widespread influence. The concept has been subjected to considerable criticism, however, in recent years. See Parsons, T., *Essays in Sociological Theory*, Free Press of Glencoe, New York, revised paperback edition, 1964, esp. his essay on 'Age and Sex in the Social Structure of the United States'. For criticisms see, for example, Shanas *et al.*, *Old People in Three Industrial Societies*, Chapters 1 and 6.

2. An influential example of this approach is Cumming, E., and Henry, W. E., *Growing Old*, Basic Books, New York, 1961.

3. For example, Wedderburn, D., 'The Financial Resources of Older People', in Shanas *et al.*, *Old People in Three Industrial Societies*, p. 367.

has been given both to comparisons between the elderly and the rest of the population and to the internal analysis of structural differences among the elderly.

How might we proceed in comparing the standards of living of the elderly with the non-elderly in society? Many more adults under than over the pensionable ages have children and other dependants whom they support on their incomes. Many more of them incur the additional expenses of going to work, including clothing or equipment as well as costs of travel. More, too, have high accommodation costs, because they are still paying for mortgages, or because they do not live in rent-controlled tenancies or in accommodation paid for by others. On the other hand, the elderly have the benefit of higher personal tax allowances and are more likely to benefit from the exclusion from tax of certain types of income from savings, and from the disregard of certain types of income, capital and capital gains, in receiving social security payments. For such reasons, comparisons of absolute gross or net incomes are not particularly appropriate. The comparison set out in Table 23.1 takes each of the points so far mentioned into account and expresses net incomes on a comparable basis. The income of the income unit, de-

Table 23.1. *Percentages and numbers of elderly*[a] *and non-elderly persons in income units with incomes above and below the state's standard of poverty.*

Net disposable income of income unit last year as % of supplementary benefit standard plus housing cost			Estimated number in population (millions)[b]	
	Elderly	Non-elderly	Elderly	Non-elderly
Under 100	20	7	1·7	3·2
100–39	44	19	3·7	8·8
140–99	17	31	1·4	14·3
200+	19	43	1·6	19·9
Total	100	100	8·2	46·2
Number	861	4,494	–	–

NOTES: [a]Women 60 and over and men 65 and over, in one-person and two-person income units, thus excluding the small number of elderly people with dependent children under 15.
[b]Excluding the non-institutionalized population (i.e. in hospital and residential homes).

fined as any person or married couple, with or without children under 15, is expressed as a percentage of the basic supplementary benefit rates prevailing at the time plus current housing cost. These rates reflect what incomes for different sizes and types of income unit are treated by society as equivalent for the purposes of securing subsistence. Work expenses and the costs of travel to work are subtracted from gross disposable income (i.e. gross income less direct taxes and national insurance contributions). It can be seen that there was a striking difference in the distribution of the elderly and the non-elderly around the state's standard of poverty. Twenty per cent, compared with 7 per cent, were living in poverty; another 44 per cent, compared with 19 per cent, were living on the margins of poverty.[1] At the other end of the income scale, more than twice as many of the non-elderly than of the elderly were living comfortably above the standard. The median income of the non-elderly was nearly twice that of the elderly. Although the elderly comprised only one sixth of the total population, they comprised one third of those in poverty, and nearly one third on the margins of poverty, by the state's standards. As the table shows, nearly 6 million of them were in this vulnerable financial situation.

The difference between elderly and non-elderly is also sharp if incomes are related to the alternative deprivation standard. As many as 54 per cent had incomes below this, compared with 21 per cent of the non-elderly, and only 9 per cent had incomes of more than 200 per cent of the standard, compared with 24 per cent (see Table A.90, Appendix Eight, page 1061).

The principal reason for the difference rests in the separation of the vast majority of the elderly from access to the rates of income obtainable in paid employment and their heavy dependence on the low rates of income obtainable through the state's social-security system. A 'pension' has come to mean an income smaller, and usually very much smaller, than a 'wage' or 'salary'. Eighty per cent of those of pensionable age were neither employed nor had been employed during the preceding year. Eleven per cent of these depended for their incomes exclusively upon state retirement pensions, and another 16 per cent exclusively upon state retirement pensions and supplementary benefits or other benefits. Many others had only small amounts of income from any other source. Altogether, over two thirds depended for more than half their incomes on state retirement pensions and supplementary benefits (Table A.91, Appendix Eight, page 1061). Even among the remaining people of pensionable age who had gained some income from employment in the preceding year, there was substantial dependence on retirement pensions, 42 per cent having more than half their income from this source.

That the rates of retirement pensions and of supplementary benefits are low, relative to earnings, and have remained low since the war, is demonstrated by Table 23.2. For the twenty-seven years between 1948 and 1975, the single person's

1. It should be noted that when the supplementary benefit standard is applied to the income of income units, more people are found below the standard than when it is applied to income of *households*, as in Chapter 7. Whether the income of the whole household reflects better than the income of different units which comprise it the consumption standards of individual members is a controversial question.

Table 23.2. *Rates of benefit as a percentage of average gross industrial earnings (males).*

Year (October)	Retirement pensions		Supplementary benefits	
	Single	Married couple	Single householder	Married couple
1948	18·8	30·4	17·4	29·0
1958	19·5	31·2	17·5	29·6
1963	20·2	32·5	19·0	31·2
1965	20·4	33·2	19·4	32·0
1967	21·1	34·2	20·1	33·0
1968	19·6	31·7	19·8	32·4
1969	18·1	29·4	18·3	30·0
1970	17·8	28·9	17·1	28·0
1971	19·4	31·4	18·8	30·6
1972	18·8	30·4	18·3	29·7
1973	18·9	30·5	19·9	31·4
1974	20·6	32·9	21·4	33·6
1975	19·5	31·7	20·5	32·2
1976	19·9	31·7	20·5	32·2

SOURCE: *Hansard*, 23 January 1973, and *Social Security Statistics, 1976*, HMSO, London, 1978, p. 216. Note that from 1973 long-term rate of supplementary benefit is taken.

rate of retirement pension, for example, ebbed and flowed between 18 and 21 per cent of average gross industrial earnings, and the rate of supplementary benefit between 17 and 21 per cent. In 1974 and 1975, despite substantial money increases in benefit rates, their relationship to gross earnings did not, because of inflation, improve. Evidence of the relatively low level of some other sources of income received by the elderly is given later. Some state pensioners obtain increments by deferring retirement, and are entitled to graduated pensions, introduced in 1961. But the amounts of the latter are very small, and their value has been eroded steadily by inflation. Even when pension increments and graduated pensions are added, few pensioners obtain much above the basic rate of pension. Thus a government survey found in 1965 that only 21 per cent of married couples and only 1 per cent of single pensioners had more than £1 above the basic rates.[1] In 1975, the basic rate of pension for the single pensioner amounted, for the year as a whole, to just under £600. According to the Family Expenditure Survey, the mean amount paid in that year to single pensioner households was only £604, to which other cash benefits, principally supplementary benefits, added £191 and earnings £52, making a total of £847.[2]

1. Ministry of Pensions and National Insurance, *Financial and Other Circumstances of Retirement Pensioners*, HMSO, London, 1966, Table III, 15.
2. Harris, R., 'A Review of the Effects of Taxes and Benefits on Household Incomes, 1961–1975', *Economic Trends*, January 1977, p. 107.

Although pensions have not increased more than fitfully in relation to gross earnings, they increased slightly during the 1960s and early 1970s, particularly in 1974–5, in relation to net earnings.[1] The failure on the part of the government to raise tax thresholds fully in relation to inflation has resulted in a higher proportion of earnings being taken in tax. It is for this reason that pensioners have experienced some improvement in their net disposable incomes relative to people of non-pensionable age. Thus, the single pensioner's disposable income, as a percentage of that of the adult non-pensioner living alone, was 43 in 1961, 46 in 1967, 46 in 1970, 45 in 1973, and 50 in 1975. For married pensioners, the corresponding percentages (that is, in relation to households with two non-pensioner adults without any dependants) were 37, 42, 41, 39 and 42.[2]

The low rate of pension is significant, not only because of the lack among many of the elderly of other substantial sources of income, due especially to their retirement from work, but because the rate has been lower, throughout the years since the war, than society's definition of a poverty standard, and lower, too, than the rates recommended as a goal in the Beveridge Report of 1942. As the figures in Table 23.2 testify, the basic rates of supplementary benefit have been nearly as high in most years as the rates of pension, and for a brief period in the late 1960s were actually higher than the rates of pension, without adding on the actual amounts paid for rent and other housing costs. Whether many people attain the social standard of a minimum income therefore depends crucially upon whether or not they apply for, and receive, appropriate supplementation of their pensions from the Supplementary Benefits Commission. More than a quarter of retirement pensioners do, in fact, receive supplementation, though whether large numbers of them could be paid more than they are, according to existing administrative rules and procedures, has become a matter of some controversy.

Other groups than the elderly depend on the supplementary benefits scheme. That scheme is also part of a more general system of means-tested, or conditional, welfare. For these reasons, the scheme and other means-tested benefits are discussed more fully in Chapters 24 and 25. Chapter 24 shows, however, that more than two thirds as many old people again as are receiving supplementary benefits are eligible to do so. Only a little over half of those eligible to receive supplementary benefits were actually receiving such benefits. The rest were spread among all age groups over the pensionable ages, and represented 1,500,000 in the total population of the United Kingdom. The chapter also finds that the reasons for low uptake rest less in the ignorance of old people of their rights and their reluctance to exercise them as in administrative difficulties of access and the conflicting functions of the system. On the one hand, the Supplementary Benefits Commission has a legal duty to meet need; on the other, they have the less clearly formulated

1. *Social Trends*, No. 7, H M S O, London, 1976, p. 107.
2. Derived from Harris, 'A Review of the Effects of Taxes and Benefits on Household Incomes', pp. 107–9.

responsibility of protecting and enforcing social values and saving the unnecessary expenditure of public monies. This seriously handicaps their discretion to add materially to the basic rates prescribed, as in reality they are, by Parliament.

The inequality in incomes between elderly and young is in some respects widened, and in others reduced, when their other resources are examined. The most important of these are assets. Asset-holdings augment living standards in various ways. Outright ownership of a home can represent the equivalent of what others have to pay in rent from their incomes. Savings can be withdrawn or valuable possessions sold to meet current living costs. Property can provide security in order to obtain loans more easily. The ownership of a car can in certain circumstances reduce travel costs or increase or maintain range and quality of activities. Our definition of assets (explained in Chapter 5, and in detail in Appendix Five) was wide and included the value of owner-occupied houses as well as cars and personal possessions like pictures and jewellery. None the less, a quarter of the elderly had no assets at all or assets of less than £25 value, and altogether more than two fifths of them less than £200. It can be seen, however, in Table 23.3

Table 23.3. *Percentages of elderly and non-elderly comprising income units, according to total net assets and readily realizable assets.*[a]

Value of assets (£)	Elderly		Non-elderly	
	Total net assets	Readily realizable assets only	Total net assets	Readily realizable assets only
Under 25	25	33	22	44
25–99	9	10	9	16
100–99	7	9	6	9
200–499	7	15	11	15
500–999	7	12	8	7
1,000–4,999	27	14	27	7
5,000–9,999	12	4	11	1
10,000+	6	3	6	1
Total	100	100	100	100
Number	750	835	3,861	4,440

NOTE: [a]For definition, see Appendix Five, page 981.

that the distribution by value was not very different among the elderly from that among the non-elderly. Assets include values, like savings, which are readily realizable, as well as values, like owner-occupied homes, which are not readily realizable. If attention is confined to the former, it can also be seen that fewer of the elderly than of the non-elderly had low values, and more of them had high values. This means that, despite relatively low net disposable incomes, more of them had assets which could be used to raise living standards. In practice, it seems that only a minority do so to any considerable extent. Thus, when we asked for information on dissaving, we found that only 13 per cent of the elderly who lived alone and 17 per cent of elderly married couples had drawn £25 or more from savings in the previous year. About 4 per cent and 8 per cent had drawn £100 or more, some of them more than £200. Altogether, only 12 per cent of the elderly had drawn savings during the year.

By contradistinction, more of the elderly than of the non-elderly (47 per cent compared with 31 per cent) possessed no assets, or virtually no assets, which could be readily realized. Relatively fewer of them had assets worth £5,000 or more. Fewer of the elderly, for example, possessed cars and other saleable assets worth over £25, and fewer lived in owner-occupied houses of relatively high value (after subtracting capital still to be repaid for mortgaged property).

As explained in Chapter 5 (pages 212–15), we attempted to find the approximate effect of assets in raising living standards by expressing them as an annuity value and adding this value to disposable incomes. The hazards involved in this enterprise have been emphasized. Because investment in owned homes cannot be liquidated to supplement income as readily as savings and investment assets, and because the imputed annual addition to income is necessarily larger for people with a relatively short expectation of life, the procedure is less satisfactory for the elderly than for the non-elderly. None the less, assets are a substantial contributory factor in the determination of real or at least potential living standards for some old people. For this reason, some crude estimate of the imputed addition to income is better than no estimate at all. Two conclusions emerge. Even when 'potential' income from assets is added, a substantial proportion of the elderly remain in poverty or on the margins of poverty; thus, when 'potential' incomes are added to net disposable incomes, the number below the state poverty standard falls from 20 to 12 per cent and the number on the margins of that standard from 44 to 26 per cent. Secondly, the situation of some elderly people is transformed from that of having low or modest incomes to that of being relatively rich; thus, when 'potential' incomes are added to disposable incomes, the number with three or more times the state poverty standard rises from 5 to 26 per cent.

If the value of employer welfare benefits in kind is brought into the picture, the inequality in living standards between elderly and non-elderly widens. One method of demonstrating this is illustrated in Table 23.4. The non-asset income of income units has been expressed as a percentage of the supplementary benefit scale rates (plus housing costs). The mean for selected age groups has then been compared, and the corresponding values for different additional types of resources have been given cumulatively.

Relative to income, the elderly gain more than the non-elderly in value of social

Table 23.4. Mean resources of income unit, for people of selected ages, as percentages of supplementary benefit scale rates plus housing costs.

Age group		Non-asset income		
		plus value employer welfare benefits in kind		
			plus annuity value of assets	
				plus value of social and personal services and goods in kind
40–49	246	258	313	376
65–9	145	146	239	272
70–79	123	123	213	244
80+	104	104	156	180

services in kind. However, it is difficult to treat these resources unequivocally as an imputed addition to income. In large measure, they reflect additional need. More of the elderly than of the non-elderly are sick and disabled, and the fact that they tend to gain more in value from free health services does not mean that they are enabled to enjoy a higher standard of living – only that they are freed from certain additional costs and anxieties that would be incurred if such services had to be paid for. But there are some services, such as subsidized meal services, which represent a subvention towards income.

The relative lack of total resources on the part of the elderly was reflected in our measures of deprivation. Significantly more of them than of the non-elderly lacked television sets, refrigerators and other household durables; had not eaten fresh meat most days of the week; had not had a summer holiday away from home in the last twelve months; had not had an afternoon or evening out in the last fortnight; and had not been out to relatives or friends in the last four weeks for a meal or a snack, and had gone for at least one day without a cooked meal in the previous fortnight (see Table 11.1, page 414). More of the elderly than of the non-elderly were also conscious of being worse off than others (Table 11.3, page 420).

We noted above that fewer of the elderly than of the non-elderly possessed substantial amounts of assets, the value of which could be readily realized. Paradoxically, many more of the elderly than of the non-elderly were in income units owning their homes outright, as Table 23.5 shows. This is certainly the most important qualification that needs to be made to the figures so far presented of inequality of living standards between elderly and non-elderly. The differences in distribution by tenure, as laid out in Table 23.5, are striking. As would be expected, more of the elderly than of the non-elderly income units had paid off

Table 23.5. *Percentages of elderly and non-elderly according to housing tenure.*

Tenure	Elderly[a]	Non-elderly
Owner-occupier: fully owned	44·9	15·4
paying mortgage	5·4	32·4
Rented: local authority	24·6	31·5
privately furnished	1·8	4·8
privately unfurnished	20·8	11·8
privately with farm/business	0·6	0·6
Rent free (mostly employer owned)	1·8	3·5
Total	100	100
Number	924	5,155

NOTE: [a]Women 60 and over, men 65 and over.

mortgages, but the proportion occupying homes owned by the household (just over 50 per cent) was none the less slightly higher than the corresponding proportion of the non-elderly.

This requires comment. In view of the rapid increase since the war in the extent of owner-occupation, one might expect the ratio between elderly and non-elderly to be reversed. Thus, in England and Wales, the number of dwellings which were owner-occupied in 1947 was only 27 per cent, in 1961, 42 per cent, in 1966, 47 per cent, and in 1971, 52 per cent.[1] Other things being equal, one would expect a higher proportion of each age cohort than of its immediate predecessor to be owner-occupiers, with the elderly tending to reflect, at any one date, the national proportion found at a date between ten and twenty years previously. That so many were outright owner-occupiers must in some part be attributable to the purchase of properties, usually of low value, like bungalows, from savings in late middle age or upon retirement, by people who had formerly lived in rented accommodation; though in some cases moves may have been prompted by inheritance. But the phenomenon must also be attributable to much higher mortality at the older ages of working-class people, particularly of semi-skilled and unskilled manual workers.

Whatever the full explanation, more of the elderly than of the non-elderly were found in fact to own their own homes. But although fewer rented council accommodation, more rented privately unfurnished accommodation. The proportion was nearly double that of the non-elderly. In Chapter 13 (pages 490–98) we showed that this sector had the worst record for housing facilities of any type of tenure. The table therefore also suggests a polarization of experience among the elderly,

1. OPCS, Social Survey Division, *The General Household Survey*, HMSO, London, 1973, pp. 91–2.

relative to the non-elderly, which can be demonstrated again and again in describing and analysing their economic and social situation. This introduces a second main theme of this chapter.

Inequality among the Elderly: Single and Married

One method of pursuing, and explaining, the inequality in incomes between elderly and non-elderly is to examine and compare different sub-groups among them. There are striking differences between the component sub-groups of the elderly. The great majority of the elderly are not in paid employment. Three quarters of these, compared with only a third of the elderly who were employed currently or for at least a period during the preceding twelve months, were found to be in, or on the margins of, poverty, according to the state's standard. Among the retired, a further difference was found between the single and the married. More than four fifths of the unmarried, widowed, and married but separated elderly were in poverty, or on the margins of poverty, compared with three fifths

Table 23.6. Percentages of elderly and non-elderly in different types of income unit that have incomes above or below the state's standard of poverty.

Net disposable income of income unit last year as % of supplementary benefit standard plus housing cost	Elderly[a]				Non-elderly	
	Not employed		Employed[b]			
	Single[c]	Married	Single[c]	Married	Single	Married (with and without children)
Under 100	26	19	14	7	14	4
100–39	56	42	30	22	10	21
140–99	11	17	32	28	21	34
200+	7	21	23	43	55	42
Total	100	100	100	100	100	100
Number	329	360	56	116	789	3,466

NOTES: [a]Women 60 and over, men 65 and over.
[b]In paid employment, even for a few hours a week, during the previous twelve months.
[c]Including unmarried, widowed, divorced and married but separated.

of the married. At the other end of the income scale, there were three times as many married as single persons with incomes of double or more than double the state's standard (Table 23.6).

The inequalities between single and married become wider when the value of assets is taken into account. Forty-four per cent of single men and 45 per cent of single women, compared with 24 per cent of married persons, had net assets of less than £100 in value (most of them having no assets at all). At the other extreme, 13 per cent and 12 per cent respectively of single men and women, compared with 23 per cent of the married, had £5,000 or more.

Among the single, there are further differences between, on the one hand, men and women, and between the unmarried and the widowed, separated or divorced, on the other. More of the men than of the women were found to have relatively high incomes, and fewer relatively low incomes (Table A.92, Appendix Eight, page 1062). Among women, widows were the most disadvantaged. Not only were more of them than of other groups living in poverty or on the margins of poverty; more had no assets or virtually no assets, and fewer possessed substantial amounts of assets (Table A.93, Appendix Eight, page 1062). According to a variety of indi-

Table 23.7. *Percentages of elderly of different sex and marital status, according to selected characteristics of their economic situation.*

Characteristic	Single men	Single women		Married men
		Unmarried	Widowed, separated or divorced	and women
1. Income below or on margins of social standard of poverty	65	69	77	53
2. Fewer than £100 assets	44	26	49	24
3. Living in house owned outright	35	51	32	53
4. Living in unfurnished rented accommodation	18	24	27	17
5. Fewer than 6 durables in list of 10 in home	49	46	50	35
	Numbers on which percentages based			
1.	59	68	266	437
2.	52	57	236	388
3.	71	79	286	499
4.	71	79	286	499
5.	71	79	286	499

cators of economic situation, widowed women were least advantaged, as Table 23.7 shows.

Society makes scant provision for women of pensionable age who are widowed. It also makes scant provision for people of advanced age. Among all men and women of pensionable age in the national sample who were found in units with incomes below or on the margins of the social standard of poverty, nearly half were widows. Of elderly women in this vulnerable financial situation, 78 per cent were widows.

Inequality among the Elderly: the Concept of the Fourth Generation

The disadvantage of elderly women as compared with elderly men, and of the single compared with the married, is partly a function of age, and more directly of the relative lack of resources and of access to resources on the part of the elderly of advanced age. A substantial proportion of the elderly are now aged 75 and over. Among the population of men aged 65 and over, and women aged 60 and over, those aged 75 and over comprised 19 per cent in 1931, 26 per cent in 1951, 29 per cent in 1971 and is expected to be 38 per cent in 2001.[1]

Most of the increase is due to a rise in the numbers of women, rather than of men, aged 75 and over. Indeed, between 1950 and 1970 the average expectation of life of men aged 65 deteriorated marginally from 12·2 years to 11·9 years, while that of women increased from 14·6 years to 15·8 years.[2] There are now $1\frac{1}{4}$ million widows aged 75 and over (and a further $1\frac{1}{2}$ million aged 65–74). Altogether there are more than twice as many women as men of 75 years of age and over. The growth in proportion of elderly widows among the elderly suggests how important it is to understand their relatively precarious economic situation, and the present methods and amounts of resources allocated.

The growing number of people of advanced age, which includes a disproportionate number of women, also coincides with the emergence in industrial society of a fourth generation on any scale. A cross-national study of the populations aged 65 and over in Britain, Denmark and the United States found that of those with children 23 per cent in both Britain and Denmark, and 40 per cent in the United States, had great-grandchildren, much larger proportions than can have been possible even twenty-five years previously.[3] This rapid increase in the 'fourth generation' can be attributed not only to greater longevity but also to earlier marriage and earlier childbearing, which reduces the average span in years between the generations.[4] For reasons of changing stratification by age, changing

1. *Social Trends*, No. 7, p. 62.

2. DHSS, *Health and Personal Social Service Statistics for England and Wales* (with summary tables for Great Britain), 1972, HMSO, London, 1973, Table 1.6.

3. Shanas *et al.*, *Old People in Three Industrial Societies*, p. 141.

4. Townsend, P., 'The Four Generation Family', in *The Social Minority*, Allen Lane, London, 1973.

family structure, and changing systems of resource distribution in societies experiencing economic growth and inflation, a distinction between a third and a fourth generation over the pensionable ages has to be made.

The present inequality in incomes and other resources between elderly men and elderly women is traceable to these demographic, social and economic factors associated with the development in the social structure on a substantial scale of a fourth generation. Men tend to have higher incomes and more of other types of resource than women. But, in the national survey, 76 per cent of them, compared with only 43 per cent of women, were married and, as we have seen, the married had more resources of different kinds than the single. More, too, of single women than of single men were of advanced age: thus, 62 per cent of women aged 60 and over were aged 70 and over, compared with only 45 per cent of men. These two structural factors underlie any of the comparisons which might be drawn between elderly men and elderly women. When an attempt is made to hold them constant, as in Table 23.8, it is still possible to show the relationship between diminishing

Table 23.8. *Percentage of single and married people of different age in income units with incomes below or on margins of the state's standard of poverty.*[a]

Age	Men			Women		
	Single	Married	All	Single	Married	All
20–39	9	24	19	29	26	26
40–49	(19)	17	17	26	13	15
50–59	(15)	15	15	41	19	24
60–64	–	19	20	66	31	46
65–69	–	48	48	76	53	63
70–79	–	67	68	74	71	73
80+	–	–	(85)	89	–	86
Numbers on which percentages based						
20–39	211	481	692	159	544	703
40–49	42	272	314	57	285	342
50–59	34	261	295	80	241	321
60–64	23	95	118	65	90	155
65–69	22	101	123	63	83	146
70–79	24	84	108	140	59	199
80+	13	14	27	66	6	72

NOTE: [a]Net disposable income of income unit below 140 per cent of supplementary benefit standard plus housing cost.

resources and advancing age.[1] This phenomenon is found in other countries.[2] The table shows that, after fluctuating around a fifth or a quarter for most of adult life, the proportion of people in poverty or on the margins of poverty rises sharply after the pensionable ages. The table also shows that the over eighties are the poorest group of all. In fact among the over eighties as many as 53 per cent were either receiving supplementary benefits or were eligible to receive them, compared with 45–46 per cent of those in their late sixties (Table A.94, Appendix Eight, page 1063).

In judging the significance of these findings about age, two questions have to be posed. We have been considering the incomes of income units, not of households, and 31 per cent of the elderly in the sample were neither living alone nor in married pairs, but were living with others – for example, elderly siblings, other adults, and married children and grandchildren. Assuming household incomes were pooled, might the living standards of the elderly be less unequally distri-

Table 23.9. Percentages of elderly people of different age living below or on the margins of the state's standard of poverty, according to three measures: unit income; household income; and net income worth.

Age	As % of supplementary benefit standard plus housing cost						
	Net disposable income last year of income unit		Net disposable income last year of household	Net income worth of household last year			
	Men	Women	Men and women	Men and women	Men	Women	Men and women
60–64	–	46	–	30	–	21	–
65–69	48	63	56	49	22	28	25
70–79	68	73	71	60	26	37	33
80+	(85)	86	86	64	–	46	39
All of pensionable age	60	65	63	53	23	31	29

1. See also Ministry of Pensions and National Insurance, *Financial and Other Circumstances of Retirement Pensioners*, HMSO, London, 1966, Chapter 2.

2. For an excellent overall analysis, see Morgan, J. N., 'The Retirement Process in the United States', Working Paper from OEO Study of Family Income Dynamics, Survey Research Center, University of Michigan, 1972; Morgan, J. N., and David, M., 'The Aged: Their Ability to Meet Medical Expenses', *Financing Health Care for the Aged*, Part I, Blue Cross Association, American Hospital Association, Chicago, Ill., 1962.

buted with advancing age? The answer is that although the incomes of other people, when pooled with those of the elderly in cases where they live in the same household, reduce the numbers living in poverty or on the margins of poverty, the benefit is spread more or less evenly among the age groups, and a marked inequality according to age remains.

Secondly, savings and other assets have not so far been taken into account, which, in theory at least, might enable those of advanced age to raise standards of consumption to levels closer to those of people of less advanced age. Assuming that the value of assets can be combined with incomes, is the effect to reduce inequality with advancing age? Again, although 'potential' incomes, when added to net disposable incomes, reduce the numbers living below or on the margins of poverty standards, the benefit is spread more or less evenly among the different age groups, and a marked inequality, according to age, remains. The effects of adopting different measures are illustrated in Table 23.9.

Social Class and Access to Resources

Inequalities between the aged in their command of resources is also a function of class position. Depending on previous occupation, some of the elderly had received much higher salaries or wages than others during active working life and had therefore enjoyed more opportunities to save, and acquire property and other possessions. Those of high occupational status had also had more access to membership of occupational pension schemes. For such reasons, as well as greater opportunity to inherit wealth, and failure on the part of the state's social policies to redress such inequalities subsequent to retirement, class position correlates with poverty.

The elderly in the sample were divided into three groups according to present or last occupation: non-manual, skilled manual and partly skilled or unskilled manual. A markedly larger proportion of manual than non-manual groups lived in households with incomes below or on the margins of the social standard of poverty. Higher proportions also lacked assets worth £200 or more, had fewer than six among a list of ten common durables in the home, and were not living in homes owned outright. When the 'potential' income of assets was added to disposable income, the proportion of non-manual groups living at poverty standards was reduced much more than the corresponding proportion of manual groups. The ownership of assets substantially widens class inequality of incomes in old age (Table 23.10).

The groups compared in Table 23.10 include elderly people living with others, as well as people living alone and in married pairs. When each of these three groups were considered separately, significantly more elderly people living alone than others were found to have resources below or on the margins of poverty,

Table 23.10. Percentages of elderly of different social class living in households and income units with resources below selected standards.

Standard	Non-manual	Skilled manual	Partly skilled and unskilled manual	Numbers on which % based Non-manual	Skilled manual	Partly skilled and unskilled manual
Net disposable household income below or on margins of poverty standard	41·7	60·6	61·6	187	203	242
Net disposable income unit income *ditto*	47·7	73·0	71·6	243	255	271
Income net worth of household below or on margins of poverty standard	9·9	36·2	42·1	172	185	214
Income net worth of income unit *ditto*	18·1	47·1	50·6	215	227	241
Unit assets of less than £200	15·4	42·2	53·0	201	199	232
Fewer than 6 durables in home in list of 10	28·3	47·3	49·6	226	207	236
Accommodation not owner-occupied	31·4	59·6	71·2	242	225	267

and significantly more elderly people living in married pairs than people sharing households with others. But in each of the three household groups the class gradient remains marked (see Table A.95, Appendix Eight, page 1063).

Low Lifelong Social Status and Poverty

Living standards in old age are not only a function of class position as signified by present occupation, last occupation prior to retirement or husband's occupation prior to widowhood. They appear also to be a function of lifelong class position. We had asked all individuals in the sample for information about the main occupation followed by their fathers. Ideally, we would have wished to analyse the relationship between own and father's (and spouse's) occupational status for each of the eight ranks discussed elsewhere in this book, but numbers in some ranks were much too small. However, there were minimally adequate numbers for the seven combinations set out in Table 24.11. When different measures of resources were applied, a difference *within* certain classes, according to father's social class, could be demonstrated. The table shows that non-manual elderly whose fathers had also had non-manual occupations tended to have more resources than those whose fathers had been in manual occupations. The reverse also applied. Again, bearing in mind the small numbers on which some of the percentages are based, there is a tendency among manual groups for resources to be higher for those whose fathers had been in skilled occupations, and to be lower for those whose fathers had been in partly skilled or unskilled occupations. Those of unskilled or partly skilled occupational status whose fathers had held comparable status were the poorest of all.

The data in the table demonstrate the sharp inequalities in wealth between elderly of different class, which have the effect of widening inequalities found between incomes. As many as a quarter of elderly people from non-manual occupations, whose fathers had also held non-manual occupations, had net assets of £10,000 or more, and a half £5,000 or more, compared with 0 per cent and 2 per cent of those at the other end of the occupational status scale. If 'potential' income, represented by the annuity value of assets, is added to net disposable incomes, then 66 per cent, compared with 6 per cent, were found to have resources of three or more times the social poverty standard.

Although the incidence of poverty is highly correlated with class position, that is not the only explanation for the existence of poverty on a disproportionate scale among the elderly. The various measures to assess living standards which we have used show that, even when class is held constant, more of the old than of the young are in poverty or on its margins. The protective mechanisms and resources of those in non-manual and in skilled manual occupations, as well as in partly skilled and unskilled occupations, are diminished in old age by the different processes of exclusion from employment, falling value of certain resources, particularly occupational pensions, in relation both to rising real incomes of the community at large and inflation, and lack of protection for women who become widowed and men and women who become disabled from the preservation of living standards relative to those of adults below pensionable age.

Withdrawal or diminution of some of the economic resources associated with class position in old age has the effect of superimposing upon the disadvantages of class the disadvantages of depressed retirement status. In an important sense, the elderly poor are an 'under-class' as well as being predominantly persons who would be deprived, whatever their age, by virtue of their class position. They share in common a particular social status – whatever their class origins. Two of

Table 23.11. *Percentages of elderly of different lifelong status who have less than, or more than, certain levels of resources.*

Own class in relation to father's class	Net disposable household income last year below or on margins of poverty standard	Net income worth of household last year below or on margins of poverty standard	Living in home not owner-occupied (outright)	Fewer than 8 of 10 selected durables in home	Net income worth of household last year three or more times poverty standard	Net unit assets of £5,000 or more	Number on which percentages are based
1. Non-manual, father likewise	41	7	26	58	66	50	96–140[a]
2. Non-manual, father manual	42	13	36	71	37	26	76–97
3. Manual, father non-manual	59	27	48	79	26	18	70–91
4. Skilled manual, father likewise	61	38	62	86	13	8	89–103
5. Skilled manual, father partly skilled or unskilled manual	62	(40)	71	81	(17)	8	48–56
6. Partly skilled or unskilled manual, father skilled	59	(34)	60	88	15	6	47–53
7. Partly skilled or unskilled manual, father likewise	63	48	75	93	6	2	145–76

NOTE: [a]The smallest number refers to column 2. Other columns approximate to the highest number.

the important steps in this process are retirement and inadequate access to occupational pensions or to the maintenance in value of such pensions, which will now be discussed.

Retirement and the Diminished Social Status of the Employed

Retirement is frequently attributed to individual characteristics, such as ill-health or infirmity and personal preference,[1] but it is more than unlikely that such factors can account for the rapid fall in proportion of men of 65 and over not in paid employment in the course of the present century. As we considered in some detail in Chapter 19 (pages 654–6), retirement has become much more common in this century. For example, while four fifths of men aged 65–9 were employed in 1921, the fraction fell to less than a fifth by 1971. The Government Actuary estimates that the number will continue to decline to about 7 per cent in the early 1980s.[2] The decline is common to industrial societies. The explanation is to be found, as we have seen, in the accommodation of social values and social policies to the changing values and organizational practices of industry. Perhaps the most fundamental generator of the decline has been society's insistence on maintaining and even increasing the relatively high rates of remuneration and other privileges of professional, managerial and other white-collar groups, during a period when it has also sought to recruit relatively greater numbers through higher education to those groups. In the context of existing social and economic institutions, particularly as they affect the national structure of incomes, these two goals are contradictory and are difficult to reconcile. That they have been reconciled is due substantially to the adoption of a policy of gradually excluding the majority of men over 65 from employment into less highly rewarded retirement, a policy which now appears to be being extended to men in the late fifties and early sixties.[3]

That retirement brings relatively lower income has been demonstrated, in relation both to adults under the pensionable ages and the small numbers of adults over the pensionable ages who continue in paid employment. That retirement brings relatively lower social status might be demonstrated at some length, with examples of the social labelling of 'pensioners' through customs like cheap afternoon tickets for the cinema, cheap travel in off-peak hours on local bus routes, cheap seaside holidays in May or October, condescending gifts of gold watches after forty or fifty years' employed service, cheap butter and government

1. Ministry of Pensions and National Insurance, *Reasons Given for Retiring or Continuing at Work*, H M S O, London, 1954.

2. Report by the Government Actuary on the Financial Provisions of the National Superannuation and Social Insurance Bill, 1969, Cmnd 4223, H M S O, London, 1969, p. 21; Report by the Government Actuary on the Financial Provisions of the Social Security Bill 1972, Cmnd 5143, H M S O, London, 1972, p. 17.

3. See Chapter 19, pages 674–5.

doles (in the early 1970s) of £10 at Christmas. That the retired recognize their depressed status might be demonstrated from evidence adduced earlier of the numbers feeling worse off than their families, neighbours and the population at large, and, in particular, worse off than at previous stages in their lives (Table 11.3, page 420).

The low status of people of pensionable age also rubs off on those who retain, or who are able to find alternative, employment. In the sample were 17 per cent of men and 12 per cent of women of pensionable age in employment. Around three fifths of both sexes worked for fewer than thirty hours a week. Many of these supplemented their pensions through paid employment. Before the war, the state financed old-age pensions and not 'retirement' pensions. The fact that since the war the state has operated a retirement rule as a condition for receipt of pension, and an earnings rule for those receiving pensions, has had the effect of reducing employment among the elderly. Persons reaching pensionable age have been faced with a choice of retiring on a pension or continuing in work without pension. Those with low earnings are not given much incentive to continue working, despite the higher rates of pension that can be earned (for men up to 70, and for women up to 65) by postponing retirement.[1] The difficulties experienced before 65 of redundancy, unemployment and work of lower status and with lower earnings also help to condition the choice made by many upon attaining the pensionable ages. After retirement, the earnings rule limits the desire to take part-time work[2] and encourages some employers to offer low wage rates.

Relatively few of the elderly in the sample remained in full-time employment. Despite working as many hours as those in middle age, their earnings were much smaller. The gross earnings of a third of these fully employed elderly, compared with only 6 per cent of men and 22 per cent of women in their forties and fifties, were below half the mean for their sex. Only a fifth, compared with two fifths of employed men and women in their forties and fifties, had gross earnings above the mean. Over three quarters of men had take-home pay of under £15 per week, while nearly three quarters of men in their thirties, forties and fifties had take-home pay of *more* than this sum. These figures show the sharp erosion of earning power among people of pensionable age, an erosion which begins in the mid and late fifties. As at younger ages, the earning power of women of pensionable age is proportionately less than that of men of these ages.

When we considered the conditions under which men and women of pensionable age worked, we found that relatively more of them than of younger workers

1. In 1968–9, a single person could earn an addition to pension of 1s. (or 5p) for every nine weeks worked beyond pensionable age. After one year, the addition would amount to just over 5s. (or 25p) – representing an addition to the single pension (£4.50) of 5½ per cent.

2. In 1968–9, the retirement pension was reduced if earnings exceeded £6.50. The earnings rule was subsequently relaxed – even allowing for inflation. In 1977 the pension was not affected until earnings exceeded £35 a week.

experienced very poor conditions, and fewer experienced good conditions.[1] Many worked outside. Relatively more were subject to very short notice. Two thirds of men aged 60–64 and three quarters aged 65 and over, compared with only a half of men aged 40–59, spent *all* their working time standing or walking about. Again, these are indicators of depressed status in the labour market, but because the number of pensionable age in the sample who were still employed was small, these are matters which would justify further investigation.

Three elements in the depression of older people's occupational and social status therefore have to be identified. Before reaching pensionable age, some men and women are made redundant and move to jobs of lower occupational status and earnings. After reaching pensionable age, the few who continue in full-time employment tend to be in jobs of low status and earnings. And those who supplement pensions with earnings from (usually part-time) employment, do so in partly skilled or unskilled roles with low status and earnings.

These three elements are, of course, conditioned by society's conception of 're-tirement', including the ages at which retirement is applied. The development of the concept of retirement has been associated with campaigns on behalf of the rights of workers when management considers they have reached the point of no longer being worth their wage, and on behalf of the rights of old people to better standards of life. But it has also been associated with pressure to exclude certain groups of workers from the bargaining process, social perceptions of failing health and physical capacity, and social interpretations of the value to the economy of workers past certain ages. Changing technology and the successive introduction of new forms of training and educational qualifications have encouraged high evaluations of the productive capacity of younger workers and low evaluation of the productive capacity of older workers. The combined effects of industrial, economic and educational reorganization seem to have led to a more rigid stratification of the population by age.[2]

Despite voluminous evidence as well as biographical anecdote of the immense variety among individuals of any given age of health, physical and mental agility, motivation, creativity and occupational performance, most societies have applied concepts of retirement to particular chronological ages. Individuals are obliged to conform or adapt to the crude rules of employment sectors and government. The chronological ages have varied historically in most societies and continue to vary across societies. In Britain in 1908, non-contributory pensions on test of means were introduced, with certain exceptions, for persons aged 70 and over. In 1925, a contributory scheme was introduced and the qualifying age reduced to 65 for both sexes. In 1940, women became entitled to pensions at 60, mainly on grounds

1. According to answers to the sequence of questions discussed on pages 437–43.
2. See, for example, the wide range of material on age stratification in Riley, M. W., Johnson, M., and Foner, A. (eds.), *Ageing and Society*, vol. 3: *A Sociology of Age Stratification*, Russell Sage Foundation, New York, 1972.

that wives are usually younger than their husbands.[1] In 1957, at a time of concern about the economic 'burden' of a growing number of pensioners, the Phillips Committee recommended the raising of the minimum age for pension by three years for both sexes, but this was not, in the event, accepted by the government.[2] In recent years, pressures have been exerted to reduce the pensionable age to 60, or even 55, for both sexes.[3] There are variations between societies in pensionable ages. In the early 1970s, the age was 70 in Ireland and 67 in Sweden for both sexes; and 60 for men and 55 for women in Italy, Hungary, Japan and the USSR. These variations are as difficult as the ages chosen at different dates in Britain to explain in terms of the onset of ill-health or incapacity among the majority of individuals.

There is no evidence that *more* people past a certain age, of, say, 65, are infirm than there were in 1920 or 1880. Indeed, the advances in many countries in the expectation of life of people at 60, as well as a large volume of indirect evidence, might be cited to suggest that more people in their sixties than in previous historical periods remain physically active, and therefore potentially productive in at least a number of respects. So the introduction of the concept of retirement and its association with particular ages in the twentieth century has to be explained more by social and economic considerations. These conspired, as I have argued, to create an underclass of pensioners.

Occupational Pensions and the Middle Class

Occupational pensions owe their development in this century largely to pressures on the part of upper and middle occupational groups to ensure that the lowered incomes and inability to get alternative employment which were imposed on, and in large measure accepted by, the working classes who reached pensionable age would not apply to them. Previously, some of the principles of the schemes had been pioneered in the public superannuation scheme for the Civil Service. This dates from an Act of 1810,[4] to provide compensation at the end of working life

1. For a historical outline of state pensions, see George, V., *Social Security: Beveridge and After*, Routledge & Kegan Paul, London, 1968, Chapter 8.

2. Like the Royal Commission on Population, the committee found that available medical and other evidence, combined with the fact that substantial numbers of people continue to work beyond the pensionable ages, 'indicate that over a wide field these do not by any means represent the limit of the working life'. See Report of the Committee on the Economic and Financial Problems of the Provision for Old Age, Cmd 9333, HMSO, London, 1954, p. 49. Other influential bodies also argued against the inflexibility of fixed pensionable or retirement ages. See, for example, the first and second Reports of the National Advisory Committee on the Employment of Older Men and Women, Cmds 8963 and 9626, HMSO, London, October 1953 and December 1955.

3. See, for example, *Sex Equality and the Pension Age*, Equal Opportunities Commission, London, 1977.

4. Raphael, M., *Pensions and Public Servants: A Study of the Origins of the British System*, Mouton & Co., Paris, 1964.

as well as security during working life for employees who were not expected, or allowed, to enjoy the rates of remuneration obtaining in the private sector. This policy helped to diminish corruption among civil servants and to create the ideology associated with public service in Britain. During the latter part of the nineteenth and the early part of the twentieth century, pension schemes were adopted in other public services. The police had to wait until 1890, teachers until 1898 and local government officers until 1922, or in some cases until 1937. Although manual employees sometimes had to wait, they were often brought into the public pension schemes on similar terms to non-manual staff. When the public sector grew in the middle of the twentieth century, a two-tier system began to be established. Partly because former private schemes were continued, the schemes for groups of manual workers in the new nationalized industries, including mineworkers and railwaymen, were based on separate principles from those on which the schemes for non-manual staff were based. The pensions for which they became eligible were very small.[1]

Private-sector pensions have to be distinguished from public-sector pensions. Occupational pension schemes have been poorer in coverage; the benefits have been maintained worse in periods of inflation; the schemes have been more diverse, and separate schemes for non-manual and manual staff have been common. While some features were borrowed from the public sector, others were introduced in conformity with the interests of industry. Pensions were introduced to encourage loyalty to the firm and prevent the loss to competitors of skilled workers – especially during 'full' employment after the war. Rules were introduced so that employees who left their employment had no right to transferability of pension rights, to the contributions paid by the employer and even any interest on the contributions which they had paid themselves. Rules were also introduced to lower the benefits paid from the funds after employees reached pension age. Thus, widows were rarely entitled to any part of a pension formerly paid to the husband, and pensions in payment were not increased until recently if the cost of living or average salaries and wages increased. But, to reconcile demands of long-service employees with pressures for promotion from younger employees as well as demands for institutional and technological change, inducements to retire early were introduced for highly paid employees. Lump sums of considerable amount were paid, say at 60, to managers, along with pensions close to the levels of final salary. The 'golden handshake' took the form of lump sums of £5,000, and sometimes much more for the highly paid, and a gold watch for skilled manual employees with long service.

One further major element in the story since the war has been the manipulation of pension schemes to avoid or offset high rates of taxation for some of the highest

1. A good source of information on the history of private as well as public occupational schemes, which has been neglected in the literature, is Rhodes, G., *Public Sector Pensions*, Allen & Unwin, London, 1965.

paid. By accepting lower salaries in their forties and fifties in exchange for high lump sums, and high pensions once they reached the age of 55 or 60, some managers and other highly paid employees could substantially reduce the taxes they would pay over a span of ten or fifteen years without any difference in cost to the employer.[1] Very considerable amounts in lump sums and pensions can sometimes be paid, in what have come to be called 'top hat' schemes. As long ago as 1954 there were cases in which the tax-free lump sum might be as much as £40,000.[2]

These features of occupational pension schemes were first revealed in stark form in Britain by the Millard Tucker Committee in 1954.[3] The committee were strangely oblivious of the remarkable differences which existed in principle between private and state schemes. The 'needs' of the elderly were perceived in relation to 'final earnings' and not 'subsistence'. The appropriate pensionable age for men was believed to be 60, or even younger, and not 65, as in the state scheme. The pension would be payable irrespective of any subsequent earnings in alternative employment, contrary to the rule in the state scheme, and so was an 'occupational' and not a 'retirement' pension. Lump sums would normally be paid once the pensionable age was reached, but no such entitlement existed in the state scheme. The Millard Tucker and Phillips Committees made no effort to reconcile the principles of the two types of scheme. Hence the charge that 'two nations' in old age were being consolidated was wholly justified.[4]

After growing rapidly after the war, occupational pension schemes have lately shown no signs of being extended to the whole employed population, and they are very unequally distributed, not only between non-manual and manual workers, but between new and long-standing pensioners. In 1936, 1·6 million employees outside the public services, or approximately 10 per cent, were covered by occupational pension schemes. If members of public-service schemes are added (including the armed services), the total was probably about 2½ million.[5]

In 1967 the Government Actuary estimated that there were 8·3 million employees in private-sector schemes, or less than half, and 3·9 million in public-sector schemes, or more than two thirds.[6] But, by 1971, the number of employees in

1. For an important historical review of ways in which pension schemes have been used to avoid tax, see Lynes, T., 'The Use of Life Assurance, Pension Schemes and Trusts for Tax Avoidance', in Titmuss, R. M., *Income Distribution and Social Change*, Allen & Unwin, London, 1962, pp. 217–29.

2. Rhodes, *Public Sector Pensions*, p. 309.

3. Report of the Committee on the Taxation Treatment of Provisions for Retirement, Cmd 9063, H M S O, London, 1954.

4. There may be developing 'the problem of two nations in old age; of greater inequalities in living standards after work than in work' – Titmuss, R. M., 'The Age of Pensions', *The Times*, 29 and 30 December 1953; see also Abel-Smith, B., and Townsend, P., *New Pensions for the Old*, Fabian Research Series No. 171, Fabian Society, London, March 1955.

5. *Ministry of Labour Gazette*, May 1938.

6. *Occupational Pension Schemes, 1971, Fourth Survey by the Government Actuary*, H M S O, London, 1972, p. 5.

private-sector schemes had fallen back to 7 million, while those in public-sector schemes rose slightly to 4·1 million. The Government Actuary went on to show that this contraction applied to manual and not non-manual workers. The number of male manual workers in schemes had contracted from 64 to 56 per cent, but had *increased* among male non-manual workers from 85 to 87 per cent. The number of female manual workers in schemes had contracted from 21 to 18 per cent, but *increased* among female non-manual workers from 53 to 56 per cent.[1] At the end of 1971, there were 2·45 million former employees and 0·5 million widows and other dependants drawing pensions from occupational schemes – over half of them in the public sector. The total of 2·95 million, representing about 32 per cent of the population of pensionable age, had grown from 1·80 million in 1963, representing 22 per cent. Forty per cent of the pensions in payment were under £3 per week, and only 18 per cent more than £10 per week. Analysis of pensions in payment showed for the private sector that an average increase of 2·5 per cent per annum had been paid over a period of ten years, compared with an average increase in retail prices of about 4·5 per cent per annum.[2]

In the survey, only 16 per cent of persons of pensionable age were receiving an occupational pension – a third of them from the government or armed services. When allowance is made for a spouse in some income units, then 26 per cent were in units receiving such a pension (38 per cent of men and 20 per cent of women).

Table 23.12. *Percentages of elderly people of manual and non-manual occupational status receiving occupational pensions of different amount.*

Amount of pension last year (£)	Non-manual			Manual		
	Single men	Single women	Married	Single men	Single women	Married
Nil	(60)	84	55	71	96	70
Under 50	(0)	0	3	8	1	6
50–99	(0)	2	3	8	1	9
100–99	(7)	6	5	8	1	7
200–99	(13)	3	5	6	0	4
300+	(20)	5	29	0	1	4
Total	100	100	100	100	100	100
Number	15	129	155	52	195	319

1. *Occupational Pension Schemes, 1971*, p. 7. Part of the contraction was attributed to a 'possible overstatement' of the 1967 totals, 'but the bulk of the fall appears to be a genuine development'.

2. ibid., pp. 13, 14 and 38.

(See also Table A.96, Appendix Eight, page 1064).[1] We also found a substantial number of people below the state's pensionable age, representing about 700,000 drawing an occupational pension from a former employer. Table 23.12 confirms that fewer elderly people of manual than of non-manual status receive pensions, and more of them receive small amounts. The relative advantage of married people as compared with single women, predominantly widows, can also be seen. This is both an effect of their younger age, and the tendency for widows to be ineligible for pensions. There was little or no evidence from the survey of a dramatic improvement taking place in either the numbers or amounts of pension received by former employees. Thus, the percentage of men aged 65–9 drawing an employer's pension was no larger than of men aged 70–79 and 80 and over (Table A.96, Appendix Eight, page 1064). And nearly a third of them continued to draw pensions of under £100 a year (Table A.97, Appendix Eight, page 1064).

Social Isolation and Access to Family Resources

We have shown that, relative to the married, the elderly who are unmarried, widowed, divorced and separated have low resources. We have also shown that, relative to the younger elderly, the elderly of advanced age have low resources. These results are largely attributable, as we have seen, to socially institutionalized rules which determine, during the course of the life-cycle, differential access to earnings from employment, differential opportunities of inheriting and accumulating assets, scope of membership of state and occupational pension schemes and changes in the value of pensions in payment. These rules are governed by class position and sex, but also by family status. Indeed, their effect is also modified in some important respects by family status and situation.

Through the institution of marriage, women are both deprived of male privileges to certain individual rights to income, and entitled to a share of the financial prerogatives of men. After reaching the pensionable age, some married women are cushioned from falling into poverty. Those whose husbands have already died or become separated from them, or whose husbands subsequently do so, are exposed to greater risks of both social isolation and financial loss. The fact that women are living increasingly longer than men at the older ages is exposing them to these risks at an advanced age. Many continue to live alone, but many find it possible to offer accommodation to a relative or are able (and encouraged) to join members of their families. After the death of the husband, there seems to be a tendency for women who are still physically active, usually in the sixties or early seventies, to go on living alone, and for the frail and usually older elderly to move into the households of others. So the phenomenon of social isolation in old age

1. In comparing these data with those from other sources (e.g. the government's *Financial and Other Circumstances of Retirement Pensioners*), it should be noted that they refer to all people of pensionable age and not just retirement pensioners.

depends, first, on how prevalent in the population are unbroken marriages, but secondly, on the structure, situation and values of the family.

In reviewing the contribution of the family to the standards of living of the elderly, the membership by single people of households of two or more people is the first question of importance. It is true that some individuals who are in multi-person households live in relatively self-contained income units. But, by definition, they live under the same roof, share the same amenities and share a common housekeeping. Many of the elderly with low incomes enjoy indirect subsidies from other household members with higher incomes. Table 23.13 shows that, when

Table 23.13. Percentages of elderly in different types of household who had resources below or on the margins of the state's standard of poverty.

Net disposable household income last year as % of supplementary benefit rates plus housing cost	Type of household		
	Living alone	Living in married pairs only	Living with others
Under 100	19	15	8
100–39	58	36	23
140+	24	49	69
Total	100	100	100
Number	219	350	130

Net income worth last year of household as % of supplementary benefit rates plus housing cost			
Under 100	10	7	1
100–39	43	16	12
140–99	12	21	31
200–99	15	25	28
300+	21	31	27
	100	100	100
	197	317	176

household incomes and assets are aggregated, the elderly who live with others are less likely to be living in poverty or on the margins of poverty than married couples, and even less likely than the elderly living alone. The phenomenon is found in each of the major social classes (Table A.95, Appendix Eight, page 1063).

The most prosperous groups were the single elderly who lived with adult children or adult children and grandchildren. This pattern of inequality according to living arrangements also applied when the range of consumer durables and values of household assets were considered separately.

Among those living alone, more women than men had low resources, even excluding the employed, but more men than women lived in homes with few consumer durables. The numbers of men in the sample who were living alone were too few to justify any differentiation by age, but, among women, more of those in their eighties than of those in their seventies, and more of the latter than of those in their sixties, had relatively low incomes and assets.

A special feature of the survey was its demonstration of the value of family contacts. We asked everyone in the sample whether they had seen any relative (not living in the same house) most or all days of the week, at least once a week, or not at all. Unfortunately, because we did not want to protract interviews which were already lengthy, we had to ask the question not for each relative but for relatives in general. As a consequence, we believe the number in the sample seeing at least

Table 23.14. *Percentages of elderly people living alone or in married pairs and seeing relatives with varying frequency who were deprived in different respects.*

Measure of deprivation	Contact with relatives outside household					
	Living alone			Living in married pairs		
	None seen weekly	At least weekly	Most or all days of week	None seen weekly	At least weekly	Most or all days of week
Net disposable income last year below state poverty standard	30	15	12	18	16	12
Net income worth last year below state poverty standard	18	5	7	9	5	7
Fewer than 4 of list of 10 consumer durables in home	18	9	8	1	2	4
Number on which percentages based	66	82	68	134	134	77

one of their relatives frequently is underestimated. However, frequency of stated contact with relatives was correlated with level of income.

Among the elderly living alone, fewer seeing relatives most or all days than not at all in the week had net disposable incomes below the state's poverty standard (Table 23.14). The difference could not be attributed to the spread of assets owned among the two groups, because the respective proportions owning small amounts of assets or none were in fact broadly similar. More of those having close contacts with relatives than not having such contacts proved to be receiving supplementary benefits and other means-tested benefits, and more received small cash incomes or gifts or income or gifts in kind. They also tended to have more consumer durables in the home. Integration with family therefore enables the elderly to gain access to discretionary social security, and in other ways to attain slightly higher standards of living. The aid takes many indirect forms rather than weekly cash payments. The elderly stay with relatives for periods of the year, visit rela-

Table 23.15. *Percentages of elderly living alone, in married pairs and with others who had various types of relationship with relatives and friends.*

Type of relationship with relatives or friends outside household	Living alone	Living in married pairs	Living with others
Seeing relative outside household most or all days of week	31	24	21
Seeing relative outside household at least weekly	38	38	36
Relative outside household – none seen weekly	31	38	43
Receives help from relative	34	13	8
Receives help from neighbour or friend	23	4	3
Receives help from relative, neighbour or friend	52	16	11
Helped in illness or emergency in last 12 months	43	25	21
Stayed at least 1 night in last 12 months with relatives	41	31	21
Stayed at least 1 night in last 12 months with friends	11	5	6
Had relative to stay at least 1 night in last 12 months	23	38	31
Had friend to stay at least 1 night in last 12 months	8	7	9
Total number on which percentages based	223	401	266

tives for meals, receive gifts of food, clothes and household goods, and benefit from a variety of free domestic and nursing services.

Among the elderly living alone, nearly a third had close contacts with relatives and more than another third saw a relative at least weekly. More of them than of the elderly living with a spouse or with others had regular help from a neighbour or friend, and more, too, had received help in illness or in an emergency, as after an accident in the home, during the previous twelve months. More, again, had stayed elsewhere with relatives or friends during the year, sometimes for lengthy periods. Fewer had had a relative or friend to stay in their own homes, but nearly a third of them had nevertheless been able to make such an arrangement in the year.

Among those living alone, more of the poor and marginally poor received help from both relatives and friends than did those with incomes substantially in excess of the poverty standard. There were no significant differences between the poor and the non-poor in the proportions staying for periods away from home and having guests to stay. The various indices suggest that between a third and a half of the elderly living alone have very close contacts with others outside the home, particularly with relatives, and can depend on them for support regularly and in emergencies. Others are in weekly contact, but perhaps a third altogether are relatively isolated and vulnerable in illness or other emergencies. Elderly married couples depend less on outside relationships, but substantial proportions get help in illness and also stay with relatives or friends. Nearly half of them have relatives or friends to stay at least occasionally during the year.

Increasing Disability and Access to Resources

We have traced the greater liability to disablement and incapacity of people of advancing age (Chapter 20). The rates for both men and women rise markedly in the fifties and tend to be higher at each successive age after 60. For men in the age groups 60–64, 65–9, 70–74, 75–9 and 80 and over, the percentages in the sample with appreciable or severe incapacity were, respectively, 10, 7, 21, 31 and 56; for women they were 18, 20, 28, 42 and 58. Among all men 60 and over the percentage was 17, and among women 31. Table 23.16 shows that those with greater degrees of incapacity tended to have smaller incomes, fewer assets and consumer durables, and were more susceptible to forms of objective deprivation.

The association between disability and deprivation among the elderly arises, of course, partly because there are at the older ages proportionately more women, and more widowed people, as well as more disabled. But disablement has a number of consequences for living standards. In the fifties and early sixties, people are compelled to withdraw from the labour market; find difficulty in securing employment; are obliged to take jobs with low earnings; begin to draw on savings; are less likely to obtain full rights to occupational pensions; withdraw from

Table 23.16. *Percentages of non-incapacitated and incapacitated people of 60 and over according to selected indices of resources and deprivation.*

Selected standard of resources/deprivation		Degree of incapacity[a]			
		None (0)	Minor (1–2)	Some (3–6)	Appreciable or severe (7+)
Income net worth of household below or on margins of poverty standard[b]	%	22	35	34	49
	base number	190	196	207	205
Fewer than 5 durables in home in list of 10[c]	%	14	19	28	39
	base number	279	265	267	265
With scores of 6 or more on deprivation index[d]	%	21	32	33	43
	base number	128	123	212	179

NOTES: [a]Defined as described in Chapter 21, pages 692 and 697.
[b]Net disposable income of household in previous year plus annuity value of assets below 100 per cent or below 140 per cent of supplementary benefit rates plus housing costs.
[c]See page 714.
[d]See page 250. Persons aged 65 and over only.

owner-occupied homes or are less likely to become owner-occupiers; and, because they spend more time at home, make heavier use of the resources of the home, foreshortening the expected life of some consumer durables. Because the sub-sample of elderly in the survey was too small to allow all the social and resources variables to be held constant, Table 23.17 gives no more than a suggestion of the outcomes. The table suggests that more older than younger people are in poverty or on the margins of poverty, *even when* disablement *and* household composition are held constant. It suggests, secondly, that more disabled than non-disabled elderly people are in poverty or on the margins of poverty, even when age *and* household composition are held constant. These two trends have important im-plications for policy.

This line of analysis naturally leads to the question of the *additional* resources which the disabled elderly need if they are to maintain living standards compar-able with the non-disabled. Only preliminary attempts have so far been made to identify these.[1] There are direct costs of the conditions and states of disablement:

1. Harris, A., *et al.*, *Income and Entitlement to Supplementary Benefit of Impaired People in Great Britain* (Part III of *Handicapped and Impaired in Great Britain*), HMSO, London, 1972, p. 8.

drugs, emollients, hearing aids, spectacles, sticks, calipers, surgical belts, wheel-
chairs, hoists, special diets, forms of transport, slip-on clothing, incontinence
pads, specially designed implements for eating, purpose-built shoes or boots,
books and newspapers in braille or with large print, breathing apparatus, non-
slip mats, ramps, handrails and so on. Some of these items are required once and
for all or occasionally, and others at regular intervals. It would be wrong to as-

*Table 23.17. Percentages of non-incapacitated and incapacitated elderly under 75
and over 75, living alone, in married pairs and with others who have relatively low
resources.*

Living arrangements, age, and degree of incapacity	Net disposable income last year below or on margins of poverty standard		Income net worth last year below or on margins of poverty standard	
	%	Base number	%	Base number
1. *Living alone under 75* with no or slight incapacity (0–2)	63	59	43	56
2. with some, appreciable or severe incapacity (3+)	76	68	53	57
3. *Living alone, 75 and over,* with no or slight incapacity (0–2)	–	16	–	14
4. with some, appreciable or severe incapacity (3+)	87	77	64	70
5. *Living in married pairs under 75,* with no or slight incapacity (0–2)	49	212	22	188
6. with some, appreciable or severe incapacity (3+)	53	156	25	139
7. *Living in married pairs 75 and over* with no or slight incapacity (0–2)	–	13	–	12
8. with some, appreciable or severe incapacity (3+)	72	50	36	47
9. *Living with others under 75,* with no or slight incapacity (0–2)	68	57	51	47
10. with some, appreciable or severe incapacity (3+)	64	44	41	39
11. *Living with others 75 and over,* with no or slight incapacity (0–2)	–	8	–	7
12. with some, appreciable or severe incapacity (3+)	82	62	58	48

sume that all of them can be or are paid for or made available without personal charge under existing health and welfare legislation. National Health Service prescriptions for the elderly are free, but some goods required or felt to be required are purchased from chemists and other sources, and in obtaining free prescriptions and free goods it is sometimes necessary to incur costs of travel or payments to others.

There are many indirect costs of disablement. Even when someone does not suffer from a condition such as diabetes or heart disease for which a particular diet is prescribed by a doctor, he may be restricted in practice to a range of foods which are difficult or costly to obtain. Someone with limited mobility may have to depend for his shopping on near-by corner shops rather than on cut-price stores and supermarkets. To maintain circulation, extra heating, or to offset pain or discomfort, cushions, hot-water bottles and electric blankets, may be required. Those who are unable to drive or to use public transport may have to depend on paying privately to get about, or at least feel obliged to offer a gift in exchange for unpaid services. Much the same applies to activities like cleaning, cooking, housekeeping, going on holiday or going to a cinema or football match. Sometimes it is argued that the extra costs of disability in old age are balanced in part by necessary restrictions in range of social activities and hence savings in various costs, including diet. This argument is difficult to sustain, however, because its assumptions are based on social observation of the disabled elderly, many of whom are obliged to restrict their activities for want of the resources to command the goods and services to compensate for or counterbalance their disabilities. The key question here is how the disabled elderly with relatively high incomes behave. They form a small proportion of the elderly population at the present time, and there were not many in our sample. For example, there were 198 people of pensionable age with appreciable or severe incapacity, and from whom we had obtained full information on income and assets. Among them were forty-two who had income net worth of more than three times the supplementary benefit standard. The activities of this small number were restricted by the inadequacy generally of services and amenities in society for the disabled. None the less, most undertook activities enjoyed by younger non-disabled people, such as going on summer holidays, staying with relatives and friends, having friends and relatives to stay, having an evening out and so on. The majority of this small group had low scores on our deprivation index.

The implications of this analysis of disability among the elderly for policy are two-fold. First, methods need to be developed of providing substitute incomes and some types of asset for those whose sources of income and means of restoring or accumulating assets have been reduced as a direct consequence of their disability. Secondly, methods need to be developed of providing levels of income and perhaps also types of assets which are *additional* to those which society has approved or can be persuaded to approve in certain circumstances for the non-disabled. The former set of proposals would make good the inequality in resources between the disabled and non-disabled. The latter set would acknowledge their additional need for resources to ensure opportunities to follow equivalent styles of living. Some concrete proposals along these lines have been set out by the Disability Alliance.[1]

Conclusion

During the twentieth century, the number of men aged 65 and over and of women aged 60 and over in the United Kingdom has increased from fewer than 3 million to over 9 million, representing 16 per cent of the population. If the income unit is taken as the unit of measurement, nearly 20 per cent in our survey, representing 1·7 million, were found to be in poverty, and 44 per cent, representing 3·7 million, on the margins of poverty, according to the state's definition. The elderly poor comprised 36 per cent of the poor.

Why are a disproportionate number of the elderly poor? The chapter's argument is that poverty in old age is a function of low levels of resources, and restricted access to resources, relative to younger people. More of the elderly than of the young or middle aged are poor because they have been excluded from employment, and therefore from the rates of income associated with employment, without adequate substitution through the state's social security system and other sources of income in old age, especially private occupational pensions. There is a dual process of deprivation, stemming fundamentally from class position, but also from changing class structure. Some old people are poor by virtue of their low life-long class position. Others are poor by virtue of society's imposition upon the elderly of 'underclass' status.

Some of our most interesting evidence concerns the economic consequences of low life-long occupational status. Those who had held jobs of low occupational status, and whose fathers' status was correspondingly low, were more likely than others to be poor in old age. Conversely, those of high status whose fathers' status was also high were least likely to be poor in old age. This double criterion of status divides the elderly into a succession of distinguishable ranks, ranging from the possession of high to the possession of low income and other resources. We traced some of the major determinants of this structure of inequality. People of high status were more likely to have benefited from high earnings; to have accumulated savings and other assets, and in particular to have become outright owner-occupiers of their homes; inherited wealth; enjoyed employer welfare benefits in kind during working life; and gained rights to occupational pensions. On the other hand, people of low status were more likely to have had low earnings; experienced long spells of unemployment and more spells of illness off

1. See, in particular, *Poverty and Disability: The Case for a Comprehensive Income Scheme for Disabled People*, Disability Alliance, London, 1975.

work; experienced insecurity of employment with no rights to occupational pensions, paid holidays and wages during sickness; had more dependants to support during working life; and lived in rented dwellings with little opportunity to enter the owner-occupied sector of housing. As a consequence, upon reaching the threshold of old age, the *private* sources of income and wealth upon which they could draw were non-existent or minimal.

Even before old age, living standards tend to become more unequal. Those of high status tend to benefit from seniority rights in their occupations, continue to receive increments of salary, complete mortgage payments on their homes, and no longer have dependants in the home. Those of low status tend to lose chances of making up basic wages with overtime earnings, or because of age or incapacity are no longer able to work long hours, and run greater risks of redundancy, unemployment and chronic sickness or disability.

In moving into old age, this process continues. People tend to separate into two groups, one anticipating a comfortable and even early retirement, the other dreading the prospect and depending almost entirely for their livelihood on the resources made available by the state through its social security system.

At this point we have to recognize two general sets of factors which affect the numbers who are distributed above and below the poverty line. First are structural factors. Irrespective of economic and social changes. fewer people continue to command, as the years go by, all the resources held immediately after retirement. Bereavement and ageing, and latterly high rates of inflation, affect living standards in particular. The incomes of the elderly relative to the young tend to diminish. Many widows are not entitled to a share of the occupational pensions received when husbands were alive; more people incur additional costs because of disabilities associated with advancing age; household goods depreciate in value; and some costs, such as the costs of accommodation, which could be provided for from joint incomes, prove to be inelastic when people are reduced to a single income.

The other set of factors derive from economic and social change. The most important changes which influence the income position of people of advancing age are changes in retirement practices, changes in provisions for incomes which are alternative to employment incomes, and changes in real incomes because of inflation and economic growth. As we have seen, 'retirement' has rapidly become associated in this century with fixed pension ages, irrespective of individual variations in health and capacity. As late as 1921, 80 per cent of men in their late sixties were in paid employment, but by 1971 the figure had declined to 16 per cent, and is expected by the Government Actuary to decline to about 7 per cent by the early 1980s. This has meant that each successive cohort reaching pensionable age has been able to depend less on employment income than its predecessor, and much has therefore hinged on alternative pensions and other resources of the state and private sector. We have argued that indirectly the low incomes associated with retirement (traced, for example, in the rates of pension summarized for the last thirty years in Table 24.3, page 789) have been a consequence of the simultaneous recruitment of more younger adults to non-manual occupations and maintenance or enhancement of the levels of remuneration received by these non-manual groups. An 'underclass' has been created in retirement.

To some extent, the spread of occupational pensions has protected some people, particularly non-manual workers, from experiencing the sharp fall in living standards which they would otherwise have experienced from their withdrawal from the labour market. For some among them, however, such a fall has been only temporary, because women who are widowed are no longer covered and because pensions in payment have not been maintained relative to increases in earnings or even prices. Some non-manual groups therefore lose their relatively advantageous position on the income scale and descend into poverty, perhaps for the first time.

Among people of manual status, protection from poverty has not been guaranteed by the levels of state retirement pensions and has depended on supplementary forms of assistance through means-tested benefits. While many obtain supplementary benefits, official and independent evidence, further confirmed by this national survey, has shown that this supplementary system of conditional welfare has not operated efficiently, and a substantial minority, at present over $1\frac{1}{4}$ million, do not obtain the supplementary aid for which they are eligible. Moreover, the additional financial costs of disability have as yet been only fitfully recognized (through such devices as the attendance allowance, the supplement for pensioners over 80, and the exceptional circumstances additions of the Supplementary Benefits Commission).

Other factors, of course, would properly play a part in any general analysis. These include the tax treatment of lump sums received upon retirement and taxation of investment and other income, changes in the values of assets which are held, and the pooling of incomes, and costs, and the provision of services within the household, family and community.

The Social Security Pensions Act 1975, which began to operate from April 1978, will not have a swift or sufficient impact on the problem. After political uncertainty and conflict throughout the 1960s and early 1970s, the Conservative party felt able to offer broad support for the measure introduced and passed by the Labour government in 1975. This provides massive subsidies for occupational pensions and reduces the contributions paid for the flat-rate scheme by those contracted out of the state earnings-related scheme. The potentialities of redistribution and a significantly higher flat-rate pension for the mass of the elderly are accordingly restricted. The additional earnings-related state pensions will grow year by year for each new cohort of pensioners reaching pensionable age, and will, after twenty years, add up to 25 per cent of revalued earnings between a minimum and a maximum. The numbers needing to obtain supplementary benefits will be reduced but not eliminated. Inequalities among old people will persist, and for many years to come the older elderly will have even lower average incomes, compared with the younger elderly, than they do at present.

That the problem of poverty in old age is massive and is continuing cannot be doubted. The policy solutions implied by our analysis clearly centre on the problem of raising the level of state retirement pensions, relative to earnings, introducing supplementary rights to income by virtue of disability and exercising more effective control and distribution of the resources hitherto so arbitrarily and unequally mobilized under the development of occupational pension schemes. Bearing in mind present and likely future pressures to lower fixed retirement ages, the problem underlying all three is that of reorganizing access to remunerated and meaningful occupation so that the elderly and disabled are less likely to be accorded unproductive and derogatory status.

24

Eligibility for Supplementary Benefit

Payments of income on test of means are an important part of the social security systems of all industrial societies. Some schemes are, of course, wider in scope and more generous than others. With the passage of the years, the schemes in some countries are broadened and improved. But because benefits are dependent on a test of means, all such schemes tend to acquire characteristics which are different from those which allocate benefits according to some other criterion – whether this is the previous payment of contributions, age, medically assessed injury or sickness or the existence of dependants. Because income may come from different sources, assessment is often complicated, and because circumstances may change, checks have to be carried out at frequent intervals. This makes such schemes expensive to administer and leads to problems of achieving uniform assessments. Although, in principle, benefits are dependent primarily on test of means, in practice they have to be governed by other considerations as well, whether someone is genuinely sick or seeking work, whether a woman is genuinely supporting children on her own and whether an elderly person is or is not the householder. This is because the act of making up income without strings would come into open conflict with the other values upon which all societies are built – for example, that incomes are earned by work, that men living as husbands with women should support them, that children living with their parents should be supported by them, and so on. For the sake of preserving its order and cohesion, society insists that these values are upheld. In different ways, benefits under means-tested schemes have to be conditional on behaviour and upon the readiness of potential recipients to submit themselves to test. The function of the schemes is as much to control behaviour as to meet need.

It is no accident that the rules of such schemes are rarely all specified exactly; or if they are specified exactly to staff, are not published; or if they are published, are inconsistently applied. On the one hand, need is difficult to define, and if laid down exactly makes difficult the payment of benefit in exceptional but appropriate instances. On the other, the fact that controls are being operated is not something that society wants to have too clearly called to attention. Suppositions are made alike by applicants and staff, myths are created and obstacles to the receipt of benefits, both real and imaginary, arise. Those who defend the 'flexibility' in meeting need which this discretionary system permits forget that the same flexibility makes for misunderstanding and uncertainty among the public and exposes them to unconscious, if not conscious, manipulation by staff on behalf of society and its approved values.

All this suggests why, in scope and amount, the coverage of such schemes is uncertain and needs to be investigated and measured. On the one hand, there are people who object to means-tested benefits on grounds that potential applicants feel stigmatized or are stigmatized, and as a consequence either do not apply for them or feel uncomfortable in drawing them. On the other, supporters of such benefits argue that they are the most efficient way of allocating scarce national resources to the poor. This chapter and the next will discuss the success of different means-tested schemes in reaching those for whom they are designed.

The History of Research on 'Take-Up'

The biggest scheme financially and in coverage is the system of supplementary benefits, administered on behalf of the Department of Health and Social Security by the Supplementary Benefits Commission. In 1968, expenditure amounted to £400 million, and the incomes of approximately 4 million persons in the United Kingdom were dependent in whole or in part on weekly payments by the commission. The rates of benefit and main conditions of eligibility are set out in Chapter 6 (pages 241–7).

During the 1950s and early 1960s, a series of research studies gradually led to the realization that large numbers of people were eligible for benefits but did not claim them. The evidence was concerned primarily with old people.[1] Government spokesmen were at first openly critical of such research, then sceptical of the findings, but finally convinced by research carried out by the Ministry of Pensions and National Insurance itself. A national survey showed that nearly a million retirement pensioners were entitled to national assistance but were not receiving assistance. Even when allowance was made for misreported income, the ministry estimated that the figure was 850,000.[2] This figure was equivalent to rather more than half those actually receiving assistance at the time. Some would have been entitled only to small weekly payments.

The design of the supplementary benefit scheme, which was introduced by the

1. Cole Wedderburn, D., with Utting, J., *The Economic Circumstances of Old People*, Codicote Press, Welwyn, 1962; Townsend, P., *The Family Life of Old People*, Routledge & Kegan Paul, London, 1957; Townsend, P., and Wedderburn, D., *The Aged in the Welfare State*, Bell, London, 1965; Report of the Committee of Inquiry into the Impact of Rates on Households (The Allen Report), Cmnd 2582, H M S O, London, 1965, p. 117.

2. Ministry of Pensions and National Insurance, *Financial and Other Circumstances of Retirement Pensioners*, H M S O, London, 1966, Tables III.2 and III.4, pp. 20 and 83–4.

government in late 1966 to replace national assistance, was partly influenced by this research. The ministry hoped to improve take-up by eliminating 'three features of the existing scheme which are misunderstood or disliked, while preserving the humanity and efficiency of its administration'.[1] People satisfying the conditions laid down in the Social Security Act and its regulations now had a specific entitlement to benefit, the procedure for claiming benefits was simplified, national insurance and assistance were linked more closely in administration, and a new long-term addition to payments was introduced. The ministry also undertook an advertising campaign. Several hundred thousand people applied within a few weeks, and government ministers were quick to claim a remarkable success.[2]

However, the extent of the success was debatable. Rates of benefit had been raised and more generous disregards for income and savings had been introduced at the same time. Careful estimates were made on the basis of information published in the government's own report on the incomes of the retired which showed that, even ignoring the more generous disregards, the increase in numbers of retirement pensioners receiving supplements between December 1965 and November 1968 'not explained by the higher assistance scale amounts only to some 100,000–200,000'.[3] No field survey was carried out subsequently by government departments to confirm or reject these estimates, and the secondary analyses of Family Expenditure Survey data undertaken by the Department of Health and Social Security did not include reports on take-up among pensioners[4] until the Supplementary Benefits Commission itself published estimates in the mid 1970s.[5] For 1974, they estimated that 560,000 retirement pensioners (excluding about 180,000 wives and other dependants) or 24 per cent of the total who were eligible for supplementary benefit were not receiving it (the total value of unclaimed benefit being £60 million). In producing this figure, the estimate of the number of

1. Ministry of Pensions and National Insurance, Ministry of Social Security Bill 1966, HMSO, London, 1966, p. 1.
2. See, for example, Houghton, D., *Paying for the Social Services*, Institute of Economic Affairs, London, 1967, p. 12; Annual Report of the Ministry of Social Security for 1966, HMSO, London, 1967, p. 53; and DHSS, *National Superannuation and Social Insurance*, HMSO, London, January 1967, p. 7.
3. Atkinson, A. B., *Poverty in Britain and the Reform of Social Security*, Cambridge University Press, 1969, pp. 75–6.
4. The Minister of Social Security announced in 1968 that secondary analysis of the extent of poverty had been launched. A report in July 1971 on two-parent families stated, 'Further studies will report on analyses of FES data covering the circumstances of families without children, one-parent families and pensioners.' See DHSS, *Two-Parent Families: A Study of Their Resources and Needs in 1968, 1969, and 1970*, Statistical Report Series No. 14, HMSO, London, 1971, p. 1.
5. Supplementary Benefits Commission, *Annual Report, 1975*, Cmnd 6615, HMSO, London, 1976, p. 52. A paper prepared by the DHSS Statistics and Research Branch, 'The Take Up of Supplementary Benefit', October 1977, develops in considerable detail the qualifications that need to be made in reaching the estimates.

people of pensionable age living on incomes below the basic supplementary benefit scale rates was reduced from about 690,000[1] to take some account of those who would not, in the event, have qualified for benefit – because they were in paid employment or had a substantial sum in savings or other capital.

Research among groups other than pensioners has not been so extensive. There had been scattered evidence of reluctance to apply for benefits.[2] A secondary analysis of the Family Expenditure Survey for 1953–4 and 1960 concluded cautiously that over 3 per cent of the people in the sample, representing about 1½ million in the total population, were living at a level 'which, *prima facie*, might have allowed them to qualify for supplementary help from the National Assistance Board'. They included about a million people dependent primarily on pensions, and half a million on other state benefits.[3] A survey in 1966 of families with two or more children, by the Ministry of Social Security, found that about two fifths of those in which the father was sick or unemployed were eligible for assistance but were not receiving it. They represented about 34,000 families (including 209,000 people). In the case of the sick, however, relatively fewer of those who had been off work for three months or more than of the short-term sick were not receiving assistance. Only a small number of fatherless families with two or more children (about 8,000, including about 32,000 people) were not receiving assistance.[4] For 1974, the Supplementary Benefits Commission estimated that altogether 350,000 families of heads under pensionable age, or 28 per cent of the total who were entitled to benefit, were not receiving it. The estimated value of unclaimed benefit was £120 million.[5]

Social Security

The evidence from the poverty survey suggests that government estimates may hitherto have been underestimates. Information about social security payments received in the previous twelve months as well as the previous week was obtained. Estimates from the sample for payments in the week previous to interview are compared with government figures in Table 24.1. Certain difficulties in comparing the two sets of figures should be borne in mind. The sample were interviewed throughout a period of twelve months in 1968–9, whereas most government estimates apply to a single date at the end of 1968. Some families approached in the survey deferred an interview because of sickness. The numbers interviewed in the

1. Central Statistical Office, *Social Trends, 1975*, H M S O, London, 1976, p. 116.
2. Marris, P., *Widows and Their Families*, Routledge & Kegan Paul, London, 1958; Shaw, L. A., and Bowerbank, M., 'Living on a State-Maintained Income', I and II, *Case Conference*, March and April 1958; Marsden, D., *Mothers Alone*, Allen Lane, London, 1969.
3. Abel-Smith, B., and Townsend, P., *The Poor and the Poorest*, Bell, London, 1965, p. 48.
4. Ministry of Social Security, *Circumstances of Families*, H M S O, London, 1967, estimated from Table A.1, p. 133.
5. Annual Report, 1975, p. 52. See also D H S S, 'The Take Up of Supplementary Benefit'.

Table 24.1. *Estimated numbers receiving social security benefits.*

Type of benefit	Estimated on basis of sample numbers[a] (000s)	Government estimates (000s)
Unemployment benefit	390	325[c]
Sickness benefit	920	994[d]
Industrial injury and war disablement pension	325	615[e]
Retirement pension	7,215[b]	7,122[f]
Widows' benefits	485	577[f]
Family allowances	4,400	4,257[f]
Supplementary benefit	2,440	2,736[g]

NOTES: [a]Except for wives receiving retirement pensions, dependants are not included.
[b]Including elderly widows misclassified as receiving widows' pensions.
[c]Average number for counts made at five separate dates in 1968–9.
[d]Average number of insured persons absent from work owing to sickness 1968–9 (estimated by Government Actuary).
[e]Britain only. In the case of industrial disablement pension, 30 September 1968.
[f]31 December 1968.
[g]November 1968.

SOURCES: DHSS, *Social Security Statistics, 1972*, HMSO, London, 1973, pp. 18, 116, 168, 196, 198, 199, 201, 202; DHSS, National Superannuation and Social Insurance Bill, 1969, Report by the Government Actuary on the Financial Provisions of the Bill, Cmnd 4223, HMSO, London, December 1969, p. 28.

sample who were currently receiving sickness benefit and supplementary benefit might otherwise have been a little higher. And elderly widows receiving retirement or old-age pensions were sometimes understandably misclassified as receiving widows' pensions. Accordingly, we have adjusted the estimates for these two categories. Despite the problems of sampling error, it is evident that the sample produced a range of social security beneficiaries in broad conformity with the numbers which would be expected.

Eligibility for Supplementary Benefits

One of our objectives in the survey was to find how many people would have been eligible for supplementary benefits but were not receiving them. A schedule was drawn up summarizing the rules which are normally applied by the Supplementary Benefits Commission. This was submitted to the commission for comment and was then amended. It is given in full in Appendix Three.[1] Two procedures

1. Since that time the Department of Health and Social Security has itself adapted SBC rates and regulations for research purposes in analysing the distribution of income. See, for example, Howe, J. R., *Two Parent Families*, DHSS Statistical Report Series No. 14, HMSO,

were then adopted. For the national survey, each questionnaire was checked by one person who was specially trained in using the schedule. For income units satisfying the broad conditions for entitlement, that is, having no one in full-time employment, he then checked whether they were receiving benefit, and, if not, whether they were eligible.

For the area surveys, the questionnaires were not only examined in the same way, but a research officer paid another visit to many households to verify the facts as given to interviewers, to explore reasons for failure to apply for benefit and offer information to enable people to apply. These follow-up visits allowed us to place greater confidence in our estimates of the numbers of eligible non-recipients. A total of seventy-two households, or 6 per cent, were singled out from the 1,177 which had already provided information for these further visits.

Table 24.2 shows the results for all four major age groups in the national sample – children, young adults, middle-aged adults and elderly. There were 6·1 per cent of people in income units currently receiving supplementary benefits.

Table 24.2. Percentages of people of different age according to eligibility of income unit for supplementary benefit.

Eligibility of income unit for supplementary benefit	0–14	15–29	30–44	45–64	65+	All ages
Unclassifiable	2·1	1·0	0·4	1·7	4·7	1·8
Could not claim (employed)	88·9	92·4	94·7	79·0	6·9	78·1
Currently receiving benefit	4·0	2·1	1·6	5·5	24·6	6·1
Ineligible (income too high)	2·1	2·8	1·9	10·9	44·7	9·6
Eligible but not receiving	2·9	1·8	1·4	2·9	19·1	4·4
Total	100	100	100	100	100	100
Number	1,543	1,254	1,104	1,438	759	6,098

The figure was, however, around 2 per cent for younger adults, 4 per cent for children, 5 per cent for the middle aged and nearly 25 per cent for the elderly. This distribution corresponded fairly well with official data (Table A.101, Appendix Eight, page 1066). There were another 4·4 per cent who were eligible for benefits but not receiving them, the figure again being much lower for people below 65 than for those of this age or older, and lower for younger adults than for children.

These proportions represented large numbers in the non-institutionalized population of the United Kingdom. The percentage of the sample currently receiving benefits represented nearly 3,400,000 people, which compares with the figure of 3,995,000 for Britain reported by the Supplementary Benefits Commis-

London, 1971; Knight, I. B., and Nixon, J. M., *Two Parent Families in Receipt of Family Income Supplement, 1972*, DHSS Statistical and Research Report Series No. 9, HMSO, London, 1975.

sion as provided for in households receiving regular weekly payments in November 1968.[1] The latter figure should be reduced by about 65,000 to exclude people in hospital, local-authority homes and hostels. The percentage of retirement pensioners (and widow pensioners aged 60 and over) receiving supplementary benefits was 25·2 compared with 28·1 per cent on December 1968 according to administrative records.[2] They represented 1,715,000, which compared with the figure of 2,044,000 retirement pensioners (and widow pensioners aged 60 and over), and another 179,000 over pensionable age who were in households receiving supplementary benefit, according to administrative records.[3]

The figure of 4·4 per cent not receiving but eligible for benefits represented 2,430,000 people, including 1,315,000 aged 65 and over, and 410,000 children. Retirement pensioners comprised the majority of eligible non-recipients. Most of the others were in the families of the unemployed, sick and disabled, as Table 24.3 shows. The corresponding figures from official reports are also given. The fact that government data are based on a 1¼ per cent sample should be noted. One would not expect the two sets of figures to be identical, but when taken with estimates of the total numbers in the population who received national insurance benefits (Table 24.1), certain conclusions may be drawn. Unlike other groups of beneficiaries, fewer retirement pensioners in the sample than would have been expected were found to be drawing supplementary benefit. Part of the difference is attributable to the inclusion in official figures of persons in hospital, residential hostels and homes, and guest houses. Part is also attributable to the difficulty of distinguishing between widows' and retirement pensions for widows in their sixties. None the less, an underestimation within the sample remains. But even if all of this were to be deducted from the figure in the final column of the table more than a million retirement pensioners would still be eligible for benefit but not receiving benefit. Our conclusion therefore is that at least 2 million people in the United Kingdom, more than half of them being retirement pensioners, were entitled to obtain supplementary benefit but were not receiving such benefit.

Although the numbers in the sample of currently unemployed and sick and disabled people off work were small, substantial fractions were assessed to be eligible for, although not receiving, supplementary benefit. There were over a third of the unemployed, one in seven of the sick and one in eight of the disabled

1. Annual Report of the Department of Health and Social Security for 1968, Cmnd 4100, HMSO, London, 1969, p. 316.
2. DHSS, *Social Security Statistics, 1974*, HMSO, London, 1975, p. 176.
3. We found that although some elderly individuals in the sample appeared to have said they were not drawing supplementary benefit when in fact they were, they had given a figure for their weekly pension which appeared to include both retirement and supplementary pension. For this reason, it should not be supposed that the figure of retirement pensioners estimated to be receiving supplementary benefit in Table 24.3 should be augmented from the final column. We believe that some at least of the missing individuals have been coded as having an income too high to be eligible for supplementary benefit.

Table 24.3. *Number of persons in income units in the United Kingdom receiving and estimated to be eligible for supplementary benefits.*

	Government estimates of numbers receiving supplementary benefit (000s of persons)	Estimated on basis of sample numbers	
		Receiving supplementary benefit (000s of persons)	Eligible for supplementary benefit but not receiving (000s of persons)
Reason for head not being at work[a]			
Retired	–	1,455	1 300
Unemployed	–	320	425
Sick	–	365	370
Disabled	–	155	35
Housewives (many units headed by lone mothers)	–	980	265
Age			
0–14	–	565	410
15–29	–	235	200
30–44	–	165	135
45–64	–	720	370
65+	–	1,700	1,315
Total	–	3,380	2,430
Type of benefit received by income unit			
Retirement pension (and widows over 60)	2,044	1,715	1,500
Widow's pension or allowance	97	120	120
Sickness or disablement benefit	385	340	365
Unemployment benefit	225	280	325
Supplementary benefit to lone parents with dependent children	548	565	160
Type of benefit received by income unit	*(000s of units)*	*(000s of units)*	*(000s of units)*
Retirement pension (and widows over 60)	–	1,465	1,045
Widow's pension or allowance	61	90	65
Sickness or disablement allowance	172	160	120
Unemployment benefit	73	90	100
Supplementary benefit to lone parents	188	170	55

NOTE: [a]Certain small categories (e.g. students, on paid and unpaid holiday) have been excluded.

SOURCES: Government estimates from DHSS, Annual Report for 1968, HMSO, London, 1969, p. 316; Report of the Committee on One-Parent Families (The Finer Report), vol. 2, pp. 313 and 316.

(Table A.98, Appendix Eight, page 1065). More than one in ten of the families of lone parents also qualified for supplementary benefit but were not receiving it.

The numbers of different types of beneficiary who were eligible for, but who did not receive, supplementary benefits can also be compared with the numbers actually receiving them. As a fraction of the numbers of units obtaining supplementary benefits, the numbers eligible for them varies between two thirds and the same number in the case of those receiving retirement pensions, widows' benefits, sickness benefits and unemployment benefits. In the case of those receiving industrial and war disablement pensions, however, relatively few income units drew supplementary benefits, and there was no evidence in the sample of anyone eligible for but not drawing them (although, as we shall see, such persons were found among the samples surveyed in the four special areas). Two qualifications need to be made. There were some households in the sample where someone was off work sick in the week preceding interview but sickness or unemployment benefit had not been paid. To reflect a real 'current' distribution, a number of short-term beneficiaries should therefore be added. Secondly, some of the unemployed not getting supplementary benefits though eligible for them may have applied but been refused because of the operation of the wage-stop.

Table 24.4. Percentages of income units with income from different state sources in previous week according to eligibility for supplementary benefit.

	Income units with income last week from				
Eligibility of income unit for supplementary benefits	Retirement pensions	Widows' benefits	Sickness benefit	Unemployment benefit	Industrial and war disablement pensions
Unclassifiable	3·6	1·6	1·0	(2·4)	(2·4)
Could not claim	3·9	62·5	21·2	(4·8)	(50·0)
Receiving supplementary benefit	27·5	15·6	14·1	(23·8)	(9·5)
Ineligible for supplementary benefit (income too high)	45·3	9·4	50·5	(42·9)	(38·1)
Eligible but not receiving	19·7	10·9	13·1	(26·2)	(0·0)
Total	100	100	100	100	100
Number	585	64	99	42	42

The existence of substantial numbers of individuals and families other than those of pensionable age who are entitled to claim supplementary benefit but are not doing so is supported by a range of research studies for the 1970s as well as the 1960s. These involve long-term sick[1] and disabled people,[2] the unemployed[3] and one-parent families.[4] Organization as well as information shortcoming have begun to be discussed.[5]

Implications of Estimated Numbers Eligible for Benefits

The estimates of numbers of people eligible for, but not receiving, supplementary benefits in the United Kingdom as a whole require some elucidation. The number of old people is considerably higher than the estimate made by the Ministry of Pensions in its survey of 1966. There are at least four reasons for this. First, during the late 1960s the number of retirement pensioners was continuing to increase disproportionately to population and to the elderly population. Secondly, higher disregards for income and assets were introduced in late 1966. Thirdly, the long-term addition initially of 45p for every retirement pensioner, which largely replaced the varying amounts previously paid to nearly three quarters of retirement pensioners receiving supplementary benefits, had the effect of lifting the 'floor' of eligibility. Fourthly, the spread of incomes of the great majority of old people covers a very small range, and even a slight change in the basic scales of supplementary benefit, relative to median or mean income, can change substantially the numbers qualifying for benefit.

If the long-term addition were excluded from the income allowed in meeting needs, the number of old people eligible for benefits but not receiving them would have been just over 1 million. If the lower disregards of income and assets had remained in force after November 1966, then the total number of old people eligible for benefits but not receiving them would have been approximately 850,000. This figure is approximately the same as that produced in the Ministry of Pensions survey of 1965, though because of the increase in numbers of retirement pensioners it represents a proportionate reduction (from 13·4 to 12·2 per cent). To conclude, the evidence from this survey suggests that the effect of introducing

1. For example, between a fifth and a quarter of people sick for six months or more had an income below 'notional supplementary benefit assessments' – Martin, J., and Morgan, M., *Prolonged Sickness and the Return to Work*, HMSO, London, 1975, p. 58.
2. Harris, A. I., *et al.*, *Income and Entitlement to Supplementary Benefit of Impaired People in Great Britain*, (vol. III of *Handicapped and Impaired in Great Britain*), HMSO, London, 1972; Smith, C. R. W., *Entitlement to Supplementary Benefit of Impaired People in Great Britain*, Office of Population Censuses and Surveys, Social Survey Division, London, 1972.
3. Estimates derived from the Family Expenditure Survey were given in *Hansard*, 20 May 1974.
4. Hunt, A., *Families and Their Needs*, Office of Population Censuses and Surveys, Social Survey Division, London, 1973. See also Bond, N., *Knowledge of Rights and Extent of Unmet Need Amongst Recipients of Supplementary Benefit*, Coventry CDP, Occasional Paper No. 4, 1971. General sources are reviewed in Lister, R., *Take-up of Means Tested Benefits*, Poverty Pamphlet No. 18, Child Poverty Action Group, London, November 1974.
5. For example, Meacher, M., *Scrounging on the Welfare*, Arrow Books, London, 1974.

supplementary benefits was to reduce the number of retirement pensioners eligible for benefit but not receiving from 13·4 to 12·2 per cent, or up to approximately 75,000. This is a modest achievement, certainly much more modest than was claimed at the time.

The estimates we have given for the unemployed not receiving benefit also require comment. Not all of them would, in practice, have received benefit had they applied. There are two factors not taken into account by our estimates. First, the wage-stop was then being applied to unemployed and temporarily sick applicants. Thus, the supplementary benefit that can be paid to an applicant was restricted to the amount of his net weekly earnings when at work. Our estimates, of course, exclude income units receiving *reduced* benefits. But they include others subject to the wage-stop who did not qualify for supplementary benefit at all, even though their incomes were less than the basic scale rates. A few of the people we interviewed had applied for benefit but had been unsuccessful for this reason.

On 25 July 1968, the Minister of Social Security also announced that the benefits for unskilled and fit single men under 45 could be terminated four weeks after they had started drawing benefit, roughly on grounds that by then it should have been possible for them to find work. Benefits for skilled men and those with families could also be terminated after four weeks' warning, though this procedure was to be applied only to those drawing benefit for at least three months. These provisions applied only to regions with low levels of unemployment.

Our estimates do not take account of these two limitations. From scrutiny of the questionnaires it would seem that up to about a third of the unemployed in the sample who were not drawing supplementary benefits, and were apparently eligible for them, might not in practice have received them on one of these grounds, had they applied.

Characteristics of the Legally Entitled

What were the characteristics of those legally entitled to, but not receiving, benefits? There are the characteristics of the income units and households of which they are members, and their characteristics as individuals. Government spokesmen have suggested in the past that substantial proportions of eligible non-recipients are old people who, although legally entitled to benefits in their own right, are in fact sharing a household with other income units and so, by implication, are sharing a much larger total household income. Our survey offered small support for this contention. As many as 67 per cent of people aged 65 and over were members of households in which there was only one income unit, and a further 25 per cent were in households with only two income units. Sixty-one per cent of the elderly non-recipients were living in households alone or in couples. Moreover, the households of nearly a third of households in which there were two or more income units had a net disposable income in the year as a whole of below or just above the supplementary benefit level. All these figures are not very different from the corresponding figures for those actually receiving benefits.

The income units who were eligible for supplementary benefits but not receiving them were spread over a large number of different types of household. Twenty per cent were, or were in, households with children. Just over a quarter of them were households consisting of man and woman only, and over another quarter were single or widowed, the great majority of them elderly, people living alone. (The numbers are given in Table A.99, Appendix Eight, p. 1065.) They show beyond any doubt that those who are living in households with other income units are a minority. The income units were also distributed as widely as income

Table 24.5. *Percentages of people in income units receiving and eligible for, but not receiving, supplementary benefits, according to certain characteristics (United Kingdom and four areas).*

	Four areas		United Kingdom		
Reason for not working last week	*Receiving*	*Eligible but not receiving*	*Receiving*	*Eligible but not receiving*	*Receiving supplementary benefit November 1968*[a]
Dependent children (incl. those aged 15–18 at school)	28·9	36·3	16·6	17·5	18·4
Unemployed	6·8	8·9	3·3	6·4	5·6
Sick	9·5	8·9	5·7	4·7	}8·1
Disabled	3·3	5·5	4·2	0·8	
Housewife (mainly lone mothers)	24·4	21·4	28·9	21·8	22·3
Retired	25·8	17·4	38·3	46·6	44·8
Other	1·4	1·5	3·0	2·1	0·7
Total	100	100	100	100	100
Age 0–14	27·5	34·3	16·6	16·8	17·6
15–44	16·5	24·4	11·8	13·8	13·8
45–64	21·9	18·4	21·2	15·3	18·9
65+	34·0	22·9	50·3	54·1	49·7
Total	100	100	100	100	100
Number	516	201	372	268	3,995,000

NOTE: [a]Britain only. Based on Tables 30–34 in Annual Report of the Department of Health and Social Security for 1968. The distribution as between housewives, retired and miscellaneous is approximate, as is implied by the corresponding figures for the population aged 65 and over. Note that S B C statistics are based on a 1¼ per cent sample of those receiving benefit.

units receiving benefits among households with heads of different ages. As might be expected of people experiencing temporary adversities, slightly more eligible non-recipients than recipients proved to be young. This was not uniform for all age groups. As many as 45 per cent, compared with 43 per cent, proved to be income units in households with heads aged 70 and over.

Table 24.5 shows certain characteristics of both the recipients and eligible non-recipients of supplementary benefit for the UK sample as a whole (the findings for the four areas are discussed later). The distributions are not markedly different. More than half of each group are aged 65 and over, more than two thirds are housewives (mostly lone mothers) or retired, and about a sixth are children. The proportions who are unemployed, sick or disabled as such, excluding their dependants, are small, but it is noticeable that the proportion of unemployed among eligible non-recipients is rather larger, and the proportion of disabled smaller, than among recipients. The final column of the table shows the corresponding administrative statistics of the Supplementary Benefits Commission (themselves based, it should be noted, on a 1¼ per cent sample of 'live cases').

Temporary and Long-term Poverty

Because incomes have a tendency to fluctuate, government spokesmen often suppose that people found in the week of a particular survey to be eligible non-recipients are not really in need or are only temporarily in need, because their incomes in the year other than in that week are adequate. There was small evidence for this supposition in the survey. Over two thirds of eligible non-recipients lived in households with net disposable incomes in the previous twelve months of less than, or only just above, the basic supplementary benefit scales. There was a majority among them living in households consisting of a single income unit, and 82 per cent of them had incomes for the year of below or just above the standard (Table 24.6). In considering the interrelationship of the two measures, it must be remembered that the basic standard takes account neither of income disregarded in the more refined 'administrative measure' nor of the long-term addition received by pensioners and younger recipients who have been receiving benefits for two years or more and are not required to register at an employment exchange. It is not surprising, therefore, that some people who are eligible on strict application of the official regulations and procedures in fact have annual incomes sometimes considerably in excess of the basic scale rates.

As a comparative measure of the resources of the different categories, we expressed income for the previous year as a percentage of the state's poverty standard for each income unit, and then averaged this percentage for the different categories. The results in Table 24.6 show that the average unit which was eligible for but not receiving supplementary benefit had a lower relative income than recipients.

Table 24.6.

Eligibility for supplementary benefit	Last year's income as a % of the state poverty standard
Receives	113·1
Not receiving but eligible	108·4
Eligible to claim but income too high	185·4
Cannot claim (in employment)	220·4

Among all income units eligible for supplementary benefits but not receiving them, approximately 20 per cent had incomes assessed at over 50p below, some of them of £1 below, the incomes which they would have been allowed under the supplementary benefits scheme, and another 20 per cent had incomes of between 25p and 50p below. Most of these income units comprised the elderly. Among those coded ineligible for supplementary benefit, a third had incomes of only up to 50p more than the income they would have been allowed.

Levels of Living of Recipients

Some of those in receipt of benefits have incomes above, and some below, the basic standard. Table 24.7 shows that over a quarter of the people in households with a single income unit had incomes in the year as a whole of less than the basic

Table 24.7. *Percentages of people in income units receiving and eligible for, but not receiving, supplementary benefits, according to the net disposable income in previous year of the households in which they lived, expressed as a percentage of supplementary benefit basic scale rates plus housing costs.*

Net disposable household income last year as % of supplementary benefit scale rates plus housing cost	Receiving			Eligible but not receiving			All neither receiving nor eligible
	1 income unit in household	2 or more units in household	All	1 income unit in household	2 or more units in household	All	
Under 100	27·5	3·5	21·4	48·2	10·0	36·8	3·4
100–19	50·2	16·5	41·6	25·6	15·7	22·6	5·7
120–39	15·0	23·5	17·2	7·9	12·9	9·4	12·8
140+	7·2	56·5	19·9	18·2	61·4	31·2	78·1
Total	100	100	100	100	100	100	100
Number	247	85	332	164	70	234	4,591

rates. Some of these had delayed applying for benefit and had lived for weeks or months on incomes below the basic scale rates. A few with high rents were not allowed full rents by the Supplementary Benefits Commission. Some were people in the families of unemployed men who were wage-stopped.

The household incomes of 50 per cent of recipients in 'single unit' households were up to 20 per cent above the basic scale rates. Many of them had small amounts of income which were disregarded. A further 15 per cent had incomes up to 40 per cent above the basic rates, and 7 per cent higher incomes still. Some were people in households in which wage-earners had been at work earlier in the year.

We also considered recipients in relation to current or last week's income. Altogether we found that 16·5 per cent of people in income units receiving supplementary benefits had an income last week of below the scale rates (Table A.100, Appendix Eight, page 1066). If the percentage is applied to the number stated by the commission to be depending on supplementary benefit at the time, then approximately 660,000 did not live at the level which appeared to be laid down in the rules attaching to the scale rates. Some were in wage-stopped families, but in other cases needs appeared to have been underassessed, or reduced allowances were being paid. The commission has itself conceded an administrative error rate of over 10 per cent, though only just over half of these are believed to be underpayments.[1] This phenomenon has been discussed in other studies[2] and will be discussed here later.

Eligibility in Four Areas

Identical questionnaires to those in the national survey were used in the surveys in Belfast, Glasgow, Neath and Salford. But they were applied only to those among the samples of the population found to belong to minority groups, or rather less than half. A shorter screening questionnaire was applied to the remainder. The percentages of the total samples found to be receiving, and not receiving but eligible for, benefit are shown in Table 24.8. They are larger but not very much larger than for the population as a whole, with the percentage of eligible non-recipients being largest in Belfast, next in Glasgow, and finally about the same in Neath and Salford.

Because levels of unemployment and disability and sickness were higher, and incomes lower, especially among the retired, the fact that more people received supplementary benefit is not unexpected. But it might be assumed that, in such poor areas, receipt of benefit would be much more an accepted part of everyday experience and that knowledge of the system would be better diffused throughout the local community. As a consequence, eligible non-recipients might be considerably fewer. The fact that they are not is therefore important.

1. Annual Report, 1975, p. 112.
2. Bond, *Knowledge of Rights and Extent of Unmet Need Amongst Recipients of Supplementary Benefit.*

But the differences between the findings for the four areas and those for the country as a whole are not very large. Perhaps this is what deserves emphasis. While low incomes are prevalent in these relatively poor communities, dependence or potential dependence upon the supplementary benefit system of the state does not seem to be so marked as is sometimes supposed. Eligibility for help because of needs that are defined by the state seems to be widely diffused.

Table 24.8. *Percentages of people of different age in four areas, according to eligibility of income unit for supplementary benefit.*

Age/area	Eligibility of income unit for supplementary benefits					Total	No.
	Unclassi-fiable	Could not claim (employed)	Currently receiving benefit	Ineligible (income too high)	Eligible but not receiving		
Age 0–14	1·5	71·5	14·0	6·4	6·7	100	1,023
15–44	0·7	83·5	6·5	5·6	3·7	100	1,320
45–64	2·2	67·7	14·7	10·7	4·8	100	777
65+	5·0	3·4	40·4	40·6	10·5	100	438
All ages	1·8	66·7	14·6	11·3	5·6	100	3,559
Area:							
Belfast	0·9	61·9	15·0	12·6	9·6	100	782
Glasgow	2·7	65·5	15·4	9·4	6·9	100	1,039
Neath	1·8	71·5	10·7	13·4	2·5	100	710
Salford	1·5	68·2	16·2	10·6	3·5	100	1,028
All areas	1·8	66·7	14·6	11·3	5·6	100	3,559

In comparing the samples from the four areas with the national sample, two points need to be made. In the four areas a higher percentage of different categories of person drawing national insurance than in the population as a whole qualified to draw, and were drawing, supplementary benefit as well (Table 24.9). And a much higher percentage of those both depending on, and eligible to depend on, supplementary benefit were children (Tables 24.5, page 834, and A.61, Appendix Eight, page 1039). Fewer of those in the country as a whole than in the four areas needed to have their contributory national insurance benefits made up to the state's minimum. Considerably more of the poor in these areas than elsewhere comprised children. Proportionately fewer of the poor were of pensionable age.

Because the interviewing was concentrated in a few areas, we decided to pay return visits to all those apparently eligible for, but not receiving, benefits. Many of these visits took place within three months of the first interviews, but for prac-

Table 24.9. Percentages of different types of national insurance beneficiaries in the United Kingdom and four areas who received, and who did not receive, but were eligible for, supplementary benefit.

Category of national insurance beneficiary	Percentage in income units receiving supplementary benefit		Percentage in income units who are eligible for but not receiving supplementary benefit	
	Four areas	UK	Four areas	UK
Retirement pensioners	43·7	25·9	13·2	˙19·7
Widows' benefits	34·6	28·0	5·9	15·2
Sickness benefit	38·2	14·1	17·3	13·1
Unemployment benefit	30·5	23·8	38·0	26·2
Industrial injury and war benefit	13·8	9·5	10·3	0·0
Total population	15·1	6·4	5·9	4·5

tical reasons some, particularly in Belfast, took place more than three months later. Some families could not be contacted because they had moved, but, as Table 24.10 shows, fifty-seven of the seventy-two households were interviewed again. The eligibility of the majority of these was confirmed.

The largest category was of retirement pensioners, about half of whom were living alone and the others with relatives. They accounted for about three fifths of households, but for more than a third of the people qualifying for benefit but not getting it. The next largest category were fathers off work because of sickness. Over half of these had only been sick for periods of less than a month, but some for much longer. The remainder were fatherless families, disabled and handicapped people and a few unemployed men with families where it seemed likely that they would receive some benefit even if they were wage-stopped, and unemployed men who had not yet applied, or reapplied, for benefit.

The average amount to which each household seemed to be entitled was £1·20 a week, not including any discretionary allowances which might have been payable. Amounts ranged from an average of 50p a week for pensioners who were householders living with relatives, and 60p for householders living alone, to £1·90 for the fathers off work sick. One old woman and one young woman off work sick had no income of their own and were at the time eligible for about £4 a week each.

After the follow-up interviews, a number of the families appeared not to be eligible for benefit. They fell into three groups: (a) unemployed men whose income resources were lower than their needs, as assessed according to the basic scales of the Supplementary Benefits Commission, but who would have been

Table 24.10. *Numbers and percentages of eligible non-recipients in four areas.*

Households/persons	Belfast	Glasgow	Neath	Salford	Four areas
Total number of households interviewed	256	361	223	337	1,177
Total number of persons in interviewed households	782	1,039	710	1,028	3,559
Percentage in income units receiving supplementary benefit	15·0	15·4	10·7	16·7	14·6
Percentage in income units eligible for but not receiving supplementary benefit	9·6	6·9	2·5	3·5	5·6
Number of households with income units eligible for but not receiving benefit and interviewed a second time[a]	24	27	9	12	72

Assessment after second interview	Number of households				
Ineligible because of wage-stop	2	4	0	2	8
Ineligible for other reasons[b]	4	5	2	3	14
Eligible	15	9	6	5	35
Non-contact	2	6[c]	1	1	10
Refusal	1	3	0	1	5

NOTES: [a]Six additional households also should have been interviewed, but they were identified only after coding, punching and computer analysis of the data had been completed.
[b]For example, an additional source of income, such as supplementary benefit, was found which had not been specified in the first interviews; or a family had, in fact, applied for, and been refused benefit, because income which we believed could have been disregarded was *not* disregarded.
[c]All in an area which had been demolished since the first interview.

'wage-stopped' at a figure below a level entitling them to supplementary benefit; (b) families who had in fact applied for benefit but had been refused on grounds which we believed might be wrong but which we felt we should accept (e.g. an employer's pension or disability pension had not been disregarded, as the regulations suggested they might have been, in the assessment); and (c) households whose circumstances or income did not, after all, qualify them to receive benefit (principally pensioners who had not specified some supplementary source of income). Our intention was to produce an estimate which would be, as near as possible, acceptable to the Supplementary Benefits Commission itself. If those who refused a second interview, or who could not be contacted, are discounted, and if the number of families ineligible for supplementary benefit only because of the wage-stop are added to families confirmed as eligible for benefit, and then compared with those families found to be ineligible, it can be seen that only one in four families failed our second test. While information supplied in these four areas must not be regarded as representative of the country as a whole, the results of our test procedure can only be regarded as tending to reinforce the national findings. The large numbers failing to claim benefit cannot be dismissed as a function of incomplete or over-hasty survey interviewing. Even if that charge were true, it would also apply to a succession of studies carried out by the government itself.[1] Among only a small minority of these very poor income units was income found to have been underestimated.

The follow-up interviews helped us to understand how some interviews can produce wrong or incomplete information. For example, the initial interview with an 81-year-old woman living alone in Salford showed that she had a retirement pension (£4·50 per week at the time), but there appeared to be some friend, neighbour or relative who came and occasionally gave her 15p or 20p in addition. At the follow-up interview it was established that the visitor was in fact an SBC officer and the elderly woman received supplementary benefit of 20p a week. Again, a woman of 64, living with a son permanently off work through sickness, appeared on the basis of the first interview to be eligible to receive a total of £6·20 but only received a pension of £4·50. At the follow-up interview she revealed she had a cleaning job for two hours a day. She would give no further details, and despite the interviewer's assurance to the contrary, persisted in believing that because she had a part-time job she was not eligible for supplementary benefit. In the absence of full information, we had to assume her income was such as to make her ineligible for benefit.

There were a few informants, mainly old people, who revealed either with order books or after questioning that they were, in fact, receiving supplementary benefit, though this had not emerged during the first interview.[2] In almost no instances was concealment deliberate, though in some instances embarrassment had caused people to imply that the total figure they gave in reply to questions about income was attributable to a pension and not also to supplementary benefit. The term 'supplementary benefit' was unfamiliar to some people. Indeed, we came across instances of people referring to 'public assistance' and even 'outdoor relief' instead of 'national assistance' (operating between 1948 and 1966). And the amount of supplementary benefit was sometimes combined in payment with a non-contributory old-age pension for some of the oldest people, so misapprehensions were understandable.

This follow-up research tends to reinforce substantial estimates of shortfalls of receipt of benefit made on the basis of the national and special area surveys. It

1. For example, the Ministry of Pensions studies of retirement pensions and families with children, and DHSS and OPCS studies in the 1970s of one-parent families, and the long-term sick and disabled.

2. It should be noted that most of the errors of the first interview were made in 'screening' interviews of short duration rather than in the full interviews held with households falling into one or more of the thirteen social minorities (and with all households in the national survey).

shows that a proportion of those initially assessed as eligible for but not receiving benefit would be ineligible, but the proportion is small and is made up in part of families who would be ineligible only because of the operation of the wage-stop. On the other hand, it should be remembered that the follow-up research was confined to the potentially eligible and, just as some errors of interviewer classification were found among them, a few errors may well have been made in classifying the potentially ineligible. This would have had the reverse effect of *increasing*, rather than *decreasing*, the estimate.

Attitudes and Circumstances of those Eligible for Benefit

About three quarters of the pensioners interviewed in the follow-up research seemed to be unaware that they might be eligible. They assumed they did not qualify because they were not destitute, had part-time earnings, owned their own houses, had savings or had help from their families. Householders living with working relatives, including sons and brothers, were, in particular, unaware of their rights. 'But I'm not on my own. I've a son (brother) working who lives with me.' When the qualifying regulations were pointed out to them, several seemed very doubtful and it seemed unlikely that they would apply.

But, as pointed out earlier, such people account for only a small proportion of eligible non-recipients. Pensioners living alone were also uninformed. Some were aware that they might get help with their rent, but believed that savings or small sources of income would disqualify them. Despite protestations to the contrary, the interviewer was sometimes regarded as being a representative of the 'welfare' and felt that explanations of failure to apply were sometimes couched politely in terms of the complexities of the system instead of distaste for it. Some pensioners reacted in traditional terms to supplementary benefit as a form of charity. As one woman in Glasgow said, 'I'll apply when I need it. As we are now we can manage. I've always been independent, but with the way things are going perhaps I'll be applying soon.'

> A widowed householder of 77 lived with a 68-year-old unmarried sister in one of the city's slum areas. The widow's pension was £5 and she appeared at the first interview to be entitled to another 60p. At the follow-up interview she claimed she had part-time earnings. She had been a corset-maker all her life and still lived over the shop, which she owned, and made corsets for her relatives. But it was unlikely that her earnings even reached 25p per week. She was well aware of her entitlement to supplementary benefit, and indeed referred to the notes circulated with her pension book. She did not regard supplementary benefit as a charity, yet said she would only apply for it when she 'needed it'. For her, such an act seemed to symbolize the end of her working life and independence.

The fathers off work sick were all unaware of their possible entitlement to benefit. At least in the areas in which we did this research, it was apparently not the policy of officials to tell men drawing sickness or unemployment benefit that they might be eligible for supplementary benefit. Instead, information was given only when requested. Some men were doubtful when told by our interviewer of their entitlement, and some were opposed to making an application because they had an unfavourable impression of the Supplementary Benefits Commission officers and procedures. Antagonism was strongest in Belfast where the wage-stop appeared to be more frequently and stringently applied and where unemployment was running highest. People in Belfast were, for example, convinced that supplementary benefit *rates* were lower than in England, and that discretion was less frequently exercised in the applicant's favour. The commission does not publish area analyses of the number of households receiving exceptional circumstances additions, exceptional needs grants, and so forth, but the commission's Northern Ireland Report shows that, in number and amount, such payments in Northern Ireland are disproportionately small.[1] The stigma of charity was also strong. One wife said, 'It sounds like superstition but your own money goes further. You can lay it out better.'

Among reasons given for not applying in all four areas was a fear that basic sickness benefit would be reduced, or that an application would lead to bureaucratic inquiries during a period of convalescence. Some people were reluctant to submit to what they regarded as distasteful procedures for comparatively small results. This was particularly true if there was more than a single income unit in the household and a member of the family was still at work, or if earnings-related supplements to national insurance benefits were expected after the first fortnight. Understandably, people confused these 'supplements' with supplementary benefit.

Most of the sick people who were eligible for supplementary benefit were temporarily in poverty, as in the following example.

> At first interview a man off work sick for just over a week showed that the total family income per week from sickness benefit and a family allowance for his second child was £9·10. His supplementary benefit entitlement worked out at £11·65. At the follow-up interview, he was back at work and revealed that he had drawn a 'sub' of £4 from the SBC to tide him over the first week until he was paid. Although this involved the loss of a day's pay because of the waiting in the office, he preferred it to asking for a 'sub' from his employer. He claimed not to have known he was eligible for supplementary benefit while sick but said he might apply if he became sick another time.

The long-term sick posed a variety of problems. Sometimes there was a straightforward refusal to apply for benefit even after many weeks on a minute income.

1. The severity of conditions in Northern Ireland and the long-term nature of adversities would suggest that more of those granted supplementary benefits should be receiving discretionary additions, either regularly or occasionally. But the reverse is, in fact, the case. In 1969, for example, only 13·2 per cent received exceptional circumstances additions, compared with 17·5 per cent in Britain. DHSS, Annual Report, 1969, Cmnd 4462, HMSO, London, p. 332; and *Northern Ireland*, SBC Report for 1969.

The first interview showed that a Salford man who had been off work for twenty-four weeks with thrombosis had a wife and six children of school or pre-school age and a total income, including family allowances, of £13·18 a week. Their entitlement appeared to be £16·25. The follow-up interview confirmed all the information obtained at the first and showed that although the couple were acutely aware of the possibility of getting some additional help, and lived only just round the corner from the offices, they refused point-blank to apply.[1]

Sometimes the people living in the household were unaware of entitlement.

A woman of 50 years of age in Glasgow was off work because of 'nerves'. She had no income whatsoever and acted as housekeeper to her unmarried brother and sister, both of whom were in paid employment. Some entitlement existed, but the exact amount depended on whether or not the SBC would treat her as 'working' for her relations. She had not worked full time since 1944, though she had done a little outwork recently as a raincoat machinist. Her basic problem was claustrophobia in factory conditions. When her father was alive she had drawn national assistance, but had sent her allowance book back when he died, a few years previously. She said in the follow-up interview that she was aware that pensions and benefits could be paid to the crippled or physically ill, but did not believe her condition made her eligible. 'The people I've seen with allowances have all been crippled, their hands all twisted up with rheumatism, or they've had bronchitis.' Two years earlier her sister had sought advice from the local Citizens' Advice Bureau after a circular had been put through the letter-box, but had been offended at the suggestion that a further application should be made to the National Assistance Board. They both felt that national assistance was degrading and that the Citizen's Advice Bureau should have helped. 'Well you have got a bit of pride left, haven't you?' she asked the interviewer. Since then they had let the matter drift. When she learned that it was possible to apply for a home visit through the Post Office she said she would apply.

This was not the most extreme case of individual entitlement.

A man of 55 living with a common-law wife in Neath had, he said, chronic bronchitis and spent his life on or near his bed. He looked like a living skeleton and could only move a few feet at a time, and with great difficulty. His only income was his sickness benefit of £4·50 per week. In better times he had bought his wife a small hairdressing business, and she had worked at this for several years but failed to stamp her insurance card. Now she had fallen ill and could work very little, with the result that the couple were living on sickness benefit for a single man, but were afraid to apply for supplementary benefit because they believed the irregularity over the stamp would be discovered.

There were a number of other kinds of household eligible for benefit but not receiving it.

A separated woman in Belfast with two illegitimate children received £5 per week from the children's father. Although this was equal to the maximum possible main-

1. From September 1971, invalidity benefit became payable instead of sickness benefit after six months' incapacity for work, and higher allowances were paid for dependants and later for claimants. But, at the end of 1971, the number of sickness beneficiaries drawing supplementary benefit was still 12·6 per cent (compared with 14·6 per cent at the end of 1970). By the end of 1974 it was 7·7 per cent. See DHSS, *Social Security Statistics, 1974*, HMSO, London, 1975, p. 176.

tenance award, it was below the supplementary benefit level. At the follow-up interview it proved that the woman was not aware that she was eligible, but she was also
reluctant to apply for benefit, since the question of her divorce and prospective
remarriage was at a delicate stage. She did not want to make relationships with her
former husband more acrimonious, nor damage her relations with the children's
father. Had she applied, the SBC would have been legally entitled, though unlikely,
to sue the father for the minimum 50p which they would have had to pay her. The
practice of the SBC in Northern Ireland was to make a wife deserted by her husband
sue him; and some informants told us that benefit was not paid until she had done so. ·

There were also three instances in which difficult decisions would have to be
taken in the event of any application. In one family a girl aged 15 stayed off work
to care for her mother who was ill and was said to need constant attention. For
six months the girl had been supported from the father's sickness benefit. A girl
of that age could not receive money in her own right from the Supplementary
Benefits Commission, and whether the commission chose to pay her a housekeeper allowance would depend on whether the family could establish that the
mother needed attention and that the daughter was suitable to provide this
attention.

In another instance, a widow worked to keep her 27-year-old son who was mentally handicapped and had never worked. She said he was 'excused paying
stamps' and was incapable of the most menial job. When the interviewer suggested the possibility of support, the widow said she was reluctant to contact
officials because they would call attention to her son's handicap.

Among the elderly, the predominant impression about their failure to obtain
supplementary benefit was one of ignorance and inability to comprehend complex rules and pride in such independence as was left to them. Among men with
families, it was one more of fear of the power and arbitrariness of official procedure and decisions. Both shied away from wearisome form-filling and queries at
offices. They were deterred by physical distances, by waiting and uncertainty, by
awesome bureaucratic procedures and by the uncomfortable and sometimes
abrasive contacts with officials or other clients which they expected. People were
visibly pleased to be told about the Post Office method of applying for a home
visit to determine eligibility. But, in general, old and young returned by one route
or another to the stigma which they felt was still implied by this system of obtaining money in need.

Attitudes of Recipients

We asked people receiving benefits who had advised them to apply and whether
they were embarrassed to have this kind of help. Among the total receiving benefits, 31 per cent said that making an application was their own idea and another
16 per cent did not know of any particular advice; but 24 per cent said a relative
or a friend had advised them, 8 per cent a 'welfare worker', 5 per cent a doctor

and 3 per cent the Post Office, leaving 13 per cent who gave miscellaneous sources. The exact question we asked of people receiving benefit was: 'Do you feel embarrassed or uncomfortable about it or do you accept it just like a pension or any other kind of income?' Table 24.11 gives the distribution of answers. The great majority were not embarrassed or uncomfortable, although some of these were over-assertive, for example: 'I've worked my guts out all my life and it's about time my country did something for me in return.' Alternatively, some were mechanical in giving their replies, as if applying for help were an automatic part of the adjustment they had had to make in their self-esteem: 'You have to take it, don't you, and get on with it? It's the only thing you can do.' A little less than a third, but rather more younger than older people, felt embarrassed or uncomfortable.

Among recipients under the pensionable ages, there was little variation among the unemployed, sick, disabled and housewives in the proportion expressing embarrassment. The fraction did not vary much around two fifths for each of these categories. And roughly as many men as women expressed embarrassment. Among the elderly, the fraction fell to about a quarter, but relatively twice as many housewives as retired married men, or two fifths compared with one fifth, expressed embarrassment. On the other hand, the proportion of women living alone in retirement who expressed embarrassment was approximately the same as of retired husbands (or one fifth). In the four special areas, fewer claimants than in the United Kingdom as a whole expressed discomfort (21 per cent compared with 29 per cent), but the distribution between the sexes and age groups followed the same pattern.

The information given here should not be regarded as offering more than a starting point. It was not our purpose to explore relationships with social security agencies,[1] and it was evident from illustrative comments that many people held

Table 24.11. Percentages of elderly and younger recipients, according to their attitudes to receiving supplementary benefit.

Whether embarrassed or uncomfortable at receiving supplementary benefit or accepting it like a pension or other income	Recipients aged 60 and over	Recipients under 60		Recipients	
		Male	Female	All	
Very embarrassed or uncomfortable	5·3	19·2	8·0	9·7	9·1
A little embarrassed	20·7	19·2	18·4	21·2	20·0
Not embarrassed	74·1	61·6	73·6	69·1	70·9
Total	100	100	100	100	100
Number	189	73	87	175	265

1. But see, for example, Meacher, *Scrounging on the Welfare.*

strong views about correct methods of procedure and treatment. All we have sought to show is that there is a wide variation in attitudes towards the receipt of benefit, which is bound to contribute to any explanation of the inefficiency of supplementary benefits as a system.

Inadequate Payments

We did not attempt to check every payment of supplementary benefit to recipients in the national and special area samples to find whether payments corresponded with needs as they were defined in regulations. However, interviewers were instructed to pass on information whenever they could, and to encourage informants to apply for additional benefits or appeal if there seemed to be grounds, *prima facie*, for doing so. There were at least ten households which subsequently applied for, and obtained, supplementary benefit, and at least twenty-five families gained additional payments as a result of asking for an account of an assessment, appealing against an assessment, or applying for an 'exceptional circumstances addition' or an 'exceptional needs grant', as they are known administratively. There may have been others about whom we did not subsequently learn. A number of cases were also taken up on behalf of interviewers by those in charge of the survey. The correspondence describing one such case is given in full in an annex to this chapter (except for one or two cuts and inconsequential changes to conceal identity), to illustrate the different issues that can arise.

The Conflicting Functions of the Supplementary Benefits Scheme

In support of other evidence,[1] the correspondence brings out how difficult it is for staff to apply Supplementary Benefits Commission rules in practice (embodied as they are in the voluminous unpublished A and AX codes); how easy it is for mistakes to be made; how strenuously the commission itself, its senior officials and its area managers, endeavour to apply the rules of the organization in what they consider to be a rational, dignified and humane way while remaining conscious of (and some would say unduly influenced by) unbridled and erroneous expressions of antipathy towards claimants on the part of many in the press and among the public; and how vainly allowances are adjusted to any, even crude, assessment of real need. Most importantly, the correspondence illustrates the conflict between the social control and poverty alleviation functions of the Supplementary Benefits Commission whereby the exercise of 'discretion' becomes self-deceiving.

Management tends to be governed more by the need to safeguard public expenditure, control abuse and ensure conformity to social norms than generously

1. In recent years perhaps the best illustrations are to be found in the exchange between David Donnison, the chairman of the S B C (from 1 October 1975), and Michael Hill, David Bull, Ruth Lister and Frank Field in *Social Work Today*, 1975–6.

to meet poverty. Thus, it is implicitly assumed that people have to be motivated towards work and self-help, and rents paid regularly, and that men must be obliged to maintain their wives and children, and women to honour the ties of formal marriage. In spite of some impulses to the contrary, the organization will tend to *delay* payment, or will underpay.[1] It will impose repayments unnecessarily or impose them over unnecessarily short periods. The payment of additional grants or allowances will more often be the result of intense pressure than of anticipatory action, and, at least for those under pensionable age, will be withdrawn unless that pressure is kept up. In other words, the commission as an organization will tend to revert to form – that is, acting more in conformity with established institutions and the views of the majority of the population than of the minority of claimants.

In the case of the Thackens (see the annex at the end of this chapter, pages 850–59), the weekly allowance was increased, and an exceptional needs payment of £30 was made in 1968. But no further lump-sum payment was made until 1972 – despite the appalling problems which any visit to the family would have disclosed – and in that year we found that the additional allowance for Mr Thacken's dietary needs was no longer being paid. This is, of course, only one unusually well-documented instance, but it is a particularly illuminating one, which might be backed up by the accumulated experience of organizations like the Citizens' Rights Office of the Child Poverty Action Group. When challenged about particular families, the commission will often respond in conformity with its poverty alleviation functions and will appear to take individual need into account. But unless the situation can be watched, it may revert to one more in conformity with principles of parsimony and control. A different example of the tendency for extensions of welfare to be impermanent is the fact that decisions of Supplementary Benefits Appeal Tribunals cannot be treated as setting precedents.[2]

Summary

This is the first of two chapters which discuss the function and success or failure of means-tested schemes in alleviating poverty. The supplementary benefits scheme is the largest of the many schemes. The chapter suggests that the scheme exists as much to control behaviour in conformity with what is regarded as

1. This can arise not only from difficulties, because of staff shortages, in administering prompt payments, but also from discrepancies between published and unpublished rules, for example the published S B C Handbook and unpublished A code. See Healy, P., 'Three Ways in which the Social Security System Misleads Claimants', *The Times*, 28 June 1976.
2. 'The law they have to administer leaves them with wide, problematic and in some areas ambiguous discretionary powers. Each tribunal is isolated from the rest, there is no second tier appeal structure and thus no body of decisions which can be referred to' – Bell, K., *Research Study on Supplementary Benefit Appeal Tribunals*, H M S O, London, 1975 p. 20.

desirable socially as to meet need. Prior to 1966, independent and government research studies had revealed that there were substantial proportions of the elderly and other groups in the population who were eligible for national assistance but not receiving it. The Social Security Act 1966 and the substitution of supplementary benefits for national assistance was believed by the government to have greatly reduced these proportions, but independent estimates had thrown doubt on official claims. Our evidence suggests that the number of people failing to claim benefit to which they were entitled was reduced by only about 75,000 (from a total conceded even officially as being in excess of 1 million).

The income units in the sample which were dependent on supplementary benefit corresponded closely in number and type with expectations based on administrative statistics in the reports of the Supplementary Benefits Commission for 1968 and 1969. But 4·4 per cent of the people in the sample, representing 2,430,000 people (comprising 410,000 children, 1,315,000 people aged 65 and over and over 700,000 other adults), seemed on the basis of a careful check to be eligible for but not receiving benefit. Further research in four poor areas, Belfast, Glasgow, Neath and Salford, where follow-up visits were paid to those found on the basis of an initial interview to be eligible for benefit but not receiving it, largely confirmed these estimates. Around half the eligible old people lived alone and not with relatives. Many of the younger families were not temporarily in poverty but had been living on a low income for the whole of the previous twelve months.

Some people did not realize that they might still qualify for help if they lived with relatives, had savings or an occupational pension, or had part-time earnings. Certainly there are severe problems in acquainting potential applicants with information about the conditions of benefit. Some people were discouraged by the procedures involved in making an application, and the waiting and questions to which they would have to submit. Others wanted to maintain their independence or to avoid the shame of pleading poverty. Their feelings were shared to a lesser extent by a substantial minority of those who received such benefits. They said they were embarrassed to receive this assistance, and some had grounds for seeking an 'exceptional needs grant' or an 'exceptional circumstances addition' but were reluctant to press their claims.

Since the survey was carried out, a more pronounced distinction has been made between 'ordinary' and 'long-term' rates of benefit. This is perhaps the most important development in the scheme. By and large, the long-term rates are paid after two years receipt of benefit, except to those who have to register for work. Retirement pensioners, however, are eligible for the 'long-term' rate from the date of their retirement. In 1974, the ordinary rate for a single householder (including rent) expressed as a percentage of *net* average earnings was 34·6, and the long-term rate was 43·5, compared with 38·6 and 41·6 respectively in 1968. In 1974, the corresponding rate for a married couple with four children (two aged under 5 and two aged between 5 and 10) was 67·2, and the long-term rate 73·6, compared with respectively 70·4 and 72·7 per cent in 1968.[1] The ordinary rate declined in relation to earnings, and the long-term rate improved slightly. However, the total number of claimants in Britain increased by 43,000 between these two years, and the total number of recipients and dependants from 3,995,000 to 4,092,000. The number of sick and disabled people with national insurance benefit declined, and the number of unemployed increased. Other changes could be listed. But, in coverage and level of provision in relation to other incomes in society, the scheme can be said to remain substantially the same as it was in 1968. In broad outline, at least, the survey conclusions would seem therefore to apply to the mid 1970s and not only the late 1960s.

Annex to Chapter 24

A man and woman in their mid thirties were visited in Salford. They had three young children. He was an epileptic and was suffering from a brain haemorrhage as well as a peptic ulcer. His wife had recovered from tuberculosis and suffered from bronchitis. Two of the three children had been ill for long periods in the recent past. They had all lived in poverty or on the margins of poverty for some years, and the house had been condemned. Certainly the roof let in water, and the back yard, into which everyone had to go to reach the W C, was a quagmire in rainy weather. (The name and address of the family below have been changed.)

26th April 1968

To The Manager
Supplementary Benefits Commission
SALFORD

(Copy also to the Permanent Secretary of the Supplementary Benefits Commission)

Dear Sir,
    You may be aware that at the present time a research team from Essex University and the London School of Economics, under the direction of Professor Abel-Smith and myself, are carrying out a survey of standards of living in Salford. This is, in fact, part of a national survey. Although social work is not the responsibility of our interviewing officers, we occasionally feel a moral duty to help certain families. Usually the interviewer can deal with this himself or herself but I should like to obtain your advice about Mr George Thacken and his family, of 14 Mulford Street, Salford. Mr Thacken has given us permission to approach you and any other body on his behalf. Mr Thacken is chronic sick and has been off work for more than six years. In exploring his resources we find that his total income from you (including rent paid) is £14·80p. This does not appear to include the automatic allowance of 45p for a person who has been sick for two years or more. I also wonder whether there is not a case for an additional discretionary allowance. As far as we can discover, Mr Thacken, who is in his mid 30s, suffers from both epilepsy and a clot on the brain and his life expectation may be unfortunately short.

1. *Hansard*, 13 February 1976, cols. 423–4.

The final point I should like to raise is the question of single grants. I understand that a grant of about £4·50 was made for shoes as well as a previous similar grant in the year for some other purchase. The living conditions of this man, his wife and his three young children are very bad and they are extremely short of furniture and other essentials. There does seem to be a *prima facie* case for a much more substantial single grant.

> Yours faithfully,
> P. T.

8th May, 1968

> Ministry of Social Security
> Salford West Area Office

Dear Sir,

Thank you for your letter dated 26th April, 1968 regarding Mr George Thacken, and his family of 14 Mulford Street, Salford.

Unfortunately we have not been able to see Mr Thacken at his home, to date, in order to investigate his circumstances, but we hope to deal with this matter in a day or so, and I will let you have a reply in due course.

> Yours faithfully,
> H. Grundy
> Manager

23rd May, 1968

> Supplementary Benefits Commission
> Ministry of Social Security
> LONDON E C 4

Dear Professor Townsend,

Thank you for sending me a copy of your letter to our local Manager about Mr George Thacken of 14 Mulford Street, Salford.

As you know the, Manager has arranged for Mr Thacken to be visited to see what additional help can be given and he will be writing to you direct about this. I understand, on the main point in your letter, that the long-term addition of 45p has been allowed in calculating Mr Thacken's Supplementary Allowance, and I have asked the Manager to let you have a detailed explanation of how the allowance is calculated.

> Yours sincerely,
> Donald Sargent
> (Permanent Secretary)

4th June, 1968

> Ministry of Social Security
> Salford West Area Office

Dear Sir,

With reference to your letter dated 26th April, 1968, regarding Mr George Thacken and his family of 14 Mulford Street, Salford, we have now looked into his circumstances and I am able to let you have the following reply.

I understand that the Secretary of the Commission has advised you that a detailed explanation of the calculation of Mr Thacken's supplementary allowance will be given to you and this information is furnished hereunder.

Weekly income taken into account

	£	p
Sickness benefit	9	90
Family allowance	1	60
Total to be taken into account	11	50

Weekly Requirements	*Amount* £ p
Claimant and wife	7 05
Children Age	
Christopher 7 years	1 50
Harriett 9 years	1 50
George 13 years	1 85
Long-term addition	0 45
Rent allowance	2 61
Total	14 96
LESS total to be taken into account	11 50
Supplementary allowance entitlement	3 45

You will see from the details overleaf that the long term addition of 45p has been allowed in the calculation, and that Mr Thacken's weekly requirements have been brought up to a total of £14·95p by the payment of supplementary allowance of £3·45p.

I must point out, however, that at the time of your survey the total weekly income was in fact £14·80 as mentioned in your letter, and the reason for this difference was that Mr Thacken agreed to a weekly deduction of 15p in order to repay an excess of benefit which he had drawn. This matter has been cleared up and he now receives a weekly supplementary allowance of £3·45p.

It has been possible to make grants to cover the cost of new clothing, and some other urgent needs, and steps are now being taken to provide a modest amount of necessary furniture.

Yours faithfully,
H. Grundy
Manager

24th June, 1968

To The Manager
Ministry of Social Security
Salford West Area Office
(Copy to Sir Donald Sargent)

Dear Mr Grundy,
    I very much appreciated your courtesy in writing such a full letter about the circumstances of Mr George Thacken. I am very glad indeed that you have found it possible to make grants to cover the cost of new clothing and some other urgent needs, including furniture. On the basis of the information I have, I am sure this is most justified.
    I must confess that there are still two points which make me uncomfortable. You mention that the sum of 15p per week was deducted as repayment of 'an excess of benefit which he had drawn'. While not knowing all the circumstances resulting in this deduction, I wonder whether such a step really is necessary with families living in such poverty as that of Mr Thacken. If an excess of benefit is ever given through some misunderstanding or some mistake on the part of an officer serving the Ministry, I am sure that the right principle would be to impose no repayment. The only instance which might give rise to doubt is one where an applicant knowingly gives false information. I would like to be assured that this was the case and whether Mr Thacken was informed of the deduction and was offered the opportunity of appealing against the decision. There must be many instances when members of your own staff and staff of offices elsewhere believe that applicants have consciously witheld information but where in practice they may be simply confused by official procedures and forms.
    The other point which disturbs me is that although Mr Thacken did in fact receive the 'long-term addition' of 45p he did not receive any additional discretionary sum. I would have thought that if ever there was a family which deserved to receive a regular additional discretionary amount, that family was Mr Thacken's. But this, as you must know, raises in question the whole problem of how the introduction of the long-term addition of 45p has changed, or ought to have changed, the Ministry's policy over discretionary payments.

Yours sincerely,
P. T.

27th June, 1968

Ministry of Social Security
Salford West Area Office

Dear Professor Townsend,
    Thank you for your letter dated 24th June, 1968, regarding Mr Thacken.
    I will look into this case with particular reference to the points you raise and will let you have a reply as soon as I am able.

Yours sincerely,
H. Grundy
Manager

9th August, 1968

Ministry of Social Security
Salford West Area Office

Dear Professor Townsend,

Thank you for your further letter of 24th June about Mr George Thacken, of 14 Mulford Street, Salford.

To enable me to clarify the first point in your letter, I should explain the Ministry's position in connection with the recovery of overpayments of supplementary benefit. Under the Ministry of Social Security Act 1966, the Ministry is entitled to recover the full amount of any excess expenditure incurred due to a person's failure to disclose a material fact. The Supplementary Benefit (Claims and Payments) Regulations provide that recipients of supplementary benefit must report information, for example, about changes in their circumstances 'at any office or place as the Commission may direct.' This is explained in notes included in the order-book, which set out the changes to be reported to the address given in the book. Mr Thacken's wife ceased work on 13th April, 1967 and this led to an increase in the dependent's sickness benefit for his wife (£2·50). He did not, however, report the change to the Supplementary Benefits Office until 16th June, 1967, and as a result he was overpaid supplementary benefit for the period 14th April 1967 to 18th June 1967. I should explain that whereas only £1·95 per week of Mrs Thacken's earnings were offset against the family's requirements in calculating the supplementary allowance paid to Mr Thacken the full dependant's sickness benefit for her would be taken into account. Normally the Ministry seeks recovery in cases such as this only where the claimant has either some disregarded income or readily available capital and, clearly, since Mr Thacken possessed no such resources the decision to seek recovery was incorrect. (In answer to the question in your letter on appeal rights, when Mr Thacken signed a form of undertaking to repay, this included a paragraph drawing his attention to his right of appeal under section 26(2) of the Act, but he did not exercise this right.)

When the decision to require the payment was recognized as being contrary to the normal practice, the deduction from benefit was stopped. By that time, £6·75 had been recovered and this fact was taken into account, among other considerations, in making the grants for clothing and furniture, to which I referred in my previous letter. The grants made for these purposes totalled £29 and there was also a payment to clear some rent arrears and to provide the family with a supply of coal (they had previously been buying coal in very small quantities at correspondingly high prices).

I can confirm that the Ministry would not normally seek to effect recovery when an overpayment of supplementary benefit was due entirely to an error on the part of a member of the Ministry's or other Government Department's Staff.

Finally, you comment on the fact that no discretionary sum over and above the long-term addition was allowed in the calculation of Mr Thacken's supplementary allowance. As you will know, the long-term addition was one of the major innovations of the Supplementary Benefits scheme and was intended to provide a margin, over and above the basic scale rate, to meet special expenses. Where the long-term addition is not payable or is insufficient to cover all the special expenses a person, or his dependants, may have, the supplementary benefit can be increased. On the information we had about Mr Thacken's circumstances, and those of his family, it appeared that any special needs were more than covered by the long-term addition but when I called at the home following receipt of your earlier letter Mrs Thacken mentioned for the first time that her husband also suffered from stomach trouble but did not take a special diet. In his own interest, I thought it best that I should have a word with his doctor, who told me that a peptic ulcer had been diagnosed and that Mr Thacken had been recommended to follow a special diet. He had, however, failed to collect the diet sheet. I therefore advised Mr Thacken to obtain his diet sheet forthwith and I have increased his supplementary allowance to enable him to meet the extra cost involved. On medical advice, the Commission take the extra expense of a diet for peptic ulcer as being 62½p a week. In Mr Thacken's case, 45p of this is provided by the long-term addition and a further addition for the balance of 17½p has been made. This has the result that, after rounding his allowance to the nearest 5p, he receives an extra 20p a week.

Yours sincerely,
H. Grundy
Manager

10th September, 1968

To The Ministry of Social Security
Salford West Area Office

Dear Mr Grundy,
    Thank you for your further information about Mr Thacken. There are a number of very disturbing points about this case, most of which affect Ministry policy rather than local administration. Although your recent inquiries have resulted in both a small increase in the weekly allowance and the payment of a lump sum, I am not sure that justice has been done.
    First, you mention that recipients must report changes in their circumstances and that Mr Thacken did not for some weeks report that when his wife ceased work, he received an increase in sickness benefit of £2·50 for a dependent wife. I find it rather astonishing for you to suggest that the responsibility for notifying a change *always* rests with the recipient. Mr Thacken might be entitled to assume that one half of the Ministry will know what the other half is doing. After all, sickness and supplementary benefit are both paid by the same organization.
    Secondly, you say that Mr Thacken was overpaid supplementary benefit for the period 14th April, 1967 to 18th June, 1967. This covers about nine weeks. Taking into account the £2·50 extra sickness benefit as against £1·95 of the wife's earnings deducted from the calculation of the family's requirements, he seems to have been overpaid around 55p per week. I would be grateful if you could confirm the details because if the amount were as low as this, then the total overpayment during the nine weeks would be about £5 – as against the sum of £6·75, which you say was 'recovered'. Irrespective of the error in seeking repayment, it seems that no check was made to ensure that too much was not repaid.
    Thirdly, you admit that 'the decision to seek recovery was incorrect'. It would follow that Mr Thacken should be reimbursed and should also receive an apology. Instead you

say the fact 'was taken into account' in making a grant for clothing and furniture. The two matters are clearly distinct in principle. Putting right the wrongful recovery of money is one thing; making a payment for need is another.

Fourthly, you say that a form signed by Mr Thacken, undertaking to repay, contained a paragraph drawing attention to his right to appeal. May I ask whether in all such cases the individual's right to appeal is specified *verbally* by officers of the Ministry? We make a mockery of individual rights unless the Ministry ensures they are called properly to the attention of persons in poverty – particularly since so many are sick, disabled or old.

Fifthly, the additional allowance of only 17½p for a special diet is absurd. You say that the introduction in 1966 of the long-term addition of 45p was to meet special expenses. This appears to deny the *general* need of those who have been sick for two years or more or who are retired for a higher rate of subsistence. There is an argument from equity which might be discussed publicly. Two men who have been off work sick for over two years will both receive the long-term addition of 45p. Yet if one has the additional expense of a special diet (which you acknowledge to be 62½p per week) you pay him only 17½p more than the other man. Moreover, in Mr Thacken's case I would ask most seriously whether there is not still a case for a further discretionary allowance, beyond that for a special diet?

Finally, I would be grateful to know the itemization of the grants which you say amount to £29. It would seem that about £22 was made available for clothing and furniture for a family of five.

Yours sincerely,
P. T.

30th September, 1968

Salford West Area Office
Salford

Dear Professor Townsend,

Thank you for your further letter dated 10th September, 1968, regarding Mr George Thacken.

I regret the delay in this acknowledgement, and wish to inform you that the matter is receiving attention.

Yours sincerely,
H. Grundy
Manager

18th November, 1968

To Ministry of Social Security
Salford West Area Office

Dear Mr Grundy,

I would be most grateful for any observations you care to make on my last letter of 10th September concerning Mr George Thacken.

Yours sincerely,
P. T.

21st November, 1968

> Ministry of Social Security
> Salford West Area Office
> Salford

Dear Professor Townsend,
  Thank you for your letter of 18th November 1968, concerning Mr George Thacken. I am very sorry that you have not yet received a full reply, and hasten to explain that in view of the questions you asked, I referred the matter to my Headquarters at London for consideration, and understand that they will be replying to you direct very shortly.

> Yours sincerely,
> H. Grundy
> Manager

16th December, 1968

> Supplementary Benefits Commission
> Department of Health and Social Security
> LONDON WC2

Dear Professor Townsend,
  You have been in correspondence with Mr Grundy, the Manager of our Salford West Office, about the case of Mr George Thacken, of 14 Mulford Street, Salford. Your most recent letter, of 10th September, raises, as you know, a number of points which concern Departmental policy and I have therefore been asked to reply. I am sorry that I have been unable to do so sooner.
  Your first comment related to the need for a claimant to report changes in his circumstances. Mr Grundy explained the provisions of the Regulations on this point and pointed out that the position is set out in some detail in the notes which the claimant is asked to read in the order-books sent to him. The claimant is requested to report changes of circumstances to the office from which the order-book was issued. Where he is in receipt of more than one benefit, and these benefits are controlled by different offices, the claimant may in practice report a change of circumstances to one office only, but it is reasonable then to expect him to give details of the various benefits he is receiving. The procedures which are followed within the Department are designed to ensure that, where possible, information reaches other offices which are known to have an interest in a case but, bearing in mind the many different benefits and pensions paid by the Department, not all of which are controlled by local offices, this is not always practicable and it is necessary to rely on reports from the individual claimant. In Mr Thacken's case, the local office which paid his sickness benefit did in fact notify the supplementary benefit office – though unfortunately somewhat belatedly – that the sickness benefit had been increased. As a result, he was interviewed right away and he then provided information about the termination of his wife's employment.
  Your second point concerned the amount by which Mr Thacken was overpaid and I do agree that there was a miscalculation. The position has been looked at again and the information on which the assessment was based has been checked in detail to ensure that

the calculation of the overpayment is correct. As a result it has been found that Mrs Thacken's earnings increased during the period and it is now calculated that the overpayment of supplementary allowance was £7·70 in respect of a period from 20th March, 1967, to 18th June, 1967. This overpayment arose for two reasons: initially because Mr Thacken did not tell the local officers that his wife's earnings had increased and subsequently because, as you know, she ceased work and the additional sickness benefit which became payable was not taken into account. A detailed week by week account of how the overpayment arose is attached to this letter.

On your third point, the Department has the right under the Act to recover any overpayment which arises because, whether fraudulently or otherwise, a person misrepresents or fails to disclose any material fact. However, where an overpayment arises in circumstances similar to those in Mr Thacken's case, a refund is normally invited only where the claimant is in a position to repay, e.g. has income which is disregarded, or savings. The refund in Mr Thacken's case was contrary to our normal practice and Mr Grundy himself apologized for this mistake when he visited Mr Thacken on 8th May last. Although I agree that it was only right and proper that this apology should have been given, it does not follow that a repayment should have been made to Mr Thacken. There was, as I have said, a statutory right to recover the money and Mr Thacken had refunded less than he had been overpaid. But because the refund had been made during a separate and subsequent period it was likely that this had contributed to the need of clothing; the question whether to repay the money he had refunded was therefore considered with the decision to award a lump sum for exceptional needs over and above the weekly benefit to meet this situation. If the £6·75 had been refunded a correspondingly smaller lump sum payment would have been necessary – because the need would have been smaller – and the overall result would have been the same.

With regard to your fourth point, which concerned the right of appeal, where a claimant agrees to refund an overpayment he not only sees, and signs, the undertaking which includes a statement concerning the right of appeal in the event of dispute, but he also retains a copy of the form.

We could not undertake to inform the claimant verbally, on every decision which carried a right of appeal – if only because so many of these decisions are issued in writing, but, as in the case of the undertaking signed by Mr Thacken, each notice does explain that the claimant has this right.

In answer to your fifth point I must first of all make it clear that the purpose of the long-term addition is not to provide a higher rate of basic subsistence. The addition is paid in recognition of the fact that people who qualify for it are likely to incur additional expenses, for example, on account of their age or illness. The addition is a means of providing for these, mainly small, expenses as and when they arise without the detailed specific inquiries which were necessary under the former national assistance scheme and which were often a source of embarrassment, particularly to the elderly. The taking into account of the long-term addition when the need for exceptional circumstances additions under paragraph 4 of Schedule 2 to the Act comes into question is laid down in paragraph 4 itself – the situation has been made clear on many occasions since the new supplementary benefits scheme started for example in the Ministry of Social Security Annual Reports for 1966 (pp. 55–56) and 1967 (page 57), and is also referred to in explanatory leaflets. Where, however, there is reason to think that a person's special expenses may be greater than 50p (the current rate of the long-term addition) our officers do, of course, make full inquiries about the actual expense so that any necessary addition can be given. In Mr Thacken's case, we have accepted that he incurs additional expense (now of 67½p a week) on account of his special diet and we have always been prepared to consider any other specific item which leads to necessary additional expenditure.

You asked, finally, to know the items covered by the lump sum payments. These amounted in total to £29 (and I am sorry that it had been suggested to you that this amount did not include the provision for fuel and rent arrears). Of this £29 payment, £2·50 was spent on second-hand furniture, £1·57½ on a stock of fuel, £3·42 on rent arrears and 50p on four pillowcases. Of the remainder, Mr Thacken spent £18·52 on clothing and obtained trousers, shoes, a raincoat, a shirt and two pairs of socks for himself; a dress and two pairs of shoes for his wife; and five pairs of socks, two pairs of trousers and four pairs of shoes for his children; in general the items purchased were somewhat cheaper than had been envisaged by our local officers. There was a balance of £2·49 unspent and Mr Thacken was advised to use this in connection with the cost of repairs to a broken window. Now that the family possess an adequate amount of clothing it should be possible for them to provide replacements from their weekly income.

I am afraid that I must end this letter on an unhappy note. We have been paying benefit to Mr Thacken on the basis that his wife has not worked since April 1967; he had signed statements about his circumstances on a number of occasions since then, including one on 1st May, 1968 in which he stated specifically that his wife was not employed and had no income apart from family allowances. We have discovered, however, that Mrs Thacken had resumed work prior to May 1968 and it is necessary that our officers should now investigate the extent of this overpayment and the circumstances in which Mr Thacken failed to advise the Department of this material change in his financial position.

Yours sincerely,
N. M. Hale

25

The Failure of Means-tested Benefits

In addition to supplementary benefits, which is the principal means-tested scheme in the United Kingdom, there are more than forty other means-tested schemes. There are higher education awards; schemes for exemption from prescription charges, dental charges and optical charges; free welfare milk and foods; free school meals; rate rebates; rent rebates; local charges for residential accommodation for the elderly and handicapped and homeless; local charges for home help, meals, day nursery, chiropody, convalescent and family planning services; school uniform and clothing grants; and maintenance allowances. Local authorities tend to vary in the way they administer some of these schemes, and even the kind of means test they apply. This chapter will show how far people living in poverty take advantage of these schemes, and in a long final section will attempt to go on to explain, and therefore to add to the discussion in the previous chapter, why some people do not receive benefits for which they are eligible.

In 1968, the government spent £421 million on supplementary benefits but the following was spent on other means-tested benefits: free school meals, about £25 million; rate rebates, £15 million, local authority rent rebates, £18 million, free welfare milk and food £7 million.[1] There were a variety of other schemes, some of which cost very little by national standards. Thus, in 1970–71, the Department of Employment made 300 grants costing £10,000 to severely disabled people to provide special aids for employment; paid 180 disabled people an allowance to assist exceptional expenses in travelling to work at a cost of £29,000; and made ten grants to disabled people to help them start a small business at a total cost of £2,000.[2]

Free School Meals

Each local authority administers a government scheme making school meals free for children of parents receiving supplementary benefits or parents whose income

1. See written answers to parliamentary questions, *Hansard*, 3 and 5 August, 3 and 9 December 1971.
2. Written answer to a parliamentary question, *Hansard*, 16 November 1971, col. 90.

is below certain limits laid down in national regulations. The limits are revised regularly, normally when supplementary benefit scales are increased. On 24 July 1967, Mr Patrick Gordon Walker announced a package of government decisions which included an increase from 5p to 7½p in the price of a school meal (from April 1968) as well as an increase in family allowances. He admitted that the government was anxious about parents who did not take up their entitlement. Later that year, a Department of Education and Science circular was sent to local-education authorities pointing out that some people failed to apply because of fear of identification of children who received free meals in the classroom. At the same time, a circular issued by the Scottish Education Department called attention to the humiliating practices adopted by some authorities. The department advised against handing out specially coloured tickets and said that, 'in no case should pupils receiving meals free be required to enter the dining-room by an entrance other than that used by paying pupils, to sit at separate tables, or to receive different meals'.[1] Whether from embarrassment or lack of information, many parents had failed to apply for free meals. A survey carried out by the Ministry of Social Security and published in 1967 showed that, in 1966, two thirds of the children of fathers in full-time work who were taking school meals were entitled to them free but were paying for them.[2] Mr Gordon Walker then sent a circular letter to all parents of school-children, reminding them that it was possible to apply for free school meals, and giving the income limits. A tear-off slip allowed potential applicants to get further information with a minimum of fuss. Although publicity had already resulted in a marked increase in numbers applying for free school meals, the circular letter had a marked initial effect. A similar exercise in May 1970 was marred by the omission of the tear-off slip.[3] The numbers for each year in England and Wales and Scotland are given in Table 25.1. The increase in 1968 is partly attributable to the temporary provision for free meals for all children in large families, irrespective of income (withdrawn from April 1969), and also to the raising of the income exemption limits. The increase in 1971 is partly attributable to a further proportionate increase in the exemption limits. But the rises in price of school meals led to a sharp reduction in the number and percentage of children taking school meals, by no means all of it temporary. Thus in England and Wales the number taking meals fell from 5,148,000 (or 68 per cent) in September 1970, to 4,161,000 (or 54 per cent) in May 1971.[4] With the exception of 1968, when the annual census was taken at the time of an influenza epidemic, a lower percentage of pupils in England and Wales than

---

1. Quoted in Lynes, T., 'The Dinner Money Problem', *Poverty*, No. 10, Spring 1969, p. 13.
2. Ministry of Social Security, *Circumstances of Families*, H M S O, London, 1967, p. 29.
3. Lynes, T., 'The Failure of Selectivity', in Bull, D. (ed.), *Family Poverty*, Duckworth, London, 1971.
4. Written answer, *Hansard*, 5 July 1971.

Table 25.1. *Numbers and percentages of school meals which are free.*

Year	England and Wales		Scotland[b]	
	Free meals	Percentage of pupils in attendance receiving free meals	Free meals	Percentage of pupils in attendance receiving free meals
1967	404,000	5·8	65,000	n.a.
1968	841,000[a]	11·7	65,000	8·3
1969	594,000	8·0	140,000	16·3
1970	627,000	8·3	96,000	11·3
1971	805,000	10·3	97,000	11·1
1972	850,000	10·7	144,000	16·6
1973	795,000	9·7	137,000	15·3
1974	750,000	9·1	130,000	14·0
1975	784,000	9·3	122,000	13·0

NOTES: [a]Including free meal to fourth and subsequent children in family irrespective of family income.
[b]Census in January in each year.

SOURCES: *Hansard*, 29 July 1975, col. 359, and 26 February 1976, col. 328; private communication, Scottish Education Department.

in Scotland received free meals. This may be due to there being more families with low incomes in Scotland, or higher take-up rates, or both.

Although the income levels up to which families are eligible to receive free school meals have broadly corresponded in the past with the supplementary benefit scales, the two sets of scales are by no means coincident. Thus, supplementary allowances but not allowances for school meals vary according to the age of each child. Again, disregarded earnings and hire-purchase commitments are treated differently in the two schemes. In the summer of 1968, a family with three children at school qualified for free school meals if family income after deducting rent and rates, fares to work, national-insurance contributions and the first £2 of the mother's earnings was less than £12·65p a week. The comparable allowance from the Supplementary Benefits Commission, however, varied according to age of school-children from £10·80p to £14·95p. In October 1972, the figures were £20·40p a week and from £16·35p to £23·95p a week respectively. There are therefore two separate and uncoordinated means tests. Some families with a net income up to 20 per cent larger than the supplementary benefit for which they would become eligible if unemployed or sick, none the less qualify for free school meals for each child. Conversely, some families with a net income up to 20 per cent smaller fail to qualify for free school meals for each child.

Although the regulations governing the administration of free school meals do not lay down a definite period over which weekly pay should be averaged to determine eligibility, in practice, local education authorities usually work on the basis of four or five weekly pay-slips, or two months for monthly paid workers. Therefore, parents whose income over the year as a whole is below the minimum scales may find their children ineligible for free school meals at times when earnings are relatively high. Parents are also under the obligation to inform the local education authority if their circumstances change. The local education authorities have a free hand in deciding the period of the award of free school meals. Usually there is a review twice a year when new application forms are issued to all families in which children are receiving meals free. Thus, not only are parents subjected to a means test at least twice yearly, but for many of them the meals represent an uncertain source of indirect income. The introduction of provision only for an annual review irrespective of changes in circumstances in April 1973[1] reduced this uncertainty – but only at the possible cost of making it less fair for that large number of families whose income fluctuates around the margins of eligibility.

Table 25.2 presents the two important sets of data about school-children in

Table 25.2. Percentages of children in different household income groups who have or do not have school meals.

Children attending school	Net disposable household income last year as % of supplementary benefit scales plus housing cost							All
	Under 100	100–19	120–39	140–59	160–99	200–99	300+	
Pays for school meals	33	44	56	50	66	66	68	58
Free school meals	52	30	16	20	1	0	2	12
Total school meals	85	75	72	69	68	66	70	70
Has meals at home	11	22	27	27	23	25	24	24
Has meals with relative	0	2	0	0	2	2	0	1
Takes sandwiches	3	1	1	2	4	6	5	4
Buys meals out	0	0	0	0	2	0	1	1
Total	100	100	100	100	100	100	100	100
Number	61	79	151	154	233	206	81	965

1. *Hansard*, 6 November 1972, col. 625.

low-income households – those not having meals and therefore either going home or taking sandwiches, and those receiving meals free. Altogether only 70 per cent of school-children get meals at school. The correlation according to income is not at all marked. Proportionately more of the poorest children have meals at school, but there are still 15 per cent who do not. Another 33 per cent of the poorest children pay for meals. Thus, only half the children in the poorest families get meals free at school.

In some respects, Table 25.2 and other tables using net household income in the previous year as a criterion may under-represent take-up by poor families of means-tested benefits, but also in some respects may over-represent take-up. These limitations must be briefly listed. As already indicated, some families classified as having incomes under 100 per cent in Table 25.2 will include children all of whom are in their teens but, because supplementary benefit scales for teenagers are higher than the corresponding meals scales, will not be eligible for free school meals, whereas some classified as having incomes of between 100 per cent and 120 per cent, all of whom have only very young children, will be eligible to receive meals. Unlike the supplementary benefits scheme, the school meals scheme is based on a means test making no allowance for the higher costs of bringing up older children. Secondly, income is calculated for the household as a whole rather than for each income unit. This is one reason why some households with an income, say, of more than 40 per cent in excess of the basic supplementary benefit scales are none the less receiving school meals free. Thirdly, the incomes of some households are irregular. Some with a low income for the year as a whole may have increased their income in, say, the past two months. Conversely, some with a high income for the year will now have tumbled to a very low income. We found that the numbers in these two groups tended to balance out, but that the means-tested scheme suffers seriously from 'assessment lag'. Thus, of all the children who were having school meals and who also were in poverty or had recent experience of poverty, 46 per cent were in families in poverty or on the margins of poverty both in the week preceding interview and for the year as a whole, but there were another 54 per cent from families in, or on, the margins of poverty, *either* in the preceding week *or* for the year as a whole. In the survey, none of the children in families tumbling the previous week into poverty or to its margins were yet receiving school meals free. All of them were still paying for meals. That is a significant finding. Finally, during the year of the survey, eligibility levels for free school meals were raised twice,[1] supplementary benefit scales were increased once, the price of school meals was increased, and from April 1968 (but for one

1. In the summer of 1968, a child in a one-child family qualified for free school meals if net family income, including family allowances, and deducting fares, rent and rates, national insurance contributions and the first 40s. of any of the mother's earnings, was less than £9.15p per week, and from October 1968, £9.75. Corresponding figures for each child in two- and three-child families were £11.10 and £11.60 and £12.65 and £13.45 respectively.

year only) all children in families with four or more children were entitled to free school meals irrespective of income.

It would be difficult to make adjustments for all the factors listed above. Since Table 25.2 is based in substantial part on incomes received prior to the introduction in October 1968 of new supplementary benefit scales, it slightly underestimates the numbers in the lowest income groups.[1] And because four-child families no longer became entitled automatically without means test to free school meals, the numbers of poor children getting free meals was in this respect higher than the numbers in subsequent years.

For these reasons, the proportion of children in the poorest income group found in the survey to be receiving school meals free will be high relative to the true figure in recent years, which therefore gives a more favourable impression of the efficiency of means tests than other criteria. Thus, the equivalent proportion of *all children who are eligible* (including all those in income groups close to the eligibility ceilings) and *of children in families whose incomes are low in a particular week rather than in the year as a whole* would be smaller. But the data none the less provide a basis for analysis and discussion.

Table 25.3 deals just with children having meals at school. Altogether, 17·4 per cent were found not to be paying for them. This figure compares with the figures of 16·8 per cent for England and Wales and 17·2 per cent for Scotland given in official censuses.[2] Only 61 per cent of the children in the poorest income group were getting meals free.[3] They comprised only just over a quarter of all children

Table 25.3. Percentages of children in different household income groups who receive free school meals.

All children taking school meals	Net disposable household income last year as % of supplementary benefit scales plus housing cost			All
	Under 100	100–39	140+	
Free	61·6	28·5	8·4	17·4
Pays	38·4	71·4	91·5	82·5
Total	100	100	100	100
Number	52	168	463	683

1. See Chapter 7, pages 274–80, for a discussion of possible adjustments.
2. *Hansard*, 14 July and 3 December 1971.
3. This was in spite of the big upsurge in claims in early 1968. The authors of a government survey carried out in 1966 concluded that, of the children having school meals, only just over 60 per cent of those who were eligible to receive them free did so. Among the children of men in full-time work, the figure was only 34 per cent. See *Circumstances of Families*, HMSO, London, 1967, Table III, 10, p. 29.

getting meals free. Indeed, a third of children receiving meals free were in households with an income more than 40 per cent above the basic supplementary benefit scales. We were also able to examine the situation of children in families actually receiving supplementary benefits, and in families of the sick and unemployed who were eligible for supplementary benefits, when both groups had meals at school. Only 86 per cent of the former and 54 per cent of the latter were receiving free school meals. This pattern applies to 1968 and the early part of 1969, and neither the official statistics about free school meals nor subsequent studies offer evidence which would lead to substantial modification. For example, a small-scale study in Islington in 1971 found that only 68 per cent of households eligible for free school meals were receiving them.[1]

We also checked the relative incomes of the households in which the children having meals at school lived. When household income in the previous year was expressed as a percentage of the mean for its type, only 49 per cent of children in households with an income less than 80 per cent of the mean were found to be having meals free.

Government estimates that between 80 and 85 per cent of children who are entitled to free school meals are receiving them must be treated with extreme scepticism.[2] These and similar estimates for other means-tested benefits seem to be inflated for the following reason. Estimates are based on the numbers and types of household found in the Family Expenditure Survey to have 'normal' incomes below particular levels. The results are then compared with the numbers receiving free meals, free welfare milk, allowances and so on. But the latter include income units with relatively low incomes in households with relatively high total incomes. They include households whose incomes are no longer low and whose eligibility for benefit may have been judged six months or more sooner. They also include households in which a child may recently have left school and so have 'lost' the right to entitlement for a second child.

There is one further point about take-up of free school meals. Fifteen per cent of children in the poorest households, and altogether 24 per cent of all children in poverty or on the margins of poverty, do not have meals at school, whether paid or free. Although some of these live in areas in which the schools lack facilities, and some of their parents actively prefer children, perhaps because there are younger children in the family, to come home for dinner, there is no doubt that some would get meals at school if they were an automatic right. This point is too often neglected in discussions about take-up.[3] Many going home will be adequate-

1. Meacher, M., *Rate Rebates: A Study of the Effectiveness of Means-Tests*, Poverty Research Series No. 1, 1972, Child Poverty Action Group, London, p. 22.
2. *Hansard*, 16 November 1971, col. 115. See also *Hansard*, 6 August 1975, col. 141.
3. There has been considerable discussion of the effect of changes in price on the number of children taking school meals, but not of the consequential effects on uptake of free meals. See, for example, Davies, B., and Reddin, M., 'School Meals and Plowden', *New Society*, May 1967.

ly fed, but, as one writer puts it, 'The question without an answer is how many children are there who are not well looked after and who may be having an inadequate diet?'[1] The withdrawal of free school milk, first for secondary children and then for school children aged 7 and over, and the further rise in the price of school meals are bound to sharpen this question.

We did, in fact, ask parents why their children did not have meals at school (see Q. 5C on page 1145). Altogether, 8 per cent said there were no facilities at school for meals, 10 per cent that meals were cheaper at home, 34 per cent that the children did not like the food, 7 per cent that the children did not have enough to eat (Table 25.4). Over a third gave other reasons. The bulk of these were ex-

Table 25.4. Reasons why children in families with different incomes do not have school meals.

Parent's reason why child does not have school meals	Net disposable household income last year as % of supplementary benefit scales plus housing cost		All children not having school meals
	Under 140	140+	
Does not like the food	19·1	38·3	33·6
Not enough to eat	11·8	5·3	6·9
No facilities at school	16·2	5·7	8·3
Cheaper at home	17·6	7·7	10·1
Other	35·3	43·1	41·2
Total	100	100	100
Number	68	209	277

pressed in terms of preference or nearness. Some parents said their children preferred to come home or go to relatives, or they preferred them to do so. Some said that the school was near by or it was convenient because they had to prepare a midday meal for themselves. Some felt they could ensure that the child had a proper amount or the right kind of food. One said her child had to have a weight-reducing diet. There were also parents who said their children attended school only for half the day, or came home because there was inadequate supervision at lunch-time, because the head believed the children should go home if the mother was not at work, and, in one case, because a child wanted to be sure that her mother was still at home.

That over a third of those not having meals at school disliked them is important. A survey of 772 meals in forty-eight infant, junior and senior schools has also thrown doubt on their size and nutritional value. On average, the meals were

1. Bender, A. E., 'Feeding the School Child', *Poverty*, No. 23, Summer 1972, p. 1.

two thirds of the size recommended. The average protein content was only just over half the target. In only four of the schools did the meals reach the calorie target set by the Department of Education and Science.[1]

Significantly more of those with incomes below or on the margins of the supplementary benefit scales than substantially above those scales, namely 18 per cent compared with 8 per cent, gave as the reason for their children not having meals at school that they were cheaper at home. Relatively more of them were said to have no facilities at school for meals, and relatively fewer were said to dislike the food.

When the families living in or on the margins of poverty are isolated, 32 per cent of the children aged under 10, 25 per cent aged between 10 and 14, and 34 per cent aged over 15 did not have school meals. Similarly, in households consisting of a man, woman and two children, 29 per cent of the children, but in households of a man, woman and four or more children and three adults with children, 33 per cent and 46 per cent respectively, did not have school meals.

After analysing different evidence, we concluded that it would be difficult to substantiate any claim to more than 60 per cent of school-children eligible for school meals at any particular time actually receiving them. Around half a million children in the United Kingdom can be said to be not receiving free school meals, though strictly eligible for them. Our estimates for 1968 varied from 450,000 to 700,000, depending on the assumptions made about the period of measurement of family income; numbers of children not taking school meals at all who would be able to take them, and would choose to take them if they were free automatically; and the time that would normally elapse after assessment and before any review.

Free Welfare Milk

Until April 1971, parents of children under 5 years of age could obtain a milk-token book which entitled them to one pint of milk at a cheap rate. In 1968, this was 4d. (or 1½p) a pint. Families receiving supplementary benefits or wages below particular levels were and remain eligible to get 'welfare' milk and foods free for each child under 5. Expectant mothers with a low income and low-income parents of a handicapped child aged 5–16, unable to attend school, could also obtain milk free. Like school meals, the means test is distinct from the test for supplementary benefits. The rules for assessing eligibility in the different schemes are uncoordinated. On 29 March 1967, about 195,000 of 215,000 children under 5 in families receiving supplementary benefits were getting free welfare milk and foods, but only about 4,800 under 5 among an unknown number eligible in wage-earning families were receiving such milk and foods.[2] The latter figure represented 1,000 *fewer* than the corresponding figure in November 1965, and not more than 4 per cent of eligible children in wage-earning families. By late 1970, the figure had

1. Bender, 'Feeding the School Child', p. 2.   2. *Hansard*, 3 July 1967.

scarcely changed.[1] In April 1971, provision for 'cheap rate' milk was abolished and the eligibility for free milk was greatly extended. Questions were asked in the survey about welfare milk. The answers show that two fifths of children in households with a net disposable income of less than the supplementary benefit level receive welfare milk free. But the proportion of all children said to be getting free milk was (at 13 per cent) between two and three times the figure suggested by administrative statistics. Some parents getting cheap milk had clearly misunderstood the question. Either they were simply reporting their dependence on the milk-token books, or they were confusing the question with free school milk. Beyond confirming the fact that the overwhelming majority of children in the families of the low paid who were entitled to free welfare milk were not getting it, the data cannot unfortunately be analysed in detail.[2] Our information suggests that, at that time, at least 450,000 children were eligible for free welfare milk, of whom the great majority were not receiving it. In 1970, it was officially estimated that 340,000 families were eligible, of whom less than 1 per cent were claiming.[3]

Although the introduction of the family income supplement scheme, with automatic entitlement to free milk on the part of those receiving benefits and heavy advertising in 1971 and 1972, greatly improved take-up, the figures have not been maintained. Up to the time of writing, it certainly remains doubtful whether as many as a quarter of the children eligible for free milk are receiving it.[4]

Educational Maintenance Allowances

The 1944 Education Act empowered local authorities to pay allowances to parents with low incomes whose children were staying on at school beyond the minimum age. Each authority makes its own definition of need, and varying amounts tend to be paid for children aged 15, 16 and 17. The scheme is very small, costing about £1¼ million a year in the late 1960s and reaching only about 20,000 children. Local authorities vary widely in the income limits which they apply.[5] A Ministry of Education Working Party recommended new scales of a £55 maximum grant

1. There were 1,500 *families* claiming free milk. *Hansard*, 1 December 1970.

2. The same problem arose in a survey undertaken by the Ministry of Social Security. 'An appreciable number who were clearly not entitled to free welfare milk said they were receiving it. It seems likely that these families were receiving welfare milk tokens but that they answered the question whether they were getting the milk free, or paying for it, incorrectly . . . The analyses did suggest, however, that very few families with fathers in full-time work were receiving free welfare milk' – *Circumstances of Families*, HMSO, London, 1967, p. 28.

3. Field, F., *An Incomes Policy for Poor Families*, Poverty Pamphlet No. 14, Child Poverty Action Group, London, 1973, p. 2.

4. Excluding families receiving supplementary benefits and family income supplement, the number claiming free milk increased to 84,000 in November 1971, but by November 1972 had already fallen again to 43,000, and during 1975 has varied between 10,000 and 12,000. See *Hansard*, 25 March 1975, col. 289.

5. See, for example, Reddin, M., in *Social Services for All?*, Fabian Society, London, 1968.

at 15, £65 at 16 and £75 at 17,[1] but in 1957 the minister reduced their figures to £40, £55 and £65. No local authority adopted generous scales, and in some areas parents whose income is too high for them to qualify for an educational maintenance allowance for a son or daughter of 17 find that in the following year, with identical income, the son or daughter may qualify for a maximum grant of £875 (1976-7) for students away from home other than in London. Research into the administration of educational maintenance allowances by others has revealed some of the anomalies characteristic of means-tested benefits in general. Whereas recipients of supplementary benefit in some local authorities are automatically entitled to maintenance allowances, working families with the same net incomes are not. Calculations of income for the purposes of assessment are inconsistent. Since there is no right of appeal, this finding is of particular importance.[2] A report of the Parliamentary Expenditure Committee in 1974 recommended that educational maintenance allowances should be mandatory and should be administered by local authorities like free school meals for the benefit of families in financial need.[3] Not until May 1976 did the Secretary of State respond and declare (on the 11th of that month in Parliament) that he could not 'contemplate any immediate action'. But in 1978 a small pilot scheme was announced.

In the survey, parents of children aged 14-18 were asked whether they had heard of educational maintenance allowances. Children of 14 were included, though not strictly eligible, because we wanted to find whether such allowances were known to their parents who were expected to advise their children whether or not to leave school at the minimum leaving age. Only 15 per cent of the parents of 14-year-olds, and only 33 per cent of the parents of 15- to 18-year-olds, had heard of these allowances. Parents of 15- to 18-year-olds were then asked whether they had applied for such an allowance. As Table 25.5 shows, only 2 per cent were found to have applied successfully (and only 1 per cent were currently receiving a maintenance allowance). Nearly as many again had applied unsuccessfully. As many as 80 per cent of parents of children of this age in the sample who were living in households in poverty or on the margins of poverty had not heard of educational maintenance allowances, and another 18 per cent had not applied. This compares with 63 and 32 per cent respectively in households with higher incomes.

No accurate information about educational maintenance allowances for years before 1971 exists. Early in that year, a special inquiry was carried out by the Department of Education and Science, which found a total of 20,121 pupils in

1. Report of a Working Party on Educational Maintenance Allowances (The Weaver Report), H M S O, London, 1957.
2. See Drabble, R., 'Education Maintenance Allowances', Poverty, No. 24, 1972, pp. 7-8; and Reddin, M., Where?, No. 72, September 1972.
3. Third Report from the Expenditure Committee, Session 1974, Educational Maintenance Allowances in the 16-18 Years Age Group, HC 306, H M S O, London, 24 July 1974, p. xii.

Table 25.5. *Percentages of parents of 15- to 18-year-olds with different income who had heard of, and applied for, educational maintenance allowance.*

Whether heard of educational maintenance allowances	Net disposable household income last year as % of supplementary benefit scales plus housing cost		All parents of 15- to 18-year-olds
	Under 140	140+	
Not heard	80·4	63·0	66·9
Heard, applied unsuccessfully	0·0	2·6	2·0
Heard, applied successfully	1·8	2·6	2·4
Heard, not applied	17·9	31·7	28·6
Total	100	100	100
Number	56	189	245

England and Wales for whom maintenance grants were being paid.[1] This compares with an equivalent estimate produced from the sample of 20,000. The results of the census, which up to the time of writing had not been repeated, showed that the average amount paid per pupil in that year differed widely – for example, from £123 in East Sussex, £117 in Wiltshire and £118 in Hillingdon, to £21 in Merthyr Tydfil, £18 in Burton-on-Trent and £26 in Harrow. Similarly, the number of pupils receiving awards as a percentage of all pupils over school-leaving age varied greatly – for example, from 16·6 per cent in West Suffolk and 14·0 per cent in Durham, to 0·4 per cent in Reading and 0·7 per cent in Barnet. In some authorities, a relatively high number of pupils receiving awards corresponded with low average amounts (e.g. in Harrow, 182 pupils received an average of £26) while, in others, relatively high amounts were given to fewer pupils (e.g. at Hillingdon nineteen pupils received an average of £118). Thus if pupils were lucky enough to qualify for an award, they could not be sure, depending on where they lived, that the amount would be sufficient to ensure that they were not still in considerable financial hardship. We estimated that if proportionately as many children in the country as a whole as in the top ten authorities received allowances, then the number in current payment would be at least six times as many, and that if the allowances were also as high as in the top ten authorities, then expenditure on educational maintenance allowances would be between £15 million and £20 million instead of £1¼ million.

School-uniform Grants

Local authorities are also empowered to pay school-uniform grants for children in their secondary schools (and for children holding free places in direct-grant

1. Written answer, *Hansard*, 16 June 1972.

schools). No information exists about the numbers in the country as a whole who receive grants. In principle, there is immense scope for such grants. A series of questions were asked in the poverty survey. We found, first of all, that just under two thirds of all primary and secondary school-children attended schools which had a school uniform. As Table 25.6 shows, the proportion varied from under a third of children in poor households to over two thirds of children in relatively prosperous households.

Table 25.6. Percentages of children in households with different income who attended schools having a school uniform.

Whether school has uniform	Net disposable income last year as a % of supplementary benefit scales plus housing cost			All households
	Under 100	100–39	140+	
No	69·0	45·2	33·2	38·8
Yes	31·0	54·8	66·8	61·2
Total	100	100	100	100
Number	58	219	566	843

We then asked whether parents knew that it was possible in many areas to apply for uniform grants. A minority did so (Table 25.7). Most of these were middle class. When we pursued the question of uniform grants with the parents of secondary school-children who were expected to wear uniforms, we found that

Table 25.7. Percentages of parents, with low and middle or high incomes, of children at secondary schools requiring uniforms who had heard of and received school-uniform grants.[a]

Whether parent had heard of school-uniform grants	Net disposable household income last year as % of supplementary benefit scales plus housing cost		All parents
	Under 140	140+	
Heard, received	2·9	0·3	1·0
Heard, no grant	42·2	49·0	47·3
Not heard	54·9	50·7	51·7
Total	100	100	100
Number	102	306	408

NOTE: [a]No scheme in Northern Ireland; therefore data are for Britain only.

only 1 per cent had received such a grant in the previous year, half of them from a local education department, and half from the Supplementary Benefits Commission. They represented only 40,000 children in the population. Some were not strictly living in poverty, though they may have been at the time of assessment. Half were middle class. Of the parents with incomes below the poverty line, 76 per cent of those with children at secondary schools which required uniforms had not heard of uniform grants and 39 per cent were actually receiving supplementary benefits. We estimate that there were 300,000 children in households with a net annual disposable income of below or just above the supplementary benefit scales who attended schools requiring uniforms. There is no evidence, then, that local authorities have even begun to provide the service envisaged in the Education Act 1944.

Rate Rebates

Following the work of the Allen Committee, the government introduced a rate rebate scheme in 1966.[1] Tenants paying rents which include rates, as well as owner-occupiers, can apply to the local-authority treasurer if their income does not exceed a particular level. In October 1968, this was £9 *gross* a week for a single householder and £11 *gross* a week for a couple, averaged over a twenty-six-week period preceding each half-year when the rates are due. The limit was raised by a further £2 a week for each dependent child.[2] Like the school-meals scheme, the benefits under this scheme are not coordinated with supplementary benefit levels. Eligibility does not, for example, depend on the age, but only on the number of children. Unlike the school meals scheme, however, there is the further anomaly in that a family with a high rent finds it no easier to qualify for rebate than a family with a low rent. Thus one family with three children and a high rent, for example, might qualify comfortably for free school meals but not rate rebates, while another family with the same number of children and an identical income, but with a lower rent, might not be eligible for either. Elderly people with low housing costs could qualify for rebates even when they are not eligible for supplementary benefit (the figure of £8, or £9 from October 1968, for a single householder, comparing with the supplementary allowance of £4·30 per week, or £4.55 from October 1968, plus an average rent of under £2). By contrast, few working families with incomes *above* supplementary benefit levels are eligible. Not only are national insurance contributions and any taxes paid counted as part of income, but such families tend to be paying higher rents or mortgage payments, and in the case of children in their teens, the supplementary benefit scales are higher than the flat-rate allowance in the rebate scheme. In 1966–7, the number

1. Report of the Committee of Inquiry into the Impact of Rates on Households (The Allen Report), Cmnd 2582, H M S O, London, 1965.
2. Before October 1968, the rates were £8, £11 and £1.50 respectively.

of ratepayers in England and Wales receiving rebates was just over 1 million, and the average amount for the year was £13·80.[1] In 1967–8, the average rebate was £15·65 (at a total national cost of £12·3 million).[2] As many as 88 per cent were believed in one town to be wholly or mainly retired.[3] Subsequent reports showed a decline in the numbers obtaining rebates, despite increases in the income limits.[4]

Table 25.8 confirms the fact that relatively more owner-occupiers than tenants have rebates – proportionately four times as many among those in poverty and on the margins of poverty. Even when households receiving supplementary bene-

Table 25.8. *Percentages of owner-occupier or tenant households in different income groups who were receiving rate rebates.*[a]

Type of tenure	Net disposable household income last year as % of supplementary benefit scales plus housing cost						All households	
	Under 100		100–39		140+			
Council and private tenants	5·7	*(6·3)*	3·5	*5·5*	1·3	*1·4*	2·3	*2·6*
Owner-occupiers	*(23·3)*	*(28·6)*	19·7	*20·8*	3·6	*3·4*	7·5	*7·3*
Tenants and owner-occupiers	12·4	*15·7*	9·3	*12·4*	2·5	*2·5*	4·8	*5·1*
	Numbers in sample							
Council and private tenants	70	*48*	255	*146*	535	*505*	860	*699*
Owner-occupiers	43	*35*	142	*120*	613	*609*	798	*764*
Tenants and owner-occupiers	113	*83*	397	*266*	1,148	*1,114*	1,658	*1,463*

NOTE: [a]Percentages and totals in italic exclude *households* receiving supplementary benefit.

fits, because their rates are covered in the payments for housing costs, are excluded, the disparity remains as large. In the survey, 74 per cent of those receiving rebates were owner-occupiers. The proportion of expenditure on rebates going to owner-occupiers is probably higher than this. There are therefore substantial numbers not receiving rebates who are eligible for them. The number of house-

1. Written answer, *Hansard*, 13 July 1967.

2. Department of the Environment, *Handbook of Statistics* (Local Government, Housing and Planning), HMSO, London, 1970, p. 5.

3. Written answer, *Hansard*, 27 October 1967. The tendency for the retired to make most use of the scheme is discussed by Nevitt, A. A., 'How Fair are Rate Rebates?', *New Society*, 10 June 1971; Bradshaw, J., and Wicks, M., 'Where Have all the Rate Rebates Gone?', *Poverty*, No. 15, 1970; and Legg, C., 'Will Rent Rebates be Claimed?', *Poverty*, No. 23, 1972.

4. See, for example, *Rate Rebates in England and Wales 1968–69*, HMSO, London, 1969; and *Rate Rebates in England and Wales 1971*, HMSO, London, 1971.

holds receiving rebates was found to correspond broadly with national administrative totals – and was equivalent to over 800,000 households in the population as a whole.[1] We estimated, after subtracting income units ineligible for rate rebates because they were dependent on supplementary benefits, that approximately 1,350,000 other households (comprising about 2¼ million people) were eligible for rebates but had not applied for them. This was higher than government estimates.[2] They included over 200,000 owner-occupiers and 800,000 tenants who were eligible for supplementary benefits but were not receiving them, and about 50,000 owner-occupiers and 250,000 tenants who were dependent on employment income.

Within the sample were 268 people in income units who were eligible for, but not receiving, supplementary benefits. All or nearly all of these could have claimed rate rebates. Only 19 per cent were in households actually receiving rate rebates, the figure being much larger for individuals in owner-occupied households (35 per cent) than for those in rent-paying households (5 per cent).[3] A detailed study in a London borough in 1971 found a very small proportion of eligible householders actually receiving rebates. An expensive advertising campaign increased the number by under 10 per cent, and 'still left three-quarters or even four-fifths of those entitled not claiming'.[4]

Rent Rebates

A number of local authorities operated rent-rebate schemes for several years before the 1972 Housing Finance Act, which introduced a national scheme of rent rebates. Eastbourne, for example, started one in 1956, but other authorities not until 1968 or 1969. These varied in scope, and the local authorities were free to determine the income limits. Almost all the local-authority schemes affected council tenants only. Table 25.9 gives a number of examples for 1968.

In the poverty survey, families in council accommodation, who accounted for over a quarter of the total sample, were asked whether the council had a differential rents or rebate scheme. Roughly a quarter of tenants could not say whether

1. The number of rate rebates awarded in England and Wales fell from 932,000 in 1966–7, to 786,000 in 1967–8, 792,000 in 1968–9, 808,000 in 1969–70, and 814,000 in 1970–71 – written answer, *Hansard*, 6 December 1971. Compare also the figure of 4·8 per cent of householders receiving rebates (Table 25.8) with the Department of the Environment's figure of 5·1 per cent for England and Wales alone for 1967–8. See *Handbook of Statistics*, p. 5.
2. In a Commons debate on 29 June 1968, the Joint Parliamentary Secretary to the Ministry of Housing estimated that the number of eligible households was 1½ million for England and Wales.
3. If expressed in terms of households and not individuals, then only 47 per cent of owner-occupiers and only 8 per cent of tenants who were eligible for, but not receiving, supplementary benefits received rate rebates.
4. Meacher, *Rate Rebates*, p. 45.

there was such a scheme, but 60 per cent said there was. They represented about 9 million people in the population as a whole. Seven per cent, equivalent to about 1 million, said their rent was reduced or they received a rebate. They comprised 360,000 households, or 320,000 if those among them who were also recipients of supplementary benefits and who had, presumably mistakenly, suggested they received a rent rebate, are excluded. This total corresponds with independent estimates. Thus the Institute of Municipal Treasurers and Accountants estimated that, in March 1968, there were 283,000 in England and Wales, and in March 1969, 298,000.[1]

Table 25.9. Selected local authorities operating rent rebate schemes (March 1968).

Local authority	Total amount of rebates granted (£)	Date scheme introduced	Number receiving rebates	Average amount of rebate granted (p)
Carlisle	5,596	Apr. 1957	729	16
Exeter	600,853	May 1965	7,443	159
Grimsby	1,425	Oct. 1964	73	34
Newcastle-upon-Tyne	75,688	Oct. 1967	4,075	36
London:				
Camden	348,000	Apr. 1965	6,969	97½
Kensington and Chelsea	293,800	Apr. 1966	3,235	175
GLC	317,992	Oct. 1965	4,526	64
Colchester	21,060	Apr. 1967	620	69
Rugby	3,066	Dec. 1967	92	57½
Truro	33,643	Apr. 1966	908	76
Margate	2,241	Apr. 1956	329	13

SOURCE: Institute of Municipal Treasurers and Accountants, 1968.

The receipt of rebate was found, not surprisingly, to correlate with income. But three points need to be registered (Table 25.10). First, although only 4 per cent of those with incomes substantially above the state poverty line were receiving rebates, they accounted for a third of the total recipients. Secondly, the proportion of people not knowing whether the council operated a rebate scheme was significantly higher at the lowest than at the highest levels of income. Thirdly, even discounting people not knowing whether there was such a scheme, the numbers not receiving rebates in areas where they operated them were very high. This remains true even when households receiving supplementary benefits are omitted from the tables. As the figures in brackets show, there are substantial proportions

1. The figures are slightly underestimated because Norwich, Oxford, Enfield, Greenwich, Neath, Yeovil and Abergele, for example, were not included. See Institute of Municipal Treasurers and Accountants, *Housing Statistics*, London, 1967–71.

Table 25.10. Percentages of people in council accommodation with different income who receive rent rebates.[a]

Relationship to council rent rebate scheme	Net disposable household income last year as % of supplementary benefit scale plus housing cost						All council tenants	
	Under 100		100–39		140+			
No council scheme	17·3	(16·4)	10·6	(7·7)	12·0	(14·1)	13·2	(12·3)
Scheme, rent reduced	11·2	(3·3)	12·4	(13·2)	3·7	(3·5)	7·0	(6·3)
Scheme, applied not reduced	1·0	(0·0)	5·7	(6·2)	3·9	(4·0)	4·3	(4·4)
Scheme neither applied nor reduced[b]	29·6	(42·6)	40·9	(43·4)	54·5	(54·9)	48·5	(51·0)
Not known if there is a scheme	40·8	(37·7)	30·3	(29·5)	23·8	(23·6)	27·0	(26·0)
Total	100	100	100	100	100	100	100	100
Number	98	(61)	491	(403)	942	(911)	1,531	(1,375)

NOTES: [a]Figures in brackets exclude recipients of supplementary benefits.
[b]Including 2, 2 and 12 respectively who did not know whether there had been any reduction or application.

of the two lowest income groups who say there is a scheme in their areas but have neither applied for a rebate nor been considered for one. Very approximately, it seemed that less than a third of those eligible for rebates in 1968–9 were getting them. This estimate is reinforced if we consider only the households in the sample who were found to be eligible for supplementary benefits but not receiving them in areas operating rent-rebate schemes. Only a fifth of people eligible for supplementary benefits and not receiving them were getting rent rebates. The remainder represented about 400,000 people (in 135,000 households) in the United Kingdom population. Since the national scheme was introduced, there has been some improvement in the council sector, but very little in the private sector.[1]

Option Mortgage Scheme

The option mortgage scheme was just beginning to operate when the survey was carried out. Owner-occupiers were asked whether they intended to apply. Intro-

1. 'Take up of rent rebates is much higher than that of rent allowances, though still a long way from the Conservative Government's original assumption of 100 per cent take up. During the first half of 1975, 70–75 per cent of those eligible were receiving a rent rebate, but only 30–35 per cent of eligible unfurnished tenants, a rent allowance. The most recent figure for furnished tenants is for 1974 when it was estimated that only about 10 per cent of those eligible were claiming' – Lister, R., 'Take-up: The Same Old Story', Poverty, No. 34, Summer 1976, pp. 5–6.

duced by the Housing Subsidies Act 1967, the scheme is designed to help people with low incomes who are buying their own homes. By taking an option mortgage, a family will normally have the rate of interest on capital outstanding reduced by 2 per cent. But entitlement to tax relief on interest is lost, and once in the scheme a borrower cannot leave it for five years, and only then in exceptional circumstances. Conditions are complex, but as a rough rule of thumb, families paying less than £80 a year in tax stand to gain by opting into the scheme. On the other hand, if they are young and their incomes rise after two or three years, they may find they derive less benefit than they would have done by remaining outside the scheme and claiming tax relief in the ordinary way. Strictly there is no test of means, but since the 'net' beneficiaries must be people in the scheme whose incomes are below a particular level (which is above the minimum taxable level), the scheme's effectiveness has to be judged in much the same way as means-tested services. The scheme began to operate from 1 April 1968. In the subsequent year, about a tenth of mortgages were option mortgages.[1] Nearly three quarters of option mortgages obtained from building societies in 1968 were for mortgages under £5,000; 84 per cent of borrowers had incomes below £1,400 per annum and 70 per cent below £1,200. A quarter were under 25 years of age, and one fifth

Table 25.11. *Option mortgages as a percentage of all building society and local-authority mortgages in Great Britain, 1968–72.*

Year	Option mortgages as % of mortgage advances on all types of dwellings by building societies		Option mortgages as % of all loans to private persons for housing purchase by local authorities	
	Percentage[a]	Number	Percentage	Number
1968[b]	8·9	20,737	15·8	3,135
1969	6·3	28,931	12·4	2,387
1970	6·5	35,175	12·8	5,558
1971	8·6	56,826	12·9	6,175
1972[c]	17·0	27,370	17·0	2,080

NOTES: [a]Average of quarterly percentages.
[b]3rd and 4th quarters only.
[c]1st quarter only.

SOURCE: Department of Environment, *Housing Statistics* (Great Britain), Nos. 16, 20, 23, 24 February 1970, February 1971, November 1971, February 1972.

1. Between April 1968 and March 1969, the number of people granted option mortgages, expressed as a percentage of all people obtaining mortgages, was 6 per cent among owner-occupiers, 11 per cent among private tenants, and 11 per cent among council tenants, the average amounts being £2,485, £2,592 and £2,389 respectively. See Department of Environment, *Housing Statistics*, 14, p. 78.

between 25 and 34. The highest proportion of option mortgage advances from building societies (38 per cent) was in the Northern, Yorkshire and Humberside and North-West regions, compared with 4 per cent in Greater London and Wales and 2 per cent in Scotland.

In the sample, 1 per cent of owner-occupiers were planning to apply or had applied, and another 0·5 per cent were uncertain. The number of potential claimants was equivalent to over 50,000 households in the population as a whole.[1] As Table 25.11 suggests, this figure is close to the actual number arranged in 1968 and the early months of 1969. However, in the sample, none of the group who probably stood most to gain from the scheme – owner-occupiers with incomes below the supplementary benefit rates – were planning to apply. The applicants were mostly in the lowish though not lowest income groups.

Explanations of Under-use

How can both the failure to apply for means-tested benefits and the variation in take-up be explained? We began to ponder this question in Chapter 24. Some factors will be common to every type of benefit, but others will be particular to certain types of benefit. In public discussion, references have been made for generations to pride, the shame of pleading poverty, ignorance of entitlement, lack of clear information and difficulty of making claims in explaining failure to come forward for benefit. While each of these deserves examination, they are expressed in such an unconnected way that attention is diverted to the shortcomings of clients from the organization and functions of means-tested schemes in society. Explanations have generally been unhelpful, becoming fragmented and individual-centred. The functional unity of the scheme or schemes has gone relatively unexamined. For example, attention has been concentrated on the difficulties people have in understanding application forms or their ignorance of conditions of eligibility. Implicitly or explicitly, their lack of education and intelligence is treated as paramount. So the policy solution is restricted in the short term to improving methods of communication, simplifying the presentation of rules and exhorting the poor to apply. Pious hopes are expressed about improving and extending educational services in the long term and strengthening popular beliefs in the values of hard work, thrift and self-help. Yet is there not something self-defeating about a scheme which can be understood or managed only by the well-educated, or which is based on rules which rigidly assume that incomes and social conditions are stable and that the opportunities to obtain paid employment are uniform? May not the shame of pleading poverty for substantial sections of the population have something to do with administrative treatment of claimants or the attitudes adopted by the media and the public towards them? And may not

1. Subsidy payments in Britain amounted to £9·2 million in 1969–70, and were estimated to be £13·5 million for 1970–71 and £15·6 million for 1971–2. See *Hansard*, 26 November 1970.

the pride which prevents or delays the retirement pensioner from applying for supplementary benefit and the parent from applying for free school meals be a necessary product, not only of the conduct expected of individual members of British society as a whole, but of the structure and values of the means-tested schemes themselves?

The general hypothesis of this chapter is that the denial or difficulty of access to resources is inherent in all means-tested services and explains under-use. The services are devices which mediate conflicting political claims for severity, on the one hand, and generosity, on the other, in the treatment of particular groups of poor people in different educational, economic and social contexts. They are essentially devices which ration and control. There is a *general* discouragement to use means-tested services which is built into their operating rules and administration by a society which sets great store by self-help and thrift. And there are specific conditions attached to the receipt of benefit which are more stringently applied to some groups than to others. Therefore the denial of access to resources operates differentially, affecting some groups more than others, and this explains some differences of uptake *within* services as well as *between* services. But under-use of some services is explained less in terms of social discrimination against, or in favour of, particular groups, than as half-hearted gestures to public recognition of need, pulling against restrictions on public expenditure demanded by taxpayers, ratepayers and a precedent-conscious bureaucracy. Very important is the fact that the rules framing eligibility themselves reflect values approved by society of residential stability, probity of marriage and the family, regular work, prompt payment of debt and conformity in general with the social order. People who live rough, disrespect marriage, do not send their children regularly to school, are particular about the kind of employment they will accept, are in arrears with their rent, dress unusually or otherwise behave unconventionally will tend to be deprived of the benefits of means-tested services, even though the process by which this happens is indirect.

Fundamental to the denial of access to resources is therefore the conflict, almost a contradiction, in means-tested services between their poverty-alleviation functions and their implicit social-control function. In every service there is an uneasy and fitful compromise between these two. The sociologist has scarcely begun to document the consequences of this conflict. It can, of course, be examined historically as well as contemporaneously, and distance from events can sometimes help us to understand the less benevolent aspects of the social services. Thus the 1834 Report on the Poor Laws is unambiguous. 'The great object of our early pauper legislation seems to have been the restraint of vagrancy.'[1] The report traces the legislation of the 15th century which required beggars who were unable to work to go to the hundred where they last lived and not beg outside that hun-

1. Report from His Majesty's Commissioners for Inquiry into the Administration and Practical Operation of the Poor Laws, B. Fellowes, London, 1834, p. 6.

dred. The legislation of the 16th century introduced compulsory charity, but the motive for its establishment was the desire to 'repress vagrancy'. The Report of 1834 itself adopted a restrictive approach, recommending the abolition of outdoor relief and the application of the workhouse test to the able-bodied. The development of policy has been governed at critical points of history less by unconditional motives of generosity towards the poor than by unbending concern for their moral good, with efforts being made to control, if not prevent, their deviance and shepherd them into unquestioning conformity with economic and social values.

There are historical phases when first one and then the other gains ascendancy. Impulses towards greater generosity are succeeded by impulses towards parsimony and control. Thus, there has been a continuing growth of concern about the needs of the elderly since the 1950s, and there were sweeping proposals both for a national superannuation scheme and an 'income guarantee' which appeared to be blocked in the mid 1960s by a mixture of economic, political and administrative objections, and the Government instead switched direction, passed the Social Security Act 1966 and established the Supplementary Benefits Commission. An attempt was made to put the principal means-tested scheme into new clothes. Inevitably it reduced the momentum in favour of an extension of universal benefits. Subsequently the increase in unemployment and the mounting hostility against immigrants and Welfare State 'scroungers' encouraged the government in a series of measures to restrict benefits for the unemployed (for example, in introducing the four-week rule and the Social Security Bill 1972) and appoint the Fisher Committee on the 'abuse' of social security benefits, notwithstanding the much more widespread and financially significant evidence of tax evasion. It could, in fact, be argued that the 'scrounger' of the late 1960s and early 1970s was a 'folk devil' created by society in moral panic, in the sense developed by Cohen.[1] Contemporary Britain remains within the grip of this restrictive mood, despite simultaneous efforts to extend and improve the income rights of such minorities as retirement pensioners, disabled people and one-parent families. There is also a parallel tendency for proposals to be made – for example, the guaranteed maintenance allowance for one-parent families proposed by the Finer Committee (discussed in Chapter 22, pages 778–81), and negative income tax and tax credit schemes – which appear at first to meet the major objections to existing means-tested schemes, but which, once they are examined and put into operational form, reproduce some of the major disadvantages of those schemes.

Some contemporary writers recognize the control functions. In the United States, for example, surprising authority has been found for the belief that public assistance is a degrading process in which 'various forms of coercion may be used to impose conditions on recipients of aid. Recipients may be harrassed by in-

1. Cohen, S., *Folk Devils and Moral Panics: The Creation of the Mods and Rockers*, MacGibbon & Kee, London, 1972.

vestigators, and their private lives may be exposed to governmental scrutiny seldom found in an open society.'[1] One critic concluded that American public assistance programmes sought (a) to relieve a segment of the deserving very poor at a minimum level of subsistence, and for as short a time per case as possible; (b) to prevent the 'undeserving' poor from gaining access to the system; (c) to minimize the impact of the system on the taxpayer, because other public expenditures are preferred that show tangible gain to the taxpayers. But, more positively, the programmes sought to provide support for those who, for good and identifiable reasons, could not now support themselves, and to increase the labour force participation rate of 'employables'.[2] Others have developed at length the view that 'expensive relief policies are designed to mute civil disorder, and restrictive ones to reinforce work norms'.[3] But the poverty alleviation and control functions of means-tested services seem to be combined in more complex fashion than this thesis suggests. For example, increased expenditure may actually increase dissatisfaction and the likelihood of disorder because, depending on its form, it may increase, or fail to decrease, inequality. And when unemployment grows, a society may actually tighten the rules of eligibility for unemployment benefit, perhaps unconsciously to comfort itself that mass unemployment is attributable more to undeserving men than an inadequate industrial and economic system.

For the United Kingdom, how would the poverty alleviation and control functions of means-tested services be analysed? An attempt will be made here to illustrate rather than substantiate the thesis. The numbers of those receiving and eligible for means-tested benefits in the survey were relatively small. Exhaustive analysis, holding different variables constant, is not feasible. Instead, I shall attempt to show how resources come to be denied, first, fitfully at *regional and area* level, then by a process of social selection according to pattern of *socialization*, *type of family* and *class*.

Regional and area variation:

Some means-tested benefits are not administered through a regional tier. Those which are, such as supplementary benefits, can be shown to vary regionally in expenditure and take-up. But the regional distribution of other means-tested services also varies, and *prima facie* it seems difficult to explain all of such variation without hypothesizing a kind of 'competitive' or 'contagious' effect among groups of adjoining local authority areas. Table 25.12 shows that the distribution

---

1. President's Commission on Income Maintenance Programs, *Poverty and Plenty*, Government Printing Office, Washington, DC, 1969, p. 50.

2. Stein, B., *On Relief: The Economics of Poverty and Public Welfare*, Basic Books, New York, 1971, pp. 23–9.

3. Piven, F. F., and Cloward, R. A., *Regulating the Poor: The Functions of Public Welfare*, Tavistock, London, 1972, p. xiii.

of means-tested benefits does not correlate consistently with the prevalence of poverty.

Contrast, for instance, the regional variations in poverty between Northern Ireland and the North-West and Greater London and the South-East. There are marked differences in the extent to which regions receive different types of means-tested benefits, such as supplementary benefit, varying from 18 per cent of people in income units in Northern Ireland and 9 per cent in Northern, Yorks and Humberside to 5 per cent in the West Midlands and the South-East and 2 per cent for Anglia and the East Midlands; and rate rebates, where 7 per cent of households in Scotland compared with 2 per cent in the West Midlands received them. The survey results also showed significant regional variation in the proportion of people in income units eligible for but not receiving supplementary benefit (the regional average being 5 per cent). In Northern Ireland there were 12 per cent, North-West 7 per cent, Scotland 6 per cent, Greater London and the South-East 3 per cent, and Anglia and the East Midlands 1 per cent. As a general rule, the higher the proportions receiving supplementary benefits in a region, the higher the proportion eligible but not receiving them.

There was also marked variation between regions in the proportions of householders obtaining rate and rent rebates (Table A.102, Appendix Eight, page 1067). However, the smallish sample numbers in several regions, and the uneven distribution of councils operating rent-rebate schemes, may to some extent account for such variation.

Smaller areas show more marked variations still. That local differences in administration may affect outcome, irrespective of differences in the composition of their populations, is evident if statistical data for different local authorities are examined. Different pairs of authorities have been selected for purposes of illustration in Table 25.13. (The data for all local authorities are listed in Table A.105 in Appendix Eight, page 1070). Some of the differences between authorities in the proportions of children having free school meals is larger than anything that the occupations, household composition, unemployment rates or earnings of their populations would suggest. Attempts in other research to account for the variation in take-up have not found that poverty is strongly correlated.[1]

There was considerable regional variation in the survey of the proportion of children not having school meals at all. For example, in Greater London, there were 59 per cent of children not having school meals because they disliked the food, and 3 per cent because they thought there was not enough to eat; the respective figures were 31 per cent and 2 per cent for the South-East, 26 per cent and 8

---

1. 'Although the proportion of children taking free school meals is positively correlated with poverty, the proportion of the variance of the free school meals rate that can be explained by the poverty correlates (low social class, large families, overcrowding, high population density and poor housing amenities) is relatively small' – Davies, B., and Williamson, V., 'School Meals – Short Fall and Poverty', *Social and Economic Administration*, January 1968.

Table 25.12. Percentages receiving different types of means-tested benefit in different regions.

Region	Percentage of people in income units in poverty or on the margins of poverty[a]	Percentage of income units receiving supplementary benefits	Percentage of children having school meals who have them free	Percentage of households receiving rate rebates	Total number in regions — People in income units	Total number in regions — School-children having meals	Households
Northern Ireland	50	18	(66)	6	282	35	86
Scotland	37	8	34	7	623	68	188
North-West	36	6	17	6	678	86	238
South-West and Wales	34	6	7	6	665	85	231
Northern, Yorks and Humberside	33	9	18	6	702	89	237
West Midlands	30	5	7	2	810	123	254
Anglia and East Midlands	29	2	20	3	621	70	183
South-East	27	5	10	6	891	130	303
Greater London	27	7	21	5	806	96	286
All regions	32	6	18	5	6,078	782	2,006

NOTE: [a]Net disposable income last year below 140 per cent of supplementary benefit scales plus housing cost.

Table 25.13. Percentages of children having free school meals in selected local authorities.

Selected local education authorities	Free meals expressed as %	
	All pupils	All meals served
Devon	16·2	24·8
Buckinghamshire	4·0	6·8
Newcastle	27·1	47·1
Wolverhampton	8·6	17·6
Ealing	9·3	15·1
Havering	4·0	8·4
Caernarvonshire	25·2	36·0
Montgomeryshire	8·6	11·4
Aberdeen	8·2	41·6
Glasgow	19·0	64·1
England and Wales	9·9	18·3
Scotland	13·4	39·6

SOURCE: Written answers, *Hansard*, 5 and 13 July 1971.

per cent for Scotland, and 23 per cent and 5 per cent for the North-West. Furthermore, 19 per cent of parents of children not having school meals in Northern Ireland and 18 per cent in Anglia and the East Midlands, compared with none in the South-West and Wales, none in the West Midlands and 5 per cent in Greater London, said that there were no facilities for school meals.

There are even more extreme variations for other means-tested benefits. Table 25.14 shows that the number of educational maintenance allowances is sometimes three, four or even more times greater in some areas than in other, fairly similar areas.

Differences between areas are not just the reflection of the policies being followed by local chief administrators, and the relative generosity or parsimony of local councils. In the case of school meals, they are partly the consequence of action in the schools themselves, by teachers, sometimes with, sometimes without, the approval or guidance of educational administrators. A survey which was carried out by the Child Poverty Action Group in 1968, after methods of administration had been supposedly reviewed by all local education authorities, found that children receiving free meals were still marked out in many areas.

Collection of dinner money in the classroom still seems to be the general rule, and this in itself rules out complete confidentiality. Reports on 11 schools in the North-East shows

Table 25.14. Percentages of older pupils receiving educational maintenance allowances.

Area	Educational maintenance allowances as % of all pupils over school-leaving age
East Suffolk	4·3
West Suffolk	16·6
Sunderland	12·9
West Bromwich	1·8
Preston	14·1
Salford	3·0
Barnet	0·7
Harrow	6·2
Denbighshire	12·5
Flintshire	1·0
England and Wales	2·2

that class teachers are collecting the money in nine of them. The school secretary collects it in one of the other two, in conditions which should ensure secrecy – 'but the boys know the free dinner children'. In the eleventh school, the money is collected in class by teachers who are members of the National Association of Schoolmasters, and by the school secretary from other children: 'either way there is no confidentiality' . . . The mother of one free dinner child wrote: 'The thing is still not anonymous – the tickets marked with a cross are known to indicate non-payment. Teachers I have spoken to all over the city say that no matter what they do – put them first, last or in the middle when asking for money on Mondays – it is still known by the other children.'[1]

Further studies in 1974 and 1975 by the Child Poverty Action Group and some of its branches show that stigmatizing practices are still common.[2]

Socialization:

As children get older, and particularly after the onset of puberty, they adopt different attitudes to their roles at school. They behave more independently of their parents and no longer stay within the routine of home life. They begin sometimes either to escape from unquestioning conformity with school values or come into open conflict with them after a period of sullen acquiescence. Precocious adulthood is more common in the working than the middle class. But this may

1. Lynes, 'The Dinner Money Problem', p. 14.
2. Field, F., *The Stigma of Free School Meals*, Welfare in Action, Child Poverty Action Group, London, October 1974; *Hungry Children*, CPAG, Leicester, 1975; *Free School Meals*, Colchester Poverty Action Group, 1975.

be part effect as well as part cause. Lack of resources shape parental attitudes towards early leaving. Working-class parents often encourage their children to leave school at the minimum leaving age. But accelerated socialization into adult working-class culture may ease the psychological adjustment of a child to the experiences of wage labour at the age of 15 and offset any possible disappointment in school achievement. Expressive middle-class values and aspirations towards high educational achievement are fostered at school, particularly grammar schools, but to a differing extent a kind of counter-culture gradually becomes more widespread. Some older pupils react against treatment as children and, among other things, avoid wearing school uniforms when they can, smoke cigarettes, dodge school meals and abscond.

This is not peculiar to working-class children, of course. Society expects all boys and girls to take more decisions for themselves as they grow older – for example, how to spend their leisure time and, important in this context, pay for themselves. It is just a fact that the sheer lack of resources and the humiliations that have to be undergone in order to obtain some of them are more likely to be experienced by working-class children. There is a strong motivation towards independence and self-help. In the working class, it is important to remember, large numbers of boys and girls of 12 years of age and older earn small amounts delivering newspapers and serving in shops at weekends. It is natural therefore that, among older children, the stigma of claiming free meals becomes stronger.

Table 25.15. Percentages of children of different age having school meals.

Age	Net disposable household income last year as a % of supplementary benefit scales	Percentage having school meals	Percentage of those having school meals who have them free	Total number of schoolchildren
5–8	Under 140	73 ⎫ 68	38 ⎫ 18	108
	140+	65 ⎭	6 ⎭	222
9–11	Under 140	76 ⎫ 71	36 ⎫ 19	88
	140+	69 ⎭	11 ⎭	188
12–13	Under 140	(77) ⎫ 79	37 ⎫ 18	39
	140+	79 ⎭	11 ⎭	102
14–15	Under 140	(83) ⎫ 76	38 ⎫ 19	35
	140+	73 ⎭	10 ⎭	93
16+	Under 140	(80) ⎫ 65	(37) ⎫ 8	10
	140+	(62) ⎭	0 ⎭	50
All ages	Under 140	76 ⎫ 71	37 ⎫ 18	280
	140+	69 ⎭	9 ⎭	655

Parents of young children feel less shame in claiming free benefits on behalf of their children than they do for themselves. But some older children feel they have a much larger share in that decision and may directly and indirectly counsel avoidance or delay. It is not unreasonable to argue that they are denied, or at least discouraged from having, access to the resources of means-tested benefits by the barriers put up by society as a whole as well as by friends and by parents. Some recognize that to claim them is a kind of confession of failure, an acceptance of dependent and subservient status.

Table 25.15 shows that there is a tendency for the proportion of older pupils having school meals to fall after reaching a peak for children of 12 and 13 in secondary schools. There is little change up to the age of 15 in the proportion having school meals who have them free. However, our data depend on information supplied usually by the parents, and not by the pupils.

Type of family:

Irrespective of technical eligibility, resources tend to be steered towards socially approved groups and denied to others. School heads are empowered to let children have meals free until an official assessment can be carried out. Educational welfare officers assess some children leniently. Children being brought up by

Table 25.16. *Percentages of children in households of different type and income who were receiving school meals.*

Type of household	Net disposable income last year as % of supplementary benefit scales	Percentage having school meals	Percentage of those having school meals who have them free	Total number of schoolchildren
Man, woman and 1 or 2 children	Under 140	75 } 65	9 } 4	60
	140+	62	2	194
Man, woman and 3 children	Under 140	(75) } 74	(9) } 3	45
	140+	74	0	95
Man, woman and 4 or more children	Under 140	73 } 76	57 } 46	98
	140+	(82)	(25)	49
3 adults and children	Under 140	(81) } 74	(17) } 12	37
	140+	73	11	212
Other households with children	Under 140	(74) } 69	(77) } 37	47
	140+	67	15	99
All households	Under 140	75 } 71	37 } 18	287
	140+	69	9	649

women alone and children in large families are more likely to attract notice and concern. On the other hand, married couples with one child or two children are more likely to be regarded by the rest of society as being able to 'stand on their own feet' and are likely to be more inhibited from applying. Our evidence showed that relatively few children in families consisting of husband and wife and up to three children under 15 received school meals free (4 per cent of one- and two-child families and 3 per cent of three-child families), but substantial proportions of families consisting of four or more children (46 per cent) and of households in which one-parent families predominated (39 per cent). Table 25.16 suggests that fewer of the low-income families among the former than of the latter received free meals.

Class:

Finally, use and under-use of means-tested services is related to social class. The correlation is, however, by no means consistent. For example, the figures in the first two columns of Table 25.17 can be compared. The lower middle class and the skilled working class seem to be less likely to apply for benefits which are felt to be stigmatizing, such as free school meals, than either the middle classes (professional, managerial and high inspectorate), on the one hand, or unskilled manual workers on the other. Among other things, the children of unskilled and partly skilled manual workers are likely to be more 'conspicuously' in need – either because of size of family or because of occupations which are publicly recognized to be low paid. They may attract more encouragement to apply from school heads, educational welfare officers and others, and also have fewer inhibitions about accepting what is seen by most occupational classes as dependent, and sometimes even humiliating status. On the other hand, many fewer of them are aware of the existence of some means-tested services.

For example, fewer of the parents of 15- to 18-year-olds who were unskilled or partly skilled manual workers than of parents belonging to professional and managerial, other non-manual and skilled manual classes had heard of educational maintenance allowances (Table A.103, Appendix Eight, page 1068).

Another factor in explanation is the special definition, or rather modification of the definition of 'need' by different organizations and local communities. Even though individual members of such organizations or communities belong to different social classes, the organization or community as a whole tends to adopt a class style. I mean, for example, that some schools attach much more importance to the 'need' for a good school meal, occasional expenditure on educational aids, the wearing of school uniforms and 'correct' moral behaviour than do other schools. Pressure is therefore brought indirectly to bear on parents to make use of means-tested services. Fewer secondary school-children of parents who were unskilled or partly skilled manual workers than of other parents were ex-

Table 25.17. *Percentages of persons of different occupational class obtaining means-tested benefits.*

Occupational class	Percentage in poverty or on the margins of poverty	Percentage of children having meals who have them free	Percentage of households receiving rate rebates	Percentage of 16- to 25-year-olds having educational grants	Total numbers			
					People in households	Children having school meals	House-holds	16- to 25-year-olds
Professional	9	4	2	(12)	299	79	111	26
Managerial	13	(9)	6	(24)	259	46	97	25
Higher supervisory	17	13	5	14	518	74	192	77
Lower supervisory	30	8	2	3	664	124	287	104
Routine non-manual	31	(6)	6	1	414	35	143	151
Skilled manual	35	18	5	2	1,686	237	637	245
Partly skilled manual	38	23	6	4	858	114	320	118
Unskilled manual	59	57	7	4	532	66	200	71
All classes	33	17	5	5	5,230	775	1,987	817

NOTE: People living in income units with net disposable household income in previous year of less than 140 per cent of supplementary benefit scales plus housing cost.

pected to wear uniforms, but nearly half were. Very few of these obtained uniform or school clothing grants (Table A.103, Appendix Eight, page 1068).

Table 25.17 also calls attention to the fact that explanations of take-up cannot be applied uniformly to all means-tested services. Compared with the proportions of working classes and middle classes in poverty or on the margins of poverty, the proportions of some middle-class groups claiming rate rebates is relatively high (Table A.104, Appendix Eight, page 1069). This is attributable to the disproportionately large number of owner-occupiers among them, and the fact that poor owner-occupiers are more likely to apply for rate rebates than are poor tenants.

Grants by local education authorities to students are a special case. This service is different from other means-tested services in certain crucial respects. It deals principally with middle-class students, and is administered in sensitive accordance with this fact. Levels of income at which families remain eligible for substantial proportion of grant are high, and rules about disregarded income are generous. Students whose parents are rich still obtain a minimum grant. Table 25.17 shows that a very substantial proportion of the 16- to 25-year-old sons and daughters of upper-middle-class parents are receiving maintenance grants.

Irrespective of the formal rules about qualifying income, this discussion shows that social factors such as type of area, type of family and occupational class, as well as the organizational and procedural features of each particular type of means test, influence level of take-up. And it is the attitudes and conceptions of administrative and professional staff and of the general public, and not only the dispositions of potential applicants, which underlie that influence.

Summary

The huge scale of unmet need is the major conclusion of the last two chapters. There are more than forty types of means-tested services in the United Kingdom. The principal scheme was discussed in Chapter 24, and some other important schemes are discussed in this chapter.[1] The different schemes were found not to be coordinated, and there were quite marked variations in the point on the income scale at which families of different composition qualified. The schemes suffered from 'assessment lag' and inability to provide for as many poor families as qualified for benefit. Government estimates of take-up were and are seriously misleading, since they include people who may have been eligible for benefit at the time of assessment but who no longer have incomes low enough to make them eligible automatically. As a consequence, a higher proportion of those in poverty or on the margins of poverty at any single time are not receiving means-tested

1. Certain provisions which were not covered in the survey, or which did not exist at the time, are reviewed by Lister, R., *Take-up of Means-Tested Benefits*, CPAG Poverty Pamphlet No. 18, November 1974.

Table 25.18. *Estimated numbers eligible for, but not receiving, benefit.*[a]

	1968	1976	1976 Percentage (take-up)
Supplementary benefit	At least 2,100,000	At least 2,000,000	60–65[b]
Free school meals	At least 450,000	At least 400,000	60
Free welfare milk	At least 400,000	At least 450,000	under 2
Educational maintenance allowances	At least 100,000	At least 130,000	under 15
School-uniform grants	At least 300,000	At least 300,000	under 5
Rate rebates	About 1,350,000 (households)	At least 1,450,000 (households)	under 25
Rent rebates	At least 500,000 (households)	At least 500,000 (households)	under 30[c]

NOTES: [a]Some of these estimates are modifications of those given earlier, for reasons discussed in the text. Except where specified, the estimates are of people in families, not claimants.
[b]The S B C estimate is 75 per cent for 1974. S B C Annual Report, 1975, p. 52.
[c]Only 20–25 per cent of eligible private unfurnished tenants, and only 10 per cent of furnished tenants, were estimated to have rent allowances. See *Hansard*, 17 February 1975, cols. 303–4.

benefits than is officially believed. Estimates from the survey and for 1976 are given in Table 25.18. The estimates for 1976 are very rough and take into account trends in recent years in official estimates of the numbers below the supplementary benefit level, changes such as the extension of the compulsory school-leaving age to 16, and government estimates of take-up (as with rent rebates and allowances).

Denial or difficulty of access to resources is inherent in means-tested services and is put forward in this chapter to explain under-use. Because there is a contradiction or conflict in the services between their poverty alleviation and social-control functions, there is a very uneven outcome. There are differences of view about which groups most need help as well as about those who most need discipline or correction. Society upholds the virtues of self-help, family support, work and thrift, and cannot therefore consistently encourage the use of means-tested services. Specific conditions are attached to the receipt of benefit which are more stringently applied to some groups than to others. Just as there are differences of view about which groups most need help, so there are about those who most need discipline, correction and discouragement. Denial or difficulty of access to resources operates unevenly. This explains some differences of uptake *within* services as well as *between* services. The chapter illustrates finally the ways in which resources come to be distributed in relation to the social structure through regional and area administration, family type and the process of socialization, and especially through social class.

26
Conclusion I: The Social Distribution of Poverty and Trends in the 1970s

The chief conclusion of this report is that poverty is more extensive than is generally or officially believed and has to be understood not only as an inevitable feature of severe social inequality but also as a particular consequence of actions by the rich to preserve and enhance their wealth and so deny it to others. Control of wealth and of the institutions created by that wealth, and therefore of the terms under which it may be generated and passed on selectively or for the general good, is therefore central to any policies designed to abolish or alleviate the condition.

This conclusion must be related to the previous analysis. One has first to plumb the full meaning of the elaborate and interconnected *structure* of society, as this book, by means of its survey data, has attempted to portray. Through direct relationships to the economy by virtue of employment and membership of professions and trade unions, and through indirect relationships by virtue of membership of income units, households, extended families and neighbourhood, community or regional, ethnic and other social groups, individuals are fitted into a highly stratified hierarchy of roles. This hierarchy is kept in being by a web of institutions of a more complex and firmly rooted kind than is generally supposed even in the work of social scientists, and yet public consciousness of the existence of a hierarchy – or at least of the ranks most relevant to their own position – is relatively acute.

But, secondly, social structures hold implications for action. The structure of severe inequality is not just an artefact of history, nor is it a necessary feature of industrial societies to which we must in substantial if not entire measure adjust. From different positions in the hierarchy many individuals act to maintain and improve economic position and status. In particular, the rich exert major control over the evolution of the class hierarchy – deciding the scope and nature of economic activity, wage and salary differentials, the terms and conditions of employment and the organization of housing finance. They play a dominant part in fashioning social policy in both the narrow and wide senses of that term, especially the identification of social objectives and needs in conformity with market priorities and hence their own perceptions and interests. Redistribution is therefore not much of a reality and the social services can increasingly be seen to serve functions which reinforce rather than reduce poverty and inequality. This is not just because of a diversification of benefits and functions but because of the arrogation to new and enlarged professions of capacity to monopolize knowledge and govern events.

Chapters 26 and 27 will therefore attempt to explain and illustrate this conclusion. This chapter will set out some of the principal findings about the 'structure' of poverty in the United Kingdom, not only as given in earlier pages from the national survey of poverty in 1968–9, but also as shown by studies and reports published in the 1970s. We will review in some detail how far the findings from the survey may be said to apply to the United Kingdom in the late 1970s. It seems appropriate to separate this more detailed material from the more general concluding discussion in Chapter 27.

The sample who were interviewed held various conceptions of poverty. Eight per cent thought of poverty as conditions in which people experienced extreme hunger or starvation, and 31 per cent as a standard of life below subsistence or which lacked or made it impossible to obtain the basic necessities of life. Another 29 per cent referred to membership of minorities, such as old-age pensioners or the unemployed, rather than to a standard of life, though for many of them that standard was implicit in such membership. Only a small percentage of the sample believed that poverty was relative and spoke of the difficulties of following ordinary activities or enjoying goods, amenities and services available to most people in society.

The most common conceptions may therefore be said to reflect the standards of subsistence institutionalized by the state, particularly for minorities covered by national-insurance benefits who are, like retirement pensioners, widows and the long-term sick and disabled, frequently the subject of policy discussion.

For operational purposes, three distinct standards or definitions were developed: the state's (or supplementary benefit) standard; the relative income standard; and the relative deprivation standard. The first represents the conventional or social standard defined in law and administrative practice, the second a level substantially and consistently below the mean income for households of each type, and the third a level of income for each type of household or income unit below which the capacity to fulfil membership of society diminishes disproportionately to income. This third standard hypothesizes a threshold on the income scale for each type of household below which deprivation increases disproportionately.

There is evidence from the survey for this hypothesis, but it is certainly not conclusive. Not all aspects of deprivation could be explored. We developed indicators of work deprivation, housing and environmental deprivation, and material and social deprivation. The indices which we used operationally were necessarily rough and, for purposes of any analysis requiring division of the data into a large number of sub-categories, the sample was restricted in size. Moreover, a threshold of generalized deprivation is hard to identify if, as a number of the chapters show, some forms of deprivation are widely distributed, especially among manual workers and their families, and are by no means coincident with each other.

Measurement of Poverty

By all three of these measures poverty was substantial. By the state's standard, there were 6·1 per cent of the sample in households, and 9·1 per cent in income units who, when their net disposable incomes were averaged over the previous twelve months, were found to be living in poverty. They represented 3,300,000 and 4,950,000 people respectively. A further 21·8 per cent in households and 23·2 per cent in income units were on the margins of poverty, representing 11,900,000 and 12,600,000 respectively. These measures were related to net disposable incomes for the twelve months prior to interview. By the state's own definition, therefore, there were between 15 and 17½ million in a population of some 55½ million who were in or near poverty. By the relative income standard, 9·2 per cent of the sample in households were in poverty and another 29·6 per cent on the margins. According to this standard, poverty is represented by incomes of less than 50 per cent of the mean for households of their type. And by the deprivation standard, 22·9 per cent of the sample in households and 25·9 per cent in income units were found to be living in poverty (representing 12,500,000 and 14,000,000 respectively).

For purposes of illustration, we investigated how many of the poor or marginally poor had assets, or employer, public social service or private benefits in kind which, in equivalent money income, would theoretically have taken them above the state's standard. Few people with low incomes owned assets of substantial value. The percentage of income units with incomes below the supplementary benefit standard fell from 9·1 to only 7·1 after the annuity value of assets, including owner-occupied housing, was added. Even after the total annual value of public social service benefits in kind – including the value of schooling, hospital and general practitioner care, employer welfare benefits and private income in kind, including the value of services as well as gifts received from others outside the household – was added, there were still 3·2 per cent with resources below the standard and 6·7 per cent on the margins.

There were 28 per cent who were below or just above the state's standard for the year as a whole, but the figure increases to 36 per cent if people who dropped to these levels for at least a short period of the year are added. During a short period, therefore, a large section of the population, and predominantly the working class, run the risk of experiencing poverty.

For longer periods than twelve months, the numbers must be higher. In his 1899, 1936 and 1950 surveys, Seebohm Rowntree called attention to the life-cycle

Table 26.1. Percentages of people in income units in or on the margins of poverty.

Category	According to the state poverty standard[a]		According to the relative deprivation standard[b]	
	Percentage in or on the margins of poverty (% in poverty in brackets)		Percentage in poverty	Number in sample for whom information complete on income and category
Professional or managerial occupational status, living alone or with spouse only and aged under 60	0	(0)	0	70
Regularly employed of professional or managerial status	5	(2)	3	112
Employed, living with wife or husband only, under 60	6	(2)	4	374
Aged 0–14, parents of professional status	7	(0)	2	98
Aged 15–39, professional status	8	(2)	3	96
Aged 40 but not over pensionable age, professional status	9	(6)	9	79
Regularly employed, non-manual status	13	(5)	9	574
Fifteen or more years of education	14	(7)	8	142
Regularly employed in previous year	16	(5)	12	1,328
Employed, no unemployment in previous year	17	(5)	13	2,320
Regularly employed, manual status	18	(4)	14	739
Aged 40 but not over pensionable age	22	(6)	16	1,392
Irish birth	23	(7)	26	74
Aged 15–39	26	(8)	19	1,759
No disability	28	(8)	20	4,152
Self-employed	28	(13)	22	172
Males	29	(8)	23	2,564
Professional or managerial status, of pensionable age	(32)	(9)	18	44
White	33	(9)	25	5,176
All persons in sample	33	(9)	26	5,309
Born in UK	33	(9)	26	5,067
Unemployed 1–9 weeks in previous year	33	(11)	29	100
Females	36	(11)	29	2,764

Table 26.1. – contd

Category	According to the state poverty standard[a]		According to the relative deprivation standard[b]	Number in
	Percentage in or on the margins of poverty (% in poverty in brackets)		Percentage in poverty	Number in sample for whom infor- mation com- plete on income and category
Aged 0–14	37	(8)	28	1,355
Non-white	38	(16)	42	144
Born West Indies, Africa, India or Pakistan	39	(18)	39	102
Unemployed 10 or more weeks in previous year	39	(18)	33	79
Minor disability	41	(14)	30	470
Not employed	46	(13)	36	2,840
Appreciable or severe disability, under pensionable age	49	(16)	50	80
Aged 15–39, unskilled manual status	54	(26)	43	131
In 1-parent family	55	(31)	48	157
Fewer than 9 years' education	60	(19)	50	391
Of pensionable age (60+ women, 55+ men)	63	(20)	54	828
In fatherless family	66	(38)	57	130
Appreciable or severe disability	67	(20)	74	314
In household of man, woman and 4 or more children	68	(21)	62	315
Of pensionable age, unskilled manual status	71	(19)	67	144
Appreciable or severe disability of pensionable age	73	(21)	82	234
Aged 0–14, parents unskilled manual status	76	(37)	77	119
Retired, living alone, aged 60 or over	82	(21)	70	130
Aged 80 or over	86	(24)	82	98
In household of man, woman and 3 or more children, unskilled manual status	89	(64)	93	73

NOTES: [a]Net disposable income in previous year of less than the supplementary benefit scale rates plus housing cost (or 100 per cent to 139 per cent being treated as 'on the margins' of that standard).
[b]Gross disposable income in previous year of less than the deprivation standard (as listed in Chapter 6, page 268).

of poverty. In the poverty survey, there were similar variations according to age. Children and the aged accounted for the great majority of those found to be living in poverty. More than a third of the children and more than half the elderly, compared with only a tenth of the middle aged, lived in households who were, by the state's standard, in poverty or on the margins of poverty. For at least some part of the life-cycle, therefore, it is likely that more than half the population experience poverty or near-poverty.

The 'structure' of poverty, as revealed in the sample survey, therefore reflects changes according to age and circumstances. Table 26.1 illustrates this structure. As can be seen, the risks of being in poverty vary dramatically according to age, employment status, family type and, especially, occupational class. The choice of poverty standard makes some, but not a lot of, difference to the ranking. The trends from applying either the state's standard or the deprivation standard are much the same. Middle-aged professional and managerial workers employed throughout the year and living alone, in married couples or with small families, were least likely to be poor. Elderly people who had been unskilled manual workers and children in the families of young unskilled manual workers, especially those with substantial experience of unemployment, sickness, or disablement and in one-parent families, were most likely to be poor.

The variation was related more to the changing position with age of people of different class origin in the economic and social hierarchy than to ethnic origin or geographical location. The percentage of people in non-white households living in poverty or on the margins of poverty was rather higher than of the population as a whole. Fewer than in the population as a whole had substantial assets, fewer were in non-manual occupations despite the high proportion who had had a lengthy education, and large numbers were deprived on different indicators.

The proportions of poor and marginally poor did not vary greatly from rural to urban areas and to conurbations. Although there were relatively more rich people in rural than other areas, there were fewer in the next rank of prosperity. Poverty and near poverty was more common in Northern Ireland, Scotland, the North-West, Wales and the South-West than elsewhere, but these conditions were to be found on a substantial scale in all regions. The sample was drawn from fifty-one constituencies: at one extreme there were ten which accounted for 32 per cent of the poor; at the other there were ten which still accounted for 10 per cent. In four poor areas located in Belfast, Glasgow, Salford and Neath, special additional surveys were carried out. The percentage living in *households* with incomes below or on the margins of the state's standard was lowest in Neath, with 27 per cent, and highest in Belfast North, with just under 50 per cent, the other two areas, Salford and Glasgow Shettleston, being intermediate, with 37 per cent and 48 per cent.

There are therefore areas with up to twice as many poor as there are in the nation as a whole. But our evidence showed how wide is the dispersion of poor people. On the one hand, the majority are not to be found in areas which even account for as much as 20 per cent of the population; on the other, there are substantial minorities of relatively prosperous people even in the poorest districts of the country.

The social distribution of poverty may now be summarized. Many people, and overwhelmingly married women and children, are not in poverty by virtue of any *personal* characteristics so much as indirectly by virtue of the labour market, wage or social security characteristics of the principal income recipient of the family unit. In this book, we have used both household and income unit as the basic 'family' units of analysis. The household and the income unit are, in fact, the same thing for about two thirds of the population. Where there are two or more units in a single household, their incomes may be pooled and the pattern of consumption treated as common to all its members. But incomes may be treated separately, and consumption may be predominantly a matter for the individual or at least sub-groups within the household. In its taxation and social security policies, the state also tends to be concerned with the income unit rather than the household.

For these reasons, the social distribution of poverty may be best summarized in terms of the population composing income units rather than households. The accompanying table (26.2) gives the distribution of the population in poverty according to the labour market, personal and other characteristics of one or more of the members of the income unit. About a third of people in poverty by the state's standard belong to income units in which someone is substantially employed. Another third belong to units in which someone is disabled or is, or has been, ill for five or more weeks, and yet another third to units in which someone is retired and of pensionable age. These are the principal groupings from which any description and explanation of poverty must proceed. If account is taken also of those with incomes on the margins of the state's standard, or, alternatively, the population are considered in terms of the relative deprivation standard, each of the first two categories assume greater importance. By the relative deprivation standard, nearly half the population in poverty are in units in which someone is employed. Certain important qualifications must be added. Readers will observe that employment, unemployment, disability, one-parent family status and retirement are not exclusive categories in the table. There is some overlapping. For example, among the people in units with an income below the state poverty line, and yet in which there was someone substantially employed, 22 per cent were also in income units in which someone (not necessarily the same person) had been disabled or ill for five weeks or more, and another 16 per cent unemployed for at least one week in the year. As many as 62 per cent in a unit with someone disabled or sick were also in a unit with someone retired. Roughly the same proportion of the people in 'retirement' units were also in 'disablement' units. These two categories overlap more substantially than any other two categories.

Table 26.2. *The distribution of poverty.*

Type of income unit	All in sample %	All in poverty by state's standard %	All in po⋯ or on ma⋯ by state' standard⋯
1. *Employed*			
(a) At least one person in unit employed last year for 1,000 hours or more	78·9	32·5	53·2
(b) At least one person in unit employed last year for 1,000 hours or more *and* with earnings of less than 90 per cent of the mean for own sex[b]	(28·3)	(16·5)	(25·4)
2. *Unemployed*			
At least one person unemployed for 1 week or more in previous year	7·3	9·1	8·0
3. *Disabled*			
(a) At least one person with some appreciable or severe disablement (scoring 3 or more on index) *or* sick 5 weeks or more	27·1	34·8	39·8
(b) At least one person with appreciable or severe disablement (scoring 7 or more on index) *or* sick 12 weeks or more in year[b]	(12·4)	(15·9)	(20·0)
4. *One-parent family*	3·0	10·5	5·2
5. *Elderly Retired*			
Not employed, of pensionable age	14·9	34·2	30·7
6. *Others*	1·9	9·1	3·6
Total[c]	(100)	(100)	(100)
N = 100 per cent	5,340	486	1,728

NOTES: [a] 'Children' in this table means dependent child under 19 living in household.
[b] 1b and 3b are placed in brackets because they are included in 1a and 3a respectively.
[c] Totals in the first five columns add to more than 100 per cent because some people fall into two or more categories.

The table also selects two sub-categories – on the one hand of the low paid among the substantially employed, and on the other of the appreciably or severely disabled. In each case, the sub-categories account for about half of those found to be in poverty. Each sub-category represents a considerable minority of the population. If we include both those on the margins of as well as under the state's poverty line, there are 4,500,000 people in units in which someone is substantially employed (that is, working a total of 1,000 hours or more in the year) and also low paid. There are 3,500,000 in units in which someone is appreciably or severely

overty ive ·ion d	Percentage in poverty by state's standard	Percentage in poverty or on margins by state's standard	Percentage in poverty by relative deprivation standard	All children in poverty by state's standard[a] %	All children in poverty or on margins by state's standard[a] %
	3·8	21·8	16·2	56·9	82·4
	(5·3)	(29·0)	(26·3)	(31·7)	(37·6)
	11·3	35·8	30·4	15·4	11·3
	11·7	47·6	44·1	19·5	25·9
	11·6	52·0	56·9	(4·1)	(9·6)
	31·5	55·0	47·5	29·3	11·3
	20·9	66·7	56·2	0	1·3
	44·0	62·0	52·6	4·1	1·5
	9·1	32·4	25·9	(100)	100
	486	1,728	5,307	123	529

disabled or has been ill for twelve or more weeks in the last twelve months. Table 26.3 gives the full estimates.

Some minorities contribute to the population in poverty out of all proportion to their numbers in the general population. As Table 26.2 shows, the elderly retired accounted for 15 per cent of the population in units, but 34 per cent of those with incomes of less than the state's standard. One-parent families accounted for only 3 per cent of the total population, but 10 per cent of those in poverty.

A higher proportion of children than of adults live in units which experience poverty or marginal poverty – 36 per cent compared with 31 per cent (or 22 per cent if the retired elderly are excluded). This figure represents 4,900,000 children under 15 (or 5,500,000 if older dependent children are added). The vast majority (over four fifths) were in units in which the adult or adults were in substantial em-

Table 26.3. *Estimated numbers in population in categories of poverty.*

Characteristic of income unit or at least 1 person in unit	Estimated numbers in income units in poverty or on the margins of poverty (by the state's standards)
Employed last year	9,400,000 (of which 4,500,000 low paid)
Unemployed last year	1,400,000
Disabled or long-term sick	7,000,000 (of which 3,500,000 appreciably or severely disabled or chronic sick)
1-parent family	900,000
Elderly retired	5,400,000
All characteristics	17,630,000

ployment, that is, working for 1,000 hours or more in the previous year. Two fifths of all children were in units in which an adult was working full time but was low paid.

Changes since 1968–9

The extent and 'structure' of poverty in the United Kingdom as established in the survey has been summarized above. Has that extent and structure changed since 1968–9? This question can be approached in terms of changes in the structure of the population, the distribution of wealth, in the levels of income gross and net of tax, the relationship of these types of income to the supplementary benefit scales, and changes in the overall structure of incomes in society.

In Table 26.4 I have listed certain indicators of change in social structure for Britain 1968–76. This shows that some minorities known to be exposed to greater risk of poverty, namely elderly pensioners and unemployed, increased disproportionately to population. The numbers of invalidity pensioners increased slightly, and the numbers of one-parent families dependent on supplementary benefit increased very sharply. The total number of families with children increased, but the number with three or more decreased, proportionately to population.

During the late 1960s and early 1970s, there appears to have been a continuation of a fall in the percentage of wealth held by the top 1 per cent, but not much change in the broad inequalities of wealth between the top 20 per cent of the population and the rest (Table 26.5). An independent study suggests that the official statistical series exaggerates the trend and offers alternative estimates showing fluctuations from year to year but no change between 1968 and 1972 in the proportion of wealth held by the top 10 per cent and top 20 per cent.[1] A sharp fall in share values in the mid 1970s, which corresponded with a decline in the shares

1. Atkinson, A. B., and Harrison, A. J., *Distribution of Personal Wealth in Britain*, Cambridge University Press, 1978, p. 159.

Table 26.4.   Selected indicators of change in social structure in the United Kingdom, 1968-76.

Social category	1968	1976	1976 as % of 1968
Total population	55,049,000	56,000,000	102
Retirement pensioners (incl. others with pensions, aged 60 and over)	7,133,000	8,617,000	121
People aged 75 and over	2,491,000	2,847,000	114
Families receiving family allowances	4,257,000	4,592,000	108
Families receiving family allowances with 3 or more children	1,766,000	1,631,000	93
Supplementary benefit recipients	2,736,000	3,050,000	111
1-parent families receiving supplementary benefits	(185,000)[a]	310,000	168
Unemployed	560,000	1,359,000	243
Unemployed receiving supplementary benefits	235,000	684,000	291
Unemployed receiving unemployment insurance benefit	331,000	617,000	186
Unemployed receiving neither supplementary nor unemployment benefits	110,000[a]	200,000	182
Recipients of supplementary benefits not eligible for long-term addition or long-term (higher) scale rate	550,000[b]	572,000[b]	104
Recipients of invalidity benefits for more than 6 months	416,000	431,000[c]	104

NOTES: [a]Estimated.
[b]Britain only.
[c]For the year 1975.
SOURCES: *Annual Abstract of Statistics*, HMSO, London, 1978, pp. 13, 67, 68, 69; *Social Security Statistics 1975*, HMSO, London, 1977; and *Social Trends*, No. 8, HMSO, London, 1977, pp. 41, 53, 65, 86, 110, 111.

of wealth of the top 1 per cent and top 5 per cent, was reversed in 1977-8, and longer-term trends are difficult to judge.

Table (26.6, below) derived from government sources, summarizes changes in level of income of different social security claimants, relative to average gross and net incomes. Clearly there have been fluctuations from year to year in the level of individual social-security benefits in relation to average gross earnings and net income. By 1974, short-term national insurance and supplementary benefits had lost ground since the late 1960s relative to gross and net income – for both single people and married couples with children. On the other hand, long-term benefits

Table 26.5. *Two versions of trends in the distribution of wealth (Britain).*

Year	Inland Revenue data series B[a]				Atkinson and Harrison (assumption B3)[b]			
	Top 1%	Top 5%	Top 10%	Top 20%	Top 1%	Top 5%	Top 10%	Top 20%
1960	38·2	64·3	76·7	89·8	34·4	60·0	72·1	83·6
1964	34·4	59·3	73·5	88·4	34·7	59·2	72·0	85·2
1966	31·8	56·7	71·8	87·8	31·0	56·1	69·9	84·2
1968	32·7	59·0	73·8	89·4	33·6	58·6	72·0	85·4
1970	29·0	56·3	70·1	89·0	30·1	54·3	69·4	84·9
1972	29·9	56·3	71·9	89·2	32·0	57·2	71·7	85·3
1974	25·3	49·9	66·0	85·5	–	–	–	–
1975[c]	23·2	46·5	62·4	81·8	–	–	–	–

NOTE: [a] Assuming that persons not covered by the Inland Revenue estimates have no wealth.
[b] Assuming that the value of certain property not accounted for by estate data but estimated by means of the balance-sheet method is distributed between the population included in the estate data and the population excluded. This is their 'central estimate'.
[c] United Kingdom.

SOURCES: Royal Commission on the Distribution of Income and Wealth, Report No. 5, *Third Report on the Standing Reference*, Cmnd 6999, HMSO, London, 1977, p. 76; Atkinson, A. B., and Harrison, A.J., *Distribution of Personal Wealth in Britain*, Cambridge University Press, 1978, p. 159.

Table 26.6. *Benefits when sick, unemployed or retired as a percentage of gross earnings and of net income (after deducting tax and national insurance contributions).*

October each year	Standard rate of sickness or unemployment benefit plus earnings related supplement				Standard rate of long-term invalidity or retirement pension			Supplementary benefit rates (including rent) as % of net income			
	Single man		Married couple with 2 children		Single man		Married couple with 2 children	Short term		Long term	
	As % gross earnings	As % net income	As % gross earnings	As % net income	As % gross earnings	As % net income	As % net income	Single person	Married couple with 2 children (aged under 5)	Single person	Married couple with 2 children (aged under 5)
1967	40·0	53·9	63·6	73·2	21·0	28·4	51·8	38·9	62·9	41·8	65·3
1968	38·9	52·9	60·9	72·8	19·6	26·6	50·6	38·6	63·3	41·6	65·8
1969	38·1	52·1	58·5	71·0	18·1	24·8	52·8	37·8	62·4	40·6	64·8
1970	38·0	53·3	58·2	72·7	17·8	25·0	48·3	37·0	61·4	39·5	63·6
1971	41·2	57·5	63·3	77·9	19·4	27·1	60·3	37·6	61·9	39·8	63·9
1972	38·4	52·3	60·2	73·7	18·8	25·7	58·4	35·3	59·6	37·6	61·6
1973	35·1	48·4	56·2	70·6	18·9	26·1	60·4	36·0	59·3	39·4	62·9
1974	33·6	48·6	54·6	70·3	20·6	28·7	67·1	34·6	60·6	43·5	67·7
1975	30·8	45·9	50·2	67·0	19·5	29·0	65·2	34·8	58·2	40·7	65·0
1976	31·1	46·7	50·7	67·3	19·9	29·8	66·2	36·0	59·0	42·0	66·1
1977	32·7	47·6	52·9	68·4	20·9	30·4	67·2	–	–	–	–

SOURCES: First 6 columns: DHSS, *Social Security Statistics, 1974,* HMSO, London, 1975, pp. 212–13; last 5 columns: *Hansard,* 13 February 1976, cols. 417 and 423. Royal Commission on the Distribution of Income and Wealth, *Report No. 6,* pp. 294 and 299–300.

either maintained or (especially in the case of invalidity benefits) gained ground, though the levels achieved by the uprating of July 1974 appear in retrospect to have been exceptional. During the high rates of inflation in the mid 1970s, values of benefits have fluctuated sharply between upratings in relation both to earnings and prices. The government attempted to maintain values through more frequent upratings – after nine and a half months (July 1974), eight and a half months (April 1975), and seven and a half months (November 1975) respectively, but by the months immediately preceding these upratings, benefits had none the less fallen very sharply in value.[1] Subsequently (November 1976, 1977 and 1978), the government has reverted to annual upratings.

During these years, successive Labour and Conservative governments introduced new measures aimed in whole or in part at helping those on low incomes. Probably the most important of these measures is the Social Security Pensions Act 1975, which came into effect in April 1978. This affects the whole population, but it will be many years before a substantial additional number of pensioners will have received earnings-related pensions large enough to remove them from the scope of the supplementary benefits scheme. In the early years, those retiring will have earned only small additional earnings-related pensions and the scheme will not come into full effect until after the year 2020. The child benefit scheme (which introduces a cash allowance for each child in the family in substitution for child tax allowances for all dependent children, and family allowances for the second and each subsequent child in the family) had begun, by 1978, to restore the losses during the mid 1970s in real value of family support, but, depending on the rate of inflation and further government decisions, it remained to be seen whether the government would act after the increase of April 1979 to lift the level of support to a markedly higher level.[2]

A Family Income Supplement scheme was introduced for the low paid with children in 1971. From the start, the numbers who applied were considerably fewer than the numbers who were estimated to be entitled. The number of two-parent families receiving this supplement reached 65,000 in June 1972, but fell sharply later that year, fluctuated around 50,000 in 1973, and fell steadily during 1974, until the figure of 32,000 was reached in that December. The number was

1. See, for example, the papers by Trinder, C., in Willmott, P. (ed.), *Sharing Inflation?*, Poverty Report 1976, Temple-Smith, London, 1976; Field, F., *The New Corporate Interest*, Poverty Pamphlet No. 23, Child Poverty Action Group, London, 1976; Disability Alliance, 'Nearly a Million Disabled People in Poverty', memorandum to the Chancellor of the Exchequer, March 1976; Lewis, P., *et al.*, *Inflation and Low Incomes*, Fabian Research Series No. 322, Fabian Society, London, August 1975.

2. In its evidence in 1977 to the Royal Commission on the Distribution of Income and Wealth, the Supplementary Benefit Commission showed that the combined value of family allowances and child tax allowances in October 1976 was substantially smaller for families, relative to net incomes, than in the early years after the introduction of family allowances in 1946.

under 30,000 in 1975, but increased in 1976 to 42,000. A government report further shows that more than a fifth of these are not strictly below the prescribed income limits at any one time – mainly because, under the rules, families qualify for supplement for twelve months irrespective of a change in their circumstances.[1] The total at the end of 1976 of 85,000 two-parent and one-parent families represents only 0·3 per cent of the labour force. The total cost, estimated at £24 million for 1977–8, represented only 1·3 per cent of the cost of supplementary benefits.[2]

New benefits, starting in 1971, were introduced for disabled people. By December 1974, 187,000 severely disabled people were receiving attendance allowance at one of two rates. Among 444,000 invalidity pensioners in 1974, 70,000 qualified for a higher rate of invalidity allowance of £2·40 per week; 72,000 a middle rate of £1·50; 224,000 a lower rate of 0·75p; and 78,000 for nothing.[3] About a half of all invalidity pensioners had an adult dependant, and a fifth a child dependant. The benefit rates for these dependants were increased in 1971. A non-contributory invalidity pension was introduced in 1975 for disabled people who had not qualified for invalidity pension, most of whom had had to rely solely on supplementary benefits. Excluding certain hospital patients receiving a pocket-money rate of benefit, 64,000 were estimated to be drawing benefit by the beginning of 1976, but 46,000 were estimated not to be receiving any net gain whatsoever. They lost in supplementary benefits what they gained in the new pension.[4] However, this pension was extended in November 1977 – to severely disabled married women. An invalid care allowance was introduced in July 1976 for single women and others who give up their jobs to care for severely disabled relatives. It is expected to be claimed by only 11,500 people, at a net cost of about £2 million a year. Finally, a mobility allowance is being introduced by stages for about 100,000 disabled people who have difficulty in walking. In 1976–7, 25,000 were estimated to be receiving it. People of pensionable age are not eligible for the allowance.

These allowances have probably reduced the numbers of disabled people living in poverty, but the government has been criticized strongly for a 'piecemeal' and, by reference to the needs, 'inadequate' programme.[5] By 1978–9, the attendance allowance, invalid care allowance, mobility allowance and non-contributory invalidity pension were expected to cost £301 million, or just over 2 per cent of the

1. Knight, I. B., and Nixon, J., *Two-Parent Families in Receipt of Family Income Supplement, 1972*, DHSS, Statistical and Research Report Series, No. 9, HMSO, London, 1975.

2. DHSS, *Social Security Statistics, 1974*, HMSO, London, 1975, pp. 62–3.

3. *The Government's Expenditure Plans 1978–79 to 1981–82*, vol. II, Cmnd 7049, HMSO, London, 1978, pp. 90–91.

4. *Hansard*, 27 February 1976, col. 380.

5. *Poverty and Disability: The Case for a Comprehensive Income Scheme for Disabled People*, Disability Alliance, London, 1975. See also *Poverty and Low Incomes Amongst Disabled People*, a submission to the Royal Commission on the Distribution of Incomes and Wealth – Lower Incomes Reference, Disability Alliance, London, 1977.

total expenditure on social security. This is almost exactly the same as the total cost of war pensions in that year.[1]

The introduction of these measures is not easy to relate to outcomes – as reflected either in estimated numbers in or on the margins of poverty, or in income distribution. I will briefly describe sources of information for each of these. First, the government has published estimates of the numbers in and near poverty for the early and mid 1970s (Table 26.7). According to these estimates, derived from the Family Expenditure Survey, the total at or around the supplementary benefit standard increased in the 1960s and declined slightly in the early 1970s before rising again in 1975–6. There is evidence from the same source (the Family Expenditure Survey) that the numbers and percentage of the population with incomes under the supplementary benefit standard or marginally above that standard, and also the numbers and percentages receiving supplementary benefit, were all higher in the early and mid 1970s than in 1960.

In the poverty survey, the number of people living in units with incomes of no more than 140 per cent of the supplementary benefit standard in 1968–9 was estimated to represent 17·6 million. A rather similar but not exactly comparable government estimate for 1976 was 14·9 million (there were 8·5 million with incomes

Table 26.7. *Government estimates of numbers in poverty* (*Family Expenditure Survey*).

Relationship to benefit standard	Britain (000s)				
	1960[a]	Dec. 1972[b]	Dec. 1974	Dec. 1975	Dec. 1976
Under supplementary benefit standard	1,260	1,780	1,410	1,840	2,280
At or not more than 10% above standard	(710)	1,120	960	1,120	1,630
Receiving supplementary benefit[c]	2,670	4,140	3,730	3,710	4,090
Total	4,640	7,040	6,100	6,670	8,000

NOTES: [a]From Abel-Smith, B., and Townsend, P., *The Poor and the Poorest*, Bell, London, 1965, pp. 40 and 44, with estimate for second line. The data are for the UK and are on a household rather than an income unit basis.
[b]Self-employed assumed to be distributed among the poor in the same proportion as the employed.
[c]This information (for 1972–6) is drawn separately from a supplementary benefit sample inquiry, and to make it consistent with the information from the FES (given in the first two lines above), people drawing supplementary benefit for less than three months are excluded. In the FES, people are categorized according to their 'normal' income and employment in the three months preceding interview.

SOURCE: For 1972–6, DHSS analyses of FES data.

1. *The Government's Expenditure Plans 1978–79 to 1981–82*, pp. 90–91.

within the range 100–39 per cent of the standard in addition to 2·3 million under the standard and 4·1 million receiving supplementary benefit).[1] At least half and perhaps most of the difference between these estimates is due to differences in representativeness of the samples and to differences of definition. As explained on pages 275–7, the numbers in some low-income groups in the Family Expenditure Survey sample have been consistently under-represented. But without a fresh study on the same basis as the poverty survey, it would be difficult to conclude whether the numbers had declined or increased. All that can be cautiously inferred is that the numbers in and near poverty cannot be substantially different in 1976 from what they were in 1968–9, though the representation of social categories among them will certainly have changed.

Another approach is to trace changes in the distribution of incomes over the whole scale. The same points in the scale are selected for different years and expressed in Table 26.8 as percentages of the median. The definition of income, selected in this case by the Royal Commission on the Distribution of Income and Wealth, is the widest definition currently used by the government, and includes the value of some employer welfare benefits and social service benefits – such as education and health. A slightly different method of looking at the distribution is given in Table 26.9. Allowing for possible fluctuations due to sampling variation, the structure would appear to have been surprisingly stable during this period of economic and industrial upheaval. Indeed, a review of the data available for the whole period 1961–73 confirmed the 'relative stability of the income distribution

Table 26.8. Quantiles as percentages of the median, United Kingdom 1968–75.

Quantile	Final income of households as % of median							
	1968	*1969*	*1970*	*1971*	*1972*	*1973*	*1974*	*1975*
Highest percentile	347	341	345	361	342	348	–	–
Highest decile	191	188	195	196	192	192	192	189
Upper quartile	142	140	145	144	143	143	145	143
Median	100	100	100	100	100	100	100	100
Lower quartile	63	62	62	61	61	62	62	62
Lowest decile	38	38	37	38	38	39	38	40

SOURCES: Central Statistical Office (based on Family Expenditure Survey). As quoted in the Royal Commission on the Distribution of Income and Wealth, Report No. 1, *Initial Report on the Standing Reference*, Cmnd 6171, HMSO, London, 1975, p. 216, and Report No. 5, *Third Report on the Standing Reference*, Cmnd 6999, HMSO, London, 1977, p. 252.

1. Tables available from the Department of Health and Social Security. The estimate excludes those dependent on supplementary benefit for less than three months. It includes all others dependent on supplementary benefit, and all other people with incomes below the appropriate supplementary benefit scales.

Table 26.9. Percentage share of final income received by given quantile groups of households, United Kingdom, 1968–75.

Quantile group (%)	Final income of households as % of total							
	1968	1969	1970	1971	1972	1973	1974	1975
Top 10	23·4	23·3	23·5	23·7	23·0	23·4	24·7	22·4
11–20	15·3	15·3	15·5	15·6	15·5	15·4	15·1	15·4
21–30	12·9	12·8	12·9	12·8	13·0	12·9	12·7	13·0
31–40	11·0	11·1	11·2	11·0	11·1	11·1	11·0	11·2
41–50	9·6	9·8	9·5	9·6	9·7	9·6	9·4	9·7
51–60	8·4	8·5	8·2	8·3	8·4	8·3	8·1	8·4
61–70	7·1	7·0	7·0	6·9	7·0	6·9	6·8	7·0
71–80	5·7	5·5	5·6	5·4	5·5	5·6	5·5	5·7
81–90	4·2	4·1	4·1	4·1	4·2	4·2	4·0	4·3
91–100	2·5	2·5	2·4	2·5	2·6	2·7	2·7	2·9

SOURCES: Central Statistical Office (based on Family Expenditure Survey). As quoted in the Royal Commission on the Distribution of Income and Wealth, Report No. 1, *Initial Report on the Standing Reference*, Cmnd 6171, HMSO, London, 1975, p. 215. For 1974, see Nissel, M., and Peretz, J., 'Effects of Taxes and Benefits on Household Income 1974', *Economic Trends*, No. 268, February 1976, p. 110; and Report No. 5, *Third Report on the Standing Reference*, Cmnd 6999, HMSO, London, 1977, p. 251.

both before, and after, standardization (for household composition)'.[1] A later government study concluded that, between 1961 and 1975, 'the inequality of final income has hardly changed'.[2] In its report in 1978 on lower incomes, the Royal Commission found that after standardizing for household composition the distribution of income remained stable between 1968 and 1976.[3]

Certain trends in income for different types of household can also be traced. Bearing in mind fluctuations from one year to another, especially in the case of relatively small sub-groups, because of sampling variation, official data do not disclose consistent changes of any magnitude.[4] At a low point in the dispersion, income was slightly lower, as a percentage of the median, in 1974 than in 1969 for six of the ten types of household, and slightly higher for the other four. At a high point in the dispersion, income was slightly higher for four of the ten types of household and slightly lower for the other six.

1. Semple, M., 'The Effect of Changes in Household Composition on the Distribution of Income 1961–73', *Economic Trends*, December 1975, p. 101.
2. Harris, R., 'A Review of the Effects of Taxes and Benefits on Household Incomes 1961–1975', *Economic Trends*, January 1977, p. 105.
3. Royal Commission on the Distribution of Income and Wealth, Report No. 6, *Lower Incomes*, Cmnd 7175, HMSO, London, 1978, p. 143.
4. See, for example, *Economic Trends* No. 254, December 1974, pp. lvii–lxiv.

Government data on trends in the distribution of resources are incomplete in a number of critical respects. Despite secondary analyses of the Family Expenditure Survey in recent years, information about changes in the composition and level of income of the poorest 20 per cent, especially the poorest 10 per cent, is sparse. Important changes have been taking place in the relationship between earnings, taxes, cash benefits and benefits in kind, especially employer welfare benefits, but these have not yet been pursued to fully articulated conclusions. Thus, articles in *Economic Trends* show that there has been widening inequality since 1960 in 'original' incomes (principally gross earnings, but also social security benefits).[1] As argued above (pages 667–70 and 902–3), this has been due not just to a relative increase in the number of social security recipients – particularly retirement pensioners, though also including one-parent families, unemployed and disabled people – but to a relative increase in the numbers of employees of professional and managerial status. With rising real incomes, there has been a disproportionate increase in taxation, among other things, to help pay for the larger numbers of social security beneficiaries. But there has also been a relative increase in the resources committed by the nation to the production of highly educated groups – principally benefiting the middle classes. There would appear as well to have been a relative increase in the share of the disposable resources of the top 5 and 10 per cent (who include most managers and professionals), represented by employer welfare benefits in kind. Contrary to the impression conveyed by data on trends in gross and net incomes reproduced by the Royal Commission on Incomes and Wealth, suggesting that 'there has been a continuing decline in the share of the top 5 per cent',[2] the percentage share of real resources (as distinct from post-tax incomes as conventionally defined) received by the top groups may have remained steady or even increased. Data on the value of employer in-kind benefits collected by the Royal Commission (not, however, added to gross or net incomes and then analysed), as well as data from the poverty survey on such benefits presented above in Chapters 5 and 12, even supports this view.

Thus, the commission quoted evidence of expansion in coverage of executive employees by occupational pension, life insurance, medical insurance, holiday entitlement and other schemes. Pension provisions at least had been 'growing as a proportion of salary for higher executives'. Share acquisition schemes and reduced interest or interest-free loans could be of 'considerable financial advantage', and fixed-term service contracts (with the first £5,000 of compensation normally being tax-free) 'might have been entered into with a view to providing em-

1. See, for example, Harris, 'The Effect of Changes in Household Composition on the Distribution of Income', p. 105.

2. Royal Commission on the Distribution of Income and Wealth, Report No. 1, *Initial Report on the Standing Reference*, p. 156. See also Report No. 5, *Third Report on the Standing Reference*, pp. 199–202.

ployees with additional benefits'.[1] The whole problem is one of understanding and measuring personal advantage as a result of access to corporate wealth. It may be hoped that the standing Royal Commission will seek to improve data on both the distribution of employer welfare benefits and wealth and the extent to which they augment cash incomes or living standards.

This discussion shows some of the respects in which the findings from the poverty survey need to be modified to take account of events in the 1970s. There have been major changes tending to increase the numbers in or near poverty – especially the substantial increase in numbers unemployed but also the relative increase in numbers of retired disabled people and those belonging to one-parent families. The fall in the early and mid 1970s in the real value of family support (both tax allowances for children and family allowances) also tended to depress more families into poverty. On the other hand, the steadily increasing participation of women in employment has improved the living standards of some low-income families and the slow decline in proportion of manual employees in the workforce will have affected the structure or at least the variability of low earnings. New social security benefits have been introduced, and the rates of other benefits such as invalidity pensions, have been increased relative to previous values. Many other influences will have played a part in balancing the forces reducing, and those increasing, numbers in or near poverty. But, as the Royal Commission say, it is none the less 'surprising' to find such underlying longer-term stability in the distribution of incomes 'in view of the considerable economic, social and demographic changes which have taken place [between 1968 and 1976]'.[2]

1. Royal Commission on the Distribution of Income and Wealth, Third Report, *Higher Incomes from Employment*, Cmnd 6383, H M S O, London, 1976, pp. 89–101.

2. Royal Commission on the Distribution of Income and Wealth, Report No. 6, *Lower Incomes*, p. 144.

27

Conclusion II: The Explanation and Elimination of Poverty

Our evidence shows that poverty is a national phenomenon which is structurally pervasive and of major dimensions. But its extent and effects tend to be greatly underestimated and its causes wrongly, or weakly, identified. Some of the reasons for this need to be traced if the resources and organizational capacities of Britain are to be harnessed on behalf of what must be regarded as a task of national regeneration.

The limitations of our data must be recognized. Any single study must be handicapped by virtue of its methodology. Some of these limitations are described in Chapter 3 (pages 111–15). By selecting a principal method of research, other methods are necessarily ignored or abbreviated. For example, the principal method used in this study was the nationally representative sample survey. This method cannot permit sufficient weight to be given to personal histories of poverty and observations of the physical, material and emotional consequences, including illness and death, of the phenomenon. Nor can an account of structural changes in the production, accumulation and distribution of resources and changes in desired and approved styles of living, which control the definition, extent and severity of poverty, be developed, except indirectly. These questions will have to be pursued more directly elsewhere.

The object of this book has been to define, measure and, in part, explain the extent of poverty in the United Kingdom. Ultimately, these three activities cannot be undertaken and described in isolation from each other. Whatever ideas and words are chosen for each of the three, they carry assumptions if not specific prescriptions for the other two. Their necessary conjunction or interaction needs to be emphasized, because that paves the way for a clearer understanding of the functions and likely success of policies to relieve or abolish poverty.

Definition of Poverty

Perceptions of poverty are one source of underestimation of its extent and severity. Individuals in any population hold different specific or general ideas of its nature. As noted earlier (Chapter 6, page 237), some people think of poverty as a condition in which families go hungry or starve, and others as a condition relative to standards enjoyed on average or by most people in society. But the majority take the view that poverty is a condition under which people are unable to obtain subsistence, or the basic necessities of life, or is a condition which applies to particular low-income minorities, such as pensioners or the unemployed.

Their conceptions reflect those held by major groups and classes in society, and indeed by the state itself, as expressed in its legislation and central and local administration. Ministerial speeches, government publications, annual reviews by the Trades Union Congress, and studies by influential voluntary associations and academic investigators could all be quoted in substantiation. In this book I have consequently treated *society's* definition of poverty as being, with certain qualifications, the basic rates paid by the Supplementary Benefits Commission to families of different composition. This is the state's poverty line or standard. The advantage of this treatment is that it can, in principle, be applied in many different societies to demonstrate the effectiveness of policy. The British supplementary benefit scheme resembles the public assistance schemes of other countries. According to the International Labour Office, there were, by 1967, forty-four countries in their list of sixty-one, ranging from Australia, through Israel, Kenya, Nicaragua, Sweden and the United States to Yugoslavia, with public assistance schemes paying cash allowances of a standard kind to poor families on test of means.[1] The standards of different countries for different types of beneficiary, and the numbers in the population having incomes of less than the prescribed amounts, can be estimated and compared.

Public opinion can therefore be sampled, or administrative practice analysed by the social scientist, to demonstrate conventional conceptions and operational definitions of poverty. Nevertheless, one country's definition is certainly not the only, and is unlikely to be an objective, definition of poverty. There are variations between societies which have to be accounted for. There are also variations within any single society in history. Thus, in Britain since 1948, the ordinary rate of national assistance or supplementary benefit for a single householder has fluctuated from 15 to 21 per cent of average male industrial earnings. There are, therefore, difficulties both in using a *social* poverty standard to make comparisons between different years in the same country and in using different national poverty standards to make comparisons between different societies. Both exercises are rewarding, only in so far as the meaning of the standards being used can be clarified in relation to the distribution of income, mean income and social structure.

The state's (and the public's) conception of subsistence poverty is different from, and more generous than, starvation poverty. Yet it is none the less a severely limited conception of need, fostered by motives of condescension and self-interest as well as duty by the rich. Ideas of 'need' are socially conditioned, and scientific substantiation of such ideas may be non-existent or insufficient. This is independent of the fact that objective needs are socially determined. Our study has sug-

1. International Labour Office, *The Cost of Social Security*, Geneva, 1969, pp. 316–22.

gested that the traditional conceptions of 'subsistence' poverty restrict people's understanding of modern social conditions as well as their willingness to act generously. On the one hand, they are encouraged to believe that 'subsistence' represents the limit of basic human needs, and this tends to restrict their assessment of what individual rights or entitlements could be introduced and guaranteed. A limited definition of need leads to a limited appreciation of rights. On the other hand, needs other than those included in the conception of 'subsistence' are denied full acknowledgement. There are goods, amenities and services which men and women are impelled to seek and do seek, and which by the tests of both subjective choice and behaviour are therefore social necessities, that have traditionally been excluded from consideration in devising poverty standards. People do not live by bread alone, and sometimes they are prepared to forego bread to meet a more pressing social need.

I have suggested that an alternative, and more objective, conception might be founded on 'relative deprivation' – by which I mean the absence or inadequacy of those diets, amenities, standards, services and activities which are common or customary in society. People are deprived of the conditions of life which ordinarily define membership of society. If they lack or are denied resources to obtain access to these conditions of life and so fulfil membership of society, they are in poverty. Deprivation can arise in any or all of the major spheres of life – at work, where the means largely determining one's position in other spheres are earned; at home, in neighbourhood and family; in travel; and in a range of social and individual activities outside work and home or neighbourhood. In principle, there could be extreme divergencies in the experience of different kinds of deprivation. In practice, there is a systematic relationship between deprivation and level of resources. The 'subsistence' approach ignores major spheres of life in which deprivation can arise. A physically efficient diet is regarded as the basis of subsistence or a national minimum, which then provides the rationale for Britain's income maintenance system. It could be argued that this preoccupation with nutritional deprivation as the centrally evident problem of meeting need in society has, first, to be extended logically to *dietary* deprivation, thereby putting stress on the *kind* of food and drink which people actually consume (and the distribution of the budgets from which they purchase it), as well as the amount and quality of nutrients which they absorb, so acknowledging the *social* definition of dietary need. Secondly, membership of society involves the satisfaction of a range of other needs which are socially defined. The necessities of life are not fixed. They are continuously being adapted and augmented as changes take place in a society and its products. Increasing stratification and a developing division of labour, as well as the growth of powerful new organizations, create, as well as reconstitute, 'need'. In particular, the rich set fashions of consumption which gradually become diffused.

When attempts are made to express these conceptions in an operational form for purposes of measurement, and then are applied, rather different conclusions about the extent and nature of the problem are reached. By the deprivation standard, more people are found to be in poverty than by the state's standard, with the implication, for example, that the scale rates of the Supplementary Benefits Commission have been drawn too low, especially for households with older children, and that they should be raised.

But the implications for the development of explanations of poverty and policies to eliminate poverty do not rest there. An attempt to apply either standard over the different periods of time to the same populations shows that, contrary to much supposition, the poor are not a separate and relatively fixed section of society. This can be demonstrated first by tracing changes during the year. At any particular time there are households who, because of demotion, unemployment, sickness, disablement, retirement or increase in dependency, have recently fallen into poverty, just as there are households who, because of promotion, engagement or re-engagement at work, recovery from sickness or decrease in dependency, have just emerged from poverty.

This affects our exposition of the nature of the phenomenon, and hence our explanation. During the early stages of the life-cycle, incomes and other resources are low; children put claims on the resources of the young adults who are their parents; the costs of housing and establishing a home are considerable; and the parents have jobs which are relatively insecure and paid below average. During middle or late middle life, a peak of prosperity is reached; the numbers of dependants and housing costs diminish just when resources actually increase or are at least maintained; earnings for a standard number of hours often increase because of promotion or seniority, and assets are accumulated or invested. In the later stages of life, there is a descent into austerity or poverty: before retirement, incomes are already reduced, and people who reach an advanced age (a) have greater needs as a consequence of disablement, (b) find that their share of the fruits of economic growth – for example, in new forms of state and occupational pension scheme – are smaller than average, and (c) tend to be less well protected than younger age groups from inflation. Assets and employer welfare benefits in particular augment the advantage of the middle aged over younger and older groups. Figure 7.2 (page 287) provides a summary of these changes over life.

From infancy onwards, therefore, the risks of being in poverty vary according to, and depend crucially upon, the employment status of adults in the income unit or household, the ratio of dependants to earners, form of tenure, value of assets, individual disablement and, related to all of these, occupational class.

Explanations of Poverty

What therefore is the explanation of widespread poverty? The theoretical approach developed in this book is one rooted in class relations. Some account has to be given of allocative principles and mechanisms and developments in the pattern of social life and consumption. In all societies, there is a crucial relationship between the production, distribution and redistribution of resources on the one hand and the creation or sponsorship of style of living on the other. One governs the resources which come to be in the control of individuals and families. The other governs the 'ordinary' conditions and expectations attaching to membership of society, the denial or lack of which represents deprivation. The two are in constant interaction and explain at any given moment historically both the level and extent of poverty.

Institutions arise to control both the production and allocation of resources. These are predominantly institutions concerned with the productive process – of capital, management and labour. Hierarchical organizations, with elaborate ranks of privilege and preferment, evolve, and induce gradations of acknowledged status and not just different levels of profit and income. The relationships typified in the productive process tend to be reproduced in the processes of distribution. Salaries might be differentiated from wages – for example, occupational welfare from public welfare – and bank deposit accounts from Post Office savings. Markets arise to correspond with different levels of wealth. But increasingly, and partly through the establishment of intermediary institutions, some processes of distribution and redistribution originate from, and are impelled by, wider or external interests and values.

The growth of organizations and associations not directly linked with production exerts considerable influence. Their relative independence may stem from their own bureaucratic or professional power, or from specialized groups of consumers whom they serve. Some agencies of the distribution of resources become separated from those of production. These interests are not necessarily more public spirited. Some writers treat agencies of the state, for example, as subordinate to the interests of a private capitalist economy. Large parts of the operations currently of the Departments of Trade, Industry, Energy, Employment, Agriculture and Prices and Consumer Protection, for example, could be so construed. But this hegemony is too crudely described and needs to be examined closely.

There are agencies of the state which are only indirectly related to the interests of capital as historically and restrictedly defined. They simultaneously serve diffuse political, intellectual or consumer interests as well as those of the private market. Sometimes they act more for self-aggrandizement than to advance the immediate interests of the market, and may act to create a larger inequality of resources and power than that which otherwise exists in a market society. Even if they are tied in principle to the fortunes of the economy, it is an economy which they are helping to shape. There are also agencies of the state which, though they can be said to be closely identified with the interests of the private market, act at least in large measure as checks on their operations and try to guide and control them. And there are agencies or groups participating in the market who are constantly seeking to modify or change it.

All this has to be borne in mind in developing an explanation of unequal earnings. The unions, the boards of the nationalized industries, and the government, principally through its incomes and fiscal policies, but also through a network of agencies like the Wages Councils and the Equal Opportunities Commission, and wage-negotiation machinery like the Whitley Council and the Review Body on Top Salaries, contribute to the evolution of the wage and salary system. It would be absurd to exclude them from any part of the explanation of inequality of earnings. One part of our task in explaining the unequal distribution of resources is therefore to trace the weight and influence of these different institutions in defining wage and salary rates and influencing decisions about increases.

It is not just a question of how incomes come to be graded or resources distributed, but how access is decided. We have to identify the rules of access which govern the scope or exclusiveness of structures, and not just the rules which control their internal differentiation. With the evolution and internal differentiation of resource systems, including the wage system, people have problems of access to these resources. The idea of admission or selection carries with it the corresponding idea of exclusion or rejection – even if that seems irrelevant or unintended. This double-sidedness of the operation of institutions which distribute resources is crucial to the explanation of poverty. There are sets of rules which, for example, control entry, define and organize queues, categorize entrants by type and determine specific amounts to which they are entitled. Others have called attention to the 'neglected' problems of access to resources in poor countries.[1] But the concept of access is also helpful in explaining the unequal distribution of resources in relatively rich countries.

The wage system itself breaks down into a differentiated structure of mini-systems. This corresponds not so much with a 'dual' as with a highly stratified labour market. Thus, as shown in Chapter 12, occupational class is correlated with graduated forms of work deprivation and with scope and value of employer welfare benefits as well as with earnings. There are elaborate rules of professional associations and trade unions, as well as of private firms and public services, including employment agencies and educational institutions, which control access of numbers and social characteristics of individuals. With each new differentiation within the system, new rules of access are devised; a new basis for establishing rights and making claims is laid, personnel appointed to supervise the application of the rules, and through the assertion of a kind of preferment excluded groups consigned to the risks of deprivation. The form taken by the hierarchy of occupational classes, the differentiated work conditions, status and fringe bene-

1. For example, Schaffer, B., and Wen-hsien, H., 'Distribution and the Theory of Access', Institute of Development Studies, University of Sussex, May 1973; Schaffer, B., 'Easiness of Access: A Concept of Queues', Institute of Development Studies, University of Sussex, 1972.

fits as well as earnings of those classes, and the institutions controlling access to different levels and sanctioning the conditions associated with each stratum, must comprise a major part of any explanation of inequality. Certainly, the survey on which this report is based confirms in some detail the existence, and surprisingly regular form, of this structure. Large sections of the population are denied access to work which has good pay, security and otherwise good conditions. Their numbers, and the relative level of resources which they do attain (or to which they fall), are a function of both the hierarchical structure which exists *above* their class and of the resources which ascending strata succeed in attracting. In this respect, therefore, the direct implication is that, if poverty is to be reduced, there must be less differentiation hierarchically of the employed population *and* a smaller proportionate share of total national resources by higher groups.

So far we have been speaking as if inequality of incomes, and the poverty of those at the foot of the scale, corresponded solely with the differentiation of the earnings system and of the work force. Two major modifications now require to be introduced. One is that people holding different positions in the occupational scale have varied numbers of dependants. The significant question is not whether they have more dependants than their wage can support, or what level of wage supports a 'reasonable' number of dependants, but why different types of dependant are denied access to a wage, or why such a high proportion of the national resources available for distribution (proportionate, that is, to the number of wage-earners) is channelled through the individual wage system rather than through the child benefit and social security systems and, say, an income scheme for married women working in the home. Children have gradually been excluded from the wage-force and compulsorily required to attend school, currently up to 16, without access to income. Their parents have rights, after the child reaches the age of 16, only to a derisory level of educational maintenance grants, and a low rate of child benefit – unless they qualify for national insurance dependants' benefit because of inability to work. Married women who stay at home receive no income other than that allowed by their husbands from the wage, irrespective of their work in bringing up children and maintaining a home and family. Their husbands are allowed additional tax relief. Other adult dependants, mostly disabled and elderly persons, are nearly all entitled to contributory or non-contributory social security benefits, but at levels which, even allowing for the numbers which a wage is sometimes expected to support, are below the wages of unskilled manual workers. These three forms of restriction of access to resources have to be traced historically. They depend on the social meanings given respectively to childhood, marriage, family and non-productive work. There are a number of possible themes. One is how the conferment of protected status can result in dependence or disprivilege among excluded groups. Another is how the over-studious definition of the rights of certain minorities can hold them back during periods of rapid economic expansion. While at a moment of time the definition of their rights may seem entirely reasonable, the inflexibility of those definitions may prove to be a disadvantage when economic and social conditions change.

A consequential modification must also be listed. A large, and proportionately increasing, section of the population are neither part of the paid workforce nor members of the households of that workforce. The great majority of them are retired elderly people living singly or in married pairs, who have no prospect or intention of returning to the workforce. Others include disabled, chronic sick and long-term unemployed people and one-parent families. The ways in which they have been denied access to paid employment, conceded incomes equivalent in value to bare subsistence, attracted specially defined low social status as minority groups, and accommodated, as a result, within the social structure as a kind of modern 'underclass', need to be traced.

The significance of minority-group status has been explored in the second half of this book, and the creation of an underclass discussed at length, particularly in relation to the elderly in Chapter 23. There are class groups among the retired population corresponding with the occupational classes of the employed population, who possess distinguishable material amenities; but superimposed on the low relative position of these different strata are the added disadvantages of being a minority group. The status of 'retirement' has been extended and has come to be rigorously enforced in the course of the twentieth century. The incomes of the vast majority of retired elderly derive from state pensions and supplementary benefits and are below the net earnings, allowing for dependants, of the lowest paid class of manual workers. Because retired people are, at a time of economic growth, denied a full share of its benefits, and because, at a time of rapid inflation, some sources of income, especially of occupational pensions, but also certain types of savings, such as National Savings, are eroded in purchasing value, some elderly people who are not in poverty in the early period of their retirement fall into poverty subsequently. Through the mechanisms of the state and occupational pension schemes and the discriminatory practices of institutions which control the allocation of real annual surplus and operate interest rates selectively their incomes fail to keep pace with the advance of others.

One further step needs to be taken in analysing resources. The unequal distribution of standards of living derives not just from the hierarchical ranking of roles in the employment system and the exclusion of certain sections of the population from that system, it derives also from resources other than earnings net of taxes or benefits and allowances paid from such taxes. On the one hand, children whose parents have considerable resources other than cash incomes, especially assets or employer welfare benefits, obtain advantages in a whole variety of ways over their peers, are more likely to gain access to the privileged sectors of education and hence reach the upper levels of the occupational hierarchy. They get a flying start as well as material help or security at subsequent critical stages of their careers. On the other hand, families with substantial resources other than cash incomes can contain debts and borrow more easily. Generally they attain higher standards of living than those without such resources. Inequality and poverty therefore originate in part in institutions perpetuating the unequal distribution of wealth and benefits and services in kind. The existing distribution of land, property and other forms of wealth, and the mechanisms for the transmission, augmentation and redistribution of such wealth, provide both a highly material and also a social framework within which the earnings system has grown up and operates. The conventions and differentials of the earnings system may themselves reflect features of the structure and transmission of wealth. Those professionals whose skills were employed by wealthy families themselves acquired high status and eventually the power to control entry to the professions and negotiate high fees and salaries.

The insistence theoretically in this book on the concept of 'resources' instead of 'incomes' therefore shifts attention from the reasons for unequal individual net earnings to the reasons for unequal distribution of total resources including wealth. Here the importance, among other things, of the inheritance over the accumulation of wealth has to be recognized. This was shown in Chapter 9 for the rich in the sample. The resilience of fortunes also has to be explained – through ingenious tax avoidance, the accumulative value of portfolios of stocks and shares, the surges and offerings of the property market and the laws of testamentary succession. The extremely unequal distribution of wealth is perhaps the single most notable feature of social conditions in the United Kingdom. That may be the key not just to the action required to obtain a more equitable earnings structure, but also to any substantial diminution of poverty. Exclusion from access to wealth, and especially from property, is perhaps the single most notable feature of the poor. In general, access to occupational class tends to be a function of class origins and family wealth.

What is the social outcome of this unequal structure of resources, and how is it legitimated? Different types and amounts of resources provide a foundation for different styles of living. Occupational classes reflect the processes of production, but, since they have unequal resources, they also reflect unequal styles of living. The term 'styles of living' has been preferred to styles of consumption because it suggests a wider and more appropriate set of activities than a term which suggests merely the ingestion of material (and implicitly *digestible*) goods. There exists a hierarchy of styles of living which reflect differential command over resources. There are, of course, threads linking behaviour and conditions of people in their capacity of producers or earners with behaviour and conditions of people in their capacity of users of resources. Level of resources reflects the style of living that can be adopted, as well as social acknowledgement of the worth of the recipients or earners of those resources. Marx put the point graphically: 'Hunger is hunger, but the hunger gratified by cooked meat eaten with a knife and fork is a different hunger from that which bolts down raw meat with the aid of hand, nail and tooth.'[1] But society has to foster citizenship and integrate its members, and not merely observe and regulate a hierarchy of life-styles. Different institutions, including the Church, the media and various professional associations, as well as the advertising agencies of private and public industry, endeavour to universalize, for example, standards of child care, the practices of marriage and family relationships, reciprocity between neighbours and the treatment of elderly, disabled and blacks. State as well as market agencies are constantly seeking to widen and change modes of consumption and behaviour. A social style of living is cultivated and recommended, in which both poor and rich are expected to participate. People low on the income scale cannot buy goods as expensive as those bought by, or live as well as, the rich, but they are presumed, none the less, to engage in the same broad scheme of consumption, customs and activities. The student of poverty is therefore concerned to trace two things. What constitutes the social style of living, and the changes which are taking place in that style, has to be described and explained. The standards which are consciously underwritten by the state, *or* established by popular expectations within the community, may be difficult or not difficult for some groups with low-ranking resources to attain. In other words, it is society which defines the nature and level of the threshold of activities and consumption which it expects its members to attain. And, by the nature of modern development, 'society' is increasingly a national rather than a regional or local society. Although the threshold style of living will tend to rise or fall in conjunction with any rise or fall in real national resources, there is no necessary or invariant connection.

The student of poverty is also concerned to identify the groups failing in different respects, not necessarily all respects, to attain the threshold of standards set explicitly or implicitly by society. The groups may be found to be deprived in one, two or more respects. In the course of Chapters 11 to 14, we examined a number of measures of deprivation and found that they were correlated with level of resources. There was provisional evidence of a threshold of poverty such that, below a particular level with allowances for composition of income unit, people were disproportionately unable to share in customary or commonly approved customs and activities.

The extent and severity of poverty is therefore a function, on the one hand, of the hierarchical and highly unequal distribution of resources, and, on the other, of the style or styles of living which are constantly being defined and redefined and which the population feels compelled, or is compelled, to emulate.

The Principles of Policy

The implications for policy remain to be sketched. In Chapter 2, three principles or models of social policy were advanced: (a) conditional welfare for the few; (b)

1. Marx, K., *Grundrisse: Foundations of the Critique of Political Economy* (seven notebooks rough-drafted in 1857–8), Penguin Books, Harmondsworth, 1973, p. 92.

minimum rights for the many; and (c) distributional justice for all. These principles were shown to be implicit in theories of inequality and poverty. In the course of the twentieth century, social policy has been dominated by one or other of the first two principles or by a mixture of both principles. One of the purposes of this book has been to call attention to at least the possibility of applying the third principle extensively in constructing policy. In the late 1960s and early 1970s, despite protestations to the contrary, successive governments invoked the first principle with renewed vigour. The limitations of this principle, especially as affecting those families in the survey who were dependent on, or eligible for, means-tested services, are discussed at length in Chapters 24 and 25. The assumptions about the scale and personal origins of poverty, as well as about the effectiveness and appropriateness of the measures taken to alleviate it, are shown to be mistaken.

The second principle is more persuasive, but falls far short of the expectations of its advocates. The assumption is not only that the hierarchical social and economic system requires generous underpinning rather than recasting, but that it *can* be so underpinned. History throws doubt on this assumption. Basic needs have tended to be defined in historical, absolute terms instead of contemporaneous, relative or social terms – and even such needs have not been met in practice. For example, Beveridge adopted the meagre definition of necessities outlined by Rowntree as a 'subsistence' basis for national insurance benefits. He intended these benefits to be at a level sufficient to guarantee subsistence without resort to means-tested supplementation. This was the cardinal principle, as he himself proclaimed it, of his plan. In over thirty years since the national insurance scheme was enacted, this principle has never been fulfilled. Governments have shrunk from fulfilling it, perhaps because of the implications for public expenditure, but more likely because of the threat that would be posed to the lower reaches of the wage system, and more generally to the kind of employment system appropriate to a capitalist or even 'mixed' economy. The 1834 Poor Law Commission's principle of less eligibility[1] lives on in the definition of levels and conditions of social security benefits.

In the Edwardian era, the introduction of universal minimum benefits represented a diminution in the severity and perhaps the scale of poverty. But this change could not be regarded as permanent. Maxima were not defined and, as the economy grew, privileged groups could continue to obtain a disproportionate share of the additional national resources that were created. Without provision for regular upward revision of *all* minima, the poor were liable to see their share of resources reduced. Alternatively, the demand on the part of the majority of the

---

1. 'The first and most essential of all conditions, a principle which we find universally admitted, even by those whose practice is at variance with it, is, that [the pauper's] situation on the whole shall not be made really or apparently so eligible as the situation of the independent labourer of the lowest class' – Report from His Majesty's Commissioners for Inquiring into the Administration and Practical Operation of the Poor Laws, Fellowes, London, 1834, p. 228.

population for 'better' styles of living as resources grew not only imposed new expectations upon the poor but left them experiencing new forms of deprivation. And, finally, the adoption of 'minima' seems to have had the effect of 'fixing' or institutionalizing the low status of certain minorities in society – rather as if this was their legitimate entitlement. At one stage of history, the application of a label to a particular group in the population seems to assist the allocation to them of resources; yet, at a later stage, the label may be a hindrance or a positive handicap, because of the stigmatizing connotations which it has in the meantime acquired. It is perhaps in this sense that the principle of minimum rights for the many, as it is applied in policy, has to be watched most carefully. Far from being the most realistic, and acceptable, method of diminishing poverty and inequality, it can turn out to be a major instrument legitimating them.

There are further difficulties about the principle. Those who seek to apply it tend to assume that the stratum of the population who are in poverty is fairly stable, and fairly small, when, as we have seen, there is constant movement into and out of poverty and, at any one stage, a very large proportion of the population who only just escape its clutches as well as a much more substantial proportion than has been appreciated in poverty. They also assume an over-simplified model of redistribution required to safeguard people against poverty, believing that a sufficient sum can be extracted in taxes from incomes and payments for goods and services to meet needs. The problem here is that, once people receive a particular sum of earnings or other income, they assume that that is the figure to which they have an inalienable right. There is bound to be some kind of limit which they will seek to set on the amount that they will allow governments to extract in taxes, whether directly or indirectly, so that the needs of the poor may be met. Moreover, as the *providers* of those taxes, they consequently expect the beneficiaries not to receive anything like the same levels of *net* income as themselves. Personal taxation as applied to the gross wage has, in practice, helped to perpetuate the inequalities in a market economy between those who have access to the wage system and those who do not.

I am suggesting that there is an in-built tension, and even contradiction, in the application of the principle of a national minimum to a market economy. A minimum is hard to establish alongside or underneath a wage-earning and property-owning hierarchy – except at a very low level. It becomes hard to maintain when the number of dependants at each end of the age-scale increases and, as a result of the economy meeting fluctuating fortunes, more people of so-called active age are made redundant or unemployed. Either wages and transfer payments alike have to be brought under the control of a statutory incomes policy, or the payment of money for goods and services has to give way to the provision of free goods and services.

The third principle of distributional justice for all reflects a more adequate theory of poverty and a better prescription of the policies required to defeat it. In this report we have found maldistribution of types as well as of amounts of resources. We have shown the large numbers of those in poverty or on its margins, the constant movement into and out of poverty, and the relationships between low income or denial of access to income and *systems* or *structures* of resources. Enlargement of access is as important as greater equality of distribution. Thus, the rights of both disabled and non-disabled people, including the elderly, to obtain gainful employment can and must be extended – by legal and social means. Wealth, including land, property and other assets, can and must be distributed more widely as well as more evenly. This can be done by the enlargement of the direct rights of the individual as well as by extending public ownership. Rights to housing, for example, should be more widely shared in the sense that the disparity between owner-occupation and tenancy should be reduced by common definition of the rights to succession and adaptation as well as to space and amenities.

Another example is incomes policy. The separation of the payment of earnings from that of social security and the lack of access of married women to cash incomes of their own would be reviewed. Income might be paid from a common, public, source or by a small number of agencies regulated by common principles. An incomes policy would be negotiated annually for workers and non-workers alike. It would therefore absorb the social security scheme, though there would continue to be direct payments as there are at present, for example, to disabled and elderly people, and child allowances drawn at the Post Office by mothers. New cash allowances would be payable to many categories of married women, by virtue of their work. With more adequate provisions in cash for many people currently labelled 'dependants' of the wage-earner or family, there could be fewer grades of payment to the 'employed' and 'self-employed' within a much smaller ratio between top and bottom of the income scale. Or perhaps the state could regulate a policy for a basic income for the entire population, leaving provision for some topping up by local or industrial negotiation. The further implication is that, given social regulation of incomes and of the distribution of other resources, the tax system would be substantially reduced as an intermediary in the allocation and reallocation of resources. Illustrations have been given in this report of different policies which might be adopted, and in this final chapter I have not attempted to reproduce recommendations listed in Chapters 12 to 25.

A transformation of work organization and social relations would be required to legitimate such changes and secure public approval for them. The hierarchy of earnings depends on an elaborate division of labour and the supervision of each grade by the personnel in an ascendant grade. The hierarchy of social class depends in substantial part on the unequal distribution of wealth, including land, housing and other property. By reorganizing production in smaller collaborative units or teams, interchanging workers or arranging spells of manual and non-manual work and dividing possessions and property more evenly, the possibilities might at least be indicated.

An effective assault on poverty would therefore include:

1. *Abolition of excessive wealth.* The wealth of the rich must be substantially reduced by different policies and a statutory definition of maximum permissible wealth in relation to the mean agreed.
2. *Abolition of excessive income.* Top salaries or wages must be substantially reduced in relation to the mean and a statutory definition of maximum permissible earnings (and income) agreed.
3. *Introduction of an equitable income structure and some breaking down of the distinction between earners and dependants.* At the logical extreme this might involve the withdrawal of personal income taxation and of the social security benefits scheme, and the payment of tax-free incomes according to a publicly agreed and controlled schedule by occupational category and skill, but also by need or dependency – which would cover a relatively narrow span of variability; together with a substantial increase in corporation or payroll taxes. A less radical and therefore less effective solution would be the adoption of a more comprehensive income policy than the policies primarily of wage restraint which have operated since the early 1960s, together with a more coordinated social security benefit scheme with higher relative levels of benefit.
4. *Abolition of unemployment.* For all over the age of compulsory education a legally enforceable right to work is needed, with a corresponding obligation on the part of employers, the government and especially local authorities, to provide alternative types of employment. This right would apply at different, including severe, levels of disablement, and would apply also to the elderly.
5. *Reorganization of employment and professional practice.* There must be further innovations in public ownership, industrial democracy and collaborative instead of hierarchical work structures; restraint on the growth of power under the guise of professional and managerial autonomy, and encouragement of self-dependence and a high level of universal education.
6. *Reorganization of community service.* There must be a corresponding growth of rights and hence responsibilities for members of local communities, with abolition of the distinction between owner-occupiers and tenants, and social-service support for the individual and family at home rather than in institutions.

It would be wrong to suggest that any of this is easy or even likely. The citadels of wealth and privilege are deeply entrenched and have shown tenacious capacity to withstand assaults, notwithstanding the gentleness of their legal, as distinct from the ferocity of their verbal, form. Yet we have observed the elaborate hierarchy of wealth and esteem, of which poverty is an integral part. If any conclusion deserves to be picked out from this report as its central message it is this, with which, some time, the British people must come to terms.

Appendix One
Methods of Sampling

Hilary Land

The sampling had a number of novel features and is described in full in this appendix. A multi-stage stratified design was used in which, with the exception of Belfast, every household had an equal probability of selection. Our aim was to achieve completed interviews with approximately 2,000 households in the United Kingdom.

The sampling procedure can be considered in four main phases:

1. The division of the United Kingdom into appropriate regions.
2. The selection of a primary area unit for sampling within each region and the selection of a suitable variable by which to stratify these units within each region.
3. The selection of suitable secondary area units within each primary area unit and the selection of a suitable stratification factor.
4. The final selection of addresses and conversion into a sample of households.

The Choice of Regions

The first question is the division of the United Kingdom into regions. Our object was to limit the number to as few as possible while preserving a representatively wide geographical spread of the eventual sample. A small number would allow reasonable methods of stratification to be applied so that about fifty areas could be selected – these fifty being about the maximum for effective and economical interviewing for an achieved sample of around 2,000 household interviews. Official statistics are usually based on the twelve standard regions of the United Kingdom or the eleven planning regions. These are identical, except for south-eastern England, as shown below.

Standard Regions

1. *South-Eastern*   Greater London, Surrey, Sussex and Kent.
2. *Eastern*   Bedfordshire, Hertfordshire, Essex, Suffolk, Norfolk, Cambridge and the Isle of Ely, Huntingdonshire.
3. *Southern*   Oxfordshire, Buckinghamshire, Berkshire, Hampshire and the Isle of Wight, Poole in Dorset.
4. *South-Western*   Gloucestershire, Wiltshire, Somerset, Dorset, Devon, Cornwall.
5. *West Midlands*   Herefordshire, Shropshire, Staffordshire, Warwickshire and Worcestershire.
6. *East Midlands*   part Derbyshire, Nottinghamshire, Lincolnshire (parts of Holland and Kesteven) Rutland, Leicestershire, Northamptonshire.

7. *North-Western*   Lancashire, Cheshire, part of Derbyshire.
8. *Yorkshire and*   West Riding of Yorkshire, East Riding of Yorkshire, Lindsay, part of
   Humberside   Lincolnshire.
9. *Northern*   Cumberland, Westmorland, Northumberland, Durham and North
                        Riding of Yorkshire.
10. *Wales*
11. *Scotland*
12. *Northern Ireland*

The Planning Regions

Regions 4 to 12 are the same as above. The South-East of England is divided differently
as follows:

South-East   Greater London, Surrey, Sussex, Kent, Essex, Bedfordshire,
                   Hertfordshire, together with all the counties included in the Southern
                   region above.
Anglia   Norfolk, Suffolk, Cambridge and Isle of Ely, Huntingdonshire.

The Family Expenditure Survey is based on the Planning Regions, except that Greater
London is treated as a separate stratum.[1]

Table A1.1. The regional distribution of population and electorate.

Region	Population (June 1966)		Electorate (March 1966)		Number of con- stituencies	Number of administra- tive areas
	Number	%	Number	%		
South-East	9,158,290	16·9	5,890,851	16·4	86	273
West Midlands	5,021,380	9·2	3,232,757	9·0	54	120
North-West	6,731,940	12·4	4,432,479	12·4	79	177
Northern and Yorkshire and Humberside	8,048,900	14·8	5,338,912	14·9	95	263
Scotland	5,190,800	9·5	3,344,859	9·3	71	372
Wales and South-West	6,320,230	11·7	4,150,882	11·6	78	353
Anglia and East Midlands	4,880,960	9·0	3,128,407	8·7	52	191
Greater London	7,913,600	14·6	5,423,849	15·1	103	33
Northern Ireland	1,469,000	2·7	902,301	2·5	12	67
Total	54,321,500	100	35,845,297	100	630	1,849

1. See *Monthly Digest of Statistics Supplement*, Appendix 1, Central Statistical Office, HMSO, London,
1968.

We decided to treat Greater London separately, and to amalgamate some of the remaining regions, so that the quantity could be reduced to an economical number. There were several ways in which pairs of regions could have been amalgamated. For our purposes, variations in incomes between regions are important and, taking the criterion of average net income before tax per capita,[1] the richest region is the South-Eastern followed by the Eastern, Southern and West Midland regions. Next are the South-West, East Midland, North-West, Yorkshire and Humberside regions, with Wales, Scotland, the Northern region and Northern Ireland the poorest. There are, of course, big variations within certain regions, for example, the Eastern regions. As a whole, the planning region of Anglia is a low-income area, but, within it, Essex is a high-income area, and Hertford is very high. We therefore decided to use the planning regions, thus including Essex and Hertford with the South-East, but also to reduce the number, for example by combining Anglia with the East Midlands. The United Kingdom was divided into nine regions, as shown in Table A1.1.

At the next stage, we divided the primary area units in each region into a maximum of three strata: rural, high-income urban and low-income urban. We selected two primary units from each stratum so that standard errors could be calculated with some degree of accuracy. This whole procedure allowed us to restrict the sample to about fifty areas, which was necessary for practical and financial reasons.

The Selection of Primary Area Units within Regions

There are two units of area commonly used for sampling purposes: (a) *local-authority administrative areas* and (b) *constituencies*. In England and Wales, the administrative areas are the Greater London boroughs, county boroughs, municipal boroughs, urban districts and rural districts. In Scotland, administrative areas are cities, burghs and district councils. In Great Britain, there are 1,782 administrative areas which vary greatly in size. The Family Expenditure Survey uses the administrative areas of Great Britain as the primary sampling units and stratifies all of them except those in the Greater London Council area into four strata:

1. Administrative areas in provincial conurbations.
2. All urban areas not in provincial conurbations.
3. Semi-rural areas.
4. Rural areas.[2]

There are 630 constituencies in the United Kingdom. They vary in size much less than administrative areas, the majority of constituencies comprising an electorate of between 50,000 and 70,000.

Our choice between administrative areas and constituencies seemed, in principle, to depend on the availability of data, first by which to stratify, and secondly by which to compare the representativeness of the selected sample. If possible, it was also important to choose units of roughly comparable size.

1. The data were based on an analysis of a personal incomes survey by the Board of Inland Revenue for 1964–5, by Coates, B. E., and Rawstron, E. M., *Guardian*, 10 April 1967.
2. For a detailed description of the sample design of the Family Expenditure Survey, see Kemsley, W. F. F., *Family Expenditure Survey – Handbook on the Sample Fieldwork and Coding Procedures*, Government Social Survey, H M S O, London, 1969, pp. 8–20.

In terms of availability of data, local-authority administrative areas seemed at first sight to be the better choice. For each county borough, each administrative county, and for urban areas with populations above 50,000, there were a lot of published data in the census reports for 1961 and elsewhere. However, for rural districts there was less information, and published data were restricted to population size, density and structure, number of households, dwellings, amenities overcrowding and tenure. Some unpublished data for 1961 were available but based on a 10 per cent sample only.

The only data actually based on constituency areas were size of electorate and voting behaviour. But this did not cause us to rule constituencies out, for we found that amalgamations of data could achieve almost the same result. Very few constituencies are in two counties (there are three partly in Greater London and partly in Hertford, Kent or Surrey). Only one county borough does not fall within a single constituency. Altogether, fifty-three of the eighty-one county boroughs in England and Wales have boundaries coinciding exactly with constituency boundaries. Moreover, the names of the boroughs, urban districts and rural districts included in each constituency are known. So the data from the census can be used for constituencies as well as for administrative areas. In both instances, however, data for individual rural districts are very limited. There were no differences between administrative areas or constituencies in availability of data for comparing the representativeness of the sample.

Administrative areas have the disadvantage, compared with constituencies, of varying greatly in population. The problem could have been overcome to some extent by amalgamating some of the smaller areas, though this would have been a complicated exercise. The final choice therefore seemed to depend on the availability of a stratification factor which would enable us to classify urban area units into high-income, middle-income and low-income areas.

The Stratification of Urban Areas

The 'J-index' has been used in previous national surveys as a stratification factor for urban areas. The J-index is the percentage of the parliamentary electorate qualified to serve as jurors.[1] Until 1967, the Family Expenditure Survey used the J-index based on the parliamentary electorate who in 1955 were qualified to serve as jurors. But, in 1963, rateable values were reassessed in England and Wales, and this reduced the power of J-index to discriminate between high- and low-income areas because the new assessment had increased the number eligible for jury service.

It was likely that, in 1968, we might still have found a high proportion of the very poor in areas where the J-index was low, but as we wanted to select a national sample *representative of all income groups*, this did not make it a suitable stratification factor for our purposes.

It was important to find, if possible, a *single* stratification factor. A composite factor could have been calculated using factors which indicate variations in the socio-economic status of an area – for example, percentage of overcrowded households, percentage of manual workers, percentage of the population under 15 years of age, and population

1. The qualification for a juror (indicated by a J against the elector's name) was to be a householder resident in premises of a rateable value of £30 or more in London and Middlesex and of £20 or more elsewhere. See Kemsley, *Family Expenditure Survey*, p. 9.

density. As we wanted to limit the number of primary unit areas to about fifty, and at the same time to make regional comparisons, it would not have been possible to stratify by several factors unless they could have been weighted in a composite index. Instead, we looked for one factor which correlated highly with factors associated with low socio-

Table A1.2. *Correlations with percentage voting left at 1964 general election for county boroughs (Britain).*

Factor	Correlation coefficient
Workers in industry as % of occupied males	+0·6
Ratio of semi and unskilled manual workers to non-manual workers	+0·8
Percentage of population under 14 years	+0·5
Percentage of population over 25 years who left school at 15 or under	+0·7
Percentage of households without exclusive use of bath	+0·6
Percentage of households living less than 1½ persons per room	−0·6
Administrative, managerial and professional workers as % of economically active males	−0·8
Percentage of population over 25 years who finished education after 17 years of age	−0·7
Retail turnover *per capita*	−0·4

economic status. Voting behaviour defined as the percentage of the electorate voting left was such a factor.[1] It is examined in Tables A1.2 and A1.3. There was a high positive correlation with factors associated with low income (high proportion of unskilled and semi-skilled workers of population leaving school early and of households without a bath),

Table A1.3. *Correlations with percentage voting left at 1964 general elections for county boroughs and counties together (Britain).*

Factor	Correlation coefficient	
	Voting left	Population density
Percentage of population over 25 years of age who finished education at 15 or sooner	+0·9	+0·5
Workers in heavy industry as % of occupied males	+0·5	+0·1
Males sick as % of economically active males	+0·5	+0·4
Percentage of households overcrowded	+0·5	+0·5
Administrative, managerial and professional workers as % of economically active males	−0·6	−0·3
Non-manual males as % of economically active males	−0·6	−0·4

1. It was put forward for explanation by Professor Durbin and Professor Stuart of the London School of Economics. Voting left was defined as all those not voting for Conservative, Independent or Liberal candidates. The correlations used in Tables 2 and 3 were calculated by Bleddyn Davies and Peter Stone.

and a high negative correlation with factors associated with high income (high proportion of managerial and professional workers and of population staying at school after the age of 17).

The correlation between socio-economic factors and voting behaviour was not as high when counties as well as county boroughs were taken into the reckoning, partly because there is a greater variation *within* such areas, which are also much larger. However, the correlation tended to be higher than between socio-economic factors and population density, a factor which we had considered using as an alternative (see Table A1.3).

Percentage of the electorate voting left at the 1964 general election was therefore chosen as the best available single stratification factor for urban areas. Since voting behaviour of local-authority administrative areas other than county boroughs or counties cannot be calculated, this meant that constituencies were necessarily chosen as the primary area units.

Rural Areas

Voting behaviour was not considered a suitable stratification factor for rural areas. In the first place, voting behaviour in very rural areas is not correlated highly with socio-economic factors. Secondly, only about 20 per cent of the population live in rural areas, so further stratification is perhaps unnecessary. Using constituencies as the primary area units, we defined a rural constituency as a constituency in which more than 50 per cent of the population lives in rural districts and in which there is no urban district or borough larger than 30,000 population. The latter criterion is added as a check against those rural districts which have been substantially urbanized since their designation 'rural'.[1]

Sampling Procedure with Primary Area Units

The constituencies in Great Britain were divided, first, into rural and urban. In Northern Ireland, we treated Belfast as one stratum and the remaining eight constituencies as another. As there were only eight rural constituencies in the West Midlands (14·4 per cent of the electorate in the region), and only three in the North-West, it was decided to ᴀmalgamate them with the nineteen rural constituencies of Northern, Yorkshire and Humberside region (forming 19·9 per cent of the electorate in the region) to form a separate stratum from which two constituencies could be chosen. In the event, both the constituencies which were selected happened to be drawn from the West Midlands region, and this means that, when amalgamated with the urban results for the regions, the West Midlands is over-represented and the Northern Yorkshire and Humberside region under-represented. It should be remembered that the probability of a household being included in the sample was the same for all households in each stratum and therefore in both these regions.

No adjustment is made in Table A1.4 for the deliberate oversampling of households in Northern Ireland. We increased the sample in order to make possible a very broad comparison of conditions in that region with conditions in regions in Britain. As stated in

1. Since 1967, the definition of 'rural area' for the Family Expenditure Survey has been based on population density and size of population of urban areas within the rural district. See Kemsley, *Family Expenditure Survey*, p. 8.

Table A1.4. *Distribution of electorate and sample in different strata in each region.*

Region	Number of constituencies	Stratum	Electorate (March 1966)		Poverty sample completed interviews	
			Number	%	Number	%
South-East	16	Rural	1,088,343	3·0	56	3·0
	24	Poor	1,630,112	4·5	82	4·3
	24	Middle	1,661,027	4·6	79	4·2
	22	Rich	1,511,369	4·2	75	4·0
	86		5,890,951	16·4[a]	292	15·5
West Midlands (urban)	24	Poor	1,410,573	3·9	78	4·1
	22	Rich	1,353,516	3·8	77	4·1
	46		2,764,089	7·7	155	8·2
North-West (urban)	26	Poor	1,384,743	3·8	73	3·9
	24	Middle	1,311,628	3·7	70	3·7
	26	Rich	1,568,473	4·4	83	4·4
	76		4,264,844	11·9[a]	226	12·0
Northern, Yorkshire and Humberside (urban)	26	Poor	1,382,301	3·9	85	4·5
	24	Middle	1,563,228	4·4	78	4·1
	26	Rich	1,332,415	3·7	62	3·3
	76		4,277,944	11·9[a]	225	11·9
Scotland	29	Rural	1,331,248	3·7	82	4·3
	22	Poor	1,046,980	2·9	50	2·7
	20	Rich	966,631	2·7	50	2·7
	71		3,344,859	9·3	182	9·7
Wales, South-West	32	Rural	1,636,625	4·6	68	3·6
	24	Poor	1,244,122	3·5	62	3·3
	22	Rich	1,270,135	3·5	84	4·4
	78		4,150,882	11·6	214	11·3
Anglia and East Midlands	20	Rural	1,243,790	3·5	67	3·6
	32	Poor} Rich}	1,884,617	5·2	95	5·0
	52		3,128,407	8·7	162	8·6
Greater London	34	Poor	1,643,438	4·6	88	4·7
	34	Middle	1,923,120	5·4	92	4·9
	35	Rich	1,857,291	5·2	91	4·8
	103		5,423,849	15·1[a]	271	14·4

Table A1.4 – contd

Region	Number of constituencies	Stratum	Electorate (March 1966) Number	%	Poverty sample completed interviews Number	%
West and North-West Midlands Northern Yorkshire and Humberside (rural)	30	Rural	1,695,207	4·7	72	3·8
Northern Ireland	4	Belfast	252,480	0·7	46	2·4
	8	Rural	649,821	1·8	41	2·2
	12		902,301	2·5	87	4·6
Total UK	630		35,845,297	100·0	1,886	100

NOTE: ªDue to rounding, figures do not add up exactly to the total.

Chapter 1, certain tables in the report describing the results from the whole UK sample have been adjusted to reflect the true proportion of households and population in Northern Ireland.

Bearing in mind the slight adjustment needing to be made for Northern Ireland, Table A1.4 shows that, for the different regions, the numbers interviewed were fairly representative. The rural parts of the West Midlands, the North-West and the Northern, Yorkshire and Humberside regions have been distinguished in the table from the urban parts of these regions because of the procedure described above.

In the regions where there are large numbers of urban constituencies – the South-East, Greater London, the North-West, Northern Yorkshire and Humberside – the constituencies were ranked in descending order of percentage voting left and divided into *three* strata denoting low-income, middle-income and high-income areas. In East Anglia and East Midlands, there were insufficient urban constituencies to justify two urban strata. The distribution of strata within each region is shown in Table A1.4 and Tables A1.4 and A1.5 compare the distribution of the electorate with that of the households in the sample who were finally interviewed. It should be noted that substantial proportions of the elec-

Table A1.5. *Percentage of households interviewed in each stratum (first stage).*

Stratum	Electorate of UK	Households in poverty survey
Rural	21·4	20·5
Low % voting left (rich)	27·5	27·7
Middle % voting left (middle)	23·2	21·9
High % voting left (poor)	27·1	27·5
(Belfast)	(0·7)	(2·4)
Total UK	100·0	100·0

torate fall into each of the four strata which were evolved: rural, rich urban, middle-income urban and poor urban. The proportions of the eventual sample who were interviewed were broadly similar. For the percentage of the electorate voting left, Table A1.6 compares the urban constituencies selected for inclusion in the sample with all urban constituencies.

Table A1.6. Distribution of primary area units.

Percentage of electorate voting left (1966)	Urban constituencies in sample (excluding Northern Ireland)		Urban constituencies in Great Britain
	Number	%	%
80 and over	1	(2·6)	4·7
70–80	3	(7·9)	12·0
60–70	9	(23·6)	19·6
50–60	10	(26·3)	29·6
40–50	9	(23·6)	21·4
30–40	5	(13·1)	10·6
Under 30	1	(2·6)	1·8
Total	38	100	100

Within each stratum constituencies were ranked in pairs in descending order of size of electorate. Using random numbers, two constituencies were selected with replacement in each stratum, with probability proportioned to size except in the event of selecting the same unit, when the opposite member of the pair was included in the sample.[1] In Northern Ireland, two constituencies were sampled in Belfast and one from the remaining rural constituencies. The full list of constituencies follows.

The Selected Constituencies

		Percentage voting left
Greater London	Woolwich East	71·6
	Islington North	65·9
	Lewisham North	53·0
	Hornchurch	52·3
	Wandsworth Streatham	45·4
	Hendon North	49·2
South-East	Thurrock	69·4
	Dartford	56·6
	S.-W. Hertfordshire	47·0
	Aylesbury	45·5
	Guildford	39·5

1. The theoretical basis of the sample design is described in a paper by Durbin. See Durbin, J., 'Estimation of Sampling Errors in Multi-Stage Surveys', London School of Economics.

			Percentage voting left
South-East – *contd*	Bournemouth W.		38·8
	New Forest	Rural	
	Lewes	Rural	
Anglia and East Midlands	Ipswich		56·4
	Leicester S.-E.		40·1
	Melton	Rural	
	Grantham	Rural	
Wales and South-West	Neath		83·9
	Bristol South		67·1
	Gloucester		42·8
	Bristol West		29·5
	Yeovil (Somerset)	Rural	
	North Devon	Rural	
West Midlands	(R) Coventry East		67·8
	(R) Birmingham Northfield		59·6
	Brierley Hill		48·8
	Oldbury and Halesowen		53·2
North-West	Newton		62·8
	Salford East		67·2
	Manchester Wythenshawe		59·7
	Bolton East		59·2
	Southport		37·2
	North Fylde		36·7
Northern and Yorkshire and Humberside	Pontefract		78·3
	Bradford East		69·4
	South Shields		64·7
	Newcastle-on-Tyne East		59·8
	Leeds N.-W.		44·4
	Haltemprice		33·7
West Midlands, North-West, Northern and Yorkshire and Humberside	South Worcestershire	Rural	
	Oswestry	Rural	
Scotland	Glasgow Shettleston		77·5
	Coatbridge and Airdrie		64·1
	(R) Aberdeen South		52·0
	(R) Edinburgh West		44·7
	Galloway	Rural	
	Kinross and W. Perthshire	Rural	
Northern Ireland	Fermanagh and South Tyrone	Rural	
	Belfast East		
	Belfast North		

R = Repeated selection, Edinburgh West and Birmingham Northfield were selected twice, so the second members of the pairs to which they belonged were selected, i.e. Aberdeen South and Coventry East.

Selection within Constituencies

Every constituency in England and Wales is made up of part of one or one borough, or several boroughs, urban districts or rural districts. There are further divisions: borough and urban districts are divided into wards, rural districts into parishes. In Scotland, the administrative districts are slightly different. There are cities, large burghs, small burghs and district councils. A constituency may consist of a number of wards in a city or large burgh, or small burghs and districts in rural areas.

The constituencies in the large conurbations may consist of only the part of a large metropolitan borough, whereas the constituencies in rural areas consist almost entirely of rural districts with one or two small boroughs or urban districts. Some urban constituencies are therefore divided into only three wards, each comprising 7,000 or 8,000 households, others into some fifteen wards, each comprising only 1,000 or 2,000 households. Rural constituencies may be divided into three or four wards and more than ninety parishes. Some parishes are very small. For example, some parishes in the constituency of South Worcestershire have a population of less than thirty. Therefore, before a selection was made, some of the very small parishes were grouped together.

Such grouping was carried out on a geographical basis. The main object was to reduce the amount of travelling to be done in rural areas. The most convenient grouping was, in most instances, based on county electoral divisions (divisions on which county council elections are based), together with the help of a map. This information was usually obtained from the clerk of each rural district council.

Stratification Factors

How could certain groups of addresses in large areas be selected? For wards and parishes, it was not possible to use voting figures from parliamentary elections since these are not given. There are several disadvantages in using voting figures in local elections. First, there is a far lower poll than in general elections, so the voting figures only refer to a small proportion of the population. Secondly, although in densely populated urban areas the distinction between parties is as clear as in national elections, in the more rural areas the distinction is blurred by the number of independent candidates. Thirdly, no data exist on how well voting behaviour in local elections correlates with characteristics associated with low income.

For wards and parishes, again, there is little information published in Census County Reports. Instead, we chose a stratification factor based on unpublished material from the 10 per cent sample of the 1961 Census obtained from the General Registrar's Office. The choice was made by looking at factors positively correlated with characteristics associated with low income and negatively correlated with those associated with high income. The best one available appeared to be the proportion of the population aged 25 years or more who had left school at the age of 15 or under. Data based on all administrative counties and county boroughs was used. The proportion of the population aged 25 and over who had left school early did not prove to be an ideal factor, because, of course, it was related in part to the age structure of the ward or groups of parishes. Few of the elderly had a lengthy schooling as children, and a population with a high propor-

Table A1.7. *Correlations with high proportion of population aged 25 and over leaving school early at 15 or under (administrative counties and county boroughs in Britain).*

Factor	Correlation coefficient
Ratio of semi-skilled and unskilled manual workers to non-manual male workers	+0·7
Infant mortality rate per 1,000 population (average for the 3 years 1960–62)	+0·5
Percentage of households overcrowded	+0·5
Non-manual male workers as % of economically active males	−0·8

tion of elderly would tend as a whole to have a relatively high proportion of early leavers. However, despite this disadvantage it remained one of the best *single* factors *available* for our purposes.

Within each constituency, rural districts were treated separately from urban districts, boroughs and wards so that the final number of selected addresses could reflect the urban/rural composition of the constituency.

The proportion of the population aged 25 and over leaving school at 15 or under was calculated for each ward and county electoral division or group of parishes. Where the proportions varied widely, the wards were grouped into two strata, and within each stratum were ranked in descending order of size. If there was little difference then the wards were treated as a single stratum and arranged in descending order of size. A similar procedure was followed in the rural areas.

A ward or county electoral division was chosen for each stratum of each constituency with probability proportional to size (measured by number of *households*, not electorate). The number of interviews allocated to this ward or county electoral division equalled the product of the total number of interviews for the constituency and the proportion of the constituency households in the particular stratum. In the constituencies where a repeated selection had occurred, i.e. Birmingham and Coventry, Edinburgh and Aberdeen, a slightly different procedure was adopted. The number of interviews allocated to each constituency was divided into two equal samples. Two independent samples of wards were chosen with probability proportional to size. It did not matter that a particular ward occurred in both samples.

The Selection of Addresses

No national sampling frame of private households exists. A sample of households is usually obtained either by sampling addresses from the published electoral registers or by sampling rateable units from the rating records. Both of these sampling frames have disadvantages from the point of view of obtaining an up-to-date sample of households. To overcome these and obtain the most complete sampling frame, we explored the possibility of using either rating records or the records on which the electoral register was based. The Home Secretary gave his permission for us to approach electoral registration officers for access to their records. This usually meant that we had access to a list of addresses which, unlike the electoral register, included dwellings which had been empty or only partly built and into which families had recently moved, as well as dwellings containing households none of whose members were eligible to vote. In effect, these lists allowed a more comprehensive and up-to-date sample to be drawn.

Rating Records

Use of rating records depended on several factors. In some areas it was possible only to have access to the valuation list. This is the main record of property in the district which local authorities are required by law to prepare and keep up to date. However, this does not mean valuation lists are rewritten every year: additions and deletions are recorded on additional pages as directed by the valuation officer of the Board of Inland Revenue. There may be some delay in the receipt of directives from the valuation officer notifying changes in value, new properties and demolitions. Although the time-lag for the addition of new buildings is not large, there can sometimes be a much greater delay in removing demolished buildings from the list, so there is the risk of including dwellings in the sample which no longer exist. Thus the valuation lists are not completely up to date, and the additional pages of amendments add considerable practical difficulties to sampling if only part of the district (i.e. one or two wards) is being sampled, since the amendments are arranged by year and not grouped by wards.

Secondly, in valuation lists a group of dwellings owned or managed by the same person or company, Crown property or council property, or a caravan site may be listed as a single entry although the total number of separate dwelling units is normally specified. For this reason, the number of units listed on a page varies considerably, making it difficult to handle large sampling intervals. To sample a large block of Crown property, for example, reference may have to be made to a separate list specifying individual dwellings, though, like the amendments, these lists may not be grouped in wards, so the sampling procedure is complicated. With a caravan site, there may be no indication of the number of occupied caravans, and although it is possible in theory to maintain equal probability of selection by interviewing *all* occupants of a rateable unit, this can have serious clustering effects when a large proportion of the sample of an area comes from one unit. It is therefore important to use a sampling frame whose units correspond as closely as possible to individual households.

Although the local authorities we approached were very cooperative, it was sometimes only possible for them to offer us use of valuation lists. In some instances, their rating lists were in the process of being computerized and therefore inaccessible for sampling purposes. In other authorities, their rating lists, being working documents, were in constant use, and it was felt that the practical problems involved in using them to draw a sample were too great. In these authorities, we explored through electoral registration offices the alternative of using the records on which the electoral register was based.

Thirdly, although access to rating lists was offered by some local authorities, they, too, were not always in a suitable form for sampling. Some rating lists had similar disadvantages to valuation lists. Amendments were often made on the relevant page, but sometimes were made on additional pages at the end. Some rating lists included council property or Crown property in single dwelling units as they occurred geographically, others listed them separately for the whole area. In the latter case, if they were grouped by wards and formed a sizeable proportion of the total number of dwelling units, it was possible to treat these dwellings as a separate stratum and sample accordingly. In some local authorities, rating lists were arranged alphabetically by streets and not grouped by wards or parishes, thus making the sampling procedure very complicated if we only wanted to sample part of the area.

Altogether it was possible to use rating records for the whole of six constituencies and for part of a further eight constituencies in England and Wales. The rating records used for sampling in this survey were usually in the form of a card index – a separate card for each separate dwelling – arranged by ward or parish. In Scotland, it was possible to use the valuation rolls in four of the constituencies because in Scotland the register of electors is compiled by the assessor appointed under the Lands Valuation Acts. This makes it possible to use the valuation roll, which is reprinted annually, as a firm base when conducting the annual canvass in connection with the preparation of the register.

The Electoral Register

In every constituency in England included in our sample with the exception of one, we were given access to the records on which the electoral register is based. Although the format of these records varied in some respects, they were much more standardized than rating records. They were invariably grouped by wards, parishes or county electoral divisions, so there was no difficulty in defining our sampling frame. As the electoral register is prepared and printed annually, amendments do not accumulate from year to year, and even if not recorded in the relevant road or street, are at least grouped by ward or parish. The problem of block ownership did not occur as the electoral register is concerned with persons eligible to vote, so each occupant of a dwelling eligible to vote is recorded. Ownership of the dwelling is irrelevant, and therefore no distinction is made between local-authority, Crown or private property. Caravan sites still posed a problem because individual caravans were not always indicated, so we assumed persons with different names lived in different caravans and included them in the sample accordingly. By using the records on which the registers were based, it was hoped to give an equal chance of inclusion in our sample of households living either at addresses which were empty or at which no one entitled to vote was living at the time the canvass was made (in September and October).

The records were kept in several forms: sets of card indexes, files of Home Office Forms A and B, canvassers' notebooks, or the published electors' Lists A, B and C. Some constituencies compiled separate records of properties empty on the qualifying date, or which were occupied by people not qualified to be included in the register and also from the Borough Engineers' records compiled a list of new properties built since the publication of the current register.

Card indexes and files of Home Office Forms A and B (the form which all electors must complete and return by the qualifying date each year) were the simplest to use. Each card or form usually represented a single home or flat, and if more than one dwelling was represented on a card or form, this was usually clear. Addresses which were empty or at which no one was entitled to vote were sometimes included as they occurred, and sometimes indexed or filed separately. It was therefore a straightforward though tedious task to ascertain the total number of separately identifiable dwellings in the selected wards, calculate the appropriate sampling fraction to give the requisite number of addresses for that ward or county electoral division and, with a random starting number, draw the sample.

Canvassers' notes usually consisted of the current register with amendments recorded on it, i.e. empty or non-elector addresses written in at appropriate points. Taking note of the additions, deletions, empty and non-elector addresses, a sample of addresses was drawn by using a random start and a sampling fraction based on the total number of addresses in the ward. In order to give each address an equal chance of selection, only addresses at which the sampling interval ended with the *first* elector listed at that address were included. In urban areas where names of electors are listed in address order by street or roads, it is very simple to ascertain the first elector, but in rural areas, electors are listed within polling districts by alphabetical order of surnames. Therefore, to establish whether the sampling interval has ended on the first entry for that address, it was necessary to search for the address among the names previously listed in the polling district.

Electors Lists A, B and C are published annually at the end of November and comprise the register currently in force (List A), a list of newly qualified electors (List B) and a list of persons from List A who are no longer qualified to be registered (List C). From List B it would be possible to identify addresses not included in the current register. In fact, we did not need to use these lists as a sampling frame. In the tiny minority of constituencies where canvassers' notes were not available, or where the electoral registration officer kept no separate record of empty or non-elector addresses, we found it easier and more thorough to ascertain the existence of addresses missing from the electoral register by reference to the rating lists.

Selection of Addresses in Northern Ireland

In Northern Ireland, the sampling procedure was slightly different. For practical and economic reasons, we had only sampled one rural constituency and took two wards in two different Belfast constituencies. To achieve approximately 100 completed interviews in Northern Ireland, we over-sampled households in Belfast so that the probability of selection for these households was three times that for households in the rest of the United Kingdom, and in Fermanagh and South Tyrone the probability was twice that for the rest of the United Kingdom.

In Belfast, we drew the sample from the electoral register as this was the most complete record of addresses suitable and accessible for use as a sampling frame. The sampling procedure was slightly more complicated because owners of business premises are entitled to an additional vote. We excluded business addresses at which no one resided, and counted only those addresses at which people were entitled to vote because they *lived* at the address, thus maintaining equal probability of selection for each household.

In the constituency of Fermanagh and South Tyrone, we also used the electoral register as a sampling frame, but were able to obtain information on empty and non-elector dwellings from the rate collectors and then include them in the sampling frame. In some of the rural areas, there were difficulties because electors are listed alphabetically by surnames and listed under a townland or village street. There were often *no* street numbers or names of houses, and therefore no way of knowing whether electors with the same name listed in a street or townland lived in the same or a different home. For the purpose of deciding whether the sampling interval ended with the *first* entry for an address, we assumed that electors with the same surname listed in the same townland or street lived in the same house.

Conversion of Address Sample into Households

By common convention, *a household* consists of either one person living alone or a group of persons living together, having some or all meals together and benefiting from a common housekeeping. There are difficulties, however. We developed the following specific rules. Persons who have resided in a household for at least four weeks and are not expected to leave shortly, and persons who have resided in a household for less than four weeks and are not expected to leave again after that period, are counted as household members. Persons living but not boarding with a household in a house or flat are counted as a separate household. But if a person living with a household eats breakfast or any other meal with the household, he or she is counted as a part of the household. Persons living in an institution or hotel (e.g. staff) are treated as forming a private household when they occupy separate quarters (even a single room) and do not depend invariably on the institution's services for meals. Broadly speaking, *residents* of boarding houses and hotels (*not* temporary guests) and *resident staff* of hospitals, welfare homes, nursing homes and schools are counted as private households for the purposes of this survey. Even though different staff may have eaten many meals together and depend on a common housekeeping, they are counted as separate households if they occupy separate sleeping accommodation.

The addresses which were sampled by the procedure described earlier contained one household, several households or none. The translation from the address sample to household sample was made on the basis that each household had an equal chance of selection subject to the following qualification. To keep the probabilities correct, each household living at an address was treated as eligible for interview. If there were two households at an address, one address, and if there were three households, two addresses, were deleted from the end of the list. However, if a large number of households lived at one address, a large proportion of the sample for that particular ward would have come from the same address, introducing bias due to clustering effects. We therefore decided to interview all households living at an address subject to a maximum of *six*. We chose a higher maximum than is usual (in the Family Expenditure Survey a maximum of three is taken), because, in constituencies with a high proportion of multi-occupied property, it was felt that six households per multi-occupied address would reflect the actual situation more closely. In Islington North, for example, the average number of electors living at an address was approximately five, which was twice the national average. Among the sample of addresses, 4·3 per cent contained two or more households. This compares with 4·5 per cent in the Family Expenditure Survey of 1967.[1]

The addresses which did not contain a household comprised those dwellings which were empty, those no longer in existence and those containing no private households. Table A1.8 shows for each region the numbers of ineffective addresses. The address lists for each area were randomly divided into quarters with the intention of interviewing a quarter of the addresses in each quarter of the year. If a household was away for the

1. Kemsley, *Family Expenditure Survey*, p. 18.

whole of a quarter (thirteen weeks), then that address was considered empty and therefore non-effective. If, however, the household was expected back within thirteen weeks, attempts were made to interview that household on its return. When no contact was made, or when no information could be obtained as to whether the household was away or not, the household was retained in the effective sample and regarded as a non-respondent. Households comprising aliens who were in this country only temporarily (e.g. members of the US Forces or the Diplomatic Corps of another country) were also excluded from the effective sample.

Table A1.8. *Sample of addresses analysed by eligibility for inclusion in the sample.*

Region	Total number of addresses issued	Address untraced	Empty	Business only	De-molished	Aliens	Ill and away	Ill at home	Away	Total number of households at effective addresses
Northern Yorkshire and Humberside	308	–	11	1	1	1	–	4	–	290
North-West	317	1	13	1	1	–	–	4	–	298
East Midlands and East Anglia	227	1	9	–	–	2	1	–	3	211
Greater London	392	–	11	–	2	–	1	2	2	376[a]
West Midlands	322	3	12	–	1	–	2	4	2	298
South-East	420	2	11	1	1	–	–	2	1	402
South-West and Wales	304	–	13	–	–	2	–	2	1	286
Scotland	248	–	10	1	–	–	–	4	3	230
Northern Ireland	109	–	3	2	–	–	–	–	–	104
Total	2,647	6	93	6	6	5	4	22	12	2,495[a]

NOTE: [a]In the final stages of interviewing, two additional households were found at an address, and there were no unvisited addresses left which could be deleted in accordance with the procedure described for multiple households in the text.

Some Limitations of the Sample

We tried to overcome the defects of the electoral register as a sampling frame by using rating lists or the records on which the electoral registers were based as soon after they had been compiled as possible. We found that, as a result, approximately only one

944 POVERTY IN THE UNITED KINGDOM

address in 100 was included in the sample which would not otherwise have been included. In view of the additional time and trouble that the use of this sampling frame entailed, both for our interviewers and local government officers, and in view of the existence of more important sources of bias, in particular that due to non-response, it is difficult to conclude that such a procedure would be justified for future surveys, at least on subjects affecting all sections of the population rather, than say, poverty or homelessness, which affect only certain sections. Our purpose had been to obtain the most reliable sample for measuring the extent of poverty, and it seemed that even if the percentage of the population 'missed' by sampling from the electoral register was very small, it might include a disproportionately large number of poor families. The poor are liable to move more frequently than others, and to use caravans or other accommodation not always listed as containing electors. We felt it was therefore right in principle to obtain a more comprehensive sample, even at the cost of extra time and effort, though 1 per cent of additional addresses is smaller than expected.

There appeared to be little difference in the extent to which rating lists contained empty or demolished property as compared with the electoral register records. Approximately 3·7 per cent of addresses drawn from the former were for these reasons noneffective, compared with 3·5 per cent overall. Only in Scotland was it valuable to have access to the valuation rolls instead of the published electoral register. Unlike the register, the valuation rolls not only list the names of electors living in a particular tenement, but also indicate the location of their dwelling, e.g. third-floor landing, flat on the right-hand side. We did not therefore have to identify the dwelling by the name of the occupants which, while straightforward if the occupants have not changed since the register was compiled, is more complicated if the occupants have moved. Moreover, we wished to emphasize that all information given to us would be treated confidentially, so it was better not to have to ask for a household by name.

Because of the minority of addresses containing more than six households, we were unable to keep the probabilities of selection strictly so that each household had an equal chance of selection. As explained, this was a compromise between slightly reducing the probability of selecting households in addresses in large multiple occupation, and the clustering effect if the entire quarterly sample for an area had been concentrated at two or three addresses.

Table A1.9. Characteristics of areas selected within constituencies.

Constituency	Total number of households 1961 (1966 in brackets)	Ward or county electoral division selected	Percentage leaving school at 15 or earlier	Number of households (1961)	Percentage distribution of households between strata
GREATER LONDON					
Woolwich E.	22,509	St Margarets	63·8	2,545	50
101	(22,790)	Slade	81·0	2,427	50
Islington North	28,079	Tufnell	75·8	11,101	100
102	(26,280)				

Table A1.9. – contd

Constituency	Total number of households 1961 (1966 in brackets)	Ward or county electoral division selected	Percentage leaving school at 15 or earlier	Number of households (1961)	Percentage distribution of households between strata
GREATER LONDON – contd					
Lewisham North 103	24,509 (23,420)	South Lee	69·9	5,808	100
Hornchurch 104	40,931 (42,600)	Upminster Hylands	58·2 80·2	4,020 3,601	34 66
Wandsworth and Streatham 105	26,094 (26,240)	Streatham Hill	63·4	7,009	100
Hendon North 106	22,853 (21,810)	Mill Hill Burnt Oak	54·2 84·1	7,638 4,502	80 20
SOUTH-EAST Thurrock 207	31,921 (34,570)	Grays Little Thurrock	84·0 79·0	5,628 2,630	59 41
Dartford 208	32,683 (34,850)	Priory R Dartford Rural West	75·4 73·4	4,001 4,853	51 49
South-West Hertfordshire 209	34,290 (34,200)	Heath Leavesden R Abbots Langley	52·9 74·1 57·5	2,925 3,006 4,607	30 42 28
Aylesbury 210	28,691 (31,710)	Aylesbury North R Haddenham and Stone R Long Crendon	79·1 64·7 75·5	2,709 1,769 1,421	47 28 25
Guildford 211	27,383 (28,560)	Merrow and Burpham Stoughton R Cranleigh	55·1 64·2 62·0	3,272 1,973 1,925	30 33 37
Bournemouth West 212	33,804 (34,010)	Central Moordown North	48·0 65·9	3,142 3,551	39 61
New Forest 213	29,439 (33,930)	Milton Central Milton North R Ringwood R Burley	56·5 64·6 56·1 70·4	1,433 1,351 3,149 3,316	20 14 31 35
Lewes 214	28,284 (31,940)	Seaford UD St Andrews R Barcombe	56·3 80·1 74·0	3,919 937 1,952	29 27 44

Table A1.9. – contd

Constituency	Total number of households 1961 (1966 in brackets)	Ward or county electoral division selected	Percentage leaving school at 15 or earlier	Number of households (1961)	Percentage distribution of households between strata
EAST ANGLIA and EAST MIDLANDS					
Ipswich	37,792	Whitton	85·5	3,102	51
315	(38,720)	Westbourne	93·5	2,578	49
Leicester South-East	22,156	Knighton	52·2	6,756	36
316	(26,880)	Spinney Hill	84·8	5,316	64
Melton	34,705	Melton Mowbray	63·9	4,937	14
317	(39,020)	R Quorndon	67·0	1,247	35
		R Rothley	77·5	2,331	51
Grantham	28,760	Sleaford East	64·2	657	11
318	(31,580)	Somerby	74·1	3,012	19
		R Swinderby	51·9	899	25
		R N. Hykeham	71·0	1,735	45
SOUTH-WEST and WALES					
Neath	21,940	Neath North	83·7	2,877	44
419	(22,060)	R Dylais Higher and Lower	90·0	2,213	23
		R Coedfranc	83·9	2,850	33
Bristol South	25,824	Hengrave	87·8	5,719	100
420	(26,940)				
Bristol West	25,969	Redland	49·8	5,645	64
421	(25,420)	Cabot	68·1	4,423	36
Gloucester	21,165	Eastgate	73·7	2,217	50
422	(27,060)	Barton	85·2	2,460	50
Yeovil	28,477	Yeovil West	70·7	1,530	17
423	(29,800)	Preston	85·3	1,801	26
		R Langport	73·9	1,796	18
		R Ilchester	72·4	3,112	39
North Devon	19,230	Lynton	60·5	523	22
424	(21,080)	Trinity	81·1	1,162	23
		R Swimbridge	67·1	1,301	30
		R South Molton	74·7	607	25
WEST MIDLANDS					
Coventry East	36,010	Lower Stoke	83·2	6,460	repeated con-stituencies
525	(38,150)	(1 × 2)			
		Longford	91·2	9,773	
		(1 × 2)			
Birmingham	35,928	Northfield (1)	79·2	14,520	
Northfield 526	(40,000)	Weobley (2)	84·0	11,675	

Table A1.9. – contd

Constituency	Total number of households 1961 (1966 in brackets)	Ward or county electoral division selected	Percentage leaving school at 15 or earlier	Number of households (1961)	Percentage distribution, of households between strata
WEST MIDLANDS – *contd*					
Brierley Hill	29,544	St John's	88·5	1,657	29
527	(40,120)	St Mary's	77·6	4,551	32
		Wombowne	79·7	3,316	39
Oldbury and	31,814	South	73·7	3,916	69
Halesowen	(32,530)	Central			
528		(Oldbury)	82·8	1,501	31
South	38,928	Malvern 4	69·0	1,037	17
Worcestershire	(29,980)	Malvern 5	58·4	1,213	14
541		R Upton Sudbury	69·5	1,165	29
		R Worndown	76·5	3,136	40
Oswestry	25,656	East	63·7	361	24
542	(23,720)	South	70·0	1,195	22
		R Ellesmere			
		Rural	68·9	1,181	23
		R Prees	61·7	1,928	31
NORTH-WEST					
Salford East	24,905	Kersal	82·0	4,872	50
629	(22,580)	Crescent	95·0	2,132	50
Manchester	32,610	Didsbury	51·5	5,676	17
Wythenshawe 630	(33,380)	Baguley	81·8	6,415	83
Bolton East	29,735	Great Lever	88·1	5,292	50
631	(29,530)	Attley Bridge	88·4	4,188	50
Southport	29,206	West	66·5	1,601	41
632	(28,910)	Birkdale North	81·7	1,798	59
Newton	31,518	Irlam	61·7	1,330	17
633	(36,350)	Wargrave	88·1	1,928	54
		R Great Sankey	73·4	1,887 ⎫	⎫ 19
		R Winwick	84·0	576 ⎭	⎭
Northfylde	26,084	Thornton			
634	(29,380)	Clevelys	72·9	1,525	36
		Thornton			
		Clevelys North	84·3	1,814	46
		R Cabus	77·9	1,498 ⎫	⎫ 18
		R Bilborrow	60·3	1,720 ⎭	⎭
NORTHERN YORKSHIRE and HUMBERSIDE					
Pontefract	26,554	Castleton	91·6	1,996	31
735	(26,110)	Half Acres	92·9	1,580	35
		South	92·1	1,109	34

Table A1.9. – contd

Constituency	Total number of households 1961 (1966 in brackets)	Ward or county electoral division selected	Percentage leaving school at 15 or earlier	Number of house- holds (1961)	Percentage distribution of households between strata
NORTHERN YORKSHIRE AND HUMBERSIDE – *contd*					
Bradford East	23,173	Lister Hills	77·3	4,254	50
736	(21,070)	East Bowling	90·6	3,755	50
Leeds North-West	35,730	Far Headingley	60·4	8,517	55
737	(37,510)	Hyde Park	77·4	5,754	45
Haltemprice	26,438	Central	62·2	5,588	21
738	(29,850)	Hessle	76·4	4,636	52
		R Part Beverley RD	–	7,134	27
Newcastle-on-Tyne	23,161	Dene	70·6	4,740	21
East 739	(22,420)	Heaton	77·4	4,975	79
South Shields	36,974	West Park	79·5	2,698	50
740	(35,600)	Cleadon Park	83·9	2,241	50
SCOTLAND					
Glasgow	28,561	Parkhead	91·0	5,592	100
943	(21,110)				
Coatbridge and	23,421	Fourth ⎱ data not		3,718	50
Airdrie 944	(24,880)	Airdrie II ⎰ available		1,238	50
Galloway and	15,687	Crossmichael	83·7	297	21
Wigtown	(17,270)	Kirkcudbright	75·4	186	26
945		R Old Luce North	61·8	332	12
		R Port Patrick	52·4	308	14
		R Kirkcudbright	56·0	807	14
		R Whithorn	82·0	315	13
Aberdeen South	28,599	Rosemount ⎱ data not		4,328	50
946	(30,050)	Rubislaw ⎰ available		4,182	50
Edinburgh West	30,604	Pilton	91·7	7,367	24
947	(31,420)	St Bernards	62·8	8,615	38
		Corstophine	62·7	7,324	38
Kinross and West	18,276	Dunblane	69·2	1,007	18
Perthshire	(15,240)	Aberfeldy	54·7	519	35
948		R Dunblane and Secroft	80·2	238	12
		R Little Dunkeld	36·3	416	11
		R Blair Atholl	28·1	414	12
		R Landward of Kinross	68·2	1,341	12

Table A1.9. – contd

Constituency	Total number of households 1961 (1966 in brackets)	Ward or county electoral division selected	Percentage leaving school at 15 or earlier	Number of house-holds (1961)	Percentage distribution of house-holds between strata
NORTHERN IRELAND					
Belfast East 849	32,900	Duncairn		10,088	50
Belfast North 850	26,303	Pottinger		13,147	50
Fermanagh and South	18,858	Enniskillen East	not stratified	830	23
851		R Augnockry		901	77
		R Fintona		967	

R = Rural

In making a selection with probability proportional to size, the measure of size should be in constant proportion to the number of final units, i.e. households. But, at the first stage, the measure of size was the electorate of the constituency, and the proportion of electorate to numbers of households varies very slightly from constituency to constituency. At the second stage, however, we did use the number of households as a measure of size in each ward or county electoral division. Any departure from the principle of a uniform overall sampling fraction was therefore small.

The Additional Samples in Four Areas

In addition to the national sample of approximately 2,000 households, concentrated studies were conducted in four areas. We aimed to choose areas within constituencies in which the proportion of low-income households would be high. These four areas, chosen from among the constituencies already included in the sample, were selected using criteria indicating that the incidence of the main types of low-income households would be well above the national average. In each area, between about 300 and 500 addresses were selected. The first interview was a screening interview to identify the following groups:

1. Families in which one parent is absent.
2. Families consisting of woman and adult dependants.
3. Families in which there are four or more dependent children.
4. Families containing an adult who has been unemployed for eight weeks (consecutively or in last twelve months).
5. Families containing an adult under 65 years of age who has been ill or injured for eight weeks (consecutively or off work for a total of eight weeks or more in last twelve months).
6. Families containing a disabled adult under 65.
7. Families containing a disabled or handicapped child (including children ill or injured for eight weeks or more).
8. Families containing a person aged 65 or over who has been bedfast or ill for thirteen weeks or more or who is otherwise severely incapacitated.

9. Families in which there are:
   (a) adult female earners (aged 21–59) earning less than £8 a week;
   (b) adult male earners (aged 21–64) earning less than £14 a week.
10. Families in which there are persons who are:
    (a) non-white;
    (b) born in Eire.

The first interview for those households who fell into one or more of these special groups was followed by a longer interview using exactly the same questionnaire as in the national sample. Approximately one in every three households in the sample fell into one or more of the special groups and was given the full interview. Thus the random national sample of households giving us information about the prevalence of poverty in its various forms was complemented by intensive studies in certain areas to find both the extent of any increase in the prevalence and how far such an increase might be linked with certain characteristics of the households.

Criteria Used for Selecting the Areas

The selection can be considered in two stages: first, the selection of the constituency, and secondly, the selection of the area within the constituency in which the households would be concentrated. The choice of the four areas was restricted to a choice from constituencies already included within the national sample because we had already collected a considerable amount of information about the characteristics of these constituencies. In addition, drawing the sample and interviewing in areas with which we had already established contact was administratively easier.

We wanted to select areas in which unemployment and low wages were particularly prevalent. This made constituencies from Northern Ireland and Scotland obvious choices. We therefore chose Belfast as one area. Glasgow Shettleston was the second 'poorest' of all the Scottish constituencies by our first stratification factor, and the 'poorest' actually selected in our sample.

The only constituency selected in the national sample in Wales was Neath, and by our first stratification factor was the 'poorest' selected in Wales and the South-West. While Neath is not the area of highest unemployment in Wales, its selection as one of the four special areas had several advantages. Due to recent pit closures in several valleys in and around the constituency of Neath, in particular the Cefn Coed colliery, the incidence of unemployment was high. The incidence of chronic sickness and disability was high: death-rates for men in Glamorgan were over 17 per cent above the national average, and in the urban districts of Glamorgan the mortality rate from bronchitis was 61 per cent above the national average (based on figures for 1960–62). In Glamorgan, 5·7 per cent of pupils received free school meals compared with 4 per cent of pupils for all counties in England and Wales in 1966. In addition, part of the constituency was rural, so that by choosing Neath as one of the four areas, we included for intensive study a rural area with problems of depopulation and unemployment.

The fourth area was chosen from our sample of English constituencies. Unemployment figures were not collected or published in a form which allowed calculations of unemployment rates for particular constituencies to be made. We might have chosen Newcastle-on-Tyne or South Shields, for example, on the grounds that they were included in an above-average unemployment region. However, these particular constituencies were not likely to be the poorest in our sample of English constituencies. By our first stratification factor, they were one of the richer constituencies in that region, and by our second stratification factor, the highest proportion of the population aged 25 or over leaving school at 15 or before in any one ward was 82 per cent in Newcastle-on-Tyne East, although in one ward of South Shields the proportion was 92 per cent. In terms of our second stratification factor, Salford East contained the ward with the highest proportion (95 per cent) leaving school at the minimum age in the whole sample. The proportion in all the other wards in the constituency, with the exception of two, was over 90 per cent. Salford had other characteristics which strengthened the case for making it the fourth special area. In the borough of Salford in 1966, 9·6 per cent of school children received free meals compared with 6·1 per cent for all English boroughs and county boroughs. The mortality rate was 46 per cent above the average for all boroughs and county boroughs in England and Wales, and was the worst (figures based on the average 1960–62). The mortality rate (for the same three years) due to bronchitis was over twice the national average, and respiratory tuberculosis rates were above average. There was therefore strong evidence that Salford would contain a higher than average proportion of low wage earners even if the unemployment rate was not the highest. We therefore chose Salford East as the fourth area.

Selection within the Four Areas

Within the chosen constituencies, one or two smaller areas comprising altogether between 6,000 and 8,000 households, preferably not crossing polling districts boundaries, or at least areas that could be identified as district communities, were chosen. The selection was based on as much information as we could obtain from published data and from local officials: rating officers, medical officers of health, education officers and housing

Table A1.10. Characteristics of the wards of Salford East.

Ward	Population density	Population	Households	Percentage leaving school at 15 or younger
Albert Park	43·9	12,831	4,154	94·7
Crescent	19·9	6,341	2,132	95·0
Kersal	18·7	15,330	4,872	82·0
Mandley Park	57·3	11,750	3,885	92·2
Ordsall Park	60·9	10,224	3,443	95·9
Regent	74·0	9,541	3,084	95·5
St Matthias	41·0	6,518	2,145	93·1
Trinity	20·4	4,396	1,190	86·1

officers. For different wards of Salford East, Table A1.10 shows the percentage who had left school at 15 or younger.

The Education Officer confirmed that St Matthias, Trinity, Crescent and Regent were among the poorest wards in this constituency, and provided the following figures on recipients of free school meals. The wards of St Matthias, Trinity, Crescent and Regent

Table A1.11. *Percentage of children receiving free meals in four wards in Salford East.*

Ward	Percentage receiving free school meals (March 1968)
St Matthias	30·2
Trinity	16·1
Crescent	15·8
Regent	22·2
Average for Salford (1966)	9·5

formed a unit of approximately 8,000 households within the constituency. On the basis of this, and the above evidence that the proportion of low income households was high, these wards were therefore selected. The choice of wards in Glasgow Shettleston was more difficult. Table A1.12 gives the percentage of adults leaving school early in three areas.

Table A1.12. *Characteristics of the wards of Glasgow Shettleston.*

Ward	Population density	Population	Households	Percentage leaving school at 15 or younger
Parkhead	21·5	17,123	5,592	91·0
Shettleston and Tollcross	37·9	44,253	13,032	88·3
Milend	67·3	29,680	9,937	94·3

The City Assessor's Office provided us with the information in Table A1.13 on rateable values and let property (based on figures for Whit Sunday 1967). In the light of this information, together with the results of the discussions our interviewer in Glasgow had with the Education Department, Health and Welfare Department and doctors in these areas, it was clear that no single ward was likely to include a substantially higher proportion of low-income households than the others. Moreover, though Shettleston and Tollcross included some of the very worst areas, this ward also included some good areas.

Table A1.13. *Rateable value and proportion of privately let homes in the wards of Glasgow Shettleston.*

Ward	Total number of households	Average rateable value	Percentage of privately rented houses	Average rateable value – privately rented
Parkhead	13,385	£33·5	25	£17·2
Shettleston and Tollcross	5,880	£34·8	24	£21·4
Milend	3,828	£18·3	55	£13·1

We therefore decided not to confine the sample to one ward, but, on the basis of local information, defined an area of approximately 5,000 households on a map which included polling districts in all three wards.

Belfast

In Belfast, we departed from the procedure adopted in other constituencies and did not confine the selection of wards to those in the constituencies chosen in the national sample, i.e. Belfast North and Belfast East. We were anxious to include the poorer areas and, if possible, select two areas: one predominantly Roman Catholic and one predominantly Protestant.

The Rates Department informed us that Shankill Ward in North Belfast and Dock Ward in East Belfast contained more property of low rateable value than other wards in Belfast. However, we compared this with figures from the Education Department on the proportion of school-children receiving free meals in each ward in Belfast. Neither Dock nor Shankill Wards had the highest proportions (9·3 per cent and 9·8 per cent respectively). The average for the whole of Belfast was 12·3 per cent, and Smithfield Ward and St George's Ward in Belfast West had the highest proportion of school-children receiving free meals: 20·7 per cent and 19·2 per cent respectively. The former was predominantly Roman Catholic, the latter Protestant, and both wards were roughly the same size and together comprised about 6,000 households.

Neath

In this constituency we decided to divide the sample into two areas: one urban and one rural.

We obtained some information from the Borough Treasurer concerning rate rebates. The percentage of rate rebate in Briton Ferry, Neath North and Neath South were 7·9,

Table A1.14. Characteristics of the wards in the constituency of Neath.

Ward	Population density	Population	Households	Percentage leaving school at 15 or younger
Briton Ferry	4·8	8,636	2,745	81·3
Neath North	7·6	8,437	2,877	73·8
Neath South	9·7	13,862	3,962	83·7

8·6 and 7·4 respectively. The Divisional Education Officer in Neath provided us with further information (based on figures relating to October 1967), and identified one polling district in Briton Ferry Ward, comprising some 600 dwellings, in which there appeared to be a concentration of low-income families. In this polling district, the birth-rate was 45 per 1,000 compared with 24 per 1,000 for the Briton Ferry Ward and 15 per 1,000 for the whole division. Seventeen per cent of the junior- and infant-school children received free meals, compared with approximately 6 per cent for the whole division. The proportion of children obtaining passes in the 11-plus examinations was much lower than for the whole division: 15 per cent compared with 25 per cent; and absenteeism was higher than average. We therefore decided to sample this polling district, together with the other polling districts of Briton Ferry Ward, sampling approximately one in ten addresses.

In the rural areas of Neath constituency we were able to obtain less information.

The Divisional Education Office was unable to supply figures to indicate an area within Neath rural district that was likely to be particularly poor. In the whole area of Dylais valley, there was a general slow process of depopulation as people drifted away from the

Table A1.15. *Characteristics of the parishes in the constituency of Neath.*

Parishes	Population density	Households	Percentage leaving school at 15 or younger
Baglan Higher Clyne Michaelston Higher	0·4	775	89·5
Neath Higher Neath Lower	0·7	1,657	84·0
Blaengurach	0·4	476	85·0
Blaenhondden	1·3	1,363	68·1
Coedfranc	2·4	2,850	83·9
Dylais Higher Dylais Lower	0·8	2,213	90·1
Resowen	0·8	897	83·4
Rhigos	0·3	555	82·7
Tonse	0·7	685	88·6
Dyffryn Clydock	1·7	885	85·8

valley to employment in the towns. In the Seven Sisters/Crynant area, for example, the primary schools were losing more 11-year-olds than they were gaining each year in 5-year-olds. It was in this area that a study of the problems of pit closures was being undertaken by social scientists at University College, Swansea.

The Housing Department of the Neath Rural District Council was very helpful, and were able to locate several streets in their housing estate at Seven Sisters which had a noticeably lower living standard than the rest of the area.

In many respects, the areas Dylais Higher and Dylais Lower were the most suitable choice for our purpose. However, it was felt locally that the recent closure of the colliery in Dylais Higher would make interviewing in that area difficult because feelings were running very high at the time. Moreover, it was feared that a survey of the area might raise false hopes that action would be taken. We therefore confined our area to one lower down the valley comprising Dylais Lower, Resolven and Crynant.

Appendix Two
Representativeness of the Sample

A summary account of the representativeness of the sample will be found in Chapter 3 (pages 109–11), and further details are given here.

The age distribution of the responding sample is compared with that of the non-institutionalized population of the United Kingdom in Table A2.1. The source of information

Table A2.1. *Distribution by age and sex of the UK population: three sources compared.*

| Age | UK total population[a] 1969 (Registrar General) | Poverty survey 1968–9 | Family Expenditure Survey 1969[b] | Percentage of each age group who were females | | |
				UK total population 1969 (Registrar General)	Poverty survey 1968–9	Family Expenditure Survey 1969
0–4	8·6	8·9	9·7	48	46	47
5–9	8·4	8·7	9·2	49	50	50
10–14	7·3	7·7	7·9	49	49	48
15–19	7·0	7·2	6·8	49	48	49
20–29	14·1	13·4	12·8	50	51	53
30–39	12·0	12·4	12·6	49	49	50
40–49	13·0	12·4	13·3	50	51	49
50–59	11·9	11·7	11·0	52	52	52
60–69	10·4	10·3	10·2	55	55	53
70–79	5·6	5·5	5·0	63	65	58
80+	1·8	1·8	1·4	71	70	69
Total	100	100	100	51	51	51
Number	54,395,000	6,045	20,744	–	–	–

NOTES: [a]Population estimates published by the Registrar General adjusted to exclude institutionalized population.
[b]The detailed breakdown is from the sub-file deposited in the Survey Archive, University of Essex, and corresponds closely to the amalgamated categories in the published report.
SOURCES: Col. 1: *Annual Abstract of Statistics, 1974*, HMSO, London, p. 7; and Census 1971, *Non-Private Households*, HMSO, London, 1974.
Col. 2: Marginals count, responding sample.
Col. 3: Survey Archive, University of Essex, and Department of Employment and Productivity, *Family Expenditure Survey*, Report for 1969, HMSO, London, 1970, p. 83.

Table A2.2. *Percentages of population, and of households, with specified characteristics – census compared with poverty survey.*

Characteristic	1966	1971	Poverty survey 1968–9
Birthplace[a] (population)			
UK	95·0	94·5	94·8
Republic of Ireland	1·4	1·3	1·4
West Indies, India, Pakistan and Africa	1·6	2·1	2·1
Other overseas	1·9	2·1	1·7
Number of persons in household 1	15·4	18·1	17·7
(households) 2	30·2	31·5	29·8
3	21·2	18·9	18·9
4	17·7	17·2	17·5
5	8·8	8·3	9·1
6+	6·6	6·0	7·0
Tenure[b] (households)			
Owner-occupied	46·3	50·4	47·2
Council rented	28·2	30·7	27·7
Privately rented and others	25·5	18·9	25·1
Households without amenities[a]			
Fixed bath	15·4	9·1	11·2
Internal W C	20·0	12·6	9·9
Households sharing amenities[a]			
Fixed bath	4·1	3·2	5·9
Internal W C	10·8	7·2	5·7

NOTES: [a]Census data for Britain only.
[b]The census distribution is based on tenure of *dwellings*, not households. Since some (mostly privately rented) dwellings are shared by two or more households, the figures are not precisely comparable with the poverty survey's findings. The figure for privately rented and other forms of tenure derived from the poverty survey would be reduced, and the other two figures slightly increased, to provide a true comparison.
SOURCES: *Social Trends*, No. 5, HMSO, London, 1974, pp. 81, 83, 162 and 165.

about the age distribution for the UK population in 1969 is the *Annual Abstract of Statistics*.[1] The numbers in each age group are given there as adding to 55,534,000. However, official estimates of population in the late 1960s were found, in the light of the results of the 1971 Census, to be too high. The revised estimate for *total* population given in the *Annual Abstract* is 55,262,000 – though, to the best of the author's knowledge, a breakdown by age has not been published. In comparing official data of age distribution with the results from the poverty survey, therefore, the number given for each age group has been slightly reduced by the same percentage to conform with this total. Secondly, on the basis of 1971 Census data for non-private households, the numbers in each age group living in hospitals, residential institutions and prisons, which were not included in the survey, have been estimated and deducted.[2] The results are given in Table A2.1, though

1. *Annual Abstract of Statistics, 1974*, HMSO, London, 1974.
2. The age-group data for these institutions have been adjusted, first, to conform with the total numbers found to be in such institutions at the 1971 Census, and secondly, to include an estimate for Northern Ireland.

it must be added that these refinements have not made much difference to the percentage distribution. For purposes of comparison, the age distribution of the responding FES sample for 1969 is also shown in the table, and it will be seen that the poverty survey sample reflects more closely than does the FES sample the proportions of the population at the youngest and oldest ages.

Fifty-one per cent of the sample were females, exactly reflecting the proportion in the population as a whole. The percentage of each age group who were females was also closely representative, as shown in the right-hand columns of Table A2.1.

From the censuses of 1966 and 1971, it is possible to select other data for purposes of comparison with the survey data. Some examples are given in Table A2.2. Because the survey occupied a period a little more than midway between the two censuses, inferences can be made from these two 'benchmarks' for the survey year – though the fact that the 1966 Census was itself based on a 10 per cent sample needs to be remembered. The survey data for birthplace and number of persons in the household compare fairly well with census data. There seems to have been some over-representation of privately rented tenures, and a slight under-representation of council-rented tenures, but this was due partly to the distribution being based on dwellings in the case of the census and households in the case of the survey. There seems to have been some under-representation of households lacking sole use of an internal WC, but about the expected representation of households lacking sole use of a fixed bath.

There are other checks on the survey data. In 1971, the General Household Survey, a representative sample survey covering England, Wales and Scotland, was launched. In that year, nearly 12,000 households provided information. Table A2.3 compares the distribution by household type with the corresponding distribution from the poverty survey. There was a close correspondence between the two sets of results. A further example is provided by estimates from the General Household Survey of the incidence of limiting

Table A2.3. *Percentage of households by type, comparing the General Household Survey with the poverty survey.*

Household type	General Household Survey (1971)	Poverty survey (1968–9)
Single person under 60	5	6
Single person 60 or over	12	12
2 adults, both under 60	14	14
2 adults, one or both 60 or over	17	17
Small families (1 or 2 adults with 1 or 2 children)	22	20
Large families	12	13
Large adult-households (3 or more adults with 1 child at most)	18	19
Total	100	100
Number	11,858	2,044

SOURCE: Office of Population Censuses and Surveys, Social Survey Division, *The General Household Survey*, Introductory Report, HMSO, London, 1973, p. 95.

long-standing illness and of the poverty survey of disablement conditions restricting activity (which are compared in Figure 20.1, page 704).

A source of comparable data other than the General Household Survey is the Family Expenditure Survey. Elsewhere in this report some examples have been given. Thus, mean gross and mean gross disposable income for different types of household are compared with the distribution derived from the Family Expenditure Survey in Table A.3 (Appendix Eight, page 993), and the percentages of total net disposable income received by quantile groups are compared in Table A.1 (Appendix Eight, page 991). The two surveys corresponded closely in the percentages of aggregate household income drawn from different sources.

Finally, the survey findings can in many different respects be compared with administrative counts and estimates. Some examples are given in Table A2.4.

Table A2.4.[a]

	Survey estimates	Government estimates
Receiving unemployment benefit	390,000	325,000
sickness benefit	920,000	994,000
industrial injury and war disablement pension	325,000	615,000
retirement pension	7,215,000	7,122,000
widows' benefits	485,000	577,000
family allowances	4,400,000	4,257,000
supplementary benefit	2,440,000	2,736,000

NOTE: [a]For source and methods, see Chapter 24, page 827.

Again on the basis of the survey, there were estimated to be 535,000 one-parent families, with 1,010,000 children, in the United Kingdom in 1968–9, compared with DHSS estimates for Britain in 1971 of 620,000 and 1,080,000 respectively (see page 755). There were 4·8 per cent of households in receipt of rate rebates. This compares with a figure of 5·1 per cent given by the Department of the Environment for 1967–8 for England and Wales only.[1] There were 17·4 per cent of school-children in the sample receiving free school meals, compared with government figures of 16·8 per cent for England and Wales and 17·2 per cent for Scotland (see page 865). An estimated 320,000 council tenants were receiving rent rebates, compared with an IMTA estimate of just under 300,000 for England and Wales (see page 876).

1. Department of the Environment, *Handbook of Statistics*, HMSO, London, 1970, p. 5.

Appendix Three
Eligibility for Supplementary Benefit

The purpose of this schedule[1] is to ascertain those who would be eligible for supplementary benefit and are not receiving it. It does not attempt to identify those who are receiving less than the full scale because they are wage-stopped or have unreasonably high rents. Wage-stopped families account for only about 2 households per 1,000 and families with unreasonably high rents only 0·5 per 1,000 (of course the schedule applies to 1968–9).

In standardizing the discretionary procedures of the Supplementary Benefits Commission and simplifying some of the provisions, use of this schedule will *overstate* the true number of income units eligible for benefit: (a) in so far as income is under-reported; and (b) in so far as no allowance is made for unreasonably high rents – which affects 2 per cent of applicants. But it will *understate* it for the following reasons:

1. We take no account of eligibility for extra allowances for diet, fuel and so on.
2. The special higher rates of benefit available to the blind, etc. are not allowed for. These rates apply to the registered blind and we have not attempted to ascertain in the questionnaire who is *registered* blind.
3. The repairs and insurance allowance for owner-occupiers varies with rateable value from a minimum of £10 per annum. We have used a standard allowance of 20p a week (approximating to £10 per annum) for *all* owner-occupiers.
4. In valuing houses, the Supplementary Benefits Commission deducts 10 per cent from the district valuers' valuation. In so far as our valuations are correct, we are in this respect over-valuing for SBC purposes. As valuations may tend to be too low, it seems appropriate not to deduct the 10 per cent.
5. In certain rare circumstances where the householder has a low income or there are dependants not at work, the attributable rent may be more favourable to the applicant than allowed for in our procedure.
6. We give no allowance for the excess of war or industrial injury, or widows' pensions over standard national insurance widows' pensions.

We have introduced a standard allowance of 25p for hire purchase. In practice, discretion is exercised depending on whether or not the article is an 'essential', for example, a cooking stove or bed, rather than a 'luxury', for example, a television.

In one respect, our assessment will not be accurate because we simply did not collect the data in the requisite form. Income from sub-tenants (as distinct from lodgers and

1. We are grateful to headquarters officers of the Supplementary Benefits Commission for commenting in great detail on the schedule before it was used. The officers are, of course, in no way responsible for any errors which remain, or for the application of the schedule.

boarders) at the same address may not be obtained (if picked up under 'other' income it will not be clearly identified). Moreover, services provided to sub-tenants are not checked. Applicants who have sub-tenants are therefore allowed the following weekly sums:

Wear and tear	£0·15
If light provided	£0·12½
If heat provided	£0·40
If accommodation furnished	£0·20

Schedule of Assessment of Eligibility for Supplementary Benefit[1]

For use with all income units in which the head (man in the case of a married couple) meets one of the following sets of criteria and was not drawing supplementary benefit in previous week, p. 18, Q. 15 (06).

(a) Head, man under 65
    Head, woman under 60, no dependent
        children in income unit,
        and unemployed   p. 6, Q. 6 (3/32/2)
        or sick or injured   (3/32/3)
(b) Head, man 65 or over
    woman 60 or over
    woman under 60 but dependent children
    man (under 65) or woman (under 60)
    disabled or handicapped   p. 6, Q. 6 (3/32/4) and under 60/65
In each case under (b) worked less than 30 hours last week p. 6, Q. 5 (3/29–30)
Add together Income
Earnings last week (1) Head of household   Main occupation
(Change from month   p. 15, Q. 1 (6/13–17 or
to week if necessary)   7/12–15)   ....
                                  p. 18, Q. 14 Casual
                                  (7/27–31)   ....
        (2) Wife   Main occupation
                              p. 15, Q. 1 (6/13–17) or
                                  7/12–15)   ....
                                  p. 18, Q. 14 Casual
                                  (7/27–31)   ....

Social Security and Maintenance Payments
(last week)   (3) Widow's pension or allowance
                p. 18, Q. 15 (7/36–37/03)   ....
        (4) Disability pension
                p. 18, Q. 15 (7/36–37/08 or 09)   ....
        (5) Other except codes 11 and 12
                p. 18, Q. 15 (lump sum grants)   ....

1. Note that the allowances were raised in October 1968. Adjustments were made in working out whether households interviewed subsequently were eligible for supplementary benefit.

	(5a) Maintenance payments reported in Q. 20, p. 20 (10/53–56)	... ...
Other income	(6) Employers' pension p. 19, Q. 19 (10/44–7)	... .
(Change from month to week where necessary)	(7) Other income *excluding* maintenance payments p. 20, Q. 20 (10/53–56)	... .
	(8) Sick pay *if sick last week only* p. 16, Q. 10 (6/72–75)	... ...

Income from capital. Add together value of assets

p. 24, Q. 2	11/42–47	....
Q. 3	11/54–58	....
Q. 4	11/65–69	....
Q. 5	11/71–75	....
Q. 9	12/31–35	....
Deduct		
Q. 13	12/54–58	....
Q. 14	12/60–62	....
Q. 15	12/63–66	....

Total value of assets
Deduct   £300

Assessable Assets

	(9) Count as income 5p per complete £25 up to £500	... ...
	12½p per complete £25 on remainder	... ...

                    Total assessable income

Income allowed for SBC purposes

(10) Up to £1 for category (a) and up to £2 from (1) above if category (b)	....
(11) Up to £2 from (2) above	....
(12) Up to total of £1 from (6), (7), (8), (9)	....
(13) Up to a total of £2 from (4)	....

Where entry under (3) allow 37½p for a first and second dependent child in income unit and 27½p for each subsequent child in income unit *providing the entry in this heading and (12) combined do not exceed £2*

(14) Up to 25p for hire purchase (p. 26, Q. 12)	....
(15) Housing cost (a) Where head of income unit *not responsible for rent*	

(10/77/5, e.g. earning child) or *living in rent-free accommodation* (p. 21, Q. 24, 10/77/4) allow 50p. But in the case of rent-free accommodation the proportion of the 50p which can be allowed is limited by the extent to which (i) in the case of those providing services (p. 23, Q. 29, 2/55/0 or 2) the amount allowed under (10) is less than £1 or £2 if appropriate (ii) in the case of those not providing services (p. 23, Q. 29, 2/55/7, 1, 3, 4) the amount allowed under (12) is less than £1 ....

(b) If only one income unit in household (i) if head of income unit is owner-occupier (p. 21, Q. 24, 10/77/X or Y). Allow weekly shares of ground rent, rates, water rates (p. 21, Q. 25, b, c, and d) plus *interest* on mortgage (Q. 25 H) plus 20p repairs and insurance allowance. (ii) If head of income unit pays rent allow rent and rates *less* 10p if lighting provided (p. 22, Q. 26 e) and *less* 62½p if centrally heated (p. 2, Q. 9, 1/37/5). But if meals provided allow total rent paid and adjust under (16) below. ....

(c) If more than one income unit in household and this income unit pays rent, calculate housing cost as in (b) (i) above. Count members of household excluding tenants but including boarders and members of family but count children under 16 as ½. Allot to income unit its proportionate share of housing cost if head of unit pays rent. For owner-occupier divide weekly share of rates plus interest: only add 20p if householder is applying for S B ....

TOTAL

£

(16) Personal allowances

If a boarder single (Commercial)	1·37½	....
If a boarder married couple	2·30	....
If a single householder (16 or over) responsible for rent, rates, etc.	4·30	....
Married couple (responsible for rent or not)	7·05	....
If *not* a householder and *not* a boarder (commercial) aged 21 or over	3·55	....
18–20	2·90	....
16–17	2·50	....
Child 11–15	1·85	....
5–10	1·50	....
Under 5	1·25	....

Special addition if person over pensionable age allow extra 0·45 ....

If head of income unit over 65 or 60 if a woman and not a boarder add 0·45 less any sum allowed under (14) above ....

Total income allowed

If Income Allowed exceeds Assessable Income the income unit would be eligible for supplementary benefit

Summary

Income allowed ....

Subtract Assessable income ....

delete one $\left\{\begin{array}{l} \text{plus} \\ \text{minus} \end{array}\right.$

Appendix Four
The Value to Families of the Social Services

with John Bond

This appendix sets out our methods of valuing public social services supplied to households. We will first discuss an official method used hitherto. The valuation of the direct and indirect benefits to families of the social services by the Central Statistical Office has become a regular feature of the analyses of successive Family Expenditure Surveys.[1] The estimates which were used by the office for 1968[2] were based on the findings of the Family Expenditure Survey in that year.[3] The surveys have been carried out annually since 1957 by the Department of Employment and Productivity. The samples for the Family Expenditure Survey do not include residents in hotels, boarding houses and other institutions, or members of the armed forces and the merchant navy who are stationed away from home for the duration of the survey. Detailed information about all forms of income, including national insurance and other cash benefits received from the state, is recorded. In addition, details of income tax and surtax paid, the type of dwelling occupied, family structure, types of education received and details of other variables affecting income and expenditure are collected. In 1968, over 7,000 households among the sample provided information.

Definitions and Methods Used by the Central Statistical Office[4]

The taxes and benefits included in the CSO estimates are divided into five groups: direct taxes, direct benefits, indirect benefits, indirect taxes on final consumer goods and services, and indirect taxes on intermediate products. We are concerned here only with direct and indirect benefits.

Direct Benefits

There are two groups of direct benefit which a household might receive: cash benefits and benefits in kind. Cash benefits include family allowances, national insurance bene-

---

1. These were published in *Economic Trends* in November 1962, February 1964, August 1966, February 1968, February 1969, February 1970 and February 1971, and additional information about low-income households in July 1968.

2. Central Statistical Office, 'The Incidence of Taxes and Social Service Benefits in 1968', *Economic Trends*, February 1970.

3. Department of Employment and Productivity, *Family Expenditure Survey*, Report for 1968, HMSO, London, 1969.

4. For a fuller account of the methods used in estimating taxes and benefits, see Nicholson, J. L., *Redistribution of Income in the United Kingdom in 1959, 1957 and 1953*, Bowes & Bowes, Cambridge, 1965; and *Economic Trends*, February 1970, pp. xxv–xxvi.

fits (pensions; sickness, unemployment, industrial injury, maternity benefits, etc.; death grants), non-contributory old-age pensions, supplementary pensions and allowances, war pensions, service grants and allowances. The value of each cash benefit (and of scholarships and education grants from public funds) is the amount stated to have been received by the household during the twelve months prior to the interview. Benefits in kind include state education, scholarships and education grants, school meals, milk and other welfare foods, school health services and national health services.

Education: the benefit of state education is taken to be the estimated average expenditure per child by public authorities according to the type of school or college attended – special schools, primary, secondary modern, other secondary and direct-grant schools, universities, colleges of advanced technology and teachers' training colleges. The value of the benefit is taken to be the same for all pupils attending any of these educational establishments, except that the benefit of secondary and direct-grant schools makes no allowance for differential expenditure on different types of school. A lower benefit is ascribed to children over 16, since a larger proportion of expenditure is allocated to children over 16. In 1968 but not in 1969,[1] children attending private schools were allotted a benefit equal to the average cost per child of either state primary or all state secondary schools.

National Health Service: detailed information about the use made by the family of the National Health Service is not collected in the Family Expenditure Survey. The values of the benefits assumed to be obtained are estimated in the following way. The current cost of maternity services is estimated separately and the average cost per birth allocated to each household reporting the receipt of national insurance maternity benefit. The values of the benefits from all other national health services combined are based on rough estimates of the differences in the extent to which these services are used by, first, children, secondly, by adults below retirement age, and thirdly, by adults above retirement age. In each case, estimates are made for males and females separately. The value of benefit assigned to each household is the average net cost to the state of providing national health services. This procedure has limitations which the Central Statistical Office recognizes. There is considerable variation in the utilization of the National Health Service, and therefore in the value to families of the service.

Indirect Benefits

The only indirect benefit which is estimated is the housing subsidy. This is defined for each local-authority dwelling as the excess of the economic rent over the actual rent paid by the tenant. For 1968, the economic rent is calculated by marking up the rateable value of the dwelling in the ratio of the total current account expenditure on all dwellings owned by the local authority to the rateable value of these dwellings. As a result, the subsidy can in exceptional cases be negative.

Limitations of the Central Statistical Office Methods of Estimating the Value of Social Services

The Central Statistical Office recognizes that the methods which have been adopted are very crude. It is difficult to know how far they distort the true picture of redistribution.

1. In 1969, fee-paying pupils to private schools were excluded. See *Economic Trends*, February 1971.

966 POVERTY IN THE UNITED KINGDOM

The problem is not just that broad estimates of value for large sections of the population, as, for example, for the National Health Service, conceal marked variations in practice between different families. It is that some types of benefit are not recognized. These include child tax allowances and tax relief on the interest included in mortgage payments, both of which have been recognized lately by successive governments to be integral features of social policy.[1] But a number of ordinary public social services are also left out of the reckoning, mainly because they do not feature in the questionnaires used in the Family Expenditure Survey. These include local-authority welfare and child-care services and legal aid.

In principle, it would be possible to develop a more searching review of the distribution of social service benefits. There are other public services which are not equally available to or utilized by all sections of the population – including public environmental facilities like playgrounds, swimming baths and libraries, passenger transport subsidies, the development of new towns and public health services. The value to families in monetary terms of these services could be worked out according to certain assumptions. The indirect value to families of certain tax concessions (as under Schedule D) could also be pursued. The definition of what are and what are not social services will always be subject to argument.[2]

Here, it is argued only that the CSO method of allocating the imputed value of social services does not reflect a sufficiently comprehensive definition of social services because certain major forms of tax relief which have clear welfare functions are excluded; and is not sufficiently refined for services as costly as health, housing and education.

The alternative method which is described below does not meet all problems. It represents merely a serious attempt to develop the CSO method further so that the distribution of social service benefits can be traced more accurately.

Alternative Methods

In costing the social services for individuals and households, we have divided benefits into two groups: direct cash benefits and direct benefits in kind. For the first group, which includes family allowance, retirement pensions, widow's pension, sickness benefit, unemployment benefit, supplementary benefit, industrial injury benefit, industrial disablement benefit, war-disability pension, maternity allowance, maternity grant, death grant, redundancy payment, school-uniform grant, educational grants and allowances, the value of each form of benefit is taken to be the amount received by each household in the previous twelve months prior to the interview. This is the same method as that used by the Central Statistical Office, but we look at a much larger range of benefits. In addition, we can trace periods of benefit in the previous year and the amounts received at different times during the year. For the second group, estimates have been made of the cash equi-

1. For example, the Labour government introduced 'clawback' (a method of reducing the value of child tax allowances to the standard rate taxpayer) when raising family allowances in 1968, and the subsequent Conservative government adopted the same terminology in discussions in Parliament about a possible further stage of 'clawback'. Again, the White Paper *Help Towards Home Ownership* represented the first official recognition that tax relief on mortgage interest materially helps a family in purchasing a house. The Treasury has also more recently acknowledged such tax relief as a policy measure to encourage owner-occupation.
2. For further discussion of the CSO definitions and methods, see Webb, A. L., and Sieve, J. E. B., *Income Redistribution and the Welfare State*, Bell, London, 1971, esp. Chapter 5.

Table A4.1. *Expenditure on health and welfare services, 1968–9 (England and Wales, Scotland) in thousands of pounds.*

Type of service	Scotland			England and Wales		
	Expenditure	Charges to recipients	Net expenditure	Expenditure	Charges to recipients	Net expenditure
	177,197	5,432	172,565	1,600,000	73,000	1,527,000
Central government services	–	–		1,364,000	–	1,364,000
Central administration	–	–	–	9,000	–	9,000
Hospitals	110,286	–	110,285	914,000	9,000	900,000
Administration of executive councils	1,175	–	1,175	10,000	–	10,000
General medical	13,134	–	13,134	120,000	–	120,000
Pharmaceutical	17,491	–	17,491	160,000	10,000	150,000
General dental	7,159	1,332	5,723	75,000	14,000	61,000
General opthalmic	2,109	823	1,286	22,000	8,000	14,000
Welfare foods	5,005	–	5,005	35,000	2,000	33,000
Other	–	–`	–	19,000	–	19,000
Local-authority services				236,000	30,000	206,000
Health centres	53	–	53	835	–	835
Day nurseries	†	†	†	5,807	2,784	3,623
Welfare clinics	2,420	–	2,420	10,431	–	10,431
Other	†	†	†	2,071	–	2,071
Midwifery	600	–	600	11,017	–	11,017
Health visiting	1,120	–	1,120	9,613	–	9,613
Home nursing	1,700	–	1,700	15,759	–	15,759
Home help	2,293	†	†	22,241	1,736	20,505
Ambulance	2,175	–	2,175	30,566	–	30,566
Mental Health	1,042	–	1,042	24,871	–	24,871
Other health services	1,449	†	†	9,414	263	9,151
Welfare services (aged)	4,776	†	†	51,848	23,970	27,878
Welfare services (handicapped)	564	†	†	9,074	220	8,854
Other welfare services	–	–	–	2,241	41	2,220

† = Figure not available.

SOURCE: Department of Health and Social Security, *Digest of Health Statistics*, Table 2.9; and Scottish Department of Health and Social Security, *Scottish Health Statistics*.

valent to each household who recorded receiving benefits from the social services. Estimates of national expenditure on social services have been calculated on the basis of the 1968–9 financial year. Strictly, the estimates should have been weighted between the financial years 1967–8 and 1968–9. Families in the sample were questioned about their incomes in the twelve months preceding each interview, and the interviews were spread from early 1968 to early 1969. The self-employed also had to be asked about incomes in the latest completed financial year for which information could be given. However, the balance of the data applies to the financial year 1968–9, and the great majority of interviews were actually carried out during that year

Health and Welfare Services

Table A4.1 gives both local-authority and central government expenditure on health and welfare services in Scotland, England and Wales. Table A4.2 gives estimates of the number of people using health and welfare services in England and Wales. Whereas the Central Statistical Office made estimates for the National Health Service as a whole, we have attempted to account for differences in the use of services. Some of the estimates are very crude because, first, the information obtained in the survey was rather general, and secondly, the detailed information about national expenditure on some individual services was not available. For example, although we obtained information about child and welfare officers' visits to families, no available detailed information concerning expenditure on these services could be traced. Other estimates are more reliable. The methods which we have adopted in making these estimates are as follows. Where estimates for the United Kingdom are not available, estimates based on England and Wales are used.

The annual value of the subsidy per person on cheap-rate and free welfare milk is estimated by dividing the net expenditure on cheap-rate milk and the gross expenditure on free welfare milk by the estimated number of individuals in receipt of the service.[1] In 1968–9, mothers with young children under 5 could obtain a pint of milk a day for 6d. a pint cheaper than retail prices. Free-milk tokens had to be claimed separately, and few parents claimed them, other than those getting supplementary benefits.

The annual value of the subsidy on welfare clinics is estimated by dividing the net expenditure by the estimated number of individuals who visited welfare clinics in 1968. The annual value of the subsidy on welfare foods such as national health orange juice and dried milk is estimated by dividing net expenditure by the estimated number of individuals in receipt of welfare foods.

The cost to the National Health Service of giving birth in hospital is estimated by taking the estimated cost per birth in a maternity hospital and adding to this the cost per birth of early discharge cases. Midwives are responsible for the care, not only of mothers and their babies born at home, but of those cases discharged early from hospital up to ten days following the birth. In 1968, midwives attended 164,477 home deliveries and 357,096 early discharge cases throughout Great Britain. Expenditure on midwifery services was divided equally by the total number of cases; 521,573.[2] This was taken to be the esti-

1. In 1969, the beneficiaries, including expectant and nursing mothers, young children up to the age of 5 years and 1 month and certain handicapped children under 16 were estimated to number 4,060,000, of whom 200,000 in large families had free entitlement. DHSS, Annual Report for 1969, Cmnd 4462, HMSO, London, pp. 19–20.
2. DHSS, Digest of Health Statistics, HMSO, London, 1970, p. 95, Table 8.1.

Table A4.2. Estimates of the number of people using health and welfare services in 1968 (*England and Wales*).

Unit/Type of health of welfare service	Number
Number of individuals in receipt of cheap-rate milk	3,560,000
Number of individuals in receipt of free welfare milk	500,000
Number of individuals using welfare clinics	1,990,000
Number of individuals receiving welfare foods through welfare clinics	1,440,000
Number of home births[a]	153,626
Number of hospital births[a]	653,107
Number of visits made by district nurses	14,270,000
Number of visits made by home help	26,280,000
Number of visits made to dentists	45,340,000
Number of individuals receiving N H S spectacles	4,690,000
Number of individuals receiving N H S hearing aids	310,000

SOURCE: [a]General Register Office, *Statistical Review of England and Wales, 1968*, Part II, H M S O, London.

mated value of home births and the estimated value of midwifery services in the case of all hospital births. This method of estimating the cost of births underestimates the cost of home deliveries while overestimating the cost of early discharge cases. Although crude, this method is more reliable than allocating for each birth an average cost per birth of all maternity services.

Table A4.3 gives the estimated cost per patient for different types of hospital in England and Wales. A cost per patient per night is estimated, and the benefit to the patient

Table A4.3. Estimated cost per in-patient week of various types of hospital, 1968–9 (*England and Wales*).

Type of hospital	Weekly cost £
Teaching hospital (London)	72·58
Teaching hospital (elsewhere)	64·56
Acute	49·38
Mainly acute	43·55
Chronic sick	21·17
Maternity	51·60
Mental illness	16·07
Mental handicap	13·49

SOURCE: D H S S, *Digest of Health Statistics*, H M S O, London, 1970, Table 2.9.

calculated by scaling up this figure according to the number of nights spent in the institution. The cost per out-patient attendance was taken to be the estimated cost per out-patient attendance at an acute non-teaching hospital[1] since we did not ask questions about the types of hospital individuals attended as out-patients. We asked only the number of visits they made.

1. D H S S, *Digest of Health Statistics*, Table 2.9.

The estimated cost of a domiciliary visit by a district nurse is calculated by dividing the net expenditure of the home nursing service by the estimated number of visits made by district nurses. The benefit to the individual or household is then estimated by scaling up the cost per visit according to the number of visits each individual claimed he had received in the previous twelve months.

An estimate of the cost per case of dental services[1] cannot be used since our data are recorded in terms of the number of visits each individual made to the dentist in the previous twelve months. An estimate of the cost per visit is made by dividing the expenditure net of fees by an estimate of the total number of visits made to dentists in 1968. A more reliable method would have been to estimate the cost per visit and subtract for those fee-paying patients the amount they spent in 1968, which would have been either £1·50 or £3. But information is not available from our survey on this. Some patients receive free treatment, such as mothers of young babies and children. In these cases, an estimate of the full cost was added.

The estimate of health service hearing aids and spectacles is made separately for those paying contributions and those not. Again estimates of the benefit to fee-paying patients is calculated by dividing total net expenditure on each service by the estimated total number in receipt of each service. The benefit to those who did not contribute is estimated

Table A4.4. *Estimated value of social services per person, England and Wales, 1968–9.*

Type of cost	Cost per person in 1968–9[a] £
Annual value of subsidy on cheap-rate milk	7·4
Annual value of subsidy on free welfare milk	10·0
Annual value of subsidy on welfare clinics	5·2
Annual value of subsidy on welfare foods	1·4
Cost per birth of home delivery	21·6
Cost per birth of hospital delivery	51·0
Cost per visit by district nurse	1·1
Cost per visit by home help (free)	0·8
Subsidy per visit by home help	0·7
Cost per patient of NHS spectacles (free)	4·7
Subsidy per patient of NHS spectacles	3·0
Cost per patient of NHS hearing aids (free) ⎫ average	21·3
Subsidy per patient of NHS hearing aids ⎬ subsidy	
Cost per visit of dental treatment (free)	1·7
Subsidy per visit of dental treatment	1·3
Cost per domiciliary visit by GP	1·8
Cost per surgery consultation by GP	0·6
Cost per out-patient visit	2·7

NOTE: [a]Annual values will, of course, average the value of goods and services received by some people for only a part of the year (e.g. families in which a child reaches 5 years of age soon after the year starts and is no longer eligible for welfare milk, as well as families in which a child is born towards the end of the year and so is eligible for such milk).

1. Estimated as £10·31 per case in 1968. See DHSS, Annual Report, 1969.

by dividing gross expenditure by the total number of individuals in receipt of the service.

An estimate of the cost per home visit and surgery consultation of health service patients is made. In 1964–5, it was found that, on average, a general practitioner took six minutes per surgery consultation, while taking on average seventeen minutes for each home visit, including travelling.[1] From this it is assumed that the average domiciliary consultation costs three times more than the average surgery consultation. In 1968–9, the average number of surgery consultations per doctor in four practices was 6,654, and the average number of domiciliary consultations per doctor in the same four practices was 1,736.[2] The average cost of one domiciliary consultation and three surgery consultations is calculated by dividing the estimate and annual expenditure per general practitioner by the average number of domiciliary plus one third of the average number of surgery consultations. This method, although admittedly crude, allows us to make estimates of the known differences in cost between surgery and domiciliary consultations. The estimated value of those services are given in Table A4.4. In estimating the value of the benefit of health and welfare services to individuals and households in our sample, only those receiving services through the state are included.

Education

The value of the benefit of state education is taken to be the average net cost per child to the public authorities under each of the following headings: special schools, nursery schools, primary schools, secondary modern schools, comprehensive schools, technical schools, state grammar schools, universities, teacher-training and other colleges of education. Estimates of the cost per pupil or student for special schools, nursery schools, primary schools, teacher-training colleges, universities and other colleges of education is calculated by dividing the net expenditure in 1967–8 by the number of full-time (full-time equivalents) pupils/students attending in 1967. Estimates of the cost per pupil of secondary modern, grammar, technical and comprehensive schools could not be made in the same way since expenditure on the individual types of school is not available. Estimates of the cost per pupil at grammar and secondary modern schools according to various age groups (under 15, 15 but not in sixth form, and sixth form) are available for grammar, comprehensive and secondary modern schools for 1966–7.[3] The cost per pupil in second-

1. Eimer, I. T. S., and Pearson, R. J. C., 'Working Time in General Practice. How General Practitioners use their Time', *British Medical Journal*, December 1966.
2. Lance, H., *Supplement to the Journal of the Royal College of General Practitioners* (forthcoming), September 1971.
3. *Hansard*, 13 February 1970. The following information has also been provided by the Department of Education and Science based on calculations for the year 1966–7 (in reply to a request from Mr M. Meacher, MP). The following calculations based on data for the *financial year 1966–7* show the relationship between costs per pupil, at various ages, in grammar, comprehensive and modern schools (£ per head (current expenditure)):

	(1) Under 15	(2) 15 not in 6th form	(3) 6th form	(4) All pupils
Grammar	125	152	236	150
Comprehensive	119	167	251	132
Secondary modern	108	185	266	114

NOTES: (a) The fairest general comparisons are those in Columns (1) and (4). The high figures for 15-year-olds and sixth-formers in secondary modern schools and, to a lesser extent, in comprehensive schools, reflects the uneconomically small groups staying on voluntarily in such schools.
(b) The figures for comprehensive schools show increased expenditure per pupil, compared with secondary modern schools. It is reasonable to expect that the cost per pupil staying on voluntarily in comprehensive schools would now be relatively lower.

ary modern schools is smaller than grammar schools. Since the ratio of teachers to pupils is similar for both grammar and technical schools, it is assumed that the cost per pupil is similar.

The ratio of pupils to teachers in comprehensive schools is higher than in grammar schools, but still less than in secondary modern schools. It was assumed that the cost per pupil at comprehensive schools is equivalent to the average cost per pupil of all secondary schools. Clearly this method of estimation is open to criticism. Yet there is little alternative open to us since the Department of Education and Science seems reluctant to obtain regular estimates of expenditure on the different types of secondary school. Until this information is available, no alternative methods can be adopted in place of the method described by the Central Statistical Office and the method put forward very tentatively here.

The value of the benefit of school meals to the household differs according to whether the meals are subsidized or free. The annual value of free school meals is estimated by dividing the gross expenditure on school meals by the number of children taking school meals. The annual value of subsidized school meals is estimated by dividing the gross expenditure on school meals by the number of children taking them and subtracting from this amount the average annual contribution families make for each child. The estimated value of school milk is calculated by dividing the gross expenditure on the school milk service by the number of children taking school milk. The estimated value of these services and the estimated cost per pupil at educational institutions are shown in Table A4.5.

Table A4.5. Annual value per person of educational services, England and Wales, 1968–9.

Type of cost		Value per person 1968–9 £
Nursery schools (cost per pupil)		63
Primary schools (cost per pupil)		90
State grammar schools (cost per pupil)	(a) under 15	144
	(b) over 15	222
Technical school (cost per pupil)	(a) under 15	144
	(b) over 15	222
Comprehensive school (cost per pupil)	(a) under 15	137
	(b) over 15	225
Secondary modern school (cost per pupil)	(a) under 15	125
	(b) over 15	257
Teacher-training college (cost per student)		751
University or college of advanced technology (cost per student)		1,219
Other college of further education		680
Adult and further education		107
Value of free school meals		27·2
Value of subsidized school meals		18·4
Value of free school milk		6·0

SOURCES: Department of Education and Science, *Statistics of Education*, vols. I, V and VI; private communication to Mr M. Meacher, MP, supplementing *Hansard*, 13 February 1970.

Housing Subsidies: Owner-occupiers

There are at least two approaches to the calculation of housing subsidies to owner-occupiers. One is to calculate the amount of tax relief given to individual households on the interest paid on their mortgages,[1] with or without the further addition of that part of any capital gain enjoyed in the year which can be attributed to such relief. The approach can be justified on grounds that the tax relief raises the capital value of houses and makes it more difficult for poorer families to obtain a house. For example, a house might have been bought in 1968–9 without tax concessions on a mortgage for an annual outgoing of £489, which would have fixed the capital price of the house and land at about £4,500–£5,000. If £489 was the maximum amount most households could afford to pay for this size of house, the price for most houses of this size would have been less than £5,200. By getting income-tax payments reduced because of their mortgage repayments, these households would have been able to afford to bid up the price of the house and contract to pay, say, £590 in mortgage repayments, knowing they would get back approximately £100 through tax concession.

We did, in fact, operationalize this approach. The amount of housing subsidy enjoyed by each owner-occupier was estimated by multiplying the amount paid in annual interest repayments on a mortgage by the standard rate of tax using information supplied in interviews about incomes and housing costs. To this sum, we added an estimate for the capital gain enjoyed by the household in the year because of the tax relief. The estimate of capital gains was calculated by multiplying the value of the house in 1968–9, as estimated by the owner (revised, where necessary, on the basis of information supplied by the interviewer), by the average percentage rise in house prices for that year. The value of tax relief was then expressed as a percentage of the household's total housing cost in the previous twelve months, and this percentage was applied to the capital gain on the house.

This method has a number of disadvantages. Those whose interest repayments are heavy in relation to the value, or the future value, of their homes are made out to be enjoying the heaviest subsidies. No account is taken, especially in the early years of repayments, of exceptional costs of repairs. And no 'subsidy' is attributed to outright owners (or for the years of occupation following repayments). In recent years, the advantages of owner-occupation in comparison with other forms of tenure have begun to be documented. In an article which compares the costs of an owner-occupier with those of a council tenant in Scotland, Hare[2] estimated that the value of buying a house in 1970 rather than renting a council house of similar standard was £298·42 after six years or £49·74 per annum. His estimates were based on the average costs facing first-time buyers assuming conservative inflation rates of 4 per cent for retail prices and 10 per cent for house prices.

Making estimates about the comparative costs of renting and owning over a six-year period is relatively simple providing one's assumptions are correct. For one particular household type, and over the period defined, it could be argued that this £298·42 represents an income from house-ownership. To try and calculate for each household in the

1. This form of subsidy was discussed by Nevitt, A. A., *Housing, Taxation and Subsidies*, Nelson, London, 1966, p. 146.
2. Hare, P. H., 'Comparing the Costs of Owning and Renting in Scotland', *Housing Review*, 22(3), 1973, pp. 113–17.

sample an income from house-ownership would rely on a good estimate of an equivalent rent for a council house in the different years that the household owned the property. Such information was not collected during interviews and estimates would be hazardous to make. If it could be done, it would then be difficult to decide how much house-ownership earned in any particular year.

A similar approach, which would use information collected during interviews, also deviates from the traditional concept of a housing subsidy and looks at the financial value of owner-occupation in terms of a 'social' subsidy. This method calculates for each household an estimate of an 'imputed income'. This could be calculated as the amount in rent that the owner-occupier would expect to pay for his house, deducting expenses for maintenance and then estimating the amount of tax which he would otherwise have had to pay on this 'income', making an allowance for interest included in any mortgage repayments.

The 'Imputed Income' Approach

With the abolition of Schedule A tax in 1963, owner-occupiers no longer had to pay tax on the imputed rent of their homes, although they still receive the tax relief on the interest element of their mortgage repayments. A man who bought a house in 1968 for £5,000 lives rent free, while the man who invested £5,000 to yield £300 gross per annum (assuming 6 per cent interest rate), the sum required to pay the rent of an identical house, would have been left after tax with only £175, since his income from investment was taxed whereas the owner-occupier's income from his investment was not. Both men would have had a gross annual income of £300 on their investment, but one paid tax of £125 and the other paid none.

Since the withdrawal of Schedule A tax in 1963, the use of the concept of 'imputed rental income' would be both comprehensive and rational. However, it poses awkward questions of principle and practice. If rent is to be calculated on a house that is owned, then this principle might be extended to other forms of property, and there is room for considerable argument as to the forms of property to which the principle should be applied. There are also real problems in agreeing values according to rateable, gross 'market' or replacement value. However, there is a case for treating housing differently from at least some other forms of property. First, it is something everyone needs. Secondly, buyers of other forms of property, such as antiques, were not, in 1968, receiving tax relief on the interest for money which they borrowed in order to purchase such property, whereas house buyers were receiving tax relief on the interest element of their mortgages. This tax relief was not originally seen as a subsidy to owner-occupiers, but since the abolition of Schedule A tax has increasingly been seen as such. Under Schedule A, the owner-occupier's taxable income was increased by an imputed rent and then lowered by the actual costs of obtaining the imputed rental income.[1]

By adopting this method in the calculation of subsidies to owner-occupiers, estimates are thereby made of the benefit to outright owner-occupiers as well as home buyers.

The subsidy to outright owner-occupiers is estimated by multiplying the value of the house by a rate of interest, deducting from this total housing cost (repairs), and applying

1. Nevitt, *Housing, Taxation and Subsidies*, p. 72.

Table A4.6. Housing subsidy of owner-occupiers in sample (outright) (£).

1 Value of house	2 Imputed rental income at 7%	3 Total housing cost (repairs)	4 2–3	5 Estimated subsidy (i.e. 33⅓% of 4)
1,500	105	50·00	55	18·33
5,800	406	90·00	316	105·33
7,000	490	125·00	365	121·67
7,500	525	140·00	385	128·33
7,800	546	90·00	456	152·00
10,000	700	275·00	415	138·33

the standard rate of tax. Table A4.6 shows the calculation of this subsidy for six outright owner-occupiers in the sample.

The subsidy to house buyers is estimated by multiplying the value of the house by a rate of interest, deducting from this an allowance for repairs and the interest element of mortgage repayments and applying the standard rate of tax. Table A4.7 shows the calculation of this subsidy for five mortgage payers.

Table A4.7. Housing subsidy of mortgage payers in sample (£).

1 Value of house	2 Imputed rental income at 7%	3 Housing costs (interest, repairs)	4 2–3	5 Estimated subsidy (i.e. 33⅓% of 4)
2,100	147	62·00	85	28·33
2,500	175	92·00	83	27·67
5,000	350	316·00	34	11·33
5,500	385	392·00	−7	–
6,500	455	159·00	296	98·67

Capital Gains

Calculating subsidies in this way can produce, as can be seen from one case in Table A4.7, some negative estimates. No allowance for the effect of capital gain has been made so far. It can be argued that, by calculating the imputed *rental* income, it would not be correct to calculate an estimate of capital gain in addition. There are two elements of capital gain. First, the element of capital gain which mortgage buyers enjoy because of the tax relief on their interest repayments. It would not seem right to include this since the principle of Schedule A tax was to increase the taxable income by the imputed rent and then lower it by the actual cost of obtaining this imputed rental income. However, it could be argued that if the tax concession was not given, and if imputed rental income was taxed without allowances being made, the house buyer would not be able to bid up the price of the property. Hence the capital-gain element still exists when tax relief is given.

The second element of capital gain is on the profits of selling the house. When an owner-occupier sells, he will normally realize considerably more than he paid for his house, even when allowance is made for retail price inflation. The house is an asset which appreciates faster than most other classes of assets.[1] It has been argued that the appreciation of house value should not be taken into account on considering housing costs. The reasoning put forward is that the 'paper profits' of house price-inflation cannot be realized because to realize them the owner-occupier must sell his house, and if he sells his house he must reinvest the profits in another house. However, as Harrington[2] has pointed out, if by owning people cannot realize a capital gain, they can avoid a capital loss. In any case, capital gains on houses are eventually realized, if only by heirs of the home owner. Also, when people do sell and have to reinvest their profits in another house, it is normally bigger or in a better neighbourhood.[3] The proceeds of the first house enable owner-occupiers to increase their housing consumption and increase appreciation on the second, more expensive, home. The exception of this pattern might be some older people who sell their houses and who do, in fact, realize their 'paper' profits by moving to a smaller house. It is, then, feasible to add to the value of housing subsidy estimated from an imputed rent an estimate of the capital gain enjoyed by owner-occupiers during the year. This could be calculated by multiplying the value of the house by an appreciation value and applying the standard rate of tax.[4] In the method put into practice, we adopted an appreciation value of 6 per cent. Therefore the 'capital-gain subsidy' was 2 per cent of the estimated market value of the home. For the examples given in Tables A4.6 and A4.7, the subsidy ranged from £42 (for the home valued at £2,100) to £200 (for the home valued at £10,000).

Housing Subsidies: Council Tenants

In calculating the value of housing subsidies to the tenants of local-authority housing, the Central Statistical Office makes a very crude estimate. These subsidies are defined for each local-authority dwelling as the excess of the estimated economic rent over the actual rent paid by the tenant. They calculate the economic rent by marking up the rateable value of the dwelling in the ratio of the total current account expenditure on all dwellings owned by the local authority to the total rateable value of those dwellings. By allocating the average subsidy per local-authority dwelling to such tenants, no allowance is made for variations between local authorities. Table A4.8 shows the differences in subsidies between local authorities in England and Wales. Table A4.9 gives similar figures for Scotland. Figures for Northern Ireland are based on the average amounts of English administrative areas.

The subsidy on local-authority housing does not go directly to the tenant. The exchequer subsidy is paid into the current account of the local-authority housing account,

1. National Economic Development Office, Building Economic Development Committee, *Low Start Mortgage Scheme*, 1972.
2. Harrington, R., *Some Fundamental Economics of the Housing Problem*, paper presented at Shelter Conference on House Purchase Finance, 1972.
3. Nationwide Building Society, *Occasional Bulletin*, 99, 1970.
4. Feasibly, one could have used a higher rate of tax to correspond with capital-gains tax in 1968.

Table A4.8. Average Exchequer and rate subsidies per dwelling on local authority housing for individual local authorities in the sample, England and Wales,[a] 1968–9.

County boroughs	Exchequer	Rate £s	Total £s
Birmingham	30·9	10·3	41·2
Bournemouth	19·1	–	19·1
Bolton	19·2	4·1	23·3
Bristol	20·9	0·1	21·0
Coventry	29·1	5·8	34·9
Gloucester	19·1	1·5	20·6
Ipswich	17·9	–	17·9
Leicester	20·5	2·2	22·7
Leeds	27·6	5·4	33·0
Manchester	27·4	7·4	34·8
Newcastle-on-Tyne	27·1	8·6	35·7
Salford	47·2	30·4	77·6
Southport	16·2	5·2	21·4
South Shields	22·1	7·7	29·8
Greater London			
Croydon	23·9	–	23·9
Enfield	35·7	9·0	44·7
Greenwich	32·9	29·6	62·5
Havering	29·5	4·8	34·3
Islington	71·4	88·9	160·3
Lewisham	42·9	69·7	112·6
Non-county boroughs			
Aylesbury	31·9	7·0	38·9
Bridgenorth	20·9	10·5	31·4
Guildford	17·5	1·2	18·7
Lymington	25·0	–	25·0
Lewes	25·6	4·7	30·3
Pontefract	26·1	–	26·1

Urban district councils	Exchequer	Rate £s	Total £s
Haltemprice	24·2	–	24·2
Lynton	15·8	–	15·8
Malvern	22·1	0·1	22·2
Melton Mowbray	20·9	2·0	22·9
Sleaford	17·7	–	17·7
Thornton Cleveleys	21·5	0·9	22·4
Thurrock	22·8	11·7	34·5
Rural district councils			
Barrow upon Soar	19·0	–	19·0
Dartford	17·8	0·2	18·0
Garstang	22·7	–	22·7
Hambledon	20·5	0·1	20·6
Melton Belvoir	20·7	2·3	23·0
Neath	20·8	10·0	30·8
North Cotswold	18·3	3·8	22·1
Northkestevern	20·0	–	20·0
Oswestry	29·0	0·9	29·9
Pershore	20·6	2·1	22·7
Ringaced and Fardingbridge	23·2	1·5	24·7
Walsingham	21·8	0·6	22·4
Warrington	18·5	4·0	22·5
Yeovil	18·5	1·3	19·8
Summary			
County boroughs	24·9	6·1	31·0
Greater London	35·9	18·4	54·3
Non-county boroughs	22·9	3·2	26·1
Urban boroughs	22·7	3·9	26·6
Rural	22·7	2·5	25·2

NOTE: [a]For ten wards, households, information concerning subsidies is not available. Figures have been estimated according to the type of administrative area.
SOURCE: Institute of Municipal Treasurers and Accountants, *Housing Statistics (England and Wales), 1968–69.*

Table A4.9. Average Exchequer and rate subsidies per dwelling on local-authority housing for individual local authorities in the sample, Scotland, 1968–9.

Cities	Exchequer subsidy £s	Rate subsidy £s	Total per dwelling
Aberdeen	986,121	1,605,050	95·8
Edinburgh	1,735,201	3,170,017	104·4
Glasgow	4,945,694	8,363,881	93·3
Large burghs			
Airdrie	315,181	760,622	126·1
Coatbridge	416,190	1,177,147	
Small burghs[a]	2,716,049	3,226,680	74·4

NOTE: [a]Figures for individual small burghs are not available. Figures have been calculated on the basis of this average figure.

SOURCE: The Institute of Municipal Treasurers and Accountants (Scottish Branch), *Rating Review*, January 1970.

along with rents and rate subsidies. It is up to each local authority how this money is spent. In practice, a higher proportion of the total subsidy will be given indirectly to tenants of modern dwellings than to the occupiers of older stock.[1] To estimate the subsidy which individual tenants receive would entail a knowledge of the economic rent of individual properties. An estimate of average economic rent is not sufficient. The true economic rent is based on the interaction of supply and demand in the short run, and not the historic cost to local authorities of providing dwellings. In the long run, economic rent is based upon the contemporary cost of replacing dwellings.[2] One method of estimating the subsidy to local-authority tenants would be to take the value of the dwelling discounting 25 per cent for pre-war houses and 10 per cent for pre-1955 houses. Taking interest, plus a fixed amount per annum for maintenance and management, we could calculate the economic rent for each dwelling. The difference between the real rent and the economic rent would be the amount of subsidy which each tenant receives. However, information was not collected in the survey about the value of local-authority housing so that our estimates are not based on this method.

A second approach would be to follow the Central Statistical Office, and for each individual dwelling weight the total subsidy to the local authority according to the rateable value of the dwelling. This method would not be very reliable, since the methods of applying rateable values to properties differ considerably from methods used to determine the amount of subsidy each local authority receives for individual dwellings from the central government. For example, pre-war housing lacking bathrooms and indoor WCs has a low rateable value, while subsidies are higher than subsidies on modern dwellings with bathroom and indoor WC where the rateable value is high. We are unable to adopt this method since we lack data about the rateable value of individual properties.

The method we have used is to allocate to each local-authority dwelling the average

1. Nevitt, *Housing, Taxation and Subsidies.*
2. Webb and Sieve, *Income Redistribution and the Welfare State*, p. 51.

subsidy, including rate subsidy, for each local authority. In this way, we have allowed for the great differences which exist between local authorities, but we have been unable to allow for differences between dwellings within each local authority. It is difficult to know how unreliable this method is.

In estimating housing subsidies, we have not made any estimate of the size of the subsidy, if any, that households living in privately rented accommodation receive. The subsidy is borne by the landlords. It is not possible to determine whether it is passed on to the tenants or not.

Appendix Five
Some Definitions

1. *Net disposable income last year*

   (a) Add earnings in fifty-two weeks previous to interview from employment, including casual and occasional earnings, earnings from second jobs, sick pay, holiday pay, commissions and bonuses, fees and payments for consultancies.

   (b) Add income from self-employment less tax, depreciation and business for the latest period of fifty-two weeks for which information is available.

   (c) Add repayments of tax received in year.

   (d) *Subtract* income tax, surtax, national insurance and graduated contributions and contributions to occupational pension schemes and subtract any tax paid direct to the Board of Inland Revenue.

   (e) Add all state social security allowances and benefits received regularly or occasionally for any periods during the fifty-two weeks preceding interview, including family allowances, retirement pensions, national insurance sickness and unemployment benefits, industrial injury benefits, industrial disablement pensions, war and widows' pensions, war disability pensions, maternity grants, death grants, redundancy payments, supplementary benefits, exceptional needs or other single grants.

   (f) Add local-authority educational maintenance allowances and grants in cash.

   (g) Add allowances in cash from relatives, including maintenance allowances from husbands or wives, children or parents, annuities through private insurance, money gifts, trade-union benefits, benefits from a friendly society, benefits under private sickness or accident insurance, income from a trust or covenant and any other source.

   (h) *Subtract* allowances to any relative outside household.

   (i) Add any pension from a former employer.

   (j) Add income in the form of interest or dividends from savings, investments, including stocks and shares.

   (k) Add receipts of rent for property including garages, and receipts from lodgers or boarders, less expenses and the estimated cost of services.

(l) Add windfalls, including an inheritance, betting or football-pool win, Premium Bond or prize (but only when these have been declared to be used for living expenses).

(m) *Subtract* expenses of going to work, including clothing or equipment allowed for tax purposes as well as cost of travel.

2. Gross income

As in 1, without subtracting (d) and (m), that is income tax, surtax and other deductions, and expenses of going to work.

3. Gross disposable income

As in 1, without subtracting (m), expenses of going to work.

4. Non-asset income (*last year*)

As in 1, without adding (j) and (k), that is, income from rent, property and investments.

5. Net assets

(a) Add readily realizable assets, namely deposits in savings and other banks, holdings of Savings Certificates, Defence Bonds and Premium Bonds, and shares and deposits in building societies and Cooperative societies; value of stocks and shares (all marketable securities whether issued by governments, municipalities, public boards or companies) and money owed (ignoring sums below £25).

(b) *Subtract*: debts, namely bank overdraft or loan, rent owed, hire-purchase debts over £25 and any personal debts over £25.

(c) Add less readily realizable assets, namely, the value of any business, farm or professional practice; owner-occupied houses and other houses, boats and caravans; cars and other saleable assets worth over £25 (jewellery, silver and antiques and pictures, but excluding household equipment).

(d) *Subtract* value of mortgages outstanding and money owed on cars.

6. Imputed income from net assets last year

Estimates were made for each income unit, starting with the total of net assets in 5. We decided to convert this total into an equivalent annuity value. First, for each adult the number of years he or she expected to live was calculated (using the Registrar General's Life Tables for each specific age). For a married couple, the longest number of years that either spouse expected to live was taken. Secondly, all assets were assumed to produce a rate of interest of 7 per cent (a figure slightly below that being applied by most building societies at the time). The value of owner-occupied flats and houses was included. This represented the estimated market value, less any capital sum remaining to be paid on a mortgage. The previous year's 'income' from the annuity was then calculated. *In an alternative measure* the annual interest (at 7 per cent) on the value of an owner-occupied house or flat, not the annuity value, was included.

7. *Imputed income from employer welfare benefits in kind*

(a) Add value of meals subsidies. The annual value of luncheon or meal vouchers was estimated by multiplying the weekly amount by the number of weeks worked by each individual in the previous twelve months. Each employee was also asked to estimate the weekly amount saved during an average week if meals were subsidized by the employer, whether in the form of cheap meals or meals eaten out and paid for by the firm. Annual values were similarly calculated.

(b) Add value of personal use of car. Employees using a firm's car were asked to estimate the value to them personally of its use. An estimate of annual values was based on answers to questions on mileage driven for personal use, make, type and value of car and miles per gallon.

(c) Add value of other goods and services in kind provided by employer – including free goods and travel (free or concessionary coal, railway tickets), medical expenses, educational fees and shares or options to purchase shares.

(d) Add value of accommodation, occupied free or subsidized. Employees were asked to estimate the annual value to them of such accommodation.

(e) Add annual value of pension rights. The current value of the pension rights which had been earned so far was calculated by taking the pension expected annually by them upon reaching pensionable age, plus any lump sum upon retirement, working out the total sum they would expect to receive in the years up to their deaths (by relating their current age to the Registrar General's tables of expectation of life). The fraction of this total sum which they had so far earned was treated as the number of years served towards pension, divided by the total number they expected to serve before retirement. Finally the total value of pension rights so far earned was converted into an annual value by dividing by the number of years they now expected to live.

(f) Add value of sick-pay rights. Average weeks of sickness for different age groups in the whole period up to retirement were calculated and multiplied by the weekly value of sick pay, less any deduction for national insurance sickness benefits. The annual value until retirement was calculated by dividing by the difference between their age and the number of years they would expect to work until retirement. Any sick pay received in the previous twelve months (already included in net disposable income) was deducted.

8. *Imputed income of social services in kind*

(a) Add the annual value of subsidy per person in households actually receiving cheap-rate or free welfare milk. The cost was estimated by dividing the net expenditure on cheap-rate milk and the gross expenditure on free welfare milk by the estimated number of individuals in receipt of the service.

(b) Add the annual value of the subsidy on welfare clinics per mother using such clinics.

(c) Add the annual value of the subsidy on welfare foods per person said to receive such foods. The annual value was estimated by dividing net expenditure by the estimated number of individuals in receipt of welfare foods.

(d) Add the cost of any birth in hospital by a woman in the household, and of any birth at home. These costs were estimated by taking the average cost per birth respectively in maternity hospitals and at home, making allowance for early discharge cases.

(e) Add the cost per night in hospital of any stay, and the cost of any out-patient attendances. The average costs of in-patient care were estimated for each type of hospital and applied according to information given by patients about the type of hospital in which they had resided. The cost per out-patient attendance was averaged for all types of hospital.

(f) Add the cost of each visit to the household by a district nurse. This was estimated by dividing the net expenditure of the home nursing service by the number of visits made by district nurses.

(g) Add the cost per dental visit. This was estimated by dividing expenditure net of fees received by an estimate of the total number of visits made to dentists in 1968.

(h) Add the cost of each home visit and surgery consultation by a doctor under the National Health Service. Average costs for each of these were worked out and applied to the information given for each member of the household about medical consultations in the previous twelve months.

(i) Add the cost of each visit by a home help for those receiving home help free, and, separately, the subsidized cost for those paying a charge.

(j) Add the annual cost of education in different types of school and college for each pupil or student attending. Information was obtained for each pupil or student of the type of school or college attended, and the average cost according to type of institution applied. In the case of grammar, technical, comprehensive and secondary modern schools, costs were estimated separately for pupils under 15 and over 15.

(k) Add the annual value of school meals for those receiving them free, and the subsidized costs for those paying for them.

(l) Add the annual value of school milk for each recipient.

(m) Add the annual subsidy value of council housing. The average subsidy, including rate subsidy, for the local authority in which the tenancy was situated was applied.

(n) Add the estimated tax foregone on imputed rental income of *home owners*. This was calculated in three steps: (i) the estimated market value of the home was multiplied by 7 per cent (the estimated rate of interest on the capital value of housing at the time); (ii) total housing cost, in the case of outright owners, and total housing cost less the last year's interest payment on the mortgage, in the case of mortgage payers, was deducted from this figure to derive 'imputed rental income'; and (iii) the standard rate of tax (33⅓ per cent) was applied to the outstanding amount. The resulting figure represents 'the notional income subsidy'.

(o) Add the estimated tax foregone on any capital gain on owner-occupied housing. This was calculated by applying a rate of capital gains tax (taken as 33⅓ per cent) to the appreciated value of the house in the previous twelve months (taken as 6 per cent in the late 1960s). The tax foregone was therefore treated as being 2 per cent of the market value of the house (or of the value paid off by the mortgagor).

9. *Private income in kind*

(a) Add the annual value of garden produce and farm produce for personal consumption. Households were asked to estimate the weekly average value, net of the costs and expenses of production.

(b) Add the rental value of consumer durables. Information was obtained about the ownership of a list of consumer durables and average rental values estimated and applied. The list included television sets, record players, radios, refrigerators, washing machines, vacuum cleaners, telephones and central heating.

(c) Add the annual value of home-help services performed by relatives and others, less the value of such services performed for others. Information was obtained about the weekly hours of home help worked by people outside the household and an amount calculated on the basis of the hourly rate paid to local authority home helps.

(d) Add the value of gifts received worth £25 or more less the value of any gifts given worth £25 or more.

10. *Total or gross disposable resources*

(a) Add net disposable income last year less income from assets (4 above).

(b) Add imputed income from net assets last year (6 above).

(c) Add imputed income from employer welfare benefits in kind (7 above).

(d) Add imputed income of public social services in kind (8 above), less tax relief on mortgage interest.

(e) Add private income in kind (9 above).

11. *Total annual housing costs*

(a) *For owner-occupiers* add annual mortgage payments (including any annual insurance payment); annual payment of rates and water rates less any rate rebate;

annual ground rent, and any payment for insurance on house or flat (but excluding any payment for insurance of contents). In cases where information is available about source and amount of loan, and term of repayment but not monthly amount of repayment, divide amount of loan by number of years of repayment and treat annual payment of mortgage as this amount plus an amount for interest, at 7 per cent. If a figure for rates has not been divided between business and private use, work out the proportion of total rooms used by the household, exclusive of business, and add this proportion of rates.

(b) *For tenants* add annual rent paid; annual payment, if any, of rates and water rates less any rate rebate. Deduct any costs of lighting, heating, meals and services that are included in the rent. Deduct net receipts from sub-letting.

Special coding instructions and schedules were developed to deal with exceptional types of tenure and instances where information for certain subsidiary types of payment or receipt (e.g. sub-letting) was incomplete.

Appendix Six
The Social Grading of Occupations

Although the Registrar General's classification of occupations was used in analysing the data from the national survey described in this report, it was not entirely suited to our purpose. By applying it, we could compare the survey material with data from the census and data from other sources, but could not easily distinguish non-manual from manual categories. An alternative eight-fold classification was adopted, which has been used more extensively in this report.

The eight-fold classification derives from a pioneering study of social class by Professor Glass and his colleagues in the early 1950s.[1] Some changes have been made, which should be explained. A seven-fold classification was described by Hall and Caradog Jones in 1950,[2] and further described by Moser and Hall in 1954.[3] The main object was to divide the Registrar General's social class III into three distinct categories. The seven classes were as follows:

(i) Professional and high administrative.
(ii) Managerial and executive.
(iii) Inspectional, supervisory and other non-manual, higher grade.
(iv) Inspectional, supervisory and other non-manual, lower grade.
(v) Skilled manual, and routine grades of non-manual.
(vi) Semi-skilled manual.
(vii) Unskilled manual.

Occupations were assigned to these seven categories, and subsequently two inquiries were carried out to validate the categorization. These were discussed by Moser and Hall.[4] People were invited to grade thirty occupations according to their social status or prestige. These thirty occupations were then used as 'reference points', first in examining the seven-fold classification, and secondly in revising it for subsequent use. A principal conclusion was that the classification should be eight-fold.

1. Glass, D. V. (ed.), *Social Mobility in Britain*, Routledge & Kegan Paul, London, 1954.
2. Hall, J., and Caradog Jones, D., 'The Social Grading of Occupations', *British Journal of Sociology*, March 1950.
3. Moser, C. A., and Hall, J. R., 'The Social Grading of Occupations', in Glass (ed.), *Social Mobility in Britain*.
4. ibid., pp. 32–46.

The seven-fold status classification is too coarse. In particular, the findings of other studies in this volume show that there are important attitude and behaviour differences between persons in the manual and non-manual sections of category (v), which in our analysis covers routine non-manual as well as skilled manual occupations. Even if recombination had subsequently proved necessary, it would have been better to have begun by treating the manual and non-manual sectors separately.[1]

The eight-fold classification was subsequently adopted in further studies.[2] In preparing our study, we therefore decided to use the classification for most of the cross-tabulations which involved a social class variable. In examining the updated list of 1,200 occupational titles available at the London School of Economics in the late 1960s, however, it became apparent that the allocation of some titles seemed to be inconsistent both with the Hall–Jones scale and with the Registrar General's 1961 classification. As Mac-Donald has explained, no account existed of the way in which the ranking of thirty occupations was used to rank many hundred more occupations.[3] It may be that the interpretation of certain key decisions was left to coding personnel, without subsequent checking. While nearly all non-manual occupations seemed to have been coded logically, discrepancies were noticed among manual occupations – among codes 6, 7 and 8. Among striking instances was the categorization of coal hewer or miner, short-distance lorry driver, crane driver, sheet-metal worker, sawyer and tree feller in class 7 (or the partly skilled category). We considered these occupations should be listed in class 6.

We took the view that, if certain occupational titles seemed to be coded inconsistently with the scale implied by the revised Hall–Jones scale *and* were coded differently from the Registrar General's occupational classification, we would alter them in favour of the latter. Although this may seem to have been an arbitrary correction of the original list, we believe it both reflected the original intentions of Professor Glass and his colleagues, and their successors, using the scale, *and* more logically related the classification to the Registrar General's classification. To obtain some estimate of the size of the problem, we drew 200 occupations at random from our sample and checked the correspondence of coding between the revised Hall–Jones list and the Registrar General's occupational classification. In 75 per cent of cases, codes 6, 7 and 8 in the former corresponded with III, IV and V in the latter. In nearly two thirds of the remaining cases, the changes (usually one category up or down) seemed justified. But we felt that some, amounting to 9 per cent of the sub-sample, should be changed in favour of the Registrar General's classification. These decisions were taken before the survey began in 1968. Had we benefited from recent work on stratification, we would probably have attempted to review the ranking of many occupations in relation to the mean years of full-time education or the income levels of those following them[4] – or other criteria. However, in view of the results re-

1. Glass, D. V., and Hall, J. R., 'A Study of Intergeneration Changes in Status', in Glass (ed.), *Social Mobility in Britain*, p. 217.
2. For example, see the outline in Oppenheim, A. N., *Questionnaire Design and Attitude Measurement*, Heinemann, London, 1966. Professor Glass has applied the scale in new research on fertility.
3. MacDonald, K., 'The Hall–Jones scale: A Note on the Interpretation of the Main British Prestige Coding', in Ridge, J. M. (ed.), *Mobility in Britain Reconsidered*, Clarendon Press, Oxford, 1974.
4. On the lines described in Blau, P. M., and Duncan, O. D., *The American Occupational Structure*, John Wiley, New York, 1967, pp. 117–28. A group of Oxford sociologists have put forward a new scale. This consists of 124 subdivisions which can be collapsed into 36, and therefore remains rather unwieldy. Some of the changes in the ranking of certain occupations (for example, technicians and lorry and coach drivers) are on the face of it puzzling and are not discussed in relation to the special survey. See Goldthorpe, J. H., and Hope, K., *The Social Grading of Occupations: A New Approach and Scale*, Clarendon Press, Oxford, 1974.

ported in this book for the scale adopted, we do not believe that the ranking of occupations would, in practice, have been very different. Of the list of some 1,200 occupational titles, we altered 121, or 10 per cent, nearly all of them by one grade only. A list of these changes, together with the original list, is obtainable on request from the author.

Appendix Seven
Note on the Adjustment of Sample Findings

The results of all sample surveys can be adjusted to take account of any departures from the true representativeness that can be traced because of sampling and response. The poverty survey poses particular problems of adjustment because interviewing was distributed over twelve months. During this period, incomes rose and rates of supplementary benefit were increased. But since the sample in each area consisted of four randomly drawn sub-samples of households which were interviewed in each quarter of the year, the results for each quarter can be compared and any cumulative results corrected for seasonal and other factors.

According to the social or government standard of poverty, 7·1 per cent of the sample households and 6·1 per cent of the sample population were living below the standard, and another 23·8 and 21·8 per cent respectively up to 40 per cent higher. These figures were adjusted to take account of the following factors:

1. *Northern Ireland.* A relatively larger sample of households was drawn in Northern Ireland so that some statements could be made about poverty in this region. Adjustments were made to all key national findings for this oversampling. As a consequence, the number in the sample living below the standard, according to their income in the previous twelve months, was reduced from 6·1 to 5·8 per cent, but those in the sample living on the margins of the standard remained at 21·8 per cent.
2. *Complete information on income.* Although information was collected for 2,050 households in the sample, information about the previous week's income was complete for only 1,808 of these, for income during the last twelve months for only 1,768. The proportion of families with different numbers of children was almost exactly the same among households giving incomplete as giving complete information, but rather more single-person households and rather fewer households containing three or four adults gave complete information. Adjustment for this factor tended to slightly reduce the numbers of households in poverty and on the margins of poverty, but leave the numbers of *people* in poverty or on its margins almost exactly the same.
3. *The supplementary benefit standard.* The net disposable income for the previous week and the previous year of households was compared with the supplementary benefit scales in force up to 7 October 1968 (plus actual housing costs). Yet a substantial part of the sample were interviewed after this date, and part of *the previous year's* income of these households was received after this date. It would have been difficult to devise and apply an appropriately weighted standard to each household. Moreover, very little

difference would be made to the results. This is partly because actual housing costs are added to the supplementary benefit scales, which themselves were increased by less than 6 per cent on 7 October 1968. In practice, households which had an income over 106 per cent of the standard before 7 October 1968 would have been over 100 per cent according to the pre-7 October standard. Adjustments were made to the results for the sample interviewed after October. Table A7.1 shows their income in the week prior to interview.

Table A7.1. Household income as percentage of S B scales plus housing cost.

	Under 100		100–39	
	Households	Population	Households	Population
Unadjusted	6·7	5·9	23·9	20·8
Adjusted	7·6	6·7	23·6	20·7

Appendix Eight
Additional Tables

Table A.1. Percentages of total net disposable income received by given quantile groups of households (CSO estimates compared with poverty survey).

Quantile group	CSO (based on FES) 1968	Poverty survey 1968–9 (individuals in households)
Top 10%	24·7	25·7
11–20%	14·9	15·0
21–30%	12·3	12·5
31–40%	10·7	10·7
41–50%	9·4	9·4
51–60%	8·4	8·2
61–70%	7·0	6·9
71–80%	5·9	5·4
81–90%	4·2	3·8
91–100%	2·5	2·4

SOURCE: Royal Commission on the Distribution of Income and Wealth, Report No. 1, *Initial Report on the Standing Reference*, Cmnd 6171, HMSO, London, Table G.13, p. 213.

Table A.2. Percentages of income in previous year of different types of household from different sources.

Type of household	Earnings from wages and salaries	Self-employment income	Income from assets	Income from sub-letting	Retirement and widows' pensions	Other state benefits	Income from non-state pensions and annuities	Income from other sources	Total %	Total No.
Man aged 60+	(38)	(5)	(5)	(0)	(31)	(6)	(14)	(1)	100	37
Man under 60	89	5	1	0	0	2	0	1	100	55
Woman aged 60+	10	0	11	3	50	17	5	2	100	190
Woman under 60	77	3	8	1	4	2	0	3	100	57
Man and woman,										
both over 60	31	4	7	2	34	4	14	2	100	166
one over 60	73	3	3	1	9	6	3	0	100	52
both under 60	88	6	1	0	0	2	1	1	100	213
Man, woman, 1 child	85	9	1	1	0	2	0	1	100	134
2 children	85	7	1	0	0	4	0	1	100	172
3 children	79	14	1	0	0	4	0	0	100	78
4+ children	(53)	(20)	(15)	(1)	(0)	(10)	(0)	(0)	100	48
3 adults	78	7	2	0	4	3	2	3	100	186
3 adults, plus children	77	11	1	0	2	3	1	3	100	126
4 adults	83	2	1	0	3	3	2	3	100	62
Others without children	69	10	3	1	8	4	2	2	100	66
Others with children	80	5	0	1	3	6	1	3	100	85
All households	75·7	7·5	2·6	0·6	5·9	4·1	1·8	1·8	100	1,769
FES 1968[a]	77·0	7·2	3·4	0·1	6·2	2·9	2·1	1·2	100	7,184

NOTE: [a]*Family Expenditure Survey*, Report for 1968, p. 81, adjusted to exclude imputed income from owner/rent-free occupancy. The FES data are not precisely comparable with the poverty survey data because (a) the former refer to the current rate of income rather than income over the whole year; (b) the former include 'normal' earnings instead of social security benefits if such benefits have been received for less than thirteen weeks; and (c) although windfalls have been excluded from the latter 'other sources of income' include a few additional sources of income, such as money gifts and profits from boarders.

Table A.3. *Mean gross and gross disposable income per annum in £s of different types of household.*

	Poverty survey[a]		Family Expenditure Survey gross disposable income[b]	
	Gross income	Gross disposable income	1967	1968
1 adult, pensioner	338	330	306	328
non-pensioner	1,025	786	661	663
All	805	716	–	–
2 adults, pensioners			466	510
non-pensioners			1,137	1,181
All	1,250	1,100	–	–
2 adults, 1 child	1,629	1,296	1,157	1,291
2 children	1,544	1,366	1,289	1,371
3 children	1,612	1,406	1,330	1,412
4+ children	1,998	1,804	1,279	1,432
3 adults	2,004	1,695	1,613	1,671
3 adults, plus 1 child	} 2,060 {	1,803	1,599	1,747
3 adults, plus 2 children			1,675	1,812
4 adults	2,250	1,966	2,134	2,172
All households	1,459	1,263	1,212	1,266

NOTES: [a]Estimates adjusted for slight over-sampling in Northern Ireland.
[b]This is the FES concept of net household income, excluding imputed income of owner-occupiers income in kind from employers and the imputed value of school meals, and milk.

SOURCE: FES figures based on data kindly supplied by the Central Statistical Office.

Table A.4. *Direct tax liability and net income at various levels of gross household income.*

Gross household income (£)	Mean gross income	Mean tax liability	Mean net income	Distribution of aggregate income	Percentage of households
	£	£	£	%	
Under 275	235	$\frac{1}{2}$	234	0·5	3·3
275–	288	3	285	0·2	0·8
300–	349	3	346	1·7	7·2
400–	447	3	441	1·5	5·0
500–	543	14	528	1·5	4·1
600–	652	41	612	1·5	3·2
700–	745	55	690	1·9	3·7
800–	856	94	763	2·7	4·5
900–	952	111	840	3·5	5·3
1,000–	1,124	149	975	9·5	12·2
1,250–	1,369	197	1,173	12·4	13·2
1,500–	1,722	280	1,442	20·6	17·3
2,000–	2,372	408	1,964	23·5	14·4
3,000–	3,608	669	2,940	11·0	4·4
5,000–	6,309	1,346	4,963	3·4	0·8
10,000–	12,074	2,995	9,079	3·8	0·5
20,000	20,596	15,410	5,186	0·8	0·1

Table A.5. *Percentages of individuals of different age, according to amount of household assets.*

Sex and age	None	Under £100	£100 -199	£200 -999	£1,000 -1,999	£2,000 -4,999	£5,000+	Total %	Total No.
Male:									
0–14	19	10	6	17	14	14	21	100	598
15–29	12	12	8	18	13	17	21	100	467
30–39	14	10	3	16	15	21	20	100	285
40–49	10	7	4	23	11	19	26	100	286
50–59	9	7	9	20	12	19	25	100	266
60–69	12	10	5	14	10	21	27	100	230
70+	10	8	10	18	6	23	25	100	117
All ages	13	9	6	18	13	18	23	100	2,249
Female:									
0–14	19	12	4	18	12	16	19	100	570
15–29	13	13	6	21	14	18	15	100	483
30–39	13	8	5	17	13	21	22	100	280
40–49	11	6	5	21	9	22	26	100	301
50–59	10	5	7	18	11	19	29	100	285
60–69	11	15	5	15	9	21	24	100	271
70+	17	10	8	17	8	21	18	100	235
All ages	14	10	6	18	11	19	21	100	2,425
Male and Female:									
0–14	19	11	5	17	13	15	20	100	1,168
15–29	12	12	7	20	14	17	18	100	950
30–39	13	9	4	17	14	21	21	100	565
40–49	11	6	5	22	10	20	26	100	587
50–59	10	6	8	18	11	19	27	100	551
60–69	12	13	5	15	10	21	25	100	501
70+	15	9	8	18	8	22	20	100	352
All ages	14	10	6	18	12	18	22	100	4,674

Table A.6. *Percentages of households according to gross disposable income, excluding and including dissaving previous year, and percentages of households in each income range who were dissaving.*

Range of income (£)	Gross disposable income last year		
	%	plus dissaving %	Percentage of each range dissaving (£25 or more)
Under 400	11·5	10·8	15·7
400–99	4·9	5·2	10·3
500–99	4·1	3·7	19·4
600–99	3·3	3·1	22·0
700–99	3·8	4·1	13·4
800–99	3·8	3·8	10·4
900–99	3·6	3·6	11·1
1,000–99	4·1	4·1	6·9
1,100–99	4·4	4·6	13·0
1,200–399	8·0	8·0	8·5
1,400–599	6·1	6·1	10·2
1,600–799	6·3	6·0	15·3
1,800–999	5·3	5·0	14·0
2,000–499	9·7	9·8	19·3
2,500+	21·3	22·0	10·3
Total	100	100	13·1
Number	1,769	1,768	1,769

Table A.7. *Percentages of people in households of different type with relatively high or relatively low incomes and resources.*

Type of household	Percentages of people in households having less than 50% or 200% or more of the mean for household type		
	Net disposable income last year	Net income worth	Gross disposable resources
1 man aged 60 or over	(19)	(48)	(40)
1 man under 60	13	14	17
1 woman aged 60 or over	6	36	41
1 woman under 60	16	26	25
Man and woman	20	22	24
including both aged 60+	15	34	33
1 aged 60+	15	20	32
both under 60	10	12	15
Man and woman, 1 child	4	5	5
2 children	8	13	12
3 children	6	11	3
4 or more children	26	25	11
3 adults	15	15	11
3 adults and children	10	14	12
4 adults	2	6	7
Other households without children	34	29	34
Other households with children	15	19	23
All households	13	17	15
Number	5,145	4,391	3,576

Table A.8. *The cumulative effect on the mean value in the previous year of the resources of different types of household.*

Type of household	Non asset income £	and property income and annuitized value of assets £	and employer fringe benefits £	and value social services in kind £	and private income in kind £	Minimum number
Single, aged under 60	726	887	962	1,043	1,095	104
Single, aged 60 and over	364	626	635	703	746	200
Man and woman, both 60 or over	739	1,137	1,157	1,271	1,332	145
Man and woman, one 60 or over	887	1,091	1,152	1,257	1,327	49
Man and woman, both under 60	1,220	1,480	1,548	1,656	1,754	229
Man and woman, 1 child	1,202	1,298	1,358	1,555	1,619	110
2 children	1,270	1,464	1,534	1,799	1,816	139
3 children	1,327	1,700	1,752	2,087	2,098	61
4 or more children	1,414	1,754	1,776	2,242	2,222	42
3 adults only	1,574	1,858	1,943	2,204	2,296	156
3 adults and children	1,702	2,018	2,123	2,543	2,640	105
4 adults only	1,830	2,234	2,249	2,652	2,806	52
Others without children	1,572	2,112	2,216	2,560	2,653	54
Others with children	1,648	2,045	2,108	2,559	2,633	71
All types	1,164	1,434	1,491	1,704	1,771	1,517

Table A.9. Percentages of heads of household of different occupational class giving different descriptions of poverty.

Description of poverty	Professional and managerial	Other non-manual	All non-manual	All manual	Skilled manual	Partly skilled and unskilled manual
Subsistence	37	37	37	29	28	29
Minority groups (e.g. pensioners, low paid)	34	30	31	29	32	24
Mismanagement	6	7	7	9	8	11
Relative with past	2	3	3	6	5	7
Relative with others	3	2	2	2	2	1
Starvation	6	5	6	9	9	9
None to describe	4	8	7	8	7	9
Other	6	7	7	9	9	9
Total	100	100	100	100	100	100
Number	200	589	789	1,077	595	482

NOTE: Unclassifiable: 194.

Table A.10. Mean score on deprivation index according to income for different types of household.

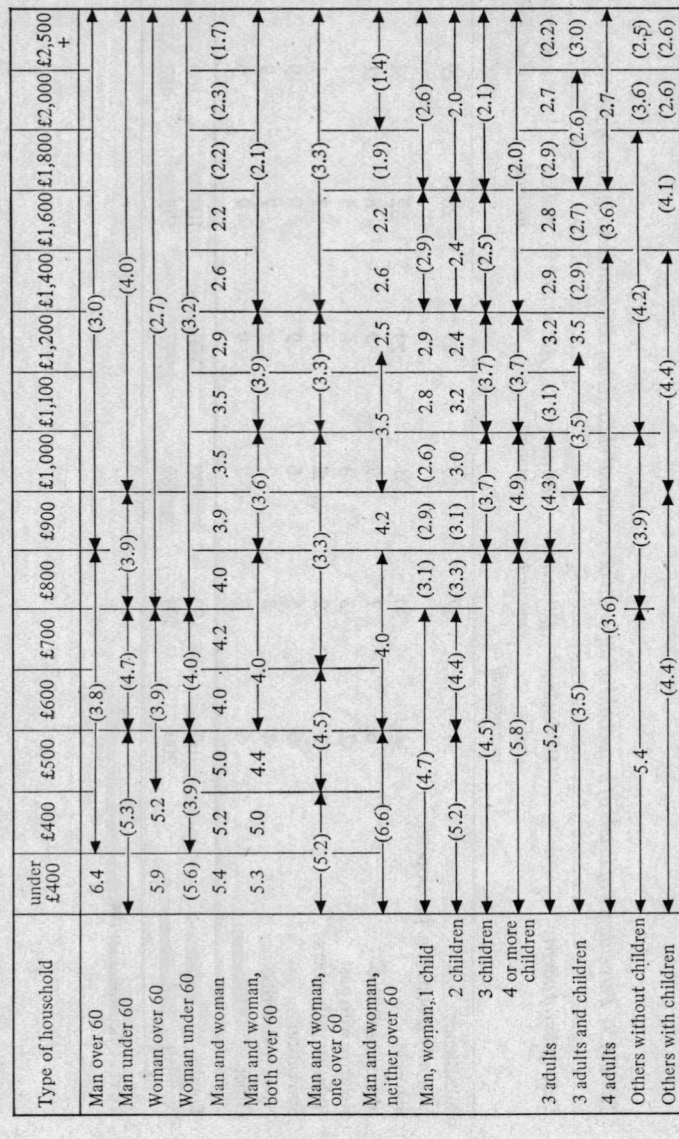

NOTE: Mean scores for fewer than ten households have not been calculated. Means for groups of households numbering 10–19 are placed in brackets.

Table A.11. *Percentages of individuals in households with net disposable incomes in previous year at different levels in relation to the supplementary benefit standard, according to their deprivation score.*

Net disposable income last year as % of supplementary benefit scales plus housing cost	Score on Deprivation Index									Total	Number	Mean score
	0	1	2	3	4	5	6	7	8			
600 or more	15	26	23	15	7	4	6	4	0	100	81	2·3
400–599	5	25	35	16	13	4	1	2	0	100	101	2·3
300–99	6	21	24	20	16	9	2	1	0	100	337	2·6
250–99	7	19	22	22	14	8	5	1	0	100	517	2·7
200–49	5	15	22	22	19	11	4	2	0	100	874	3·0
180–99	3	17	18	19	17	15	6	3	2	100	506	3·2
160–79	5	17	19	21	16	11	5	4	2	100	567	3·1
140–59	1	8	16	18	17	16	12	8	3	100	523	4·0
120–39	3	7	18	20	18	11	12	8	3	100	611	3·8
100–19	0	3	10	14	19	15	17	12	9	100	420	4·8
80–99	0	5	10	11	14	15	16	16	12	100	236	5·0
Under 80	0	1	11	6	10	12	21	11	26	100	80	5·6
All incomes	4	13	19	19	17	12	8	5	3	100	4,853	3.5

Table A.12. *Household food expenditure as percentage of average declared net family income (1968).*

Type of household	£33 and over	£19–32	Under £19
Man and woman (both under 55)	14·3	19·2	26·1
Man and woman, 1 child	18·6	25·6	33·7
2 children	19·5	27·2	37·1
3 children	21·0	30·6	38·0
4 or more children	(22·2)	33·1	42·7
adolescents only	17·7	23·9	29·0
adolescents and children	20·9	28·9	33·0

SOURCE: *Household Food Consumption and Expenditure: 1968*, HMSO, London, 1970, p. 57.

Table A.13. *Mean deprivation score for the non-disabled and disabled at different ranges of income.*

Range of income	Mean deprivation index score		Number of persons	
	Little or no disability	Disabled	Little or no disability	Disabled
	Single person 60+			
Under £400	5·3	6·3	64	93
400–499	4·5	5·5	17	19
500–699	3·0	}3·9{	11	12
700+	3·2		12	
All ranges	4·7	6·0	104	124
	Man and woman			
Under £600	5·3	5·0	86	46
600–799	4·4	4·8	94	53
800–899	3·6	5·3	60	18
900–1,099	3·7	3·7	116	24
1,100–599	2·8	3·1	286	32
1,600+	2·0	2·9	118	10
All ranges	3·4	4·3	760	183

Table A.14. *Percentages of households with net disposable income in previous week and previous year, expressed as a percentage of state's poverty standard.*

Net disposable income last week as % of state's poverty standard	Net disposable income last year as % of state's poverty standard						
	Under 100	100–19	120–39	140–79	180–249	250+	All ranges
Under 100	5·1	0·7	0·9	0·6	0·5	0·4	8·2
100–19	1·7	9·6	0·7	0·6	0·2	0·1	12·9
120–39	0·1	1·5	7·4	1·6	0·4	0·1	11·0
140–79	0·2	0·4	2·4	12·8	2·4	0·7	18·9
180–249	0·0	0·3	0·5	4·6	20·7	3·1	29·2
250+	0·0	0·0	0·0	0·4	2·7	16·7	19·8
All ranges	7·1	12·4	11·9	20·5	26·9	21·2	100

Table A.15a. *Percentages of households of different size having a net disposable income in previous week and previous year of less than the supplementary benefit scales plus housing cost, or less than 40 per cent higher.*

%	Number of persons in household with net disposable income last week					Number of persons in household with net disposable income last year				
	1	*2*	*3*	*4*	*5*	*1*	*2*	*3*	*4*	*5*
250+	14	26	25	17	17	13	28	27	18	18
200–49	9	21	25	22	17	9	22	23	19	13
180–99	6	10	15	12	11	5	7	15	12	10
160–79	7	8	9	12	15	8	8	9	17	12
140–59	7	8	8	14	12	7	7	8	12	16
120–39	10	10	8	13	14	10	10	10	14	16
110–19	20	4	3	3	4	17	4	3	4	3
100–9	14	6	3	3	3	15	6	3	2	4
90–99	6	3	1	1	3	6	3	1	1	2
80–89	3	1	1	0	1	4	2	1	0	4
Under 80	4	3	2	2	2	5	2	0	1	1
Total	100	100	100	100	100	100	100	100	100	100
Number	345	539	337	306	281	338	528	330	300	273

Table A.15b. *Percentages of people in households containing different numbers of income units, according to net disposable household income in previous year.*

Income as % of supplementary benefit scales plus housing cost	Number of income units in household			
	1	*2*	*3*	*4+*
300+	9	14	16	3
200–99	25	33	35	52
160–99	20	27	26	17
140–59	13	7	13	8
120–39	15	8	6	9
100–19	11	6	1	5
Under 100	8	3	3	6
Total	100	100	100	100
Number	3,417	1,102	448	193

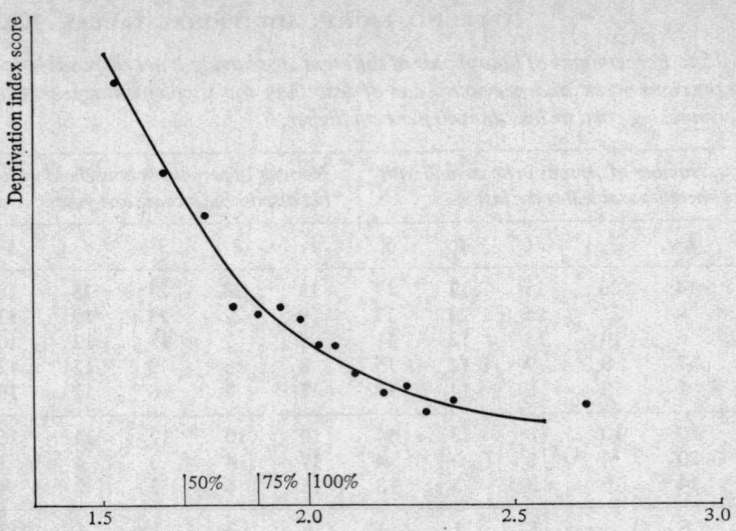

Figure A.1. *Modal deprivation by logarithm of income as percentage of mean for household type.*

Table A.16. *Percentages and estimated population in poverty in different regions.*

Regions	Income unit with net disposable income last year under or just above state poverty standard			
	Under %	Just above[a] %	Estimated number of persons in 000s	
			Under	Just above[a]
Greater London	8	19	570	1,380
South-East	6	21	490	1,770
Anglia and East Midlands	11	18	585	980
South-West and Wales	8	26	440	1,480
West Midlands	8	22	595	1,565
North West	9	27	570	1,695
Northern Yorks and Humberside	10	23	585	1,390
Northern Ireland	18	31	460	775
Scotland	9	29	490	1,655
Rural	9	21	890	2,010
Urban	8	25	1,885	6,195
Conurban	10	22	1,970	4,465

NOTE: [a]100–39 per cent of standard.

Table A.17. Percentage of households of different type with net disposable income below or just above the state's standard in previous week and previous year.

Type of household	Net disposable household income as % of supplementary benefit rates plus housing cost						Total	No.
	Under 100 last week and last year	100–39 last week and last year	Under 100 or 100–39 last week and last year	Under 100 or 100–39 only last week	Under 100 or 100–39 only on average last year	140 or more last week and last year		
Man over 60	(6)	(42)	(0)	(6)	(11)	(36)	100	36
Man under 60	5	2	2	2	3	86	100	57
Woman over 60	14	56	5	3	1	21	100	175
Woman under 60	6	19	4	2	9	61	100	54
Man and woman	5	16	4	2	3	70	100	457
Man and woman, both over 60	9	27	7	4	7	45	100	161
Man and woman, one under 60	5	25	4	2	0	64	100	55
Man and woman, both under 60	2	5	1	0	1	90	100	202
Man, woman, 1 child	2	14	2	4	5	74	100	118
2 children	2	18	2	9	6	63	100	148
3 children	2	19	2	8	11	59	100	64
4 or more children	(9)	(38)	(7)	(18)	(2)	(27)	100	45
3 adults	2	8	4	2	4	80	100	167
3 adults plus children	3	10	4	1	5	77	100	117
4 adults	3	3	0	5	5	83	100	59
Others without children	5	10	2	5	7	72	100	60
Others with children	9	14	5	5	1	65	100	77
All types	5	19	3	4	4	64	100	1,634

Table A.18. Percentages of persons, according to gross disposable income and income net worth of income units expressed as a percentage of the deprivation standard.

Percentage of deprivation standard	Gross disposable income	Income net worth
250+	11·6	20·1
200–49	9·3	11·0
180–99	6·6	8·2
160–79	8·0	9·8
140–59	12·5	10·1
120–39	13·0	10·3
110–19	6·4	4·6
100–9	7·4	6·4
90–99	6·3	5·5
80–89	6·5	4·5
Under 80	12·4	9·6
Total	100	100
Number	5,289	4,576

Table A.19. *Percentages of households of different type having a net disposable income in previous year of less than 50 per cent and 80 per cent of the mean for their type.*

Household type	Last year		
	Under 50 % of mean	50–79 % of mean	Total no. = 100 %
Man aged 60+	(15·8)	(44·8)	37
Man under 60	9·1	30·8	55
Woman aged 60+	1·0	38·8	190
Woman under 60	12·3	28·1	57
Man and woman	18·2	23·2	472
Man and woman, both over 60	13·3	36·8	166
Man and woman, one over 60	13·5	25·0	52
Man and woman, both under 60	7·0	26·3	213
Man and woman, 1 child	0·7	31·4	134
2 children	3·5	33·7	172
3 children	2·6	34·6	78
4 or more children	(17·8)	(54·4)	48
3 adults	11·3	25·2	186
3 adults, plus children	4·9	37·1	126
4 adults	1·6	21·9	62
Others without children	22·8	14·5	66
Others with children	10·5	14·5	85
All types	9·2	29·6	1,768

Table A.20. Percentages of households of different type according to housing costs per annum.

Type of household	Housing costs per annum							
	Under £50	£50–99	£100–49	£150–99	£200–99	£300+	Total	No.
Man aged 60+	36	33	19	5	5	2	100	42
Man under 60	27	19	24	16	11	2	100	62
Woman aged 60+	33	39	16	7	3	1	100	200
Woman under 60	22	25	27	18	5	3	100	60
Man and woman	27	28	15	10	12	7	100	543
Man and woman, 1 child	9	12	16	21	26	16	100	152
2 children	10	11	20	20	21	17	100	191
3 children	9	17	22	21	18	13	100	90
4 or more children	9	22	31	13	9	16	100	55
3 adults	23	27	23	14	7	5	100	225
3 adults, plus children	20	12	19	22	19	8	100	155
4 adults	17	22	19	18	10	13	100	87
Others without children	27	33	16	5	10	10	100	82
Others with children	13	16	23	24	17	7	100	105
All types	21	24	19	15	13	8	100	2,049

Table A.21. Housing cost as percentage of household income, for different types of household.

Type of household	Housing cost as % of net disposable income last year						Mean housing cost, as % of mean household income
	Under 5	5–9	10–19	20+	Total	No.	
Man aged 60+	16	19	30	35	100	37	17
Man under 60	15	20	29	36	100	55	16
Woman aged 60+	5	15	32	49	100	190	25
Woman under 60	12	16	33	39	100	57	17
Man and woman	21	24	34	21	100	472	13
Man and woman, 1 child	9	14	31	35	100	134	16
2 children	8	17	35	28	100	172	15
3 children	8	20	32	20	100	78	14
4 or more children	8	25	40	19	100	48	14
3 adults	32	34	27	5	100	186	8
3 adults, plus children	25	18	40	9	100	126	10
4 adults	26	44	21	10	100	62	8
Others without children	35	30	18	12	100	66	10
Others with children	25	33	18	19	100	85	17
All types	18	23	35	24	100	1,768	14

Table A.22. *Mean income, assets and income net worth of quantile groups of households ranked according to income net worth expressed as a percentage of the state's poverty standard, compared with mean income, assets and income net worth of quantile groups ranked according to income, assets and income net worth respectively.*

Quantile	Mean net disposable income last year	Mean net assets	Income net worth	Ranked according to income: disposable income last year	Ranked according to net assets: mean net assets	Ranked according to net worth: income net worth
			Ranked according to income net worth as % of household supplementary benefit standard:			
%	£	£	£	£	£	£
Top 1%	4,498	62,654	9,571	7,567	94,696	11,611
2–5	2,491	18,419	3,674	3,095	19,654	4,045
6–10	1,719	9,059	2,368	2,297	10,703	2,755
11–20	1,560	5,185	1,913	1,840	6,534	2,136
21–30	1,394	3,576	1,640	1,530	4,188	1,727
31–40	1,354	2,851	1,555	1,309	2,645	1,476
41–50	1,171	2,235	1,325	1,151	1,521	1,264
51–60	1,106	1,431	1,206	998	780	1,108
61–70	954	1,019	1,021	839	331	939
71–80	855	894	914	665	121	766
81–90	674	502	708	461	25	553
91–95	483	99	491	344	0	392
96–100	420	31	423	253	−561	293

NOTE: The value of owner-occupied housing is represented in the third and last columns of this table only by an imputed rental 'income' of 7 per cent on the capital.

Table A.23. *Age distribution of the rich.*[a]

Age	Top 1%	Next 4%	Next 5%	All top 10%	All samples
0–14	28	17	16	18	25
15–29	17	15	18	17	20
30–49	18	28	27	26	25
50–64	18	22	28	24	17
65–79	15	17	9	13	11
80+	4	1	2	2	2
Total	100	100	100	100	100
Number	54	146	193	393	4,320

NOTE: [a]Households ranked on criteria of non-asset income in previous year plus annuitized value of assets expressed as a percentage of the government poverty standard.

Table A.24. *Persons in richest and poorest households, according to household type.*

Type of household	Persons	
	Richest 5% of households[a]	Poorest 5% of households[a]
Single person under 60	7	4
Single person over 60	4	14
Man and woman, both under 60	12	12
one under 60	2	2
both over 60	11	4
Man and woman, 1 child	2	0
2 children	7	7
3 children	6	3
4 or more children	7	24
3 adults	16	0
3 adults, plus children	10	7
4 adults	4	0
Others without children	8	4
Others with children	6	19
Total	100	100
Number of persons	181	183

NOTE: [a]Defined in terms of income net worth of households in previous year as percentage of state poverty standard (see Chapter 9, page 357).

Table A.25. *Percentages of men and women*[a] *with different years of education according to principal factor believed to determine social class.*

Principal factor believed to determine class	Number of years education					
	Men Up to 8	9	10	11	12–14	15 or more
Job	26	21	24	18	18	21
Education	8	9	7	14	12	14
Family	15	17	14	12	14	16
Way of life	29	29	28	32	33	21
Money	16	18	19	12	13	10
Other	2	4	4	6	4	6
Don't know	4	2	4	4	6	11
Total	100	100	100	100	100	100
Number	156	610	361	160	121	62
	Women					
Job	12	12	13	11	10	23
Education	11	8	10	11	20	22
Family	26	21	19	21	22	19
Way of life	28	37	31	34	29	16
Money	18	16	22	15	10	5
Other	3	4	2	5	6	12
Don't know	1	2	2	2	3	3
Total	100	100	100	100	100	100
Number	180	690	100	197	167	64

NOTE: [a]Chief wage-earners or heads of households and housewives only.

Table A.26. *Percentages of men and women of different occupational class saying they were middle class, according to selected characteristics.*

Selected characteristics	Men		Women	
	Non-manual	Manual	Non-manual	Manual
Father non-manual	70	25	74	33
manual	48	16	49	23
Education under 10 years	41	16	50	23
10 years	52	20	55	26
11 or more years	77	37	77	47
Home rented from council	33	17	35	21
owned	65	23	68	34
Church not attended in last year	55	17	54	23
attended in last month	63	21	68	30
Net income worth below 50% of mean	48	12	46	18
110–99% of mean	68	31	73	38
200% or more of mean	81	–	80	–
	Number			
Father non-manual	312	198	382	222
manual	264	644	338	728
Education under 10 years	214	580	262	641
10 years	120	251	177	241
11 or more years	277	70	333	94
Home rented from council	75	358	104	400
owned	432	323	518	342
Church not attended in last year	271	516	266	482
attended in last month	175	213	238	218
Net income worth below 50% of mean	48	162	96	238
110–99% of mean	222	119	244	118
200% or more of mean	80	12	97	10

Table A.27. *Percentages of manual and non-manual chief wage-earners or heads of households and housewives with different net income worth who designated themselves as middle class.*

		Percentage designating themselves middle class				
		Net income worth as % of the mean of each household type				
		Under 50	50–89	90–109	110–99	200+
Male:	manual	12	15	22	31	–
	non-manual	(48)	45	53	68	81
Female:	manual	18	24	33	38	–
	non-manual	46	51	60	73	80
		Total numbers on which percentages based				
Male:	manual	162	477	141	119	12
	non-manual	48	165	107	222	80
Female:	manual	238	501	138	118	10
	non-manual	96	219	132	244	97

Table A.28. *Percentages of chief wage-earners and housewives living in households with different numbers of durables in a list of ten who felt deprived in none or one or more of five different respects.*

Number out of total of 5 expressions of deprivation	Number of selected list of 10 durables in household			
	0–3	4–5	6–7	8+
None	28	33	42	53
1–2	37	38	41	35
3–5	35	28	17	12
Total	100	100	100	100
Number	200	406	665	752

LIST OF DURABLES: television, record player, radio, refrigerator, washing machine, vacuum cleaner, telephone, central heating, armchairs, easy chairs for each member of the household, and living-room carpet.

Table A.29. Percentages of chief wage-earners or heads of households saying they felt poor always, sometimes and never, whose household incomes were below and above the mean of their type.

Net disposable household income as % of the mean of household type	Always poor	Sometimes poor	Never poor
Under 60	43	32	13
60–99	45	50	42
100–99	10	14	26
200+	1	4	18
Total	100	100	100
Number	153	328	1,344

Table A.30. Percentages of chief wage-earners or heads of households saying they found it difficult and not difficult managing on their incomes whose household incomes were below and above the state's standard of poverty.

Net disposable household income as % of supplementary benefit scale plus housing cost	Difficult to manage		Not difficult	
Under 100	14	(11)	5	(4)
100–39	39	(35)	16	(15)
140+	47	(54)	78	(81)
Total	100	(100)	100	(100)
Number	558	(1,577)	1,294	(3,541)

NOTE: Percentages in brackets apply to all persons in such households.

Table A.31. *Percentages of people in households having net income worth in previous year (and total resources) below and above the mean of their type who had different numbers of durables in a selected list of ten.*[a]

Number of durables in household	Total net income worth (total resources in brackets)									
	Under 50		50–89		100–9		110–99		200+	
0–3	14	(18)	5	(4)	0	(2)	0	(1)	0	(0)
4–5	38	(41)	24	(26)	10	(10)	5	(9)	5	(3)
6–7	38	(33)	41	(43)	37	(34)	23	(22)	14	(16)
8–10	11	(8)	30	(26)	53	(54)	72	(68)	81	(81)
Total	100	(100)	100	(100)	100	(100)	100	(100)	100	(100)
Number	446	(373)	1,859	(1,450)	744	(555)	874	(932)	229	(228)

NOTE: [a]See page 1014.

Table A.32. Percentages of employed men of different occupational class according to their place of work.

Place of work	Pro-fessional	Mana-gerial	Supervisory High	Supervisory Low	Routine non-manual	All non-manual	Skilled manual	Partly skilled manual	Unskilled manual	All manual
Mainly outdoors, 1 place of work	2	0	3	3	4	3	11	7	35	14
Mainly outdoors, 2 or more places	3	2	8	7	8	6	15	11	27	16
Transport	2	6	5	2	8	4	11	11	2	10
Mainly indoors, 1 place of work	75	74	68	74	72	72	44	62	30	47
Mainly indoors, 2 or more places	8	7	8	6	3	7	9	2	1	6
Both indoors and outdoors	10	11	8	7	5	8	10	6	5	8
Total	100	100	100	100	100	100	100	100	100	100
Number	61	53	156	149	101	520	569	269	153	991

Table A.33. Percentages of employed men and women of different social class according to the fraction of working time spent standing or walking about.

Fraction of working time spent standing or walking about	Professional	Managerial	Supervisory High	Supervisory Low	Routine non-manual	Skilled manual	Partly skilled manual	Unskilled manual
Men: All or nearly all	2	16	27	28	32	69	79	89
At least half but not all	34	28	36	20	14	11	15	9
Less than half but at least a quarter	23	32	12	13	12	5	2	2
Some but less than a quarter	26	12	10	13	16	6	2	1
Little or none	15	12	15	26	26	8	2	0
Total	100	100	100	100	100	100	100	100
Number	61	50	156	148	100	561	261	150
Women: All or nearly all	–	–	45	34	26	(67)	55	(87)
At least half but not all	–	–	31	21	9	(20)	11	(6)
Less than half but at least a quarter	–	–	6	1	6	(0)	4	(3)
Some but less than a quarter	–	–	8	10	13	(2)	7	(0)
Little or none	–	–	9	34	45	(11)	23	(3)
Total	–	–	100	100	100	100	100	100
Number	4	12	77	71	267	45	161	31

Table A.34. *Percentages of employed men and women of different age according to the fraction of working time spent standing or walking about.*

Fraction of working time spent standing or walking	Age							
	15–19	20–29	30–39	40–49	50–59	60–64	65+	All ages
Men:								
All or nearly all	71	58	52	55	52	67	(74)	57
At least half but not all	11	15	19	17	18	16	(19)	17
Less than half but at least a quarter	3	6	9	9	11	6	(0)	8
Some but less than a quarter	5	9	9	7	8	4	(4)	8
Little or none	9	11	11	11	10	7	(4)	10
Total	100	100	100	100	100	100	100	100
Number	119	352	330	297	261	103	27	1,489
Women:								
All or nearly all	32	37	44	46	55	(46)		42
At least half but not all	11	16	17	15	12	(14)		15
Less than half but at least a quarter	4	4	7	5	4	(4)		5
Some but less than a quarter	15	10	7	5	12	(4)		10
Little or none	37	32	26	28	16	(32)		29
Total	100	100	100	100	100	100		100
Number	104	212	101	134	91	28		670

Table A.35. *Percentages of employed men and women of different occupational class according to their times of work in day.*

Starting and finishing times of work last week	Men				Women[a]	
	Non-manual		Manual		Non-manual	Manual
	Professional and managerial	Other	Skilled	Other		
Before 8 a.m. to 6 p.m. (or earlier)	7	10	33	37	3	19
Before 8 a.m. to after 6 p.m.	8	6	9	9	3	2
8 a.m. (or after) to 6 p.m. or earlier	49	59	40	32	73	57
8 a.m. (or after) to after 6 p.m.	20	10	8	7	8	7
After 6 p.m. to 8 a.m. (or earlier)	2	1	4	5	2	4
No regular pattern last week	15	14	7	9	11	11
Total	100	100	100	100	100	100
Number	156	480	525	400	514	383

NOTE: [a]Since there were only twenty-one women of professional and managerial class and fifty-four of skilled manual class, they have been combined respectively with other non-manual and manual classes.

Table A.36. *Percentages of employed men and women of different occupational class according to number of hours worked in previous week.*

	Men				Women[a]	
	Non-manual		Manual		Non-manual	Manual
Number of hours	Professional and managerial	Other	Skilled	Other		
0–9	1	1	1	1	3	11
10–19	1	2	1	1	7	16
20–29	3	1	1	4	15	21
30–39	40	32	7	6	40	16
40–49	35	48	67	65	31	32
50–59	11	11	14	17	2	2
60 or more	9	5	9	6	1	1
Total	100	100	100	100	100	100
Number	105	399	521	403	472	379

NOTE: [a]Since there were only fifteen women of professional and managerial class, and fifty-four of skilled manual class, they have been combined respectively with other non-manual and manual classes.

Table A.37. *Percentages of male and female workers[a] of different occupational class, according to number of weeks of unemployment or sickness in previous twelve months.*

Number of weeks	Men			Women[b]		
	Professional and managerial	Other non-manual	Skilled manual	Partly skilled and unskilled manual	Non-manual	Manual
Unemployed						
0	100	95	93	88	96	94
1–2	0	1	3	2	0	2
3–4	0	1	2	2	1	0
5–9	0	1	1	2	1	2
10–19	0	1	1	4	1	1
20+	0	1	1	3	1	1
Total	100	100	100	100	100	100
Number	167	509	589	452	603	454
Sick or disabled						
0	81	74	68	68	71	69
1–2	13	14	15	14	17	15
3–4	1	6	8	7	5	8
5–9	3	3	5	6	3	5
10–19	1	1	2	4	2	2
20+	1	1	3	2	0	1
Total	100	100	100	100	100	100
Number	167	507	592	448	602	455

NOTES: [a]Including self-employed.
[b]Since there were only twenty-seven women of professional or managerial class, and sixty-two of skilled manual class, they have been combined respectively with other non-manual and manual classes.

Table A.38. Percentages of employed men and women of different occupational class working different numbers of weeks in the previous twelve months.

Men

Number of weeks at work	Professional	Managerial	Supervisory High	Supervisory Low	Routine non-manual	All non-manual	Skilled manual	Partly skilled manual	Unskilled manual	All manual
Under 12	2	2	1	1	6	2	1	2	6	2
13–26	2	6	1	0	1	1	4	3	8	4
27–40	8	26	9	6	7	9	5	9	15	8
41–2	0	2	2	2	6	2	3	2	2	3
43–4	2	4	2	4	3	3	4	2	2	3
45–6	10	9	9	7	7	8	7	7	5	7
47–8	39	17	22	22	21	23	16	11	9	13
49–52	39	35	54	57	50	50	60	63	53	60
Total	100	100	100	100	100	100	100	100	100	100
Number	62	54	158	155	106	535	584	284	169	1,037

Women

Number of weeks at work	Professional	Managerial	Supervisory High	Supervisory Low	Routine non-manual	All non-manual	Skilled manual	Partly skilled manual	Unskilled manual	All manual
Under 13	–	–	9	4	6	6	8	8	11	9
13–26	–	–	10	2	7	6	11	8	5	8
27–40	–	–	41	9	11	17	13	15	11	13
41–2	–	–	4	1	3	3	2	6	2	4
43–4	–	–	2	9	4	4	5	3	3	3
45–6	–	–	9	7	6	7	3	8	2	6
47–8	–	–	12	26	13	15	13	12	11	12
49–42	–	–	13	42	49	41	45	40	55	45
Total	–	–	100	100	100	100	100	100	100	100
Number	5	16	92	89	356	558	62	254	132	448

Table A.39. *Percentages of employed and self-employed men and women, according to number of hours worked in previous twelve months.*

Number of hours worked in last 12 months	Men		Women	
	Self-employed	Employed	Self-employed	Employed
2,800 or more	34	7	12	1
2,600–799	10	4	0	1
2,400–599	12	9	10	2
2,200–399	11	13	10	2
2,000–199	9	26	6	13
1,800–999	6	21	8	21
1,400–799	12	13	29	20
1,000–399	5	4	8	17
Under 1,000	3	3	18	23
Total	100	100	100	100
Number	146	1,399	51	772

Table A.40. *Percentages of employed population working indoors and outdoors lacking certain amenities.*

Amenities lacking indoors	%	Amenities lacking outdoors	%
Insufficient heating in winter	11	No dry and warm place to shelter in heavy rain	19
No tea or coffee available (whether charged or not)	8	No tea or coffee available (whether charged or not)	31
No flush WC	3		
No facilities for washing and changing	7	No lavatory (incl. earth closet or chemical closet)	15
No place to buy lunch or eat sandwiches	14	No facilities for washing	29
No place for coat and other articles without risk of loss	17	No indoor place to eat sandwiches or midday meal	20
No place for personal articles which can be locked	34	No safe and dry place for coat and other articles	38
No first-aid box or facilities	4	No first-aid box or facilities	10
Impossible to make and receive at least one personal telephone call a day	26	Impossible to make and receive at least one personal telephone call a day	47
No control over lighting over work	42		
Total number	1,631–76	Total number[a]	165–9

NOTE: [a]Data obtained only from persons working mainly at one place of work outdoors.

Table A.41. Percentages of employed men and women of different class working indoors, and working either indoors or outdoors, according to their working conditions.

Working conditions	Men working indoors									
	Pro-fessional	Mana-gerial	Supervisory High	Supervisory Low	Routine non-manual	All non-manual	Skilled	Partly skilled	Unskilled	All manual
Very poor	0	(4)	2	3	5	3	14	5	12	11
Poor	2	(8)	5	3	4	4	13	16	14	14
Adequate	5	(22)	23	20	38	22	32	38	43	35
Good	93	(65)	70	74	53	71	41	42	30	40
Total	100	100	100	100	100	100	100	100	100	100
Number	57	49	131	131	81	449	359	189	56	604
Men working indoors and outdoors[a]										
Very poor	0	(4)	2	5	8	4	15	9	12	13
Poor	2	(8)	4	5	3	4	14	18	28	17
Adequate	5	(22)	20	18	37	21	27	32	24	28
Good	93	(66)	74	73	53	71	44	41	36	42
Total	100	100	100	100	100	100	100	100	100	100
Number	60	50	146	146	93	497	508	238	150	896
Women working indoors[b]										
Very poor	–	–	7	4	4	5	(9)	8	(3)	8
Poor	–	–	7	6	8	7	(9)	12	(24)	13
Adequate	–	–	17	32	29	27	(34)	46	(42)	43
Good	–	–	69	57	58	60	(48)	34	(30)	36
Total	–	–	100	100	100	100	100	100	100	100
Number	4	12	71	68	266	421	44	148	33	225

NOTES: [a]Conditions of men working outdoors in more than one place of work assumed to be distributed in the same proportion as of men working outdoors in one place. Men working in transport excluded.
[b]Only eighteen women in the sample were working outdoors.

Table A.42. *Percentages of non-manual and manual male and female employees with and without entitlement to pay in sickness, according to weeks off work because of sickness in previous twelve months.*

Weeks off work sick in last year	Men				Women			
	Entitled to sick pay:				Entitled to sick pay:			
	yes		no		yes		no	
	Non-manual	Manual	Non-manual	Manual	Non-manual	Manual	Non-manua	Manual
0	75	66	83	68	61	54	85	62
1–2	15	16	12	13	24	24	8	18
3–4	5	9	0	7	6	12	5	9
5–9	2	5	3	6	5	10	1	7
10 or more	1	4	2	7	4	1	1	4
Total	100	100	100	100	100	100	100	100
Number	447	468	64	468	406	84	84	137

Table A.43. *Percentages of employed men and women of non-manual and manual status, who had subsidized meals.*

Type of subsidized meal	Men			Women		
	Non-manual	Manual	All	Non-manual	Manual	All
Provided by employer at below restaurant prices	23	18	20	28	21	29
Paid on account charged to employer	7	2	3	2	1	2
Luncheon vouchers	5	2	3	7	1	5
None	65	78	74	63	77	64
Total	100	100	100	100	100	100
Number	517	977	1,504	354	296	661

Table A.44. Percentages of employed men and women of different occupational class, according to number of weeks of paid holiday during the previous twelve months.

Number of weeks paid holiday	Men				Women	
	Non-manual		Manual		Non-manual	Manual
	Professional and managerial	Other	Skilled	Other		
0	23	14	11	19	25	32
1–2	19	34	66	62	38	53
3–4	40	44	21	18	26	11
5–9	9	5	2	0	5	1
10–19	10	3	0	1	6	4
Total	100	100	100	100	100	100
Number	167	507	591	444	602	452

Table A.45. Percentages of employed people in poverty, on the margins of poverty and not in poverty, according to paid and unpaid holidays.

Whether paid or unpaid holidays in year	Net disposable household income as % of supplementary benefit rates plus housing costs			
	Under 100	100–39	140+	All
No holiday	53	26	12	15
Unpaid	8	6	5	5
Paid	37	67	79	77
Both unpaid and paid	2	2	4	3
Total	100	100	100	100
Number	51	296	1,996	2,343

Table A.46. *Percentages of male and female employees with different degrees of total work deprivation, according to overall job satisfaction.*

Job satisfaction (index)[a]	Men – total work deprivation (index)[b]			
	None or slight (0–2)	Substantial (3–4)	Severe (5+)	All
Satisfied (all 4 respects)	44	37	24	38
Fairly satisfied (satisfied or neutral all 4)	19	22	20	20
Dissatisfied in 1 respect	26	23	28	25
Dissatisfied in 2 or more respects	11	17	28	16
Total	100	100	100	100
Number	653	443	217	1,313
	Women			
Satisfied (all 4 respects)	55	49	(30)	51
Fairly satisfied (satisfied or neutral all 4)	17	22	(20)	19
Dissatisfied in 1 respect	21	17	(27)	20
Dissatisfied in 2 or more respects	7	11	(22)	9
Total	100	100	100	100
Number	363	219	40	622

NOTES: [a]Satisfaction with facilities, security, pay and nature of job.
[b]As defined on page 461.

Table A.47. *Percentages of households with too few, enough or more than enough bedrooms who wanted more rooms or fewer rooms.*

Need expressed for additional or fewer rooms	Number of bedrooms by bedroom standard				
	2 or more too few	1 too few	Enough	1 too many	2 or more too many
2 or more rooms wanted	(39)	34	10	4	2
1 bedroom wanted	(21)	28	14	4	0
1 living room (or bathroom) wanted	(6)	5	9	7	3
Enough rooms	(34)	33	64	76	68
1, 2 or more rooms fewer	(0)	1	3	9	27
Total	100	100	100	100	100
Number	38	145	629	656	302

Table A.48. *Percentages of households of different type with different numbers of rooms usually heated in winter.*

Rooms usually heated in winter	Type of household				
	Single person	Man and woman	Man, woman and children	Others without children	Others with children
None or only 1	64	44	36	32	43
2 rooms in accommodation with 4 or more rooms	17	26	26	32	23
Others	19	30	38	36	34
Total	100	100	100	100	100
Number	351	529	476	256	384

Table A.49. *Percentages of households of different tenure according to household type.*

Household type	Owner-occupier		Rented				Rent free (mainly through employment)	All types
	Fully owned	Paying mortgage	Local authority	Privately furnished	Privately unfurnished			
Man or woman, under 60	5	3	4	32	7		13	6
Man or woman, over 60	16	1	13	6	23		4	12
Man and woman	36	21	22	21	31		28	26
Man, woman and children	5	44	26	21	17		24	24
Other households without children	28	15	18	13	16		13	19
Other households with children	10	16	16	7	7		18	13
Total	100	100	100	100	100		100	100
Number	474	477	559	109	323		68	2,022

Table A.50. *Percentages of people in different types of tenure and at different levels of income with at least three forms of housing deprivation.*

Type of tenure	Net disposable household income last year as % of supplementary benefit scale plus housing costs		
	Under 100	100–39	140+
Renting, council	48	10	8
Renting, private	47	35	27
Owner-occupier	1	11	2
	Total number of people in categories		
Renting, council	98	477	954
Renting, private	91	183	660
Owner-occupier	102	400	1,869

Table A.51. *Percentages of people in households with low, average, and high net income worth and of different tenure who possessed eight or more durables and fittings in a selected list of ten.*[a]

Type of tenure	Net income worth as % of mean of household type				
	Under 50	50–89	90–109	110–99	200+
Owner-occupier	13	38	64	77	82
Council tenant	8	30	38	55	–
Private tenant	3	18	30	51	–
Total number of people in:					
Owner-occupation	55	624	437	668	204
Council tenancies	207	756	191	85	4
Privately rented tenancies	146	393	100	94	21

NOTE: [a]The ten were television, radio, refrigerator, washing machine, vacuum cleaner, telephone, record player, central heating, upholstered chairs for each person, living-room carpet.

Table A.52. *Percentages of individuals in households of different occupational class with multiple types of poor housing.*

Number of types of poor housing[a]	Occupational class of household							
	Professional	Managerial	Higher supervisory	Lower supervisory	Routine non-manual	Skilled manual	Semi-skilled manual	Unskilled manual
None	74	58	59	52	30	32	25	17
1	20	32	33	34	45	35	35	37
2	5	6	5	9	15	21	25	20
3	–	1	2	4	9	9	12	21
4	–	2	1	–	1	2	3	4
Total	100	100	100	100	100	100	100	100
Number	289	236	497	628	363	1,555	817	482

NOTE: [a]The five types are: structural defects, inadequate housing facilities, insufficient bedrooms, only one room (or no rooms) heated in winter and insufficient internal play space for children aged 1–10.

Table A.53. *Percentages of households in different forms of tenure, according to the level of their annual incomes in relation to the state's poverty standard.*

Net disposable household income as % of supplementary benefit scale rates plus housing cost	Type of tenure				
	Owner-occupiers		Council tenants	Private tenants	
	Fully owned	Paying mortgages		Furnished	Unfurnished
Under 100	9	2	6	11	10
100–39	21	15	35	16	27
140–99	21	36	33	32	26
200–99	26	37	22	28	31
300+	23	9	3	13	5
Total	100	100	100	100	100
Number	394	411	488	102	295

Table A.54. *Mean absolute housing costs (£ per annum)[a] of households according to region and type of tenure (including repairs and before deducting for tax relief).*

Region	Owner-occupiers		Council tenants	Private tenants		All[b]	No.
	Fully owned	Paying mortgages		Furnished	Unfurnished		
Greater London	111	351	190	217	181	219	276
South-East	95	375	161	(191)	157	200	293
West Midlands	83	294	157	(298)	(123)	176	246
Anglia and East Midlands	106	281	143	(182)	(126)	176	174
Northern, Yorks and Humberside	80	306	152	(166)	118	158	222
North-West	68	242	129	(250)	112	138	230
South-West and Wales	88	251	145	(219)	107	137	225
Scotland	99	(279)	112	(111)	70	109	189
Northern Ireland	70	(197)	86	(97)	45	77	82

NOTES: [a] Means based on fewer than twenty households are placed in brackets.
[b] Including other tenures.

Table A.55. *Percentages of people living in homes with gardens of different size whose children, aged 5–10, did not have a safe place to play near by and with some or a lot of air pollution.*

	Size of garden or yard		
Whether safe place to play, and air sometimes or always polluted	SMALL *No sole use or too small for household to sit in sun (under 10 feet square)*	MEDIUM *Over 10 feet square, but not as large in size as tennis court*	LARGE *Equivalent in size to tennis court or larger*
Neither safe to play nor unpolluted	24	16	5
Not safe to play but unpolluted	17	21	21
Safe to play but polluted	31	11	6
Both safe to play and unpolluted	28	52	69
Total	100	100	100
Number	96	328	196

Table A.56. *Percentages of poor, marginally poor and non-poor[a] of different occupational class with some or a lot of air pollution and having insufficient garden space.*

Class	Air always or sometimes dirty, smoky or foul-smelling			
	Poor	*Marginally poor*	*Non-poor*	
Professional and managerial	–	(31)	16	
Other non-manual	25	18	21	
Skilled manual	35	22	34	
Partly skilled and unskilled manual	43	26	38	
	No sole use of garden or yard or too small to sit out in sun			
Professional and managerial	–	(22)	10	
Other non-manual	18	24	16	
Skilled manual	36	22	21	
Partly skilled and unskilled manual	26	31	29	
	Number			
Professional and managerial	10	40	501	
Other non-manual	73	253	1,211	
Skilled manual	104	408	1,125	
Partly skilled and unskilled manual	117	399	808	

NOTE: [a]Net disposable household income in previous year less than, 100–39 per cent of, or 140 per cent or more of the supplementary benefit scales plus housing costs.

Table A.57. *Percentages of people with low, medium and high net income worth who experienced different forms of environmental deprivation.*

Form of environmental deprivation	Net income worth as % of mean of household type				
	Under 50	50–89	90–119	110–99	200+
No sole use of garden	41	26	18	12	8
Garden or yard too small for household to sit in sun	14	11	8	3	3
No safe place near by for children aged 1–4 to play	55	40	30	26	12
No safe place near by for children aged 5–10	39	32	38	34	14
Air always or sometimes polluted	32	32	31	16	16
Number	514	1,984	748	873	236

Table A.58. Percentages of people of different age in different regions who were poor or marginally poor.

Region	Percentage of those of different age living in units with net disposable incomes last year of less than, or no more than 40% above, the state's poverty standard			
	Aged 0–14	15–39	40–59	60
Greater London	30	20	14	52
South-East	26	24	14	49
Anglia and East Midlands	35	27	14	44
South-West and Wales	35	25	21	67
West Midlands	33	25	15	62
North-West	38	31	19	56
Northern, Yorks and Humberside	38	21	17	61
Northern Ireland	62	28	43	74
Scotland	45	29	21	62

Table A.59. Percentages of people of different age in different regions who were poor or marginally poor.

Type of area	Percentage of those of different age living in units with net disposable incomes last year of less than, or no more than 40% above, the state's poverty standard			
	Aged 0–14	15–39	40–59	60+
Rural	28	24	24	58
Urban	35	28	16	59
Conurban	41	26	17	57

1038 POVERTY IN THE UNITED KINGDOM

Table A.60. *Rank order of constituencies according to proportion of individuals living in households who were in poverty or on the margins of poverty (with percentage of persons in manual worker households in brackets).*

Fermanagh and Tyrone	66	(50)	Ipswich	26	(65)
South Shields	46	(72)	Bristol South	25	(65)
North Devon	45	(54)	South-West Herts.	23	(43)
Galloway	45	(60)	Lewisham North	23	(48)
North Fylde	41	(58)	Lewes	23	(29)
Salford East	41	(79)	Pontefract	23	(62)
Gloucester	41	(68)	Southport	22	(47)
Coatbridge and Airdrie	38	(78)	Haltemprice	22	(34)
Bolton East	37	(55)	Melton	22	(60)
Woolwich East	37	(58)	Brierley Hill	20	(48)
South Worcestershire	36	(43)	Islington North	19	(57)
Neath	35	(66)	Grantham	19	(56)
New Forest	34	(65)	Edinburgh West	18	(58)
Manchester Wythenshawe	33	(50)	Guildford	18	(27)
Glasgow Shettleston	33	(79)	Birmingham, Northfield	18	(60)
Bradford East	32	(81)	Hornchurch	17	(38)
Oswestry	32	(64)	Newcastle East	17	(39)
Leeds North-West	31	(47)	Bristol West	16	(25)
Leicester South-East	31	(61)	Yeovil	16	(54)
Aylesbury	30	(67)	Oldbury and Halesowen	15	(55)
Coventry East	29	(75)	Belfast East	15	(81)
Belfast North	29	(63)	Aberdeen South	14	(36)
Wandsworth/Streatham	29	(50)	Kinross	13	(48)
Newton	27	(60)	Hendon North	13	(25)
Thurrock	26	(50)	Dartford	12	(58)
Bournemouth North	26	(46)			

NOTE: No individual figure should be regarded as reliable for the constituency in question. Sampling error will be high on the small number of interviews conducted in individual constituencies. The purpose of the table is to show the *kind* of constituencies which tend to be found towards the top, or towards the bottom, of a ranking by poverty.

Table A.61. Percentages of people living below or on the margins of the state's standard of poverty, according to their age and type of household (four areas and UK).

Age	Percentage living below or on margins of state standard		Number of base	
	Four areas	*UK*	*Four areas*	*UK*
0–14	51	34	943	1,322
15–25	31	17	472	692
25–44	34	24	696	1,309
45–64	29	18	658	1,161
65+	68	56	399	629
All ages	42	28	3,168	5,113
Household type				
Single person under 60	46	21	76	111
Single person 60 or over	79	75	169	227
Man and woman	38	26	484	940
Man, woman and 1 child	29	21	259	402
2 children	29	30	344	687
3 children	65	31	217	389
4 or more children	64	(69)	299	309
3 adults	19	14	237	554
3 adults and children	57	14	249	603
4 adults	19	8	137	245
Others without children	34	23	116	183
Others with children	46	31	458	476

Table A.62. *Percentages of households belonging to different numbers of social minorities who had incomes below, just above and substantially above the state's standard.*

Number of social minorities to which household belongs	Net disposable income last year as % of supplementary benefit scales plus housing cost				
	Under 100	*100–39*	*140+*	*Total*	*No.*
None	5·0	22·6	72·3	100	911
1	8·7	25·3	66·0	100	577
2	7·4	24·2	68·4	100	215
3 or more	15·4	30·8	53·8	100	65
All	7·0	24·0	69·1	100	1,768

	Net disposable income last week as % of supplementary benefit scales plus housing cost				
	Under 100	*100–39*	*140+*	*Total*	*No.*
None	5·8	22·5	71·7	100	925
1	6·1	25·9	68·1	100	595
2	7·7	22·7	69·5	100	220
3 or more	18·2	27·3	54·5	100	66
All	6·6	23·8	69·6	100	1,806

Table A.63. *Percentages of persons in certain social minorities according to occupational class of household.*

Occupational class of head of household	Characteristic of household			
	Large family	Non-white	Born in Eire	All households in survey
Professional, managerial and higher supervisory	19	8	22	21
Lower supervisory and routine non-manual	12	14	13	22
Skilled manual	32	35	30	31
Partly skilled and unskilled manual	37	43	36	26
Total	100	100	100	100
Number	565	170	156	5,310

Table A.64. *Percentages of the currently employed and non-employed, according to weeks of unemployment in the previous twelve months, who were in units living in poverty or on the margins of poverty.*

Income last year of income unit as % of supplementary benefit scale rates plus housing cost	Weeks unemployed in previous 12 months					
	Currently employed			Currently non-employed[a]		
	None	1–9	10+	None	1–9	10+
Under 100	4	9	(10)	8	(17)	(22)
100–39	12	17	(21)	15	(33)	(22)
140–99	28	31	(42)	32	(20)	(17)
200–99	38	29	(21)	29	(27)	(25)
300+	18	14	(5)	16	(3)	(14)
Total	100	100	100	100	100	100
Number	2,105	70	38	212	30	36

NOTE: [a]Having worked at least one week in the year or being unemployed and registered for work throughout the year.

Table A.65. *Gross average weekly earnings and gross year's earnings of adult employees as a percentage of the mean and median.*

Earnings as %	Full-time men, 21 and over				Full-time women, 18 and over			
	Gross average weekly earnings		Gross year's earnings		Gross average weekly earnings		Gross year's earnings	
	as % median	as % mean	as % median	as % mean	as % median	as % mean	as % median	as % mean
Under 60	4·1	11·0	5·4	12·2	9·6	19·7	13·3	19·7
60–79	18·0	29·6	17·8	28·2	19·7	22·3	17·3	21·5
80–99	27·6	26·0	26·8	25·8	18·9	19·1	19·1	20·5
100–19	20·4	15·6	20·1	15·9	15·3	16·5	15·5	15·5
120–39	12·6	7·4	12·5	7·2	14·1	9·8	15·3	10·0
140–59	6·4	3·5	6·5	3·5	8·0	2·6	8·2	2·8
160–99	5·6	3·3	5·0	3·3	6·2	5·2	4·8	4·6
200–99	3·4	2·4	3·7	2·1	6·0	3·4	6·0	3·6
300+	1·8	1·3	2·2	1·7	2·2	1·4	2·4	1·8
Total	100	100	100	100	100	100	100	100
Number	1,186	1,186	1,186	502	502	502	502	502
Amount median/mean	£21·4	£24·3	£1,087	£1,254	£11·3	£13·4	£587	£675

NOTE: Employees only.

Table A.66. *Percentages of men and women with different earnings according to their total deprivation at work.*

Work deprivation index	Gross earnings last week as % of the mean						
	Men						
	Under 50	50– 59	60– 79	80– 99	100– 119	120– 199	200+
0–2	35	38	34	45	53	65	95
3–4	42	39	43	36	34	24	3
5+	23	23	23	19	13	12	2
Total	100	100	100	100	100	100	100
Number	119	77	349	365	234	248	60
	Women						
0–2	55	(41)	50	53	66	77	(90)
3–4	38	(41)	40	43	28	21	(10)
5+	7	(18)	10	4	6	1	(0)
Total	100	100	100	100	100	100	100
Number	89	44	149	134	83	142	39

Table A.67. Percentages of men and women of different occupational class and earnings working indoors with poor or adequate but not good work conditions.

Percentage of gross earnings last year	Men				Women	Manual
	Non-manual		Manual		Non-manual	
	Professional or managerial	Other	Skilled	Other	(supervisory or routine only)[a]	(chiefly the partly skilled)
Under 80	–	43	68	59	43	65
80–99	–	24	59	66	43	(56)
100–19	–	24	53	(62)	35	(59)
120+	22	27	(52)	–	33	–
All percentages	20	31	60	61	39	63
			Number			
Under 80	4	99	113	140	107	109
80–99	4	81	118	44	69	43
100–19	6	66	60	29	52	22
120+	79	60	40	12	97	17
All percentages	93	306	331	225	325	191

NOTE: [a]There were only eleven women in professional or managerial occupations in the sample who could be classified according to their working conditions indoors.

Table A.68. *Percentages of men and women of different occupational class and earnings who worked unsocial hours (before 8 a.m. or at night).*

Gross earnings last year as % of mean	Men				Women	
	Non-manual		Manual		Non-manual	Manual
	Professional or managerial	Other	Skilled	Other	(supervisory or routine only)[a]	(chiefly the partly skilled)
Under 80	–	21	40	54	6	32
80–99	–	12	48	53	4	(55)
100–19	–	19	49	(66)	2	(57)
120+	15	18	59	(65)	6	(46)
All percentages	16	18	47	56	6	41
			Number			
Under 80	9	154	177	224	116	107
80–99	5	101	164	77	72	40
100–19	11	92	85	32	53	21
120+	121	72	64	23	102	24
All percentages	146	419	490	356	343	192

NOTE: [a]Only fifteen professional or managerial women employees were in the sample.

Table A.69. *Percentages of men and women of different occupational class and earnings who were entitled to one week's notice or less.*

Percentage of gross earnings last year	Men				Women	
	Non-manual		Manual		Non-manual	Manual
	Professional or managerial	Other	Skilled	Other	(supervisory or routine only)	(chiefly the partly skilled)
Under 80	–	39	56	66	57	75
80–99	–	14	50	55	50	(75)
100–19	–	15	41	(51)	29	(76)
120+	5	13	45	(59)	13	(60)
All percentages	4	22	52	62	37	73
			Number			
Under 80	2	115	179	223	106	100
80–99	3	91	165	84	64	44
100–19	7	78	88	37	56	21
120+	81	68	58	22	102	25
All percentages	93	352	490	366	328	190

Table A.70. *Percentages of male and female employees of different age according to their weekly gross earnings.*

Gross weekly earnings	Men aged −19	20–29	30–39	40–49	50–59	60+
Under £12	67	6	3	4	4	12
£12 and under £14	14	9	3	3	7	9
£14 and under £16	7	8	6	8	10	19
£16 and under £20	8	27	21	21	28	25
£20 and under £24	2	21	22	19	18	14
£24 and under £28	1	13	16	16	11	11
£28 and under £40	1	13	19	17	14	6
£40 or over	0	3	10	12	8	4
Total	100	100	100	100	100	100
Number	101	351	338	322	285	127
	Women					
Under £6	15	6	9	10	11	(25)
£6 and under £8	36	5	6	14	19	(4)
£8 and under £10	25	13	13	25	18	(29)
£10 and under £12	18	21	14	11	17	(11)
£12 and under £14	3	18	10	10	6	(4)
£14 and under £20	2	31	29	14	19	(14)
£20 and under £28	0	4	13	8	7	(4)
£28 and under £40	0	2	4	4	1	(11)
£40 or over	0	0	1	3	1	0
Total	100	100	100	100	100	10
Number	88	175	89	126	88	28

Table A.71. *Percentages of males and females of different age with scores of one or more, and seven or more, on the incapacity index.*

Age	Males		Females		Total number	
	Score of 1 or more	Score of 7 or more	Score of 1 or more	Score of 7 or more	Males	Females
10–14	2·6	0·0	3·1	1·8	233	222
15–19	3·2	0·5	1·4	0·9	222	213
20–24	2·4	0·5	5·0	0·5	205	219
25–29	3·6	0·5	8·5	0·0	194	201
30–34	3·8	1·0	7·0	0·0	184	171
35–39	8·0	1·0	12·2	1·0	200	197
40–44	13·4	2·4	20·7	1·6	164	188
45–49	14·9	3·0	21·3	3·0	202	202
50–54	27·1	3·5	37·8	7·4	140	188
55–59	37·7	9·0	43·8	6·9	204	185
60–64	44·0	9·8	62·5	17·7	141	176
65–69	67·6	6·9	79·4	19·9	148	165
70–74	76·8	21·5	87·3	27·9	69	118
75–79	(81·2)	(31·5)	90·9	42·3	48	99
80–84	(96·0)	(56·0)	(95·7)	(57·6)	25	47

Table A.72. Number and percentage of people with severe, appreciable and some incapacity who are of different age.

| Age | Estimated number in UK (000s) | | | | | | Percentage of all with some, appreciable or severe incapacity (scores of 3 or more) | | |
| | Severe and appreciable incapacity (scores of 7 and over) | | | Some, appreciable and severe incapacity (scores 3 and over) | | | | | |
	Males	Females	Males and females	Males	Females	Males and females	Males	Females	Males and females
10–39	80	95	175	265	320	585	10·5	7·2	8·3
40–49	80	70	150	250	330	580	9·7	7·4	8·2
50–59	200	220	420	260	630	1,090	18·0	14·1	15·5
60–64	120	285	405	320	600	920	12·6	13·5	13·2
65–9	100	295	395	415	665	1,080	16·2	14·9	15·4
70–79	275	655	930	600	1,310	1,910	23·5	29·4	27·3
80+	185	435	620	240	605	845	9·4	13·5	12·1
All ages	1,040	2,055	3,095	2,550	4,460	7,010	100	100	100

NOTE: Population estimates rounded to nearest 5,000.

1050 POVERTY IN THE UNITED KINGDOM

Table A.73. *Percentages of males and females of different ages who have trouble with one or more disablement conditions and have a marked or specific restriction of activity (in brackets).*

Age	Males		Females		Males and females		Total numbers in sample Males	Females
0–9	7·1	(2·0)	4·7	(1·8)	5·9	(1·9)	540	502
10–19	5·3	(3·4)	5·5	(2·5)	5·4	(2·9)	452	433
20–29	10·4	(4·1)	13·4	(8·4)	12·0	(6·2)	389	407
30–39	15·7	(6·1)	19·5	(11·1)	17·5	(8·5)	378	360
40–49	18·0	(7·8)	24·4	(14·1)	21·3	(11·1)	360	381
50–59	34·2	(18·6)	32·3	(20·4)	33·2	(19·6)	329	363
60–69	46·5	(24·3)	50·0	(27·4)	48·4	(25·9)	276	339
70–79	60·5	(38·9)	65·7	(38·7)	63·9	(35·7)	113	209
80+	(70·0)	(58·1)	80·9	(58·3)	77·8	(58·3)	31	72
All ages	20·5	(9·9)	25·3	(14·3)	23·0	(12·2)	2,868	3,066

NOTE: [a]Information covering restriction of activity.

Table A.74. *Numbers and percentages of people with one or more disablement conditions which limit activities, according to age.*

Age	Estimated number (000s) in non-institutionalized population (UK) Males	Females	Males and females	Percentage of those with disablement condition who were of different age Males	Females	Males and females
Under 10	100	85	185	3·9	2·1	2·8
10–14	55	25	80	2·1	0·7	1·2
15–19	85	75	160	3·2	1·8	2·4
20–29	150	310	460	5·7	7·8	6·9
30–39	215	370	585	8·1	9·1	8·7
40–49	265	490	755	9·9	12·3	11·4
50–59	570	670	1,240	21·6	16·9	18·7
60–64	320	455	775	12·0	11·4	11·7
65–9	310	395	705	11·7	9·8	10·5
70–79	410	745	1,155	15·5	18·5	17·3
80+	170	380	550	6·4	9·6	8·3
All ages	2,650	4,000	6,650	100	100	100

NOTE: Population estimates rounded to nearest 5,000.

Table A.75. *Percentages of males and females of different age and occupational class with one or more disablement conditions which limited their activities (percentages on base of under 50 in brackets).*

Occupational class[a]	Males					Females				
	0–19	20–39	40–59	60+	All ages	0–19	20–39	40–59	60+	All ages
Professional	1·3	(5·0)	(2·4)	[b]	4·6	1·5	(4·4)	(22·7)	[b]	9·8
Managerial	0·0	(2·8)	(9·7)	[b]	6·3	(4·1)	(12·8)	(9·8)	[b]	10·3
Higher inspectorate	2·1	2·4	12·7	(30·0)	7·7	1·2	7·2	9·6	(30·0)	9·2
Lower inspectorate	1·6	5·4	9·2	(24·4)	7·4	0·7	9·3	8·8	42·4	11·5
Routine non-manual	1·8	(2·3)	(23·1)	[b]	10·4	4·2	5·6	17·2	27·2	12·1
Skilled manual	3·2	4·3	12·5	33·9	9·8	1·8	8·9	16·4	38·2	14·7
Partly skilled manual	3·7	7·5	14·0	30·1	11·2	1·4	13·7	26·4	33·0	16·9
Unskilled manual	2·1	11·8	20·3	31·6	15·9	3·8	20·0	21·7	33·3	20·1

NOTES: [a]Occupational class of head of households or chief wage-earner.
[b]Percentage not given because base is under 30.

Table A.76. *Percentages of non-incapacitated and incapacitated at different age living in housing without sole use of four basic amenities.[a]*

Age	Degree of incapacity (score)			
	None (0)	Minor (1–2)	Some (3–6)	Appreciable or severe (7+)
20–29	20		(18)	
30–49	15	18	18	(32)
50–59	15	18	16	22
60+	21	20	29	27
All ages	18	22	25	26
Numbers of all ages	4,877	536	435	350

NOTE: [a]Scoring 4 or more on index of amenities. Scoring 1 for shared use, 2 for no use of indoor WC, sink, bath and cooker.

Table A.77. Percentages of non-incapacitated and incapacitated with household incomes above and below the state's standard of poverty who said they were poor all of the time or sometimes.

Net disposable income last year as % of supplementary benefit scales plus housing cost	Degree of incapacity			
	None (0)	Minor (1–2)	Some (3–6)	Appreciable or severe (7+)
Under 100	40	42	41	44
100–39	47	45	53	53
140+	17	20	21	22
All	24	29	34	37
Total	4,777	536	435	350

Table A.78. *Percentages and estimated total population of men and women who were ill for different periods (four measures of illness).*

Definition and period of illness	Percentage		Estimated no. in population (000s)	
	Men	Women	Men	Women
Number of weeks off work ill in last 52[a]				
None	71·5	71·1	11,385	7,011
1–2	14·0	15·5	2,223	1,530
3–9	10·6	10·1	1,692	999
10–19	2·1	2·4	342	234
20+	1·8	0·8	288	81
Total	100	100	15,930	9,855
Number	1,770[a]	1,095[a]	–	–
Number of weeks of current illness				
None, or less than 1	96·6	96·7	25,550	27,030
1–9	1·8	2·1	475	585
10–19	0·5	0·2	135	55
20+	1·1	1·0	290	280
Total	100	100	26,450	27,950
Number	2,923	3,116	–	–
Days ill in bed last 12 months				
None	71·3	66·8	18,860	18,660
1–19	25·6	29·5	6,760	8,240
20–49	2·5	3·1	660	880
50–149	0·3	0·3	90	100
150+	0·3	0·3	80	70
Total	100	100	26,450	27,950
Number	2,954	3,144	–	–
Years since chronic illness or condition started[b]				
Under 5	33·6	37·3	745	985
5–9	19·1	19·5	425	515
10–19	21·2	21·3	470	560
20 or more	26·1	22·0	580	580
Total	100	100[b]	2,220	2,640
Number	241[b]	287[b]	–	–

NOTES: [a]Employed and self-employed only.
[b]Only those aged 15–64 with any long-term illness or condition.

Table A.79. *Percentages of men and women with and without a disablement condition who were currently ill for different periods.*

Weeks' illness off work or confined to house	Number of disablement conditions					
	Men			Women		
	None	1	2 or more	None	1	2 or more
None or less than 1	97·7	89·8	80·6	97·5	93·6	83·7
1	1·0	1·8	1·6	1·5	2·0	1·0
2–4	0·4	0·9	0·0	0·3	0·6	0·0
5–9	0·2	1·3	1·6	0·2	0·3	2·0
10–19	0·3	2·2	3·2	0·1	0·9	2·0
20+	0·5	4·0	12·9	0·4	2·6	11·2
Total	100	100	100	100	100	100
Number	2,600	226	62	2,638	343	98

Table A.80. *Estimated numbers in population (000s) who are both disabled or incapacitated and have been ill for long periods.*

Disablement condition	Weeks of current illness[a]		
	None	Under 10 weeks	10 weeks or over
None	46,615	850	290
1 or more	5,980	220	445
Incapacity			
None (0)	32,730	545	75
Minor (1–2)	4,730	65	45
Some (3–6)	3,635	100	175
Appreciable or severe (7+)	2,465	180	410

NOTE: [a]Using the specific criteria of ill off work or school or ill confined to bed or house. Note that the measure of incapacity was not applied to children under the age of 10.

Table A.81. Percentages and estimated numbers of men and women of different age and employment status during previous twelve months who were incapacitated or non-incapacitated.

Degree of incapacity

| | Employed (or self-employed) | | | | | | Not employed | | | | | |
| | Men | | | Women | | | Men | | | Women | | |
Age	None 0	Minor 1-2	Some 3+	None 0	Minor 1-2	Some 3+	None 0	Minor 1-2	Some 3+	None 0	Minor 1-2	Some 3+
15-19	97	1	2	99	0	1	97	1	1	98	0	2
20-29	97	1	2	95	3	3	–	–	3	91	4	4
30-39	95	3	2	89	7	5	–	–	5	91	7	2
40-49	87	6	6	81	11	7	–	–	7	75	12	13
50-59	70	19	11	68	19	13	(19)	(9)	13	51	24	25
60-64	59	20	20	(47)	(29)	(25)	(30)	(15)	(25)	31	26	43
65+	42	32	26	(32)	(34)	(34)	25	29	(34)	12	21	66
All ages	85	8	6	82	10	8	41	18	8	53	16	40
No. in sample	1,486	146	113	887	109	85	158	70	85	1,568	310	154

Estimated number in population (000s)[a]

| | Employed (or self-employed) | | | | | | Not employed | | | | | |
| | Men | | | Women | | | Men | | | Women | | |
Age	None 0	Minor 1-2	Some 3+	None 0	Minor 1-2	Some 3+	None 0	Minor 1-2	Some 3+	None 0	Minor 1-2	Some 3+
15-19	1,155	10	25	1,055	0	10	815	10	20	825	0	20
20-29	3,410	35	55	2,235	65	65	110	0	20	1,310	65	65
30-39	3,300	110	65	1,485	110	80	10	0	25	1,520	110	35
40-49	2,830	210	200	1,895	255	175	25	0	45	890	145	155
50-59	2,025	560	310	1,135	320	220	35	20	135	870	405	420
60-64	640	220	220	210	120	110	55	25	100	365	310	515
65+	255	190	155	110	120	120	395	585	1,065	460	805	2,500
All ages	13,620	1,340	1,035	8,130	1,000	780	1,450	640	1,410	6,240	1,840	3,710

NOTE: [a]Estimated to nearest 5,000.

Table A.82. Percentages of employed, self-employed and non-employed of different age with a disablement condition.

Age	Employed[a]		Self-employed[a]		Non-employed	
	%	Total number of that age	%	Total number of that age	%	Total number of that age
15–19	3	240	} (12)	25 {	4	183
20–29	5	604			9	170
30–39	6	499	15	54	14	184
40–49	9	547	2	56	24	139
50–59	16	435	16	55	28	202
60–69	23	214	} (20)	30 {	28	374
70+	32	25			30	394
All ages	11	2,564	12	220	25	1,646

NOTE: [a]For at least one week in previous twelve months.

Table A.83. Percentages of men[a] with and without a disablement condition with earnings for previous week in relation to the mean.

Earnings last week as % of mean	Disablement condition	
	None	One or more conditions
Under 60	7	14
60–79	24	30
80–99	27	25
100–39	28	21
140–99	9	7
200+	5	2
Total	100	100
Number	1,202	123

NOTE: [a]Aged 20 and over and employed for 30 or more hours in previous week.

Table A.84. *Percentages of non-incapacitated and incapacitated full-time[a] male and female employees with different average gross earnings.*

Gross earnings per week of employment last year	Degree of incapacity		
	Men		
	None (0)	Minor (1–2)	Some, appreciable or severe (3+)
Under £15	11	17	25
£15–24	54	58	51
£25–34	23	18	20
£35+	11	6	5
Total	100	100	100
Number	1,093	103	64
	Women		
Under £10	34	(43)	(59)
£10–14	38	(34)	(22)
£15–19	17	(20)	(15)
£20+	11	(3)	(4)
Total	100	100	100
Number	452	35	27

NOTE: [a]Thirty hours a week or more.

1058 POVERTY IN THE UNITED KINGDOM

Table A.85. *Percentages of non-incapacitated and incapacitated who worked different numbers of hours in previous week.*

Number of hours worked last week	Degree of incapacity			
	Men			
	None (0)	Minor (1-2)	Some or appreciable (3+)	Any degree (1+)
Under 30	4	5	24	13
30–39	16	9	11	10
40–49	54	58	48	54
50+	26	28	17	23
Total	100	100	100	100
Number	1,180	122	89	211
	Women			
Under 30	6	(2)	(20)	11
30–39	44	(45)	(26)	36
40–49	45	(45)	(43)	44
50+	6	(7)	(11)	9
Total	100	100	100	100
Number	484	40	35	75

Table A.86. *Percentages of people of different age in income units with incomes above and below the state's poverty standard, according to the level of incapacity of the most incapacitated member of the income unit.*

	Percentage whose income was below or on the margins of the state's poverty standard[a]			
Age	No one incapacitated (scores 0 only)	At least 1 with minor incapacity (1–2)	At least 1 with some incapacity (3–6)	At least 1 with appreciable or severe incapacity (7+)
0–14	35·0	35·1	48·0	(52·9)
15–29	23·8	26·0	36·0	b
30–44	22·8	26·6	38·3	b
45–59	12·2	14·9	27·0	44·6
60+	41·3	53·8	59·1	68·6

NOTE: [a]Less than 140 per cent of supplementary benefit scale rates plus housing cost.
[b]Base smaller than 20.

Table A.87. *Percentages of children living in income units with and without an incapacitated child who were below and above the state's standard of poverty.*

	Children, aged 10–14		Children, aged 0–14	
Net disposable income last year as % of supplementary benefit rates plus housing cost	No child incapacitated (0)	At least 1 child with minor, some or severe incapacity (scores 1 or more)	No child with disablement condition	At least 1 child in unit with disablement condition
Under 100	5·3	(20·0)	7·9	16·7
100–39	27·7	(40·0)	27·8	35·0
140–99	32·7	(28·6)	36·8	18·3
200+	34·3	(11·4)	27·5	30·0
Total	100	100	100	100
Number	376	35	1,304	60

Table A.88. *Percentages of children in the United Kingdom and in four special areas, according to the presence in the household of their natural parents.*

Parental status	United Kingdom		Four poor areas	
	No.	%	No.	%
Mother only present	92	5·5	91	9·9
Father only present	23	1·4	5	0·5
Natural mother, legal stepfather	15	0·9		
Natural mother, accepted stepfather	7	0·4		
Natural father, legal stepmother	6	0·4		
Neither parent present, but both alive	8	0·5	824	89·6
Neither parent present, father alive	4	0·2		
Neither parent present, mother alive	3	0·2		
Both parents present, not married	5	0·3		
Both parents present, married	1,509	90·3		
	1,672	100·0	920	100·0

Table A.89. *Percentages of individuals in one-parent families in the United Kingdom and in four special areas, according to income in relation to the poverty standard.*

Net disposable household income last year as % of supplementary benefit rates plus housing cost	United Kingdom	Four poor areas
Under 100	23	29
100–39	22	21
140–99	32	34
200+	22	17
Total	100	100
Number	154	192

Table A.90. *Percentages and estimated number of elderly persons (of pensionable age) in income units with incomes above and below the deprivation standard.*

Gross disposable income as percentage of the deprivation standard	Elderly	Non-elderly	Estimated number in population (000,000s)	
			Elderly	Non-elderly
Under 100	54	21	4·4	9·7
100–99	37	55	3·0	25·4
200+	9	24	0·7	11·0
Total	100	100	8·2	46·2
Number	828	4,437	–	–

Table A.91. *Percentages of employed and non-employed elderly[a] according to percentage of incomes from retirement pensions and supplementary benefits.*

Percentage of income derived from retirement pensions and/or supplementary benefits	Percentage of elderly[a] in single-person and two-person income units	
	Not employed	Employed[b]
100	24	1
90–99	20	1
70–89	12	12
50–69	12	27
20–49	16	21
10–19	2	5
Under 10	14	33
Total	100	100
Number	689	172

NOTES: [a]Women 60 and over; men 65 and over.
[b]In paid employment, even for a few hours a week, during the previous twelve months.

Table A.92. Percentages of people of pensionable age and different marital status in income units with incomes above and below the state's standard of poverty.

Net disposable income of income units as % of supplementary benefit standard plus housing costs	Single men	Single women		Married men and women
		Unmarried	Widowed, divorced and separated	
Under 100	19	25	23	16
100–39	46	44	54	37
140–99	17	19	14	20
200+	19	12	9	27
Total	100	100	100	100
Number	59	68	266	437

Table A.93. Percentages of people of pensionable age and different marital status in income units, according to value of net assets.

Value of assets (£)	Single men	Single women		Married men and women	Single and married men and women
		Unmarried	Widowed, divorced and separated		
Under 25	38	12	39	17	25
25–49	2	4	3	3	3
50–99	4	11	7	4	5
100–99	12	7	6	6	7
200–499	10	9	9	7	8
500–999	2	10	5	7	6
1,000–4,999	19	33	20	33	28
5,000–9,999	10	11	8	14	12
10,000+	4	4	2	9	6
Total	100	100	100	100	100
Number	52	57	236	388	733

Table A.94. Percentages of elderly people of different age who received, or were eligible to receive, supplementary benefits.

Age	Received	Eligible to receive	Total number in age group
60–64	19·1	11·5	157
65–9	27·2	18·7	235
70–74	18·4	26·6	158
75–9	32·9	15·7	140
80+	34·6	18·7	107
All ages	25·8	18·3	797

Table A.95. Percentages of elderly in different social classes and types of household who had resources below or on the margins of the state's standard of poverty.

Household membership	Net disposable household income last year below 140% of supplementary benefit rates plus housing cost		
	Non-manual	Skilled manual	Partly skilled and unskilled manual
Living alone	59	85	85
Married couples	35	55	61
Living with others	(28)	(29)	41
	Net income worth last year of household below 140% of supplementary benefit rates plus housing cost		
Living alone	24	62	65
Married couples	4	26	38
Living with others	(3)	(9)	(28)

Table A.96. *Percentages of men and women of different age in income units receiving an employer's pension.*

Receiving employer's pension	Age							
	Under 70		70–79		80+		All ages	
	Men	Women	Men	Women	Men	Women	Men	Women
No	62	77	62	82	(62)	90	62	80
Yes	38	23	38	18	(38)	10	38	20
Total	100	100	100	100	100	100	100	100
Number	147	341	117	216	34	77	298	634

Table A.97. *Percentages of men and women of pensionable age, according to the annual value of employer's pension received by the income unit.*

Amount of employer's pension per annum (£)	Men		Women	
	Under 70	70 and over	Under 70	70 and over
Nil	63	64	79	85
Under 50	5	5	3	2
50–99	6	8	4	3
100–99	6	7	4	4
200–99	8	3	4	1
300+	12	13	7	5
Total	100	100	100	100
Number	147	151	341	293

Table A.98. Percentages of heads of income units not in paid employment in the previous week according to eligibility to supplementary benefits.

Eligibility of income unit for supplementary benefits	Unemployed	Sick	Disabled	Housewives	Retired
Unclassifiable	1·9	3·2	(3·1)	3·0	5·3
Could not claim	0·0	10·6	(6·2)	16·9	2·6
Currently receiving benefit	24·5	21·3	(50·0)	41·0	25·2
Ineligible for supplementary benefit (income too high)	35·8	50·0	(28·1)	24·7	47·0
Eligible but not receiving	37·7	14·9	(12·5)	14·5	19·9
Total	100	100	100	100	100
Number	53	94	32	166	508

Table A.99. Percentages of income units receiving and eligible for, but not receiving supplementary benefits, according to type of household.

Type of household	Receiving		Eligible but not receiving	
	%	No.	%	No.
Man aged 60+	5·5	14	4·2	7
Man under 60	0·4	1	0·6	1
Woman aged 60+	40·6	104	23·5	39
Woman under 60	1·6	4	1·2	2
Man and woman, head under pensionable age	3·9	10	2·4	4
Man and woman, head of pensionable age or over	14·5	37	25·3	46
Man and woman, 1 child	0·8	2	1·2	2
2 children	1·6	4	1·8	3
3 children	0·0	0	0·0	0
4 or more children	1·2	3	2·4	4
3 adults	9·4	24	12·7	21
3 adults plus children	3·5	9	5·4	9
4 adults	3·9	10	4·8	8
Others without children	6·6	17	5·4	9
Others with children	6·6	17	9·0	15
All types	100	256	100	166

Table A.100. *Percentages of people in income units with incomes for previous week expressed as a percentage of the supplementary benefit standard.*

Type of social security received by unit	Incomes last week				
	Under 100	100–39	140 or more	Total	Number
Retirement pension	21·0	46·7	33·3	100	713
Widows' benefit (under 60)	(14·6)	(25·0)	(60·4)	100	48
Unemployment insurance benefit	(28·2)	(20·5)	(51·3)	100	39
Sickness benefit	9·1	39·8	51·1	100	88
War and industrial injury disablement pension	(0·0)	(25·8)	(74·2)	100	31
Supplementary benefit	16·5	72·7	10·8	100	249

Table A.101. *Percentages of men and of women receiving supplementary benefit who were of different age.*

Age	Britain: DHSS estimates[a]		Survey estimates	
	Males	Females	Males	Females
Under 29	8·6	6·4	11·7	5·4
30–39	6·2	4·2	5·2	5·4
40–49	7·9	4·5	5·2	2·7
50–59	9·8	6·9	16·9	5·4
60–64	9·2	10·2	3·9	15·6
65–69	21·5	15·5	36·4	13·4
70–79	27·2	34·3	14·3	34·9
80+	9·5	17·8	6·5	17·2
Total	100	100	100	100
Number	966,000	1,671,000	77	186

NOTE: [a]Sample of 1 in 80 cases.

SOURCE: DHSS, *Social Security Statistics, 1972*, HMSO, London, 1973, pp. 154–5.

Table A.102. *Percentages of households receiving rate and rent rebates in different regions.*

Region	Percentage of owner-occupiers getting rate rebates	Percentage of rent payers getting rate rebates	Percentage of council households getting rent rebates	Total households		
				Owner-occupiers	Private tenants	Council tenants[a]
Northern Ireland	(6·3)	1·9	(0·0)	32	53	–
North-West	8·6	0·8	13·5	128	109	52
South-West and Wales	8·4	3·6	(20·0)	107	111	45
Scotland	(2·3)	8·0	9·5	43	125	63
Northern, Yorks and Humberside	10·2	1·8	(4·8)	118	112	42
West Midlands	5·1	0·0	6·5	118	135	92
Anglia and East Midlands	2·9	1·3	(0·0)	104	78	29
South-East	6·9	2·6	14·9	175	116	74
Greater London	8·1	1·5	8·0	136	136	50
All regions	7·0	2·5	9·9	961	975	456

NOTE: [a]Excluding households who answered 'no scheme'.

Table A.103. *Percentages of secondary school children of different occupational class not requiring uniforms, and percentages of parents knowing about educational maintenance allowances.*

Occupational class	Percentage of children at secondary schools not requiring uniform[a]	Percentage of 15- to 18-year-olds whose parents had heard of educational maintenance allowances	Total numbers Children at secondary school[a] (excl. Northern Ireland)	All children 15–18
Professional	31	} 47	75	21
Managerial	(33)		48	19
Higher inspectorate	28	} 35	72	26
Lower inspectorate	49		126	41
Routine non-manual	(37)		49	40
Skilled manual	44 *1·4*	} 21	250 *139*	77
Partly skilled manual	53 *2·9*		148 *67*	40
Unskilled manual	52 *3·1*		67 *32*	31
All classes	44 *1·1*	33	835 *471*	295

NOTE: [a] Percentages and totals in italics are those at schools with uniforms receiving grants and number at schools with uniform.

Table A.104. Percentages of households in different occupational classes receiving rate and rent rebates.

Occupational class	Percentage of owner-occupiers getting rate rebates	Percentage of rent payers getting rate rebates	Percentage of council households getting rent rebates	Owner-occupiers	Total households Private tenants	Council tenants[a]
Professional	1·1	} 7·2	} 6·2	89	14	–
Managerial	3·3			61	24	3
Higher inspectorate	5·8			138	45	13
Lower inspectorate	1·7	3·3		179	91	34
Routine non-manual	12·9	1·6		62	61	31
Skilled manual	8·4	2·4	7·8	239	372	179
Partly skilled manual	13·7	2·8	10·9	102	212	110
Unskilled manual	(18·6)	4·9	18·5	43	143	65
All classes	7·0	3·3	9·9	913	962	435

NOTE: [a]Excluding households who answered 'no scheme'.

Table A.105. *Pupils taking midday meals and having free meals (local education authorities, Britain, May 1971).*

	Day pupils taking midday meals	Percentage of pupils present	Free meals as % of total meals served
England			
Bedfordshire	25,845	5·2	9·0
Berkshire	45,667	4·4	7·8
Buckinghamshire	55,608	4·0	6·8
Cambridgeshire and Isle of Ely	22,301	6·7	11·9
Cheshire	87,417	7·7	13·6
Cornwall	24,965	14·5	24·0
Cumberland	24,701	13·0	16·8
Derbyshire	50,995	7·6	13·7
Devon	28,990	16·2	24·8
Dorset	22,483	10·1	19·1
Durham	53,347	13·9	26·7
Essex	81,206	5·6	11·9
Gloucestershire	47,391	7·4	12·7
Hampshire	79,900	6·6	12·3
Herefordshire	14,395	11·9	15·7
Hertfordshire	92,045	5·6	8·8
Huntingdon and Peterborough	18,326	7·5	13·0
Isle of Wight	5,979	10·6	21·1
Kent	109,169	8·2	13·7
Lancashire	189,535	9·7	17·2
Leicestershire	40,086	4·5	7·5
Lincolnshire –			
Holland	6,665	8·9	18·1
Kesteven	12,774	7·0	12·4
Lindsey	35,644	10·1	16·0
Norfolk	33,878	9·5	15·5
Northamptonshire	22,229	6·2	13·3
Northumberland	39,306	13·8	22·2
Nottinghamshire	54,938	6·8	11·7
Oxfordshire	21,623	5·5	10·2
Rutland	2,198	2·0	3·9
Shropshire (Salop)	30,092	9·5	14·5
Somerset	45,891	8·8	14·4
Staffordshire	54,053	7·2	13·8
Suffolk, East	17,246	7·7	13·7
Suffolk, West	10,934	7·5	14·7
Surrey	81,278	4·4	7·1
Sussex, East	27,672	8·6	14·6

Table A.105. – contd

	Day pupils taking midday meals	Percentage of pupils present	Free meals as % of total meals served
England – contd			
Sussex, West	34,592	8·4	14·5
Warwickshire	55,442	6·9	11·7
Westmorland	8,023	6·6	8·1
Wiltshire	34,529	6·8	14·0
Worcestershire	38,800	5·4	8·8
Yorkshire –			
East Riding	18,676	7·4	13·9
North Riding	28,254	11·2	16·2
West Riding	139,388	10·5	18·3
County boroughs			
Barnsley	4,531	13·5	28·4
Barrow-in-Furness	2,839	9·4	26·7
Bath	5,437	9·9	17·8
Birkenhead	8,224	15·2	29·0
Birmingham	62,264	11·4	24·3
Blackburn	6,365	13·2	24·0
Blackpool	9,744	14·5	22·7
Bolton	12,150	13·3	21·8
Bootle	3,176	12·6	36·9
Bournemouth	7,817	12·3	21·6
Bradford	15,272	15·9	34·9
Brighton	9,802	15·1	24·6
Bristol	24,980	10·4	21·2
Burnley	5,226	12·6	25·2
Burton-upon-Trent	2,616	7·3	22·3
Bury	4,068	11·0	21·9
Canterbury	3,882	11·3	16·3
Carlisle	4,643	12·1	24·5
Chester	4,543	9·3	18·9
Coventry	27,402	8·1	14·8
Darlington	6,275	12·7	23·5
Derby	14,064	8·8	18·3
Dewsbury	3,187	15·9	31·8
Doncaster	6,721	9·8	18·1
Dudley	8,562	4·6	13·3
Eastbourne	3,680	9·9	17·8
Exeter	4,938	15·3	28·7
Gateshead	3,873	20·5	44·2

Table A.105. – contd

	Day pupils taking midday meals	Percentage of pupils present	Free meals as % of total meals served
County boroughs – contd			
Gloucester	7,367	9·9	18·7
Great Yarmouth	2,627	11·2	27·9
Grimsby	7,450	10·8	19·5
Halifax	8,060	16·4	23·7
Hartlepool	5,314	12·6	31·4
Hastings	3,997	15·2	25·8
Huddersfield	12,107	10·8	16·6
Ipswich	5,692	7·7	21·2
Kingston-upon-Hull	9,675	13·3	40·9
Leeds	37,580	13·7	22·5
Leicester	18,469	7·1	15·8
Lincoln	5,543	12·4	22·2
Liverpool	28,922	12·9	32·3
Luton	13,520	7·5	14·3
Manchester	35,870	22·2	37·0
Newcastle-upon-Tyne	10,361	27·1	47·1
Northampton	7,026	5·6	14·4
Norwich	5,819	13·3	29·0
Nottingham	12,921	14·4	36·4
Oldham	5,866	18·9	36·4
Oxford	7,707	9·5	16·9
Plymouth	13,840	11·1	24·5
Portsmouth	7,532	12·5	33·3
Preston	6,789	18·4	31·7
Reading	10,113	11·0	19·0
Rochdale	6,751	14·0	24·8
Rotherham	6,150	10·4	20·2
St Helens	6,244	11·6	24·6
Salford	7,073	19·0	37·8
Sheffield	7,555	9·5	22·0
Solihull	10,640	3·0	5·0
Southampton	13,024	9·5	20·7
Southend-on-sea	9,420	8·8	18·1
Southport	4,768	11·1	21·9
South Shields	2,355	13·2	49·5
Stockport	9,026	11·8	22·7
Stoke-on-Trent	18,602	11·3	21·1
Sunderland	7,765	15·0	43·8
Teesside	35,138	14·5	25·1

Table A.105. – contd

	Day pupils taking midday meals	Percentage of pupils present	Free meals as % of total meals served
County boroughs – contd			
Torbay	6,103	17·4	27·1
Tynemouth	3,403	14·7	35·4
Wakefield	3,717	12·8	23·8
Wallasey	4,330	11·6	30·7
Walsall	10,676	8·8	21·1
Warley	7,869	9·1	22·6
Warrington	4,060	10·9	24·3
West Bromwich	8,092	8·7	23·4
Wigan	5,024	12·7	24·8
Wolverhampton	18,942	8·6	17·6
Worcester	6,136	7·1	12·8
York	4,723	10·4	28·2
London boroughs			
Barking	6,777	8·7	23·9
Barnet	23,031	5·8	9·5
Bexley	17,686	4·0	6·9
Brent	19,328	8·3	14·4
Bromley	25,795	5·1	8·1
Croydon	20,354	7·3	15·4
Ealing	21,474	9·3	15·1
Enfield	18,717	5·1	9·4
Haringey	15,949	9·4	16·8
Harrow	14,482	4·0	7·5
Havering	17,697	4·0	8·4
Hillingdon	19,915	4·2	7·2
Hounslow	14,244	5·9	11·1
Kingston-upon-Thames	10,109	5·0	8·5
Merton	10,919	6·2	11·7
Newham	11,159	6·5	17·6
Redbridge	14,459	4·4	8·9
Richmond-upon-Thames	11,090	5·3	8·9
Sutton	11,567	5·0	8·7
Waltham Forest	11,916	6·6	15·2
London	140,648	16·5	30·4
Wales			
Anglesey	4,993	17·5	26·4
Breconshire	4,121	15·4	24·9
Caernarvonshire	8,160	25·2	36·0

Table A.105. – contd

	Day pupils taking midday meals	Percentage of pupils present	Free meals as % of total meals served
Wales – contd			
Cardiganshire	5,088	14·5	20·7
Carmarthenshire	12,291	11·4	19·0
Denbighshire	11,670	14·1	26·3
Flintshire	8,548	8·1	22·0
Glamorgan	40,114	11·0	25·3
Merioneth	3,054	16·7	24·0
Monmouthshire	16,795	9·1	24·7
Montgomeryshire	4,897	8·6	11·4
Pembrokeshire	6,503	16·9	31·0
Radnorshire	1,771	12·3	17·4
Cardiff	10,682	14·5	39·3
Merthyr Tydfil	2,047	14·3	39·4
Newport (Mon.)	4,652	10·4	31·0
Swansea	6,673	15·6	39·0
Scotland			
Burghs			
Aberdeen	5,498	8·2	41·6
Dundee	10,169	13·6	44·2
Edinburgh	22,797	15·7	45·2
Glasgow	45,578	19·0	64·1
Counties			
Aberdeen	10,028	8·3	19·5
Angus	4,643	9·2	30·1
Argyll	4,146	8·2	17·2
Ayr	23,243	12·2	33·4
Banff	3,319	14·7	35·6
Berwick	1,465	12·4	28·8
Bute	742	11·3	28·8
Caithness	1,795	13·2	42·7
Clackmannan	2,438	12·7	42·2
Dumfries	6,327	16·8	38·5
Dunbarton	14,777	11·3	33·2
East Lothian	3,222	9·8	29·1
Fife	20,596	12·6	35·6
Inverness	6,450	15·1	36·3
Kincardine	2,267	11·9	22·7
Kirkcudbright	2,638	10·1	18·2
Lanark	36,718	13·4	42·8

Table A.105 – contd

	Day pupils taking midday meals	Percentage of pupils present	Free meals as % of total meals served
Counties – contd			
Midlothian	7,461	8·0	27·3
Moray and Nairn	3,874	9·6	25·8
Orkney	1,484	16·9	32·7
Peebles	714	8·4	23·5
Perth and Kinross	8,143	8·0	19·6
Renfrew	23,588	12·6	34·9
Ross and Cromarty	5,861	24·5	43·4
Roxburgh	2,428	9·1	24·3
Selkirk	949	7·7	27·9
Stirling	9,105	9·1	37·3
Sutherland	1,566	17·7	25·5
West Lothian	5,131	8·6	34·0
Wigtown	3,054	23·2	39·7
Zetland	1,839	14·1	21·3

Appendix Nine
Commentary on the Survey and the
Questionnaire

(This was prepared before the start of fieldwork as a guide to interviewers and others)

Beginning with the notable work of Charles Booth, Seebohm Rowntree and A. L. Bowley at the turn of the century, the investigation of living standards and of poverty has always had an important place in the social sciences in Britain. But a comprehensive national survey has never been carried out. Such a survey is now to be carried out by a team of research workers based on the Department of Sociology at the University of Essex and the Department of Social Administration at the London School of Economics. The work is financed by the Joseph Rowntree Memorial Trust and is guided by an advisory committee consisting of representatives of the trust, senior personnel of government departments and academic experts in nutrition, statistics and social science, under the chairmanship of Professor Richard M. Titmuss. Professor A. Stuart and Professor J. Durbin have given considerable help with the special problems of sampling.

The first object of the survey is to estimate the numbers in the population living at different levels of living, particularly the numbers living in or on the margins of poverty. The second object is to find what are the characteristics and problems of families and persons with low levels of living and thus begin to explain why they are poor.

Method of Approach

Our own pilot work and other research studies have shown that families living on low incomes are far less homogeneous than has been supposed hitherto. Fatherless families, families dependent on low earnings, families with a chronically sick or disabled adult and families with an unemployed head have problems which are very different from each other as well as those which are common. Even within these groups there are big differences, as between widows and separated wives within the category of fatherless families, for example. We have come to the conclusion that, in defining people's needs in modern society and finding how low standards of living might begin to be measured and explained, five steps are necessary.

1. *Living standards among families of each type need to be compared.* We want to be able to distinguish problems which are attributable to poverty rather than family circumstances or social status. In judging at what point families have resources which are

adequate for the activities and purchases of food which are customary in society, we must have good information for families of the same type with relatively high incomes.

2. *Living standards of families with relatively low incomes of each type need to be compared with the living standards of families of average composition and income.*

3. *Variations in living standards over time have to be assessed.* A distinction must be drawn between short-term or occasional and chronic poverty, whether due to some combination of family size, rent and low earnings or to absence of earnings (fatherlessness, unemployment, sickness or disability) or to irregular employment.

4. *Variations in people's access to the social services and in their environmental facilities and facilities at work also have to be assessed as aspects of living standards.* A distinction has to be drawn between partial and total poverty. A family with a very low income may be found living in a modern council house, the father working in good factory conditions and the children of the family attending a newly built school. Paradoxes in living conditions of this kind are increasingly characteristic of societies in which the big corporation and a highly developed 'Welfare State' are found.

5. *The effectiveness of the social services which aim at helping the poor has to be established.* We have to check on the extent to which some families apply for certain benefits – for example, free school meals and welfare milk.

In addition to trying to measure and explain low levels of living as found at present, we will study the use of those services which might help to prevent certain types of poverty, now and in the future, particularly longer-term poverty. Thus we are interested in those occupations which are low paid; the effectiveness of education, apprenticeship, job placement, training, retraining and rehabilitation services; savings, fringe benefits and private insurance; housing and rent policies; and health, welfare and family planning services.

Survey design and procedure

A random sample of about 2,500 dwellings from fifty-one sample constituencies throughout the United Kingdom will be drawn and the households living in those dwellings will be approached for an interview. In many instances a subsequent call may have to be made to interview a husband or another earner so that full information for the household may be collected. Since information is required not only about the household but also about each individual member of the household, the length of the interview will tend to vary even more widely than is usual in surveys. Many of the interviewers will assist in drawing addresses from rating and other lists for inclusion in the sample, following a procedure which has been carefully laid down. The interviews will be spread over twelve months in four stages.

The Questionnaire: General

The importance of minorities

The purpose of many surveys is to obtain information about 'ordinary' families. If the questions are found not to fit unusual or uncommon households, or if there are difficulties in undertaking an interview, no special measures are taken by those in charge of the work and by the interviewers. In this survey, however, we are particularly concerned to obtain information from representatives of every minority in the country. People who are poor have very assorted circumstances: some are disabled and others are old, have large numbers of children, have been unable to learn to read and write, are immigrants and so on. The more unusual a person, the harder the interviewer should endeavour to obtain reliable information. We have tried to allow therefore in the design of the questionnaire for diverse circumstances, and we have adopted a form of layout which records answers which apply to each individual living in the household as well as to the household as a whole. But the interviewer should use discretion in making notes to elucidate certain answers and also to collect any information not covered by the questionnaire which seems to be important in arriving at a reliable picture of the individual's or the household's resources.

Information about non-respondents is also more important to collect than in many other surveys. Relatively more of the sick, the aged and those with large numbers of children are likely to have difficulty in granting an interview. Yet relatively more of them are likely to be poor. We must ensure that our estimates of the incidence of poverty are not weakened by lack of information about non-respondents in the sample. We are, therefore, instructing interviewers to do all that is humanly possible to record vital information about the composition of the household, housing amenities and other matters.

The importance of the distinction between total and partial poverty

For reasons given earlier, we must find to what extent families with low monetary incomes *also* have poor resources in other respects – housing and living facilities, capital assets, fringe benefits and occupational facilities and access to the social services. Groups of questions have to be asked about each of these aspects of living standards, and some attempts made to estimate their total value to the individual and to the household.

The importance of the distinction between short-term and long-term poverty

At the time of interview, some families may have very low incomes through recent adversity such as sickness or bereavement. They will not have been 'poor' for very long, and some of them will not be 'poor' for much longer. In giving estimates of the incidence of poverty, we must be able to specify how many people have been poor for long and short periods. It is, of course, difficult to collect information about income at any date in the past, so we confine ourselves to groups of questions designed to establish the current income (i.e. last week), the average income (i.e. during the last year), together with information about certain abrupt changes in recent years in employment status.

Three measures of poverty

In the survey we envisage applying three measures of poverty:

1. Comparisons with supplementary benefit levels as used by the government in its own survey.

2. Comparisons with average levels of living (median, for example, and mean income of different types of household and mean disposable personal income).
3. An attempt to identify deprivation on the basis of inability to participate in even a substantial number of the activities and customs followed by the majority of the population of the United Kingdom (see Section IX below).

The Questionnaire: Sections 1—9

Section I: Housing and living facilities

The first aim in this section is to establish more carefully than is usual the exact composition of the household, taking particular account of visitors and members of the household who may be temporarily or indefinitely away, such as men working at sea or in the transport services.

The second aim is to obtain various measures of poor housing:

1. Adequacy of basic facilities of dwelling.
2. Degree of overcrowding.
3. Deficiency of bedrooms.
4. Overall facilities of household.
5. Degree of satisfaction with living facilities and environment.

Overcrowding will be measured first by applying the census definition. The total number of rooms is divided by the total number of persons in the household and the resulting ratio will be worked out. We will also use a slight modification of the bedroom deficiency index devised by P. G. Gray of the Government Social Survey and used in a survey for the Plowden Committee. This index is calculated by comparing the number of bedrooms in the household with the following standard:

1. Each married couple must have one bedroom.
2. Any other person over 21 must have a bedroom.
3. Any two persons of the same sex aged 10–20 must have a bedroom. If any remaining person aged 10–20 cannot be paired with a child of under 10 of the same sex, then he or she must have a bedroom.
4. Any two remaining children under 10 must have a bedroom. Any child remaining must be given an additional room.

We have introduced the following small modifications: (a) if an infant of under one year is left after the standard is applied he or she is not assumed to require an additional room; (b) households comprising more than four persons and any other households with three or more children are assumed to require a minimum of two living rooms, including the kitchen only if it is big enough for the household to eat in, before calculating how many rooms are left for sleeping in.

In developing a 'household amenities index' we have simply listed ten items which are now widely available in British homes. Ideally we would have wished to have taken more account of furnishings, wall coverings and curtaining, but these vary so widely in substance and quality that it is difficult to be both objective and meaningful.

Section II: Employment

This section has two special aims. One is to build up a picture of each individual's 'work-record' over the previous twelve months. Low standards of living are often caused by intermittent sickness or unemployment or by spells of casual employment, for example. The situation at the time of the interview may not be representative of the pattern of work during the year, and that is primarily why we are seeking information about the latter.

The second is to find what educational experience people have had, so that we may analyse better the relation between education and standards of living.

Section III: Occupational facilities and fringe benefits

This is an experimental section designed to indicate the nature and adequacy of people's working environment and whether the individual benefits provided by the employer are a substantial supplement to earnings. Since a large part of adult life is passed at places of employment, we are concerned to explore whether there are people who experience squalor at work as well as at home. And poverty at work can be real even when poverty is unknown at home.

We aim, first, to find what facilities are provided for indoor and outdoor employment, beyond those which are necessary for the particular type of employment (e.g. machines, vehicles, blackboards). We appreciate that some of the questions may be inappropriate for people working in certain types of employment, and our attention should be called to this if necessary.

We aim, secondly, to provide statistical information about the number and character-istics of people who are eligible and ineligible for different fringe benefits. Some people may not have had any sick pay in the past year and yet they are entitled to it. Again, many people are expecting eventually to receive an occupational pension. Such matters as these can make a big difference to the 'security' of people's living standards, particularly in middle age. The problem is that individuals, particularly when they are young, are often hazy about the exact benefits they expect to receive. The questions are designed to elicit minimum information.

The third aim is to give exact information about the value of fringe benefits in kind which have actually been received during the year. This will allow us to calculate how important these benefits are to certain kinds of people, including the poor. (It should be noted that questions about fringe benefits in the form of income in kind are included in this section, but that questions about fringe benefits in the form of cash income are in-cluded, for convenience, in the subsequent Section V.)

Section IV: Current monetary income

This series of questions forms a centrepiece to the questionnaire and aims to establish what was the total cash income in (a) the previous week and (b) the previous twelve months from any source of each income unit in the household. There are four groups of questions – on earnings, income of self-employed, government social security benefits, and miscellaneous sources of income. For convenience, certain questions on 'windfall' income, from sales, capital gains or loans which has been used for ordinary living expenses, and income from interest and dividends has been included in Section V as 'Savings and Assets'. More than in any other section of the questionnaire, the questions are derived from previous surveys – particularly the income schedule of the Ministry of Labour's Family Expenditure Survey, but also the cross-national survey on old people and the Ministry of Social Security's survey of families. The questions break new ground in the sense of (a) making searching inquiries of each income recipient in the household and not only the head of household or those in full-time employment; (b) widening the definition of cash income to include capital gains and receipts which have been used for ordinary living expenses during the year; (c) paying particular attention to earnings from occasional spare-time and second jobs; and (d) establishing forms of income for any part of the previous twelve months so that we can give figures for income 'last year' as well as 'last week'. Income in kind is left to Section VIII of the questionnaire. Broadly, the definition of income elaborated by Simons, Kaldor and the Minority of the Royal Commission on Taxation (Kaldor, Woodcock and Bullock) is favoured.[1]

Income of a household does not include payments received by one member of a household from another, e.g. housekeeping, wages of domestic servant. Some of these exchanges are explored in Section IX. Amounts of income should not be entered more than once in different places or in different columns. Providing income is listed under the individual income recipient, it will then be possible both to add up a total income for the household as a whole and a total income for each income unit (i.e. a married couple or an adult over the age of 15 who is an independent income 'recipient'). It will sometimes be necessary to extract the personal income of an income unit (e.g. retirement pensioners, young persons at work) from the information about the household as a whole in order to analyse the adequacy, say, of social security benefits or compare information from the sample with data collected by the Board of Inland Revenue.

We have also incorporated in this section, for convenience of the interviewer, certain questions aiming to obtain an accurate figure of housing costs (and house value), so that household income, less rents and other costs of housing, can be compared with supplementary benefit levels.

Section V: Savings and assets

This section aims to establish estimates of the total value of savings and assets owned by the household (the value of an owner-occupied house has already been estimated in Section IV where, for convenience, a question was added to other questions about rent, rates and amenities). This will allow us to calculate how many poor families have 'reserves' of any kind. It will also allow us to 'correct' information about income levels, so that we get closer to a true picture of levels of living.

The questions are directed first at savings and second at property – both housing and household or personal possessions. We do not attempt to estimate the value of goods in everyday household use, but only articles worth £25 or more which could be sold if necessary to raise money.

1. Simons, H., *Personal Income Taxation*, Chicago, 1938, pp. 49–50; Kaldor, N., *An Expenditure Tax*, Allen & Unwin, London, 1955; Final Report of the Royal Commission on Taxation, Cmnd 9474, HMSO, London, 1955, pp. 355–6.

Section VI: Health and disability

Our object here is to discover and measure the numbers of persons who are lightly or severely disabled so that we can assess their living standards. We employ two methods which are based on extensive pilot work. One is to ask whether anyone in the household is suffering from anything affecting limbs, chest or lungs, nerves, etc. The other is to ask whether the individuals in the household (aged 10 and over) can undertake certain specific activities without difficulty, including washing down, tying a knot in string, negotiating stairs and going shopping. The coding is arranged so that a 'score' (of 0–18) can be given for each individual which will crudely reflect his capacity to undertake ordinary personal and household activities.

The two methods used in combination will allow us to make estimates of the numbers and kinds of person in the population who are disabled and, in conjunction with income, will make it possible to generalize about the standards of living of households in which one or more of the members are disabled.

Section VII: Social services

Here there are two objects: to find which social services are utilized by different kinds of family, including the poor, and to make approximate estimates of the total 'subsidy' (i.e. money value) received by families from the government and the local authorities via the social services.

The answers will allow generalizations to be made about the numbers and kinds of eligible families not taking up certain kinds of welfare benefits, e.g. free school meals, welfare milk and educational maintenance allowances. In a minority of cases, it may be very difficult to build up a reliable estimate, e.g. the number of consultations with a doctor in the previous twelve months, but such questions have been found in other research to produce fairly reliable results in general. Again, we are not attempting to get comprehensive data, but only to get such data as we can about the costlier services.

Section VIII: Private income in kind

The aim of this section is, first, to obtain an estimate of the value of goods and services received in the previous twelve months from persons other than an employer, i.e. relatives and friends, as a contribution to the level of living. The second aim is to be able to describe the characteristics of individuals and of households receiving considerable income in kind. The third aim is to discover to what extent households are self-sufficient in the sense of depending upon their own resources, i.e. income and services, and not upon goods and services supplied from outside the household. (Note that, for convenience, a question about the value of the produce of garden, smallholding, allotment or farm was included in Section IV.)

All previous experience of asking questions about the receipt of income in kind shows that *general* questions produce gross underestimates of such income. If you try to ask about relationships and exchanges with specific persons or organizations, fuller information is likely to be supplied. Because of the wide variation in age, the *kind* of persons likely to be providing gifts and help will also vary widely. All this explains the approach adopted at the start. We recognize that the method might be more detailed than it is.

Questions are asked about services performed for others and by others for the household. This is unusual. Yet it is likely that some poor families with a good network of support from friends and relatives are able to maintain a comfortable standard of living. By contrast, there are likely to be middle-income families who are rather isolated and therefore stretched to the limit in, say, rearing young children, either because there is little unpaid help available, or because they have to pay to get the help they need. The value of unpaid services may be greater than of goods in kind to many families. And trying to give estimates of them will also, to some extent, reveal the 'compensations' of the poor.

Section IX: Style of living

In this final section there are two main objects. The first is to find whether members of the household participate in ordinary cultural and spare-time activities (like going away on holiday, having an evening out regularly and going to sports meetings or club meetings) and have ordinary diets, including milk and fresh meat. The second is to find what internal arrangements are made within the household for financial responsibility for the housekeeping and paying the rent and bills.

We hope the answers will allow us to justify drawing a 'poverty line' at a particular level of income or of resources and so give objective precision to the major aim of the whole survey to define and measure the extent of poverty. Although there are wide variations in cultural pursuits within any society, we suspect that participation in those which are common tends, statistically to diminish rapidly below a certain level of income, or of resources, for each type of household. It is, however, difficult in survey conditions to gain even an outline of some families' 'style of living'. Customs and activities are extraordinarily diverse. We cannot claim to be comprehensive, but only to be using some useful indicators.

We also hope that the answers will allow us to identify certain kinds of deprivation among families. Our pilot work has shown that some families and some persons, particularly housewives, go without meals or rarely or never have an evening out because of low income.

QUESTIONNAIRE ON HOUSEHOLD RESOURCES
&
STANDARDS OF LIVING IN THE UNITED KINGDOM
1968-69

I   Housing and Living Facilities

II   Employment

III   Occupational Facilities and Fringe Benefits

IV   Current Monetary Income

V   Assets and Savings

VI   Health and Disability

VII   Social Services

VIII   Private Income in Kind

IX   Style of Living

A Survey carried out from the University of Essex
and the University of London (L.S.E.)

Queries should be addressed to: Miss Sheila Benson
Skepper House
13 Endsleigh Street
London WCI

FOR OFFICE USE

INTRODUCTION

(a) IF INFORMANT WILLING TO GIVE INTERVIEW

proceed to Q. 1 at the beginning of the Housing Section and when the interview is finished complete the Summary at the beginning of the questionnaire.

(b) IF A FIRM REFUSAL

(and no other adult member of the household is likely to give an interview now or at a later date) encourage the informant at least to answer the questions on your Summary sheets. Information on these sheets giving:

(i) the reference number of the household

(ii) the date of call(s)

(iii) the reasons why no interview was obtainable (in addition to the notes on your record sheet) must be provided in all instances.

Finally, leave a copy of our introductory letter and send us the Summary sheets as soon as possible.

(c) IF PUT OFF AT FIRST CONTACT

(because of illness, domestic emergency, etc.) then having made sure that no other adult member of the household is free to give an interview (unless of course circumstances clearly dictate that this enquiry should **not** be made), leave the introductory letter and go immediately for fear of jeopardising a later interview, asking only when a second call might be convenient. Use your record sheet to note the date and result of this first contact.

IF PUT OFF AGAIN AT SECOND CONTACT

then try at least to obtain the answers to the questions in the Summary sheets, preferably taking replies from someone in the household but, failing that, from an external source.

At this point we rely on your discretion to decide whether

(a) the household's response should be regarded as a disguised refusal (in which case return Summary sheets and complete your record sheet accordingly); or

(b) an interview is probably obtainable at a third call, in which case retain the Summary sheets for the time being (they can be destroyed if you obtain an interview at the third visit or returned to us if you are put off a third time).

If you are in any doubt then consult the London Office or Regional Supervisor about the advisability of a third call.

C.I.C.

	1	2	3	4	5	6	7	8	9
SERIAL NUMBER								0	1

Name of Interviewer...

Date(s) of interview(s)..   Length of interview(s) ....

or contacts ....

....

....

Total actual interviewing time...............................

Form of introduction

" My name is X. I'm from Essex/London University. We're preparing a report (writing a book) about standards of living in Britain today and how families manage. We think it's important for the Government and everyone else to know what the facts really are. We're hoping to talk to about 3,000 families throughout the country and I'd be very grateful if you could help us by answering some questions. All our information is, of course, strictly confidential."

SUMMARY : COMPLETE AFTER INTERVIEW

1. Interview carried out — 10
- at first call — X
- at second call — Y
- at third or later call — 0

2. Information for household — 11
- complete — skip to Q. 3 — X
- incomplete — answer 2a — Y

(a) Sections incomplete (CODE ALL THAT APPLY)
- Housing — 1
- Employment — 2
- Occupational — 3
- Income — 4
- Assets — 5
- Health — 6
- Soc. Services — 7
- Inc. in kind — 8
- Style of living — 9

(b) Reasons if incomplete — 12
- ill/disabled — X
- does not know information — Y
- unwilling to give information — 0
- other (specify) — 1
  ....
  ....

3. Which sections were answered in whole or in part by which persons on the household? (CODE ALL THAT APPLY AS LISTED IN Q'AIRE (Some Sections may be listed twice))

Write Section 1, 2, 3, etc.

Informant	13
2nd member	14
3rd	15
4th	16
5th	17
6th	18
Other (specify)	19

4. Type of Accomm.
- Semi or detached house or bungalow — 20
- Ter. h'se or bungalow — X
- Self-con. flat in block — Y
- Self-con. flat in house — 0
- Self-con. flat attached to shop/business — 1
- Room(s): furnished — 2
- Other (specify) — 3
- — 4
  ....
  ....

5. Number of other households at address — 21
- None — 0

6. Household living on — 22
- ground — X
- basement floor — Y
- 1st floor — 1
- 2nd floor — 2
- 3rd floor — 3
- 4th floor — 4
- 5th or above — 5
- Specify

  (Answer 6a)

(a) Is there a lift in the building?
- Yes — 6
- No — 7

7. Is there an internal or external flight of at least 4 steps or stairs to the dwelling entrance? — 23
- Yes — 8
- No — 9

(i)

HOUSING AND LIVING FACILITIES

General

Information recorded by the interviewer on the left of the main column is needed so that the circumstances of the household may be fully understood by those in the office but it may not be required for computer-analysis.

QUESTION 1 — Rooms

No room should be listed twice. Bedsitters should be listed as bedrooms and not also as living-rooms. Do not count a scullery or a hall or a bathroom as a room. The total number of living and dining and bedrooms should not include a kitchen if it is not large enough for a family to eat in. You will see that there are two numbered boxes in the column in which to write the numbers of bedrooms and total numbers of rooms. Each is for each digit in the total: Thus, if there are 9 or fewer rooms the number should be written in the right-hand box and " O " should be written in the left-hand box. If there are, say, 13 rooms, then " 1 " should be written in the left-hand and " 3 " in the right hand box. This will help us to avoid mistakes in transfering information to the computer.

QUESTION 2 — Additional or fewer rooms

Define " room " as above.

QUESTION 4

A water closet flushed by water. Chemical or earth closets are not included, nor are flush water closets which can only be reached by going outdoors across a yard, even if under cover.

QUESTION 5

A garden is any space at the front or back of the house where it is possible to grow something. A yard is an outdoor space which is covered in concrete, asphalt, etc., where there are no plants or lawn other than in boxes or barrels (if any).

If you have already seen the garden it may be unnecessary to ask the second part of the question, for it may be possible to code 3, 4 or 5. But be sure that you are taking back as well as front garden into the reckoning. Add the two together in estimating size.

SECTION 1   HOUSING AND LIVING FACILITIES

I'd like to start by asking a few questions about your house/flat

1(a) How many rooms are there - I mean for the sole use of the household?

number of living and dining-rooms (excluding bed-sitter)

number of kitchens

Is the kitchen large enough to eat in?   Yes | 1 |
No | 2 | `24 | 25`

*number of bedrooms (including bed-sitter)   `26 | 27`

*total number of living and dining and bedrooms (including kitchen if large enough to eat in)

(b) How many of these rooms are usually heated during the evenings in winter (whether by coal, gas or electric, paraffin stove or central heating)?   `28 | 29`

DK   `X`

2. Would you and your family like to have more rooms or fewer rooms in the home?   `30`

CODE ONE ONLY

X*	more than one room extra	X
Y	an extra bedroom	Y
0	an extra living room	0
1	number of rooms about right	1
2	one room fewer	2
3	two or more rooms fewer	3
4	DK	4

3. Is electricity laid on?

yes, power points and lighting	5
yes, lighting only	6
No	7
DK	8

4. Has the household the sole or shared use of the following INDOOR facilities?   `31`

PROMPT CODE ALL THAT APPLY

(a) A flush W.C.*	X yes, sole use	X
	Y yes, shared	Y
	0 none	0
(b) A sink or washbasin and cold water tap	1 yes, sole use	1
	2 yes, shared	2
	3 none	3
(c) A fixed bath or shower	4 yes, sole use	4
	5 yes, shared	5
	6 none	6
(d) A gas or electric cooker	7 yes, sole use	7
	8 yes, shared	8
	9 none	9

5. Does the household have the sole use or shared use of a garden or yard?   `32`

CODE ONE ONLY

X	sole use garden	X
Y	sole use yard	Y
0	shared garden	0
1	shared yard	1
2	neither garden nor yard	2

ASK Q. 5(a)

SKIP TO Q.6.

(a) Is it - too small for the household to sit in the sun (e.g. smaller than 10 feet x 10 feet)   `3`

CODE ONE ONLY

- at least big enough for the household to sit in the sun, but not equal in size to a tennis court   `4`

- substantial in size (e.g. equal in size to a tennis court or bigger)   `5`

6. One or two other questions about living here. Do you find the air in this neighbourhood clean or is it dirty, smoky or foul-smelling?   `33`

always dirty, smoky, foul-smelling	X
sometimes dirty, smoky or foul-smelling	Y
not dirty, smoky or foul-smelling	0
DK	1

1

QUESTION 8(d) — Length of housing problem

Number of years should not include any period before the age of 21.

QUESTION 9 — Structural defects

Note that the need for redecoration and refurnishing is not included. Informants may vary in their interpretation of a " defect " (for example, a woman living in a modern house may complain of small damp spots on the walls) but apart from discouraging people from regarding minor blemishes as defects you should accept what informants say.

QUESTION 9

Television: combined television, radio and record-playing sets may be listed under separate headings.

Central heating: uniform heating throughout dwelling (or part of dwelling) occupied by household.

2a

7. Does the house/flat have any structural defects?   `34`

PROMPT	rising damp, damp walls or ceilings	1	Yes ASK Q.7(a)
	loose brick-work/plaster	2	no } SKIP TO
	roof which leaks in heavy rain	3	DK } Q. 8.
	badly-fitting windows or doors which do not open or close	4	
	broken floorboards, stairs	5	
	other _____	6	

`X Y 0`

(a) Do you feel any of these are a danger to your health or of anyone in the household?

Yes   `1`
No   `2`
DK   `3`

8. Would you say you (and the family) have a serious housing problem?   `35`

Yes   ASK Q.8(a)   `X`
No }   SKIP TO Q.8(b)   `Y`
DK }   `0`

(a) What sort of problem is the worst?

	1 overcrowding	`1`
	2 inadequate basic facilities	SKIP `2`
	3 damp accommodation	TO `3`
CODE ONE ONLY	4 other structural defects	Q.9 `4`
	5 need to move elsewhere	`5`
	6 other (specify)	`6`

(b) Have you ever had a serious housing problem (since you were 21)?

Yes   ASK 8(c)   `7`
No }   `8`
DK }   SKIP TO Q.9.   `9`

(c) What sort of problem was the worst?   `36`

X overcrowding   `X`
Y inadequate basic facilities   `Y`
0 damp accommodation   `0`
1 other structural defects   `1`
2 need to move elsewhere   `2`
3 other (specify)_____   `3`

(d) How long did it last?

under 2 years   `4`
2 and less than 5 years   `5`
5 and less than 9 years   `6`
10 or more   `7`

9. Which of the following items do you have in the household?   `37`

	X television	`X`
	Y record player	`Y`
	0 radio	`0`
PROMPT CODE	1 refrigerator	`1`
ALL THAT	2 washing machine	`2`
APPLY	3 vacuum cleaner	`3`
	4 telephone	`4`
	*5 central heating	`5`
	6 enough upholstered arm-chairs, easy chairs or settees for every member of family plus one visitor	`6`
	7 carpet covering all or nearly all floor in main sitting room	`7`
	8 DK one or more items (specify)	`8`
	9 None	`9`

QUESTION 10

At this point put any christian name of informant in first box on back flap, then christian names of all other adults and children in household. In complex households always list children immediately after their parent(s) or guardian(s). Otherwise, in the case, say, of a married couple and adolescent children you may find it easiest to list according to age: first the wife who is, say 54, husband 55, children 26, 24, 20, 17 and 14. When you write in information throughout the questionnaire please keep rigorously to the particular column for each named person in the household. Specifically " household " information is recorded in the first column. The informant's answers about himself should always be entered in the next column. The list of members under Q. 10 may have to be later modified according to who is temporarily residing in the household or who is temporarily away. This should be checked carefully. **Boarders** of more than four weeks residence should be recorded as members of the household; lodgers and sub-tenants will require separate questionnaires.

** HOUSEHOLD TYPE

On the back of the questionnaire you will find a code list of household compositions. When you are checking the questionnaire put the appropriate code for this household in the box allocated under the double asterisk

Definition of a Household

A private household comprises one person living alone or a group of persons living together, having some or all meals together and benefiting from a common housekeeping. Persons who have resided in the household for at least four weeks and are not expected to leave shortly, and persons who have resided in the household for less than four weeks but are not expected to leave again after that period, should be listed as members. Persons who are felt to be members of the household but are away (e.g. students or men at work) should only be included if they have been away for less than 13 weeks and are expected back within the total period of 13 weeks (code under 10(d)).

QUESTION 10(e)

Age-group: code as below

0 — 1	01
2 — 4	02
5 — 9	03
10 — 14	04
15 — 19	05
20 — 29	06
30 — 39	07
40 — 49	08
50 — 59	09
60 — 64	10
65 — 69	11
70 — 79	12
80 and over	13
DK	X
NA	Y

QUESTION 10(d)

Code reasons as below

Hospital/nursing Home/convalescent Home	1
Staying with relative or friend	2
Otherwise away on holiday	3
In armed services/merchant navy	4
Otherwise working away from home	5
Prison, approved school, Borstal, detention, etc.	6
Children's Home or foster home	7
Boarding school, college, university	8
Other (specify)	9

QUESTION 10(f) — Court order

A maintenance order secured through the courts. If no action has been taken to confirm the separation then code 1; in this situation at least the spouse in the household accepts that man and wife are not living together and there is no immediate prospect of them so doing.

QUESTION 11

If answer yes, complete other parts of question and amend Q. 10 if someone included in answers to that question who proves in fact to be a temporary visitor or guest (i.e. who has stayed less than 4 weeks and not expected to stay for total period longer than 4 weeks).

QUESTION 11(a)

If there is more than one visitor enter information for all in box or on this left hand page.

QUESTION 11(f) Code as follows:

Relative staying without payment	1
Friend staying without payment	2
Relative staying with payment	3
Friend staying with payment	4
Other person staying with payment	5
Other (e.g. nurse/student —specify)	6

QUESTION 12

If any person is felt to belong to the household and is expected to return to it after a total absence of less than thirteen weeks (e.g. at University, in hospital, at work, staying with relatives), then the interviewer should include such a person in the replies to Q. 10. But the information should also be recorded here in Q.12.

QUESTION 12(h) Prompt and code as follows:

Hospital/nursing/convalescent/residential Home	1
Staying with relative or friend	2
Otherwise away on holiday	3
In armed services/merchant navy	4
At boarding school, college or university	5
Otherwise working away from home	6
Approved school/Borstal/detention centre, etc.	7
Children's Home/foster home	8
Prison	9
Other (specify)	x

3a

10. Now I would like to ask some questions about each person living here at present: I mean someone living here for more than a month, or someone here less than that but expected to stay longer than a month.

(a) First of all, can you tell me how many persons aged 15 and over there are? | Total persons in household

– And how many children under 15?

(b) And now can you tell me who they all are?

DESCRIBE RELATIONSHIP TO INFORMANT IN EACH COLUMN
(e.g. husband, son or other relationships between members)
LIST NAMES AND AGES ON BACK FLAP FOR REFERENCE

          related to informant
          not related to informant

          male
          female

(c) Was he/she here last night or was he/she   Yes, here SKIP TO Q.10(e)
away – staying with a relative or because   Not here ASK Q.10(d)
of work, for example?

(d) Why not? *
                      CODE
                      REASON

(e) How old are you (is he/she last birthday)? *   code age-group
(f) Are you (is he/she) married or unmarried?

        X unmarried
        Y married, present last night   SKIP TO Q.11
        0 married, away last night
        1 married, separated – no court order   ASK Q. 10(g)
        2 married, separated – court order   ASK Q. 10(h)
        3 divorced
        4 widowed   ASK Q. 10(i)

(g) How long is it since your husband/wife was at home?
OR (h) How long is it since you were living   years if 1 or more
together as man and wife?   less than 1 year, more
than 3 months
(i) How long is it since you were widowed?   3 months or less

        * CODE HOUSEHOLD TYPE (THREE DIGITS)

11. Is there anyone staying with you who doesn't usually live here or who will be living here for less than a month altogether – a visitor, say?
        yes   ASK Q.11(a)
        no   SKIP TO Q.12

(a) What is his relationship to you?
(b) Sex?
(c) Age?   CODE AGE-GROUP
(d) How long has he/she lived here?
(e) How much longer do you expect him to stay?
(f) What is his/her reason for staying/living here?
    * CODE REASON

12. You have told me who lives here. Can I just check whether

(a) Any of the adults living here have   yes, dependent child   ASK Q.
any dependent children who are away   yes, adult   12(c)
at present?
(b) Any adult member is away at present   no, neither child   SKIP TO
– in hospital, at college or on   nor adult   Q.13
holiday, for example?   DK

(c) What is his relationship to you?
(d) Sex?
(e) Age?   CODE AGE-GROUP
(f) How long has he been away?
(g) How much longer do you expect him to be away? (in weeks)
(h) Why is he/she away at present?
    * CODE REASON
(i) IF CHILD. Does any adult in the household help to pay for his/her keep? Who?
(j) About how much a week does he pay?

1	2	3	4	5	6	7	8	9
.							0	3

Inft	2nd	3rd	4th	5th	6th	7	8	9	10
10-11	10-11	10-11	10-11	10-11	10-11	10-11	10-11	10-11	10-11
01	02	03	04	05	06	07	08	09	10
12	12	12	12	12	12	12	12	12	12
X	X	X	X	X	X	X	X	X	X
Y	Y	Y	Y	Y	Y	Y	Y	Y	Y
0	0	0	0	0	0	0	0	0	0
1	1	1	1	1	1	1	1	1	1
2	2	2	2	2	2	2	2	2	2
3	3	3	3	3	3	3	3	3	3
13	13	13	13	13	13	13	13	13	13
14 15	14 15	14 15	14 15	14 15	14 15	14 15	14 15	14 15	14 15
16	16	16	16	16	16	16	16	16	16
X	X	X	X	X	X	X	X	X	X
Y	Y	Y	Y	Y	Y	Y	Y	Y	Y
0	0	0	0	0	0	0	0	0	0
1	1	1	1	1	1	1	1	1	1
2	2	2	2	2	2	2	2	2	2
3	3	3	3	3	3	3	3	3	3
4	4	4	4	4	4	4	4	4	4
17 18	17 18	17 18	17 18	17 18	17 18	17 18	17 18	17 18	17 18
X	X	X	X	X	X	X	X	X	X
Y	Y	Y	Y	Y	Y	Y	Y	Y	Y

** 38 39 40

41
X
Y

0
1

2
3

3

QUESTION 13(a)

" Marriage ": include common law marriage if in fact revealed by informant.

QUESTION 13(b)

Code whereabouts of parents only in terms of the replies so far given (or given later) by the informant. Direct questions might seem to be very offensive **and they must be avoided.** Indirect questions will be helpful according to the circumstances. For example, it may transpire that one child is the half-sister of another. It would then be very reasonable to ask " How are they related? " Or when it becomes obvious that one parent is not present, it would be reasonable to ask " Does John see his father regularly? "

" Accepted stepfather " or " Accepted stepmother " describes a man or woman not legally married to the natural mother or father of the child(ren) who has been in the household for at least 13 weeks and who is clearly accepted by the informant as the " stepfather " or " stepmother " of the child(ren) living in the household, albeit not accepted by law in this role.

QUESTION 14(a)   Play within easy reach

This means that the mother can rush to a tearful child within, say, 30 seconds of hearing a wail. A " safe place " could of course include the garden.

4a

13. ASK ALL WITH CHILDREN OR WITH CHILDREN LIVING TEMPORARILY AWAY
(IF NONE SKIP TO Q.17)
We have to check on adopted children or step-children. Have you or
your husband/wife been married before?

		Inft	2nd	3rd	4th	5th	6th	7	8	9	10
		19	19	19	19	19	19	19	19	19	19
X yes, married twice or more	IF ANY CODED ASK Q.13(a)	X	X	X	X	X	X	X	X	X	X
Y no, married once		Y	Y	Y	Y	Y	Y	Y	Y	Y	Y
0 never married or too young	SKIP to Q.13(b)	0	0	0	0	0	0	0	0	0	0
1 married DK times		1	1	1	1	1	1	1	1	1	1
2 does not apply		2	2	2	2	2	2	2	2	2	2
(a) Is the child (are any of the children) in the	3 yes	3 •	3	3	3	3	3	3	3	3	3
household from a previous marriage?	4 no	4	4	4	4	4	4	4	4	4	4
CODE EACH CHILD	5 DK	5	5	5	5	5	5	5	5	5	5
(b) Is the child (are any of the children) an	6 yes, adopted	6	6	6	6	6	6	6	6	6	6
adopted or foster child?	7 yes, foster	7	7	7	7	7	7	7	7	7	7
	8 no	8	8	8	8	8	8	8	8	8	8
CODE EACH CHILD	9 DK	9	9	9	9	9	9	9	9	9	9
		20	20	20	20	20	20	20	20	20	20
INTERVIEWER: NOTE ANY	X both (natural) parents present: married	X	X	X	X	X	X	X	X	X	X
HELPFUL INFORMATION	Y : not married	Y	Y	Y	Y	Y	Y	Y	Y	Y	Y
BELOW AND CODE FOR EACH	0 mother present: and legal stepfather	0	0	0	0	0	0	0	0	0	0
DEPENDENT CHILD	1 : and accepted stepfather*	1	1	1	1	1	1	1	1	1	1
	2 father present: and legal stepmother	2	2	2	2	2	2	2	2	2	2
	3 : and accepted stepmother*	3	3	3	3	3	3	3	3	3	3
	4 mother present only	4	4	4	4	4	4	4	4	4	4
	5 father present only	5	5	5	5	5	5	5	5	5	5
	6 neither present: both alive	6	6	6	6	6	6	6	6	6	6
	7 neither present: father alive	7	7	7	7	7	7	7	7	7	7
	8 neither present: mother alive	8	8	8	8	8	8	8	8	8	8
	9 neither present: neither alive	9	9	9	9	9	9	9	9	9	9
		21	21	21	21	21	21	21	21	21	21
	X DK	X	X	X	X	X	X	X	X	X	X

14. ASK ALL WITH CHILD AGED 1 - 4
Is there a safe place for him/her to play within easy reach of
the home?

	Inft	2nd	3rd	4th	5th	6th	7	8	9	10
Y yes	Y	Y	Y	Y	Y	Y	Y	Y	Y	Y
0 no	0	0	0	0	0	0	0	0	0	0
1 DK	1	1	1	1	1	1	1	1	1	1
2 does not apply	2	2	2	2	2	2	2	2	2	2

15. ASK ALL WITH CHILDREN AGED 5 - 10
Is there a safe place nearby to which he/she can go unaccompanied
to play?

	Inft	2nd	3rd	4th	5th	6th	7	8	9	10
3 yes	3	3	3	3	3	3	3	3	3	3
4 no	4	4	4	4	4	4	4	4	4	4
5 DK	5	5	5	5	5	5	5	5	5	5
6 does not apply	6	6	6	6	6	6	6	6	6	6
	22	22	22	22	22	22	22	22	22	22

16. ASK ALL WITH CHILDREN AGED 1 - 10
Do the children have enough good places to play indoors without
troubling the neighbours?

	Inft	2nd	3rd	4th	5th	6th	7	8	9	10
X no, not enough space and annoys neighbours	X	X	X	X	X	X	•X	X	X	X
Y no, not enough space	Y	Y	Y	Y	Y	Y	Y	Y	Y	Y
0 no, enough space but annoys neighbours	0	0	0	0	0	0	0	0	0	0
1 yes	1	1	1	1	1	1	1	1	1	1
2 DK	2	2	2	2	2	2	2	2	2	2
3 does not apply	3	3	3	3	3	3	3	3	3	3
	23	23	23	23	23	23	23	23	23	23

17. ASK ALL
How long have each of you in the household lived at this
address?

	Inft	2nd	3rd	4th	5th	6th	7	8	9	10
Y all life	Y	Y	Y	Y	Y	Y	Y	Y	Y	Y
0 less than 3 months	0	0	0	0	0	0	0	0	0	0
1 3 months and less than 6 months	1	1	1	1	1	1	1	1	1	1
2 6 months and less than 1 year	2	2	2	2	2	2	2	2	2	2
3 1 year and less than 2 years	3	3	3	3	3	3	3	3	3	3
4 2 years and less than 5 years	4	4	4	4	4	4	4	4	4	4
5 5 years and less than 15 years	5	5	5	5	5	5	5	5	5	5
6 15 years or more	6	6	6	6	6	6	6	6	6	6
7 DK	7	7	7	7	7	7	7	7	7	7
	24	24	24	24	24	24	24	24	24	24

ASK Q.17(a) / SKIP TO Q.18 (for codes 1, 2 and 3 / for the others)

(a) How many times have each of you moved in the past two years?

	Inft	2nd	3rd	4th	5th	6th	7	8	9	10
1 once	1	1	1	1	1	1	1	1	1	1
2 twice	2	2	2	2	2	2	2	2	2	2
3 three times	3	3	3	3	3	3	3	3	3	3
4 four times	4	4	4	4	4	4	4	4	4	4
5 five times	5	5	5	5	5	5	5	5	5	5
6 six or more times	6	6	6	6	6	6	6	6	6	6
7 DK	7	7	7	7	7	7	7	7	7	7

QUESTION 18 Birthplace

Note that some coloured persons (especially children) will have been born in UK.

QUESTION 18(b) Non-white

We are seeking to distinguish between coloured and non-coloured immigrants. Listen carefully to the informant when he or she is answering for other members of the household about country of origin and years of residence. You should base your codes on observation together with inferences from what you are told in the interviews. When you have not observed a particular member of the household and **there is reasonable cause** for asking whether he or she is coloured (e.g. because statements have been made about an external country of birth, or you are working in an immigrant area), you may ask " Is he/she coloured? " If this question would seem tactless do not ask but code " DK white/non-white ". In general, people of African, Indian, Asian or Arab origin should be coded as non-white, in that our society at large tends to classify such people as " coloured ". Those of European origin should in general be coded as white.

Some difficulties will inevitably be encountered (an Arab informant who looks European) but the majorities of such difficulties should be solved by learning the country of origin. A minority will remain (e.g. the man born in France who may or may not be an Indian or a Tunisian Arab) and we must rely on the interviewer obtaining the best information possible.

5a

18. Can you tell me if there is anyone in the household who was born outside the United Kingdom (that is England, Scotland, Wales and Northern Ireland)?

     X born outside UK   ASK Q.18(a)
     Y born inside UK   }
     0 DK   ASK Q.18(b)

(a) What is your country of origin?

     1 Irish Republic
     2 West Indies
     3 India
     4 Pakistan
     5 Africa
     6 Europe (other than Irish Republic)
     7 Other (specify) _____

(b) How many years have you lived in the United Kingdom?

     X less than 2 years
     Y 2 years and less than 5 years
     0 5 years and less than 20 years
     1 20 years or more

(c)   DO   {2 white
      NOT   {3 non-white
      ASK   {4 DK white/non-white

Inft	2nd	3rd	4th	5th	6th	7	8	9	10
25	25	25	25	25	25	25	25	25	25
X	X	X	X	X	X	X	X	X	X
Y	Y	Y	Y	Y	Y	Y	Y	Y	Y
0	0	0	0	0	0	0	0	0	0
1	1	1	1	1	1	1	1	1	1
2	2	2	2	2	2	2	2	2	2
3	3	3	3	3	3	3	3	3	3
4	4	4	4	4	4	4	4	4	4
5	5	5	5	5	5	5	5	5	5
6	6	6	6	6	6	6	6	6	6
7	7	7	7	7	7	7	7	7	7
26	26	26	26	26	26	26	26	26	26
X	X	X	X	X	X	X	X	X	X
Y	Y	Y	Y	Y	Y	Y	Y	Y	Y
0	0	0	0	0	0	0	0	0	0
1	1	1	1	1	1	1	1	1	1
2	2	2	2	2	2	2	2	2	2
3	3	3	3	3	3	3	3	3	3
4	4	4	4	4	4	4	4	4	4

SECTION II EMPLOYMENT

General

This section and the next (Occupational Facilities) should normally be asked of each adult earner in the household. If you happen to be interviewing the housewife during the day you should ask these questions as they apply to herself (and also to any children and adult dependants — e.g. elderly widowed mother) and then a separate (shorter) interview with the husband (and any other adult earner who is not available at the time of the first interview) to ask him for answers to this section, to the section on occupational facilities, to the questions on earnings in Section IV and any other questions which cannot be answered by the housewife.

QUESTION 1 Attended paid employment

All persons working for gain. If a housewife, retired person or even a schoolchild works a few hours for pay each week, he or she should be included. Also count man who is not at his main occupation (and even who may be thought of as unemployable) but who has pay from a minor job. We will be able to check in analysis. Our purpose is not to miss casual earnings and supplementary sources of income.

QUESTION 2 Two jobs

If a person does some kind of job for a different employer or on own behalf in his " spare " time this counts as a second job. Even if it is the same kind of job but is separately paid for (e.g. decorator working in spare time for himself) it should be counted as second job.

QUESTION 3 House or flat

Includes house combined with business premises or farm; but the question has been introduced primarily to cater for women home-workers on piece rates. Note that it refers to any second as well as the principal job.

QUESTION 4 Starting and finishing work times

The question applies to last week. Ignore variations in working hours from week to week. If working times were the same on at least three days of the week regard them as " usual ". If there were two shifts (e.g. morning and evening), list according to starting time of the first and finishing time of the second, and note fact on left.

QUESTION 5 Aid in calculating hours of work

The table below assumes a 5-day week and 1 hour for lunch. Note that each digit should be put in each separate part of the box (i.e. one digit under No. 29 and the other under No. 30).

Starting time	Finishing time			
	4.30 p.m.	5.00 p.m.	5.30 p.m.	6.00 p.m.
7.00 a.m.	42½	45	47½	50
7.30 a.m.	40	42½	45	47½
8.00 a.m.	37½	40	42½	45
8.30 a.m.	35	37½	40	42½
9.00 a.m.	32½	35	37½	40
9.30 a.m.	30	32½	35	35½
10.00 a.m.	27½	30	32½	35

QUESTION 6 NOT AT WORK

Note that this question must also be answered for persons working last week for **less than 30 hours Unemployed:** as distinct from " off sick " or temporarily off work (e.g. on holiday). The replies will be, for example: " I lost my job "; " I'm out of a job "; " There was redundancy at the firm so I'm out of work for the moment ". Sometimes a person may say he is both unemployed AND sick or disabled, or it may for other reasons be difficult to specify just one code. Accept the best answer given by the informant even if you observe that someone who says he is unemployed is obviously sick or disabled (and vice-versa). Later questions are designed to establish whether or not he is seeking work and whether or not he is chronically sick or disabled.

Unpaid holiday

Part of our purpose in asking if holidays are unpaid is to ensure that 5 is not coded rather than the underlying reasons coded as 7, 8 or 9. Distinguishing between paid and unpaid holidays introduces complications but may be worthwhile (a) for the opportunity afforded to probe the reasons an unpaid holiday is being taken and (b) later when calculating weeks not at work in previous year.

SECTION II   EMPLOYMENT

1. Can you tell me who in the household was at work last week, for any number of hours, however few?

  attended paid employment, or self employed *
  not attending paid employment } SKIP TO Q.6
  DK

2. Just the one job, or more than one? I mean did you do any spare-time or regular paid work? *
  one job
  two or more jobs

3. Is the work carried out here in the house or flat? *
  yes, main/only occupation
  yes, secondary occupation(s) only
  no

4. What was the usual hour at which you started and finished work each day last week? *

CODE ONE X worked from before 8 am to 6 pm (or earlier)
ONLY ON Y before 8 am and finished after 6 pm
BASIS OF 0 8 am (or after) to 6 pm (or earlier)
ANSWER 1 8 am (or after) and finished after 6 pm
  2 after 6 pm to 8 am (or earlier)
  3 no usual hour of starting and/or finishing

5. Can you tell me the total number of hours you worked last week (counting all jobs for which you received pay)? Insert number*
IF WORKED LESS THAN 30 HOURS ASK Q.5(a) DK
IF WORKED 30 HOURS OR MORE SKIP TO Q.8

(a) When did you last work 30 hours X less than 6 months ago
or more in a week? Y 6 months and less than 1 year ago
  0 1 and less than 3 years
  1 3 and less than 10 years
  2 10 or more years
  3 never
  4 DK

(b) Would you work more hours if 5 yes, unconditionally
such a job were available? 6 yes, with reservations
 CODE ONE ONLY 7 no, would not wish to
 ON BASIS OF ANSWER 8 no, could not do so
  9 DK

6. IF NOT AT WORK LAST WEEK OR WORKING LESS THAN 30 HOURS
Why weren't you at work last week? X housewife
OR Why weren't you at work full-time? Y retired
  0 student
  1 pre-school or school child SKIP TO NEXT SECTION
PROMPT * 2 unemployed
  3 sick or injured
CODE ONE 4 disabled or handicapped
ONLY 5 paid holiday
  * 6 unpaid holiday
  7 not working because: school holidays
  8 : caring for someone ill
  9 : deputising for house-wife

  X other (specify)_____
  Y DK

	1nft	2nd	3rd	4th	5th	6th	7	8	9	10
	27	27	27	27	27	27	27	27	27	27
	X Y 0	X Y 0	X Y 0	X Y 0	X Y 0	X Y 0	X Y 0	X Y 0	X Y 0	X Y 0
	1 2	1 2	1 2	1 2	1 2	1 2	1 2	1 2	1 2	1 2
	3 4 5	3 4 5	3 4 5	3 4 5	3 4 5	3 4 5	3 4 5	3 4 5	3 4 5	3 4 5
	28	28	28	28	28	28	28	28	28	28
	X Y 0 1 2 3	X Y 0 1 2 3	X Y 0 1 2 3	X Y 0 1 2 3	X Y 0 1 2 3	X Y 0 1 2 3	X Y 0 1 2 3	X Y 0 1 2 3	X Y 0 1 2 3	X Y 0 1 2 3
	29 30	29 30	29 30	29 30	29 30	29 30	29 30	29 30	29 30	29 30
	1 X 31	1 X 31	1 X 31	1 X 31	1 X 31	1 X 31	1 X 31	1 X 31	1 X 31	1 X 31
	X Y 0 1 2 3 4	X Y 0 1 2 3 4	X Y 0 1 2 3 4	X Y 0 1 2 3 4	X Y 0 1 2 3 4	X Y 0 1 2 3 4	X Y 0 1 2 3 4	X Y 0 1 2 3 4	X Y 0 1 2 3 4	X Y 0 1 2 3 4
	5 6 7 8 9	5 6 7 8 9	5 6 7 8 9	5 6 7 8 9	5 6 7 8 9	5 6 7 8 9	5 6 7 8 9	5 6 7 8 9	5 6 7 8 9	5 6 7 8 9
	32	32	32	32	32	32	32	32	32	32
	X Y 0 1 2 3 4 5 6 7 8 9	X Y 0 1 2 3 4 5 6 7 8 9	X Y 0 1 2 3 4 5 6 7 8 9	X Y 0 1 2 3 4 5 6 7 8 9	X Y 0 1 2 3 4 5 6 7 8 9	X Y 0 1 2 3 4 5 6 7 8 9	X Y 0 1 2 3 4 5 6 7 8 9	X Y 0 1 2 3 4 5 6 7 8 9	X Y 0 1 2 3 4 5 6 7 8 9	X Y 0 1 2 3 4 5 6 7 8 9
	33	33	33	33	33	33	33	33	33	33
	X Y	X Y	X Y	X Y	X Y	X Y	X Y	X Y	X Y	X Y

6

QUESTION 7(b)   Last Occupation

Write in the occupation on the left of the columns. Identify the person to whom the information applies in the little box (i.e. Inf or 2nd or 3rd etc.) This will both allow you to enter information for a second or third person if that proves to be applicable and for the office to code in the right column(s) on the basis of your information.

QUESTION 7(c)   Looking for work

You will find yourself asking retired persons as well as unemployed and other persons this question. Sometimes it will be entirely applicable because persons who have been retired by their employers or have automatically ceased employment upon reaching a pensionable age of, say, 60, may in fact be seeking alternative work. It may even be applicable for some persons in their seventies and eighties. But sometimes it will plainly be inapplicable to frail persons of extreme age, especially women. In this case code " NO " and skip to Q. 8. When in doubt, however, you should ask the question.

7. IF NOT AT WORK LAST WEEK
Are you at work this week?

    0 yes, attending paid employment   SKIP TO Q.8
    1 no   ASK Q.7(a)

(a) How long is it since you were at work?

    2 never paid employment   SKIP TO Q.15
    3 less than 6 months   }
    4 6 months and less than 1 year } SKIP TO Q.8
    5 1 and less than 3 years
    6 3 and less than 10 years   } ASK Q.7(b)
    7 10 years or more   }
    8 DK

(b) What was your last paid occupation? And the employer's (or own) business? *

    WRITE IN ANSWER: IF UNSPECIFIC ASK What do you do?

(c) Are you looking for work? *   yes   ASK Q.7(d)
                        no }
                        DK } SKIP TO Q.8

(d) Are you registered at the Employment Exchange?   no ASK Q.7(e)
                        yes }
                        DK } SKIP TO Q.7(f)

(e) Why not?   WRITE IN ANSWER

(f) Have you looked in the papers for any jobs that looked suitable for you?   yes
                                       no
                                       DK

(g) Are there any other kind of things you have done lately to try to get a job?   WRITE IN ANSWER

Inft	2nd	3rd	4th	5th	6th	7	8	9	10
0	0	0	0	0	0	0	0	0	0
1	1	1	1	1	1	1	1	1	1
2	2	2	2	2	2	2	2	2	2
3	3	3	3	3	3	3	3	3	3
4	4	4	4	4	4	4	4	4	4
5	5	5	5	5	5	5	5	5	5
6	6	6	6	6	6	6	6	6	6
7	7	7	7	7	7	7	7	7	7
8	8	8	8	8	8	8	8	8	8
34	34	34	34	34	34	34	34	34	34
35	35	35	35	35	35	35	35	35	35
X	X	X	X	X	X	X	X	X	X
Y	Y	Y	Y	Y	Y	Y	Y	Y	Y
0	0	0	0	0	0	0	0	0	0
1	1	1	1	1	1	1	1	1	1
2	2	2	2	2	2	2	2	2	2
3	3	3	3	3	3	3	3	3	3
36	36	36	36	36	36	36	36	36	36
4	4	4	4	4	4	4	4	4	4
5	5	5	5	5	5	5	5	5	5
6	6	6	6	6	6	6	6	6	6

QUESTION 8 Work record

Our aim is to trace persons whose work record is not full and to establish both numbers of weeks off work and numbers of weeks in which fewer than 30 hours were worked.

Weeks off work in year

The procedure is first to ask the general question about numbers of weeks off work. Some informants will be uncertain of the right answer. They can be encouraged by prompts about the last spell off work for **unemployment**, then **sickness** and so on down the list. Whenever it is clear they are going back more than 12 months you should move on to the next eventuality on the list. In the appropriate column note the number of weeks for **all** spells of unemployment, sickness, etc. You must record " O " in all open boxes when the person has had no spell off work for that reason. You may ignore the codes " X " and " Y " under each open box. They are for office use. For easy reference you can record each spell off work alongside the months listed below. (You may in rare instances interview persons, say, who had five or six spells off work through sickness and may need to show some rough working to arrive at the right total. (Please leave any rough working in case of queries.)

List member of household (informant, 2nd, 3rd) and weeks off work and reason

January..	July..
February...	August...
March..	September..
April...	October..
May..	November..
June..	December...

Some informants may have a quick answer for the first general question (usually because they have a very full or almost empty record of work in the year). You should nonetheless use the same procedure of asking about each type of eventuality and each spell off work as a check. If an informant says he hasn't been off work except for "just odd days because of colds and so on " ASK How much would it amount to over the past twelve months — one week, two weeks? AND CODE ACCORDINGLY. For informants (e.g. housewives or students) who have only worked for a few weeks in the year, you may find it quicker to establish first how long they were at work.

As with so many other questions about " the last twelve months " in this questionnaire, informants will often find it helpful if you encourage them to think forwards from a date exactly a year ago.

8. FOR ALL WORKING AT LEAST ONE WEEK DURING PAST 12 MONTHS
About how many weeks have your been off work for any reason in the past 12 months? – I mean for sickness, unemployment and so on, but also paid and unpaid holidays. *

PROMPT ACCORDING TO REPLY:

For Instance, when were you last off work sick? And how long did it last?
(IF WITHIN YEAR: And the time before that?)

PROMPT FROM LIST AND WRITE IN TOTAL WEEKS ALL SPELLS OFF WORK

WRITE IN TOTAL NUMBER OF WEEKS

unemployment

sickness or injury ____

disability or handicap ____

holiday: paid ____

holiday: unpaid ____

not working because of school holidays ____

caring for someone who is ill ____

deputising for housewife ____

resuming duties as housewife ____

stopped work upon marriage or for honeymoon ____

for childbirth ____

retirement ____

taking up or resuming full-time study ____

other (specify) ____

off work, reason not known, or reason not given ____

(a) CHECK. So you had ____ weeks not working altogether in the past 12 months?   WRITE IN total weeks not working

total weeks working

(b) In the total you have given me of the weeks worked, how many were there (approximately) in which you worked less than 30 hours?   WRITE IN NUMBER

(c) Have you ever had a spell off work continuously for as long as 8 weeks or more because of

PROMPT   sickness   yes
unemployment   yes
anything else (specify) ____ yes
no
DK

(d) FOR THOSE WHO HAVE HAD 8 WEEKS OR MORE CONSECUTIVELY OFF WORK, DURING THE LAST 12 MONTHS FOR REASONS OF SICKNESS, INJURY, OR DISABILITY
Would you say that the work you were doing was responsible in any way for your being off work?   yes ASK Q.8(e)
no
DK } SKIP TO Q.9
DNA

(e) How was that?   WRITE ANSWER BELOW

	Intt	2nd	3rd	4th	5th	6th	7	8	9	10
	37	37	37	37	37	37	37	37	37	37
	X Y	X Y	X Y	X Y	X Y	X Y	X Y	X Y	X Y	X Y
	38	38	38	38	38	38	38	38	38	38
	X Y	X Y	X Y	X Y	X Y	X Y	X Y	X Y	X Y	X Y
	39	39	39	39	39	39	39	39	39	39
	X Y	X Y	X Y	X Y	X Y	X Y	X Y	X Y	X Y	X Y
	40	40	40	40	40	40	40	40	40	40
	X Y	X Y	X Y	X Y	X Y	X Y	X Y	X Y	X Y	X Y
	41	41	41	41	41	41	41	41	41	41
	X Y	X Y	X Y	X Y	X Y	X Y	X Y	X Y	X Y	X Y
	42	42	42	42	42	42	42	42	42	42
	X Y	X Y	X Y	X Y	X Y	X Y	X Y	X Y	X Y	X Y
	43	43	43	43	43	43	43	43	43	43
	X Y	X Y	X Y	X Y	X Y	X Y	X Y	X Y	X Y	X Y
	44	44	44	44	44	44	44	44	44	44
	X Y	X Y	X Y	X Y	X Y	X Y	X Y	X Y	X Y	X Y
	45	45	45	45	45	45	45	45	45	45
	X Y	X Y	X Y	X Y	X Y	X Y	X Y	X Y	X Y	X Y
	46	46	46	46	46	46	46	46	46	46
	X Y	X Y	X Y	X Y	X Y	X Y	X Y	X Y	X Y	X Y
	47	47	47	47	47	47	47	47	47	47
	X Y	X Y	X Y	X Y	X Y	X Y	X Y	X Y	X Y	X Y
	48	48	48	48	48	48	48	48	48	48
	X Y	X Y	X Y	X Y	X Y	X Y	X Y	X Y	X Y	X Y
	49	49	49	49	49	49	49	49	49	49
	X Y	X Y	X Y	X Y	X Y	X Y	X Y	X Y	X Y	X Y
	50	50	50	50	50	50	50	50	50	50
	X Y	X Y	X Y	X Y	X Y	X Y	X Y	X Y	X Y	X Y
	51	51	51	51	51	51	51	51	51	51
	X Y	X Y	X Y	X Y	X Y	X Y	X Y	X Y	X Y	X Y
	52 ¦ 53	52 ¦ 53	52 ¦ 53	52 ¦ 53	52 ¦ 53	52 ¦ 53	52¦53	52¦53	52¦53	52¦53
	54 ¦ 55	54 ¦ 55	54 ¦ 55	54 ¦ 55	54 ¦ 55	54 ¦ 55	54¦55	54¦55	54¦55	54¦55
	56 ¦ 57	56 ¦ 57	56 ¦ 57	56 ¦ 57	56 ¦ 57	56 ¦ 57	56¦57	56¦57	56¦57	56¦57
	58	58	58	58	58	58	58	58	58	58
	X Y O 1 2	X Y O 1 2	X Y O 1 2	X Y O 1 2	X Y O 1 2	X Y O 1 2	X Y O 1 2	X Y O 1 2	X Y O 1 2	X Y O 1 2
	3 4 5 6	3 4 5 6	3 4 5 6	3 4 5 6	3 4 5 6	3 4 5 6	3 4 5 6	3 4 5 6	3 4 5 6	3 4 5 6

8

QUESTION 9

Exclude Bank Holidays in counting up holiday entitlement. List number of weeks to nearest week. Do not insert "½".

QUESTION 10   Occupation

See instructions above for Q. 7(b). Start by recording member of household in left-hand box (informant, 2nd, 3rd, etc.) and then carefully note occupation and industry or business. The office will code in the right-hand columns on the basis of your information. Avoid all vague terms, e.g. "engineer". If you find the answer too general or difficult to understand always ask "What do you do?" and write in the answer. In many households there will be only one or two persons who have been at work in the past twelve months. If necessary you can use all the space in the box just for one or two persons, providing it is clear to which person(s) the information applies.

QUESTION 11   Change of Job

Note that sub-questions (a) - (d) apply only to persons changing their jobs less than five years previously.

11(c). IRU, etc., means Industrial Rehabilitation Unit or any other Government training centre.

QUESTION 12   Training Course

Our object is to check on men taking a re-training or training course, whether or not they changed their job. Some men may have taken a course and gone back to their former job or employers. Others may be unemployed and yet have taken such a course.

QUESTION 13   Fall in Earnings

You may be asked what you mean by "big" fall. Accept whatever the informant thinks is big. Put the information in the box, including the approximate earnings previously as well as the subsequent earnings and code the extent of the fall in the right-hand columns.

9a

9. You've told me how many weeks paid holiday you took last year.
How many weeks are you entitled to (excluding Bank Holidays)?

* number of weeks

10. What is your occupation? (or last occupation IF AT WORK DURING
LAST 12 MONTHS)

WRITE IN   MAIN JOB   AND EMPLOYER'S (OR OWN)
BUSINESS

SECOND JOB

IF REPLY UNSPECIFIC ASK "What do you do?"

11. When did you last change your job? *

	X less than 5 years ago	ASK Q.11(a)
	Y more than 5 years ago	SKIP TO Q.12

(a) Did you change   0 for health reasons?
It →   1 because you were made redundant?
PROMPT   CODE   2 or for other reasons?
ONE ONLY   3 DK
          9 Never
(b) Can you tell me how it came about?

WRITE IN ANSWER

(c) Did you have any retraining?   in-service training
                          attending IRU, etc
              other (specify)

                          none
(d) How did you find or hear   2 labour exchange
about your present job?   3 advertisement
                  4 recommendation by relative
                  5 inquired about possible vacancy
                  6 recommended by friend
       7 other (specify)

12. FOR MEN AGED 30-64 ONLY
Can I just check. Have you been on a trade, industrial rehabilitation or Government training course of any kind in the last 5 years
(whether or not you have changed your job)? *   yes   ASK Q.12(a)
                              no
                              DK   SKIP TO Q.13
                              DNA
(a) Who arranged it?   Government
                     employer
                     armed services
              other (specify)
(b) How long did it last?   number of weeks
(c) Did it help you to get a better job?   yes
                          no
                          DK

13. Have you ever experienced a big fall in earnings?
                     yes   ASK Q.13(a)
                     no
                     cannot remember   SKIP TO Q.14
       CODE APPROXIMATE PERCENTAGE FALL IN EARNINGS
(a) When?   (b) Why?   (c) from how much to how much?
       year
       19   under 10%
       19   10 - 19%
       19   20 - 49%
                              50% or over

	1nft	2nd	3rd	4th	5th	6th	7	8	9	10
	59	59	59	59	59	59	59	59	59	59
	X Y	X Y	X Y	X Y	X Y	X Y	X Y	X Y	X Y	X Y
	60	60	60	60	60	60	60	60	60	60
	61	61	61	61	61	61	61	61	61	61
	X Y 0 1 2 3 9	X Y 0 1 2 3 9	X Y 0 1 2 3 9	X Y 0 1 2 3 9	X Y 0 1 2 3 9	X Y 0 1 2 3 9	X Y 0 1 2 3 9	X Y 0 1 2 3 9	X Y 0 1 2 3 9	X Y 0 1 2 3 9
	62	62	62	62	62	62	62	62	62	62
	X Y 0 1 2 3 4 5 6 7	X Y 0 1 2 3 4 5 6 7	X Y 0 1 2 3 4 5 6 7	X Y 0 1 2 3 4 5 6 7	X Y 0 1 2 3 4 5 6 7	X Y 0 1 2 3 4 5 6 7	X Y 0 1 2 3 4 5 6 7	X Y 0 1 2 3 4 5 6 7	X Y 0 1 2 3 4 5 6 7	X Y 0 1 2 3 4 5 6 7
	63	63	63	63	63	63	63	63	63	63
	X Y 0 1 2 3 4 5	X Y 0 1 2 3 4 5	X Y 0 1 2 3 4 5	X Y 0 1 2 3 4 5	X Y 0 1 2 3 4 5	X Y 0 1 2 3 4 5	X Y 0 1 2 3 4 5	X Y 0 1 2 3 4 5	X Y 0 1 2 3 4 5	X Y 0 1 2 3 4 5
	64 65	64 65	64 65	64 65	64 65	64 65	64 65	64 65	64 65	64 65
	X Y 0	X Y 0	X Y 0	X Y 0	X Y 0	X Y 0	X Y 0	X Y 0	X Y 0	X Y 0
	66	66	66	66	66	66	66	66	66	66
	X Y 0	X Y 0	X Y 0	X Y 0	X Y 0	X Y 0	X Y 0	X Y 0	X Y 0	X Y 0
	1 2 3 4	1 2 3 4	1 2 3 4	1 2 3 4	1 2 3 4	1 2 3 4	1 2 3 4	1 2 3 4	1 2 3 4	1 2 3 4

9

QUESTION 14 Best job

If you are asked "What do you mean by 'best'?" you should say "It is up to you to decide" (adding, but only if necessary, "whether it's best because of the money, the people, the job in itself or anything else"). of course there will be people who give a mixture of reasons. Code the one they treat as most important. If they are undecided code DK.

QUESTION 15

A few persons — e.g. students — may have worked for part of the last year, or may work every Saturday and still be in full-time education. We will be asking about them later. Code them as still in full-time education.

QUESTION 15(a) Years of full-time education

The question is worded so that if someone has missed a year's schooling because of illness, say, between the ages of 5 and 14, he can adjust his answer accordingly. You can check (or aid other informants trying to reach an answer) by deducting five years from the leaving age and then asking if the result allows for any absence because of hospitalisation, war evacuation, military service, or any other reason. Note that full-time education can be provided in hospital. Only deduct a year if ALL of it was spent out of school. When writing in leaving age and number of years education remember again to insert each digit.

QUESTION 16 Manual Workers

If you are in doubt from what you have been told about a man's job whether it is manual ask, "How do you do your work? Is it mostly heavy work, or operating a machine or mostly with your hands?" If he indicates any of these ask Q. 16. If still in doubt ask the question and write a note.

QUESTION 17(a) Husband's occupation

Follow same procedure as above under Question 10. It will be even more necessary to probe for the exact type of job. Encourage the woman to tell you what her husband did, since the answer is most important for us in classifying occupational status.

10a

4(a) ASK ALL   What was the best job you have ever had in your life?

WRITE IN JOB AND EMPLOYER'S (OR OWN) BUSINESS

present job ⎤ ASK
a previous job ⎦ Q.14 (b)
DK ⎱ SKIP TO Q. 15
DNA ⎰

(b) Why was/is it the best?*

CODE ONE ONLY

X highest paid
Y best job in itself
0 best company at work
1 easiest
2 Other (SPECIFY)
3 DK

(c) How old were you then?

CODE ALL THAT APPLY

4 all working life
5 person in teens or twenties
6 person in thirties
7 person in forties
8 person in fifties
9 person in sixties or seventies

5. ASK ALL   How old were you when you left school (or college) and were able to work full-time?
   SKIP
   *still in full-time education → TO NEXT SECTION
   leaving age

(a) How many years of full-time education did you have altogether?
   *number of years

6. FOR MEN WHO ARE MANUAL WORKERS ONLY
   Have you completed an apprenticeship?
   yes → ASK Q. 15(a)
   no ⎱ SKIP
   DK ⎰
   DNA

(a) What was it?
   ─ WRITE IN ANSWER ─

   And for how many years?

   number of years

7(a) FOR SEPARATED, DIVORCED AND WIDOWED WOMEN ONLY
   What was your husband's last occupation?*
   does not apply
   DK

   WRITE IN MAIN JOB AND EMPLOYER'S (OR OWN) BUSINESS

   IF REPLY UNSPECIFIC ASK "What did he do?"

(b) When you separated from/lost your husband would you say you were financially worse off as a result?
   yes
   no
   DK

   FOR SEPARATED AND DIVORCED WOMEN ONLY
(c) Did he leave you or did you leave him?
   husband left
   wife left
   mutual separation
   DK

(d) Did you stay in the home where you had lived together?
   yes
   no
   DK

   FOR DIVORCED WOMEN ONLY
(e) How long was it between the time you were living together as man and wife and the time when your divorce finally came through?   Number of years
   DK

	1st	2nd	3rd	4th	5th	6th	7	8	9	10
	67	67	67	67	67	67	67	67	67	67
	X Y	X Y	X Y	X Y	X Y	X Y	X Y	X Y	X Y	X Y
	0 1	0 1	0 1	0 1	0 1	0 1	0 1	0 1	0 1	0 1
	68	68	68	68	68	68	68	68	68	68
	X Y 0 1 2 3	X Y 0 1 2 3	X Y 0 1 2 3	X Y 0 1 2 3	X Y 0 1 2 3	X Y 0 1 2 3	X Y 0 1 2 3	X Y 0 1 2 3	X Y 0 1 2 3	X Y 0 1 2 3
	4 5 6 7 8 9	4 5 6 7 8 9	4 5 6 7 8 9	4 5 6 7 8 9	4 5 6 7 8 9	4 5 6 7 8 9	4 5 6 7 8 9	4 5 6 7 8 9	4 5 6 7 8 9	4 5 6 7 8 9
	69 70	69 70	69 70	69 70	69 70	69 70	69 70	69 70	69 70	69 70
	X	X	X	X	X	X	X	X	X	X
	71 72	71 72	71 72	71 72	71 72	71 72	71 72	71 72	71 72	71 72
	73	73	73	73	73	73	73	73	73	73
	X Y 0 1	X Y 0 1	X Y 0 1	X Y 0 1	X Y 0 1	X Y 0 1	X Y 0 1	X Y 0 1	X Y 0 1	X Y 0 1
	74	74	74	74	74	74	74	74	74	74
	75	75	75	75	75	75	75	75	75	75
	X Y	X Y	X Y	X Y	X Y	X Y	X Y	X Y	X Y	X Y
	76	76	76	76	76	76	76	76	76	76
	X Y 0	X Y 0	X Y 0	X Y 0	X Y 0	X Y 0	X Y 0	X Y 0	X Y 0	X Y 0
	1 2 3 4	1 2 3 4	1 2 3 4	1 2 3 4	1 2 3 4	1 2 3 4	1 2 3 4	1 2 3 4	1 2 3 4	1 2 3 4
	5 6 7	5 6 7	5 6 7	5 6 7	5 6 7	5 6 7	5 6 7	5 6 7	5 6 7	5 6 7
	77	77	77	77	77	77	77	77	77	77
	X	X	X	X	X	X	X	X	X	X

OCCUPATIONAL FACILITIES AND FRINGE BENEFITS

General

Our intention is to invite anyone who has been working full-time to tell us about working conditions and fringe benefits. This will include anyone currently sick or unemployed who has been in full-time work in the last 12 months.

NORMALLY QUESTIONS SHOULD NOT BE ASKED ON SOMEONE ELSE'S BEHALF: THEY SHOULD BE ADDRESSED TO THE PERSON IN OR RECENTLY IN A PARTICULAR EMPLOYMENT.

But if two brothers, or husband and wife, work in the same factory or if otherwise the informant has good reason for knowing the employment conditions, then the interviewer may exercise discretion.

QUESTION 1 Outdoors

In determining whether mainly outdoors, you should find whether proportion of working time spent outdoors exceeds 50 per cent. Those working outdoors but under cover (e.g. some dock labourers and railway porters) should be counted as outdoors. Where conditions have changed, the question should be applied to the most recent conditions (e.g. last week at work).

QUESTION 2 Facilities

We are interested only in facilities provided by the employer. Disregard provisions and facilities which may happen to be available but which are not provided by the employer (e.g. garage hand who uses W.C. and washing facilities in neighbouring shop, or printer's apprentice who nips into local café for tea). For someone currently sick or unemployed the questions apply to the last job he held during the previous 12 months.

Facilities for washing Note that there must be hot water, soap and towel if "yes" is to be coded. Include liquid soap and paper towels in definition if necessary.

QUESTIONS 2 and 3 Writing in questions which do not apply

Working conditions vary widely and it is impossible to devise questions which fit them all. If you are satisfied that the answer yes or no to a particular question is meaningless or inappropriate DO NOT CODE alongside the item but write in underneath how many of the 8 or 10 items do not apply.

QUESTION 3 Sufficient Heating

The test is whether the informant feels cold at his work more often than the occasional instance of there being a heating breakdown or a really big freeze.

Facilities for washing Note that there must be hot water, soap, towel and mirror if "yes" is to be coded. You may count liquid soap as "soap" and paper towels and even a hand drying machine as equivalent to a towel if necessary.

Place for lunch Eating at bench or desk does not count.

Place to keep clothes e.g. cupboard, locker, wardrobe, hook in small room, etc. The wording should make clear that we are interested both in a place where clothes can be kept and one where they will be reasonably safe.

11a

C.I.C.

1	2	3	4	5	6	7	8	9	
							0	4	
Inft	2nd	3rd	4th	5th	6th	7	8	9	10
10-11	10-11	10-11	10-11	10-11	10-11	10-11	10-11	10-11	10-11
01	02	03	04	05	06	07	08	09	10
12	12	12	12	12	12	12	12	12	12

SECTION III   OCCUPATIONAL FACILITIES AND FRINGE
BENEFITS

ONLY FOR EMPLOYEES WORKING 30 HOURS A WEEK OR MORE FOR AT LEAST ONE
WEEK IN PREVIOUS 12 MONTHS

self-employed, Does Not Apply   SKIP TO Q.14
otherwise Does Not Apply

X	X	X	X	X	X	X	X	X	X
Y	Y	Y	Y	Y	Y	Y	Y	Y	Y

• I'd like to ask you a few questions about your work. Do you work
outdoors or indoors? *

0	mainly outdoors – one or mainly one place of work ASK Q.2
1	– different places of work
2	– transport travelling } SKIP TO Q.4
3	mainly indoors – one or mainly one place of work } SKIP
4	– different places of work TO Q.3
5	about as much indoors as outdoors

0	0	0	0	0	0	0	0	0	0
1	1	1	1	1	1	1	1	1	1
2	2	2	2	2	2	2	2	2	2
3	3	3	3	3	3	3	3	3	3
4	4	4	4	4	4	4	4	4	4
5	5	5	5	5	5	5	5	5	5
13	13	13	13	13	13	13	13	13	13

• FOR THOSE WORKING MAINLY OUTDOORS (Code 0 in Q.1)
How many of the following does your employer provide at your
main) place of work? (CODE ALL THAT APPLY)

(i)   dry and warm place to shelter in heavy rain   yes / no
(ii)   tea or coffee during day (whether charged or not)   yes / no
(iii) lavatory (I mean WC, earth closet or chemical closet) yes / no
• (iv) facilities for washing, including hot water, soap and yes / no
       towel
• (v) indoor place to eat sandwiches or midday meal   yes / no
(vi)   safe and dry place (e.g. cupboard or locker) for coat, yes / no
       spare set of clothes, personal articles
(vii) first aid box or facilities   yes / no
(viii) Is it possible to make and receive at least one   yes / no
       personal telephone call per day?

       facilities at work too varied to say for any of these } SKIP
       WRITE IN HOW MANY OF 8 ITEMS DO NOT APPLY   TO Q.4

X	X	X	X	X	X	X	X	X	X
Y	Y	Y	Y	Y	Y	Y	Y	Y	Y
0	0	0	0	0	0	0	0	0	0
1	1	1	1	1	1	1	1	1	1
2	2	2	2	2	2	2	2	2	2
3	3	3	3	3	3	3	3	3	3
4	4	4	4	4	4	4	4	4	4
5	5	5	5	5	5	5	5	5	5
6	6	6	6	6	6	6	6	6	6
7	7	7	7	7	7	7	7	7	7
8	8	8	8	8	8	8	8	8	8
9	9	9	9	9	9	9	9	9	9
14	14	14	14	14	14	14	14	14	14
X	X	X	X	X	X	X	X	X	X
Y	Y	Y	Y	Y	Y	Y	Y	Y	Y
0	0	0	0	0	0	0	0	0	0
1	1	1	1	1	1	1	1	1	1
15	15	15	15	15	15	15	15	15	15
X	X	X	X	X	X	X	X	X	X
16	16	16	16	16	16	16	16	16	16

3. FOR THOSE WORKING (MAINLY) INDOORS (Codes 3,4 and 5 in Q.1)
How many of the following does your employer provide at work?
(CODE ALL THAT APPLY)

• (i) sufficient heating in winter for you to be warm at work yes / no
(ii)   tea or coffee (whether charged or not)   yes / no
(iii) indoor flush WC   yes / no
• (iv) facilities for washing and changing, including hot water, yes / no
       soap, towel and mirror
• (v) place to buy lunch or eat own sandwiches (whether used or yes / no
       not)
• (vi) place to keep coat and spare set of clothes without risk yes / no
       of loss
(vii) place for small personal articles which can be locked   yes / no
(viii) first aid box or facilities   yes / no
(ix)   Is it possible to make and receive at least one personal yes / no
       telephone call per day?
(x)   lighting which an individual can increase or reduce,   yes / no
       (e.g. light over work)

       facilities at work too varied to say for any of these
       WRITE IN HOW MANY OF 10 ITEMS DO NOT APPLY

X	X	X	X	X	X	X	X	X	X
Y	Y	Y	Y	Y	Y	Y	Y	Y	Y
0	0	0	0	0	0	0	0	0	0
1	1	1	1	1	1	1	1	1	1
2	2	2	2	2	2	2	2	2	2
3	3	3	3	3	3	3	3	3	3
4	4	4	4	4	4	4	4	4	4
5	5	5	5	5	5	5	5	5	5
6	6	6	6	6	6	6	6	6	6
7	7	7	7	7	7	7	7	7	7
8	8	8	8	8	8	8	8	8	8
9	9	9	9	9	9	9	9	9	9
17	17	17	17	17	17	17	17	17	17
X	X	X	X	X	X	X	X	X	X
Y	Y	Y	Y	Y	Y	Y	Y	Y	Y
0	0	0	0	0	0	0	0	0	0
1	1	1	1	1	1	1	1	1	1
2	2	2	2	2	2	2	2	2	2
3	3	3	3	3	3	3	3	3	3
4	4	4	4	4	4	4	4	4	4
5	5	5	5	5	5	5	5	5	5
18	18	18	18	18	18	18	18	18	18
X	X	X	X	X	X	X	X	X	X
19	19	19	19	19	19	19	19	19	19

4. Roughly for how much of your working time do you stand or walk
about?

X   very little or none
Y   some but less than ¼ of working time
0   at least ¼ but less than ½ of working time
1   at least ½ but not all of working time
2   all or nearly all the time
3   DK

X	X	X	X	X	X	X	X	X	X
Y	Y	Y	Y	Y	Y	Y	Y	Y	Y
0	0	0	0	0	0	0	0	0	0
1	1	1	1	1	1	1	1	1	1
2	2	2	2	2	2	2	2	2	2
3	3	3	3	3	3	3	3	3	3

QUESTION 5
Note that the recent Industrial Employment Act gives employers the responsibility of notifying employees about certain terms of service. Many employees will have received some kind of notification.

QUESTION 6   Whether sick pay
Include only when employer pays **cash** directly to an employee who is sick. Contributions towards medical care costs come under Q. 11. Ideally we would like to have details of sick pay expected and length of time employer is expected to go on paying. (Sometimes a man is paid one proportion of pay for 3 months and then a lower proportion for a further 3 months.) Many informants, however, will not know and you should do your best to get a general idea at least of the **starting level** for the first month, recording underneath more specific information if known.
Sick pay amount What should be entered here is costs paid by employer. Sickness benefit should not be included even though employers contribute towards it. Earnings means **earnings before tax.**

QUESTION 7   Pension
Include any type of occupational pension, contributory or non-contributory, funded or unfunded.

QUESTION 7a   Employee's contribution
Note that we are not attempting to establish what the employer pays, because many informants will not know. We require amount paid (preferably) or per cent of earnings before tax: many schemes are not of the type that the employer pays a fixed proportion of earnings. In these instances, code "None" or "Does not apply", according to the information you are given. When given a percentage note that it may be calculated on basic wages rather than earnings and you should note this so that we can adjust the figure in the office. Estimate the proportion of normal earnings the previous contribution amounts to — correct to nearest percentage point unless respondent names half a percentage point.

QUESTION 7b   Pensionable age
That is, the age at which the pension is first payable.

QUESTION 7c   Years towards pension
Do not count any years towards another pension in a previous employment unless those years have been accepted by the present employer as counting towards the pension from his employment.

QUESTION 7d   Amount of pension
The question refers to the total occupational pension, though part of the cost may be paid by the informant. If the informant knows more details about his entitlement enter information in box (e.g. two-thirds of salary in last 5 years of service).

QUESTION 8   Meal vouchers
You may have to build up towards the average weekly value by asking "How much is each voucher worth?", "How many do you use in an average week?". Generally vouchers are additional to wage or salary but sometimes the employer will include them on a pay slip as part of earnings received. Watch that you do not count their value both here and later under net earnings.

QUESTION 9   Subsidised meals
Meals include drinks that may accompany them though we think it might cause offence to ask this in a formal question. We are interested to learn of anything from subsidised canteen meals to expense account lunches and dinners.

QUESTION 9a   Saving on meals
Note that we are seeking an estimate of the difference between the actual cost to the employee and what he would have spent in the ordinary way if there were no subsidised canteen or restaurant available, or if his work did not allow him to charge the cost of outside meals. We are not seeking an estimate of the real value of the meals. Since some employees may not spend more outside on a poorer meal than they spend inside for a subsidised one, some entries may be "O" shillings.

12a

	Inft	2nd	3rd	4th	5th	6th	INTERVIEWER: INSERT "07" "08" IF 7th, 8th MEMBER	
	01	02	03	04	05	06		
	19 cont	19 cont	19 cont	19 cont	19 cont	19 cont	19 cont	19 cont

How much notice are you entitled to? *
- 4 week
- 5 fortnight
- 6 month
- 7 more than month
- 8 none
- 9 DK

4	4	4	4	4	4	4	4
5	5	5	5	5	5	5	5
6	6	6	6	6	6	6	6
7	7	7	7	7	7	7	7
8	8	8	8	8	8	8	8
9	9	9	9	9	9	9	9
20	20	20	20	20	20	20	20

If you were sick would you receive any money from your employer? *
- yes — ASK Q.6(a)
- no } SKIP TO Q.7
- DK }

X	X	X	X	X	X	X	X
Y	Y	Y	Y	Y	Y	Y	Y
0	0	0	0	0	0	0	0

a) Would the total amount for the first month of sickness, excluding any sickness benefit, amount to –
- 2/3 or more of normal earnings
- between 1/3 and 2/3
- less than 1/3 *
- DK

WRITE IN AMOUNT PER WK/MTH & DURATION IF KNOWN — OFFICE USE ONLY

1	1	1	1	1	1	1	1
2	2	2	2	2	2	2	2
3	3	3	3	3	3	3	3
4	4	4	4	4	4	4	4
21-25	21-25	21-25	21-25	21-25	21-25	21-25	21-25

If you stay in your present job until you retire, will you receive a pension from your employment?
- yes — ASK Q.7(a)
- no } SKIP TO Q.8
- DK }

26	26	26	26	26	26	26	26
X	X	X	X	X	X	X	X
Y	Y	Y	Y	Y	Y	Y	Y
0	0	0	0	0	0	0	0

a) How much (or what proportion of your normal earnings) do you pay? *
WRITE IN AMOUNT (OR %) PER WK/MTH
- none
- does not apply
- DK

OFFICE USE ONLY

1	1	1	1	1	1	1	1
2	2	2	2	2	2	2	2
3	3	3	3	3	3	3	3
27-31	27-31	27-31	27-31	27-31	27-31	27-31	27-31

b) At what age can you take the pension? *
- X 55
- Y 60
- 0 62
- 1 65
- 2 67
- 3 70
- 4 other
- 5 DK

32	32	32	32	32	32	32	32
X	X	X	X	X	X	X	X
Y	Y	Y	Y	Y	Y	Y	Y
0	0	0	0	0	0	0	0
1	1	1	1	1	1	1	1
2	2	2	2	2	2	2	2
3	3	3	3	3	3	3	3
4	4	4	4	4	4	4	4
5	5	5	5	5	5	5	5
33-34	33-34	33-34	33-34	33-34	33-34	33-34	33-34

c) How many years counting towards pension have you served? *

35	35	35	35	35	35	35	35
X	X	X	X	X	X	X	X
Y	Y	Y	Y	Y	Y	Y	Y
0	0	0	0	0	0	0	0
1	1	1	1	1	1	1	1
2	2	2	2	2	2	2	2
36-40	36-40	36-40	36-40	36-40	36-40	36-40	36-40

d) What proportion of your final earnings (i.e. before retirement) do you expect to receive in pension (not counting the state retirement or graduated pension)?
- 2 to full
- 1 but less than 2
- 1 but less than 1
- under 1
- DK

WRITE IN AMOUNT PER WK OR PER YR IF KNOWN

OFFICE USE ONLY

e) Is there a lump sum in addition?
- yes — ASK Q.7(f)
- no } SKIP TO Q.8
- DK }

41	41	41	41	41	41	41	41
X	X	X	X	X	X	X	X
Y	Y	Y	Y	Y	Y	Y	Y
0	0	0	0	0	0	0	0
42-46	42-46	42-46	42-46	42-46	42-46	42-46	42-46

f) How much (what proportion of your final year's earnings) is in a lump sum?
WRITE IN AMOUNT OR %

OFFICE USE ONLY

Do you receive meal vouchers from your employer that are additional to your wage/salary? *
- yes — ASK Q.8(a)
- no } SKIP TO Q.9
- DK }

47	47	47	47	47	47	47	47
X	X	X	X	X	X	X	X
Y	Y	Y	Y	Y	Y	Y	Y
0	0	0	0	0	0	0	0
48-49	48-49	48-49	48-49	48-49	48-49	48-49	48-49

a) How much are they worth to you in an average working week?
ENTER WEEKLY VALUE IN SHILLINGS

| 50 | 50 | 50 | 50 | 50 | 50 | 50 | 50 |

Do you ever have any meals
- provided by your employer below ordinary restaurant prices? } ASK
- paid for on an account chargeable to your employer? * } Q.9(a)
- neither provided cheaply nor paid for
- DK } SKIP TO Q.10

X	X	X	X	X	X	X	X
Y	Y	Y	Y	Y	Y	Y	Y
0	0	0	0	0	0	0	0
1	1	1	1	1	1	1	1
51-52	51-52	51-52	51-52	51-52	51-52	51-52	51-52

a) How much do you think this saves you in an average working week if otherwise you had to buy all your meals in the ordinary way for yourself? *
ENTER WEEKLY VALUE IN SHILLINGS

QUESTION 10   Personal use

Includes transport to and from work.

QUESTION 10a   Normal repairs

Excludes repairs caused by negligence of informant or family. **Make and type** — e.g. Vauxhall Cresta, Saloon or Morris 15 cwt. van. The description should be enough for us to look up its second-hand value as a check on the value.

QUESTION 10d   Driver

This is a polite way of ascertaining whether the car is chauffeur-driven. Thus Code X includes self, family, friends and other employees driving for pleasure and not because they are paid to drive the respondent around.

QUESTION 11   Other benefits

Read the prompts slowly: they are carefully drafted to cover the perks of both senior and junior staff. **The goods** may vary from free or subsidised coal given to miners to discounts on goods bought or free vegetables, seeds or seedlings. Don't hesitate to pursue it further according to occupations of informants. **Transport** may be free leisure travel given to railway or bus employees or paid holidays given to senior executives. Note this section is supplementary to the use of a vehicle in Q. 10. **Medical expenses** may be premiums to insurance agencies for private medical care or the direct payment of doctors' bills. **Education** can range from free tennis lessons or typing lessons to payment of public school fees. **Shares in the company** can be given free or below market value.

ENCOURAGE THE INFORMANT to add items under the various headings together and give time for this to be done. We are interested to know what it would cost to buy these things privately even though the employee might not have chosen to do so (e.g. the employee might have used the Health Service if his employer did not pay for him to have private medical care).

"How much a year are these things worth altogether?"

The point here is that some kinds of entries will be money saved, say, on goods and services which the informant would have had to pay for, whereas other entries will involve things he would never have afforded or thought about. Our aim is to discover what equivalent in extra income would be needed if he did the same things but had to bear the full cost himself.

QUESTION 13   Satisfaction with job

The questions are laid out in a form which equally encourage positive or negative answers. You may shorten the question to " Are you satisfied or dissatisfied with ——" providing the informant seems to be genuinely weighing the alternatives.

Facilities at work means facilities as asked under Q. 3 earlier.

13a

10. Have you the use sometimes for personal purposes of a car or van owned by your employer? *

              yes   ASK Q.10(a)
              no   SKIP TO Q.11
              DK

(a) Does your employer pay
    – road tax
    – insurance
    – petrol
    – normal repairs
    – none of above

(b) What is the vehicle's

(i) approximate current value **(ii)** make and type **(iii)** year **(iv)** m.p.g.?

WRITE IN ANSWERS

    _____ 19 ____
    _____ 19 ____
    _____ 19 ____

(c) What proportion of the mileage do you use for personal purposes (including transport to work)? And roughly how many miles would that be in a year?

WRITE IN ANSWER

    _____ % _____ miles
    _____ % _____ miles   OFFICE USE ONLY
    _____ % _____ miles

(d) Do you drive it yourself when using it for personal purposes or does another employee of the firm (paid by the firm) drive it?
    self or family
    other employee

11. Does your employer provide you with anything else which is of value to you which you have not already told me about?

    any goods free or at reduced prices (e.g. free/concessionary coal or railway tickets)
    travel other than for work
    medical expenses (including medical insurance)
    educational expenses – for your children
PROMPT   educational expenses – for yourself
    shares or options to purchase shares
    life insurance
    loans or grants towards purchase of car
    other (SPECIFY) _____
    none of these
IF ANY RECORDED
Roughly how much a year are these things worth to you altogether? I mean, how much more would you have to spend if you had bought the same things yourself?

WRITE IN ESTIMATES FOR ITEMS   ENTER TOTAL ANNUAL ESTIMATE IN £'s

12. Are you a member of a Trade Union or a professional association?
    yes, trade union
    yes, professional association
    no
    DK

13. Can I just ask whether you are satisfied or dissatisfied with some of the things connected with your work – *

(a) Are you satisfied / neither satisfied nor dissatisfied / or dissatisfied – with the pay? DK

(b) Are you satisfied / neither satisfied nor dissatisfied / or dissatisfied – with facilities at work (e.g. heating, canteen)? DK

(c) Are you satisfied / neither satisfied or dissatisfied / or dissatisfied – with the security of the job (I mean amount of notice and prospect of keeping job)? DK

(d) Are you satisfied / neither satisfied nor dissatisfied / or dissatisfied – with the job itself? DK   SKIP TO NEXT SECTION

Inft	2nd	3rd	4th	5th	6th	7	8	9	10
53	53	53	53	53	53	53	53	53	53
X	X	X	X	X	X	X	X	X	X
Y	Y	Y	Y	Y	Y	Y	Y	Y	Y
O	O	O	O	O	O	O	O	O	O
1	1	1	1	1	1	1	1	1	1
2	2	2	2	2	2	2	2	2	2
3	3	3	3	3	3	3	3	3	3
4	4	4	4	4	4	4	4	4	4
5	5	5	5	5	5	5	5	5	5
54-56	54-56	54-56	54-56	54-56	54-56	5456	5456	5456	5456
X	X	X	X	X	X	X	X	X	X
Y	Y	Y	Y	Y	Y	Y	Y	Y	Y
57	57	57	57	57	57	57	57	57	57
X	X	X	X	X	X	X	X	X	X
Y	Y	Y	Y	Y	Y	Y	Y	Y	Y
0	0	0	0	0	0	0	0	0	0
1	1	1	1	1	1	1	1	1	1
2	2	2	2	2	2	2	2	2	2
3	3	3	3	3	3	3	3	3	3
4	4	4	4	4	4	4	4	4	4
5	5	5	5	5	5	5	5	5	5
6	6	6	6	6	6	6	6	6	6
9	9	9	9	9	9	9	9	9	9
58-61	58-61	58-61	58-61	58-61	58-61	5861	5861	5861	5861
62	62	62	62	62	62	62	62	62	62
X	X	X	X	X	X	X	X	X	X
Y	Y	Y	Y	Y	Y	Y	Y	Y	Y
0	0	0	0	0	0	0	0	0	0
1	1	1	1	1	1	1	1	1	1
63	63	63	63	63	63	63	63	63	63
X	X	X	X	X	X	X	X	X	X
Y	Y	Y	Y	Y	Y	Y	Y	Y	Y
0	0	0	0	0	0	0	0	0	0
1	1	1	1	1	1	1	1	1	1
2	2	2	2	2	2	2	2	2	2
3	3	3	3	3	3	3	3	3	3
4	4	4	4	4	4	4	4	4	4
5	5	5	5	5	5	5	5	5	5
6	6	6	6	6	6	6	6	6	6
7	7	7	7	7	7	7	7	7	7
8	8	8	8	8	8	8	8	8	8
9	9	9	9	9	9	9	9	9	9
64	64	64	64	64	64	64	64	64	64
X	X	X	X	X	X	X	X	X	X
Y	Y	Y	Y	Y	Y	Y	Y	Y	Y
0	0	0	0	0	0	0	0	0	0
1	1	1	1	1	1	1	1	1	1

13

QUESTION 16   Pension

Only include if a pension scheme has been worked out in relation to the business, or is available from an insurance company or another body, because of the nature of the business or self-employment. Note that provision is made in a series of questions on this page for entries to be made in the office (Qs 16a, 16b, 17a, 18c). Much depends, however, on the information you can provide in boxes on the left, leaving us to make necessary calculations.

QUESTION 19   Cheap goods and services

You should normally expect positive answers. A garage-owner may be able to purchase a car and run it well below ordinary retail prices. A grocer will obtain household stores cheaply. An insurance company sometimes reduces certain premiums. A small-holder may receive supplies cheaply in exchange for produce at market costs. There are exchange arrangements between people in different trades. It will, of course, be difficult to explore all these things properly but Q. 19a conveys our object and you should probe carefully whenever possible.

QUESTION 20   Tax savings because of combined home and business

The real incomes of many self-employed persons tend to be under-estimated. Their difficulties are not always easy to explain to the tax authorities and in practice low real incomes and insecure incomes are compensated because part of housing and other costs can be offset against tax. Ask the questions openly and straightforwardly.

If informants seem doubtful about answering, say: "We have nothing at all to do with the tax people. We know it is difficult for you to divide costs between the business and yourself. But we also know that even if they have more problems many self-employed persons can live a little more cheaply than people getting a salary. I wonder whether you'd mind guessing how much more cheaply — I mean because of savings of tax".

14a

1	2	3	4	5	6	7	8	9

FOR THE SELF-EMPLOYED ONLY

14. Do you work indoors or outdoors?
mainly outdoors
mainly indoors
about as much indoors as outdoors

15. Roughly for how much of your working time do you stand or walk about?
very little
some but less than ¼ of working time
→ at least ¼ but less than ½ working time
all or nearly all the time
DK
x at least ½ (code 6)

16. Do you have provision for a private pension through your employment? yes ASK Q.16(a)
no } SKIP TO Q.17
DK }

(a) How much, or what proportion of your normal earnings, do you pay?
WRITE IN AMOUNT (OR %) PER WEEK/MONTH
OFFICE USE ONLY

(b) What proportion of your final earnings (i.e. before retirement) do you expect to receive in pension (not counting the State pension) and in a lump sum?
¾ to full
½ but less than ¾
¼ but less than ½
under ¼
DK
WRITE IN AMOUNT PER WK/YR AND LUMP SUM IF KNOWN
OFFICE USE ONLY

17. Have you made private provision for cash benefits in sickness? yes ASK Q.17(a)
no } SKIP TO Q.18
DK }

(a) How much do you expect to receive for the first month of sickness?
WRITE IN AMOUNT (OR %) AND DURATION IF KNOWN
OFFICE USE ONLY

18. Does your business include a car or vehicle which you or a member of the family are able to use sometimes yes ASK Q.18(a)
for personal purposes? no } SKIP TO Q.19
DK }

(a) Does your business pay for
road tax
insurance
petrol
normal repairs
none of above
CODE ALL THAT APPLY

(b) What is the vehicle's
(i) approximate current value (ii) make and type (iii) year (iv) m.p.g.
19

(c) What proportion of the mileage do you use for personal purposes (including transport to work)? And roughly how many miles would that be in a year?
WRITE IN ANSWER ___ % ___ miles OFFICE USE

19. Because of your business are you able to buy anything more cheaply - I mean goods and services for yourself and your family. For example -
travel other than for work
medical expenses (or insurance)
educational expenses for children
educational expenses for self
other (SPECIFY)

(a) IF ANY RECORDED Roughly how much a year are these worth to you altogether? I mean how much more would you have had to spend if you had bought everything outside your business?
WRITE IN APPROX ANNUAL AMT IN £'s

20. Is your home and business in the same premises? yes ASK Q.20(a)
no SKIP TO NEXT SECTION

(a) Are you able to offset against tax any of your (family's) accommodation, lighting or heating, telephone charges, etc? yes ASK Q.20(b)
no } SKIP TO NEXT SECTION
DK } NEXT SECTION

(b) Roughly how much a year would you say this helped you?
WRITE AMOUNT IN £'s

	Inft	2nd	3rd	4th	INTERVIEWER: CODE 05, 06, etc IF 5th,6th etc MEMBER OF HOUSEHOLD
	10-11	10-11	10-11	10-11	10-11 10-11
	01	02	03	04	
	12	12	12	12	12 ·12
	X	X	X	X	X X
	Y	Y	Y	Y	Y Y
	0	0	0	0	0 0
	1	1	1	1	1 1
	2	2	2	2	2 2
	3	3	3	3	3 3
	4	4	4	4	4 4
	5	5	5	5	5 5
	13	13	13	13	13 13
	X	X	X	X	X X
	Y	Y	Y	Y	Y Y
	0	0	0	0	0 0
	14-18	14-18	14-18	14-18	14-18 14-18
	£ s	£ s	£ s	£ s	£ s £ s
	19	19	19	19	19 19
	X	X	X	X	X X
	Y	Y	Y	Y	Y Y
	0	0	0	0	0 0
	1	1	1	1	1 1
	2	2	2	2	2 2
	20-24	20-24	20-24	20-24	20-24 20-24
	£ s	£ s	£ s	£ s	£ s £ s
	25	25	25	25	25 25
	X	X	X	X	X X
	Y	Y	Y	Y	Y Y
	0	0	0	0	0 0
	26-30	26-30	26-30	26-30	26-30 26-30
	£ s	£ s	£ s	£ s	£ s £ s
	31	31	31	31	31 31
	X	X	X	X	X X
	Y	Y	Y	Y	Y Y
	0	0	0	0	0 0
	1	1	1	1	1 1
	2	2	2	2	2 2
	3	3	3	3	3 3
	4	4	4	4	4 4
	5	5	5	5	5 5
	32-36	32-36	32-36	32-36	32-36 32-36
	£ s	£ s	£ s	£ s	£ s £ s
	37	37	37	37	37 37
	X	X	X	X	X X
	Y	Y	Y	Y	Y Y
	0	0	0	0	0 0
	1	1	1	1	1 1
	2	2	2	2	2 2
	38-40	38-40	38-40	38-40	38-40 38-40
	£	£	£	£	£ £
	41	41	41	41	41 41
	X	X	X	X	X X
	Y	Y	Y	Y	Y Y
	0	0	0	0	0 0
	1	1	1	1	1 1
	2	2	2	2	2 2
	42-44	42-44	42-44	42-44	42-44 42-44
	£	£	£	£	£ £

14

CURRENT MONETARY INCOME

General

This section asks questions in turn of the employed, the self-employed and then everyone, including those who are not employed. Our object is to obtain reliable estimates of income, before and after tax, for each income unit in the household, both for " last week " and " the last 12 months "

Income Unit

This is any person aged 15 or over, or if in full-time education any person aged 19 or over, together with wife or husband (if she or he has one) and children under 15 (or aged 16-18 if in full-time education), if any. According to this definition a man, wife, and children aged under 15 count as one income unit, but a middle-aged widow and a son who is a university student, or an elderly widow and a single daughter of 40, count as two income units. A household consisting of man and wife with three single children who are all over 15 years of age and who are at work counts as four income units.

Allocating Income

Usually amounts of income can be entered in the appropriate column, according to the person receiving it. Do not enter any income twice. Do not, for example, enter a particular amount both for the wife and the husband. Nor need you split up any amount part of which is payable for a dependent wife or child. Thus, do not attempt to divide up the total of family allowances; enter the total in the wife's column and enter an amount for sickness benefit, say, even if it includes sums for the wife and children, in the husband's column (if indeed it is he who receives it).

Gross and Net

In the first question you carefully ask for the last pay net of deductions and go on in the second question to establish what these deductions are. The answers to both questions effectively give gross and net earnings for the last period for which pay was received and you can build up further information in the questions that follow. You should be conscious of this distinction throughout the section. It will not always be possible to get information both for income after tax and income before tax. Remember that if you cannot get an answer for one you may be able to get it for the other. Make a note whenever you can. We can calculate in the office.

Last 12 months

Though you start by finding what was the last amount of pay received it is very important also to find what was the average pay during the previous 12 months and gradually build up the total income received by the income unit and the household in those months. You have already filled in a work-record and this will help you to answer several of the questions in the section.

QUESTION 1 Last earnings

Remember to check earnings for each member of the household, even those of a wife who had a job for only a few weeks in the year, a young son who works only on Saturdays, and a retired man with a part-time job. Second or subsidiary earnings are dealt with in Q. 14. Note that each digit is ruled off from the next. Insert " O " in any column which does not apply. Please note also that we have allowed wider columns on these income pages so that you have enough room to write in figures. But note that you will have to indicate which member of the household received any income if you are obliged to use a fifth or sixth column.

QUESTION 2 Deductions

Don't forget that a total is better than nothing. If the informant is uncertain say, " I believe it is on your pay slip " and encourage him or her to check. We have asked you to put a tick if in fact you are shown a slip or the informant reads off the amounts. As before, the small boxes on the left are for you to identify the member of the household: " Inf." " 2nd " " 3rd ", etc.

National Insurance contributions

A male employee ordinarily pays 15s. 8d. and a female employee 13s. 2d. per week, although note that a married women can elect to pay only 7d. per week to cover industrial injuries benefits. Boys under 18 pay 10s. 1d. and girls 8s. 5d. per week. Persons over 18 who are contracted out of the graduated pension scheme pay a higher flat rate insurance contribution of 18s. 1d. (men), 14s. 8d. (women).

Graduated pension contributions

The employee contributes 4¼ per cent of each pound of gross weekly earnings between the ninth and the eighteenth, i.e. approximately 11¾d. for each of these pounds, plus ⅓ per cent for each pound between the 19th and the 30th, i.e. rather more than 1d. for each of these pounds. In fact a man with gross weekly earnings of £9 pays nothing, one with £13 pays 4s. 0d., one with £21 pays 9s. 0d., and one with £30, 9s. 9d. About one person in every five, however, is contracted out of the graduated pension scheme, but such persons nonetheless pay ⅓ per cent on each pound of gross earnings between the ninth and the 30th, or a maximum of 2s. 1d.

QUESTION 3 Highest and lowest

Check the number of weeks worked by turning up the work record. Some people's earnings will have varied only in one or two weeks of the year and it will not be difficult for you to establish an average in (b). Remember Q. 3(b) is very important. Other people's earnings may have varied widely, either because of changes of job or variations in overtime. Do not include variations due to holidays or sickness. If it is difficult to arrive at an average write in the box or in the margins, e.g. 10 weeks @ £15 10s., six weeks @ £18 15s. and 23 weeks @ £24 11s. We will work out the rest. Do not include weeks of holiday or sickness, which are explored later.

QUESTION 4 Bonuses

If a commission or bonus has been included in Q. 3 do not now amend the answer to that question. If the information is given for the first time write the amount in the box and also strike out " Before " or " After " Tax as appropriate.

15a

C.I.C.

					0	6

Inft	2nd	3rd	4th		INTERVIEWER: CODE 05, 06, etc IF 5th, 6th,etc MEMBER OF HOUSEHOLD
10-11	10-11	10-11	10-11	10-11	10-11
01	02	03	04		
12	12	12	12	12	12
1 2 3 4	1 2 3 4	1 2 3 4	1 2 3 4	1 2 3 4	1 2 3 4
7 8 9	7 8 9	7 8 9	7 8 9	7 8 9	7 8 9
13-17 £ s	13-17 £ s	13-17 £ s	13-17 £ s	13-17 £ s	13-17 £ s

SECTION IV   CURRENT MONETARY INCOME

FOR THOSE IN PAID EMPLOYMENT LAST WEEK OR AT LEAST ONE WEEK DURING PREVIOUS 52 WEEKS (WORK RECORD p.7)

CODE MEMBERSHIP OF INCOME UNIT

employed   ASK Q.1
self-employed   SKIP TO Q.11
not employed during year SKIP TO Q.15

1. How much did you receive in wages or salary the last time you were paid, including overtime, bonus, commission, tips, etc. and after all deductions from pay, such as income tax and national insurance - I mean total take-home pay from your main occupation? If you received a repayment of income tax don't count that in. *

SHOW FLASHCARD 2 ONLY IF NECESSARY. WRITE EXACT AMOUNT WHERE POSSIBLE.
                                        DK
                                        Does Not Apply

(a) What period did this cover?   week
                                   month
                                   other (SPECIFY)____
(b) How long ago was the last day   less than a month
which this period covered?   1 month and less than 3 months
                                   3 months and less than 6 months
                                   6 months and less than 12 months

2. How much was deducted
   for *   £ s £ s £ s £ s
- Income tax
- national insurance and
  grad. pension contribs.*   total
- other things such as sports   deductions:
  clubs, subscriptions to   amount
  hospitals, private pension   (INSERT
  payments   "0" IF NONE)
  SPECIFY   TICK IF
                                                  DOCUMENTS
                                                  SEEN
CHECK So your last pay before
tax amounted altogether to:____

3. You have already told me you have had   (FROM WORK RECORD)
weeks in work in the last 12 months. Some people's pay varies."
Can you tell me what was your highest   rate of pay did not vary SKIP
pay and what was your lowest pay in   to Q.4
those weeks?   highest ASK Q.3(a)

(a) IF HIGHEST AND LOWEST. Can you   lowest ASK Q. 3(a)
    tell me why your earnings have varied -
through change of job, overtime or anything else?
                                       CODE ONE ONLY
WRITE IN ANSWER AND CODE MAIN REASON ----   change of job
                                             rise in pay
                                             overtime
                                             short working wk
                                             other
(b) What would you say was your average (take-home) pay (per week or
per month) for those weeks of work, taking the year as a whole?

(c) IF WEEKLY PAID. What is your basic weekly rate of pay - I mean
before any deductions?
                                       amount
                                       DK
                                       Does Not Apply

4. Have you received any additions to pay (at
   Christmas) or occasional commissions or bonuses yes ASK Q.4(a)
that you haven't already included in what you have no } SKIP TO Q.5
told me?   DK }
(a) How much extra did you get like this during the last 52 weeks?

WRITE IN ANSWER
                    before/after tax
                    before/after tax

18 X Y O	18 X Y O	18 X Y O	18 X Y O	18 X Y O	18 X Y O
1 2 3 4	1 2 3 4	1 2 3 4	1 2 3 4	1 2 3 4	1 2 3 4
19-23 £ s	19-23 £ s	19-23 £ s	19-23 £ s	19-23 £ s	19-23 £ s
29-33 £ s	29-33 £ s	29-33 £ s	29-33 £ s	29-33 £ s	29-33 £ s
34-38 £ s	34-38 £ s	34-38 £ s	34-38 £ s	34-38 £ s	34-38 £ s
39 X Y O I 2	39 X Y O I 2	39 X Y O I 2	39 X Y O I 2	39 X Y O I 2	39 X Y O I 2
40-44 £ s	40-44 £ s	40-44 £ s	40-44 £ s	40-44 £ s	40-44 £ s
45-48 £ s	45-48 £ s	45-48 £ s	45-48 £ s	45-48 £ s	45-48 £ s
49 X Y O	49 X Y O	49 X Y O	49 X Y O	49 X Y O	49 X Y O

15

QUESTION 8

Obtain an estimate of total cost by the normal transport used. Some people who drive cars will offer their estimate of real cost but in such cases write in as indicated the average weekly mileage to and from work (not during work). In other instances assume 6d. per mile for all small cars (i.e. under 12 h.p.) and 8d. per mile for larger vehicles.

5 miles @ 6d. = 2s. 6d.	5 miles @ 8d. = 3s. 4d.
10 miles @ 6d. = 5s. 0d.	10 miles @ 8d. = 6s. 8d.
50 miles @ 6d. = 25s. 0d.	50 miles @ 8d. = 33s. 4d.
100 miles @ 6d. = 50s. 0d.	100 miles @ 8d. = 66s. 8d.

QUESTION 9 Holiday pay

Be careful not to include pay received simultaneously with holiday pay for any week of work. Remember that many wage earners only receive the basic wage during holidays, which is usually much lower than average earnings.

QUESTION 10 Sick pay

There are several practices. (1) Some employers (e.g. public services) automatically deduct national insurance sickness benefit for the worker and his dependants from pay during sickness (or sometimes expect him to report what sickness benefit he receives so that it may be deducted from later amounts of sick pay or even from the first weeks of earnings after recovery from sickness). (2) Others (mainly smaller private firms) deduct only the sickness benefit for the worker, ignoring what he may get for his dependants. (3) Still others deduct nothing for any sickness benefit for which a worker may be eligible. In the last two cases it might seem that the worker will be better off in sickness than at work. This is true for some, particularly salaried earners, but remember that if any employer pays anything to a wage-earner in sickness rarely does it exceed the basic wage. His average earnings may be much higher. (4) When the level of sick pay is small no deductions may be made for any sickness benefit.
Changes in sick pay after the first weeks

In rare instances of persons who have been sick more than a few weeks the rate of sick pay will have changed. If the average is difficult to estimate write in the amounts thus: 4 weeks @ £10, 4 @ £5 10s., etc. After deductions of tax, etc. Note if only the amount of pay before deductions is known.

QUESTION 11 Income of self-employed

The income of the self-employed is sometimes difficult to ascertain. Four alternative methods of questioning that have been found to be helpful in previous research are listed. Our first aim is to find the figure for annual income before tax. Thus Q. 11 A(iv) is the crucial one and if you can get the answer to this do not press unduly for the answers to the preceding questions, but they are helpful in establishing that (iv) is in fact the figure you want. The alternative aim (if you cannot achieve the first) is to seek the amount obtained from the business, either Method B — net profit including money taken out for own use, or Method C, the sums actually taken out for personal use. Method D should only be tried if all else fails, and frankly, is not of much help. An accurate figure for income is important and you should if necessary take time to establish it. Method D " Turnover " = total receipts from sale of goods and services, less any discount allowed.

16a

	1nft	2nd	3rd	4th	INTERVIEWER: CODE 05, 06, etc. IF 5th, 6th

5. Income tax is usually deducted from your pay. Have you received a repayment of tax in the last 12 months? yes ASK Q. 5(a) / no, DK } SKIP TO Q.6

(a) How much altogether? (TICK IF DOCUMENTS SEEN ☐)

6. Did you pay any income tax or surtax direct to the tax authorities last year? yes ASK Q.6(a) / no, DK } SKIP TO Q.7

(a) How much altogether? (TICK IF DOCUMENTS SEEN ☐)

7. Have you any expenses in going to work which are allowed for tax purposes, such as special clothing, laundry or use of equipment?
(a) How much a week are these expenses? yes ASK Q.7(a) / no, DK } SKIP TO Q.8

ADD SUB-ITEMS HERE IF NECESSARY
laundry / special clothing / use of tools / other (SPECIFY)   estimated total per week in shillings

8. How much does it cost you to travel to and from work each week? (NOTE MILEAGE IF CAR _____)* AMOUNT IN SHILLINGS WRITE "0" IF NOTHING

9. You have told me you had _____ weeks (FROM WORK RECORD) of paid holiday last year. How much pay after deductions did you receive on average per week? same as average earnings WRITE "0" IF NOTHING average per week

10. FOR THOSE WITH ONE OR MORE WEEKS SICKNESS IN PREVIOUS 12 MONTHS You've told me you had _____ weeks (FROM WORK RECORD) of sickness. How much pay, after deductions, did you receive on average per week? I mean not including any sickness benefit.* same as average earnings average per week

EMPLOYED - SKIP TO Q.14

11. ASK SELF-EMPLOYED USE APPROPRIATE METHOD *

METHOD A How much was your income for the most recent 12 months period for which you can give the income before tax or the profit from the business? I mean the amount assessed for tax after deducting depreciation allowances and business or practice expenses from the total. DK, DNA } TRY METHOD B

(i) What was the total income before allowance and tax? £
(ii) How much depreciation?
(iii) How much business or practice expenses were allowable for tax purposes?
* (iv) So the net assessable income was
(v) 12 months period FROM/TO

METHOD B How much net profit before tax do you get from the business including money taken out for your own use, after deducting all expenses and wages? DK, DNA } TRY METHOD C

12 months period FROM/TO

(cont/...)

16

QUESTION 12   Income tax

The informant will often know the approximate amount because profits or income from business fall under Schedule D. But we ask 12b to check that the informant is not including tax which is allowed for in other questions. For example, elsewhere we establish net income from dividends, but if **here** the informant adds £100, say, to the figure for tax to take account of tax on dividends deducted at source, we risk deducting the £100 **twice by** deducting it here as well. You should be warned that for this and other reasons the net income of the self-employed tends to be underestimated. **Weekly National Insurance contribution**

Self-employed men pay 21s. per week. Self-employed women pay 17s. 3d. per week. Boys and girls under 18 pay 11s. 10d. and 10s. 1d. respectively.

QUESTION 13   Fluctuation in Income

The self-employed will often have an income that fluctuates throughout the year — especially those on low incomes. For example, the scrap dealer or stall-holder may not do as well in the winter as he does in the summer. The professional architect and the free-lance photographer may be paid at very irregular intervals. We are particularly interested in fluctuations which may produce hardship for a household which is usually prosperous. But remember that though **income** may fluctuate (e.g. in winter, for a shop-keeper or free-lance interviewer the same amounts per month may be drawn out of the bank or spent. Living standards are not necessarily affected.

17a

11. (cont)

METHOD C   Do you draw sums of money regularly from the business for your own use?   DK } TRY METHOD D   DNA }

(I) How much do you usually take out?   £   £   £   £
(II) How often is that?
(III) So the total taken out for your own use in the past 12 months was
(IV) What was the remaining profit from the business?
(V) So the net assessable income before tax was

METHOD D   What was the total turnover* of the business during the most recent period of 12 months for which you have figures?   £   £   £   £

12 months period FROM/TO _____

OFFICE USE ONLY   net assessable income before tax

12.   FOR SELF-EMPLOYED ONLY
Have you paid any income tax   X yes   ASK Q.12(a)
or surtax in the last 12 months?   Y no }   SKIP TO Q.13
                                    O DK }
                                    I Does Not Apply SKIP TO Q.14

                                       £   £   £   £

(a) How much   Income tax?
               surtax?
(b) Does this income tax include amounts deducted at source on income, such as share dividends or a pension?
               Amount, if any
(c) Did you receive any refunds of income tax or surtax in the last 12 months?
               Amount income tax, if any
               Amount surtax, if any
(d) What is your weekly National Insurance contribution? *

OFFICE USE ONLY   net annual income after tax

13.   FOR SELF-EMPLOYED ONLY
Has your income fluctuated   X yes, considerably } ASK Q.13(a)
in the last 12 months?   Y yes, a little   }
                               O no }
                               I DK } SKIP TO Q.14
                               2 Does Not Apply

(a) Why has it varied?

WRITE IN ANSWER AND CODE MAIN REASON   CODE ONE ONLY
                                            change of job
                                            seasonal variation
                                            varying fortunes of business
                                            other

(b) Has this affected your standard of living? Have you experienced any period of hardship in these 12 months?

WRITE IN ANSWER AND CODE IF HARDSHIP   CODE ONE ONLY
                                            standard affected
                                            – yes, hardship
                                            – no hardship
                                            – DK, hardship
                                            standard not affected
                                            DK

	1nft	2nd	3rd	4th	INTERVIEWER: CODE 05, 06, etc, IF 5th, 6th MEMBERS OF HOUSEHOLD
	12-15	12-15	12-15	12-15	12-15	12-15
	16	16	16	16	16	16
	X	X	X	X	X	X
	Y	Y	Y	Y	Y	Y
	O	O	O	O	O	O
	I	I	I	I	I	I
	21-24	21-24	21-24	21-24	21-24	21-24
	25	25	25	25	25	25
	X	X	X	X	X	X
	Y	Y	Y	Y	Y	Y
	O	O	O	O	O	O
	I	I	I	I	I	I
	2	2	2	2	2	2
	5	5	5	5	5	5
	6	6	6	6	6	6
	7	7	7	7	7	7
	8	8	8	8	8	8
	26	26	26	26	26	26
	X	X	X	X	X	X
	Y	Y	Y	Y	Y	Y
	O	O	O	O	O	O
	I	I	I	I	I	I
	2	2	2	2	2	2

QUESTION 14   Second job

This will have been established in the earlier section on Employment. Repeat the question because earnings from subsidiary occupations tend to be forgotten. For example, painters and decorators may have done one remunerative weekend job for a few weeks several months earlier in the year. A gardener may have done some intensive paid work for various local people in the evenings and weekends of the summer months. Or a university lecturer may have had a remunerative consultancy or a series of well-paid broadcasts at some point in the year. **Remember that extra earnings from a source other than usual employment may not be thought of as a second job.** You should probe for all kinds of additional earnings, depending on the nature of the usual employment.

QUESTION 15

This is laid out as concisely as possible on one page and you are asked to ring 01, 02, 03, etc., as appropriate and then to enter the rates per week and amounts below, carefully writing in the code " 01 " (i.e. Family Allowances) " 02 " (i.e. Retirement Pension) and so on so that we are clearly aware of the allowances to which the amounts refer.

Amounts will sometimes be joint — e.g. retirement pension for man and wife — or will be for several members of the household — e.g. sickness benefit for man and wife and children. In these instances the amount should be entered (if necessary, after the interview) in **one column** only, under that member of household receiving the payment. Wherever possible encourage informants (especially when elderly) to show you the allowance or pension book.

CODE 01 Family Allowances

	First child	Second	Third	Fourth & subsequent
up to April 1968	nil	8s.	10s.	15s.
after April 1968	nil	15s.	17s.	17s.

counting children under 15 or up to 19 if still in full-time education or college or an apprentice on low wages.

CODE 02   Retirement Pension

Note that the actual amounts vary widely. Increased pensions are paid if retirement is deferred. There are now in addition small graduated state pensions (averaging about 3s.) and pensions may be reduced because of earnings or a deficient contribution record. Note that some of these points also apply to other benefits. Pensions and supplementary benefits can be combined in a single payment. You will be prompting for supplementary benefit and wherever possible we should like you to list the amount separately (as well as the fact that it is being received). But whenever the rate given to you exceeds the standard rate below you should check the reason.

Single person (husband)	£4 10s. 0d.
Wife's income	£2 16s. 0d.
1st dependent child	£1 5s. 0d.
2nd dependent child	17s. 0d.

CODE 03   Standard Widow's Pension

Note: not the widow's allowance which is paid for the first 26 weeks after widowhood.

Widow or widowed mother	£4 10s. 0d.
1st dependent child	£2 2s. 6d.
2nd child	£1 14s. 6d.
3rd and subsequent child	£1 12s. 6d.

Depending on the circumstances of the death of the husband (armed service and so on) widows' pensions may differ in size. Note that family allowances are received in addition to dependent children's allowances.

Widow's Allowance: Widow £6 7s., children as for widow's pension

CODE 04 and 05 Sickness Benefit and Unemployment Benefit

Sickness benefit is often paid for periods other than a week. Find what was the last payment and for how many days (excluding Sundays). A payment for 6 days, excluding Sunday, makes up a " week's " benefit. Note that an earnings-related supplement may be paid in addition to the flat rate benefits listed below. Moreover, these benefit rates depend on the contribution record.

Single person	£4 10s. 0d.
Married woman	£2 16s. 0d.
1st dependent child	£1 5s. 0d.
Each subsequent child	17s. 0d.

CODE 06   Supplementary Benefit

The former " national assistance ". Rent is sometimes paid direct to the landlord by the Supplementary Benefits Commission. There is a check later that the amount is known and counted as income.

CODE 07   Industrial Injury Benefit

£6 7s. 0d. (with additions for dependants) is payable for the first 26 weeks after injury after which the injured person goes before a Board to have his injury assessed for an individual disablement pension.

CODES 08 and 09   Industrial and Disablement Pensions

The 100 per cent rate is £7 12s. 0d. (with additions for dependants). **CODE 09:** Note that these are war pensions, not service pensions included under occupational pensions later in Q. 19.

CODE 10   Maternity Allowance

The standard rate of maternity allowance is £4 a week. It is paid to women who have been paying full national insurance contributions. It begins 11 weeks before the expected confinement and ends after the sixth week following it.

CODE 11   Maternity Grant

This grant is £22 either for home or hospital confinement.

CODE 12   Single Grant

This is officially described as an exceptional needs grant. The Ministry of Social Security has replaced the former National Assistance Board and you may need to explain " a grant from the Assistance ". Probe carefully for this for all income units who are not employed, whether or not they receive supplementary benefit. A large number of people obtain single grants, e.g. for spectacles or dentures, even though they are not normally eligible to receive supplementary benefit. Note also that since you are asking about a period of 12 months there will be instances of people now in work who obtained a grant at an earlier point in the year.

18a

14. FOR ALL EMPLOYED AND SELF-EMPLOYED
(a) Can you tell me how much you earned   * not earning from second job
In a second job or in casual earnings   last wk
last week?   amount before/after tax
                                                              last wk

(b) How much would you say you earned altogether for a second job or in
casual and part-time earnings during the last 12 months — whether or not
you had such earnings last week? I mean in addition
to earnings you told me about earlier, and including   nothing
fees and consultancies, and deducting any expenses.   WRITE IN
                                                  ESTIMATED AMOUNT
                                              before/after tax

15. FOR ALL
Now I'd like to ask about pensions, allowances or benefits from the
Government. Do you receive or have you received in the last 12 months a

38–	01	Family allowance
50–	02	Retirement (old age) pension
62–	03	Widows pension or allowance (including war and widowed mother)
C08–12	* 04	Sickness benefit
C08–24	05	Unemployment benefit
C08–36	* 06	Supplementary benefit (national assistance)
C08–48	07	Industrial injury benefit
C08–60	08	Industrial disablement pension
C09–12	09	War disability pension
C09–24	10	Maternity allowance
C09–36	11	Maternity grant
C09–48	12	Death grant
C09–60	13	Redundancy payment (from Ministry of Labour)
C10–12	14	A single grant (for clothing or other special needs from the Ministry of Social Security)
C10–24	15	Other (SPECIFY)
	16	None of these SKIP TO Q.17

IF ANY CODED INSERT CODE IN COLUMN

AND ASK
  (a) Did you receive it for last week?   yes
                                                              no
  (b) How much a week do (did) you receive and for how many
        weeks have (did) you receive(d) that rate?

WRITE IN ANSWER   WRITE IN AMT
rate per week   LAST WEEK
number of weeks   OFFICE:
                                            wkly average
previous rate per wk   OFFICE:
number of weeks   yrly total
single amt if any   INSERT CODE

2nd Benefit
WRITE IN ANSWER   WRITE IN AMT
rate per week   LAST WEEK
number of weeks   OFFICE:
                                            wkly average
previous rate per wk   OFFICE:
number of weeks   yrly total
single amt if any   INSERT CODE

3rd Benefit
WRITE IN ANSWER   WRITE IN AMT
rate per week   LAST WEEK
number of weeks   OFFICE:
                                            wkly average
previous rate per wk   OFFICE:
number of weeks   yrly total
single amt if any   INSERT CODE

4th Benefit
WRITE IN BENEFIT AND
ANY FURTHER AMOUNTS   OFFICE:
AS NECESSARY

	1nft		2nd		3rd		4th		INTERVIEWER: CODE 05, 06, etc. IF 5th, 6th MEMBERS OF HOUSEHOLD	
	27–31		27–31		27–31		27–31		27–31	27–31
		X		X		X		X		X		X
	£	s	£	s	£	s	£	s	£	s	£	s
	32–35		32–35		32–35		32–35		32–35	32–35
		X		X		X		X		X		X
	£		£		£		£		£		£
	36–37		36–37		36–37		36–37		36–37	36–37
	0 1	0 2	0 1	0 2	0 1	0 2	0 1	0 2	0 1	0 2	0 1	0 2
	0 3	0 4	0 3	0 4	0 3	0 4	0 3	0 4	0 3	0 4	0 3	0 4
	0 5	0 6	0 5	0 6	0 5	0 6	0 5	0 6	0 5	0 6	0 5	0 6
	0 7	0 8	0 7	0 8	0 7	0 8	0 7	0 8	0 7	0 8	0 7	0 8
	0 9	1 0	0 9	1 0	0 9	1 0	0 9	1 0	0 9	1 0	0 9	1 0
	1 1	1 2	1 1	1 2	1 1	1 2	1 1	1 2	1 1	1 2	1 1	1 2
	1 3	1 4	1 3	1 4	1 3	1 4	1 3	1 4	1 3	1 4	1 3	1 4
	1 5	1 6	1 5	1 6	1 5	1 6	1 5	1 6	1 5	1 6	1 5	1 6
	X Y		X Y		X Y		X Y		X Y		X Y
	£	s	£	s	£	s	£	s	£	s	£	s
	£	s	£	s	£	s	£	s	£	s	£	s
	£	s	£	s	£	s	£	s	£	s	£	s

18

QUESTION 16 Supplementary Benefit

It is most important that you should not overlook anyone who may be receiving or who has received supplementary benefit. There are two problems. One is, as noted above, that an informant may neglect to tell you that a standard benefit, like retirement pension and sickness benefit, is in fact supplemented. The other is that the official term " supplementary benefit " is fairly new. You may therefore have to prompt " supplementary assistance? ", ' national assistance? " or " public assistance? "

QUESTION 16(c) Rent paid by Supplementary Benefits Commission

If the rent is in fact paid by the S.B.C. we shall be asking later how much that is.

QUESTION 17 Single Grant

A single payment may be made to meet an exceptional need — such as bedding, clothing or household equipment. It may also be made to meet charges for glasses, dentures or dental treatment obtained through the National Health Service.

QUESTION 18 Income in last year at work

Note that you have already asked how many years it is since such a man last worked (in Section II). Now you are asking for the actual year when last at work, and, if it is 1955 or a later year, for the wage and household income. Do not neglect to find the composition of the household at that time (for example, write: man, wife and adult single son, or, man, wife and wife's widowed mother). We realise memories may be faulty but most people remember the last occasion they were at work and we are anxious (for retired and disabled persons, for example) to get a rough estimate of their fall in income upon giving up work. In the office we shall of course allow for average wage increases in the intervening years in interpreting the information you collect.

QUESTION 19 Employer's pension

The question is in a form which allows for the possibility of an ex-policeman, ex-serviceman or ex-civil servant drawing a pension though still holding a subsequent job. Service pensions should be included here but not war pensions, which have been covered in Q. 15. As before: Strike out Before or After Tax as appropriate.

19a

	1nft	2nd	3rd	4th	INTERVIEWER: CODE 05, 06, IF 5th, 6th MEMBERS OF HOUSEHOLD

16. IF SUPPLEMENTARY BENEFIT RECEIVED LAST YEAR (CODE 06 Q.15)
   * Did anyone advise you to apply for supplementary benefit (national assistance) or was it your own idea?

	1nft	2nd	3rd	4th		
	36	36	36	36	36	36

X yes, advised ASK Q.16(a)
Y no, own idea } SKIP TO Q.17
O DK
1 Does Not Apply

(a) Who was it? _____
2 doctor
3 welfare worker
4 post office
5 relative
6 friend
7 other (SPECIFY)_____

	1nft	2nd	3rd	4th		
	X Y O 1	X Y .O 1	X Y O ·1	X Y O 1	X Y O 1	X Y O 1
	2 3 4 5 6 7	2 3 4 5 6 7	2 3 4 5 6 7	2 3 4 5 6 7	2 3 4 5 6 7	2 3 4 5 6 7

(b) IF CURRENTLY RECEIVING SUPPLEMENTARY BENEFIT
Do you feel embarrassed or uncomfortable about getting it or do you accept it just like a pension or any other kind of income?
very embarrassed or uncomfortable) ASK
a little embarrassed } Q.16
not embarrassed (c)
DK
Does Not Apply SKIP TO Q.17

	37	37	37	37	37	37
	X Y O 1 2	X Y O 1 2	X Y O 1 2	X Y O 1 2	X Y O 1 2	X Y O 1 2

(c) Do you pay the rent yourself or do you have an arrangement with "the supplementary" (or national assistance office) to pay it direct to the landlord?
Does Not Apply
paid by housewife
paid by Supplementary Benefits Commission

	3 4 5	3 4 5	3 4 5	3 4 5	3 4 5	3 4 5

17. IF SINGLE GRANT(S) RECEIVED LAST YEAR FROM MINISTRY (CODE 15,Q.15)
  * Can you tell me how you came to get this and how much it is for? each grant?

WRITE IN ANSWER   Does Not Apply

	6	6	6	6	6	6

18. FOR MEN AGED 18 AND OVER NEITHER IN PAID EMPLOYMENT NOR SELF-EMPLOYED IN LAST 12 MONTHS.
In what year did you last work full-time (that is, 30 hours or more in a week)?
WRITE IN Year 19____
IF 1955 OR LATER ASK Q.18(a)
IF 1954 OR EARLIER SKIP TO Q.19
never } SKIP TO Q.19
Does Not Apply

	38	38	38	38	38	38
	X Y O 1	X Y O 1	X Y O 1	X Y O 1	X Y O 1	X Y O 1

(a) What were your earnings in the last week you worked full-time, after deductions?
(b) And roughly what would you say was the total income of the household in that week?
(c) Were the members of the household then the same as they are today?
(d) IF DIFFERENT. Who were in the household then? *
same 1 same 1
different 2 different 2
OFFICE USE ONLY

	39-42	39-42	39-42	39-42	39-42	39-42

19. FOR ALL. Have you received in the last 12 months a pension from a former employer?
yes, central or local govt, armed forces) ASK
yes, other employer's pensions }Q.19(a)
no)
DK) SKIP TO Q.20

	43	43	43	43	43	43
	X Y O 1	X Y O 1	X Y O 1	X Y· O 1	X Y O 1	X Y O 1

(a) How much?
per week ____ bef/aft tax ____ bef/aft tax OFFICE amt
OR per month ____ USE last
AND total ONLY week
last 12 months ____ bef/aft tax ____ bef/aft tax
Payment last wk 1 1 OFFICE amt
Payment not USE last
received last wk 2 2 ONLY year

	44-47	44-47	44-47	44-47	44-47	44-47
	48-51	48-51	48-51	48-51	48-51	48-51

(b) How many years did you serve for pension?

19

QUESTION 20 Miscellaneous allowances and cash income

The various kinds of income have been laid out as compactly as possible but remember that two or more may need to be coded and you should prompt carefully. Underneath describe the type of allowance (so that we know to which code a particular amount refers) and the amount per week or per month. Ring either " 1 " or " 2 " depending on whether the allowance did in fact cover last week and strike out " Before " or "After " tax as appropriate. Make sure that in the case of allowances of husbands temporarily away from home that you have not already written in his earnings earlier as a member of the household. If you have do not write in any amount he pays. All we want here is any income which is not covered by earlier entries.

QUESTION 20(b) Allowances for separated and divorced wives

Some wives receive money direct from their husbands (or via the court). Others have court orders but these are signed over to the Supplementary Benefits Commission, which collects the money and pays the mother a standard weekly allowance. We therefore want to avoid counting the amount in Q. 20 if that amount is already included in the figure for supplementary benefit listed under Q. 15. We also want to be able to sort out irregular payments of both money from court orders and supplementary benefit. Check carefully in all these instances and write a note if anything needs clarification. Fatherless families form a small proportion of the total sample of households. Where money from court orders is paid irregularly and the mother claims weekly from the Supplementary Benefits Office she might not always claim the full amount, or may delay her claim in which case she loses benefit. Check to see if such loss is occurring.

QUESTION 21 Allowances and sums paid to others

This question complements some of the sub-questions in Q. 20. Here we are concerned to find out about all cash payments or allowances amounting to at least 10s. a week or £25 a year. Note that married children frequently pay rent or bills for elderly parents and old people sometimes make considerable cash gifts to their children. Examples are payments for grandchildren's clothing or holidays, payment of T.V. rentals and licence, cash gift for car.

QUESTION 22 Tax relief

Our object is to gain further evidence about reciprocal aid but also to help us in interpreting the figures for earnings and deductions given earlier. Note that you are not expected to probe for amounts.

QUESTION 23

Property income is considerable for a small percentage of informants and tends to be of two types: income from only one or two houses and income from a range of properties. With a few people considerable time may need to be spent on getting a reliable answer to this question. Net income after tax may not be known so we deliberately seek gross income before tax, then expenses, and only finally income after tax. You may not be able to get the third but make sure you get a figure for the first. It may also be difficult to secure a figure for expenses of rates and repairs but remember that property-owners will often know the total sums entered on their income tax returns. It may even be helpful to remind informants of this: " I mean the total like that in your income tax return — gross income less expenses." Note that many owner-occupiers and tenants rent rooms and flats to others in their accommodation. Do not count the rent from a boarder living in the household.

20a

20. ASK ALL
Have you received any of the following in the last 12 months?

PROMPT VERY CAREFULLY, CODE ALL THAT APPLY AND ASK Q.20(a) FOR ALL.
TICK IF DOCUMENTS SEEN [ ]

X An annuity (e.g. through private insurance) (N.B. NOT DIVIDENDS)
Y A gratuity or a lump sum like an employer's redundancy payment or a gift on retirement or marriage?
0 Income from trust or covenant
1 Money from a court order or voluntary payment from the children's father (NOT FORCES ALLOTMENT) ASK Q.20(a) and (b)
2 Allowances from relatives who are members of armed forces or merchant navy away from home
3 Other allowances from husbands and others temporarily away from home
4 Regular cash help or allowances from grandparents, parents, children or other relatives or from friends
5 A money gift of more than £25 (or 10s. a week) from any of your family, relatives or friends
6 Trade Union benefits (e.g. pension, sick or strike pay)
7 Friendly Society, voluntary society or British Legion benefits
8 Any other benefits under private sickness or accident insurance
9 None of these   SKIP TO Q.21

a) How much? # [ ]
ame of allowance
mount per week
R   per month   ___ bef/aft tax ___ bef/aft tax ___ bef/aft tax   OFF amt USE last ONLY week
ND total last
12 months   ___ bef/aft tax ___ bef/aft tax ___ bef/aft tax
ayment last wk   I   I   I   OFF USE last ONLY year
ayment not
received last wk   2   2   2

b) FOR SEPARATED AND DIVORCED OR UNMARRIED MOTHERS (OR WIFE'S CHILDREN OF A PREVIOUS MARRIAGE IF UNDER 16) WHO ARE RECEIVING MONEY FROM A COURT ORDER AND SUPPLEMENTARY BENEFIT.
ay I just check? Is the court order received   collected by informant
y you or collected by the Supplementary Benefits   collected by S.B.C.
commission (National Assistance office)? *   DK
WRITE IN ANY COMMENT ABOUT REGULARITY AND   Does Not Apply
MANNER OF RECEIPT OF INCOME

21. FOR ALL. From your income are you supporting or helping anyone elsewhere? I mean an allowance to a parent, child, relative or former wife, for example, of at least 10s. a week, or occasional cash gifts or paying a bill amounting   yes ASK Q.21(a)
to at least £25 a year? * [ ] [ ] no) SKIP TO Q.22
                                    DK)
a) Who to?
b) How much per wk?   OFFICE amt
c) Was there a pay-   USE last
ent last week? yes   ONLY week
               no
                    2   2   2
d) How much in single
ayments altogether   OFFICE amt
ast year?   USE last
                                       ONLY year

22. Did you receive any tax relief last year for
X the support of a relative other than your wife and children
Y someone to look after the house or children (other than wife or relative)
0 any type of covenant to pay for the education of a relative
1 life insurance
2 none of above
3 DK

23. Have you received any income from property -- renting out a house flat or room (even adjoining your own   yes ASK Q.23(a)
ouse or flat) in the last 12 months? no) SKIP TO Q.24
                                       DK)
a) How many different rents
ave you received?
b) About how much was the ross amount you received in he last 12 mths before tax?
c) How much did your expenses ome to? (incl. paying for ates and repairs)
pprox. income after tax   OFFICE amt
f known)   USE last
                                       ONLY year

Inft	2nd	3rd	4th	INTERVIEWER: CODE 05, 06, etc. IF 5th, 6th MEMBERS OF HOUSEHOLD	
52	52	52	52	52	52
X	X	X	X	X	X
Y	Y	Y	Y	Y	Y
0	0	0	0	0	0
I	I	I	I	I	I
2	2	2	2	2	2
3	3	3	3	3	3
4	4	4	4	4	4
5	5	5	5	5	5
6	6	6	6	6	6
7	7	7	7	7	7
8	8	8	8	8	8
9	9	9	9	9	9
53-56	53-56	53-56	53-56	53-56	53-56
57-60	57-60	57-60	57-60	57-60	57-60
61	61	61	61	61	61
X	X	X	X	X	X
Y	Y	Y	Y	Y	Y
0	0	0	0	0	0
I	I	I	I	I	I
62	62	62	62	62	62
X	X	X	X	X	X
Y	Y	Y	Y	Y	Y
0	0	0	0	0	0
63-66	63-66	63-66	63-66	63-66	63-66
67-70	67-70	67-70	67-70	67-70	67-70
71	71	71	71	71	71
X	X	X	X	X	X
Y	Y	Y	Y	Y	Y
0	0	0	0	0	0
1	1	1	1	1	1
2	2	2	2	2	2
3	3	3	3	3	3
72	72	72	72	72	72
X	X	X	X	X	X
Y	Y	Y	Y	Y	Y
0	0	0	0	0	0
					•
73-76	73-76	73-76	73-76	73-76	73-76

QUESTION 25(a)   Private and business accommodation

Count as " business " accommodation any accommodation which counts for purposes of offsetting tax. This may include a study room for some teachers, for example.

QUESTION 25(e)   Rate rebate or reduction

Note that many councils pay rebates twice a year.

QUESTION 25(h)   Mortgage

The informant may know the total sum paid in the previous year but not the division of the sum between interest and repayments of principal. Yet it is essential for us to find how much of the peyment represents capital repayments and how much interest payments, because otherwise we cannot work out housing costs which are comparable with costs incurred by households paying rent. In many instances a monthly or annual payment slip will show the two amounts and the informant should be encouraged to look this up. Note that if the informant still **cannot** give you the answer we have provided certain questions on the right-hand side of the page which will allow us to make a reliable estimate. You should note certain details in the

(a)   source of loan or mortgage;
(b)   term of repayment;
(c)   number of years paid;
(d)   amount of loan.

Please make special note if the repayment of a mortgage is covered by an endowment policy and note the amount and frequency of the premium. As elsewhere put a tick in the small box or make a note if you are fortunate enough to be shown documents.

QUESTION 25(i)   Value of house/flat

Ask for an estimate and only show Flashcard No. 3 if the informant hesitates in giving an answer and you judge that it would be appropriate. Always insert the code number as given on the Flashcard, even if you also obtain an exact estimate.

QUESTION 25(l)   Government's Mortgage Scheme

Note that, broadly, this is advantageous only to a householder with relatively low income who does not expect to pay tax at the standard rate in the foreseeable future.

	Inft	2nd	3rd	4th	INTERVIEWER: CODE 05, 06, etc. IF 5th, 6th	
	77	77	77	77	77	77
	X	X	X	X	X	X
	Y	Y	Y	Y	Y	Y
	0	0	0	0	0	0
	1	1	1	1	1	1
	2	2	2	2	2	2
	3	3	3	3	3	3
	4	4	4	4	4	4
	5	5	5	5	5	5
	6	6	6	6	6	6

1	2	3	4	5	6	7	8	9
							0.	2

24. Is this house/flat rented or owned (i.e. by the householder)?

X	Owner occupied:	fully owned }	ASK Q.25
Y		paying mortgage }	
0	Rented:	from local council	
1		privately — furnished	
2		privately — unfurnished	} SKIP TO Q.26
3		privately — with farm, business premises	
4	Rent free:	because of present or previous employment }	SKIP
5		for reasons other than employment }	TO Q.28
6	DK	SKIP TO Q.29	

25. IF HOUSEHOLDER IS OWNER OCCUPIER

(a) Does the dwelling include business as
well as private accommodation?
Does Not Apply SKIP TO Q.26
yes ASK Q.25(a)(i)
no SKIP TO Q.25(b)

`10` X Y O

(a)(i) How many rooms are used for business? number ____
(b) How much ground rent, feu duty (Scotland)
chief rent, do you pay? amount £ ____
(c) How much did you pay last year in rates? amount £ ____
(d) How much in water rates (if not
included in (c))? amount £ ____
(e) Do you get a reduction under the rates rebate scheme? yes / no / DK

`11`

IF YES How much is it per year ____

`X Y O 1 2`

(f) Have you already deducted this figure from the amount
you have just given me for rates? yes / no
(g) When did you buy this house? 19__

MORTGAGE PAYERS ONLY
£ s d
(h) What is the total monthly payment? ____ OFFICE total
* How much of this is interest? ____ USE annual
And how much capital repayments? ____ ONLY housing cost

`12-15`

Other, if any (e.g. insurance premium
on building) SPECIFY ____ OFFICE USE ONLY

`16-19`

ASK ALL (i.e. FULLY OWNING AND PAYING MORTGAGE)
(i) How much do you estimate your house (and garden) to be worth at
present? SHOW FLASHCARD NO.3 *
WRITE IN YOUR ESTIMATE informant's estimate £ ____ range code
IF DIFFERENT interviewer's estimate £ ____ OFFICE
AND NOTE REASON USE ONLY

`20`

`21-25`
£

Do you pay an insurance premium on the house or flat (not contents)?
annual premium £ ____ insured value of house in hundreds
of pounds

`26-28`

(j) Has your employer helped you with a loan or grant
in purchasing your house? yes / no
IF YES grant: How much?
loan: At what interest rate?

`29`
X Y

(k) How much have you spent in the last 12 months for alterations,
decorations or repairs to your home (not business, and including paint
and tools for work by self)? Total £ ____
DESCRIBE ITEMS IF NECESSARY AND COSTS

____

(l) Are you applying for a mortgage under the Government's new option
mortgage scheme? *
yes / no / DK } SKIP TO Q.30

`30`
X Y O

IF TOTAL CANNOT BE DIVIDED
ASK:
Source of loan ____
Term of repayment ____
Number of years paid ____
Amount of loan ____
TICK IF DOCUMENTS SEEN [ ]
IF AMOUNTS FOR BUSINESS/FARM AND
HOME CANNOT BE SEPARATED
NOTE HERE:
estimated value of house/business ____
insured value of house/business (building) ____
"   "   (contents) ____

21

QUESTION 27(a)

Our object is to try to find what rent might be paid in normal circumstances in that area for such accommodation. We have asked you to make an estimate in the light of your knowledge of the area if the informant cannot make such an estimate.

QUESTION 28(a) Years on list

Sometimes the tenant will have taken on a tenancy from a member of the family who has died or moved away. Code "inherited tenancy" in all instances except that of a woman who has become the tenant through the death or absence of her husband.

QUESTION 28(d) Reason for obtaining council accommodation

Interpret "inheriting tenancy" as above. Although more than one reason may be advanced code what the informant considers to be the chief one.

QUESTION 28(e) Rent reduction or rebate

Broadly three types of scheme have been introduced. Some councils operate an automatic differential rents scheme and some informants may have their rents reduced initially upon the introduction of the scheme. But in this sort of scheme most people will not know whether or not their rents are "reduced". The second scheme is one where the tenant has to apply for a reduction of rent he expects to pay in the future, upon test of means. The third scheme is one where the tenant applies for a rebate of rent paid in the past, on test of means. We are primarily concerned with the second and third schemes here.

22a

26. IF HOUSEHOLDER PAYS RENT

Does Not Apply

(a) How much do you pay a week in rent?

(b) Do you have a rent holiday?
yes 1   no of wks rent   OFFICE   total
no 2   paid in year   USE   rent
                  ONLY   last year

(c) Do you pay rates in addition?

    IF YES   amount general rates last yr _____   yes
            amount water rates last yr _____   no
                                         DK

(d) Have you had a rates rebate?   yes

    IF YES (I) How much was it? _____ SPECIFY PERIOD _____   no
       (II) Did you get it as a lump sum payment   DK
       or was it deducted from your rates or   deducted from rent
       rent?   deducted from rates
                                     lump sum payment

(e) Does your rent include: lighting 1   other service or commodity 5
                       gas   2   electric power   6
PROMPT AND CODE ANY   coal   3   none of these   7
   THAT APPLY   meals   4   DK   8

(f) How much have you spent in the last 12 months for alterations,
decorations or repairs (including paint or tools for work by yourself)?
                               Total £ _____
DESCRIBE ITEMS IF NECESSARY AND COSTS _____   OFFICE   total
                                     USE   annual
                                     ONLY   housing
                                           cost

27. IF HOUSEHOLDER RENTS PRIVATELY

                             Does Not Apply SKIP TO Q.28
(a) Is this accommodation owned   Y   yes   ASK Q.27(a)(I)
by your employer?   0   no } SKIP TO Q.27(b)
                               1   DK }
IF YES (I) Do you pay less than it   2   yes   ASK Q.27(a)(II)
would cost if you rented it in the   3   no } SKIP TO Q.27(b)
ordinary way?   4   DK }

IF YES (II) How much extra rent per year would you
expect to pay if you were renting it privately? *   extra rent per yr
   GIVE YOUR ESTIMATE IF INFORMANT UNCERTAIN   £ _____

(III) Would you have to leave this house/flat if you
stopped working for him or when you retire?   yes
                                                 no
                                                 DK

(b) Are you on a council housing list?
               1   yes, entire household } ASK Q.27(b)(I)
               2   yes, part of household }
                       3   no } SKIP TO Q.30
                       4   DK }

                       (I) How long?   number of years

28. IF HOUSEHOLDER RENTS FROM COUNCIL

                       Does Not Apply   SKIP TO Q.30
(a) How long were you (the tenant) on the
list before getting council accommodation?   inherited tenancy
                                        DK
                                        number of years

(b) When was this house/flat built?   before war
                                        1946-1954
                                        1955 or later
                                        DK

(c) How long have you been living in council accommodation?   years

(d) Why did you get a council house/flat when   X   inherited tenancy
you did? Was it because you reached the top   Y   bad housing
of the list or were there other reasons?   0   health of member of family
                                    1   overcrowding
            PROMPT   CODE   2   other (SPECIFY)
                    ONE   3   solely top of list
                    ONLY   4   DK

(e) Do you know if the council operates a differential rents or rent
rebate scheme to adjust rents to needs?   yes   ASK Q.28(e)(I)
                                       no } SKIP TO Q.30
                                       DK }

(f) Have you had your rent reduced or   rent reduced { ASK Q.28(e)
obtained a rebate, or have you applied   applied, no rent reduction) (II)
but not had a reduction or a rebate?   not applied   SKIP TO
                                       other (SPECIFY) } Q.30
                                       DK

(II) Do you know by how much? _____

Right margin coding column:

Code ref	Values
31-34	X / £ s
35-37	£
38	X Y O
	1 2 3 4 5 6
39-42	
43	X Y O 1 2 3 4
44-46	£
47	X Y O
	1 2 3 4
48	
49	X Y O
50	X Y O 1
51-52	
53	X Y O 1 2 3 4
54	X Y O
	1 2 3 4 5

22

QUESTION 29(c) Estimate of market rent

Proceed as for Q. 27(a)

QUESTION 30(a) Income from lodgers or boarders

Be careful not to obtain an inflated total. Amounts may vary according to numbers of boarders and, if necessary, write down separate amounts on this page. If the informant has difficulty in producing an average per week or total in year, obtain last week's GROSS income (taking into account number of boarders) and then work back to get an estimate for the year.

QUESTION 30(c) Net income

Carefully prompt for services and the cost of providing these services so that you can make an estimate of NET income — "profit" as some people will understand it. In some instances you will have to write down figures for gross amount received and an estimate of the cost of different services. If the informant does not know what his net income has been, make an estimate on the basis of what he tells you about gross payments and cost of services and expenses. Try to obtain a figure net of any tax paid. As before, note that if you cannot do this, you can strike out "after" tax in the box provided. We are asking you to provide a figure both for last week and last year. There may be changes in income (due to loss or arrival of boarders) during the year which are revealed in interview. Remember also that costs may be as great or even greater than receipts. In these cases write in "O" and make a note.

QUESTION 32 Value of own food or poultry

Try to obtain a weekly average of the value of using own garden, allotment and farm produce. Do not waste too much time on produce amounting in value to less than 10s. a week. Be careful not to give an inflated estimate of the saving. Husbands sometimes exaggerate the value of what they grow in a large garden. What you want is an estimate of what it would cost in the shops to purchase the kind of produce consumed in the home which is grown by the household, LESS all expenses. For a small-holding or farm this means taking account of purchases of stock or seed, wages, payments of fuel bills, etc., in the same way as earlier you explored the income of the self-employed.

QUESTION 33 Total income last year

In some instances you may have difficulty with an informant who, though willing to answer other questions, is unwilling to answer questions on income, or an informant who is vague or uncertain about details. By adopting a matter of fact approach or by coming back to these questions after dealing with the rest of the questionnaire in an interview, you may overcome the difficulty If the questions remain unanswered, try the question here as given, adding any other explanation according to your individual style or to the circumstances of the situation. Show the Flash-card and the do your best to arrive at a specific amount. Also do your best to check: "Does that include family allowances, pensions, etc.?" You may be surprised sometimes to find that the informant gradually unends and is prepared to answer many preceding questions. You should also do your best to check whether the total given includes other income units in the household. Try to establish totals for these units in the same way.

23a

29. IF HOUSEHOLDER LIVES RENT FREE

(a) Do you give any services
In return for living rent free?

Does Not Apply   SKIP TO Q.30
employer owns: no services beyond
                employment
relative or friend owns: no services
               : some extra services
               : some extra services
other (SPECIFY) _____
DK

WRITE IN NATURE OF SERVICES

(b) How much do you pay in rates?   amt gen. rates last yr £ _____
                                    amt water rates last yr £ _____

(c) How much rent would you say someone would have to pay in this area
for a house/flat like this?   estimated rent per year _____
GIVE YOUR ESTIMATE IF INFORMANT UNCERTAIN £ _____ per year

(d) How much have you spent in the last 12 months for alterations,
decorations or repairs (including paint or tools for work by yourself)?
                                            Total £

DESCRIBE ITEMS IF NECESSARY AND COSTS
_____ _____   OFFICE   total annual
_____ _____   USE   housing
_____ _____   ONLY   costs

30. FOR ALL
Do you receive any payments from lodgers or boarders?

                          yes, lodger(s) }
                          yes, boarder(s)} ASK Q.30(a)
                          no } SKIP TO Q.31
                          DK

(a) About how much have you received in the last 12 months before
allowing for expenses?
       per week _____ OR total in last year* _____

(b) Do you provide any of the following services without additional
charge?
PROMPT =   light   1 breakfast and one meal 4 laundry 7
CODE ALL ; heat   2 all meals   5 other   8
THAT APPLY breakfast only 3 cleaning   6 none   9

(c) Can you say how much income you get each week last wk [bef/aft] tax
after allowing for the cost of providing these
services and paying tax? *
                          total last yr [bef/aft] tax
                                        (in £'s only)

31. Is there a garage attached to the accommodation or do you own or
rent one elsewhere?   yes, attached }
                             yes, elsewhere } ASK Q.31(a)
                             no } SKIP TO Q.32
                             DK

(a) Have you sub-let the garage separately yes 1   amount last wk
in the last 12 months?   no   2
    IF YES How much do you get per week
           after deducting expenses?   total last yr (in £'s only)

32. Do you grow any of your own food or
keep poultry either in the garden or yes, own ground/garden) ASK
grounds by the home or elsewhere? *   yes, allotment, etc   } Q.
                                      elsewhere   ) 32(a)
                                      no } SKIP TO Q.33
                                      DK

(a) How much a week on average do you think you and
your family by eating or using the things you grow - I mean the
price in the shops of the things you use at home, but deducting all
your costs and expenses?   amount
NOTE ANY VARIATION IN YEAR _____ per week

33. ASK ONLY IF INCOME INFORMATION INCOMPLETE *
                              Does Not Apply
Even though it may be difficult to go into details I wonder if you
would mind looking at this card (SHOW FLASHCARD NO.2) and indicating
the number that best tells us the total income, after deductions of
tax and national insurance, from all sources of yourself and your
family in the last year. It is most important for us to have an idea
of the total.   range code
PROBE FOR SEPARATE INCOME UNITS
                              * total last year
                                  (£'s only)

	55 X Y 0 1 2 3 4
	56-58 £
	59-61

	Inft	2nd	3rd	4th		INTERVIEWER: CODE 05, 06, etc. IF 5th, 6th MEMBERS OF HOUSEHOLD
1 2 3 4 5 6 7 8 9	10-11	10-11	10-11	10-11	10-11	10-11
	01	02	03	04		
	12	12	12	12	12	12
	X	X	X	X	X	X
	Y	Y	Y	Y	Y	Y
	0	0	0	0	0	0
	1	1	1	1	1	1
	13-16 £ s	13-16 £ s	13-16 £ s	13-16 £ s	13-16 £ s	13-16 £ s
	17-20 £	17-20 £	17-20 £	17-20 £	17-20 £	17-20 £
	21	21	21	21	21	21
	X	X	X	X	X	X
	Y	Y	Y	Y	Y	Y
	0	0	0	0	0	0
	1	1	1	1	1	1
	22-25 £ s	22-25 £ s	22-25 £ s	22-25 £ s	22-25 £ s	22-25 £ s
	26-28 £	26-28 £	26-28 £	26-28 £	26-28 £	26-28 £
	29	29	29	29	29	29
	X	X	X	X	X	X
	Y	Y	Y	Y	Y	Y
	0	0	0	0	0	0
	1	1	1	1	1	1
	30-33 £ s	30-33 £ s	30-33 £ s	30-33 £ s	30-33 £ s	30-33 £ s
	34-35 X	34-35 X	34-35 X	34-35 X	34-35 X	34-35 X
	36-39	36-39	36-39	36-39	36-39	36-39

23

V SAVINGS AND ASSETS

QUESTION 1 Personal

This excludes a business bank account which is covered by Q. 4. Avoid double-counting the same bank balance or assets when questioning husband and wife.

QUESTION 2 Savings

Note that you should proceed by prompting all items to see how many are appropriate, then try to establish a total and then establish totals for each item only as a check or if necessary. Care should be taken to avoid double-counting. If the informant is hesitant or confused repeat the question to make sure he or she knows what kind of savings you are referring to and THEN show Flashcard No. 4 to get the total. Then try to obtain an absolute total rather than a range. For example, you could ask: " Would you say the figure was at the top end or the lower end of that range — nearer X or nearer Y? "

QUESTION 2(c) Interest

Try to establish the amounts the informant receives in the form he receives it — that is, before tax is deducted or after it has been deducted at source. In difficult instances you need not waste time converting a " before tax " total into " after tax " so long as you make plain what it is. We will do that work in the office.

QUESTION 3 Value of stocks and shares

This question of the value of stocks and shares is crucial and every encouragement should be used to obtain an answer. Some informants simply will not know. Remember that brokers sometimes send an annual valuation. If there is considerable uncertainty, tactfully suggest or imply that it would be very helpful to know and take any opportunity to see the valuation or to leave a note (and s.a.e.) so that a more reliable estimate can be made and either you can pick it up at a second call or ask for it to be sent on.

QUESTION 3(b) Interest

Proceed as in Q. 2c above. Mostly amounts will be received after tax has been deducted.

QUESTION 4

This is to cover any type of business which is owned in part or in whole by the informant. Being a director does not necessarily mean owner-ship. The answer to this question should not duplicate the answer to the previous question. Shares come under Q. 3. This is to cover such things as shops, professional practices and small businesses of every kind except limited companies. In all cases make sure that money in the business, bank account and stocks are borne in mind when the valuation is made. When the business (e.g. shop or farm) is run from the owner occupier's dwelling, the value of the dwelling will often have been included in the answer to this question (i.e. Q. 25 in Section V). UNDER NO CIRCUMSTANCES MUST THE DWELLING BE COUNTED TWICE. The valuation should be on the assumption that the informant had to sell but was in no great hurry. A year or even more could be taken to find a purchaser. The valuation should NOT be made on the basis of: " What would you take for your business? " — that is, when the informant has to be persuaded to sell. NOTE that vehicles should be included in the valuation of a business — say of a haulage contractor, a cab owner or even a building contractor or window cleaner.

QUESTION 5 Other property

Remember that some people use two houses. Others have houses which they rent off to others. This last is not uncommon among elderly people who may be very poor themselves. A " boat " may include anything from a luxury yacht to a small rowing boat.

24a

V SAVINGS AND ASSETS

1. ASK ALL
Have you a personal bank account? *

         yes ASK Q.1(a)
         no }
         DK } SKIP TO Q.2
(a) Is it joint husband/wife?   joint
           exclusive

2. (a) Have you any money in: * WRITE IN IDENTIFICATION NUMBERS
CODE ON RIGHT, ASK Q.2(b) AND WRITE IN SUB-TOTALS BELOW ONLY IF
NECESSARY

X	Bank Deposit Account	
Y	Post Office Savings Bank	
0	Trustee Savings Bank	
1	The Co-op	
2	Any other Savings Bank	
3	Shares or deposits in Building Society	
4	Savings Certificates	
5	Defence Bonds	
6	Premium Bonds	
7	Any other (SPECIFY)	
8	None of these SKIP TO Q.3	
9	DK	

PROMPT AND CODE ALL THAT APPLY

(b) How much have you in all
these kinds of savings Total _____
altogether? WRITE TOTAL AMOUNTS
         ALSO ON RIGHT
IF INFORMANT RELUCTANT TO NAME A FIGURE/APPEARS NOT TO KNOW/ IS SHY/
LOOKS OFFENDED: SHOW FLASHCARD NO.4   WRITE IN
                RANGE CODE
(c) During the last 12 months how much in interest altogether have you
received or been credited with from these kinds of savings?
         total in last 12 months before/after tax
          IF APPROPRIATE SHOW FLASHCARD NO.5
SPECIFY ITEMS AND SUB-TOTALS BELOW ONLY IF NECESSARY

_____ bef/aft tax
_____ bef/aft tax
_____ bef/aft tax
_____ bef/aft tax
_____ bef/aft tax

3. Have you any stocks or shares (or any other
kinds of bonds or savings)? *   yes ASK Q.3(a)
           no }
           DK } SKIP TO Q.4
(a) What would you estimate to be their present value
altogether? IF INFORMANT RELUCTANT TO NAME A FIGURE/
APPEARS NOT TO KNOW/IS SHY/LOOKS OFFENDED SHOW FLASHCARD total value
NO.4 AND WRITE IN RANGE CODE   in £'s

               range code
(b) During the last 12 months how much in dividends and interest
altogether have you received or been credited with?
          total in last 12 months
IF APPROPRIATE SHOW FLASHCARD NO.5   before/after tax

4. Have you a business, farm or professional practice?
         yes ASK Q.4(a)
         no } SKIP TO Q.5
         DK }
(a) What do you estimate it (or your share of it)
had to be sold, including any vehicles owned by the business? *
IF COMBINED BUSINESS/HOUSE OR FLAT PROMPT:
Not including the value of the accommodation
you and your family occupy.   total value
IF APPROPRIATE SHOW FLASHCARD NO.3   in £'s

5. Do you own a house other than this
which I've already asked about, or yes, including house(s) } ASK
land which is not included along with yes, not incl. house(s) } Q.5(a)
this house? Or a caravan or boat? * no } SKIP TO Q.6.
           DK }
(a) What do you estimate is the present value of those assets?

   IF APPROPRIATE SHOW FLASHCARD NO.3   total value
               in £'s

Inft	2nd	3rd	4th	INTERVIEWER: CODE 05, 06 etc. IF 5th, 6th MEMBERS OF HOUSEHOLD	
40	40	40	40	40	40
X	X	X	X	X	X
Y	Y	Y	Y	Y	Y
0	0	0	0	0	0
1	1	1	1	1	1
2	2	2	2	2	2
41	41	41	41	41	41
X	X	X	X	X	X
Y	Y	Y	Y	Y	Y
0	0	0	0	0	0
1	1	1	1	1	1
2	2	2	2	2	2
3	3	3	3	3	3
4	4	4	4	4	4
5	5	5	5	5	5
6	6	6	6	6	6
7	7	7	7	7	7
8	8	8	8	8	8
9	9	9	9	9	9
42–47	42–47	42–47	42–47	42–47	42–47
£	£	£	£	£	£
48	48	48	48	48	48
49–52	49–52	49–52	49–52	49–52	49–52
£	£	£	£	£	£
53	53	53	53	53	53
X	X	X	X	X	X
Y	Y	Y	Y	Y	Y
0	0	0	0	0	0
54–58	54–58	54–58	54–58	54–58	54–58
£	£	£	£	£	£
59	59	59	59	59	59
60–63	60–63	60–63	60–63	60–63	60–63
£	£	£	£	£	£
64	64	64	64	64	64
X	X	X	X	X	X
Y	Y	Y	Y	Y	Y
0	0	0	0	0	0
65–69	65–69	65–69	65–69	65–69	65–69
£	£	£	£	£	£
70	70	70	70	70	70
X	X	X	X	X	X
Y	Y	Y	Y	Y	Y
0	0	0	0	0	0
1	1	1	1	1	1
71–75	71–75	71–75	71–75	71–75	71–75
£	£	£	£	£	£

QUESTION 6a Cars, Vans

Note that in Section II you will have noted any car owned by the business or firm and whether it is also used privately. Do not count this car here also but find out whether there is a second car — e.g. wife's. If informant unable to value a vehicle note instead its make, type and year of manufacture to enable us to look up its value.

QUESTION 6c Debts on vehicles

Note that the question does not apply only to payments which are over-due but to the total sum still owing. You will usually have difficulty in excluding interest from the amount owed. If the amount owed is estimated at less than £50 record the sum and do not take up time making sure that the interest is deducted. But if the amount owed including the interest element is £50 or more ask for the details listed under (c). We will then make an estimate in the office.

QUESTION 7 Life Insurance

If there is more than one policy add up the payments and, if necessary, note any difference in frequency or years of payment. Note that our main object is to establish the equivalent current value in cash of policies they hold. The majority of households will hold policies of little current value and you will see that if they pay less than 10s. a week we do not ask for any details.

QUESTION 8 Value of saleable assets

Please note that we do not envisage that goods in everyday use — beds, blankets, basic furniture, crockery, clothes — need to be valued. We are interested only in items of value that could be sold without serious detri-ment to the household and its daily life if some ready cash was badly needed. Jewellery, furs, stamp collections, works of art, antiques, and collections of books, might be sold and we need to obtain an approximate estimate of their total current worth. Naturally enough we cannot expect precise valuations and you will find the minimum value of £25 for an article (or a group of articles — e.g. a number of pieces of jewellery) helpful in avoiding protracted discussion of the value of articles used every day in the home.

QUESTION 9 Other assets

Rarely will there be any kind of asset not covered by our other ques-tions. But by asking this general question you may be given information that belongs in the answer to another question. The informant may have misunderstood a question. But be careful not to include an item here which is already covered elsewhere.

QUESTIONS 10 & 11 General assets sold and windfalls

It may be difficult for you to secure an estimate of money raised or spent on " ordinary living expenses " but you will find that our object is fairly clear and once you understand it you can probe for an estimate. We do not want information about sums of money invested in new assets, in replacing old assets (e.g. property, including houses and cars) and in savings, but only information about sums of money spent in the ordinary way on housekeeping, food, clothing, and entertainment. An estimate is better than nothing. Note that we are not asking you to waste time checking small amounts of less than £25.

QUESTION 10 Assets sold in last 12 months

Some people, especially the elderly, will have sold some of their assets in the last 12 months to bolster a low income. This can be an important contribution to their standard of living. Savings—Note that each item should be prompted carefully, especially to persons who have already told you they have sizeable amounts in savings, stocks and shares, etc. Note that we are not interested in this question in total sums which amount to less than £25 in the 12 months. Nor are we interested in amounts that may have been saved from income and spent in the same year (e.g. savings for Christmas or a holiday).

Partial use of sales or savings for living expenses—In some cases property might have been sold, say, and part of the money spent but part of it saved. Try to get a total estimate only of the sum spent on ordinary living expenses.

25a

	1	2	3	4	5	6	7	8	9		
									1	2	

6. Do you own a car, van or motorcycle (apart from business vehicles already asked for)?

- X car
- Y two or more cars } ASK Q.6(a)
- O van
- 1 motor-cycle
- 2 other (SPECIFY) _____
- 3 no } SKIP TO Q.7
- 4 DK }

(a) What would it (they) sell for?   total value in £'s
IF TOTAL MORE THAN £250 ASK:

(b) Do you owe any money on it (them)?
I mean are you paying back a loan or making HP payments?   yes ASK Q.6(c) / no / DK } SKIP TO Q.7

(c) How much do you owe, excluding interest? *   total owed in £'s
IF DK OR UNCERTAIN ASK:

Original price _____   Amount each repayment _____
Deposit _____   No. of repayments made _____   No. still to make _____

7. Have you a life insurance, endowment insurance or death benefit policy?   yes ASK Q.7(a) / no / DK } SKIP TO Q.8

(a) Do you pay 10s. a week or more altogether?   yes ASK Q.7(b) / no / DK } SKIP TO Q.8

TICK IF DOCUMENTS SEEN

(b) How much do you pay?

(c) How many years have you paid?

(d) What is the total sum for which you are insured?   DK estimated total in £'s

8. If you needed to raise money in a hurry have you any personal possessions worth £25 or more which you could sell - and about how much are they worth altogether? I don't mean ordinary household equipment, furniture and clothing. I mean things you might do without if you had to - like jewellery, silver and antiques.   yes / no / DK

WRITE IN ITEMS AND ADD AMTS IF NECESSARY   total saleable assets in £'s

9. May I just check: Is there any other property or savings you own which you have not told me about?   yes ASK Q.9(a) / no / DK } SKIP TO Q.10

(a) What?

(b) How much is it worth?   total value in £'s

10. Have you in fact sold or borrowed anything worth £25 or more, or drawn out £25 or more of savings during the last 12 months to meet ordinary living expenses? I don't mean money to buy a house or other property, like a car, or to put into savings but money for rent, housekeeping, food, clothing and leisure. For example, have you

- X Sold property (including house, caravan, etc)?
- Y Raised a loan on property or a life insurance policy?
- PROMPT 0 Sold personal possessions (e.g. jewellery)? } ASK Q.10(a)
- ALL 1 Sold stocks or shares?
- THAT 2 Drawn savings?
- APPLY 3 Otherwise sold assets or borrowed money?
- 4 None of these }
- 5 DK } SKIP TO Q.11

(a) About how much did you raise altogether for these purposes?

SPECIFY ITEMS AND ADD AMOUNTS IF NECESSARY   total cash to meet expenses in £'s

Coding grid

	Inft	2nd	3rd	4th	INTERVIEWER: CODE 05, 06, etc. IF 5th, 6th MEMBERS OF HOUSEHOLD	
	10-11	10-11	10-11	10-11	10-11	10-11
	01	02	03	04		
	12	12	12	12	12	12
Q.6	X Y 0 1 2 3 4	X Y 0 1 2 3 4	X Y 0 1 2 3 4	X Y 0 1 2 3 4	X Y 0 1 2 3 4	X Y 0 1 2 3 4
	13-16 £	13-16 £	13-16 £	13-16 £	13-16 £	13-16 £
	17-20 X Y 0 £	17-20 X Y 0 £	17-20 X Y 0 £	17-20 X Y 0 £	17-20 X Y 0 £	17-20 X Y 0 £
Q.7	21 X Y 0 1 2 3	21 X Y 0 1 2 3	21 X Y 0 1 2 3	21 X Y 0 1 2 3	21 X Y 0 1 2 3	21 X Y 0 1 2 3
	22-25 X £	22-25 X £	22-25 X £	22-25 X £	22-25 X £	22-25 X £
	26-30 X Y 0 £	26-30 X Y 0 £	26-30 X Y 0 £	26-30 X Y 0 £	26-30 X Y 0 £	26-30 X Y 0 £
Q.9	31-35 X Y 0 £	31-35 X Y 0 £	31-35 X Y 0 £	31-35 X Y 0 £	31-35 X Y 0 £	31-35 X Y 0 £
Q.10	36 X Y 0 1 2 3 4 5	36 X Y 0 1 2 3 4 5	36 X Y 0 1 2 3 4 5	36 X Y 0 1 2 3 4 5	36 X Y 0 1 2 3 4 5	36 X Y 0 1 2 3 4 5
	37-41 £	37-41 £	37-41 £	37-41 £	37-41 £	37-41 £

25

QUESTION 11   "Windfalls"

The procedure is the same as in the last question (Q. 10). Remember that for some people an occasional windfall is the only hope they have of getting out of debt, and please make a note if you come across any interesting example.

QUESTION 12   Hire purchase

The informant may know neither the total amounts nor the amounts less interest which are owed. If the total is less than £25 simply write it in and do not waste time asking detailed questions about original price, etc. Otherwise ask each of the questions and tick the box if any documents are seen. Sometimes there may be several large items and you may need to use the margins on the page for any additional notes. Remember that we are concerned to establish the total owed altogether, less interest, and so long as this can be estimated you should not be concerned to take up time with every subsidiary question. If you cannot get the informant to give an estimate of the total owed less interest and succeed only in answering the questions under (a) you can leave to the office the job of estimating and writing in the total.

QUESTION 14   Rent or mortgage arrears

As elsewhere, remember to write in an amount in only one column (not in two columns, e.g. wife and husband). The amount should be debited to the person who normally pays the rent or the mortgage payments. Do not trouble to calculate the exact total amount owed. You have asked about the weekly or monthly payments earlier and so long as you tell us the number of payments (and whether weekly or monthly) we can calculate the figure in the office.

QUESTION 17   Total assets

Like the question at the end of the Income section, this question is designed to be used when an informant does not wish to go into detail or finds great difficulty, either in the first or in a subsequent interview, in answering preceding questions. Encourage him or her to help you gain at least a broad estimate of total assets, but remember this includes the value of any owner-occupied house, a car, the surrender value of any life insurance policy and personal possessions of value, as well as any savings or stocks and shares. Again, try to get a separate estimate for each income unit in the household, and if the informant shows willingness to go back to the preceding detailed questions encourage him to do so. Try if you can to get the informant to give an exact figure rather than a range.

26a

11. Apart from what you have told me about already have you received any other money amounting to £25 or more in the last 12 months which was spent on ordinary living expenses (rather than saved or used to buy property, like a house or a car) such as:

PROMPT	an inheritance	amount
AND CODE	betting or football pool win	
ALL THAT	premium bond or prize	
APPLY	other (SPECIFY)	
ON THE	none of these	
RIGHT	DK	

total gained in £'s

12. May I just check on debts or loans? Are you making hire purchase payments on personal possessions, for example on furniture and household appliances?

(a) How much altogether do you have to pay, excluding interest? *
yes — ASK Q.12(a)
no / DK — SKIP TO Q.13

IF DK OR UNCERTAIN ASK:
Original price
Deposit paid
Amount of each repayment
No. of repayments made
No. of repayments still to make

TICK IF DOCUMENTS SEEN
INTERVIEWER OR OFFICE total owed in £'s

13. FOR ALL WITH PERSONAL BANK ACCOUNT (Q.1)
Have you an overdraft on any personal bank account?
yes — ASK Q.13(a)
no
DK
Does Not Apply — SKIP TO Q.14

(a) How much is the overdraft, including any loan? total in £'s

14. FOR ALL PAYING RENT OR MORTGAGE
Are you behind with your rent/payments?
yes — ASK Q.14(a)
no
DK
Does Not Apply — SKIP TO Q.15

(a) How many weeks/payments (or total amount)? OFFICE: total arrears in £'s

15. Apart from what you have told me do you owe anyone any money — say £25 or more?
yes — ASK Q.15(a)
no / DK — SKIP TO Q.16

(a) How much? total in £'s

16. Does anyone owe you any money — say £25 or more?
yes — ASK Q.16(a)
no / DK — SKIP TO Q.17

(a) How much? total in £'s

17. IF SAVINGS AND ASSETS INFORMATION INCOMPLETE ASK:
It may be difficult to give any details but I wonder if you would mind looking at this card (SHOW FLASHCARD NO.4) and telling me which number best indicates the total value of any savings, property (including house and car) and personal possessions you may have?
DNA range code

PROBE FOR SEPARATE INCOME UNITS

total value in £'s if volunteered

1st	2nd	3rd	4th	INTERVIEWER: CODE 05, 06, etc. IF 5th, 6th MEMBERS OF HOUSEHOLD
42	42	42	42	42 42
X Y O 1 2 3	X Y O 1 2 3	X Y O 1 2 3	X Y O 1 2 3	X Y O 1 2 3	X Y O 1 2 3
43-47 £	43-47 £	43-47 £	43-47 £	43-47 £	43-47 £
48	48	48	48	48	48
X Y O	X Y O	X Y O	X Y O	X Y O	X Y O
49-52 £	49-52 £	49-52 £	49-52 £	49-52 £	49-52 £
53	53	53	53	53	53
X Y O 1	X Y O 1	X Y O 1	X Y O 1	X Y O 1	X Y O 1
54-58 £	54-58 £	54-58 £	54-58 £	54-58 £	54-58 £
59	59	59	59	59	59
X Y O 1	X Y O 1	X Y O 1	X Y O 1	X Y O 1	X Y O 1
60-62 £	60-62 £	60-62 £	60-62 £	60-62 £	60-62 £
63-66 X Y O £	63-66 X Y O £	63-66 X Y O £	66-66 X Y O £	63-66 X Y O £	63-66 X Y O £
67-70 X Y O £	67-70 X Y O £	67-70 X Y O £	67-70 X Y O £	67-70 X Y O £	67-70 X Y O £
71	71	71	71	71	71
X	X	X	X	X	X
72-76 £	72-76 £	72-76 £	72-76 £	72-76 £	72-76 £

VI HEALTH AND DISABILITY

QUESTION 1 Health

Do not probe for the names of disabling illnesses or conditions, unless the informant happens to mention them.

QUESTION 2 Unwell today

Note that the emphasis is on " today " and that you are instructed to complete the questionnaire as if all questions applied to the date when you first made contact with the household. This means that if you have postponed an interview because of illness you should ask all the questions about the day you first called.

QUESTION 2a Off work

Check with the work record (page 8) where weeks off work will have been established. But here the information is needed as the basis for general questions about current illness and disability.

QUESTION 2a (i) & b (i) Number of weeks

If more than a year write " 52 ". If the informant cannot be sure of the exact number and there is uncertainty whether it is less or more than eight weeks seek confirmation of the exact period from the individual concerned at a second call if necessary.

QUESTION 2c Regularly

That is, at least once a month for the past three months in connection with the present illness or disability.

QUESTION 3 Condition affecting activity

This question is designed to prepare the ground for the all-important Q. 7. You are not asked to trace every conceivable disability or condition from which people may suffer. Many of them, anyway, will not know diagnostic terms even if you ask them. Instead, you ask about conditions which restrict activity, show Flashcard No. 6 (which is nearly the same list as prompted verbally) and code any part of the body or faculty with which " trouble " is reported. You do not explore all possible effects but only a few examples of effects in which we are particularly interested. Remember you are only trying to find out about certain conditions, not every condition.

Nerves

Pay particular attention to the need to prompt for any trouble with " nerves ".

Reading ordinary print

Note that your code " No " only if a person cannot read print in a newspaper. Do not code " No " if a person merely has difficulty. For someone who cannot read interpret the question as " seeing " print in newspaper. We are interested at this point in sight not literacy.

Hearing

Note that if an informant does not admit difficulty with hearing but it is observed, you can code accordingly.

27a

VI HEALTH AND DISABILITY

I would like to ask a few questions about the health of yourself and the other members of the household.

1. How would you describe the health of each person living here? Generally, is it good for your (this/her) age, fair or poor?
good for age
fair for age
poor for age
DK

2. Is anyone in the family ill or unwell today? *
yes ASK Q.2(a)
no} SKIP TO Q.3
DK}

(a) Are you (is he/she)
5 off work? *}
6 off school?} ASK Q.2(a)(i)
7 neither off work nor off school} SKIP
8 Does Not Apply (e.g. housewife, TO
small child)} Q.2(b)

(i) How many weeks?
less than one
number *

(b) Are you (is he/she) confined to bed or to the house?
(i) For how many weeks continuously?
yes ASK Q.2(b)(i)
no SKIP TO Q.2(c)
less than one
number *

(c) Are you (is he/she) seeing a doctor regularly?
yes
no
DK

(d) What is the illness? WRITE IN ANSWER

3. Do you (does he/she) suffer from any condition which prevents you (him/her) from doing things which an ordinary person of the same age might expect to do? SHOW FLASHCARD NO.6 For example, do you have trouble with

	X	your chest or lungs ? ASK Q.3(a)
PROMPT	Y	your back or spine ?
	0	your joints ? ASK Q.3(b)
AND	*1	your nerves ? ASK Q.3(c)
CODE	2	your sight ? ASK Q.3(d)
ALL	3	your hearing ? ASK Q.3(e)
	4	your speech ? ASK Q.3(f)
THAT	5	fits or blackouts ?
	6	diabetes ? }SKIP
APPLY	7	a mental handicap (apart from nerves) ? }TO
	8	anything else important (SPECIFY) }Q.4
	9	DK
	X	none of these

(a) For example, do you become breathless or have any pain or fits of coughing when you hurry? yes no
(b) For example, do you have any difficulty in moving freely and fully and using your hands? yes no
(c)(i) Are you affected, for example
- by depression or weeping so that you can't face your work or mix with other people?
- by getting in a rage with other people? PROMPT AND
- by being unable to concentrate? CODE ALL
- by sleeping badly? THAT APPLY
- none of these

(ii) Are you seeing a doctor about it or having treatment for it? yes no
IF NO Do you think you should see the doctor about it? yes no
(d) For example, can you read ordinary print in a newspaper (even with glasses)? yes no
(e) Do you have difficulty hearing ordinary conversation? yes no but observed *
no
(f) Do you have difficulty joining in ordinary conversation with people outside the family? yes no

1	2	3	4	5	6	7	8	9	
							1	3	
Inft	2nd	3rd	4th	5th	6th	7	8	9	10
10-11	10-11	10-11	10-11	10-11	10-11	10-11	10-11	10-11	10-11
01	02	03	04	05	06	07	08	09	10
12	12	12	12	12	12	12	12	12	12
X	X	X	X	X	X	X	X	X	X
Y	Y	Y	Y	Y	Y	Y	Y	Y	Y
O	O	O	O	O	O	O	O	O	O
1	1	1	1	1	1	1	1	1	1
2	2	2	2	2	2	2	2	2	2
3	3	3	3	3	3	3	3	3	3
4	4	4	4	4	4	4	4	4	4
5	5	5	5	5	5	5	5	5	5
6	6	6	6	6	6	6	6	6	6
7	7	7	7	7	7	7	7	7	7
8	8	8	8	8	8	8	8	8	8
13-14	13-14	13-14	13-14	13-14	13-14	13-14	13-14	13-14	13-14
X	X	X	X	X	X	X	X	X	X
15-16	15-16	15-16	15-16	15-16	15-16	15-16	15-16	15-16	15-16
X	X	X	X	X	X	X	X	X	X
Y	Y	Y	Y	Y	Y	Y	Y	Y	Y
O	O	O	O	O	O	O	O	O	O
17	17	17	17	17	17	17	17	17	17
X	X	X	X	X	X	X	X	X	X
Y	Y	Y	Y	Y	Y	Y	Y	Y	Y
O	O	O	O	O	O	O	O	O	O
18	18	18	18	18	18	18	18	18	
X	X	X	X	X	X	X	X	X	
Y	Y	Y	Y	Y	Y	Y	Y	Y	
O	O	O	O	O	O	O	O	O	
1	1	1	1	1	1	1	1	1	
2	2	2	2	2	2	2	2	2	
3	3	3	3	3	3	3	3	3	
4	4	4	4	4	4	4	4	4	
5	5	5	5	5	5	5	5	5	
6	6	6	6	6	6	6	6	6	
7	7	7	7	7	7	7	7	7	
8	8	8	8	8	8	8	8	8	
9	9	9	9	9	9	9	9	9	
19	19	19	19	19	19	19	19	19	
X	X	X	X	X	X	X	X	X	
Y	Y	Y	Y	Y	Y	Y	Y	Y	
O	O	O	O	O	O	O	O	O	
1	1	1	1	1	1	1	1	1	
2	2	2	2	2	2	2	2	2	
3	3	3	3	3	3	3	3	3	
4	4	4	4	4	4	4	4	4	
5	5	5	5	5	5	5	5	5	
6	6	6	6	6	6	6	6	6	
7	7	7	7	7	7	7	7	7	
20	20	20	20	20	20	20	20	20	
X	X	X	X	X	X	X	X	X	
Y	Y	Y	Y	Y	Y	Y	Y	Y	
O	O	O	O	O	O	O	O	O	
1	1	1	1	1	1	1	1	1	
2	2	2	2	2	2	2	2	2	
3	3	3	3	3	3	3	3	3	
4	4	4	4	4	4	4	4	4	
5	5	5	5	5	5	5	5	5	
6	6	6	6	6	6	6	6	6	
7	7	7	7	7	7	7	7	7	
8	8	8	8	8	8	8	8	8	

QUESTION 4 Special schools & centres

This question is asked only of persons who have been ill and off work or confined to bed or the house for eight weeks or more continuously, and those who are coded for any item in Question 3.

QUESTION 5 Date of onset of sickness or disabling condition

Our object is to establish the year of onset but the question is worded ' first have any condition " so as to allow for the fact that some conditions develop out of others. For persons with a disabling condition you ask, in effect, when all the trouble started.

Previous occupation

In the section on Employment you have already asked for the last occupation of everyone not now at work (p. 7). Some people change their occupation because of a disabling condition before finally being obliged to give up work. You should probe for the (previous) occupation which people had before any history of illness or disability started.

QUESTION 6 Mobility

You should code people according to their **usual** mobility, taking no account of a temporary illness or injury. " Usual mobility " may be interpreted as " for at least eight weeks and unlikely to become more mobile in the immediate future " or " for less than eight weeks but unlikely to become more mobile within at least that total period." Someone who spends most of the time in bed and needs help to get out to sit in a chair is defined as bedfast. Someone who can get out of his bed into a chair or wheelchair and who can walk indoors but not even a few yards outdoors without help is defined as housebound. The test is whether someone can walk on his own (without the assistance or company of any other person — though with or without sticks or crutches).

QUESTION 7 Incapacity

In prompting this series of questions you may find it simplest to ask the question without the variation in brackets, unless it seems appropriate. Remember you are asking whether they have any difficulty in doing X. Sometimes certain questions will not apply to particular people or to particular situations. You will meet people who do not (or say they do not) wash down, negotiate stairs (living in bungalows), go shopping and do housework (especially some men). The question should then be asked in terms of " But would you have any difficulty in doing X if you had to? " The codes 0, 1, 2 are listed in increasing order of difficulty and you should check that you ring one of them for each item.

QUESTION 7e

It would be insensitive and unnecessary to ask questions about the daily activities of the bedfast. They are therefore excluded from this question and the rest of the series. You may encounter other people (e.g. advanced obesity) of whom it is clear that they cannot do certain activities. You may refrain from putting questions to them. The same is true of any situations in which the questions are likely to cause great distress. BUT AS A GENERAL RULE QUESTIONS 7 (e) to (i) SHOULD BE ASKED FOR ALL OTHER THAN THE BEDFAST AND CHAIRFAST.

QUESTIONS 8 & 9 Variation in incapacity

These questions explore whether the pattern of answers to Question 7 is permanent. Question 8 seeks any indication of seasonal variations (e.g. bronchitis) and Question 9 day-to-day variations in the effects of disability.

4. FOR THOSE WITH ANY LONG-TERM ILLNESS (8 WEEKS OR MORE - Q.2(a)8(b))
AND ANY CONDITION (Q.3)
Do you attend - a special training or occupational treatment centre?
- a special school?
- a disabled person's club?
- any other club, school or centre because of your health?
- no club, school or centre?
Does Not Apply   LONG-TERM SKIP TO Q.6

5. FOR THOSE AGED 15-64 WITH ANY LONG-TERM ILLNESS OR CONDITION
(a) When did you first become sick or have any condition? *
[ ]   Does Not Apply SKIP TO Q.6
    19____   19____WRITE IN NUMBER OF YEARS AGO
(b) What was your occupation then? Was it the last occupation you had
(which you have already told   never had paid employment   ]SKIP
me about (p.7) or a previous   condition started in last job held]TO Q.6
one?   condition started in previous job ASK
                                                                  Q.5(c)
(c) What was that previous job? WRITE IN OCCUPATION AND EMPLOYER'S
                                        (OWN) BUSINESS
[ ] _____
[ ] _____

6. ASK ALL. Is there anyone living here who is *
X - usually confined to bed or needs help to get out of bed and sit
    in a chair?
Y - not confined to bed but cannot walk unaided a few yards outdoors
    without help?
O - neither of these
I - DK

7. ASK OF ALL EXCEPT CHILDREN UNDER 10
* Do you or would you have any   Does Not Apply SKIP TO Q.9
difficulty (or find it troublesome, CODE O = no difficulty
exhausting or worrying)   CODE I = has/would have difficulty
                                     CODE 2 = cannot do task
(a) washing down (whether in bath or not)?

(b) removing a jug, say, from an overhead shelf?

(c) tying a good knot in string?

(d) cutting toenails?

NOW CONTINUE FOR ALL EXCEPT CHILDREN UNDER 10 AND THE BEDFAST
                                Does Not Apply SKIP TO Q.8
(e) running to catch a bus?

(f) going up and downstairs?

(g) going shopping AND carrying a full basket of shopping in each hand?
AND NOW CONTINUE FOR ALL EXCEPT CHILDREN UNDER 16 AND THE BEDFAST
                                Does Not Apply SKIP TO Q.8
(h) doing heavy housework, like washing floors and cleaning windows?

(i) preparing a hot meal?

        Dont Know for any or all of these

8. Are there any other periods of the year when you might give
different answers to these questions (i.e. in Q.7) about
ordinary activities? *   yes ASK Q.8(a)
                                  no]
                                  DK] SKIP TO Q.9
(a) In those periods would you find any of the activities
                - much more difficult?
                - more difficult?
                - easier?
                - much easier?

9. ASK ALL CODED I or 2 FOR ANY ITEM IN Q.7
Would you say you vary from week to week or day to day   yes
In having difficulty with any of these activities?   no
                                                         DK
                                                         DNA

10. FOR HOUSEWIFE ONLY
Do you feel tired - all the time?
                  - sometimes?
                  - rarely or never?
                              DK
                              DNA

Row	Inft	2nd	3rd	4th	5th	6th	7	8	9	10
21	X Y 0 I 2 3	X Y 0 I 2 3	X Y 0 I 2 3	X Y 0 I 2 3	X Y 0 I 2 3	X Y 0 I 2 3	X Y 0 I 2 3	X Y 0 I 2 3	X Y 0 I 2 3	X Y 0 I 2 3
22-23	X	X	X	X	X	X	X	X	X	X
24	X Y 0	X Y 0	X Y 0	X Y 0	X Y 0	X Y 0	X Y 0	X Y 0	X Y 0	X Y 0
25	X Y 0 I	X Y 0 I	X Y 0 I	X Y 0 I	X Y 0 I	X Y 0 I	X Y 0 I	X Y 0 I	X Y 0 I	X Y 0 I
26	X	X	X	X	X	X	X	X	X	X
26	0 I 2	0 I 2	0 I 2	0 I 2	0 I 2	0 I 2	0 I 2	0 I 2	0 I 2	0 I 2
27	0 I 2	0 I 2	0 I 2	0 I 2	0 I 2	0 I 2	0 I 2	0 I 2	0 I 2	0 I 2
28	0 I 2	0 I 2	0 I 2	0 I 2	0 I 2	0 I 2	0 I 2	0 I 2	0 I 2	0 I 2
29	0 I 2	0 I 2	0 I 2	0 I 2	0 I 2	0 I 2	0 I 2	0 I 2	0 I 2	0 I 2
30	0 I 2	0 I 2	0 I 2	0 I 2	0 I 2	0 I 2	0 I 2	0 I 2	0 I 2	0 I 2
(X Y 0 I)	X Y 0 I	X Y 0 I	X Y 0 I	X Y 0 I	X Y 0 I	X Y 0 I	X Y 0 I	X Y 0 I	X Y 0 I	X Y 0 I
31	0 I 2	0 I 2	0 I 2	0 I 2	0 I 2	0 I 2	0 I 2	0 I 2	0 I 2	0 I 2
32	0 I 2	0 I 2	0 I 2	0 I 2	0 I 2	0 I 2	0 I 2	0 I 2	0 I 2	0 I 2
33	X	X	X	X	X	X	X	X	X	X
33	0 I 2	0 I 2	0 I 2	0 I 2	0 I 2	0 I 2	0 I 2	0 I 2	0 I 2	0 I 2
34	0 I 2	0 I 2	0 I 2	0 I 2	0 I 2	0 I 2	0 I 2	0 I 2	0 I 2	0 I 2
35	X	X	X	X	X	X	X	X	X	X
	Y 0 I 2 3 4 5	Y 0 I 2 3 4 5	Y 0 I 2 3 4 5	Y 0 I 2 3 4 5	Y 0 I 2 3 4 5	Y 0 I 2 3 4 5	Y 0 I 2 3 4 5	Y 0 I 2 3 4 5	Y 0 I 2 3 4 5	Y 0 I 2 3 4 5
36	X Y 0 I	X Y 0 I	X Y 0 I	X Y 0 I	X Y 0 I	X Y 0 I	X Y 0 I	X Y 0 I	X Y 0 I	X Y 0 I
37	X Y 0 I 2	X Y 0 I 2	X Y 0 I 2	X Y 0 I 2	X Y 0 I 2	X Y 0 I 2	X Y 0 I 2	X Y 0 I 2	X Y 0 I 2	X Y 0 I 2

VII SOCIAL SERVICES

General

It is assumed that the housewife will normally be the informant. It is also assumed that she will generally be the "parent" to whom many of the questions are addressed. If in fact there is another mother in the household with a child then you may accept answers by a proxy (i.e. the housewife). You should also use your discretion about the housewife's ability to answer questions about the visits to hospital, doctor or dentist by each member of the household. If she plainly does not know or is uncertain you should check the appropriate questions when you come to ask earners in the household Sections II, III & IV. If this still does not involve the right members of the household you must check directly with them. Remember to code carefully since the questions vary as to whom they apply. We have repeated instructions at the head of each question to help you.

QUESTION 1 Welfare milk

Tokens are obtained from the Ministry of Social Security and handed to the milkman. All families with children under 5 can obtain a pint of milk for each child for each day for 6d. per pint cheaper than retail prices. Free milk tokens have to be claimed separately, and few parents claim them (other than those getting supplementary benefits).

QUESTION 2

Child welfare clinics are provided by local authority health departments. A visit to an ordinary hospital out-patient department does not count. Cod liver oil and orange juice are the main goods which may be purchased below normal shop prices. "Ever visited" means for the informant herself to obtain advice concerning herself or her child or to obtain goods. Accompanying another mother does not count.

QUESTION 3 Baby in hospital

It is possible there may be two mothers in the household.
On the National Health means **free** in a National Health Service hospital contracted to the N.H.S.

QUESTION 4 Type of school

Write in the name of each school on the left. The parent will usually know the type of school but if he or she does not or is doubtful the interviewer may know. If in doubt please verify from the Education Department or a teacher who knows about the local schools. If the child is aged 16 or over and is at an institute, college or school (of commerce, for example), list under Q. 12.

Type	Maintained day nursery, nursery school or class	1
of	Private nursery school or nursery class	2
School	State primary school	3
	Private primary/preparatory school	4
	Secondary modern/elementary/non-grammar denominational	5
	Comprehensive	6
	Technical school, Central, Intermediate	7
	State grammar	8
	Private or "public" school (secondary)	9
	Other (SPECIFY)	0

Whether built pre- or post-1940

Again, the parent may not know or may be unsure. Check if necessary.

QUESTION 5 School meals

Normally means when neither sick nor in the holidays. Did the child last week have school meals if attending school? If not attending school, when last attending school. Free school meals are provided to poorer children on a means test basis.

QUESTION 5(c) No facilities

There really are schools which do not offer school meals either because they lack dining space or there are too many children for the space available or for other reasons.

QUESTION 7 Days absent from school

Absences due to visiting an out-patient department or a dentist should not be counted.

QUESTION 8 Boarding school

If the child boards at a school which is primarily a day school code the answer "yes".

29a

VII SOCIAL SERVICES

FOR CHILDREN UNDER 5 (i.e. TO MOTHER OR PERSON CARING FOR CHILD)
Not under 5, DNA   SKIP TO Q.4
1. Do you get welfare milk * for him/her - at the cheaper rate
                                         - free
                                         or not at all?
                                         DK

2. ASK MOTHER OF CHILD UNDER 5   CODE (EACH) MOTHER ONLY
   Have you visited the child   X Does Not Apply
   welfare clinic in the last year   Y Visited and obtained goods } SKIP
   and obtained anything there   O Visited but not obtained goods TO
   for the children?   I DK   } Q.3
                                     2 Goods obtained but not visited) ASK
                                     3 Neither visited nor goods   ) Q.2(a)
                                                          obtained
(a) Have you ever visited the clinic?   yes
                                                    no
                                                    DK

3. ASK MOTHER OF CHILD UNDER 5   CODE (EACH) MOTHER
   Did you have your last baby in hospital   Does Not Apply SKIP
   or at home?   Home   TO
                                             DK   Q.4
                                             Hospital ASK Q.3(a)
(a) Was it on the National Health? *   yes
                                                   no
                                                   DK

4. ASK PARENTS OF CHILDREN AT SCHOOL   CODE EACH CHILD
   What school does your child attend?   Does Not Apply SKIP TO Q.9
   WRITE IN NAME   * CODE TYPE FROM LIST OPPOSITE

   [   ]   * CODE WHETHER BUILT PRE-1940
   [   ]   BUILT 1940 OR LATER
   [   ]

5. ASK PARENTS OF CHILDREN AT SCHOOL   CODE EACH CHILD
   Does he/she normally take meals   yes, always or nearly always) ASK
   at school? *   yes, but sometimes at home } Q.5
                                     or elsewhere   ) (a)
                                     no   ASK Q.5(b)
                                     DK   SKIP TO Q.6
(a) Does he/she pay for the meals or get them free?   pays } SKIP TO
                                                      free } Q.6
                                                      DK
(b) What does he/she normally do?   has meals at home
    PROMPT   has meals with relative
                                      takes sandwiches
                                      buys meals out
              Anything else? other (SPECIFY) _____

(c) Why doesn't he/she have meals   * No facilities at school?
    at school?   Cheaper at home?
                        Child doesn't like type of food?
                                        Not enough to eat?
              Anything else? (SPECIFY) _____

6. ASK PARENT OF CHILDREN AT SCHOOL   CODE EACH CHILD
   Does he/she have free milk at school?   yes
                                                     no
                                                     DK

7. ASK PARENT OF CHILDREN AT SCHOOL
   Did he/she miss any days off school last term for any reason
   besides sickness* such as - going out with someone in the family?
   PROMPT AND CODE   - helping at home?
   ALL THAT APPLY   - having no dry shoes or a raincoat to put on?
                              - anything else? (SPECIFY)
                              DK

8. ASK PARENT OF CHILDREN AT SCHOOL   CODE EACH CHILD
   Does he/she go to a boarding school?   yes ASK Q.8(a)
                                          no } SKIP TO Q.9
                                          DK }
(a) Who pays the fees?   local Education Dept.
                          paid privately
                  other SPECIFY _____

Inft	2nd	3rd	4th	5th	6th	7	8	9	10
38	38	38	38	38	38	38	38	38	38
X	X	X	X	X	X	X	X	X	X
Y	Y	Y	Y	Y	Y	Y	Y	Y	Y
O	O	O	O	O	O	O	O	O	O
I	I	I	I	I	I	I	I	I	I
2	2	2	2	2	2	2	2	2	2
39	39	39	39	39	39	39	39	39	39
X	X	X	X	X	X.	X	X	X	X
Y	Y	Y	Y	Y	Y	Y	Y	Y	Y
O	O	O	O	O	O	O	O	O	O
I	I	I	I	I	I	I	I	I	I
2	2	2	2	2	2	2	2	2	2
3	3	3	3	3	3	3	3	3	3
40	40	40	40	40	40	40	40	40	40
X	X	X	X	X	X	X	X	X	X
Y	Y	Y	Y	Y	Y	Y	Y	Y	Y
O	O	O	O	O	O	O	O	O	O
I	I	I	I	I	I	I	I	I	I
2	2	2	2	2	2	2	2	2	2
3	3	3	3	3	3	3	3	3	3
4	4	4	4	4	4	4	4	4	4
41	41	41	41	41	41	41	41	41	41
X	X	X	X	X	X	X	X	X	X
X	X	X	X	X	X	X	X	X	X
Y	Y	Y	Y	Y	Y	Y	Y	Y	Y
42	42	42	42	42	42	42	42	42	42
X	X	X	X	X	X	X	X	X	X
Y	Y	Y	Y	Y	Y	Y	Y	Y	Y
O	O	O	O	O	O	O	O	O	O
I	I	I	I	I	I	I	I	I	I
2	2	2	2	2	2	2	2	2	2
3	3	3	3	3	3	3	3	3	3
4	4	4	4	4	4	4	4	4	4
5	5	5	5	5	5	5	5	5	5
6	6	6	6	6	6	6	6	6	6
7	7	7	7	7	7	7	7	7	7
8	8	8	8	8	8	8	8	8	8
9	9	9	9	9	9	9	9	9	9
43	43	43	43	43	43	43	43	43	43
X	X	X	X	X	X	X	X	X	X
Y	Y	Y	Y	Y	Y	Y	Y	Y	Y
O	O	O	O	O	O	O	O	O	O
I	I	I	I	I	I	I	I	I	I
2	2	2	2	2	2	2	2	2	2
3	3	3	3	3	3	3	3	3	3
4	4	4	4	4	4	4	4	4	4
5	5	5	5	5	5	5	5	5	5
44	44	44	44	44	44	44	44	44	44
X	X	X	X	X	X	X	X	X	X
Y	Y	Y	Y	Y	Y	Y	Y	Y	Y
O	O	O	O	O	O	O	O	O	O
I	I	I	I	I	I	I	I	I	I
2	2	2	2	2	2	2	2	2	2
45	45	45	45	45	45	45	45	45	45
X	X	X	X	X	X	X	X	X	X
Y	Y	Y	Y	Y	Y	Y	Y	Y	Y
O	O	O	O	O	O	O	O	O	O
I	I	I	I	I	I	I	I	I	I
2	2	2	2	2	2	2	2	2	2
3	3	3	3	3	3	3	3	3	3

QUESTION 9

Uniform grants are available to poorer children in State schools on a means test basis. The grant can be in kind: a parent may be given a voucher or a letter to take to a special shop. NOTE that the question is addressed ONLY TO ONE OF THE PARENTS OF THE CHILD OR CHILDREN. Very uncommonly there will be two sets of parents and children in the household. ONE parent of the second family should also be asked the question. ONLY complete the column alongside Qs. 10a and 10b for the parent in question. If the parent says the grant was made by the Supplementary Benefits Commission check whether you have already included the amount in Q. 15 (code 14) of the Income Section. If not, include the amount here. Remember to code parent only.

QUESTION 10   Costs of going to school

We are interested not only in fees paid to private or " public " schools but in some kinds of cost met by parents of children in State schools. Fees include payments for music lessons. School outings — We are interested only in payments for outings or school holidays organised by the school or a school club which the child went on.

QUESTION 11

Educational maintenance allowances are provided by local authorities for poorer children attending school between the ages of 15 and 18 on a means test basis. We ask parents of 14-year-olds whether they have heard about them to find whether this is taken into account in the decision to leave school. We are also interested in applications which were refused or which were made and the child did not in the end continue at school after the minimum leaving age.

QUESTION 12   Type of college

Teacher training college	1
College of Education	2
Technical college	3
University	4
College or School of Commerce	5
Art college	6
Domestic Science college	7
Evening Institute	8
Secretarial college	9
Other: SPECIFY	0

As with " school " the informant may not know the type and the interviewer may be able to code on the basis of the name supplied. Or he should check on the basis of that name. Part time DAY study means attendance during normal working hours when the student or pupil works for a salary or wage, however small, or, if he has no job, attendance during the morning or afternoon.

QUESTION 12 (d) & 12 (g)   Fees and cash from others

Code source of help but if the amount has been included in the Income section earlier (i.e. Q. 20 of that section) make a note, drawing our attention to the fact.

30a

	Intt	2nd	3rd	4th	5th	6th	INTERVIEWER: CODE 07, 08, etc. IF 7th, 8th MEMBERS

9. ASK PARENT WITH CHILD(REN) AT SCHOOL   CODE EACH CHILD
Does the school have a uniform?
  X yes ASK Q.9(a)
  Y no } SKIP TO Q.10
  0 DK }

(a) Do you know that uniform grants can be obtained for some secondary school children? *
  1 Does Not Apply SKIP TO Q.11
  2 yes ASK Q.9(b)   CODE INFOR-
  3 no SKIP TO Q.10 MANT ONLY

(b) Have you had one during the last 12 months?   •
  CODE INFORMANT ONLY
  4 yes, local ed. dept.} ASK
  5 yes, SBC or other } Q.9(c)
  6 no

(c) For how much?   WRITE IN AMOUNT TO NEAREST £ FOR RECIPIENT ONLY

Intt	2nd	3rd	4th	5th	6th		
46	46	46	46	46	46	46	46
X	X	X	X	X	X	X	X
Y	Y	Y	Y	Y	Y	Y	Y
0	0	0	0	0	0	0	0
1	1	1	1	1	1	1	1
2	2	2	2	2	2	2	2
3	3	3	3	3	3	3	3
4	4	4	4	4	4	4	4
5	5	5	5	5	5	5	5
6	6	6	6	6	6	6	6
47-48	47-48	47-48	47-48	47-48	47-48	47-48	47-48
£	£	£	£	£	£	£	£

10. ASK PARENT WITH CHILD(REN) AT SCHOOL   WRITE IN AMT FOR EACH CHILD
Does it cost you anything to have your children at school? *
- In fees you pay to the school?   WRITE IN AMT IN £'s PER YEAR

49-51	49-51	49-51	49-51	49-51	49-51	49-51	49-51
£	£	£	£	£	£	£	£

- In materials for classes (e.g. cooking, carpentry, books) per year?   AMT IN £'s

52-53	52-53	52-53	52-53	52-53	52-53	52-53	52-53
£	£	£	£	£	£	£	£

- school holidays/outings (per year)?   AMT IN £'s

54-55	54-55	54-55	54-55	54-55	54-55	54-55	54-55
£	£	£	£	£	£	£	£

- more than 5s. per week (per child) in bus or train fares?   SHILLINGS PER WEEK
  none of these
  DK

56-57	56-57	56-57	56-57	56-57	56-57	56-57	56-57
s	s	s	s	s	s	s	s
58	58	58	58	58	58	58	58
X	X	X	X	X	X	X	X
Y	Y	Y	Y	Y	Y	Y	Y

11. ASK PARENT OF CHILD(REN) AGED 14-18 (WHETHER CHILDREN AT SCHOOL OR NOT)
Have you heard of educational maintenance allowances? *
  CODE INFORMANT ONLY
  X yes ASK Q.11(a)
  Y no } SKIP TO Q.12
  0 DK }
  1 Does Not Apply

(a) IF CHILD(REN) AGED 15-18 Did you apply for a maintenance allowance for him/her and were you successful?
  2 yes, successful } ASK Q.11(b)
  3 yes, unsuccessful }
  4 no } SKIP TO Q.12
  5 DNA (AGED 14) }

(b) Are you (or the child) currently receiving an allowance?
  6 yes ASK Q.11(c)
  7 no SKIP TO Q.12

(c) How much a year does it amount to?   WRITE IN AMT IN £'s

59	59	59	59	59	59	59	59
X	X	X	X	X	X	X	X
Y	Y	Y	Y	Y	Y	Y	Y
0	0	0	0	0	0	0	0
1	1	1	1	1	1	1	1
2	2	2	2	2	2	2	2
3	3	3	3	3	3	3	3
4	4	4	4	4	4	4	4
5	5	5	5	5	5	5	5
6	6	6	6	6	6	6	6
7	7	7	7	7	7	7	7
60-62	60-62	60-62	60-62	60-62	60-62	60-62	60-62
£	£	£	£	£	£	£	£

12. ASK ABOUT ALL AGED 16-25
Does he/she still go to school, university or technical college, or is he/she still taking any other kind of educational course?
  CODE PERSONS AGED 16-25
  X Does Not Apply } SKIP TO
  Y no } Q.13
  0 DK }
  1 yes ASK Q.12(a)

(a) Is this
  - full-time?
  - part-time by day?
  - part-time by evening?

63	63	63	63	63	63	63	63
X	X	X	X	X	X	X	X
Y	Y	Y	Y	Y	Y	Y	Y
0	0	0	0	0	0	0	0
1	1	1	1	1	1	1	1
2	2	2	2	2	2	2	2
3	3	3	3	3	3	3	3
4	4	4	4	4	4	4	4
64	64	64	64	64	64	64	64

(b) Which college/course?   CODE TYPE * FROM LIST OPPOSITE

(c) How much a year does he/she obtain in any grant?   WRITE IN AMT IN £'s

65-67	65-67	65-67	65-67	65-67	65-67	65-67	65-67
£	£	£	£	£	£	£	£

(d) Are any fees paid (in addition) by
  X - him/herself or his/her parents?
  Y - someone else in the household? } ASK
  0 - a relative living elsewhere? } Q.12
  1 - someone else (SPECIFY)___ } (e)
  2 DK }
  3 none of these } SKIP TO Q.12(f)

(e) How much in the last 12 months? *   WRITE IN AMT IN £'s

68	68	68	68	68	68	68	68
X	X	X	X	X	X	X	X
Y	Y	Y	Y	Y	Y	Y	Y
0	0	0	0	0	0	0	0
1	1	1	1	1	1	1	1
2	2	2	2	2	2	2	2
3	3	3	3	3	3	3	3
69-71	69-71	69-71	69-71	69-71	69-71	69-71	69-71
£	£	£	£	£	£	£	£

(f) Does he/she get any help privately - I mean full keep or an allowance for example from
  X - you (parents)? } ASK
  Y - someone else in household } Q.12
  0 - a relative living elsewhere? } (g)
  1 - someone else (SPECIFY)___
  2 DK }
  3 none } SKIP TO Q.13

72	72	72	72	72	72	72	72
X	X	X	X	X	X	X	X
Y	Y	Y	Y	Y	Y	Y	Y
0	0	0	0	0	0	0	0
1	1	1	1	1	1	1	1
2	2	2	2	2	2	2	2
3	3	3	3	3	3	3	3
73-75	73-75	73-75	73-75	73-75	73-75	73-75	73-75
£	£	£	£	£	£	£	£

(g) How much altogether in the last 12 months? * WRITE IN AMT IN £'s

30

QUESTION 13

NHS means free, wholly paid for by the National Health Service. Private and amenity (paying) beds in NHS hospitals should be coded as private.

QUESTION 13(b)   Number of nights

If a person has had two or more spells in hospital add the total number of nights together.

QUESTION 13(c)   Name of hospital

This will be used in the office to code type of hospital.

QUESTION 14

Ill in bed means actually in bed for at least half the day.

QUESTION 15

Visits by and to a doctor will include calls when a person is no longer in bed but up and about. The questions are not, therefore, dependent on the answer yes to Q. 14. When the household is large and/or when there have been several visits it may take you a little time to obtain a reliable answer. Remember that in cases of difficulty it is usually best to approach the answer by asking: " When did you last see your doctor? " "And when was the time before that? " " So that means you saw your doctor seven times altogether in the last 12 months? " Remember that we want to count each consultation, even if there are two consultations on one day or on succeeding days. Remember also to include locums and other (alternative) doctor seen in this period.

QUESTION 15(c)   Visits paid for

If the informant is a wife who makes a visit to her NHS doctor and pays later for the pill, which he prescribes, this should still be counted as a NHS visit.

QUESTION 16   Spectacles

Most people pay in part for spectacles even under the NHS but some obtain them free by paying and then claiming a refund on test of means (by the SBC).

QUESTION 18 Doctor at hospital

It is the number of occasions we want to know, not the number of doctors seen at the hospital.

Visits to dentist

Remember to ask number of visits, not number of courses of treatment.

Home help

We are interested only in the use of a local council's Home Help Service.

Someone from the Welfare

We mean a social worker or officer fro ma Council health, welfare or children's department who is concerned with some aspect of family welfare. Include a health visitor, say, but not an officer from the Supplementary Benefits Commission or someone from a voluntary organisation — like the WVS or Salvation Army.

QUESTION 18(a)   Paying a dentist

The point is that very poor people can get free dentures and do not have to pay the £1 for a course of treatment.

QUESTION 18(b)   Home help

Some councils charge for a home help's service on test of means.

31a

	2	3	4	5	6	7	8 9	
							1 4	

	Inft	2nd	3rd	4th	5th	6th	INTERVIEWER: CODE 07, 08, etc. IF 7th, 8th MEMBER OR HOUSEHOLD	

13. ASK ALL
Have you spent any period in a hospital or nursing Home overnight during the last 12 months?

CODE ALL IN HOUSEHOLD   yes ASK Q.13(a)
no } SKIP TO Q.14
DK

	10-11	10-11	10-11	10-11	10-11	10-11	10-11	10-11
	01	02	03	04	05	06		
	12	12	12	12	12	12	12	12
	X	X	X	X	X	X	X	X
	Y	Y	Y	Y	Y	Y	Y	Y
	0	0	0	0	0	0	0	0

(a) Was it on the National Health?   ✱ NHS   private

	1	1	1	1	1	1	1	1
	2	2	2	2	2	2	2	2

(b) How many nights altogether?   WRITE IN NUMBER
(c) What was its name?

	13-15	13-15	13-15	13-15	13-15	13-15	13-15	13-15

OFFICE USE ONLY:
HOSPITAL TYPE

	16	16	16	16	16	16	16	16

	17	17	17	17	17	17	17	17

14. ASK ALL. Have you been ill in bed* at home for even a day during the last year?   X yes, ill or bedfast at present } ASK Q.14a
Y yes, ill previously
O no
CODE ALL IN HOUSEHOLD   I DK

	X	X	X	X	X	X	X	X
	Y	Y	Y	Y	Y	Y	Y	Y
	0	0	0	0	0	0	0	0
	I	I	I	I	I	I	I	I

(a) How many days altogether (i.e. in bed)?   WRITE IN NUMBER OF DAYS

	18-20	18-20	18-20	18-20	18-20	18-20	18-20	18-20

(b) When you were (last) ill in bed, were you visited by a doctor or a district nurse?   X yes, doctor
Y yes, nurse
CODE ALL THAT APPLY   O no
I DK.

	21	21	21	21	21	21	21	21
	X	X	X	X	X	X	X	X
	Y	Y	Y	Y	Y	Y	Y	Y
	0	0	0	0	0	0	0	0
	I	I	I	I	I	I	I	I

15. ASK ALL.
(a) How many times did a doctor visit you during the last 12 months?   CODE ALL   number: home

	22-23	22-23	22-23	22-23	22-23	22-23	22-23	22-23

(b) How many times did you visit a doctor during the last 12 months – I mean in a surgery – not in a hospital or out-patients? *   number: surgery

	24-25	24-25	24-25	24-25	24-25	24-25	24-25	24-25

IF ANY VISITS (c) Were these visits on the National Health?   NHS
paid *
NHS and paid

	26	26	26	26	26	26	26	26
	X	X	X	X	X	X	X	X
	Y	Y	Y	Y	Y	Y	Y	Y
	0	0	0	0	0	0	0	0

16. ASK ALL. Have you obtained a pair of spectacles on the National Health or privately in the last year?
X yes, NHS lenses and frames
Y yes, NHS lenses OR frames } ASK Q.16(a)
O yes, private
I no } SKIP TO Q.17
2 DK
(a) Did you pay anything for them?   3 yes
4 no

	27	27	27	27	27	27	27	27
	X	X	X	X	X	X	X	X
	Y	Y	Y	Y	Y	Y	Y	Y
	0	0	0	0	0	0	0	0
	I	I	I	I	I	I	I	I
	2	2	2	2	2	2	2	2
	3	3	3	3	3	3	3	3
	4	4	4	4	4	4	4	4

17. ASK ALL. Do you possess a National Health Service or a private hearing aid?   CODE ALL THAT APPLY
yes, NHS
yes, private
no
DK

	5	5	5	5	5	5	5	5
	6	6	6	6	6	6	6	6
	7	7	7	7	7	7	7	7
	8	8	8	8	8	8	8	8

18. ASK ALL. During the last 12 months have you   WRITE IN NO. OF VISITS FOR EACH PERSON
– visited a doctor at a hospital? IF YES How many times? *

	28-29	28-29	28-29	28-29	28-29	28-29	28-29	28-29

PROMPT AND WRITE IN NUMBER OF VISITS IF ANY
– visited a dentist? IF YES How many times? ✱ASK Q.18(a)

	30-31	30-31	30-31	30-31	30-31	30-31	30-31	30-31

– been visited by a district nurse? IF YES How many times?

	32-33	32-33	32-33	32-33	32-33	32-33	32-33	32-33

– been visited by a council home help?* IF YES How many times? ASK.Q.18(b)

	34-35	34-35	34-35	34-35	34-35	34-35	34-35	34-35

– been visited by someone from the welfare, such as a welfare officer, or a children's officer? * IF YES How many times?

	36-37	36-37	36-37	36-37	36-37	36-37	36-37	36-37

– been visited by anyone else from the NHS or the welfare (SPECIFY)_____ IF YES How many times?

	38-39	38-39	38-39	38-39	38-39	38-39	38-39	38-39

none of these
DK
(a) IF DENTIST VISITED Did you have to pay? ✱   yes
no
DK
(b) IF VISITS BY HOME HELP Did you pay anything? ✱   yes
no
DK

	40	40	40	40	40	40	40	40
	X	X	X	X	X	X	X	X
	Y	Y	Y	Y	Y	Y	Y	Y
	0	0	0	0	0	0	0	0
	1	1	1	1	1	1	1	1
	2	2	2	2	2	2	2	2
	3	3	3	3	3	3	3	3
	4	4	4	4	4	4	4	4
	5	5	5	5	5	5	5	5

31

VIII   INCOME IN KIND

General

This section aims to discover the major exchanges of services and gifts between the household and relatives or friends living elsewhere. One major problem is that people ordinarily take for granted the exchanges between themselves and their closest relatives. When being asked questions about " help " and " gifts " a housewife may not think of her mother, or her husband's mother, who lives nearby. A grandfather may not think of his daily activity of seeing a grandchild home from school. The first question is designed to help overcome this problem. You should remember that **most** households in the UK have frequent contact with a relative (either of a wife or a husband or of both) living elsewhere in the locality. Remember that independently of his wife a husband may see someone in his family (eg: his mother or a brother at work) every day. It will be very unusual if you make no entry in the box alonside Q. 1, so probe for likely relatives (eg: parents in the case of young and middle-aged people, brothers and sisters in the case of unmarried people, sons and daughters in the case of the elderly). In the remaining questions the contacts with such relatives are a likely indication of a flow of services or small gifts. Note that earning members of the household should normally be asked these questions independently of the housewife.

QUESTION 1   Relatives seen frequently

The question is designed to establish the existence of the relatives who have the most frequent contact with members of the household. Note that you ask " any of your family or a relative ". The alternative wording will help to avoid information about really close relatives — eg: parents and children — who are thought of as " family " or even as members of a common household rather than as " relatives ". By " most " days in the week is meant at least four of the seven days.

QUESTION 2   Help given

The unspoken assumption in the question is that these must be **unpaid** services. Prompt the items in the list carefully, emphasising those which are appropriate to the age or social situation of different members of the household. Make direct reference to the relatives listed in Q. 1. For example: " You say you see your mother every day. Do you do any of these things for her? And what about your sister? " Note that you prompt **also** for help given to friends and neighbours.

Hours

If two or three different services are undertaken, add together the informant's estimates of the time taken. Since the services are unpaid you should not expect informants to be able to give more than an approximate estimate of the time taken (that is, the time spent in the performance of the job, not interruptions for tea and conversations, etc).

QUESTION 3   Help received

The question reverses Q. 2 and proceed as in that question. Check in whatever way seems appropriate to establish the unpaid services being performed for members of the household. Again the question should be repeated for relatives seen frequently. " You've told me you see your mother every day. Does she do any of these things for you? " Two separate people might do the cleaning, for example. Add the hours together.

VIII   INCOME IN KIND

FOR ALL

1. Now I'd like to ask about any help you give or receive from your family and friends.

Do you see any of your family or a relative who doesn't live here most days in the week or at least once a week? I mean, for example, your mother, your husband's mother, a married sister or brother, son or daughter? I'm thinking especially of any of your own family or in-laws living near. *

WRITE IN RELATIVES SEEN

	daily or almost every day	at least once a week

CODE ONE ONLY
- seen one or more relatives most or all days in week
- seen one or more relatives at least weekly
- no relatives or none seen weekly
- DK

2. Do you regularly help anyone – a friend, a neighbour or someone in the family (PROMPT RELATIVES IN Q.1) – by doing things for them for example *

PROMPT AND CODE ALL THAT APPLY – MENTIONING AGAIN THE RELATIVES IN Q.1
- minding children and taking them out?
- preparing meals for a child or someone in the family, a friend or an old person?
- shopping?
- helping to arrange money matters?
- laundry or washing?
- cleaning?
- looking after/dressing them?
- driving to work, school or elsewhere?
- gardening?
- anything else? (SPECIFY)_____

CODE ALL THAT APPLY
- yes, helps relative
- yes, helps friend/neighbour
- no, help not given
- DK

IF ANY HELP GIVEN About how many hours a week altogether would you say you spend doing (all) these things? WRITE IN TOTAL* HOURS

3. Does anyone – a friend, a neighbour or someone in the family (PROMPT RELATIVES IN Q.1) – help you or anyone living with you by doing things for you, for example *

PROMPT AND CODE ALL THAT APPLY – MENTIONING AGAIN THE RELATIVES IN Q.1
- minding children and taking them out?
- preparing meals for you (your husband, children)?
- shopping?
- helping to arrange money matters?
- laundry or washing?
- cleaning?
- looking after you (your husband, children)?
- driving you (husband, children) to work, school or elsewhere?
- gardening?
- anything else? (SPECIFY)_____

CODE ALL THAT APPLY
- yes, a relative helps
- yes, a friend/neighbour helps
- no, no-one helps
- DK

IF ANY PERSON RECEIVES ANY HELP About how many hours a week altogether would you say they spent doing (all) those things? WRITE IN TOTAL *

1nft	2nd	3rd	4th	5th	6th	7	8	9	10
41	41	41	41	41	41	41	41	41	41
X	X	X	X	X	X	X	X	X	X
Y	Y	Y	Y	Y	Y	Y	Y	Y	Y
0	0	0	0	0	0	0	0	0	0
1	1	1	1	1	1	1	1	1	1
42	42	42	42	42	42	42	42	42	42
X	X	X	X	X	X	X	X	X	X
Y	Y	Y	Y	Y	Y	Y	Y	Y	Y
0	0	0	0	0	0	0	0	0	0
1	1	1	1	1	1	1	1	1	1
2	2	2	2	2	2	2	2	2	2
3	3	3	3	3	3	3	3	3	3
4	4	4	4	4	4	4	4	4	4
5	5	5	5	5	5	5	5	5	5
6	6	6	6	6	6	6	6	6	6
7	7	7	7	7	7	7	7	7	7
43	43	43	43	43	43	43	43	43	43
X	X	X	X	X	X	X	X	X	X
Y	Y	Y	Y	Y	Y	Y	Y	Y	Y
0	0	0	0	0	0	0	0	0	0
1	1	1	1	1	1	1	1	1	1
44-45	44-45	44-45	44-45	44-45	44-45	44-45	44-45	44-45	44-45
46	46	46	46	46	46	46	46	46	46
X	X	X	X	X	X	X	X	X	X
Y	Y	Y	Y	Y	Y	Y	Y	Y	Y
0	0	0	0	0	0	0	0	0	0
1	1	1	1	1	1	1	1	1	1
2	2	2	2	2	2	2	2	2	2
3	3	3	3	3	3	3	3	3	3
4	4	4	4	4	4	4	4	4	4
5	5	5	5	5	5	5	5	5	5
6	6	6	6	6	6	6	6	6	6
7	7	7	7	7	7	7	7	7	7
47	47	47	47	47	47	47	47	47	47
X	X	X	X	X	X	X	X	X	X
Y	Y	Y	Y	Y	Y	Y	Y	Y	Y
0	0	0	0	0	0	0	0	0	0
1	1	1	1	1	1	1	1	1	1
48-49	48-49	48-49	48-49	48-49	48-49	48-49	48-49	48-49	48-49

32

QUESTION 4 Emergency help

Since this is rather a general question specific acts may be forgotten. Probe as seems appropriate in the light of previous answers. Most people have occasional help from family or friends in the neighbourhood.

QUESTION 5 Gifts regularly made

This is the counterpart of Q. 2, dealing with gifts or commodities rather than services. Again repeat the question in reference to relatives seen often. Note that a meal that is given is distinct from the service of preparing a meal (prompted in Q. 2). Obtain the best total estimate that you can of the worth of these gifts, however rough.

QUESTION 6 Occasional gifts made

We do not wish to waste time on occasional gifts of a value of less than £25.

QUESTION 7 Gifts (regularly) received

This is the counterpart of Q. 3. Refer to relatives seen frequently and repeat the question. Note that meals consumed should also be coded in this question. The service (of preparing them) was included under Q. 3. Probe according to the answers made previously.

QUESTION 8 Occasional gifts received

Do not waste time inquiring about gifts of a value of less than £25.

33a

ASK HOUSEWIFE ONLY
4.(a) If someone in the household were ill, or you were in any kind of trouble - burning your hand, or all the lights fusing, or the water pipes bursting - could you count on help from anyone, a relative or friend, say, living near or elsewhere?
yes
no
DK
Does Not Apply

(b) Have you had such help in the last 12 months
PROMPT
- a little?
- some?
- a lot?
- none?
DK

5. FOR ALL AGED 15 AND OVER
Apart from helping people, do you regularly give things - I don't mean money - to anyone, a friend, a neighbour or someone in the family (PROMPT RELATIVES IN Q.1) - things like sweets for children, ice-cream, cigarettes, any meals for family visitors or food (cakes, chicken) groceries, beer, wine, flowers or clothing?
yes - gifts to relative } ASK
yes - gifts to neighbour/friend } Q.5(a)
no gifts made
DK } SKIP TO Q.6
Does Not Apply

(a) How much a week would you say the things you give would cost if someone bought them in the shops?
DK
WRITE IN AMOUNT IN SHILLINGS

FOR ALL AGED 15 and OVER
6(a) May I check on any larger gifts you have made to anyone - a friend, a neighbour or someone in the family (PROMPT RELATIVES IN Q.1) - during the last 12 months, such as a TV set, radio, carpet, jewellery, car or house? Have you made any gifts worth altogether £25 or more?
none or less than £25
DK
Does Not Apply
£25 or more   WRITE IN AMOUNT IN £'s

(b) And have you made any really large gifts - say, worth £100 or more - previously in the last 5 years, such as jewellery, a car or a house?
yes   ASK Q.6(c)
no
DK } SKIP TO Q.7

(c) How much would these gifts be worth altogether? WRITE IN AMOUNT IN £'s

FOR ALL AGED 15 AND OVER
7. Does anyone - a friend, neighbour or someone in the family (PROMPT RELATIVES IN Q.1) - give you things - I don't mean money - like sweets for the children, ice-cream, cigarettes, meals when you visit, or food, groceries, beer, wine, flowers or clothing?
yes - gifts from relative } ASK
yes - gifts from neighbour/friend } Q.7(a)
no
DK } SKIP TO Q.8
DNA

(a) How much a week would you say the things you receive would cost if someone bought them in the shops?
DK
WRITE IN AMOUNT IN SHILLINGS

FOR ALL AGED 15 AND OVER
8.(a) May I check on any larger gifts you may have received from anyone - a friend, a neighbour or someone in the family (PROMPT RELATIVES IN Q.1) - during the last 12 months - such as a TV set, radio, carpet, jewellery, car or house? Have you received any gifts worth altogether £25 or more?
none or less than £25
DK
Does Not Apply
£25 or more   WRITE IN AMOUNT IN £'s

(b) And have you received any really large gifts - say, worth £100 or more - previously in the last 5 years, such as jewellery, a car or a house?
yes   ASK Q.8(c)
no
DK } SKIP TO Q.9

(c) How much would these gifts be worth altogether? WRITE IN AMOUNT IN £'s

1st†	2nd	3rd	4th	INTERVIEWER: CODE 05, 06, etc. IF 5th, 6th MEMBERS OF HOUSEHOLD	
50	50	50	50	50	50
X Y 0 1	X Y 0 1	X Y 0 1	X Y 0 1	X Y 0 1	X Y 0 1
2 3 4 5 6	2 3 4 5 6	2 3 4 5 6	2 3 4 5 6	2 3 4 5 6	2 3 4 5 6
51	51	51	51	51	51
X Y 0 1 2	X Y 0 1 2	X Y 0 1 2	X Y 0 1 2	X Y 0 1 2	X Y 0 1 2
52-54 X	52-54 X	52-54 X	52-54 X	52-54 X	52-54 X
55-58	55-58	55-58	55-58	55-58	55-58
X Y 0 £	X Y 0 £	X Y 0 £	X Y 0 £	X Y 0 £	X Y 0 £
59-62	59-62	59-62	59-62	59-62	59-62
X Y 0 £	X Y 0 £	X Y 0 £	X Y 0 £	X Y 0 £	X Y 0 £
63	63	63	63	63	63
X Y 0 1 2	X Y 0 1 2	X Y 0 1 2	X Y 0 1 2	X Y 0 1 2	X Y 0 1 2
64-66 X	64-66 X	64-66 X	64-66 X	64-66 X	64-66 X
67-70	67-70	67-70	67-70	67-70	67-70
X Y 0 £	X Y 0 £	X Y 0 £	X Y 0 £	X Y 0 £	X Y 0 £
71-74	71-74	71-74	71-74	71-74	71-74
X Y 0 £	X Y 0 £	X Y 0 £	X Y 0 £	X Y 0 £	X Y 0 £

33

QUESTION 9 Staying overnight

The question concentrates on holidays and stays which are directly or indirectly paid for or subsidised by relatives and friends. It may be difficult to obtain an estimate of saving. We have in mind not only the instance of holiday but also an elderly person or a child staying with a member of the family for a lengthy period of the year during a time of loneliness or financial difficulty. Note that space allows only 8 columns on this page. In the unlikely event of interviewing in a household with 9 or 10 persons write in the details for the 9th and 10th persons lower on the page.

QUESTION 9 (b) Saving

Note that there are two alternatives in the question. The saving from staying in a relative's or a friend's home should be estimated in terms of the comparable cost of living at home. The saving from being taken on holiday should be estimated in terms of the cost of going on holiday on one's own.

QUESTION 10 Visitors

This question reverses Q. 9 but estimates of cost should be written into the column allocated for the housewife.

	1	2	3	4	5	6	7	8	9
								1	5

OR ALL

Have you stayed overnight with relatives or friends (on holiday or
otherwise) in the last year, either without paying or not paying
he full cost? Or has anyone taken you on holiday or lent you a house
- a cottage of their own in which to stay?

    yes, relatives) ASK Q.9(a)
    yes, friends }
    no }
    DK } SKIP TO Q.10

a) How many nights altogether in the year?   WRITE IN NUMBER

F STAYING 30 NIGHTS OR MORE
b) How much a week do you think you saved
compared with what you would have spent
f you had stopped at home or had to pay
he cost of the holiday yourself?

    Does Not Apply
    nothing
    DK
    APPROXIMATE SAVINGS IN
    SHILLINGS PER WEEK

0. Has anyone stayed overnight with you in the last 12 months,
either without paying or not paying full costs? Or have you
aken anyone on holiday or lent them
place of your own in which to stay?

    yes, relatives) ASK Q.10(a)
    yes, friends }
    no }
    DK } SKIP TO NEXT SECTION

a) How many nights altogether in the year?   WRITE IN NUMBER

STAYING 30 NIGHTS OR MORE
b) How much a week more do you
hink this cost compared with
hat you would have usually spent
llowing for anything they may
ave paid you)?

    WRITE IN AMOUNT IN COLUMN
    FOR HOUSEWIFE ONLY
    Does Not Apply
    nothing
    DK
    APPROXIMATE ADDITIONAL
    COST IN SHILLINGS PER
    WK

Inft	2nd	3rd	4th	5th	6th	INTERVIEWER: CODE 07, 08, etc. IF 7th, 8th MEMBERS OF HOUSEHOLD	
10-11	10-11	10-11	10-11	10-11	10-11	10-11	10-11
01	02	03	04	05	06		
12	12	12	12	12	12	12	12
X Y 0 1	X Y 0 1	X Y 0 1	X Y 0 1	X Y 0 1	X Y 0 1	X Y 0	X Y 0
13-15	13-15	13-15	13-15	13-15	13-15	13-15	13-15
16-18	16-18	16-18	16-18	16-18	16-18	16-18	16-18
X Y 0	X Y 0	X Y 0	X Y 0	X Y 0	X Y 0	X Y 0	X Y 0
19	19	19	19	19	19	19	9
X Y 0 1	X Y 0 1	X Y 0 1	X Y 0 1	X Y 0 1	X Y 0 1	X Y 0 1	X Y 0 1
20-22	20-22	20-22	20-22	20-22	20-22	20-22	20-22
23-25	23-25	23-25	23-25	23-25	23-25	23-25	23-25
X Y 0	X Y 0	X Y 0	X Y 0	X Y 0	X Y 0	X Y 0	X Y 0

IX STYLE OF LIVING

This section aims to find out some ways in which people spend their time, how they manage on their incomes, what kinds of things they buy and do, and how they feel about their situation. Most of the questions are pre-coded (but interviewers are urged to write any interesting comments on the blank spaces in the questionnaire or on the back). It is hoped that the answers will put some flesh on the income skeleton you have painstakingly built up in the rest of the questionnaire.

QUESTION 1   Holidays

Note that this question immediately follows Questions 9 and 10 of Section VIII. Question 9 of Section VIII refers only to staying in the homes of relatives and friends or being subsidised by them on a joint holiday. Question 1 in this section applies to all "holidays" (as understood by the informant) which are away from home, excluding only those which were spent actually in the homes of relatives or friends. If there was more than one holiday add together their duration and code accordingly in Question 1 (a).

QUESTION 2   Meals out

Care should be taken because people may forget meals which were incidental to the visit. By "snack" you should understand something more than a biscuit and cup of tea, say at least a sandwich. Note that in this question and in later questions there are certain persons whom it is not expected you should code. Thus children under the age of 15 should be coded DNA.

QUESTION 3   Friends to meals

Note that it is possible to code both " Yes, relative " and " Yes, friend ".

QUESTION 4   Friends in to play

There are few simple questions which can be asked about the child's own standard of living and social life. Some homes are too poor for the child to bring his friends in, so stress in the house.

QUESTION 5   Afternoons and evenings out

The key point is entertainment for which someone spends money (youth clubs require entrance and weekly fees; scouts, guides, etc., require uniform and 'bus fares for outings). Examples of leisure-time activities will vary according to the age of the person to whom the question is addressed and you should probe accordingly. (Note that while we do not ask for amounts of expenditure we try to find the relative frequency of all forms of entertainments so that we can see how it varies with income.)

QUESTION 6   Church

Accept any religious sect or denomination which may be mentioned.

IX STYLE OF LIVING

...nally, I'd like to ask a few questions about the kind of things you do your leisure-time and in managing at home.

R ALL
Apart from staying with family or friends in their homes have you had a holiday away from home in e last 12 months? *

yes ASK Q.1(a)
no } SKIP TO Q.2
DK }

) For how long?

less than a week
one week (7 nights)
more than 1 week, less than 3 weeks
3 weeks and less than 5 wks
5 weeks or more

R ALL AGED 15 AND OVER   CODE ALL AGED 15 AND OVER
I've been asking about seeing relatives. Have you been out in the last 4 weeks to friends or other ...mbers of the family for a meal or snack? *

yes
no
DK
Does Not Apply

R ALL AGED 15 AND OVER   CODE ALL AGED 15 AND OVER
, Or have any of your family or friends come here for a meal or snack during e last four weeks?

yes, relative *
yes, friend *
no
DK
Does Not Apply

SK PARENT OF CHILDREN AGED 3-14   CODE CHILDREN AGED 3-14
, What about your child(ren)? Has he/she had a friend to play (or to tea) here n the house during the last four weeks?

Does Not Apply SKIP TO Q.5
yes
no
DK

OR ALL
. Have you had an afternoon or evening out in the last fortnight for your entertainment, something that cost money? * For example, ave you been to

PROMPT	X	a cinema or theatre?	
AND	Y	a football match or other sports meeting?	
CODE	0	a pub or club mainly for having drinks?	ASK
ALL	1	a social club (old people's, youth, sports, working men's, church social)?	Q.5(a)
THAT	2	dancing?	
APPLY	3	bingo?	
	4	other (SPECIFY)	

5 none of these   ASK Q. 5(b)
6 DK
7 under 3 years old or others, Does Not Apply } SKIP TO Q.6

a) So how many afternoons or evenings out have you had in the last fortnight?   CODE NUMBER
SKIP TO Q.6

b) Why haven't you had an evening out?   X no desire to
CODE ONE ONLY   Y not enough money
0 cannot leave children (or other)
1 ill
2 full social life in other ways
3 other (SPECIFY)
4 DK

FOR ALL
5. Have you been to church (or Sunday School)

X – during the last four weeks?
Y – not during the last four weeks but during the last year } ASK Q.6(a)
0 – not in the last year
1 DK } SKIP TO Q.7
2 Does Not Apply

(a) Which denomination do you belong to?
Church of England
Roman Catholic
Non-conformists (Baptists, Methodists, Wesleyans, etc)
"Sectarians" (Plymouth Brethren, Salvation Army,
Jehovah's Witnesses)
other (SPECIFY)

	Inft	2nd	3rd	4th	5th	6th	7	8	9	10
	26	26	26	26	26	26	26	26	26	26
	X	X	X	X	X	X	X	X	X	X
	Y	Y	Y	Y	Y	Y	Y	Y	Y	Y
	0	0	0	0	0	0	0	0	0	0
	1	1	1	1	1	1	1	1	1	1
	2	2	2	2	2	2	2	2	2	2
	3	3	3	3	3	3	3	3	3	3
	4	4	4	4	4	4	4	4	4	4
	5	5	5	5	5	5	5	5	5	5
	27	27	27	27	27	27	27	27	27	27
	X	X	X	X	X	X	X	X	X	X
	Y	Y	Y	Y	Y	Y	Y	Y	Y	Y
	0	0	0	0	0	0	0	0	0	0
	1	1	1	1	1	1	1	1	1	1
	28	28	28	28	28	28	28	28	28	28
	X	X	X	X	X	X	X	X	X	X
	Y	Y	Y	Y	Y	Y	Y	Y	Y	Y
	0	0	0	0	0	0	0	0	0	0
	1	1	1	1	1	1	1	1	1	1
	2	2	2	2	2	2	2	2	2	2
	29	29	29	29	29	29	29	29	29	29
	X	X	X	X	X	X	X	X	X	X
	Y	Y	Y	Y	Y	Y	Y	Y	Y	Y
	0	0	0	0	0	0	0	0	0	0
	1	1	1	1	1	1	1	1	1	1
	30	30	30	30	30	30	30	30	30	30
	X	X	X	X	X	X	X	X	X	X
	Y	Y	Y	Y	Y	Y	Y	Y	Y	Y
	0	0	0	0	0	0	0	0	0	0
	1	1	1	1	1	1	1	1	1	1
	2	2	2	2	2	2	2	2	2	2
	3	3	3	3	3	3	3	3	3	3
	4	4	4	4	4	4	4	4	4	4
	5	5	5	5	5	5	5	5	5	5
	6	6	6	6	6	6	6	6	6	6
	7	7	7	7	7	7	7	7	7	7
	31-32	31-32	31-32	31-32	31-32	31-32	3132	3132	3132	3132
	33	33	33	33	33	33	33	33	33	33
	X	X	X	X	X	X	X	X	X	X
	Y	Y	Y	Y	Y	Y	Y	Y	Y	Y
	0	0	0	0	0	0	0	0	0	0
	1	1	1	1	1	1	1	1	1	1
	2	2	2	2	2	2	2	2	2	2
	3	3	3	3	3	3	3	3	3	3
	4	4	4	4	4	4	4	4	4	4
	34	34	34	34	34	34	34	34	34	34
	X	X	X	X	X	X	X	X	X	X
	Y	Y	Y	Y	Y	Y	Y	Y	Y	Y
	0	0	0	0	0	0	0	0	0	0
	1	1	1	1	1	1	1	1	1	1
	2	2	2	2	2	2	2	2	2	2
	3	3	3	3	3	3	3	3	3	3
	4	4	4	4	4	4	4	4	4	4
	5	5	5	5	5	5	5	5	5	5
	6	6	6	6	6	6	6	6	6	6
	7	7	7	7	7	7	7	7	7	7

QUESTION 7   Food

Actual nutritional levels cannot be established by an interview of this kind, but it is hoped that these questions will show very roughly (i) whether a family member goes short of food occasionally, (ii) whether the family is able to buy relatively expensive foods frequently, (iii) whether any member of the family goes short of food occasionally, and (iv) to what extent patterns of food consumption vary with income.

(a)   Cooked breakfast

Many women do not eat breakfast. **Bacon and eggs** is only an example. Others would be boiled or fried egg, haddock, kipper, etc. But not porridge, toast, fried bread or potatoes (the distinction is between carbohydrates and other foods).

(b)   No cooked meal

Stress the whole day. A heavy breakfast but nothing later, or a heavy meal at supper-time will not count as going without a cooked meal during the day.

(c)   Fresh meat

This will be difficult for households where children have school dinners, or members of the household eat canteen meals. It would be reasonable to code such persons " Yes " in the absence of any better information. It is highly possible that some housewives may have very little fresh meat (defined to include chicken, chops, frozen meat of any kind but not corned beef, tinner meat, boiled ham or sausages). Care is needed as meat-eating is probably over-stated, and when there is meat the men in the household and not the women may have it.

QUESTION 8 (a)   Joint

Accept what the informant understands by a joint.

QUESTION 8 (b) and (c)   Milk

Do not include school milk (a correction for this will be made in the office). Check for extra milk at weekends. Include sterilised milk (" stera ") as fresh. Some houses buy milk in powder or liquid in tins for babies too, but do not attempt to assess the quantities of this. Just make a note that it is bought.

QUESTION 9 (b)   Clothing

Clothing cheques are " Provident " cheques and the like where a cheque for £1, for example, entitles a person to shop at certain shops and repayment is made at 1s. in the £1 for 21 weeks. Clubs include any kind of arrangement through a catalogue, shop, or door-to-door salesman.

QUESTION 9 (c) and (d)   Spending on clothing clubs

Some clubs include coal and furniture as well as clothes; try to get an estimate of the proportion of money spent on clothes. Informants often give a maximum figure, when in fact they miss or only pay something on account.

QUESTION 11   Adequate footwear

Includes state of repair as well as fit. Plimsolls and sandals in winter are not adequate, nor are boots alone adequate for summer. Plastic sandals are coded not adequate, unless there are other shoes.

QUESTION 12   Smoking, pools and betting

Smoking is often underestimated in surveys. By asking quantities we hope to be able to work out roughly the expenditure. Note if cigars and not cigarettes. Take care to make betting seem a very common activity (which it is, of course), since information may not readily be forthcoming in the context of all these questions on shortages.

QUESTION 13   Christmas

Make sure that the sum you have is the **extra** expense on top of normal housekeeping for the household unit.

Inft	2nd	3rd	4th	5th	6th	7	8	9	10
35	35	35	35	35	35	35	35	35	35

FOR ALL CODE ALL
7. Now could I ask a few questions about food? (a) Do you have a cooked breakfast most days? I mean four or more days a week — things like bacon and egg (not porridge or toast)? *
- yes
- no
- DK
- Does Not Apply

X	X	X	X	X	X	X	X	X	X
Y	Y	Y	Y	Y	Y	Y	Y	Y	Y
0	0	0	0	0	0	0	0	0	0
1	1	1	1	1	1	1	1	1	1

(b) During the last two weeks was there a day when you ate no cooked meal at all (I mean from getting up to going to bed)? *
- yes
- no
- DK
- Does Not Apply

2	2	2	2	2	2	2	2	2	2
3	3	3	3	3	3	3	3	3	3
4	4	4	4	4	4	4	4	4	4
5	5	5	5	5	5	5	5	5	5

(c) Do you have fresh meat most days, I mean four or more days a week (not sausages, bacon or boiled ham) – either here or in your meals out? CHECK ANSWER ESPECIALLY CAREFULLY FOR HOUSEWIFE
- yes
- no
- DK
- Does Not Apply

6	6	6	6	6	6	6	6	6	6
7	7	7	7	7	7	7	7	7	7
8	8	8	8	8	8	8	8	8	8
9	9	9	9	9	9	9	9	9	9

ASK HOUSEWIFE ONLY CODE HOUSEHOLD ONLY
8. (a) Do you normally have a Sunday joint (i.e. 3 weeks out of 4)?
- yes
- no
- DK

50
X
Y
0

(b) How many pints do you usually take for the family (everyone in the household) in a whole week, including any extra at weekends and fresh milk bought from a shop? *
- no. of pints in week
- OFFICE USE ONLY

51–52
53–54

(c) And do you buy tinned or powdered milk as well?
- yes
- no
- DK

55
X
Y
0

ASK HOUSEWIFE ONLY CODE HOUSEHOLD ONLY
9. (a) Do you ever buy second-hand clothing from a shop or a stall, for yourself or others in the household?
CODE ONE ONLY
- often
- sometimes
- never
- DK

56
X
Y
0
1

(b) Do you buy any of your clothing or shoes through clubs or clothing cheques? *
- yes ASK Q.9(c)
- no } SKIP TO Q.10
- DK }

2
3
4

(c) About how much do you spend on clothing clubs per week?
- WRITE IN AMOUNT IN SHILLINGS

57–58

(d) Do you ever miss payments or pay less than the full amount?
- regularly
- not often
- no
- DK

59
X
Y
0
1

ASK HOUSEWIFE ONLY CODE HOUSEWIFE ONLY
10. Have you had a new winter coat in the last 3 years (i.e. 3 winters)?
- Does Not Apply SKIP TO Q.11
- yes
- no
- DK

36	36	36	36	36	36	36	36	36	36
X	X	X	X	X	X	X	X	X	X
Y	Y	Y	Y	Y	Y	Y	Y	Y	Y
0	0	0	0	0	0	0	0	0	0
1	1	1	1	1	1	1	1	1	1

FOR ALL CODE ALL HOUSEHOLD
11. Has everyone got adequate footwear for fine weather AND if it rains?
- yes
- no
- DK
- Does Not Apply

2	2	2	2	2	2	2	2	2	2
3	3	3	3	3	3	3	3	3	3
4	4	4	4	4	4	4	4	4	4
5	5	5	5	5	5	5	5	5	5

37	37	37	37	37	37	37	37	37	37

FOR ALL
12. Can you tell me whether you
- X – smoke? * IF YES, ASK Q.12(a)
- Y – buy a daily newspaper
- 0 – regularly do the football pools (in season)? } SKIP TO
- 1 – regularly have a flutter on the horses or dogs? } Q.13
- 2 none of these
- 3 DK
- 4 Does Not Apply

(a) How many cigarettes/ozs of tobacco a week? *

X	X	X	X	X	X	X	X	X	X
Y	Y	Y	Y	Y	Y	Y	Y	Y	Y
0	0	0	0	0	0	0	0	0	0
1	1	1	1	1	1	1	1	1	1
2	2	2	2	2	2	2	2	2	2
3	3	3	3	3	3	3	3	3	3
4	4	4	4	4	4	4	4	4	4

☐ ___ cigs/ozs ☐ ___ cigs/ozs   OFFICE
☐ ___ cigs/ozs ☐ ___ cigs/ozs   USE

60–61

ASK HOUSEWIFE CODE HOUSEHOLD ONLY
13. About how much did you (and your family) spend altogether last Christmas – I mean extra to the usual housekeeping – on presents, food, entertainment, everything? *

Estimate in £'s

62–64

QUESTION 14 Fuel

Everyone forgets to order coal. Stress " through lack of money ".

QUESTION 15 Birthday parties

Again the emphasis is on the expense and the experience of bringing the child's friends into the home, so stress that we don't mean just a family party.

QUESTION 17 (a) Social class

This question requires the views of both chief wage-earner (head of household) and housewife. By " chief wage-earner " we mean the person upon whose earnings the housekeeping income primarily depends. By " Head of Household " we have in mind the alternative person to be questioned if there is no chief wage-earner, e.g. a husband who is a retirement pensioner, or a widowed mother (who may be the tenant) living with her widowed daughter (the housewife) and grandchildren. As far as possible the views on social class should be sought from each person independently. If both are present take the question stage by stage, making sure both answer before passing on. The question asks first for a self-rating, which must be written down. At this stage avoid putting names of classes into people's heads. People often hesitate awkwardly, so try to get the informant to say what class she thinks she belongs to or " is nearest to ". Prompt by repeating the question carefully, and say " It's what you think ", implying (which is true) that everyone has their own idea and each is equally valid. Do not strain to get an answer if one is not easily forthcoming. Do not assume the informant will pick one class only. Multiple choices of " middle and working " or " professional and working " are allowed.

QUESTION 17 (b) Determinant of class

Code housewife and chief wage-earner only. Next, to give us a clue as to what the informant is using as a reference point and scale we ask, in effect, the informant's idea of what determines " class ". Try to get the most important one only.

QUESTION 17 (c) Names of classes

Third, the informant is presented with a flash-card (this is why husband and wife should if possible be interviewed separately, since otherwise the second person may be unduly influenced). Code one item only. If informant wants (again) to say " None ", say ' Well, I've got to put something down, which would you think was nearest? " This rating is the most important bit of the question. Do not be puzzled if the wife gives a different answer from the husband. This is quite common.

QUESTION 17 (d) Father's main occupation

That is, the occupation held for most of the time (not necessarily the most recent).

QUESTION 18 Well off

Four comparisons are made in this series of questions—with relatives, with other people (note—of the same age) in locality, with the average in the country and finally in the context of time. Prompt carefully and remember that you might get a different response for one comparison than for another.

	1st††	2nd	3rd	4th	5th	6th	7	8	9	10

FOR ALL   CODE ALL IN HOUSEHOLD
14. Have you ever been short of fuel during the last year through lack of money? I mean have you had to go without a fire on a cold day, or go to bed early to keep warm or light the fire late because of lack of coal?
yes / no / DK / DNA

	38	38	38	38	38	38	38	38	38	38
	X	X	X	X	X	X	X	X	X	X
	Y	Y	Y	Y	Y	Y	Y	Y	Y	Y
	0	0	0	0	0	0	0	0	0	0
	I	I	I	I	I	I	I	I	I	I

ASK PARENT OF CHILD AGED 3-14   CODE ALL CHILDREN 3-14
15. What about your son's/daughter's last birthday? Did he/she have a party with friends (not just brothers and sisters)? *
Does Not Apply SKIP TO Q.16 / yes / no / DK

	39	39	39	39	39	39	39	39	39	39
	X	X	X	X	X	X	X	X	X	X
	Y	Y	Y	Y	Y	Y	Y	Y	Y	Y
	0	0	0	0	0	0	0	0	0	0
	I	I	I	I	I	I	I	I	I	I

ASK PARENT OF CHILD AGED 3-14
16. How much altogether does he/she get in pocket money per week, i.e. only from persons living in the household)?
nothing   WRITE IN EST. AMT. IN SHILLINGS

	40-41	40-41	40-41	40-41	40-41	40-41	4041	4041	4041	4041
	X	X	X	X	X	X	X	X	X	X

ASK HOUSEWIFE AND CHIEF WAGE EARNER/HEAD OF HOUSEHOLD
17. (a) You hear of people talking about social class. If you were asked what social class you belong to, what would you say? *
PROMPT BY REPEATING THE QUESTION AND SAY It's what you say; everyone has their own view. What would be the name of the class you belong to or are nearest to? *
WRITE IN ANSWER

	42	42	42	42	42	42	42	42	42	42

    CODE HOUSEWIFE AND C.W.E. ONLY
(b) What decides what class you're in? * Is it mainly
Does Not Apply SKIP TO Q.19
Y - job? / 0 - education? / 1 - the family you're born into? / 2 - your way of life? / 3 - money? / 4 - other (SPECIFY) / 5 DK
PROMPT AND CODE ONE ONLY

	43	43	43	43	43	43	43	43	43	43
	X	X	X	X	X	X	X	X	X	X
	Y	Y	Y	Y	Y	Y	Y	Y	Y	Y
	0	0	0	0	0	0	0	0	0	0
	1	1	1	1	1	1	1	1	1	1
	2	2	2	2	2	2	2	2	2	2
	3	3	3	3	3	3	3	3	3	3
	4	4	4	4	4	4	4	4	4	4
	5	5	5	5	5	5	5	5	5	5

(c) I have a card which has some names of classes written on it. Could you please look and say which of these you belong to?
SHOW FLASHCARD NO.7 *
X upper middle / Y middle / 0 lower middle / 1 upper working / 2 working / 3 poor / 4 DK / 5 none

	44	44	44	44	44	44	44	44	44	44
	X	X	X	X	X	X	X	X	X	X
	Y	Y	Y	Y	Y	Y	Y	Y	Y	Y
	0	0	0	0	0	0	0	0	0	0
	1	1	1	1	1	1	1	1	1	1
	2	2	2	2	2	2	2	2	2	2
	3	3	3	3	3	3	3	3	3	3
	4	4	4	4	4	4	4	4	4	4
	5	5	5	5	5	5	5	5	5	5

(d) Some people think it goes by what your father's job was. Could you tell me your father's main job in life? And the employer's (or own) business?
WRITE IN ANSWER. IF UNSPECIFIC ASK What did he do?

	45	45	45	45	45	45	45	45	45	45

ASK HOUSEWIFE AND CHIEF WAGE EARNER/H.O.H.   CODE H'WIFE AND C.W.E. ONLY
18. * (a) How well off do you feel these days on your income? For example, compared with the rest of your family (I mean the relatives who don't live here) would you say you are
PROMPT AND CODE ONE ONLY
X better off? / Y about the same? / 0 worse off? / I DK

(b) Compared with other people round here of your age would you say you are
2 better off? / 3 about the same? / 4 worse off? / 5 DK

(c) Compared with the average in the country would you say you are
X better off? / Y about the same? / 0 worse off? / I DK

(d) On the whole is your situation getting better or worse? Are you
2 better off than ever? / 3 worse off than ever? / 4 have known better and worse times? / 5 about the same as ever? / 6 DK

	46	46	46	46	46	46	46	46	46	46
	X	X	X	X	X	X	X	X	X	X
	Y	Y	Y	Y	Y	Y	Y	Y	Y	Y
	0	0	0	0	0	0	0	0	0	0
	I	I	I	I	I	I	I	I	I	I
	2	2	2	2	2	2	2	2	2	2
	3	3	3	3	3	3	3	3	3	3
	4	4	4	4	4	4	4	4	4	4
	5	5	5	5	5	5	5	5	5	5
	47	47	47	47	47	47	47	47	47	47
	X	X	X	X	X	X	X	X	X	X
	Y	Y	Y	Y	Y	Y	Y	Y	Y	Y
	0	0	0	0	-Y	0	0	0	0	0
	I	I	I	I	0	I	I	I	I	I
	2	2	2	2	I	2	2	2	2	2
	3	3	3	3	2	3	3	3	3	3
					3					
	4	4	4	4	4	4	4	4	4	4
	5	5	5	5	5	5	5	5	5	5
	6	6	6	6	6	6	6	6	6	6

37

QUESTION 19   Housekeeping and board

The question refers to ALL INCOME RECIPIENTS including pensioners, as well as earners, who contribute to the housekeeping expenses. Be careful that you probe for everyone in the house, including adolescent earners. Sometimes the actual sum available for housekeeping will be quite different from that suggested by the total income of the household. The husband or teenagers may retain quite large sums not only for their own use but because the pattern of responsibility in one household for expenditure may be different from that in another household which has the same composition. Housekeeping can be a touchy point if both husband and wife are present, and it is perhaps best dealt with by interviewing one of them on their own (the housewife preferably) and, if possible, checking later with the other (the husband). If both husband and wife are present avoid expressing any surprise or criticism if you think the housekeeping is small. Also avoid indicating any opinion on the question of whether wage-earners should pay bills. Try to imply that all arrangements are equally possible. We have listed the common ones, but there will be others. REMEMBER TO CODE EACH INCOME RECIPIENT.

QUESTION 19 (b)   Money back

This can be daily fares, insurances or clubs paid, dinner money, or simply " spending money ". Some teenagers hand over their wages but get clothing bought. Usually this question will apply to teenagers, but some husbands may get money from the housekeeping for their cigarettes and beer mid-week.

QUESTION 19 (c)   Payment of housekeeping bills

Often the husband will pay some larger bills, but alternatively he may pay housekeeping but expect to " help out " if a heavy bill comes in. We realise that an estimate may be rough but try to get an average contribution. Teenage children may buy food as " treats " for the household from the money they retain. Again try for an average.

QUESTION 20   Long-term saving

We are not interested in asking here whether the informant has savings (that was asked in Section V). Nor are we interested here in asking for short-term saving. Instead the question explores whether at the present time the informant manages to put aside savings for a long-term objective.

QUESTION 21   Ten years ago

To give us some idea of fluctuating fortunes we ask what things were like ten years ago. Some persons aged 35 or over will have been at home in their parents' households ten years ago and therefore we have to find what was the composition of the household. In any case, we require an estimate of the total money flowing into the household, and the number of adults and children that were supported at that time. Give the informant time to recollect. And check that income includes pensions, family allowances, etc. Fortunately, the informant will already have some idea of what you are after from the detailed questions asked earlier.

ASK HOUSEWIFE AND INCOME RECIPIENT
19. How do you arrange the payment of housekeeping (and board-money)?
Here are some of the ways we've come across. Can you tell me how you arrange things? Does he/she * CODE ALL INCOME RECIPIENTS

PROMPT FOR ALL INCOME RECIPIENTS AND CODE ONE ONLY
X – give a fixed amount for housekeeping (or board)?
Y – give an amount which varies depending on earnings?
0 – give entire wage (earnings), receiving back money for fares, pocket money, etc?
1 – give entire wage (earnings) after first taking out fares, pocket money, etc?
2 – pay earnings (wage) into a joint bank account?
3 – have no fixed arrangement?
4 – any other arrangement (SPECIFY)

5 DK
6 Does Not Apply } SKIP TO Q.20

(a) And how much for housekeeping (board) would you say he/she gives on average per week? WRITE IN AMOUNT (IN DONOR'S COLUMN)

(b) May I just check? About how much on average does he/she receive back through the week out of the housekeeping (for meals out, or entertainment or payment of clubs, insurances, etc.)? * WRITE IN EST. AMOUNT (IN DONOR'S COLUMN) — nothing

(c) And roughly how much on average per week would you say he/she pays from the money he/she keeps for household bills (I mean for electricity, gas, coal, rent, rates, H.P., TV, curtains, bedlinen)? * WRITE IN EST. AMOUNT (IN DONOR'S COLUMN) — nothing

ASK HOUSEWIFE CODE EACH INCOME RECIPIENT
20. Do you (and your husband) manage to save, not just for holidays or Christmas or for buying things, but for a rainy day, or retirement, say? *
yes
no
DK
Does Not Apply

ASK CHIEF WAGE EARNER OR HEAD OF HOUSEHOLD IF AGED 35 OR OVER CODE C.W.E. OR H.O.H ONLY
21. Does Not Apply SKIP TO Q.22
(a) Do you think you were as well off, say, ten years ago – that is, in 1957/58?
yes
no
DK

(b) Can you just tell me who were the members of your family (household) then? * WRITE IN NOS. ADULTS

WRITE IN NOS. CHILDREN (11–14)

WRITE IN NOS. CHILDREN (0–10)

(c) And roughly how much was the total family (household) income to support you – Including any pensions, family allowances, wife's earnings, everything? * estimated weekly income of household in 1957/58

ASK CHIEF WAGE EARNER OR HEAD OF HOUSEHOLD (OF ANY AGE) CODE C.W.E. OR H.O.H ONLY
22. Do you find it specially difficult to manage on your income? Does Not Apply SKIP TO Q.23
yes
no
DK

1nft	2nd	3rd	4th	INTERVIEWER: CODE 05, 06, etc. IF 5th, 6th MEMBERS OF HOUSEHOLD	
48	48	48	48	48	48
X Y	X Y	X Y	X Y	X Y	X Y
0	0	0	0	0	0
1 2 3 4	1 2 3 4	1 2 3 4	1 2 3 4	1 2 3 4	1 2 3 4
5 6	5 6	5 6	5 6	5 6	5 6
49–52 £ s	49–52 £ s	49–52 £ s	49–52 £ s	49–52 £ s	49–52 £ s
53–56 X £ s	53–56 X £ s	53–56 X £ s	53–56 X £ s	53–56 X £ s	53–56 X £ s
57–60 X £ s	57–60 X £ s	57–60 X £ s	57–60 X £ s	57–60 X £ s	57–60 X £ s
61	61	61	61	61	61
X Y 0 1	X Y 0 1	X Y 0 1	X Y 0 1	X Y 0 1	X Y 0 1
2 3 4 5	2 3 4 5	2 3 4 5	2 3 4 5	2 3 4 5	2 3 4 5
62	62	62	62	62	62
63	63	63	63	63	63
64	64	64	64	64	64
65–69 £ s	65–69 £ s	65–69 £ s	65–69 £ s	65–69 £ s	65–69 £ s
70	70	70	70	70	70
X Y 0 1	X Y 0 1	X Y 0 1	X Y 0 1	X Y 0 1	X Y 0 1

QUESTION 23   Poor now

Stress **genuinely** and try to avoid facetiousness at this point. Question 23 (a) explores what the informant understands by feeling " poor ". If the word " poor " seems inappropriate use the alternative " very hard up ".

QUESTION 24   Poverty

Stress the word " poverty ". Do not explain what you think it means if you are asked. Seek from the informant his definition and write it in the box as clearly as you can.

QUESTION 25   Voting

Ask for those old enough to have voted in the last election (March 1965). We are not concerned who they voted for (although they will probably say) but would like to know if they are sufficiently involved to vote at all. Be careful to reassure people that this is confidential and as far as you are concerned non-voting is blameless—many people consider that voting is legally compulsory or morally obligatory and so voting figures are over-estimated. Try to get a clear recollection by fixing the incident (time of day, who they went with) if necessary. Stress **National**, not local elections.

QUESTION 26   Action on poverty

We are interested in what the informant thinks can be done. Give as full an answer as possible.

Please write in any additional notes.

ASK CHIEF WAGE EARNER/H.O.H.   CODE C.W.E./H.O.H. ONLY
23.✱ Do you think you could GENUINELY say
   you are poor now? ──   X Does Not Apply SKIP TO Q.24

       PROMPT AND CODE   Y all the time ⎤ ASK Q.23(a)
       ONE ONLY   0 sometimes   ⎦
                           1 never ⎤ SKIP TO Q.24
                           2 DK   ⎦

(a) Do you feel poor at any of these times   3 at weekends
    or in any of these situations?   4 mid-week
    PROMPT AND   5 at Christmas
    CODE ALL THAT   6 with some of your friends
    APPLY   7 with some of your relatives
                           8 with some of the people round here
                        ── 9 other (SPECIFY)

FOR CHIEF WAGE EARNER/H.O.H.   CODE C.W.E./H.O.H. ONLY
24. (a) There's been a lot of talk about   Does Not Apply SKIP TO
    poverty. Do you think there's such a   Q.25
    thing as REAL poverty these days? ✱   yes
                                             no
(b) What would you describe as poverty?   DK
 ┌─ WRITE IN ANSWER

(c) Would you say that if people are in poverty its mainly

       X - their own fault?
       Y - the Government's fault?
       0 - the fault of their education?
   PROMPT 1 - the fault of industry not providing the right jobs?
   AND CODE 2 - anything else? (SPECIFY)
   ONE ONLY
       3 - a combination of (some of) these?
       4 - none of these?
       5 DK

ASK CHIEF WAGE EARNER/H.O.H. ABOUT ALL AGED 23 AND OVER
25. Do you mind telling me if you voted in the last   CODE
    General Election (I don't mean who you voted for,   ALL AGED
    just whether you voted)? ✱   23 & OVER
                                             yes, voted
                                             no
                                             DK
                                             DNA
ASK CHIEF WAGE EARNER/H.O.H.   CODE C.W.E./H.O.H. ONLY
26. If there is poverty what do you think   nothing
    can be done about it?   DK
 ┌─ WRITE IN ANSWER

	1nft	2nd	3rd	4th	5th	6th	7	8	9	10
	71	71	71	71	71	71	71	71	71	71
	X	X	X	X	X	X	X	X	X	X
	Y	Y	Y	Y	Y	Y	Y	Y	Y	Y
	0	0	0	0	0	0	0	0	0	0
	1	1	1	1	1	1	1	1	1	1
	2	2	2	2	2	2	2	2	2	2
	3	3	3	3	3	3	3	3	3	3
	4	4	4	4	4	4	4	4	4	4
	5	5	5	5	5	5	5	5	5	5
	6	6	6	6	6	6	6	6	6	6
	7	7	7	7	7	7	7	7	7	7
	8	8	8	8	8	8	8	8	8	8
	9	9	9	9	9	9	9	9	9	9
	72	72	72	72	72	72	72	72	72	72
	X	X	X	X	X	X	X	X	X	X
	Y	Y	Y	Y	Y	Y	Y	Y	Y	Y
	0	0	0	0	0	0	0	0	0	0
	1	1	1	1	1	11	1	1	1	1
	73	73	73	73	73	73	73	73	73	73
	X	X	X	X	X	X	X	X	X	X
	Y	Y	Y	Y	Y	Y	Y	Y	Y	Y
	0	0	0	0	0	0	0	0	0	0
	1	1	1	1	1	1	1	1	1	1
	2	2	2	2	2	2	2	2	2	2
	3	3	3	3	3	3	3	3	3	3
	4	4	4	4	4	4	4	4	4	4
	5	5	5	5	5	5	5	5	5	5
	74	74	74	74	74	74	74	74	74	74
	X	X	X	X	X	X	X	X	X	X
	Y	Y	Y	Y	Y	Y	Y	Y	Y	Y
	0	0	0	0	0	0	0	0	0	0
	1	1	1	1	1	1	1	1	1	1
	75	75	75	75	75	75	75	75	75	75
	X	X	X	X	X	X	X	X	X	X
	Y	Y	Y	Y	Y	Y	Y	Y	Y	Y

39

METHOD OF CHECKING MINORITY GROUPS MEMBERSHIP OF WHICH TO BE CODED ON INSIDE BACK COVER

(a) Households in which there is a child, one of whose parents is not resident. Page 4. Question 13 (b) code 4 or 5.

(b) Households consisting of a woman and adult dependent

This is a difficult group to define—the main thing to remember is that we are looking for a household where a woman either with her earnings or income from government benefits or from stocks, shares, etc., is partly or wholly supporting an adult male or female (usually related to her), who has a smaller income than she has. There will be no males in full-time employment in this household. Consider household composition (page 3, Question 10 (b)) and also employment (page 6, dependents are coded Y for Question 1 and the woman is coded X for Question 1). If the woman is not employed (i.e. coded Y in Q. 1, page 6) then you should check income from employer's pension (page 19, Question 19, coded X or Y), annuity, trust, allowance, etc. (page 20, Question 20, coded X Y 0 1 2 4 5 6 7 or 8), property (page 20, Question 23, coded X), lodgers or boarders (page 23, Question 30, coded X or Y), and stocks and shares (page 24, Question 3 (b)). If the dependent adult receives government allowances or pensions (page 18, Question 15), then the amount received should be less than any allowance or benefit together with any earnings the woman receives.

(c) Households in which there are five or more dependent children

The best check is whether any informant receives 48s. or more in family allowances (up to April 1968) or any informant receives 66s. or more in family allowances (after April 1968). See page 18, Question 15.

(d) Households in which there is an adult who has been unemployed for eight weeks or more (consecutively or in last 12 months)

See page 8, Question 8 and Question 8 (a) and page 7, Question 7 (c) should be coded X or Question 7 (d) should be coded 2.

(e) Households in which there is an adult under 65 who has been ill or injured for eight weeks or more (consecutively or in the last 12 months)

See page 8, Question 8 and Question 8 (a) and page 6, Question 6, code 3. Note that page 27, Question 2 (a) or Question 2 (b) shows eight weeks off work or school or confined to bed or house.)

(f) Households in which there is a disabled adult under 65

See page 28, Question 7. Any household containing an adult for whom enough codes 1 and 2 ringed to add to a total of 5 or more or an adult for whom at least one item in Question 7 is coded 1 or 2 and who is coded " Yes " to any of Questions 3 (a), (b), (c), (e) or (f) or " No " to Question 3 (d). Do not include a person coded positively for one or more of the prompts in Question 3 (i.e. chest, lungs, back, joints, etc.) unless he or she is also coded " Yes " in one of the questions 3 (a), (b), (c), (e), (f) or " No " for Question 3 (d). Borderline disabled. See page 28, Question 7, if coded 1, 2, 3 or 4 for at least one item or page 27, Question 3, if any of the questions (a) - (f) is coded " Yes " or page 28, Question 8, the answer given as " much more difficult ".

(g) Households containing a disabled child or handicapped child (including children ill or injured for eight weeks or more)

A family with a child 15 years or under for whom the following answers were given: page 27, Question 2 (a), code 6 and 8 weeks or more away from school or page 27, Question 2 (b) code X and 8 weeks or more confined to bed or home, or page 27 Question 3, suffering from " nerves " and coded X or 0 for Question 3 (c) (ii), or page 28, Question 4, coded X, Y, 0, 1 or 2.

(h) Households containing a person aged 65 or over who has been bedfast or ill for 8 weeks or more or who is otherwise severely handicapped.

A family with an old person aged 65 or over for whom the following answers apply: page 27, Question 2 (b) code X and 8 weeks or more confined to bed or house, or page 28, Question 6, code X, or page 28, Question 7, enough codes 1 or 2 ringed to add to a total of 9 or more.

(i) Households in which there are: (a) earners, none earning £12 a week or more; (b) adult male earners (aged 21 to 64) earning less than £14 a week

(a) See page 15, Question 3 (b), no adult earning more than £12 a week.
(b) See page 15, Question 3 (b) not earning more than £14 a week.

(j) Immigrant families

Households containing one or more adults born in Eire or non-white (whether born overseas or in this country). Eire, see page 5, Question 18 code X for any adult and Question 18 (a), code 1. Non-white, see page 5, Question 18 (b), code 3, or code 4 and Question 18, code X, plus Question 18 (a), codes 2, 3, 4, 5 (and 7, if appropriate).

40a

MEMBERS OF HOUSEHOLD

	.Inft.	2nd	3rd	4th	5th	6th	7th	8th	9th	10th
Christian name for reference only										
	65-66	65-66	65-66	65-66	65-66	65-66				
Age last birthday										

INTERVIEWER PLEASE CODE ALL THAT APPLY AFTER INTERVIEW

			67
(a)	Household in which there is a child, one of whose parents is not resident		X
(b)	Household consisting of woman and adult dependants		Y
(c)	Household in which there are five or more dependent children		0
(d)	Household containing an adult who has been unemployed for eight weeks (consecutively or in last 12 months)		1
(e)	Household containing an adult under 65 years of age who has been ill or injured for eight weeks (consecutively or in last 12 months)		2
(f)	Household containing a disabled adult under 65 (a) disabled		3
	(b) borderline disabled		4
(g)	Household containing a disabled or handicapped child (including child ill or injured for eight weeks or more)		5
(h)	Household containing a person aged 65 or over who has been bedfast or ill for eight weeks or more or who is otherwise severely incapacitated		6
(i)	Household in which there are (a) earners, none earning £12 a week or more		7
	(b) adult male earners (aged 21 to 64) earning less than £14 a week		8
(j)	Household in which there are persons who are (a) non-white		68 / X
	(b) born in Eire		Y

COMPOSITION OF HOUSEHOLD: CODES (Q. 10, p. 3)

One generation
Man alone: aged 60 or over	101
Man alone: aged under 60	102
Woman alone: aged 60 or over	103
Woman alone: aged under 60	104
Husband and wife: both aged 60 or over	105
Husband and wife: at least one aged under 60	106
Husband and wife: both under 60	107
Man and woman: otherwise related	108
Man and woman: unrelated	109
Two or more men only: related	110
Two or more men only: unrelated	111
Two or more women only: related	112
Two or more women only: unrelated	113
Other (SPECIFY)	114

Two generation
Man, wife: + 1 child under 15	201
Man, wife: + 2 children both under 15	202
Man, wife: + 3 children all under 15	203
Man, wife: + 4 or more children all under 15	204
Man, wife: + children, at least 1 under 15 and at least 1 over 15, none married	205
Man, wife: + children all aged 15-24, none married	206
Man, wife: + children all over 15, at least 1 aged 25 or over, none married	207
Man and one child under 15	208
Man and two children both under 15	209
Man and three or more children under 15	210
Man and children at least one under and one over 15, none married	211
Man and children all aged 15-24, none married	212
Man and children all over 15 at least one 25 or over, none married	213
Woman: and one child under 15	214
Woman: and two children both under 15	215
Woman: and three or more children under 15	216
Woman: and children, at least one under and one over 15, none married	217
Woman: and children, all aged 15-24, none married	218
Woman: and children all over 15, at least one 25 or over, none married	219
Man: and widowed or separated son	220

Man: and widowed or separated daughter	221
Woman: and widowed or separated son	222
Woman: and widowed or separated daughter	223
Otherwise two generations: all related	224
Otherwise two generations: at least one person not related to any other	225
Other (SPECIFY)	226

Three generation
Man, son and d-in-law, grandchildren: all under 15	301
Man, son and d-in-law, grandchildren: at least one under 15 and one over 15	302
Man, daughter & son-in-law, grandchildren: all under 15	303
Man, daughter and son-in-law, grandchildren: at least one under 15 and one over 15	304
Woman, son and d-in-law, grandchildren: all under 15	305
Woman, son and d-in-law, grandchildren: at least one under 15, one over 15	306
Woman, daughter and son-in-law, grandchildren: all under 15	307
Woman, daughter and son-in-law, grandchildren: at least one under 15	308
Married couple, married child and child-in-law, grandchildren under 15	309
Otherwise 3-generations: —all persons related, at least one child under 15	310
—at least one child over 15	311
—all persons related	312
—unrelated	313
Other (SPECIFY)	314

Four generation
DESCRIBE COMPOSITION BELOW	401

40

Appendix Eleven
Statistical Tests

A range of statistical tests were available with the SPSS programmes for use with the PDP 10 computer at the University of Essex in the latter stages of the preparation of this report, and we computed chi-square, lamda (asymmetric) and gamma when a number of sets of tables were printed. Chi-square is used in inferential statistics as a basis for a test of significance called the chi-square test. It has the advantage of working for nominal variables and compares expected with actual cell frequencies. The larger the values of chi-square (and the fewer the degrees of freedom), the greater is the probability of a relationship between two variables. When the computed chi-square is large, it does not mean that there is a strong relationship between the variables. It merely means that we can be more confident about rejecting the null hypothesis and concluding that the variables are related. Lamda is another measure of association suitable for nominal variables. Lamda is a measure of the proportionate reduction of error in predicting modal values from knowing not only the distribution of a dependent variable but of the way that dependent variable is distributed within the categories of an independent variable. It varies in magnitude from 0·0 to +1·0. Unlike chi-square it *is* a measure of the strength of a relationship. Gamma is a third measure of association, suitable for ordinal data, and measures the proportionate reduction in errors in predicting the ranking of pairs drawn from both of two variables when the known distribution is compared with a random distribution. It varies in magnitude from −1·0 to +1·0.

All statistical tests require care, because assumptions are made in applying them. Thus, in the computation of chi-square it is assumed that the data analysed are a simple random sample of the population, that the observations are independent, that no expected frequency in the contingency table being analysed will be less than 5, and that the underlying distribution of the computed chi-square statistic is continuous.[1] The poverty survey was not based on a simple random sample but, especially in view of the evidence on representativeness, has been assumed to be so for purposes of statistical testing. This assumption has been made in much other research.

An example is given in Table A11.1. Our object in this example is not simply to test the strength of the association between two variables, but to find whether the association between occupational class and income net worth is stronger than between occupational class and net disposable income, and by how much. The gamma test shows that the association is stronger, and markedly so.

1. Examples of the warnings that need to be observed in using tests are given in Loether, H. J., and McTavish, D. G., *Inferential Statistics for Sociologists: An Introduction*, Allyn & Bacon, Boston, 1974, Chapter 8.

Table A11.1. Percentages and number of chief wage-earners or heads of households and housewives of different occupational class, according to the net disposable income and income net worth of the income unit, expressed as a percentage of the state's poverty standard (married couples only).

Income/income net worth as % of supplementary benefit scale plus housing cost	Professional	Managerial	Supervisory		Routine non-manual	Skilled manual	Partly skilled manual	Unskilled manual
			High	Low				
A. Net disposable income of income unit								
Under 140	6	7	8	18	15	24	27	48
140–99	13	15	30	30	29	35	35	18
200+	81	77	62	52	55	42	38	34
Total	100	100	100	100	100	100	100	100
Number	106	80	192	230	112	682	306	172
B. Income net worth								
Under 140	7		3	6	5	15	20	41
140–99	6		13	15	30	31	29	17
200+	87		83	79	64	54	50	42
Total	100	100	100	100	100	100	100	100
Number	106	80	192	230	112	682	306	172

NOTE: Income units which did not give information about *both* A *and* B in full have been excluded from this table.

TESTS: Gamma A = −0·327   B = −0·415

Lamda   A = 0·024 with income dependent   B = 0·0000 with income dependent
          = 0·0000 with class dependent   = 0·0000 with class dependent

Chi-square = 200·05 with 14 degrees of freedom   = 264·365 with 14 degrees of freedom
          (or significant at 0·0001 level)   (or significant at 0·0001 level)

Appendix Twelve
Method of Adjusting Distribution of Assets

(See Chapter 9, Table 9.1, page 342)

In Chapter 5 we compared aggregate figures for assets (grossed up from sample) with Inland Revenue figures. We can also compare these estimates with balance-sheet estimates produced by Revell and Tomkins. Allowing for certain problems of definition, our estimates for dwellings plus land and other buildings, and even consumer durables, seem broadly to reflect estimates of aggregate national value. But our estimates are much too low for savings and stocks and shares.

There is reason to believe that our estimates of percentage shares of wealth are too low for the top groups, i.e. the top 1 per cent, next 4 per cent and, possibly, next 4 per cent. There are three contributory reasons:

1. On the basis of the information we collected about non-respondents (Chapter 3), it seems that slightly *more* non-respondents than respondents were wealthy. However, our information does not suggest that this was more than a slight deficiency.
2. Among respondents, more of the rich than of middle-income and poor groups did not give complete information. First, we produced tables showing what numbers and percentages of different groups of households ranked by income were not counted as complete for assets. Secondly, we produced a special print-out for every household in the sample, ranked by household net disposable income and such income expressed as a percentage of supplementary benefit scale rates. Moreover, some of the rich households rejected from the analysis of assets had disclosed enough information about a variety of questions to allow a *minimum* estimate of their wealth to be given. There were three, for example, with a minimum of between £118,000 and £131,000 each, and another three with between £50,000 and £100,000. Even without adding any allowance to these estimates, their reintroduction into the rankings would have the effect of increasing the percentage share of the top 5 per cent.
3. Values of assets were underestimated by our informants. Often we are sure that this was because questioning should have been more detailed for wealthy informants. We do not believe underestimation was proportionally uniform from top to bottom of the income scale. Thus 82 per cent of the aggregate value of stocks and shares admitted to be held by the sample was held by the top 5 per cent. The corresponding figure for savings was 27 per cent. These two categories of asset were substantially underestimated.

The first of these sources of underestimation of the percentage share of riches held by the top 5 per cent seems to be small and will be ignored. There is no basis on which an adjustment can be made.

The second is more promising. There were 1,764 households with complete information for income, and 1,533 *of these* complete for assets. This means that 13 per cent were incomplete. But twenty-six of the 100 top-ranking households for income gave incomplete information on assets. We replaced half of these, and entered the incomplete information for their assets.

Finally, we made some allowance for underestimation. We assumed that the underestimation of stocks and shares and of savings was proportionally uniform for the percentage ranks into which they had been distributed, namely, the top 1 per cent, next 4 per cent, next 5 per cent, next 10 per cent, and so on.

Table A12.1.

	Unadjusted sample aggregates	Including 13 additional rich households	Adjusting for stocks, shares and savings	Percentage of adjusted aggregate net assets
Top 1%	1,515,143	1,765,000 (adding £250,000)	2,615,000	26·0
2–5%	1,277,533	1,698,000 (adding £420,000)	2,498,000	24·9
6–10%	866,949	927,000 (adding £60,000)	1,287,000	12·8
11–20%	1,071,536	1,122,000 (adding £50,000)	1,532,000	15·3
21–100%	1,512,118	1,522,000 (adding £10,000)	2,112,000	21·0
	6,243,279	7,034,000	10,044,000	100·0

The adjustments are shown in Table A12.1 (used as a basis for the third column of Table 9.1, page 342). This gives a mean of £6,107. National wealth would therefore on this basis be approximately £115,000 million for 1968–9.

Thirteen added (but therefore displacing others at the foot of each of the percentage groups):

£131,000
121,000
119,000
75,000
52,000
48,000
(45,000)
(45,000)
36,000
30,000
(30,000)
(30,000)
(30,000)
———
792,000

sum = £6,243,000 = 1,630 *sample*
£7,035,000 = 1,643 adjusted sample

includes   £952,000 savings (× 2·7)
£702,000 stocks and shares (× 3·0)
But should include £2,570,000 savings
£2,106,000 stocks and shares
∴ additional £1,618,000
£1,404,000

has been divided as follows:		Multipliers		Multipliers
Top 1%	£200,000	(0·06)	£650,000	(0·43)
next 4%	£300,000	(0·16)	£500,000	(0·37)
next 5%	£240,000	(0·15)	£120,000	(0·10)
next 10%	£350,000	(0·22)	£60,000	(0·05)
bottom 80%	£520,000	(0·41)	£70,000	(0·05)
	£1,610,000	(1·00)	£1,400,000	(1·00)

Appendix Thirteen
Multiple Deprivation

Before compiling a summary index of material and social deprivation set out in Chapter 6 (page 250), we had examined answers to a large number of questions on different aspects of deprivation. This appendix sets out a fuller list, grouped under particular headings. (Some of the principal forms of deprivation are discussed in Chapters 11–14.) Correlation coefficients are given for individual items (and collectively) in relation to net disposable income expressed first as a percentage of the state's poverty standard and secondly as a percentage of the deprivation standard. Both standards have the effect of taking composition of income unit and relativity to other units into account. Two conclusions may be drawn. The relationship between most (as many as forty-two) indicators of deprivation and income (as measured in these two ways) is highly significant. And the correlation between indicators and the deprivation standard is generally closer than between indicators and the state's poverty standard (in only eight of the sixty instances was the size of the latter coefficient larger).

Form of deprivation		*Pearson coefficient* net disposable income of income unit	
		as % supplementary benefit standard	as % deprivation standard
Dietary	1. At least one day without cooked meal in last two weeks	0·0241 (S = ·041)	0·0220 (S = ·055)
	2. No fresh meat most days of week	0·1453 (S = ·001)	0·1546 (S = ·001)
	3. School child does not have school meals	0·1345 (S = ·001)	0·1170 (S = ·001)
	4. Has not had cooked breakfast most days of the week	0·0577 (S = ·001)	0·0603 (S = ·001)
	5. Household does not have a Sunday joint three weeks in four	0·1011 (S = ·001)	0·1030 (S = ·001)
	6. Fewer than three pints of milk per person per week	0·0272 (S = ·024)	0·0359 (S = ·004)

Clothing	7. Inadequate footwear for both wet and fine weather	0·0765 (S = ·001)	0·0766 (S = ·001)
	8. Income unit buys second-hand clothes often or sometimes	0·1080 (S = ·001)	0·0759 (S = ·001)
	9. Income unit misses clothing club payments often or sometimes	0·1247 (S = ·001)	0·1563 (S = ·001)
	10. (Married women) No new winter coat in last three years	0·1720 (S = ·001)	0·1812 (S = ·001)
Fuel and light	11. No electricity or light only (not power)	0·0527 (S = ·001)	0·0666 (S = ·001)
	12. Short of fuel sometimes or often	0·1267 (S = ·001)	0·1334 (S = .001)
	13. No central heating	0·0379 (S = ·003)	0·0711 (S = ·001)
	14. No rooms heated (or only one)	0·1566 (S = ·001)	0·1831 (S = ·001)
Household facilities	15. No TV	0·0003 (S = ·491)	0·0030 (S = ·413)
	16. No refrigerator	0·0666 (S = ·001)	0·878 (S = ·001)
	17. No telephone	0·0793 (S = ·001)	0·1105 (S = ·001)
	18. No record player	0·0544 (S = ·001)	0·0709 (S = ·001)
	19. No radio	0·0029 (S = ·415)	0·0054 (S = ·347)
	20. No washing machine	0·0347 (S = ·006)	0·0384 (S = ·003)
	21. No vacuum cleaner	0·0410 (S = ·001)	0·0525 (S = ·001)
	22. No carpet	0·0119 (S = ·193)	0·0204 (S = ·068)
	23. No armchair	0·0066 (S = ·314)	0·0147 (S = ·142)
Housing conditions and amenities	24. No sole use of four amenities (indoor WC, sink or washbasin, bath or shower, and cooker)	0·0905 (S = ·001)	0·1339 (S = ·001)
	25. Structural defects	0·0713 (S = ·001)	0·1012 (S = ·001)
	26. Structural defects believed dangerous to health	0·1366 (S = ·001)	0·1597 (S = ·001)
	27. Overcrowded (in terms of number of bedrooms)	0·0771 (S = ·001)	0·0993 (S = ·001)

Conditions at work (severity, security, amenities and welfare benefits)	28. Works mainly or entirely outdoors	0·0060 (S = ·392)	0·0422 (S = ·026)
	29. Stands or walks at work all the time	0·0540 (S = ·008)	0·0814 (S = ·001)
	30. Working fifty or more hours last week	0·0180 (S = ·197)	0·0085 (S = ·344)
	31. At work before 8 a.m. or working at night	0·0315 (S = ·069)	0·0069 (S.= ·373)
	32. Poor outdoor amenities of work (see page 438)	0·1214 (S = ·069)	0·0972 (S = ·119)
	33. Poor indoor amenities of work (page 438)	0·0546 (S = ·016)	0·0646 (S = ·006)
	34. Unemployed for two weeks or more during previous twelve months	0·0584 (S = ·002)	0·0723 (S = ·001)
	35. Subject to one week's entitlement to notice or less	0·0800 (S = ·001)	0·1244 (S = ·001)
	36. No wages or salary during sickness	0·0964 (S = ·001)	0·1314 (S = ·001)
	37. Paid holidays of two weeks or less	0·1286 (S = ·001)	0·1413 (S = ·001)
	38. No meals paid or subsidized by employer	0·0351 (S = ·060)	0·0598 (S = ·004)
	39. No entitlement to occupational pension	0·1259 (S = ·001)	0·1758 (S = ·001)
Health	40. Health poor or fair	0·0926 (S = ·001)	0·1202 (S = ·001)
	41. Sick from work five or more weeks last year	0·0437 (S = ·015)	0·0574 (S = ·002)
	42. Ill in bed fourteen days or more last year	0·0930 (S = ·001)	0·1122 (S = ·001)
	43. Has disability condition	0·0830 (S = ·001)	0·0973 (S = ·001)
	44. Has some or severe disability	0·1076 (S = ·001)	0·1323 (S = ·001)
Educational	45. Fewer than ten years' education	0·1019 (S = ·001)	0·1523 (S = ·001)
Environmental	46. No garden or yard, or shared	0·0614 (S = ·001)	0·0806 (S = ·001)
	47. If garden, too small to sit in	0·0455 (S = ·001)	0·0703 (S = ·001)
	48. Air dirty or foul smelling	0·0688 (S = ·001)	0·0869 (S = ·001)
	49. No safe place for child (1–4) to play	0·1132 (S = ·010)	0·1132 (S = ·010)

	50. No safe place for child (5–10) to play	0·0641 (S = ·068)	0·0463 (S = ·141)
Family	51. Difficulties indoors for child to play	0·1829 (S = ·001)	0·2025 (S = ·141)
	52. Child not had friend in to play in last four weeks	0·0919 (S = ·001)	0·1178 (S = ·001)
	53. Child not had party last birthday	0·1163 (S = ·001)	0·1299 (S = ·001)
	54. Household spent less than additional £10 last Christmas	0·1637 (S = ·001)	0·1763 (S = ·001)
Recreational	55. No afternoons or evenings out in last two weeks	0·0950 (S = ·001)	0·1136 (S = ·001)
	56. No holiday in last twelve months away from home	0·1704 (S = ·001)	0·2019 (S = ·001)
Social	57. No emergency help available, e.g. illness	0·0209 (S = ·190)	0·0175 (S = ·231)
	58. No one coming to meal or snack in last four weeks	0·0555 (S = ·001)	0·0816 (S = ·001)
	59. Not been out to meal or snack with relatives or friends in last four weeks	0·0723 (S = ·001)	0·0961 (S = ·001)
	60. Moved house at least twice in last two years	0·0085 (S = ·267)	0·0585 (S = ·001)

Multiple Deprivation	0·2177 (S = ·001)	0·2808 (S = ·001)

NOTE: According to both the state's poverty standard and the deprivation standard, the size of the coefficient was larger when net income worth plus the value of employer welfare benefits in kind was substituted for net disposable income. For example, the coefficient for multiple deprivation and net income worth plus the value of employer welfare benefits in kind as a percentage of the deprivation standard was 0.3304 compared with the figure of 0.2808 given above.

List of References

1. General Publications

ABEL-SMITH, B., AND TOWNSEND, P., *New Pensions for the Old*, Fabian Research Series No. 171, London, March 1955.

ABEL-SMITH, B., AND TOWNSEND, P., *The Poor and the Poorest*, Bell, London, 1965.

AIGNER, D. J., 'A Comment on Problems in Making Inferences from the Coleman Report', *American Sociological Review*, vol. 35, No. 2, April 1970.

AITCHISON, J., AND BROWN, J. A. C., *The Lognormal Distribution*, Cambridge University Press, 1957.

ALLAN, K. H., AND CINSKY, M. E., 'General Characteristics of the Disabled Population', *Social Security Survey of the Disabled: 1966*, Report No. 19, US Department of Health, Education and Welfare, Office of Research and Statistics, July 1972.

ANDERSEN, B. R., *Fysisk Handicappede i Danmark* (The Physically Handicapped in Denmark), vol. 2, Report No. 16 of the Danish National Institute of Social Research, Copenhagen, 1964.

ATKINSON, A. B., *The Economics of Inequality*, Clarendon Press, Oxford, 1975.

ATKINSON, A. B., 'Low Pay and the Cycle of Poverty', in Field, F. (ed.), *Low Pay*, Arrow Books, London, 1973.

ATKINSON, A. B., 'On the Measurement of Inequality', *Journal of Economic Theory*, September 1970.

ATKINSON, A. B., *Poverty in Britain and the Reform of Social Security*, Cambridge University Press, 1969.

ATKINSON, A. B., 'The Reform of Wealth Taxes in Britain', *Political Quarterly*, January 1971.

ATKINSON, A. B. (ed.), *Wealth, Income and Inequality*, Penguin Books, Harmondsworth, 1973.

ATKINSON, A. B., *Unequal Shares: The Distribution of Wealth in Britain*, Allen Lane, London, 1972.

ATKINSON, A. B., *The Economics of Inequality*, Clarendon Press, Oxford, 1975.

ATKINSON, A. B., AND HARRISON, A. J., 'Wealth Distribution and Investment Income in Britain', *Review of Income and Wealth*, June 1974.

ATKINSON, A. B., AND HARRISON, A. J., *Distribution of Personal Wealth in Britain*, Cambridge University Press, 1978.

BAGLEY, C., *The Cost of a Child: Problems in the Relief and Measurement of Poverty*, Institute of Psychiatry, London, 1969.

BALDWIN, S., *Disabled Children: Counting the Costs*, Disability Alliance, London, 1977.

BALL, M., 'Owner Occupation', in Edwards, M., *et al.* (eds.), *Housing and Class in Britain*, Political Economy of Housing Workshop of the Conference of Socialist Economists, University of Sussex, 1976.

BALOGH, T., *Labour and Inflation*, Fabian Tract No. 403, Fabian Society, London, October 1970.

BARAN, P., AND SWEEZY, P., *Monopoly Capital*, Monthly Review Press, New York, 1966.

BARNA, T., *The Redistribution of Income through Public Finance in 1937*, Clarendon Press, Oxford, 1945.

BARNES, J. H., AND LUCAS, H., *Positive Discrimination in Education: Individuals, Groups and Institutions*, ILEA, London, 1973.

BARRATT BROWN, M., *et al.*, *Full Employment*, Spokesman Books, London, 1978.

BARRON, R., AND NORRIS, G., *Studies of Poverty among the Subemployed*, unpublished SSRC Report, 1976.

BARRON, R., AND NORRIS, G., 'Sexual Divisions and the Dual Labour Market', in Barker, D. L., and Allen, S. (eds.), *Dependence and Exploitation in Work and Marriage*, Longman, London, 1976.

BARTEN, A. P., 'Family Composition, Prices and Expenditure Patterns', *Econometric Analysis for National Economic Planning*, Butterworth, London, 1964.

BATSON, E., *The Poverty Line in Salisbury*, University of Cape Town, 1945.

BATSON, E., *Social Survey of Cape Town*, Reports of the School of Social Science and Social Administration, University of Cape Town, 1941–4.

BECHHOFER, F., 'Occupation', in STACEY, M. (ed.), *Comparability in Social Research*, Heinemann, London, 1969.

BECKER, G. S., *Human Capital*, National Bureau of Economic Research, New York, 1964.

BELL, LADY FLORENCE, *At the Works*, Nelson, London, 1911.

BENDER, A. E., 'Feeding the School Child', *Poverty*, No. 23, Summer 1972.

BENJAMIN, B., 'Tuberculosis and Social Conditions in the Metropolitan Boroughs of London', *British Journal of Tuberculosis*, 47, 1953.

BENNETT, A. E., GARRAD, J., AND HALIL, T., 'Chronic Disease and Disability in the Community: A Prevalence Study', *British Medical Journal*, 26 September 1970.

BETTISON, D. S., 'The Poverty Datum Line in Central Africa', *Rhodes Livingston Journal*, No. 27, 1960.

BLANDY, R., 'The Welfare Analysis of Fertility Reduction', *Economic Journal*, March 1974.

BLAU, P. M., AND DUNCAN, O. D., *The American Occupational Structure*, John Wiley, New York, 1967.

BLUESTONE, B., 'The Tripartite Economy', *Poverty and Human Resources Abstracts*, July–August 1970.

BLUESTONE, B., 'The Tripartite Economy: Labor Markets and the Working Poor', *Poverty and Human Resources Abstracts*, July–August 1970.

BLUESTONE, B., MURPHY, W., AND STEVENSON, M., *Low Wages and the Working Poor*, Institute of Labor and Industrial Relations, University of Michigan – Wayne State University, October 1971.

BODDY, M., 'Building Societies and Owner Occupation', in Edwards, M., *et al.* (eds.), *Housing and Class in Britain*, Political Economy of Housing Workshop of the Conference of Socialist Economists, University of Sussex, 1976.

BODDY, M., 'Building Societies and the Social Formation', *Transactions of the Institute of British Geographers*, 1975.

BOOTH, C., *The Aged Poor: Condition*, Macmillan, London, 1894.

BOOTH, C., *Life and Labour of the People in London*, Macmillan, London (17-vol. edition), 1903. (Original volume on East London published 1889).

BOOTH, C., *Old Age Pensions and the Aged Poor*, Macmillan, London, 1899.

BOOTH, C., *Pauperism: A Picture; and the Endowment of Old Age: An Argument*, Macmillan, London, 1892.

BORIS ALLAN, G. J., 'Simplicity in Path Analysis', *Sociology*, May 1974.

BOSANQUET, N., *Low Pay: An International Comparison of Patterns and Policies*, OECD, Paris, 1973.

BOSANQUET, N., AND DOERINGER, R., 'Is there a Dual Labour Market in Britain?', *Economic Journal*, 1973.

BOSANQUET, N., AND STANDING, G., 'Government and Unemployment, 1966–1970: A Study of Policy and Evidence', *British Journal of Industrial Relations*, 1972.

BOSANQUET, N., AND STEPHENS, R. J., 'Another Look at Low Pay': *Journal of Social Policy*, July 1972.

BOTT, E., *Family Network and Social Class*, Tavistock Publications, London, 1957.

BOUDON, R., *The Logic of Sociological Explanation*, Penguin Books, Harmondsworth, 1974.

BOWLEY, A. L., *Wages and Income in the United Kingdom Since 1860*, Cambridge University Press, 1937.

BOWLEY, A. L., AND BURNETT-HURST, A. R., *Livelihood and Poverty, A Study in the Economic and Social Conditions of Working Class Households in Northampton, Warrington, Stanley, Reading (and Bolton)*, King, London, 1915.

BOWLEY, A. L., AND HOGG, M. H., *Has Poverty Diminished?*, King, London, 1925.

BOWMAN, M. J., in FELLNER, W., AND HALEY, B. F. (eds.), *Readings in the Theory of Income Distribution*, Allen & Unwin, London, 1950.

BRADSHAW, J., *The Financial Needs of Disabled Children*, Disability Alliance, London, 1975.

BRADSHAW, J., AND WICKS, M., 'Where Have All the Rate Rebates Gone?', *Poverty*, No. 15, 1970.

BRIDGES, B., 'Net Worth of the Aged'. *Research and Statistics Note*, US Department of Health, Education and Welfare, September 1967.

TEN BROEK, J., AND MATSON, F. W., 'The Disabled and the Law of Welfare', *California Law Review*, vol. 54, No. 2, May 1966.

BROWN, C. V., AND DAWSON, D. A., *Personal Taxation, Incentives and Tax Reform*, Political and Economic Planning, London, January 1969.

BROWN, G. W., *et al.*, *Schizophrenia and Social Care*, Oxford University Press, 1966.

BROWN, M., *Sweated Labour: A Study of Homework*, Low Pay Unit, London, 1974.

BROWN, M., *Low Pay in Hotels and Catering*, Low Pay Unit, London, 1975.

BUCKLE, J. R., *Work and Housing of Impaired Persons in Great Britain*, HMSO, London, 1971.

BURNS, T., 'The Study of Consumer Behaviour: A Sociological View', *Archives of European Sociology*, VII, 1966.

CAIN, G. G., 'The Challenge of Dual and Radical Theories of the Labour Market to Orthodox Theory', *Proceedings of the American Economic Association*, May 1975.

CAIN, G. G., AND WATTS, H. W., 'Problems in Making Policy Inferences from the Coleman Report', *American Sociological Review*, vol. 35, No. 2, April 1970.

CAPLOVITZ, D., *The Poor Pay More*, Free Press, New York, 1963.

CAPLOW, T., *The Sociology of Work*, McGraw-Hill, New York, 1954.

CARADOG JONES, D., *Social Survey of Merseyside*, Liverpool, 1934.

CARTTER, A. M., *The Redistribution of Income in Post War Britain, A Study of the Effects of the Central Government Fiscal Programme in 1948–49*, Yale University Press, 1955.

CENTERS, R., *The Psychology of Social Classes*, Princeton University Press, 1949.

CHAMPERNOWNE, D. G., 'A Model of Income Distribution', *Economic Journal*, vol. 63, 1953.

CHAPMAN, D., *The Home and Social Status*, Routledge & Kegan Paul, London, 1955.

CLARK, R. M., *Canadian Issues: Essays in Honour of Henry F. Angus*, University of Toronto Press, 1962.

COATES, K., AND SILBURN, R., *Poverty: the Forgotten Englishmen*, Penguin Books, Harmondsworth, 1970.

COHEN, M., 'Some Alternative Measures of Sub-employment', *US Bureau of Labor Statistics*, 9 September 1968.

COHEN, S., *Folk Devils and Moral Panics: The Creation of the Mods and Rockers*, MacGibbon & Kee, London, 1972.

COLE WEDDERBURN, D., WITH UTTING, J., *The Economic Circumstances of Old People*, Codicote Press, Welwyn, 1962.

COLEMAN, J. S., 'Reply to Cain and Watts', *American Sociological Review*, vol. 35, No. 2, April 1970.

COLEMAN, J. S., CAMPBELL, E. Q., HOBSON, C. F., MCPARTLAND, J., AND MOOD, A. M., *Equality of Educational Opportunity*, US Office of Education, Washington DC, 1966.

COLLINS, D., 'The Introduction of Old Age Pensions in Great Britain', *Historical Journal*, VIII, 2, 1965.

COLQUHOUN, P., *On Destitution*, Hatchard, London, 1806.

CRAIG, C., *Men in Manufacturing Industry*, Department of Applied Economics, Cambridge, 1969.

CROWDER, N. D., 'A Critique of Duncan's Stratification Research', *Sociology*, No. 1, January 1974.

CSEH-SZOMBATHY, L., AND ANDORKA, R., *Situation and Problems of the Pensioners of Budapest*, Central Statistical Office, Research Group for Population Studies, 1965–6.

CULLINGWORTH, J. B., *English Housing Trends*, Bell, London, 1965.

CUMMING, E., AND HENRY, W. E., *Growing Old*, Basic Books, New York, 1961.

CUTRIGHT, P., 'Income Distribution: A Cross-National Analysis', *Social Forces*, December 1967.

DANIEL, W. W., *A National Survey of the Unemployed*, Political and Economic Planning, Broadsheet No. 546, October 1974.

DAVIES, B., *Social Needs and Resources in Local Services*, Michael Joseph, London, 1968.

DAVIES, B., 'Territorial Injustice', *New Society*, 13 May 1976.

DAVIES, B., AND REDDIN, M., 'School Meals and Plowden', *New Society*, May 1967.

DAVIES, B., AND WILLIAMSON, V., 'School Meals – Short Fall and Poverty', *Social and Economic Administration*, January 1968.

DAVIES, M., *Life in an English Village*, London, 1909.

DAVIS, K., AND MOORE, W. E., 'Some Principles of Stratification', *American Sociological Review*, April 1945.

DAW, R. H., in *Journal of the Institute of Actuaries*, 1971.

DEBEAUVAIS, M., *Comparative Study of Educational Expenditure and its Trends in OECD Countries since 1950*, Background Study No. 2, Conference on Policies for Educational Growth, OECD, 1970.

DENNIS, N., *People and Planning: the Sociology of Housing in Sunderland*, Faber and Faber, London, 1971.

DOERINGER, P. B., AND PIORE, M. J., *Internal Labor Markets and Manpower Analysis*, Heath Lexington Books, Lexington, Mass., 1971.

DOLL, PROFESSOR SIR RICHARD, 'Monitoring the National Health Service', *Proceedings of the Royal Society of Medicine*, vol. 66, August 1973.

DONNISON, D., 'Policies for Priority Areas', *Journal of Social Policy*, vol. 3.

DONNISON, D., *Housing Policy Since the War*, Codicote Press, Welwyn, 1962.

DOREIAN, P., AND STOCKMAN, N., 'A Critique of the Multidimensional Approach to Stratification', *Sociological Review*, 17, 1969.

DOUGLAS, J. D. (ed.), *The Relevance of Sociology*, Appleton-Century-Crofts, New York, 1970.

DOUGLAS, J. W. B., AND SIMPSON, H., *Milbank Memorial Fund Quarterly*, vol. 42, 1964.

DRABBLE, R., 'Education Maintenance Allowances', *Poverty*, No. 24, 1972.

DUBOIS, W. E. B., *The Philadelphia Negro*, Schocken Books, New York, 1967.

DUNCAN, G., 'Non-Pecuniary Work Rewards', in Morgan, J. N. (ed.), *Five Thousand American Families – Patterns of Economic Progress*, Survey Research Center, Institute for Social Research, University of Michigan, vol. II, 1974.

DUNCAN, T. L. C., *Measuring Housing Quality: A Study of Methods*, Occasional Paper No. 20, Centre for Urban and Regional Studies, University of Birmingham, 1971.

DURKHEIM, E., *The Division of Labour*, The Free Press, Glencoe, 1964.

DURWIN, J. V. G. A., AND PASSMORE, R., *Energy, Work and Leisure*, Heinemann, London, 1967.

EDDING, F., 'Expenditure on Education: Statistics and Comments', in Robinson, E. A. G., and Vaizey, J. E. (eds.), *The Economics of Education*, Macmillan, London, 1966.

ELKS, L., *The Wage Stop*, Child Poverty Action Group, London, 1974.

ENGEL, E., 'Die Lebenskasten belgischer Arbeiter – Familien früher und jetzt', *International Statistical Institute Bulletin*, No. 9, 1895.

ENGELS, F., *The Condition of the Working Class in England*, Panther Books, London, 1969.

EPSTEIN, L. A., 'Income of the Aged in 1962: First Findings of the 1963 Survey of the Aged', *Social Security Bulletin*, XXVII, March 1964.

FALK, N., AND MARTINOS, H., *Inner City*, Fabian Society, London, May 1975.

FARNDALE, J. (ed.), *Trends in Social Welfare*, Pergamon Press, Oxford, 1965.

FERMAN, L. A., *et al.*, *Jobs and Negroes*, University of Michigan Press, 1968.

FIEGEHEN, G. C., LANSLEY, P. S., AND SMITH, A. D., *Poverty and Progress in Britain 1953–73*, Cambridge University Press, 1977.

FIELD, F., *An Incomes Policy for Poor Families*, Child Poverty Action Group, London, 1973.

FIELD, F., *Low Pay*, Arrow Books, London, 1973.

FIELD, F., '70 Years On: A New Report on Homeworking', *Low Pay Bulletin*, August–October 1976.

FIELD, F., *The New Corporate Interest*, Poverty Pamphlet No. 23, London, Child Poverty Action Group, London, 1976.

FIELD, F. (ed.), *The Conscript Army: A Study of Britain's Unemployed*, Routledge & Kegan Paul, London, 1977.

FIELD, F., MEACHER, M., AND POND, C., *To Him Who Hath*, Penguin Books, Harmondsworth, 1977.

FISK, T., AND JONES, K., *Regional Development*, Fabian Society, London, 1972.

FORSYTH, G., *Doctors and State Medicine: A Study of the British Health Service*, Pitman, London, 1966.

FREIDSON, E., 'Disability as Social Deviance', in Sussman, M. B. (ed.), *Sociology and Rehabilitation*, Penguin Books, Harmondsworth, 1968.

FUCHS, V. F., 'Differentials in Hourly Wages between Men and Women', *Monthly Labor Review*, May 1971.

GALENSON, W., AND LIPSET, S. M. (eds.), *Labor and Trade Unionism*, Wiley, New York, 1960.

GALLAWAY, L. E., 'On the Importance of "Picking One's Parents"', *Quarterly Review of Economics and Business*, VI, No. 2 (Summer 1966).

GALTUNG, J., *Theory and Methods of Social Research*, Allen & Unwin, London, 1967.

GANS, H., *The Urban Villagers*, Free Press, New York, 1962.

GANS, H., 'The Positive Functions of Poverty', *American Journal of Sociology*, 78, No. 2, 1973.

GEORGE, V., *Social Security: Beveridge and After*, Routledge & Kegan Paul, London, 1968.

GEORGE, V., *Social Security and Society*, Routledge & Kegan Paul, London, 1973.

GEORGE, V., AND WILDING, P., *Motherless Families*, Routledge & Kegan Paul, London, 1972.

GERMANI, G., MAR, J. M., PEARSE, A., in Hauser, P. (ed.), *Urbanization in Latin America*, Unesco, Paris, 1961.

GERTH, H., AND MILLS, C. W., *From Max Weber: Essays in Sociology*, Oxford University Press, 1946.

GIBRAT, R., *Les Inégalités Économiques*, Librairie du Recueil Sirey, Paris, 1931.

GIFFEN, R., 'The Progress of the Working Classes in the Last Half Century', *Essays in Finance* (2nd edn), 1887.

GINZBERG, E., 'The Occupational Adjustment of 1000 Selectees', *American Sociological Review*, 1943.

GLASS, D. V. (ed.), *Social Mobility in Britain*, Routledge & Kegan Paul, London, 1954.

GLAZER, N., AND MOYNIHAN, D. P., *Beyond the Melting Pot*, MIT Press and Harvard University Press, 1963.

GOFFMAN, E., *Stigma: Notes on the Management of Spoiled Identity*, Penguin Books, Harmondsworth, 1968.

GOLDBERG, E. M., AND MORRISON, S. L., 'Schizophrenia and Social Class', *British Journal of Psychiatry*, 1963.

GOLDTHORPE, J. H., 'Social Inequality and Social Integration in Modern Britain', *Advancement of Science*, December 1969.

GOLDTHORPE, J. H., AND HOPE, K., 'Occupational Grading and Occupational Prestige', *The Analysis of Social Mobility: Methods and Approaches*, Clarendon Press, Oxford, 1972.

GOLDTHORPE, J. H., AND HOPE, K., *The Social Grading of Occupations*, Clarendon Press, Oxford, 1974.

GOLDTHORPE, J. H., LOCKWOOD, D., BECHHOFER, F., AND PLATT, J., *The Affluent Worker: Industrial Attitudes and Behaviour*, Cambridge University Press, 1968.

GOLDTHORPE, J. H., LOCKWOOD, D., BECHHOFER, F., AND PLATT, J., *The Affluent Worker in the Class Structure*, Cambridge University Press, 1969.

GOLDSTEIN, H., 'Factors Influencing the Height of Seven Year Old Children – Results from the National Child Development Study', *Human Biology*, vol. 43, 1971.

GORDON, D. M., *Theories of Poverty and Underemployment*, Lexington Books, Lexington, Mass., 1972.

GOULDNER, A., 'The Sociologist as Partisan: Sociology and the Welfare State', in Douglas, J. D. (ed.), *The Relevance of Sociology*, Appleton-Century-Crofts, New York, 1970.

GRAY, P., AND GEE, F. A., *A Quality Check of the 1966 Ten Per Cent Sample Census of England and Wales*, Social Survey Division, OPCS, HMSO, London, 1972.

GRAY, P. G., AND RUSSELL, R., *The Housing Situation in 1960*, Social Survey, SS319, Central Office of Information, May 1962.

GREAVES, J. P., AND HOLLINGSWORTH, D. F., in *World Review of Nutrition and Dietetics*, VI, 1966.

GREER, R., *Building Societies?*, Fabian Society, London, 1974.

GREGORY, P., *Polluted Homes*, Bell, London, 1965.

HABER, L. D. 'Prevalence of Disability among Non-Institutionalized Adults under Age 65: 1966 Survey of Disabled Adults', *Research and Statistics Notes*, US Department of Health, Education and Welfare, Social Security Administration, Office of Research and Statistics, 20 February 1968.

HALL, J., AND JONES, D. CARADOG, 'Social Grading of Occupations', *British Journal of Sociology*, March 1950.

HARBURY, C. D., 'Inheritance and the Distribution of Personal Wealth in Britain', *Economic Journal*, December 1962.

HARBURY, C., AND MCMAHON, P., 'Inheritance and Characteristics of Top Wealth Leavers in Britain', *Economic Journal*, September 1973.

HARCOURT, A., HARPER, R. J. A., AND SHAVER, S., *The Melbourne Poverty Survey: Further Notes on Methods and Results*, Technical Paper No. 3, Institute of Applied Economic and Social Research, University of Melbourne, May 1972.

HARE, P. H., 'Comparing the Costs of Owning and Renting in Scotland', *Housing Review*, April 1973.

HARRINGTON, M., *The Other America*, Penguin Books, Harmondsworth, 1962.

HARRIS, A. I., ASSISTED BY CLAUSEN, R., *Social Welfare for the Elderly: A Study of Thirteen Local Authority Areas in England, Wales and Scotland*, vol. 1, HMSO, London, 1968.

HARRIS, A. I. ASSISTED BY CLAUSEN, R., *Labour Mobility in Great Britain 1953–63*, Government Social Survey, SS333, March 1966.

HARRIS, A. I., WITH COX, E., AND SMITH, C. R. W., *Handicapped and Impaired in Great Britain*, HMSO, London, 1971.

HARRIS, A. I., SMITH, C. R. W., AND HEAD, E., *Income and Entitlement to Supplementary Benefit of Impaired People in Great Britain*, HMSO, London, 1972.

HARRIS, R., 'A Review of the Effects of Taxes and Benefits on Household Incomes, 1961–1975', *Economic Trends*, January 1977.

HART, J. T., 'Data on Occupational Mortality, 1959–63', *Lancet*, 22 January 1972.

HAUSER, M. M., AND BURROWS, P., *The Economics of Unemployment Insurance*, University of York Studies in Economics, No. 3, Allen & Unwin, London, 1969.

HENDERSON, A. M., 'The Cost of a Family', *Review of Economic Studies, 1949–50*, vol. XVII.

HENDERSON, R. F., HARCOURT, A., AND HARPER, R. J. A., *People in Poverty: A Melbourne Survey*, Cheshire, Melbourne, 1970.

HERRICK, N. Q., AND QUINN, R. P., 'The Working Conditions Survey as a source of Social Indicators', *Monthly Labor Review*, April 1971.

HERZOG, E., 'Some Assumptions about the Poor', *Social Service Review*, December 1963.

HICKS, J. R., *The Theory of Wages*, Macmillan, London, 1935.

HILL, M. J., HARRISON, R. M., SARGEANT, A. V., AND TALBOT, V., *Men Out of Work: A Study of Unemployment in Three English Towns*, Cambridge University Press, 1973.

HILL, O., *Homes of the London Poor* (2nd edn), Macmillan, London, 1883.

HILL, T. P., 'Incomes, Savings and Net Worth – the Savings Surveys of 1952–54', *Bulletin of the Oxford University Institute of Statistics*, XVII, 1955.

HILLER, P., 'Variations in Everyday Conceptual Components of Class', *Sociology*, May 1975.

HOBSBAWM, E. J., 'Poverty', in Sills, D. L. (ed.), *New International Encyclopaedia of the Social Sciences*, vol. 12, Macmillan, London, 1968.

HOLMANS, A. E., 'The Growth of Public Expenditure in the United Kingdom since 1950', *Manchester School of Economic and Social Studies*, December 1968.

HOLTERMANN, S., 'Census Indicators of Urban Deprivation', Working Note No. 6, Great Britain, Department of the Environment, February 1975; and an amended version in *Social Trends*, No. 6, HMSO, London, 1976.

HOUGHTON, D., *Paying for the Social Services*, Institute of Economic Affairs, London, 1967.

HOWE, J. R., *Two Parent Families: A Study of their Resources and Needs in 1968, 1969 and 1970*, Statistical Report Series No. 14, HMSO, London, 1971.

HUGHES, D., *How Psychiatric Patients Manage Out of Hospital*, Disability Alliance, London, 1978.

HUGHES, J., 'The Increase in Inequality', *New Statesman*, 8 November 1968.

HUNT, A., WITH FOX, J., AND MORGAN, M., *Families and their Needs, with Particular Reference to One Parent Families*, HMSO, London, 1973.

JACKSON, D., AND FINK, A., 'Assets, Liabilities and Poverty', *Social and Economic Administration*, 1971.

JACO, E. G. (ed.), *Patients, Physicians and Illness*, Free Press, New York, 1958.

JAEHNIG, W., 'Seeking Out the Disabled', *Yearbook on Social Policy, 1973*, Routledge & Kegan Paul, London, 1973.

JEFFERYS, M., MILLARD, J. B., HYMAN, M., AND WARREN, M. D., 'A Set of Tests for Measuring Motor Impairment in Prevalence Studies', *Journal of Chronic Diseases*, vol. 22, 1964.

JEPHCOTT, P., *Homes in High Flats*, Oliver & Boyd, London, 1971.

KARN, V., *Priorities for Local Authority Mortgage Lending: A Case Study of Birmingham*, Centre for Urban and Regional Studies Research Memorandum, 52, 1976.

KEMSLEY, W. F. F., *Family Expenditure Survey: Handbook on the Sample, Fieldwork and Coding Procedures*, HMSO, London, 1969.

KEMSLEY, W. F. F., 'Family Expenditure Survey: A Study of Differential Response Based on a Comparison of the 1971 Sample with the Census', *Statistical News*, November 1975.

KERR, C., 'The Balkanization of Labour Markets', in Bakke, E. W. (ed.), *Labor Mobility and Economic Opportunity*, John Wiley, New York, 1954.

KINCAID, J. C., *Poverty and Equality in Britain*, Penguin Books, Harmondsworth, 1973.

KINNERSLY, P., *The Hazards of Work: How to Fight Them*, Workers' Handbook No. 1, Pluto Press, London, 1973.

KNIGHT, I. B., AND NIXON, J., *Two Parent Families in Receipt of Family Income Supplement, 1972*, DHSS Statistical and Research Report Series No. 9, HMSO, London, 1975.

KNIGHT, R., 'Changes in the Occupational Structure of the Working Population', *Journal of the Royal Statistical Society*, vol. 130, part 3.

KUZNETS, S., 'Quantitative Aspects of Economic Growth of Nations: VIII Distribution of Income by Size', *Economic Development and Cultural Change*, 11 January 1963.

LABBENS, J., *La Condition sous prolétarienne*, Bureau de Recherches Sociales, Paris, 1965.

LABBENS, J., *Reflections on the Concept of a Culture of Poverty*, International Committee on Poverty Research, Bureau de Recherches Sociales, Paris, 1966.

LAING, S., *National Distress: Its Causes and Remedies*, Longmans, Green, London, 1844.

LAMBERT, R., *Nutrition in Britain, 1950–60*, Codicote Press, Welwyn, 1964.

LAMPMAN, R. J., 'The Share of Top Wealth-Holders in National Wealth 1922–1956', *Review of Economic Statistics*, 1959.

LAND, H., *Large Families in London*, Bell, London, 1969.

LANGLEY, K. M., 'The Distribution of Private Capital 1950–51', *Bulletin of the Oxford University Institute of Statistics*, 1954.

LANSLEY, S., AND FIEGEHEN, G., *Housing Allowances and Inequality*, Fabian Society, London, 1973.

LEBERGOTT, S., 'The Shape of the Income Distribution', *American Economic Review*, 1959.

LEGG, C., 'Will Rent Rebates be Claimed?', *Poverty*, No. 23, 1972.

LE GROS CLARK, F., AND DUNNE, A. C., *Ageing in Industry*, Nuffield Foundation, London, 1955.

LEIBENSTEIN, H., 'An Interpretation of the Economic Theory of Fertility: Promising Path or Blind Alley?', *Journal of the Economics of Literature*, June 1974.

LEWIS, O., *Life in a Mexican Village: Tepoztlán Restudied*, University of Illinois, 1951.

LEWIS, O., *The Children of Sánchez*, Penguin Books, Harmondsworth, 1964.

LEWIS, O., 'Urbanisation without Breakdown: A Case Study', in Heath, D. B., and Adams, R. N. (eds.), *Contemporary Cultures and Societies of Latin America*, Random House, New York, 1965.

LEWIS, O., *La Vida*, Panther Books, London, 1968.

LEWIS, O., 'Rejoinder to Critics' in *Cultural Anthropology*, April–June 1969.

LEWIS, P., *et al.*, *Inflation and Low Incomes*, Fabian Research Series No. 322, Fabian Society, London, August 1975.

LIDBETTER, E. J., *Heredity and the Social Problem Group*, Arnold, London, 1933.

LISTER, R., *The Take-up of Means Tested Benefits*, Child Poverty Action Group, London, 1974.

LISTER, R., *Social Security: The Case for Reform*, Child Poverty Action Group, London, 1975.

LISTER, R., 'Take-up: The Same Old Story', *Poverty*, No. 34, Summer 1976.

LITTLE, A., 'Schools: Targets and Methods', in Glennerster, H., and Hatch, S. (eds.), *Positive Discrimination and Inequality*, Fabian Society, London, March 1974.

LUNDBERG, F., *The Rich and the Super-Rich*, Nelson, London, 1969.

LYDALL, H. F., *British Incomes and Savings*, Blackwell, Oxford, 1955.

LYDALL, H. F., 'The Long-Term Trend in the Size Distribution of Income', *Journal of the Royal Statistical Society*, Series A (General), 122, Part 1, 1959.

LYDALL, H., *The Structure of Earnings*, Oxford University Press, 1968.

LYDALL, H., AND LANSING, J. B., 'A Comparison of the Distribution of Personal Income and Wealth in the United States and Great Britain', *American Economic Review*, March 1959.

LYDALL, H. F., AND TIPPING, D. G., 'The Distribution of Personal Wealth in Britain', *Bulletin of the Oxford University Institute of Statistics*, XXIII, 1961.

LYNES, T., 'The Use of Life Assurance, Pension Schemes and Trusts for Tax Avoidance', in Titmuss, R. M., *Income Distribution and Social Change*, Allen & Unwin, London, 1962.

LYNES, T., 'The Dinner Money Problem', *Poverty*, No. 10, Spring 1969.

LYNES, T., 'The Failure of Selectivity', in Bull, D. (ed.), *Family Poverty*, Duckworth, London, 1971.

LYNES, T., 'Clawback', in Bull, D. (ed.), *Family Poverty*, Duckworth, London, 1971.

MAASDORP, G., AND HUMPHREYS, A. S. B. (eds.), *From Shanty Town to Township: An Economic Study of African Poverty and Rehousing in a South African City*, Juta, Capetown, 1975.

MACEWEN, A., 'Stability and Change in a Shanty Town', *Sociology*, January 1972.

MACKAY, D., *et al.*, *Labour Markets under Different Employment Conditions*, Allen & Unwin, London, 1971.

MANN, M., 'Economic Determinism and Structural Change', University of Essex, unpublished paper, March 1974.

MARRIS, P., *Widows and Their Families*, Routledge & Kegan Paul, London, 1958.

MARRIS, P., AND REIN, M., *Dilemmas of Social Reform: Poverty and Community Action in the United States*, Routledge & Kegan Paul, London, 1967.

MARSDEN, D., *Mothers Alone: Poverty and the Fatherless Family*, Allen Lane, London, 1969 (rev. edn, Penguin Books, Harmondsworth, 1973).

MARSDEN, D., AND DUFF, E., *Workless*, Penguin Books, Harmondsworth, 1975.

MARX, K., *Capital*, Lawrence & Wishart, London, 1970 and 1972.

MARX, K., *Grundisse: Foundations of the Critique of Political Economy* (seven notebooks rough-drafted in 1857–8), Penguin Books, Harmondsworth, 1973.

MASTERMAN, C., *The Condition of England*, Methuen, London, 1960 (originally published 1909).

MAURICE, R., *National Accounts Statistics: Sources and Methods*, Central Statistical Office, HMSO, London, 1969.

MCCLEMENTS, L. D., 'Equivalence Scales for Children', Department of Health and Social Security, July 1975. (Also *Journal of Public Economics*, no. 8, 1977).

MCCRONE, G., *Regional Policy in Britain*, Allen & Unwin, London, 1969.

MEACHER, M., *Rate Rebates: A Study of the Effectiveness of Means-Tests*, Child Poverty Action Group, London, 1972.

MEACHER, M., *Scrounging on the Welfare: The Scandal of the Four Week Rule*, Arrow Books, London, 1974.

MEACHER, M., 'Wealth: Labour's Achilles Heel', in Bosanquet, N., and Townsend, P., *Labour and Inequality*, Fabian Society, London, 1971.

MEADE, J. E., *Efficiency, Equality and the Ownership of Property*, Allen & Unwin, London, 1964.

MECHANIC, D., 'The Concept of Illness Behaviour', *Journal of Chronic Diseases*, vol. 15, 1962.

MECHANIC, D., 'Response Factors in Illness: The Study of Illness Behaviour', *Social Psychiatry*, vol. 1, August 1966.

MEDHURST, F., AND LEWIS, J. P., *Urban Decay: An Analysis and a Policy*, Macmillan, London, 1969.

MERTON, R. K., *Social Theory and Social Structure* (revised edn), Glencoe, Illinois, 1957.

MILLER, F. J. W., *et al.*, *Growing up in Newcastle-upon-Tyne*, Oxford University Press, 1960.

MILLER, H. P., *Income of the American People*, John Wiley, New York, 1955.

MILLER, S. M., AND ROBY, P., 'Poverty: Changing Social Stratification', in Townsend, P. (ed.), *The Concept of Poverty*, Heinemann, London, 1970.

MILLER, S. M., AND ROBY, P., *The Future of Inequality*, Basic Books, New York, 1970.

MILLS, C. W., *The Power Elite*, Oxford University Press, 1959.

MORGAN, E. V., *Personal Savings and Wealth in Britain*, an EAG Business Research Study, Financial Times, London, 1975.

MORGAN, J. N., 'The Anatomy of Income Distribution', *Review of Economics and Statistics*, XLIV, August 1962.

MORGAN, J. N., 'The Retirement Process in the United States', working paper from

OEO, Study of Family Income Dynamics, Survey Research Center, University of Michigan, 1972.

MORGAN, J. N., MARTIN, D. M., COHEN, W., AND BRAZER, H. E., *Income and Welfare in the United States*, McGraw-Hill, New York, 1962.

MORGAN, J. N., AND DAVID, M., 'The Aged: Their Ability to Meet Medical Expenses', *Financing Health Care for the Aged*, Part I, Blue Cross Association, American Hospital Association, Chicago, Illinois, 1962.

MORRIS, J. N., 'Health and Social Class', *Lancet*, 7 February 1959.

MOSER, C. A., AND HALL, J. R., 'The Social Grading of Occupations', in Glass, D. V. (ed.), *Social Mobility in Britain*, Routledge & Kegan Paul, London, 1954.

MOSER, C. A., AND SCOTT, W., *British Towns: A Statistical Study of their Social and Economic Differences*, Oliver & Boyd, London, 1961.

MOULY, J., 'Wage Determination: Institutional Aspects', *International Labour Review*, November 1967.

MOYNIHAN, D. P., *The Negro Family: The Case for National Action*, US Department of Labor, Washington DC, 1965.

MOYNIHAN, D. P., *Maximum Feasible Misunderstanding: Community Action in the War on Poverty*, Arkville Press, New York, 1969.

MUELLBAUER, J., 'Testing the Barten Model of Household Composition Effects and the Cost of Children', *Economic Journal*, September 1977.

MURRAY, J., 'Potential Income from Assets: Findings of the 1963 Survey of the Aged', *Social Security Bulletin* (US Department of Health, Education and Welfare), December 1964.

MYRDAL, G., *Objectivity in Social Research*, Duckworth, London, 1970.

NAGI, S. Z., 'Some Conceptual Issues in Disability and Rehabilitation', in Sussman, M. B. (ed.), *Sociology and Rehabilitation*, American Sociological Association, Washington DC, 1966.

NEVITT, A. A., *Fair Deal for Householders*, Fabian Research Series No. 297, Fabian Society, London, 1971.

NEVITT, A. A., 'How Fair are Rate Rebates?', *New Society*, 10 June 1971.

NEWBY, H., *The Deferential Worker*, Allen Lane, London, 1977.

NEWBY, H., 'Tied Cottage Reform', *British Journal of Law and Society*, Summer 1977.

NICHOLSON, J. L., 'Variations in Working Class Family Expenditure', *Journal of the Royal Statistical Society* (Series A), vol. 112, 1949.

NICHOLSON, J. L., *Redistribution of Income in the United Kingdom in 1959, 1957, and 1953*, Bowes & Bowes, Cambridge, 1965.

NICHOLSON, J. L., 'Appraisal of Different Methods of Estimating Equivalence Scales and their Results', *Review of Income and Wealth*, 1976.

NICHOLSON, R. J., 'The Distribution of Personal Income', *Lloyds Bank Review*, January 1967.

NORRIS, G., 'Employment Participation and Household Incomes in Two Local Authorities in England'; and 'Subemployment Amongst Men', evidence submitted to the Royal Commission on the Distribution of Income and Wealth, 1977.

ORNATI, O., *Poverty Amid Affluence*, Twentieth Century Fund, New York, 1966.

ORSHANSKY, M., 'Counting the Poor: Another Look at the Poverty Profile', *Social Security Bulletin*, vol. 28, January 1965.

ORSHANSKY, M., 'Who Was Poor in 1966?', *Research and Statistics Note*, US Department of Health and Education and Welfare, 6 December 1967.

ORSHANSKY, M., 'How Poverty is Measured', *Monthly Labor Review*, February 1969.

ORWELL, G., *The Road to Wigan Pier*, Gollancz, London, 1936.

PAGANI, A., *La Linea Della Poverta*, Collana di Scienze Sociali, Edizioni ANEA, Milano, 1960.

PAHL, R. E., 'The Rural Urban Continuum', *Readings in Urban Sociology*, Pergamon, Oxford, 1968.

PAHL, R. E., 'Poverty and the Urban System', in Chisholm, M., and Manners, G., (eds.), *Spatial Problems of the British Economy*, Cambridge University Press, 1971.

PAISH, F. W., 'The Real Incidence of Personal Taxation', *Lloyds Bank Review*, 43, 1957.

PARKER, R. A., *The Housing Finance Act and Council Tenants*, Poverty Pamphlet No. 9, Child Poverty Action Group, London, 1972.

PARKIN, F., *Class, Inequality and Political Order*, MacGibbon & Kee, London, 1971.

PARSONS, T., *Essays in Sociological Theory*, The Free Press of Glencoe, New York, 1964.

PASAMANICK, B., LILIENFELD, A., AND ROGERS, M. E., *Prenatal and Perinatal Factors in the Development of Childhood Behaviour Disorders*, Johns Hopkins University, School of Hygiene, 1957.

PASSMORE, R., NICOL, D. M., AND NARAYANA, RAO M., WITH BEATON, G. H., AND DEMAYER, E. M., *Handbook on Human Nutritional Requirements*, WHO, Geneva, 1974.

PEACOCK, A., AND SHANNON, R., 'The Welfare State and the Redistribution of Income', *Westminster Bank Review*, August 1968.

PIACHAUD, D., *Do the Poor Pay More?*, Child Poverty Action Group, London, 1974.

PIGOU, A. C., *The Economics of Welfare* (4th edn), Macmillan, London, 1932.

PIVEN, F. F., AND CLOWARD, R. A., *Regulating the Poor: The Functions of Public Welfare*, Tavistock Publications, London, 1972.

PODULUK, J. R., *Income Distribution and Poverty in Canada, 1967*, Dominion Bureau of Statistics, 1968.

POLANYI, G., AND WOOD, J. B., *How Much Inequality?*, Institute of Economic Affairs, London, 1974.

POND, C., *The Low Pay Bulletin*, Nos. 1 and 5, Low Pay Unit, London, 1974 and 1976.

PRAIS, S. J., 'The Estimation of Equivalent Adult Scales from Family Budgets', *Economic Journal*, December 1953.

PRAIS, S. J., AND HOUTHAKKER, H. S., *The Analysis of Family Budgets*, Department of Applied Economics Monograph 4, Cambridge University Press, 1955.

PREST, A. R., AND STARK, T., 'Some Aspects of Income Distribution in the UK since World War II', *Manchester School*, vol. 35, 1967.

PROJECTOR, D. S., AND WEISS, G. S., *Survey of Financial Characteristics of Consumers*, Washington Board of Governors of the Federal Reserve System, 1966.

RANADIVE, K. R., 'The Equality of Incomes in India', *Bulletin of the Oxford Institute of Statistics*, May 1965.

RAPHAEL, M., *Pensions and Public Servants: A Study of the Origins of the British System*, Mouton, Paris, 1964.

REDDIN, M., 'Local Authority Means-Tested Services', in Townsend, P., *et al.*, *Social Services for All?*, Fabian Society, London, 1968.

REDDIN, M., *Where?*, No. 72, September 1972.

REDER, M. W., 'The Theory of Occupational Wage Differentials', in McCormick, B. J., and Owen Smith, E. (eds.), *The Labour Market*, Penguin Books, Harmondsworth, 1968.

REEVES, P., *Round About a Pound a Week*, Bell, London, 1913.

REID, G. L., AND ROBERTSON, D. J., *Fringe Benefits, Labour Costs and Social Security*, Allen & Unwin, London, 1965.

REUBENS, B. G., *The Hard to Employ: European Programs*, Columbia University Press, 1970.

REVELL, J., 'Changes in the Social Distribution of Property in Britain During the Twentieth Century', *Actes du Troisième Congrès International d'Histoire Économique*, 1965.

REVELL, J., HOCKLEY, G., AND MOYLE, J., *The Wealth of the Nation*, Cambridge University Press, 1967.

REVELL, J., AND TOMKINS, C., *Personal Wealth and Finance in Wales*, Welsh Council, 1974.

REX, J., AND MOORE, R., *Race, Community and Conflict*, Oxford University Press, 1967.

RHODES, G., *Public Sector Pensions*, Allen & Unwin, London, 1965.

RICARDO, D., *The Principles of Taxation and Political Economy*, Dent, London, 1821.

RICHARDSON, H. W., *Elements of Regional Economics*, Penguin Books, Harmondsworth, 1969.

RILEY, M. W., JOHNSON, M., AND FONER, A. (eds.), *Ageing and Society*, vol. 3: *A Sociology of Age Stratification*, Russell Sage Foundation, New York, 1972.

ROBINSON, D., 'Low Paid Workers and Incomes Policy', *Bulletin of the Oxford University Institute of Economics and Statistics*, vol. 29, February 1967.

ROBINSON, D., *Local Labour Markets and Wage Structures*, Gower Press, London, 1970.

ROSE, H., *The Housing Problem*, Heinemann, London, 1968.

ROSE, M. E., *The Relief of Poverty: 1834–1914*, Macmillan, London, 1972.

ROSSI, P. H., AND BLUM, A. D., in Moynihan, D. P. (ed.), *On Understanding Poverty*, Basic Books, New York, 1968.

ROUTH, G., *Occupation and Pay in Great Britain 1906–60*, Cambridge University Press, 1965.

ROWNTREE, B. SEEBOHM, *Poverty: A Study of Town Life*, Macmillan, London, 1901.

ROWNTREE, B. S., *The Human Needs of Labour*, Nelson, London, 1918 (rev. edn, Longmans, Green, London, 1937).

ROWNTREE, B. S., *Poverty and Progress*, Longmans, Green, London, 1941.

ROWNTREE, B. S., AND LASKER, B., *Unemployment: A Social Survey*, Macmillan, London, 1911.

ROWNTREE, B. S., AND LAVERS, G. R., *Poverty and the Welfare State: A Third Social Survey of York dealing only with Economic Questions*, Longmans, Green, London, 1951.

ROY, A. D., 'The Distribution of Earnings and of Individual Output', and 'A Further Statistical Note on the Distribution of Individual Output', *Economic Journal*, vol. 60, 1950.

ROY, A. D., 'Some Thoughts on the Distribution of Earnings', *Oxford Economic Papers*, vol. 3, 1951.

RUNCIMAN, W. G., 'Embourgeoisement, Self-Rated Class and Party Preference', *Sociological Review*, vol. 12, No. 2, July 1964.

RUNCIMAN, W. G., *Relative Deprivation and Social Justice*, Routledge & Kegan Paul, London, 1966.

RUSSETT, B. M., *et al.*, *World Handbook of Political and Social Indicators*, Yale University Press, 1964.

RUTHERFORD, R. S. G., 'Income Distributions: A New Model', *Econometrica*, vol. 23, 1955.

SAINSBURY, S., *Registered as Disabled*, Bell, London, 1970.

SAINSBURY, S., *Measuring Disability*, Bell, London, 1974.

SBOROWSKI, M., 'Cultural Components in Responses to Pain', *Journal of Social Issues*, vol. 8, 1952.

SCHAFFER, B., 'Easiness of Access: A Concept of Queues', Institute of Development Studies, University of Sussex, 1972.

SCHAFFER, B., AND WEN-HSIEN, H., 'The Distribution and the Theory of Access', Institute of Development Studies, University of Sussex, May 1973.

SCHORR, A. L., *Slums and Social Insecurity*, Nelson, London, 1964.

SCHORR, A. L., 'The Non-Culture of Poverty', *American Journal of Orthopsychiatry*, vol. 34, No. 5, 1964.

SCHORR, A. L. (ed.), *Jubilee for Our Times: A Practical Program for Income Equality*, Columbia University Press, 1977.

SCHWARTZ, R. D., 'Functional Alternatives to Inequality', *American Sociological Review*, April 1955.

SCOTT, J. A., 'Gastro-enteritism in Infancy', *British Journal of Preventive and Social Medicine*, October 1953.

SEERS, D., *The Levelling of Incomes Since 1938*, Blackwell, Oxford, 1951.

SEERS, D., 'Has the Distribution of Income Become More Unequal?', *Bulletin of the Oxford University Institute of Statistics*, February 1956.

SEERS, D., *The Levelling of Incomes Since 1938*, Blackwell, Oxford, 1957.

SEMPLE, M., 'The Effect of Changes in Household Composition on the Distribution of Income 1961–73', *Economic Trends*, December 1975.

SENECA, J. H., AND TAUSSIG, M. K., 'Family Equivalence Scales and Personal Income Tax Exemptions for Children', *Review of Economics and Statistics*, August 1971.

SHANAS, E., *et al.*, *Old People in Three Industrial Societies*, Routledge & Kegan Paul, London, 1968.

SHAW, L. A., AND BOWERBANK, M., 'Living on a State-Maintained Income', *Case Conference*, I and II, March and April 1958.

SINFIELD, A., *The Long-Term Unemployed*, OECD, Paris, 1968.

SINFIELD, A., *Unemployed in Shields* (unpublished mimeographed report), University of Essex, 1967.

SINFIELD, A., 'The Social Costs of Unemployment', in Jones, K. (ed.), *Yearbook of Social Policy in Britain 1976*, Routledge & Kegan Paul, London, 1978.

SINGH, R., 'On the Determination of Economics of Scale in Household Composition', *International Economic Review*, June 1972.

SMITH, A., *An Inquiry into the Natural Causes of the Wealth of Nations*, Ward, Lock, London, 1812 (originally published 1776).

SMITH, D., *The Facts of Racial Disadvantage*, Political and Economic Planning, London, 1976.

SOUTAR, M. S., WILKINS, E. H., AND FLORENCE, P., *Nutrition and Size of Family*, London, 1942.

SPICER, C. C., AND LIPWORTH, L., *Regional and Social Factors in Infant Mortality*, GRO Studies on Medical and Population Subjects No. 19, HMSO, London, 1966.

STACEY, M., *Tradition and Change: A Study of Banbury*, Oxford University Press, 1960.

STAEHLE, H., 'Ability, Wages and Income', *Review of Economic Statistics*, 1943.

STANWORTH, P., AND GIDDENS, A., *Elites and Power in British Society*, Cambridge University Press, 1974.

STARK, T., *The Distribution of Personal Income in the United Kingdom 1949–1963*, Cambridge University Press, 1972.

STEIN, B., *On Relief: The Economics of Poverty and Public Welfare*, Basic Books, New York, 1971.

STEIN, L., 'Tuberculosis and the "Social Complex" in Glasgow', *British Journal of Social Medicine*, January 1952.

STEIN, R., 'Sub-employment Measures', *US Bureau of Labor Statistics*, 7 May 1969.

STOUFFER, S. A., *et al.*, *The American Soldier*, Princeton, 1949.

STRAW, K. H., 'Consumers' Net Worth: the 1953 Savings Survey', *Bulletin of the Oxford University Institute of Statistics*, XVIII, 1956.

TAIRA, K., 'Consumer Preferences, Poverty Norms and Extent of Poverty', *Quarterly Review of Economics and Business*, 1969.

THUROW, L. C., *Poverty and Discrimination*, Brookings Institution, Washington DC, 1969.

TIPPING, D. G., 'Price Changes and Income Distribution', *Applied Statistics*, No. 1, 1970.

TITMUSS, R. M., *Birth, Poverty and Wealth: A Study of Infant Mortality*, Hamish Hamilton Medical Books, London, 1943.

TITMUSS, R. M., 'The Age of Pensions', *The Times*, 29 and 30 December 1953.

TITMUSS, R. M., *Essays on the Welfare State*, Allen & Unwin, London, 1958.

TITMUSS, R. M., *Income Distribution and Social Change*, Allen & Unwin, London, 1962.

TODD, J. E., AND JONES, L. M., *Matrimonial Property*, OPCS, HMSO, London, 1972.

TOUT, H., *The Standard of Living in Bristol*, Bristol, 1938.

TOWNSEND, P., 'The Meaning of Poverty', *British Journal of Sociology*, June 1954.

TOWNSEND, P., *The Family Life of Old People*, Routledge & Kegan Paul, London, 1957.

TOWNSEND, P., *The Last Refuge*, Routledge & Kegan Paul, London, 1962.

TOWNSEND, P., *The Disabled in Society*, Greater London Association for the Disabled, London, 1967.

TOWNSEND, P., 'Measures and Explanations of Poverty in High Income and Low Income Countries: The Problems of Operationalizing the Concepts of Development, Class and Poverty', *The Concept of Poverty*, Heinemann, London, 1970.

TOWNSEND, P., 'The Problems of Social Growth', *The Times*, 9 March 1971.

TOWNSEND, P., *The Scope and Limitations of Means-Tested Social Services in Britain*, Proceedings of the Manchester Statistical Society, 29 March 1972.

TOWNSEND, P., 'The Four Generation Family' in *The Social Minority*, Allen Lane, London, 1973.

TOWNSEND, P., 'The Needs of the Elderly and the Planning of Hospitals' in *The Needs of the Elderly*, Exeter University, 1973.

TOWNSEND, P., 'Inequality and the Health Service', *Lancet*, 15 June 1974.

TOWNSEND, P., AND WEDDERBURN, D., *The Aged in the Welfare State*, Bell, London, 1965.

TOWNSEND, P., AND BOSANQUET, N., (eds.), *Labour and Inequality*, Fabian Society, London, 1972.

TRINDER, C., 'Sharing Inflation?', in Willmott, P. (ed.), *Poverty Report 1976*, Temple Smith, London, 1976.

TRIST, E. L., HIGGIN, G. W., MURRAY, H., AND POLLOCK, A. B., *Organizational Choice: Capabilities of Groups at the Coal Face under Changing Technologies*, Tavistock, London, 1963.

TURNER, H. A., AND ZOETEWEIJ, H., *Prices, Wages and Incomes Policies in Industrialized Market Economies*, International Labour Office, Geneva, 1966.

TUNNARD, J., *No Father, No Home?*, Child Poverty Action Group, London, 1976.

WACHTEL, H. M., 'Looking at Poverty from a Radical Perspective', *Review of Radical Political Economics*, Summer 1971. (Also reprinted in Roby, P. (ed.), *The Poverty Establishment*, Prentice-Hall, Englewood Cliffs, 1974.)

WALKER, C. R., AND GUEST, R. H., *The Man on the Assembly Line*, Harvard University Press, 1952.

WEBB, A. L., AND SIEVE, J. E. B., *Income Distribution and the Welfare State*, Bell, London, 1971.

WEBB, B., *My Apprenticeship* (2nd edn), Longmans, Green, London, 1926.

WEBER, M., *The Theory of Social and Economic Organization* (edited by Talcott Parsons), Free Press, New York, 1964.

WEBER, M., *Economy and Society*, vol. 2, New York, 1968.

WEDDERBURN, D., 'The Financial Resources of Older People', in Shanas, E., *Old People in Three Industrial Societies*, Routledge & Kegan Paul, London, 1968.

WEDDERBURN, D., 'Workplace Inequality', *New Society*, 5 April 1970.

WEDDERBURN, D., WITH UTTING, J., *The Economic Circumstances of Old People*, Codicote, Welwyn, 1962.

WEDDERBURN, D., AND CRAIG, C., 'Relative Deprivation in Work', in Wedderburn, D., (ed.), *Poverty, Inequality and Class Structure*, Cambridge University Press, 1974.

WEDEL, J., 'Social Security and Economic Integration II', *International Labour Review*, December 1970.

WEISBROD, B. A., AND HANSEN, W. L., 'An Income-Net Worth Approach to Measuring Economic Welfare', *American Economic Review*, vol. LVIII, No. 5, December 1968.

WELFORD, J., *Skill and Age: An Experimental Approach*, Nuffield Foundation, Oxford University Press, 1961.

WESOLOWSKI, W., 'Some Notes on the Functional Theory of Stratification', in Bendix, R., and Lipset, S. M., *Class, Status and Power* (2nd edn), Free Press, New York, 1966.

WILLMOTT, P., AND YOUNG, M., *Family and Class in a London Suburb*, Routledge & Kegan Paul, London, 1960.

WILSON, N. A. B., *On the Quality of Working Life*, Department of Employment, Manpower Papers No. 7, HMSO, London, 1973.

WINYARD, S., *Policing Low Wages*, Low Pay Unit, London, 1976.
WOODWARD, J., *Industrial Organization: Theory and Practice*, Oxford University Press, 1965.
WOOLF, M., *The Housing Survey in England and Wales*, Social Survey, SS372, Ministry of Housing and Local Government, March 1967.
WOOTTON, B., *The Social Foundations of Wages Policy*, Allen & Unwin, London, 1955 (2nd edn 1962).
WOOTTON, B., *Social Science and Social Pathology*, Allen & Unwin, London, 1959.
WOOTTON, B., *In a World I Never Made*, Allen & Unwin, London, 1967.
WOOTTON, B., *Incomes Policy: An Inquest and a Proposal*, Davis-Poynter, London, 1974.
WYNN, M., *Family Policy*, Michael Joseph, London, 1970.

2. Command Papers

Report of the Commissioners Appointed to Inquire into the Working of the Factory and Workshop Acts, C. 1443, HMSO, London, 1876.
Final Report of the Departmental Committee Appointed to Inquire into and Report upon Certain Miscellaneous Dangerous Trades, C. 9509, HMSO, London, 1899.
Social Insurance and Allied Services (The Beveridge Report), Cmd 6404, HMSO, London, 1942.
Statement on Personal Incomes, Costs and Prices, Cmd 7321, HMSO, London, 1948.
Board of Inland Revenue, *92nd Annual Report*, Cmd 8052, HMSO, London, 1950.
Report of the Committee on the Taxation Treatment of Provisions for Retirement, Cmd 9063, HMSO, London, 1954.
Report of the Committee on the Economic and Financial Problems of the Provision for Old Age, Cmd 9333, HMSO, London, 1954.
Report of the Royal Commission on Taxation, Cmd 9474, HMSO, London, 1955.
Reports of the National Advisory Committee on the Employment of Older Men and Women, Cmds 8963 and 9628, HMSO, London, October 1953 and December 1955.
Report of the Commission on Doctors' and Dentists' Remuneration (The Pilkington Report), Cmnd 939, HMSO, London, 1960.
Report of the Royal Commission on the Police, Cmnd 1222, HMSO, London, 1960.
Report of the Committee of Inquiry into the Impact of Rates on Households (The Allen Report), Cmnd 2582, HMSO, London, 1965.
Report of the Committee on Housing in Greater London, (The Milner Holland Committee), Cmnd 2605, HMSO, London, 1965.
Prices and Incomes Policy, Cmnd 2639, HMSO, London, 1965.
Report of the Committee on the Assessment of Disablement (The McCorquodale Report), Cmnd 2847, HMSO, London, December 1965.
Prices and Incomes Standstill: Period of Severe Restraint, Cmnd 3150, HMSO, London, November 1966.
National Board for Prices and Incomes, *Pay of Workers in Agriculture in England and Wales*, Report No. 25, Cmnd 3199, HMSO, London, 1967.
Pay of Workers in the Retail Drapery, Outfitting and Footwear Trades, Report No. 27, Cmnd 3224, March 1967.

Productivity, Prices and Incomes Policy in 1968 and 1969, Cmnd 3590, HMSO, London, 1968.

Report of the Royal Commission on Trade Unions and Employers' Associations, 1965–68, Cmnd 3623, HMSO, London, 1968.

Department of Health and Social Security, Annual Report for the Year 1968, Cmnd 4100, HMSO, London.

Department of Health and Social Security, Report by the Government Actuary on the Financial Provisions of the National Superannuation and Social Insurance Bill, 1969, Cmnd 4223, HMSO, London.

Productivity, Prices and Incomes Policy After 1969, Cmnd 4237, December 1969.

Annual Report of the Chief Inspector of Factories for 1969, Cmnd 4461, HMSO, London.

Department of Health and Social Security, Annual Report for 1969, Cmnd 4462, HMSO, London.

National Board for Prices and Incomes, *Hours of Work, Overtime and Shift Working*, Cmnd 4554, HMSO, London, 1970.

Pay and Conditions in the Contract Cleaning Trade, Report No. 168, Cmnd 4637, HMSO, London, 1971.

National Board for Prices and Incomes, *The Pay and Conditions of Service of Ancillary Workers in the National Health Service*, Report No. 166, Cmnd 4644, H MSO, London, April 1971.

National Board for Prices and Incomes, *The Pay and Conditions of Service of Workers in the Laundry and Dry Cleaning Industry*, Report No. 167, Cmnd 4647, HMSO, London, April 1971.

National Board for Prices and Incomes, *General Problems of Low Pay*, Report No. 169, Cmnd 4648, HMSO, London, 1971.

Report by the Government Actuary on the Financial Provision of the Social Security Bill 1972, Cmnd 5143, HMSO, London, 1972.

Unemployment Statistics, Report of an Inter-Departmental Working Party, Cmnd 5157, HMSO, London, November 1972.

Reports of the Review Body on Top Salaries, Cmnd 4836, 5001, 5372, 5595 and 5846, HMSO, London, December 1971–4.

Safety and Health at Work (The Robens Committee), Cmnd 5034, HMSO, London, 1972.

Report of the Committee on One Parent Families (The Finer Report), Cmnd 5629, HMSO, London, July 1974.

Wealth Tax, Cmnd 5704, HMSO, London, 1974.

Capital Transfer Tax, Cmnd 5705, HMSO, London, 1974.

Report on Top Salaries, Review Body on Top Salaries, Report No. 6, Cmnd 5846, HMSO, London, 1975.

Royal Commission on the Distribution of Income and Wealth, Report No. 1, *Initial Report on the Standing Reference*, Cmnd 6171, HMSO, London, July 1975.

Royal Commission on the Distribution of Income and Wealth, Third Report, *Higher Incomes from Employment*, Cmnd 6383, HMSO, London, 1976.

Royal Commission on the Distribution of Income and Wealth, Report No. 4, *Second Report on the Standing Reference*, Cmnd 6626, HMSO, London, 1976.

Royal Commission on the Distribution of Income and Wealth, Report No. 5, *Third Report on the Standing Reference*, Cmnd 6999, H M S O, London, 1977.

Royal Commission on the Distribution of Income and Wealth, Report No. 6, *Low Incomes*, Cmnd 7175, H M S O, London, 1978.

Public Expenditure to 1979–80, Cmnd 6393, H M S O, London, February 1976.

The Government's Expenditure Plans 1978–9 to 1981–82, Cmnd 7049, H M S O, London, February 1978.

3. Other Government Publications

Board of Inland Revenue, *Inland Revenue Statistics, 1971*, H M S O, London, 1972.

Board of Inland Revenue, Reports of the Commissioners of H M Inland Revenue, 1960–61 to 1967–8.

Central Advisory Council for Education (England), *Children and Their Primary Schools*, H M S O, London, 1967.

Central Statistical Office, *Social Trends*, Nos 1–8, H M S O, London, 1970–77.

Community Relations Commission, *Some of My Best Friends . . . A Report on Race Relations Attitudes*, London, 1976.

Community Relations Commission, *Urban Deprivation, Racial Inequality and Social Policy*, H M S O, London, 1977.

Department of Employment and Productivity, Disabled Persons (Employment) Act 1944.

Department of Employment and Productivity, 'Employment Changes in Certain Less Skilled Occupations, 1961–66', *Employment and Productivity Gazette*, April 1969.

Department of Employment and Productivity, 'Results of a New Survey of Earnings in September 1968', *Employment and Productivity Gazette*, May 1969 and June 1969.

Department of Employment and Productivity, *Employment and Productivity Gazette*, May 1969.

Department of Employment and Productivity, *A National Minimum Wage: An Inquiry*, H M S O, London, 1969.

Department of Employment and Productivity, *Ryhope: A Pit Closes*, H M S O, London, 1970.

Department of Employment and Productivity, *New Earnings Survey, 1968*, H M S O, London, 1970, and subsequent reports of the New Earnings Survey 1970–76, H M S O, London.

Department of Employment and Productivity, 'People and Jobs', *Department of Employment Gazette*, December 1971.

Department of Employment and Productivity, 'Characteristics of the Unemployed: Sample Survey, June 1973', *Department of Employment Gazette*, March 1974.

Department of Employment and Productivity, *Family Expenditure Survey*, Reports, H M S O, London, 1953–4 and 1957–76.

Department of Employment and Productivity, *The Quota Scheme for Disabled People*, Consultative Document, 1973.

Department of the Environment, *Rate Rebates in England and Wales 1968–69*, H M S O, London, 1969.

Department of the Environment, *Handbook of Statistics* (Local Government, Housing, and Planning), HMSO, London, 1970.

Department of the Environment, *Rate Rebates in England and Wales 1971*, HMSO, London, 1971.

Department of the Environment, *Housing Policy*, HMSO, London, 1977.

Department of the Environment, Area Improvement Note 10, *The Use of Indicators for Area Action*, Housing Act 1974, HMSO, London, 1975.

Department of Health and Social Security, *National Superannuation and Social Insurance*, HMSO, London, January 1967.

Department of Health and Social Security, *Recommended Intakes of Nutrients for the United Kingdom*, Reports on Public Health and Medical Subjects, No. 120, HMSO, London, 1969.

Department of Health and Social Security, Interim Report on Vitamin D by the Panel on Child Nutrition, HMSO, London, 1970.

Department of Health and Social Security, *Occupational Pension Schemes 1971: Fourth Survey by the Government Actuary*, HMSO, London, 1972.

Department of Health and Social Security, *Health and Personal Social Service Statistics for England and Wales* (with summary tables for Great Britain), 1972, HMSO, London, 1973.

Department of Health and Social Security, *Social Security Statistics* (Reports for 1974–6), HMSO, London.

Department of Health and Social Security, Report No. 10 on Health and Social Subjects, *A Nutrition Survey of Pre-School Children, 1967–68*, HMSO, London, 1975.

General Register Office, *Classification of Occupations, 1960*, HMSO, London, 1960.

General Register Office, *Registrar General's Decennial Supplement, England and Wales 1961: Occupational Mortality Tables*, HMSO, London, 1971.

'House Conditions Survey, England and Wales, 1976', *Economic Trends*, No. 175, HMSO, London, 1968.

Ministry of Agriculture, *Domestic Food Consumption, 1950*, HMSO, London, 1962.

Ministry of Agriculture, *Household Food Consumption and Expenditure*, (Reports 1950–74), HMSO, London.

Ministry of Housing and Local Government, *The Density of Residential Areas*, HMSO, London, 1952.

Ministry of Housing and Local Government, *Homes for Today and Tomorrow*, HMSO, London, 1961.

Ministry of Housing and Local Government, *The Deeplish Study: Improvement Possibilities in a District of Rochdale*, HMSO, London, 1966.

Ministry of Housing, Central Housing Advisory Committee, *Our Older Homes: A Call for Action*, HMSO, London, 1966.

Ministry of Housing and Local Government, *Council Housing, Purposes, Procedures and Priorities*, Ninth Report of the Housing Management Sub-Committee of the Central Housing Advisory Committee, Ministry of Housing and Local Government, London, 1969.

Ministry of Labour, *Ministry of Labour Gazette*, April 1961 and June 1961.

Ministry of Labour, 'Characteristics of the Unemployed 1961', *Ministry of Labour Gazette*, April and September 1962.

Ministry of Labour, *Sick Pay Schemes*, Report of a Committee of the National Joint Advisory Council on Occupational Sick Pay Schemes, HMSO, London, 1964.

Ministry of Labour, 'Enquiry into the Characteristics of the Unemployed', October 1964, *Ministry of Labour Gazette*, November 1965.

Ministry of Labour, *Statistics on Incomes, Prices, Employment and Production*, No. 18, September 1966.

Ministry of Pensions and National Insurance, *Reasons Given for Retiring or Continuing at Work*, HMSO, London, 1954.

Ministry of Pensions and National Insurance, Report on an Enquiry into the Incidence of Incapacity for Work, HMSO, London, 1964.

Ministry of Pensions and National Insurance, Report of an Enquiry into the Incidence of Incapacity for Work, Part I: *Scope and Characteristics of Employers' Sick Pay Schemes*, HMSO, London, 1964.

Ministry of Pensions and National Insurance, 'Occupational Pensions – Memorandum by the Government Actuary's Department in Ministry of Pensions and National Insurance', *Financial Circumstances of Retirement Pensioners*, HMSO, London, 1966.

Ministry of Pensions and National Insurance, Ministry of Social Security Bill 1966, HMSO, London, 1966.

Ministry of Social Security, Annual Report of the Ministry of Social Security for 1966, HMSO, London, 1967.

Ministry of Social Security, *Circumstances of Families*, HMSO, London, 1967.

Office of Population Censuses and Surveys, *Classification of Occupations, 1970*, HMSO, London, 1970.

Office of Population Censuses and Surveys, *The General Household Survey*, Introductory Report and later reports, HMSO, London, 1973–5.

Recommended Intakes of Nutrients for the United Kingdom, Reports on Public Health and Medical Subjects No. 120, HMSO, London, 1969.

Registrar General's Decennial Supplement, England and Wales, 1961, *Occupational Mortality Tables*, HMSO, London, 1971.

Report from His Majesty's Commissioners for Inquiry into the Administration and Practical Operation of the Poor Laws, B. Fellowes, London, 1834.

Report of a Working Party on Education Maintenance Allowances (Chairman Mr T. Weaver), HMSO, London, 1957.

Scotland's Older Houses (The Cullingworth Report), HMSO, Edinburgh, 1967.

Scottish Home and Health Department, Joint Working Party on the Integration of Medical Work, *Towards an Integrated Child Health Service*, HMSO, Edinburgh, 1973.

Social Science Research Council and Department of Health and Social Security, *Approaches to Research on Transmitted Deprivation*, 16 April 1973.

Supplementary Benefits Commission, *Administration of the Wage Stop*, Report by the Supplementary Benefits Commission to the Minister of Social Security, HMSO, London, 1967.

4. Other Publications

Australian Government, *Poverty in Australia*, Interim Report of the Australian Government's Commission of Inquiry into Poverty, March 1974, Canberra.

Carnegie UK Trust, *Handicapped Children and Their Families*, Carnegie United Kingdom Trust, Dunfermline, 1974.

Child Poverty Action Group, *Memorandum to the Prime Minister*, 1965.

Child Poverty Action Group, *Poverty*, 1966–77.

Community Development Project, *The National Community Development Project*, Inter-Project Report 1973, CDP Information and Intelligence Unit, February 1974.

Counter Information Services, *Your Money and Your Life: Insurance Companies and Pension Funds*, London, 1974.

The Cost of the Social Services, 1938–1952, Planning No. 354, June 1953.

Department of Economic and Social Affairs, United Nations, *Social Policy and the Distribution of Income in the Nation*, New York, 1969.

Disability Alliance, *Poverty and Disability: The Case for a Comprehensive Income Scheme for Disabled People*, London, 1975.

Disability Alliance, 'Nearly a Million Disabled People in Poverty', Memorandum to the Chancellor of the Exchequer, March 1976.

'House Buying: Mortgage or Endowment', *The Times*, 7 January 1967.

'How Life Assurance can help with House Purchase', *Insurance Mail*, February 1964.

Institute of Municipal Treasurers and Accountants, *Housing Statistics*, London, 1967–71.

International Labour Office, *The Cost of Social Security*, Geneva, 1969.

International Labour Office, *The Cost of Social Security 1964–66*, Geneva, 1971.

Labour Party, *Labour's Social Strategy*, August 1969.

The 1964 Economic Report of the President, US Government Printing Office, Washington DC, 1964.

Organization for Economic Cooperation and Development, *Public Expenditure on Income Maintenance Programmes*, Studies in Resource Allocation No. 3, OECD, Paris, July 1976.

Office of Health Economics, *Malnutrition in the 1960s?*, Office of Health Economics, London, 1967.

'Political and Economic Planning', *Poverty: Ten Years after Beveridge*, Planning No. 344, 1952.

President's Commission on Income Maintenance Programs, *Poverty and Plenty*, Government Printing Office, Washington DC, 1969.

Royal College of Physicians, Report of the Committee on Accidental Hypothermia, Royal College of Physicians, London, 1966.

The Senate of Canada, *Proceedings of the Special Senate Committee on Poverty*, 24 and 26 February 1970.

Social Security in the Nordic Countries, Statistical Reports on the Nordic Countries, 16, Copenhagen, 1970.

United Nations, *Economic Survey of Europe in 1956*, Geneva, 1957.

United States, Department of Commerce, *Social Indicators 1973*, The 1970 Manpower Report of the President, Social and Economic Statistics Administration, US Department of Commerce, Government Printing Office, Washington DC, 1974.

US Department of Health, Education and Welfare, *Monthly Cost Standards for Basic Needs Used by States for Specified Types of Old Age Assistance Cases and Families Receiving Aid to Families with Dependent Children, January 1965*, Department of Health,

Education and Welfare Administration, Bureau of Family Services, Division of Program Statistics and Analysis, August 1965.

US Department of Health, Education and Welfare, *The Measure of Poverty*, A Report to Congress as Mandated by the Education Amendments of 1974, US Government Printing Office, Washington DC, April 1976.

US Department of Labor, Bureau of Labor Statistics, *Monthly Labor Review*, March 1965, April 1967 and September 1970.

Index

For ease of reference, the index has been divided into two sections, the first (pages 1203–1211) comprising general topics, the second (pages 1212–1216) names of persons referred to in the text and footnotes.

Figures in italics indicate page references to tables only. Where treatment is continuous (e.g. 144–7), or where information is also given in the main text, tables are not specifically indicated.

General Index

Acts of Parliament, *see individual Acts*
Agricultural Safety Inspectorate, 434
Alkali and Clean Air Inspectorate, 434
Allen Committee, 873
annuity values, 212–13, 214, 282, 295, 347, *362*, 390, *391*, 406–7, 713, 792
Argentina, 142
area deprivation, 284, *487*, 536, 543–64, 837–42, 882–6; *see also* deprivation
assets: definition, 981; at different ages, *995*; in different types of household, 205–10; disabled and, 712–13; distribution of, 144–7, 199–205, 1170–72; inequality and, 215; living standards and, 144, 199, 215–16, 218, 223; relation to income, 210–15; studies of, 96–8; *see also* annuity values; benefits; income; private income in kind; resources; social services
Australia: income distribution, 43, 138, 142; poverty in, 41–2

Belfast, research in, 93, 104, 107–8, 548, 553–5, 558–9, 950, 953
Belgium, 654–5
benefits, *see* employer welfare benefits; family allowances; Family Income Supplement; fringe benefits; means-tested benefits; national assistance; social security; social services; supplementary benefit
Beveridge Report (1942), 32, 63, 161, 243, 790, 923
Blue Books, 191, 193, 154n, 184n
Board of Inland Revenue, *see* Inland Revenue, Board of
Brazil, 43
British Journal of Sociology, 25
British Medical Association, 167, 168, 169
British Rail, 459
Building Societies Association, 511

Canada, 138, 142
capital gains, 120, 124
capitalism, 79
Central Statistical Office (CSO): assessment of social service values, 157, 158, 219, 964; data on incomes, 19, 22, 23, 123, 124, *125*, 175, 178, 184, 191, 193; on tax, 148, 341
Ceylon, 43
Charity Organization Society, 62
Child Poverty Action Group, 29, 151, 780, 848, 885, 886
Children: % in poverty, 285–7; and eligibility for supplementary benefit, 830, 838; and environmental deprivation, *533*, 538, 540–41; and housing deprivation, 486–9, 502–3; families with children in poverty, 288–91; and means-tested benefits, 860–73; *see also* handicapped children; one-parent families; large families
Chile, 43
Chronic illness, 722–4
Chronically Sick and Disabled Persons Act (1970), 693
Circumstances of Families survey (1966), 165
Citizens' Advice Bureau, 844
Citizens' Rights Office, 848
classes: 'class structuration', 87–92; conflict between, 20; earnings contrasted, 142–4; and economic circumstances, 385–9; environmental deprivation and, *533*, 542; evolution of (Marx), 80; factors believed to determine, 377–81, *1012–13*; housing deprivation, 503, 515–17; images of, 371–7; and income distribution, 78, 133, 142; and life-style, 369–412; and means-tested benefits, 889–90; and poverty, 293–5, 394, *406*, 409–12, 555–6; problems of measuring, 370–71; resources, command over, 389–94; social grading, 986–8; social

Classes – *contd*
  mobility, 400–409; social and
  occupational, 381–5; work deprivation,
  443–4; *see also* occupational classes;
  managerial workers; manual workers;
  professional workers
clerical workers, 134, 135, 136, 140
collective bargaining, 84
Commission for Industrial Relations, 634
commissions of inquiry, 39
Community Development Project, 544
Contract of Employment Act (1963), 439, 469
convention and 'relative' poverty, 50–52
council tenants: access to council housing,
  519–22; environmental deprivation,
  539–40; housing costs, 506–14; housing
  deprivation, 490–98; 501, 502; and
  poverty, *549*; rate rebates, 874; rent
  rebates, 875–7
'cycle of deprivation', 70–71; *see also*
  deprivation
Czechoslovakia, 43

Defence Bonds, 199, *202, 203*
Denmark, 654–5 705, 797
departments, government, *see individual
  departments*
'dependent' population, 19–20; *see also*
  disabled, the; old people; retired, the;
  unemployed, the
deprivation: *see also* area deprivation;
  inequality; multiple deprivation; poor
  areas; poverty
  OF ENVIRONMENT, 529–42, *1034–5*;
    measures of, 531–2, 541; multiple,
    532–5; need for concept of, 529–31;
    occupational class and, *533*, 542;
    poverty and, 538–41, 542; regional, 536,
    541, *551*, 552; social characteristics of
    deprived, 535–8
  IN HOUSING, 476–528; different indices
    of, 479–86; explanations of, 524–6, 528;
    and household type, 487–9, 492; and
    housing costs, 503–14; and housing
    market, 490–98; occupational class and,
    503, 515–17; regional, 486–7; relation
    to low income, 498–503; social
    perceptions of, 478–9; and types of
    tenure, 501, 514–24
  AT WORK, 432–75; changing problems,
    435–6, 468–70; and character of job,
    444–52; concept of, 437–43; conditions
    at work, 96, 453–5, *1017–28, 1043–6*,
    difficulty in measuring, 433–5; and
    earnings, 463–5, *1043*; index of, 461–3;
    and job satisfaction, 470–74; and
    occupational class, 443–4; poverty and,
    466–8; and security, 452–3; and self-

employed, 465–6; various occupations
    and, 436–7; *see also* employer welfare
    benefits; fringe benefits
  GENERAL TOPICS: 'cycle of', 70–71;
    denials of poverty, 425–7; deprivation
    index, 249–62, *439, 716, 1000*; dietary,
    clothing, health, educational and
    recreational deprivation, 1173–6; forms
    (objective), 413–18; objective/subjective,
    413–31; objective and lack of income,
    430–31; subjective (do people *feel*
    deprived?), 418–22; subjective and
    disablement, 716–17; subjective and
    income, 423–4; subjective perceptions
    of poverty, 427–30
deprivation standard, 267–71, 271–4,
  893–900
differentials, 19
Disability Alliance, 819
disabled, the: ages of, *1048–51, 1056*;
  assessment, need for new approach,
  693–5; chronic illness or invalidity,
  722–4, *1053–4*; concept and definition
  of, 686–93; and deprivation, 714–17,
  1001; earnings of, *1056–8*; employment
  disadvantages, 727–33, 735, 739; home
  difficulties, 717–22; housewives, 733–4;
  increase with age, 705–9; low official
  estimates, 699–705; low pay, *636, 639*;
  low social status, 709–11; mental illness,
  725–7; new benefits (1971), 906–7;
  numbers, 695–9; in poverty, 305–10,
  311–12, 315, 318, 319, 322, 323, 328–9,
  331–2, 334–5, 711–14, 723–4, 726–7,
  734–8, *897, 898, 1052*; as social
  minority, 567, 569, *570*, 571, *573*, 574–5,
  576, *577*, 587; and supplementary
  benefit, *830*, 832, *834*, 835, 837, 839, 846;
  and unemployment, *592*, 599, 605
Disablement Income Group, 733
distribution of earnings, 19–21; deficiency
  of government statistics, 21–3; in
  different countries, 43–6, 76; and dual
  labour market, 77–9; economic factors
  and, 71–7; (1938–68), 160–66; social
  factors and, 81; *see also* earnings;
  incomes; inequality; low paid, the;
  resources; rich, the
dual labour market, 77–8
Dudley Committee, 477

earnings: occupational and class structure
  related to, 142–4; occupations
  contrasted, 133–6; in other countries,
  138–9; 142; structure, 139–42; wages/
  salaries, 133–4; women's, 136, *137, 138*,
  141; *see also* distribution; income;
  low paid, the; rich, the

economic theory and poverty, 71–7
Economic Trends, 19, 23, 127, 148n, 149n,
    150n, 154n, 159n, 219n, 478n, 480n,
    493n, 530n, 789n, 909n, 910n, 911, 964n,
    965n
Economists Advisory Group Business
    Research Study, 339
Education Act (1944), 869, 873
Education and Science, Department of, 861,
    868, 870
Education Ministry of, 869
Eire, people born in, 313–15, 321–2, 569,
    570, 571, 573, 577, 579, 580–81, 587, *896*
electoral registers, 100
employer welfare benefits, 152–3, 215–18,
    225, 228, 232–3, *362,* 386–9, 390, 455–61,
    678–80, 982; *see also* fringe benefits
Employment and Productivity, Department
    of: and disabled, 694, 729; and earnings
    distribution, 139, 338, 571; and low-paid
    623, 634, 650; and older workers, 661,
    675; salary index, 133–4; and
    unemployment, 110–11, 590, 591, 596,
    610, 614, 616; and working conditions,
    435; *see also* Family Expenditure Survey
Environment, Department of the, 530
environment, deprivation of, *see under*
    deprivation
Equal Opportunities Commission, 918
equivalence, problems of concept of, 262–7
Essex, University of, 25, 26, 28, 29, 93
ethnic minorities, 53, 59, 566; *see also* Eire,
    people born in; immigrants; non-whites
Explosives Inspectorate, 434

facilities at work, *see* deprivation at work
Factory Act, 433
Factory Inspectorates, 433–5
family allowances, 150, 151, 156, 161, 162–3,
    306–7, 314, 320, 322, 326, 330, 332;
    numbers receiving, *903*
Family Expenditure Survey (1957–76): data
    on incomes, 19, 22, 25, 41, 94, 95, 124,
    125, 126–8, 133, 134, 141, 142, 148, 180,
    181, 182, 183, 184, 187, 189, 195, 196,
    232, 245, 263, 266, 621–3, *624,* 866, *992,*
    993; housing costs, 299, 504, 508;
    J-Index, 930; numbers in poverty, 160,
    161, 165, 275, 907, 908, 911; pensioners,
    789; purpose, 338; response, 104, *108,*
    109; sampling procedure, 942; and
    supplementary benefit, 825, 826, and
    value of social services, 157, 219, 964,
    966
Family Income Supplement, 619, 906;
    failure of, 633–4, 648; and one-parent
    families, 763

Finer Committee, 754–5, 758, 759, 761, 775,
    778, 782, 881
Fisher Committee, 881
food expenditure, 263, *1001*; *see also*
    nutrition
France, 138, 142, 156, 654–5
fringe benefits: importance as proportion of
    total resources, 45, *89,* 90, 124; living
    standards and, 54, 55; older workers
    and, 678–9; questionnaire and, 94, 111;
    value of, 386, 387, *391, 393;* and work
    conditions, 48, 437, 438, *439, 441, 442,*
    455–61; *see also* employer welfare
    benefits
functionalism, 83–5
functions of poverty, 85–7, 922

General Household Survey, 23, 174n, 381n,
    456n, 477n, 480, 481n, 484n, 495n, 496n,
    520n, 596, 597n, 605n, 612n, 703, *704,*
    705n, 757, 758n, 794n, 957, 958
Germany: income distribution, 138;
    % poverty in, 42; taxation, 148
Gini coefficient, 229, 343
Glasgow, research in, 93, 104, 107–8, 950,
    952
Government Social Survey, 26, 101, 484,
    701, 703
Guillebaud Committee, 155

Hall-Jones scale, 370, 987
handicapped children, 740–52; estimates of
    numbers, 740–42; examples, 746–50;
    forms of handicap, 742–5; need for
    further evidence, 750–52; poverty
    among, 745–6, 750, *1059*; *see also*
    disabled, the
Hansard, 152n, 523n, 544n, 675n, 729n, 848n,
    860n, 861n, 863n, 865n, 866n, 868n,
    869n, 871n, 874n, 879n, 907n, 971n
health: public services, 218, 219, 223, *967,*
    968–71; significance in relation to
    poverty, 170–74; *see also* disabled, the;
    Health and Social Security, Department
    of; National Health Service; nutrition
Health and Safety at Work Act, 434
Health and Safety Executive, 434, 435
Health and Social Security, Department of:
    and deprivation cycle, 70; and disabled,
    724, 736; and handicapped children,
    740–41; incomes data, 191; nutrition,
    51, 168; and one-parent families, 754–5,
    756, 757, 763, 958; poverty standard,
    241, 246; unemployed, 608, 612; *see also*
    National Health Service; social security;
    supplementary benefit
Health Economics, Office of, 167

Household Conditions Survey, 480, 529
households, different types of: assets of, 205–10; as basis for assessing wealth distribution, 341, 345–7, 360–66; incomes of, 193–8, 910, *992–3, 996–7, 1000, 1003, 1005, 1007, 1010,* and poverty, 267–70, 290–91, 298; resources of, 282–3, *998;* size related to poverty, *163,* 276–8; supplementary benefit, *1065; see also* council tenants; housing costs; owner-occupation; tenure
housing: costs, 503–14, *984–5, 1008, 1009;* market, 490–98; subsidies, 973–9 *(see also* rate rebates; rent rebates); values, 97; *see also* deprivation in housing; households; tenure
Housing Acts, 479, 480, 481, 544
Housing and Local Government, Ministry of, 529, 531
Housing Finance Act (1972), 522, 875
Housing Subsidies Act (1967), 878
Hungary, 43, 807

immigrants, 321–2, 335–6, 579, 616; numbers in poverty, *897; see also* Eire, people born in; ethnic minorities; non-whites
incomes: definitions of, 45, 180–93, 980–84; and deprivation, 271, 423–4, 425, 430–31, *1006, 1036;* different household types, 193–8; difficulty in assessing, 54–5; of disabled and long-term sick, 711–14, 723–4, 729–33; incomes policy, 128–32, 925; 'income unit', 302; income units and distribution of poverty, 900–901; of old people, 787–93, 798–800, 819, 820–21; of one-parent families, 759–63; questionnaire and, 94–5, 98, 111; survey of (1938–68), 117–28; of various households, *991–3, 997, 1000, 1002–3, 1005, 1007, 1010;* and wealth, 230–32; *see also* assets; benefits; distribution; earnings; Family Expenditure Survey; private income in kind; resources; taxation
India, 43
inequality: characteristics of, 18; deficiency of documentation, 21–3; and economic factors, 71–7; functionalism and, 83–5; relation of poverty to, 33, 43–6; sociological approaches, 80–83; survey of incomes (1938–68), 117–76; *see also* class; deprivation; occupational class
infant mortality, 170–72
Inland Revenue, Board of, 117, 119, 122, 124, 133, 146, 178, 184–5, 191, 201, 203, 205, 232, 338, 339
Inner London Education Authority, 559

International Labour Office, 914
interviewing, 101–4; *see also* poverty survey; questionnaire
Italy, 654–5, 807

Japan, 654–5, 807
Joseph Rowntree Memorial Trust, 25–6, 752

Labour, Ministry of, 133, 139
large families, 289–91, 487, 527, 569–71, *579,* 584–6
life-styles, *see* style of living
living standards: changes (1938–68), 117; compared in different societies, 225–6, 248
London School of Economics, 28
low paid, the, 618–51; case-history, 643–5; concept of low pay, 618–21; correlates of low pay, 635–9; dual labour market theory, 645–8, 650–51; failure of Family Income Supplement, 633–4; fluctuations in manual pay, 639–42; instability of pay and conditions, 642; lowest decile, 621–4; as % of mean, 625–8; policy towards, 648–9; and poverty, 316–17 326, 329–31, 629–33; Wages Councils, 634–5

McCorquodale Committee on the Assessment of the Disabled, 693–4
managerial workers: age, 665, 669; conception of poverty, *999;* and deprivation, *400, 414–16,* 418, 419, *420–21, 533,* 538, *540, 1035;* and disablement, *710;* earnings of, 134, 135, 140, *141, 386, 387, 464;* growth of, 19–20 142–3; housing, *482–3,* 515–17, *1032;* large families, *585;* occupational classification, *382–3;* and poverty, *292,* 293, *408, 555, 896;* resources, *362;* unemployment, 601–2; working conditions, 443, *451, 453, 462, 1017–18, 1020–23, 1025, 1027, 1044–6*
manual workers: accident rates, 469; age, 665, 666, 667–8, 675; assets, 145, *362,* 390–94, 407; and class, 380, 382, 404, *1014;* conception of poverty, *999;* deprivation, *414–16,* 418, *420–21;* deprivation at work, 443, 444–52, *462,* 468; disablement, 710; earnings, 133–9, *464;* environmental deprivation, *533,* 538, *540, 1035;* fluctuations in pay, 639–42; fringe benefits, 152–3, 387, 388, 455–61, 678–9; housing, *482–3,* 515–17, *1032;* instability of pay and conditions, 642; job satisfaction, *471,* 472, *473,* 474; job security, 452–3; large families, *585;*

life-styles, 389–90, 419; means-tested
   benefits, 889–90; numbers in poverty,
   292, 293–5, 296–7, 408, 555, 896;
   pensions, 457, 458–9, 808, 810;
   proportion of, 43, 385–6; resources
   in old age, 800–801, 802, 803, 821;
   social mobility, 400–408; unemployment
   601–2, 603; and wealth, 361; working
   conditions, 455, 1017–18, 1020–23,
   1025–7, 1044–6
'marketability', 231, 340
means-tested benefits: educational
   maintenance allowances, 869–71, 885,
   886, 889, 891, 892; failure of, 860–92;
   free school meals, 860–68, 883–6, 887–9,
   892, 952, 953, 972, 1070–75; free
   welfare milk, 868–9, 892; numbers
   eligible but not receiving, 892; and
   occupational class, 1068–9; option
   mortgage scheme, 877–9; rate rebates,
   873–5, 883, 884, 891, 892; rent rebates,
   875–7, 883, 884, 892; school uniform
   grants, 871–3, 892; under-use,
   explanations of: class, 889–91; regional
   and area variation, 882–6; socialization,
   886–8; type of family, 888–9
means tests, 242; and supplementary
   benefit, 823
men, activity rates, 658–61; earnings, 217–18,
   624–9, 638, 641, characteristics of
   employed, 636, 639; differences from
   women in employment, 661–80;
   disablement, 695–9, 705–8; differences
   from women in occupational class and
   work conditions, 382, 438–4, 451–61,
   464, 467, 471, 473; % in poverty, 285;
   % of older men compared with older
   women in poverty, 796–800; differences,
   from women in unemployment, 591–3,
   611–12; perceptions of class, 375, 378
mental illness, 725–7
Mexico, 43, 67
middle-class values and poverty, 67–8
Millard Tucker Committee, 809
Mines and Quarries Inspectorate, 434
minimum-wage legislation, 138–9
Ministries, government, see individual
   ministries
'minority group theory', 64–5; see also
   social minorities
mortality, 170–72, 436–7
multinational companies, 79
multiple deprivation, 422–3, 425–6, 501–3,
   535, 1173–6; see also deprivation

national assistance, 161, 163, 176
National Assistance Board, 41, 243, 844
National Board for Prices and Incomes, 129,
   130–32, 138–9, 142, 153, 176; and the
   low paid, 619, 621, 623, 624
National Child Development Study, 174,
   741, 743
National Children's Bureau, 741
National Coal Board, 459
National Food Survey, 52, 167, 168
National Health Service, 55, 136, 155, 189,
   245, 751, 818, 965, 967, 968–71
National Incomes Commission, 132
National Savings, 95, 96, 122, 920
Neath, research in, 93, 104, 107–8, 950, 953–4
Netherlands, the, 138, 142, 156, 654
New Earnings Survey of the Department of
   Employment, 19, 111, 133, 445, 571n,
   621–3, 624, 625, 634, 641, 642, 675n,
   676, 681
New Zealand, 138, 142, 156
non-whites, 569, 570, 571, 573, 575, 577, 579,
   580, 582–4, 587, 897
Norway, 654–5
Nuclear Installations Inspectorate, 434
nutrition: needs, 33, 34–7, 39, 51–2, 264–5;
   trends, 167–9

occupational class: and area deprivation,
   535; composition, 291; and deprivation
   of environment, 533, 540; and
   disablement, 710; and the dual labour
   market, 645–8; and earnings, 638; and
   means-tested benefits, 889–91;
   measurement, 369–71; and poverty,
   291–4, 916; and subjective and objective
   class, 381–412; and resources in old age,
   800–804; and unemployment, 601–3,
   615; and trends in employment, 661–71;
   and wealth, 359–63; see also class
OECD (Organization for Economic
   Cooperation and Development), 38, 42
Offices, government, see individual offices
Offices, Shops and Railway Premises Act,
   434
older workers, 652–84; activity rates,
   658–61; earnings rates, 675–8;
   employment record, 661–3; fringe
   benefits and work conditions, 678–80;
   incapacity and age, 663–5; skill,
   training and education, 665–7; trend to
   retirement and explanations, 654–8;
   trends in social class, 667–71; types of
   industry and employment, 671–5; who
   are they? 652–4; women, 680–82
old people, 784–822; assets, 791–2, 796, 800,
   1062; concept of 4th generation, 797–9;
   deprivation, 793, 1061; income, 1061–2;
   increasing disability and relation to
   resources, 815–19; inequality among
   elderly, 795–800; inequality elderly/

Old people – *contd*
young, 786–95; occupational pensions, 807–11; pensions, 788–90; policy implications, 818–19, 822; poverty and, 784–6, *1061*–3; retirement and social status, 804–7; social class and resources, 800–804, 819–20; social isolation and family resources, 811–15; supplementary benefit, *1062–3*; tenure, 793–5; *see also* older workers; retired, the

one-parent families: alternative policies, 778–81, 783; committee on, 754; consequences of poverty, 768–71; disadvantages of, 753–4, 771–3, 781; and Family Income Supplement, 763, 779; income rights, 773–5; living standards, 764–8, 775–6; married parents, 777–8; non-poor, 764, 785; numbers, 754–9; in poor areas, 554, 655; and poverty, 313, 322–3, 327–8, 759–63, 781, *1060*; as social minority, 566, 568, *570*, *571*, 572, *573*, 575, 576, *577*, 578; and supplementary benefit, 832

option mortgages scheme, 877–9

owner-occupation: access to, 514–19; and calculation of resources, 177, 181, 207, 225, 229, 295, 347, 367; capital gains, 975–6; deprivation and, *491*, 493–4, 495, 496–8, 501, 502, 539–40; elderly and, 793–4; housing costs, *300*, 504, 506–14; housing subsidies, 220, 874–5, 877–9, 973–4; 'imputed income', 974–5; and occupational class, *396*, 398; and poverty, 246, 283, *549*; proportions, 490; the rich and, 350–51

Oxford University Institute of Statistics, 145, 339

Pareto's Law, 72–3
Parker Morris Committee, 477, 485
Parker Morris standards. 52
Pearson Commission, 752
pensions: disablement, 193; occupational, 152–3, 216, 345, 457–9, 807–11, 820, 821; retirement, 788–90, 805, 806–7, 821–2; and supplementary benefit, 831; and trend towards retirement, 656–7, 675; widows', 765, 773; *see also* benefits; disabled, the; old people; retired, the
Pensions and National Insurance, Ministry of, 164, 456, 678, 824, 832
Phillips Committee, 807, 809
Pilkington Commission, 81
Plowden Report, 544
policy: on employment, 610–14, 616; incomes, 128–32; poverty, 62–4, 922–6; *see also* social policy
poor areas: areas of high deprivation, 553–8;

conception of, 543–5, 563–4; incidence of poverty, 545–8; persistence of, 558–9; regions, 545–8, 563; regional differences, 550–53; rural/urban, *546*, 549–50; theory of area poverty, 559–63; *see also* poverty: DISTRIBUTION
Poor Laws, 62, 63
Population Censuses and Surveys, Office of, 23, 26
Post Office Savings Bank, 201, 202, 203
poverty: *see also* deprivation; inequality; poor areas; poverty survey

DEFINITIONS AND THEORIES: 'cycle of deprivation', 70–71; defined as deprivation, 31–3; definitions, subjective and social, 237–41, 270, 913–16, *1014, 1016*; dual labour market and radical theories, 77–9; economic theory and, 71–7; evidence, inadequacy of, 39–43; explanations, 916–22; forms of deprivation, 48–9; functionalism, 83–5; functions of, 85–7; minority group theory, 64–5, 238; as mismanagement, 239; policy, 62–4, 922–6; poverty line, 57, 267; relative deprivation, 31, 46–9, 50–53, 248–62, 272–5, 281, 287, 299, 301–3, *395*, 893–4, 915–16; relative income standard, 247–8, 280, 290; sociological approaches, 80–83; short and long-term, 56, 275–6; state's standard, 241–7, 270, 272–5, 278–80, 282 284, 893–901, 914–15 (*see also* supplementary benefit); 'subculture of', 65–70; subsistence, 32–9, 238; theories of, 61–92; total/partial, 56

DISTRIBUTION: changes since 1968–9, 902–12; and conceptions of, 893–4; estimated numbers in various regions, *1004*; families with children, 288–90, 291; households, different types, 262–7, 290–91; measurement, 894–901; % in, *1039*; regional, 284, *1037–40*

EFFECTS ON INDIVIDUALS: chronically sick, 332–3; disabled, 305–10, 311–12, 315, 318, 319, 322, 323, 328–9, 331–2, 334–5, 711–14, 723–4, 726–7, 734–8, *897, 898, 1052*; gipsies, 324–5; immigrants, 321–2, *897*; low paid, 316–17, 326, 329–31, 629–33; one-parent families, 313, 327–8, 335–6, 759–63 768–71, 781, *1060*; retired people, 310–11, 323–4, 328–9, 333–4, 784–6, *1061–3*; unemployed, 313–15, 324–5, 588–617, *897, 898, 1041*

FACTORS INFLUENCING: birthplace and colour, 291; distribution of income and benefits, 160–66; employment status, 291–2, 293–5, *406*; population, 285–8;

see also assets; benefits; classes; households; housing; income; resources
poverty survey: interviewing, 101–4; limitations, 111–13; method of approach, 1076–7; obtaining representative sample, 98–100, 109–11; response, 104–8; survey method, 113–15; see also questionnaire; sampling
Premium Bonds, 199, 201, *202, 203*
pressure groups, 63
private income in kind, *89,* 223–4, 228, 233, 312, 343, *362, 391*; definition, 984
private tenacies; access to, 522–4; environmental deprivation and, 539–40
professional workers: age, 665, 668–9; conception of poverty, *999;* and deprivation, *400, 414–16,* 418, 419, *420–21, 533,* 538, *540, 1035;* and disablement, *710;* earnings, 134, 135, *386, 387, 464;* growth of, 19–20, 142–3; housing, *482–3,* 515–17, *1032;* large families, *585;* means-tested benefits, 889–90; occupational classification, *382–3;* and poverty, *292,* 293, *408, 555, 896;* resources, *362;* social class, 382; unemployment, 601–2; working conditions, 153, 443, *451, 453, 462, 1017–18, 1020–23, 1025, 1027, 1044–6*
property values, 97
Public Attitudes Surveys, 27
Public Health and Housing Acts, 51, 477
public sector wages, 136

questionnaire, 94–8; reproduced, 1084–167; structure, 1077–83

Radiochemical Inspectorate, 434
rate rebates, 873–5, 883, *884,* 891, *892, 1067, 1069*
rate support grant, 561
Redundancy Payments Act, 469
relative deprivation, 31, 46–9, 50–53, 248–62, 270–71, 272–5, 281, 287, 299, 301–3, *395,* 893–4, 915–16
relative income standard, 247–8, 280, 290
rent rebates, 875–7, 883, *884, 892, 1067, 1069*
research into poverty, see poverty survey
resources: concept and distribution, 88–91, 98, 177–236, 916–26; definitions, 116, 984; in different countries, 90; difficulty in assessing, 177–8; inequality of distribution, 55–7, 60, 81, 82–3, 87–92, 227–9, 232–3; interrelationship of, 225–32; and living standards, 174–6; occupational class and, 389–94; recipient units, 179–80; types of, 55–6, 88–9; see also annuity values; assets; benefits; distribution; income; private income in kind; rich, the
Retail Price Index, 54, 510
retired, the: assets, 199, 214; attitude of poor to, 428; in deprived areas, 558; effects of poverty on, 310–11, 323–4, 328–9, 333–4; numbers, *902;* numbers in poverty, 91, 161, 163–4, 293, *897–8;* and supplementary benefit, 244, 824, 825–6, 829, *830,* 832–3, *834,* 837, 839, 842, 846; trend towards retirement and explanations, 144, 654–8, 665; see also old people
Review Body on Top Salaries, 649, 918
rich, the: age distribution, *1011;* compared with the poor, 357–9; concepts of riches, 338–40; definition of the rich and examples, 347–57; income and wealth-holding, 341–7, 368; power élite or ruling class? 363–4; sources of wealth, 364–5; wealth and class, 359–63, 893
Robens Committee, 434–6
Royal Commission on Doctor's and Dentist's Remuneration, 128, 129, 619
Royal Commission on the Distribution of Income and Wealth, 17, 21, 123–4, 175, 181, 199, 230–31, 340, 342, 345, 908–9, 911, *991*

Salford, research in, 93, 104, 107–8, 950–52
sampling: adjustment of findings, 989–90; choice of regions, 927–9; of units within regions, 929–30, 949; limitations, 943–4; representativeness, 955–8; rural areas, 932, 937, 938; sampling procedure, 98–100, 932–54; selection of addresses, 938–43, *944–9;* stratification of urban areas, 930–32, 937–8; see also poverty survey; questionnaire
savings, 201, 202, 316, 317, 329, 791, 792
Savings Certificates, 199, *202, 203*
Scottish Education Department, 861
Scottish Home and Health Department, 740
self-employed, the, 182, 189, 191, 193, 291, *292, 396, 896, 1024*
shanty-town dwellers, 68
shift-work, 439, 445, 468
social minorities: 565–87; characteristics of the poor, 576–8; concept of, 91–2; definitions, 566–8; examples, 568–72, 578–86; incomes, 572–6; occupational class, 575–6; see also disabled, the; ethnic minorities; immigrants; large families; low paid; non-whites; old people; one-parent families; unemployed, the; women with adult dependants

social mobility, 400–409
social policy: for dealing with poverty, 62–4;
    and definition of poverty, 32;
    redistributive effects of, 218–19; and
    upper non-manual groups, 20
social security: benefits for disabled, 735–6;
    for elderly, 788; invalidity benefit, 737;
    numbers receiving, 826–7; rationale for
    benefits, 32, 34; sickness benefit, 216,
    225; see also family allowances; Family
    Income Supplement; Health and Social
    Security, Department of; means-tested
    benefits; national assistance; pensions;
    supplementary benefit
Social Security Act, 825, 881
Social Security, Ministry of, 41, 321, 332, 826
Social Security Pensions Act (1975), 821, 906
social services: allocation of subsidies, 128;
    as assets, 218–23; direct and indirect
    benefits, 964–5; education, 971–2;
    expenditure on, 154–5, 156–7, 220;
    housing subsidies to owner-occupiers,
    973–6; to council tenants, 976–9; and
    imputed income, 982–4; and inequality,
    154–5, 157–60; manual/non-manual
    workers, 390, 412; value to different
    households, 89, 98, 126, 159, 343, 362,
    391, 393, 964–79; see also benefits;
    health; National Health Service; rate
    rebates; rent rebates; social security
social structure, 17–21, 893–912
Social Trends, 41, 108n, 110n, 152n, 154n,
    174n, 176n, 465n, 524n, 551n, 658n,
    662n, 699n, 784n, 790n, 797n, 826n,
    902n
Society for the Single Woman and Her
    Dependants, 578
Spencer Marketing Research Services, 27,
    104
state's poverty standard, 241–7, 270, 272–5,
    278–80, 282, 284, 893–901, 914–15; see
    also supplementary benefit
statistical tests, 1168–9
style of living: change in, 18; defining, 54,
    58–60; concept and relationship to
    poverty, 921–2; in different countries,
    45; and inequality of resources, 921–2;
    and occupational class, 369–412; and the
    rich, 366–7; what constitutes
    deprivation? 57–8, 149–53; variation in,
    54, 57, 247; see also deprivation index;
    households; living standards; multiple
    deprivation
'subculture of poverty', 65–70, 71
subsistence, see under poverty: DEFINITIONS
    AND THEORIES
supplementary benefit: attitudes and
    circumstances of eligible, 842–5; of

recipients, 845–7; characteristics of
    legally entitled, 833–5; conflicting
    functions, 847–59; and deprivation, 501,
    504, 538; and elderly, 788–9, 790–91,
    799, 821; eligibility for, 823–59, 959–63;
    eligibility in four areas, 837–42, 849;
    grants, 182, 322, 327; and housing
    subsidies, 299, 306, 316; inadequate
    payments, 847–59; and incomes of
    minorities, 572–3, 576; numbers
    receiving, 902, 1066; one-parent families,
    759, 761, 762, 763, 765, 766–7, 774–5,
    778–9; regional variations, 882, 883;
    research into eligibility and receipt,
    827–33, 892; into 'take-up', 824–6;
    scales of payment 166, 242–4, 245, 246,
    260, 264, 266, 268–70, 271, 272, 278,
    279, 283, 287, 289, 292, 295, 296, 307,
    308, 311, 312, 313, 314, 316, 320, 322–5
    passim, 330, 332, 334, 335, 338, 359, 389
Survey of Personal Incomes (Inland Revenue),
    124, 338
Sweden: income distribution, 138, 142, 156;
    % poverty in, 42, 57; retirement, 654–5,
    807

tax: allowances, 150–52, 158, 219, 220; in
    different countries, 149; and dispersion
    of incomes, 147–50; and employer
    welfare benefits, 215–16; evasion, 45,
    119, 122; (1938–50), 117, 118, 119
tenure: different types, 105, 490–98, 504, 956,
    1030–32; employer-subsidized, 460;
    and environmental deprivation, 539–40;
    and housing costs, 300, 506–14, 1033;
    Irish and, 581; large families, 585–6;
    non-whites, 582–3; see also council
    tenants; housing; owner-occupation;
    private tenancies
Trades Union Congress, 270, 625, 914
trade unions, 58, 63, 68, 77, 78, 215, 398, 433,
    603, 604, 618, 637, 646, 918
Tudor Walters Committee, 477
Tunbridge Committee, 752

unemployed, the: characteristics of, 603–7;
    discontinuous employment, 590–95;
    employment policy and, 610–14, 616;
    grades, 589–90; income support for,
    607–10; levels, 595–601, 615; numbers,
    143–4, 902; numbers in poverty, 897–8;
    occupational class and, 601–3; relation
    of unemployment to poverty, 588–617;
    as social minority, 567, 569, 570–71, 572
    573, 575, 576, 577; and supplementary
    benefit, 829, 830, 831, 832, 834, 835, 837,
    839, 846
United States: disability in, 704–5; elderly,

797; income distribution, 76, 138, 142; means-tested benefits, 881–2; poverty in, 32–3, 34–6, 37, 39, 41, 42, 47, 57; retirement, 654–5; spending units, *146*; taxation, 148; wealth distribution, 145
USSR, 807

wage bargaining, 128–9, 131
wages, *see* earnings, income
Wages Councils, 130, 131, 142, 270, 634–5, 648, 918
work: deprivation at, *see* deprivation at work; *see also* managerial, manual *and* professional workers; unemployed, the
work-incentive schemes, 432
wealth: and class, 359–63; conceptual problems, 230–32; and income, 341–7, 368; institutional structure, 365–6; methods of assessing distribution,

339–40; sources, 364–5; *see also* assets; income; resources; rich, the
Whitley Council, 918
Wilberforce Committee, 619
Willink Commission, 128
women: with adult dependants, 568–9, *570*, *573*, *575*, *577*, 578–9, 587; disabled housewives, 733–4; earnings, 136, *137*, *138*, 141, 143, 620–21, 625, *626*, 627–8, 631; economic position of, 389; employer welfare benefits, 217–18, 232–3; income distribution, 187; occupational pensions, 458–9; and older workers, 674–5, 680–82, 683; % in poverty, 285, *414*, *416*; self-employed, 465; unemployment, 602–3; working conditions, 438–9, 443, 444, *446*, 447, 451–61, *464*, *467*, *471*, *473*
World Health Organization (WHO), 52

Index of Names

Abel-Smith, Brian, 25, 26, 27–8, 29, 49n, 93n, 120n, 160n, 162n, 242n, 245n, 247n, 262n, 273n, 588n, 809n, 826n
Adams, Faith, 27
Adams, R. N., 69n
Aigner, D. J., 113n
Aitchison, J., 73n
Allan, K. H., 691n, 705n
Almes, Mrs K., 27
Amery, Julian, 478n
Andersen, B. R., 705n
Andorka, R., 785n
Armstrong, Sir William, 458
Atkinson, A. B., 21, 28, 43, 44, 77n, 120, 123, 124, 147, 203n, 242n, 266n, 275n, 339n, 342, 343n, 366n, 631n, 645n, 825n, 902n
Atwater, W. O., 33
Avens, Angela, 27

Bagley, Christopher, 26, 93n, 243n, 262n, 264n
Baguley, Mrs, 27
Bakke, E. W., 645n
Baldwin, S., 617n
Ball, M., 513n
Balogh, T., 132n
Baran, P., 79n
Barber, B., 83
Barna, 218
Barnes, J. H., 560n
Barratt Brown, M., 617n
Barron, Richard, 28, 647n
Barten, A. P., 262n
Batson, E., 34n
Batson, Geoffrey, 40n, 41n
Beaton, G. H., 52n
Bechhofer, F., 373n, 381n, 410n, 452m, 470n

Becker, G. S., 646n
Bell, Colin, 28
Bell, Lady F., 33n
Bell, K., 848n
Bender, A. E., 867n
Bendix, R., 83n
Benjamin, B., 39n
Bennett, A. E., 704n
Benson, Sheila, 26, 29
Benton, Grace, 27
Best, Sue, 29
Bettison, D. S., 34n
Beveridge, Sir William (later Lord Beveridge), 34, 619, 923
Blandy, R., 262n
Blau, P., 113n, 371n, 987n
Blauner, R., 472n
Bluestone, B., 78n, 635n, 648n
Blum, Z. D., 68
Boddy, M., 513n, 515n
Bond, John, 28, 964
Bond, N., 832n, 837n
Booth, Charles, 25, 40n, 62, 565n, 784n
Boris Allan, G. J., 113n
Bosanquet, N., 78n, 147n, 469n, 513n, 596n, 635n, 646n, 648n
Bott, E., 373n
Boudon, R., 113n
Bowerbank, M., 164n, 826n
Bowley, A. L., 32, 33n, 34n, 40n, 41n
Bowman, M. J., 81n
Bradshaw, J., 742n, 750n, 874n
Brazer, H. E., 99n
Brown, C. V., 148n
Brown, George, 130
Brown, G. W., 40n

Brown, J. A. C., 73n
Brown, Marie, 26, 27, 29, 465n, 559, 634n
Buckle, J. R., 685n
Bull, D., 151n, 847n, 861n
Bunning, Mrs J., 27
Burnett, Mrs, 27
Burnett-Hurst, A. R., 33n, 40n
Burns, Tom, 58
Burrows, P., 614n

Cain, G. G., 79n, 113n
Callaghan, James, 544n
Campbell, E. Q., 113n
Campion, H., 144–5
Canvin, R. W., 696n
Caplovitz, D., 175
Caplow, T., 652n
Carney, Mollie, 27
Carstairs, V., 696n
Carter, H., 70n, 71n
Cartter, A. M., 118n, 218
Centers, R., 373n
Chamberlain, R. N., 751n
Champernowne, D. G., 73
Chapman, D., 530n
Chapman, Paul, 27
Chapple, Sheila, 27
Cinsky, M. E., 691n, 705n
Clark, R. M., 264n
Clausen, R., 703n
Cloward, R. A., 882n
Cluley, Mrs E. M., 27
Coates, B. E., 929n
Coates, K., 79n
Cohen, M., 589n
Cohen, S., 881
Cohen, W., 99n
Coleman, James, 113
Collier, Peter, 27
Collins, D., 784n

Colquhoun, P., 62n
Cordani, Andrea, 27
Coulson, Mrs P., 27
Coverdale, A. G., 266n
Cowell, Marjorie, 28
Cox, E., 685n
Craig, C., 444n, 446n
Crossley, J. R., 139n
Crossman, Richard, 27
Crouch, C., 513n
Crowder, N. D., 113n
Cseh-Szombathy, L., 785n
Cullen, J., 27
Cullingworth, J. B., 492n
Cumming, E., 786n
Cutright, P., 84

Daniel, W. W., 612n
David, M., 799n
Davie, R., 741n
Davies, B., 40n
Davies, M., 33n
Davis, Kingsley, 83, 84, 86, 87
Daw, R. H., 174n
Dawson, D. A., 148n
Debeauvais, M., 156n
Demayer, E. M., 52n
Dennis, N., 543n
Doeringer, P. B., 78n, 646n
Doll, Prof. Sir R., 171n
Donnison, D., 492n, 847n
Doreian, P., 82n
Doughty, Mrs M. L., 27
Douglas, J. D., 47n
Douglas, J. W. B., 174n
Dubois, W. E. B., 40n
Duncan, O., 113n, 371n, 987n
Duncan, T. L. C., 530n
Dunlop, Dr, 33
Dunne, A. C., 652n
Durbin, J., 26, 99n, 931n, 935n
Durkheim, E., 652n
Durwin, J. V. G. A., 51n

Eckstein, H. B., 751n
Edding, F., 156n
Eden, Sir Frederick, 410–11
Edwards, M., 513n
Eimer, I. T. S., 971n
Elks, L., 608n
Engel, E., 263n
Engels, F., 39, 263
Epstein, L. A., 784n

Faherty, Michael, 27
Faherty, Zara, 27

Falk, N., 562n
Farndale, J., 685m
Fellner, W., 81n
Feltell, Mrs, 27
Ferge, Susan, 28
Ferman, L. A., 78n, 646n
Ferri, E., 770n
Fiegehen, G. C., 19n, 39n, 41n, 266n, 267n, 275n, 513n
Field, F., 29, 150n, 366n, 617n, 847n, 869n, 886n, 903n
Fink, A., 212n,
Fisk, T., 561n
Florence, P., 34n
Foner, A., 806n
Ford, Marion, 27
Ford, Peter, 29
Forsyth, G., 129n
Fraser, Rhoda, 27
Friedson, E., 686n
Fuchs, V. F., 76n

Galenson, W., 472n
Gallaway, L. E., 69n
Galtung, J., 56, 114n
Gans, H., 85, 86, 87n, 543n
Garrad, J., 704n
Gatt, Jim, 27
Gee, F. A., 485n
George, David Lloyd, 151
George, V., 79n, 753n, 754n, 759h, 772n, 776n, 807n
Germani, G., 68n
Gerth, H., 58n
Gibrat, R., 73n
Giddens, Anthony, 91n, 363n
Giffen, R., 62n
Giles, Roger, 27
Ginzberg, E., 77
Glass, D. V., 293, 370n, 751n, 986, 987
Glastonbury, B., 773n
Glazer, Nathan, 69n
Glennerster, H., 559n
Godber, Sir George, 169
Goffman, E., 566n, 686n
Goldberg, E. M., 40n
Golden, Mrs E. Y., 27
Goldstein, H., 174n
Goldthorpe, J. H., 90n, 370n, 371, 373n, 410n, 452n, 470n, 472n, 474n, 987n
Gordon, D. M., 74, 76n, 78n, 90n
Gordon Walker, Patrick, 861

Gouldner, A., 47n
Gray, F., 522n
Gray, P. G., 484n, 485n
Greaves, J. P., 167n
Greer, R., 490n, 513n, 515n
Gregory, P., 477n
Greve, J., 773n
Groom, Doreen, 27
Guest, R. H., 432n

Haber, J. D., 690n, 704n
Haberhauer, Marion, 29
Haley, B. F., 81n
Halil, T., 704n
Hall, J., 381n, 986
Halpern, Ron, 27
Hansen, W. L., 212n, 213n
Harbury, Colin, 21n, 28, 361, 364n
Harcourt, A., 41n
Hare, P. H., 513n, 973
Harper, R. J. A., 41n
Harrington, M., 66n
Harrington, R., 976n
Harris, A. I., 381n, 452n, 685n, 695n, 698n, 699n, 700n, 701n, 702n, 703n, 714n, 733n, 816n, 832n
Harris, R., 19n, 789n, 910n, 911n
Harrison, Alan J., 21n, 28, 147, 203n, 339n, 902n
Harrison, R. M., 605n, 606n
Hart, J. J., 170n, 173n
Hart, P., 262n
Hatch, S., 559n
Hauser, M. M., 614n
Hauser, P., 68n
Hawthorn, Geoffrey, 28, 70n, 71n
Head, E., 685n
Healy, P., 848n
Heath, D. B., 69n
Henderson, A. M., 34n
Henderson, R. F., 41n
Henry, W. E., 786n
Herrick, N. Q., 435n
Hersee, Doreen, 27
Herzog, Elizabeth, 69n
Hicks, J. R., 81
Higgin, G. W., 432n
Hill, M. J., 605n, 606n, 614n, 847n
Hill, T. P., 145n
Hiller, P., 373n
Hinchcliffe, Andrew, 27
Hobsbawm, E. J., 263n
Hobson, C. F., 113n

Hockley, G., 146n
Hogg, M. H., 34n
Holden, Phil, 28
Holland, Walter, 688n
Hollingsworth, D. F., 167n
Holmans, A. E., 156n
Holtermann, Sally, 560
Hope, K., 370n, 371, 987n
Hosier, Mrs, 27
Houghton, D., 825n
Houthakker, H. S., 262n
Howe, J. R., 165n, 246n, 247n, 827n
Hughes, David, 28, 727n
Hughes, J., 121
Humphrey, Michael, 685n
Humphreys, A. S. B., 41n
Hunt, A., 753n, 754n, 761n, 773n, 776n, 832n
Hunt, Sir Joseph, 562
Hunt, P., 571n
Hyman, M., 702n

Jackson, D., 212n
Jackson, Mrs, 28
Jaco, E. G., 687n
Jacobsen, Colin, 27
Jaehnig, W., 693n, 744n
Jefferys, Margot, 688n, 702n
Jephcott, P., 477n
Johnson, M., 806n
Jones, D. Caradog, 40n, 293, 381n, 986
Jones, Inez, 27
Jones, K., 561n, 617n, 693n
Jones, L. M., 364n
Joseph, Sir Keith, 70, 71

Kaldor, N., 178, 1081n
Kalimo, E., 174n
Karn, V., 525n
Kemsley, W. F. F., 95, 108n, 109n, 929n, 932n, 942n
Kerr, C., 645n
Kerr, Hugh, 27
Kincaid, J. C., 79n
Kinnersly, P., 432n
Knight, Mrs B., 27
Knight, I. B., 634n, 828n, 906n
Kuznets, S., 43n

Labbens, J., 68n
Laing, S., 543n
Lambert, Royston, 167
Lampman, R. J., 147n
Lance, H., 971n

Land, Hilary, 17n, 26, 28, 93n, 164n, 165n, 584n, 927
Langley, K. M., 146n
Lansing, J. B., 57n
Lansley, P. S., 19n, 39n, 41n, 266n, 267n, 275n, 513n
Lasker, B., 647n
Laudanska, Stasia, 27
Lavers, G. R., 34n, 160
Lebergott, S., 73n
Legg, C., 874n
Le Gros Clark, F., 652n
Levy, M. J., 83
Lewis, J. P., 530n
Lewis, Oscar, 65, 66–70
Lewis, P., 906n
Lidbetter, E. J., 71n
Liebenstein, H., 262n
Lilienfeld, A., 39n
Lipset, S. M., 83n, 472n
Lipworth, L., 170n
Lister, R., 832n, 847n, 877n, 891n
Little, A., 559n
Lockwood, David, 28, 373n, 410n, 452n, 470n
Longman, Ford, 26
Lucas, H., 560n
Lundberg, F., 364n
Lydall, Harold, 43, 45n, 57n, 74, 75–7, 96, 97, 118, 119, 121, 122, 138, 142, 145n, 146n, 152, 180n, 196n, 205n, 339n, 627n
Lynes, Tony, 28, 151n, 809n, 861n, 886n

Maasdorp, G., 41n
Macarthy, John, 28
McCannagh, Ian, 27
McClements, L. D., 266n
McCormick, B. J., 645n
McCowen, P., 727n
McCrone, G., 561n
MacDonald, K., 987
MacEwen, A., 68n
McGregor, O. R., 774n, 775n
Mackay, D., 645n
MacMahon, P., 364n
Macmillan, Harold, 478
Macnab, G. H., 751n
McPartland, J., 113n
Malthus, T. R., 81
Mann, M., 399n
Mar, J. M., 68n
Marcuse, Joy, 27
Marris, P., 164n, 543n, 826n

Marsden, Dennis, 17n, 26, 28, 29, 56n, 93n, 164n, 753, 757n, 766n, 775n, 776n, 779n, 826n
Marsh, David, 26
Marshall, R., 753n, 776n
Martin, D. M., 99n
Martin, J., 724n, 832n
Martin, Mrs J., 27
Martinos, H., 562n
Marx, Karl, 61, 80, 81, 82, 87, 411n, 432n, 921
Mason, Tim, 28
Masterman, C., 39
Matson, F. W., 687n
Maurice, R., 193n
Mayhew, Henry, 65n
Meacher, M., 147n, 150n, 366n, 608n, 832n, 846n, 866n, 875n
Meade, J. E., 339n
Mechanic, D., 687n
Medhurst, F., 530n
Merton, R. K., 47, 85
Millard, J. B., 702n
Miller, F. J. W., 40n, 740n
Miller, H. P., 73n
Miller, S. M., 82n, 247n
Mills, C., Wright, 58n, 363
Mills, G., 262n
Mood, A. M., 113n
Moore, F. G., 27
Moore, R., 580n
Moore, W. E., 83, 84, 86, 87
Morgan, E. V., 339n
Morgan, J. N., 69n, 72n, 99n, 219n, 637n, 799n
Morgan, M., 724n, 832n
Morgan, Wendy, 29
Morris, J. N., 170
Morris, P., 777n
Morrison, M., 696n
Morrison, S. L., 40n
Moser, C. A., 40n, 382n, 986
Mouly, J., 140n
Moyle, J., 146n
Moynihan, D. P., 68n, 69n, 543n
Muellbauer, J., 263n
Murphy, W., 635n, 648n
Murray, H., 432n
Murray, J., 212n
Myrdal, Gunnar, 45n

Nagi, S. Z., 686n
Narayana, Rao M., 52n
Nevitt, A. A., 28, 513n, 874n, 973n, 974n, 978n

ewby, H., 460n, 551n
icholson, J. L., 26, 126n, 148, 150n, 219, 262n, 263, 964n
cholson, R. J., 122, 123
col, B. M., 52n
ssel, M., 909n
xon, J. M., 634n, 828n, 906n
orman, Jill, 29
orris, G., 28, 615n, 647n
yman, Jennifer, 28
yman, K., 174n

Hare, Hazel, 28
penheim, A. N., 987n
nati, O., 161n
shansky, Molly, 35, 36, 37, 41n, 264n, 784n
well, George, 39
ven Smith, E., 645n

ckman, J., 743n
gani, A., 40n
hl, R. E., 543n, 674n
ish, F. W., 118, 119
rker, Mrs H. T., 27
rker, R. A., 522n
rkin, Frank, 82n
rsons, Talcott, 83, 786n
samanick, B., 39n
ssmore, R., 51n, 52n
ttison, Mrs M. B., 27
achey, Linda, 29
acock, A., 219n, 220n
arse, A., 68n
arson, N. G., 696n
arson, R. J. C., 971n
retz, J., 909n
achaud, D., 175
gou, A. C., 73n
lay, P. N., 34n
re, M. J., 78n, 646n
ven, F. F., 882n
itt, J., 373n, 410n, 452n, 470n
duluk, J. R., 34n
lanyi, G., 364n
llock, A. B., 432n
nd, C., 150n, 175, 366n
wer, M., 743n
ais, S. J., 262n
est, A. R., 122–3, 262n
nce, Betty, 27
ejector, D. S., 212n
rola, T., 174n
e, Chris, 27

Quinn, R. P., 435n

Ragg, Nicholas, 28
Ranadive, K. R., 43n
Raphael, M., 807n
Rattee, Pam, 27
Rawlings, Brenda, 27
Rawlings, H. E., 751n
Rawstron, E. M., 929n
Reddin, M., 866n, 869n, 870n
Reder, M. W., 645n
Reeves, P., 33n
Reid, G. L., 153n, 455n, 461n
Rein, M., 543n
Restron, Joy, 27
Reubens, B. G., 614n
Revell, J., 146n, 339n
Rex, J., 580n
Rhodes, G., 808n, 809n
Ricardo, D., 71, 80
Richard, H. W., 561n
Ridge, J. M., 987n
Riley, M. W., 806n
Roberts, Gwilym, 675n
Roberts, Robert, 559
Robertson, D. J., 153n, 455n, 461n
Robinson, Derek, 133, 645n
Robinson, E. A. G., 156n
Robinson, H., 770n
Roby, P., 79n, 82n, 247n
Rogers, M. E., 39n
Rose, H., 492n
Rose, M. E., 62n
Rossi, P. H., 68
Routh, Guy, 19, 134, 139n, 140
Rowell, Sandra, 29
Rowntree, Jean, 26
Rowntree, Seebohm, 25, 32, 33–4, 38, 40n, 41n, 50, 56, 62, 64, 160, 161, 264n, 565n, 588, 618, 647n, 895
Roy, A. D., 73n, 74
Runciman, W. G., 47, 82n, 145n, 452n
Russell, R., 484n
Russett, B. M., 43n
Rutherford, R. S. G., 74n
Rutter, M., 742n

Sainsbury, Sally, 28, 663n, 685n, 688n, 690n, 691n
Sargeant, A. V., 605n, 606n
Sargent, Sir Donald, 26
Sawyer, Lucianne, 685n
Schaffer, B., 918n

Schorr, A. L., 32n, 68n, 79n, 530n
Schwartz, R. D., 84n
Scott, J. A., 40n
Scott, W., 40n
Seers, D., 118n, 121n, 133
Semple, M., 126–7, 910
Seneca, J. H., 262n
Shanas, E., 653n, 657n, 663n, 690n, 784n, 786n
Shannon, R., 219n, 220n
Shaver, S., 41n
Shaw, L. A., 164n, 826n
Sieve, J. E. B., 154n, 219n, 966n, 978n
Sievers, K., 174n
Silburn, R., 79n
Simons, H., 1081n
Simpson, H., 174n
Sinfield, Adrian, 26, 29, 93n, 611n, 612n, 617n, 660n
Singh, Gurmukh, 28
Singh, R., 262n
Smith, A. D., 19n, 38n, 39n, 41n, 266n, 267n, 275n
Smith, Adam, 32n, 80, 338
Smith, C. R. W., 685n, 832n
Smith, D., 584n
Sorbie, Mrs, 27
Soutar, M. S., 34n
Spence, J., 740n
Spencer, Jim, 28
Spicer, C. C., 170n
Stacey, M., 58n
Staehle, H., 73n
Standing, G., 596n
Stanworth, P., 363n
Stark, T., 122–3, 262n
Stein, B., 882n
Stein, L., 40n
Stein, R., 589n
Stephens, R. J., 635n
Stevenson, M., 635n, 648n
Stevenson, T. H. C., 369n
Stewart, M., 126n
Stockman, N., 82n
Stone, M., 518n
Stouffer, S. A., 47
Straw, K. H., 145n
Stuart, Alan, 26
Sussman, M. B., 686n
Sweezy, P., 79n

Taira, K., 242n
Talbot, V., 605n, 606n,
Taussig, M. K., 262n
Taylor, Mrs E., 27
Ten Broek, J., 687n

Thatcher, A. R., 19, 139n, 141n
Thompson, E., 65n
Thurow, L. C., 74, 635n
Tipping, D. G., 146n, 175, 205n
Titmuss, Richard, 21, 26, 118, 119n, 122, 124, 152, 170n, 185n, 809n
Tizard, J., 742n
Todd, J. E., 364n
Tout, H., 40n
Townsend, Joy, 29
Townsend, Peter, 17n, 48n, 56n, 71n, 82n, 93n, 120n, 126n, 147n, 160n, 162n, 163n, 173n, 220n, 242n, 245n, 247n, 262n, 264n, 273n, 469n, 513n, 524n, 588n, 609n, 685n, 690n, 696n, 703n, 780n, 784n, 797n, 809n, 824n, 826n
Townsend, Ruth, 29
Travis, Keith, 27
Trinder, C., 21n, 906n
Trist, E. L., 432n
Tunnard, J., 515n
Turner, H. A., 132n

Utting, J., 163n, 784n, 824n

Vaizey, J. E., 156n
Valentine, C. A., 67n, 69n
Van Slooten, R., 266n
Veit-Wilson, John, 26, 685n
Vinen, Susan, 27

Wachtel, H. M., 79n
Walker, Alan, 28, 29, 522n, 744n
Walker, C. R., 432n
Wallis, Roy, 28, 69n
Warren, Michael, 688n, 702n
Watts, H. W., 113n
Webb, A. L., 154n, 219n, 966n, 978n
Webb, Beatrice, 62n
Weber, Max, 57–8, 80, 82, 367, 399n
Wedderburn, Dorothy, 26, 29, 48n, 123n, 150n, 163n, 443n, 444n, 446n, 469n, 703n, 784n, 786n, 824n
Wedel, J., 156n
Weisbrod, B. A., 212n, 213n
Weiss, G. S., 212n
Welford, J., 667n
Wen-hsien, H., 918n
Wesolowski, W., 83n, 84
Whitmore, K., 742n
Wicks, M., 874n
Widdett, Mrs V., 27

Wilder, J., 727n
Wilding, P., 753n, 754n, 759n, 772n, 776n
Wilkins, E. H., 34n
Williams, Janet, 27
Williamson, V., 883n
Willmott, P., 58n, 906n
Wilson, N. A. B., 435n
Winyard, Steve, 29, 634n, 648n
Wolf, M., 513n
Wood, J. B., 364n
Woodward, J., 432n
Woolf, M., 484n
Wootton, Barbara, 29, 70n, 71n, 128n, 129, 374n, 645, 648
Worgan, Mrs H., 27
Worthington, Joan, 27
Wynn, M., 243n, 262n, 754, 759, 773n

Yarrow, L., 751n
Yeo, E., 65n
Young, Sir Hilton, 478n
Young, M., 58n
Younghusband, Dame Eileen, 743n, 751
Yudkin, John, 26

Zborowski, M., 687n